I.P. at 40^{00}

$20.$ ^{\underline{oo}}

I.P. at 40$^{\underline{00}}$

WORDS
TO RHYME WITH

WORDS
TO
RHYME WITH

For Poets and Song Writers

Including a Primer of Prosody; a List of More Than 80,000 Words That Rhyme; a Glossary Defining 9,000 of the More Eccentric Rhyming Words; and a Variety of Exemplary Verses, One of Which Does Not Rhyme at All

WILLARD R. ESPY

MACMILLAN
PRESS
Reference Books

First edition published by Facts On File, New York 1986.

This edition first published 1986 by
THE MACMILLAN PRESS LTD
London and Basingstoke

Associated companies in Auckland, Delhi, Dublin, Gaborone, Hamburg, Harare, Hong Kong, Johannesburg, Kuala Lumpur, Lagos, Manzini, Melbourne, Mexico City, Nairobi, New York, Singapore, Tokyo

British Library Cataloguing in Publication Data

Espy, Willard R.
    Words To Rhyme With: A Rhyming Dictionary.
        1. English Language   Rhyme
    Dictionaries
    I. Title
    423′.1   PE1519

ISBN 0-333-46426-9

Printed in the United States of America

YOU'D BE A POET, BUT
YOU HEAR IT'S TOUGH?

You'd be a poet, but you hear it's tough?
   No problem. Just be strict about one rule:
No high-flown words, unless your aim is fluff;
   The hard thought needs the naked syllable.
For giggles, gauds like *pseudoantidis-*
   establishment fulfill the purpose well;
But when you go for guts, the big words miss:
   Trade *"pandemonic regions"* in for *"hell."*

. . . *Important* poems? Oh . . . excuse the snort . . .
   Sack scansion, then—and grammar, sense, and rhyme.
They only lie around to spoil the sport—
   They're potholes on the road to the sublime.

And poets with important things to say
Don't write Important Poems anyway.

Books by Willard R. Espy

Bold New Program
The Game of Words
Omak Me Yours Tonight
Oysterville: Roads to Grandpa's Village
An Almanac of Words at Play
Another Almanac of Words at Play
A Children's Almanac of Words at Play
The Life and Works of Mr. Anonymous
O Thou Improper, Thou Uncommon Noun
Say It Me Way
Have a Word on Me
Espygrams
The Garden of Eloquence
Word Puzzles
Words to Rhyme With

Contents

When People Tell You Writing Verse Is Tough	*v*		*Doublet*	*39*
Author's note	*viii*		*Ormonym*	*39*
Acknowledgments	*x*		*Homonym Couplet*	*39*
Introduction	*1*		*ESPYramids*	*40*
Rhythm and meter	*2*		*Pangrammic couplet*	*40*
Enjambment	*3*		*Univocalic verse*	*41*
Rhyme	**4**		*Lipogrammatic verse*	*41*
The stanza	**7**		*Acrostic verse*	*41*
The metric line	**10**		*Limerick with palindromic verse*	*42*
Forms of lyric verse	**18**		*Abbreviation verse*	*43*
Sonnet	*18*		*Digital verse*	*43*
Shakespearean sonnet	*19*		*Alphabetic verse*	*43*
Ottava Rima	*19*		*Parthenogenetic verse*	*44*
Terza Rima	*19*		*Symbols and signs*	*45*
Rhyming sestina	*20*		*Acronymic verse*	*46*
Ballade	*21*		*Grammar verse*	*47*
Ballade with double refrain	*22*		*Macaronic verse*	*49*
Chant Royal	*23*			
Triolet	*25*		**Caution: identicals do not rhyme**	**50**
Rondel	*25*		**How to use the list of rhyming words**	**53**
Rondelet	*25*		**Single rhymes, with stress on the last syllables**	**59**
Roundel	*26*		**Double rhymes, with stress on the next to the last syllable**	**179**
Rondeau	*26*		**Triple rhymes, with stress on the second syllable before the last**	**423**
Rondeau redoublé	*27*			
Villanelle	*28*			
Kyrielle	*29*			
Ode	*30*		**The glossary**	**551**
Sapphic	*30*		**How Dreka's blotting-case fathered a glossary**	**551**
Haiku	*31*			
Pantoum	*31*		**How to use the glossary**	**554**
Ballad	*32*		**Pronunciation key**	**554**
Venus and Adonis stanza	*33*		**Appendix A: Meaning of the number keys**	**647**
Spenserian stanza	*33*			
Elegy	*33*		**Appendix B: Additional words ending in -mancy**	**648**
Limerick	*34*			
Clerihew	*34*		**Appendix C: Additional words ending in -mania**	**649**
Double dactyl	*35*			
Chain verse	*35*		**Appendix D: Additional words ending in -phobia**	**651**
Epigram	*36*			
Word play in rhyme	**37**		**Index of first lines**	**655**
Procrustean (impossible) rhyme	*37*			
Mosaic rhyme	*37*			
Anagram verse	*38*			

Author's Note

It is not unusual for the writers of handbooks like this one to slip in few verses of their own making. I have gone a bit further than that. In this book I resurrect no moth-eaten old lines from such has-beens as Shakespeare or Milton. With the exception of one borrowed quatrain from the Latin and a contributed verse consisting of two one-letter words in two lines, *all* the verses are my own. Most of those in the early chapters have been published before (some appear here in slightly modified form); most of those in the rhyming list, and I think all those in the glossary, were written specially for this book.

Mind you, these are not POems. They are jingles—nominies—doggerel—amphigories. They should serve to remind you that one need not be a Poet with a capital P to have a capital time putting rhymes together. They should also challenge you to prove that at least you can rhyme better than *that*.

W. R. E.

To Charles F. Dery: a Dedication

Some sleepers, myself included, occasionally dream in color; but of my acquaintance, only Charles F. Dery admits to dreaming regularly in puns. In the example he described most recently, a young woman turns down his offer of a canoe ride: ''I hear,'' she explains, ''that you are a big tipper.''

That Charles, in his eighties, continues to pun even when asleep is itself enough to justify this dedication, but I have a defensive reason for it as well. He is a person of deadly critical faculties, sometimes loosely leashed; a few appreciative words written now may save me from having to read a twenty-page letter, with footnotes, listing just the more egregious errors he has uncovered in his first half-hour with WORDS TO RHYME WITH.

The preceding paragraph was a joke, Charles, I owe you this dedication because when it comes to choosing the right word for the occasion you are the quickest draw in the West. You are, moreover, the person who provided me with not one rhyme for ''purple'' but two, both from Scotland—first *hirple,* meaning ''gimpy,'' and then the glorious *curple,* meaning ''horse's ass.'' Language for you is both a mistress to embrace and a divinity to worship. I have found you a peerless guide to the magical world of words at play, and count you a dear friend to boot.

Thank you, Charles.

W.R.E.

Acknowledgments

WORDS TO RHYME WITH aches from every ill rhyming guide produced by an amateur, more or less single-handedly, is heir to Misspellings, mised rhymes, misplaced stresses and the like abound. I should have hired a crew.

Still others were present, or almost so, at the creation, most of them without relaizing it. I cannot think of a way to blame them for my errors, but at least they should share the credit for any redeeming features you find here.

Steven Wortman, for instance, turned over the first earth for this book back in 1981. I gave him as many different rhyming dictionaries as I could find in the bookstores, and he tirelessly and expertly collated the rhymes.

So the authors of those rhyming dictionaries are in some measure the authors of this one. I do not remember who they all were, but I do recall Burges Johnson, who wrote *New Rhyming Dictionary and Poet's Handbook* (1931), Clement Wood, author of *The Complete Rhyming Dictionary and Poet's Craft Book* (1934), and Frances Stillman, whose *The Poet's Manual and Rhyming Dictionary* appeared in England in 1966. More recently I found unexpected words in *The Penguin Rhyming Dictionary* (1985), by Rosalind Fergusson.

I next leafed through *The American Heritage Dictionary* (1969), a top-drawer reference at university level. From there I proceeded to four unabridged dictionaries: *The Encyclopaedic Dictionary* (1896), which is less comprehensive than today's mastodons, but lends comfort by its admirably simple phonetic system; *Webster's New International Dictionary,* Second Edition (1959); *Webster's Third New International Dictionary* (1961, with addenda in 1981); and *The Oxford English Dictionary* (1970, with supplements through SCZ).

I watched for additional words in the course of my general reading. Since many were too new on the scene to show up in my regular references, I checked their bona fides in *The Barnhart Dictionary of New English Words Since 1963* and *The Second Barnhart Dictionary of New English Words,* both by Clarence L. Barnhart, Sol Steinmetz, and Robert K. Reinhart; *The Morrow Book of New Words,* by N. H. and S. K. Mager; and Merriam-Webster's *9,000 Words,* a supplement to the Third.

Three teeming sources of outré terms were *Words,* by Paul Dickson; *Mrs. Byrne's Dictionary of Unusual, Obscure, and Preposterous Words,* by Josefa Heifetz Byrne; and *Hobble-de-hoy, The Wor Game for Geniuses,* by Elizabeth Seymour. The extra words ending in -mancy in Appendix B are from *Words.* Those ending in *-mania* and *-phobia* (Appendices C and D) are from a remarkable collection, still unpublished as I write, by Rudy Ondrijka.

Richard E. Priest volunteered over drinks one day the elegant locution *sesquitricentennial,* meaning "four hundred and fiftieth." I out to William Cole a persuasive rationale for taking all the trouble this book required. He pointed out that tens and tens of thousands of poets nowadays shun rhyme as if it were herpes. They will need *Words to Rhyme With* to know which words to avoid.

Jan McDonald typed the glossary. The speed of her word processor matches that of the space shuttle, and she appears incapable of hitting the wrong key. Recalcitrant words (*hippopotomonstrosesquipedalian* is a minor example) flowed flawlessly from her fingers, along with their phonetic equivalents (in this instance, *hip.o.pot'o.mons'tro.ses'kwi.pi.dāl'yun*).

x

I extend warm thanks to Steven Wortman; to Burges Johnson and Clement Wood (though they can scarcely be still alive); to Frances Stillman, Rosaline Fergusson, and Elizabeth Seymour; to the compilers of the rhyming dictionaries I have forgotten; to those responsible for the other standard dictionaries on my list; to Messrs. Barnhart, Steinmetz, Reinhart, and Mager (though I have only initials for the given names of the Magers; perhaps they are Madams or Mademoiselles); to Mrs. Byrne, Mr. Dickson, and Mr. Ondrijka; to Richard Priest; to Bill Cole; and to Jan McDonald.

And especially, to Louise. For better or worse, she once said. For better or worse, this book could not have been completed without her.

Espy Verses from Earlier Books

My thanks to the following publishers for permission to use the verses indicated:

Bramhall House, *The Game of Words:* A Dream of Couth; Applesauce; Drinking Song; Looking Glass Logic; New Words for an Old Saw; Noel, Noel; Oops! You Almost Picked Up the Check; On an Aging Prude; Passion's a Personal Perception; Singular Singulars, Peculiar Plurals; The Cry of a Cat's a Meow; Venereally Speaking; Words in Labor.

Doubleday & Company, *Say It My Way:* Although Informal Speech Is Free; Get That "Get;" Grammatical Usage for Stompers; Graveyard Square; I'd Say in Retrospect; My Idol, Your Idle; On a Distinguished Victorian Poet Who Never Pronounced His Name the Same Way Twice; On the Correct Use of Lie and Lay; Polonius to Laertes: a Grammatical Farewell; The Heaving of Her Maiden Breast; To a Young Lady Who Asked Me to "Do" Her in a Thumbnail Sketch.

Clarkson N. Potter, *An Almanac of Words at Play:* A Classical Education; A Mouse of My Acquaintance; A Positive Reaction; Bless These Sheep; E Pluribus Unum; Facsimile of a Love Song; Forecast, Chilly; Haikus Show IQ's; Identity Problem in the Mammoth Caves; I Love You to Infinity; In-Riddle; I Scarce Recall; Love's a Game; Macaulay Tells Us; My Amnesty to All; Never Emberlucock or Impurgalize Your Spirits With These Vain Thoughts and Idle Concepts; Pre-Parental Plaint; Some May Promise Riches; The Mrs. Kr. Mr.; There Are Numerous Locutions to Express the Idea of Never; The Susurrant Schwa; To a Praying Mantis; To a Young Poetess; Typesetting Tarradiddle; When Charon Ferries Me Across the Styx; Wild Boars and Lions Haul Admetus' Car.

Clarkson N. Potter, *Another Almanac of Words at Play:* A Pest Iamb, Anapest Rick Ballad Was; Brooklyn Love Song; Centripetal, Centrifugal; Charles Dickens and the Devil; Concede, My Own; Consider Now the Quark; Elegy for My Late Friend and Tailor, Canio Saluzzi: For Isaac Asimov; For Planets Forsaken; Grammar in Extremis; Had I Butt Nude; I Have a Little Philtrum; I Was a Stranger; I Was Prodigal with Time; Kitchy-koo; Larva, Pupa, Imago; Let Us Wonder, While We Loiter; Love Song; Manon? Mais Non; My Chinese Miss; Now, a Little While; Ode to an Elevator; On Joseph Brodsky's Contention; On the Hermit Crab; Our Love Will Never Dwindle, Being Never; Resquiescat in Pace; Round (a Roundelet); Scratch That Mudblower—One Love-Maiden to Go; The Active and the Passive Voice; There Ought to Be a Law; There's Seldom Been a Man I Knew; They Were As Fed Horses in the Morning; To God the Praise; Up-and-Down Counting Song.

Clarkson N. Potter, *A Children's Almanac of Words at Play:* The Pygmy Race Were Little Guys; Incident in a World's Series Game.

Harper & Row, *The Garden of Eloquence:* ''Alliteration's Artful Aid;'' Don't Tell Me No Grammatic Rules; If Love Be Fine, As Some Pretend; O Mangy Cat, O Scruffy Cat.

Simon & Schuster, *Have a Word on Me:* A Man in Our Town, Cal Y-clempt; A Certain Paris Avocat; Bactrian Camels Have Two Humps; Don Juan at College; Forgotten Words Are Mighty Hard to Rhyme; God Argues Constantly With Me; I Find It Curiositive; I Would I Were a Polyglot; Jogger, Jog; Veritas Mutatur.

Introduction

She warn't particular; she could write about anything you choose to give her to write about just so it was sadful. Every time a man died, or a woman died, or a child died, she would be on hand with her "tribute" before he was cold. She called them tributes. The neighbors said it was the doctor first, then Emmeline, then the undertaker—the undertaker never got in ahead of Emmeline but once, and then she hung fire on a rhyme for the dead person's name which was Whistler. She warn't ever the same after that; she never complained, but she kinder pined away and did not live long.

—Mark Twain

Mark Twain was a rigidly honest man, so beyond doubt Emmeline did indeed die of grief for want of a rhyme.

It is for addicts like Emmeline and me that one editor after another has cobbled together rhyming lists, generally preceded by a treatise on the craft (though not necessarily the art) of versification. But these lists can never be entirely satisfactory. Many words simply refuse to rhyme, even under torture; yet you would need a wheelbarrow to transport the hundreds of thousands that do have rhyming matches. So though I believe this book contains more rhyming words than any of its contemporaries, it does not pretend to be complete—not to mention that up to the last minute I was still thinking of obvious words I had missed, while you are bound to think of equally obvious words still missing.

Books of this genre often carry the rather showy word-pair "Rhyming Dictionary" in the title; but in the sense that I understand the term, they are not dictionaries at all. A distinguishing feature of a dictionary, as far as I am concerned, is that it defines its entries. Rhyming dictionaries never do. That is why my collection has to rest content with the humbler name *Words to Rhyme With*, even though it does introduce a glossary defining a smattering (sadly, that was all there turned out to be room for) of the more exotic specimens.

Checking on meanings was a process full of astonishments. Dictionary definitions are generally clear, and sometimes curt. Occasionally they labor, like a 1917 Ford climbing a steep hill. And once in awhile they thrill, like a fine line of poetry. But often they do become a bit prosy. The definition of *aubesic,* for instance, is likely to be on the order of "utilitarian; common in thought or taste; vocational; breadwinning." Yet one dictionary got to the heart of the matter in just four words: "Smacking of the workshop." Sheer genius!

Definitions repeatedly take me by surprise. *Pettitoes,* for instance, are the feet of a pig, often used as food, but they have no etymological connection with the toes of their last syllable at all; the word descends from two Middle French forebears meaning "little goose," and was first applied to goose giblets.

I know now that an *arter* is a worm that bores into wood; that *Aepyornis* is a genus of extinct birds that laid eggs thirteen inches long (the fabulous gillygaloo lays *square* eggs); that *storge* denotes instinctive parental affection; that the *arui* is an *aoudad;* and that the aoudad is a wild sheep of North Africa which may be the chamois mentioned in the Old Testament.

I even learned something about my own nickname, which is *Wede*. But before telling you the meaning, I must explain how I received the name.

Nearly seventy years ago, in my fifth or sixth year, I became for one matchless summer the worshipful slave of a ten-year-old boy whose family had just settled in our village.*

---

*Its name is Oysterville, and it is located in the southwestern corner of the state of Washington.

Not just his slave—his shadow. Day after day I trotted at his heels—through the marshes and woodlands; across the salt hay meadows; onto the mudflats at the edge of the bay; and, when the tide was low enough, out across the hard gray corduroyed sand.

The name of my idol was *Aquila*, pronounced a.*kwil′*a; and perhaps because of an echo between that and my own name, *Willard*, the neighbors began referring to us as if we were a monster with two joined bodies: "Aquila-and-Willard." When Aquila announced that he preferred to be called *Quede* (I have no idea why), they immediately nicknamed me to match, and we became "Quede-and-Wede."

Nearly a lifetime later, as I was leafing through Webster's Second to confirm some rhyming word, my eye fell on my own name:

wede (wēd), adj. Shriveled.

The description was accurate enough, but I turned to *The Oxford English Dictionary* in search of something kinder. Here is what I found:

wede (wēd), v. intr. 1. To be or become mad.
2. To be wild with anger or desire; to rage.

As for quede, it too was waiting for me in both dictionaries. It means (or did, for, like wede, it is now obsolete) "evil; also, an evil person; specif., the Devil."

So now I know whose footsteps I began to walk in at the early age of five.

Even if you never have occasion to rhyme with words like *quede* and *wede* and *arter* and *Aepyornis* and *storge* and *arui* and *aoudad*, it is comforting to know that they are there, no less at your service than *love* and *dove* and *June* and *moon*.

Only God can make a poet, and for his own good reasons He makes one but seldom. If He has such a destiny in mind for you, I hope the pages ahead may provide a few shortcuts along the way. But do not expect me to be consistent. In the poem that opens this book, for instance, I plump for the use of simple words, and mean it. But if only a complicated word can express what is in your head and heart, you have no choice but to use it. In the trivia which is my own substitute for poetry the fact that a word is long and complicated may indeed be its only asset.

Since I have yet to experience Poetic Afflatus, I cannot possibly define it, much less communicate it. This book simply sets down certain basics of rhyme and metrics; demonstrates that even the noblest forms of poetry run risks when in hands that are mostly thumbs; and goes on and on listing rhyming words until you will find them coming out of your ears. If we are both lucky, some day the right ones will also start coming out of your pen, and you will find yourself saying something that the world needs to hear, in the one way in the world that it should be said.

In my wildest dreams I cannot conceive of a poet employing some of the words in the list that follows. Nonetheless, they do rhyme. Even if *Words to Rhyme With* had been around in time, though, it could not have saved Emmeline's life. There is no rhyme for Whistler.

Rhythm and Meter

Rhythm is where poetry starts. Rhythm is older than speech; older than sound; older than the stars themselves. The Big Bang ushered it in. Rhythm is the heartbeat of the universe.

In prosody, which some dictionaries describe as the science of versification, rhythm is codified as *meter,* the regular beat of accent, or stress. Syllables are grouped in metrical units called feet, each a single accented syllable, generally combined with one or more that are unaccented. The way in which the feet are arranged determines the meter of a line. It is not intended that metrical rules should be slavishly followed—rocking-horse meter is widely scorned, though it may be tolerated for whistlers-in-rhyme such as I—but a good poet knows meter in his head and feels rhythm in his blood. If ever he violates their canons he does so deliberately, knowing exactly the purpose he is seeking to achieve. If he disobeys the king, it is only to serve him more faithfully.

The most widely used metric feet in our poetry are:

• The *iambic,* an unaccented (or unstressed, or short) syllable followed by an accented (or stressed, or long*) syllable. (. ' : De.*ny* him. *not.*)

• The *trochaic,* an accented followed by an unaccented syllable (' . : *Ho.*ly *Fa.*ther, *bless.* me).

• The *anapestic,* two unaccented syllables followed by an accented syllable (. . ' : Un.re.*tur.*ning is *Time*).

• The *dactylic,* an accented syllable followed by two unaccented syllables (' . . : *Al.*ice is *beau.*ti.ful).

• The *amphibrachic,* an accented syllable dividing two unaccented syllables (. ' . : Un.*cer.*tain.ly *walk.*ing).

Less usual are the *spondaic,* with two or more accented syllables in succession (' ' : *Fields, streams, skies I know; Death not yet*), and the *pyrrhic,* consisting of two or more unaccented syllables—so difficult to cut away from the attending stressed syllables that I cannot think offhand of an example that clearly makes the point. It is all but impossible to make a string of unstressed syllables; one of them will seize power. The merest hint of a shift in emphasis can alter the beat of a line. It can turn a trochee into an iamb (*fish.*wife into fish.*wife*) or an iamb into a trochee (in.*sult* into *in.*sult). And it frequently does.

Once formal meter is ingrained in you, it may be helpful at times not simply to change emphasis within a line, but even to add or drop part or all of a foot. But never take such a liberty by mistake. The rule is, master meter, *then* maneuver it.

ENJAMBMENT

(Enjambment, from Old French *enjamber,* "to straddle," is the run-on of a sentence or idea from one line or couplet of a poem to the next.)

Enjambment doesn't—say who may—	No—the problem is that it
Start at mid-tide, either way	Doesn't know the place to quit;
Flowing (as if poetry	On and on it rushes, beckoned
First should lap about the knee;	From the first line to the second,
Thence with climbing moon should rise,	From the second to the third,
Drowning inch by inch the thighs,	Shunning the concluding word,
Navel, nipples, nape, and crown;	Past the fourth line, fifth, and so on,
Then again come ebbing down,	Always one more line to grow on,
All returning, till below	Till, though ardor's undiminished,
It at last reveals the toe)—	It expires; enjambment's finished.

---

*The stressed part of a foot is sometimes also called the *thesis,* and the remainder the *arsis,* after corresponding Greek words that translate loosely as the heavier and the lighter part. But *arsis,* signifying literally "raising," was mistaken by some to apply to a raised or loudened voice, so the meaning of the two words is frequently reversed. You will avoid confusion by avoiding their use.

Rhyme

The beat of sound in poetry is always accounted as meter, but balance between sounds is not always accounted as rhyme. Rhyme as it is presently defined was unknown to the ancient Greeks, nor is there evidence of it in classic Latin poetry. It appeared in church Latin around 200 A.D., and took a thousand years to seep through Europe. Our Anglo-Saxon forebears preferred alliteration—the repetition of the opening sounds of accented syllables, as in Shakespeare's "Full fathoms five thy father lies." My home encyclopedia describes alliteration as the "jingle of like beginnings;" rhyme, in Milton's phrase, is "the jingling sound of like endings." His definition has a patronizing echo; though immortal poetry has been written in rhyme, there have been and continue to be poets who consider it beneath their dignity to employ it for serious business. If there must be any association at all between the sound of one word or another, they prefer that it be more oblique, as in assonance and consonance (see below).*

Blank verse—generally iambic pentameter—discards rhyme but not meter. Free verse, the favorite of many modern poets, drops them both. But neither is a threatened species. Writers will continue to produce some of our finest poetry in rhyme; and in the field of light verse it stands alone.

Types of Rhyme

Rhyme, says the dictionary, is

> The correspondence, in two or more words or verses, of terminal sounds beginning with an accented vowel, which, in modern English usage, must be preceded by different consonantal sounds, or by a consonant in one case and none in the other.

In traditional rhymed verse, the rhyme is carried by the last foot of the line. The briefest possible rhyming foot is a semi-iamb, a single stressed syllable, as in

> *Fly'*
> *High'!*

But the usual iambic (or single, or masculine) rhyming foot is made of two syllables, with the accent on the second:

> Don't *fly'*
> Too *high'*!†

A two-syllable rhyming foot with the accent on the first syllable is a trochaic (or double, or feminine) rhyme:

> *Pret'*ty
> *Kit'*ty'!

Even if the remainder of the line is iambic, or of some other beat, the final rhyming foot can be made trochaic by adding an unaccented syllable:

> His *moth'*er *said'*, "Son, *do'* not *wan'*der
> Out *yon'*der."

---

*A caution here. I have admitted words to this book that rhyme technically, but deplorably. You would have to be in desperate straits, for instance, to rhyme *tolerable* with *babble*. The result would probably not be tolerable, though it would be babble.

†Stressed syllables here are underlined and followed by ('). Unstressed syllables are not underlined.

A triple (or dactylic) rhyming foot has three syllables, with the accent on the first:

*Crick'*e.ty, *lick'*e.ty,
*Ma'*s are per.*snick'*e.ty.

The list of rhyming words in this book is divided into the foregoing three categories—single, double, and triple. The rhymes are traditional; that is, the accented vowels match exactly, and the unaccented syllables are similar enough not to jar the ear. Once conventional rhyming is second nature to you, you may wish to vary the position of the rhyming foot in the line or among lines to meet special needs. Here are some of the possibilities:

•   *Random* rhyme, which goes beyond the common practice of alternating rhymed and unrhymed lines, instead mixing them irregularly;
•   *Initial* rhyme, occurring at the beginning instead of the end of the line;
•   *Interior* rhyme, occurring within the line;
•   *Cross* rhyme, in which the rhyming sound at the end of one line is matched somewhere inside another.

Or, if you are acting deliberately and with full awareness of the risks, you may experiment with various sorts of *near*-rhyme, including the following:

•   *Identicals.* These match the sound of the consonant as well as the vowel, though they are seldom simply repetitions of the same word:
    Praise, prays; bard, barred; coral, choral.
•   *Consonance.* Here not the sound of the vowel in the stressed syllable but instead that of the opening and closing consonants makes the match:
    Tick, tack, tuck, tock; hit, hat, hot, hut.
•   *Consonantal rhyme.* This matches only the sound that ends the syllable, whether accented or unaccented:
    Easy, busy; fast, waste; missing, bussing.
•   *Assonance.* This simply echoes a vowel sound within a line:
    Old bones move slowly.
•   *Vowel rhyme.* Here only the vowel sounds of the rhyming feet correspond:
    Age, rail, take; blue, move, flute.
•   *Smothered (imperfect) rhyme.* The match is between an accented and an unaccented syllable:
    Bring, going; beaten, pen; hardly, foresee.
•   *Unaccented rhyme.* The match is between the final unaccented syllables:
    Faster, mover, killer; happy, pretty, chummy.
•   *Half-rhyme.* The rhyming foot ends in one or more unaccented syllables, but only the stressed syllable has a match:
    Differ, fifth; cavern, ravenous.
•   *Spelling* (or *sight*) *rhyme.* The spellings but not the sound of the stressed vowels match:
    Woman, Roman; love, grove.

And if none of these ways of rhyming hits the mark for you, you can always make up your own rhyming words:

BACTRIAN CAMELS HAVE TWO HUMPS

I met on a tram in exotic Siam
    (Known as *tramela* out in Siamela)
Three Campbellite camels—a sire, dam, and lamb
    (In Siamese, *Camela famila*).

The sire was Ben-Amelel-Ben-Abraham,
A suitable name for a Bactrian cam
   (Which is Siamese shorthand for *camela*).
The femme of the cam was a well-trodden dam

Whom tram-trippers taunted as *Bactrian mam*
   On account of her uberous mammila.
The lamb of the Campbellite camels was Pam,
   Though sometimes she answered to Pamela.

And what has becam of that Camela fam
Since they traveled away on their Siamese tram?
I know not—and frankly, I don't give a damn,
   Or even a Siamese dammela.

To lengthen *tram* to *tramela* and *cam* to *camela*—to shorten *camel* to *cam, mammal* to *mam, family* to *fam, became* to *becam*—these are deliberate breaches of contract with the English language. As with the alteration of a metric beat, it is perfectly acceptable to abuse the language for effect—but only if you are fully aware of the abuse yourself, and are sure that the reader will recognize it as intentional.

There are two other ways to rhyme, one quite usual and the other rare except as sheer artifice. The usual way is called *mosaic* rhyme. It matches one word against two, or occasionally more:

tiller, kill her; queenly, green lea; Ohio, I owe

Mosaic matches come readily to mind. Be sure, though, that the mosaic is a true rhyme. *Tiller* does not rhyme with *ill sir; queenly* does not rhyme with *green tea; Ohio* does not rhyme with *I know*.

The less common way is *Procrustean*, or *impossible*, rhyme, which may stretch words, chop them up, or squeeze several into one to make a match, as the mythical giant Procrustes rearranged the length of his victims to fit them to his bed.

You will find, beginning on page 37, verses built around these two rhyming tricks. But since such rhymes consist of either more than one word, or less than one, they are not included in the list of rhyming words.

Any sort of off-rhyme, if used with knowledge and sensitivity, increases the range and vocabulary of poetry. But so do the widely varying arrangements available in conventional rhyme schemes, as we are about to see.

I do not know if there is a name for spellings that change their sound, and so their rhyme, from one word to the next, but there should be. Among such perverse spellings, the syllable -ough has perhaps provided more grist than any other to versifiers. According to circumstance, it is pronounced at least five ways—as *uff, ow, oh, off,* or *oo:*

ON A DISTINGUISHED VICTORIAN POET WHO NEVER
PRONOUNCED HIS NAME THE SAME WAY TWICE

I seldom stretch beneath a bough
To browse on lines of Arthur Clough.
His work seems rather dated, though
Victorians loved Arthur Clough.
In fact, they could not get enough

Of poems penned by Arthur Clough;
While I—I groan, I snort, I cough
When forced to slog through Arthur Clough.
And I am glad that I am through
With this review of Arthur Clough.

(The ghost of Mr. Clough—who pronounced his name *cluf*—will forgive me for any apparent unkindness; the fact is that critics recall his works with respect. I did not mean to be mean; it was the fault of the rhyme.)

The Stanza

A stanza is a series of rhythmic lines that, put together, make up a poem. (*Stanza* and *verse* are sometimes used interchangeably, though verse may also mean either a complete poem or metric writing in general.) If the poem consists of two or more stanzas, they are divided by spaces. A stanza must contain at least two lines to make a rhymed unit; any greater number is permitted. The rhyme scheme, meter, and length of the line are up to the poet.

Couplet—Two Lines

A poem may consist of a single couplet:

INSPIRATION

The bard who Hippocrene* for gin gave up
Saw empty couplets gush from empty cup.

Couplets, not necessarily set apart as stanzas, can be building blocks for poems of any length. If two rhymed lines in iambic hexameter form a self-contained verse unit, expressing a complete thought, they are a *heroic couplet.* (The two lines above do not make a heroic couplet because they are written in pentameter—five syllables—instead of hexameter—six.)

I said earlier that the continuation of a sentence or idea from one couplet to the next is *enjambment.* The verse below starts to enjamb in the third stanza.

A PUP BY ANY OTHER NAME

Ah, Chloe, the animal kingdom's a-teem
With litters that turn out not quite what they seem:

For a cow has a *calf,* but the calf of a mare
Is a *foal,* and a *cub* is the foal of a bear;

A *fawn* is the cub of a deer, while the fawn
Of a beaver's a *kitten;* and, carrying on,

The kit of a sheep is a *lamb,* and the lamb
Of a wolf is a *whelp,* while the whelp of Madame

Is a *babe,* and the babe of a dog is a *pup,*
And I thought for a while this would wind the thing up,

But the pup of a goat is a *kid,* and—ah, Chloe—
What else is a kangaroo's kid but a *joey?*

Triplet (Tercet)—Three Lines

Except in *terza rima,* where they are strung together with a rhyme scheme of a b a, b c b, c d c, and so on, you can rhyme triplets any way you like. If a single triplet makes up a complete poem, you will have to rhyme it a a a, though, unless you are willing to leave one line unrhymed:

---

*Hippocrene, a legendary fountain on Mount Helicon, sprang up when Pegasus, the winged steed of the Muses, struck the earth with his hoof. The water from this fountain is said to provide inspiration for poets.

THE BRIEFER THE BETTER

For Jim's scant thought no style could be too terse;
A couplet were too long, a triplet worse;
Jim just might justify a one-line verse.

Quatrain—Four Lines

The quatrain is frequently a self-contained poem, though as often it is one stanza in a series. It may be written so that only the second and fourth lines rhyme: a b c b. Generally, though, it consists of two couplets (a a b b), called a *rubai*, or of lines rhyming a b a b, as in the two following examples:

THE HEAVING OF HER MAIDEN BREAST

The heaving of her maiden breast
   Had to be seen to be believed.
The boat lurched down another crest—
   And up she heaved.

ME VS. GOD

God holds a dialogue with me
   With which we both are growing fed up.
Says He to I, says I to He,
   "Oh, *shed*dup! *Shed*dup! *Shed*dup! *Shed*dup!"

Quintet—Five Lines

As the number of lines in a stanza increases, so does the potential number of rhyme schemes. The scheme here is a b a a b, and the subject is forgotten positives—words that reverse their meanings if you knock away their negative prefix.

A DREAM OF COUTH

I dreamt of a corrigible, nocuous youth,
   Gainly, gruntled, and kempt;
A mayed and a sidious fellow, forsooth—
Ordinate, effable, shevelled, and couth;
   A delible fellow I dreamt.

(If you play with forgotten positives, remember that the prefix *in-* does not always mean *not*. *Inflammable* means the same as *flammable*. *In-* may mean *in* or *into*, as in *innate, insert*. It may indicate intensive action, as in *inosculate*.)

Sextet—Six Lines

A sextet could run a a a b b b; or a b a b a b; or a b c a b c—oh, there is no need to bother listing all the possibilities. This one is a a b b c c.

Pygmy. *One of a nation fabled to be only three spans high, and after long wars to have been destroyed by the cranes.*—Johnson's Dictionary

Pygmies? Weren't they little guys,
Only three hand spans in size?
Yes—and they had pygmy brains
Not to know those giant cranes
Could beat them standing on one leg,
And still take time to lay an egg.

Septet—Seven Lines

There are too many possible rhyme variations in a seven-line stanza to bother listing them all. The verse that follows runs a b a a b a b.

THERE'S SELDOM BEEN A MAN I KNEW

There's seldom been a man I knew
    Who struck me as a pest.
Of women, there were quite a few.
Yet when I take the longer view,
    The women worked out best.
Those rare exceptions—one or two—
    Made up for all the rest.

Octave—Eight Lines

An octave can be rhymed as four couplets, or two quatrains, or two tercets and a couplet, or—well, here it has only three rhyming lines, a - a - a, and really consists of four lines split in two.

HOW MANY ANGELS CAN DANCE ON THE HEAD OF A PIN?
(Medieval Church argument)

If you're ab-
    le to spin
On the Head
    of a Pin,
You must be
    an An-
gel—or *ter-*
    ribly thin.

Nine-line Stanza

The rhyme scheme in this example is a b c c b B a B B.*

KITCHY-KOO

My dear's dear kitchy-koo am I,
    As she is my dear kitchy-koo.
What tears one kitchy-koo would shed
If t'other kitchy-koo were dead!
    And yet grief's freshets often do
    Wash up another kitchy-koo.
(I hear my kitchy-koo reply:
    "They do; they do,
    Kitchy-koo.")

Ten-line Stanza

The example consists of five rhyming couplets.

WILD BOARS AND LIONS

Wild boars and lions haul Admetus' car.
White horses seven pull the Morning Star.
Gold panthers lead bright Bacchus on his way;

---

*A capitalized letter represents a refrain line, or, as here, the repetition of part of a line.

Gemmed peacocks Juno's chariot convey.
By chastened lions Cybele is drawn,
And antlered stags tug fair Diana on.
Behind her wingèd dragons Ceres travels,
And flights of doves bear Venus to her revels.
Sea horses carry their thalassic lord.
    I drive a Ford.

The Metric Line

You have seen that the beat of iambic verse is da *da;* of trochaic, *da* da; of anapestic, da da *da;* of dactylic, *da* da da; of amphibrachic, da *da* da. I may also have suggested—if so, it is worth repeating—that lines in any meter will almost never scan perfectly when read aloud with normal emphasis. That is a good thing; an unaltering beat would be unbearably monotonous. Look at Elizabeth Barrett Browning's famous line:

How do I love thee? Let me count the ways.

That is iambic pentameter—in theory, five da *da* beats in a row. Forced into Procrustes's bed, it would come out like this:

How *do* I *love* thee? *Let* me *count* the *ways.*

But in fact that line is not iambic at all. It is lucky even to be a pentameter, with five feet, no more, no less; Mrs. Browning, like any other sensible poet, would not have hesitated to add or drop a syllable or so for the greater glory of the line. It begins, in my ear, with a dactyl, continues with three trochees, and concludes with a long iamb. The reader adjusts the stress automatically to the sense of the message, while allowing maximum sweetness to the flow of sound.

Yet it is considered an iambic line. So are Shakespeare's pentameters, any one of which co-opts the beat most suitable for the moment within the overall iambic framework.

The Beat and Length of Poetic Lines

A metric foot is a single beat of sound requiring a stressed syllable (except for those ridiculous pyrrhics, which don't count). It may have one, two, or more unstressed syllables, or it may have none.

A line of poetry comprising a single foot is a *monometer.* Two feet make a *dimeter;* three, a *trimeter;* four, a *tetrameter;* five, a *pentameter;* six, a *hexameter;* seven, a *heptameter.* And that is as far as there is any likely reason to go.

Lines come in all the metric beats that have been mentioned. Here are iambic, trochaic, anapestic, and dactylic examples:

Monometer:
Iambic:	A *gain* (or simply *gain*).
Trochaic:	*Ho'*ly.
Anapestic:	In the *night.*
Dactylic:	*Bear'*a.ble.

Dimeter:
Iambic:	They *fled* a.*way.*
Trochaic:	*Feet* that *stum'*ble.
Anapestic:	In a *song* that she *sang.*
Dactylic:	*El.*ea.nor *Roo'*se.velt.

Trimeter:
  Iambic: I *watched* a *sink'*ing *star.*
  Trochaic: *Fa'*ther, *call* the *doc'*tor.
  Anapestic: When the *dark* shall turn *bright* as the *day.*
  Dactylic: *Why* does the *teach'*er keep *shout'*ing so?

Tetrameter:
  Iambic: The *crows* have *fall'*en *si'*lent now.
  Trochaic: *In* the *ram'*age *of* the *elm* tree.
  Anapestic: And the *ech'*o now *fades* in the *streets;* he is *gone.*
  Dactylic: *Cor'*al sand *un'*der them, *pur'*ple sky *o'*ver them.

Pentameter:
  Iambic: I *know* one *won'*der *that* will *nev'*er *cease.*
  Trochaic: *Then* the *tel'*e.*phone'* will *cease* to *jin'*gle.
  Anapestic: Do not *speak* in that *voice;* it will *troub'*le the *wom'*en a.*sleep.*
  Dactylic: *No,* I'm a.*fraid* I'm not *read'*y to *give* to that *char'*i.ty.

Hexameter:
  Iambic: The *riv'*er *wat'*er *is* no *long'*er *run'*ning *clear.*
  Trochaic: *Sis'*ters, *let* us *raise* a *cup* to *ab'*sent *Ma.*ry.
  Anapestic: We were *walk'*ing on *cob'*bles; I *think* that my *feet* will be *ach*ing to.*mor.*row.
  Dactylic: *Call* in the *preach'*er; I *sud'*den.ly *wish* to be *wed'*ded to *Jon'*a.than.

Heptameter:
  Iambic: Men *looked* at *him,* and *by* their *look* he *knew* he *neared* the *end.*
  Trochaic: *What* is *on* this *eve'*ning's *tel'*e.*vis'*ion *that's* worth *watch'*ing?
  Anapestic: Though I *find* it a *long* and un.*like'*ly ac.*count,* yet I *some*how be.*lieve* it is *true.*
  Dactylic: *Out* of the *pas'*sion of *Le'*da, there's *on'*ly a *feath'*er re.*main'*ing for *mem'*o.ry.

Not many poets have composed consistently graceful lines in dactylic heptameter. To try is excellent training, though, and you have as good a chance as anyone else of being the one who succeeds.

Shown below are verses in the four most common metric beats, ranging in length from one metric foot to seven.

Monometer: A One-Foot Line

Since a single metric foot is the shortest poetic line, while a one-syllable, one-letter word is the shortest metric foot, a matching pair of one-letter words is the shortest possible rhyming verse. Here is such a verse—though it must be admitted that for the sake of understanding I had to give it an unusually long title.

> A BRIEF AND SOMEWHAT UNGRACIOUS EXCHANGE BETWEEN
> THE BRITISH AMBASSADOR'S WIFE, WHO SPEAKS NO SPANISH,
> AND THE SPANISH AMBASSADOR'S WIFE, WHO SPEAKS NO
> ENGLISH, DURING A COURTESY CALL BY THE LATTER UPON
> THE FORMER: WRITTEN ON THE ASSUMPTION THAT MY
> READERS KNOW THE SOUND OF THE SPANISH WORD FOR "YES"
>
> "T?"
> "C."*

---

*Charles F. Dery brought to my attention a similar summation in which a youth, gazing awed at the star-studded firmament and sensing his own insignificance, murmurs: "I . . .
Y?"

A twelve-line verse in iambic monometer:

TO A YOUNG WOMAN WHO REFUSES TO DIET

> No hu-
> man eyes
> Dare view
> Your size
>
> Lest day
> And night
> They stay
> Shut tight
>
> From hor-
> ror at
> Such store
> Of fat.

These eighteen lines are in anapestic monometer:

WE CAN'T SEEM TO GET IT THROUGH OUR HEADS

> If a boy
> Understood,
> He'd *enjoy*
> Being good.
>   The complaint
>   Is, he ain't.
>
> And the same,
> It applies
> Both to dames
> And to guys:
>   What a saint
>   Is, they ain't.
>
> Yes, if *I*
> Understood,
> I might try
> Being good;
>   But I don't,
>   So I won't.

Eight lines of amphibrachic monometer:

EVENHANDEDNESS

> On Sundays
> You pray, in
> Your quest for
> Salvation.
> On Mondays
> You stray, in
> Your zest for
> Temptation.

Dimeter: A Two-Foot Line

This four-line dimeter is trochaic:

TO A SOAP OPERA ADDICT

You there, watching
Lights and shadows—
Which are good-os?
Which are bad-os?

Dimeters and monometers alternate in this iambic verse.

SLOWLY DIM THE SUNSET CLOUDS

The fire, the ash
   Take turn:
Now flame and flash,
   Now urn.

What leagues we rose
   We tell
By counting those
   We fell.

Trimeter: A Line of Three Metric Feet

Does a stalagmite build up from the floor of a damp cave and a stalactite build down from the roof, or is it the other way around? This twelve-line iambic trimeter (. ′ . ′ .′) was supposed to fix the distinction in my mind once and for all—but I still forget.

IDENTITY PROBLEM IN THE MAMMOTH CAVES

O pendant stalactite,
   Deposit crystalline,
Insensate troglodyte
   Shaped of accreted brine,

Aspire you still to pierce
   That upright stalagmite
Who in a million years
   Your love cannot requite?

And if indeed your drip
   With ardor one day fill her,
And bring you lip to lip,
   And make you two one pillar . . .

Then how can you be sure,
   O pendant stalactite,
If you are you, or her—
   Stalactite-stalagmite?

THERE ARE NUMEROUS LOCUTIONS TO EXPRESS THE NOTION OF 'NEVER'

When all the world grows honest;
When the Yellow River's clear;
When Calais meets with Dover,
Do you suppose, my dear,

I shall forget I've lost you? . . .
Not until St. Tib's eve,
Not for a year of Sundays
Shall I forbear to grieve—

Till noon strikes Narrowdale; till
Latter Lammas dawns;
Till Queen Dick reigns; till Fridays
Arrive in pairs like swans;

Till the Greek calends, and the
Conversion of the Jews.
I'll mourn you till the coming
Of the Cocqcigrues.

O SOME MAY PROMISE RICHES

O some may promise riches
And some may promise ease
But I will deck my darling
In suns and galaxies.

Upon her finger, Lyra's
Ring Nebula she'll wear;
Against her throat, the Cluster
In Berenice's Hair.

Rosette in Montesoros
Her bosom shall adorn,
And Veil of Cygnus hide her
Upon her wedding morn.

O some may promise riches
And some may promise ease
But I will deck my darling
In suns and galaxies.

The verse that follows is in trochaic trimeter (′ . ′ . ′ .):

LARVA, PUPA, IMAGO

When I was a larva,
  Giddily I'd chortle,
"When I'm big I'll carve a
  Monument immortal."

When I was a pupa,
  Though more realistic,
Still I hoped to scoop a
  Funeral statistic.

Now, a worn imago,
  I do not declare
My advanced lumbago,
  Knowing none will care.

Tetrameter: A Line of Four Metric Feet

You may vary the number of feet in the lines of a verse according to any fixed pattern you choose. Four of the six trochaic lines below are tetrameter; two are trimeter.

NEIGH NEIGH, NEIGHBOR

They were as fed horses in the morning; every
one neighed after his neighbor's wife.—Jeremiah V:8.

After neighbors' wives you neigh?
    Neighbors' wives are fine—
Sorrel, chestnut, dapple gray,
Rolling neighing in the hay.
Neigh then, neighbor, neigh—but nay!—
    Neigh not after mine.

Overall, this tetrameter is anapestic, though some lines drop the last unstressed syllable.

I WOULD I WERE A POLYGLOT

I would that my palate were pat in
    Icelandic and Persian and Greek;
I would I were fluent in Latin,
    Instead of deplorably weak.

I'm sure it would help me to win you
    If polyglot hints I could spin
Of trading Herculean sinew
    For secret Lilithean sin.

Italian, Hungarian, Spanish,
    Might win me the right to caress you;
But English itself seems to vanish
    Whenever I try to address you.

    I barely can toast,
    "Hey, kid, you're the most!"

These time-honored similes arrive in dactylic tetrameter:

FACSIMILE OF A LOVE SONG

Mute as a mackerel, darling, I am;
You're fit as a fiddle, and gay as a lamb.
You're clean as a whistle; I'm ugly as sin.
I'm fat as a hog, you're as neat as a pin.
You're brave as a lion, I'm deaf as an adder;
You're brown as a berry, I'm mad as a hatter.

My ducky, my darling, the love of my life,
You're free as the wind, and as sharp as a knife.
I'm blind as a bat; you are sly as a fox.
You're pert as a sparrow; I'm dumb as an ox.
You're plump as a partridge, as sweet as a rose;
I'm flat as a flounder, and plain as my nose.

So come, let us marry, and dance in the lane
As merry as crickets, and righter than rain!
Our days will be brighter than rainbows are bright;
Our hearts will be lighter than feathers are light.
Our love will be surer than shooting is sure—
And we shall be poorer than churchmice are poor.

Each line of this amphibrachic tetrameter has an extra unaccented syllable:

FUNGIBLE: INTERCHANGEABLE, REPLACEABLE.

One fury alone has God found inexpungeable;
The wrath of a woman who finds herself fungible.

Iambic tetrameter:

OUR LOVE WILL NEVER DWINDLE, BEING NEVER

Our love will never dwindle, being never;
    It could not be so dear if it could be.
The babe that never was is ours forever;
    There is no need to set the wild deer free.

I know a country with nor dawn nor setting;
    No summer there, nor winter; spring, nor fall;
No memories are there, and no forgetting;
    The people there breathe barely, if at all.

Pentameter: A Line of Five Metric Feet

Iambic pentameter remains the most used line in English-language verse. Here are two examples of it:

TO A PRAYING MANTIS, STANDING IN THE NEED OF PRAYER

(The female mantis consumes her mate during copulation.)

The Male (or Lesser) Praying Mantis is
A victim of romantic fantasies.
He cries, "My angel, let me prove
My insect life well lost for love!"
He takes her in his mantis arms;
He soothes her virginal alarms—
Pours all his love and longing in her,
While she is having him for dinner.
He reassures her that they'll wed;
Meanwhile, she's gnawing off his head.
He soothes her gastric pains with Borax
As she is gnawing at his thorax;
And when there's nothing left above,
Still doth the Lower Mantis love.

This system, as needs scarcely saying,
Breeds little Mantises . . . all praying.

Hexameter: A Line of Six Metric Feet

The most familiar hexameter is the Alexandrine, an iambic line which is a standard unit in French poetry, and usually deals with weightier subjects than the one considered below.

MY CHINESE MISS

My Chinese Miss is dainty as a Chinese fan;
The fare she serves is manna for the inner man.
Her breath is aromatic as her Chinese tea;
My Chinese Miss is won ton dumpling soup to me.

She dips into my heart as chopsticks dip in bowls;
Her lashes flutter when I praise her lobster rolls.
Her breasts are silken, tenderer than egg foo yong—
No Peking duck could match the savor of her tongue.

When I depart this feasting, sated is my need:
No dream remains of mooshi pork, or soup seaweed;
Of birdnest soup, or sweet and sour, or moo gai pen.
(How soon I'm starving for my Chinese Miss again!)

Heptameter: A Line of Seven Metric Feet

Iambic heptameter:

A MATTER OF ETIQUETTE

I've knocked her to the sidewalk and I've taken all she's got;
I can't make up my mind if I should stomp on her or not.
Such delicate decisions aggravate us muggers most—
There's not a word about them in my Emily Post.

Trochaic heptameter:
The following verse plays with *venereal nouns*—collective nouns, that is, covering groups of animals (in this case wildfowl) that men hunt for sport. The word venereal goes back to Venus, who was goddess of both love and the hunt.

VENEREALLY SPEAKING

Tarantara, tarantara, off the hunters ride,
Off to bag a nye of pheasants—failing that, a hide;
Stalking here a plump of wildfowl, there a spring of teal;
Seeking out a sord of mallards for their evening meal.

Tarantara, tarantara, home the hunters straggle,
With of choughs a chattering, and with of geese a gaggle;
Overhead, of geese a skein, a company of widgeons;
Underfoot, a trip of dotterel. On the sidewalk—pigeons.

You may venture to put a precise name to the meter of the following heptametric verse; I would rather not.

A MOUSE OF MY ACQUAINTANCE

A mouse of my acquaintance in seven days was fed
Twice twenty thousand swordfish, and *that mouse is dead*.
The mercury in swordfish is an enemy to dread;
He ate twice twenty thousand, and *that mouse is dead*.

His sister gnawed through pizzas (I am told one million four);
There's talk of botulism—and *that sister is no more*.
Their brother downed ten thousand turkeys lined with pesticide;
It took a week to kill him, but *that poor mouse died*.

So stay away from hormones, and from salmonella too;
Be impolite to cyclamates, and DDT eschew;
For additives and chemicals can kill you just like *that*—
Though (confidentially) those mice were done in by the cat.

Forms of Lyric Verse

Reading poetry has something in common with taking a Rohrschach test—what you bring out tells considerable about what you took in. But a poem also provides a glimpse of the poet, and perhaps not always what he thought he was showing you. The self-revelation may not be quite so evident when the work is epic, spreading heroic happenings over a huge canvas, or narrative, telling a more human story in a briefer compass, or dramatic, with characters speaking for themselves, or even satirical, jeering at human folly, as it is in the lyric poem, which deliberately opens to daylight very private feelings. Even if one wishes to, it is hard to lie successfully in a lyric poem—except perhaps to oneself. If a lie does convince the reader, it is probably because it reveals a truth by accident. And mawkishness and sentimentality show through like pentimento through overlaid painting.

The traditional verse forms that follow are generally associated with lyric poetry. It may seem in dubious taste to serve jug wine from such splendid bottles; but at least the bottles *are* splendid.

Most of the best-known lyric forms in English are imports, and most of the best-known imports are from Italy and France.

From Italy

Four Italian forms that have long been at home in English are the sonnet, ottava rima, terza rima, and the rhyming sestina.

The Sonnet

The sonnet is a fourteen-line poem in iambic pentameter, broken by stanzas and thought development into two movements—the octet, of eight lines, and the sestet, of six. But there may be only one movement, or there may be more than two; and the separations may be either sharp or blurred. The original rhyme scheme, still common, is a - b - b - a, a - b - b - a, c - d - e, c - d - e, with sometimes a shift in the sestet to c - d - c, d - c - d.

Milton used the Italian rhyme scheme for his sonnets, but not the arbitrary division of thoughts. The following verse is structured in the Miltonic fashion.

WHEN CHARON FERRIES ME ACROSS THE STYX

When Charon ferries me across the Styx,
  And Cerberus confines me with the dead,
  Pray, Boswell, carve some legend at my head.
Say that I sharpened Machiavelli's tricks;
Out-Croesused Croesus with my golden bricks;
  That tides obeyed me in Canute's bestead;
  That Casanova envied me in bed
As Newman paled beside me in the flicks.

Pray, Boswell, tell the waiting world that I
  Awhile to Joan was Darby, and awhile
To Damon, Pythias; and, pray, recall
There was the steel of Caesar in my eye,
  And Aristotle's wisdom in my smile.
What—can't you think of anything at all?

The Shakespearean Sonnet

The rhyme scheme of the sonnet form that carries Shakespeare's name is a - b - a - b, c - d - c - d, e - f - e - f, g - g. The thought may take a turn at the beginning of the sestet, but this is not required. The octet here enjambs into the sestet.

POLONIUS TO LAERTES: A GRAMMATICAL FAREWELL

Aboard, Laertes, and my blessing carry;
  And let these precepts in thy memory sit
When judging thy familiars. Be thou chary
  Of tongues that scuff in slipshod counterfeit,
With words all unproportioned to their thought;
  Ill-said is no less ill because intangible.
Give every man thy ear, but count him naught

  Who *friable* equates with *frangible;*
For *friable* is foreordained to crumble,
  While *frangible* is brittle, and must shatter.
From trope to trope do men, like drunkards, stumble,
  And make of synonyms identic matter.

Reserve thy love for the grammatic few.
I wouldn't count on more than one or two.

Ottava Rima

Ottava Rima has six lines rhyming a - b - a - b - a - b, followed by a rhyming couplet. Any meter will do. The example below is based on the conclusion of one of Chaucer's *Canterbury Tales,* in which a knight of King Arthur's court is condemned to die unless he can find an answer to the query, "What does a woman like best?" After hunting vainly far and near, he throws himself in desperation on the mercy of a stooped and withered crone:

HANDSOME IS AS HANDSOME DOES

He said, "Thou art ugly as e'er man did see;
  The bloom of thy nineties must seem long ago.
Yet rather than perish I'll marry with thee
  If thou halt my hanging by letting me know,
What is it a woman likes best?"
              Answered she,
"To have her own way."—And in answering, lo!
She threw her disguise off, and—son of a bitch!—
Proved beautiful, youthful, indulgent, and rich.

Terza Rima

Terza Rima is a series of three-line stanzas in chain rhyme: a - b - a, b - c - b, c - d - c, and so on. It may be as brief as two stanzas, or as long as Dante's *Divine Comedy.* The usual meter in English is iambic pentameter, and the final stanza is a quatrain instead of a triplet. The first line of the quatrain generally rhymes with the middle line of the preceding triplet as well as with the third line of the quatrain. The second and fourth lines rhyme with each other.

LOVE SONG (MULTO CON CORPORE)

THE WAYS   How do I love thee? Let me count the ways:
OF LOVE   From top to toe, with torso in between.
           Some days heels over head, and other days

THE GEOG-   Head over heels. No neck of land's as green
RAPHY OF   As your neck is; no arm of sea's as blue
LOVE   As your arm is; no hill's brow so serene

                As is your brow . . . Your headland's noble, too . . .
                  The widest river mouth is not so wide
                As your dear mouth . . .

THE COM-   Ah, men of mighty thew
PETITION
THAT LOVE   And jutting chin have wooed you—been denied!
ENGENDERS   Dare I, of lesser kidney, catch your ear?
                Dare jellied backbone swim against such tide?

                I have no stomach for the fray, I fear;
                  I'm lily-livered, yellow-bellied, weak.
                I'd only put my foot in it, my dear,

THE PITY   By begging for your hand—I lack the cheek.
NEEDED   Yet let your bowels of compassion start!
FOR LOVE   Lend me a leg up! Quickly!—else I seek
                A toehold in some softer, warmer heart.

The Rhyming Sestina

The sestina, a favorite form of Dante and Petrarch, comprises six six-line stanzas followed by a three-line envoy—thirty-nine lines in all. The last word of each stanza becomes the last word of the first line in the next, with a placement of end words throughout in a rigid pattern. Classically (though not in my example), the word repetition replaces rhyme. The end words are arranged in the following order:

Stanza 1. a - b - c - d - e - f
Stanza 2. f - a - e - b - d - c
Stanza 3. c - f - d - a - b - e
Stanza 4. e - c - b - f - a - d
Stanza 5. b - d - f - e - c - a

THE BANKRUPT'S SERENADE

1.

My television set is snowing snow;
   The snow is snowing television sets.
The lambent moon is on the wane, and lo!
   The wane is on the moon. Wan parapets
Have ceased to pet their paras, for they know
   Our debts repay us as we pay our debts.

2.

They said you only loved me for my debts;
   Yet flake on flake we snowed when we were snow
Who now are mooning wanes and parapets
   And television sets. You murmured low,
"Ah, sunsets, moonsets, hensets! Ah, the sets!"
   None know but nuns, and nuns will never know.

3.

But if a nun dun nuns, will I not know?
   Not I, for I am done with duns and debts,
And done with parapetting in the snow.

Moon on, fair wane! Be petulant, dear pets!
My lows have cattled—let my cattle low;
     My fortunes rise; my television sets.

4.

Dear love, you trounced me, matches, games, and sets.
     You parapetted, but your eyes said no.
Behind my back you dallied with my debts,
     While television sets were snowing snow;
You stroked the parapets of parapets
     While on the moon the wanes crooned sweet and low.

5.

I hear the lambent moon start up below;
     Above me soar the television sets;
The duns are nunning duns amid the snow;
     You stroll in from the garden with my debts
To bring me tidings I am loath to know:
     The paras have forsook their parapets.

6.

Alas, the paras! and alas! the pets!
     The wane is on the moon and you, and lo!
The snow is snowing television sets.
     The nuns are dunning all the nuns they know.
With lowered gaze you stand, distilling debts.
     The television set is snowing snow.

ENVOY

White is the snow upon the parapets;
     The television sets no more, for lo!
Tha pale nuns know that you have paid my debts.

From France

Represented below are ten examples of French verse forms, all with refrains and rigid rhyme schemes. Iambic pentameter is commonly used except in the triolet; but in most cases the poet may take his choice of meter.

The Ballade

The ballade, perhaps the earliest French form to win the English heart, consists of three eight-line stanzas followed by a four-line envoy—twenty-eight lines in all. The last line of the first stanza reappears as the last line of each succeeding stanza. The rhyme scheme is a - b - a - b - b - c - b - C for the principal stanzas, and b - c - b - C for the four-line envoy. The verse below is in iambic tetrameter.

MANON? MAIS NON*

HOW YOU TRICKED ME INTO ATTENDING AN OPERA WRITTEN BY PUCCINI (OR WAS IT MASSENET?)

Aida relish cymbal-smack,
     Horn-sweetness, shrill of piccolo
(To savor these, how Offenbach
To Bach and Offenbach I go!) . . .
     Or don't. I HATE *Manon Lescaut.*
(You said, "Lescaut to hear Manon.
     I've Boito tickets, second row . . . .")
Manon Lescaut a mauvais ton.

_____

Manon? Mais Non was prompted by a series of formidable puns which Boris Randolph contributed to *Word Ways*, the magazine of recreational linguistics.

HOW I DOZED AND
DREAMED OF MANON
(OR WAS IT MANON
LESCAUT?)

I go. Of Korsakov, and hack,
    As old men Lakme must; I blow
My nose, and doze. I'm in the sack
    From Faust plucked string to last *bravo*.
    I dream I'm Chopin up that shmo
Puccini; *c'est un sal cochon.*
    Most art (Mozart, say) leaves a glow;
Manon Lescaut a mauvais ton.

HOW I REFLECTED
POSTLUDALLY ON
THESE MATTERS . . .

Manon is Verdi vulgar pack
    Hangs out. If Massenet should throw
A Mass in A, I'd lead the claque.
    (Giovanni hear Giovanni? So
    Do I. It's really *comme il faut,*
Quite Gudenov.) *Alors, allons!*
    Indeed, I only hate one show:
Manon Lescaut a mauvais ton.

ENVOY

AND THE MORAL
I DREW.

Prince, best of Gluck! . . .
                    One final *mot:*
    The opera is mostly *bon.*
For Bizet folk, though, one's *de trop:*
    Manon Lescaut a mauvais ton.

Ballade with a Double Refrain

The ballade with a double refrain has three eight-line stanzas and a four-line envoy, like the ballad, but two refrain lines rather than one. The first appears in the fourth line of each stanza and the second line of the envoy, and the second in the final line of the stanzas and the envoy, thus: a - b - a - B - b - c - b - C, a - b - a - B - b - c - b - C, a - b - a - B - b - c -b - C, b - B - c - C. This specimen is in anapestic tetrameter.

WHEN THE WHOLE BLAMED CABOODLE HAS GONE UP THE SPOUT

When the whole blamed caboodle has gone up the spout;
    When you reckon you've fizzled, and flunked out, and so on;
When your hash has been settled, your string has run out,
    And you figure there's nothing much else left to go on;
When the coin of the realm is the coin that you're low on;
    When you look like a goner, a blooming galoot,
And your dishes are busted, save one to eat crow on—
    Let's clink glasses, my brother, and toss back a snoot.

You have kept your eyes skinned, you have gandered about,
    You have never said die, nor your row ceased to hoe on;
You have hefted your ax, you have tickled your trout,
    And you figure there's nothing much else left to go on;
You have taken life's wallops, and one more to grow on,
    And you've shut up, and buttoned your lip, and stayed mute.
Say, you're just the fellow I'll wager my dough on—
    Let's clink glasses, my buddy, and toss back a snoot.

So it's root, hog, or die—and you're sore in the snout?
    And it seems a coon's age since you last had a glow on?
And you're feeling knee-high to a skeeter, no doubt,
    And you figure there's nothing much else left to go on?

Well, I'll risk a simoleon, win, place, or show on
  My surmise you'll be dancing soon, playing your flute.
For you'll light a fire yet, pal; you've embers to blow on—
  Let's clink glasses, good buddy, and toss back a snoot.

ENVOY

Oh, you know you can't stop it; time's river will flow on,
And you figure there's nothing much else left to go on;
But I've got a prescription that chaws at the root:
Lesh clink glashes, ole buddy, an' tosh back a shnoot.

The Chant Royal

The chant royal, developed in medieval France, was popularized in English about a hundred years ago. It has five eleven-line stanzas and a five-line envoy, sixty lines in all. The stanzas are rhymed a - b - a - b - c - d - d - e - d - E, with the last line of each stanza as the refrain. The five-line envoy is rhymed d - d - e - d - E. The variant that follows has ten lines to a stanza, rhyming a - b - a - b - c - d - d - e - d - E, with the d - d - e - d - E envoy as before. The obsolete words are from *Poplollies and Bellibones,* by Susan Sperling.

FORGOTTEN WORDS ARE MIGHTY HARD TO RHYME

Quoth I to me, "A chant royal I'll dite,
  With much ado of words long laid away,
And make windsuckers of the bards who cite
  The sloomy phrases of the present day.
My song, though it encompass but a page,
  Will man illume from April bud till snow—
A song all merry-sorry, con and pro."
  (I would have pulled it off, too, given time,
Except for one small catch that didn't show:
  Forgotten words are mighty hard to rhyme.)

Ah, hadavist, in younghede, when from night
  There dawned abluscent some fair morn in May
(The word for dawning, 'sparrowfart,' won't quite
  Work in here)—hadavist, I say,
That I would ever by stoopgallant age
  Be shabbed, adushed, pitchkettled, suggiled so,
I'd not have been so redmod! Could I know?—
  One scantling piece of outwit's all that I'm
Still sure of, after all this catch-and-throw:
  Forgotten words are mighty hard to rhyme.

In younghede ne'er a thrip gave I for blight
  Of cark or ribble; I was ycore, gay;
I matched boonfellows hum for hum, each wight
  By eelpots aimcried, till we'd swerve and sway,
Turngiddy. Blashy ale could not assuage
  My thirst, nor kill-priest, even.
No Lothario

Could overpass me on Poplolly Row.
  A fairhead who eyebit me in my prime
Soon shared my donge. (The meaning's clear, although
  Forgotten words are mighty hard to rhyme.)

Fair draggle-tails once spurred my appetite;
   Then walking morts and drossels shared my play.
Bedswerver, smellsmock, housebreak was I hight—
   Poop-noddy at poop-noddy. Now I pray
That other fonkins reach safe anchorage—
   Find bellibone, straight-fingered, to bestow
True love, till truehead in their own hearts grow.
   Still, umbecasting friends who scrowward climb,
I'm swerked by mubblefubbles. Wit grows slow;
   Forgotten words are mighty hard to rhyme.

Dim on the wong at cockshut falls the light;
   Birds' sleepy croodles cease. Not long to stay . . .
Once nesh as open-tide, I now affright;
   I'm lennow, spittle-ready—samdead clay,
One clutched bell-penny left of all my wage.
   Acclumsied now, I dare no more the scrow,
But look downsteepy to the Pit below.
   Ah, hadavist! . . Yet silly is the chime;
Such squiddle is no longer apropos.
   Forgotten words are mighty hard to rhyme.

ENVOY

About me ghosts of old bawdreaminy blow;
   Eldnyng is gone, and flerd is long *de trop*.
Yet eaubruche pleased me well; I see no crime
In looking back with a ''Bravissimo!''
   (Forgotten words are mighty hard to rhyme.)

Glossary of obsolete terms in ''Forgotten Words Are Mighty Hard to Rhyme''

Windsucker. Covetous, envious person.
Sloomy. Lazy, dull, sleepy.
Merry-sorry. Part cheerful, part despondent.
Hadavist. Had I but known.
Younghede. Youth.
Abluscent. Cleansing, purifying.
Stoopgallant. That which humbles (the great).
Shab. To get rid of.
Adush. To cause to fall heavily.
Pitchkettle. Puzzle.
Suggil. To beat black and blue, defame.
Redmod. Hasty, rash.
Scantling. Scanty.
Outwit. Knowledge.
Thrip. A snap of the fingers.
Cark. Care, distress.
Ribble. Wrinkle, furrow.
Ycore. Chosen, elect.
Boonfellow. Warm companion.
Hum. A mixture of beer or ale and spirits.
Aimcry. Encourage.
Turngiddy. Drunk.
Blashy. Thin, weak.
Kill-priest. Port wine; any strong drink.
Fairhead. A beautiful woman.
Eyebite. To wink at.
Donge. Bed.
Draggle-tail. A wanton, a prostitute.

Mort. A harlot, a loose woman.
Drossel. A slut, hussy.
Bedswerver. An unfaithful husband.
Housebreak. A home wrecker.
Smellsmock. A licentious man.
Poop-noddy. A fool; also, the game of love.
Fonkin. A little fool.
Bellibone. A fair and good maiden.
Umbecast. To ponder.
Scrow. Sky.
Swerked. Troubled.
Mubblefubbles. Melancholy.
Wong. Moor.
Cockshut. Dusk.
Croodle. Cheeping.
Nesh. Fresh, young.
Open-tide. Spring.
Lennow. Flabby, limp.
Spittle. Hospital for indigents, lepers, etc.
Samdead. Half-dead.
Bell-penny. Money saved for one's funeral.
Acclumsied. Physically impaired, paralyzed.
Downsteepy. Precipitous.
Squiddle. Time-wasting chatter.
Bawdreaminy. Bawdry; unchastity; lewdness.
Eldnyng. Anxiety.
Flerd. Deceit, fraud.
Eaubruche. Adultery.

The Triolet

The triolet is an eight-line verse. Lines 7 and 8 repeat lines 1 and 2; line 1 is also repeated as line 4. The rhyme scheme is a - b - A - a - b - A - B; the metric system is iambic tetrameter.

ECHOING TRIOLET

O try, O try a triolet!—
    O try, O try! O try, O try
A triolet to win your pet!
O try, O try a triolet!—
What if the triolet's all wet?—
    The trial yet will catch her eye.
O try, O try a triolet!
    O try, O try! O try, O try!

IF LOVE BE FINE

If love be fine, as some contend,
    The lady's not for burning.
What blame is hers who love doth lend
If love be fine, as some contend?
The sin is when the kisses end—
    The fault in love is spurning.
If love be fine, as some pretend,
    The lady's not for burning.

The Rondel

The rondel, an outgrowth of the triolet, commonly nowadays has thirteen or fourteen lines, two rhymes, two stanzas, and a one- or two-line refrain. This is in iambic pentameter, rhyming A - B - b - a - a - b - A - B, a - b - b - a - A:

I WAS A STRANGER

"I was a stranger, and you took me in."
    So spake the Christ; and you seemed kind as He.
    When I was hungered, short of do-re-mi,
You offered introductions—credit—gin—
The shirt from off your back, come lose, come win;
    Your eyes were wet from selfless sympathy.
"I was a stranger, and you took me in."
    So spake the Christ; and you seemed kind as He.

I woke next morning, gulped down aspirin,
    And found you gone, and gone your charity . . .
    Also my wallet, credit cards, and key.
It's odd, in fact, that I still have my skin.
I was a stranger, and you took me in.

The Rondelet

The rondelet, a verse of seven lines, generally has a purport similar to a tickle on the inner elbow, or the dropped handkerchief of your great-great Aunt Jane. The rhyme scheme is A - b - A - a - b - b - A.

ROUND

. . . then she from laving
emerges fragrant misty and unkissed
  then she from laving
emerges and my heart is not behaving
and how can I refrain or she resist
and afterward anew the fragrant mist
  then she from laving . . .

The Roundel

The roundel, an eleven-line verse derived from the rondel, was introduced into English verse in the nineteenth century by Algernon Swinburne. The usual rhyme scheme is a - b - a - B, b - a - b - a - b - a - B. The fourth and eleventh lines form the refrain, a repetition of the first two syllables of the opening line. Except for the refrain, the first of the roundels that follow is in iambic pentameter, and the second in iambic tetrameter.

TO A YOUNG LADY WHO ASKED ME
TO "DO" HER IN A THUMBNAIL SKETCH

What? Do you in a thumbnail sketch? I may go
  Too far, my dear; perhaps I'll kick your shin.
Suppose I say you're often a virago?
  What? Do you in?

  Suppose I say how shamelessly you sin—
How far from paths of virtue you agley go?—
  How incoherent in your cups you've been—
Your speech verbose, your logic a farrago?
  All right, though, if you wish it . . . I'll begin.
But . . . do you really *mean* it when you say "Go"?
  What? Do you in?

The key word in the roundel below begged to be punned on, and I can't resist that sort of thing.

TO A CRITIC

To die a critic will be tough;
  Hell yawns for you, you shmo, you schnook.
No ebony is black enough
  To dye a critic.

You brushed off my phonetics book—
  Dismissed it as a bit of fluff.
Look here, you nincompoop—it took
  Me midnight oil to write that stuff;—
To range from schwa and printer's hook
  To circumflex; from macron gruff
    To diacritic.

The Rondeau

There are thirteen rhyming lines in the rondeau, with part of the first line used twice as a refrain. My verse is in iambic tetrameter, but pentameter is more usual. The rhyme scheme is a - a - b - b - a - a - b - R; a - b - a - R.

HOW SAD, HOW SAD!

How sad, how sad that I must say
I shall not save the world today!
Just yesterday that wasn't true;
I knew exactly what to do
To end society's decay
And keep the atom bomb at bay
And make pollution fade away.
Today I fell in love with you.
            How sad, how sad!
Let victims weep, let villains prey!
Though all the earth's in disarray,
Let it go hang—who cares? We two
Will trade our kisses anyway.
            (How sad, how sad!)

The following version of the rondeau has seventeen rhyming lines in five stanzas, of which the last four conclude with a steadily shrinking refrain. The rhyme is a - a - b - b - a; a - a - b - R; a - a - b - R; a - a - b - R; a - a - b - R.

OOPS! YOU ALMOST PICKED UP THE CHECK!

"I'll pay for lunch this time," I hear you say,
"So join me in the best . . . What's good today?
Fresh *Escargots?* . . . *Saumon? Palourdes Farcies?* . . .
Coquille Saint-Jacques? . . . or *Jambon de Paris?* . . .
Bisque de Homard? Or *Soupe de Trois Filets?*

"Délices de sole, perhaps, for *entremets?* . . .
Quiche? Fruits de Mer? . . . or *Foie de Veau Sauté?*
Escallopines de Veau? . . . The treat's on me;
I'll pay for lunch this time." (I bet!)

"And then . . . *Filet mignon?* Or *Demi-Grain Grillé?* . . .
Chateaubriand? . . . *Paillard de Boeuf Vert-Pré?* . . .
With *Haut-Brion?* . . . Or *Haut-Lafitte?* Feel free:
I'll pay for lunch this time.

"We'll finish with . . . say *Mousse?* Or *Crêpes Flambées?*
And *Café Filtre,* after *Pousse-café?*"
(Again you murmur, reassuringly:
"I'll pay for lunch.")

But having lunched with you before, I'll stay
With toast and tea, and count my cash. The way
The record reads, it's sure as sure can be
I'll pay.

The Rondeau Redoublé

The rondeau redoublé has five quatrains of four iambic pentameter lines each, with a sixth of three iambic pentameter lines followed by an iambic dimeter. The first line of the first stanza recurs as the last line of the second; the second line of the first stanza as the last line of the third; the third line of the first stanza as the last line of the fourth; and the fourth line of the first stanza as the last line of the fifth. The last line of the sixth, concluding stanza repeats the opening of the first line of the first stanza. A bit complicated, but fun.

The following rondeau redoublé runs through several idiomatic uses of the word "get."

GET THAT "GET"!

Get gets around. *Get* also gets the air;
   Gets after; gets it in the neck; gets set.
Get gets off easy . . . back at . . . in my hair.
   Prince, marvel at all these: the get of *get!*

Get gets a wiggle on; gets off the ground; gets wet;
   Gets wise to; gets the gate; gets here; gets there;
Gets wind of . . . words in edgewise . . . even with. You bet,
   Get gets around! *Get* also gets the air.

Get gets a load of; gets ahead; gets square;
   Gets on the ball (I've hardly started yet).
Get gets the worst of; sometimes gets unfair;
   Gets after; gets it in the neck; gets set.

Get gets my number; gets me in a fret;
   Gets on my nerves . . . a move on . . . tells me where
I get off; gets a rise out of; gets met.
   Get gets off easy . . . back at . . . in my hair.

Get gets along; gets by; gets lost; gets rare;
   Gets better . . . down to cases . . . in a sweat . . .
The jump on . . . to first base . . . me down . . . a threat.
   Prince, marvel at all these: the get of *get!*

Get gets my back up; gets me into debt.
   Get gets the ax . . . the feel of . . . gets unbear-
Able . . . the picture . . . in a pet . . .
   Me off. *Get* even gets the clothes I wear.
     Get gets around.

The Villanelle

Villanelle is the diminutive of a Latin word for "rustic," and the form was first used for country songs. It is made up of five tercets and a final quatrain—a total of nineteen lines. Lines one and three of the first tercet are refrain lines, repeated alternately as the last lines of the succeeding stanzas. The final four-line stanza closes with the two refrain lines. The rhyme scheme is A^1 - b - A^2, a - b - A^1, a - b - A^2, a - b - A^1, a - b - A^2, a - b - A^1, A^2.

The first of the following villanelles is in trochaic tetrameter, the second in dactylic tetrameter.

GRAVEYARD SQUARE

None recalls that I am there,
So sedately do I lie
On the hill in Graveyard Square.

Tranquil is the mouse's lair
In the moss above my thigh;
None recalls that I am there.

Each intent on his affair,
Snake and mole and hare go by
On the hill in Graveyard Square.

Earth, diaphanous as air,
Opens heaven to my eye:
None recalls that I am there.

> Cherubim raise wings in prayer,
> Unsuspecting how I spy;
> None recalls that I am there
> On the hill in Graveyard Square.

WAS BACCHUS A BOIL VEXING JUPITER'S THIGH?

Never emberlucock or inpuregafize your spirits
with these vain thoughts and idle concepts.
—Rabelais

Bacchus a boil vexing Jupiter's thigh? . . .
Gargantua, wax formed in Gargamelle's ear?
(And where did we hail from ourselves, you and I?)

A heel burst its blister for Roquetaillade's cry;
From nurse's old slipper did Crocmosh appear.
(Was Bacchus a boil vexing Jupiter's thigh?)

When Castor and Pollux hatched, Leda clucked, "My!
Some gossips may hint that a swan has been here!"
(And where did we hail from ourselves, you and I?)

With myrrh bark the dad of Adonis did lie;
Minerva popped out of a migraine chimere.
(Was Bacchus a boil vexing Jupiter's thigh?)

Jehovah shaped Eve from the rib of her guy,
While Venus from foam undertook her career.
(And where did we hail from ourselves, you and I?)

We call for the Author, but hear no reply;
The future is mist, and the past is unclear.
Was Bacchus a boil vexing Jupiter's thigh?
And where did we hail from ourselves, you and I?

The Kyrielle

The kyrielle, which originated in medieval France, is from *kyrie eleison* (Greek, "Lord have mercy"), part of a short liturgy used especially at the beginning of the Mass in the Eastern and Roman churches. The words are repeated several times. Often used in hymns but by no means confined to them, the kyrielle consists of any number of four-line stanzas, the first three lines in iambic tetrameter and the fourth (which is unchanged throughout the verse) generally in iambic dimeter. The rhyme scheme is a - a - b - B.

TO GOD THE PRAISE

When I was keen and young as you,
I laid the world out to renew.
I laid it out, and there it lays—
To God the praise.

When I was new and young and dense,
My friends deplored my want of sense.
But, sense is silliness these days—
To God the praise.

Confounded by my flabby thighs,
They urged me on to exercise.
Their obsequies my spirits raise—
To God the praise.

No Jack more dearly loved his Jill
Than I loved mine. I love her still:
Love unrequited ne'er decays.
To God the praise.

My wife and I do well agree,
For she sees little hope for me;
And there is much in what she says.
To God the praise.

From Greece

The Ode

In ancient Greece, the ode, unrhymed, had a *strophe,* during which the chorus moved to the left side of the stage; an *antistrophe,* during which it moved back to the right; and an *epode,* or aftersong, during which it stood still. Today any dignified lyric may be styled an ode, providing there is constant progress in the stanzas toward a conclusion.

The following verse is not dignified; it is an ode simply because I chose to name it so.

ODE TO AN ELEVATOR

Capricious, upsy-downsy sweet,
  My patience with thy presence crown!
Pray, when thy rising I entreat,
No more, dear love, rush past my feet
  Down!

Behold, thy button burneth bright,
  A signal thou wilt be here soon—
If not today, if not tonight,
Anon—perhaps when clappers smite
  Noon.

I hear thee coming! Praise to thee,
  And praise to God, and praise to luck!—
(Though well I know that presently,
'Twixt Six and Seven, I shall be
  Stuck.)

Thy door slides open. Slightly squiffed,
  I sense too late the empty draft.
A lesser lover would be miffed
To step in lift, and find but lift
  Shaft.

No tears for me I pray thee shed;
  Drain not for me the hemlock cup.
But I adjure thee from the dead—
When next I press thy button, head
  Up.

The Sapphic

The verse form associated with the Greek poet Sappho, who flourished around 600 B.C., is a series of four-line stanzas. The first three lines are now variant trochaic pentameter (the third foot is a dactyl), while the fourth pairs a dactyl and a trochee. The form is traditionally without rhyme, so no example was needed in this book; but there was a specimen in my files, so here it is. There is nothing to prevent you from developing a rhyme scheme for your own sapphic.

SCRATCH THAT MUDBLOWER; ONE LOVE-MAIDEN TO GO

*Research having demonstrated that diners will not order
fishes with ugly names, the National Marine Fisheries Service
is seeking to make the names more attractive.*—The Wall Street Journal

Toadfish, croaker, hogsucker, safely swimming;
Harmless, care-free mudblower, spurned by humans—
Keep those names! they save you from being eaten—
    Flaunted on menus.

Ratfish, gag, grunt, viperfish, pray you never
Turn to "lovefish, honeyfish, poached in parsley"!
Menus offer "love-maiden" just to render
    Mudblower tempting.

From Japan: the Haiku

The haiku is a Japanese verse form of seventeen syllables making three lines, with five syllables in the first, seven in the second, and five in the third. There is no rhyme. To the Japanese it is an allusive form, leaving much unsaid. Perhaps they do not use it in jest, as is done here:

HAIKUS SHOW I.Q.'S

Haikus show I. Q.'s:
High I. Q.'s try haikus. Low
I. Q.'s—no haikus.*

From the East Indies: The Pantoum

The pantoum is a Malay verse form popularized by Victor Hugo in the nineteenth century, and since widely imitated in both French and English. The stanzas are indefinite in number, rhyming a - b - a - b; the second and fourth lines of each stanza are repeated as the first and third of the next, and the fourth line of the final stanza is identical with the first line of the first.

This pantoum is in iambic tetrameter:

CONSIDER NOW THE QUARK

Consider now the Quark, which is
    A Concept sub-atomical.
No man alive has seen its phiz;
    Perhaps it isn't Is at all.

A Concept sub-atomical
    Too tenuous I find to prove.
Perhaps it isn't Is at all.
    This goes for Hate, and also Love.

Too tenuous I find to prove
    The Sun, the Shadow, and the Wind.
This goes for Hate, and also Love,
    And other matters of the kind.

The Sun, the Shadow, and the Wind—
    The Dream, the Doing, the Despair,

---

*Frank Johnson says I have it backward; *low* I. Q.'s write haikus.

And other matters of the kind
    I find are proven best in prayer.

The Dream, the Doing, the Despair,
    And other matters, being His,
I find are proven best in prayer.
    Consider now the Quark, which Is.

Local Products

The Ballad

Some English-language verse forms have kissing kin but no sure forebears in other languages. The ballad, for instance, may be related to the French ballade, but its temperament is Scottish. It is a fairly short poem, tending to four-line stanzas, which often tells a violent story. The meter and rhyme scheme are not fixed. The most popular line is iambic tetrameter, used in the sad and fictitious tale about Rick Ballad that follows.

When I first met the real Rick Ballad he was considerably overweight; the floor of his office was said to have required a series of reinforcements. But the last time I dined with him he had lost more than a hundred pounds and was still losing, as a result of restricting his ingestion to a mysterious white powder stirred in water. His entrees in this verse are all of prosodic origin.

A PEST IAMB, ANAPEST RICK BALLAD WAS

(Or, a Ballad in a Sad Cafe)

Rick Ballad (God him pity!)
    Set out one night to dine.
His menu was a Ditty
    In Galliambic line.

His soup was Virelaic;
    His cocktail, Dipodee;
His Spondee was Alcaic,
His Distych, Ditrochee.

He took a pinch of Rhythm,
    Of Ode and Dithyramb,
And mixing Rondeaus with 'em
    He seasoned his Iamb.

He ordered baked Sestinas,
    And half-baked Doggerel;
He licked his Lyric clean as
    A Sapphic Kyrielle.

He flavored Terza Rima
    With Pastoral and Thesis,
And Chant Royal with cream—a
    Bucolic Diaeresis.

His Tercet was a salad
    Of Sonnet and Cinquain.
"Ballade too," ordered Ballad,
    "And Double the Refrain."

Verse Onomatopoeian,
    Szysigium to taste,
Enlarged unendingly an
    Enjambe-ment of waist.

Still Ballad gorged on Dactyl,
  While Trochee and Molossus
Still down his maw were packed till
  He out-colossed Colossus.

(Colossus fell, and wallowed.
  So, too, poor Ballad fell;
And, dying, left unswallowed
  His final Villanelle.)

The Venus and Adonis Stanza

Shakespeare wrote *Venus and Adonis* in a series of six-line stanzas rhyming a - b - a - b - c - c. Though the prototype was in iambic pentameter, Venus and Adonis stanzas now employ a variety of poetic lines.

I HAVE LONE AND LEVEL SANDS OF MY OWN, SHELLEY

Now may the heavens open up, and pour
  Into the desert of my mind, a rain
Of smarts . . . gray matter . . . "two and two make four"—
  A drench of brain!
What wit bloomed here before some early drought
  Parched it out!

The Spenserian Stanza

The Spenserian stanza, developed by the poet for the *Faerie Queen,* is made up of eight lines in iambic pentameter and a ninth in iambic hexameter, rhyming a - b - a - b - c - b - c - c.

The example below was inspired, if that is the word, by the Graeae sisters, three old sea deities of Greek mythology named Pephredo, Deino, and Enyo. Their hair was gray and straggly from birth, their shape was that of a swan, and they possessed among them but one eye and one tooth, which they passed back and forth.

You have probably read, as I have, poems that seem to suffer the ailments of the Graeaes: blindness the blacker by contrast with isolated flashes of vision; insights that might be meaty, if only a tooth were provided for chewing them.

A REFLECTION THAT BORROWS TROPES FROM CURRENT POEMS

The Graeaes' dreadful eye gets twenty-twenty
  On Aesculapius's chart.* That eye
Must serve for all three sisters, but sees plenty:
  Streaked-yellow urine dulling in the sky . . .
Robe like a door ajar . . . twigs stripped in rain . . .
  Legs under-tucked in grief . . . breasts brushing by . . .
Sees plenty, but cannot inform the brain—
The Graeaes shake dim heads, and pass it round again.

The Elegy

The elegy, first "a poem composed in elegiac couplets," is now any mournful poem, especially one lamenting the dead. Here the first, second, third, fifth, sixth, and seventh lines of the octet are iambic tetrameter; the fourth and eighth are iambic pentameter. The sestet alternates between iambic tetrameter and iambic trimeter.

---

*Aesculapius, son of Apollo, was the god of healing, and doubtless practiced ophthalmology among other specialties.

ELEGY FOR MY LATE FRIEND AND TAILOR, CANIO SALUZZI

As spread my waistful span (io),
You never failed, dear Canio,
To prove clothes make the man (io),
   However dropsical his lower part.
Your camouflaging suits (zi)
My ev'ry bulge confute (zi);
Saluto-te, Saluzzi,
Past master of the thread-and-needle art!

You're called aloft, to furbelow
   Our Lord Emmanuel.
Unhid henceforth must be my slow,
   Sure embonpointal swell.
Yet I am comforted to know
   That God is tailored well.

The Limerick

The limerick, though perhaps associated with a medieval Latin verse form, was popularized by Edward Lear in the nineteenth century; some speculate that the name corrupts Lear-ick. More often it is attributed to the refrain "Will you come up to Limerick" (an Irish county and city), said to have been sung between extemporized verses at convivial Irish gatherings. Limericks are judged by the elegance of their structure, the wittiness of their conceits, and often by their ribaldry. There are five lines, and the rhyme scheme is a - a - b - b - a. The first, second, and fifth lines have three feet each—an iamb and two anapests. The third and fourth have one iamb and one anapest each.

FOR ISAAC ASIMOV, WHO NEVER THOUGHT
OF HIMSELF AS A COCKNEY

A Cockney named I. Asimov,
As 'is trousers 'e started to doff,
   Said, "My lydy friends yawn
   W'en I 'as 'em on,
But w'istle w'en I 'as 'em off."

ON JOSEPH BRODSKY'S CONTENTION THAT
NINETY PERCENT OF THE BEST LYRIC POETRY
IS WRITTEN FOLLOWING SEXUAL INTERCOURSE

A poetry writer named Brodsky
Came up with this theory oddsky:
   The best odes to sweetum
   Emerge post-coitum.
(From some folks. The rest of us nodsky.)

The Clerihew

The clerihew, created at the dawn of this century by the English journalist Edmund Clerihew Bentley, consists of two couplets of uneven length and scansion, the first line referring to some individual and the remainder reporting on him (or her). The intent is humorous, and the result often (but, as with the limerick, not always) funny.

DON JUAN AT COLLEGE

Don Juan
Carried on
Till they switched him from Biology
To Abnormal Psychology.

INCIDENT IN A WORLD SERIES GAME

Babe Ruth
Generally told the truth.
When he pointed over the wall
That's where he hit the ball.

The Double Dactyl

Perhaps half a century after the invention of the clerihew it was joined by another new verse form, the double dactyl. Anthony Hecht and Paul Pascal developed the device, and Mr. Hecht, with John Hollander, wrote the first examples. It has two stanzas of four lines each, each line a double dactyl, except that the last line of each stanza is truncated. Nonsense syllables make up the first line; a name, the second; a single word, the sixth. The third, fifth and seventh develop the theme, and the fourth and eighth are rhyme lines.

A DOUBLE DACTYL FOR HECHT, ECT.

Scribble a dribble a
Hecht on you Hollander
Pascal vobiscum you
Lyrical three!

Write me a poem in
Proceleusmaticus;*
Then I'll admit you are
Better than me.

LOOKING GLASS LOGIC

Tweedledum Tweedledee
Alice in Wonderland
First she was tiny and
Then she was tall;

Animal arguments
Anthropomorphical
Were not persuasive to
Alice at all.

Chain Verse

Chain (or *echoing*) verse repeats sounds in a fixed pattern. The following sonnet returns to the last sound of each preceding line in the first sound of the next.

I SCARCE RECALL

I scarce recall when first you said hello.
"Hello!" said I, too young to realize

---

* A poetic foot of four short syllables (pyrrhics), impractical in English.

Lies were your vade mecum. (Spiders so
  Sew webs, and lie in wait for hapless flies.)

Flies time so fast? Why is it I can know
  No more that lying lovelight in your eyes?
I scarce recall . . . it was so long ago . . .
  A golden time, before I grew too wise.

Why's wisdom executioner of youth?
  You thought I left because you lied. Not I!
I left when you began to tell the truth:
  Truth comes too dear for coinless youth to buy.

By lies I might regain you, after all.
Although . . . so long ago . . . I scarce recall.

The Epigram

An epigram is a pithy saying in either prose or verse. A translation from the Latin describes it this way:

> The qualities rare in a bee that we meet
>   In an epigram never should fail;
> The body should always be little and sweet,
>   And a sting should be left in its tail.

The epigrams below are intended not to instruct but to amuse.

TO A YOUNG POETESS

You're beautiful, you're sweet,
  But, God!—
How your iambic feet
  Plod!

LOVE'S A GAME

Love's a game
  Indeed, my pet;
I think its name
  Is Russian Roulette.

PAMPHLET FROM THE RIGHT TO LIFE FOUNDATION

To abort little Willy
Is silly.
That's what war
Is for.

MACAULAY TELLS US

Macaulay tells us Byron's rules of life
Were: Hate your neighbor; love your
  neighbor's wife.

ON AN AGING PRUDE

She who, when young and fair,
Would wink men up the stair,
Now, old and ugly, locks
The door where no man knocks.

Word Play In Rhyme

All poetry, even the most serious—not to say all literature, and indeed all verbal communication—requires word play for maximum effectiveness. Every rhetorical device, from metaphor to hyperbole to tmesis, is word play. When the purpose of the exercise is simply to amuse or divert, as is the case with most of the verses here, it is permissible to mispronounce, to split a word in two for a rhyme (Procrustean verse), to rhyme one word with two (mosaic verse), and to use any of the other devices that follow, along with many that I have not mentioned.

Procrustean (Impossible) Rhyme

There are no conventional rhymes for many words. As mentioned earlier, however, it is frequently possible to rhyme them by the method Procrustes used on his victims—stretching them if they were too short to fit his bed, and lopping something off if they were too long. Here the chopping process was used:

THE UNRHYMABLE WORD	THE RHYME
Month	It is unth- inkable to find A rhyme for month Except this special kind.

Orange	The four eng-
	    ineers
	Wore orange
	    Brassieres.*

Oblige	Love's lost its glow?
	    No need to lie; j-
	ust tell me ''go!''
	    And I'll oblige.

Silver	If Pegasus
	Were but a bus
	    That any man could board,
	I might distil Ver-
	ona's silver
	    Beauty in a word.

Mosaic Rhyme

Mosaic rhyming, the match of one word with two or more, increases the rhyming potential of many words, and makes some available that otherwise would have no rhyme at all. With a few exceptions, however, my rhyming list does not include mosaics.

---

*This rhyme would not have worked before women began moving into jobs once reserved for men.

HOW ARIADNE BECAME DIFFERENTLY-ABLED

The dryad Ariadne used for play den
A cypress tree. When youths strolled by she'd note 'em,
And (quite unlike a proper blushing maiden)
Would downward swoop, and grab 'em by the scrotum.

They flocked to sample what that dryad's swoop meant;
She added lovers not as you and I add,
By ones or twos or threes, but by aggroupment;
She was the cypress grove's most active dryad

Until she pulled a tendon.
                                        Hence this sad ode.
Our discombobulated Ariadne
No longer swoops in love from bower shadowed;
She sits above and poultices her bad knee.

How sad for one who's wantoned from the cradle!
No more a light of love! No more a gay dish!
Below, youths pant galore, yet she must stay dull!
With all that fire inside, must act old-maidish!

(A dryad, being amorously matchless,
Needs quantity to show her what the French meant
By ''Vive la difference!'' When doomed to catch less,
She's very apt to die of the retrenchment.)

Anagram Verse

   Anagrams are words which, by rearrangement of the letters, form other words. They
can be the basis of puzzle verses:

DRINKING SONG

He **** for gold,
   As I for ale;
I've **** of this;
   Of that has he.
For me a kiss
   **** Holy Grail;
He'd go cuckold
   To **** a fee.
Yet, ****! I wist
   (And I'd **** bail)
He'd pay fourfold
   To be like me.

   The anagrams: opts, pots, tops, spot, stop, post.

PRE-PARENTAL PLAINT

When I ******* to be a father,
You ******* my willingness to bother.
Now I *******, for I foresee
You'll leave the ******* to me.

   The missing words: aspired, praised, despair, dia-
pers.

The Doublet

Doublets are variants of anagram verse built around a series of missing words of which each differs from its predecessor by a single letter. The last word of the series contrasts in meaning with the first. Here is a nursery rhyme redone as a doublet:

SOLOMON GRUNDY

Solomon Grundy, Monday ****,
Tuesday orphaned, lone and ****,
Wednesday begged the **** relent,
Thursday 'neath his **** still bent,
Friday on the **** fell ill,
Saturday **** and signed his will.
Sunday final rites were said:
Solomon Grundy, he was ****.

> The missing words: born, lorn, Lord, load, road, read, dead.

Ormonym

Verbatim, the language quarterly, defines "ormonym" as "a verbal pair of charade sentences, as 'some others I've seen' and 'some mothers I've seen.' " Here the verbal pair is a verbal quartet.

WANTED: AN UNDERSTANDING

Insinuate
That you, as I, impatient moan,
Nor longer can (so tumid grown
In breath, in blood, in pore, in pate,
In sinew) wait!

Vow you've nipped apples of your own
In sin! (You ate
Your share, I'm bound!) Admit it, mate!—
In sin you wait.

Homonym Couplet

Words that sound alike but have a different spelling and meaning are homonyms. You are supposed to guess the homonyms indicated by asterisks in the following couplets:

1.

Dammed be that beast who, as he ***** on others,
Gives ****** to God, and ***** all beasts be brothers.

2.

Say, **** man in thy ***** cot,
Art ****** pleased with thy lowly lot?

3.

I met a wise antelope, born in a zoo;
And I wish that I knew what that *** *** ****.

> 1. Preys, praise, prays.
> 2. Holy, holey, wholly.
> 3. New, gnu, knew.

ESPYramids

In ESPYramids, another variant of the anagram verse, the first missing word consists of one letter. An added letter makes the next word in the sequence, and the accumulation continues throughout the verse, letters being rearranged as required to make each new word. Or the process may be reversed, going from a long word down. An ESPYramid:

JUST BRAGGING, REALLY

Though *, well gone ** ***, may ****,
''O tyrant Death, where is thy *****?''
The ****** of wicked things I've done
Makes ******* out my sins no fun.
There's but a ******** chance at best
That I will pass my final test.
For all my *********, I've mounting
Concern about that Last Accounting.

The missing words: I, in, gin, sing, sting, string, sorting, sporting, posturing. The verse in the clear:

Though I, well gone in gin, may sing,
''O tyrant Death, where is thy sting?''
The string of wicked things I've done
Makes sorting out my sins no fun.
There's but a sporting chance at best
That I will pass my final test.
For all my posturing, I've mounting
Concern about that Last Accounting.

TO AN IDIOT WHO SEES THE BEST IN EVERYTHING

Would * saw proof of God's restraint
** rank defects by Him deviced!—
In ***, saw gold!—in ****, saw *****!—
A ****, ** daub of mud and sand!—
** *****, a treasure underpriced!—
Plain ******, ** errant atoms!—and
* ******, ** every **********!

The missing words: I; in; tin; snit; saint; star; in; In trash; charts, in; A Christ, in; Antichrist. The verse in the clear:

Would *I* saw proof of God's restraint
In rank defects by Him deviced!—
In tin, saw gold!—in snit, saw saint!—
A star, in daub of mud and sand!—
In trash, a treasure underpriced!—
Plain charts, in errant atoms!—and
A Christ, in every Antichrist!

Pangrammic Couplet

A pangram is a passage containing all twenty-six letters of the alphabet with a minimum of repetitions. As the number of letters shrinks, it becomes increasingly difficult to create a sensible line, and there are few comprehensible pangrams of fewer than twenty-eight letters. ''The quick brown fox jumps over the lazy dog,'' used as a touch-typing exercise, has thirty-five. It is almost impossible to create a sensible verse in that brief a compass. This pangram verse has seventy letters:

GOD BE HIS JUDGE

God be his judge: that passive, zealous Quaker
Who first yields Country, Kindred next; then Maker.

Univocalic Verse

A univocalic verse restricts itself to a single vowel, in this case *e:*

BLESS THESE SHEEP

Blessed Shepherd,
Bless these sheep;
Bless the shepherdess.
Gentle the bell-
wether keep;
Shelter send them,
Send them sleep;
Send them blessedness.

Lipogrammatic Verse

A lipogram bars entry to some one of the five vowels. But that does not mean, as you will see in three of the four verses below, that the *sound* of the vowel has to be forgone.

No A:

My weight, sir, you must not survey.
No, weigh me not—no weigh, no weigh.

No E:

Said Ann, "Kiss not, sir—any
Would quickly turn to many."
And all that happy night
I found that Ann was right.

No I:

Why doth the eyeless fellow cry? . . .
Would you not cry, had you no eye?

No U:

A needless vowel this—it's heard
E'en when not written in a word,
As in *eschew, kerchoo,* and *who;*
And *drew, anew,* and *interview.*
I now declare this vowel moot,
And ban it from the alphaboot.

Acrostic Verse

An acrostic verse is one in which certain letters, read in sequence, form a name, motto, or message. Though the acrostic letters are usually the first in each line, they may be anywhere in it, so long as the pattern is consistent. The acrostic below is a holiday greeting.

NOW, A LITTLE WHILE

Now, a little while,
From the care and cark,
Something like a smile
Shimmers in the dark.

Zephyr's scented art
  Dwindles rime and snow;
In a melted heart,
  Softly, flowers grow.

Joy, a moment now,
  Thumps old Sorrow's side;
Under festive bough
  Nemesis has died.

Brief, by iron laws,
  Though this magic be,
Unbeliever, pause:
  Pagan, bend your knee.

Zest as keen as this
  Pricks the sullen soul;
Vast polarities
  Blend in vaster whole.

Mark—the night is through.
Memory must do.

(You could waste a deal of time looking for the key here, but once you know it the message is simple to decipher. Simply replace the first letter of each line with the letter that precedes it in the alphabet, and read down; you have MERRY CHRISTMAS TO YOU ALL.)

Words, not letters, are the acrostic units in the verse below.

FORECAST: CHILLY

Time befriends
  For brief space—
Warm days sends;
  Clothes in grace

Man and maid.
  This I wot:
Looks must fade,
  Like or not.

One is not
  Long here, chums;
Cold from hot,
  Winter comes.

(If you take the first word of each line one after another, they read: TIME FOR WARM CLOTHES, MAN: THIS LOOKS LIKE ONE LONG COLD WINTER.)

Limerick with Palindrome

A palindrome is a passage that reads the same from left to right or right to left. Some fanatics have written palindromes pages long, generally conveying little except perhaps a mood. In this limerick, the palindrome takes up only the last line.

PASSION'S A PERSONAL PERCEPTION

Meg's fashion in passion, though warm, 'll
Strike some as a trifle too formal.
  In the midst of a bout
  She's been heard to cry out,
"La, Mr. O'Neill, lie normal!"

Abbreviation Verse

THE MRS. KR. MR. (A ROUND)

The Mrs. kr. Mr.
Then how her Mr. kr.!
He kr. kr. kr.
Until he raised a blr.
The blr. killed his Mrs.
Then how he mr. krs.!
He. mr. mr. mr.
Until he kr. sr.
He covered her with krs.
Till she became his Mrs.
The Mrs. kr. Mr.
(and so on and on)

Digital Verse

A digital verse replaces suitable words or syllables with digits:

UP-AND-DOWN COUNTING SONG

Up   Dear ewe, dear lamb, I've *1* thee; we
        Shall *2*tle through the fields together.
      With *3*d and pipe we'll jubilee;
      We'll gambol back and *4*th in glee;
      If *5* thy heart, I'll bellow, "Whee!"
        However *6* the weather.
      In *7*th heaven I with thee
      Shall culmin*8* our ecstasy;
      Dear ewe be*9*, thou'rt tied to me,
        And *10*der is the tether.

Down   Yet I confess, I *10*d to see
        (When *9* no more am certain whether
      This herb we *8* doth still agree—
      Somehow it tastes less *7*ly)
      That class*6* sense says thou shouldst flee
        (If *5* agreed) to new bellwether,
      With him to *4*age. It may be,
      From oath *3*leased, love grows more free—
      Although (*2* change my simile)
        It's shrunk to *1* pin-feather.

Alphabetic verse

The first line of an alphabetical verse starts with A, the second with B, and so on through the twenty-six letters. The verses are often lists—of flowers, say, or beasts, rivers, countries—and in some of the more difficult examples several items are named to a line, each with the same opening letter. (In the example below, check the second word rather than the first in each indented line.)

THE ALPHABETIC CIRCUS WHERE THE BEASTS ALL SIT AND RHYME

I'll meet you at the circus where the beasts all sit and rhyme;
The keepers sing in sonnets, and admission is a dime.
   The Addis, a skink, can make lepers feel fine;
   The Balisaur, badger, is nosed like a swine;

The *Chil,* or the Indian kite, is a hawk;
The *Dikkop*'s a curlew with dikkopy squawk;
The *Essling*'s a salmon that isn't full-grown;
The *Fitchet*'s a polecat you don't want to own;
The *Gundi*'s a rodent as long as your hand;
The *Hassar*'s a catfish that walks on the land;
The *Inia*'s seven feet long—and a whale;
The *Jako*'s a parrot, and gray beak to tail;
The *Koi* is a carp from a Japanese bay;
The *Lindo*'s a tanager, bright as the day;
The *Maha* is monkey and deer—two in one;
The *Naja*'s a serpent that kills just for fun;
Orignal's a moose, with great antlers like saws;
The *Pia*'s a rabbit-like creature that gnaws;
The *Quica*'s a possum that sighs in its sleep;
The *Rosella*'s a parrakeet, also a sheep;
The *Simbil*'s a bronzy-backed stork with white belly;
The *Tua*'s a bird that eats honey and jelly;
The *Urva*'s a mongoose, the crab-eating kind;
The *Vison*'s a mink with fur coats on its mind;
The *Wou-wou*'s a gibbon that calls out ''Wow-wow;''
The *Xerus,* a squirrel, resides on a bough;
The *Yabu*'s a pony that's bred for hard wear;
Zyzzogeton, a leaf hopper, ends the affair.
I'll meet you at the circus where the beasts all sit and rhyme;
The keepers sing in sonnets, and admission is a dime.

Parthenogenetic Verse

Some words contain briefer near-equivalents within themselves, as in the instances that follow:

WORDS IN LABOR

I met some swollen words one day,
   As full of roe as sturgeons;
For certain in a family way,
   Yet innocent as virgins.

Parthenogenesis, they swore,
   Had stocked their inner shelves,
And all those nascent words in store
   Were carbons of themselves.

Lo! when at last their babies came,
   They were indeed the spit
Of their mamás; each given name
   Was ample proof of it:

For *Aberrate* did *Err* produce,
   And *Slithered* mothered *Slid,*
And *Utilize* gave suck to *Use,*
   And *Cut* was *Curtail*'s kid.

The child of *Jocularity*
   Was aptly christened *Joy,*
While *Masculine*'s was instantly
   Named *Male,* as fits a boy.

Transgression called her daughter *Sin*,
    And *Matches'* child was *Mates;*
Container's twins were *Can* and *Tin,*
    And *Prattles'* wee one, *Prates.*

So *Rascal*'s from *Rapscallion* born,
    So *Rules* from *Regulates;*
What babe, as *Rest* from *Respite*'s torn,
    Vacates Evacuates?

Now *Calumnies* is nursing *Lies;*
    Encourage, Urge doth hug;
Rage safe in arms of *Rampage* lies,
    And *Struggle* mothers *Tug.*

The letters of the shorter italicized words above are drawn from the longer ones, and appear in the same order. Below, letters from words are juggled to make shorter ones of different meaning.

EVE'S DREAM

In your demeanor there's a dream, dear friend,
    That leads to sorrow. Dreams hold something sad:
In dream, a part of Eden is Eden's end,
    And part of Adam is mad.

Demeanor—dream
Dreams—sad
Eden—end
Adam—mad

IN-RIDDLE

I was recently warned by a girl in Algeria
    There was peace in Hepaticae, war in Wisteria.
I put her in halter, that girl in Algeria;
    She wasn't insane, but she was in hysteria.

Algeria, girl
Hepaticae, peace
Wisteria, war
Halter, her
Hysteria, she

Symbols and Signs

Some signs and symbols are given exact equivalents in words. These can be fitted into verses easily enough, as you will see from the example below. Whether the effort is worthwhile is another question.

I LOVE YOU TO ∞ (±A°)

I am ♂ and you are ♀;
Amorous war shall rage between us—
War in which, as ♂, my *f*
Is to orbit toward ♂
While ℛ you pretend,
And ☊ to my end.
A ♀ knows dissatisfaction
A ⇌
Since (as always in these wars)

♀ → at last to ♂:
My Σ of love you'll give again
× eight or ten.

(Many dictionaries have lists of signs and symbols
with definitions. Just in case yours does not, here is the
above verse with the symbols translated.)

I LOVE YOU TO INFINITY (PLUS OR MINUS A DEGREE)

I am Mars and you are Venus;
Amorous war shall rage between us—
War in which, as male, my function
Is to orbit toward conjunction,
While reluctance you pretend,
And opposition to my end.
A female knows dissatisfaction
A reversible reaction
Since (as always in these wars)
Venus yields at last to Mars;
My sum of love you'll give again
Multiplied by eight or ten.

TYPESETTING TARRADIDDLE

Friend John, whose (:) was removed,
When asked why he had lately proved
So free of caution and of fear,
Said, "I've no (*), my dear."

A schwa, indicated in dictionaries by ∂, is a vowel so unstressed that it loses its identity of sound:

THE SUSURRANT SCHWA

The ∂ on his diurn∂l rounds
Is min∂s all but min∂r sounds;
Yet may, phonet∂c∂sts ∂gree
Transmit a wide v∂ri∂ty
Of aud∂ble ph∂nom∂na:
A∂, E∂, I∂, O∂ . . .
U∂.

Acronyms in Verse

Many tantalizing acronyms (words formed of initial letters) can be matched in rhyme, but a sizable number cannot. It seems a shame that low poets cannot rhyme SNAFU (Situation Normal, All Fucked-Up); or SUBFU (Situation Unchanged, Still Fucked-Up); or TARFU (Things Are Really Fucked-Up); or SAPFU (Surpassing All Previous Fuck-Ups). Of the acronyms in the fuck-up team that have come to my attention, only FUBB (Fucked-Up Beyond Belief) lends itself to conventional rhyme:

The Lord said, "Stop complaining, bub;
Your situation's normal: FUBB."

Some acronyms were not eligible for my rhyming list because they match only mosaic rhymes. It takes two words, for instance, to rhyme POTUS (President of the United States):

> The opposition candidate
>   Reviles the current POTUS
> And calls the union's normal state
>   "The mess this POTUS got us."

But many acronyms do make standard rhymes—the Federal Register alone must contain scores of them. The fact is that I did not think of making a special search for acronyms until the book was almost ready to be set in type. I apologize.

Grammar Verse

Grammar, a subject larded with oddities and vagaries, offers fine resource material for light poetry (though perhaps one should avoid writing grammar verses when in a tense mood).

E PLURIBUS UNUM

The spelling of certain words ending in *s* does not change between singular and plural. For instance:

> The drunken Species homeward reels,
> Or reel; it sets the mind ajar
> That species is and Species are.
>
> A Congeries of conger eels
> Is either are or is a bunch;
> Are either is or are for lunch.
>
> A Shambles of new-slaughtered seals
> Is either are or is deplorable;
> Are either is or are abhorrable.
>
> No Kudos for this verse, one feels,
> Is either are or is in view;
> Nor is, are, it, he, she, they, due.

THE ACTIVE AND THE PASSIVE VOICE

> One acts, one's acted on. (I ment-
>   ion this re subjects of a sent-
> ence.) Subjects that commit an act
>   Are Male. This need not mean attract-
> ive (no!) but *prominent*,
>   With bulging Biceps; it's a fact
> That virile symbols make a dent
>   In ladies who enjoy a gent.
>   *Wherefore rejoice,*
> O Subjects of the Active Voice!
>
> Not so the subject of the Pass-
>   ive Voice; she is not corded round with mass-
> ive muscles, being of the lact-
>   ic or mammalian sort, well stacked,
> And virgin—till, like any lass,
>   She's acted on with her consent.
>   *Wherefore rejoice,*
> O Subjects of the Passive Voice!

SINGULAR SINGULARS, PECULIAR PLURALS

How singular some old words are!
I know two with *no* singular:
Agenda, marginalia, both
Are always plural, 'pon my oath.*

The opposite's the case to greet us
In *propaganda* and *coitus;*
Upon these never sets the sun,
And yet of each there's only one.
Phantasmagoria, likewise,
Pervades, yet never multiplies.

Strata pluralizes *stratum;*
Ultimata, ultimatum;
Why are *nostrums* then not *nostra?*
Why speak I not then from *rostra?*
Thus my *datum* grows to *data,*
My *erratum* to *errata.*

Child, put this on your next agenda:
Pudendum's half of two *pudenda.*

ALTHOUGH INFORMAL SPEECH IS FREE (A RONDEL)

Although informal speech is free,
   It isn't quite as free as air.
You *must* not say: ''This here''; ''That there'';
   ''I don't need nothing''; ''Maybe me

And him can come''; ''When we was three'';
   ''He don't.'' . . . You *must*n't! Don't you *dare!*—
Although informal speech is free,
   It isn't quite as free as air.

''Now you have did it!'' *must* not be,
   And ''irregardless'' gets the air.
''He done''; ''I seen''—another pair

To sweep away with the debris
(Although informal speech is free).

TRIOLET IN PRAISE OF AIN'T

My tongue can't handle 'amn't I'—
   I opt instead for 'ain't.'
Though 'am I not' is worth a try,
My tongue can't handle 'amn't I,'
And though I am a rugged guy,
   'Aren't I' makes me faint.
My tongue can't handle 'amn't I'—
   I opt instead for 'ain't.'

---

*But *agenda,* though plural in form, takes a singular verb.

ON THE CORRECT USE OF LIE AND LAY

Lie down once more where once we kissed,
    While I the laws of lie and lay
Lay down. Lie where we lay—and list,
    Here where you lay and lied, dear Kay;
Lie down once more where once we kissed.

Where with a hundred lads you'd lain,
    You swore to lie with me for aye.
You laid sweet ambush to my brain:
    You lay; lied; laid one more lad prey
Where with a hundred lads you'd lain.

GRAMMATICAL USAGE FOR STOMPERS

When stomping victims in a mugging,
    Attack the proper zone:
The belly if the victim's *supine,*
    The spine if he is *prone.*

GRAMMAR IN EXTREMIS

The vows that I exchanged with she
Were broken soon by both of we.
(The sacred love of you and I
May also wither by-and-by.)

    (The third line of the above verse is from a prize-winning poem printed in the Pittsburgh Press.)

Macaronic Verse

A macaronic is a verse, like this one, that stirs two or more languages together for the fun of it:

QUESTION DE FOI

An aging Paris *avocat*
    (An atheist, *bien entendu*),
        When asked about his point of view
On birthday number *soixante-trois,*
    Replied, "I find that *plus en plus*
        Je ne crois pas
            Que je ne crois pas."

Here is the simple English of it, with a rhyming change in the last three lines:

A QUESTION OF FAITH

An aging lawyer of Paree,
    To atheism long inclined,
        When asked if he had changed his mind
On reaching birthday sixty-three,
    Said, "I increasingly perceive
        That I don't believe
            That I don't believe."

This is not exactly a macaronic, but it contains the first words that used to be taught to students of Latin:

A CLASSICAL EDUCATION

The Latin teacher need not explicate
Amo, amas
To Latin students who will conjugate
After class.

Caution: Identicals Do Not Rhyme

In preparing *Words to Rhyme With*, I compared my word lists ad nauseam with those in comparable books, and am grateful for valuable entries that I might have missed otherwise. It was puzzling, however, to find that many rhyming dictionaries list identicals as if they were rhymes. Rhymes are not identicals; they are terminal sounds, beginning with an accented vowel, that are preceded by different consonantal sounds, or by a consonant in one case and none in the other. Hundreds of words end in *-phobia*, for instance, but they are included in this book only because of the existence of one rhyming word, *obeah*, meaning "a kind of voodoo religion once common in the British West Indies, or a priest of it." Scores of words end in *-lagnia*, which means erotic arousal, but they do not appear here because *-lagnia* has no rhyme.

One of my favorite handbooks for rhymesters points out that its list contains the following words that "have no rhyming mates." But it does not explain why, that being the case, the words are in the list at all:

aitch, H	fugue	swoln
bilge	gulf, engulf	sylph
bulb	month	torsk
coif	morgue	twelfth
culm	peart	plagued, unplagued
cusp	poulp	warmth
doth	scarce	wharves
film	spoilt	wolf
		wolves

(It is even more curious that this same list of unrhymables includes other words that in fact do rhyme—among them *avenge*, which rhymes with *Stonehenge*; *bourne*, which in one accepted pronunciation rhymes with *mourn* and in another with *horn*; *forge*, which rhymes with *gorge*; *lounge*, which rhymes with *scrounge*; *mauve*, which rhymes with *rove*; *porch*, which rhymes with *torch*; *pork*, which rhymes with *fork*; *rouge*, which rhymes with *gamboge*; and *sauce*, which rhymes with *toss*.

(A recent rhyming dictionary aimed especially at lyricists similarly lists legitimate rhyming words as unrhymables. Among them are *chaos*, which rhymes with *Laos*; *donkey*, which rhymes with *honky*; *obese*, which rhymes with *niece*; *torture*, which rhymes with *scorcher*; *roguish*, which rhymes with *voguish*; *chartreuse*, which rhymes with *Betelgeuse*; *consummate*, which rhymes with *grummet*; *coffin*, which rhymes with *dauphin* (and, according to dictionaries which treat the *i* as a schwa, with *often* and *soften* as well); *cuckold*, which rhymes with *chuckled*; *ogre*, which rhymes with *maugre* (archaic in some senses and obsolete in others, but absolutely valid); and even *moldy*, which must bring *golden oldy* to the mind of many lyricists.

(Many more unrhymables that in fact rhyme might be cited, but these suffice for my point: if you are doubtful, check. Remember that many words have more than one correct pronunciation, and that any pronunciation accepted by any standard dictionary is legitimate. If you find me saying a word has no legitimate rhyme, make me prove it.)

Back to identicals. Here are some from just one rhyming dictionary—and a superior dictionary, at that:

BAL'AN-SING	balancing, counterbalancing, overbalancing, unbalancing
BANGKMENT	bankment, embankment
BEZLER	bezzler, embezzler
DONA	belladonna, donna, Madonna, prima donna
DUKTIL	ductile, inductile, productile
DUK'TER-Ē	deductory, inductory, introductory, manuductory, reproductory
DŪSMENT	deducement, inducement, producement, superinducement
EM'I-NENS	eminence, preeminence, supereminence
ENTRANS	entrance, entrants
EPIK	epic, monoepic, orthoepic
ETHNIK	ethnic, holoethnic
FĀ'SED-LĒ	barefacedly, shamefacedly
FĀ'SI-ENT	facient, calefacient, liquefacient
FOOT'ED-NES	bigfootedness, duckfootedness, clubfootedness, splayfootedness
FURMANS	affirmance, disaffirmance, confirmance, reaffirmance
FUR'MA-TIV	affirmative, disaffirmative, confirmative, reaffirmative
GASTRIK	digastric, gastric, hypogastric, perigastric
GRĒ'A-BL	agreeable, disagreeable
HAR'TED-LĒ	bigheartedly, downheartedly, hardheartedly, kindheartedly, lightheartedly, lionheartedly, simpleheartedly
HAR'TED-NES	bigheartedness, downheartedness, hardheartedness, kindheartedness, lightheartedness, lionheartedness, simpleheartedness
HER'I-TANS	disinheritance, heritance, inheritance
HĒ'SIV-LĒ	adhesively, inhesively, cohesively
JEKTMENT	dejectment, ejectment, injectment, projectment, rejectment
JUJMENT	adjudgment, judgment, misjudgment, prejudgment, rejudgment
JUNGK'TIV-LĒ	adjunctively, disjunctively, conjunctively, subjunctively
KAL'I-BER	caliber, calibre, calabur, Excalibur
KARPAL	intercarpal, carpal, metacarpal
KLIV'I-TUS	acclivitous, declivitous, proclivitous
KON'SŪ-LAR	consular, non-consular, pro-consular, vice-consular
KOSTIK	caustic, costic
KRĒ'SHUN-AL	concretional, secretional
KUL'CHER-IST	agriculturalist, floriculturalist, horticulturalist, apiculturalist
KUM'BEN-SĒ	incumbency, decumbency, recumbency
KUMBENT	accument, decumbent, incumbent, procumbent, recumbent, superincumbent
KUR'ENT-LĒ	concurrently, currently, recurrently
KWIZ'I-TIV	acquisitive, disquisitive, inquisitive, uninquisitive
LAB'O-RĀT	elaborate, collaborate
LAT'ER-AL	collateral, quadrilateral, lateral, multilateral, plurilateral, unilateral
LEKTRIK	analectric, dielectric, electric, idiolectric
LIS'I-TUS	felicitous, solicitous
MĒ'DI-ĀT	immediate, intermediate, mediate
MIS'I-BL	admissible, permissible

MORFĒ	geomorphy, metamorphy, zoomorphy
NACH′ER-AL	natural, preternatural, supernatural, unnatural
NIF′I-SENT	magnificent, munificent
NOUNS′MENT	announcement, denouncement, pronouncement, renouncement
PARTMENT	apartment, department, impartment, compartment
PASH′UN-IT	dispassionate, impassionate, incompassionate, compassionate, passionate
PET′A-LUS	apetalous, petalous, polypetalous
POS′I-TR	depositor, expositor, compositor, ovipositor, repositor, transpositor
PRAN′DI-AL	anteprandial, postprandial, prandial
PRĒ′SHI-ĀT	appreciate, depreciate
PRES′E-DEN-SĒ	antiprecedency, precedency (these words do *not* rhyme with hesitancy, presidency)
PUB′LI-KAN	publican, republican
PUGNANT	oppugnant, repugnant, unrepugnant
PUMIS	pomace, pumace, pumice
RAD′I-KAL	radical, sporadical, unradical
RĀ′DI-ĀT	erradiate, irradiate, radiate
RĒ′JEN-SĒ	regency, vice-regency
RĪPNES	deadripeness, overripeness, ripeness, underripeness
RUPSHUN	abruption, disruption, eruption, interruption, corruption
RUP′TIV-LĒ	disruptively, interruptively, corruptively
SEN′SHI-ENT	assentient, dissentient, insentient, consentient, presentient
SEP′SHUN-AL	exceptional, conceptional, unexceptional
SEP′TI-BL	acceptable, deceptible, perceptible, receptible, susceptible
SHAD′Ō-ING	foreshadowing, overshadowing, shadowing
SIK′LI-KAL	bicyclical, encyclical, cyclical
SIL′I-KA	basilica, silica
SIM′I-LĒ	dissimile, facsimile, simile
SIP′I-ENT	appercipient, desipient, incipient, insipient, percipient
SKRIP′SHUN-AL	inscriptional, conscriptional, transcriptional
SKRIPTIV	descriptive, prescriptive, circumscriptive
SKUCHUN	escutcheon, scutcheon, unscutcheon
SPIK′Ū-US	inconspicuous, conspicuous, perspicuous, transpicuous
SPONDENT	despondent, co-respondent, correspondent
STRUKCHER	constructure, structure, substructure, superstructure
TAG′O-NIZM	antagonism, protagonism
TEM′PO-RAL	atemporal, extemporal, supertemporal, temporal
TEN′Ū-ĀT	attenuate, extenuate, tenuate
THER′A-PĒ	autotherapy, balneotherapy, hydrotherapy, radiotherapy, psychotherapy, theotherapy
TŌ′TAL-ER	teetotaler, totaler
TRAN′SI-TIV	intransitive, transitive
TRENCHMENT	entrenchment, retrenchment, trenchment
VELUP	develop, envelop, underdevelop
VIN′SI-BL	evincible, invincible, convincible
VĪ′TA-LĪZ	devitalize, revitalize, vitalize
VUR′SI-TĒ	adversity, diversity, perversity, university
VUR′TIZ-MENT	advertisement, divertissement

You will find none of these identicals in my rhyming list. I hope, though I cannot guarantee, that you will find no others either.

How to Use the List of Rhyming Words

The Sets, Subsets, and Categories

The rhyming words ahead are divided into three sets: single, or masculine rhymes (accented on the last syllable); double, or feminine rhymes (accented on the syllable before the last); and triple, or dactylic, rhymes (accented usually on the syllable before the syllable before the last, but occasionally even on the one before that).

Each of the three sets is divided into five subsets, one for each vowel—A, E, I, O, and U.

The subsets are broken down into phonetically alphabetized categories, with headings. These category headings are the *mother rhymes*.

The Subcategories

Each mother rhyme broods over a clutch of subcategories. If the mother rhyme happens to be itself one of a rhyming set, it is relisted as the first of the subcategories, this way:

Ā

Ā   a, aye, DNA, dossier, habitué, Coué, couturier, roturier, roué

The other subcategories then follow in the alphabetical order of their opening sounds:

BĀ   bay, bey, Bombay, dapple bay, disobey, flambé, obey
BLĀ   criblé, seinsemblers
BRĀ   brae, bray

and so on.

Note: a mother rhyme that is also one of a rhyming set is always the first subcategory to be listed, whatever its opening sound:

UNDER

UNDER   down under, hereunder, thereunder, under
BLUNDER   blunder
BUNDER   bunder
DUNDER   dunder

and so on.

The Pronunciation and Order of Vowels

The usual sounds of stressed vowels are indicated as follows:

Ā	as in	*gate*
Â	as in	*air*
A	as in	*pat*
Ä	as in	*part, swaddle*
Ē	as in	*beet*

E	as in	*bet*
Ī	as in	*kite*
I	as in	*kit*
ÎR	as in	*ear*
Ō	as in	*coat*
Ô	as in	*caught*
O	as in	*hot*
ŌŌ	as in	*chew*
OO	as in	*foot*
OU	as in	*out*
Ū	as in	*cute*
U	as in	*cut, curt*

(A slightly different phonetic system is employed for the glossary. A guide to it appears there.)

Ū, ŌŌ

Ū in the rhyming syllables of some words has the sound of Ū, in other words the sound of ŌŌ, and in still other words either sound. Dictionaries disagree, moreover, on which words fit these categories. To add to the confusion, Ū is pronounced YŌŌ, and is so itself a rhyme for ŌŌ. Rather than give two listings for all the words which may be pronounced either way, I list each in the category which seems most appropriate to me (sometimes in both), and refer the reader from one category to the other.

The Order of Categories and Subcategories

Within each set of vowels—A, E, I, O, or U—the category headings, or mother rhymes, are listed in the alphabetical order of the *closing* consonant sound of the heading: Ā, ĀB, AB, ÄB, ABD, ACH, ACHT, etc. The order of the subcategory headings is determined by the *opening* sound of the rhyming syllable: BĀ, BLĀ, BRĀ, etc.

Headings Are Spelled Phonetically

Sound and spellings in the headings need not correspond. The word *precise*, for instance, is listed in the category ĪS and the subcategory SĪS, because though the rhyming syllable -*cise* begins with the *letter c*, it begins with the *sound s*. The word *colt* appears in the category ŌLT and the subcategory KŌLT; in this case, the *c* is pronounced like a *k*.

The Spelling of Consonants in the Headings of Categories and Subcategories

The phonetic spelling	The consonant	Sounded as in
B	**b**	*b*oy, am*b*ivalent
BL	**bl**	*bl*ack
BR	**br**	*br*and, am*br*osia
CH	**ch**	*ch*art, en*ch*ant
D	**d**	*d*ay, a*d*ore
F	**f, ph**	*f*amily, a*ph*asis
G	**g**	*g*ood, a*g*o
GL	**gl**	*gl*orious, a*gl*ey
GR	**gr**	*gr*eat, di*gr*ess
H	**h**	*h*appy, ab*h*or
HW	**wh**	*wh*ite, a*wh*ile

J	g, j	in*g*est, *j*est
K	c, ch, k	*c*at, al*ch*emy, *k*itten
KL	chl, cl, kl	*chl*orine, *cl*atter, *kl*ieg
KR	chr, cr, kr	*Chr*istian, *cr*est, *kr*aken
KW	qu	*qu*it, re*qu*ite
L	l	*l*engthy, a*l*low
M	m	*m*ayhem, ad*m*issible
N	GN, KN, MN, N	*gn*ostic, *kn*owledge, *mn*e-monics, *n*othing
P	p	*p*assage, re*p*el
PL	pl	im*pl*acable, *pl*easant
PR	pr	*pr*ominent, im*pr*ovident
R	r	*r*affish, meteo*r*ology
S	c, ps, s	re*c*eipt, *ps*ychology, *s*ong
SH	ch, s, sh	para*ch*ute, in*s*ure, *sh*ame
SK	sc, sk	*sc*out, *sk*irt
SKR	scr	*scr*ibe, sub*scr*iption
SKW	squ	*squ*iggle
SM	sm	*sm*attering
SN	sn	*sn*eer
SP	sp	*sp*acious, in*sp*issate
ST	st	*st*ill
STR	str	*str*ong
T	pht, pt, t	*pht*hisic, *pt*armigan, *t*oil
TH (as in thin)	th	*th*in, a*th*irst
TH (as in then)	th	*th*en, *th*ese
THR	thr	*thr*eaten
THW	thw	*thw*ack
TR	tr	*tr*easure, en*tr*eat
TW	tw	*tw*addle, be*tw*een
V	v	*v*arious, in*v*est
W	w	*w*on, *o*ne
Y	y	*y*oung, un*y*ielding
Z	z, s, ss, x	*z*eal, re*s*olve, di*ss*olve, e*x*ert
ZH	g	in*g*enue

Order of Words in a Subcategory

Since the rhyming element provides no guide for allocating words within any one subcategory—all the words being identical in that respect—their position is established instead by their opening sounds, as here:

> **BELĒ** belly, *gorbelly, whitebelly,* ca-sus belli, *potbelly, redbelly, shadbelly, slowbelly,* tenter-belly, yellowbelly*

---

*Words in the rhyming list may be italicized if the vowel sound is not an exact match for others in the category. In the ŌRTH category, for instance, *fourth* is italicized because it would appear under ŌRTH if there were any other ŌRTH words. Under URV, *hors d'oeuvres* is italicized as an incorrect pronunciation. More commonly, words are italicized when the normal stress has been either advanced or put back by one or two syllables to force a match with others in the same category. The word snowdrift, for instance, is correctly accented on the penultimate, but may be made a single rhyme by pushing the accent forward:

> On winter evenings don't get squiffed:
> You may wind up in a *snowdrift.*

Make such metric liberties the exception rather than the rule.

I have used initial letters to facilitate the location of rhyming words when a subcategory runs over ten or so entries. It may be useful to give an example of how the system works:

> **FĀST** *A* angel-faced, apple-faced, *B* baby-faced, *baldfaced, bare-faced, bold-faced, BR* brazen-faced, *D* defaced, dirty-faced, *dish-faced, doughfaced, E* ef-faced, *F* faced, furrow-faced, *FR* freckle-faced, *H hard-faced,* hatchet-faced, *horse-faced, HW whey-faced, J* Janus-faced, *KL clean-faced, L lean-faced,* lily-faced, *M* mottle-faced, *P pale-faced,* paper-faced, *pie-faced,* pickle-faced, pimple-faced, pippin-faced, pudding-faced, *pug-faced, PL* platter-faced, *plump-faced, R* refaced, *SH shame-faced, SM* smooth-faced, *smug-faced, T* tallow-faced, *two-faced, TR* triple-faced, *U* undefaced, unshamefaced, *V* vinegar-faced, *W* weasel-faced, wizen-faced

How to Locate Multi-Syllabled Words in a Subcategory

The rhyming element of a word establishes its category and subcategory, and its opening sound dictates its general position within the subcategory. But where a subcategory is a long one with long words, several of them may have the same opening sound. In that event, the specific position of a word depends on the overall sound of its non-rhyming part. Take these DĀSHUN words beginning with I:

> **I** infeudation, ingravidation, incommo-dation, intimidation, inundation, inval-idation

All six words begin with in- and end with -dation. Their sequence is determined by the opening sounds of the syllables in between: in*F*eudation, in*GR*avitation, in*K*ommodation, in*T*imidation, in*U*ndation, in*V*alidation.

Unstressed Vowels in the Phonetic Headings

A vowel that is unstressed but distinctly pronounced goes into the phonetic heading unchanged:

> **BRŌŌTISH**   brutish
> **DEDHED**   deadhead

Unstressed Vowels with Variant Pronunciations

When an unstressed vowel has a pronunciation not usually associated with it, the spelling of the heading changes accordingly:

> **ŪSIJ**   usage

Vowels That Substitute for Schwas

Many unaccented syllables are so lightly stressed that their vowel sound is indeterminate. The pronunciation of *mammary,* for instance, does not reveal whether the second vowel is an *a, e, i, o,* or *u.* Dictionaries indicate this vague sound by a schwa (∂). Instead of a schwa, a single handy vowel is used in each phonetic head or subhead of my rhyming list to represent that faint sound, even though it may be represented by different vowels in some of the words themselves. Suppose, for instance, that you are checking the word hobbit, and turn to OBIT. You will find

OBIT

(See **OBET**)

and under OBET there will be the subcategories

GOBET   gobbet
HOBET   hobbit

Similarly, if you look for *bodice* under ODIS, you will find

ODIS

(See **ODES**)

and, under ODES,

BODES   bodice
GODES   goddess

If a word ends in a faint vowel sound followed by -l, the vowel may be dropped from the phonetic listing altogether:

MODL

MODL   model
TODL   toddle

Plurals Formed by Adding -s or -es

The rhyming list seldom has categories confined to plurals formed by the addition of -s or -es, though such plurals appear as rhymes for other words.

Words Formed by the Addition of Suffixes

When words formed by adding the suffixes -ed, -er, -ful, -fully, -ing, -ish, -less, -let, -ment, or -ous to other words are not separately categorized, an entry directs the reader to the appropriate rhyme category to do his own suffixing.

Omission of Archaic -est and -eth as Suffixes

There are no separate listings of verbs with the archaic suffixes -est and -eth (runnest, runneth).

Other Omissions of Suffixed Words

With a few exceptions, there are no separate listings of words ending in the suffixes -like or -some, or of adjectives made superlative by the addition of -est.

A Passing Note on Pronunciation

Your dictionary on occasion gives several pronunciations for the same word; unless it adds a caveat, it accepts them all. The order in which they happen to appear is unimportant; after all, there is no way to avoid having one pronunciation or another come first. Some words therefore appear in more than one place in the rhyming list.

Unless italicized, all the rhyme sounds listed in this book are accepted by some standard dictionary.

Regional Accents

Pronunciation, especially in informal speech, varies from one locality to another. There are parts of the United States where any distinction between the sounds of *Mary, merry,* and *marry,* for instance, defies detection by the human ear. Such localisms are not included in this book; here, *Mary* rhymes with *airy, marry* with *tarry,* and *merry* with *very.* There is no reason not to use a local pronunciation as a rhyme, as long as you are aware of what you are doing; fine poets have done so. But you will generally be better off if you go by the dictionary.

Syllabification

In the list of single rhymes there is no need to divide category headings into syllables, since they have only one. Nor do I show the division between the two syllables in the headings of double rhymes, the emphasis being always on the first syllable; for rhyming purposes, the question of whether the second syllable happens to begin with a consonant or a vowel is irrelevant.

In the triple rhyme list, however, I do indicate syllabification; it would be confusing not to in, say, JELUSLĒ (jealously) or THROPIKAL (philanthropical). Here the rhyming emphasis is indicated by a (') following the accented syllable, and the other syllables are separated by (-): JEL'US-LĒ, THROP'I-KAL.

The words within categories are not syllabified or phoneticized; the rhyme has already been established, and to throw in phonetic markings would simply make the sledding harder for the reader.

Proper Names

I have used proper names sparingly as rhymes, and have tried (not altogether successfully) to confine myself to those of some historic, topical, or literary significance. I could not resist *Steven,* since it was the only rhyme for *even.* I also rhymed *Nilot* with *pilot* (a Nilot is a native of the Nile), and would have rhymed *hylism* with *Carlislism* if my wife had not put her foot down.

Italics

Imperfect rhymes are italicized in the list of rhyming words.

SINGLE RHYMES

(Words of one syllable, or words accented on
the final syllable. Also called *iambic*, or *masculine*, rhymes.)

Ā

Ā	A, aye, DNA, dossier, habitué, Coué, couturier, plié, roturier, roué
BĀ	bay, bey, Bombay, bombé, dapple bay, disobey, flambé, obey
BLĀ	criblé, seinsemblers
BRĀ	brae, bray
DĀ	*A* alackaday, Ascension Day, *B* bidet, *birthday, D* D-day, day, démodé, *doomsday, E* everyday, *F firstday, FR Friday, G* good-day, *H half-day, heyday, high-day,* holiday, *I* intraday, *J* Judgment Day, *KR* Christmas Day, *KW* quarter day, *L* Labor Day, lackaday, Lord's day, *M* market day, *Mayday, midday, N noonday, P payday, PL playday, S* settling-day, seventh-day, *someday,* sundae, *Sunday, T* today, *Tuesday, TH Thursday, TR* trysting-day, *W* wedding day, *weekday,* welladay, *Wednesday,* workaday, *workday,* working day, *Y* yesterday
DRĀ	dray
DYĀ	boulevardier
FĀ	buffet, café, fay, fey, coryphée, ofay, au fait, auto-da-fé, parfait, pousse-café, rechauffé, Santa Fe
FLĀ	flay, soufflé
FRĀ	affray, defray, frae, fray
GĀ	assagai, distingué, gay, *margay, nosegay,* toujours gai
GLĀ	agley, gley
GRĀ	dapple-gray, emigré, gray, hodden-gray, iron-gray, *lean-gray,* silver-gray
GWĀ	ngwee
HĀ	hae, hay, hey, hey-hey
HWĀ	whey
JĀ	*deejay,* jay, popinjay
KĀ	*B* Biscay, bouquet, *D* decay, *K* cay, communiqué, *KR* croquet, *M* manqué, *O* okay, *P* parquet, piquet, *R* risqué, roquet, *S* sobriquet, *T* tokay, tourniquet
KLĀ	bouclé, bouclée, clay, fire clay, pipe clay, roman à clef
KYĀ	perruquier

LĀ	*A* allay, *B* belay, Beaujolais, Bordelais, *D* delay, *F* forelay, forlay, *H* haole, *I* inlay, interlay, *K* cabriolet, kantele, coulée *L* lai, lay, *M Malay,* Mandalay, melee, mislay, *O* olé, outlay, overlay, *P* parlay, Pelée, pis-aller, pourparler, *R* Rabelais, relay, reveillé, rissolé, rokelay, roundelay, *U* underlay, *unlay, uplay, V* virelay, *W* waylay
MĀ	dismay, entremets, gamay, gourmet, consommé, lamé, macramé, may, May, resumé, Salomé
NĀ	acharné, déraciné, estaminet, Hogmanay, cloisonné, matinée, nae, nay, née, neigh, Dubonnet, massinet, raisonné
PĀ	dead pay, épée, épopée, Gaspé, coupé, mortpay, overpay, pay, prepay, repay, strathspey, Taipei, toupée, toupet, underpay
PLĀ	*B* byplay, *D* display, *endplay, F* fair play, *foreplay,* photoplay, foul play, fun play, *H* horse play, *I* interplay, *M* misplay, *O* overplay, *P* Passion play, *PL* play, *R* replay, *S* satyr play, *SKR screenplay, ST* stage play, *U* underplay, *W wordplay*
PRĀ	bepray, pray, prey, repray, unpray
PYĀ	passepied
RĀ	*A* array, *B* beray, beret, bewray, *D* disarray, *F* foray, *G* green beret, *H* hip-hip-hooray, hooray, hurray, *M* Monterey, moray, *MW* moiré, *P* purée, *R* ray, re, *S* soirée, *ST* sting ray, *X* x-ray
SĀ	*A* assay, *D* déclassé, divorcé, divorcée, *E* essay, *F* fiancé, fiancée, foresay, *G* gainsay, *GL* glacé, *H hearsay, PL* plissé, *L* lycée, *M* matelassé, missay, *N* naysay, *P* passé, per se, *PL* plissé, *PR* presay, *R* retroussé, *S* say, *soothsay, U* undersay, unsay
SHĀ	attaché, brochet, cachet, cliché, couchée, crochet,

	papier-maché, recherché, ricochet, sachet, sashay, shay, touché
SKRĀ	scray
SLĀ	bob sleigh, slay, sleigh, sley
SPĀ	spay, strathspey
SPLĀ	splay
SPRĀ	auto-spray, bespray, featherspray, respray, spray
STĀ	astay, *backstay, bobstay, forestay, jackstay, mainstay, outstay,* overstay, stay, *upstay*
STRĀ	astray, distrait, estray, stray, windlestrae
SWĀ	sway, swing and sway
TĀ	tay, paté, volupté, velouté
THĀ	Cathay, they
TRĀ	*ashtray,* betray, distrait, distray, entrée, estray, outré, portray, tray, trey
TYĀ	métier
VĀ	inveigh, convey, corvée, névé, oy vay, pavé, purvey, resurvey, survey, chevet
WĀ	*A* airway, archway, aweigh, *B* beltway, byway, *BR* breakway, bridleway, Broadway, *D* doorway, *DR* driveway, *E* expressway, entryway, *F fairway, footway, FR freeway, G* Galloway, *Galway, gangway, gateway,* getaway, *guideway, H halfway, hatchway, headway, highway, K* cableway, *causeway, cogway,* cutaway, *KL clearway, KR* crossway, *cruiseway, L leeway, M* midway, *Midway,* Milky Way, motorway, *N Norway, O* overweigh, *outway,* outweigh, *P* passageway, *pathway, R railway, roadway,* runaway, *runway, S seaway,* cycle way, *someway, subway, SK skidway, SL slipway, SP speedway,* spillway, *ST stairway,* steerageway, *sternway,* stowaway, *STR* straightaway, *straightway, T* takeaway, *tideway,* towaway, *TH* that-a-way, thereaway, *THR throughway, TR* tramway,

U underway, under way, underweigh, *W walkway,* waterway, way, wellaway, wey

YĀ atelier, employé, employée, espalier, grandgoussier, métayer, Montgolfier, Olivier, Parmentier, plumassier, Récamier, roturier, soigné, sommelier, chevalier, yea

ZĀ blasé, exposé, espasé, San José

ZHĀ negligee, protegé

Ä

Ä a, aa, ah

BÄ aba, baa, baah, bah, bas, *Casbah, Poobah,* sis-boom-bah

BLÄ blah

BRÄ algebra, bra, chapeaubras, vertebra

CHÄ cha-cha, cha-cha-cha

DÄ andromeda, da, dada, *houdah, howdah, purdah*

DRÄ clepsydra

FÄ apocrypha, do re mi fa, fa

FRWÄ sangfroid

FWÄ paté de foie

GÄ aga, budgereegah, Dégas, ga, *nougat*

GLÄ verglas

GRÄ paté de foie gras

HÄ aha, ha, ha-ha, taiaha

HWÄ Taniwha

KÄ abaca, basilica, Jataka, majolica, ka, replica, sciatica, silica

KLÄ éclat

KWÄ qua, quaa

LÄ *A* alala, *F* formula, *H* holla, *K* cabala, qabbalah, cupola, *L* la, lala, *N* nebula, *OO* oolala, *P* parabola, peninsula, pyrola, *R* ranula, *SP* spatula, sporabola, *T* tarantula, tarentola, *TR* tralala, *V viola*

MÄ *amah,* anathema, Aceldama, grandmamma, ma, maa, mama, mamma, palama, Panama, cinema

MWÄ moi

NÄ alumina, phenomena, guarana, quadrumana, na, nah, padsamana, prolegomena, retina

PÄ faux pas, n'est-ce-pas, oompah, pa, pah, papa, pas

PWÄ petits pois

RÄ *A* acara, *B* baccarat, *E* ephemera, et cetera, *H* Hegira, hurrah, *J* genera, *K* camera, carnivora, cholera, *L* last hurrah, *M* mandragora, *O* opera, *PL plethora, R* Ra, rah, rah-rah

SÄ sah, yassah, yessah

SHÄ padishah, *pasha,* shah

SHVÄ schwa

SKÄ ska

SPÄ spa

SWÄ peau de soie, soie

TÄ Al Fatah, automata, incognita, coup d'état, taffeta, t'a, ta, taa, Ptah, ta-ta

THÄ Golgotha

TRÄ orchestra

TWÄ patois

VÄ baklava

WÄ wa, waah, wah

YÄ ja, Jah, yah, yaya, yeah

ZÄ huzza

ZHWÄ bourgeois, joie

ĀB

BĀB babe, foster-babe, *scarebabe*

GRĀB outgrabe

LĀB astrolabe, cosmolabe

AB

AB abb, Joab, Moab

BAB bab, baobab

BLAB blab

BRAB brab

DAB bedab, dab, dhabb

DRAB drab

FAB fab, confab, prefab

FRAB frab

GAB baffle-gab, gab

GRAB grab

JAB jab

KAB cab, pedicab, taxicab

KRAB crab

LAB lab, *Skylab*

MAB mab, Mab

NAB knab, nab

RAB rab

SHAB shab

SKAB scab

SLAB slab

STAB stab

TAB *eartab,* tab

ÄB

BÄB wooer-bab

LÄB jelab

SKWÄB squab

SWÄB swab

WÄB jawab

(See **OB**)

ÄBD

SWABD swabbed

(See **OB,** add *-ed* where appropriate.)

ACH

BACH bach, batch

BRACH brach

HACH hatch, *crosshatch, nuthatch*

KACH catch, *seacatch*

KLACH kaffeeklatsch, coffee klatch

KRACH cratch

LACH latch, *potlatch,* unlatch

MACH match, mismatch, overmatch, rematch, shooting match, undermatch

NACH natch

PACH dispatch, *crosspatch,* patch, *tolpatch*

RACH rach, ratch

SKACH scatch

SKRACH scratch

SLACH slatch

SMACH smatch

SNACH snatch

TACH attach, detach, tache

THACH thatch

ÄCH

(See **OCH**)

ACHT

HACHT hatched

TACHT attached, detached, semi-detached

(See **ACH,** add *-ed* where appropriate.)

ĀD

ĀD ade, aid, aide, co-aid, *Band-Aid,* first-aid, *hand-*

aid, ginger-ade, lemonade, *limeade,* orangeade

BĀD bade, bayed, forbade, gambade, obeyed
BLĀD blade, Damascus blade, grass blade, *twayblade*
BRĀD abrade, abraid, braid, brayed, unbraid, upbraid
DĀD brandade
FĀD fade
FLĀD flayed, unflayed
FRĀD afraid, defrayed, unafraid
GĀD brigade, dragade, renegade
GLĀD everglade, glade, *moonglade*
GRĀD *A* aggrade, *B* Belgrade, *D* degrade, downgrade, *GR* grade, grayed, *P* palmigrade, *PL* plantigrade, *R* rectigrade, regrade, regrayed, retrograde, *S* Centigrade, *T* taligrade, tardigrade, *U* ungrayed
HĀD hade
HWĀD wheyed
JĀD bejade, jade
KĀD *A* alcaide, ambuscade, appliquéd, arcade, *B* barricade, *BL* blockade, *BR* brocade, *D* decade, decayed, *E* escalade, estacade, *F* falcade, *FR* frescade, *K* cade, cascade, cavalcade, cockade, Medicaid, *S* saccade, *ST* stockade
LĀD *A* accolade, allayed, *D* deep-laid, defilade, delayed, *E* enfilade, escalade, *F* fusillade, *GR* grillade, *I* inlaid, interlaid, *L* lade, laid, *M* marmalade, *O* overlaid, *P* parlayed, pistolade, *R* relade, relaid, relayed, *U* underlaid, unlade, unlaid
MĀD *B* barmaid, bondmaid, *BR* bridesmaid, *CH* chambermaid, *D* dairy maid, dismayed, *H* handmade, *handmaid,* homemade, *housemaid, M* made, maid, *mermaid,* meter maid, *milkmaid, N* newmade, nursemaid, *O* old maid, *P* pomade, *R* ready-made, remade, *S* sea maid, self-made, serving maid, *U* undismayed, unmade
NĀD *B* bastinade, *DR* dragonnade, *E* esplanade,

F fanfaronade, *FL* flanconnade, *G* gabionade, gasconade, *GR* grenade, *H* harlequinade, *K* cannonade, carbonade, carronade, cassonade, colonnade, cottonade, *L* lemonade, *M* marinade, *N* nayed, neighed, *P* panade, pasquinade, *PR* promenade, *S* serenade, citronade, *STR* strephonade
PĀD *A* apaid, *E* escapade, estrapade, *G* gallopade, *KR* croupade, *O* overpaid, *P* paid, postpaid, *PR* prepaid, *R* repaid, *U* underpaid, unpaid, unrepaid, wellpaid
PLĀD displayed, overplayed, plaid, played, underplayed, undisplayed, unplayed
PRĀD prayed, preyed, unprayed, unpreyed
RĀD *A* arrayed, *B* bewrayed, *D* disarrayed, *J* gingerade, *M* masquerade, *P* parade, *R* raid, rayed, *SH* charade, *T* tirade, *U* unarrayed, unrayed
SĀD *A* ambassade, assayed, *E* essayed, *GL* glacéed, glissade, *H* harquebusade, *KR* crusade, *P* palisade, passade, pesade, *T* torsade, *U* unassayed, unessayed
SHĀD crocheted, *eyeshade, nightshade,* overshade, ricocheted, *sunshade,* shade
SLĀD slade, sleighed
SPĀD spade, spayed, unspayed
SPLĀD splayed
SPRĀD besprayed, resprayed, sprayed, unsprayed
STĀD overstayed, stade, staid, stayed, unstaid
STRĀD balustrade, estrayed, strayed
SWĀD dissuade, overpersuade, persuade, repersuade, suede, swayed, unswayed
TĀD rodomontade, sautéed
THĀD they'd
TRĀD betrayed, fair trade, free trade, portrayed, retrad trade
VĀD evade, invade, conveyed, pervade, purveyed, surveyed
WĀD overweighed, reweighed, unweighed, wade, weighed

(See **Ā,** add *-ed* where appropriate.)

AD

AD A ad, add, *D* dyad, Dunciad, *DR* dryad, *E* ennead, *G* Gilead, *GW* gwynniad, *H* hamadryad, *I* Iliad, *J* jeremiad, *K* chiliad, Columbiad, *L* Lusiad, *M* myriad, *N* Naiad, *O* ogdoad, Olympiad, oread, *R* re-add, superadd, *TR* triad
BAD aubade, bad, bade, forbade, *Sinbad,* unforbade
BLAD blad
BRAD brad
CHAD Chad
DAD alidad, aoudad, Baghdad, bedad, dad, granddad, Trinidad
FAD fad
GAD begad, egad, gad
GLAD glad
GRAD grad, Leningrad, Petrograd, undergrad
HAD Galahad, had
KAD cad
KLAD *E* y-clad, *H* heavy-clad, *I* ironclad, ivy-clad, *KL* clad, *M* mail-clad, *moss-clad, P* pine-clad, *U* unclad, *W* winter-clad
LAD lad, reculade, cephalad
MAD hebdomad, *nomad,* mad
PAD *footpad,* helipad, *kneepad,* launching pad, pad, shoulder pad, tongue pad
PLAD plaid
RAD rad
SAD *dorsad, hexad,* sad
SHAD shad
SKAD scad
TAD *heptad, octad,* tad
TRAD trad

ÄD

ÄD ahed, ohed and ahed, oohed and ahed
BÄD baaed, aubade
HÄD jihad
KÄD falcade
KWÄD quad
LÄD ballade, remolade, remoulade, roulade
MÄD pomade, chamade
NÄD esplanade, promenade
PÄD gallopade
RÄD hurrahed, kamerad, saraad
SÄD façade, glissade, lancepesade

SHÄD	psha'd
SKWÄD	death squad, squad
TÄD	metad, rodomontade
TRÄD	estrade
VÄD	couvade
WÄD	wad
YÄD	noyade, oeillade
ZÄD	huzzahed

(See **Ä,** add *-ed* where appropriate; see also **OD.**)

ĀDZ

ĀDZ	aids, Aids

ADZ

(See **ĀD,** add -s where appropriate.)

ADZ	ads, adze, Lusiads
SKADZ	scads

(See **AD,** add *-s* where appropriate.)

ĀF

CHĀF	chafe, enchafe, rechafe
KĀF	kef
SĀF	*fail-safe, jail-safe,* safe, unsafe, vouchsafe
STRĀF	strafe
WĀF	waif

AF

AF	aff
BAF	baff
CHAF	chaff, chiff-chaff
DAF	daff
DRAF	draff
FAF	faff
GAF	gaff, gaffe, penny gaff, shandy-gaff
GRAF	*A* agraffe, actinograph, allograph, anagraph, areograph, *B* barograph, *D* diagraph, dictograph, *E* electrocardiograph, electograph, epigraph, *F* phonograph, photograph, *FR* phraseograph, *GR* graf, graph, *H* hagiograph, hectograph, heliograph, hydrograph, holograph, homograph, *I* ideograph, eidograph, *K* calligraph, cardiograph, caraunograph, kymograph, kindergraph, choreograph, coronograph, *KR* chronograph, cryptograph, *L* lithograph, logograph, *M* macrograph, mechanograph, melograph, mimeograph, myograph, myocardiograph, monograph, *N* nephograph, pneumograph, *O* oleograph, ondograph, opisthograph, autograph, autoradiograph, *P* paleograph, pantograph, paragraph, perigraph, pictograph, polygraph, *PL* pluviograph, *R* radiograph, rexograph, *S* serigraph, sillograph, seismograph, cinematograph, *SF* sphygmograph, *SH* shadowgraph, seismograph, *SP* spectrograph, spectroheliograph, spirograph, *ST* stathmograph, stenograph, stereograph, stylograph, *T* tachograph, telegraph, telephotograph, *TH* thermograph, *TR* trigraph, *Z* xylograph, zincograph
SKAF	bathyscaph
SKLAF	sclaff
STAF	*distaff, Falstaff, flagstaff,* half-staff, *gibstaff,* quarterstaff, overstaff, *pikestaff, plowstaff, tipstaff,* understaff
TAF	bibliotaph, epitaph, cenotaph
YAF	yaff

ÄF

HÄF	behalf, better half, half, half-and-half
KÄF	calf, Kaf, moon calf
KWÄF	quaff
LÄF	belly laugh, *horselaugh,* laugh
RÄF	giraffe, carafe, *riffraff*
STRÄF	strafe

ĀFT

CHĀFT	chafed
SĀFT	vouchsafed
STRĀFT	strafed

AFT

AFT	aft
BAFT	abaft, baffed
CHAFT	chaffed
DAFT	daft, daffed
DRAFT	draft, overdraft, redraft
GAFT	gaffed, ungaffed
GRAFT	allograft, engraft, photographed, graft, graphed, ingraft, lithographed, autographed, paragraphed, telegraphed
HAFT	haft
KRAFT	*A* aircraft, antiaircraft, *F* folkcraft, *H* handcraft, handicraft, hovercraft, *KR* Chriscraft, craft, *M* metalcraft, *mooncraft, N* needlecraft, *PR* priestcraft, *R* rivercraft, *S* seacraft, *ST* stagecraft, starcraft, *W* witchcraft, woodcraft
RAFT	raft
SHAFT	shaft
STAFT	overstaffed, restaffed, staffed, understaffed

(See **AF,** add *-ed* where appropriate.)

ÄFT

DRÄFT	draft, draught, overdraft. redraft
KWÄFT	quaffed
LÄFT	laughed
WÄFT	awaft, waft

ĀG

HĀG	Hague
NĀG	fainaigue
PLĀG	plague
PRĀG	Prague
VĀG	stravag, vague

AG

BAG	*B* bag, *beanbag, D* debag, *F feedbag, FL fleabag, H handbag, K* carpetbag, *kitbag, M mailbag,* moneybag, *N nosebag, P* postbag, *R ragbag, ratbag, S* saddlebag, *W windbag, workbag*
BRAG	brag, Fort Bragg
DAG	dag
DRAG	drag, wallydrag

FAG	fag, fish fag	**KĀJ**	discage, encage, cage,	**FLĀK**	flake, *cornflake, snowflake*
FLAG	battle flag, flag		uncage	**FRĀK**	frake
FRAG	frag	**MĀJ**	mage	**HĀK**	haik, hake
GAG	gag	**PĀJ**	*footpage,* op-ed page,	**JĀK**	jake
HAG	demihag, fag hag, hag,		page, rampage, repage	**KĀK**	*B beefcake, FR friedcake,*
	hellhag, night hag, old hag	**RĀJ**	enrage, outrage, rage		*fruitcake, GR griddlecake,*
JAG	*adjag,* jag	**SĀJ**	Osage, *presage,* sage,		*H* havercake, hoe cake,
KAG	cag		unsage		honey cake, *J* johnnycake,
KRAG	crag	**STĀJ**	backstage, downstage,		*K* cake, coffee cake,
KWAG	quag		forestage, center stage,		*cupcake, N* nutcake, *O*
LAG	jet lag, lag		stage, upstage		oatcake, *P* pancake, piece
MAG	mag	**SWĀJ**	assuage, swage		of cake, *S* seed cake, *SH*
NAG	Brobdignag, knag, nag	**WĀJ**	wage		*shortcake, T* tea cake, *W*
RAG	bullyrag, chew the rag, on				wedding cake
	the rag, rag, rowlyrag,	(See **IJ.**)		**KRĀK**	crake, water crake
	shag-rag			**KWĀK**	earthquake, *moonquake,*
SAG	sag				quake, *seaquake*
SHAG	abishag, shag	**AJ**		**LĀK**	lake
SKAG	skag			**MĀK**	make, on the make,
SKRAG	scrag	**BAJ**	badge		remake, unmake
SLAG	slag	**FAJ**	fadge	**PĀK**	opaque, radiopaque
SNAG	snag	**HAJ**	hadj	**RĀK**	afterrake, *muckrake,* rake
SPRAG	sprag	**KAJ**	cadge	**SĀK**	forsake, *keepsake,*
STAG	stag				*namesake,* sake
SWAG	swag			**SHĀK**	*handshake,* shake, sheik
TAG	ragtag, tag	**ÄJ**		**SLĀK**	aslake, slake
VAG	vag			**SNĀK**	*blacksnake,* garter snake,
WAG	*chinwag,* scalawag, wag,	(See **ÄZH**)			coral snake, milk snake,
	wagwag, wigwag				rattlesnake, ribbon snake,
ZAG	zag, *zigzag*				snake, water snake
		ĀJD		**SPĀK**	forespake, spake
				STĀK	*beefsteak, grubstake,*
ÄG		**ĀJD**	aged		mistake, stake, steak,
		GĀJD	disengaged, engaged,		*sweepstake, vealsteak*
BLÄG	blague		gauged	**STRĀK**	strake
PRÄG	Prague	**KĀJD**	encaged, caged	**TĀK**	betake, *intake,* mistake,
TÄG	*qualtagh*	**PĀJD**	paged, rampaged, repaged		overtake, partake, retake,
		RĀJD	enraged, outraged, raged		take, undertake, uptake,
		STĀJD	restaged, staged, unstaged		wapentake
AGD		**SWĀJD**	assuaged	**TRĀK**	traik
		WĀJD	waged	**VĀK**	*thalweg*
(See **AG,** add *-ed* where appropriate.)				**WĀK**	awake, kittiwake, rewake,
					robin-wake, wake
ĀGZ		**ĀK**			
				AK	
PLĀGZ	plagues	**ĀK**	ache, *backache,* bellyache,		
VĀGZ	gyrovagues		*earache, headache,*	**AK**	*A* aphrodisiac, ack-ack,
			heartache, stomach-ache,		ammoniac, amnesiac, *B*
			toothache		bivouac, *D* demoniac,
ĀJ		**BĀK**	bake, *hardbake, clambake,*		dipsomaniac, *Dyak,*
			sunbake		Dionysiac, *E* egomaniac,
ĀJ	age, mid-age, middle age,	**BRĀK**	*B* barley brake, *BR* brake,		elegiac, *H* haemophiliac,
	old age, over-age, under-		break, *D daybreak, F*		hypochondriac, *I* ileac,
	age		*firebreak, H handbrake,*		iliac, insomniac, *K*
FĀJ	alliaphage, anthropophage,		*heartbreak, J jailbreak, K*		cardiac, Kodiak, *KL*
	bacteriophage,		*canebrake,* coffee-break, *L*		kleptomaniac, *M* maniac,
	paedophage, theophage,		lunch break, *O outbreak, P*		megalomaniac,
	xylophage		parabrake, *U upbreak, W*		monomaniac, *N*
FRĀJ	saxifrage		waterbreak, *windbreak,*		nymphomaniac, *O* oomiak,
GĀJ	disengage, engage, gage,		*wordbreak*		*P* pyromaniac, Pontiac, *S*
	gauge, *greengage,*	**DRĀK**	drake, firedrake,		sacroiliac, sal ammoniac,
	reengage, weather gauge		mandrake, sheldrake		
		FĀK	fake		

	coeliac, symposiac, *Z* zodiac
BAK	*A* aback, *B* bac, back, *bareback,* biofeedback, *D diamondback, dieback, DR drawback, F* feedback, fiddleback, *fullback, FL flashback, G* giveback, *GR* greenback, *H* hatchback, halfback, hardback, horseback, huckaback, humpback, hunchback, *K* kickback, comeback, cutback, *KW* quarterback, quillback, *L* laid-back, leaseback, leatherback, *M mossback, O* outback, *P* paperback, pickaback, piggyback, pickaback, *pinchback, puffback, R* razorback, *SPL* splashback, *ST* stickleback, *SW switchback, T tieback, tumbak, TH throwback, W wetback, Z zweiback*
BLAK	black, *boneblack, bootblack, lampblack, shoeblack*
BRAK	amphibrach, brach, bricabrac, ladybrac, tetrabrach
CHAK	chak
DAK	dak, *Kodak, sandak*
FLAK	*flicflac,* flack, flak
HAK	hack, hard hack, tacamahak
HWAK	*bullwhack, bushwhack, paddy-whack,* whack
JAK	*A* amberjack, applejack, *B bootblack, BL* blackjack, *FL* flapjack, *H* hijack, *HW* whipjack, *J* jack, *KR* crackerjack, *crossjack, L* leatherjack, lumberjack, *M muntjac, N* natterjack, *SK skipjack, skyjack, SL* slapjack, *SM* smokejack, *ST* steeplejack, *Y* yellowjack, Union Jack
KAK	ipecac, macaque
KLAK	clack, claque
KRAK	*jimcrack,* crack, thundercrack, *wisecrack*
KWAK	quack
LAK	alack, *kulak,* lac, lack, lakh, shellac
MAK	mac, mack, *sumac, Tarmac,* yashmak
NAK	almanac, coronach, knack, nievie-nievie-nick-nack, Pasternak, Sassenach

PAK	*backpack, daypack, gopak, calpac, mudpack,* naughty-pack, unpack, wool pack
PLAK	plack, plaque
RAK	anorak, hayrack, rack, rickrack, sea wrack, serac, *Shadrach,* tamarack, wrack
SAK	*D* doodlesack, *G* gunnysack, *GR* gripsack, *H* Hackensack, haversack, hopsack, *K* cul-de-sac, *M* mailsack, *N* knapsack, *O* ovisack, *R* ransack, rucksack, *S* sac, sack, sadsack, *W* woolsack
SHAK	shack
SLAK	forslack, slack
SMAK	smack
SNAK	snack
STAK	*haystack, smokestack,* stack
TAK	attack, hackmatack, hard tack, *thumbtack,* tack, *ticktack*
THRAK	thrack
THWAK	thwack
TRAK	*backtrack, racetrack, sidetrack,* track
VAK	*Czechoslovak, Slovak*
WAK	Sarawak, Waac, Wac, wack
YAK	cattle-yak, coulibiac, yack, yak, yakkity-yak
ZAK	*Anzac, Balzac, Muzak, ziczac*

ÄK

KÄK	macaque
LÄK	lac
RÄK	Iraq
TÄK	chittak, *qualtagh*
WÄK	Sarawak

(See **OK**)

AKS

AKS	ax, axe, battleax, battleaxe, coax, pickax, poleax
DAKS	*addaks,* Adirondacks
FAKS	facts, fax, Halifax
FLAKS	flacks, flax, *toadflax*
JAKS	*Ajax*
LAKS	Analax, lax, *smilax,* parallax, relax, unlax
MAKS	*anticlimax,* Betamax, Blue Max, *climax, Lomax,* minimax, *subclimax*

NAKS	*Fornax*
PAKS	packs, pax, repacks, unpacks
RAKS	*borax, hyrax, styrax, storax, thorax*
SAKS	sacks, sax, Tay-Sachs
SLAKS	slacks
TAKS	attacks, excise tax, income tax, overtax, sales tax, *syntax,* supertax, *surtax,* tacks, tax, undertax
THRAKS	*anthrax,* thrax
WAKS	beeswax, bewax, *earwax,* sealing wax, unwax, wax
ZAKS	zax

(See **AK**, add *-s* where appropriate.)

ĀKT

(See **ĀK**, add *-d* where appropriate.)

AKT

AKT	abreact, act, enact, entr'acte, coact, counteract, overact, overreact, react, reenact, retroact, underact, underreact
BAKT	backed, *humpbacked, hunchbacked,* rebacked, saddle-backed, *stoopbacked,* unbacked
BRAKT	bract
DAKT	redact, autodidact
FAKT	artifact, fact, in fact, matter-of-fact
FRAKT	defract, diffract, fract, infract, catophract, refract
HAKT	hacked, unhacked
PAKT	*epact,* impact, compact, pact
RAKT	cataract, racked, wracked, tesseract
SAKT	resacked, retransact, sacked, transact
STRAKT	abstract, reabstract
SWAKT	swacked
TAKT	attacked, intact, contact, reattacked, recontact, tact, unattacked
TRAKT	attract, detract, distract, extract, contract, protract, retract, subtract, tracked, tract, untracked
ZAKT	exact, inexact, transact

(See **AK**, add *-ed* where appropriate.)

ĀL

ĀL	ail, ale, ginger ale
BĀL	Baal, bail, bale
BRĀL	brail, Braille
DĀL	*Airedale*, Chippendale, dale, *quardeel*, merdaille
DRĀL	drail
DWĀL	dwale
FĀL	fail, *pass-fail*
FLĀL	flail
FRĀL	frail
GĀL	farthingale, gale, galingale, martingale, nightingale, regale
GRĀL	engrail, grail, Holy Grail
HĀL	all hail, exhale, hail, hale, ylahayll, inhale
HWĀL	whale, *narwhale*
JĀL	engaol, enjail, gaol, jail, ungaol, unjail
KĀL	kail, kale, percale
KWĀL	quail
LĀL	Hallel
MĀL	*blackmail*, camail, mail, male, remail
NĀL	*agnail*, fingernail, *hangnail, hobnail*, canaille, nail, tenaille, *thumbnail, toenail, treenail*
PĀL	bepale, dead pale, *deathpale*, empale, impale, pail, pale
RĀL	derail, *guardrail, handrail, cograil, landrail*, monorail, rail, serail, *taffrail*
SĀL	*A* a-sail, assail, *F foresail, H headsail*, wholesale, *L lugsail, M mainsail, O* outsail, *R* resail, *resale, S* sail, sale, *SK skysail, SP spritsail, ST staysail, T topsail, TR trysail*, tresaiel, *W* wassail
SHĀL	shale
SKĀL	enscale, in scale, scale, sliding scale
SKWĀL	squail
SNĀL	snail
SPĀL	spale
STĀL	stale
SWĀL	swale
TĀL	*A* aventail, *B bangtail*, betail, *boattail, bobtail, bucktail, BR broadtail, D* detail, disentail, *dovetail, DR* draggletail, *E* entail, *F* fairytale, *fantail, fishtail, forktail, foxtail, H hairtail*, hightail, *horntail, K cat-tail, coattail, cocktail*,

	coontail, cottontail, curtail, *O oxtail, P pigtail, pintail*, ponytail, *R* retail, *S* scissor-tail, *swordtail, SH shavetail, sheartail, short-tail, SPR sprittail, SW* swallowtail, *T* tael, tail, taille, tale, tattletale, *telltale*, teetertail, *TH thorntail, TR* trundletail, *V ventail, W wagtail*
THĀL	they'll
THRĀL	thrail
TRĀL	entrail, *contrail*, off-trail, trail
VĀL	*A* avail, *E* envail, *I* intervale, inveil, *K* countervail, *O* overvail, *P* paravail, *PR* prevail, *TR* travail, *U* unveil, *V* vail, vale, veil
WĀL	bewail, wail, wale
YĀL	Yale
ZĀL	grisaille

AL

AL	*A* accentual, aerial, allodial, alluvial, amatorial, ambrosial, annual, antediluvial, arboreal, asexual, *B* baronial, bestial, bisexual, boreal, *D* dictatorial, diluvial, *E* effectual, empyreal, ethereal, eventual, expurgatorial, *F* phantasmagorial, ferial, fiducial, finial, funereal, *GR* gradual, *H* habitual, hernial, hymeneal, *I* immaterial, immemorial, imperial, incorporeal, individual, industrial, ineffectual, infusorial, initial, inquisitorial, intellectual, *J* genial, gerundial, jovial, *K* casual, collegial, colloquial, commercial, congenial, conjugial, connubial, consanguineal, consistorial, continual, conventual, cordial, corporeal, *KW* quadrennial, *M* magisterial, marsupial, memorial, menstrual, mercurial, microbial, ministerial, mutual, *N* nectareal, novendial, *P*

	participial, patrimonial, pedestrial, perennial, perpetual, pictorial, post-prandial, punctual, purpureal, *PR* preceptorial, primordial, *R* remedial, residual, *S* sartorial, sensual, seigneurial, serial, sexual, sidereal, *SP* splenial, *T* textual, terrestrial, territorial, tertial, testimonial, *TR* transsexual, trivial, *U* uxorial, unusual, *V* ventriloquial, vestigial, vicarial, victorial, virtual, visual, *Y* usual
BAL	bal, Hannibal, cabal, cannibal
BRAL	cerebral, vertebral
DAL	antipodal, iridal, quadrupedal, pyramidal
FAL	apocryphal
GAL	agal, gal, conjugal, madrigal, Portugal, Senegal
GRAL	integral
KAL	*A* academical, acritical, alchemical, alexipharmical, alexiterical, alphabetical, algebraical, alkalimetrical, allegorical, analytical, analogical, anarchical, anatomical, angelical, antarctical, anthological, antithetical, apical, apologetical, apostolical, arithmetical, archaeological, arsenical, ascetical, astrological, atypical, atmospherical, asthmatical *B* Babylonical, bacchical, bacteriological, balsamical, barometrical, basilical, beatifical, biblical, bibliophilical, bibliographical, bibliomanical, biographical, biological, botanical, bureaucratical, *BR* Brahmanical, *CH* cherubical, *D* deistical, democratical, demoniacal, demonological, despotical, diabolical, diaphonical, diagraphical, diacritical, dialectical, dialogical, dialogistical, diametrical, didactical, dietetical, dynamical, diplomatical, dipsomaniacal, dogmatical,

dolorifical, dominical, *DR* dramatical, dropsical, Druidical, *E* egoistical, egotistical, eccentrical, exegetical, exoterical, exotical, extrinsical, ecumenical, equivocal, electrical, elegiacal, ellipitical, emblematical, emphatical, empirical, endemical, energetical, enigmatical, encomiastical, encyclical, encyclopedical, enthusiastical, epical, epidemical, epigrammatical, episodical, epithetical, erotical, esoterical, aesthetical, esthetical, ethical, ethnical, ethnological, etymological, evangelical, *F* fanatical, phantasmagorical, fantastical, Pharisaical, pharmaceutical, farcical, philanthropical, philological, philosophical, finical, physical, physiological, forensical, photographical, *FR* phrenological, *G* galvanical, *GR* graphical, grammatical, *H* harmonical, Hebraical, helical, hemispherical, heretical, hermitical, heroical, hierarchical, hygienical, historical, hyperbolical, hypercritical, hypochondriacal, hypocritical, hysterical, *HW* whimsical, *I* identical, idiotical, illogical, immechanical, inimical, ironical, *J* genealogical, generical, jesuitical, juridical, *K* cacophonical, Calvinistical, canonical, caracal, characteristical, cardical, cartographical, categorical, catholical, casuistical, chemical, chimerical, codical, coxcombical, conical, conventical, cortical, caustical, cosmetical, cosmical, cubical, *KL* classical, clerical, climactical, climatological, clinical, *KR* critical, cryptical, chronological, *KW* quizzical, *L*

lackadaisical, laical, lethargical, Levitical, lyrical, liturgical, logical, locale, *M* magnifical, majestical, magical, maniacal, mathematical, medical, mechanical, metaphysical, metaphorical, methodical, Methodistical, metical, metrical, microscopical, misanthropical, mystical, mythical, mythological, monarchical, musical, *N* nymphical, nonclassical, nonsensical, nautical, pneumatological, numerical, *O* oneirocritical, optical, oratorical, *P* parabolical, paradisiacal, parasitical, parenthetical, pathetical, pathological, patronymical, pedagogical, pedantical, penological, periphrastical, periodical, pietistical, pyramidical, piratical, pyrotechnical, poetical, polemical, political, pontifical, puritanical, *PL* platonical, *PR* pragmatical, practical, problematical, prophetical, *R* radical, rhapsodical, reciprocal, rhetorical, rhythmical, rheumatical, *S* sabbatical, satanical, satirical, scenical, centrical, seraphical, cervical, sybaritical, psychiatrical, psychical, cyclical, psychological, cylindrical, cynical, symbolical, symmetrical, synchronical, synodical, synonymical, synoptical, synthetical, systematical, schismatical, soritical, *SF* spherical, *SK* schismatical, *SP* spasmodical, sporadical, *ST* stoical, *STR* strategical, *T* tactical, technical, technicological, technological, typical, typographical, tyrannical, topical, topographical, *TH* theoretical, *TR* tragical, tropical, *U* umbilical, unethical, uncanonical, *V* vatical, veridical, vertical, vesical, vortical, *Y* euphemistical, euphonical,

KWAL
MAL

NAL

Eucharistical, eulogistical, *Z* zodiacal, zoological ventriloqual animal, decimal, hexidecimal, infinitesimal, quadragesimal, lachrymal, millesimal, minimal, shamal, synonymal *A* aboriginal, adhesional, affectional, antiphonal, arsenal, *B* bacchanal, banal, *D* decanal, denominational, descensional, destinal, devotional, diagonal, diaconal, digressional, discretional, divisional, doctrinal, duodecimal, *E* educational, echinal, expansional, exceptional, emotional, evolutional, *F* phenomenal, fictional, functional, *FR* fractional, *H* hexagonal, heptagonal, *I* imaginal, imitational, impersonal, indigenal, inguinal, inspirational, institutional, instructional, insurrectional, intentional, interjectional, international, intercessional, intestinal, *J* geminal, germinal, *K* cardinal, carcinal, communal, complexional, conditional, confessional, congressional, conclusional, constitutional, contradictional, conventional, conversational, convulsional, *KR* criminal, *L* longitudinal, *M* machinal, marginal, matinal, matronal, matutinal, medicinal, meridional, missional, *N* national, nominal, notional, *O* occasional, octagonal, optional, original, *P* partitional, passional, patronal, pentagonal, personal, polygonal, *PR* precautional, probational, professional, progressional, proportional, processional, provisional, *R* rational, rationale, regional, recessional, retinal, *S* sensational, seasonal, synchronal, circumlocutional, *ST* staminal, *T* terminal, tympanal, torsional, *TR* traditional, trigonal, *V* vaginal, viminal, virginal, visional, volitional, *Y* urinal

PAL   Episcopal, municipal, pal, principal

RAL   *A* admiral, agricultural, anchoral, arbocultural, architectural, *D* doctoral, *E* ephemeral, extemporal, *F* falderal, federal, femoral, funeral, *G* geyseral, guttural, *H* horticultural, *I* inaugural, *J* general, gestural, *K* cantoral, carnivoral, collateral, chorale, corral, *L* literal, littoral, *M* magistral, mayoral, mensural, mineral, morale, *N* natural, *P* pastoral, pastorale, pastural, peripheral, pictural, postural, *PR* preceptoral, *S* several, supernatural, sutural, *SH* chapparal, *SK* sculptural, *SKR* scriptural, *T* tellural, temporal, textural, *TR* tragicomipastoral, *V* vesperal, visceral

SAL   Provençale, sal, salle, quetzal

SHAL   seneschal, shall

TAL   *D* digital, *H* hospital, *K* capital, *M* marital, *N* nepotal, *O* orbital, *P* palatal, pedestal, pivotal, *SK* skeletal, *V* vegetal

VAL   festival, interval, carnival, travale

ÄL

BÄL   Baal
DÄL   dal
FÄL   rafale
HÄL   mahal, Taj Mahal
KÄL   jacal
KRÄL   kraal
MÄL   grand mal
RÄL   rale

ĀLD

ĀLD   ailed

(See **ĀL,** add *-d* or *-ed* where appropriate.)

ALD

BALD   caballed
PALD   palled
RALD   emerald, corralled

ALK

ALK   alk
FALK   catafalque
KALK   calk
TALK   talc

ALKS

FALKS   falx, catafalques
KALKS   calx

(See **ALK,** add *-s* where appropriate.)

ALP

ALP   alp
GALP   galp
PALP   palp
SKALP   auriscalp, scalp

ALPS

ALPS   Alps

(See **ALP,** add *-s* where appropriate.)

ALT

ALT   alt
SHALT   shalt

ALV

SALV   salve
VALV   bivalve, priming valve, safety valve, valve, univalve

ĀLZ

ĀLZ   ails
SĀLZ   Marseilles, sails, sales
WĀLZ   Wales

(See **ĀL,** add *-s* where appropriate.)

ĀM

ĀM   aim
BLĀM   blame
DĀM   dame

DRĀM   melodrame
FĀM   defame, disfame, fame
FLĀM   aflame, flame, inflame
FRĀM   *airframe, doorframe,* frame
GĀM   *endgame,* game, videogame, *war-game*
HĀM   hame
KĀM   became, came, kame, overcame
KLĀM   acclaim, declaim, disclaim, exclaim, claim, counterclaim, *quitclaim,* proclaim, reclaim
KRĀM   *crème de la crème*
LĀM   lame
MĀM   maim
NĀM   *byname, forename,* misname, name, *nickname,* rename, *surname,* unname
SĀM   same, self-same, Sejm
SHĀM   ashame, shame
TĀM   entame, tame, untame

AM

AM   ad nauseam, am, Iamb, choriamb, Kayam, Siam
BAM   Alabam', bam, wham-bam
CHAM   cham
DAM   Amsterdam, *beldam,* dam, damn, goddamn, *grandam,* grande dame, cofferdam, madame, *milldam,* Rotterdam
DRAM   drachm, dram, dramme
FLAM   flam, *flimflam,* oriflamme
FRAM   diaphragm
GAM   gam, gamb
GRAM   *A* anagram, aerogram, *B* barogram, *D* dactylogram, diagram, *E* echocardiogram, electrocardiogram, electroencephalogram, encephalogram, epigram, *F* phonogram, photogram, *FR* phraseogram, *GR* gram, gramme, *H* hexagram, hectogram, *H* hierogram, histogram, *I* ideogram, ichnogram, *K* cablegram, candygram, kilogram, *KR* cryptogram, chronogram, *L* lexigram, lipogram, logogram, *M* melogram, milligram, *N* nephogram, pneumencephalogram, *P* pangram, paragram, parallelogram,

	pelmatogram, *PR program, R* roentgenogram, *S* centigram, sonogram, *ST* stereogram, *T tangram,* telegram, tetragram
HAM	Abraham, Birmingham, ham, Nottingham
HWAM	wham, *whimwham*
JAM	demijambe, *doorjamb,* enjamb, jam, jamb, *jimjam*
KAM	cam
KLAM	hardshell clam, clam, littleneck clam, mud clam, razor clam, softshell clam, steamer clam
KRAM	cram
LAM	lam, lamb
MAM	ma'am, Mam
NAM	Vietnam
PAM	pam
PRAM	pram
RAM	battering ram, dithyramb, marjoram, ram, rhamn
SAM	Assam, cheong-sam, *Samsam,* Uncle Sam
SHAM	sham
SHRAM	shram
SKAM	scam
SKRAM	scram
SLAM	slam
SPAM	Spam
SWAM	swam
TAM	tam, *tamtam*
TRAM	tram
YAM	yam, Omar Khayyam
ZAM	alakazam, Nizam, shazam, zam

ÄM

ÄM	ame, ad nauseam
BÄM	balm, embalm
BRÄM	parabrahm
DÄM	Madame
GWÄM	Guam
KÄM	calm
KWÄM	qualm
LÄM	Islam, salaam
MÄM	hammam, imam, malm
NÄM	withernam
PÄM	impalm, palm
SÄM	psalm
WÄM	walm
YÄM	Omar Khayyam

AMB

AMB	iamb, choriamb
GAMB	gamb, gambe

JAMB	enjamb
RAMB	dithyramb

ĀMD

(See **ĀM,** add *-ed* or *-d* where appropriate.)

AMD

(See **AM,** add *-ed* where appropriate.)

AMP

AMP	amp
CHAMP	champ
DAMP	afterdamp, *blackdamp, chokedamp,* damp, *deathdamp, firedamp, whitedamp, minedamp*
GAMP	gamp, guimpe
KAMP	decamp, encamp, camp
KLAMP	clamp, unclamp
KRAMP	cramp
LAMP	*blowlamp,* Davy lamp, electric lamp, gas lamp, kerosene lamp, lamp, safety lamp, signal lamp
PAMP	*slampamp*
RAMP	ramp
SAMP	samp
SKAMP	scamp
STAMP	*backstamp,* enstamp, restamp, stamp
TAMP	tamp, retamp
TRAMP	tramp
VAMP	revamp, vamp
HWAMP	whamp
YAMP	yamp

ÄMP

PÄMP	*slampamp*
SWÄMP	swamp

(See **OMP**)

AMPT

DAMPT	damped

(See **AMP,** add *-ed* where appropriate.)

ÄMPT

SWÄMPT	swamped

(See **OMP,** add *-ed* where appropriate.)

ĀMZ

(See **ĀM,** add *-s* where appropriate.)

ÄMZ

AMZ	alms

(See **ÄM,** add *-s* where appropriate.)

ĀN

ĀN	ain, Aisne, ane, eigne, inane
BĀN	bane, *bugbane, fleabane, henbane, herbbane,* inurbane, *cowbane, ratsbane,* urbane, *wolfsbane*
BLĀN	blain, *chilblain*
BRĀN	brain, *endbrain,* featherbrain, *forebrain, hindbrain, lamebrain, membrane, midbrain,* scatterbrain
CHĀN	chain, enchain, interchain, rechain, unchain
DĀN	Dane, deign, demimondaine, disdain, foreordain, intermundane, kadein, coordain, mundane, ordain, preordain, reordain, transmundane
DRĀN	*braindrain,* drain, *subdrain*
FĀN	*A* allophane, aerophane, areophane, *D* diaphane, *F* fain, fane, feign, *H* hydrophane, *L* lithophane, *M* misfeign, *PR* profane, *S* cellophane, Sinn Fein
FRĀN	refrain
GĀN	again, gain, gaine, regain
GRĀN	against the grain, engrain, grain, *grosgrain,* ingrain, *crossgrain, migraine*
KĀN	arcane, Biscayne, Duquesne, hurricane, Cain, cane, cocaine, Cockaigne, chicane, procaine, cinquain, sugar cane
KRĀN	crane, water crane, Ukraine
LĀN	chamberlain, delaine, lain, laine, lane, porcelain, chatelain, chatelaine
MĀN	*A* amain, *CH* chow mein, *D* demesne, domain, *H* humane, *I* immane,

PĀN inhumane, *J* germane, *L* legerdemain, *M* main, Maine, mane, *mortmain, R* remain, romaine, *SH* Charlemagne, *T* ptomaine elecampane, frangipane, campaign, campane, counterpane, *marchpane,* pain, pane, *propane,* Champaign, champagne, windowpane

PLĀN *A* aeroplane, *airplane,* aquaplane, *B* biplane, *E* explain, emplane, *H* hydroplane, *J* gyroplane, *K* complain, *M* monoplane, multiplane, *P* peneplain, pursuit plane, *PL* plain, plane, *S* sailplane, seaplane, *SH* Champlain, *SK* skiplane, *T* taxiplane, *tailplane, TR* triplane, *V* volplane, *W* warplane

RĀN *A* arraign, acid rain, *B* Bahrain, borane, *BR* bridle rein, *CH* check-rein, *D* darrein, *F* forane, *I* interreign, *KW* quatrain, *L* Lorraine, *M* mediterrane, moraine, *R* rain, reign, rein, *S* souterrain, subterrane, suzerain, *T* terrain, terrane, *U* unrein, *V* viceraine

SĀN Hussein, insane, sain, sane, seine, Seine, *sixain*

SKĀN skein

SLĀN slain

SPĀN Spain

SPRĀN sprain

STĀN abstain, bestain, *bloodstain,* distain, *tearstain*

STRĀN Andromeda strain, *eyestrain,* constrain, overstrain, restrain, strain

TRĀN distrain

SWĀN boatswain, coxswain, swain

TĀN *A* appertain, ascertain, attain, *B* butane, *D* detain, *E* entertain, *K* contain, curtein, *M* maintain, *O* obtain, *octane, P* pertain, *R* retain, *S* sextain, soutane, sustain, *SH* chevrotain, *T* ta'en, tain, *U* ultramontane

THĀN bower thane, *ethane, methane,* thane, thegn

TRĀN detrain, distrain, down train, entrain, hovertrain, pleasure train, Pontchartrain, quatrain, train, uptrain

TWĀN atwain, twain

VĀN paravane, vain, vane, vein, vervain, weather vane

WĀN Gawain, *cordwain,* wain, wane

ZĀN quatorzain, zain

AN

AN an, yuan, Yuan, abecedarian (see **UN** for additional words, ending in the final syllable -an, which normally carry the principal stress on the antepenult and a secondary stress on the final syllable. They become single rhymes if the principal stress is shifted to the final syllable: Acadian, guardian, Zoroastrian, etc.)

BAN ban, cabane, Caliban, corban

BRAN bran

CHAN chan

DAN echinidan, foo young dan, harridan, *Houdan,* Mohammedan, oppidan, Ramadan, randan, redan, Sedan, shandrydan, Sudan

FAN fan, turbofan

FLAN flan

GAN *Afghan,* began, hooligan, cardigan, larrigan, Michigan, mulligan, origan, suffragan, ptarmigan, tsigane, wanigan, yataghan

GRAN gran

HAN Han

KAN *A* African, American, Anglican, astrakhan, *B* balmacaan, barbican, barracan, basilican, billycan, *D* Dominican, *G* Gallican, *I* indican, *K* can, khan, cancan, *M* Mexican, *O* oil can, *P* pecan, pelican, pemmican, publican, *R* republican, Republican, rubican, *U* ugly American, *V* Vatican

KLAN clan, Klan

KRAN cran

LAN gamelan, castellan, Catalan, Milan, ortolan, *tolan, yulan*

MAN *A adman, amman,* aircraftsman, *airman, almsman,* artilleryman, *B* backwoodsman, *bailsman, bandman, bandsman, bankman, bargeman, barman, batman,* Bat Man, *batsman, beadsman, bellman,* best man, *billman, birdman, boatman, bondman, bondsman, bookman, bowman,* Bushman, *BR brakeman, CH chantman, chapman, checkman,* Chinaman, *churchman, D* dairyman, deliveryman, *dirgeman, dolesman,* dollyman, *dolman,* Dutchman, *DR draftsman, dragman,* dragoman, *drayman, F ferryman, fireman,* fisherman, *foeman, footman,* foremostman, fugleman, *FL flagman, flyman, floorman, FR freeman,* Frenchman, *freshman, frontiersman, G gangsman, guardsman,* gunman, *GR groomsman, H hangman, headman, headsman, helmsman,* henchman, *herdsman,* highwayman, *hodman, horseman, huntsman,* husbandman, *HW* wherryman, *I* Isle of Man, infantryman, Englishman, Irishman, *iceman, J* gentleman, *jibman,* jinrikiman, journeyman, juryman, *K cabman, cageman, campman, carman, cayman,* kibblerman, *kinsman,* coachman, *cogman,* Cornishman, *cowman,* countryman, *KL clansman, Klansman,* clergyman, *clubman, KR craftsman, crewman, KW* quarryman, quarterman, *L* lady's man, *landsman, leadman, leadsman,* lighterman, *lineman, linesman, liveryman, lockman,* longshoreman, *M madman,* man, *marksman, meatman,* medicine man, merchantman, *merman, merryman, messman,*

middleman, midshipman,
militiaman, *milkman,*
millman, minuteman,
Mussulman, *N* nobleman,
Norman, Norseman,
Northman, O alderman,
oarsman, odd man,
oddsman, oilman,
Orangeman, ottoman,
outman, overman, *P* Pac-
man, packman, passman,
pegman, penman,
peterman, *pitman,*
postman, Pullman, *PL*
playman, plowman, *PR*
pressman, *R* ragman,
ranchman, reman,
rifleman, *roadman,*
rodman, Roman, *S*
sailorman, *salesman,*
sandman, seaman,
selectman, signalman,
songman, swordman,
swordsman, subman,
superman, Superman, *SH*
sheepman, shipman,
shopman, shoreman,
shoresman, showman, *SK*
schoolman, Scotchman,
Scotsman, *SL*
slaughterman, *SP*
spearman, spoilsman,
spokesman, sportsman, *ST*
statesman, stockman, *SW*
swagman, switchman, *T*
talesman, talisman,
tallyman, *tapeman,*
tipman, tollman, toman,
top man, *townsman,*
tubman, tugman, tupman,
TR tradesman, *trainman,*
trencherman, *tribesman, U*
unman, *V* vestryman, *W*
wardman, watchman,
waterman, *wayman,*
Welchman, *Welshman,*
wireman, wise man,
woman, woodman,
woodsman, workman, Y
yachtsman, yeggman,
yeoman

NAN Hainan, nan, Hunan, Tainan

PAN *B* bedpan, *BR* brainpan, *D*
deadpan, dustpan, *FR*
frying pan, *H* hardpan, *J*
jampan, Japan, *K* cocopan,
KL claypan, *M* marzipan,
Matapan, *N* kneepan, *P*
pan, Pan, panne, *sampan,*
Saipan, sapan, *SH* Chopin,
T taipan, TR tragopan,
trepan, *W* warming pan

PLAN plan, rataplan, replan
RAN Aldeberan, also-ran,
foreran, furan, Iran,
catamaran, Koran,
Lutheran, outran, overran,
ran, Teheran, trimaran,
veteran
SKAN *cat-scan,* scan
SKRAN scran
SPAN inspan, life span, outspan,
span, spick-and-span, *wing*
span
STAN Afghanistan, Pakistan,
Turkestan
TAN *B* Bataan, *F* fantan, *K*
caftan, cosmopolitan, *M*
metropolitan, *N*
Neapolitan, *O* orangutan,
P Powhatan, puritan,
Puritan, *R* rattan, rheotan,
S sacristan, Samaritan,
sumpitan, *suntan, SH*
charlatan, *T* tan,
topopolitan, *Y* Yucatan
THAN than
VAN divan, caravan, cordovan,
luggage van, pavan, prison
van, van
YAN shintiyan
ZAN artisan, bartizan, fusain,
courtesan, Lausanne,
partisan, nonpartisan,
Parmesan, ptisane, tisane

ÄN

ÄN liane, t'ai chi ch'uan
BÄN autobahn
CHÄN machan
CHWÄN t'ai chi ch'uan
DÄN maidan
DWÄN macedoine
GÄN tzigane
KÄN Genghis Khan, khan,
macan, pecan
MÄN Oman, toman
RÄN buran, Iran, Koran
STÄN Turkestan
SWÄN swan
TÄN Bataan, caftan, soutane,
Wotan
VÄN pavane
WÄN wan
ZÄN Parmesan, tisane

(See **ON**)

ANCH

BLANCH blanch

BRANCH anabranch, branch,
disbranch, rebranch
FLANCH flanch
GANCH ganch
LANCH avalanche
RANCH horse ranch, cattle ranch,
ranch
SCRANCH scranch
STANCH stanch

ÄNCH

BLÄNCH carte blanche
HÄNCH haunch
KRÄNCH craunch
LÄNCH launch
MÄNCH manche
PÄNCH paunch
STÄNCH stanch, staunch

(See **ÔNCH**)

ÄNCHT

LÄNCHT launched

(See **ÄNCH,** add *-ed* where appropriate.)

ĀND

BRĀND *B* bird-brained, *BR*
brained, *F* feather-brained,
H hare-brained, *hot-*
brained, M muddy-
brained, R rattle-brained,
SH shatter-brained, *SK*
scatter-brained
STĀND blood-stained, stained,
travel-stained

(See **ĀN,** add *-d* or *-ed* where
appropriate.)

AND

AND and, Chateaubriand,
waniand
BAND *A* aband, *armband, B*
band, banned, bellyband,
BR breastband, browband,
D disband, *H* hatband,
headband, I imband, *N*
neckband, noseband, *K*
contraband, *R* rainband,
wristband, S saraband, *SP*
spaceband, SW sweatband,
TR trainband, *W*
waistband, waveband

BLAND	bland
BRAND	brand, *firebrand*
DAND	dand, deodand
FAND	fanned, refanned
GLAND	gland, goat gland, monkey gland
GRAND	grand, integrand, Rio Grande
HAND	*A* afterhand, *B* backhand, behindhand, *BR* bridlehand, *E* even hand, *F* fine Italian hand, *forehand*, four-in-hand, *H* hand, *hothand, L longhand, M* master hand, minute hand, *O* offhand, overhand, *S* secondhand, second hand, *SH shorthand, ST* stagehand, *U* underhand, unhand, upperhand
KAND	canned, multiplicand, Samarkand
KLAND	clanned
LAND	*A* abbeyland, *B* borderland, *D* Disneyland, *DR dreamland, E* eland, *F* fairyland, *farmland*, fatherland, *GR grassland*, Greenland, *H* headland, *heartland*, hinterland, Holy Land, *homeland, I* inland, *KR* crownland, *KW* Queensland, *L* land, *Lapland*, lotus land, *lowland, M mainland, midland, moorland*, motherland, *N* never-never land, no man's land, *northland, O* overland, *R* Rhineland, *T* toyland, *U* upland, *W* wasteland, woodland
MAND	*D* demand, *F full-manned, H half-manned, I ill-manned, K* command, confirmand, countermand, *M* manned, *R* remand, reprimand, *S* self-command, summand, *U* unmanned
NAND	ordinand
PAND	expand, panned, repand
PLAND	planned
RAND	rand
SAND	ampersand, analysand, *greensand, quicksand,* sand
SKAND	rescanned, scanned, unscanned
SPAND	respanned, spanned, unspanned
STAND	*bandstand, bedstand, grandstand, handstand,*

	inkstand, kickstand, lampstand, newsstand, stablestand, stand, understand, *washstand,* withstand
STRAND	strand
TAND	retanned, tanned, untanned
VAND	revanned, vanned

ÄND

(See **OND**)

ANG

BANG	bang, bhang, Big Bang, gang bang, gobang, interrobang, probang, shebang
DANG	dang, yardang
FANG	defang, fang, unfang
GANG	gang, gangue, *holmgang, outgang, oxgang, sirgang*
HANG	hang, overhang, uphang
HWANG	whang
KANG	cangue
KLANG	clang, reclang
KYANG	kiang
LANG	lang
MANG	mang, siamang
NANG	Penang
PANG	pang, trepang
PRANG	prang
RANG	boomerang, harangue, meringue, rang, serang
SANG	pisang, resang, sang
SLANG	*boomslang,* slang
SPANG	spang
SPRANG	resprang, sprang
STANG	stang
SWANG	swang
TANG	*mustang,* orangutang, sea tang, tang
TWANG	twang
VANG	vang
WANG	burrawang
YANG	Pyongyang, yang

ÄNG

FÄNG	*yesterfang*
TSVÄNG	*zugzwang*

ANGD

FANGD	bi-fanged, defanged, fanged, unfanged

(See **ANG,** add *-ed* where appropriate.)

ANGK

ANGK	ankh
BANGK	banc, bank, data bank, embank, *claybank,* mountebank, river bank, *sandbank,* savings bank
BLANGK	blank, Mont Blanc, point-blank
BRANGK	brank
CHANGK	chank
DANGK	dank
DRANGK	drank, outdrank
FLANGK	flank, outflank
FRANGK	franc, frank, Frank
HANGK	hank
KLANGK	clank, reclank
KRANGK	crank, recrank
LANGK	lank
PANGK	hanky-pank
PLANGK	*gangplank,* plank
PRANGK	prank
RANGK	disrank, enrank, outrank, rank
SANGK	sank
SHANGK	*foreshank, greenshank, redshank,* shank, *sheepshank, scrimshank*
SHRANGK	reshrank, shrank
SLANGK	slank
SPANGK	spank
STANGK	outstank, stank
SWANGK	swank
TANGK	antitank, tank, water tank
THANGK	thank
TRANGK	trank
TWANGK	twank
YANGK	yank, Yank

ANGKS

BANGKS	*Fairbanks*
BRANGKS	branks
LANGKS	*phalanx,* lanx
MANGKS	Manx
SHANGKS	bonyshanks, *longshanks,* spindleshanks
THANGKS	thanks
YANGKS	yanks, Yanks

(See **ANGK,** add *-s* where appropriate.)

ANGKT

SANGKT	sacrosanct, sanct

(See **ANGK,** add *-ed* where appropriate.)

ĀNJ

CHĀNJ	change, exchange, interchange,

	counterchange, shortchange
GRĀNJ	grange
MĀNJ	mange
RĀNJ	arrange, derange, disarrange, enrange, prearrange, range, rearrange
STRĀNJ	estrange, strange

ANJ

FLANJ	flange
GANJ	gange
LANJ	phalange
RANJ	*orange,* sporange

ANS

ANS	*A* anse, *appliance, D* discontinuance, *I* insouciance, irradiance, issuance, *K* continuance, *KL* clairvoyance, *L* luxuriance, *P* permeance, perpetuance, *pursuance, R* radiance, *S* seance, suppliance, *V* variance
BANS	*disturbance*
BRANS	*encumbrance, remembrance*
CHANS	bechance, chance, mischance, perchance
DANS	*ascendance, avoidance,* barn dance, break dance, dance, death dance, folk dance, *impedance,* country dance, courting dance, mating dance, *misguidance,* square dance, tap dance, witch dance
FRANS	France
GANS	arrogance, elegance, extravagance, inelegance
GLANS	glance, side glance
HANS	enhance, hance, hanse
JANS	*allegiance*
KANS	askance, insignificance, significance
LANS	ambulance, demilance, fer-de-lance, jubilance, lance, nonchalance, petulance, sibilance, simulance, vigilance
MANS	manse, romance
NANS	*A* appurtenance, assonance, *D* discountenance, dissonance, dominance, *F*

	finance, *G* governance, *H* high finance, *I* inconsonance, *K* consonance, countenance, *M* maintenance, *N* nance, *O* ordinance, *PR* predominance, preordinance, provenance, *R* repugnance, resonance, *S* sustenance
PANS	expanse
PRANS	prance
RANS	*A aberrance, D* deliverance, *E* exuberance, *F* furtherance, *I* ignorance, intemperance, intolerance, *PR* preponderance, protuberance, *R* rance, *S* severance, sufferance, *T* temperance, tolerance, *U* utterance, *V* vociferance
SANS	impuissance, *complaisance, conversance,* puissance, reconnaisance
SKANS	askance
STANS	*inconstance,* circumstance, stance
TANS	*A acceptance, D* disinheritance, *E* exorbitance, *expectance, H* heritance, *I inductance,* inhabitance, inhabitants, inheritance, *K* concomitance, *conductance, O* oscitance, *PR* precipitance, *R reluctance, remonstrance, repentance*
TRANS	entrance, penetrance, recalcitrance, *remonstrance,* trance, outrance
VANS	advance, irrelevance, relevance
ZANS	*defeasance, complaisance, malfeasance, obeisance,* recognizance

(See **ANT,** add -*s* where appropriate.)

ÄNS

ÄNS	insouciance, nuance, seance
BLÄNS	vraisemblance
FRÄNS	France
LÄNS	fer-de-lance, lance, nonchalance
SÄNS	Renaissance
TRÄNS	outrance

ĀNT

ĀNT	ain't
DĀNT	daint
FĀNT	faint, feint
HĀNT	hain't
KWĀNT	acquaint, quaint
MĀNT	mayn't
PĀNT	bepaint, depaint, *greasepaint,* paint, repaint
PLĀNT	complaint, plaint
RĀNT	Geraint
SĀNT	besaint, ensaint, enceinte, saint, unsaint
STRĀNT	constraint, restraint, self-restraint, straint, unconstraint
TĀNT	attaint, taint, 'tain't
TRĀNT	distraint

ANT

ANT	*A* ant, aunt, attenuant, *D* depreciant, *FL* fluctuant, *G* grand-aunt, great-aunt (etc.), *I* insouciant, irradiant, issuant, *K* continuant, *L* luxuriant, *M* menstruant, miscreant, *O* officiant, otiant, *P* permeant, *PR* procreant, *R* recreant, renunciant, resiant, *V* variant
BANT	bant, Corybant
BRANT	brant, celebrant, *Rembrandt*
CHANT	chant, disenchant, enchant
DANT	commandant, confidant, confidante, consolidant
FANT	elephant, hierophant, oliphant, sycophant, *triumphant*
GANT	*A* arrogant, *E* elegant, extravagant, *I* inelegant, irrigant, *K* congregant, *L* litigant, *M* mitigant, *O* obligant, *S* suffragant, *T* termagant
GRANT	block grant, emigrant, grant, immigrant, integrant
KANT	*A* abdicant, albicant, applicant, askant, *D* decant, dedicant, dodecant, descant, desiccant, *E* exsiccant, *F* fabricant, formicant, *I* imprecant, indicant, insignificant, intoxicant, *K* can't, cant, Kant, communicant, *coruscant, L* lubricant, *M* mendicant, *R* radicant,

recant, resiccant, *S* safricant, significant, supplicant, *T* toxicant, *V* vesicant

KWANT quant

LANT *A* ambulant, articulant, *FL* flagellant, *G* gallant, *GR* gratulant, *I* impetulant, *J* jubilant, *K* capitulant, coagulant, congratulant, cumulant, *L* lant, *M* matriculant, *N* nonchalant, *O* osculant, *P* periculant, petulant, postulant, *R* revelant, *S* sibilant, scintillant, circulant, circumvolant, *ST* stimulant, *STR* stridulant, *T* tintinnabulant, *TR* tremolant, *U* ululant, undulant, *V* vigilant

MANT adamant, *informant*

NANT *A* agglutinant, appurtenant, assonant, *D* determinant, discriminant, dissonant, dominant, *F* fulminant, *H* horrisonant, *I* illuminant, imaginant, inconsonant, *J* germinant, *K* conglutinant, consonant, culminant, covenant, *L* luminant, *O* ordinant, *PR* predominant, *R* revenant, resonant, ruminant

PANT anticipant, pant, Sacripant

PLANT deplant, *eggplant*, implant, *pieplant*, plant, replant, supplant, transplant

RANT *A* adulterant, agglomerant, alterant, ameliorant, *D* decolorant, deodorant, discolorant, *E* expectorant, exuberant, *F* figurant, figurante, fulturant, *I* ignorant, intolerant, itinerant, *K* cormorant, corroborant, cauterant, colorant, courant, courante, *M* mensurant, *O* obscurant, odorant, *PR* preponderant, protuberant, *R* rant, refrigerant, reiterant, reverberant, *T* tolerant, *V* vociferant

SANT enceinte, impuissant, *complaisant, conversant,* puissant, recusant

SHANT shan't

SKANT askant, scant

SLANT aslant, slant

TANT *A* adjutant, annuitant, *D* debutante, dilettante, *disputant, E* executant, exorbitant, extant, *H*

habitant, hebetant, hesitant, *I important,* inhabitant, incogitant, *inconstant,* irritant, *K* combatant, comitant, concomitant, *KR* crepitant, *M* militant, ministrant, *O* oscitant, *PR* precipitant, Protestant, *R* regurgitant, registrant, resuscitant, *V* vegetant, visitant

TRANT administrant, penetrant, recalcitrant, registrant

VANT gallivant, innovant, irrelevant, levant, Levant, pickedevant, poursuivant, relevant

ZANT bezant, incognizant, cognizant, *complaisant,* corposant

ÄNT

ÄNT aunt, grand-aunt, great-aunt (etc.)

DÄNT confidant, confidante

KÄNT can't, Kant

KWÄNT quant

LÄNT gallant, nonchalant

NÄNT revenant

RÄNT courant, courante, rente

SHÄNT shan't

TÄNT debutant, debutante, detente, dilettant, dilettante

VÄNT cidevant

WÄNT want

YÄNT ondoyant

(See **ONT**)

ÄNTS

SPRÄNTS spraints

(See **ÄNT,** add -*s* where appropriate.)

ANTS

ANTS ants

HANTS Hants

PANTS fancy-pants, pants

(See **ANS;** also **ANT,** add -*s* where appropriate.)

ÄNTS

KRÄNTS Liederkrantz

(See **ÄNT,** add -*s* where appropriate.)

ANZ

BANZ banns

KANZ Louis Quinze

(See **AN,** add -*s* where appropriate.)

ĀP

ĀP ape, naked ape

CHĀP chape

DRĀP bedrape, drape, undrape

GĀP agape, gape

GRĀP graip, grape

JĀP jape

KĀP escape, fire escape, cape, uncape

KRĀP crape, crepe

NĀP nape

PĀP pape

RĀP *broomrape,* rape

SHĀP misshape, reshape, shape, *shipshape,* transshape, unshape

SKĀP escape, *inscape, cloudscape, landscape, seascape,* scape, *skyscape, townscape,* waterscape

SKRĀP rescrape, scrape

SWĀP swape

TĀP *nametape,* audiotape, red-tape, tape, untape, videotape

TRĀP trape

AP

BAP bap

CHAP chap, old chap, young chap

DAP dap

DRAP drap

FLAP *earflap,* flap, *flipflap*

FRAP frap, unfrap

GAP agape, gap, gape, stopgap

HAP hap, mayhap, mishap

JAP Jap

KAP *ASCAP, BL* blackcap, *bluecap, F* foolscap, forage cap, *H* handicap, *hubcap, HW* whitecap, *I* icecap, *K* cap, *M* madcap, mobcap, *N* kneecap, nightcap, *P* percussion cap, *R* redcap, recap, *SK* skullcap, *SN* snowcap, *T* toecap, *U* uncap, *W* wishing cap

KLAP afterclap, beclap, clap, thunderclap

KRAP	crap
LAP	*burlap, dewlap, halflap, catlap,* lap, Lapp, overlap, semordnilap, unlap
MAP	photomap, map
NAP	genapp, genappe, *horsenap, catnap, kidnap,* knap, nap, nappe, *surnap*
PAP	pap, genipap
RAP	enwrap, *giftwrap,* rap, wrap, unwrap
SAP	homo sap, sap, *winesap*
SKRAP	scrap
SLAP	*backslap,* reslap, slap
SNAP	resnap, snap, unsnap
STRAP	bestrap, *blackstrap, checkstrap, jockstrap,* restrap, shoulder strap, strap, unstrap, *watchstrap*
TAP	heel tap, retap, tap, water tap
TRAP	*D deathtrap, E entrap, F firetrap, FL fleatrap, flytrap, KL claptrap, M mantrap, mousetrap, R rat trap, rattletrap, S sun trap, TR trap, untrap*
YAP	lagniappe, yap, yapp
ZAP	zap

ÄP

(See OP)

ĀPS

NĀPS	jackanapes
TRĀPS	traipse

(See AP, add *-s* where appropriate.)

APS

APS	apse
CHAPS	chaps, pettichaps
HAPS	haps, perhaps
KRAPS	craps
LAPS	elapse, illapse, interlapse, collapse, lapse, *prolapse,* relapse
NAPS	*synapse*
SHNAPS	schnapps

(See AP, *add -s* where appropriate.)

ĀPT

(See ĀP, *add -d* where appropriate.)

APT

APT	apt, inapt, periapt
CHAPT	chapped, unchapped
DAPT	adapt, maladapt
KAPT	capped, *moss-capped, snow-capped*
RAPT	enrapt, rapt, wrapped
STRAPT	bestrapped, restrapped, strapped, unstrapped

(See AP, add *-ped* where appropriate.)

ÂR

ÂR	*A* air, Aire, Ayr, Eir, e'er, ere, eyre, heir, *H* howe'er, *HW* whate'er, whatsoe'er, whene'er, whensoe'er, where'er, wheresoe'er, *J* jardiniere, *K* co-heir, *M* mid-air, *P* portiere, *PL* plein-air, *PR* premiere, *V* vivandiere
BÂR	*B* bare, bear, *bugbear, F* forbear, *forebear, K* Camembert, *cudbear, M* misbear, *O* overbear, *THR* threadbare, *U* underbear, upbear
BLÂR	blare
CHÂR	*armchair,* chair, chare, *highchair, wheelchair, pushchair,* rocking chair, sedan chair,
DÂR	bedare, dare, Kildare, outdare
FÂR	*A* affair, *CH* chargé d'affaires, *F fanfare,* fair, fare, *fieldfare, funfare, K* county fair, *L laissez-faire, M Mayfair,* misfare, *S* savoir faire, *ST* state fair, *TH* thoroughfare, *U* unfair, *V* Vanity Fair, *W warfare,* welfare
FLÂR	flair, flare
FRÂR	*confrère*
GÂR	gair, gare
GLÂR	beglare, glair, glare
HÂR	hair, hare, *horsehair,* camelhair, maidenhair, *mohair,* unhair
HWÂR	*elsewhere,* anywhere, everywhere, where, *nowhere, somewhere,* otherwhere
KÂR	aftercare, devil-may-care, care, Medicare, natal care, prenatal care
KLÂR	declare, eclair, undeclare

KWÂR	quair
LÂR	capillaire, lair
MÂR	mal de mer, mare, mayor, *nightmare*
NÂR	*B* billionaire, *D* debonair, doctrinaire, *K* commissionaire, concessionaire, *KW* questionnaire, *M* millionaire, *N* ne'er, *TR* trillionaire, *V* vin ordinaire
NYÂR	jardiniere
PÂR	disrepair, impair, compare, au pair, pair, pare, pear, prickly pear, repair
PRÂR	prayer
RÂR	rare
SÂR	*corsair*
SHÂR	share, joint share, crop share, *plowshare,* porte-cochere, torchère
SKÂR	rescare, scare, unscare
SKWÂR	*foursquare, headsquare,* resquare, square, T square, unsquare
SNÂR	ensnare, resnare, snare, unsnare
SPÂR	despair, spare
STÂR	*backstair,* front stair, cocklestair, outstare, spiral stair, stare, upstare
SWÂR	forswear, outswear, sware, swear, unswear
TÂR	parterre, pied-à-terre, proletaire, solitaire, tare, tear, up-tear, Voltaire
THÂR	their, there
VÂR	revers, vair, vare
WÂR	*A* aware, *B* beware, *D* Delaware, *E* earthenware, *F firmware, footwear, GL glassware, H hardware, hornware, L liveware, M menswear, N neckwear, nightwear, O outwear,* overwear, *R rainware, redware, S* silverware, *software, SP sportswear, ST stemware, stoneware, T* tableware, *tinware, TR treenware, U* unaware, underwear, *W* ware, wear
YÂR	Gruyère, tuyère, mamelière, meunière, yair, yare
ZÂR	misère
ZHÂR	étagère, fourragère

ÄR

ÄR	antiar, aar, are, foliar, gangliar, jaguar, caviar

BÄR	A axlebar, B bar, *busbar*, D debar, disbar, *durbar*, DR drawbar, E embar, H handlebar, I isallobar, isobar, KR crossbar, *crowbar*, M Malabar, millibar, R rollbar, S saddlebar, centibar, cinnabar, SH shacklebar, T *towbar*, U unbar, upbar, W Wunderbar, Z Zanzibar		

vermicular, vernacular, versicular, Y uvular

LWÄR	couloir, Loire
MÄR	jacamar, maar, mar, Palomar, cymar, tintamarre
MWÄR	aide memoire, armoire, memoir, moire
NÄR	dinar, canard, *columnar*, gnar, knar, narr, laminar, seminar, *sonar*, thenar
NWÄR	bête noire, Renoir, rouge et noire
PÄR	par, parr
SÄR	commissar, *pulsar*
SKÄR	rescar, scar, unscar
SPÄR	*feldspar,* spar, unspar
STÄR	*daystar, earthstar,* evening star, falling star, instar, *lonestar, lodestar,* morning star, north star, pilot star, *polestar,* star, sunstar, *Telstar*
TÄR	avatar, guitar, kantar, catarrh, katar, scimitar, sitar, tahr, tar
STRÄR	registrar
TSÄR	tsar
TWÄR	abattoir, escritoire, repertoire
VÄR	bolivar, Bolivar, *boulevard,* cultivar, *louvar,* Navarre, samovar
VWÄR	devoir, au revoir, reservoir
WÄR	peignoir
YÄR	boyar, sillar, Wanderjahr
ZÄR	bazaar, bizarre, hussar, czar

BWÄR	pourboire
CHÄR	char
DÄR	dar, deodar, havildar, haznadar, hospodar, jemadar, calendar, objet d'art, *radar, sirdar,* subahdar, tahsildar, zamindar
DWÄR	boudoir
FÄR	afar, far, insofar, so far, *shophar*
GÄR	budgerigar, gar, segar, cigar, *Trafalgar,* vinegar
JÄR	ajar, jar, *nightjar*
KÄR	B boxcar, CH chukar, J jaunting car, gyrocar, K car, L Lascar, M motorcar, O autocar, R railway car, S sidecar, sircar, SH shikar, STR streetcar, T turbocar, TR trocar, trolley car
KWÄR	quar
LÄR	A angular, animalcular, acetabular, annular, axillar, B binocular, D dissimilar, E escolar, F fabular, funicular, FL flagellar, GL glandular, globular, I incunabular, insular, irregular, J jocular, jugular, K capsular, consular, cunabular, KR crepuscular, KW quadrangular, L lamellar, M modular, molecular, monocular, N nebular, O ocular, ovular, P particular, perpendicular, popular, R regular, S secular, similar, simular, singular, circular, somnambular, SF spherular, SK scapular, schedular, SP spatular, spectacular, ST stellular, T tabernacular, tabular, tesselar, tintinnabular, titular, tonsilar, torcular, tubular, tutelar, TR triangular, V valvular, vascular, vehicular,

ÄRB

ÄRB	*coarb*
BÄRB	barb, rhubarb
DÄRB	darb
GÄRB	garb
TÄRB	pantarbe
YÄRB	yarb

ÄRBD

(See **ÄRB,** add *-ed* where appropriate.)

ÄRCH

ÄRCH	arch, inarch, overarch
LÄRCH	larch
MÄRCH	dead march, *frogmarch,* countermarch, march, outmarch, overmarch, remark, route march
PÄRCH	parch
STÄRCH	*cornstarch,* starch

ÂRD

ÂRD	aired, heired, co-heired, un-heired
BÂRD	bared, rebared, unbared
CHÂRD	chaired, rechaired, unchaired
DÂRD	dared, redared, undared
FÂRD	fared
FLÂRD	flared, reflared
HÂRD	BL black-haired, blond-haired, F fair-haired, G golden-haired, GR gray-haired, K curly-haired, R raven-haired, *red-haired,* S silver-haired, *ST straight-haired,* T Titian-haired
KÂRD	cared, uncared
KLÂRD	declared, redeclared, undeclared
LÂRD	laird, laired
PÂRD	impaired, paired, prepared, repaired, unimpaired, unpaired, unprepared, unrepaired
SHÂRD	reshared, shared, unshared
SNÂRD	ensnared, snared
SPÂRD	despaired, spared, unspared
STÂRD	stared, outstared

(See **ÂR,** add *-d* or *-ed* where appropriate.)

ÄRD

ÄRD	milliard
BÄRD	bard, barred, bombard, debarred, close-barred
CHÄRD	chard, charred
FÄRD	fard
GÄRD	A afterguard, Asgard, avant-garde, B bodyguard, BL blackguard, D disregard, E enguard, G guard, K Kierkegaard, L laggard, lifeguard, M mudguard, N noseguard, R regard, rearguard, S safeguard, V vanguard
HÄRD	blowhard, die-hard, hard
JÄRD	jarred
KÄRD	birthday card, discard, file card, Jacquard, calling card, card, placard, postal card, postcard, racecard, report card, scorecard, timecard, wedding card
LÄRD	Abelard, foulard, interlard, lard, poulard
MÄRD	marred, remarred, unmarred

NÄRD	canard, gnarred, communard, knarred, nard, Reynard, *spikenard*
PÄRD	camelopard, pard
SÄRD	*brassard, mansard,* sard
SHÄRD	shard
SKÄRD	rescarred, scarred, unscarred
STÄRD	bestarred, evil-starred, ill-starred, starred
TÄRD	dynamitard, petard, retard, retarred, tarred, untarred
VÄRD	boulevard
YÄRD	*B* backyard, barnyard, boneyard, *BR* brickyard, *CH* chickenyard, *churchyard, D* dockyard, dooryard, *F* foreyard, *FR* front yard, *GR* graveyard, *H* hopyard, *J* junkyard, *K* kaleyard, courtyard, *L* lumberyard, *M* milliard, Montagnard, *P* poultry yard, *S* Savoyard, *SH* shipyard, *ST* steelyard, stockyard, *T* tiltyard, timberyard, *V* vineyard, *Y* yard

(See **ÄR**, add *-ed* or *-red* where appropriate.)

ÄRF

ÄRF	*headscarf,* arf, 'arf-and-'arf
BÄRF	barf
LÄRF	larf
SKÄRF	scarf
ZÄRF	zarf

ÄRJ

BÄRJ	barge
CHÄRJ	charge, discharge, encharge, countercharge, overcharge, recharge, supercharge, *surcharge,* uncharge, undercharge
LÄRJ	enlarge, large, reënlarge
MÄRJ	lithomarge, marge, sea marge
SÄRJ	sarge
SPÄRJ	sparge
TÄRJ	targe
THÄRJ	litharge

ÄRJD

LÄRJD	unenlarged

(See **ÄRJ**, add *-d* where appropriate.)

ÄRK

ÄRK	arc, ark, Asiarch, *diarch,* ecclesiarch, heresiarch, gymnasiarch, matriarch, Noah's ark, patriarch, symposiarch
BÄRK	bark, barque, debark, disembark, embark, ironbark, paperbark, *shagbark, shellbark, snakebark, soapbark, tanbark*
DÄRK	bedark, dark, endark
GÄRK	oligarch
HÄRK	hark
KÄRK	cark
KLÄRK	clerk
KWÄRK	quark
LÄRK	lark, meadowlark, *mudlark, sealark, skylark, titlark, woodlark*
MÄRK	*B* birthmark, Bismarck, bookmark, *D* Denmark, *E* earmark, easy mark, *F* fingermark, *Finnmark,* footmark, *FL* floodmark, *H* hallmark, *K* countermark, *L* landmark, *M* marc, mark, marque, Monomark, *O* ostmark, *P* pockmark, postmark, *PL* platemark, *PR* pressmark, *R* remark, remarque, *Reichsmark, S* sitzmark, *T* telemark, *tidemark, touchmark, TH* thumbmark, *TR* trademark, *W* watermark
NÄRK	*anarch, ethnarch, irenarch, monarch,* knark, narc, nark
PÄRK	amusement park, ball park, dispark, *eparch, hipparch,* impark, park, repark, *toparch,* unpark
RÄRK	hierarch, *Petrarch, tetrarch, xerarch*
SÄRK	*exarch,* sark
SHÄRK	blacktip shark, blue shark, bullhead shark, dog shark, dusky shark, hammerhead shark, white shark, *landshark,* leopard shark, porbeagle shark, shark, shovelhead shark
SPÄRK	spark
STÄRK	stark
VÄRK	*aardvark*
YÄRK	yark
ZÄRK	*Ozark*

ÄRKS

ÄRKS	Marx

(See **ÄRK**, add *-s* where appropriate.)

ÄRKT

(See **ÄRK**, add *-ed* where appropriate.)

ÄRL

FÄRL	farl
HÄRL	harl
JÄRL	jarl
KÄRL	*housecarl,* carl
MÄRL	Albemarle, marl
NÄRL	gnarl
PÄRL	imparl
SNÄRL	snarl, unsnarl

ÄRM

ÄRM	*A* arm, axle arm, *D* disarm, *F* firearm, forearm, *I* inarm, *KR* crossarm, *O* overarm, *R* rearm, *S* sidearm, *U* unarm, underarm, *Y* yardarm
BÄRM	barm
CHÄRM	becharm, charm, decharm, disencharm, counter-charm, love charm, uncharm
DÄRM	gendarme
FÄRM	aquafarm, farm, county farm, poor farm
HÄRM	harm, unharm
LÄRM	alarm, false alarm
MÄRM	marm, *schoolmarm*
SMÄRM	smarm
THÄRM	tharm
ZÄRM	gisarme

ÂRN

BÂRN	bairn
DÂRN	moderne
KÂRN	cairn, *Pitcairn*

ÄRN

BÄRN	barn, imbarn
DÄRN	darn, goldarn, goshdarn
KÄRN	incarn, lucarne
LÄRN	l'arn

MÄRN	Marne
SÄRN	consarn
TÄRN	tarn
YÄRN	yarn

ÄRND

(See **ÄRN,** add *-ed* where appropriate.)

ÄRP

HÄRP	harp, Irish harp, Jew's harp, claviharp
KÄRP	archicarp, endocarp, epicarp, escarp, carp, mesocarp, monocarp, pericarp, *syncarp,* cystocarp
SHÄRP	*cardsharp,* sharp
SKÄRP	escarp, counterscarp, scarp
TÄRP	tarp
ZÄRP	zarp

ÄRS

ÄRS	arse
FÄRS	farce
GÄRS	garce
KÄRS	carse
PÄRS	parse
SPÄRS	sparse

ÄRSH

HÄRSH	harsh
MÄRSH	démarche, marsh

ÄRT

ÄRT	art, modern art, op art, pop art, state-of-the-art, video art (etc.)
BÄRT	Bart
CHÄRT	chart, flip chart, rechart, unchart
DÄRT	dart, indart
FÄRT	fart, sparrowfart
HÄRT	*Bernhardt, faintheart, flintheart, greenheart,* hart, heart, lionheart, *stoutheart, sweetheart,* unheart
KÄRT	à la carte, cart, quarte, Descartes, *dogcart, dumpcart, gocart,* uncart, watercart
KLÄRT	clart
MÄRT	jumart, mart
PÄRT	apart, depart, dispart,

	forepart, impart, counterpart, *mouthpart,* part, *rampart,* repart
SÄRT	assart, Mozart, sart
SMÄRT	outsmart, smart
STÄRT	astart, head start, *kick start,* restart, *redstart, upstart*
TÄRT	apple tart, sugar tart, tart

ÄRTH

GÄRTH	*fishgarth,* garth, *Hogarth*
HÄRTH	hearth
SWÄRTH	swarth

ÄRTS

ÄRTS	arts
SMÄRTS	smarts, street-smarts

(See **ÄRT,** add *-s* where appropriate.)

ÄRV

KÄRV	carve
LÄRV	larve
STÄRV	starve
VÄRV	varve

ÂRZ

STÂRS	*backstairs, downstairs,* front stairs, stairs, *upstairs*
WÂRS	unawares, unbewares, unwares

(See **ÂR,** add *-s* where appropriate.)

ÄRZ

MÄRZ	Mars

(See **ÄR,** add *-s* where appropriate.)

ĀS

ĀS	*ambsace,* ace, casease, nuclease, protease, ribonuclease
BĀS	abase, base, bass, debase, free base, *wheelbase,* contrabass, octobass, *subbase, surbase*
BRĀS	brace, embrace, *mainbrace,* unbrace, underbrace, *vambrace*

CHĀS	chase, enchase, steeplechase
DĀS	dace, dais, oxidase, peptidase, *vendace*
FĀS	*A* aface, angel face, *B* baby face, *boldface,* boniface, *BL* blackface, *D* deface, *E* efface, *F* face, *FR* frogface, *HW* wheyface, *I* interface, *K* catface, *O* outface, *P* paleface, pigface, *PL* platterface, *R* reface, *typeface*
GRĀS	begrace, disgrace, grace, *scapegrace*
KĀS	*B* basket case, *bookcase, BR* briefcase, *E* endcase, encase, *K* cardcase, case, *KR* crankcase, *N* notecase, nut-case, *S* seedcase, *SH* showcase, *SL* slipcase, *SM* smearcase, *ST* staircase, *T* test case, *typecase, U* uncase, *W* watchcase, *Y* ukase
KLĀS	orthoclase, periclase
KRĀS	*sucrase*
LĀS	bootlace, enlace, interlace, catalase, Queen Anne's lace, lace, *Lovelace,* populace, relace, cellulase, *shoelace,* unlace
MĀS	grimace, mace, Mace
NĀS	*tenace*
PĀS	apace, *footpace,* carapace, quarterpace, *lipace,* outpace, pace
PLĀS	*birthplace,* displace, *fireplace,* hiding place, commonplace, marketplace, misplace, place, plaice, replace, resting place, *showplace,* trysting place
RĀS	*B* boat race, *CH* channel race, chariot race, *D* dog race, *DR* drag race, *E* erase, *F* foot race, *H* headrace, horse race, *I* in media res, *L* land race, *M* mile race, millrace, marathon race, *O* auto race, *R* race, res, rat race, *S* sack race, *T* tail race, *TH* three-legged race (etc.)
SĀS	*Alsace*
SPĀS	aerospace, *airspace, backspace,* breathing space, inner space, hyperspace, interspace, outer space, space
TĀS	anatase, phosphatase,

	invertase, *lactase, maltase, pectase*
THRĀS	Samothrace, Thrace
TRĀS	retrace, trace
VĀS	transvase, vase

AS

AS	alias, ass, Boreas, habeas, *jackass,* paterfamilias, pancreas, Pythias
BAS	anabas, bass, contrabass, octobass, rubasse
BRAS	brass, brasse
FAS	volte-face
FRAS	frass, sassafras
GAS	bagasse, degas, fougasse, gas, megass, noble gas, *syngas*
GLAS	*FL* flint glass, *G* gallowglass, *GL* glass, *I* isinglass, *eyeglass, L* looking glass, *M* magnifying glass, minute glass, *O* object glass, *hourglass, SP* spyglass, *ST* stained glass, *W* waterglass, weatherglass
GRAS	aftergrass, *eelgrass,* grass, coup de grace, *crabgrass,* peppergrass, sparrowgrass
KAS	*fracas*
KLAS	declass, *first-class,* class, middle class, outclass, reclass, second-class, *third-class,* underclass, upperclass, working class
KRAS	crass, hippocras
LAS	alas, lass
MAS	*A* admass, Allhallowmas, amass, *B* biomass, *D* damasse, *E* en masse, *GR* groundmass, *H* Hallowmas, *K camass,* Candlemas, *KR* Christmas, *L* land mass, *M* Martinmas, mass, Mass, Michaelmas, *R* remass
NAS	vinasse
PAS	impasse, Khyber Pass, overpass, pass, repass, surpass, *trespass,* underpass, Eurailpass
RAS	*arras,* harass, cuirass, morass, wrasse, terrasse
SAS	Alsace, sass
STRAS	strass
TAS	demitasse, tarantass, tass, Tass, tasse
VAS	kavass, crevasse, vas
YAS	paillasse
ZAS	rosace

ÄS

GRÄS	coup de grace
KLÄS	declass, *first-class,* class, middle class, outclass, reclass, second-class, *third-class,* underclass, upperclass, working class
KVÄS	kvass
LÄS	alas
PÄS	Khyber Pass, overpass, pass, repass, underpass, Eurailpass
TÄS	demitasse

ASH

ASH	ash, mountain ash, weeping ash
BASH	abash, bash, *earbash,* calabash, squabash, *Wabash*
BLASH	blash
BRASH	brash
DASH	balderdash, bedash, interdash, pebble-dash, rondache, *slapdash,* spatterdash, splatterdash
FASH	fash
FLASH	photoflash, flash, Syncroflash
GASH	gash
HASH	hache, rehash
KASH	encache, encash, cache, cash
KLASH	clash
KRASH	crash
LASH	*backlash, frontlash, goulash, whiplash, eyelash,* calash, lash, *throatlash,* unlash
MASH	*quamash,* mash, *mishmash, shamash*
NASH	gnash, panache
PASH	apache, Apache, calipash, pash
PLASH	plash
RASH	rash
SASH	sash
SLASH	slash
SMASH	smash
SNASH	snash
SPLASH	splash
STASH	stash
TASH	mustache, patache, pistache, soutache, sabretache, succotash, tash
THRASH	thrash
TRASH	trash
VASH	*chichevache*

ASK

ASK	ask
BASK	bask, Basque
FLASK	flask, hip flask, powder flask
HASK	hask
KASK	cask, casque, watercask
MASK	antimask, antimasque, antic-mask, antic-masque, bemask, mask, masque, remask, unmask
TASK	overtask, task

ÄSK

ÄSK	ask
BÄSK	bask
FLÄSK	flask, hip flask, powder flask
KÄSK	cask, watercask
MÄSK	antimask, antimasque, antic-mask, antic-masque, bemask, mask, masque, remask, unmask
TÄSK	overtask, task

ASKT

ASKT	asked, unasked

(See **ASK,** add *-ed* where appropriate.)

ÄSKT	asked, unasked

(See **ÄSK,** add *-ed* where appropriate.)

ASP

ASP	asp
GASP	agasp, gasp
GRASP	engrasp, grasp
HASP	hasp, rehasp, unhasp
KLASP	enclasp, *handclasp,* clasp, reclasp, unclasp
RASP	rasp

ASPT

(See **ASP,** add *-ed* where appropriate.)

ĀST

ĀST	aced
BĀST	abased, based, baste, debased, lambaste, self-abased

BRĀST braced, embraced, unbraced, unembraced

CHĀST chased, chaste, unchased, unchaste

FĀST *A* angel-faced, apple-faced, *B* baby-faced, *baldfaced, barefaced,* bold-faced, *BR* brazen-faced, *D* defaced, dirty-faced, *dish-faced, doughfaced,* double-faced, *E* effaced, *F* faced, furrow-faced, *FR* freckle-faced, *H* hard-faced, hatchet-faced, *horse-faced, HW* whey-faced, *J* Janus-faced, *KL* clean-faced, *L* lean-faced, lily-faced, *M* mottle-faced, *P* pale-faced, paper-faced, *pie-faced,* pickle-faced, pimple-faced, pippin-faced, pudding-faced, *pug-faced, PL* platter-faced, *plump-faced, R* refaced, *SH* shamefaced, *SM* smooth-faced, smug-faced, *T* tallow-faced, *two-faced, TR* triple-faced, *U* undefaced, *unshamefaced, V* vinegar-faced, *W* weasel-faced, wizen-faced

GRĀST disgraced, graced, undisgraced, ungraced, well-graced

HĀST haste, *posthaste*

KĀST encased, cased, uncased

LĀST enlaced, interlaced, laced, relaced, straitlaced, unlaced

MĀST grimaced

PĀST impaste, leaden-paced, outpaced, paced, paste, *slow-paced, snail-paced, toothpaste,* thorough-paced

PLĀST displaced, misplaced, placed, replaced, unplaced

SNĀST snaste

SPĀST interspaced, spaced, respaced, unspaced

TĀST after-taste, distaste, *foretaste,* taste

TRĀST retraced, traced, untraced

WĀST pantywaist, waist, waste

AST

AST bucoliast, ecdysiast, ecclesiast, elegiast, encomiast, enthusiast, gymnasiast, orgiast, scholiast, symposiast, cineast, *tight-assed*

BAST bast, *bombast*

BLAST blast, erythroblast, counterblast, lymphoblast, mesoblast, neuroblast, osteoblast, *sandblast, stormblast*

DAST dast

FAST *Belfast, breakfast,* emberfast, fast, *handfast, headfast, holdfast,* colorfast, *makefast, sitfast, sunfast, steadfast,* unfast

FNAST fnast

FRAST metaphrast, paraphrast

GAST aghast, flabbergast, gassed, gast

HAST hast

KAST *BR* broadcast, *D* dicast, *die-cast,* downcast, *F* forecast, *H* half-caste, high-caste, *K* cablecast, cast, caste, *L low-caste, M* miscast, *molecast, N* newscast, *O* opencast, outcast, overcast, *PR* precast, *R* recast, *rough-cast, S* simulcast, *SP* sportscast, *T* telecast, *typecast, U* undercast, under-caste, upcast, *W wormcast*

KLAST iconoclast, idoloclast, classed, osteoclast, outclassed, reclassed, theoclast, unclassed

LAST agelast, *ballast,* last, *oblast,* outlast, *portlast*

MAST *A* amassed, *D* dismast, *durmast, F* foremast, *H* half-mast, *J* jiggermast, jury mast, *M mainmast,* massed, mast, mizzen mast, *R* remassed, remast, *T topmast, U* unmassed, unmast

NAST *dynast, gymnast,* nast

PAST passed, past, repassed, repast, surpassed, *trispast,* unsurpassed

PLAST leucoplast, chloroplast, metaplast, protoplast

RAST harassed, pederast

SAST sassed, resassed

SNAST snast

SPAST antispast, *trispast*

TAST *fantast, phantast, peltast*

TRAST contrast

VAST avast, devast, vast

(See **AS,** add *-ed* where appropriate.)

ÄST

(See **OST**)

ĀT

ĀT *A* ate, ait, eight, eyot, abbreviate, absinthiate, affiliate, accentuate, actuate, aculeate, alleviate, ammoniate, ampliate, annunciate, appreciate, appropriate, asphyxiate, associate, attenuate, aviate, *B* benzoate, bifoliate, *BR* brachiate, *D* debulliate, defoliate, delineate, denunciate, depreciate, deviate, differentiate, dimidiate, disaffiliate, disambiguate, disassociate, discalceate, dissociate, *E* effectuate, exfodiate, exfoliate, excalceate, excruciate, expropriate, enucleate, enunciate, eradiate, evacuate, evaluate, eventuate, excoriate, expatiate, expatriate, expiate, extenuate, exuviate, *F* fasciate, figure-eight, filiate, foliate, *FL* floriate, fluctuate, *FR* free-associate, fructuate, *GL* gladiate, glaciate, *GR* graduate, *H* habituate, humiliate, *I* ideate, immateriate, impropriate, inchoate, increate, individuate, inebriate, infatuate, infuriate, ingratiate, initiate, insatiate, insinuate, instantiate, irradiate, *K* chalybeate, calumniate, caseate, cochleate, conciliate, consociate, *KR* create, *KW* quadrifoliate, *L* labiate, laciniate, lixiviate, lineolate, licentiate, luxuriate, *M* maleate, marsupiate, mediate, menstruate, miscreate, *N* negotiate, nauseate, novitiate, nucleate, *O* obganiate, obviate, officiate, oleate, opiate, aureate, overate, *P* palliate, permeate, perpetuate, pileate, poet

laureate, pogoniate,
potentiate, punctuate, *PR*
professoriate, procreate,
propitiate, provinciate, *R*
radiate, recreate,
remediate, renegotiate,
repatriate, repudiate,
retaliate, *S* sagaciate,
satiate, seriate, sinuate,
circumstantiate, situate,
substantiate, superannuate,
SP spoliate, *T* tenuate,
tertiate, toluate, *TR*
transsubstantiate, *U*
uncreate, *V* vacuate,
valuate, variate, vicariate,
vitiate

BĀT *A* abate, approbate,
acerbate, *B* bait, bate,
bilobate, *D* debate, *E*
exacerbate, *HW* whitebait,
I incubate, *K* cohobate,
conglobate, *KR* crowbait,
L lowbait, *M* makebate,
masturbate, *PR* probate,
rebate, reprobate, *S*
celibate, *ST* stereobate,
stylobate

BRĀT elucubrate, invertebrate,
calibrate, lucubrate,
obtenebrate, palpebrate,
celebrate, cerebrate,
vertebrate

DĀT *A* accommodate, afterdate,
antedate, *BL* blind date, *D*
date, *decaudate, denudate,*
depredate, dilapidate,
double date, Dutch date, *E*
exheredate, elucidate, *FL*
fluoridate, *GR gradate, I*
ingravidate, inlapidate,
interdate, intimidate,
inundate, invalidate, *K*
candidate, consolidate,
cuspidate, *KL* chlamydate,
L lapidate, liquidate, *M*
misdate, *O* oxidate,
outdate, *P* postdate, *PR*
predate, *R* redate,
rhipidate, *S* sedate, *V*
validate, vanadate

DRĀT *dehydrate*
FĀT fate, fete, caliphate
FLĀT deflate, efflate, inflate,
conflate, sufflate
FRĀT affreight, freight
GĀT *A* ablegate, abnegate,
abrogate, aggregate,
arrogate, *B* billingsgate, *D*
delegate, derogate,
desegregate, disgregate,
divagate, *E* expurgate,

extravagate, erugate, *F*
fumigate, fustigate, *FL*
floodgate, G gait, gate, *H*
homologate, *I* instigate,
interrogate, investigate,
irrigate, irrugate, *K*
castigate, colligate,
congregate, conjugate,
corrugate, *L* levigate,
litigate, *M* mitigate, *N*
navigate, negate, *O*
objurgate, obligate,
obrogate, *PR* promulgate,
propagate, *R* relegate,
religate, runagate, *S*
seagate, segregate,
sejugate, circumnavigate,
subjugate, subrogate,
suffumigate, supererogate,
T tailgate, V variegate,
vitiligate, *vulgate, W*
Watergate

GRĀT denigrate, disintegrate,
emigrate, grate, great,
immigrate, *ingrate,*
integrate, *migrate,*
redintegrate, regrate,
transmigrate

HĀT hate, *self-hate*
KĀT *A* abdicate, ablocate,
adjudicate, advocate,
allocate, altercate,
applicate, apricate, *B*
bifurcate, *bisulcate, D*
dedicate, defecate,
decorticate, delicate,
demarcate, deprecate,
desecate, desiccate,
detoxicate, diagnosticate,
dislocate, divaricate,
domesticate, duplicate, *E*
educate, excommunicate,
expiscate, explicate,
exsiccate, extricate,
equivocate, elasticate,
embrocate, eradicate, *F*
fabricate, *falcate,*
fimbricate, formicate,
fornicate, *H* hypothecate, *I*
imbricate, implicate,
imprecate, improlificate,
indicate, infuscate,
inculcate, intoxicate,
invocate, irradicate, *K*
Californicate, canonicate,
collocate, communicate,
complicate, confiscate,
conspurcate, corticate,
coruscate, *KW*
quadruplicate,
quintuplicate, *L* locate,
loricate, lubricate, *M*

masticate, medicate,
mendicate, metricate,
multiplicate, muricate, *N*
nidificate, nostrificate, *O*
obfuscate, authenticate, *P*
pontificate, *PL placate, PR*
predicate, prefabricate,
prevaricate, prognosticate,
R radicate, rededicate,
reduplicate, relocate,
resiccate, reciprocate,
revindicate, rubricate,
rusticate, *S* syllabicate,
syndicate, silicate,
sophisticate, suffocate,
sulcate, supplicate,
suricate, *SK* scholasticate,
SP spiflicate, *T* tunicate,
TR translocate, U urticate,
V vacate, vellicate,
vesicate, vindicate

KRĀT deconsecrate, desecrate,
execrate, consecrate,
obsecrate, crate, krait,
recrate, uncrate

KWĀT antiquate, equate, *liquate,*
torquate

LĀT *A* absquatulate, adulate,
accumulate, alveolate,
ambulate, angulate,
annihilate, annulate,
apostolate, articulate,
assibilate, acidulate,
assimilate, *B* barbellate,
belate, bimaculate,
binoculate, *D* de-escalate,
deflocculate, *decollate,*
delate, depilate,
depopulate, depucelate,
desolate, dilate,
disarticulate,
discombobulate,
dissimilate, dissimulate, *E*
ejaculate, exoculate,
expostulate, exsibilate,
extrapolate, exungulate,
elate, emasculate, emulate,
encapsulate, epilate,
escalate, ethylate, etiolate,
F faveolate, fellate,
phenolate, foliolate,
formulate, funambulate,
FL flagellate, flocculate,
GR granulate, *I* immolate,
infibulate, incastellate,
inoculate, insolate,
insulate, interpolate,
interrelate, intumulate,
invigilate, inviolate,
isolate, *J* gesticulate,
jubilate, jugulate, *K*
calculate, campanulate,

cannulate, cancellate,
cantillate, capitulate,
capsulate, carboxylate,
cardinalate, coagulate,
collate, confabulate,
congratulate, constellate,
consulate, copulate,
corniculate, correlate,
cucullate, cumulate,
cupulate, *KR* crenellate,
crenulate, *L* lamellate,
lanceolate, late, legislate,
lingulate, lunulate, *M*
machicolate, mammilate,
manipulate, matriculate,
mentulate, miscalculate,
mistranslate, modulate,
morcellate, methylate,
mutilate, *N* nasillate,
nodulate, nucleolate, *O*
obambulate, oblate,
obnubilate, obvallate,
oxalate, oppilate, ocellate,
oscillate, osculate, ovulate,
P peculate, pendulate,
peninsulate, perambulate,
percolate, poculate,
populate, postulate,
pullulate, pustulate, *R*
regulate, recapitulate,
relate, repullulate,
reticulate, *S* salicylate,
sibilate, simulate,
scintillate,
circumambulate,
somnambulate, circulate,
sublate, substaquilate,
suggilate, succulate, *SF*
sphacelate, spherulate, *SK*
scutellate, *SKR*
scrobiculate, *SP* speculate,
sporulate, *ST* stellulate,
stimulate, stipulate, *STR*
strangulate, stridulate, *T*
tabulate, tasselate, titillate,
tubulate, tumulate, *TR*
translate, triangulate, *U*
ululate, undulate, ungulate,
ustulate, *V* vacillate,
vassalate, ventilate,
vermiculate, vinculate,
violate, virgulate

MĀT   *A* acclamate, acclimate,
amalgamate, animate,
approximate, *B* bunkmate,
CH checkmate, *D*
decimate, desquamate,
despumate, desublimate,
dichromate, diplomate, *E*
estimate, *F* first mate, *G*
guesstimate, *GL* glutamate,
H helpmate, hindermate, *I*

inanimate, infumate,
intimate, *K* casemate,
collimate, *comate,*
consummate, conformate,
KL classmate, *KR* cremate,
L legitimate, *M* mate,
messmate, metrobomate,
mismate, *O* optimate,
automate, *P* palamate,
palmate, penultimate,
perhiemate, *PL* playmate,
PR proximate, *S* second
mate, cyclamate,
sublimate, *SH shipmate,*
SK schoolmate, ST
stalemate, T tentmate, TH
third mate, *TR*
trenchermate, *U*
underestimate

NĀT   *A* abominate, agglutinate,
acuminate, alienate,
alternate, aluminate,
amirrate, ammonate,
arsenate, assassinate,
assonate, *B* bicarbonate,
bipinnate, D deaminate,
deglutinate, decaffeinate,
decarbonate,
decontaminate, declinate,
delaminate, denominate,
deracinate, desalinate,
designate, destinate,
detonate, devirginate,
discriminate, disseminate,
dominate, donate, *E*
echinate, explanate,
exsanguinate, exterminate,
extortionate, eliminate,
emanate, emarginate,
enate, evaginate, *F*
fascinate, foreordinate,
fulminate, functionate, *FL*
fluorinate, *FR* fractionate,
GL glutinate, *H*
hallucinate, hibernate,
hydrogenate, hyphenate, *I*
illuminate, immarginate,
impassionate, impersonate,
impregnate, indoctrinate,
ingeminate, ingerminate,
incatenate, incriminate,
inquinnate, innate,
inornate, inseminate,
interlaminate, interminate,
intonate, invaginate, *J*
gelatinate, geminate,
germinate, juvenate, *K*
cachinnate, cacuminate,
carbonate, carinate,
catenate, coadunate,
comminate, conditionate,
conglutinate, concatenate,

consternate, contaminate,
coordinate, coronate,
culminate, *KL* chlorinate,
KR criminate, *KW*
quaternate, *L* laminate,
lancinate, Latinate, *M*
machinate, marinate,
marginate, missionate, *N*
neonate, nominate, *O*
obsignate, oxygenate,
alternate, ordinate,
originate, ornate, *P*
paginate, patinate,
patronate, pectinate,
pepsinate, peregrinate,
perendinate,
permanganate, personate,
pollinate, pulvinate, *PR*
predestinate, predesignate,
predominate, procrastinate,
R raffinate, ratiocinate,
rejuvenate, reclinate,
recriminate, repristinate,
resinate, resonate,
ruminate, *S* saginate,
septenate, septentrionate,
cybernate, cincinnate,
circinate, succinate,
sultanate, supinate, *ST*
stellionate, *T* terminate,
tubicinate, turbinate, *TR*
trutinate, *U* uncinate, *V*
vaccinate, vaticinate,
vertiginate, *Y* urinate

PĀT   *A* adipate, anticipate, *D*
dissipate, dunderpate, *E*
exculpate, extirpate,
emancipate, episcopate, *K*
constipate, *M* mancipate, *P*
participate, pate, *R* rattle-
pate, *S* syncopate

PLĀT   *A* armorplate, *BR*
breastplate, D dial plate, *E*
electroplate, *F* fashion
plate, *K* contemplate,
copperplate, *N* nickelplate,
PL plait, plate, *S*
silverplate, *U* unplait

PRĀT   constuprate, prate
RĀT   *A* adulterate, advesperate,
aerate, agglomerate,
acculturate, accelerate,
alliterate, ameliorate,
annumerate, acerate,
aspirate, asseverate, *B*
berate, biforate, *birth-rate,*
D death rate, deblaterate,
decolorate, decorate,
degenerate, deliberate,
decelerate, decerebrate,
desiderate, deteriorate,
directorate, *E* edulcorate,

exaggerate, exasperate, exenterate, exhilirate, exaugurate, exonerate, expectorate, equilibrate, equiponderate, elaborate, electorate, enumerate, evaporate, eviscerate, *F* federate, figurate, *firstrate*, fulgurate, *H* hederate, *I* immensurate, imperforate, indurate, incarcerate, incorporate, inaugurate, incinerate, intenerate, intenurate, invigorate, irate, iterate, itinerate, *J* generate, *K* camphorate, chelicerate, collaborate, commemorate, commensurate, commiserate, confederate, conglomerate, concelebrate, considerate, contriturate, cooperate, corporate, corroborate, *cut-rate, KW* quatuorvirate, *L* lacerate, levirate, liberate, literate, *M* macerate, micturate, moderate, *N* narrate, numerate, *O* obdurate, obliterate, obturate, augurate, operate, oppignorate, orate, overrate, *P* pastorate, perforate, perorate, pignorate, *picrate*, purpurate, *PR* preponderate, presbyterate, proliferate, prorate, protectorate, protuberate, *R* rate, redecorate, refrigerate, reiterate, regenerate, rectorate, recuperate, remunerate, reverberate, *S* saccharate, saturate, second-rate, scelerate, separate, coelenterate, cicurate, sororate, sulphurate, suppurate, susurrate, *ST* stearate, *T* tellurate, tolerate, *TH* third-rate, *TR* transliterate, triturate, triumvirate, *U* ulcerate, underrate, *V* venerate, verberate, vituperate, viscerate, vociferate, *W* water rate

SĀT extravasate, improvisate, *inspissate*, compensate, condensate, marquisate, pulsate, sate, *sensate*, tergiversate

SKĀT *cheapskate*, roller skate, skate

SLĀT slate

SPĀT spate

STĀT *D downstate, E* estate, *I* instate, interstate, *M* misstate, *O* overstate, *R* reinstate, restate, *S* solid-state, *ST* state, steady-state, *U* understate, unstate, *upstate*

STRĀT *D* defenestrate, demonstrate, *F* fenestrate, *FR frustrate, I* illustrate, *K* capistrate, *M* magistrate, *O* orchestrate, *PR prostrate, R* registrate, *remonstrate, S* sequestrate, *STR* straight, strait

TĀT *A* acetate, acutate, agitate, amputate, annotate, *apostate, B bidentate, D* debilitate, *degustate*, decapitate, decrepitate, *decurtate, delectate, dentate*, devastate, digitate, dictate, dissertate, disorientate, *E edentate*, excogitate, exorbitate, *eructate*, estate, *F* facilitate, felicitate, *G* gurgitate, *GR* gravitate, *H* habilitate, hebetate, hesitate, *I* imitate, ingurgitate, incapacitate, interdigitate, *intestate*, inusitate, irritate, *J gestate, K* capacitate, capitate, cogitate, commentate, connotate, *costate, KR* crepitate, *KW* quantitate, *L* levitate, limitate, *M* meditate, militate, *N* necessitate, nictitate, *notate, O occultate*, orientate, oscitate, auscultate, ostentate, *P* palpitate, permutate, potentate, *PR* premeditate, precipitate, *prostate, R* regurgitate, rehabilitate, resuscitate, revegetate, rotate, *S* sagittate, sanitate, segmentate, subacetate, supputate, *T* testate, tête-à-tête, *TR* tridentate, tridigitate, *V* vegetate

THWĀT thwaite

TRĀT *A* administrate, arbitrate, *D* distrait, *I* impenetrate, impetrate, infiltrate, *K* concentrate, *M* magistrate,

O orchestrate, *P* penetrate, perpetrate, portrait, *R* recalcitrate, *S citrate, TR* trait

VĀT *A* aggravate, activate, *D* deactivate, depravate, deprivate, derivate, *E* excavate, elevate, enervate, estivate, *I* inactivate, *incurvate*, innervate, innovate, insalivate, *K* captivate, coacervate, cultivate, *M* motivate, *N nervate, R* radioactivate, reactivate, recaptivate, reclivate, *recurvate*, renovate, *S* salivate, *T* titivate

WĀT *A* await, *B* bantamweight, *D deadweight, F* featherweight, *H* heavyweight, hundredweight, *K* counterweight, *L lightweight, M* middleweight, *O* overweight, *P* paperweight, pennyweight, *U* underweight, *W* wait, weight, welterweight

AT

AT *A* at, *D Duat, H* hereat, *HW* whereat, *K* caveat, commissariat, *KR* croat, *L* lariat, *PR* proletariat, *S* salariat, secretariat, *TH* thereat

BAT *A* acrobat, *B* bat, *bullbat, BR* brickbat, *D* dingbat, *E esbat, FL* flitterbat, *FR fruitbat, H* hurlbat, *K* combat, *N* numbat, *S sabbat, W* wombat

BLAT blat

BRAT brat, *firebrat*

CHAT *backchat*, chat, *chitchat*, fallowchat, *furze-chat, grasschat, whinchat, stonechat, woodchat*, waterchat, yellow-breasted chat

DAT dis and dat, *concordat*

DRAT drat

FAT butterfat, fat, marrowfat

FLAT aflat, flat

FRAT frat

GAT begat, forgat, gat, *nougat*

HAT hat, high-hat, sunhat, *tophat*, unhat

KAT	*B bearcat, bobcat, F fatcat, H hellcat, hepcat, K* cat, kat, kitty-cat, cool cat, *KR* Krazy Kat, *M* Magnificat, *meerkat, mudcat, muscat, P polecat,* pussycat, *R requiescat, S* civet cat, *T* tabby cat, *tipcat, tomcat, W wildcat*
KRAT	*A* aristocrat, *B* bureaucrat, *D* democrat, Democrat, *H* hierocrat, *I* isocrat, *J* gerontocrat, gynaeocrat, *M* meritocrat, monocrat, nomocrat, *O* ochiocrat, autocrat, *P* pantisocrat, pornocrat, *PL* plutocrat, *R* rheocrat, *T* technocrat, timocrat, ptochocrat, *TH* theocrat
LAT	lat, cervelat
MAT	anastigmat, diplomat, doormat, format, Laundromat, mat, matte, automat
NAT	assignat, gnat
PAT	bepat, cowpat, pat, patte, pit-a-pat
PLAT	plait, plat, Platte
PRAT	dandiprat, prat
RAT	Ararat, rat, *muskrat,* Surat, water rat, ziggurat
SAT	Intelsat, *comsat,* sat
SHAT	shat
SKAT	scat, skat
SLAT	slat
SPAT	spat
SPLAT	splat
SPRAT	sprat, Jack Spratt
STAT	*A* aerostat, *B* barostat, *F* photostat, *H* heliostat, haemostat, hydrostat, *K* chemostat, *KL* clinostat, *P* pyrostat, *R* rheostat, *TH* thermostat
TAT	aegrotat, habitat, ratatat, ratatattat, tit-for-tat, tat
VAT	cravat, savate, vat
ZAT	xat

ÄT

BÄT	*esbat*
BWÄT	boite
DÄT	iddat
GÄT	ghat
HWÄT	what
KWÄT	*cumquat, kumquat*
RÄT	ziarat
SKWÄT	resquat, squat
SWÄT	swat

| WÄT | Duat, giga-watt, kilowatt, megawatt, watt |
| YÄT | yacht, land yacht, motor yacht, Rubaiyat, sailing yacht, sand yacht, steam yacht |

(See OT)

ĀTH (as in bathe)

BĀTH	bathe
LĀTH	lathe
RĀTH	raith, rathe
SKĀTH	scathe
SNĀTH	snathe
SPĀTH	spathe
SWĀTH	swathe, unswathe

ĀTH (as in faith)

FĀTH	faith, i'faith, misfaith, unfaith
GRĀTH	graith
RĀTH	waterwraith, wraith

ATH

BATH	bath, Bath
GATH	Gath
HATH	hath
LATH	lath
MATH	aftermath, philomath, math, opsimath, polymath
NATH	chaetognath, plectognath
PATH	allopath, bridle path, *footpath,* physiopath, homeopath, naturopath, neuropath, osteopath, path, psychopath, sociopath
RATH	rath, wrath
SNATH	snath

ĀTS

| GĀTS | othergates |
| YĀTS | Yeats |

(See ĀT, add *-s* where appropriate.)

ATS

| KATS | dogs-and-cats |

(See AT, add *-s* where appropriate.)

ÄTS

| SÄTS | ersatz |

(See ÄT, add *-s* where appropriate.)

ĀV

BRĀV	brave, outbrave
GĀV	forgave, gave, misgave
GLĀV	glaive, *portglaive*
GRĀV	*burgrave,* engrave, photograve, grave, ingrave, *landgrave, margrave,* ungrave, *waldgrave*
HĀV	behave, misbehave
KĀV	biconcave, encave, concave, cave
KLĀV	angusticlave, *exclave, enclave, conclave,* autoclave
KRĀV	crave
KWĀV	quave
LĀV	belave, lave, unlave
NĀV	antenave, knave, nave
PĀV	impave, pave, repave, unpave
PRĀV	deprave
RĀV	rave
SĀV	save
SHĀV	aftershave, shave, *spokeshave*
SLĀV	beslave, enslave, galley slave, slave, wage slave
STĀV	stave
SWĀV	suave
THĀV	they've
THRĀV	thrave
TRĀV	architrave, trave
WĀV	microwave, *shortwave,* tidal wave, waive, wave

AV

HAV	halve, have
KAV	calve
LAV	lav
SAV	salve
SLAV	slav, Yugoslav

ÄV

HÄV	halve
KÄV	calve
SÄV	salve
SLÄV	Slav, Yugoslav
SWÄV	suave

ĀVD

(See **ĀV,** add *-d* where appropriate.)

AVD

(See AV, add *-d* where appropriate.)

ÄVD

(See **ÄV,** add *-d* where appropriate.)

ĀZ

ĀZ	liaise
BĀZ	baize, bays
BLĀZ	ablaze, beacon blaze, blaze, emblaze, outblaze, upblaze
BRĀZ	braise, braze
DĀZ	adaze, bedaze, days, daze, hollandaise, nowadays, oxidase, thenadays
DRĀZ	drays
FĀZ	anaphase, *diphase,* faze, phase, metaphase, polyphase, *prophase,* telephase
FLĀZ	flays, reflays
FRĀZ	fraise, phrase, metaphrase, paraphrase, rephrase, unphrase
GĀZ	gaze, ingaze, outgaze, *stargaze,* upgaze
GLĀZ	glaze, overglaze, underglaze, unglaze, reglaze
GRĀZ	graze
HĀZ	haze
JĀZ	jays
KĀZ	ukase
KLĀZ	clays
KRĀZ	craze, *sucrase*
LĀZ	Bordelaise, lase, lays, laze, malaise, Marseillaise
MĀZ	amaze, bemaze, maize, maze, *mizmaze,* wondermaze
NĀZ	béarnaise, lyonnaise, mayonnaise, naze, polonaise
PRĀZ	*A* appraise, *B* bepraise, *D* dispraise, *O* overpraise, *KR* chrysoprase, *PR* praise, prase, *R* reappraise, repraise, *S* self-praise, *U* underpraise, unpraise
RĀZ	*E* erase, *x-rays, G* gamma rays, *M* morays, mores, *R* raise, rase, rays, raze, reraise, rerase, reraze, *U* unraise, unrase, unraze, upraise
SĀZ	écossaise
SHĀZ	chaise
STĀZ	stays
VĀZ	vase
WĀZ	*edgeways, endways, lengthways, leastways, longways, always, sideways,* wase, ways
YĀZ	Marseillaise

(See **Ā,** add *-s* where appropriate.)

AZ

AZ	as, Boaz, whereas
HAZ	has
JAZ	jazz
PAZ	*topaz*
RAZ	razz
TAZ	razzmatazz
TRAZ	Alcatraz
ZAZ	bizzazz, pizzazz

ÄZ

ÄZ	ahs, ohs and ahs
BLÄZ	the blahs
MÄZ	mamas, mas
PÄZ	La Paz
SWÄZ	vichyssoise
VÄZ	vase

(See **Ä,** add *-s* where appropriate.)

ĀZD

(See **ĀZ,** add *-ed* where appropriate.)

AZD

(See **AZ,** add *-ed* where appropriate.)

ĀZH

BĀZH	beige
GRĀZH	greige
NĀZH	manège
TĀZH	cortege

ÄZH

ÄZH	*peage*
DÄZH	bavardage, sondage

FÄZH	staffage
FLÄZH	camouflage, marouflage, persiflage
KÄZH	bocage, carucage
LÄZH	fuselage, collage, moulage
NÄZH	badinage, espionage, griffonage, counterespionage, ménage
PÄZH	découpage
PLÄZH	plage
RÄZH	barrage, effleurage, entourage, garage, mirage, raj, swataj
SÄZH	corsage, massage, saj, vernissage
TÄZH	décolletage, photomontage, frottage, cabotage, curettage, matelotage, montage, potage, reportage, sabotage, taj
TRÄZH	arbitrage
VÄZH	esclavage, gavage, lavage
YÄZH	maquillage, torpillage

AZM

AZM	demoniasm, enthusiasm, chiliasm, miasm, orgiasm, schediasm
GAZM	orgasm
KAZM	chasm, sarcasm
KLAZM	biblioclasm, iconoclasm, cataclasm
NAZM	pleonasm
PAZM	empasm
PLAZM	bioplasm, ectoplasm, endoplasm, cataplasm, metaplasm, neoplasm, plasm, protoplasm, cytoplasm
SPAZM	blepharospasm, graphospasm, chirospasm, spasm
TAZM	phantasm

Ē

Ē	*A* advowee, amicus curiae, arrowy, *B* B and B, B and D, B and E, billowy, *D* Danae, diploë, *DR* drawee, *E* E, *F* facetiae, furrowy, *I* interviewee, *K* cooee, *M* meadowy, mildewy, minutiae, *P* payee, pillowy, *R* reliquiae, *S* sinewy, *SH* shadowy, *W* willowy

BĒ   *A* A.B., Araby, *B* baby, B, be, bee, B and B, *bawbee*, bumblebee, *BR* bribee, *FR* Frisbee, *H* honeybee, humblebee, *J* jacoby, jambee, *K* Koochahbee, *KW* queen bee, *N* Niobe, *R* and B, *S* sassaby, cenoby, *SK* scarabee, *W* wallaby

BLĒ   blea

BRĒ   barleybree, bree, Brie, debris, vertebrae

CHĒ   chee, *chee-chee*, chincherinchee, debauchee, *litchi*, vouchee

DĒ   *A* accidie, *B* B.V.D., B and D, bastardy, Burgundy, *CH* Chaldee, chickadee, *D* D, Dee, D.D., dipody, dispondee, *F* fiddlededee, fundee, *GR* grandee, *H* hymnody, *J* jeopardy, *K* Chaldee, *killdee*, comedy, custodee, custody, *L* L.L.D., Lombardy, *M* M.D., malady, melody, monody, *N* Normandy, *O* organdy, *P* parody, perfidy, Ph. D., Picardy, *PR* prosody, *R* R and D, rhapsody, remedy, *S* psalmody, C.O.D., subsidy, *SP spondee, ST* standee, *TH* theody, *THR* threnody, *TR* tragedy, tripody, *TW* Tweedledee, *V* vendee

DRĒ   dree, heraldry

FĒ   *A* ach-y-fi, anaglyphy, antistrophe, apostrophe, atrophy, *B* biographee, biography, *D* dactylography, dystrophy, *E* ethnography, *F* fee, phi, feoffee, philosophy, photography, *H* hagiography, *J* geography, *K* catastrophe, coryphee, *KR* cryptography, *M* misophy, *P* paleography, pornography, *R* ratafee, *STR strophe, T* tachygraphy, telegraphy, topography, *TH* theosophy, *Y* uranography, *Z* xyloglyphy, xylography

FLĒ   flea, flee

FRĒ   duty-free, enfree, fancy-free, free, heart-free, *carefree*, unfree

GĒ   ghee, whangee, muggee, Portugee, *thuggee*

GLĒ   glee

GRĒ   agree, degree, disagree, filigree, *grigri*, mistigris, pedigree, *puggree*, third degree

HĒ   bohea, he, hehee, takahe, tehee

HWĒ   whee

JĒ   *A* agee, *algae*, allergy, analogy, anthropology, apogee, apology, astrology, *B* bacteriology, bargee, biology, *burgee, D* dactylology, demology, demonology, dermatology, dilogy, dyslogy, doxology, *E* effigy, ecology, elegy, embryology, endocrinology, energy, epistemology, ethnology, ethology, *F* physiology, *Fuji, G* galiongee, *J* G, gee, genealogy, geology, *K* cardiology, *KR* criminology, chronology, cryptology, *L* laryngology, lethargy, liturgy, *M metallurgy,* misology, mortgagee, morphology, mythology, *N* nomology, neurology, *O* obligee, ophthalmology, *ogee,* onycophagy, otology, *P* pathology, panurgy, perigee, pili, pongee, *PL* pledgee, *PR* prodigy, proctology, *R* refugee, *S* salvagee, psychology, psychurgy, sylloge, synergy, syzygy, sociology, *SH shoji, SKW* squeegee, *STR* strategy, *T* telenergy, telurgy, typology, *TH* theurgy, *TR* trilogy, *U* eulogy, *Z* zymurgy, zoology

KĒ   *A* anarchy, *Bacchae, CH* Cherokee, *G* garlicky, *H* hillocky, hummocky, *K* cay, key, chi, colicky, *L latchkey, M* maquis, Manichee, marquee,

master key, monarchy, naumochy, *P* panicky, *passkey, R raki, S* synarchy, synecdoche, *T turnkey, TH* thelymachy, *TR trochee, W* Waikiki, *Z* xenodochy

KRĒ   decree, Cree, cushlamochree

KWĒ   *BL* blandiloquy, *BR* breviloquy, *D* dentiloquy, dulciloquy, *FL* flexiloquy, *G* gastriloquy, *I* inauiloquy, *K* colloquy, *M* multiloquy, *O* obloquy, *P* pectoroloquy, *PL* pleniloquy, *S* sanctiloquy, soliloquy, somniloquy, *ST* stultiloquy, *SW* suaviloquy, *T* tolutiloquy, *TR* tristiloquy, *V* vaniloquy, veritriloquy, veriloquy

LĒ   *A* advisedly, alee, Annabel Lee, anomaly, appellee, *B* bailee, belee, *D* diastole, *E* enrollee, *F* facsimile, *FL* fleur-de-lis, *G* Galilee, *H* homily, hyperbole, *I* infulae, Italy, *J* jubilee, *L* lapis lazuli, lee, li, libelee, *M mallee, P* parolee, *S* Cybele, Sicily, simile, systole, *SH* shirallee, *SK* skillagalee, *TH* Thermopylae, Thessaly

[See also adverbs composed of a noun plus *-ly* (fatherly, motherly, etc.) or of an adjective plus *-ly* (absorbingly, abusively, etc.)]

MĒ   *A* agronomy, academy, alchemy, anatomy, anthroponomy, antimony, appendectomy, astronomy, atomy, *B* balsamy, bigamy, bonhomie, *BL* blasphemy, blossomy, *D* dichotomy, dittamy, deuterogamy, Deuteronomy, *E* economy, endogamy, enemy, epitome, *F* physiognomy, *FL* phlebotomy, *I* infamy, *J* jessamy, *K* confirmee, *L* lobotomy, *M* me, mi, monogamy, *N* neurotomy, *O* occamy, autonomy, *P* polygamy, *S* syntomy, sodomy, *T* taxonomy, teknonymy, Ptolemy, *TH thermae, TR* trichotomy, *Z* zootomy

NĒ *A* abandonee, aborigine, Agapemone, agony, accompany, Albany, alienee, aknee, anemone, Antigone, assignee, *B* balcony, bargainee, barony, Bimini, bouquet garni, botany, *BR* bryony, *CH* Chinee, designee, destiny, dysphony, distrainee, dominie, donee, *E* ebony, examinee, epiphany, *F* felony, *G* Gethsemane, *GL* gluttony, *GW* guarani, Guarani, *H* harmony, hegemony, *I ignominy,* irony, *J* Japanee, Germany, jinni, *K* cacophony, calumny, *kidney,* kitcheny, *koine,* colony, company, consignee, cottony, cushiony, *KR* crimsony, *L* laryngophony, litany, *M macaroni,* mahogany, Melpomene, misogyny, monotony, mutiny, muttony, *N* knee, Mnemosyne, nominee, nominy, *O* optionee, *P* pantemone, *patrimony,* Persephone, petitionee, pawnee, Pawnee, *PR* progeny, *R rani,* Romany, *S* Saxony, symphony, simony, *SH* Shawnee, *SKR* scrutiny, *ST* stephane, *T* telegony, tiffany, Tiffany, townee, tyranny, Tuscany, *TR* distrainee, trainee, *U* oniony, *V* villainy, *Y* euphony, Euphrosyne

PĒ *A* agape, allotropy, apocope, *CH* chick-pea, *D* diacope, *E* entropy, epopee, escapee, *F* philanthropy, physianthropy, *H* hydrotherapy, *J* jalopy, *K* calipee, calliope, canopy,

cap-a-pie, *cowpea, M* microscopy, misanthropy, *P* P, pea, pee, penotherapy, *R* R.S.V.P., rapee, rappee, recipe, rupee, *S* psychotherapy, *SH charpie, T* tapis, *tepee,* teratoscopy, topee, toupee, *TH* thalassotherapy, therapy, *W* wampee, *Y* yippee, *Z* zomotherapy

PRĒ belesprit, esprit

RĒ *A* adultery, alimentary, anniversary, archery, armory, artery, artillery, *B* bain-marie, bakery, Barbary, battery, beggary, bijouterie, *boree,* bottomry, boundary, *BR* bravery, bribery, brodery, broidery, *CH* chancery, chickaree, chicory, *D* debauchery, delivery, demonry, devilry, diary, directory, discovery, dissatisfactory, dissuasory, dungaree, *DR* drapery, drudgery, *E* effrontery, equerry, extempore, extrasensory, elementary, elusory, embroidery, enginery, *F* factory, faerie, feathery, fernery, fiery, phylactery, phyllery, finery, foppery, forestry, forgery, *FL* flattery, flowery, flummery, *FR* frippery, *G* gallery, gaucherie, *GR grivoiserie, H* heathery, heraldry, hickory, history, hostelry, husbandry, *I* ikary, illusory, imagery, infirmary, inlagary, injury, in re, ivory, *J* jamboree, gendarmery, jigamaree, jewelry, jugglery, *K* calorie, Calvary, caravansari, *cartulary,* cavalry, kedgeree, commandery, complementary, complimentary, compulsory, conferee, contradictory, *contrary,* corroboree, cautery, causerie, *KW* quackery,

quandary, quaternary, *L library,* lingerie, livery, lottery, luxury, lusory, *M* machinery, masonry, mastery, memory, mercury, minauderie, mystery, misery, mockery, mummery, *N* knavery, notary, nursery, *O* augury, honoree, *P* palmary, parliamentary, penury, peppery, perfumery, perfunctory, perjury, popery, potagerie, potpourri, *puggree, PR* precursory, priory, professory, prudery, *R* rotary, raillery, rapparee, recovery, rectory, referee, refractory, receptory, revelry, reverie, ribaldry, rivalry, robbery, roguery, rockery, rookery, rosary, *rosemary,* rotisserie, rudimentary, *S* salary, sangaree, satisfactory, savagery, savory, sectary, scenery, seigniory, senary, sensory, century, serrurerie, silvery, sirree, sorcery, summary, summery, *SH* chicanery, chivalry, charivari, shivaree, shivery, sugary, *SK* sculduddery, skullduggery, *SL* slavery, slippery, *SN* snuggery, *ST* stingaree, *T* Tartary, Terpsichore, testamentary, tomfoolery, *TH* theory, thievery, thundery, *TR* transferee, tracery, treachery, trickery, trumpery, *U* unsavory, upholstery, *V vagary,* vaccary, valedictory, vapory, *W* waggery, watery, wintery, witchery, *Y* yessirree, yeomanry, usury, *Z* zephyry, zythepsary, zoopery

SĒ *A* abbacy, abstinency, adequacy, addressee, advocacy, agency, accountancy, acceptancy, accuracy, apostasy, ardency, argosy,

aristocracy, asea, assie,
ascendancy, assessee,
assis, *B* Baltic Sea,
bankruptcy, belligerency,
big C, buoyancy, *BL*
blatancy, *BR* brilliancy,
CH China Sea, *D*
Debussy, delegacy,
delicacy, delinquency,
democracy, dependency,
diplomacy, discordancy,
discourtesy, discrepancy,
divorcee, *E* effeminacy,
efficiency, expectancy,
expediency, excellency,
ecstasy, embassy, emcee,
emergency, endorsee,
episcopacy, *F* fallacy,
fantasy, Pharisee,
pharmacy, farci,
federacy, femcee,
fervency, foresee, *FL*
flagrancy, flatulency,
flippancy, fluency, *FR*
fragrancy, frequency,
fricassee, *G* galaxy, *H*
heresy, hesitancy,
hypocrisy, Holy See, *I*
idiocy, idiosyncrasy,
illiteracy, immaculacy,
immediacy, impendency,
impenitency,
impermanency,
impertinacy,
importunacy, impudency,
inadequacy,
inadvertency, inaccuracy,
indelicacy,
independency,
indecency, inebriacy,
inefficacy, infancy,
inclemency,
incompetency,
inconsistency,
incipiency, insufficiency,
insurgency, intestacy,
intimacy, intricacy,
irradiancy, irrelevancy,
irritancy, *J* jactancy,
jealousy, *K* cadency,
candidacy, captaincy,
cogency, colonelcy,
competency, compliancy,
confederacy,
conservancy,
consistency, consonancy,
conspiracy, constancy,
constituency,
conveniency, co-
respondency, corpulency,
courtesy, curacy, *KL*
clemency, cliency, *KR*

Christmasy, *L* lambency,
latency, legacy,
legitimacy, leniency,
leprosy, lessee, licensee,
literacy, luxuriancy,
lunacy, lucency, *M*
magistracy, malignancy,
minstrelsy, mordancy, *N*
nascency, negligency,
nomancy, normalcy, *O*
obduracy, obstinacy,
Odyssey, omnipotency,
oscitancy, autopsy,
oversea, oversee, *P*
papacy, *Parsee,*
peccancy, pendency,
penitency, permanency,
petulancy, piquancy,
piracy, poesy,
poignancy, policy,
potency, pungency,
pernancy, *PL* pleurisy,
pliancy, *PR* pregnancy,
prelacy, preponderancy,
précis, primacy, privacy,
promisee, prophecy,
proficiency, profligacy,
proliferacy, prominency,
promisee, *R* regency,
regeneracy, recadency,
recalcitrancy,
recumbency, releasee,
relevancy, renascency,
renitency, repellency,
resplendency, romancy,
S Sadducee, saliency,
sans souci, C, sea, see,
seducee, secrecy,
celibacy, sycophancy,
sycee, *sightsee,*
solvency, sonancy,
subsistency, sufficiency,
succulency, supremacy,
surfacy, sycee,
surgeoncy, *ST* stagnancy,
T tangency, tenancy,
tendency, Tennessee, *TH*
theocracy, *TR* truancy,
truculency, *U* undersea,
unforesee, urgency, *V*
vagrancy, vacancy,
valency, valiancy,
verdancy, *Y* euphrasy

SHĒ
banshee, buckshee,
debauchee, flourishy,
garnishee, kamichi,
rubbishy, she, shea,
shee, ski, *chichi*

SHRĒ sri
SKĒ hydroski, ski
SKRĒ scree
SMĒ smee

SNĒ snee, snickersnee
SPRĒ esprit, joie d'esprit, jeu
d'esprit, spree
STĒ mestee, mustee
TĒ *A* ability, absentee,
absorptivity, absurdity,
adaptability, adversity,
advisability, affability,
affinity, agility, acclivity,
acridity, activity,
actuality, alacrity,
allottee, ambiguity,
amenability, amenity,
amiability, amicability,
amity, amnesty,
amputee, anxiety,
animosity, anonymity,
antiquity, annuity,
applicability, appointee,
aridity, acerbity, acidity,
assiduity, asperity,
attensity, atrocity,
avidity, *B* barbarity,
benignity, biggety,
bootee, *BR* brevity,
brutality, *CH*
changeability, charity,
chastity, *D* debility,
dedicatee, deformity,
deity, dexterity,
dextrality, density,
deportee, depravity,
deputy, devotee, dignity,
dimity, dynasty,
dishonesty, disparity,
dissimilarity, distributee,
diversity, divinity,
domesticity, docility,
dubiety, duplicity, *DR*
draftee, *E* extremity,
equality, equanimity,
equity, elasticity, electee,
electricity, enmity,
enormity, entity,
eternity, E.T., *F* faculty,
falsity, familiarity,
facility, fatality, fatuity,
fecundity, felicity,
ferocity, fertility,
festivity, fidelity, fidgety,
fixity, formality, fortuity,
futility, futurity, *FR*
fragility, fraternity,
frigidity, frivolity,
frugality, *G* gaiety,
garrulity, giftee, goatee,
guarantee, guaranty, *GR*
gratuity, gravity, *H*
hatchety, heredity, high
tea, hilarity, hospitality,
hostility, humanity,
humidity, humility, *I*

identity, imbecility,
immaturity, immensity,
immodesty, immorality,
immortality, immunity,
imparity, impassivity,
impecuniosity,
impetuosity, impiety,
importunity, impropriety,
impunity, impurity,
inability, indignity,
individuality, inductee,
inferiority, infinity,
iniquity, incapacity,
incomparability,
incompatibility,
incomprehensibility,
incongruity, incredulity,
intensity, *J* generosity,
geniality, gentility,
jollity, juvenility, *K*
calamity, capability,
capacity, captivity,
carroty, cavity, casualty,
coatee, collectivity,
comity, *committee,*
commodity, community,
complexity, complicity,
conformity, concavity,
consanguinity,
contiguity, *contrasty,*
convexity, covenantee,
cupidity, curiosity, Q.T.,
KR creativity, credulity,
Christianity, crotchety,
crudity, cruelty, *KW*
quality, quantity,
quiddity, quoddity, *L*
laity, laxity, legality,
legatee, lenity, levity,
liberality, liberty,
limpidity, lubricity,
luminosity, lucidity, *M*
magnanimity, maggoty,
majesty, majority,
manatee, mestee,
modesty, moeity,
morality, mortality,
mustee, mutuality, *N*
nativity, nebulosity,
nicety, nonentity,
normality, nudity,
neutrality, *O* objectivity,
audacity, ophelimity,
omneity, austerity,
authenticity, authority, *P*
parity, parvanimity,
passivity, patentee,
permittee, personality,
pertinacity, piety,
picotee, polarity,
poverty, puberty,
pupilarity, *PR* pravity,

presentee, privity,
probability, proclivity,
prolixity, propensity,
property, propinquity,
propriety, prudibundity,
R radioactivity,
relativity, reliability,
remittee, repartee,
receptivity, russety, *S*
sacristy, sanctiminity,
sanctity, security,
celebrity, celerity,
sensibility, sensitivity,
certainty, servility,
settee, seventy,
similarity, simultaneity,
sincerity, synonymity,
syntality, civility,
sovereignty, subtlety,
pseudonymity, surdity,
suttee, *SHR* shrievalty,
SK scarcity, *SN* snippety,
SP sparsity, spigotty,
spiralty, spontaneity, *T*
T, tea, tee, temerity,
tensity, typothetae, titi,
torpidity, totality, tutee,
TR trepidity, trinity,
trinkety, triviality,
trumpety, trustee, *U*
uberty, unity, utility, *V*
velleity, velvety,
viraginity, virginity, *W*
warrantee, warranty,
witchety, *Y* unanimity
A allopathy, antipathy,
apathy, *D* dyspathy, *E*
empathy, *H* homeopathy,
S sympathy, *T* telepathy,
timothy, *TH* the, thee, *Y*
eupathy

THĒ

THRĒ
TRĒ
three, twenty-three (etc.)
A ancestry, apple tree
(and other trees), artistry,
axletree, *B* barratry,
bigotry, bijouterie, *D*
deviltry, doubletree, *E*
errantry, *F* physiolatry,
forestry, *G* gallantry,
gallows tree, *gumtree, H*
harlotry, harvestry, *HW*
whiffletree, whippletree,
I idolatry, industry,
infantry, *J* geometry, *K*
chemistry, coquetry,
coventry, *KR*
craniometry, Christmas
tree, *M* mantletree,
merchantry, ministry, *N*
knight-errantry, *O*
honesty, *P* pageantry,
palmistry, pedantry,

peasantry, poetry, *PL*
pleasantry, *S* saddletree,
sequestree, psychiatry,
psychometry, symmetry,
sophistry, *SH shoetree, T*
tapestry, telemetry,
tenantry, *TH*
thalassochemistry, *TR*
tree, trestletree, *W*
wapiti, weeping tree

TWĒ	étui
VĒ	anchovy, levee, lucivee, *maulvee, mulvee,* Muscovy, eau de vie, pont-levis, c'est la vie, TV, vee, vis-a-vis
WĒ	*awiwi,* ennui, *peewee,* sallowy, yellowy
YĒ	employee, fedayee, cuir-bouilli, payee, ye
ZĒ	advisee, bourgeoisie, chimpanzee, DMZ, devisee, fusee, razee, recognizee, Z, Zuyder Zee
ZHĒ	bougie

ĒB

DĒB	dieb
FĒB	ephebe
GLĒB	glebe

BENTLEY CLERIHEW

Of Clerihew Bentley.
Speak reverently.
First name—a verse;
Second—a hearse.

GRĒB	grebe
PLĒB	plebe

EB

EB	ebb
BEB	*cubeb,* zibeb
BLEB	bleb
DEB	*ardeb,* deb, subdeb
KEB	keb
NEB	neb, *nebneb*
PLEB	pleb
REB	Johnny Reb, reb
WEB	*cobweb,* web
YEB	uayeb

EBD

EBD	ebbed
NEBD	nebbed
WEBD	cobwebbed, webbed

ĒCH

ĒCH	each
BĒCH	beach, beech
BLĒCH	bleach, rebleach, unbleach
BRĒCH	breach, breech, *housebreach, spousebreach,* unbreech
FLĒCH	fleech
KĒCH	keach, keech
LĒCH	*horseleech,* leach, leech
MĒCH	meech
PĒCH	appeach, peach, impeach
PLĒCH	pleach
PRĒCH	preach, repreach
RĒCH	forereach, *headreach,* outreach, overreach, reach
SĒCH	beseech
SKRĒCH	screech
SLĒCH	sleech
SPĒCH	speech
TĒCH	teach, unteach

ECH

ECH	etch, photo-etch, re-etch
FECH	fetch
FLECH	fletch
KECH	ketch
KLECH	cletch
KVECH	kvetch
KWECH	quetch, quetsch
LECH	lech, letch
RECH	retch, wretch, reretch
SKECH	sketch
STRECH	outstretch, stretch, restretch
TECH	mistetch, tetch
VECH	bitter vetch, vetch

ĒCHT

BLĒCHT	bleached
RĒCHT	piobaireachd

(See **ĒCH,** add *-ed* where appropriate.)

ECHT

(See **ECH,** add *-ed* where appropriate.)

ĒD

BĒD	bead, Bede
BLĒD	bleed, *nosebleed*
BRĒD	brede, breed, *halfbreed,*

inbreed, interbreed, *crossbreed,* outbreed, upbreed

DĒD	deed, indeed, Candide, misdeed
FĒD	feed, handfeed, off his feed, overfeed, spoonfeed, underfeed, unfeed, winterfeed, eutrophied
FLĒD	flead, fleaed, unfleaed
FRĒD	enfreed, freed, *Siegfried,* unfreed
GLĒD	glede, gleed
GRĒD	agreed, degreed, disagreed, filigreed, greed, pedigreed, undegreed, unpedigreed
HĒD	he'd, heed, *Lockheed*
KĒD	keyed, rekeyed, unkeyed
LĒD	*fairlead,* lead, mislead, Nibelungenlied, uplead
KWĒD	quede, Quede
MĒD	Ganymede, mead, Mede, meed, Runnymede
NĒD	ennead, knead, kneed, need, *knock-kneed*
PĒD	impede, capripede, millipede, peed, centipede, cirripede, stampede, velocipede
PLĒD	implead, interplead, misplead, plead
RĒD	bourride, jereed, copyread, *lip-read,* misread, *O* outread, overread, *PR* proofread, *R* read, rede, reed, refereed, reread, *S* sight-read, *SP* speed-read
SĒD	*A* accede, *axseed,* aniseed, antecede, *B* birdseed, *E* epicede, exceed, *FL* flaxseed, *H* hayseed, *I* intercede, Jamshid, *K* concede, cottonseed, *L* linseed, *M* moonseed, *O* allseed, *P* pumpkinseed, *PR* precede, proceed, *R* rapeseed, recede, reseed, retrocede, *S* secede, cede, seed, succeed, supersede, *ST* stickseed, *W* wormseed
SHĒD	Haroun al-Rashid, she'd
SKRĒD	screed
SNĒD	snead
SPĒD	*airspeed,* Godspeed, *groundspeed,* outspeed, speed
SPRĒD	spreed

STĒD	steed
SWĒD	Swede
TĒD	guaranteed, propertied, reguaranteed, reteed, tead, teaed, teed, unguaranteed, unteed
THRĒD	threed
TRĒD	treed, retreed, untreed
TWĒD	tweed
WĒD	*B* beggarweed, bugleweed, *CH* chickweed, *E* ennuied, *F* fireweed, *G* goutweed, gulfweed, *H* hogweed, *K* colicweed, cottonweed, *L* locoweed, *M* mayweed, milkweed, musquashweed, *N* knapweed, knotweed, *P* pigweed, pickerelweed, pokeweed, pondweed, *R* ragweed, *S* seaweed, silverweed, *T* stickweed, *T* tumbleweed, *W* waterweed, we'd, wede, weed
YĒD	yede

(See **E,** add *-d* where appropriate.)

ED

ED	coed, continuèd, op-ed, sorrowèd, wearièd, winnowèd
BED	*A* abed, *B* bed, *CH* childbed, *D* deathbed, *E* embed, *F* featherbed, *FL* flowerbed, *H* hotbed, *I* imbed, *P* pissabed, *R* riverbed, *roadbed, S* seedbed, surbed, *SL* slugabed, *TR* trucklebed, trundlebed, *W* waterbed
BRED	*B* beebread, *BL* blackbread, *BR* bread, bred, *brownbread, H* highbread, homebred, wholewheat bread, *HW* white bread, *I* inbred, *J* gingerbread, *KR* crispbread, crossbred, *L* lowbred, *O* overbred, *P* pilot bread, pita bread, *purebred, R* raisin bread, *S* sourbread, *SH* shortbread, shortening bread, *shewbread, SW* sweetbread, *TH* thoroughbred, *TR*

truebred, U unbred, underbred, *W* well-bred, *Y* yeast bread

DED bediamonded, dead, diamonded, garlanded, heralded, jeoparded, shepherded

DRED adread, dread

FED fed, *fullfed, milkfed,* overfed, underfed, unfed, well-fed

FLED fled

HED *A* ahead, *airhead,* arrowhead, *B* behead, *bighead,* billethead, *bonehead, bowhead,* bufflehead, *bulkhead, bullhead,* bullethead, *BL blackhead, blockhead,* blunderhead, *CH* chucklehead, *D deadhead, death's-head,* dunderhead, *DR* dragonhead, *drophead, drumhead, E* egghead, emptyhead, *F fathead,* featherhead, fiddlehead, figurehead, *forehead,* fountainhead, *FL flathead, G* gilthead, go-ahead, *godhead, goodhead, GR greenhead, H* hammerhead, *hardhead,* head, *hogshead,* Holyhead, *hophead, hothead, K* cathead, copperhead, *KR crosshead, L* letterhead, leatherhead, loggerhead, *M* maidenhead, marblehead, *masthead, N* nailhead, niggerhead, knucklehead, *O* overhead, *P* pinhead, poppyhead, *pothead, R railhead, ramhead, redhead, roundhead,* rudderhead, *S* sorehead, *SH* sheepshead, shovelhead, *SK* skinhead, *SL* sleepyhead, *SP spearhead, springhead, ST stairhead, steelhead, T* timberhead, *towhead, TH* thunderhead, *TR trundlehead, U* unhead, *W warhead, wellhead,* woodenhead, woolly-head

JED ravagèd, jed

KED ked, sheep-ked

LED lead, led, misled, unlead, unled, jolie-laide

MED med, pre-med

PED *A* aliped, *B* biped, *BR* breviped, *F* fissiped, *K* cheliped, *KW* quadruped, *M* maxilliped, milliped, *moped,* multiped, *O* octoped, *P* palmiped, paralleloped, ped, pinnatiped, pinniped, *PL* planiped, plumiped, *R* remiped, *S* semiped, serriped, soliped, *T* taliped, *U* uniped

PLED pled

RED Ethelred, boxy red, infrared, misread, outread, read, red, redd, reread, unread

SED *aforesaid, foresaid,* gainsaid, resaid, said, unsaid

SHED *bloodshed,* shed, *snowshed,* watershed, *woodshed*

SHRED shred

SLED *bobsled,* sled

SNED snead

SPED sped, unsped, well-sped

SPRED *bedspread,* bespread, outspread, overspread, spread, underspread, *well-spread, widespread*

STED bedstead, bestead, *farmstead, homestead,* instead, *roadstead,* stead, *oersted*

TED *A* attributed, *B* ballasted, barren-spirited, base-spirited, bigoted, bold-spirited, bonneted, *BR* breakfasted, *D* discomfited, discomforted, discredited, disinherited, disquieted, dispirited, distributed, *E* exhibited, *F* faceted, fine-spirited, forfeited, *G* gay-spirited, *H* helmeted, high-spirited, *I* inhabited, inherited, inspirited, *K* carpeted, contributed, coveted, *KR* crescented, *KW* quieted, *L* light-spirited, limited, low-spirited, *M* mean-spirited, merited, *P* patented, pirated, poor-spirited, public-spirited, *PR* profited, prohibited, *S*

signeted, soft-spirited, *SP* spirited, *T* talented, ted, tenanted, turreted, *U* unballasted, unbonneted, uninhabited, uninhibited, unlimited, unmerited, unprofited, unrespited, untenanted, unvisited, *V* visited, *W* weak-spirited

THRED *goldthread, packthread,* thread, rethread, unthread

TRED retread, tread

WED rewed, unwed, wed

YED yed

ZED zed

ĒDZ

BĒDZ beads, worry beads

(See **ĒD,** add *-s* where appropriate.)

ĒF

ĒF naïf

BĒF beef

BRĒF brief, debrief

CHĒF chief, handkerchief, neckerchief

DĒF deaf, deef, redif

FĒF enfeoff, fief, feoff

GRĒF grief

LĒF *B* bas-relief, belief, *BR broadleaf, D* demirelief, disbelief, *FL flyleaf, G goldleaf, I* interleaf, *KL cloverleaf, L* leaf, lief, *M* misbelief, *O* overleaf, *R* relief, *TH thickleaf, U* unbelief, *V velvetleaf*

NĒF hanif, neif, neife

RĒF kharif, reef, reif, shereef, tashrif, Tenerife

SĒF massif

SHĒF sheaf

TĒF aperitif, leitmotif, motif, chetif

THĒF infangthief, outfangthief, thief, utfangthief

EF

EF F, eff, ef, Kiev, Prokofiev

DEF deaf

FEF enfeoff, feoff

JEF jeff

KEF kef

92

SINGLE RHYMES; EFT

KLEF	clef
LEF	lev
NEF	*Brezhnev,* nef
REF	ref
SEF	UNICEF
SHEF	chef
TEF	tef

EFT

EFT	eft
DEFT	deft
FEFT	enfeoffed, feoffed, unfeoffed
HEFT	heft
HWEFT	wheft
JEFT	jeffed
KLEFT	cleft, klepht
LEFT	aleft, left, New Left, ultraleft
REFT	bereft, reft
THEFT	theft
WEFT	weft

ĒG

BRĒG	brigue
GRĒG	Grieg
KLĒG	klieg
KRĒG	*blitzkrieg, sitzkrieg*
LĒG	league, *colleague*
NĒG	banig, renege
PĒG	peag
SKĒG	skeeg
TĒG	fatigue, squeteague
TRĒG	intrigue
ZHĒG	gigue

EG

EG	boiled egg, duck egg, egg, goose egg (etc.)
BEG	beg, filibeg
DREG	dreg
GLEG	gleg
KEG	keg, *muskeg*
KLEG	cleg, kleg
LEG	*blackleg, bootleg, bowleg, dogleg, foreleg,* leg, *pegleg, proleg*
MEG	*nutmeg*
NEG	renege
PEG	peg, repeg, unpeg, Winnipeg
REG	reg
SEG	seg
SKEG	skeg
SNEG	sneg
TEG	teg
YEG	yegg

ĒGD

NĒGD	reneged

(See **ĒG,** add *-d* where appropriate.)

EGD

EGD	egged
LEGD	bow-legged
NEGD	reneged

(See **EG,** add *-ed* or *-ged* where appropriate.)

EGZ

LEGZ	legs, sea legs

(See **EG,** add *-s* where appropriate.)

ĒJ

LĒJ	liege
SĒJ	besiege, siege

EJ

EJ	cutting edge, featheredge, edge, razor's edge, re-edge, *straightedge,* unedge
DREJ	dredge
FLEJ	fledge
HEJ	enhedge, hedge
KEJ	kedge
KLEJ	cledge
LEJ	allege, ledge, privilege, sacrilege, sortilege
PLEJ	*frankpledge,* impledge, interpledge, pledge, repledge

PUZZLE FOR GRAMMARIANS AND MORALISTS

I find it curiositive
  My good intentionals despite,
That I am just as positive
  When I am wrong as when I'm right.

SEJ	sedge
SKEJ	skedge
SLEJ	sledge
TEJ	tedge
WEJ	wedge

EJD

EJD	edged, double-edged

(See **EJ,** add *-d* where appropriate.)

ĒK

ĒK	eke, caique, saic
BĒK	beak, beek, *grosbeak, halfbeak,* Mozambique, stickybeak
BLĒK	bleak
CHĒK	cheek, chic, radical chic
FĒK	feak
FRĒK	ecofreak, freak, Jesus freak
GĒK	geek
GLĒK	gleek
GRĒK	fenugreek, Greek
KĒK	keek
KLĒK	cleek, clique
KRĒK	creak, creek
LĒK	aleak, Belleek, houseleek, leak, leek, oblique, relique, silique
MĒK	comique, meak, meek
NĒK	clinique, Martinique, technique, unique
PĒK	*A* afterpeak, apeak, apeek, *CH* Chesapeake, *D* demipeak, *F* forepeak, *N* noddypeak, *P* peak, peek, Peke, pique, *R* repique, *W* widow's peak
RĒK	areek, perique, wreak, reek
SĒK	hide-and-seek, cacique, reseek, seek, Sikh
SHĒK	radical chic, chic, sheik
SHRĒK	shriek
SKRĒK	screak
SKWĒK	asqueak, bubble and squeak, *pipsqueak,* squeak
SLĒK	sleek, unsleek
SNĒK	sneak
SPĒK	bespeak, forespeak, *newspeak,* speak, unspeak
STRĒK	streak
TĒK	*A* antique, *B* batik, boutique, *J* geopolitik, *KR* critique, *M* mystique, *N* novantique, *P* politique, *PL* plastique, *PR* pratique, *R* Realpolitik, *T* teak, *TR* triptyque
TWĒK	tweak
WĒK	Holy Week, *midweek,* Passion Week, weak, week, yesterweek

ZĒK bezique, physique, cazique

EK

EK home-ec
BEK beck, Kennebec, *crombec*, Quebec, *pinchbeck, rebec, xebec*
BREK brek
CHEK blank check, bodycheck, check, cheque, Czech, *hatcheck, coatcheck,* countercheck, crosscheck, overcheck, recheck, *raincheck,* rubber check
DEK afterdeck, bedeck, deck, *foredeck,* quarterdeck, *sandek,* undeck
DREK dreck
FEK feck
FLEK fleck
GEK geck
HEK heck, by heck
KEK keck
KLEK cleck
LEK *cromlech,* lech, Lech, leck, lek
NEK *B* bottleneck, *BL blackneck, BR breakneck, KR crookneck, crewneck, L* leatherneck, *N* neck, nek, neck-and-neck, *R redneck, rollneck, roughneck,* rubberneck, *wryneck, SW* swanneck, *T* turtle-neck
PEK *henpeck, kopek, OPEC,* peck, repeck, sapek, Tehuantepec
REK bewreck, plane wreck, reck, *shipwreck, tenrec,* train wreck (etc.)
SEK *cusec, parsec,* sec
SHEK Chiang Kai-shek
SNEK sneck
SPEK *flyspeck,* spec, speck
TEK *Aztec,* discotheque, *conteck,* Mixtec, tec, tech, teck, *Toltec*
TREK Star Trek, trek
YEK yech, yecch

ĒKS

ĒKS eeks
BRĒKS breeks

LĒKS leeks
SĒKS maxixe, seeks

(See **ĒK,** add -*s* where appropriate.)

EKS

EKS ex, x
BEKS becks, *ibex, vibex*
DEKS bedecks, decks, *index, caudex, codex, subindex*
FEKS faex, pontifex, spinifex, tubifex
FLEKS *B* biflex, *D* deflects, deflex, *FL* flecks, flex, *I* inflects, inflex, *J* genuflects, genuflex, *R* reflects, *reflex,* retroflex, *S* circumflex
HEKS hex
KEKS kex
LEKS *ilex, isolex,* lex, *aulex, pollex, silex, scolex,* telex
MEKS Mex, *remex, cimex, Tex-Mex*
NEKS annex, disannex, *Kleenex,* connects, *connex*
PEKS *apex,* haruspex, *auspex*
PLEKS *D* diplex, duplex, *G* googolplex, *I* interrex, *K* complex, contraplex, *KW* quadruplex, *M* multiplex, *N* nulliplex, *P* perplex, *PL* plex, *S* simplex, *TR* triplex, *V* veniplex
PREKS prex
REKS *murex, Pyrex,* rex
SEKS desex, *Essex,* fair sex, homosex, intersex, Middlesex, sex, supersex, unisex, unsex, weaker sex
SPEKS *Perspex,* specs, spex
TEKS *dentex, cortex, latex, vertex, vortex*
THEKS *narthex*
VEKS biconvex, convex, vex, unvex
YEKS yex

(See **EK,** add -*s* where appropriate.)

EKST

FLEKST flexed, genuflexed
HEKST hexed
NEKST annexed, next
PLEKST perplexed, unperplexed

SEKST oversexed, sexed, sext, undersexed, unsexed
TEKST *context, pretext,* text
VEKST unvexed, vexed

ĒKT

ĒKT eked
CHĒKT apple-cheeked, cheeked, cherry-cheeked, *pale-cheeked, pink-cheeked, rosy-cheeked*
STRĒKT *ring-streaked,* streaked

(See **ĒK,** add -*ed* where appropriate.)

EKT

BEKT becked
CHEKT checked, unchecked
DEKT bedecked, decked, *pandect*
FEKT *A* affect, aftereffect, *D* defect, disaffect, disinfect, *E* effect, *F* photoelectric effect, *GR* greenhouse effect, *I* infect, *K* confect, *M* misaffect, *P* perfect, *PR* prefect, *R* refect, ripple effect
FLEKT deflect, flecked, flect, inflect, genuflect, reflect, circumflect
GLEKT benign neglect, neglect
JEKT *A* abject, adject, *D* deject, disject, *E* eject, *I* inject, interject, introject, *K* conject, *O* object, *PR* project, *R* reject, retroject, *S* subject, *TR* traject
LEKT *A* acrolect, analect, *B* basilect, *D* dialect, *E* elect, *I* idiolect, intellect, *K* collect, *N* non-elect, *PR* pre-elect, prelect, *R* re-elect, recollect, *S* select
NEKT disconnect, *goosenecked,* interconnect, connect, *crooknecked,* necked, reconnect
PEKT *aspect,* expect, *henpecked,* pecked, *prospect*
PLEKT complect
REKT *A* arrect, *D* direct, *E* erect, *I* indirect, incorrect, insurrect, *K*

correct, *M* misdirect, *P* porrect, *R* wrecked, resurrect, rewrecked, *U* unwrecked

SEKT bisect, dissect, exsect, *insect,* intersect, quadrisect, sect, transect, trisect, vivisect

SPEKT *D* disrespect, *E* expect, *I* inspect, introspect, *R* respect, retrospect, *S* self-respect, circumspect, suspect, *SP* specked, spect, 'spect, *U* unspecked

TEKT architect, detect, contect, obtect, overprotect, protect, underprotect, undetect, unprotect

TREKT trekked

(See **EK,** add *-ed* where appropriate.)

ĒL

ĒL eel, langue d'oïl

BĒL *A* abeal, abele, *B* beal, beele, *D* deshabille, dishabille, *I* immobile, *L* locomobile, *M mobile, Mobile, O* automobile, *S* cebil, *SN* snowmobile, traymobile

DĒL deal, deil, ideal, interdeal, misdeal, ordeal, redeal, misdeal, undeal, urodele

FĒL feal, feel, feil, forefeel, Israfil, refeel

GWĒL aiguille

HĒL *allheal,* heal, heel, he'll, *clownheel,* Tarheel

HWĒL *B* balance wheel, big wheel, *BR* breastwheel, *D* dial wheel, *DR* driving wheel, *FL flywheel, FR freewheel, G gearwheel, HW* wheal, wheel, *K cartwheel, cogwheel, M millwheel, P* paddlewheel, *pinwheel*

JĒL jeel, jheel, jhil, congeal, recongeal, uncongeal

KRĒL creel

LĒL allele, leal, leel, Lille

MĒL *B* barley meal, *F fistmele, H havermele, wholemeal, I inchmeal, K* Camille, camomile, *cornmeal, L* landmil, *M* meal, mil, *O* oatmeal, *P*

piecemeal, *SHL* schlemiel, *ST stoundmeal, SW sweetmeal*

NĒL anele, anneal, cochineal, manchineel, kneel, neele, chenille

PĒL appeal, ylespil, peal, peel, repeal, repeel, thunderpeal

RĒL baril, *newsreel,* real, reel, surreal, toril, unreal, unreel

SĒL endocoele, enseal, goldenseal, imbecile, conceal, neurocoele, privy seal, ceil, seal, seel, cystocele, unseal

SHĒL sheal, sheel, she'll

SKĒL skeel

SKWĒL squeal

SPĒL *bonspiel,* festspiel, glockenspiel, *kriegspiel,* speel, spiel

STĒL steal, steel, unsteel

SWĒL sweal

TĒL bastille, *datil,* infantile, genteel, castille, Castille, cockateel, manteel, pastille, shabby genteel, teal, teil, til

THĒL thee'll

TWĒL tweel, tuille

VĒL bidonville, reveal, veal

WĒL commonweal, weal, weel, we'll

ZĒL cacozeal, zeal

EL

EL A. W. O. L., el, ell, *L,* Emmanuel, Immanuel, materiel, Noel, ruelle, spirituel, vielle

BEL *B* bar bell, bel, bell, belle, bonibel, bonnibell, *BL* bluebell, *D* decibel,

THE ELEVATOR OPERATOR-OPERATED
ELEVATOR

When you sin, friend, know that later
You'll meet Charon, operator
Of an ancient elevator.
    It goes down to Hades' crater;
It goes up to your Creator.
Charon sets the indicator.
        Ponder well that antiquated
        Manually operated
    Elevator operator's
Elevator operator-
Operated elevator!

deathbell, dinner bell, *doorbell, dumbbell, E* evening bell, *G* gabelle, *H handbell, harebell,* heatherbell, Isabel, *J* Jezebel, *K* Canterbury bell, *corbeil, cowbell, KL* claribel, *M* mirabelle, morning bell, *N* Nobel, *P* passing bell, *R* rebel, *S* sacring bell, sanctus bell, school bell, sunset bell, *V* vesper bell

DEL *A* aludel, asphodel, *D* dell, *FR* fricandel, *H* hirondelle, *I* infidel, *K* cadelle, cordelle, *R* rondel, rondelle, *S* sardel, sardelle, citadel, *SH* chandelle, *Z* zinfandel

DWEL dwell, indwell

FEL Astrophel, befell, fell, refell

HEL Hel, hell

JEL aerogel, hydrogel, gel, jell, plasmagel

KEL kell

KVEL kvell

KWEL quell

LEL *hallel,* parallel

MEL bechamel, oenomel, philomel, hydromel, jumel, calomel, caramel, Carmel, mel, mell, pall-mall, pell-mell

NEL *F* fontanel, fustanel, *FR* fresnel, *J* jargonelle, *K* quenelle, Cornell, *KR* crenelle, *M* mangonel, *N* knell, *O* organelle, *P* parnel, Parnell, personnel, petronel, pimpernel, *PR* prunelle, *R* ritornel, *S* sentinel, *SP* spinel, *V* villanelle

PEL appel, dispel, expel, impel, compel, lapel, pell, propel, rappel, repel, *scalpel*

REL aquarelle, amerelle, doggerel, cockerel, jurel, mackerel, morel, nonpareil, pickerel, rel, Sacheverell, chanterelle

SEL *E* excel, encell, *F* filoselle, ficelle, photocell, *H* hardsell, *HW* white cell, *I* involucel, *K* carousel, carrousel, *M* marcel, *N* nacelle, *O* outsell,

	oversell, *P* pedicel, pennoncelle, pucelle, *R* radicel, red cell, resell, *S* sarcel, sarcelle, cell, sell, solar cell, *U* undersell, unicell
SHEL	*bombshell, eggshell,* cockleshell, nutshell, seashell, shell, tortoise shell, unshell
SMEL	smell
SNEL	snell
SPEL	love spell, misspell, respell, spell, unspell
STREL	pipistrel
SWEL	*groundswell,* swell, upswell
TEL	*A* artel, *B* bagatelle, *BR* bretelle, brocatelle, *D* dentelle, *F* foretell, *H* hotel, *I* immortelle, *K* cartel, *KL* clientele, *M* maitre d'hotel, moschatel, motel, muscatel, *R* retell, *T* tell
VEL	divel, caravel, Ravel, Tavel
WEL	*bridewell,* farewell, *inkwell, Cromwell, speedwell, stairwell,* unwell, well
YEL	yell
ZEL	demoiselle, gazelle, mademoiselle, Moselle

ELB

ELB	elb
SKELB	skelb

ELCH

BELCH	belch
KWELCH	quelch
SKWELCH	squelch
WELCH	welch, Welch

ĒLD

BĒLD	bield
FĒLD	*A* afield, *airfield, B* battlefield, *CH* chesterfield, *F* field, *H* harvest field, *HW* wheat field, *I infield, K canfield, coal field, corn field, L* left field, *M midfield,* minifield, *O* oil field, *outfield, R* right

	field, *SH* sheffield, *SK* Scofield, *SN* snowfield, *SPR* Springfield, *U* urnfield
HĒLD	heald, heeled, hield, well-heeled
SHĒLD	enshield, shield, *windshield*
WĒLD	weald, wield
YĒLD	yield

(See **EL,** add *-ed* where appropriate.)

ELD

ELD	eld
BELD	belled, rebelled, unbelled
FYELD	fjeld
GELD	*Danegeld,* geld
HELD	beheld, held, unbeheld, upheld, withheld
KELD	keld
LELD	paralleled, unparalleled
MELD	meld
PELD	dispelled, expelled, impelled, compelled, misspelled, pelled, propelled, repelled, spelled
YELD	yeld, yelled

(See **EL,** add *-ed* where appropriate.)

ELF

ELF	elf
DELF	delf, *didelf*
GWELF	Guelph
PELF	pelf
SELF	herself, himself, itself, myself, ourself, self, thyself, oneself, yourself
SHELF	closet shelf, mantel shelf, shelf, wall shelf (etc.)
SKELF	skelf

ELFT

DELFT	delft, Delft
PELFT	pelfed

ELK

ELK	elk
HWELK	whelk
YELK	yelk

ELM

ELM	elm, *wych-elm*
HELM	ahelm, dishelm, helm, unhelm, weatherhelm, *Wilhelm*
HWELM	whelm, overwhelm, underwhelm
RELM	realm

ELP

HELP	help, self-help
HWELP	whelp, *yarwhelp*
KELP	kelp
SKELP	skelp
SWELP	swelp
YELP	yelp

ELT

BELT	belt, *blackbelt, borscht belt,* rain belt, sun belt, unbelt
DELT	dealt, misdealt, undealt
DWELT	dwelt, undwelt
FELT	felt, *heartfelt, homefelt,* underfelt, unfelt, veldt
GELT	*Danegelt,* gelt, *Trinkgelt*
KELT	Celt, kelt, Kelt
MELT	melt, remelt
NELT	knelt
PELT	pelt
SELT	celt, Celt
SMELT	smelt
SPELT	misspelt, spelt, unspelt
SVELT	svelte
VELT	*backveld,* Roosevelt, veld, veldt, *zuurveldt*
WELT	welt

ELTH

HELTH	health
STELTH	stealth
WELTH	commonwealth, wealth

ELTS

(See **ELT,** add *-s* where appropriate.)

ELV

DELV	delve
HELV	helve
SHELV	shelve
TWELV	twelve

ELZ

NELZ	Dardanelles
SHELZ	Seychelles

(See **EL,** add *-s* where appropriate.)

ĒM

ĒM	eme
BĒM	abeam, beam, embeam, *hornbeam, whitebeam, crossbeam, moonbeam, sunbeam*
BRĒM	bream
DĒM	addeem, adeem, academe, deem, deme, Hasidim, misdeem, redeem
DRĒM	*daydream,* dream
FĒM	blaspheme, *grapheme, morpheme,* telepheme
FLĒM	fleam
FRĒM	fream
GLĒM	agleam, gleam, weathergleam
HĒM	haem
KĒM	hakim, hyporcheme
KRĒM	cream, *icecream*
KWĒM	queme
LĒM	leam
MĒM	*sememe*
NĒM	*phoneme,* neem, *toneme*
PRĒM	supreme
RĒM	*bireme,* quinquereme, ream, reem, rheme, riem, reream, *spireme, trireme*
SĒM	beseem, berseem, enseam, *glosseme, lexeme, oxime, raceme,* seam, seem, unbeseem, unseam
SKĒM	rescheme, scheme
SKRĒM	escrime, scream
STĒM	disesteem, esteem, self-esteem, steam
STRĒM	*downstream, headstream, mainstream, midstream, millstream, slipstream,* stream, *upstream*
TĒM	eroteme, esteem, semanteme, *septime,* centime, team, teem
THĒM	anatheme, theme
TRĒM	extreme, monotreme
YĒM	yeme
ZHĒM	regime

EM

EM	em, 'em, m, requiem
BLEM	periblem
DEM	anadem, bediadem, diadem, condemn, *modem,* recondemn
FEM	feme, femme
FLEM	phlegm
HEM	ahem, Bethlehem, hem, *mayhem*
JEM	begem, Brummagem, gem, stratagem
KEM	Yquem, kemb
KLEM	clem
KREM	crème, crème de la crème
LEM	*golem, xylem*
MEM	mem
NEM	ad hominem
REM	ad rem, in rem, theorem
SEM	*semsem*
SHEM	Shem
STEM	*pipestem,* stem
TEM	contemn, pro tem
THEM	apothegm, apothem, them
WEM	wem

ĒMD

(See **ĒM,** add *-d* or *-ed* where appropriate.)

EMD

DEMD	diademed
FREMD	fremd

(See **EM,** add *-med* or *-ed* where appropriate.)

EMP

HEMP	hemp
KEMP	kemp
TEMP	temp

EMPT

EMPT	empt, coempt, preempt
DEMPT	adempt
DREMPT	adreamt, dreamt, undreamt
KEMPT	kempt, unkempt
REMPT	dirempt
TEMPT	attempt, contempt, self-contempt, tempt
ZEMPT	exempt

EMZ

TEMZ	temse, Thames

(See **EM,** add *-s* where appropriate.)

ĒN

ĒN	ean, e'en, goode'en, Hallowe'en, narceine, cysteine, toluene
BĒN	bean, been, *buckbean,* gombeen, *has-been,* jellybean, shebeen, terebene
CHĒN	Balanchine, Capuchin
DĒN	*A* Aberdeen, almandine, *BR* brigandine, *D* dean, dene, dudeen, *G* gabardine, gardeen, Gunga Din, *GR* gradine, grenadine, *I* indene, incarnadine, *K codeine, KR* crapaudine, *P* piperidine, *S* sardine, sourdine, undine
FĒN	dauphine, *phosphene, phosphine,* Josephine, caffeine, *morphine,* toxaphene, trephine
GĒN	*Begin,* Beguine, gean, carrageen
GLĒN	glean, reglean
GRĒN	*A* aquagreen, *B* bowling green, *E* evergreen, *G* gangrene, *GR grassgreen,* green, *L* long green, *M* mythogreen, *P* peagreen, peregrine, putting green, *S sea-green, SH* shagreen, chagrin, *W* wintergreen
HĒN	fellaheen
HWĒN	wheen
JĒN	*A* alpigene, *E* epigene, *F phosgene,* photogene, *G* gazogene, *H* heterogene, hygiene, hypogene, *I* indigene, *J* gene, jean, *KW* quadragene, *M* mutator gene, *O* aubergine, *P* polygene, porphyrogene, *S* sagene, seltzogene, supergene
KĒN	achene, buckeen, damaskene, keen, nankeen, palankeen, palanquin, sakeen, *takin,* Tolkien
KLĒN	clean, come clean, Mr. Clean, super-clean, ultraclean, unclean
KRĒN	Hippocrene
KWĒN	closet queen, *cuckquean,* quean, queen
LĒN	*A* anilene, *B* baleen, bandoline, *F* philhellene,

MĒN *G* gasoline, Ghibelline, *H* Hellene, *K choline,* colleen, *KR* crinoline, *L* lean, lien, *M* magdalene, malines, moulleen, mousseline, *N* naphthalene, *O* opaline, *PR* praline, proline, *SK* scalene, *SKW squalene,* *T* tourmaline, *TH* phthalein, *U* uplean, *V* valine, vaseline

ammine, bellarmine, *bromine,* bemean, dexemphetamine, demean, demesne, dopamine, physostigmene, gamine, imine, mean, mesne, mien, misdemean, spodumine

NĒN Lenin, mavourneen, mezzanine, quinine, shoneen, cyanine, *strychnine,* torpinene

PĒN alpeen, atropine, chopine, Philippine, pean, peen, reserpine, scalpeen, spalpeen, *terpene*

PRĒN isoprene, preen

RĒN *A* aquamarine, Algerine, anserine, *B* bismarine, butterine, dourine, *F* figurine, *FL* fluorine, *K* careen, kittereen, *KL chlorine, M* marine, margarine, mazarine, moreen, *N* Nazarene, nectarine, *O* oleomargarine, *P* Palmyrene, pelerine, pyrene, pistareen, *R* reen, rosmarine, *purine,* *S* serene, cismarine, submarine, subterrene, superterrene, *SKW* squidgereen, *SM* smithereen, *T* tambourine, tangerine, terrene, terrine, tureen, *TR* transmarine, *U* ultramarine, *W* wolverine

SĒN *A* arsine, *D* damascene, *E* Eocene, epicene, Essene, *F* fantocine, fascine, foreseen, *GL* glassine, *K* kerosene, *M* Miocene, *N* Nicene, *O* obscene, overseen, *R* Racine, *S* scene, seen, psittacine, *U* unforeseen, unseen, *V* vaccine

SFĒN sphene

SHĒN arsheen, dasheen, Capuchin, machine, praying machine, sheen, voting machine

SKĒN skean

SKRĒN bescreen, multiscreen, rescreen, screen, split screen, unscreen, *windscreen*

SPLĒN spleen

STĒN mangosteen, stean, steen

TĒN *A* Argentine, eighteen, *B* barkentine, Byzantine, bottine, *BR* brigantine, brilliantine, *D dentine,* duvetyn, *F* fifteen, fourteen, *FL* Florentine, *G* galantine, guillotine, *J* gelatine, *K* canteen, Constantine, costean, *KL* clementine, *KR* chryselephantine, *KW* quarantine, quarentene, *L* lateen, libertine, lovertine, *N* nicotine, nineteen, *O* Augustine, *P* patine, pentene, poteen, potheen, *PR* pre-teen, *protein,* pristine, *R* ratteen, ratine, routine, *S* sateen, serpentine, seventeen, sixteen, *Sistine, cystine,* subroutine, *T* teen, tontine, turbitteen, *TH* thirteen, *U* umpteen, *V* velveteen

THĒN ornithene, polythene

THRĒN threne

TRĒN latrine, thestreen, treen, *vitrine,* yestreen

TWĒN atween, between, go-between, therebetween, 'tween

VĒN advene, intervene, contravene, convene, margravine, *nervine,* olivine, prevene, ravine, Slovene, subvene, supervene, visne

WĒN overween, wean, ween

YĒN yean

ZĒN benzene, benzine, bombazine, chlorobenzene, cuisine, limousine, magazine, nitrobenzene, organzine

EN

EN Darien, equestrienne, julienne, cayenne, comedienne, en, n, Parisienne, persienne, Cheyenne, Tyrolienne, tragedienne, Valenciennes

BEN ben, *benben,* benn, Big Ben

CHEN chen

DEN Ardennes, den, quarenden

FEN fen

GEN again, born-again

GLEN glen

HEN *grayhen,* hen, *moorhen, peahen,* prairie hen, *sagehen,* turkeyhen, water hen

HWEN when

JEN endogen, exogen, estrogen, halogen, gen, carcinogen, kratogen, nitrogen, oxygen, pathogen, sagene

KEN beken, ken

LEN madeleine, madrilene, Magdalen

MEN *A* aldermen, amen, *B* Bushmen, *H* horsemen, *I* Englishmen, *J* gentlemen, *M* men, *N* Norsemen, Northmen, *P* partimen, party men, *R* regimen, *S* seamen, semen, cyclamen, *SP* specimen, *T* tequmen

PEN ballpoint pen, brevipen, *bullpen,* fountain pen, impen, *cowpen,* pen, *pigpen, playpen,* poison pen, unpen

REN wren, viceraine

SEN samisen, Saracen, sen, *sensen,* Sun Yat-sen

SHEN Shen

SKEN sken

STEN Sten

TEN ten

THEN then

WEN wen

VYEN varsovieane

YEN doyenne, Cayenne, yen

ZEN denizen, citizen, Zen

ENCH

BENCH bench, disbench, carpenter's bench, unbench, *workbench*

BLENCH blench

DRENCH bedrench, drench, redrench

FLENCH	flench
FRENCH	French, un-French
KENCH	kench
KLENCH	clench, unclench
KWENCH	quench, unquench
MENCH	mensch, Uebermensch, Untermensch
RENCH	monkey wrench, wrench
SKWENCH	squench
STENCH	stench
TENCH	tench
TRENCH	entrench, intrench, retrench, trench
WENCH	*oldwench,* wench

ENCHT

BENCHT	benched

(See **ENCH,** add *-ed* where appropriate.)

ĒND

FĒND	archfiend, fiend

(See **ĒN,** add *-ed* where appropriate.)

END

END	end, gable end, Land's End, minuend, tag end, upend
BEND	*backbend,* bend, *prebend,* rebend, South Bend, unbend
BLEND	blend, blende, *hornblende,* interblend, *pitchblende*
DEND	addend, dividend
FEND	defend, fend, forfend, offend, weatherfend
FREND	befriend, *boyfriend,* friend, *girlfriend,* ladyfriend
HEND	apprehend, comprehend, misapprehend, miscomprehend, reprehend, subtrahend
KEND	kenned, unkenned
LEND	lend
MEND	amend, emend, discommend, commend, mend, recommend, remend
PEND	*A* append, *D* depend, *E* expend, *I* impend, *K* *compend, P* pend, penned, perpend, *PR* prepend, *ST stipend, U* unpenned, *V* vilipend

REND	rend, rerend, reverend
SEND	ascend, descend, *godsend,* condescend, scend, send, transcend, upsend
SHEND	shend
SPEND	expend, misspend, spend, suspend
STEND	extend, coextend, ostend, Ostend
TEND	*A* attend, *D* distend, *I* intend, *K* coextend, contend, *P* portend, *PR* pretend, *R* repetend, *S* subtend, superintend, *T* tend
TREND	trend
VEND	vend
WEND	wend
ZEND	Zend

(See **EN,** add *-ed* or *-ned* where appropriate.)

ENG

DRENG	dreng, drengh
KRENG	kreng
SHENG	sheng

ENGTH

LENGTH	length
STRENGTH	strength

ENJ

HENJ	*Stonehenge*
VENJ	avenge, revenge

ENS

ENS	*A* affluence, *D* disobedience, *E* ebullience, effluence, expedience, experience, ense, *I* inexpedience, inexperience, influence, incongruence, inconvenience, insipience, issuance, *K* confluence, congruence, continuance, convenience, *M* mellifluence, *N* nescience, *O* obedience, audience, omniscience, *P*

percipience, *PR* prescience, prurience, *R* refluence, resilience, *S* salience, sapience, subservience

DENS	*A* accidence, accidents, *D* dense, diffidence, dissidence, *E* evidence, *I* improvidence, impudence, incidence, *K* coincidence, condense, confidence, *N* nonresidence, nonresidents, *PR* providence, Providence, *R* recondense, residence, residents, *S* self-confidence, subsidence
FENS	defense, fence, offense, self-defense
FLENS	flense
HENS	hence, herehence
HWENS	whence
JENS	diligence, exigence, indigence, intelligence, negligence
KWENS	blandiloquence, breviloquence, eloquence, grandiloquence, inconsequence, consequence, magniloquence
LENS	*B* benevolence, *E* equivalence, equivalents, excellence, *FL* flatulence, flocculence, *FR* fraudulence, *I* imprevalence, indolence, insolence, insomnolence, *K* condolence, corpulence, *KW* *quantivalence, L* lutulence, *M* malevolence, *O* opulence, *P* pestilence, purulence, *PR* prevalence, *R* redolence, *S* somnolence, succulence, *T* temulence, turbulence, *TR* truculence, *V* violence, virulence
MENS	immense, commence, mense, recommence, vehemence
NENS	*A* abstinence, *E* eminence, *I* immanence, imminence, impermanence, impertinence, incontinence, *K*

PENS
continence, *P* permanence, pertinence, *PR* preeminence, prominence, *S* supereminence dispense, expense, pence, prepense, propense, recompense, *sixpence, twopence, threepence*

RENS
B belligerence, *D* deference, difference, *I* indifference, inference, irreverence, *K* conference, *PR* preference, *R* reference, reverence, *S* circumference

SENS
B beneficence, *FR* frankincense, *I* incense, innocence, *K* commonsense, concupiscence, *M* magnificence, munificence, *N nonsense, R* reticence, *S* cense, sense

SPENS
spence, suspense

TENS
A appetence, *I* impenitence, impotence, inappetence, incompetence, incompetents, intense, intents, *K* competence, *O* omnipotence, *P* penitence, *PL* plenipotence, *PR* pretense, *S* subtense, *T* tense

THENS
thence

ENSH

(See ENCH)

ENST

ENST
experienced, inexperienced, influenced, uninfluenced

DENST
evidenced, condensed, recondensed, uncondensed

FENST
fenced, unfenced

FLENST
flensed, unflensed

GENST
against, 'gainst

MENST
commenced, recommenced

NENST
anenst, fornenst

PENST
dispensed, recompensed, unrecompensed

RENST
cross-referenced, referenced, reverenced, unreferenced, unreverenced

SENST
incensed, censed, sensed, unsensed

ENT

ENT
A affluent, accipient, ambient, aperient, *D* diffluent, diluent, disobedient, disorient, *E* effluent, expedient, emollient, esurient, *GR* gradient, *I* inexpedient, influent, ingredient, incongruent, inconvenient, insentient, incipient, interfluent, *K* confluent, congruent, constituent, convenient, *L* lenient, *M* mellifluent, *O* obedient, obstruent, audient, orient, *P* parturient, percipient, *PR* prescient, profluent, prurient, *R* recipient, refluent, resilient, *S* salient, sapient, sentient, circumambient, circumfluent, subservient, substituent

BENT
bent, *hellbent,* unbent

BLENT
blent, unblent

BRENT
brent

DENT
A accident, *D* dent, diffident, dissident, *E* evident, *I* improvident, impudent, incident, incoincident, indent, *K* coincident, confident, *O* occident, *PR* precedent, president, provident, *R* resident, *S* subsident

FENT
fent

GENT
Ghent

HENT
attrahent, hent, contrahent, revehent

JENT
diligent, dirigent, exigent, gent, indigent, intelligent, intransigent, corrigent, negligent, transigent

KENT
Kent

KWENT
acquent, eloquent, frequent, grandiloquent, inconsequent, consequent, magniloquent, subsequent

LENT
B benevolent, *E* excellent, equivalent, esculent, *FL* flatulent, flocculent, *FR* fraudulent, *I* indolent, insolent, *K* corpulent, *KW* querulent, *L* leant, lent, Lent, luculent, lutulent, *M* malevolent, muculent, *O* opulent, *P* pestilent, purulent, *PR* prevalent, *R* redolent, relent, *S* somnolent, succulent, *T* turbulent, *TR* truculent, *V* vinolent, violent, virulent

MENT
A abandonment, abolishment, admeasurement, admonishment, advertisement, affamishment, affranchisement, aggrandizement, acknowledgment, accomplishment, accouterment, aliment, ament, apportionment, arbitrament, argument, armament, astonishment, *B* babblement, banishment, battlement, bedevilment, bedizenment, beleaguerment, bemuddlement, betterment, bewilderment, botherment, BL blandishment, blazonment, blemishment, *BR* brabblement, *CH* chastisement, cherishment, *D* dazzlement, decrement, dement, demolishment, decipherment, detriment, development, devilment, diminishment, dimplement, disablement, disarmament, disfigurement, disfranchisement, discouragement, disparagement, dispiritment, distinguishment, divertissement, document, *E* excrement, experiment,

extinguishment, element, embarrassment, embattlement, embellishment, embezzlement, embitterment, emblazonment, embodiment, emolument, empanelment, enablement, endangerment, endeavorment, enfeeblement, enfranchisement, encompassment, encouragement, enlightenment, ennoblement, enravishment, entanglement, envelopment, environment, envisagement, establishment, *F* famishment, ferment, fibrocement, filament, firmament, foment, foremeant, fosterment, *FR* fragment, franchisement, *G* garnishment, government, *H* habiliment, harassment, hereditament, *I* impediment, imperilment, implement, impoverishment, imprisonment, increment, instrument, integument, inveiglement, *K* *comment,* complement, compliment, condiment, *L* lament, languishment, lavishment, ligament, lineament, liniment, *M* management, medicament, meant, merriment, measurement, monument, muniment, *N* nourishment, nutriment,

O augment, ornament, *P* parliament, pediment, pesterment, punishment, *PR* prattlement, predicament, premonishment, presentiment, *R* ravishment, regiment, recrement, relinquishment, replenishment, revelment, rudiment, *S* sacrament, sediment, cement, sentiment, cerement, settlement, supplement, *T* tegument, temperament, tenement, testament, torment, tournament, *TR* tremblement, *U* unmeant, *V* vanishment, vanquishment, vehement, *W* wanderment, well-meant, wilderment, wonderment, worriment

NENT *A* abstinent, anent, *E* eminent, *F* fornent, *I* immanent, imminent, impermanent, impertinent, incontinent, *K* continent, *P* permanent, pertinent, *PR* preeminent, prominent, *R* remanent, *S* supereminent, *TH* thereanent

PENT pent, repent, unpent
RENT afferent, belligerent, deferent, different, efferent, indifferent, irreverent, preferent, rent, reverent
SENT *A* absent, accent, ascent, assent, *B* beneficent, *D* descent, dissent, docent, *H* heaven-sent, *I* innocent, *K* concent, consent, *M* magnificent, maleficent, missent, munificent, *P* percent, *R* re-sent, reticent, *S* cent, scent, sent, *U* unsent
SKLENT sklent
SPENT forespent, misspent, overspent, spent, underspent, unspent, well-spent
SPRENT besprent, sprent, unsprent
STENT stent
TENT *A* appetent, attent, *D* detent, discontent,

distent, *E* extent, *I* ignipotent, ill-content, impenitent, impotent, incompetent, intent, *K* competent, content, *M* malcontent, miscontent, *O* omnipotent, ostent, *P* penitent, *portent,* *PL* plenipotent, *T* tent, *U* untent, *W* well-content
VENT *advent,* event, invent, non-event, prevent, circumvent, pseudo-event, *sirvente,* vent
WENT overwent, underwent, went
ZENT misrepresent, present, represent, resent

ĒNTH

GRĒNTH greenth
TĒNTH eighteenth, fifteenth, fourteenth (etc.)

ENTS

MENTS accouterments
TENTS contents, tents

(See **ENS**)

ĒNZ

GRĒNZ greens
RĒNZ smithereens
TĒNZ teens

(See **ĒN,** add *-s* where appropriate.)

ENZ

ENZ ens
BLENZ *Coblenz*
JENZ gens
LENZ lens
SENZ Vincennes

(See **EN,** add *-s* where appropriate.)

ĒP

BĒP beep
BLĒP bleep
CHĒP cheap, cheep
DĒP adeep, deep, down deep
GRĒP la grippe

HĒP	aheap, heap, *scrapheap*
JĒP	jeep
KĒP	keep, *upkeep*
KLĒP	clepe
KRĒP	creep
LĒP	leap, leep, outleap, overleap
NĒP	neap, neep
PĒP	Little Bopeep, peep
RĒP	cassareep, reap, rereap
SĒP	enseep, seep
SHĒP	sheep
SLĒP	asleep, beauty sleep, outsleep, oversleep, sleep, unasleep
SNĒP	sneap
STĒP	steep
SWĒP	chimneysweep, ensweep, clean sweep, *peesweep,* sweep, upsweep
TĒP	teap
THRĒP	threap, threep
TRĒP	estrepe
WĒP	beweep, outweep, *peesweep,* weep

EP

EP	Dieppe
HEP	hep, not hep
KEP	kep
PEP	pep
PREP	prep
REP	demirep, rep
SEP	cep
SHEP	shep
SHLEP	schlep
SKEP	skep
STEP	*D doorstep, F* first step, *footstep,* giant step, *I instep, K catstep, KW quickstep, M* misstep, *O* overstep, *S sidestep, ST stairstep,* step, steppe, *T two-step, W* one-step

EPS

SEPS	janiceps

(See **EP,** add *-s* where appropriate.)

ĒPT

BĒPT	beeped

(See **ĒP,** add *-ed* where appropriate.)

EPT

EPT	ept, inept
DEPT	adept
KEPT	kept, unkept
KLEPT	biblioklept, y-clept
KREPT	crept
LEPT	leapt, nympholept
NEPT	inept
PEPT	pepped
SEPT	accept, discept, except, incept, intercept, intussuscept, *concept, percept, precept, preconcept,* recept, sept, suscept, *transept*
SLEPT	slept
STEPT	stepped, unstepped
SWEPT	*backswept,* swept, unswept, *windswept*
THREPT	mammothrept
WEPT	wept, unwept

ĒR

(See **ÎR**)

ER

ER	err
HER	Herr
TER	parterre
YER	rivière, vivandière

(See **ÂR**)

ĒRD

(See **ÎRD**)

ĒRS

(See **ÎRS**)

ĒRZ

(See **ÎRZ**)

ĒS

BĒS	obese
ĒS	Thais
FLĒS	fleece
GĒS	geese
GRĒS	ambergris, degrease, grease, grece, Greece, verdigris
KRĒS	decrease, increase, crease, creese, kris, recrease, uncrease

LĒS	coulisse, lease, lis, pelisse, police, prelease, release, re-lease, sublease, valise
MĒS	semese
NĒS	nes, nese, Nice, niece
PĒS	*A* afterpiece, apiece, *B* battlepiece, *CH* chimneypiece, *E earpiece, endpiece, F fieldpiece,* fowling piece, *FR* frontispiece, *H hairpiece, I eyepiece, K codpiece,* cornerpiece, *KR crosspiece, crownpiece, M* mantelpiece, masterpiece, *mouthpiece, N* neckpiece, *O* altarpiece, *P* peace, piece, pocketpiece, *R* repiece, *S* centerpiece, *SH showpiece, T tailpiece, timepiece*
PRĒS	caprice
RĒS	cerise, reese
SĒS	decease, cassis, predecease, cease, surcease
TĒS	atis, métis
TRĒS	cantatrice

ES

(See also additional nouns made feminine by adding *-ess,* e.g., shepherdess, stewardess.)

ES	acquiesce, Es, s, SOS, quiesce
BES	bes, Bes, bouillabaisse
BLES	bless, noblesse, rebless, unbless
CHES	chess
DES	dess, frondesce, incandesce
DRES	*A* address, ambassadress, *D* diving dress, *DR* dress, *F* full dress, *G* gala dress, *H headdress, M* maladdress, *N nightdress, O* overdress, *R* readdress, redress, *sundress, U* underdress, undress
FES	fess, 'fess, fesse, confess, profess
GES	foreguess, guess, reguess
GRES	aggress, digress, *egress, ingress, congress,* regress, retrogress, transgress

HES	Hesse
JES	jess, largess, rejess, turgesce, unjess
KRES	accresce, cress, mustard cress, pennycress, water cress
KWES	deliquesce, liquesce
LES	coalesce, convalesce, less, nevertheless, nonetheless, obsolesce, opalesce, recalesce, reconvalesce, unless

(See appropriate nouns, add -less: e.g., blemishless, bodiless, etc.)

MES	intumesce, *kermes,* mess, tumesce
NES	baroness, Dungeness, evanesce, finesse, canoness, luminesce, nes, ness, Ness, pythoness, rejuvenesce

(See appropriate adjectives, add -ness: e.g. *fleetness, quickness,* beeriness, holiness, etc.)

PES	compesce, satrapess
PRES	decompress, depress, express, impress, compress, letterpress, oppress, press, recompress, repress, suppress, *winepress*
RES	archeress, duress, effloresce, fluoresce, phosphoresce, caress, manageress, votaress

(See also nouns ending in *r* made feminine by adding the suffix -ess, e.g., mayoress.)

SES	*abscess, access,* assess, cess, excess, obsess, precess, *princess,* process, reassess, recess, sess, success
STRES	overstress, prestress, stress, understress
TES	giantess, poetess, politesse
TRES	ancestress, distress, editress, executress, idolatress, inheritress, comfortress, ministress, monitress, tress, *votress*
VES	effervesce
YES	yes
ZES	dispossess, possess, prepossess, repossess

ĒSH

BĒSH	babiche
FĒSH	affiche, fiche, microfiche, ultrafiche
KĒSH	quiche
LĒSH	leash, releash, unleash
MĒSH	miche
NĒSH	niche
RĒSH	nouveau riche
SNĒSH	sneesh
TĒSH	pastiche, postiche, potiche, *schottische*

ESH

BESH	bobêche, tête-bêche
FLESH	flesh, flèche, *horseflesh,* parfleche
FRESH	afresh, fresh, refresh, unfresh
KRESH	crèche
LESH	calèche
MESH	enmesh, mesh, syncromesh, unmesh
NESH	nesh
SESH	secesh
THRESH	rethresh, thresh

ESK

ESK	Junoesque, Kafkaesque, Rubensesque, statuesque
BESK	arabesque
DESK	desk, reading desk, writing desk
LESK	burlesque, naturalesque
NESK	Romanesque
RESK	barbaresque, humoresque, Moresque, picaresque, picturesque, plateresque, chivalresque, sculpturesque
TESK	blottesque, Dantesque, grotesque, gigantesque, soldatesque

ĒST

ĒST	east, northeast, southeast
BĒST	beast, hartebeest, wildebeest
DĒST	modiste
FĒST	*beanfeast,* feast, harvest feast, wedding feast
FLĒST	fleeced, unfleeced
GĒST	geest
GRĒST	greased, regreased, ungreased

JĒST	aubergiste
KĒST	keest
KRĒST	decreased, increased, recreased, uncreased
KWĒST	queest
LĒST	leased, least, overpoliced, policed, released, subleased, underpoliced, unleased
PĒST	pieced, piste, repieced
PRĒST	archpriest, priest, unpriest
SĒST	deceased, ceased
SNĒST	sneest
TĒST	artiste, batiste, teest
VĒST	arriviste
YĒST	yeast
ZHĒST	aubergiste

(See ĒS, add -d where appropriate.)

EST

EST	acquiesced, EST, SOS-ed, Trieste

(For the superlative degree of appropriate one- and two-syllable adjectives, add -est, e.g., *blackest,* prettiest.)

BEST	best, second-best
BLEST	blessed, blest, unblessed, unblest
BREST	abreast, *blackbreast,* breast, Brest, *redbreast,* unbreast
CHEST	chest
DEST	incandesced
DREST	addressed, dressed, overdressed, readdressed, redressed, underdressed, well-dressed, undressed, unredressed
FEST	disinfest, fessed, fest, *gabfest,* infest, confessed, counterfessed, manifest

GEST	guessed, guest, unguessed
GREST	digressed, progressed, regressed, retrogressed, transgressed
HEST	alkahest, behest, hest
JEST	almagest, beau geste, digest, egest, ingest, gest, geste, jest, congest, predigest, redigest, suggest
KREST	*firecrest, goldcrest,* increst, crest, undercrest
KWEST	acquest, bequest, deliquesced, *inquest,* quest, request
LEST	coalesced, convalesced, lest, molest, opalesced, recalesced, celeste
MEST	messed, unmessed
NEST	funeste, luminesced, nest
PEST	anapest, Budapest, impest, rinderpest, pest
PREST	*A* appressed, *D* depressed, *I* impressed, imprest, *K* compressed, *O* oppressed, *PR* pressed, *R* recompressed, repressed, *S* suppressed, *U* unimpressed, uncompressed, unpressed, unsuppressed
REST	*A armrest,* arrest, *B bookrest,* Bucharest, *D* disinterest, *E* effloresced, Everest, *F footrest,* phosphoresced, *FL* fluoresced, *H headrest, I* interest, *K* caressed, *N kniferest, O* au reste, *R* rest, wrest, *U* uninterested, uninterest, unrest
SEST	alceste, assessed, *incest,* obsessed, palimpsest, reassessed, recessed, cessed, unassessed
STREST	distressed, overstressed, prestressed, stressed, unstressed
TEST	attest, detest, contest, obtest, pretest, protest, retest, test
TREST	golden-tressed, raven-tressed, tressed, untressed
VEST	devest, divest, effervesced, invest, reinvest, revest, undervest, vest
WEST	Key West, midwest, northwest, southwest, west
YEST	yessed
ZEST	dispossessed, possessed, prepossessed, repossessed, self-possessed, unprepossessed, unpossessed, zest

(See **ES,** add *-d* or *-ed* where appropriate.)

ĒT

ĒT	eat, overeat, undereat
BĒT	beat, beet, *browbeat, deadbeat, downbeat, drumbeat, heartbeat, offbeat,* sugar beet, *upbeat*
BLĒT	bleat
CHĒT	cheat, cheet, escheat, recheat
FĒT	defeat, effete, feat, feet, Lafitte
FLĒT	fleet
FRĒT	afreet, freit
GLĒT	gleet
GRĒT	greet, congreet
HĒT	dead heat, heat, overheat, preheat, reheat, superheat, underheat, unheat
HWĒT	*buckwheat, wholewheat,* wheat
JĒT	exegete, munjeet, vegete
KĒT	keet, lorrikeet, mesquite, parakeet, polychaete, spirochete
KLĒT	cleat, cleete, paraclete
KRĒT	accrete, discreet, discrete, excrete, indiscreet, concrete, Crete, secrete
KWĒT	queet
LĒT	*athlete,* delete, elite, leat, leet, obsolete
MĒT	dead meat, *forcemeat,* fresh meat, gamete, *helpmeet,* meat, meet, mete, *mincemeat, pigmeat,* raw meat, *sweetmeat,* unmeet
NĒT	neat, proxenete
PĒT	compete, peat, repeat
PLĒT	deplete, incomplete, complete, pleat, replete, uncomplete
RĒT	afreet, marguerite, Masorete, terete
SĒT	*D* deceit, disseat, *I* inficete, *J* judgment seat,

	K catbird seat, conceit, county seat, country seat, *M* mercy seat, *PR* preconceit, *R* receipt, reseat, *S* cete, Cete, seat, self-deceit, self-conceit, *U* unseat
SHĒT	balance sheet, *broadsheet, dustsheet, foresheet, freesheet, groundsheet, clipsheet,* mainsheet, sheet, *slipsheet,* winding sheet
SKĒT	skeet, skete
SLĒT	sleet
STRĒT	*backstreet, bystreet, downstreet,* easy street, estreat, street, *upstreet*
SWĒT	bittersweet, bridal suite, honey-sweet, mansuete, meadowsweet, presidential suite, royal suite, sunnysweet, suite, sweet, unsweet
TĒT	petite, teat
THĒT	*aesthete,* thesmothete
TRĒT	Dutch treat, entreat, estreat, ill-treat, maltreat, mistreat, retreat, treat
TWĒT	tweet
VĒT	aquavit
WĒT	*peetweet,* weet
ZĒT	carte de visite

ET

ET	*A* ariette, *D* duet, *E* et, *H* historiette, *L* lariat, layette, *M* minuet, *O* oubliette, *P* pirouette, *S* serviette, silhouette, *ST* statuette, storiette, *W* winceyette
BET	abet, alphabet, barbette, bet, quodlibet, Tibet
BLET	blet
BRET	bret, soubrette, umbrette
DET	bidet, debt, indebt, judgment debt, cadet, muscadet, vedette
FET	estafette, fet, fète, mofette, *Tophet*
FLET	flet
FRET	fret, frett, frette, interfret
GET	baguet, baguette, beget, forget, get, misbeget, unget
GRET	aigrette, *egret,* regret, vinaigrette
HET	het
HWET	whet

JET   *fanjet,* jet, georgette, jumbo jet, *rainjet,* suffragette, turbojet

KET   *B* banquette, *BL* blanquette, *BR* briquette, *D* diskette, *E* enquete, etiquette, *J* jockette, *K* casquette, ket, khet, coquet, coquette, *KR* croquette, *M* maquette, moquette, *P* paroket, piquet, *PL* plaquette, *R* Rockette, *SN* snackette, *T* tourniquet

KWET   quet

LET   *A* ailette, alette, amulet, *BR* briolette, *E* aiguillette, epaulet, *FL* flageolet, flannelette, *G* galette, *GL* globulet, *I* inlet, *K* cassolette, Colette, coverlet, *L* landaulet, let, Lett, *M* mantelet, *martlet,* medalet, *N* novelette, *O* omelet, oreillet, *outlet,* *R* rigolette, rivulet, rondolet, roulette, *S* sublet, *SK* squelette, *T* toilette, *TR* triolet, *V* violet, *Z* zonulet

MET   allumette, fumette, calumet, *kismet,* met, Met, plumette, well-met

NET   *A* alkanet, *B* ballonet, baronet, bassinet, bayonet, benet, bobbinet, burgonet, *BR* brunette, *D* dinette, *dragnet,* *F* falconet, *fishnet,* *H* hairnet, *J* genet, *K* canzonet, carcanet, castanet, kitchenette, cornet, coronet, *KL* clarinet, *L* lansquenet, lorgnette, luncheonette, lunette, *M* marionette, martinet, maisonette, midinette, mignonette, minionette, mosquito net, *N* net, nonet, *P* pianette, *R* remanet, *S* sarcenet, saxcornet, satinet, *SH* chansonette, *ST* stockinet, *T* tabinet, tournette, *V* vignette, villanette, *W* wagonette

PET   parapet, pet, pipette, salopette

PRET   mpret, pret

RET   *A* amourette, anchoret, *B* bachelorette, banneret, barrette, burette, *F* farmerette, formeret, *FL* fleurette, floweret, *I* imaret, *K* collaret, curet, curette, *L* lazaret, lenneret, leatherette, leveret, Launderette, *M* majorette, minaret, *P* Pierrette, pillaret, *R* ret, *S* cellaret, cigarette, solleret, *SH* chevrette, *SP* spinneret, *SW* swimmeret, *T* tabaret, taboret, *U* usherette

SET   *A* anisette, *asset,* avocet, *B* backset, beset, *boneset, D* dancette, dead set, *deepset, F* facette, *farset,* film set, forset, fossette, photoset, *H* handset, *headset, I* ill-set, inset, interset, *K* cassette, *KR* crossette, crystal set, *KW* quickset, lettterset, *M* marquisette, marmoset, *moonset,* musette, *O* offset, *onset, outset,* overset, *P* pincette, poussette, *R* reset, *S* salicet, set, sett, scilicet, somerset, Somerset, subset, *sunset, SH* sharp-set, chemisette, *SM* smart set, *T* typeset, *TH* thick-set, *U* underset, unset, upset, *V* videlicet

SHET   brochette, flechette, fourchette, couchette, clochette, *planchet,* planchette, plushette, pochette, ricochet, shet, trebuchet

SKET   sket

STET   stet

SWET   sweat

TET   quartet, quintet, motet, octet, septet, sestet, sextet, tête-a-tête

THET   epithet

THRET   threat, triple threat

TRET   tret

VET   brevet, corvette, curvet, cuvette, minivet, olivet, revet, vet

VYET   Viet

WET   all wet, bewet, unwet, wet

YET   lorgnette, nyet, oreillet, paillette, vignette, vilayet, yet, yette

ZET   anisette, gazette, grisette, crepe suzette, marmoset, musette, noisette, rosette, chemisette

ĒTH

(th as in with)

ĒTH   ythe
HĒTH   heath
KWĒTH   bequeath
LĒTH   philalethe
NĒTH   beneath, neath, 'neath, underneath
SHĒTH   sheath
SNĒTH   sneath, sneeth
RĒTH   wreath
S̄HĒTH   sheath
TĒTH   *eyeteeth,* monteith, teeth

ĒTH

(th as in this)

BRĒTH   breathe, imbreathe, inbreathe, outbreathe
KWĒTH   bequeath, quethe
RĒTH   enwreathe, wreathe
SĒTH   seethe
SHĒTH   sheathe, ensheathe, unsheathe
SMĒTH   smeeth
TĒTH   teethe

ETH

(th as in thin)

ETH   eightieth, fiftieth, fortieth, ninetieth, seventieth, sixtieth, thirtieth, twentieth (etc.)
BETH   Macbeth
BRETH   breath
DETH   death, megadeath
LETH   shibboleth
PLETH   isopleth
SETH   saith, seth

(Archaic suffix *-eth* may be added to verbs.)

ĒTHD

BRĒTHD   breathed

(See **ĒTH,** add *-ed* where appropriate.)

ĒV

ĒV   eave, eve, Eve, Christmas Eve, naive,

	New Year's Eve, yestereve	
BĒV	beeve	
BRĒV	breve, semibreve	
CHĒV	achieve, cheve, overachieve, underachieve	
DĒV	deave, Khedive	
GRĒV	aggrieve, greave, grieve, *Congreve*	
HĒV	heave, upheave	
KĒV	keeve	
KLĒV	cleave, cleeve, cleve, uncleave	
KWĒV	queeve	
LĒV	believe, disbelieve, interleave, leave, lieve, make-believe, relieve, unbelieve	
NĒV	nieve	
PĒV	peeve	
PRĒV	reprieve, unreprieve	
RĒV	bereave, *portreeve,* reave, reeve, reve	
SĒV	*A* apperceive, *D* deceive, *K* conceive, *M* misconceive, *P* perceive, *PR* preconceive, preperceive, *R* reconceive, reperceive, receive, *S* seave, *U* undeceive	
SHĒV	sheave	
SKRĒV	screeve	
SLĒV	*shirtsleeve,* sleave, sleeve	
STĒV	steeve	
TĒV	recitative	
THĒV	thieve	
TRĒV	retrieve	
VĒV	qui vive	
WĒV	interweave, inweave, reweave, unweave, weave, we've	

ĒVD

CHĒVD	achieved

(See **ĒV,** add *-d* where appropriate.)

ĒZ

ĒZ	ease, heartsease, unease
BĒZ	bise
BRĒZ	breeze, land breeze, sea breeze
CHĒZ	cheese, Big Cheese, head cheese, *nipcheese,* Swiss cheese (etc.)

DĒZ	antipodes, Atlantides, BVD's, galliardise, Hesperides, Caryatides, Maimonides, Pleiades, tiddledies, Eumenides
FĒZ	feaze, feeze
FLĒZ	fleas
FNĒZ	fnese
FRĒZ	antifreeze, enfreeze, freeze, frieze, nuclear freeze, cheval de frise, unfreeze
GĒZ	koksaghyz, Portuguese
GRĒZ	grease
HĒZ	heeze, he's
HWĒZ	wheeze
JĒZ	jeez
KĒZ	quais, keys, marquise
KLĒZ	Androcles, Damocles, Periclese
LĒZ	*B* Belize, Bengalese, *H* Hercules, *I* isosceles, *J* journalese, *K* cablese, *L* leas, lees, *M* Mephistopheles, *N* Nepalese, *S* Senegalese, Singhalese, *T* Tyrolese, *V* valise
MĒZ	acadamese, Annamese, Assamese, Burmese, demise, camise, mease, mise, remise, chemise, Siamese
NĒZ	*A* aborigines, Aragonese, *B* bee's knees, Bolognese, *CH* Chinese, *D* Diogenes, *H* Havanese, *J* Japanese, Javanese, *K* Cantonese, chersonese, *M* manganese, Milanese, *N* knees, neese, neeze, nese, *P* pekinese, Pekinese, Pyrenees, Polonese, *V* Veronese, Viennese
PĒZ	appease, peas, pease, trapeze
PLĒZ	displease, please
PRĒZ	imprese
RĒZ	computerese, congeries, Navarrese, reeze, cerise, sububeres
SĒZ	*A* analyses, antitheses, assise, *D* disseize, *H* hypothesese, *I* interstices, *P* periphrases, *R* reseize, *S* seas, sees, seize, syntheses, *V* vortices
SKWĒZ	squeeze
SLĒZ	sleaze

SNĒZ	sneeze
PLĒZ	displease, pleas, please
TĒZ	betise, D. T.'s, Maltese, tease, Socrates, sottise
THĒZ	these
TWĒZ	tweeze
VĒZ	Genevese
WĒZ	weeze
ZĒZ	disease

(See **Ē,** add *-s* where appropriate.)

EZ

EZ	Suez
FEZ	fez
MEZ	*kermes*
NEZ	knez
PREZ	prez
REZ	Juarez
SEZ	écossaise, says, sez
TEZ	Cortes
YEZ	yez

ĒZD

LĒZD	lesed

(See **ĒZ,** add *-d* where appropriate.)

EZH

BEZH	beige
NEZH	manège
REZH	barège
TEZH	cortege

Ī

Ī	*B* bigeye, bindy-eye, *buckeye, BL* black eye, blind eye, *D* dead-eye, *E* eagle eye, evil eye, *F* fish-eye, FR* frog-eye, *G* goldeneye, *goldeye, H* Helvetii, *I* ai, ay, aye, eye, I, aye-aye, *J* genii, *K* cat's eye, *cockeye, M mooneye, N* naked eye, nuclei, *O* oxeye, *P* peepeye, pink-eye, *PR* private eye, *R* radii, red-eye, *S* sock-eye, *SH* shiai, *sheep's-eye, shut-eye, T* tiger's-eye, *W walleye,* weather eye
BĪ	*A* alibi, *B* buy, by, bye, by-and-by, bye-bye, by-the-by, *F* flyby, forby,

foreby, *G go-by,* goodbye, *H* hereby, hushaby, *HW* whereby, *I* incubi, *L* lullaby, *N* nearby, *O* overbuy, *P* passerby, *R rabbi,* rockaby, *S* syllabi, succubi, *ST standby,* stander-by, *TH* thereby, *U* underbuy

BLĪ bly

DĪ ao dai, bedye, die, dye, do-or-die, overdye, redye, sine die, undye

DRĪ adry, dry, high-and-dry

FĪ *A* acrify, alacrify, alkalify, acetify, acidify, amplify, angelify, Anglify, arefy, argufy, *B* basify, beatify, bonify, beautify, *BR* brutify, *CH* churchify, *D* daintify, damnify, dandify, defy, dehumanify, deify, declassify, demystify, demythify, demulsify, denazify, detoxify, diabolify, dignify, disqualify, dissatisfy, diversify, divinify, dulcify, duplify, *E* edify, exemplify, electrify, emulsify, esterify, *F* falsify, fie, fie-fie, phi, fortify, *FR* Frenchify, fructify, *G* gasify, *GL* glorify, *GR* gratify, *H* hi-fi, horrify, humanify, humidify, humify, *I* identify, indemnify, intensify, interstratify, *J* jellify, gentrify, jollify, justify, *K* calcify, carnify, casefy, codify, cockneyfy, chondrify, *KL* clarify, classify, *KR* crucify, *KW* qualify, quantify, *L* labefy, ladyfy, lapidify, lenify, lignify, liquefy, lubrify, *M* madefy, magnify, matrify, micrify, minify, mystify, mythify, modify, mollify, mortify, mummify, mundify, *N* Nazify, nidify, nigrify, nitrify, notify, nullify, *O* objectify, obstupefy, aurify, ossify, oversimplify, *P* pacify, personify, petrify, pinguefy, purify, putrefy, *PL* planefy, *PR* preachify, presignify, prettify, *R* ramify, rarefy, ratify, reify, regentrify, rectify,

remodify, reunify, revivify, rigidify, rubify, *S* saccharify, saxify, salify, salsify, sanctify, sanguify, sanify, saponify, satisfy, certify, sci-fi, signify, syllabify, simplify, citify, solemnify, solidify, subjectify, *SF* spherify, *SK* scarify, scorify, *SP* speechify, specify, *ST* steelify, stellify, stiltify, stultify, stupefy, *STR* stratify, *T* tabefy, tepefy, terrify, testify, typify, torpify, torrefy, tumefy, *TR* transmogrify, *U* uglify, *V* verify, versify, vilify, vitrify, vivify, *Y* unify

FLĪ *B* bobfly, botfly, butterfly, *BL* blackfly, blowfly, *D* damselfly, dobsonfly, *DR* dragonfly, *F* firefly, *FL* fly, *G* gadfly, gallfly, *GR* greenfly, *H* horsefly, housefly, *K* catchfly, *M* Mayfly, *O* outfly, overfly, *S* sandfly, *SH* shoofly, *U* underfly

FRĪ french fry, fry, small fry

GĪ assegai, fall guy, *gilgai, gilguy,* guy, *nilgei,* wise guy

GWĪ Paraguay, Uruguay

HĪ heigh, hi, hie, high, knee-high, on a high, riding high, shanghai, Shanghai, sky-high, ultrahigh

HWĪ why, kowhai

JĪ anthropophagi

KĪ akaakai, *bronchi, haikai,* chi, rocaille .

KLĪ cly

KRĪ decry, descry, cry, outcry

LĪ *A* alkali, ally, antalkali, *B* belie, *D* disally, *F* forlie, *H* jai alai, *J* July, *K* quillai, *L* lapis lazuli, lazuli, lie, lye, Lorelei, *M* misally, mislie, *O* outlie, overlie, *R* re-ally, rely, *U* underlie, *V* vox populi

MĪ demi, demy, haeremai, my

NĪ *alumnae, alumni,* Anno Domini, decani, deny, Gemini, nigh, nye, redeny, termini

PĪ apple pie, blackberry pie, espy, humble pie, *magpie,* mince pie, *nanpie,* occupy, peach pie, pi, pie, *porkpie, potpie,* preoccupy, sea pie,

shoofly pie, umble pie (etc.)

PLĪ apply, imply, comply, misapply, multiply, oversupply, ply, reply, supply, undersupply

PRĪ pry, repry

RĪ awry, caravanserai, wry, rye, samurai, serai

SHĪ *cockshy,* shy, unshy, *workshy*

SĪ assai, prophesy, psi, scye, sigh, Versailles

SKĪ *bluesky,* blue sky, ensky, cloudy sky, sky, Skye

SKRĪ descry, scry

SLĪ sly

SNĪ sny, snye

SPĪ bespy, counterspy, spatrify, spy, weatherspy

SPRĪ spry, unspry

STĪ *pigsty,* sty

THĪ thigh, thy

SWĪ swy

TĪ *bowtie, hogtie, necktie,* tie, Thai, untie

TRĪ atry, retry, try

VĪ outvie, vie

WĪ wye, Y

ĪB

BĪB imbibe

BRĪB bribe

JĪB gibe, gybe, jibe

KĪB kibe

SKRĪB *A* ascribe, *D* describe, *E* escribe, *I* inscribe, interscribe, *K* conscribe, *P* perscribe, *PR* prescribe, proscribe, *S* circumscribe, subscribe, superscribe, *SKR* scribe, *TR* transcribe

TRĪB diatribe, tribe

VĪB vibe

IB

BIB bib, bibb

CHIB chib

DIB dib

DRIB drib

FIB fib

GIB gib

GLIB glib

JIB jib

KRIB *corncrib,* crib

KWIB quib

LIB ad lib, gay lib, lib, women's lib

NIB	nib	
RIB	*midrib, sparerib,* rib	
SIB	sib	
SKWIB	squib	
SNIB	snib	

ĪBD

BĪBD   imbibed

(See **ĪB,** add *-d* where appropriate.)

IBD

RIBD   rock-ribbed

(See **IB,** add *-bed* where appropriate.)

ĪBZ

VĪBZ   vibes

(See **ĪB,** add *-s* where appropriate.)

IBZ

DIBZ	dibs, my dibs, your dibs
NIBZ	his nibs, nibs

(See **IB,** add *-s* where appropriate.)

ICH

ICH	itch
BICH	bitch, sonofabitch
BRICH	britch
DICH	ditch
FICH	fitch
FLICH	flitch
GLICH	glitch
HICH	hitch, unhitch
HWICH	which
KICH	kitsch
KWICH	quitch
LICH	lich
MICH	miche, mitch
NICH	niche
PICH	overpitch, pitch
RICH	enrich, rich, unrich
SICH	sich
SKICH	skitch
SKRICH	scritch
SMICH	smritch
SNICH	snitch
STICH	*backstitch, chainstitch, featherstitch, hemstitch, whipstitch, catstitch,* restitch, saddlestitch, *seamstitch,* stitch, unstitch
SWICH	switch, unswitch
TWICH	twitch
VICH	czarevitch
WICH	bewitch, witch

ICHT

ICHT   itched

(See **ICH,** add *-ed* where appropriate.)

ĪD

ĪD	*A* almond-eyed, Argus-eyed, *B* buck-eyed, *BL* black-eyed, blear-eyed, blue-eyed, *BR* bright-eyed, brown-eyed, *D* dioxide, *dove-eyed, dull-eyed, E* eagle-eyed, evil-eyed, *F* full-eyed, *G* goggle-eyed, *GR* green-eyed, *H* hazel-eyed, hawk-eyed, *I* eyed, I'd, ide, *K* calf-eyed, cat-eyed, cockeyed, *KL* clear-eyed, *KR* crosseyed, *L* lynx-eyed, *M* meek-eyed, misty-eyed, *monoxide, N* narrow-eyed, *O* ox-eyed, *oxide,* open-eyed, oroide, owl-eyed, *P* pale-eyed, *peroxide, pie-eyed, pink-eyed, pop-eyed, R* red-eyed, round-eyed, *S* soft-eyed, *SKW* squint-eyed, *SL* slant-eyed, sloe-eyed, *SN* snake-eyed, *W* wide-eyed, wall-eyed, *Y* yellow-eyed
BĪD	abide, bide, *carbide*
BRĪD	bride, child bride
CHĪD	chide
DĪD	died, dyed, double-dyed, iodide, redyed, *tie-dyed,* undyed
DRĪD	*anhydride,* dried, dryed, *hydride,* overdried, redried, underdried, undried
FĪD	*B* beatified, bona fide, beautified, *D* defied, deified, decalcified, dignified, dissatisfied, *disulfide,* diversified, dulcified, *E* edified, electrified, emulsified, *F* fortified, *phosfide, FR* fructified, *GL* glorified, *GR* gratified, *I* identified, intensified, *J* justified, *K* confide, countrified, *KL* classified, *KR* crucified, *KW* qualified, *L* liquefied, *M* magnified, mystified, modified, mollified, mortified, *N* notified, nullified, *O* ossified, overqualified, *P* pacified, petrified, purified, putrefied, *R* rarefied, ratified, rectified, revivified, *S* sanctified, saponified, satisfied, self-satisfied, certified, citified, solidified, *sulphide, SK* scarified, scorified, *SP* specified, *ST* stultified, stupefied, *STR* stratified, *T* tepefied, terrified, testified, torrefied, tumefied, *TR* trisulfide, *U* (prefix *un* to obtain negative of appropriate words in the FĪD category—unbeatified, unbeautified, etc.), *V* versified, vitrified, vivified
FRĪD	fried, refried, unfried
GĪD	guide, guyed, misguide, *waveguide*
GLĪD	glide
GRĪD	gride
HĪD	aldehyde, acetaldehyde, benzaldehyde, formaldehyde, hide, hied, *horsehide, cowhide, oxhide, rawhide*
KLĪD	*nuclide,* ophicleide
KRĪD	decried, cried
LĪD	acetanilide, acetylide, allied, belied, *bolide,* elide, collide, lied, misallied, unallied, unbelied
MĪD	bromide, nicotinamide, polyamide, cyanimide, sodamide, sulphanilamide, sulphonamide, tolbutamide
NĪD	actinide, arsenide, denied, ferrocyanide, isocyanide, lanthanide, nide, platinocyanide, cyanide, uranide
PĪD	occupied, pied, preoccupied, unoccupied
PLĪD	applied, misapplied, multiplied, reapplied, replied, supplied, unapplied, unsupplied
PRĪD	pride, self-pride

RĪD *A* arride, *B* boride, *D* deride, *dichloride, dioxide,* disaccharide, deuteride, *FL* fluoride, *H* hydrochloride, *KL* chloride, *M* monosaccharide, *N* night-ride, *nitride, O* outride, override, *R* ride, *S* saccharide, *T* telluride, *tetrachloride, TR* trichloride, trisaccharide, *Y* ureide

SĪD *A* aborticide, acaricide, algicide, alongside, aside, *B backside,* bactericide, Barmecide, *bedside,* beside, biocide, *BL* blindside, blind side, *BR* broadside, brookside, *D* decide, deicide, dimethysulphoxide, *diopside,* dissatisfied, *downside, E* ecocide, excide, *epoxide, ethoxide, F* felicide, feticide, filicide, *fireside, foreside,* fungicide, *FL* flip side, *FR* fratricide, *GL* glycoside, glucoside, *H* herbicide, heroicide, herpicide, Heaviside, *hillside, hydroxide, hydrosulphide,* homicide, *I* infanticide, insecticide, inside, ironside, *J* genocide, germicide, giganticide, *K* quayside, coincide, countryside, *L lakeside,* lapicide, larvicide, liberticide, *M* magnicide, Merseyside, *methoxide,* miticide, *monoxide,* monstricide, mountainside, multicide, *N nearside,* nematocide, *nightside,* nucleoside, *O* oxide, oceanside, offside, onside, autocide, outside, override, *P* parasiticide, parenticide, parricide, patricide, *peroxide,* pesticide, piscicide, Port Said, *PR* prophesied, prolecide, *R* regicide, reprophesied, *ringside,* riverside, rodenticide, *S seaside,* cephalocide, side, silicide, silverside, sororicide, subside, cervicide, suicide, *superoxide,* SL slickenside, *SP* spermicide, *ST*

stateside, stillicide, *T* taeniacide, tyrannicide, *topside, TR* trioxide, uxoricide, underside, unprophesied, *upside, V* vaticide, verbicide, vermicide, vulpicide, *W* waterside, *wayside,* weatherside

SKRĪD descried, escried, scride, scried, undescried

SLĪD *backslide, landslide,* slide

SNĪD snide

SPĪD espied, spied, respied, unspied

STRĪD astride, bestride, outstride, stride

TĪD *A* Ascensciontide, *B* Bartholomewtide, betide, *D* dispeptide, *E* Eastertide, ebbtide, Embertide, eventide, *F* phosphatide, *FL* flood tide, *H* Hallowtide, high tide, *HW* Whitsuntide, *KR* Christmastide, *L* Lammastide, lee tide, low tide, *M mercaptide,* Michaelmastide, morning tide, *N* neap tide, noon tide, nucleotide, Allhallowtide, *P* Passiontide, *peptide,* polynucleotide, polypeptide, *R* retied, *riptide, SH* Shrovetide, *SP springtide, T* tide, tied, *TW Twelfthtide, U* unbetide, undertied, untied, *W* weathertide, *Y* Yuletide

TRĪD *nitride,* tried, untried, well-tried

VĪD divide, provide, redivide, reprovide, subdivide

WĪD countrywide, nationwide, citywide, statewide, wide, worldwide

ZĪD *azide,* chlorothiazide, preside, reside

(See **Ī,** change -*y* to -*ied* or add -*d* where appropriate.)

ID

ID id
BID bid, forbid, outbid, overbid, rebid, unbid, underbid, unforbid
BRID colubrid

CHID chid
DID athodyd, did, katydid, outdid, overdid, pyralidid, undid
DRID Madrid
FID *aphid, bifid,* fid, quadrifid, multifid, *trifid*
GID gid
GRID grid
HID hid, rehid, unhid
HWID whid
KID kid
KWID quid, tertium quid
LID annelid, invalid, *eyelid,* lid
MID amid, mid, pyramid
NID hominid, prehominid, serranid, cyprinid
PID elapid
RID rid
SID Cid
SKID askid, skid, *tailskid*
SKWID squid
SLID slid
STRID strid
THRID thrid, unthrid
TID hydatid, chromatid, spermatid, tid
TRID eupatrid
VID *kid-vid*

ĪDZ

ĪDZ Ides
SĪDZ besides, insides, Ironsides, slickensides, sobersides

(See **ĪD,** add -*s* where appropriate.)

ĪF

FĪF fife
KĪF kife
LĪF afterlife, half-life, *highlife,* larger-than-life, *nightlife,* life, pro-life, *still-life, wildlife*
NĪF bowie knife, *drawknife, jackknife, claspknife,* knife, paperknife, *penknife,* pocketknife, steak knife

---

NOEL, NOEL

Virgin Mary, meek and mum,
Dominus is in thy tum.
What a jolly *jeu d'ésprit*—
Christ beneath the Christmas tree!

RĪF	rife, *wakerife*
STRĪF	*loosestrife*, strife
WĪF	*alewife*, *fishwife*, *goodwife*, *housewife*, *lairwife*, *midwife*, *oldwife*, puddingwife, sweetiewife, wife

IF

IF	if
BIF	biff
CHIF	handkerchief, neckerchief
DIF	diff
FIF	pfiff
GLIF	anaglyph, gliff, glyph, hieroglyph, lithoglyph, petroglyph
GRIF	griff, griffe, griph, hippogriff, logogriph
HWIF	whiff
JIF	jiff
KIF	kif
KLIF	cliff, undercliff
KWIF	quiff
MIF	miff
NIF	niff
PIF	piff
RIF	eriff, *midriff*, Rif, riff, Tenerife
SIF	Sif
SKIF	skiff
SNIF	sniff
SPIF	spiff
STIF	bindle stiff, lucky stiff, stiff
TIF	positif, tiff
WIF	wiff
ZIF	ziff

IFS

ZIFS	ziffs

(See **IF**, add *-s* where appropriate.)

IFT

BIFT	biffed
DRIFT	adrift, drift, *snowdrift*, *spindrift*, *spoondrift*
GIFT	gift
HWIFT	whiffed
KLIFT	cliffed
LIFT	*airlift*, heli-lift, lift, ski lift, topping lift, uplift
MIFT	miffed
RIFT	rift
SHIFT	*gearshift*, *makeshift*, shift
SHRIFT	*festschrift*, short shrift, shrift, spiegelschrift
SIFT	resift, sift

SKWIFT	squiffed, unsquiffed
SNIFT	sniffed
SPIFFED	spiffed
SWIFT	chimney swift, swift, Tom Swift
TIFT	tift
THRIFT	*spendthrift*, thrift

(See **IF**, add *-ed* where appropriate.)

IG

BIG	big, bigg, Mr. Big
BRIG	brig, brigg
DIG	dig, infra dig, *shindig*
FIG	fig, honey fig, caprifig
FRIG	frig, Frigg
GIG	*fishgig*, *fizgig*, gig, whirligig
GRIG	grig
HWIG	whig, Whig
JIG	jig, majig, rejig, thingamajig
KRIG	crig
NIG	nig, renege
PIG	*bushpig*, guinea pig, male chauvinist pig, pig
PRIG	prig
RIG	outrig, rig, wrig, thimblerig, unrig
SIG	cig
SNIG	snig
SPIG	spig
SPRIG	sprig
SWIG	swig
THIG	thig
TIG	tig, tyg
TRIG	trig
TWIG	twig
WIG	bewig, *bigwig*, *earwig*, whirliwig, periwig, wig
ZIG	zig

IGD

RIGD	full-rigged, jury-rigged, square-rigged

(See **IG**, add *-ged* where appropriate.)

IGZ

DIGZ	digs

(See **IG**, add *-s* where appropriate.)

IJ

IJ	acreage, ferriage, foliage, *image*, lineage, verbiage, *voyage*

BRIJ	abridge, bridge, rebridge, unbridge
DIJ	brigandage
FIJ	fidge
FRIJ	saxifrage
LIJ	*D* diallage, *E* ensilage, *F* fortilage, *K* cartilage, curtilage, *M* mucilage, *P* pupilage, *PR* privilege, *S* sortilage, *T* tutelage, *V* vassalage
MIJ	*image*, midge, pilgrimage
NIJ	*A* alienage, appanage, *B* badinage, baronage, *E* espionage, *G* gallonage, *K* commonage, concubinage, *M* matronage, *N* nidge, *O* orphanage, *P* parsonage, patronage, peonage, personage, *S* siphonage, *V* villeinage, vicinage
PIJ	equipage
RIJ	*A* acreage, anchorage, average, *B* beverage, *BR* brokerage, *F* foliage, fosterage, *FL* flowerage, *H* harborage, hemorrhage, *K* Coleridge, cooperage, coverage, *KW* quarterage, *L* leverage, lineage, *O* overage, *P* pastorage, pasturage, pilferage, porterage, *PL* plunderage, *R* ridge, *S* cellarage, seigneurage, sewerage, *T* telpherage, tutorage, *U* upridge, *V* vicarage, *W* waterage
SIJ	surplusage
SKWIJ	squidge
SMIJ	smidge
TIJ	agiotage, armitage, heritage, hermitage, hospitage, clientage, parentage, pilotage
TRIJ	arbitrage

(Words in which a penultimate stressed syllable is followed by *-age*—drayage or *assemblage*, for instance—may be rhymed with *-ij* by shifting the accent to the last syllable, but in most instances the result is shameful. I have omitted such words here.)

ĪK

ĪK	Van Eyk
BĪK	bike, minibike, motorbike
DĪK	dike, dyke, *Klondike*, Vandyke, Vandyck
FĪK	fike, fyke

GRĪK	grike
HĪK	haik, Haikh, hike, *hitchhike*
KĪK	kike
LĪK	*A* alike, *antlike, apelike, B* belike, *beelike,* businesslike, *BR* brotherlike, *CH childlike, D deathlike,* dislike, *doglike, DR dreamlike, G* godlike, *ghostlike, GL* glasslike, *H hairlike,* homelike, husbandlike, *J* gemlike, *K catlike,* kinglike, *KR Christlike, KW queenlike, L ladylike,* lifelike, like, lookalike, *M* maidenlike, *manlike,* mislike, *P peasantlike, piglike, R ratlike, S* seedlike, swordlike, suchlike, susulike, *SH* sheeplike, *SN snakelike, SP* sportsmanlike, *ST* starlike, *SW swanlike, U* unalike, unlike, *W warlike,* wifelike, winglike, womanlike (etc.)
MĪK	mike
PĪK	boardingpike, *garpike,* pike, pyke, *turnpike*
RĪK	Reich
SĪK	psych, sike
SHRĪK	shrike
SPĪK	*handspike,* marlinspike, spike
STRĪK	strike, *ten-strike*
TĪK	tyke
TRĪK	trike

IK

IK	ich, ick, ik, ichthyic
BIK	Arabic, *iambic*
BRIK	*airbrick,* brick, *firebrick, red-brick*
CHIK	allocochick, chic, chick, *dabchick,* holluschick, *peachick*
DIK	benedick, Benedick, dick, *dik-dik, sandik*
FLIK	flick, *skin-flick*
HIK	hic, hick
KIK	kick, *sidekick, trochaic*
KLIK	click, click-click
KRIK	creek, crick
KWIK	doublequick, quick
LIK	*bootlick, dactylic,* Catholic, *cowlick,* lick, *relic*
MIK	*comic,* mick

NIK	arsenic, kinnikinnick, nick, *eugenic*
PIK	handpick, *nutpick,* pic, pick, *toothpick,* Waterpick
PRIK	*pinprick,* prick
RIK	*A* archbishopric, *B* bishopric, *H hayrick, K* choleric, *L limerick, M* maverick, *PL plethoric, R* rhetoric, rick, wrick, *SH* chivalric, *T tumeric,* turmeric
SHRIK	schrik
SHTIK	shtick, schtick
SIK	*A airsick, BR brainsick, H* heartsick, homesick, *K carsick, L landsick,* lovesick, *M moonsick, S* seasick, sic, sick, *SP spacesick*

LET US WONDER, WHILE WE LOITER

Let us wonder, while we loiter,
Which of us will die of goiter;
Which of stone or dysentery;
Which of rheum or beriberi;
Which of grippe or diarrhea,
Nettle rash, or pyorrhea;
Which of us turn turvy topsy,
Victim of paretic dropsy.
Be it pox or whooping cough,
Something's bound to bear us off.
All we know is, we're in trouble:
Barman, make my next one double.

SLIK	slick
SNIK	snick
SPIK	spick
STIK	*B* bestick, *BR broomstick, CH chapstick,* chopstick, *D* dipstick, *DR drumstick, F* fiddlestick, *GR greenstick, K* candlestick, *L lipstick, M matchstick, metestick, maulstick,* monostich, *N* knobstick, nonstick, *P* pentastich, *pigstick, S* singlestick, *swordstick, SL* slapstick, *ST* stich, stick, swizzle stick, *T telestich,* tetrastich, *U unstick, W* walkingstick, *Y yardstick*
STRIK	strick
THIK	thick
TIK	*anapestic,* arithmetic, heretic, impolitic, cosmopolitic, lunatic, politic, ricky-tick, tic, tick, *triptych*
TRIK	dirty trick, gastrotrich, *metric,* overtrick, trick, undertrick

VIK	Old Vic, Reykjavik
WIK	bailiwick, *Brunswick,* candlewick, *lampwick, Warwick,* wick

IKS

FIKS	*A* adfix, affix, antefix, *F* fix, *I* infix, *K* confix, *KR* crucifix, *KW* quick fix, *P* postfix, *PR* prefix, pre-fix, *R* refix, *S suffix,* superfix, *TR* transfix
LIKS	prolix
MIKS	admix, immix, intermix, commix, mix, overmix, undermix
NIKS	acronyx, nix, Nyx
PIKS	picks, pix, pyx
RIKS	apteryx, archaeopterics, rix, Vercingetorix
SIKS	eighty-six, six, ninety-six (etc.)
STIKS	*chopsticks,* fiddlesticks, Styx
TRIKS	*aviatrix,* dirty tricks, executrix, inheritrix, cicatrix

(See **IK,** add *-s* where appropriate.)

IKST

TWIKST	betwixt, 'twixt

(See **IKS,** add *-ed* where appropriate.)

IKT

DIKT	addict, benedict, *edict,* interdict, contradict, maledict, predict
FLIKT	afflict, inflict, conflict
LIKT	delict, derelict, *relict*
MIKT	apomict
PIKT	depict, Pict
STRIKT	astrict, derestrict, constrict, overstrict, restrict, strict, understrict
VIKT	evict, convict

(See **IK,** add *-ed* where appropriate.)

ĪL

ĪL	aisle, I'll, isle
BĪL	atrabile, bile
CHĪL	chile

DĪL   *aedile,* crocodile, *merdaille*

FĪL   *A* Anglophile, *B*
bibliophile, *D* defile,
demophile, discophile, *E*
aelurophile, eosinnophile,
ergophile, *F* file, photofile,
FR Francophile, *G*
Gallophile, gastrophile, *H*
halophile, hippophile,
homophile, *I* Italophile, *J*
Japanophile,
Germanophile,
gynotikolobomassophile,
M myrmecophile,
mesophile, *N* nailfile,
Negrophile, *O* audiophile,
P paper file, paedophile,
pyrophile, *PR profile, R*
refile, rheophile,
Russophile, *S* psychophile,
psychrophile, cinephile,
single file, *SL* Slavophile,
SP spermophile, *T*
typophile, Turkophile, *TH*
theophile, thermophile, *Z*
xenophile, Zionophile,
zoophile

GĪL   beguile, guile, gyle
HĪL   heil
HWĪL   awhile, erewhile,
erstwhile, meanwhile,
otherwhile, somewhile,
therewhile, while,
worthwhile
KĪL   kyle
LĪL   Carlisle, lisle
MĪL   camomile, mile
NĪL   enisle, campanile,
juvenile, Nile, *senile*
PĪL   aeolipile, micropyle,
compile, pile, recompile,
repile, *stockpile,*
thermopile, unpile,
woodpile, up-pile, voltaic
pile
RĪL   puerile, rile
SĪL   domicile, ensile, exile,
reconcile, sile
SMĪL   smile
SPĪL   spile
STĪL   *A* amphiprostyle, *D*
decastyle, diastyle,
dodecastyle, *E* epistyle, *FR
freestyle, H hairstyle, M*
hypostyle, *L* life style, *M*
menostyle, *P* pentastyle,
peristyle, polystyle, *R*
restyle, *S* cyclostyle, *ST*
stile, style, *T turnstile, Y*
urostyle
TĪL   *F* fertile, *futile, H hostile, I*
infantile, *J* gentile, *M*

---

mercantile, *P* pulsatile, *R
reptile, rutile, S* saxatile,
septile, T tile, *V* versatile,
vibratile, volatile

TRĪL   acrylonitrile
VĪL   revile, vile
WĪL   weil, wile
ZĪL   *exile,* resile

(See ĪAL)

IL

IL   ill
BIL   *B* bill, *boatbill, BL
blackbill, bluebill, BR
broadbill, brownbill, D*
deshabille, dishabille,
dollar bill, *duckbill, H
handbill, hawksbill,
hornbill, KR cranesbill,
crossbill, PL playbill, R*
razorbill, *redbill, wrybill,
SH shoebill, shortbill, SP
spoonbill, ST storksbill,
TH thornbill, TW twibil, W
waxbill, waybill, Y*
yellowbill
BRIL   brill
CHIL   chil, chill
DIL   daffodil, dill, cacodyl,
piccadill, spadille
DRIL   drill, escadrille, espadrille,
quadrille, *mandrill*
FIL   *A* Anglophil, *D* demophil,
E eosinnophil, *F* fill,
phytophil, fulfil, fulfill, *KL*
cladophyll, chlorophyll,
monophyll, *N* neutrophil,
O overfill, *R* refill, *SKL*
sclerophyll, *SP* sporophyll,
U underfill, unfill, *Z*
xanthophyll
FRIL   befrill, frill
GIL   gill, *bluegill, scrodgill*
GRIL   grill, grille
HIL   *anthill,* downhill, *dunghill,
foothill,* hill, *molehill,
uphill*
JIL   aspergill, gill, jill
KIL   kil, kill, kiln, limekiln,
rekill, winterkill
KWIL   quill
LIL   li'l, lill
MIL   De Mille, *flourmill,
gristmill,* mil, powdermill,
cement mill, *sawmill,
steelmill, treadmill,*
watermill, *windmill*
NIL   juvenile, manille, nil,
thionyl, uranyl

PIL   minipill, morning-after
pill, pill
PRIL   prill
RIL   puerile, rill
SHIL   shill
SHRIL   shrill
SIL   domicile, *doorsill,
groundsill, headsill,*
imbecile, codicil, sill,
verticil, windowsill
SKIL   skill
SKWIL   squill
SPIL   overspill, spill
STIL   bestill, instill, reinstill,
standstill, still, stock-still
SWIL   *pigswill,* swill
THIL   thill
THRIL   enthrill, thrill
TIL   *A* acetyl, *D* distill, *I*
infantile, intertill, *K* coutil,
M mercantile, *O* overtill, *P*
pastille, pulsatile, *R* retill,
T 'til, till, tormentil, *TH*
thereuntil, *U* until, untill,
V versatile, vibratile,
volatile
TRIL   trill
TWIL   'twill, twill
VIL   Amityville, *dullsville,*
Evansville, Louisville,
Oysterville, Seville (etc.),
vill, ville, vaudeville
VRIL   vrille
WIL   free will, goodwill,
whippoorwill, ill will,
poorwill, self-will, will
ZIL   Brazil, frazil, zill

ILCH

FILCH   filch
MILCH   milch
PILCH   pilch
ZILCH   zilch

ĪLD

CHĪLD   brain child, child, childe,
flower child, foster child,
*godchild, grandchild,
lovechild, manchild,*
unchild
FĪLD   defiled, enfiled, filed,
profiled, refiled, undefiled,
unfiled
MĪLD   mild
WĪLD   hog wild, wild, Wilde

(See ĪL, add -*d* where appropriate.)

ILD

BILD	build, jerry-build, rebuild, unbilled, unbuild, upbuild
GILD	begild, gild, guild, octogild, regild, ungild, *wergild*
HILD	*Brunhild*
WILD	self-willed, strong-willed, unwilled, weak-willed, willed

(See **IL,** add *-ed* where appropriate.)

ILK

ILK	ilk
BILK	bilk
HWILK	whilk
MILK	milk
SILK	silk

ILS

GRILS	grilse

(See **ILT,** add *-s* where appropriate.)

ILT

BILT	built, frigate-built, jerry-built, clinker-built, clipper-built, rebuilt, unbuilt, Vanderbilt, well-built
GILT	begilt, gilt, guilt, regilt, ungilt
HILT	hilt
JILT	jilt, rejilt
KILT	kilt
KWILT	quilt, requilt
LILT	lilt
MILT	milt
SILT	silt, resilt, unsilt
SPILT	respilt, spilt, unspilt
STILT	stilt
TILT	retilt, tilt, untilt, uptilt
WILT	wilt

ILTH

ILTH	illth
FILTH	filth
SPILTH	spilth
TILTH	tilth

ĪLZ

HWĪLZ	erewhiles

(See **ĪL,** add *-s* where appropriate.)

ĪM

ĪM	I'm
BLĪM	sublime
CHĪM	chime, rechime
DĪM	dime, disme, nickel-and-dime, paradigm
GĪM	gime
GRĪM	begrime, grime
KĪM	isocheim, chyme, mesenchyme
KLĪM	climb, clime, upclimb
KRĪM	crime
LĪM	belime, *birdlime, brooklime, quicklime,* lime, Lyme
MĪM	mime, pantomime
PRĪM	overprime, prime, underprime
RĪM	berhyme, rhyme, rime
SĪM	cyme, sime
SLĪM	beslime, slime
TĪM	*A aforetime,* aftertime, *B bedtime, betime, BR breathing time, D daytime, downtime, E eaning time,* eating time, *F foretime, full-time, H halftime,* harvest time, haying time, *L lifetime, longtime, M* maritime, *meantime, midtime,* mistime, *N nighttime, noontime, O* overtime, *P pairing time, part-time, pastime,* peacetime, *PL playtime, PR prime time, R ragtime, S seedtime, sometime,* summertime, suppertime, *SP springtime, T thyme,* time, *two-time, U* undertime, *W wintertime, Y yeaning time*
ZĪM	*enzyme, co-enzyme,* lysozyme

IM

IM	Ephraim
BIM	bim, cherubim
BRIM	brim, *broadbrim*
CHIM	chimb
DIM	bedim, dim, Hasidim, paradigm
DRIM	Sanhedrim
FIM	seraphim
FRIM	frim
GLIM	glim
GRIM	grim, Grimm, grimme
HIM	him, hymn
HWIM	whim

JIM	gym
KRIM	crim
KWIM	quim
LIM	dislimb, dislimn, enlimn, *forelimb,* limb, limn, prelim
MIM	mim
NIM	*A* aconym, acronym, allonym, ananym, anonym, anthroponym, antonym, *E* eponym, exonym, *H* heteronym, homonym, *M* metonym, *N* nim, nimb, *O* ormonym, *S* synonym, pseudonym, *T* toponym, *U* undernim
PRIM	prim
RIM	borborygm, interim, *corymb,* rim
SHIM	shim
SKIM	skim
SKRIM	scrim
SLIM	slim
SWIM	swim
TIM	Tiny Tim
TRIM	betrim, retrim, trim, untrim
VIM	vim
ZIM	zimb

ĪMD

CHĪMD	chimed

(See **ĪM,** add *-d* where appropriate.)

IMD

BRIMD	brimmed

(See **IM,** add *-med* where appropriate.)

IMF

LIMF	endolymph, lymph
NIMF	nymph, paranymph, sea nymph, water nymph, wood nymph

IMP

IMP	imp
BLIMP	blimp
CHIMP	chimp
GIMP	gimp
GRIMP	grimp
JIMP	jimp
KRIMP	crimp

LIMP	limp
MIMP	mimp
PIMP	pimp
PLIMP	plimp
PRIMP	primp
SHRIMP	shrimp
SIMP	simp
SKIMP	skimp
SKRIMP	scrimp
TIMP	tymp
WIMP	wimp

IMPS

GLIMPS	glimpse

(See **IMP,** add -s where appropriate.)

ĪMZ

TĪMZ	betimes, oftentimes, *off-times,* oft-times, sometimes

(See **ĪM,** add -s where appropriate.)

ĪN

ĪN	eyn
BĪN	bine, cannabine, carabine, *carbine,* columbine, combine, concubine, *Sabine, turbine, woodbine*
BRĪN	brine, colubrine

PESSIMISM

(The mysterious celestial entities called quasars are receding at 90% of the speed of light.)

I saw quasars in the night
Leaving at the speed of light.
Why so hurried fared they?
Something must have scared they.

CHĪN	chine
DĪN	*A* alcidine, almandine, anodine, aerodyne, *D* dine, dyne, *H* heterodyne, *hirundine, I* indign, incarnadine, *K* kadein, condign, *M* muscadine, *N nundine, P* paludine, *S* celandine
FĪN	affine, define, fine, confine, refine, superfine, trephine
HWĪN	whine
JĪN	jine

KĪN	kine
KLĪN	decline, disincline, incline, monocline, recline
KRĪN	crine, volucrine
KWĪN	*equine*
LĪN	*A* align, *airline,* aquiline, alkaline, antalkaline, acervuline, *B* baseline, *beeline,* berylline, *byline, bowline,* borderline, bottom line, *D* dateline, *deadline,* dyaline, disalign, *F* feline, figuline, *fishline, FR* fringilline, *G* guideline, *H* hairline, headline, hemline, hyaline, *I* induline, inquiline, interline, *K* caballine, *carline, cauline* coraline, *coastline, KL* clothesline, *KR* crossline, crystalline, *L* lifeline, limicoline, line, *loadline, M* malign, metalline, *moline,* musteline, *N* neckline, *O* opaline, *outline, P* penduline, petaline, *pipeline, R* realign, *red-line, S saline,* sepaline, sibyline, *sideline,* suilline, *SH shoreline, SK skyline, SN* snowline, *STR streamline,T* tapeline, timberline, *towline, touchline, tump-line,* tourmaline, *TR tramline, U* underline, unline, *V* vituline, *W waistline,* waterline, *Z* zibeline
MĪN	*D damine, G* gold mine, *I* intermine, *K* calamine, calcimine, *carmine,* countermine, *M* mine, *P* powdermine, *S* sycamine, *U* undermine
NĪN	*A* Apennine, asinine, *B* benign, *E* eburnine, *F* falconine, Fescennine, *K canine, KW* quinine, *L* leonine, *N* nine, *P* pavonine, *R* ranine, *S* saturnine, ciconine, *U* unbenign
PĪN	*A Alpine, E* elapine, *L lupine, O* opine, *P* pine, porcupine, *PR* Proserpine, *R* repine, resupine, *S* cisalpine, subalpine, supine, *U* unsupine, *V vespine, vulpine*
RĪN	*A* adulterine, anserine, azurine, *D* dirhine, *E*

	estuarine, extrauterine, *F ferine,* intrauterine, *K caprine,* catarrhine, *L* lemurine, leporine, *M* mesorhine, monorhine, *murrhine, P* passerine, piperine, *PL* platyrrhine, *R* Rhine, riverine, *S* saccharine, sapphirine, satyrine, sciurine, *cedrine,* turnverein, *V* viperine, viverrine, vulturine, *W* wolverine, *Y* uterine
SHĪN	ashine, beshine, Gegenschein, monkeyshine, *moonshine,* outshine, *sunshine,* shine, *shoeshine, starshine*
SHRĪN	enshrine, shrine
SĪN	*A* assign, *E* ensign, *F phocine, H* havercine, hystricine, *hircine, I* insigne, *K* calcine, consign, co-sign, *cosine,* countersign, *L* limacine, *O* auld lang syne, omphacine, *P* piscine, porcine, *R* reconsign, *S* sign, sine, syne, tsine, *sinsyne,* psittacine, soricine, subsign, *TH* thylacine, *U* undersign, *ursine*
SPĪN	spine
SPLĪN	spline
STĪN	*Einstein, Epstein,* Eisenstein, Frankenstein, Hammerstein, Liechtenstein, Rubinstein, stein, styan, Wittgenstein
STRĪN	strine
SWĪN	Gadarene swine, swine
THĪN	hyacinthine, labyrinthine, thine
TĪN	*A* adamantine, agatine, amethystine, anatine, argentine, Argentine, *B* Byzantine, *BR* brigantine, *D* diamantine, *E* eglantine, elephantine, *F* Philistine, *FL* Florentine, *I* infantine, *K* Constantine, *L* lacertine, Levantine, libertine, *M* matutine, *P* palatine, Palestine, *S* serotine, serpentine, *cisplatine, T* tine, Tyne, turpentine, *TR* transpontine, Tridentine, *V* valentine, vespertine
TRĪN	accipitrine, trine
TWĪN	disentwine, entwine, intertwine, overtwine, retwine, twine, untwine

114

SINGLE RHYMES; IN

VĪN	aberdevine, *bovine,* divine, *grapevine,* keelivine, *ovine,* provine, *cervine,* subdivine, vine
WĪN	apple wine, brandywine, cherry wine, dandelion wine, Essenwein, May wine, red wine, white wine, wine
ZĪN	design, Auld Lang Syne, lang syne, redesign, resign

IN

IN	Bedouin, benzoin, fibroin, heroin, heroine, herein, wherein, whipper-in, in, inn, genuine, caffeine, all-in, therein, within
BIN	*B* been, bin, *dustbin, GL globin, H hasbeen, hemoglobin, J jacobin,* Jacobin, *K* carabine, colobin
BRIN	brin, *fibrin*
CHIN	chin, tchin, Capuchin, matachin
DIN	*Aladdin,* almandine, amidin, din, *hirundine,* incarnadine, codeine, *morindin,* muscadine, *Odin,* paladin
DRIN	Benzedrine, ephedrin, Sanhedrin
FIN	*B* bowfin, *BL* blackfin, *D dauphin, dolphin, E elfin, F* fin, Finn, *M* Mickey Finn, *P* paraffin, *R ragamuffin, redfin, THR threadfin*
GIN	begin
GLIN	glin
GRIN	agrin, grin, Lohengrin, peregrine
HWIN	whin
JIN	*engine,* gin, gyn, jin, *margin,* origin, tchin, *virgin,* waringin
KIN	*A* akin, *B* baldachin, billikin, birdikin, bodikin, *bodkin,* baldachin, bootikin, *buskin, BL bloodkin, D* dunnakin, *F* finikin, *GR grimalkin, K* cannikin, *catkin,* kilderkin, kin, *L lambkin,* lambrequin, larrikin, *M* manikin, mannequin, minikin, *N napkin,* nipperkin, *P* pannikin, Pekin, *R* ramekin, *S* sooterkin, *SP* spilikin

KRIN	crin
KWIN	*Algonquin,* harlequin, quin, lambrequin
LIN	*A* adrenaline, aquiline, alkaline, amygdalin, analine, *B* bandoline, berlin, Berlin, botulin, *CH* chamberlain, *chaplain, DR drumlin, E* encephalin, *F* folliculin, formalin, *FR* francolin, *G* Ghibbeline, gobelin, Gobelin, *GL* globuline, *H* hyaline, *I* immunoglobulin, insulin, *J* javelin, *K* caballine, kaolin, capelin, capeline, *carline, cauline, colin, collin, colline,* coralline, cuculine, *KR* crinoline, crystalline, crotaline, *L* lanoline, lin, linn, lupulin, *M mafflin,* mandolin, *N* noradrenaline, *O* opaline, *P* petaline, porcelain, *R* ravelin, *S* cephaline, syballine, cipolin, *SH* chevaline, *T* ptyaline, tourmaline, *U* Ursuline, *V* vaseline, violin, *Z* zeppelin
MIN	*A* albumin, amphetamine, antihystamine, arsphenamine, *B* Benjamin, *H* Ho Chi Minh, *I illumine, J* jessamine, *M* maximin, Min, *PR* provitamin, *S* sycamine, *TH* thiamine, *V* Vietminh, vitamin
NIN	agglutinin, feminine, *legnine,* Lenin, melanin, mezzanine, pavonine, *rennin, tannin*
PIN	*A* atropine, *B* belaying pin, *breastpin, CH* chinkapin, chinquapin, *H* hairpin, hatpin, *I* inchpin, *K* calepin, *kingpin, KR crankpin, L lapin,* linchpin, *N* ninepin, *P* pin, *pippin, pushpin, R* repin, *S* safety pin, *SK* sculpin, *ST* stickpin, *T* tenpin, terrapin, *tiepin, TH* thoroughpin, *U* underpin, unpin, *W* wankapin
PLIN	discipline, indiscipline
RIN	*A* adulterine, alizarin, anserine, aspirin, aventurine, *B* bacterin, *E* elaterin, *F* fiorin, *G* gorgerin, *GL* glycerine, *H* heparin, *K* corinne,

	coumarin, culverin, *L* luciferin, *M* mandarin, margarine, muscarine, *N* nectarine, nitroglycerin, *P* porphyrin, *S* sapphirine, saccharine, Sanhedrin, sovereign, suberin, *T* tamarin, tambourin, Turin, *V* viperine, vulturine, *W* warfarin
SHIN	Capuchin, shin
SIN	*D* damassin, *K* characin, kerasine, *KL* clavecin, *M* moccasin, mortal sin, *O* omphacine, *R* re-sin, *S* sin, *SP* spassadin, *T* tocsin, *toxin, U* unsin, *W Wisconsin*
SKIN	*B* bearskin, buckskin, *D deerskin, doeskin,* foreskin, *K* calfskin, *kidskin, L* lambskin, *M moleskin, O* oilskin, *P* pigskin, *R* redskin, reskin, *Rumpelstiltskin, S* sealskin, *SH* sharkskin, sheepskin, *SK* scarfskin, skin, *SN snakeskin, T* tigerskin, *U* onionskin (etc.)
SPIN	*backspin,* respin, *sidespin,* spin, *tailspin, topspin*
THIN	*absinthin, absinthine,* lecithin, sympathin, thick-and-thin, thin
TIN	*A* agatine, argentine, asbestine, astatine, *B* Byzantine, bulletin, *F* Philistine, *FL* Florentine, *I* infantine, *intestine, J* gelatin, *K* keratin, *KR* chromatin, *KW* quercitin, *L* libertine, *N* nicotine, *P* palmatin, *PR* precipitin, *R Rasputin, T* tin, *TR* travertine, *V* vespertine
TRIN	*alabastrine, alpestrine*
TWIN	twin
VIN	alevin, Angevin
WIN	win
YIN	yang and yin, yin
ZIN	*rosin*

INCH

INCH	half-inch, inch, quarter-inch
CHINCH	chinch
DINCH	dinch
FINCH	*bullfinch, chaffinch,* fallow finch, finch, *goldfinch, grassfinch, greatfinch,*

greenfinch, hawfinch,
redfinch

FLINCH	flinch
KINCH	kinch
KLINCH	clinch, unclinch
PINCH	bepinch, pinch
SINCH	recinch, cinch, uncinch
SKWINCH	squinch
WINCH	winch

ĪND

BĪND	bearbind, bind, inbind, cowbind, rebind, spellbind, unbind, underbind, upbind
BLĪND	blind, half-blind, color-blind, purblind, sandblind, snowblind, unblind
FĪND	affined, find, refind, refined, unrefined
GRĪND	greasy grind, grind, regrind
HĪND	ahind, behind, hind
KĪND	gavelkind, humankind, kind, mankind, unkind, womankind
KLĪND	enclined, inclined
LĪND	aligned, lined, nonaligned, realigned, relined, streamlined, unaligned, unlined
MĪND	mastermind, mind, remind
RĪND	rind, rynd
SĪND	re-signed, signed, undersigned, unsigned
TWĪND	intertwined, twined, untwined
WĪND	enwind, overwind, rewind, unwind, upwind, wind
ZĪND	resigned, unresigned

(See ĪN, add -d where appropriate.)

IND

IND	Ind
FIND	finned
KIND	wunderkind
LIND	lind, lynde
RIND	tamarind
SIND	abscind, exscind, prescind, rescind, sind
SKIND	reskinned, skinned, thick-skinned, thin-skinned, unskinned
TIND	retinned, tinned, untinned
WIND	downwind, east wind, forewind, headwind, whirlwind, crosswind, north wind, solar wind, south wind, stormwind, tailwind, upwind, west wind, woodwind, wind

(See IN, add -ed where appropriate.)

ING

ING	A arguing, B bandying, bellowing, bellringing, burying, billowing, busying, bullying, BL blarneying, CH churchgoing, D dallying, dairying, dishallowing, E echoing, elbowing, embodying, empitying, emptying, envying, F fancying, farrowing, following, falsifying, foregoing, foreshadowing, FL flurrying, H hallowing, harrowing, horseshoeing, HW whinnying, I ing, ingrowing, issuing, J jollying, journeying, K candying, carrying, continuing, copying, curtsying, KW querying, quarrying, quartering, L lazying, lobbying, M marrying, monkeying, mudslinging, N narrowing, O ongoing, outgoing, overshadowing, P parrying, partying, pitying, puttying, R rallying, rescuing, S sallying, seagoing, sightseeing, soothsaying, sorrowing, SH shadowing, SW swallowing, T tallying, tarrying, toadying, U undervaluing, unpitying, upbringing, V valuing, varying, volleying, W wearying, wellbeing, winnowing, worrying, Y yellowing (etc.)
BING	bing
BRING	bring
CHING	ching, Ching
DING	ding, forwarding, freestanding, garlanding, hazarding, heralding, jeoparding, outstanding, placarding, scaffolding, shepherding, smallholding, wingding
FING	triumphing
FLING	fling, refling

GING	ging
JING	CH challenging, D damaging, discouraging, disparaging, E encouraging, envisaging, F foraging, M managing, mismanaging, P pillaging, R ravaging, S savaging, SK scavenging, V voyaging
KING	A a la king, B barracking, beking, BR breathtaking, DR dressmaking, E earthshaking, F fairy king, finicking, H heartbreaking, housebreaking, K king, M mafficking, N Nanking, painstaking, pigsticking, sea king, sleepwalking, unking, trafficking
KLING	cling, recling
LING	A appareling, atheling, B barreling, bedeviling, bepummeling, beveling, bitterling, CH changeling, channeling, chiseling, chitterling, D daughterling, dialing, ding-a-ling, dueling, dukeling, DR driveling, E easterling, enameling, entrameling, F fingerling, fosterling, G gamboling, GR graveling, groveling, grueling, H hosteling, K canceling, caroling, caviling, cudgeling, KW quarreling, L labeling, leveling, libeling, ling, M marshaling, marveling, modeling, N naveling, O outrivaling, P paneling, pedaling, penciling, R reveling, rivaling, SN sniveling, SP spiraling, ST stenciling, STR stripling, T tasseling, tingaling, tinseling, toweling, tunneling, TR traveling, U underling, unraveling, unrivaling, wassailing
MING	daydreaming, Ming, slumming
NING	A abandoning, actioning, awakening, B bargaining, betokening, burdening, BL blackening, blazoning, BR broadening, CH chastening, D darkening, deadening, deafening, destining, determining, E examining, emblazoning, emboldening,

enheartening, envisaging, *evening*, *F* fashioning, fastening, fattening, foretokening, *FR* freshening, *G* gammoning, gardening, *GL* gladdening, *H* happening, hardening, heartening, hastening, *I* imagining, imprisoning, ironing, *K* cannoning, compassioning, conditioning, cautioning, *KR* christening, *KW* questioning, *L* lessening, ling, listening, livening, *M* maddening, mentioning, moistening, *O* auctioning, omening, opening, overburdening, *P* pardoning, passioning, pensioning, *PR* predestining, *R* rationing, ravening, reckoning, reasoning, roughening, *S* saddening, sanctioning, seasoning, sickening, softening, *SL* slackening, *SM* smartening, *ST* stationing, stiffening, *STR* strengthening, *SW* sweetening, *T* toughening, *TH* thickening, *THR* threatening, *U* unreasoning, *V* visioning, *W* wakening, wantoning, weakening, widening

PING bookkeeping, galloping, housekeeping, larruping, ping, Peiping, *piping*, showjumping, walloping, worshiping

RING *A* altering, angering, answering, armoring, ashlaring, *B* badgering, bantering, barbering, battering, beflattering, beggaring, belaboring, beleaguering, belecturing, bepowdering, bescattering, beslabbering, beslobbering, *besmearing*, bespattering, bewildering, bickering, bolstering, butchering, *bullring*, *BL* blathering, blistering, blithering, blubbering, blundering, blustering, *CH* chartering, chattering, cheeseparing, *D* deciphering, differing, dickering, disfavoring, dishonoring, displeasuring,

dissevering, doddering doctoring, dowering, *E* enamoring, enharboring, encumbering, enring, entering, *F* factoring, faltering, favoring, featuring, festering, feathering, *financing*, fingering, forgathering, *forgetting*, furnishing, furthering, *FL* flattering, flavoring, flickering, flittering, flowering, flustering, fluttering, *FR* fracturing, *G* gathering, guttering, *GL* glimmering, glittering, glowering, *H* hammering, hampering, hankering, harboring, hollering, hovering, humoring, hungering, *HW* whimpering, whispering, *I* indenturing, incumbering, *J* jabbering, gesturing, *K* cankering, cantering, capering, capturing, catering, cockering, coloring, conjecturing, conjuring, conquering, considering, covering, cowering, culturing, cumbering, *KL* clambering, clamoring, clattering, clustering, cluttering, *KW* quavering, quivering, quartering, *L* layering, laboring, lacquering, lathering, latticing, lecturing, lettering, liquoring, lingering, littering, long-suffering, lowering, lumbering, *M* manufacturing, martyring, meandering, measuring, mirroring, motoring, mouthwatering, murdering, murmuring, mustering, mothering, muttering, *N* neighboring, numbering, *O* offering, auguring, occasioning, opening, ordering, outnumbering, overmastering, overpowering, overtowering, *P* pampering, pandering, pattering, perishing, perjuring, pestering, picturing, pilfering, paltering, pondering, posturing, pottering,

powering, puttering, *PL* plastering, pleasuring, plundering, *PR* promising, prospering, *R* rapturing, recovering, remembering, rendering, ring, wring, roistering, rubbering, rupturing, *S* savoring, *seafaring*, seal ring, self-catering, centering, severing, ciphering, signet ring, silvering, simmering, simpering, sistering, soldering, solacing, soldiering, suffering, summering, sundering, *SH* shattering, sheepraising, sheepshearing, shimmering, shivering, shouldering, showering, shuddering, sugaring, shuttering, *SK* scampering, scattering, *SL* slandering, slobbering, slaughtering, slumbering, *SM* smattering, smoldering, *SP* spattering, *SPL* spluttering, *ST* staggering, stammering, stuttering, *SW* sweltering, *T* tampering, tapering, tempering, timbering, tittering, tottering, towering, *TH* thundering, *U* unflattering, unfaltering, unmurmuring, unremembering, unslumbering, unwandering, unwavering, upholstering, ushering, uttering, *V* vaporing, venturing, *W* wandering, wavering, weathering, westering, wintering, woolgathering, wondering, watering

SHING *A* admonishing accomplishing, astonishing, *B* banishing, burnishing, *BL* blandishing, blemishing, *BR* brandishing, brattishing, *D* diminishing, disestablishing, distinguishing, *E* embarrassing, embellishing, enravishing, establishing, *F* famishing, finishing, furnishing, *FL* flourishing, *G* garnishing, conveyancing, *L* languishing, lavishing, *N* nourishing, *P* perishing,

	polishing, publishing, punishing, *R* ravishing, rubbishing, *T* tarnishing, *U* unperishing, *V* vanishing, vanquishing, varnishing
SING	*B* balancing, besing, buttressing, *E* embarrassing, *F* focussing, *H* harassing, *K* canvassing, conveyancing, *KL* climaxing, *KR* Christmasing, *L* latticing, *M* menacing, *O* outbalancing, overbalancing, *P* purchasing, purposing, *PR* practicing, promising, *S* sing, singh, Sing-Sing, *U* unpromising, *W* witnessing
SLING	sling, unsling
SPRING	*A* aspring, *dayspring, DR* driving spring, *H* handspring, hairspring, headspring, L lifespring, M mainspring, O offspring, S* silent spring, *SPR* spring, *W* weeping spring, *watchspring*
STING	afforesting, ballasting, breakfasting, foresting, harvesting, sting
STRING	*bowstring*, string
SWING	*beeswing*, full swing, swing
THING	anything, everything, *plaything*
TING	*B* balloting, bonneting, buffeting, *BL* blanketing, *BR* bracketing, *D* dieting, discrediting, dispiriting, disquieting, distributing, *E* exhibiting, *F* fagoting, fidgeting, forfeiting, *I* inhabiting, inheriting, inhibiting, inspiriting, *J* junketing, *K* carpeting, comforting, contributing, coveting, *KR* crediting, *KW* quieting, *L* limiting, *M* marketing, meriting, *O* auditing, *P* patenting, picketing, *PR* prohibiting, *R* racketing, riveting, *S* surfeiting, *SP* spiriting, spirketing, *T* ting, *U* unmeriting, *V* velveting, visiting
WING	angel wing, *batwing,* bird wing, eagle wing, *forewing,* gull wing, hawk wing, *clearwing, lapwing, lacewing, redwing,*

	underwing, unwing, waxwing, wing
ZING	stargazing, zing (and present participles of appropriate verbs ending in the sound of *z*)

(You may always add *-ing* to verbs ending in an unstressed syllable to make a masculine rhyme. If *-ing* is added to a verb ending in a stressed syllable, it is technically possible to make a masculine rhyme by shifting the stress to the *-ing.* Such forced rhymes should be italicized in this list, and are seldom felicitous.)

INGD

DINGD	dinged
KINGD	bekinged, kinged, unkinged
LINGD	tingalinged
PINGD	pinged
RINGD	enringed, ringed, unringed
STRINGD	restringed, stringed, unstringed
WINGD	angel-winged, *bird-winged,* eagle-winged, *hawk-winged* (etc.), unwinged, winged
ZINGD	zinged

INGK

INGK	ink, Inc.
BLINGK	blink, *iceblink, snowblink*
BRINGK	brink
CHINGK	chink
DINGK	dink, rinky-dink
DRINGK	drink, strong drink
FINGK	fink, *ratfink*
GINGK	gink
GLINGK	glink
JINGK	jink, perjink
KINGK	kink
KLINGK	clink
KWINGK	quink
LINGK	bobolink, enlink, interlink, link, Maeterlinck, relink, unlink
MINGK	mink
PINGK	meadowpink, pink, *pincpinc,* sea pink
PLINGK	plink
PRINGK	prink
RINGK	oxyrhynch, rink
SHRINGK	shrink
SINGK	countersink, cinque, sink
SKINGK	skink
SLINGK	slink

SPINGK	spink
STINGK	stink
SWINGK	swink
THINGK	bethink, doublethink, forethink, outthink, rethink, think
TINGK	tink
TRINGK	trink
TWINGK	twink
WINGK	chewink, *hoodwink,* jinnywink, tiddlywink, wink
ZINGK	zinc

INGKS

JINGKS	high jinks, jinx
LINGKS	links, lynx
MINGKS	minx
PINGKS	*salpinx*
SFINGKS	androsphinx, hieracosphinx, criosphinx, sphinx
THINGKS	methinks, thinks
WINGKS	pilliwinks, tiddlywinks

(See **INGK,** add *-s* where appropriate.)

INGKT

INGKT	inked, reinked, uninked
SINGKT	discinct, *precinct,* succinct
STINGKT	instinct
TINGKT	distinct, extinct, indistinct, tinct

(See **INGK,** add *-ed* where appropriate.)

INGZ

STRINGZ	apron strings, leading strings, strings

(See **ING,** add *-s* where appropriate.)

INJ

BINJ	binge
DINJ	dinge
FRINJ	befringe, fringe, infringe
HINJ	hinge, rehinge, unhinge
HWINJ	whinge
KRINJ	cringe
PINJ	impinge
RINJ	syringe
SINJ	singe
SKRINJ	scringe
SPRINJ	springe

STRINJ astringe, constringe, obstringe, perstringe
SWINJ swinge
TINJ attinge, tinge
TWINJ atwinge, twinge

INJD

FRINJD befringed

(See **INJ,** add *-d* where appropriate.)

INS

BLINS blintz
CHINS chinse, chintz
KWINS quince
MINS mince
PRINS Black Prince, fairy prince, frog prince, merchant prince, prince, student prince, unprince
RINS rinse, rerinse, unrinse
SINS since
VINS evince, convince
WINS wince

(See **INT,** add *-s* where appropriate.)

ĪNT

HĪNT ahint, behint
JĪNT jint
PĪNT half pint, cuckoopint, pint

INT

BINT bint
DINT dint
FLINT flint, *gunflint, skinflint*
GLINT glint
HINT hint
JINT septuagint
KWINT quint
LINT lint
MINT *horsemint,* calamint, *catmint,* calamint, mint, peppermint, sodamint, *spearmint*
PRINT *BL blueprint, F fingerprint, footprint, H hoofprint, I* imprint, *M* microprint, misprint, *N newsprint, O offprint, P* palm print, *S* surprint, *TH thumbprint, U* unprint, *V voiceprint, W woodprint*
SKWINT asquint, squint

SPLINT splint, resplint, unsplint
SPRINT sprint, resprint
STINT stint
SWINT suint
TINT aquatint, mezzotint, monotint, tint
VINT vint

INTH

BINTH terebinth
MINTH *helminth*
PLINTH plinth
RINTH *Corinth,* labyrinth
SINTH *absinthe,* hyacinth, colocynth

ĪNTS

HĪNTS Heinz
JĪNTS jints
PĪNTS *halfpints,* pints

INTS

BLINTS blintz
PRINTS prince, prints

(See **INS**; see **INT,** add *-s* where appropriate.)

ĪNZ

NĪNZ Apennines, baseball nines, nines

(See **ĪN,** add *-s* where appropriate.)

INZ

KINZ ods bodikins, spoffokins
KWINZ quinse
SHINZ shins, widdershins, withershins
SKINZ *buckskins, moleskins*
PINS candlepins, *ninepins,* pins, *tenpins*
WINZ winze

(See **IN,** add *-s* where appropriate.)

ĪP

BLĪP blype
GRĪP gripe
HĪP hipe, hype

KĪP kipe
KLĪP clype
PĪP *B bagpipe, BL blowpipe, D downpipe, DR drainpipe, H hornpipe, hawsepipe, I* Indian pipe, *L liripipe, P* Panpipe, pitchpipe, pipe, *ST standpipe,* stovepipe, *T tailpipe, W* windpipe

My mother used to encourage the young people of our village to continue their education. One paid her a visit years later to say thanks. "If it hadn't been for you," he told her, "I would never have known the importance of pronouncination."

PRONOUNCINATION SEPARATES THE HOMINID* FROM THE HOMINOID⁺

The hominid avoids
Saying 'woids'
When he means 'words.'
Saying 'woids' for 'words'
Is for the birds
(Not the 'boids'),
And for hominoids
(Not hominids—
Unless the hominids
Are on the skids.)

* Man.
⁺ Manlike, but not man.

RĪP dead ripe, overripe, *rareripe,* ripe, underripe, unripe
SLĪP slype
SNĪP guttersnipe, *jacksnipe,* snipe
STĪP stipe
STRĪP pinstripe, restripe, stripe, unstripe
SWĪP *sideswipe,* swipe
TĪP *A* antitype, archetype, *B biotype, D* daguerrotype, *E ectype,* electrotype, *F* phenotype, phototype, *GR* graphotype, *H* heliotype, holotype, *J* genotype, *K* karyotype, collotype, countertype, *L* linotype, logotype, *M* megatype, monotype, *O* autotype, *PR* prototype, *R* retype, cyanotype, somatotype, *subtype, ST* stereotype, *T* teletype, *tintype,* type
TRĪP tripe
WĪP prewipe, rewipe, unwipe, wipe, wype

IP

BIP bip
BLIP blip

CHIP	chip
DIP	dip, redip
DRIP	adrip, drip
FLIP	flip, sherry flip
GIP	gip
GRIP	grip, grippe, *handgrip, hairgrip*
HIP	hip, hyp, *rosehip*
HWIP	*bullwhip, horsewhip, coachwhip,* whip
JIP	gip, gyp
KIP	kip
KLIP	clip, reclip, inclip, unclip
KWIP	equip, quip, reequip
LIP	fat lip, *harelip,* lip, underlip, upper lip
NIP	*catnip,* nip, pogonip
PIP	apple pip, pip
RIP	rip, unrip
SHIP	*A* administratorship, agentship, acquaintanceship, *amidship,* apprenticeship, *airship, heirship,* archonship, *B* babyship, bachelorship, battleship, *CH* chairmanship, championship, chancellorship, chaplainship, chieftainship, churchmanship, *D* deaconship, demonship, *DR* draughtsmanship, *E* eldership, electorship, emperorship, ensignship, *F* farmership, fathership, fellowship, *fireship, FL* flagship, *FR* friendship, *G* guardianship, good-fellowship, governorship, *H* hardship, headship, *J* generalship, jockeyship, *judgeship,* justiceship, *K* cardinalship, *kingship, kinship,* collectorship, commandership, companionship, comradeship, consortship, consulship, controllership, copartnership, *courtship,* cousinship, *KL* clanship, *KR* craftsmanship, creatorship, *KW* queenship, questorship, *L* ladyship, leadership, legislatorship, lectureship, librarianship, *lightship, longship, lordship, M* mayorship, marksmanship, marshalship, mastership, membership, Messiahship, *midship, N* neighborship,

noviceship, *O* aldermanship, authorship, ownership, *P* paintership, partisanship, partnership, pastorship, penmanship, *PR* praetorship, preachership, prelateship, probationship, professorship, proprietorship, *R* rajahship, wranglership, rangership, readership, regentship, recordership, rectorship, relationship, reship, *S* sailingship, *saintship,* secretaryship, sextonship, seamanship, censorship, *sibship,* citizenship, sizarship, swordsmanship, sultanship, sonship, survivorship, *SH* sheriffship, ship, surety-ship, *SK* scholarship, *SP* spaceship, speakership, sponsorship, sportsmanship, *ST* statesmanship, *steamship,* stewardship, studentship, *T township, TR* training ship, trans-ship, treasure ship, *troopship,* trusteeship, *U* umpireship, unship, upmanship, *V* viceroyship, virtuosoship, *W* wingmanship, wardenship, *wardship, warship,* watermanship, one-upmanship, workmanship, *worship*

SIP	sip
SKIP	skip
SKRIP	scrip
SLIP	*gymslip, cowslip, landslip, nonslip, sideslip,* slip, underslip
SNIP	snip
STRIP	*airstrip,* bumper strip, outstrip, strip, unstrip, weatherstrip
THRIP	thrip
TIP	tip
TRIP	atrip, business trip, head trip, *cantrip,* pleasure trip, trip
YIP	yip
ZIP	rezip, unzip, zip

ĪPS

KRĪPS	cripes
YĪPS	yipes

(See **ĪP,** add *-s* where appropriate.)

IPS

CHIPS	buffalo chips, chips, fish and chips, in the chips, potato chips
KLIPS	eclipse, partial eclipse, total eclipse
LIPS	Apocalypse, ellipse
SNIPS	resnips, snips, unsnips
SHIPS	*amidships, midships,* reships, ships, unships
THRIPS	thrips

(See **IP,** add *-s* where appropriate.)

ĪPT

GRIPY	griped

(See **ĪP,** add *-d* where appropriate.)

IPT

KRIPT	decrypt, encrypt, crypt, uncrypt
LIPT	apocalypt, *hare-lipped, close-lipped,* lipped, *pale-lipped, red-lipped, stiff-lipped*
SKRIPT	conscript, manuscript, nondescript, *postscript, prescript, proscript,* script, *subscript,* superscript, telescript, *typescript, transcript*

(See **IP,** add *-ped* where appropriate.)

ĪR

ĪR	ire
BĪR	byre
BRĪR	briar, brier
DĪR	dier, dire, dyer
FĪR	*A* afire, *B backfire,* beaconfire, *bonfire, BL blackfire, BR brushfire, D* death fire, *F* fire, *foxfire,* forest fire, *G* galley fire, *gunfire, GR* granophyre, *H* hellfire, *K* campfire, *camphire,* coal fire, *KR* crossfire, *L* lamprophyre, *M* melaphyre, misfire, *N needfire, P* peat fire, *portfire, R* retrofire, *S*

sapphire, signal fire, SH
shellfire, SP spitfire, SW
swamp fire, W *wildfire,*
wood fire

FRĪR friar, fryer
HĪR hire, rehire
JĪR gyre
KWĪR acquire, antechoir,
enquire, esquire, inquire,
choir, quire, require,
retrochoir
LĪR liar, lyre
MĪR admire, bemire, *quagmire,*
mire, *pismire*
PĪR *empire,* pyr, pyre, *umpire*
PLĪR plier, plyer
PRĪR prior, pryer
SHĪR shire
SĪR *belsire, grandsire,* sire
SKWĪR squire, unsquire
SPĪR aspire, expire, inspire,
conspire, perspire, respire,
spire, suspire, transpire
TĪR attire, entire, flat tire,
overtire, retire, *satire,* tire,
Tyre
VĪR envire, vire
WĪR *barbwire,* barbed wire,
haywire, rewire, *tripwire,*
unwire, wire
ZĪR desire

(See ĪER)

ÎR

ÎR ear, ere, madrier,
wheatear, rabbit's ear
BÎR beer, bier, gambier, ginger
beer, light beer, near beer,
shillibeer
BLÎR blear
CHÎR cheer, upcheer
DÎR B balladeer, bayadere,
belvedere, bombardier, BR
brigadier, D dear, deer, E
endear, F fallow deer, GR
grenadier, H halberdier, K
killdeer, commandeer,
nadir, P petardeer,
petardier, R reindeer, V
voir dire
DRÎR drear
FÎR fear, fere, interfere,
isodiaphere
FLÎR fleer
GÎR bevel gear, *footgear,*
friction gear, gear, gir,
headgear, regear, running
gear, ungear
HÎR adhere, hear, here, inhere,

cohere, Mynheer, mishear,
overhear
JÎR jeer, Tangier
KÎR fakir, kier
KLÎR chanticleer, clear, reclear,
unclear
KWÎR queer, lequear, perqueer
LÎR B bandoleer, bandolier, F
fusilier, G gaselier,
gondolier, K camelier,
cavalier, King Lear, L
lavaliere, lear, Lear, leer,
P pedalier, pistoleer, SH
chandelier, chevalier
MÎR A actinomere, amir,
antimere, BL blastomere, E
emeer, emir, epimere, K
kerseymere, M meer,
mere, metamere, mir, PR
premier, S centromere, SH
chimere, V Vermeer
NÎR A anear, B bioengineer,
buccaneer, D denier,
domineer, E electioneer,
engineer, G gonfalonier, I
Indianeer, J jardiniere, K
cannoneer, carabineer,
carabinier, caravaneer,
carbineer, M mountaineer,
muffineer, mutineer, N
near, neer, O auctioneer, P
palfrenier, pioneer,
pontonier, S souvenir,
sermoneer, SH chiffonier,
SKR scrutineer, SL
sloganeer, SP
specksioneer, T timoneer,
V veneer
PÎR appear, diapir, disappear,
compear, compeer, outpeer,
peer, pier, pir, reappear
RÎR arrear, Fenrir, career, rear,
uprear, vancourier
SFÎR A aerosphere,
anthrosphere, atmosphere,
B barysphere, bathysphere,
biosphere, E ecosphere,
exosphere, F photosphere,
H hemisphere,
hydrosphere, I insphere, L
lithosphere, M
magnetosphere,
mesosphere, ionosphere, P
perisphere, PL planisphere,
R rhizosphere, S
centrosphere, SF sphere,
STR stratosphere, TH
thermosphere, TR
troposphere, U
undersphere, unsphere
SHÎR cashier, shear, sheer,
tabasheer

SÎR A adiposere, agricere,
Aesir, E ensear, F
financier, I insincere, K
caboceer, KW cuirassier, L
Landseer, PL plancier, S
sear, seer, cere, sincere,
xerosere
SKÎR skeer
SKLÎR sclere
SMÎR asmear, besmear, resmear,
smear, unsmear
SNÎR sneer
SPÎR *Shakespeare,* spear
STÎR austere, oversteer, steer,
stere, understeer
THÎR dinothere, isothere,
chalicothere, titanothere,
uintathere
TÎR CH charioteer, FR frontier,
G gadgeteer, garreteer,
gazetteer, H haltere, K
corsetier, KR crocheteer,
M *muleteer,* musketeer, P
pamphleteer, pulpiteer,
puppeteer, PR privateer,
profiteer, R racketeer,
rocketeer, S circuiteer,
sonneteer, T targeteer,
tear, teer, tier, Tyr, V
volunteer
VÎR brevier, Guinivere, clavier,
persevere, revere, revers,
severe, veer, vire
WÎR *wasteweir,* weir, we're
YÎR *leapyear, lightyear,
midyear,* year, yesteryear
ZÎR brassiere, grand vizier,
vizier

ĪRD

FĪRD *all-fired, backfired* (etc.)

(See ĪR, add d where appropriate.)

ÎRD

ÎRD eared, *flap-eared, flop-
eared, lop-eared*
BÎRD beard, *Blackbeard,
Bluebeard, goatsbeard,
graybeard, redbeard,
treebeard*
FÎRD afeard, feared, fyrd, much
feared, unfeared
WÎRD weird

(See ÎR, add -ed where appropriate.)

ÎRS

FÎRS	fierce, unfierce
PÎRS	pierce, transpierce
TÎRS	tierce

ÎRZ

JÎRZ	Algiers, Tangiers
SHÎRZ	shears, sheers

(See **ÎR,** add -s where appropriate.)

ĪS

ĪS	black ice, choc-ice, de-ice, dry ice, ice, camphor ice
BĪS	bice
DĪS	dice, paradise
FĪS	fice, human sacrifice, sacrifice, self-sacrifice, suffice
GRĪS	grice
LĪS	beggar's lice, body lice, head lice, lice
MĪS	church mice, field mice, country mice, mice, city mice, *titmice*
NĪS	gneiss, nice, overnice
PĪS	pice
PRĪS	*half-price, off-price,* price, reprice, underprice, unprice
RĪS	rais, rice
SĪS	imprecise, concise, precise, sice, syce
SLĪS	slice
SPĪS	*allspice,* bespice, speiss, spice
SPLĪS	resplice, splice, unsplice
TĪS	entice, tice
THRĪS	thrice
TRĪS	trice
TWĪS	twice
VĪS	advice, device, intrauterine device, edelweiss, vice, vise

IS

BIS	abyss, bis, cannabis
BLIS	bliss
DIS	dis, Dis, diss, hendiadys, *Charybdis,* cowardice, magadis, prejudice
FIS	artifice, benefice, edifice, orifice, sacrifice
FRIS	dentifrice

GRIS	ambergris, mistigris, verdigris
HIS	dehisce, hiss
KIS	butterfly kiss, chocolate kiss, French kiss, Judas kiss, kiss, rekiss, soul kiss
KRIS	kris, Kriss
KWIS	cuisse, quis
LIS	*A* acropolis, Annapolis, *F* fortalice, *G* Gallipolis, *H* Heliopolis, *I* Indianapolis, *K* cosmopolis, *KR* chrysalis, *L* lis, liss, *M* megalopolis, metropolis, Minneapolis, *N* necropolis, *P* Persepolis, *S* syphilis
MIS	amiss, Artemis, dynamis, dismiss, epididymis, fideicommiss, miss, Miss, remiss, submiss
NIS	reminisce
PIS	piss, precipice
PRIS	priss
RIS	avarice, Phalaris, licorice, sui generis
SIS	*A* abiogenesis, adipogenesis, aphaeresis, aphesis, agenesis, amoebiasis, anabasis, analysis, anamorphosis, anthropogenesis, anthropomorphisis, antiphrasis, antithesis, apodosis, apophysis, apotheosis, ascariasis, atelectasis, *B* bacteriolysis, bilharziasis, biogenesis, biolysis, biosynthesis, *BR* bronchiectasis, *D* dialysis, diaeresis, diastysis, diathesis, dichastasis, *E* ectogenesis, elephantiasis, electroanalysis, electrodialysis, electrolysis, emesis, emphasis, entasis, epiphysis, *F* filariasis, photokinesis, photosynthesis, *GL* glycolisis, *H* haematiogenesis, haematemisis, haemodialysis, haemolysis, hypostasis, histogenesis, histolysis, hypothesis, holophrasis, *J* genesis, *K* catabasis, katabesis, catalysis, *KE* cryptanalysis, *L* leishmaniasis, lithiasis, *M* metabasis, metamorphosis, metastisis, metathesis, myasis, myariasis, microanalysis, morphogenesis, *N* nemesis, pneumatolysis, *O* osteogenesis, oogenesis, osteoclasis, autholysis, *P* parabasis, paragenesis, paralysis, parasynthesis, parathesis, parenthesis, parthenogenesis, pathogenesis, paedomorphosis, periphrasis, *S* satyriasis, psychoanalysis, psychogenesis, *psychokinesis,* synthesis, sis, siss, cytolysis, psoriasis, *SP* spermatogenesis, sporogenesis, *T* telekinesis, taeniasis, tycolisis, *TH* thermogenesis, thermolysis, phthiriasis, *TR* trichiasis, trypanosomiasis, *Y* urinalysis, *Z* xenogenesis
STIS	armistice, *interstice*
SWIS	Swiss
TIS	abatis, clematis
THIS	this
TRIS	cockatrice, cicatrice
VIS	vis
WIS	iwis, wis, y-wis
YIS	yisse

ISH

ISH	babyish, dowdyish, Cockneyish, ogreish, willowish, yellowish
BISH	bish
DISH	chafing dish, dish
FISH	*A* amberfish, angelfish, *B* barberfish, *batfish, BL* blackfish, blowfish, bluefish, *D* damselfish, devilfish, dogfish, *F* filefish, fish, *FL* flatfish, flying fish, *FR* frogfish, *G* garfish, goldfish, *GR* greenfish, *H* hogfish, *HW* whitefish, *J* jellyfish, jewfish, *K* catfish, killfish, killifish, kingfish, codfish, cowfish, cuttlefish, *KL* clingfish, *KR* crawfish, crayfish, *M* mayfish, monkfish, *O* oarfish, *P* pilotfish, *PL* plowfish, *R* ratfish, redfish, ribbonfish, rockfish, *S* sailfish,

sawfish, saltfish, swordfish, silverfish, SH shellfish, ST starfish, stingfish, stockfish, T tilefish, TR trunkfish, W weakfish (etc.)

GISH	gish
GWISH	*anguish*
HWISH	whish
KISH	kish
ISH	ish
JISH	orangeish
LISH	devilish, lish
NISH	heathenish, kittenish, mammonish, knish, vixenish, womanish
PISH	pish
RISH	*B* bitterish, *F* feverish, *G* gibberish, *I* impoverish, *J* gibberish, *KL* cleverish, *KW* quakerish, *L* lickerish, *T* tigerish, *V* vaporish, viperish, vulturish, *W* waterish
SHISH	shish
SKWISH	squish
SLISH	slish
SWISH	swish
TISH	tish, *schottische, Scottish*
WISH	death wish, rewish, unwish, wish

(The suffix *-ish* may be added to any suitable noun or adjective, many not listed here, to make a rhyme.)

ISK

BISK	bisque
BRISK	brisk
DISK	disc, disk, floppy disk, condensed disk
FISK	fisc
FRISK	frisk
HWISK	whisk
LISK	basilisk, lisk, obelisk, odalisque
PISK	pisk
RISK	asterisk, risk, tamarisk
SISK	francisc
TISK	tisk

ISP

HWISP	whisp
KRISP	crisp
LISP	lisp
RISP	rerisp, risp
WISP	will-o'-the-wisp, wisp

ĪST

ĪST	iced, uniced
GĪST	poltergeist, *Weltgeist, Zeitgeist*
HĪST	heist
KRĪST	antichrist, Christ
LĪST	beliced, liced

(See **ĪS,** add *-d* where appropriate.)

IST

IST	*A* altruist, archaist, atheist, *B* banjoist, *E* egoist, essayist, *H* hobbyist, Hebraist, *I* ist, *J* jingoist, Judaist, *K* casuist, copyist, *L* lobbyist, *M* Maoist, *O* oboist, *PR* prosaist, *S* soloist, *SH* Shintoist, *T* Taoist, *TR* tritheist, *U* ultraist, *V* vacuist, *Y* euphuist
BIST	Arabist
BRIST	equilibrist
DIST	*B* balladist, *K* chiropodist, concordist, *M* melodist, Methodist, monodist, *P* parodist, *PR* prejudiced, *R* rhapsodist, *S* psalmodist, synodist, *T* Talmudist, *THR* threnodist, *U* unprejudiced
FIST	*B* beneficed, *F* philosophist, fist, fyst, photographist, *J* gymnosophist, *K* chirographist, *P* pacifist, *puckfist, SP* specifist, *ST* steganographist, stenographist, *T* telegraphist, typographist, topographist, *TH* theosophist
FRIST	frist
GLIST	glist
GRIST	grist
HIST	hissed, hist
HWIST	whist, bridge whist
JIST	*A* agist, allergist, apologist, archaeologist, *B* biologist, *D* demonologist, dialogist, *E* ecclesiologist, electrobiologist, elegist, entomologist, etymologist, *F* pharmacologist, philologist, physiologist, fossilologist, *FR* phrenologist, *GR* graphologist, *J* genealogist, geologist, gynecologist, gist, jist, *K* campanologist, conchologist, *KR* chronologist, *L* lithologist, liturgist, *M* martyrologist, metallurgist, meteorologist, mineralogist, mythologist, *N* necrologist, neologist, pneumatologist, *O* ophthalmologist, ornithologist, *P* pathologist, penologist, petrologist, *R* radiologist, *S* psychologist, synergist, Sinologist, seismologist, sociologist, suffragist, *STR* strategist, *T* technologist, teleologist, toxicologist, tautologist, *TH* theologist, *Y* ufologist, eulogist, *Z* zoologist
KIST	anarchist, bekissed, catechist, kissed, cist, kist, masochist, monachist, monarchist, rekissed, Sinarquist, unkissed
KRIST	theomicrist
KWIST	quist, ventriloquist
LIST	*A* agricolist, agriculturalist, alist, analyst, animalculist, annalist, annualist, anticatalyst, aeralist, *B* bibliophilist, bibliopolist, bicyclist, bimetallist, biocatalyst, *D* dactylist, devotionalist, dialist, dualist, duelist, *E* educationalist, existentialist, experimentalist, externalist, enamelist, enlist, environmentalist, Aeolist, eternalist, evangelist, *F* fabulist, fatalist, federalist, philatelist, finalist, financialist, formalist, fossilist, feudalist, funambulist, futilist, *GL* glacialist, *H* herbalist, hyperbolist, *I* idealist, immaterialist, immoralist, immortalist, imperialist, individualist, industrialist, instrumentalist, intellectualist, internationalist, *J* generalist, journalist, *K* cabalist, capitalist, catalyst, commercialist,

congregationalist,
constitutionalist,
controversialist,
conventionalist,
conversationalist, choralist,
KL classicalist, *KW*
querulist, *L* libelist,
liberalist, list, Liszt,
literalist, loyalist, *M*
maximalist, managerialist,
martialist, materialist,
medalist, medievalist,
memorialist, metalist,
minimalist, ministerialist,
monopolist, moralist,
nationalist, naturalist,
nihilist, nominalist,
novelist, *O* oculist,
orientalist, *automobilist, P*
panelist, parabolist,
pedalist, populist, pugilist,
PL pluralist, *PR*
proverbialist, provincialist,
R racialist, rationalist,
realist, removalist,
revivalist, ritualist,
royalist, ruralist, *S*
sexualist, semifinalist,
sensationalist, sensualist,
sentimentalist, centralist,
sibylist, psychoanalyst,
cymbalist, symbolist,
somnambulist, socialist,
surrealist, *SKR*
scripturalist, *SP* specialist,
spiritualist, *T* textualist, *TR*
traditionalist,
transcendentalist, *V* violist,
vitalist, vocabulist,
vocalist, verbalist, *Y*
universalist, *Z* zoophilist

MIST *A* academist, alchemist,
anatomist, animist,
antinomist, atomist, *B*
bemist, bigamist, *D*
dismissed, dynamist,
deuterogamist, *E*
economist, epitomist, *F*
physiognomist, *FL*
phlebotomist, *L*
lachrymist, legitimist, *M*
misogamist, missed, mist,
monogamist, *O*
ophthalmist, optimist, *P*
pessimist, polygamist, *S*
ceremist, synonymist, *U*
undismissed, unmissed, *V*
volumist, *Z* zoötomist

NIST *A* abolitionist, abortionist,
agonist, accompanist,
actionist, alienist, Alpinist,
antagonist, *B* botanist,

Bourbonist, *BR*
Brahmanist, *D* Darwinist,
degenerationist,
delusionist, demonist,
destinist, destructionist,
determinist, devotionist,
Deuteragonist, *E*
educationist, exhibitionist,
exclusionist, excursionist,
expansionist,
Expressionist, extensionist,
elocutionist,
emancipationist,
evolutionist, *F* factionist,
feminist, phenomenist,
fictionist, Philhellenist, *G*
galvanist, *H* harmonist,
hedonist, Hellenist,
hygienist, humanist, *I*
illusionist, imitationist,
immersionist,
impressionist,
indeterminist,
inspirationist,
insurrectionist,
interventionist, *K*
Calvinist, canonist,
coalitionist, colonist,
columnist, communionist,
communist, Communist,
Confucionist,
conservationist,
constitutionist,
constructionist, loose
constructionist, strict
constructionist,
contortionist,
conversationalist,
conversationist, co-
religionist, corruptionist,
KR cremationist, *L*
Latinist, lutanist, *M*
Malthusianist, mammonist,
mechanist, miscellanist,
misogynist, modernist, *N*
Napoleonist, mnemonist,
Neo-expressionist,
Neoplatonist, notionist,
nutritionist, *O*
obstructionist, opinionist,
opportunist, oppositionist,
organist, Orleanist, *P* pan-
Hellenist, passionist,
pianist, perfectionist,
percussionist, pythonist,
post-impressionist, *PL*
platonist, *PR* precisionist,
progressionist,
prohibitionist,
projectionist, protagonist,
protectionist, *R* reactionist,
religionist, reminisced,

repudiationist, receptionist,
revelationist, revisionist,
revolutionist,
resurrectionist, Romanist,
S salvationist, satanist,
saturnist, segregationist,
secessionist, symphonist,
circumlocutionist,
Sorbonnist, *SH* Shamanist,
chauvinist, *T* telephonist,
terminist, timpanist,
tobacconist, *TR* trade
unionist, traditionist,
trombonist, *U* urbanist, *V*
vacationist, vaccinist,
Vaticanist, vivisectionist,
visionist, volumnist,
vulcanist, *Y* eudemonist,
unionist, *Z* Zionist

PIST *E* emancipist, *F*
philanthropist,
physiotherapist, *L*
landscapist, *M*
misanthropist, *P* pissed, *R*
radiotherapist, *S* syncopist,
TH theophilanthropist,
therapist, *Z* xenoepist

PRIST
RIST prissed
A aphorist, agriculturist,
aquarist, allegorist,
amorist, aorist, apiarist,
arborist, arborculturist,
armorist, artillerist, *B*
behaviorist, *D* diarist,
disinterest, *E* Everest, *FL*
floriculturist, *GL*
glossarist, *H* horticulturist,
humorist, *I* interest, *K*
caricaturist, colorist,
culturist, *L* laborist,
Lazarist, lepidopterist, *M*
mannerist, mesmerist,
militarist, motorist, *N*
naturist, *O* augurist,
ocularist, *P* particularist,
posturist, *PL* plagiarist,
pleasurist, *PR* preterist, *R*
rapturist, rigorist, rist,
wrist, *S* satirist, secularist,
singularist, solarist,
summarist, *SK* Scripturist,
T terrorist, *TH* theorist, *V*
votarist, *Y* Eucharist

SHIST
SIST schist
A Anglicist, assist, *B*
biblicist, *BL* blastocyst, *E*
exorcist, empiricist,
encyst, ethicist, *F*
pharmacist, physicist, *H*
hydrocyst, *I* insist, *J*
genetecist, *K* consist, *KL*
classicist, *L* lyricist, *M*

macrocyst, mythicist, mosaicist, *N* nematocyst, *P* persist, polemicist, publicist, *PR* progressist, *R* romanticist, *S* synthesist, cist, sissed, sist, cyst, solecist, solipsist, subsist, supremacist, *SP* sporocyst, *ST* statocyst, *T* technicist, *TR* trichocyst

THIST allopathist, amethyst, antipathist, apathist, sympathist, telepathist

TIST *A* Adventist, anagrammatist, anaesthetist, *apocalyptist,* *D* despotist, diplomatist, dogmatist, *DR* dramatist, *E* egotist, experimentist, enigmatist, epigrammatist, *F* phoneticist, phonetist, *H* hereditist, hypnotist, *KW* quietist, *M* magnetist, melodramatist, *N* narcotist, nepotist, numismatist, *O* *occultist,* automatist, *P* pietist, portraitist, *PR* pragmatist, prelatist, presentist, problematist, *S* Semitist, separatist, scientist, syncretist, systematist, *SH* schoenobatist, *SK* schematist, *ST* stigmatist, *Z* zealotist

TRIST hexametrist, optometrist, pedometrist, psychiatrist, symmetrist, tryst

TWIST atwist, entwist, intertwist, twist, untwist

VIST activist, archivist, Bolshevist, Menshevist, passivist, positivist, subjectivist

WIST wist

ZIST desist, exist, co-exist, pre-exist, resist, xyst

ĪT

ĪT Shiite, *troostite,* Trotskyite
BĪT *backbite,* bight, bite, byte, *fleabite,* Jacobite, kilo-byte, Moabite, Niobite, Rechabite, cenobite, *snakebite,* trilobite
BLĪT blight, blite
BRĪT bright, *eyebright*
DĪT *B* bedight, *D* dight, dite, *E* expedite, extradite, endite, erudite, *H* heulandite,

hermaphrodite, *I* indite, incondite, K condite, *cordite, L lyddite, M* meropodite, *P* pentlandite, *podite, R* recondite, *S* synodite, *TR* troglodyte
DRĪT achondrite, alexandrite, archimandrite, dendrite
FĪT *A* aerophyte, *B* bullfight, *BR* bryophyte, *D* dermophyte, *dogfight, E* ectophyte, endophyte, entophyte, epiphyte, *F* *fistfight,* fight, fite, *G* *gunfight, GR* graphite, *H* hanifite, hydrophyte, *J* geophyte, *K cockfight, KR* cryophite, *L* lithophyte, *M* mesophyte, microphyte, *N* neophyte, *O* osteophyte, *ophite, PR* prizefight, *S* sea fight, sciophyte, *sulphite,* *STR* street fight, *T* turfite, *Z* zoophyte
FLĪT flight, flite, overflight
FRĪT affright, fright, night fright, stage fright
GĪT annabergite
HĪT Fahrenheit, height, hight
HWĪT *bobwhite,* Heppelwhite, *lintwhite, offwhite, snow-white,* white
JĪT anthropophagite, eclogite
KĪT Amalekite, box kite, *hellkite,* kite, malachite, omphalopsychite
KLĪT heteroclite
KRĪT krait
KWĪT quite, not quite, requite
LĪT *A* aerolite, acolyte, actinolite, alight, amphibolite, ampelite, apophyllite, argillite, *B* Baalite, *D daylight, deadlight,* delight, *DR droplight, E* electrolyte, entomolite, *F fanlight, phonolite, footlight, FL flashlight, floodlight, G* gaslight, gastrophilite, *go-light, GR* grapholite, granulite, graptolite, green light, *H half-light,* halite, *haplite,* harbor light, *headlight, highlight,* hyalite, *hoplite, I* ichnolite, impolite, Ishmaelite, Islamite, Israelite, *K* candlelight, Carmelite, chiastolite, killer satellite, kimberlite, coprolite, corallite, cosmopolite, *KR*

cryolite, chrysolite, crystallite, crocidolite, *KW* quarterlight, *L lamplight,* lazulite, lepidolite, limelight, light, lite, *M marlite,* menilite, metabolite, microlight, monophylite, *moonlight, N* natrolite, nephelite, *nightlight,* novaculite, nummulite, *O* oolite, *P* pyrophyllite, polite, *PR* pre-Raphaelite, prophylite, proselyte, *R* Raphaelite, *redlight,* red light, relight, rhyolite, *S* satellite, sea light, cellulite, siderolite, *searchlight, sidelight,* signal light, socialite, *sunlight, SF* spherulite, *SK* scapolite, *skylight, SP spotlight, ST starlight, stylite,* styolite, *stoplight, STR streetlight,* stromatolite, *T* tachylyte, *taillight,* tantalite, toxophilite, topazolite, *TH* theodolite, *TR* traffic light, *TW twilight, V* variolite, ventriculite, *Y* uralite, *Z* zeolite, zoolite

MĪT *A* Adamite, Adullamite, *B* bedlamite, Bethlehemite, *BR bromite, D* dynamite, dolomite, *E* Edomite, Elamite, eremite, *G* Gothamite, *H Hamite,* hellgrammite, Hiramite, *I* Islamite, Itacolumite, *K* calamite, catamite, *M* midshipmite, might, mite, Moslemite, *PR* pre-Adamite, *S Semite,* sodomite, *somite, ST* stalagmite, *T* termite, *W* widow's mite, wolframite

NĪT *A* Aaronite, aconite, alunite, Ammonite, amazonite, arenite, *B* Babylonite, belemnite, beknight, benight, bentonite, *bornite, birthnight,* day and night, disunite, *E* Ebionite, ebonite, *F finite, fortnight, G* gadolinite, good night, white knight, *I ichnite,* ignite, ilmenite, *K* Canaanite, kaolinite, *KR crinite, KW* quarternight, *L lignite,* limonite, *M* Mammonite, manganite,

Maronite, melanite, Midianite, midnight, monzonite, morganite, *N* nephelinite, knight, night, *O* austenite, autunite, overnight, *R* re-ignite, retinite, reunite, rhodonite, *S* selenite, *sennight,* cyanite, syenite, sylvanite, suburbanite, *Sunnite, SM* smithsonite, *STR* strontionite, *T* taconite, tonight, *U* unknight, urbanite, *V* vulcanite, *Y* unite, uraninite, uranite, yesternight, *W* wulfenite

PLĪT plight

RĪT *A* anchorite, aright, azurite, alright, all right, *B* *barite, birthright, bookwright, D* dolerite, *downright, E* enwrite, erythrite, yperite, *F* *forthright,* phosphorite, *G* garnierite, geyserite, *ghostwrite, GR* grossularite, *HW* *wheelwright, K cartwright,* copyright, cordierite, *L* laborite, Labradorite, laterite, Lazarite, lazurite, *M* margarite, meteorite, *millwright,* Minorite, *N* Naderite, Nazarite, New Right, *O* outright, overright, overwrite, ozocerite, *P* pyrite, *PL* playwright, plowright, *R* radical right, right, rite, write, *S* sybarite, siderite, *SH* shipwright, *T* tenorite, *typewrite, U* underwrite, unright, unwrite, *upright, W* wainwright

SĪT *A* Adamsite, accite, andesite, anorthosite, anthracite, *B bombsight,* boracite, *D* dyophysite, dissight, *E* excite, erythrocyte, *F* phagocyte, *felsite, foresight, H* haemocyte, *hindsight, I* incite, *insight, eyesight, J* jarosite, *K* chalcocite, *calcyte,* kamacite, *KW quartzite, L* lymphocyte, lewisite, leucocyte, *M* macrocyte, marcasite, martensite, microcyte, monophosyte, *O* on-site, oocyte, outasight, oversight, *P* parasite,

pargasite, *PL* plebiscite, *R* recite, *S* second sight, cite, sight, site, *SK* scolecite, *SP* spermatocyte, *U* unsight, *V* variscite

SKĪT blatherskite, skite

SLĪT sleight, slight

SMĪT smite, resmite

SNĪT snite

SPĪT despite, spite

SPRĪT spright, sprite, watersprite

TĪT *A airtight,* albertite, apatite, appetite, *B* *bipartite, G* goniatite, *GR* granitite, *H* hematite, *I* ilmenitite, *KL* clematite, *L* *latite, M* magnetite, *multipartite, P partite,* peridotite, *R* ratite, *S* celestite, *SK* skintight, *SP* spessartite, *ST* stalactite, *sticktight, T* tight, tite, *TR* *transvestite, tripartite, U* uptight, *W* watertight

TRĪT attrite, contrite, trite

TWĪT twite

VĪT invite, *Levite,* moldavite, Muscovite, reinvite

WĪT wight, Wight, wite

IT

IT *A* appropriate, *B* baccalaureate, *I* immediate, inappropriate, intermediate, it, *J* Jesuit, *K* *collegiate, KW* quadrifoliate, *PR* professoriate, *R* roseate, *S* secretariat, *TR* trifoliate

BIT bit, bitt, forebitt, giga-bit, kilo-bit, mega-bit, *tidbit, titbit,* unbit, wait-a-bit

BRIT brit, Brit

CHIT chit

DIT dit, ditt

FIT befit, benefit, fit, phit, *comfit,* counterfeit, misfit, outfit, palafitte, refit, retrofit, unfit

FLIT flit

FRIT frit

GIT git, profligate

GRIT grit

HIT hit

HWIT whit

KIT delicate, indelicate, intricate, kit, contortuplicate, quadruplicate, quintuplicate, centuplicate,

septemplicate, certificate, triplicate

KLIT clit

KRIT hypocrite

KWIT adequate, acquit, inadequate, quit, *quitquit*

LIT alit, bimaculate, chocolate, disconsolate, immaculate, inarticulate, inviolate, lit, *moonlit,* relit, *starlit, sunlit, twilit,* unlit

MIT *A* admit, antepenultimate, approximate, *D* demit, *E* emit, *I* illegitimate, immit, intermit, intimate, intromit, *K* commit, compromit, *L* legitimate, *M* manumit, mit, mitt, *O* omit, *P* permit, *PR* pretermit, proximate, *R* recommit, remit, *S* submit, *TR* transmit, *U* ultimate

NIT *A* affectionate, *B* beknit, *D* definite, determinate, diaconate, dispassionate, disproportionate, *E* effeminate, *F* fortunate, *I* impassionate, importunate, indeterminate, indiscriminate, infinite, incompassionate, inordinate, insubordinate, interknit, *K* compassionate, coordinate, *KL* close-knit, *N* knit, nit, *O* obstinate, alternate, *P* passionate, *PR* proportionate, *R* reknit, *S* subalternate, subordinate, *T* tight-knit, *U* unaffectionate, unfortunate, unknit

PIT *armpit, ashpit, coalpit, cockpit,* pit, pitt, *pitpit,* rifle pit, *shilpit, tarpit*

PLIT quadruplet, quintuplet

RIT *A* accurate, *D* daywrit, degenerate, deliberate, desparate, disparate, doctorate, *E* elaborate, *F* favorite, *I* illiterate, immoderate, inaccurate, incommensurate, inconsiderate, intemperate, inveterate, *K* commensurate, considerate, corporate, *PR* preterite, *R* rewrit, rit, writ, *S* separate, *T* temperate, *U* unwrit

SIT *insensate,* outsit, plebiscite, cit, sit

SHIT beshit, *bullshit, horseshit* (etc.), shit

SKIT	skit
SKWIT	squit
SLIT	slit
SHMIT	Messerschmitt
SMIT	smit
SPIT	*lickspit,* spit, *turnspit*
SPLIT	lickety-split, split
SPRIT	*bowsprit,* sprit
TIT	*bluetit,* tit, precipitate, *tomtit*

EVE, FEAR NOT

Eve, fear not lest through my dissent
   Our Eden be attacked;
Your theory most diffident
   I take as given fact.
Your inclinations and aversions
   Are magnified in me;
Your laws are as the Medes' and Persians'
   (Until we disagree).

TWIT	twit
VIT	aquavit
WIT	afterwit, *dimwit, godwit, halfwit,* motherwit, nimblewit, *nitwit,* outwit, to wit, thimblewit, unwit, wit, *wantwit*
ZIT	apposite, exquisite, inapposite, composite, opposite, perquisite, prerequisite, requisite, unopposite, zit

(Unstressed *-ate, -et, -it* following a stressed syllable *(striate, magnet, exit)* may be rhymed with *it,* but with little satisfaction.)

ITH

(**TH** as in *then*)

BLĪTH	blithe
LĪTH	lithe
RĪTH	writhe
SĪTH	scythe, sithe
STĪTH	stythe
TĪTH	tithe
WĪTH	withe, wythe

ITH

(**TH** as in *thin*)

BRITH	B'nai B'rith
FRITH	frith
GRITH	grith
KITH	kith
KRITH	crith
LITH	*A* aerolith, acrolith,

anthropolith, *B* batholith, *E* eolith, *G* gastrolith, *GR* granolith, *K* cactolith, coccolith, *L* lactolith, lith, *M* megalith, microlith, monolith, *N* neolith, *P* paleolith, *R* regolith, *ST* statolith, *TR* trilith, *Y* urolith, *Z* xenolith

MITH	engastrimyth, epimyth, Grecian myth, myth, Nordic myth, Roman myth
PITH	pith
SITH	sith
SMITH	arrowsmith, *blacksmith, goldsmith, gunsmith, whitesmith,* coppersmith, *locksmith,* silversmith, smith, *tinsmith, tunesmith,* wordsmith
WITH	forthwith, herewith, wherewith, therewith, with, withe, wythe

ĪTS

BRĪTS	brights
HWĪTS	whites
LĪTS	*footlights,* lights
MĪTS	Dolomites
NĪTS	anights, nights
RĪTS	rights, wrights, to-rights
TĪTS	tights

(See **ĪT,** add *-s* where appropriate.)

ITS

BLITS	blitz
GLITS	glitz
GRITS	grits
KWITS	quits
PITS	pits, the pits
RITS	Ritz
SHNITS	schnitz
SITS	sits
SPITS	spits, spitz
VITS	slivovitz
WITS	Horowitz, wits

(See **IT,** add *-s* where appropriate.)

ĪV

ĪV	I've
CHĪV	chive
DĪV	dive, *endive,* high dive, *high-dive, nose-dive,* power dive, redive, swan dive

DRĪV	chain drive, drive, outdrive, overdrive
FĪV	five, spoil five
HĪV	*beehive,* hive, rehive, unhive
JĪV	gyve, jive, *ogive,* ungyve
KLĪV	clive
LĪV	alive, live, unalive
NĪV	connive
PRĪV	deprive, redeprive
RĪV	arrive, derive, rive, rearrive, rederive
SHĪV	shive
SHRĪV	shrive
SKĪV	skive
STĪV	stive
STRĪV	strive
SWĪV	swive
THRĪV	thrive
TRĪV	contrive
VĪV	convive, redivive, revive, survive
WĪV	wive

IV

CHIV	chiv
DIV	div, *gerundive*
FLIV	fliv
GIV	forgive, give, misgive
LIV	live, outlive, overlive, relive
SHIV	shiv
SIV	purposive, sieve
SPIV	spiv
TIV	*A* ablative, additive, admonitive, adversative, affirmative, affricative, agglutinative, accumulative, accusative, acquisitive, alliterative, alternative, amative, appellative, applicative, appreciative, argumentative, associative, attributive, *D* definitive, declarative, decorative, deliberative, demonstrative, denominative, denotative, depurative, derivative, derogative, desiderative, desiccative, determinative, diapositive, diminutive, dispensative, disputative, distributive, donative, dormative, durative, *E* educative, executive, exhibitive, exclamative, explicative, expletive,

elative, electropositive,
evocative, *F* factitive,
facultative, figurative,
fixative, formative,
photosensitive, fugitive,
FR frequentative, fricative,
H hypersensitive, *I*
illustrative, imaginative,
imitative, impeditive,
imperative, imputative,
inappreciative, indicative,
infinitive, informative,
initiative, incarnative,
inchoative, inquisitive,
inoperative, insensitive,
intensative, interpretive,
interrogative, intransitive,
intuitive, irrelative, *J*
genitive, judicative, *K*
calculative, calmative,
carminative, coagulative,
coercitive, *cogitative,*
combative, combinative,
commemorative,
communicative,
commutative, comparative,
compellative,
compensative, competitive,
complimentative,
compulsative, conative,
confirmative, consecutive,
conservative, conciliative,
consultative,
contemplative,
continuative, contributive,
cooperative, corporative,
correlative, causative,
cumulative, curative, *KW*
qualitative, quantitative,
quidditive, quietive, *L*
laxative, lenitive,
laudative, locative,
lucrative, *M* manipulative,
meditative, mercative,
multiplicative, N narrative,
negative, neoconservative,
nominative,
noncooperative, normative,
nutritive, *O* auditive,
augmentative, *alterative,*
operative, optative,
authoritative, P partitive,
pejorative, performative,
portative, positive,
postoperative, postpositive,
pulsative, punitive,
purgative, putative, *PR*
premonitive, preparative,
prepositive, prerogative,
preteritive, preventative,
preservative, primitive,
privative, probative,

prohibitive, provocative, *R*
radiosensitive, rebarbative,
reformative, relative,
remunerative, reparative,
recitative, restorative,
retributive, reverberative,
rotative, *ruminative, S*
sanative, sedative,
secretive, semblative,
sensitive, separative,
significative, siccative,
substantive, superlative,
suppositive, suppurative,
SP speculative, *T* talkative,
tentative, *TR* transitive, *U*
ulcerative,
undemonstrative,
uncommunicative, *V*
vegetative, vetative,
vibrative, vituperative,
vocative, volative, *Y*
unitive

ĪVD

LĪVD long-lived, short-lived

(See **ĪV,** add *-d* where appropriate.)

ĪZ

ĪZ angel eyes, archaize, asses'
eyes, atheize, bright eyes,
dandyize, eyes, Hebraize,
Judaize, sheep's eyes,
twaddleize, euphuize
CHĪZ *disfranchise, enfranchise*
DĪZ *A* aggrandize, anodize, *B*
balladize, bastardize, *D*
dastardize, deoxidize,
faradize, *FL* fluidize, *G*
gormandize, *H* hybridize, *I*
iodize, iridize, *J*
jeopardize, *KL* chloridize,
L liquidize, *M* melodize,
merchandise, methodize, *O*
oxidize, *P* paradise, *PR*
propagandize, *R*
rhapsodize, ruggedize *S*
psalmodize, subsidize, *SH*
sherardize, *ST* standardize
FĪZ *anthropomorphize,*
apostrophize, philosophize,
sacrifice, theosophize
GĪZ disguise, guise
JĪZ *A* analogize, anthologize,
apologize, astrologize, *B*
battologize, *D*
demythologize, dialogize,
doxologize, *E* elegize,

energize, entomologize,
etymologize, *H*
homologize, *J* genealogize,
geologize, *L* lethargize, *M*
mythologize, *N* neologize,
S psychologize, syllogize,
T tautologize, *TH*
theologize, *Y* eulogize
KĪZ catechize

MY AMNESTY TO ALL, EXCEPT

My amnesty to all
    The poor, imperfect throng,
Excepting just one pest:
    The man who has the gall
To say, when things go wrong,
    "I meant it for the best."

KWĪZ colloquize, soliloquize,
ventriloquize
LĪZ *A* actualize, alcoholize,
alkalize, ambrosialize,
analyze, annalize,
animalize, arterialize,
artificialize, *B* banalize,
bestialize, *BR* breathalyze,
brutalize, *CH* channelize,
D dematerialize,
demineralize, demobilize,
demoralize, denationalize,
denaturalize,
departmentalize,
depersonalize, desexualize,
decentralize, decimalize,
destabilize, devilize,
devitalize, diabolize,
dialyze, digitalize, dualize,
E editorialize,
experimentalize,
externalize, equalize,
electrolyze, etherealize,
evangelize, *F* fabulize,
fictionalize, finalize,
focalize, formalize,
formulize, fossilize,
feudalize, *FR* fractionalize,
fraternize, *G* gospelize,
gutturalize, *H* hydrolyze,
hyperbolize, hospitalize, *I*
idealize, illegalize,
immaterialize, immobilize,
immortalize, imperialize,
impersonalize,
individualize, industrialize,
initialize, institutionalize,
intellectualize, internalize,
internationalize,
irrationalize, *J* generalize,
journalize, *K* canalize,
cannibalize, capitalize,

caramelize, cardinalize,
catalyze, coalize,
communalize,
compartmentalize,
conceptualize,
conventionalize, *KR*
crystallize, *KW*
quintessentialize, *L*
legalize, liberalize,
localize, *M* martialize,
materialize, memorialize,
mercurialize, metabolize,
metagrobolize, metallize,   **NĪZ**
mineralize, mobilize,
modelize, mongrelize,
monopolize, moralize,
mortalize, mutualize, *N*
nationalize, naturalize,
nasalize, normalize,
novelize, neutralize, *O*
obelize, occidentalize,
opalize, orientalize, *P*
palatalize, papalize,
parabolize, parallelize,
paralyze, participialize,
patronize, penalize,
personalize, potentialize,
PL pluralize, *PR*
professionalize,
proverbialize,
provincialize, *R* radicalize,
racialize, rationalize,
realize, recrystallize,
revitalize, ritualize,
royalize, ruralize,
Russianize, *S* sectionalize,
sexualize, sensualize,
sentimentalize, centralize,
sepulchralize, serialize,
signalize, psychoanalyze,
symbolize, synchronize,
civilize, solubilize,
socialize, substantialize,
subtilize, *SK* scandalize,
SKR scrupulize, *SP*
specialize, spiritualize, *ST*
stabilize, sterilize, *T*
tantalize, territorialize,
testimonialize, totalize, *TH*
thermalize, *TR* tranquilize,
trivialize, *V* vandalize,
verbalize, vernalize,
visualize, vitalize,
vocalize, volatilize, *Y*
universalize, utilize
MĪZ   *A* alchemize, amalgamize,
anatomize, astronomize,
atomize, *BR* bromize, *D*
demise, *E* economize,
emblemize, epitomize, *F*
physiognomize, *FL*
phlebotomize, *I* infamize,

Islamize, itemize, *K*
compromise, customize, *L*
legitimize, lobotomize, *M*
macadamize, maximize,
manumize, minimize, *O*
optimize, autotomize, *P*
pessimize, pilgrimize,
polygamize, *PR* premise,
presurmise, *R* randomize,
racemize, remise, *S*
synonymize, surmise, *V*
victimize, *Y* euphemize
A adonize, Africanize,
agonize, agrarianize,
albumenize, aluminize,
Americanize, androgenize,
antagonize, attitudinize, *B*
bituminize, Balkanize,
botanize, *D* dehumanize,
decarbonize, decolonize,
demonize, deoxygenize,
detonize, dichotomize,
disillusionize, disorganize,
E ebonize, Edenize,
effeminize, economize,
excursionize, *F* feminize,
FR fractionize, fraternize,
G galvanize, gorgonize,
GL glutenize, gluttonize, *H*
harmonize, heathenize,
Hellenize, histrionize,
homogenize, humanize, *I*
impatronize, immunize,
ionize, ironize, Italianize,
J jargonize, gelatinize,
Germanize, *K* canonize,
caponize, carbonize,
keratinize, kyanize,
cognize, colonize,
communize, cauponize,
cosmopolitanize, *KR*
Christianize, *L* Latinize,
lionize, Londonize, *M*
macadamize, mammonize,
mangonize, matronize,
mechanize, modernize,
Mohammedanize, *N*
nitrogenize, *O* oxygenize,
opsonize, organize,
Australianize, Austrianize,
P paganize, patronize,
pavonize, pedestrianize,
peptonize, personize,
pollenize, Puritanize, *PL*
platinize, platitudinize,
Platonize, plebeianize, *PR*
preconize, *R* recognize,
rejuvenize, reorganize,
republicanize,
revolutionize,
resurrectionize, Romanize,
S sectarianize, sermonize,

PĪZ

PRĪZ

RĪZ

symphonize, simonize,
cinchonize, synchronize,
Socinianize, solemnize,
suburbanize, *SK*
skeletonize, *SKR*
scrutinize, *T* tetanize,
Timonize, tyrannize,
Teutonize, *TR* trichonize,
U urbanize, *V* villainize,
volcanize, vulcanize, *W*
wantonize, westernize,
womanize, *Y* euphonize,
unionize, Europeanize
philanthropize, philippize,
misanthropize, penelopize,
pize, sinapize, syncopize,
euripize
apprise, emprise,
enterprise, comprise,
misprize, prise, prize,
reprise, surprise,
underprise
A aphorize, allegorize,
arise, *B* barbarize,
bowdlerize, burglarize, *D*
decolorize, demilitarize,
demonetarize,
denuclearize, deodorize,
depressurize, desulphurize,
E extemporize, exteriorize,
etherize, *F* factorize,
familiarize, formularize,
FL fletcherize, *GL*
glamorize, *GR* grangerize,
H heterize, *I* isomerize, *J*
jennerize, *K* characterize,
categorize, catheterize,
chimerize, computerize,
containerize,
contemporize, cauterize, *M*
marmarize, memorize,
mercerize, mesmerize,
militarize, miniaturize,
moisturize, *moonrise,*
motorize, *N* notarize, *O*
augurize, authorize, *P*
panegyrize, particularize,
pasteurize, peculiarize,
polarize, polymerize,
pauperize, popularize,
pulverize, *PL* plagiarize,
PR pressurize, proctorize,
R rapturize, regularize,
rhetorize, revalorize, rise,
rubberize, *S* saccharize,
satirize, secularize,
seigniorize, seniorize,
silverize, singularize,
circularize, slenderize,
soberize, solarize,
suberize, sulphurize,
summarize, *sunrise, T*

tabularize, temporize, tenderize, terrorize, *TH* theorize, transistorize, *U* uprise, *V* valorize, vaporize, vulgarize

SĪZ   *A* Anglicize, apotheosize, assize, atticize, *D* depoliticize, domesticize, *E* excise, exercise, exorcise, ecstasize, emblematicize, emphasize, ethicize, *F* fanaticize, fantasize, photosynthesize, *G* Gallicize, Gothicize, *H* hypostasize, hypothesize, *I* incise, italicize, *K* capsize, Catholicize, *KL* classicize, *KR* criticize, *L* laicize, *M* metastasize, metathesize, mythicize, *O* ostracize, *outsize, oversize, P* parenthesize, poeticize, politicize, publicize, *PL* plasticize, *R* resize, romanticize, *S* Sinicize, *synopsize*, synthesize, circumcise, size, *SK* skepticize, Scotticize, *T* Turkicize

SPĪZ   despise
THĪZ   empathize, sympathize, telepathize, thighs
TĪZ   *A* advertise, agatize, acclimatize, achromatize, alphabetize, amortize, anagrammatize, anathematize, anesthetize, appetize, apostatize, aromatize, athetize, *B* baptize, bureaucratize, *CH* chastise, *D* dehypnotize, demagnetize, democratize, demonetize, denarcotize, deputize, desensitize, diatize, digitize, dogmatize, *DR* dramatize, *E* egotize, emblematize, enigmatize, epigrammatize, *F* photosensitize, *H* hypersensitize, hypnotize, hyposensitize, hypostatize, *K* concretize, concertize, *KL* climatize, *L* legitimatize, *M* magnetize, mediatize, mediocratize, melodramatize, monetize, *N* narcotize, *O* operatize, automatize, *P* parasitize, poetize, *PR* pragmatize, prelatize, prioritize, proselytize, Protestantize,

R remonetize, *S* sanitize, sensitize, syncretize, synthesize, systematize, schismatize, sonnetize, sovietize, *SK* schematize, *ST* stigmatize, *TR* traumatize
TRĪZ   idolatrize, geometrize, cicatrize, retries, tries·
VĪZ   advise, devise, improvise, collectivize, revise, supervise, televise
WĪZ   *A* afterwise, *anticlockwise, B bookwise, E edgewise, endwise,* anywise, *K* contrariwise, copywise, cornerwise, counterclockwise, *KL clockwise, KR crabwise,* crescentwise, *crosswise, L likewise, M moneywise, N nowise, O* overwise, *P* pennywise, *S sidewise, somewise, SL slantwise, ST stagewise, TR travelwise, U* unwise, otherwise, *W* weatherwise, *widthwise,* wise, *Z* zigzagwise

(See **Ī**, add *-s* or change *-y* to *-ies* where appropriate.)

IZ

IZ	is
BIZ	biz, show biz
DIZ	Cadiz
FIZ	fizz, phiz, golden fizz, gin fizz, rum fizz, silver fizz
FRIZ	frizz
HIZ	his
HWIZ	gee whiz, whiz
JIZ	gizz
KWIZ	quiz
MIZ	Ms.
RIZ	riz
SIZ	sizz
SKWIZ	squiz
SWIZ	swizz
TIZ	'tis
VIZ	vis, viz
WIZ	wis, wiz
ZIZ	zizz

ĪZD

ĪZD   dandyized

(See **ĪZ** add *-ed* where appropriate.)

IZD

FIZD   fizzed

(See **IZ,** add *-ed* or *-zed* where appropriate.)

IZM

IZM   *A* absenteeism, allotheism, altruism, archaism, asteism, atheism, *B* babyism, Bahaism, bitheism, bogeyism, boobyism, bowwowism, *BL* bluestockingism, *D* deism, Dadaism, dandyism, dichroism, ditheism, *E* egoism, egotheism, echoism, *F* fairyism, fideism, physitheism, fogeyism, *FL* flunkeyism, *G* Ghandiism, ghettoism, *H* Hebraism, henotheism, heraism, heroism, hylozoism, Hinduism, *I* Englishism, Irishism, ism, *J* jingoism, jockeyism, Judaism, *K* kathenotheism, Cockneyism, *L* ladyism, Lamaism, Lamarckism, locoism, *M* Maoism, Mazdaism, McCarthyism, *misoneism,* Mithraism, monotheism, Mosaism, monkeyism, *O* ogreism, *P* pantheism, polytheism, powwowism, puppyism, *PR* Prosaism, *R* rowdyism, *S* Sivaism, sutteeism, *SH* Shintoism, *T* Taoism, Titoism, Toryism, *TH theism, TR* trichroism, tritheism, Trotskyism, *truism, U* ultraism, untruism, *Y* Yankeeism, euphuism, *Z* xanthachroism, zanyism
BIZM   abysm, *cubism,* syllabism
BRIZM   tenebrism
DIZM   abecedism, braggardism, hyperthyroidism, hypothyroidism, invalidism, iodism, Lollardism, Methodism, monadism
FIZM   *A* anthropomorphism, *B biomorphism, DW dwarfism, E endomorphism, F*

philosophism, *M*
mechanomorphism,
metamorphism, O
Orphism, *P* pacifism,
polymorphism, S
sapphism, SK scaphism

JIZM *A* antilogism, *D* dialogism,
E energism, *I* imagism, *J*
geophagism, jism, *L*
liturgism, *M*
meconophagism, *N*
neologism, *P* paralogism,
portmontologism, *S*
savagism, psychologism,
syllogism, synergism, *Y*
eulogism

KIZM anarchism, catechism,
masochism, monarchism,
sadomasochism,
sinarquism, *tychism*

KLIZM cataclysm
KRIZM chrism
KWIZM grandiloquism,
somniloquism,
ventriloquism

LIZM *A* agriculturalism,
accidentalism, alcoholism,
anabolism, animalism,
anomalism, *B Baalism,*
behavioralism,
bibliophilism,
bibliopolism, bimetallism,
botulism, *BR* brutalism, *D*
denominationalism,
departmentalism, devilism,
diabolism, digitalism,
dualism, *E* ebullism,
existentialism,
experimentalism,
externalism, embolism,
emotionalism,
environmentalism,
etherealism,
ethnophaulism,
evangelism, *F* fatalism,
federalism,
phenomenalism, finalism,
physicalism, formalism,
formulism, fossilism,
feudalism,
fundamentalism,
functionalism, *FR*
frivolism, frugalism, *H*
hyperbolism, *I* idealism,
eidolism, immaterialism,
immobilism, imperialism,
individualism,
industrialism, infantilism,
institutionalism,
instrumentalism,
intellectualism,
internationalism, *J*

gentilism, journalism, *K*
cabalism, cannibalism,
capitalism, carnalism,
catabolism, colloquialism,
colonialism,
commercialism,
communalism,
congregationalism,
conceptualism,
constitutionalism,
controversialism,
conventionalism, *KL*
classicalism, clericalism,
chloralism, *L* legalism,
liberalism, literalism,
localism, loyalism, *M*
materialism, medievalism,
Mendelism, mentalism,
mercantilism,
mercurialism, metabolism,
myalism, mongolianism,
monometallism,
monopolism, moralism,
municipalism, *N*
nationalism, naturalism,
necrophilism, nihilism,
neutralism, *O*
occasionalism,
operationalism, *P*
papalism, parallelism,
paternalism, personalism,
petalism, pointillism,
puerilism, pugilism, *PL*
pluralism, *PR* pre-
Raphaelism, probabilism,
professionalism,
proverbialism,
provincialism, *R*
radicalism, racialism,
rationalism, realism,
reformism, regionalism,
representationalism,
revivalism, ritualism,
rhopalism, royalism,
ruralism, *S*
sacramentalism,
sacerdotalism,
sensationalism,
sensualism,
sentimentalism, centralism,
servilism, symetallism,
syndicalism, symbolism,
sciolism, somnambulism,
somnolism, socialism,
supernaturalism,
surrealism, *SK* scopelism,
scoundrelism, *SKR*
scripturalism, *SP*
specialism, spiritualism,
ST structuralism, *T*
textualism, territorialism,
ptyalism, *THR*

thromboembolism, *TR*
traditionalism,
transsexualism,
transcendentalism,
tribalism, *traulism,*
troilism, V vandalism,
vanillism, verbalism,
virilism, vitalism,
vocalism, *Y* universalism,
Z Zoilism, zoophilism

MIZM *A* academism, *alarmism,*
anatomism, animism,
atomism, *D* dynamism,
dysphemism, *I* Islamism,
K cacophemism, *L*
legitimism, *M* Muslimism,
O optimism, *P* pessimism,
T totemism, *TR*
transformism, *U*
euphemism

NIZM *A* abolitionism,
abstractionism,
Africanism, agonism,
agrarianism, actinism,
albinism, alienism,
alpinism, Americanism,
anachronism, Anglicanism,
Anglo-Saxonism,
antagonism,
antidisestablishmentarianism,
antifeminism,
antiquarianism, Arianism,
asynchronism,
associationism, *B*
bacchanalianism,
Bohemianism,
Bourbonism, Buckmanism,
BR Brahmanism, *D*
Daltonism, Darwinism,
demonianism, demonism,
destinism, deviationism,
determinism, divisionism,
E exhibitionism,
expansionism,
expressionism,
equestrianism, eonism,
epicureanism, Erastianism,
establishmentarianism,
evolutionism, *F*
Fabianism, feminism,
Fenianism, phenomenism,
philanthropinism,
philhellenism, philistinism,
foreignism, *G* Galenism,
Gallicanism, galvanism,
GR grobianism, *H*
hedonism, Hellenism,
hereditarianism,
heathenism, Hibernianism,
hyperinsulinism,
histrionism, hooliganism,
humanism,

humanitarianism, *I*
Ibsenism, illuminism,
illusionism, immersionism,
impressionism,
indeterminism,
inflationism,
infralapsarianism,
infusionism, isolationism,
Italianism, *J* Jansenism,
Germanism, *K* Calvinism,
Canadianism, cocainism,
communism,
Confucianism, *KL*
cledonism, *KR*
creationism, cretinism, *L*
laconism, Latinism,
latitudinarianism,
Leninism, lesbianism,
libertinism, lionism,
Londonism, *M*
Mahometanism,
mammonism, mancinism,
McLuhanism, mechanism,
microorganism,
millenarianism,
minimifidianism,
misotramontanism,
modernism,
Mohammedanism,
monogenism, Montanism,
morphinism, Mormonism,
multitudinism,
Munchausenism, *N*
Neoimpressionism,
Neoplatonism,
necessarianism,
necessitarianism,
Nestorianism, nicotinism,
nonunionism, *O* onanism,
opportunism, organism,
Australianism,
Austrianism, *P* paganism,
parachronism,
parliamentarianism,
patricianism, pianism,
pedestrianism,
Pelagianism, pelmanism,
peonism, perfectionism,
pythonism,
postimpressionism,
Puritanism, *PL* Platonism,
plebianism, *PR*
predestinarianism,
Presbyterianism,
precisionism,
presentationism,
prohibitionism,
prochronism,
proletarianism,
protectionism, *R*
rabbinism, religionism,
republicanism,

restorationism,
revisionism, revolutionism,
Romanism, ruffianism, *S*
sabbatarianism, Saint-
Simonism, Satanism,
Saturnism,
sacramentarianism,
secessionism,
servomechanism,
synchronism, Syrianism,
socianism,
pseudoantidisestablishment-
    arianism,
SH shamanism,
charlatanism, Shavianism,
chauvinism, *SP*
spadonism, *ST* Stalinism,
STR strychninism, *SW*
Swedenborgianism, *T*
Timonism, Titanism,
tokenism, Teutonism, *TR*
traducianism,
Tractarianism, *U*
ultraantidesestablishment-
    arianism,
ultramontanism,
undinism, *V* Vaticanism,
vegetarianism, volcanism,
W westernism, *Y*
eudemonism, euphuism,
uniformitarianism,
Unitarianism, unionism
uranism, utilitarianism,
utopianism, *Z* Zionism,
Zoroastrianism
escapism, malapropism,
priapism, sinapism
pentaprism, prism
A adiaphorism,
adventurism, aphorism,
algorism, allegorism,
allomerism,
altrigenderism,
amateurism, anachronism,
aneurism, Archie
Bunkerism, asterism, *B*
bachelorism, barbarism,
behaviorism, bowdlerism,
bovarysm, *BL* bloomerism,
E Epicurism, etherism, *F*
phalansterism, futurism, *G*
Gongorism, *H* hetaearism,
hypocorism, historism,
Hitlerism, humorism, *I*
incendiarism, isomerism,
K characterism,
consumerism,
counterterrorism, *KW*
Quakerism, *L* laborism,
Lutherism, *M* mannerism,
metamerism, mesmerism,
mycterism, militarism, *N*

naturism, *O* odonterism, *P*
particularism, pasteurism,
peculiarism, pismerism,
pauperism, *PL* plagiarism,
R rigorism, *S* secularism,
Caesarism, psithurism,
solarism, *SP* spoonerism, *T*
terrorism, tigerism,
tautomerism, *TH* theorism,
V vampirism, *verism,*
vernacularism, vulturism,
vulgarism, *Y* euhemerism
fetishism, Englishism,
Irishism

A agnosticism,
academicism, Anglicism,
asceticism, Atticism,
athleticism, Asiaticism, *BR*
Briticism, *D* demoniacism,
dichromaticism, *E*
eclecticism, ecclesiastism,
exorcism, exoticism,
electicism, empiricism,
eroticism, esotericism,
aestheticism, *F* phallicism,
fanaticism, fantasticism,
philanthropicism,
physicism, *G* Gothicism,
GR grammaticism, *H*
Hibernicism,
hypercriticism,
hypochondriacism,
Hispanicism, historicism,
histrionicism, *I* Italicism,
K Catholicism,
Kukluxicism, *KL*
classicism, *KR* criticism,
KW quixoticism, *L*
laconicism, lyricism,
logicism, *M Marxism,*
merycism metacism,
metricism, mysticism,
mytacism, monasticism, *N*
narcissism, neoclassicism,
neoplasticism, Gnosticism,
neuroticism, *O* ostracism,
P paroxysm, peripaticism,
publicism, *R* romanticism,
S cynicism, Sinicism,
schism, solecism,
solipsism, *SK* skepticism,
scholasticism, Scotticism,
ST stoicism, *T*
Teutonicism, *V* vorticism,
W witticism
agathism, erethism
A absolutism, Adamitism,
achromatism,
anathematism, animatism,
anti-Semitism,
astigmatism, *B*
Bonapartism, *CH*

PIZM

PRIZM
RIZM

SHIZM

SIZM

THIZM
TIZM

chartism, D democratism,
despotism, diamagnetism,
dicrotism, dilettantism,
diplomatism, dogmatism,
Docetism, *E* egotism,
exquisitism,
electromagnetism,
ergotism, *F* favoritism,
ferromagnetism,
fortuitism, *GR*
grammatism, *H* helotism,
H hylactism, hypnotism,
homoerotism, *I* idiotism,
ignorantism, immanentism,
indifferentism,
ipsedixitism, *J*
geomagnetism, Jesuitism,
gigantism, *K* charientism,
cataglottism, conservatism,
corybantism, *KW* quietism,
M maritodespotism,
magnetism, mithradatism,
monochromatism, *mutism,*
N narcotism, nepotism, *O*
obscurantism, *occultism,*
automatism, *P*
paramagnetism,
parasigmatism, patriotism,
pedantism, pietism,
pyrrhotism, pithiatism, *PR*
pragmatism, prelatism,
Protestantism, *R*
rheumatism, *S* sabbatism,
Semitism, separatism,
scientism, cynicism,
syncretism, syntheratism,
systematism, Sovietism,
suprematism, *SK*
schematism, *ST*
stigmatism, *T* tarantism,
teratism, *TR* traumatism, *U*
uxorodespotism,
ultimatism, ultramontism,
V virvestitism, *W* wegotism

TRIZM *androcentrism,*
egocentrism,
ethnocentrism,
polycentrism

VIZM *A* activism, atavism, *B*
Bolshevism, *I* intensivism,
K collectivism,
constructivism, *M*
Menshevism, *N* nativism,
negativism, *O* objectivism,
P passivism,
perspectivism, positivism,
PR primitivism,
progressivism, *R*
relativism, recidivism, *S*
subjectivism

WIZM *Yahwism*
ZIZM *Spinozism*

Ō

Ō *A* adagio, A.F.L.–C.I.O.,
Antonio, arpeggio, *B*
billy-o, bocaccio,
Boccaccio, borachio,
Borachio, Borneo, *BR*
braggadocio, *CH* cheerio,
D deario, *E* ex officio,
embryo, etaerio, *F*
fabliau, fellatio, folio, *H*
histrio, *I* imbroglio,
impresario, intaglio, *K*
k.o., kayo, cameo,
capriccio, *carabao,* curio,
L Lothario, *M*
Montevideo, mustachio,
N nuncio, *O* O, oe, oh,
owe, audio, oleo, olio,
Ontario, oratorio, *P* patio,
pistachio, Pinocchio,
portfolio, punctilio, *PR*
presidio, *R* radio, ratio,
rodeo, Romeo, *S*
scenario, seraglio,
solfeggio, *SK* Scorpio, *ST*
stereo, studio, *T* tetrao, *V*
vibrio, video, vireo

BLŌ blow, *by-blow,* death
blow, counterblow,
pueblo, tableau

BŌ *B* beau, 'bo, 'boe, bow, *E*
embow, *G gazabo,*
gazebo, J jabot, jambeau,
KR crossbow, *L* long
bow, *O* oboe, oxbow, *R*
rainbow, S sabot,
saddlebow

CHŌ Chou, *gazpacho, honcho,*
macho, poncho, Sancho

DŌ bandeau, Bordeaux,
dado, dido, Dido, dildo,
doe, doh, dough, do-si-
do, rideau, rondeau, *rondo*

FŌ Defoe, foe, comme il
faut, *Sappho*

FLŌ aflow, *airflow,* floe, flow,
ice floe, *inflow, outflow,*
overflow

FRŌ fro, froe, to-and-fro
GLŌ afterglow, aglow,
alpenglow, *earthglow,*
glow, counterglow,
moonglow, starglow,
sunglow

GŌ *A* ago, archipelago, *argot,*
E escargot, *F* forgo,
forego, *G* Galapago, go, *I*
indigo, *L* long ago, *O*
outgo, T touch-and-go, *U*
undergo, *V* Van Gogh,
vertigo, gigot

GRŌ grow, ingrow, intergrow,
outgrow, overgrow,
upgrow

HŌ *A* Arapaho, *H* heigh-ho,
ho, hoe, *M* mahoe, *I*
Idaho, *N* Navaho,
Navajo, *O* oho, *S* Soho, *T*
tallyho, tuckahoe, *W*
westward ho

HWŌ whoa
JŌ adagio, *banjo,* G. I. Joe
KŌ *A* angelico, *B* bunko, *H*
haricot, *J* Jericho, *K*
calico, cantico, ko, Ko,
coquelicot, *coco, cocoa,*
M magnifico, medico,
Mexico, *moko, moko-*
moko, P persico, politico,
portico, *R* rococo, *S*
simpatico, *U* unco

KRŌ *cockcrow,* cro, crow,
escrow, Jim Crow,
overcrow, *pilcrow,*
scarecrow

KWŌ in statu quo, quid pro
quo, quo, status quo
KYŌ *Tokyo*
LŌ *A* alow, *B* below, bibelot,
bombolo, buffalo,
bummalo, bungalow, *BR*
brigalow, *D* diabolo, *F*
furbelow, *H* hallo, hello,
hullo, *J* gigolo, *K*
cachalot, cattalo, *L* lo,
low, *M* matelot,
Michelangelo, *P* pedalo,
piccolo, pomelo, *R*
rouleau, rumbelow, *S*
cembalo, cymbalo, *T*
tableau, tangelo, *TR*
tremolo

MŌ *A* alamo, Alamo,
altissimo, *B* bon mot *BR*
bravissimo, *D* dynamo,
dulcissimo, duodecimo, *E*
Eskimo, *F* fortissimo, *H*
half a mo', *haymow,*
homo, J generalissimo,
Geronimo, *K* kokomo, *M*
mho, mo, mot, mow, *P*
paramo, pianissimo, *PR*
proximo, *S* centissimo,
TW twelvemo', *U* ultimo

NŌ domino, foreknow, know,
no, pompano, tonneau,
unknow

PŌ apropos, *depot,* entrepot,
gapo, kakapo,
malapropos, po, Poe,
chapeau

PYŌ papiopio
PRŌ pro, semipro

RŌ	*A* arow, *B* bureau, *D* Death Row, *H* hedgerow, hetero, *J* genro, *K* carot, *P* Pernod, Pierrot, *R* rho, ro, roe, row, Rotten Row, *S* serow, Cicero, *SK* Skid Row, *T* tarot, *W* windrow
SHMŌ	schmo, shmo
SHŌ	*D* dogshow, *F* fashion show, foreshow, *G* girlie show, *H* horseshow, *M* motion-picture show, *P* peepshow, *S* sideshow, *SH* shew, sho', show, *ST* styleshow
SKRŌ	scrow
SLŌ	sloe, slow
SNŌ	besnow, snow
SŌ	how so, Curacao, oversow, resew, resow, Rousseau, sew, so, so-and-so, *so-so*, sow, trousseau, Tussaud
STŌ	bestow, stow
STRŌ	bestrow, strow
THŌ	although, *litho*, though
THRŌ	death throe, *downthrow*, overthrow, rethrow, throe, throw, *upthrow*
TŌ	*A* atiptoe, *B* bateau, *G* gateau, *H* hammertoe, *I* incognito, *K* cabatoe, couteau, *M* manito, manteau, mistletoe, *P* paletot, *potato*, portmanteau, *PL* plateau, *SH* chateau, *T* tick-tack-toe, timbertoe, *tomato*, *tiptoe*, toe, tow, *U* undertow, *W* Watteau
TRŌ	de trop, trow
WŌ	wo, woe
YŌ	imbroglio, intaglio, maillot, seraglio, *yoyo*
ZŌ	dzo

Ô

Ô	aw, awe, overawe
BÔ	usquebaugh
BRÔ	braw
CHÔ	chaw
DÔ	dauw, daw, *jackdaw, landau*
DRÔ	draw, overdraw, redraw, undraw, withdraw
FLÔ	flaw
FÔ	faugh, guffaw
GÔ	gaw, *gewgaw*
HÔ	heehaw, haw, hawhaw
JÔ	jaw, *flapjaw, crackjaw, lockjaw, underjaw*

KLÔ	*dew-claw*, clappermaclaw, claw, crab claw, lobster claw
KÔ	caw, macaw
KRÔ	craw
LÔ	*B* by-law, *BR* brother-in-law, *D* daughter-in-law, *F* father-in-law, *I* in-law, *L* law, *M* mother-in-law, *O* outlaw, *P* pilau, pilaw, *S* sister-in-law, son-in-law, *SK* scofflaw
MÔ	maw
NÔ	begnaw, mackinaw, gnaw, naw
PÔ	*foxpaw, forepaw, papaw,* paw, *pawpaw, southpaw*
RÔ	hurrah, raw
SHÔ	*kickshaw, cumshaw, rickshaw,* pshaw, Shaw, scrimshaw, wappenschaw
SKÔ	scaw
SKWÔ	squaw
SLÔ	cole slaw, overslaugh, slaw
SMÔ	sma'
SÔ	Arkansas, *bowsaw, bucksaw,* buzz saw, *chainsaw,* chickasaw, Chickasaw, foresaw, *hacksaw, handsaw, whipsaw, jigsaw,* oversaw, saw, seesaw
SPÔ	spa
STRÔ	*bedstraw,* windlestraw, straw
TÔ	tau, taw, Wichita
THÔ	thaw
THRÔ	thraw
WÔ	williwaw, waw
YÔ	yaw

ŌB

ŌB	aube
DŌB	daube
FŌB	Anglophobe, aerophobe, demophobe, photofobe, Francophobe, Germanophobe, Negrophobe, Russophobe (etc.)
GLŌB	englobe, globe, conglobe, 'round the globe
JŌB	Job
KRŌB	*microbe*
LŌB	*earlobe,* lobe
PRŌB	probe, reprobe, unprobe
RŌB	aerobe, *bathrobe,* disrobe, enrobe, rerobe, robe, unrobe, *wardrobe*
STRŌB	strobe

ÔB

DÔB	bedaub, daub, redaub
GÔB	gaub
WÔB	nawab

OB

BLOB	blob
BOB	bob, earbob, cabob, nabob, shishkabob, skibob, thingumabob, thingumbob
BROB	brob
FOB	fob, *watchfob*
GLOB	glob
GOB	gob
HOB	hob
JOB	job
KOB	*kincob,* cob, kob, *corncob*
KWOB	quab
LOB	lob
MOB	demob, mob
NOB	hob-and-nob, *hobnob,* knob, nob
ROB	*carob,* rob
SKOB	scob
SKWOB	squab
SLOB	slob
SNOB	snob
SOB	sob
STOB	stob
SWOB	swab
THROB	athrob, *heartthrob,* throb
YOB	yob

OBZ

BOBZ	ods bobs
GLOBZ	globs
GOBZ	gobs
SKOBZ	scobs

(See **OB,** add -*s* where appropriate.)

ŌCH

BRŌCH	abroach, broach, brooch
KŌCH	encoach, coach, *mailcoach,* motorcoach, *slowcoach,* stagecoach
KRŌCH	encroach, croche
LŌCH	loach
PŌCH	poach
PRŌCH	approach, reproach, self-reproach
RŌCH	caroche, *cockroach,* roach
SNŌCH	snoach

ÔCH

BÔCH	debauch
NÔCH	nautch, pootly-nauch
WÔCH	anchor watch, *deathwatch, dogwatch,* harbor watch, larboard watch, night watch, outwatch, starboard watch, watch

OCH

BLOCH	blotch
BOCH	botch
GOCH	gotch
HOCH	hotch
KROCH	crotch
NOCH	notch, topnotch
POCH	*hotchpotch*
ROCH	rotch, rotche
SKOCH	*hopscotch,* scotch, Scotch
SPLOCH	splotch
SWOCH	swatch
WOCH	death watch, digital watch, *dogwatch, nightwatch,* overwatch, *wristwatch, stopwatch,* watch

ŌCHT

BRŌCHT	broached

(See **ŌCH,** add *-ed* where appropriate.)

ÔCHT

BÔCHT	debauched

(See **ÔCH,** add *-ed* where appropriate.)

OCHT

BLOTCHT	blotched

(See **OCH,** add *-ed* where appropriate.)

ŌD

ŌD	ode, ohed, owed, unowed
BŌD	abode, bode, forebode
GŌD	goad
HŌD	hoed
KŌD	area code, decode, encode, genetic code,

code, Morse code, postal code, zip code

LŌD	*B boatload, FR freeload, WH whipload, K carload, L* load, lode, *O* overload, *P payload, R* reload, *SH shipload, TR truckload U* unload, *W* workload
MŌD	a la mode, alamode, discommode, incommode, commode, mode
NŌD	*anode,* antinode, internode, node, palinode, staminode
PLŌD	explode, implode
PŌD	antipode, *epode,* hemipode, lycopode, megapode
RŌD	*byroad,* bridle road, erode, high road, *highroad, inroad,* corrode, low road, middle-of-the-road, Nesselrode, *railroad,* road, rode
SHŌD	shoad, shode, showed
SŌD	episode, resewed, resowed, sewed, sowed
SPŌD	spode
STŌD	bestowed, stowed, rebestowed, restowed, unbestowed, unstowed
STRŌD	bestrode, strode
THŌD	hydathode
TŌD	horned toad, nematode, pigeon-toed, retoed, retowed, toad, toed, towed, trematode, untoed
WŌD	woad
ZŌD	episode

(See **Ō,** add *-d* or *-ed* where appropriate.)

ÔD

ÔD	awed, over-awed, unawed
BÔD	baud, bawd, kilobaud
BRÔD	abroad, broad
FRÔD	defraud, fraud
GÔD	gaud
JÔD	glass-jawed, iron-jawed, steel-jawed, water-jawed
LÔD	belaud, laud, relaud
MÔD	maud
PLÔD	applaud, reapplaud
RÔD	maraud
YÔD	yaud, yauld

(See **Ô,** add *-ed* where appropriate.)

OD

OD	Hesiod, od, Od, odd
BOD	bod, Ichabod
GOD	demigod, god, God, river god, sea god
HOD	hod
KLOD	clod
KOD	Cape Cod, cod, *lingcod,* ostracod, *tomcod*
KWOD	quod
MOD	mod
NOD	*nid-nod,* nod
PLOD	plod
POD	*A* amphipod, anglepod, anthropod, arthropod, *BR* brachiopod, branchiopod, *D* decapod, diplopod, *G* gastropod, *H* hexapod, *K* chenopod, cheetopod, chilopod, copepod, *L* landing pod, *M* megapod, *O* octopod, ornithopod, *P* peapod, pod, polypod, *PL* platypod, *R* rhizopod, *S* cephalopod, sauropod, pseudopod, *SK* scaphopod, *T* pteropod, tetrapod, tylopod, *TH* theropod, *Y* unipod
PROD	prod, reprod
ROD	Aaron's rod, divining rod, emerod, goldenrod, *hotrod,* curling rod, *Nimrod,* piston rod, *pushrod, ramrod,* rod
SHOD	dry-shod, reshod, roughshod, shod, *slipshod,* unshod
SKROD	scrod
SKWOD	squad
SNOD	snod
SOD	sod
TOD	tod
TROD	retrod, trod, untrod
VOD	eisteddfod
WOD	*tightwad,* wad, wod

ŌDZ

RŌDZ	Rhodes

(See **ŌD,** add *-s* where appropriate.)

ODZ

ODZ	emerods, odds

(See **OD,** add *-s* where appropriate.)

ŌF

ŌF	oaf
GŌF	goaf
KŌF	koph, qoph

ROYAL LAP-YAP

By Louis' side in royal tumbril,
How woefully his lapdog wailed!—
Not for the King to be beheaded,
But for the Dog to be curtailed.

LŌF	*breadloaf,* half a loaf, quarterloaf, loaf, sugarloaf
STRŌF	monostrophe
TŌF	toph
TRŌF	limitrophe

ÔF

CHÔF	Gorbachev, Khrushchev
KÔF	*chincough,* whooping cough, cough, Nabakov, Rimsky-Korsakov
MÔF	maugh
NÔF	Romanov
TÔF	Molotov
TRÔF	trough

OF

OF	*brush-off, cast-off, kick-off,* kick off, off, *rip-off,* rip off, *send-off, takeoff, wave-off*
DOF	doff
GLOF	glof
GOF	goff, golf
KOF	coff
KWOF	quaff
NOF	gnoff, Rachmaninoff, Stroganoff
PROF	prof
SHROF	shroff
SKOF	scoff
SOF	bibliosoph, philosoph, soph
TOF	toff

OFT

OFT	oft
KROFT	croft, undercroft
LOFT	aloft, *hayloft, cockloft,* loft

SOFT	soft
TOFT	toft

(See **OF,** add *-ed* where appropriate.)

ŌG

BŌG	bogue, disembogue
BRŌG	brogue
DRŌG	drogh, drogue
LŌG	collogue
RŌG	pirogue, prorogue, rogue
SHŌG	pishogue
THŌG	kitthoge
TŌG	togue
TRŌG	trogue
VŌG	vogue

ÔG

MÔG	maug
SHÔG	*pishaug*

OG

OG	Og
BOG	bog, embog
BROG	brog
CHOG	Patchogue
DOG	attack-dog, *bird-dog, bulldog,* dog, *fog-dog, fire-dog, hangdog,* hot dog, hound dog, coach dog, mad dog, police dog, prairie dog, *seadog,* sun dog, *sheepdog,* underdog, *watchdog* (etc.)
FLOG	flog, reflog
FOG	befog, defog, fog, megafog, peasoup fog, pettifog
FROG	*bullfrog,* frog, *leapfrog*
GLOG	glogg
GOG	*A* agog, *D* demagogue, *E* emmenagogue, *F* physagogue, *FL* phlegmagogue, *G* galactagogue, gog, Gog, Gog and Magog, Gogmagog, *goosegog, H* haemagogue, hydragogue, holagogue, *L* logogogue, *M Magog,* mystagogue, *O* osmagogue, *P* pedagogue, *S* sialagogue, synagogue, *Z* xenagogue
GROG	grog
HOG	*groundhog, hedgehog,* hog, *quahog,* road hog,

	sandhog, seahog, shearhog, warthog
JOG	jog
KLOG	clog, reclog, unclog
KOG	cog, incog
KWOG	quag
LOG	*A* analogue, apologue, *B* backlog, *D* decalogue, dialogue, duologue, *E* eclogue, epilogue, *F* philologue, *GR* grammalogue, *H* homologue, horologue, *K* catalogue, *L* Lincoln log, log, *loglog, M* melologue, myriologue, *N* necrologue, *P* putlog, *PR* prologue, *S* sinologue, *T* Tagalog, *TH* theologue, *TR* travelogue, trialogue
MOG	mog
NOG	*eggnog, crannog,* nog
POG	pogge
PROG	prog
SHOG	shog
SKROG	scrog
SLOG	footslog, slog
SMOG	smog
SNOG	snog
SOG	sog
TOG	*tautog,* tog
TROG	trog
WOG	golliwog, polliwog, wog

OGD

BOGD	bogged

(See **OG,** add *-ged* where appropriate.)

OI

OI	oi, oy
BOI	*A* attaboy, altar boy, *B* batboy, boy, buoy, *bellboy, bellbuoy,* ball boy, *BR* breeches buoy, *CH* charity boy, *D dayboy, doughboy, footboy, H* highboy, *hautboy, hallboy, houseboy, HW* whistlebuoy, *K carboy, callboy,* cowboy, *KW choirboy, L liftboy, linkboy,* loblolly boy, *lowboy, M* maccaboy, mama's boy, *messboy, O* hautboy, oh boy, *P pageboy,* paperboy,

	postboy, potboy, PL playboy, plowboy, S sonobuoy, SK schoolboy, ST stableboy, T tallboy, tomboy, Y yellowboy
CHOI	bok choy, *pakchoi*
FOY	foy
GOI	goi, goy
HOI	ahoy, hobberdehoy, hobble-de-hoy, hoy
JOI	enjoy, joy, *killjoy,* montjoy, overjoy
KLOI	cloy
KOI	decoy, coy, koi
KWOI	Iroquois
LOI	alloy, hoi polloi, kumbaloi, loy, permalloy, saveloy
MOI	moy
NOI	annoy, Hanoi, Illinois
PLOI	deploy, employ, ploy, redeploy, reemploy
POI	avoirdupois, charpoi, poi, *sepoy, teapoy*
ROI	corduroy, Rob Roy, viceroy
SOI	paduasoy, soy
STOI	*Tolstoi*
STROI	destroy, search-and-destroy, stroy
TOI	toy
TROI	troy, Troy
VOI	*envoy,* convoy, cunjevoi, lenvoi, savoy, Savoy, travois, travoy
ZOI	*borzoi*

OID

OID	blennioid, gobioid, histioid, *hyoid,* ichthyoid, cardioid, ophioid, *ooid,* osteoid, *pyoid,* scorpioid, *zooid*
BOID	amoeboid, buoyed, *globoid, cuboid,* rebuoyed, *rhomboid,* scaraboid, *stromboid,* unbuoyed
BROID	*fibroid, lambroid, scombroid*
DOID	*gadoid, lambdoid,* pyramidoid
DROID	*android, dendroid, octahedroid, polyhedroid, salamandroid, cylindroid, tetrahedroid*
FOID	*didelphoid, lymphoid, paratyphoid, scaphoid, typhoid, xiphoid*
FROID	Freud

GOID	algoid, fungoid, spongoid, tringoid
GROID	congroid, Negroid
JOID	enjoyed, joyed, overjoyed
KLOID	epicycloid, cloyed, cycloid, uncloyed
KOID	A alopecoid, anthracoid, D discoid, F fucoid, H helicoid, J gynaecoid, K coracoid, KR cricoid, L lumbricoid, M maskoid, mineralocorticoid, mycoid, mucoid, muscoid, O autacoid, P percoid, pinacoid, PL placoid, S sarcoid, cercopithecoid, cysticercoid, T toxicoid, TR trichoid, trochoid, V viscoid
KROID	cancroid, melanochroid, chancroid, xanthocroid
KWOID	equoid
LOID	A alkaloid, alloyed, amygdaloid, amyloid, D dactyloid, E encephaloid, eripsyloid, F phylloid, H haloid, haploid, hyaloid, hyperboloid, hypsiloid, K keloid, colloid, condyloid, coralloid, cotyloid, cuculoid, KR crystalloid, M meloid, metalloid, myeloid, myloid, mongoloid, N nautiloid, O omphaloid, opaloid, P paraboloid, petaloid, R reptiloid, S cephaloid, celluloid, sepaloid, sialoid, SK squaloid, ST styloid, T tabloid, tentaculoid, tuberculoid, TR triploid, U unalloyed, V varioloid, varicelloid, Z xyloid
MOID	dermoid, desmoid, entomoid, ethmoid, comoid, prismoid, sigmoid, cymoid, sphygmoid
NOID	A adenoid, actinoid, albuminoid, annoyed, arachnid, B balanoid, bioflavinoid, BL blennoid, DR drepanoid, E echinoid, G ganoid, GL glenoid, H hypnoid, hominoid, humanoid, J gelatinoid, K carotinoid, catenoid, conoid, coronoid, KL clenoid, KR crinoid, L lunoid, M melanoid, N nanoid, O ochinoid, P paranoid, PL

	platinoid, R resinoid, S salmonoid, cynoid, cyprinoid, solenoid, SF sphenoid, SK scorpaenoid, SP spinoid, T ctenoid, tetanoid
PLOID	deployed, *diploid,* employed, misemployed, ployed, redeployed, reemployed, underemployed, undeployed, unemployed, *euploid*
POID	anthropoid, *lipoid,* polypoid, *trappoid, vespoid*
ROID	A acaroid, amberoid, aneroid, ankyroid, antheroid, asteroid, B bacteroid, D diphtheroid, H hemorrhoid, hemispheroid, hysteroid, K chorioid, *choroid,* corticosteroid, L lamuroid, *laroid,* lemuroid, liparoid, M meteoroid, N nephroid, O ochroid, P parathyroid, polaroid, porphyroid, R rhinoceroid, roid, S saccharoid, sciuroid, SF *spheroid,* SK scleroid, SP spiroid, ST steroid, T pteroid, toroid, TH *theroid,* thyroid
SLOID	sloyd
SOID	*ellipsoid, emulsoid,* Caucasoid, sinusoid, *cissoid, suspensoid, schizoid, toxoid, ursoid*
STROID	destroyed, redestroyed, undestroyed
THOID	*acanthoid, lithoid,* ornithoid
TOID	A allantoid, *archtoid,* D *deltoid, dentoid,* E *elephantoid, epileptoid,* GR granitoid, H hematoid, herpetoid, *histoid,* K keratoid, L lacertoid, *lentoid,* M *mastoid,* N nematoid, O *odontoid,* P pachydermatoid, parotoid, PL planetoid, PR prismatoid, R rheumatoid, S cestoid, cystoid, T teratoid, toyed
TROID	*astroid, centroid*
VOID	avoid, devoid, convoyed, obovoid, *ovoid,* void
ZOID	*rhizoid,* trapezoid

(See **OI,** add *-ed* where appropriate.)

OIL

OIL	enoil, lubricating oil, oil, snake oil
BOIL	aboil, boil, *gumboil, hardboil, parboil*
BROIL	broil, disembroil, embroil, rebroil, reembroil
DOIL	langue d'oïl
FOIL	quatrefoil, counterfoil, multifoil, cinquefoil, silverfoil, tin foil, *trefoil*
GOIL	*gargoyle,* goyle
KOIL	accoil, coil, recoil, uncoil, upcoil
MOIL	moil, moyle, *turmoil*
NOIL	noil
POIL	poil
ROIL	roil
SOIL	assoil, soil, *subsoil, topsoil,* undersoil
SPOIL	despoil, spoil, unspoil
STROIL	stroil
TOIL	entoil, estoile, overtoil, toil, toile
VOIL	voile

OILD

OILD	oiled

(See **OIL,** add *-ed* where appropriate.)

OIN

FOIN	*sainfoin*
GOIN	Burgoyne
GROIN	groin, groyne
JOIN	*A* adjoin, *D* disjoin, *E* enjoin, *I* interjoin, *J* join, *K* conjoin, *M* misjoin, *R* rejoin, *S* sejoin, subjoin, surrejoin, unjoin
KOIN	coigne, coin, quoin, recoin
KWOIN	quoin
LOIN	eloign, loin, purloin, *sirloin,* tenderloin
MOIN	almoign, Des Moines, frankalmoigne
POIN	talapoin
SOIN	essoin

OIND

POIND	poind

(See **OIN,** add *-ed* where appropriate.)

OINT

OINT	adjoint, disjoint, dowel joint, hinge joint, hip joint, joint, conjoint, knee joint (etc.)
NOINT	anoint, reanoint
POINT	*B* ballpoint, *BL* bluepoint, *BR* breakpoint, brownie point, *CH* checkpoint, *D* disappoint, *DR* drypoint, *E* embonpoint, *G* gunpoint, *K* counterpoint, coverpoint, *M* midpoint, *N* needlepoint, *knickpoint, P* pinpoint, point, *pourpoint, R* reappoint, repoint, *S* silverpoint, *ST* standpoint, *V* viewpoint, *W* West Point

OINTZ

JOINTZ	disjoints, joints (etc.)

(See **OINT,** add *-s* where appropriate.)

OIS

CHOIS	choice, fielder's choice, first choice, Hobson's choice, last choice, pro-choice, second choice, *top-choice*
JOIS	James Joyce, rejoice
ROIS	Rolls-Royce
VOIS	*invoice,* outvoice, revoice, unvoice, voice

OIST

FOIST	foist, refoist
HOIST	hoist, rehoist
JOIST	joist, rejoiced, unrejoiced
MOIST	moist
VOIST	*loud-voiced, low-voiced, shrill-voiced,* unvoiced

OIT

DOIT	doit
DROIT	adroit, droit, maladroit
KOIT	dacoit, coit
KWOIT	quoit
MOIT	moit
PLOIT	exploit, reexploit
TOIT	hoity-toit, toit
TROIT	Detroit

OITS

KROITS	hakenkreuz
KWOITS	quoits

(See **OIT,** add *-s* where appropriate.)

OIZ

FROIZ	froise
NOIZ	erminois, noise
POIZ	avoirdupois, equipoise, counterpoise, poise

(See **OI,** add *-s* where appropriate.)

ŌJ

BŌJ	gamboge
DŌJ	doge
LŌJ	horologe, loge

OJ

BOJ	bodge
DOJ	dodge
HOJ	hodge
LOJ	dislodge, horologe, lodge, relodge, unlodge
MOJ	modge
PLOJ	plodge
POJ	*hodgepodge,* podge
SPLOJ	splodge
STOJ	stodge
WOJ	wodge

OJD

BOJD	bodged

(See **OJ,** add *-d* where appropriate.)

ŌK

ŌK	black oak, British oak, evergreen oak, holm oak, white oak, English oak, oak, oke, pickled oak, pin oak, post oak, red oak, scrub oak (etc.)
BLŌK	bloke
BRŌK	broke, dead broke, go for broke, outbroke, unbroke, upbroke
CHŌK	artichoke, choke
DŌK	doke, okeydoke
FŌK	folk, gentlefolk, *kinfolk, kinsfolk,* countryfolk,

	little folk, *menfolk,*
	seafolk, townfolk,
	townsfolk, tradesfolk,
	womenfolk, workfolk
HŌK	hoke
JŌK	joke
KLŌK	cloak, mourning cloak,
	recloak, uncloak
KŌK	decoke, coak, coke
KRŌK	croak
LŌK	loke
MŌK	moch, moke
NŌK	Roanoke
PŌK	mopoke, pig-in-a-poke,
	poke, *shitepoke, slowpoke*
RŌK	baroque, roque
SLŌK	sloke
SMŌK	smoke, besmoke, smoke
SŌK	asoak, soak, soke
SPŌK	bespoke, forespoke,
	forspoke, respoke, spoke,
	unspoke
STŌK	stoke
STRŌK	*B backstroke, BR*
	breaststroke, D
	deathstroke, H
	handstroke, heartstroke,
	K keystroke,
	counterstroke, *M*
	masterstroke, *O*
	overstroke, *S sidestroke,*
	sunstroke, STR stroke, *TH*
	thunderstroke, *U*
	understroke, upstroke
TŌK	toke, toque
TRŌK	troke
VŌK	equivoke, equivoque,
	evoke, invoke, convoke,
	provoke, revoke
WŌK	awoke, rewoke, woke
YŌK	reyoke, unyoke, yoke,
	yolk

ÔK

ÔK	auk, awk
BÔK	balk, baulk
CHÔK	chalk
DÔK	dawk
GÔK	gawk, Van Gogh
HÔK	fish hawk, *goshawk,*
	hawk, *Mohawk,*
	newshawk, nighthawk,
	sparrow hawk,
	winklehawk (etc.)
JÔK	jauk
KÔK	calk
KWÔK	quawk
LÔK	lawk
MÔK	maugh, mawk
PÔK	pawk

RÔK	baroque
SKWÔK	squawk
STÔK	*beanstalk, leafstalk,*
	cornstalk, stalk
TÔK	baby-talk, back talk,
	black-talk, girl-talk,
	crosss talk, *man-talk,*
	man-to-man talk,
	shoptalk, table-talk, talk,
	woman-talk
WÔK	*boardwalk, jaywalk,*
	cakewalk, catwalk,
	crosswalk, outwalk,
	overwalk, ropewalk,
	sheepwalk, sidewalk,
	sleepwalk, spacewalk,
	walk

OK

OK	Antioch, och
BLOK	auction block, bloc,
	block, *breechblock,*
	butcher block,
	chockablock, en bloc,
	roadblock, city block,
	stumbling block, unblock
BOK	*blesbok, blaubok,* bock,
	bontebok, *grysbok,*
	gemsbok, klipbok,
	rhebok, sjambok,
	springbok, steinbok
BROK	broch, brock
CHOK	chock, *forechock*
DOK	*burdock,* doc, dock,
	langue d'oc, Medoc,
	spatterdock, undock
FLOK	flock
FROK	defrock, frock, unfrock
GOK	Van Gogh
GROK	grok
HOK	ad hoc, *ham-hock,* hock,
	hollyhock, *Mohock*
JOK	jock
KLOK	eight-day clock,
	biological clock, body
	clock, clock
KOK	*A acock, angekok, B*
	Bangkok, bibcock, billy
	cock, ball cock, *BL*
	blackcock, G gamecock,
	gocock, H half-cock,
	haycock, K cock, *M*
	moorcock, P peacock,
	petcock, pinchcock,
	poppycock, *PR princock,*
	S seacock, SH shittlecock,
	shuttlecock, *SP*
	spatchcock, spitchcock,
	ST stopcock, T
	turkeycock, *turncock, W*
	weathercock, *woodcock*

KROK	crock
LOK	*A airlock, B* belock, *CH*
	charlock, D daglock,
	deadlock, *E elflock, F*
	fetlock, fetterlock,
	firelock, forelock, FL
	flintlock, G gavelock,
	gunlock, H havelock,
	headlock, hemlock, *I*
	interlock, *L loch,* lock,
	lough, *lovelock, M*
	Moloch, O oarlock, P
	padlock, percussion lock,
	picklock, R relock,
	wristlock, rowlock, SH
	Sherlock, Shylock, U
	unlock, *W wedlock, warlock*
MOK	amok, bemock, moch,
	mock
NOK	*monadnock, knock,* nock
PLOK	plock
POK	*kapok,* pock, *yapok*
ROK	*A acid rock, B bedrock, H*
	hard rock, *L lavarock,*
	Little Rock, *P* Painted
	Rock, punk rock, *R*
	ragarock, rimrock, roc,
	rock, *SH shamrock, TR*
	traprock, W weeping rock
SHLOK	schlock
SHOK	*foreshock,* shock
SMOK	smock
SOK	soc, sock, *windsock*
STOK	*A alpenstock, B bitstock,*
	BL bloodstock, D
	diestock, DR drillstock, G
	gapingstock, *HW*
	whisperstock, *L*
	laughingstock, linstock,
	livestock, O overstock, *P*
	penstock, R restock,
	rootstock, ST stock, *T*
	tailstock, U understock,
	unstock
TOK	tick-tock, tock,
	Vladivostok
WOK	jabberwock, wok
YOK	yock

ŌKS

| **HŌKS** | hoax |
| **KŌKS** | coax |

(See **ŌK**, add *-s* where appropriate.)

ÔKS

| **LÔKS** | lawks |

(See **ÔK,** add *-s* where appropriate.)

OKS

OKS	*musk-ox*, ox
BOKS	*A* abox, *B* ballot box, *bandbox*, box, *CH* chatterbox, *G* gearbox, gogglebox, *H* hatbox, horsebox, *I* idiot box, *icebox*, *J* jukebox, *KR* Christmas box, *L* loosebox, *M* matchbox, mailbox, *O* honor box, *P* paddlebox, *paintbox*, *pillbox*, pillar box, *postbox*, powder box, *S* saltbox, signal box, soapbox, soundbox, *SH* shooting box, *SN* snuffbox, *STR strongbox*, *T* tinderbox, *W workbox*
DOKS	*boondocks*, philodox, heterodox, homodox, orthodox, paradox, *redox*, unorthodox
FLOKS	phlox
FOKS	fox, outfox
GROKS	groks
KOKS	cox, *princox*
LOKS	bladderlocks, Goldilocks, locks, lox
NOKS	equinox, Fort Knox, hard knocks, knocks, Nox
POKS	chickenpox, *cowpox*, pox, *smallpox*, *swinepox*
SOKS	socks, sox
TOKS	detox
VOKS	vox

(See **OK**, add *-s* where appropriate.)

ŌKT

CHŌKT	choked

(See **Ō K**, add *-d* where appropriate.)

OKT

GROKT	grokked
KOKT	decoct, concoct, recoct

(See **OK**, add *-ed* where appropriate.)

ŌL

ŌL	*A* apiole, ariole, arteriole, *BR* bronchiole, *D* dariole, *F* foliole, *GL* gloriole, glory 'ole, *K* cabriole, capriole, cariole, *KR* creole, Creole, *O* ol', 'ole, aureole, oriole, ostiole, *P* petiole, *S* centriole, *SH* Sheol, *V* vacuole, variole
BŌL	*A* amphibole, *B* bole, boll, bowl, *E* embowl, *F* fishbowl, *K* carambole, Cotton Bowl, *O* obole, *P* punchbowl, *R* rocambole, Rose Bowl, *S* Super Bowl, *SH* Sugar Bowl (etc.), *SW* swillbowl, *W* wassail bowl
DŌL	dhole, dole, farandole, *indole*, girandole, condole
DRŌL	droll
FŌL	foal
GŌL	de Gaulle, goal, segol
HŌL	*A* armhole, *B* borehole, bunghole, buttonhole, *BL* black hole, blowhole, *F* foxhole, *FR* frijol, *GL* gloryhole, *H* heart-whole, hell-whole, hole, whole, eyehole, *K* keyhole, cubbyhole, *L* loophole, *M* manhole, Mohole, *N* kneehole, knothole, *O* augur hole, *P* peephole, personhole, pigeonhole, pinhole, porthole, pothole, *SK* scupperhole, *SW* swimminghole, *T* tophole, *U* unwhole
JŌL	cajole, jole
KŌL	arvicole, bricole, charcoal, caracole, clearcole, coal, cole, kohl, latebricole, pratincole
MŌL	mole, septimole
NŌL	jobbernowl, knoll, Seminole
NYŌL	guignol, carmagnole, croquignole
PŌL	*B* bargepole, beanpole, bibliopole, *E* edipol, *F* fishing pole, *FL flagpole*, *K* catchpole, *M* Maypole, metropole, *P* pole, Pole, poll, *R* rantipole, *ridgepole*, *T* tadpole, telephone pole
ROL	*A* azarole, *B* banderole, *bankroll*, barcarole, *bedroll*, *E* enroll, escarole, *F* fumarole, furole, fusarole, *J* jellyroll, *K* casserole, *L* logroll, *M* multirole, *P* parole, *payroll*, PR profiterole, *R* reroll, rigamarole, rigmarole, rock-and-roll, role, roll, *SKW* squatarole, *U* unroll, uproll, *V* virole
SHŌL	shoal, shole
SKŌL	skoal
SKRŌL	enscroll, inscroll, scroll
SŌL	*A* anisole, *E* ensoul, *H* half-sole, *I* insole, insoul, *J* girasole, *K* camisole, console, *O* oversoul, *R* resole, rissole, *S* Seoul, sol, sole, soul, *T* turnsole, *U* unsole, unsoul
STŌL	stole
STRŌL	stroll
THŌL	thole
TŌL	extol, extoll, pistole, *sestole*, citole, sotol, tole, toll
TRŌL	decontrol, comptrol, control, patrol, recontrol, remote control, self-control, troll
VŌL	vole
YŌL	guignol, carmagnole, croquignole
ZŌL	thiazole

ÔL

ÔL	*BR* brad-awl, *FR* free-for-all, *H* hold-all, *HW* wherewithal, *K* catchall, carry-all, *M* Montreal, *O* all, all-in-all, awl, overall, *TH* therewithal, *W* withal
BÔL	*B* ball, bawl, *baseball*, basketball, *BL* blackball, *E* emery ball, *F fireball*, *football*, foul ball, *H* handball, hairball, highball, *I* eyeball, *K* cannonball, *M* masked ball, *meatball*, *mothball*, *N* netball, *O* oddball, *P* pinball, punchball, *R* wrecking-ball, *SKR screwball*, *SN* snowball, *V* volleyball
BRÔL	brawl
DRÔL	drawl
FÔL	*B* befall, *D downfall*, *E* evenfall, *F* fall, *footfall*, *FR freefall*, *K* catfall, *L* landfall, *N* nightfall, *O* overfall, *P* pitfall, *PR pratfall*, *R* rainfall, *SH*

	shortfall, SN *snowfall,* W waterfall, *windfall*
GÔL	Bengal, glass gall, gall, Gaul, *nutgall, spurgall, windgall*
HÔL	A alcohol, B banquet hall, D dance hall, G gasohol, *guildhall,* H hall, haul, HW Whitehall, J judgment hall, K keelhaul, O overhaul, T *townhall*
KÔL	*birdcall, catcall,* call, caul, miscall, nudicaul, protocol, recall, trumpet call
KRÔL	crawl, kraal
MÔL	bemaul, mall, maul
PÔL	appall, Nepal, pall, pawl, St. Paul
SHÔL	shawl
SKÔL	scall
SKRÔL	scrawl
SKWÔL	squall
SMÔL	small
SÔL	Saul, tattersall
SPÔL	spall, spawl
SPRÔL	sprawl, urban sprawl
STÔL	*bookstall, boxstall,* fingerstall, *footstall,* forestall, install, reinstall, stall, *thumbstall*
THRÔL	bethrall, disenthrall, enthrall, thrall
TÔL	atoll, tall
TRÔL	trawl
VÔL	devall
WÔL	Berlin wall, Chinese wall, Hadrian's wall, caterwaul, *Cornwall,* off the wall, sea wall, *stonewall,* wall
YÔL	yawl

OL

OL	vitriol
DOL	baby doll, dol, doll, rag doll
GOL	Bengal
HOL	alcohol
KOL	col, guaiacol, protocol
LOL	loll, trollol
MOL	gun moll, moll
NOL	ethanol, mestranol, methanol, eugenol
POL	Interpol, Nepal, pol, poll
ROL	folderol
SOL	aerosol, entresol, girasol, *consol,* creosol, lithosol, parasol, planosol, plasmasol, regosol, sol
TOL	amatol, xylotol

ŌLD

ŌLD	*age-old,* old
BŌLD	bold, bowled, *kobold,* overbold, overbowled, semibold
FŌLD	A *eightfold,* B *bifold, billfold,* BL *blindfold,* E enfold, F *fivefold,* foaled, fold, *fourfold,* G *gatefold,* H *hundredfold,* I *infold,* interfold, M *manifold, multifold,* N *ninefold,* R refoaled, refold, S *centerfold, sevenfold, sixfold,* SH *sheepfold,* T *tenfold, twofold,* TH thousandfold, *threefold* (etc.), U unfold
GŌLD	Acapulco gold, fool's gold, gold, good as gold, marigold, spun gold
HŌLD	A *afterhold, ahold,* anchor hold, B behold, F *foothold,* FR *freehold,* H *handhold,* hold, *household,* K *copyhold,* L *leasehold,* O *on hold,* P pigeonholed, ST *stokehold,* STR *stranglehold, stronghold,* T *to have and to hold, toehold,* THR *threshold,* U uphold, W withhold
JŌLD	cajoled
KŌLD	acold, ice cold, coaled, cold, stone cold
MŌLD	bullet mold, butter mold, button mold, leaf mold, mold, mould, pudding mold, remold, remould, salad mold
PŌLD	polled, repolled, unpolled
RŌLD	paroled, reparoled, rolled, rerolled, unparoled, unrolled
SHŌLD	shoaled
SKŌLD	rescold, reskoaled, scold, skoaled
SŌLD	F *full-soled,* H *half-soled, high-souled,* KW *quarter-soled,* O *oversold,* S sold, soled, souled, U *undersouled,* unsold, unsoled, unsouled
STŌLD	sable-stoled, stoled
TŌLD	foretold, retold, told, tolled, *twice-told,* untold, untolled
WŌLD	wold

(See ŌL, add *-d* or *-ed* where appropriate.)

ÔLD

ÔLD	auld
BÔLD	bald, *kobold, piebald, skewballed*
HÔLD	hauled, close-hauled, rehauled, unhauled
SKÔLD	rescald, scald

(See ÔL, add *-ed* where appropriate.)

ÔLS

FÔLS	defaults, false, faults
HÔLS	halse, halts
VÔLS	valse, envaults, vaults
SÔLS	assaults, old salts, salts, somersaults
WÔLS	waltz
ZÔLS	exalts

ŌLT

BŌLT	B bolt, D *deadbolt,* F *fishbolt,* I *eyebolt,* K *kingbolt,* L lightning bolt, R rebolt, *ringbolt, wringbolt,* SH *shacklebolt,* TH thunderbolt, U unbolt
DŌLT	dolt
HŌLT	holt
JŌLT	jolt
KŌLT	colt, Colt, wood colt
MŌLT	molt, moult
PŌLT	poult
SMŌLT	smolt
VŌLT	demivolt, lavolt, millivolt, revolt, teravolt, volt

ÔLT

BÔLT	Balt, *cobalt*
FÔLT	*asphalt,* default, fault, *no-fault*
GÔLT	gault
HÔLT	halt, *stringhalt*
MÔLT	malt
SMÔLT	smalt
SÔLT	assault, *basalt,* oxysalt, old salt, salt, sea salt, somersault, pseudosalt
SPÔLT	spalt
VÔLT	envault, vault
ZÔLT	exalt

ÔLTS

FÔLTS	false
VÔLTS	valse
WÔLTS	waltz

(See **ÔLT,** add -s where appropriate.)

OLV

SOLV	absolve, dissolve, resolve, solve, unsolve
VOLV	devolve, evolve, intervolve, involve, convolve, obvolve, revolve, circumvolve
ZOLV	absolve, dissolve, exolve, resolve

OLVD

(See **OLV,** add -d where appropriate.)

ŌM

ŌM	oam, ohm, om
BŌM	abohm, *Beerbohm*
BRŌM	brome
DŌM	astrodrome, dom, dome, endome, *radome*, semidome, Teapot Dome
DRŌM	aerodrome, acrodrome, aquadrome, hippodrome, cosmodrome, autodrome, palindrome, *syndrome*, velodrome
FŌM	afoam, befoam, foam, *seafoam*
GLŌM	gloam, glome
HŌM	animal home, at home, harvest home, heaume, holm, home, motor home, nobody home, tumblehome
KLŌM	clomb
KŌM	*backcomb*, honeycomb, catacomb, *cockscomb*, *coxcomb*, comb, currycomb
KRŌM	heliochrome, haemochrome, chrome, metallochrome, monochrome, polychrome, urochrome
LŌM	loam, Salome, shalom
MŌM	mome
NŌM	gastronome, genome, gnome, metronome, Nome

PŌM	pome
RŌM	roam, rom, Rome
SLŌM	sloam
SŌM	endosome, chromosome, leptosome, microsome, monosome, autosome, ribosome, centrosome, schistosome
STŌM	monostome, cyclostome
STRŌM	*brostrome*
TŌM	apotome, dermatome, hecatomb, macrotome, microtome, tome

ÔM

ÔM	aum
DÔM	prudhomme
GÔM	gaum
HÔM	haulm
MÔM	imaum, Maugham
SHÔM	shawm

OM

OM	axiom, om
BOM	atom bomb, bomb, *firebomb*, gas bomb, h-bomb, hydrogen bomb, car bomb, laser bomb, mail bomb, neutron bomb, time bomb
DOM	dom, domn
FROM	from, therefrom, wherefrom
GLOM	glom
GROM	pogrom
GWOM	Guam
HOM	hom
KOM	intercom, non-com, *syncom*, *sit-com*
KWOM	qualm
LOM	coulomb
MOM	cardimom, mam, mom
PLOM	aplomb
POM	pom, *pompom*
PROM	prom
ROM	rhomb
STROM	*maelstrom*, stromb
WOM	*wigwam*

(See **ÄM**)

OMB

OMB	chiliomb
ROMB	rhomb
STROMB	stromb

ŌMD

DŌMD	domed, endomed
FŌMD	befoamed, enfoamed, foamed
KŌMD	combed, recombed, uncombed
RŌMD	roamed

OMD

BOMD	bombed
GLOMD	glommed

OMP

CHOMP	chomp
KLOMP	clomp
KOMP	comp
POMP	pomp
ROMP	romp
STOMP	stomp
SWOMP	swamp
TROMP	tromp, trompe

OMPT

KOMPT	compt
PROMPT	prompt
SWOMPT	swamped

(See **OMP,** add ed where appropriate.)

ŌN

ŌN	disown, own, reown
BLŌN	blown, *flyblown, fresh-blown, full-blown, outblown,* overblown, unblown, weatherblown, *windblown*
BŌN	A aitchbone, anklebone, B backbone, bellibone, Beaune, bone, BR breastbone, CH cheekbone, F fishbone, funnybone, H herringbone, hipbone, HW whalebone, I icebone, J jawbone, K carbon, collarbone, cuttlebone, M marrowbone, N knucklebone, SH shinbone, TH thighbone, TR trombone, W wishbone

DŌN condone, methadone, recondone, uncondone

DRŌN drone, ladrone, padrone

FLŌN flown, *high-flown*, reflown, unflown

FŌN *A* allophone, Anglophone, *D* Dictaphone, *E earphone*, electrophone, *F* phone, *FR* Francophone, *GR* graphophone, gramophone, *H headphone*, heckelphone, hydrophone, homophone, *I* interphone, *K* chordophone, *M* megaphone, mellophone, microphone, *O* audiphone, *P* pyrophone, polyphone, *R* radiophone, *S* saxophone, sousaphone, *V* vibraphone, vitaphone, *Y* euphone, *Z* xylophone

GŌN epigone

GRŌN begroan, *full-grown, grass-grown*, groan, grown, *half-grown, ingrown, moss-grown*, overgrown, undergrown, ungrown

HŌN hone

KLŌN *anticyclone*, clone, *cyclone*

KŌN cone, ochone, rincon, silicone

KRŌN crone

LŌN alone, Boulogne, cologne, Cologne, colon, loan, lone, eau de cologne, prednisolone, reloan

MŌN bemoan, pheromone, *hormone*, moan, mown, remown, unmown

NŌN butanone, foreknown, Ionone, known, none, rotenone, sine qua non, unbeknown, unforeknown, unknown

PŌN Abipon, depone, dispone, interpone, Capone, *cornpone*, pone, postpone, propone, repone

PRŌN accident-prone, dependency-prone, prone

RŌN aldosterone, androsterone, coumarone, progesterone, Rhone, roan, rone, chaperon, cicerone, testosterone, Tyrone

SHŌN foreshown, outshone, reshown, shone, shown, unshown

SKŌN scone

SŌN ecdysone, cortisone, prednisone, presewn, presown, resewn, resown, sewn, sone, sown, unsewn, unsown

STŌN *B* bilestone, birthstone, *BL* bloodstone, *BR brimstone, E* end stone, *F* philosopher's stone, foundation stone, *FL flagstone, FR* freestone, *G* gallstone, *GR* gravestone, grindstone, *H* hailstone, headstone, hearthstone, holystone, *HW* whetstone, *I* imposing stone, *J* gemstone, *K* keystone, cobblestone, *copestone*, cornerstone, *curbstone, KL* clingstone, *L limestone, loadstone, lodestone, M* milestone, millstone, moonstone, *R rhinestone*, rottenstone, *S sandstone, soapstone, ST* staddlestone, stone, *T tilestone*, toadstone, *tombstone*, touchstone, *TH* thunderstone (etc.)

THRŌN dethrone, enthrone, overthrown, rethrone, rethrown, throne, thrown, unthrone, unthrown

TŌN *A* acetone, atone, *B* barbitone, baritone, barytone, *D* dial tone, duotone, *E* ecotone, *F* phenobarbitone, *H halftone*, whole tone, *I* intone, isotone, *KW* quarter tone, *M* monotone, *O* overtone, *P peptone, S* sacaton, semitone, *T* tone, *two-tone, TR* tritone, *U* undertone

ZŌN *endzone*, enzone, *ozone*, zone

ÔN

ÔN awn

BÔN bawn

BRÔN brawn

DÔN dawn

DRÔN drawn, indrawn, overdrawn, redrawn, underdrawn, undrawn, withdrawn

FÔN faun, fawn, plafond

GÔN *bygone, foregone*, gone

KÔN leprechaun

LÔN lawn

PÔN impawn, pawn, repawn

PRÔN prawn

RÔN raun

THÔN omadhaun

SÔN sawn

THÔN omadhaun

TÔN quinton

YÔN yawn

ON

ON *A* Albion, alluvion, amphibion, Anacreon, *B* bion, *E* enchiridion, Endymion, *G* gabion, galleon, *H* halcyon, hanger-on, hangers-on, hereon, Hyperion, *HW* whereon, *K* campion, carry-on, carryings-on, *L* Laocoön, *M* melodeon, melodion, *N* Napoleon, *O* oblivion, on, *P* pantheon, *TH* thereon, walker-on

BON Audubon, bon, *bonbon*

DON *B* boustrophedon, *D* don, *GL* glyptodon, *I* iguanodon, *K* Corydon, *M* Macedon, mastodon, myrmidon, celadon, *SF* sphenadon, *ST* stegedon, *Y* Euroclydon

FON antiphon, Bellerophon, phon, harmoniphon, colophon, *chiffon, euphon*, Xenophon

FRON Neophron

GON *A* agone, *B* begone, *bygone, D* Dagon, decagon, dodecagon, doggone, *E* estragon, *F* foregone, *G* gone, *GL* glucagon, *H* hexagon, heptagon, *I* isogon, *M* martagon, *N* nonagon, *O* octagon, oxygon, Oregon, *P* paragon, parergon, pentagon, Pentagon, perigon, polygon, *PR* protagon, *S* Saigon, *T* tarragon, tetragon, trimetragon, *U* ucalegon, undecagon, undergone, *W* woebegone

JON demijohn, john, John, Littlejohn, Prester John

KON	*A archon, B basilicon, E* etymologicon, *H* harmonicon, helicon, Helicon, *I* idioticon, irenicon, *K* catholicon, con, khan, *L* lexicon, *M* melodicon, *O* onomasticon, opticon, orthicon, *P* panopticon, pantechnicon, *R* Rubicon, *S* sciopticon, silicon, synonymicon, *SH* chaconne, *ST* stereopticon, *T* technicon, *V* vidicon, *Y* Yukon		*K* cacemphaton, Canton, *KR* cretonne, crouton, *M* magneton, megaton, *O* automaton, *P* polysyndeton, *PR proton,* *W* won ton	**MOND**	beau monde, demimonde, Garamond, monde
				POND	fish pond, *millpond,* pond, skating pond
		TRON	anatron, balatron, *electron,* elytron, phytotron, *neutron,* positron, cyclotron, tevatron	**ROND**	rond, ronde
				SKOND	abscond
				SOND	dropsonde, radiosonde, sonde
		VON	elevon, von	**SPOND**	despond, correspond, respond
		WON	won	**WOND**	wand, *yardwand*
		YON	boeuf Bourguignon, filet mignon, sabayon, yon	**YOND**	beyond
KRON	omicron, pentacron			**ZOND**	zond
LON	*A* Avalon, *B* Babylon, *CH* chillon, *E* echelon, encephalon, epsilon, etalon, *G* gonfalon, *I* eidolon, *K* carillon, *M* mamelon, mesencephalon *P* papillon, petalon, *S* salon, Ceylon, *U* upsilon	**ZON**	amazon, Amazon, Barbizon, benison, borazon, cabezon, liaison, Luzon, orison		
				# ONG	
		(See also **ÄN**)			
				BONG	bong, billabong
		# ÔNCH		**CHONG**	*souchong*
				DONG	*dingdong,* dong, quandong
MON	etymon, hoot mon, kikumon, mon, Pergamon	**FLÔNCH**	flaunch	**FLONG**	flong
		HÔNCH	haunch	**FONG**	underfong
NON	*A* anon, argenon, *D* dies non, *G* guenon, gonfanon, *N ninon,* noumenon, *O* olecranon, organon, *P* Parthenon, perispomenon, *PR* prolegomenon, *S* sine qua non, *T* tympanon, *TH* theologoumenon, trimenon	**KRÔNCH**	craunch	**GONG**	*bogong, dugong,* gong, wobbegong
		LÔNCH	launch, relaunch, unlaunch	**JONG**	kurrajong, mah-jong
		PÔNCH	paunch	**KONG**	Hong Kong, King Kong, Viet Cong
		RÔNCH	raunch	**LONG**	*A* all along, along, *B* belong, *D daylong, E endlong,* ere long, *F* furlong, *H headlong, K kalong, kampong, L lifelong, livelong,* long, *N nightlong, O oblong,* overlong, *PR* prolong, *S sidelong,* so long, *SH* chaise longue
		STÔNCH	staunch		
		# ŌND			
		MŌND	beau monde, demimonde, haut monde, moaned, unmoaned		
				NONG	nong, scuppernong
PON	hereupon, whereupon, jupon, coupon, put upon, thereupon, upon	(See **ŌN,** add *-ed* where appropriate.)		**PONG**	*pingpong,* pong
				PRONG	prong
		# ÔND		**RONG**	barong, binturong, wrong, sarong
RON	*A* Acheron, aileron, *D* diatesseron, *E* ephemeron, enteron, *F* fanfaron, *H* hapteron, hexameron, hyperon, *I* interferon, *M* megaron, mesenteron, *N* nychthemoron, *neuron, O* Oberon, operon, *P* Percheron, *PR* prolegeron, *Z* xeromyron	**MÔND**	maund	**SHONG**	souchong
				SONG	aftersong, battle song, drinking song, evensong, cradlesong, love song, morning song, *plainsong, singsong,* song, undersong
		(See **ÔN,** add *-ed* where appropriate.)			
		# OND			
SHON	cabochon			**STRONG**	*headstrong,* strong
SKON	scone	**BLOND**	blond, blonde	**THONG**	*diphthong,* monophthong, thong, *triphthong*
SON	Alençon, parison, Tucson, venison	**BOND**	bond, James Bond, pair bond, vagabond		
				THRONG	throng
SWON	swan	**DOND**	donned	**TONG**	paktong, tong
THON	marathon, omadhaun, ornithon, telethon, trilithon	**FOND**	fond, overfond, plafond, underfond, unfond	**WONG**	currawong, *morwong,* wong
				YONG	foo yong
		FROND	frond		
TON	*A* abaton, *antiproton,* asyndeton, *B* baryton, baton, *F phaeton,* feuilleton, *H* hyperbaton,	**GOND**	paragoned, unparagoned	# ONGD	
		KOND	conned, seconde, unconned	**BONGD**	bonged
				(See **ONG,** add *-ed* where appropriate.)	

ONGK

BONGK	bonk
BRONGK	bronc
DONGK	zedonk
GONGK	gonk
HONGK	honk
KLONGK	clonk
KONGK	conch, conk, konk, *triconch*
KRONGK	cronk
KWONGK	quonk
PLONGK	plonk
SKWONGK	squonk
STONGK	stonk
TONGK	honky-tonk, tonk
ZONGK	zonk

ONGKS

BRONGKS	Bronx

(See **ONGK,** add *-s* where appropriate.)

ONGKT

ZONGKT	zonked

(See **ONGK,** add *-ed* where appropriate.)

ONS

BONS	bonce
FONS	fonts
NONS	nonce
PONS	ponce
SKONS	ensconce, sconce
SPONS	response

(See **ONT,** add *-s* where appropriate.)

ŌNT

DŌNT	don't
WŌNT	won't

ÔNT

DÔNT	daunt, undaunt
FLÔNT	flaunt, reflaunt
GÔNT	gaunt
HÔNT	haunt, rehaunt
JÔNT	jaunt
MÔNT	romaunt
TÔNT	ataunt, taunt
VÔNT	avaunt, vaunt
WÔNT	want

ONT

ONT	halobiont, symbiont
DONT	acrodont, mastodont, xanthodont
FONT	font
KWONT	quant
MONT	*Beaumont, Piedmont,* Vermont
PLONT	*diplont*
PONT	Hellespont, pont
WONT	want, wont
ZONT	*schizont*

ŌNZ

BŌNZ	bones, funnybones, *crossbones,* lazybones, rolling the bones, *sawbones*
JŌNZ	Davy Jones, jones
NŌNZ	nones

(See **ŌN,** add *-s* where appropriate.)

ONZ

BONZ	bonze
BRONZ	bronze
FONZ	fons
FRONZ	frons
GONZ	*bygones*
JONZ	St. John's, long johns
PONZ	pons

(See **ON,** add *-s* where appropriate.)

OO

OO	oo, ooh, *spreeuw,* toodle-oo
BLOO	blew, blue, *skyblue,* true-blue
BOO	*A* aboo, Abou, abu, *B baboo, babu,* bamboo, boo, *booboo,* bugaboo, *E* ynambu, *G* gamdeboo, *J* jigaboo, *K* caribou, *M* Malibu, marabou, *P* peekaboo, *T* taboo, tabu, *U* urabu, *Y* yabu, *Z zebu*
BROO	barley-broo, brew, broo, *Hebrew,* imbrue, witch's brew
CHOO	chew, choo-choo, eschew, catechu, kerchoo, *Manchu*
DOO	*A* ado, amadou, *B* billet-doux, CH chandoo, *D* derring-do, didgerydoo, do, *doo-doo,* fordo, *F* foredo, *H* hairdo, Hindu, howdy-do, *hoodoo,* honeydew, *hoodoo, J* jadu, *K* cockadoodledoo, kudu, *M* misdo, *O* outdo, overdo, *R* redo, residue, *SK* skiddoo, *T* teledu, toodledoo, to-do, twenty-three skidoo, *U* underdo, undo, *V voodoo, W* well-to-do
DROO	drew, withdrew
FLOO	flew, flu, flue
FOO	Dien Bien Phu, fou, phoo, *phoo-phoo,* Corfu, kung fu, mafoo, mafu, snafu, succes fou, *wamefu,* widdifow
FROO	*froufrou*
GLOO	glue, igloo, reglue, unglue
GOO	burgoo, goo, *goo-goo,* gout, ragout
GROO	grew, gru, grue, outgrew, overgrew
HOO	*A* ahoo, ahu, *B* ballyhoo, boo-hoo, *H* who, hoo-hoo, Who's Who, *T* to-whit-to-hoo, *W* wahoo, *Y* yahoo, yoo-hoo
HWOO	to-whit-to-whoo
JOO	acajou, ejoo, Ju, Jew, juju, kinkajou, sapajou
KLOO	clew, clue, unclue
KOO	*aku, baku,* bill and coo, bunraku, Daikoku, coo, coup, coochy-coo, *coocoo, cuckoo,* worricow
KROO	accrew, accrue, *aircrew,* ecru, crew, cru, motley crew, premier cru
LOO	*B baloo, G* gardyloo, gillygaloo, *H* halloo, *Honolulu,* hullabaloo, *I* igloo, *K* calalu, *L* lieu, loo, *looloo, lulu,* lulliloo, *O* ormolu, *P* pililoo, poilu, *S* skip to my Lou, *V* view halloo, *W* Waterloo, *Z Zulu*

NEW WORDS FOR AN OLD SAW

I love the girls who don't,
  I love the girls who do;
But best, the girls who say, "I don't . . .
  But maybe . . . just for you . . ."

MŌŌ — emu, imu, moo, moue, mu, *muumuu*, tinamou, *umu*

NŌŌ — *A* anew, *D* detinue, *E* entre nous, *F* foreknew, *H* hoochinoo, *I* ingenue, *J* genu, *K* canoe, *N* gnu, new, *P* parvenu, *R* revenue, *T* Tippecanoe, *V* Vishnu

PLŌŌ — plew

PŌŌ — *hoopoe, coypu, cockapoo,* napoo, poo, pooh, pooh-pooh, shampoo, shapoo

RŌŌ — *B* buckaroo, buroo, *G* garoo, gillaroo, guru, *J* jabiru, jackaroo, jackeroo, *K* kaberu, kangaroo, karroo, *L* loup-garou, *M* meadow rue, *Nehru, P* Peru, potoroo, *R* roo, roux, rue, *SW* switcheroo, *W* wallaroo, wanderoo

SHŌŌ — *F* fichu, *G* gumshoe, *H* horseshoe, *K* cachou, cashew, cashoo, *O* old shoe, overshoe, *SO* softshoe, *SH* chou, choux, shoe, shoo, *SN* snowshoe, *U* unshoe

SHRŌŌ — beshrew, shrew

SKRŌŌ — *airscrew, corkscrew,* screw, *thumbscrew,* unscrew, *woodscrew*

SLŌŌ — slew, sloo, slough, slue

SŌŌ — ensue, *jujitsu,* lasso, pursue, Sioux, sou, sue, *susu*

SPRŌŌ — sprew, sprue

STRŌŌ — bestrew, construe, misconstrue, overstrew, reconstrue, strew, strue, unconstrue

THRŌŌ — overthrew, see through, threw, through, wirrasthru

TŌŌ — *B* Bantu, battue, *E* et tu, *H* hereinto, *hereto,* hereunto, hitherto, *HW* whereinto, whereto, whereunto, *I impromptu, into,* in transitu, *J* Gentoo, *K* cockatoo, *L lean-to, M* manitou, *onto, P* passe partout, *S* set-to, surtout, *T* tattoo, Timbuctu, to, too, two, tutu, *TH* thereto, thereunto, thitherto, *U unto, V* virtu

TRŌŌ — true, untrue

VŌŌ — kivu, parlez-voo, rendezvous

WŌŌ — woo, woowoo, Wu

YŌŌ — bayou, *W,* gayyou, *IOU* Vayu, ewe, *U* yew, you

ZŌŌ — bazoo, Kalamazoo, cousu, kazoo, razoo, zoo, *zoozoo,* Zu

ZHŌŌ — bijou

(See Ū)

ŌŌB

BŌŌB — boob, haboob
DŌŌB — doob
JŌŌB — jube, *jujube*
LŌŌB — loob, lube
RŌŌB — hey Rube, rube

ŌŌCH

ŌŌCH — ooch
BRŌŌCH — brooch
HŌŌCH — hooch
KŌŌCH — hoochy-cooch
MŌŌCH — mooch, mouch, Scaramouch
PŌŌCH — pooch, putsch
SMŌŌCH — smooch

ŌŌD

BRŌŌD — abrood, brood
DŌŌD — dude, subdued
FŌŌD — food, *wholefood, seafood,* soul food
JŌŌD — St. Jude
KLŌŌD — exclude, include, conclude, occlude, preclude, seclude
KŌŌD — Likud
KRŌŌD — crude
LŌŌD — allude, delude, elude, illude, interlude, collude, Quaalude, 'lude
MŌŌD — almud, mood
NŌŌD — nude
PŌŌD — pood
PRŌŌD — prude
RŌŌD — rood, rude
SHŌŌD — shoed, shood
SHRŌŌD — shrewd
SLŌŌD — slewed
SNŌŌD — snood
SŌŌD — transude
TŌŌD — *A* altitude, amplitude, aptitude, asuetude, attitude, *B* beatitude, *D* decrepitude, definitude, desuetude, disquietude, dissimilitude, *E* exactitude, eptitude, *F* fortitude, *GR* gratitude, gravitude, *H* habitude, hebetude, *I* inaptitude, inexactitude, ineptitude, infinitude, ingratitude, inquietude, incertitude, insuetude, *K* consuetude, correctitude, *KR* crassitude, *KW* quietude, *L* lassitude, latitude, lentitude, lippitude, longitude, *M* magnitude, mansuetude, mollitude, multitude, *N* necessitude, nigritude, *O* omnitude, *P* pinguitude, pulchritude, *PL* platitude, plenitude, *PR* promptitude, *R* rectitude, *S* sanctitude, senectitude, serenitude, certitude, servitude, similitude, solicitude, solitude, *SP* spissitude, *ST* stewed, stude, *T* torpitude, turpitude, *V* vastitude, verisimilitude, vicissitude

TRŌŌD — detrude, extrude, intrude, obtrude, protrude, retrude, subtrude

WŌŌD — rewooed, unwooed, wooed

YŌŌD — you'd

ZŌŌD — exude

(See ŪD)

OOD

GOOD — good
HOOD — *A* adulthood, angelhood, *B* babyhood, *boyhood, BR* brotherhood, *D* deaconhood, *F* fatherhood, falsehood, foolhardihood, *G girlhood, godhood, H* hardihood, hood, *J* gentlemanhood, *K* kinglihood, kittenhood, *L* ladyhood, likelihood, livelihood, *M* maidenhood, *manhood,* matronhood, *monkhood, monkshood,* motherhood, *N* neighborhood, *knighthood, O* orphanhood, *P* parenthood, *PR*

priesthood, R Robin
Hood, S sainthood,
selfhood, sisterhood, SP
spinsterhood, U unhood,
unlikelihood, W
widowerhood,
widowhood, womanhood

KOOD	could
MOOD	Talmud
SHOOD	should
STOOD	misunderstood, stood, understood, withstood
WOOD	A applewood, B baywood, beachwood, beechwood, bentwood, bitterwood, bogwood, boxwood, buttonwood, BL blackwood, BR brushwood, CH cherry- wood, D deadwood, dyewood, dogwood, DR driftwood, E eaglewood, F firewood, G gumwood, H hardwood, heartwood, Hollywood, HW whitewood, I ironwood, K candlewood, kingwood, cordwood, cottonwood, L legwood, leatherwood, M matchwood, milkwood, O orangewood, P pearwood, peachwood, peckerwood, pulpwood, purplewood, PL plastic wood, plywood, R redwood, ribbonwood, rosewood, S sandalwood, sappanwood, sapwood, satinwood, softwood, summerwood, southernwood, SKR scrubwood, SPR springwood, T teakwood, touch wood, touchwood, U underwood, W Wedgwood, wildwood, wood, would, wormwood, Z zebrawood (etc.)

$\overline{OO}$F

$\overline{OO}$F	oof, ouf, ouphe
B$\overline{OO}$F	boof, opera bouffe
D$\overline{OO}$F	shadoof
G$\overline{OO}$F	goof
GR$\overline{OO}$F	agroof
H$\overline{OO}$F	behoof, hoof, cloven-hoof
KL$\overline{OO}$F	kloof
L$\overline{OO}$F	aloof, loof
P$\overline{OO}$F	poof, pouf, whiffenpoof
PR$\overline{OO}$F	B bulletproof, D disproof,

F fireproof, foolproof, FL
flameproof, K
counterproof, M
mothproof, PR proof, R
rainproof, reproof,
rustproof, S sunproof, SH
shatterproof, shellproof,
shockproof, showerproof,
SK skidproof, ST
stormproof, W waterproof

R$\overline{OO}$F	gable roof, mansard roof, composition roof, reroof, roof, shingle roof, thatch roof, tile roof, unroof
SP$\overline{OO}$F	spoof
T$\overline{OO}$F	Tartuffe
W$\overline{OO}$F	woof, woof-woof, wowf

(See $\overline{U}$F)

$\overline{OO}$F

$\overline{OO}$F	oof
H$\overline{OO}$F	hoof, cloven-hoof
R$\overline{OO}$F	gable roof, composition roof, mansard roof, reroof, roof, shingle roof, thatch roof, tile roof, unroof
W$\overline{OO}$F	woof, woof-woof

$\overline{OO}$FT

(See $\overline{OO}$F, add -ed where appropriate.)

$\overline{OO}$G

B$\overline{OO}$G	boog

(See $\overline{U}$G)

$\overline{OO}$J

B$\overline{OO}$J	bouge, gamboge
L$\overline{OO}$J	luge
R$\overline{OO}$J	rouge
SKR$\overline{OO}$J	Scrooge, scrouge
ST$\overline{OO}$J	stooge

(See $\overline{U}$J, $\overline{OO}$ZH)

$\overline{OO}$K

B$\overline{OO}$K	bambuk, chibouk, rebuke
CH$\overline{OO}$K	caoutchouc
D$\overline{OO}$K	archduke, douc, duke
FL$\overline{OO}$K	fluke
G$\overline{OO}$K	gobbledygook, gook

J$\overline{OO}$K	jouk, juke
K$\overline{OO}$K	kook
L$\overline{OO}$K	Mameluke
N$\overline{OO}$K	Nanook
R$\overline{OO}$K	charuk, Farouk, peruke, seruke
SH$\overline{OO}$K	sheugh
SN$\overline{OO}$K	snoek, snook
S$\overline{OO}$K	sook
SP$\overline{OO}$K	spook
ST$\overline{OO}$K	stook
T$\overline{OO}$K	Heptateuch, Hexateuch, Octateuch, Pentateuch, tuque
Z$\overline{OO}$K	bashibazouk

(See $\overline{U}$K)

OOK

BOOK	A account book, appointment book, B bankbook, boobook, book, BL bluebook, CH chapbook, checkbook, D daybook, FL flybook, H handbook, hymnbook, K commonplace book, cookbook, copybook, L logbook, M minute book, N notebook, P paperback book, paperbook, passbook, pocketbook, PR prayerbook, S sambuk, songbook, SK sketchbook, SKR scrapbook, ST studbook, storybook, T textbook, W workbook
BROOK	Beaverbrook, Bolingbroke, brook, donnybrook, running brook
DOOK	fonduk
HOOK	billhook, boathook, buttonhook, fishhook, grapplehook, hook, rehook, tenterhook, unhook
KOOK	fancy cook, French cook, cook, cuck, overcook, pastry cook, plain cook, undercook
KROOK	crook
LOOK	look, outlook, overlook, uplook
NOOK	Chinook, inglenook, gerenuk, nook
PLOOK	plook
POOK	Volapuk
ROOK	rook

SHNOOK	schnook	
SHOOK	shook	
SOOK	forsook, *nainsook*	
TOOK	betook, mistook, overtook, partook, took, undertook	

OOKS

ZOOKS	gadzooks, odzooks

(See OOK, add *-s* where appropriate.)

OOKT

SOOKT	witzelsucht

(See OOK, add *-ed* where appropriate.)

OOL

BOOL	babul, boule, boulle, Istambul, Stambul
BROOL	brool
DOOL	*chandul,* hierodule
DROOL	drool, *chondrule*
FOOL	April fool, befool, fool, nobody's fool, poor fool, *tomfool*
GOOL	ghoul, gool
HOOL	who'll
JOOL	jhool, joule
KOOL	jokul, cool, supercool
MOOL	mool
NOOL	gallinule
POOL	*ampoule,* charity pool, dirty pool, *whirlpool,* gene pool, car pool, Liverpool, office pool, pool, pul, *cesspool,* swimming pool
ROOL	*ferrule, ferule,* misrule, rule, *spherule*
SHOOL	shul
SKOOL	boarding school, charity school, grammar school, high school, kindergarten school, nursery school, *playschool, preschool,* primary school, sabbath school, summer school, Sunday school, school
SOOL	pasul
SPOOL	spool
STOOL	*barstool,* ducking stool, *footstool,* stool
TOOL	retool, tool, tulle
YOOL	Yule

OOL

BOOL	*A* abominable, achievable, adaptable, adjustable, admirable, admissible, adorable, advisable, affable, affordable, agreeable, acceptable, accessible, accountable, actionable, alienable, allowable, amenable, amiable, amicable, answerable, applicable, appreciable, approachable, arable, arrestable, arguable, attainable, attemptable, attributable, available, avoidable, *B* bailable, bankable, bearable, beddable, believable, beatable, biddable, biodegradable, buhl, bull, *bulbul, BR* brakable, breakable, *CH* changeable, chargeable, charitable, chasuble, *D* damnable, debatable, deductible, defensible, definable, degradable, delectable, demonstrable, deniable, dependable, deplorable, depreciable, describable, despicable, destructible, detachable, detectable, determinable, detestable, devisable, desirable, differentiable, digestible, dirigible, disagreeable, dislikable, dishonorable, disreputable, discernible, dissociable, dispensable, disposable, distinguishable, disputable, divisible, doable, dowable, dubitable, durable, dutiable, *DR* drinkable, *E* edible, educable, effable, effaceable, execrable, exigible, excusable, exhaustible, expandable, expansible, expectable, expendable, explainable, explicable, expressible, excitable, extendible, extensible, extinguishable, extraditable, extricable, equable, equitable, eligible, employable, endurable, enjoyable, enviable, eradicable, erasable, estimable, eatable, *F* fallible, fashionable, fathomable, favorable, feasible, finable, fordable, forgettable, forgivable, formidable, foreseeable, forcible, fusible, *FL* flammable, flexible, *FR* friable, *G* gullible, governable, *H* habitable, heritable, horrible, hospitable, *I* identifiable, illegible, imaginable, immensurable, immeasurable, immiscible, immovable, immutable, impalpable, impassable, impeachable, impeccable, impenetrable, imperishable, impermeable, impermissible, imperceptible, imperturbable, implacable, implausible, imponderable, impossible impracticable, impregnable, impressionable, improbable, improvable, imputable, inadmissible, inadvisable, inalienable, inaccessible, inapplicable, inappreciable, indelible, indemonstrable, indecipherable, indescribable, indestructible, indigestible, indiscernible, indispensable, indissoluble, indisputable, indistinguishable, indictable, indivisible, indomitable, indubitable, ineducable, ineffable, ineffaceable, inexcusable, inexorable, inexhaustible, inexpressible, inextinguishable, inextricable, inequitable, ineligible, ineluctable, ineradicable, inescapable, inestimable, inevitable, infallible, inflammable, inflatable, inflexible, infrangible, infusible, inhospitable, inimitable, incalculable, incapable,

inclinable, incoercible, incombustible, incommunicable, incommutable, incomparable, incompatible, incomprehensible, incomputable, inconceivable, inconsiderable, inconsolable, incontestable, incontrovertible, inconvertible, inconvincible, incorrigible, incorruptible, incredible, inculpable, incurable, inaudible, inalterable, inoculable, inoperable, insatiable, insensible, innumerable, inseparable, inscrutable, insoluble, insufferable, insuperable, insupportable, insupposable, insuppressible, insurable, insurmountable, intangible, intelligible, interchangeable, interminable, intolerable, intractable, invaluable, invariable, inviable, invincible, inviolable, invisible, irascible, irredeemable, irreducible, irrefrangible, irrefutable, irreconcilable, irrecoverable, irrecusable, irreparable, irreplaceable, irreproachable, irresponsible, irretrievable, irreversible, irresistible, irresolvable, irritable, *J* generable, justifiable, justiciable, *K* calculable, capable, kissable, combustible, comfortable, commendable, commensurable, comestible, communicable, commutable, conceivable, considerable, constable, consumable, contemptible, contestable, controllable, conversable, convertible, convincible, corrigible, corruptible, culpable, curable, *KL* classifiable, *KR* credible,

creditable, crucible, *KW* quantifiable, quenchable, questionable, quotable, *L* laughable, lamentable, legible, leviable, liable, liftable, likable, litigable, laudable, lockable, lovable, *M* magnifiable, malleable, manageable, maneuverable, marketable, marriageable, medicable, memorable, mendable, mensurable, merchantable, measurable, miscible, mistakable, mitigable, miserable, modifiable, monosyllable, movable, mutable, *N* navigable, negligible, negotiable, knowledgeable, nonflammable, nonreturnable, notable, notifiable, noticeable, *O* objectionable, obtainable, observable, audible, alterable, omissible, honorable, operable, opposable, ostensible, *P* payable, palatable, palpable, parable, pardonable, passable, peccable, pensionable, perishable, perfectible, permissible, perceptible, personable, peaceable, pitiable, portable, possible, potable, punishable, purchasable, permeable, *PL* playable, placable, pleasurable, pliable, plausible, *PR* practicable, praisable, predictable, preferable, pregnable, preventable, presentable, presumable, printable, probable, producible, profitable, programmable, procurable, pronounceable, provable, *R* rateable, reachable, readable, realizable, redeemable, redoubtable, reducible, refillable, refrangible, refundable, regrettable, regulable, recognizable, recommendable, reconcilable, recordable, rectifiable, reliable, remarkable, removable,

renewable, repairable, reparable, repeatable, replaceable, reprehensible, reproachable, reputable, resaleable, rescissible, resoluble, respectable, responsible, retractable, retrievable, returnable, reversible, revocable, rewardable, resistible, reasonable, risible, *S* salvageable, satiable, saturable, semipermeable, sensible, seasonable, circumnavigable, syllable, sinkable, Sitting Bull, sizable, sociable, suable, submersible, suggestible, superable, supportable, surmountable, certifiable, serviceable, susceptible, suitable, *SK* scalable, *SP* sparable, specifiable, *ST* stoppable, *STR* stretchable, *T* taxable, tangible, teachable, tenable, tensible, terminable, tearable, terrible, tithable, tolerable, touchable, tunable, *TH* thinkable, *TR* tractable, transferable, traceable, triable, *U* unaccountable, unacceptable, unanswerable, unapproachable, unassailable, unattainable, unavailable, unavoidable, unbearable, unbelievable, unbendable, unbrakable, unbreakable, undeniable, understandable, undesirable, undrinkable, unexplainable, unemployable, unenviable, unfathomable, unfavorable, unforgettable, unforgivable, unforeseeable, ungovernable, unimaginable, unimpeachable, unintelligible, uncomfortable, unconscionable, uncontrollable, unconvincible, unquestionable,

unmatchable,
unmentionable,
unmistakable,
unknowable,
unobtainable,
unpredictable,
unpreventable,
unpresentable,
unprintable,
unpronounceable,
unreadable,
unrecognizable,
unreliable, unreasonable,
unseasonable,
unshakable, unsinkable,
unsociable, unstoppable,
unsuitable, untearable,
unteachable, untenable,
unthinkable, untouchable,
untranslatable,
unutterable, unweighable,
unwearable,
unwarrantable, *V*
valuable, variable,
vegetable, vendible,
venerable, verifiable,
veritable, viable, vincible,
visible, visual, vocable,
voluble, vulnerable, *W*
weighable, wearable,
willable, warrantable,
washable, workable

DOOL *chandul*
FOOL *A armful, artful, B*
baneful, bashful, bellyful,
bodeful, bookful,
bountiful, *bowlful,*
boastful, bountiful,
beautiful, *BL blameful,*
blissful, BR brimful, CH
cheerful, D delightful,
deceitful, disgraceful,
disrespectful, distasteful,
distrustful, doleful,
doubtful, dutiful, DR
dreadful, E earful,
eventful, F fanciful,
fateful, faithful, fearful,
fitful, forgetful, forkful,
forceful, full, *FL*
flavorful, *FR fretful,*
frightful, fruitful, G
gainful, guileful, GL
gleeful, GR graceful,
grateful, H half-full,
handful, harmful, hateful,
heedful, helpful,
healthful, hopeful,
hurtful, I eyeful, J joyful,
K careful, cartful,
caseful, colorful, *cupful,*
KW quiverful, quarter-

full, *L lawful, lustful, M*
manful, masterful,
meaningful, merciful,
mindful, mouthful,
mournful, mirthful, N
needful, needleful,
neglectful, O awful, P
painful, peaceful, pitiful,
pocketful, *potful,*
powerful, purposeful, *PL*
playful, plateful,
plentiful, *PR prayerful, R*
wrathful, regardful,
regretful, remindful,
remorseful, reproachful,
respectful, revengeful,
resentful, resourceful,
roomful, ruthful, S
sackful, sinful, songful,
soulful, successful, SH
shameful, SK skilful,
skinful, scornful, SL
slothful, SP spiteful, ST
stealthful, STR stressful,
T tactful, tankful, tasteful,
tuneful, TH thankful,
thimbleful, thoughtful, TR
trustful, U uneventful,
unfaithful, ungrateful,
unlawful, unmerciful,
unmindful, W wakeful,
wasteful, weariful, wilful,
windful, wishful, woeful,
wonderful, worshipful, *Y*
useful

KOOL *B barnacle, BR bricole, K*
canticle, coracle, *KR*
chronicle, *M* miracle,
monocle, *O* obstacle,
oracle, *P* pinnacle, *T*
testicle, *V* vehicle, versicle
POOL principal, principle, pull
WOOL abb wool, cotton wool,
lamb's wool, wool

O̅O̅M

· O̅O̅M oom
BLOOM abloom, checkerbloom,
embloom, rebloom
BOOM baby boom, boom, jib
boom, kaboom, sonic
boom
BROOM broom, brougham,
whiskbroom
DOOM doom, doum, foredoom,
predoom, redoom
FLOOM flume
FOOM perfume
GLOOM begloom, engloom,
gloom, glume

GOOM ghoom, legume
GROOM *bridegroom,* groom,
ungroom
HOOM whom
JOOM joom
KOOM coom, coomb, cwm
LOOM *broadloom, heirloom,*
illume, loom, powerloom,
reloom, relume
MOOM simoom
NOOM neume
PLOOM beplume, deplume,
displume, filoplume, nom
de plume, plume,
unplume

ROOM *A* anteroom, *B ballroom,*
barroom, bathroom,
bedroom, boardroom,
boxroom, D darkroom,
dining room, *DR* drawing
room, dressing room, *E*
elbowroom, *G*
guardroom, gunroom, GR
greenroom, grillroom, H
headroom, houseroom, K
coatroom, coffeeroom,
cookroom, courtroom, KL
classroom, cloakroom, L
living room, lumber
room, *M* meeting room,
mushroom, PL playroom,
R reading room, rheum,
room, *S salesroom,*
searoom, sitting room,
sunroom, SH showroom,
SP spare room, *ST*
stateroom, stockroom,
storeroom, STR
strongroom, T taproom,
tearoom, V varoom, *W*
wareroom, withdrawing
room, *workroom, washroom*
SOOM assume, consume, soum,
subsume
SPOOM spume
TOOM disentomb, entomb,
hecatomb, Khartoum,
costume, pantoum, tomb,
toom, untomb, womb-to-
tomb
VROOM vroom
WOOM enwomb, womb, woom
ZOOM bazoom, presume,
resume, zoom

(See Ū̅M)

O̅O̅MD

(See O̅O̅M, Ū̅M, add *-ed*, where appropriate.)

OͦͦN

OͦͦN	triune
BLOͦͦN	doubloon
BOͦͦN	baboon, boon, Daniel Boone
BROͦͦN	gombroon
DOͦͦN	bridoon, doon, dune, cardoon, rigadoon
DROͦͦN	gadroon, quadroon, spadroon
FOͦͦN	buffoon, typhoon
GOͦͦN	dragoon, goon, lagoon, Rangoon
HOͦͦN	cohune
JOͦͦN	jejune, June
KOͦͦN	barracoon, cacoon, cocoon, coon, raccoon, rockoon, tycoon
KROͦͦN	croon
LOͦͦN	apolune, balloon, demilune, galloon, loon, lune, pantaloon, perilune, saloon, shalloon, walloon, Walloon
MOͦͦN	*F* full moon, *G* gibbous moon, *H* half moon, harvest moon, honeymoon, *KW* quarter moon, *M* moon, *N* new moon, *O* old moon, *S* sickle moon, simoon, *W* waxing moon, waning moon
NOͦͦN	afternoon, *forenoon, highnoon, midnoon,* noon
POͦͦN	harpoon, lampoon, poon, tampoon
PROͦͦN	prune
ROͦͦN	floroon, Cameroon, macaroon, maroon, octoroon, picaroon, rune, seroon, Scandaroon, vinegarroon
SHOͦͦN	shoon
SKOͦͦN	scoon
SOͦͦN	bassoon, eftsoon, gossoon, matzoon, monsoon, oversoon, soon
SPOͦͦN	dessert spoon, Great Horned Spoon, coffee spoon, runcible spoon, silver spoon, spoon, tablespoon, *teaspoon*
STROͦͦN	bestrewn, overstrewn, strewn
SWOͦͦN	aswoon, reswoon, swoon
TOͦͦN	*A* altun, *F* festoon, *FR* frigatoon, *I* inopportune, *K* cantoon, cartoon, coquetoon, *M* musketoon, *O* opportune, *P* pontoon,

	PL platoon, *R* ratoon, *S* saskatoon, Saskatoon, *SP* spittoon, spontoon, *T* testoon, toon
TROͦͦN	quintroon, patroon, poltroon
WOͦͦN	woon
YOͦͦN	picayune

(See **Ŭ̄N**)

OͦͦND

BOͦͦND	Bund
HOͦͦND	*dachshund*
LOͦͦND	Lund
HOͦͦND	Mahound
WOͦͦND	wound

(See **OͦͦN**, **Ŭ̄N**, add *-ed* where appropriate.)

OͦͦNZ

ROͦͦNZ	Cameroons
SOͦͦNZ	eftsoons

(See **OͦͦN**, **Ŭ̄N**, add *-s* where appropriate.)

OͦͦP

BLOͦͦP	bloop
BOͦͦP	Betty Boop, boop
DOͦͦP	boop-boop-a-doop, dupe
DROͦͦP	adroop, droop, drupe
GOͦͦP	goop
GROͦͦP	aggroup, group, regroup, *subgroup*
HOͦͦP	cock-a-hoop, hoop, unhoop
HWOͦͦP	whoop
KLOͦͦP	cloop
KOͦͦP	chicken coop, *hen-coop,* coop, coup, coupe, recoup
KROͦͦP	croup, Krupp
LOͦͦP	Guadeloupe, cantaloupe, loop, loupe, loop-the-loop, saloop, unloop
POͦͦP	liripoop, nincompoop, poop, twiddlepoop
ROͦͦP	roup
SKOͦͦP	scoop
SKROͦͦP	scroop
SLOͦͦP	sloop
SNOͦͦP	snoop
SOͦͦP	soup, soupe, supe
STOͦͦP	stoep, stoop, stoup, stupe

SWOͦͦP	*downswoop,* swoop, *upswoop*
TROͦͦP	troop, troupe
WOͦͦP	Woop Woop

(See **Ŭ̄P**)

OͦͦPS

OͦͦPS	oops
HWOͦͦPS	whoops
WOͦͦPS	woops

(See **OͦͦP**, **Ŭ̄P**, add *-s* where appropriate.)

OͦͦR

MOͦͦR	affaire, d'amour, amour
ZHOͦͦR	plat du jour, toujours

OOR

BLOOR	doublure
BOOR	Boer, boor, tambour
CHOOR	abature, amateur, aperture, armature, *BR* briature, *D* discomfiture, divestiture, *E* expenditure, entablature, *F* forfeiture, furniture, *G* garmenture, garniture, *I* immature, investiture, *J* judicature, *K* calenture, camerature, candidature, caricature, comfiture, confiture, coverture, curvature, *KL* climature, *KW* quadrature, *L* ligature, literature, *M* mature, miniature, *O* overture, *P* portraiture, *PR* premature, primogeniture, *S* secundogeniture, sepulture, signature, *T* tablature, temperature, *V* vestiture
DOOR	dour, endure, perdure, perendure, pompadour, tandoor, troubadour
JOOR	abjure, adjure, conjure, *injure*
LOOR	allure, colure, condylure, lure, chevelure, velours, velure
KOOR	concours
MOOR	armure, blackamoor, *Dartmoor, Exmoor,*

	moor, Moor, paramour, unmoor
NOOR	Kohinhoor, manure
POOR	poor
ROOR	parure, Ruhr
SHOOR	assure, brochure, embouchure, ensure, hachure, insure, co-insure, cocksure, commissure, reassure, reinsure, cynosure, unsure
SKYOOR	clair-obscure, obscure
TOOR	detour, *contour*
TYOOR	(see CHOOR)
YOOR	voyeur, you're
ZHOOR	voyageur

ŌORD

CHOORD	caricatured
DOORD	endured, perdured, perendured
GOORD	gourd
JOORD	abjured, adjured, conjured, *injured*
LOORD	allured, lured
MOORD	moored, remoored, unmoored
SHOORD	assured, ensured, insured, reassured, reinsured
TOORD	detoured, *contoured*

(See URD.)

ŌOS

BOOS	boose, caboose, calaboose, camboose
DOOS	adduce, deduce, educe, induce, conduce, douce, obduce, produce, traduce,
GOOS	golden goose, goose, mongoose, silly goose, wayzgoose
JOOS	juice, *verjuice*
KLOOS	occluse, recluse
KOOS	*couscous*
KROOS	crouse, cruse
LOOS	*footloose*, cut loose, let loose, loose, *sooloos*, Toulouse, unloose
MOOS	moose, mousse, vamoose
NOOS	burnoose, hangman's noose, hypotenuse, noose, nous, *slipnoose*
POOS	papoose, pouce
ROOS	ceruse, charlotte russe
SLOOS	sluice, unsluice
SPROOS	spruce
STROOS	abstruse

TOOS	obtuse, retuse
TROOS	truce
YOOS	cayuse
ZOOS	Zeus

(See ŪS)

ŌOSH

BOOSH	bouche, debouch, tarboosh
DOOSH	douche, kiddush
GOOSH	syagush
HWOOSH	whoosh
LOOSH	louche
MOOSH	gobe-mouche, mouche, Scaramouch
POOSH	capuche
ROOSH	barouche, farouche, ruche
TOOSH	cartouche
WOOSH	woosh
ZOOSH	zuche

OOSH

BOOSH	*A* ambush, *B* bushbush, bush, buttonbush, *BL* blackberry bush, blueberry bush, *BR* bramblebush, brittlebush, *D* dogbush, *F* fetterbush, *forebush, FL* flannelbush, *G* gallbush, goatbush, *H* hobblebush, hollybush, *horsebush, J* jewbush, *K* kinksbush, coffee bush, currant bush, *L* loganberry bush, *lotebush, M* maybush, *N* needlebush, *P* peabush, pepperbush, *pearlbush, pinbush, R* raspberry bush, *S* saltbush, soldierbush, *SH* shadbush, sugarbush, *SKW* squawbush, *SM* smokebush, *SP* spicebush, *TW* twinebush (etc.)
KOOSH	cush
POOSH	push
SHOOSH	shoosh
SWOOSH	swoosh

ŌOST

BOOST	boost, deboost
BROOST	browst
GOOST	langouste
JOOST	joust

PROOST	Proust
ROOST	roost, roust

(See ŌOS, add *-d* where appropriate.)

ŌOT

BOOT	boot, *freeboot, jackboot, marabout, overboot,* unboot
BROOT	bruit, brute, imbrute
DOOT	folie de doute
FLOOT	flute
FROOT	*breadfruit,* first fruit, forbidden fruit, fruit, gallows fruit, *grapefruit, jackfruit,* passion fruit
HOOT	hoot, cahoot, mahout
JOOT	jute
KLOOT	cloot, clute
KOOT	baldicoot, bandicoot, coot
KROOT	croute, recruit
LOOT	*A* absolute, *D* dilute, dissolute, *E* elute, *G* galoot, *I* involute, irresolute, *K* consolute, convolute, *L* loot, lute, *O* obvolute, *P* pollute, *R* resolute, revolute, *S* salute, solute, *V* volute
MOOT	*folkmoot,* Malamute, moot
NOOT	Canute, comminute
ROOT	*A* arrowroot, *B* Beirut, *beetroot, birthroot, BR breadroot,* briarroot, *CH* cheroot, *E* enroot, en route, *K* coralroot, crinkleroot, *M* musquashroot, *O* orrisroot, auto-route, *P* puttyroot, *R* redroot, root, route, *S* seroot, *SN snakeroot, T* taproot, unroot, uproot
SHOOT	bumbershoot, *offshoot,* outshoot, overshoot, parachute, chute, undershoot, upshoot
SKOOT	scoot
SLOOT	sloot, sluit
SMOOT	smoot
SNOOT	snoot
SOOT	*B* birthday suit, *H* hirsute, *L* lawsuit, *P* pantsuit, pursuit, *PL* playsuit, *S* soot, suit, *sunsuit, SP* spacesuit, *SW* swimsuit, *TR tracksuit, W* wetsuit, *Z zootsuit*
TOOT	astute, destitute, institute,

constitute, prostitute,
rooty-toot, substitute,
toot, toot-toot, tute

(See ŪT)

OOT

FOOT	*A* afoot, *B* barefoot, Bigfoot, *BL* Blackfoot, *F* fanfoot, finfoot, foalfoot, foot, *FL* flatfoot, forefoot, *G* goosefoot, *H* hotfoot, *K* cocksfoot, coltsfoot, *KL* clubfoot, *KR* crossfoot, crowfoot, *L* lobefoot, *O* autofoot, outfoot, *P* padfoot, pussyfoot, *SP* spadefoot, *T* tenderfoot, *U* underfoot, *W* webfoot
POOT	*input*, cajuput, kaput, autoput, *output*, put, *throughput*
SOOT	soot

OŌTH

(**TH** as in ''then'')

SMOŌTH	besmooth, resmooth, unsmooth
SOŌTH	resoothe, soothe, unsoothe

OŌTH

(**TH** as in ''thin'')

BOŌTH	booth, polling booth, voting booth
KOŌTH	couth, uncouth
KROŌTH	crwth
LOŌTH	Duluth, *thuluth*
MOŌTH	vermouth
ROŌTH	ruth, Ruth
SLOŌTH	sleuth
SMOŌTH	smeuth
SOŌTH	forsooth, sooth
STROŌTH	'strewth, 'struth
TOŌTH	*backtooth, bucktooth, dogtooth, eyetooth,* tooth, wisdom tooth
TROŌTH	truth, untruth
YOŌTH	youth

OŌTHD

(**TH** as in ''then'')

SMOŌTHD	besmoothed, resmoothed, unsmoothed
SOŌTHD	resoothed, soothed, unsoothed

OŌTS

WOŌTS	wootz

(See OŌT, add *-s* where appropriate.)

OOTS

BOOTS	kibbutz
FOOTS	foots, hotfoots, pussyfoots
POOTS	puts
SOOTS	soots

OŌV

GROŌV	groove, ingroove, in-the-groove, microgroove
HOŌV	behoove, who've
MOŌV	amove, countermove, move, on-the-move, remove
PROŌV	approve, disapprove, disprove, improve, prove, reprove
YOŌV	you've

OŌZ

OŌZ	ooze
BLOŌZ	blues, the blues
BOŌZ	boos, booze, rambooze
BROŌZ	bruise
CHOŌZ	choose
DROŌZ	druse, Druse
FLOŌZ	flews, flues
HOŌZ	who's, whose
JOŌZ	Betelgeuse, Jews
KROŌZ	crews, cruise, cruse, Santa Cruz, Vera Cruz
LOŌZ	lose, relose, Toulouse
POŌZ	pouze
ROŌZ	peruse, roose, ruse
SHMOŌZ	schmooze
SHOŌZ	shoes, shoos, reshoes, reshoos, unshoes
SNOŌZ	snooze
THOŌZ	enthuse
TOŌZ	tattoos
TROŌZ	trews
YOŌZ	use, youse

(See ŪZ; see OŌ, add *-s* where appropriate.)

OŌZD

OŌZD	oozed

(See OŌZ, add *-d* where appropriate.)

OŌZH

BOŌZH	gamboge
BROŌZH	Bruges
LOŌZH	luge
ROŌZH	rouge
VOŌZH	vouge

ŌP

ŌP	myope, ope, reope
DŌP	dope, rope-a-dope
GRŌP	agrope, grope
HŌP	Cape of Good Hope, hope
KŌP	cope
LŌP	antelope, elope, envelope, interlope, cantaloupe, lope
MŌP	mope
NŌP	nope
PŌP	antipope, dispope, pope, protopope, unpope
RŌP	*dragrope*, phalarope, *footrope, jumprope, manrope, pyrope,* rope, roup, *skiprope, tightrope, towrope*
SKŌP	*A* amnioscope, astroscope, *B* bioscope, *D* dipleidoscope, *E* electroscope, episcope, *G* galvanoscope, *H* helioscope, hydroscope, horoscope, *J* gyroscope, *L* laparoscope, *M* microscope, *P* periscope, polariscope, polemoscope, *PR* proctoscope, *R* radarscope, *S* seismoscope, *SK* scope, *SP* spectroscope, *ST* stereoscope, stethoscope, *T* telescope, *TH* thermoscope, zoopraxiscope
SLŌP	aslope, slope
SŌP	*sandsoap*, soft-soap, soap, sope
STŌP	stope
THRŌP	philanthrope, lycanthrope, misanthrope
TŌP	isotope, *metope*, radioisotope, taupe, tope
TRŌP	allotrope, trope, zootrope

OP

OP	*coin-op, co-op*, op
BLOP	blop

BOP	bop, diddly-bop, diddy-bop, Cu-bop
CHOP	chop, chop-chop, karate-chop
DOP	dop
DROP	*airdrop*, bedrop, *dewdrop*, drop, *eardrop*, *eavesdrop*, *gumdrop*, paradrop, *raindrop*, *snowdrop*, *teardrop*
FLOP	*flipflop*, flippity-flop, flop
FOP	fop
GLOP	glop
GOP	gape, gop
HOP	*barhop*, *bellhop*, *hedgehop*, hippity-hop, hop, *carhop*, table-hop
HWOP	whop
KLOP	clip-clop, clop, clop-clop, clippety-clop
KOP	bull cop, cop, kop, motor cop, traffic cop
KROP	after-crop, bumper crop, intercrop, crop, *outcrop*, overcrop, riding crop, *sharecrop*, *stonecrop*
KWOP	quop
LOP	alop, lop, *orlop*
MOP	mop, remop, *rollmop*
NOP	knop
PLOP	plop
POP	gingerpop, *joypop*, lollipop, pop, soda pop
PROP	agitprop, prop, reprop, turboprop, underprop, unprop
SHOP	barbershop, *bookshop*, coffeeshop, *pawnshop*, shop, *sweatshop*, *sweetshop*, *teashop*, *workshop*
SKOP	scop
SLOP	aslop, *slipslop*, slop
SOP	asop, milksop, *sweetsop*
STOP	*backstop*, estop, *fullstop*, nonstop, reststop, shortstop, stop, unstop
STROP	strop
SWOP	swap
TOP	atop, big top, *blacktop*, flat-top, foretop, hardtop, housetop, carrot top, maintop, mizzentop, netop, overtop, *pop-top*, redtop, tiptop, top
WOP	wop

OPS

CHOPS	chops, *lambchops*, *porkchops*, slobber-chops, *vealchops*

KOPS	copse

(See **OP**, add -*s* where appropriate.)

ŌPT

(See **ŌP**, add -*d* where appropriate.)

OPT

(See **OP**, add -*ped* where appropriate.)

OPT

OPT	co-opt

(See **OP**, add -*ped* where appropriate.)

ŌR

(See **ÔR**, add -*ed* where appropriate.)

BŌR	boar, Boer, *chokebore*, bore, forbore, forebore, hellebore, *smoothbore*
CHŌR	chore
DŌR	*A* adore, *B* backdoor, bandore, battledore, *D* death's door, door, dor, dumbledore, *E* Ecuador, *I* indoor, *K* commodore, corridor, cuspidor, *L* Labrador, louis d'or, *M* matador, mirador, mogadore, moidore, *O* open-door, *outdoor*, *P* picador, Polydore, *S* Salvador, *ST* stevedore, *T* toreador, *TR* trapdoor, troubador
DRŌR	drawer
FLŌR	first floor, fifth floor, floor, fourth floor, ground floor, second floor (etc.), underfloor, upper floor
FŌR	*A* afore, *B* before, *F* fore, for, four, *H* hereinbefore, heretofore, *HW* wherefor, *wherefore*, *M* metaphor, *P* petit four, pinafore, *S* semaphore, *T* two-by-four, *TH* therefor, *therefore*, theretofore
GŌR	gore, obligor
HŌR	abhor, hoar, whore, Lahore
KŌR	*A* albacore, apple core, *D* décor, *E* encore, *H* hardcore, *K* core, corps, manticore, *markhor*, *R* rotten to the core, *S* softcore, *T* terpsichore

KRŌR	crore
LŌR	*booklore*, *folklore*, galore, counsellor, lor, lore, vice chancellor
MŌR	Baltimore, evermore, furthermore, *claymore*, mohr, moire, more, mor, nevermore, paramour, sagamore, sycamore, sophomore
NŌR	assignor, ignore, nor, pundonor
PLŌR	deplore, explore, implore
PŌR	blastopore, *downpour*, madrepore, millepore, nullipore, outpour, pore, pour, rapport, Singapore
RŌR	furore, *outroar*, roar, *uproar*
SHŌR	alongshore, ashore, foreshore, inshore, lee shore, *longshore*, offshore, onshore, *seashore*, shore, weathershore
SKŌR	*fourscore*, overscore, score, *twoscore*, *threescore* (etc.), underscore
SNŌR	snore
SŌR	*B* bedsore, *F* footsore, *H* heartsore, *I* eyesore, *K* canker sore, *coldsore*, *L* lessor, *O* outsoar, *PR* promisor, soar, sore, upsoar
SPLŌR	splore
SPŌR	archespore, spore
STŌR	*drugstore*, candy store (etc.)
SWŌR	forswore, reswore, swore
TŌR	apparitor, guarantor, imperator, legator, patentor, tore, torr, warrantor
VŌR	frugivore, herbivore, insectivore, carnivore, omnivore
WŌR	outwore, rewore, wore
YŌR	yore
ZŌR	bezoar

ÔR

(See **ŌR**, add -*ed* where appropriate.)

BÔR	Dukhobor
DÔR	corridor, cuspidor, louis d'or, matador, mirador, picador, Salvador, toreador, troubador
FÔR	for, metaphor, therefor, *therefore*

KÔR décor, encore

LÔR chancellor, councillor, counsellor, vice chancellor

NÔR nor, pundonor

SÔR balisaur, dinosaur, dolichosaur, hedrosaur, ichthyosaur, lessor, megalosaur, plesiosaur, teleosaur, tyrannosaur

SKÔR scaur

THÔR Thor

TÔR apparitor, guarantor, legator, tor (see TUR for words ending in -tor but pronounced -ter)

VÔR frugivore, herbivore, carnivore, omnivore

WÔR man-of-war, outwore, *postwar*, prewar, rewore, tug-of-war, war, wore

YÔR señor, yore, your

ZÔR bezoar, recognizor

(See **UR** for words ending in -or but pronounced -ur.)

ÔRB

ÔRB orb, disorb, inorb
FÔRB forb
KÔRB corbe
SÔRB absorb, reabsorb, resorb, sorb

ÔRBD

ÔRBD orbed, disorbed, inorbed
SÔRBD absorbed, reabsorbed, resorbed, sorbed

ÔRCH

PÔRCH back porch, front porch, porch
SKÔRCH scorch
TÔRCH torch

ÔRCHT

PÔRCHT porched
SKÔRCHT scorched
TÔRCHT torched

ŌRD

ŌRD oared, ord
BŌRD A aboard, B beaverboard, Big Board, *billboard*, board, bord, *backboard, buckboard*, BL *blackboard, blockboard,* BR breadboard, CH chairman of the board, checkerboard, chessboard, *cheeseboard, chipboard, chalkboard,* D dartboard, dashboard, diving board, *duckboard,* DR draftboard, F fiberboard, fingerboard, *fireboard, footboard,* FL *flashboard, floorboard,* FR freeboard, H headboard, I inboard, ironing board, K cardboard, keyboard, corkboard, KL clapboard, clapperboard, *clipboard,* L leeboard, M matchboard, millboard, mortarboard, O outboard, overboard, P paperboard, *pasteboard, pegboard,* PL plasterboard, S seaboard, centerboard, *sideboard, signboard, surfboard,* SH shipboard, shuffleboard, SK skateboard, *scaleboard, scoreboard,* SKR scraperboard, SM smorgasbord, *SPL splashboard, SPR springboard, STR stringboard, strawboard,* SW switchboard, T tailboard, W weatherboard, ouija board, *wallboard*

DŌRD adored, doored, *four-doored* (etc.), *close-doored,* open-doored
FŌRD afford, ford, Ford
GŌRD gored, gourd, ungored
HŌRD hoard, horde, whored, unhoard
KŌRD cored
PLŌRD deplored, explored, implored, undeplored, unexplored, unimplored
PŌRD pored, poured
SHŌRD shored
SKŌRD scored, rescored, unscored
SNŌRD snored
SŌRD *broadsword,* sord, sword
TŌRD toward, untoward

(See **ŌR,** add -ed where appropriate.)

ÔRD

HÔRD abhorred
KÔRD A accord, D disaccord, discord, E encored, H harmonichord, harpsichord, hexichord, *HW whipcord,* K *concord,* chord, cord, *KL* clavichord, L lyrichord, M masterchord, misericord, monochord, N needlecord,, notochord, R record, ripcord T tetrachord, Y urochord
LÔRD belord, *landlord,* lord, milord, overlord, unlord, *warlord*
NYÔRD Njord
SWÔRD *greensward,* sward
WÔRD award, reward, ward, warred

ÔRF

ÔRF orf, orfe
DÔRF Dusseldorf, *Waldorf*
DWÔRF dwarf, white dwarf, red dwarf
HWÔRF wharf
KÔRF corf
MÔRF A allomorph, B bimorph, D dimorph, E ephememorph, ectomorph, enantiomorph, endomorph, H hystricomorph, I isomorph, J gynandromorph, M mesamorph, morph, P paramorph, perimorph, polymorph, R rhizomorph, S pseudomorph, *TR trimorph*
SWÔRF swarf

ÔRG

ÔRG orgue
BÔRG borg, Swedenborg
MÔRG morgue

ÔRJ

FÔRJ forge
GÔRJ disengorge, disgorge, engorge, gorge, overgorge, regorge

JÔRJ   St. George
KÔRJ   corge

ÔRJD

(See **ÔRJ**, add *-d* where appropriate.)

ÔRK

ÔRK	orc
DÔRK	dork
FÔRK	fork, *hayfork, pitchfork,* tuning fork, weeding fork
GÔRK	gork
KÔRK	cork, corke, recork, uncork
KWÔRK	quark
NÔRK	nork
PÔRK	morepork, pork, roast pork, salt pork
SPÔRK	spork
STÔRK	stork
TÔRK	torque
YÔRK	New York, york, York

ÔRKT

(See **ÔRK**, add *-ed* where appropriate.)

ÔRL

ÔRL	orle
HWÔRL	whorl
KWÔRL	quarl
SHÔRL	schorl, shorl

ÔRM

DÔRM	dorm
FÔRM	*A* aeriform, aquiform, aliform, anguiform, anguilliform, acinaciform, aciniform, *B biform,* boculiform, bursiform, *BR* bromoform, *D* deform, deiform, dendriform, dentiform, digitiform, diversiform, dolabriform, *E* electroform, ensiform, eruciform, *F* falciform, fibriform, filiform, form, forme, fungiform, fusiform, *FL* floriform, *FR freeform, G* gasiform, *H* hamiform, harengiform, hederiform, hippocrepiform, *I* inform, iodoform, ypsilliform, *K*

cheliform, Cominform, conform, cordiform, coroniform, cubiform, cuculiform, cucumiform, cuneiform, *KL* chloroform, *KR* cribriform, cruciform, *L landform,* lentiform, ligniform, linguiform, *M* misform, misinform, moniliform, multiform, *N* napiform, nitrochloriform, *O* oriform, oviform, *P* panduriform, pediform, perform, piliform, pyriform, pisiform, poculiform, *PL platform,* plexiform, *R* ramiform, reform, remiform, reniform, *S* salverform, selliform, *SK* scobiform, scutiform, *SKR* scrotiform, *SKW* squaliform, *ST* stelliform, *STR* stromboliform, *T* tectiform, tauriform, turdiform, *TR* transform, *U* unform, uniform, unciform, *V* variform, vermiform, verruciform, vitriform, vulviform, *W waveform, Y* uniform

GÔRM	*cairngorm*
KÔRM	corm
NÔRM	norm
STÔRM	*B* barnstorm, bestorm, *BR* brainstorm, *F* firestorm, *H* hailstorm, *I* ice storm, *R* rainstorm, *S* sandstorm, *SL* sleetstorm, *SN* snowstorm, *ST* storm, *TH* thunderstorm, *W* windstorm
SWÔRM	aswarm, swarm, upswarm
WÔRM	*lukewarm,* rewarm, sunny warm, unwarm, warm

ÔRMD

(See **ÔRM**, add *-ed* where appropriate.)

ŌRN

MŌRN   mourn

(See **ÔRN**)

ÔRN

BÔRN   *A airborne, B* born, *CH chairborne, E earthborn,*

F first-born, forborne, *FR freeborn, H* heaven-born, heliborne, *high-born, I* inborn, *KL cloud-born, cloud-borne, L* lowborn, *N* newborn, night-born, *O* autumn-born, *R* reborn, *S sea-born, sea-borne,* suborn, summer-born, *SH shardborn, SPR* spring-*born, ST stillborn, TR true-born, U* unborn, *V* virgin-born, *W* winter-born, winterbourne, waterborne

DÔRN	adorn, disadorn, dorn, readorn, unadorn
HÔRN	*A* alpenhorn, *alphorn, althorn, D* dehorn, dishorn, *DR* drinking-horn, *F* foghorn, *FL* flugelhorn, *FR* French horn, *GR* greenhorn, *H* horn, hunting horn, *I* inkhorn, *K* Cape Horn, *cowhorn, KR crumhorn, L leghorn, longhorn, M* Matterhorn, *P* powderhorn, *PR priming horn, pronghorn, S saxhorn, SH shoehorn, shorthorn, ST staghorn, stinkhorn, T tinhorn*
KÔRN	*acorn,* barleycorn, *bicorn,* candycorn, Capricorn, cavicorn, clavicorn, corn, lamellicorn, longicorn, peppercorn, *popcorn, tricorn,* unicorn
LÔRN	forlorn, lorn, *lovelorn*
MÔRN	midmorn, morn, yestermorn
NÔRN	Norn
PÔRN	hard porn, kiddie porn, porn, soft porn
SHÔRN	shorn, reshorn, unshorn
SKÔRN	bescorn, scorn, self-scorn
SÔRN	sorn
SWÔRN	forsworn, sworn, unsworn
THÔRN	*blackthorn, buckthorn, hawthorn,* thorn
TÔRN	betorn, torn, untorn
WÔRN	*F footworn,* forewarn, *K careworn, O* outworn, *R* rewarn, *S seaworn, T timeworn, toilworn, W waveworn, wayworn,* weatherworn, warn, worn, waterworn

(See **ŌRN**)

ÔRND

(See ÔRN, add -ed where appropriate.)

ÔRP

DÔRP	dorp
GÔRP	gorp
LÔRP	australorp
THÔRP	thorp
TÔRP	torp
WÔRP	*moldwarp*, time warp, warp

ÔRPS

KÔRPS	corpse

(See ÔRP, add -s where appropriate.)

ŌRS

FŌRS	enforce, force, inforce, perforce, reinforce, tour de force
KŌRS	damp course, discourse, *forecourse*, intercourse, *concourse*, coarse, course, *racecourse*, recourse, water-course
SŌRS	resource, source
VŌRS	divorce

ÔRS

DÔRS	endorse, indorse
GÔRS	gorse
HÔRS	*CH* charley horse, *D* dead horse, *DR drayhorse*, *H* hobbyhorse, hoarse, horse, *K carthorse*, *cockhorse*, *KR* Crazy Horse, *P packhorse*, *R racehorse*, rocking horse, *S* seahorse, sawhorse, *ST* stalkinghorse, *studhorse*, *U* unhorse, *W* walkinghorse, warhorse, wooden horse, *workhorse*
KÔRS	discourse, *forecourse*, intercourse, *concourse*, coarse, corse, course, *race course*, recourse, water-course
MÔRS	Morse, premorse, remorse
NÔRS	Norse
SÔRS	resource, source
TÔRS	torse

TRÔRS	antrorse, dextrorse, extrorse, introrse, retrorse, sinistrorse
VÔRS	divorce
ZÔRS	resource

ŌRST

(See ŌRS, add -d where appropriate)

ÔRST

(See ÔRS, add -d where appropriate.)

ŌRT

FŌRT	forte, pianoforte
KŌRT	decourt, *forecourt*, county court, court

ÔRT

ÔRT	ort
BÔRT	abort, bort
DÔRT	kankedort
FÔRT	fort, *hillfort*
HÔRT	dehort
KÔRT	Agincourt, escort, *forecourt*, county court, court
KWÔRT	quart
MÔRT	amort, mort
PÔRT	*A* airport, aport, *D* davenport, deport, disport, *E* export, *H* heliport, hoverport, *I* import, *inport*, *J* jetport, *K* carport, comport, *L* life-support, *M* misreport, *N* nonsupport, *Newport*, *O* outport, *P* passport, port, purport, *R* rapport, re-export, reimport, report, *S* sally port, *seaport*, support, *SP spaceport*, *TR* transport
RÔRT	rort
SHÔRT	short, ultrashort
SNÔRT	snort
SÔRT	assort, consort, re-sort, sort, unsort
SPÔRT	*spoilsport*, sport
SWÔRT	swart
THWÔRT	athwart, thwart
TÔRT	distort, extort, intort, contort, retort, tort, torte
VÔRT	cavort
WÔRT	wart, worry wart
ZÔRT	exhort, resort

ÔRTH

FÔRTH	forth, *fourth*, henceforth, setter-forth, thenceforth
MÔRTH	morth
NÔRTH	north
SWÔRTH	swarth

ÔRTS

KWÔRTS	*biquartz*, quarts, quartz, rose quartz

(See ÔRT, add -s where appropriate.)

ŌRZ

DŌRZ	door, indoors, outdoors
FŌRZ	fours, all fours, plus fours
YŌRZ	all yours, yours

(See ŌR, add -s where appropriate.)

ÔRZ

DRÔRZ	drawers
TÔRZ	Louis Quatorze, quatorze
YÔRZ	all yours, yours
ZÔRZ	Azores

(See ÔR, add -s where appropriate.)

ŌS

ŌS	os, foliose, grandiose, caseose, otiose
BŌS	boce, *gibbose, globose, ribose*, thrombose, verbose
DŌS	dose, nodose, overdose, underdose
DYŌS	adios
GŌS	rugose, strigose
GRŌS	engross, gross
HŌS	*chaparajos*
KLŌS	close
KŌS	arkose, bellicose, *floccose, glucose*, jocose, cose, kos, metempsychose, varicose, ventricose, verrucose, *viscose*
KRŌS	necrose
LŌS	*A* alose, amylose, ankylose, annulose, *F filose*, *K* capillose, *N* nodulose, *P pilose, R*

ramose, ramulose,
rimose, rugulose, S
cymose, supulose,
surculose, *SKW*
squamulose, *ST*,
stimulose, stupulose, *TR*
tremellose

VERITAS MUTATUR

Of truths I knew,
Not one or two,
But quite a few
    (In fact, a bunch)
Have proved untrue.
    I have a hunch
The things I know
Today may go
That road also;
    Most folks must munch
    Roast crow for lunch.

MŌS	albumose, lachrymose, *mammose, osmose,* racemose
NŌS	anthracnose, diagnose, farinose, pruinose, raffinose, *spinose, venose,* uliqinose
PŌS	adipose
RŌS	aggerose, erose, morose, mulierose, operose, saccharose, *squarrose, torose, virose*
SHŌS	chausses
SŌS	soce
STŌS	stowce
TŌS	keratose, comatose, sarmentose, setose, tomentose

ÔS

HÔS	hawse
SÔS	applesauce, sauce

OS

OS	os
BOS	Bos, boss, emboss
DOS	doss
DROS	dross
FLOS	floss, candyfloss
FOS	fosse, *vanfoss*
GLOS	gloss, isogloss
GOS	mishbegoss
JOS	joss
KOS	cos, coss
KROS	*A* across, *D* doublecross, *F* fiery cross, *I* incross,

intercross, *KR* crisscross, *christcross,* cross, crosse, *L* lacrosse, *M* motocross, *O* outcross, autocross, *R* rallycross, rosy cross, *U* uncross, *W* weeping cross

LOS	krobylos, loss
MOS	moss, sea moss
PROS	pross
ROS	kaross, rhinoceros, ross
SOS	soss
STOS	stoss
TOS	toss, Thanatos
TROS	albatross

ŌSH

ŌSH	brioche
BŌSH	Boche
FŌSH	Foch
GŌSH	gauche
KLŌSH	cloche
LŌSH	guilloche
RŌSH	caroche

OSH

OSH	brioche
BOSH	Boche, bosch, bosh, debosh, *kibosh*
FROSH	frosh
GOSH	gosh
HOSH	cohosh
JOSH	josh
KOSH	cosh
KWOSH	quash, *musquash*
LOSH	galosh, tikolosh
NOSH	nosh
POSH	posh
SKWOSH	squash
SLOSH	slosh
SOSH	sosh
SPLOSH	splosh
SWOSH	swash
TOSH	mackintosh, tosh
WOSH	*A* awash, *B* backwash, bellywash, bewash, Bosnywash, *BR* brainwash, *H* hogwash, *HW* whitewash, *I* eyewash, *M* mouthwash, *O* outwash, *R* rewash, *S* siwash, Siwash, *U* unwash, *W* wishwash, wash

OSHT

SKWOSHT	squashed

(See **OSH,** add *-ed* where appropriate.)

OSK

OSK	kiosk
BOSK	Bosc, bosk, imbosk
MOSK	abelmosk, mosque

OSP

NOSP	knosp
WOSP	galliwasp, wasp

ŌST

ŌST	oast
BŌST	boast
DŌST	dosed, redosed, undosed
GŌST	ghost
GRŌST	engrossed, grossed
HŌST	host, *no-host*
KŌST	Gold Coast, coast, *seacoast*
MŌST	*A* aftermost, almost, *B* *backmost,* bettermost, bottommost, *E* easternmost, *endmost, F* farthermost, *foremost,* furthermost, *H* headmost, hindermost, *hindmost,* hithermost, *I inmost,* innermost, *L* lowermost, *M* midmost, most, *N* nethermost, northernmost, northermost, *O* outermost, *R* rearmost, *S* centermost, southernmost, southermost, *T topmost, U* undermost, *upmost,* uppermost, *utmost,* uttermost, *W* westermost, westernmost
NŌST	diagnosed
PŌST	*B bedpost, D doorpost, F* fingerpost, *G gatepost, guidepost, H* hitchingpost, *HW* whipping-post, *I impost, K compost, L lamppost,* letterpost, *M milepost, O outpost, P* post, poste, *R* riposte, *S signpost,* soundpost
RŌST	*ribroast,* roast
TŌST	*milquetoast,* toast

(See **ŌS,** add *-d* where appropriate.)

ÔST

FÔST	faust, infaust

KÔST — hippocaust, hypocaust, holocaust
ZÔST — exhaust

OST

OST — teleost
BOST — bossed, cabossed, embossed, imbost
DOST — adossed, dossed
FOST — fossed
FROST — befrost, defrost, frost, *hoarfrost,* Jack Frost, permafrost
GLOST — glossed, reglossed, unglossed
JOST — jossed
KOST — accost, *alecost,* cost, Pentecost
KROST — double-crossed, *criss-crossed,* crossed, recrossed, uncrossed
LOST — lost, relost, unlost
MOST — enmossed, mossed
NOST — anagnost, bibliognost, geognost
SOST — sossed
TOST — betossed, *sea-tossed,* tempest-tossed, tossed, untossed
WOST — wast

ŌT

ŌT — oat, nesiote
BLŌT — bloat
BŌT — *B* banana boat, boat, *F ferryboat, G* gunboat, *H houseboat, HW whaleboat, L lifeboat, longboat, M manbote,* motorboat, *P* pilot boat, power boat, *R riverboat, rowboat, S sailboat,* sea boat, *SH ship's boat, showboat, SP speedboat, ST steamboat, SW swingboat*
DŌT — anecdote, antidote, dote, epidote, lepidote, table d'hôte
FLŌT — afloat, *bobfloat,* float, refloat
FŌT — telephote
GLŌT — gloat
GŌT — billygoat, goat, mountain goat, nanny goat, old goat, redingote, *scapegoat, zygote*
GRŌT — groat

KŌT — *Ä* entrecote, *D dovecote, GR greatcoat, H housecoat, K* coat, cote, *O* overcoat, *P* petticoat, *R* raincoat, recoat, *redcoat, S surcoat, SH sheepcote, T topcoat,* turncoat, *U* undercoat, *W waistcoat,* wyliecoat
KWŌT — bequote, misquote, overquote, quote, requote, underquote, unquote
LŌT — matelote, papillote, pardalote
MŌT — demote, emote, *folkmote,* gemot, commote, moat, mote, promote, remote, witenagemot
NŌT — denote, *footnote, gracenote, keynote,* connote, note, *woodnote*
PLŌT — ploat
PŌT — capote, *compote,* pote
RŌT — garrote, rewrote, rote, wrote, underwrote
SHŌT — shoat, shote
SKŌT — scote
SLŌT — slote
SMŌT — smote, resmote
SŌT — creosote
STŌT — stoat, stote
THRŌT — *bluethroat, whitethroat, cutthroat, starthroat,* throat
TŌT — *aptote,* asymptote, *diptote,* Thoth, tote, *triptote*
TRŌT — throat
VŌT — devote, outvote, redevote, revote, vote

ÔT

ÔT — aught, ought
BÔT — bought, *dear-bought,* rebought
BRÔT — brought, upbrought
FLÔT — flaught
FÔT — fought, *hard-fought,* refought, unfought
FRÔT — fraught, unfraught
GÔT — ghat, ghaut
KÔT — caught, recaught, uncaught, upcaught
NÔT — aeronaut, aquanaut, argonaut, Argonaut, astronaut, *dreadnought, fearnought,* hydronaut, juggernaut, cosmonaut, naught, nought

RÔT — inwrought, overwrought, rewrought, underwrought, unwrought, upwrought, wrought
SLÔT — *onslaught*
SÔT — besought, resought, sought, unbesought, unsought
THÔT — *aforethought,* afterthought, bethought, *forethought,* free thought, merrythought, methought, rethought, thought, unthought
TÔT — retaught, self-taught, taught, taut, untaught, untaut
TRÔT — distraut

OT

OT — *CH* chariot, cheviot, *G* galiot, *H* heriot, *I* idiot, Iscariot, *K* compatriot, *P* patriot, *S* Sciot, *SH* cheviot
BLOT — blot, inkblot, simblot
BOT — *abbott,* bot, bott, *robot*
DOT — dot, microdot, peridot, polka-dot, Wyandotte
FOT — phot
GLOT — *diglot,* glot, heptaglot, hexaglot, microglot, monoglot, pentaglot, polyglot, tessaraglot
GOT — *A* argot, *B* begot, *E* ergot, *F fagot,* faggot, first-begot, forgot, *G ghat,* got, *H hard-got, I ill-got,* ingot, *L* larigot, last-begot, *M misbegot, SP spigot, U* unbegot, unforgot, ungot
GROT — grot
HOT — fiery hot, hot, white-hot, red-hot
HWOT — somewhat, what
JOT — jot
KLOT — *bloodclot,* clot
KOT — apricot, boycott, *dovecot,* haricot, carrycot, cocotte, cot, *mascot,* massicot, persicot, *plumcot*
KWOT — aliquot, *kumquot, loquot, Pequot*
LOT — *A* allot, *B billot, E* eschalot, *feedlot, H Helot, K* cachalot, calotte, Camelot, culotte, *L* Lancelot, lot, Lot, *M* matelotte, melilot, *O*

	ocelot, *S* sans-culotte, *SH* shallot, Shalotte, *T tillot*, *Z* zealot
MOT	bergamot, guillemot, mot, motte, *motmot*, witenagemot
NOT	*B* bowknot, *F* forget-me-not, *G* Gordian knot, *GR* granny knot, *H* Huguenot, *HW whatnot*, *J* juggernaut, *K* cannot, *L loveknot*, *N* knot, not, *R* reef knot, reknot, *SH* shoulderknot, *SKW* square knot, *SL* slipknot, *T topknot*, *U* unknot
PLOT	*grassplot*, complot, counterplot, plot, subplot, underplot
POT	*CH* chimneypot, *D dashpot, despot, F firepot, fusspot, FL fleshpot*, flowerpot, *G* galipot, gallipot, *GL* glue pot, *H hotchpot, hotpot, I inkpot, J jackpot, K catchpot*, coffeepot, *KR crackpot, M monkeypot*, *N* nelipot, *P* pot, pott, *R* repot, *S sexpot, SK skilpot, ST stinkpot, stockpot, T* talipot, *teapot, tin-pot, tosspot, trampot*
ROT	dry rot, *garrot*, garrote, *parrot*, rot, tommyrot
SHOT	*B* bowshot, buckshot, *BL bloodshot, CH* cheap shot, *E* earshot, *F foreshot, G* gunshot, *GR* grapeshot, *H hipshot, I* eyeshot, *L longshot, M moonshot, O* overshot, *P potshot, S* sighting shot, *SH* shot, shott, *SL slapshot, slingshot, SN snapshot, U* undershot, *upshot*
SKOT	Scot, Scott, *wainscot*
SKWOT	asquat, squat, resquat
SLOT	slot
SNOT	snot
SOT	besot, sot
SPOT	beauty spot, forty-sport, heli-spot, hot spot, *nightspot*, plague spot, spot, *sunspot*
STOT	stot
SWOT	swat, swot
TOT	Hottentot, tot
TROT	*dogtrot, foxtrot, jogtrot*, trot, turkeytrot

VOT	gavotte
WOT	kilowatt, megawatt, terawatt, watt, wot
YOT	yacht

ŌTH

(**TH** as in "then")

KLŌTH	clothe, reclothe, unclothe
LŌTH	loathe
TRŌTH	betroth

ŌTH

(**TH** as in "thin")

ŌTH	oath
BŌTH	both
GRŌTH	aftergrowth, growth, *ingrowth, outgrowth*, overgrowth, *regrowth*, undergrowth, zero growth
KWŌTH	quoth
LŌTH	loath
MŌTH	behemoth
RŌTH	wroth
SLŌTH	sloth
THŌTH	Thoth
TRŌTH	betroth, troth, untroth

OTH

(**TH** as in "thin")

BROTH	barley broth, broth
FROTH	froth
GOTH	Goth, Ostrogoth, Visigoth
KLOTH	*B* backcloth, breechcloth, *BR* broadcloth, *CH* cheesecloth, *D* dishcloth, *H* haircloth, *KL* cloth, *L* loincloth, *N* neckcloth, *O* oilcloth, *P* pilot cloth, *S* saddle cloth, *sackcloth*, *sailcloth, cerecloth*
MOTH	behemoth, moth
ROTH	wroth
SWOTH	swath
TROTH	troth

OTS

HOTS	hots, the hots
TROTS	trots, the trots

(See **OT,** add *-s* where appropriate.)

OU

OU	luau, meow, miaow, ow
BOU	bough, bow, golden bough

BROU	brow, *highbrow, eyebrow, lowbrow, middlebrow*, overbrow
CHOU	chou, ciao, *chowchow*, Foochow, Soochow
DOU	disendow, dhow, endow, *landau*, tou
FROU	frau, frow, *hausfrau*
GOU	*hoosegow*
HOU	and how, anyhow, how, *knowhow, somehow*
JOU	jhow
KOU	brown cow, cow, Krakow
LOU	allow, disallow, Lao, *lau-lau*, pilau, reallow
MOU	*haymow*, Mau Mau, mow
NOU	enow, erenow, how now, now, *unau*
PLOU	plough, plow, *snowplough, snowplow*, upplough, upplow
POU	pow
PROU	prow
ROU	row
SKOU	scow
SLOU	slough
SOU	sough, sow
SWOU	swow
THOU	thou
TOU	*kowtow*, tao, tau
VOU	avow, disavow, reavow, vow
WOU	bow-wow, *pow-wow*, wow
YOU	snarleyyow, yow

OUCH

OUCH	ouch
GROUCH	grouch
KOUCH	couch
KROUCH	crouch
MOUCH	Scaramouch
POUCH	pouch
SLOUCH	slouch
VOUCH	avouch, vouch

OUCHT

GROUCHT	grouched

(See **OUCH,** add *-ed* where appropriate.)

OUD

BOUD	bowed, unbowed
DOUD	dowd, endowed, well-endowed
FOUD	foud

KLOUD becloud, encloud, intercloud, cloud, overcloud, recloud, thundercloud, uncloud
KROUD crowd, overcrowd
LOUD aloud, allowed, loud, reallowed
PROUD proud, *purseproud*
SHOUD showd
SHROUD beshroud, disenshroud, enshroud, reshroud, shroud, unshroud
SOUD Ibn-Saud
STROUD stroud
VOUD avowed, reavowed, revowed, vowed

(See **OU**, add *-ed* where appropriate.)

OUJ

GOUJ gouge
SKROUJ scrouge

OUL

OUL night owl, owl, screech owl
BOUL bowel, disembowel
DOUL *dowel*, dowl
FOUL afowl, befoul, foul, fowl, guinea fowl, *moorfowl, peafowl, seafowl, wildfowl,* waterfowl
GROUL growl
HOUL behowl, howl
JOUL jowl
KOUL encowl, cowl, cowle, uncowl
PROUL prowl
SKOUL scowl
YOUL yowl

(See **OUEL**)

OULD

(See **OUL, OUEL,** add-*ed* where appropriate.)

OUN

BROUN brown, embrown, *nutbrown*
DOUN *A* adown, *BR breakdown,* bring down, *D* down, *G godown,* goose-down, *H* hand-me-down, *hoedown,*
I eiderdown, *K comedown, countdown, L lowdown, M markdown,* meltdown, moondown, *P* Piltdown, putdown, *R* reach-me-down, rubdown, *S* sundown, *SH* shakedown, showdown, shutdown, *SL slowdown, SPL splashdown, SW swan's-down, T touchdown,* tumbledown, *TH thistledown, U* upside-down
DROUN drown
FROUN frown
GOUN evening gown, gown, *nightgown,* regown, town and gown, ungown
KLOUN clown
KROUN decrown, discrown, crown, recrown, uncrown
NOUN *adnoun,* noun, *pronoun,* renown
TOUN Chinatown, *downtown,* cabbagetown, *crosstown, midtown, Motown,* shantytown, town, *uptown*

OUND

BOUND *A* abound, *B* bound, *BR brassbound, E earthbound,* eastbound, *F fogbound, H* hellbound, heavenbound, *hidebound, homebound, hoofbound, housebound, I* inbound, ironbound, icebound, *K casebound, KL clothbound, N northbound, O* outbound, outward-bound, *R* rebound, *S* southbound, super-abound, *SN snowbound, SP* spellbound, *ST stormbound, STR strikebound, U* unbound, *W* westbound, windbound
DOUND redound
FOUND *dumbfound,* found, confound, profound, refound, unfound
GROUND *A aboveground,* aground, *B* background, burial ground, burying ground, *F fairground, fine-ground, GR* ground, *H* high ground, holy ground,
K coarse-ground, *L* lost ground, *M* medium-ground, middle ground, *O* overground, *PL playground,* pleasure ground, *R* reground, *SP sportsground, U* underground, unground, *V* vantage ground
HOUND *B* bearhound, boarhound, boozehound, *BL* bloodhound, *D* deerhound, *DR draghound, E* elkhound, *F* foxhound, *GR* grayhound, grewhound, *H* hellhound, horehound, hound, *M* Mahound, *SL sleuth-hound, SM* smut-hound, *ST* staghound, *W wolfhound*
KROUND crowned, wreath-crowned, recrowned, uncrowned
MOUND mound
NOUND renowned, unrenowned
POUND decompound, expound, impound, compound, *geepound,* pound, propound
ROUND around, merry-go-round, round, surround, wraparound
SOUND infrasound, re-sound, sound, ultrasound, unsound
STOUND astound, stound
SWOUND swound
WOUND rewound, series-wound, shunt-wound, unwound, wound
ZOUND resound

(See **OUN,** add *-ed* where appropriate.)

OUNDZ

HOUNDZ *wishhounds, yethhounds*
ZOUNDZ zounds

(See **OUND,** add *-s* where appropriate.)

OUNJ

LOUNJ lounge
SKROUNJ scrounge

OUNS

OUNS ounce
BOUNS bounce

FLOUNS	flounce
FROUNS	frounce
JOUNS	jounce
NOUNS	announce, denounce, enounce, mispronounce, pronounce, renounce
POUNS	pounce
ROUNS	rounce
TROUNS	trounce

(See **OUNT,** add -s.)

OUNT

FOUNT	fount
KOUNT	account, discount, count, miscount, recount, *viscount,* uncount
MOUNT	amount, demount, dismount, catamount, mount, paramount, remount, *seamount,* surmount, tantamount, unmount

OUNZ

(See **OUN,** add -s where appropriate.)

OUR

OUR	evil hour, lucky hour, hour, our, unlucky hour
BOUR	bower, embower
DOUR	dour, dower
FLOUR	deflower, flour, flower, gillyflower, cauliflower, *cornflower, mayflower, moonflower,* passionflower, reflower, *wallflower*
GOUR	gaur
HOUR	Eisenhower
KOUR	cower
LAUR	lour, *safflower*
POUR	empower, hydropower, *horsepower, manpower,* overpower, power, superpower, *willpower*
SHOUR	rain shower, summer shower, shower, thundershower
SKOUR	bescour, rescour, scour
SOUR	besour, resour, sour
STOUR	stour
TOUR	*churchtower,* tower, *watchtower*
VOUR	devour, redevour

(See **OU,** add -er for imperfect rhymes; also see **OUER.**)

OURD

(See **OUR,** add -ed where appropriate.)

OUS

BLOUS	blouse
BOUS	bouse
CHOUS	chiaus, chouse
DOUS	douse
GOUS	degauss, gauss
GROUS	grouse, *sandgrouse, woodgrouse*
HOUS	*A* alehouse, almshouse, *B* bakehouse, bathhouse, backhouse, birdhouse, bawdy house, *Bauhaus, boathouse, bughouse, CH* chapter house, charnel house, charterhouse, *D dosshouse, doghouse, F farmhouse, FR* frat house, *G* guardhouse, gatehouse, guesthouse, *GL* glasshouse, *GR* greenhouse, *H* halfway house, henhouse, *whorehouse, hothouse,* house, *J* jailhouse, *K* cathouse, cookhouse, countinghouse, *courthouse,* customhouse, *KL* clubhouse, *L* lighthouse, *M* madhouse, *O* outhouse, *P* penthouse, *poorhouse,* porterhouse, *pothouse,* powerhouse, public house, *PL playhouse,* pleasure house, *PR* prison house, *R* roadhouse, roundhouse, *S* safe house, summerhouse, *SK schoolhouse, SL* slaughterhouse, *SP* sporting house, *ST* steakhouse, statehouse, storehouse, *T* teahouse, tollhouse, *W* warehouse, *Wodehouse,* workhouse
LOUS	book louse, delouse, louse, wood louse
MOUS	*CH* churchmouse, *D dormouse, F fieldmouse, FL* Fliedermaus, flindermouse, flittermouse, *K* country mouse, *M* Mickey Mouse, mouse, *R reremouse, S* city mouse, *T titmouse,* town mouse

NOUS	nous
SHOUS	shouse
SKOUS	*lobscouse,* scouse
SOUS	souse
SPOUS	spouse
STROUS	Strauss

OUST

OUST	oust
BROUST	browst
FOUST	Faust
FROUST	frowst
JOUST	joust
ROUST	roust

(See **OUS,** add -d where appropriate.)

OUT

OUT	*BL* blackout, *BR brownout, D* diner-out, *dugout, DR* dropout, *F fallout, H* hangout, hereout, *holdout,* hole out, *HW* whereout, *I* in-and-out, *K* cookout, *L lookout, lock-out, N* knockout, *O* out, owt, out-and-out, *P* pig out, *R rainout, SH* shutout, *SP* spaced out, *ST* stakeout, *T takeout,* turnout, *TH* thereout, throughout, *TR tryout, W* walkout, without
BOUT	*A* about, *B* bout, *DR* drinking bout, *G* gadabout, *H* hereabout, *HW* whereabout, whirlabout, *N* knockabout, *R* rightabout, roundabout, roustabout, runabout, *ST* stirabout, *TH* thereabout
DOUT	doubt, misdoubt, redoubt
DROUT	drought
FLOUT	flout
GOUT	gout
GROUT	grout
HOUT	mahout
KLOUT	*breechclout,* clout
KROUT	kraut, sauerkraut
LOUT	*ablaut,* lout, *umlaut*
NOUT	knout, nowt
POUT	*eelpout,* pout
ROUT	derout, rout
SHOUT	beshout, shout
SKOUT	boy scout, girl scout, scout

SMOUT	smout
SNOUT	snout
SPOUT	bespout, *downspout*, spout, waterspout
SPROUT	sprout, resprout
STOUT	stout, stylish stout
TOUT	tout
TROUT	trout
VOUT	devout, undevout

OUTH

DROUTH	drouth
MOUTH	*B* bemouth, *badmouth*, *bigmouth*, *BL* blabbermouth, *CH* chiselmouth, *FL* flutemouth, *FR* frogmouth, *H* hand and mouth, hand to mouth, *hardmouth*, *K* cottonmouth, *KL* closemouth, *L loudmouth*, *M* mouth, *SN* snakemouth, warmouth
SOUTH	south

OUZ

BLOUZ	blouse
BOUZ	bouse
BROUZ	browse
DOUZ	douse, dowse
DROUZ	drowse
HOUZ	house, rehouse, unhouse
MOUZ	mouse
POUZ	disespouse, espouse
ROUZ	arouse, carouse, rouse, uprouse
SMOUZ	smouse
SOUZ	souse
SPOUZ	bespouse, disespouse, espouse, spouse
TOUZ	touse, towse
TROUZ	trouse

(See **OU**, add -*s* where appropriate.)

OUZD

BOUZD	boused

(See **OUZ**, add -*d* where appropriate.)

ŌV

DŌV	dove
DRŌV	drove
GRŌV	grove, *mangrove*
HŌV	behove, hove
JŌV	apojove, Jove, perijove
KLŌV	clove
KŌV	*alcove*, cove
MŌV	gemauve, mauve
RŌV	rove
SHRŌV	shrove, Shrove
STŌV	stove
STRŌV	strove
THRŌV	throve
TRŌV	treasure trove, trove
WŌV	interwove, inwove, rewove, wove

ŌVZ

LŌVZ	loaves

(See **ŌV**, add -*s* where appropriate.)

ŌZ

BŌZ	beaux
BRŌZ	brose
CHŌZ	chose
DŌZ	*bulldoze*, doze
FŌZ	*metamorphose*
FRŌZ	froze, refroze, unfroze
GLŌZ	glose, glows, gloze
HŌZ	*half-hose*, hose, pantyhose
KLŌZ	disclose, enclose, foreclose, inclose, interclose, close, clothes, *parclose*, reclose, *smallclothes*, unclose
KŌZ	coze
KRŌZ	croze
MŌZ	anastomose
NŌZ	bladdernose, *bluenose*, bottlenose, diagnose, dominoes, *hooknose*, pug nose, shovelnose, snub nose
PŌZ	*A* appose, *D* decompose, depose, discompose, dispose, *E* expose, *I* impose, indispose, infrapose, interpose, *J* juxtapose, *K* compose, *O* oppose, overexpose, *P* pose, *PR* predispose, presuppose, propose, *R* recompose, repose, resuppose, *S* superpose, suppose, *TR* transpose, *U* underexpose
PRŌZ	prose
RŌZ	*A* arose, *BR* bramble rose, *D* damask rose, dog rose, *G* guelder-rose, *I* Irish rose, *M* moss rose, *PR* primrose, *R* rambling rose, *rockrose*, rose, *SW* sweetheart rose, *T* tearose, tuberose, *W* wild rose, York rose (etc.)
SHŌZ	quelquechose, shows
SKWŌZ	squoze
THŌZ	those
THRŌZ	throes, throws
TŌZ	pettitoes, toze

(See **Ō**, add -*s*, -*es* where appropriate.)

ÔZ

GÔZ	gauze, geegaws
HÔZ	hawse
JÔZ	jaws, lantern jaws
KLÔZ	clause, claws, Santa Claus
KÔZ	because, cause
PLÔZ	applause
PÔZ	aeropause, diapause, magnetopause, menopause, mesopause, pause, paws, stratopause
STRÔZ	*jackstraws*, straws
TÔZ	taws, tawse
VÔZ	vase
YÔZ	yaws

(See **Ô**, add -*s* where appropriate.)

OZ

BOZ	Boz
KOZ	cos
KWOZ	quoz
TWOZ	'twas
WOZ	was

ŌZD

(See **ŌZ**, add -*d* where appropriate.)

ŌZH

BŌZH	gamboge
LŌZH	éloge, loge
MŌZH	Limoges

Ū

Ū	bayou, B.T.U., I.O.U., ewe, U, yew, you

BŪ imbue, reimbue

DŪ *A* adieu, *B* bedew, bienentendu, bon dieu, *D* dew, *E* endew, endue, *F* fondue, *H* honeydew, *I* indew, *M* malentendu, mountain dew, *N* night dew, *O* overdue, *P* perdu, perdue, Purdue, *PR* prie-dieu, *R* residue, *S* sous-entendu, subdue, *sundew*, *U* undue, *V* vendue, *Z* Xanadu

FŪ feu, feverfew, few, phew, *curfew*

HŪ hew, hue, whew, clerihew, rough-hew

KŪ curlicue, cue, queue, kyu, purlicue, ratamacue

LŪ *curlew,* lieu, poilu, *purlieu*

MŪ *emu,* immew, mew, sea mew, unmew

NŪ *A* anew, avenue, *D* detinue, *E* enew, *F* foreknew, *K continue, N* gnu, knew, new, nu, *P* parvenu, *R* renew, retinue, revenue, *V venue*

PŪ conspue, pew, pugh, rompu

SKŪ askew, skew, unskew

SMŪ smeu, smew

SPŪ spew

STŪ beef stew, Irish stew, stew

SŪ ensue, resue, sue

THŪ thew

TŪ battue, tew, *virtue*

VŪ bird's-eye view, interview, overview, *preview, purview,* review, view

YŪ senryu

(See **OO**)

HAD I BUTT NUDE

Had I butt nude,
Had I but seed,
Would I have dude
The dids I deed?

ŪB

TŪB breathing tube, inner tube, tube

(See **OOB**)

UB

BLUB blub
BUB Beelzebub, bub, *hubbub,* sillabub, syllabub, trillibub
CHUB chub
DRUB drub
DUB dub, *flubdub,* rub-a-dub
FLUB flub
FUB fub
GLUB glub, glub-glub
GRUB grub
HUB hub
KLUB battle club, business club, Kiwanis club, country club, club, lunch club, men's club, *nightclub,* Rotary club, social club, war club, women's club
KUB cub
NUB knub, nub
PUB pub
RUB rub
SHRUB shrub, *subshrub*
SKRUB scrub
SLUB slub
SNUB snub
STUB stub
SUB sub
TUB *bathtub,* tub, *washtub*

UBD

(See **UB,** add *-ed* where appropriate.)

ŪCH

(See **OOCH**)

UCH

DUCH Dutch
HUCH hutch
KLUCH clutch
KRUCH crutch
KUCH cutch
MUCH forasmuch, inasmuch, insomuch, much, mutch, overmuch
RUCH rutch
SKUCH scutch
SMUCH smutch
SUCH *nonesuch,* such
TUCH master touch, Midas touch, retouch, soft touch, touch, untouch

UCHT

(See **UCH,** add *-ed* where appropriate.)

ŪD

DŪD dude
FŪD feud
HŪD many-hued, rainbow-hued, sombre-hued
LŪD collude, interlude, lewd, *prelude, postlude,* unlewd
NŪD denude, half nude, nude, renewed, unrenewed
STŪD stewed, stude
SŪD exude, transude
THŪD thewed
TŪD *A* altitude, amplitude, aptitude, asuetude, attitude, *B* beatitude, *D* decrepitude, definitude, desuetude, disquietude, dissimilitude, *E* eptitude, exactitude, *GR* gratitude, *H* habitude, hebetude, *I* inaptitude, inexactitude, ineptitude, infinitude, ingratitude, inquietude, incertitude, insuetude, *K* consuetude, correctitude, *KR* crassitude, *KW* quietude, *L* lassitude, latitude, lenitude, lentitude, lippitude, longitude, *M* magnitude, mansuetude, mollitude, multitude, *N* necessitude, negritude, nigritude, *O* omnitude, *P* pinguitude, pulchritude, *PL* platitude, plenitude, *PR* promptitude, *R* rectitude, *S* sanctitude, senectitude, serenitude, certitude, servitude, similitude, solicitude, solitude, *SP* spissitude, *T* torpitude, turpitude, *V* vastitude, verisimilitude, vicissitude
ZŪD exude

(See **OOD**; see **Ū**, add *-ed* or *-d* where appropriate.)

UD

BLUD blood, *lifeblood, oxblood,* 'sblood
BUD bud, disbud, *redbud, rosebud* (etc.)
DUD dud, fuddydud
FLUD flood, photoflood
FUD fud
KRUD crud

KUD	cud
LUD	lud, m' lud
MUD	mud
PUD	pud
RUD	rud, rudd
SHUD	shud
SKUD	scud
SPUD	spud
STUD	bestud, stud, unstud
SUD	sud, sudd
THUD	thud

ŪF

(See **OOF**)

UF

BLUF	bluff, Council Bluff, Red Bluff
BUF	blindman's-buff, buff, counterbuff, rebuff
CHUF	chough, chuff
DRUF	*dandruff*
DUF	duff, Macduff, plum duff
FLUF	fluff
FUF	fuff
GRUF	gruff
GUF	guff
HUF	huff
HWUF	whuff
KLUF	clough
KUF	becuff, fisticuff, *handcuff,* handicuff, cuff, off-the-cuff, on the cuff, uncuff
LUF	luff
MUF	*earmuff,* muff
NUF	enough
PLUF	pluff
PUF	bepuff, *creampuff, wheatpuff,* powderpuff, puff
RUF	*crossruff,* rough, ruff, *woodruff*
SKRUF	scruff
SKUF	scuff
SLUF	slough, sluff
SNUF	besnuff, snuff
STUF	*breadstuff, dyestuff, foodstuff,* garden stuff, *greenstuff,* overstuff, stuff, unstuff
SUF	sough
TUF	tough, tuff

ŪFT

(See **OOF**, add *-ed* where appropriate.)

UFT

SKUFT	scuffed, scuft
TUFT	candytuft, tuft

(See **UF,** add *-ed* where appropriate.)

ŪG

FŪG	fugue

(See **OOG**)

UG

UG	ugh
BUG	*bedbug,* bug, debug, doodlebug, *firebug, humbug,* jitterbug, ladybug, litterbug, *redbug,* spittlebug, tumblebug
CHUG	chug
DRUG	drug
DUG	dug
FUG	fug
GLUG	glug
HUG	*bearhug,* bunny hug, hug
JUG	jug
LUG	lug
MUG	mug
PLUG	*earplug, noseplug,* plug, unplug
PUG	pug
RUG	rug
SHRUG	shrug
SLUG	forslug, slug
SMUG	smug
SNUG	snug
THUG	thug
TRUG	trug
TUG	tug
VUG	vug

UGD

(See **UG,** add *-ged* where appropriate.)

ŪJ

FŪJ	deonifuge, dolorifuge, febrifuge, insectifuge, calcifuge, centrifuge, subterfuge, taenifuge, *transfuge,* vermifuge
HŪJ	huge

(See **OOJ**)

UJ

BLUJ	bludge
BUJ	budge
DRUJ	drudge
FUJ	fudge
GRUJ	begrudge, grudge
JUJ	adjudge, forejudge, forjudge, judge, misjudge, prejudge, rejudge
MUJ	mudge
NUJ	nudge
PUJ	pudge
RUJ	rudge
SLUJ	sludge
SMUJ	smudge
TRUJ	trudge

UJD

JUJD	ill-judged, unjudged, well-judged

(See **UJ,** add *-d* where appropriate.)

ŪK

ŪK	uke, yeuk, yewk, yuke
BŪK	rebuke, sambuke
NŪK	antinuke, nuke, *pro-nuke*
PŪK	puke

> *GENESIS*
>
> It all just happened? No intent?
> Then let us pray to Accident.

TŪK	Heptateuch, Hexateuch, Octateuch, Pentateuch, tuke

(See **OOK**)

UK

BUK	*blackbuck,* buck, *bushbuck, jumbuck,* huckabuck, megabuck, *prongbuck, reedbuck, roebuck, sawbuck, springbuck,* waterbuck
CHUK	chuck, *woodchuck*
DUK	beduck, dead duck, Donald Duck, duck, lame duck, *shelduck*
FUK	fuck
GLUK	gluck
GUK	guck

HUK	huck
KLUK	dumb cluck, cluck
KRUK	cruck
KUK	cuck
LUK	beginner's luck, chuck-a-luck, dumb luck, ill-luck, Lady Luck, luck, misluck, *mukluk, potluck*
MUK	amuck, high muck-a-muck, muck
NUK	Canuck
PLUK	pluck
PUK	puck, Puck, Volapuk
RUK	laverock, ruck, rukh, sumbooruk
SHMUK	shmuck
SHUK	shuck
STRUK	*dumbstruck,* horror-struck, *moonstruck, awe-struck, stagestruck,* struck, *sunstruck,* terror-struck, thunderstruck, wonderstruck
STUK	stuck, unstuck
SUK	suck
TRUK	truck
TUK	Friar Tuck, nip and tuck, tuck
YUK	yuk

UKS

DUKS	dux, *redux*
FLUKS	flux, *influx*
KRUKS	crux
LUKS	de luxe, lux, Lux
MUKS	mucks, mux
SHUKS	shucks
TUKS	tux
YUKS	yucks

(See **UK,** add -*s* where appropriate.)

UKT

DUKT	*A* abduct, aqueduct, *D* deduct, duct, *E* educt, *F* fumiduct, *I* induct, *K* conduct, *M* misconduct, *O* obduct, oviduct, *PR* product, *R* reduct, *S* circumduct, subduct, *V* viaduct
FRUKT	usufruct
LUKT	reluct
PLUKT	plucked, unplucked, well-plucked
RUKT	eruct
STRUKT	destruct, instruct, construct, misconstruct,

obstruct, reconstruct, self-destruct, substruct, superstruct

(See **UK,** add -*ed* where appropriate.)

ŪL

ŪL	Yule
BŪL	buhl, Istanbul, *jambul,* vestibule
DŪL	dual, duel, hierodule
GŪL	gule
KŪL	*macule,* molecule, reticule, ridicule, vermicule, verricule
MŪL	mewl, mule
NŪL	*newel, renewal*
PŪL	pule
SKŪL	*ulcuscule*

(See $\overline{\text{OOL}}$, $\overline{\text{OOEL}}$, **ŪAL.**)

UL

DUL	dull
GUL	gull, hooded gull, Mogul, *seagull*
HUL	ahull, dehull, hull, multihull
KUL	caracul, cull
LUL	lull
MUL	mull
NUL	annul, disannul, null
SKUL	*numskull,* scull, skull
STUL	stull
SUL	sull
TRUL	trull
WUL	wull

ULCH

GULCH	gulch
KULCH	culch, cultch
MULCH	mulch

ULD

(See **UL,** add -*ed* where appropriate.)

ULJ

BULJ	bulge
DULJ	indulge, overindulge, reindulge
FULJ	effulge
MULJ	promulge
VULJ	divulge

ULJD

(See **ULJ,** add -*d* where appropriate.)

ULK

BULK	bulk
HULK	hulk
MULK	mulk
SKULK	skulk
SULK	sulk

ULKT

MULKT	mulct

(See **ULK,** add -*ed* where appropriate.)

ULM

KULM	culm
MULM	mulm
STULM	stulm

ULP

GULP	gulp
KULP	culp
PULP	pulp
SKULP	sculp

ULPT

GULPT	gulped
PULPT	golden-pulped, *soft-pulped, sweet-pulped*
SKULPT	sculped, sculpt

ULS

BULS	bulse
DULS	dulce, dulse
MULS	mulse
PULS	appulse, expulse, *impulse,* pulse, repulse
SULS	insulse
VULS	avulse, convulse, revulse

(See **ULT,** add -*s* where appropriate.)

ULT

DULT	adult, indult, subadult, unadult
KULT	difficult, incult, cult, occult

NULT	antepenult, penult
PULT	catapult
SULT	insult, juriconsult, consult, reinsult, reconsult
ZULT	exult, result

ŪLZ

GŪLZ	gules

(See **ŪL**, **OOL**; add *-s* where appropriate.)

ŪM

ŪM	Fiume
FŪM	fume, perfume
GŪM	legume
HŪM	exhume, inhume
LŪM	illume, reillume, relume
NŪM	neume
SPŪM	spume
SŪM	assume, consume, reassume, subsume
ZŪM	exhume, presume, resume

(See **OOM**)

UM

UM	*A* absinthium, agonium, Actium, allium, aluminum, alluvium, ammonium, ante meridium, anthurium, atrium, *B* Byzantium, *BR* brachium, *D* delphinium, dentalium, disequilibrium, decennium, deliquium, delirium, *E* effluvium, equilibrium, exordium, Elysium, emporium, encomium, epigastrium, epicardium, epithalamium, Eryngium, *F* fermium, *FR*

francium, *G* gallium, *H* hafnium, harmonium, helium, hypogastrium, hypochondrium, holmium, horreum, *I* idiomindium, ischium, yttrium, *J* geranium, gymnasium, *K* cadmium, calcium, cambium, caputium, castoreum, colloquium, columbium, compendium, consortium, contagium, *KR* cranium, crematorium, chromium, *KW* quadrivium, quinquennium, *L* labium, lithium, linoleum, *M* martyrium, medium, menstruum, millennium, moratorium, mutuum, *N* nasturtium, natatorium, nephridium, *O* odeum, auditorium, odium, opium, opprobrium, opsonium, orpheum, osmium, ostium, otium, *P* palladium, pallium, pandemonium, pelargonium, pericardium, petroleum, podium, polonium, post meridiem, potassium, *PL* plutonium, *PR* premium, presidium, principium, proscenium, protium, *R* radium, residuum, *S* sanatorium, selenium, cerulium, coerulium, sestertium, silphium, symposium, sodium, *SK* scandium, *SP* sporangium, *ST* stadium, stibium, studium, *STR* stramonium, strontium, *T* tedium, tellurium, terrium, titanium, terbium, *TH* thallium, thulium, *TR* triennium, trillium, triodium, *U* um, um-um, euphonium, erbium, *V* vacuum, valium, vitium, vivarium, *Y* uranium, *Z* xenodochium

BRUM	cerebrum
BUM	bum, stumblebum
CHUM	chum
DRUM	bass drum, drum, *eardrum, humdrum, conundrum,* kettledrum, *panjandrum*
DUM	*A* heirdom, *B* Bumbledom, *D* dogdom, dukedom, dumb, *dumbdumb, dumdum, E* earldom, *FL*

flunkeydom, *H* halidom, heathendom, *whoredom, K kingdom,* Cockneydom, *KR* Christendom, *M* martyrdom, *O* officialdom, oppidum, *PR prudhomme, R* rascaldom, rebeldom, *S* sardoodledum, Saxondom, solidum, *serfdom, TW* Tweedledum

FRUM	from, wherefrom, therefrom
FUM	fee-fi-fo-fum
GLUM	glum
GRUM	grum
GUM	begum, bubblegum, chewing gum, gum, *subgum*
HUM	ho-hum, hum
KRUM	crum, crumb
KUM	become, *income,* capsicum, misbecome, modicum, *outcome,* overcome, succumb, vaticum, viaticum, unicum
LUM	coagulum, curriculum, lum, pabulum, pendulum, seculum, septulum, scybalum, symbolum, cingulum, sertulum
MUM	chrysanthemum, *quadrimum,* maximum, minimum, mum, optimum
NUM	aluminum, benumb, labdanum, laudanum, molybdenum, numb, platinum, tympanum
PLUM	plum, plumb, replumb, sugar plum, unplumb
RUM	rhumb, rum, theorum
SKRUM	scrum
SKUM	scum
SLUM	slum
SNUM	snum
STRUM	strum
STUM	stum
SUM	*A* adventuresome, *B* bothersome, burdensome, *DR* drearisome, *F foursome, FR* frolicsome, *G* gamblesome, *GR gruesome, H* wholesome, horrorsome, humorsome, *I* intermeddlesome, *K* cuddlesome, cumbersome, *KW* quarrelsome, quietsome, *L lonesome, M* meddlesome, mettlesome, *N* nettlesome, *O* awesome, *R* wranglesome, *S* some, sum, *T twosome, toothsome, THR threesome*

(etc.), *TR* troublesome, *U* ugglesome, *V* venturesome, *W* wearisome, worrisome, *Z* zero sum

SWUM swum
THRUM thrum
THUM green thumb, thumb
TUM accubitum, acquisitum, ad libitum, adytum, debitum, cognitum, compitum, placitum, tum, *tum-tum,* zibetum
YUM yum-yum, *Yum-Yum*
ZUM zum

Ū̄MD

(See **ŪM, OOM,** add -*d* or -*ed* where appropriate.)

UMD

(See **UM,** add -*ed* or -*med* where appropriate.)

UMF

UMF umph
GRUMF grumph
HUMF humph

UMP

UMP ump
BUMP bump
CHUMP chump
DUMP dump
FLUMP flump
FRUMP frump
GLUMP glump
GRUMP grump
HUMP hump
JUMP *broadjump, highjump,* jump, running jump, standing jump
KLUMP clump
KRUMP crump
LUMP lump
MUMP mump
PLUMP plump
PUMP pump
RUMP rump
SKRUMP scrump
SLUMP slump
STUMP stump
SUMP sump
THUMP bethump, thump
TRUMP *no-trump,* overtrump, trump, undertrump

TUMP tump
WUMP *mugwump,* wump
ZUMP gazump

UMPS

BUMPS *goosebumps*
MUMPS mumps

(See **UMP,** add -*s* where appropriate.)

ŪN

ŪN triune
BŪN tribune
HŪN hewn, rehewn, *rough-hewn,* unhewn
KŪN lacune
LŪN lune
MŪN immune, intercommune, commune
PŪN impugn, oppugn, repugn
TŪN attune, entune, inopportune, importune, looney-tune, *Neptune,* opportune, retune, tune, untune
YŪN picayune, triune

(See **OON**)

UN

UN *A* abecedarian, Acadian, acanthropterygian, accordion, acromion, Alabamian, alabastrian, Albanian, Albion, Alexandrian, Algonquian, Algerian, alien, alluvian, amatorian, Amazonian, amoebian, Amerindian, amphibian, amphictyon, Amphitrion, amnion, Anatolian, Anglian, antediluvean, antemeridian, anthelion, anthemion, antiquarian, Appalachian, aphelion, apian, apiarian, Apollonian, apocynthion, Arian, Aristotelian, Arcadian, Archimedean, Armenian, artesian, Arthurian, ascidian, Atlantean, avian, *B* Babylonian, bacchanalian, Baconian, bactrian, Barbadian, barbarian, basion, bastian, bastion, batrachian, Bavarian, Belgian, Bezonian, Bohemian, Bulgarian, *BR* Brazilian, Briarean, *CH* champion, Czechoslovakian, Chaucerian, *D* Darien, Darwinian, Delphian, demibastion, Dickensian, diluvian, Dionysian, disciplinarian, Deucalion, durian, *DR* Dravidian, *E* Edwardian, equestrian, Elysian, *empyrean,* epilimnion, Episcopalian, Erachtheion, etesian, Ethiopian, Etonian, *F* Fallopian, favonian, Fenian, Fijian, fustian, *FR* Phrygian, Freudian, fruitarian, *G* gabion, galleon, gammadian, ganglion, guardian, gargantuan, Gideon, Gilbertian, gonion, Gordian, gorgonian, *GR* grammarian, Gratian, *H* Hadrian, halcyon, Haitian, Herculean, Hesperian, Hessian, Hibernian, historian, holothurian, humanitarian, *I* Icarian, Ilion, Indian, infralapsarian, inion, Iranian, *J* Georgian, Johnsonian, Jordanian, Jovian, *K* Caducean, Caledonian, callipygian, Cambrian, chameleon, camion, campion, Canadian, Cantabrigian, Caribbean, carnelian, Carolingian, carrion, Carpathian, Carthaginian, Carthusian, Caspian, Castilian, chelonian, Caucasian, collodeon, Columbian, Comanchean, comedian, commentarian, chorion, Corinthian, custodian, *KL* clarion, *KR* Christadelphian, crocodilian, criterion, Cromwellian, crossopterygian, *KW* quarrion, quaternion, Quintilion, quotidian, *L* labyrinthian, Lamarckian, lampion, Lancastrian, Lacedaemonian, lacertilian, latitudinarian,

Latvian, lesbian,
libertarian, librarian,
Libyan, limitarian,
Lithuanian, Liverpudian,
Lothian, Lucian, *M*
Machiavellian,
Maximillian,
malacopterygian,
Malaysian, Malthusian,
mammalian, Marxian,
Macedonian, median,
Mediterranean,
Melanesian, melodeon,
meridian, Merovingian,
metatherion, mezerion,
Midlothian, millenarian,
Mississippian,
mitochondrian, Mongolian,
Moravian, morion,
Morovingian, *N* Napoleon,
nasion, nectarean,
nemertean, Neptunian,
Nigerian, nickelodeon,
Noachian, nonagenarian,
Northumbrian, Nubian,
nullifidian, Newtonian, *O*
oblivion, obsidian,
Augustinian, Ogygian,
Oxonian, Octavian,
octogenarian, Olympian,
Aurelian, Orcadian,
ornithischian, Orwellian,
Ossian, Australian,
Austrian, authoritarian,
ovarian, *P* pagurian,
pampean, Panamerican,
pantheon, parhelion,
Parisian, Parthian,
pedestrian, Pelion,
Pennsylvanian, perihelion,
Peruvian, pericynthion,
Pierian, Pygmalion,
Pickwickian, Pythian,
Polynesian, Pomeranian,
pomeridian, postdiluvian,
postmeridian, *PL*
planarian, platitudinarian,
Plutonian, *PR*
predestinarian,
prehistorian, Presbyterian,
pretorian, proboscidian,
Procrustean, proletarian,
promethean, prosimian,
protean, protheriean, *R*
Rabelaisian, rampion,
riparian, Rhodesian,
Rhodian, Rotarian, ruffian,
Rumanian, Ruthenian, *S*
Sabbatarian, sabellian,
saffian, sacramentarian,
Salientian, samian,
Sardinian, selachian,

seminarian,
sesquipedalian, Siberian,
Cyclopean, centenarian,
Cimmerian, Cyprian,
Syrian, Circassian,
caecilian, Sicilian,
Sisyphean, solifidian,
saurian, Socinian,
subterranean, Sumerian,
supralapsarian, *SH*
Shakespearean, Shavian,
Shoshonean, *SK* Scandian,
scorpion, *SM* Smithsonian,
ST stentorian, steradian,
Stygian, *T* tallion,
tampion, Tasmanian,
tellurian, tellurion,
Tertullian, tinean,
Tyrrhenian, Tyrian,
Tocharion, turion, *TH*
theologian, thespian,
Thessalonian, *TR*
tragedian, Transylvanian,
U Umbrian, *V* Wagnerian,
Valentinian, valerian,
valetudinarian, Valkyrian,
vegetarian, Venusian,
Vespasian, veterinarian,
vesuvian, vaudevillian,
vulgarian, Vulcanian, *W*
Wagnerian, Wesleyan, *Y*
ubiquitarian, Yugoslavian,
Ukrainian, Jungian,
unitarian, Uranian,
eutherian, utilitarian,
utopian, *Z* Zyrian,
Zoroastrian (compare UN
with AN)

BUN   bonne, bun, honeybun,
             hotcross bun, raisin bun

DUN   *D* done, dun, *F* foredone, *I*
             ill-done, *KL* clarendon, *M*
             myrmidon, *O* outdone,
             overdone, *R* redone, *U*
             underdone, undone, *W*
             well-done

FUN   fun, colophon

GUN   *A* airgun, *B* BB gun,
             begun, *G* Gatling gun,
             gun, *H* handgun, *M*
             machine gun, minute gun,
             P paragon, percussion gun,
             popgun, SH shotgun, U
             unbegun

HUN   hon, Hun

KUN   helicon, Helicon,
             pantechnicon

LUN   gonfalon, Sally Lunn

MUN   cardamon, cinnamon

NUN   phenomenon, none, nun,
             Parthenon, prolegomenon,
             unnun

PUN   pun

RUN   Bull Run, forerun, *hard-
             run, millrun,* Oberon,
             outrun, overrun, rerun,
             run, underrun

SHUN   shun

SPUN   *finespun, homespun,* spun

STUN   stun

SUN   *F* foster son, *G* garrison,
             GR grandson, *HW
             Whitsun, J* jettison, *K*
             caparison, comparison, *O*
             orison, *S* son, sun, sunn,
             ST stepson, *T* Tennyson, *V*
             venison, *Y* unison

TUN   Chesterton, Galveston,
             kiloton, megaton,
             simpleton, singleton,
             skeleton, skimmington,
             ton, tonne, tun,
             Washington, Wellington

WUN   A-1, anyone, everyone,
             hard-won, number one,
             rewon, someone, unwon,
             one, won

ZUN   amazon, Amazon, benison

UNCH

BRUNCH   brunch
BUNCH   bunch, honeybunch
HUNCH   hunch
KLUNCH   clunch
KRUNCH   crunch
LUNCH   box lunch, free lunch, heavy
              lunch, light lunch, lunch
MUNCH   munch
NUNCH   nunch
PUNCH   punch
RUNCH   runch
SKRUNCH   scrunch

$\overline{U}ND$

(See $\overline{OOND}$. See $\overline{OON}$, add *-ed* where appropriate. See $\overline{U}N$, add *-d* where appropriate.)

UND

BUND   bund, bundh, errabund,
             cummerbund, moribund
FUND   fund, refund, re-fund,
             slush fund
KUND   rubicund, verecund
MUND   immund, mund
TUND   obrotund, obtund, orotund,
             retund, rotund

(See **UN,** add *-ned* where appropriate.)

UNG

BRUNG	brung
BUNG	bung
DUNG	dung
FLUNG	flung
HUNG	hung, overhung, underhung, unhung, well-hung
KLUNG	clung
LUNG	lung, *one-lung*
MUNG	among, hereamong, whereamong, mung, thereamong
PUNG	pung
RUNG	bewrung, rung, wrung, unrung, unwrung, wither-wrung
SLUNG	slung, underslung, unslung
SPRUNG	sprung, unsprung, upsprung
STRUNG	*hamstrung*, highly strung, *highstrung*, overstrung, strung, unstrung
STUNG	stung, unstung
SUNG	sung, unsung
SWUNG	swung, upswung
TUNG	betongue, *bluetongue*, mother tongue, *ox-tongue*, *shantung*, tongue
YUNG	young

UNGD

BUNGD	bunged
LUNGD	iron-lunged, leather-lunged, loud-lunged
TUNGD	*B* betongued, *bell-tongued*, *BL* black-tongued, *PL* pleasant-tongued, *S* silver-tongued, *soft-tongued*, *SH* sharp-tongued, *SHR* shrill-tongued, *T* tongued, *TH* thick-tongued, *TR* trumpet-tongued

UNGK

UNGK	unc, unk
BLUNGK	blunk
BUNGK	bunk, debunk
CHUNGK	chunk
DRUNGK	drunk
DUNGK	dunk
FLUNGK	flunk
FUNGK	duddyfunk, funk
GUNGK	gunk
HUNGK	hunk
JUNGK	junk
KLUNGK	kinclunk, clunk

LUNGK	lunk
MUNGK	*chipmunk*, monk
NUNGK	*quidnunc*, nunc
PLUNGK	kerplunk, plunk
PUNGK	punk
SHRUNGK	*preshrunk*, shrunk
SKUNGK	skunk
SLUNGK	slunk
SPUNGK	spunk
STUNGK	stunk
SUNGK	sunk
TRUNGK	steamer trunk, *treetrunk*, trunk
TUNGK	tunk
PUNGKT	compunct

UNGKT

FUNGKT	defunct
JUNGKT	*adjunct*, disjunct, injunct, junked, conjunct

(See **UNGK,** add *-ed* where appropriate.)

UNGST

MUNGST	amongst

(See verbs in **UNG,** add *-'st* for archaic usage.)

UNJ

BLUNJ	blunge
GRUNJ	grunge
GUNJ	gunge
LUNJ	allonge, longe, lunge, muskellunge
PLUNJ	plunge
PUNJ	expunge
SKUNJ	scunge
SPUNJ	sponge

UNJD

(See **UNJ,** add *-ed* where appropriate.)

UNS

BUNS	bunce
DUNS	dunce
WUNS	once

(See **UNT,** add *-s* where appropriate.)

PARADOX

Illogic I abhor;
  And yet I have to own
That I've forgotten more
  Than I have ever known.

UNT

UNT	*exeunt*
BLUNT	blunt
BRUNT	brunt
BUNT	bunt
DUNT	dunt
FRUNT	affront, afront, *bifront*, *breakfront, forefront*, front, confront, *seafront*, up front
GRUNT	grunt
HUNT	*deerhunt*, Easter egg hunt, *elkhunt*, pheasant hunt, *foxhunt*, hunt, *manhunt*, staghunt, witchhunt (etc.)
LUNT	lunt
KUNT	cunt
PUNT	punt
RUNT	runt
SHUNT	shunt
SPRUNT	sprunt
STUNT	stunt
WUNT	wont, wun't

ŪP

DŪP	dupe
STŪP	stupe

(See $\overline{OO}$P)

UP

UP	*B* backup, batter-up, *BL* blow-up, *BR* break-up, *CH* check-up, chin up, *F* fed up, *G* get-up, giddy-up, *H* hard-up, hiccup, *K* keyed-up, cock-up, *KL* closeup, *L* lash-up, let-up, lock-up, *M* makeup, *P* pick-up, pull-up, push-up, *R* rip-up, roundup, *S* setup, setter-up, *sunup*, *SL* slap up, *T* teacup, tip-up, toss-up, *U* up, up-and-up, *W* wickiup, *wind-up*
DUP	dup
GUP	gup
HUP	hup
KRUP	Krupp
KUP	buttercup, grace cup, *grease-cup, hiccup*, hiccough, eyecup, cup, loving cup, stirrup cup, *teacup*, wassail cup
PUP	pup
SKUP	scup
SUP	sup

TUP	tup		
YUP	yup		

UPT

RUPT   abrupt, *bankrupt,* disrupt, erupt, incorrupt, interrupt, irrupt, corrupt, uncorrupt

(See **UP,** add *-ped* where appropriate.)

ŪR

ŪR	ewer, inure, you're
DŪR	dure, endure, perdure, perendure
FŪR	coiffure
HŪR	hewer
KŪR	epicure, insecure, cure, manicure, pedicure, procure, secure, sinecure, water cure
LŪR	allure, chevelure, colure, condylure, lure, velure
MŪR	demure, immure, mure
NŪR	manure, revenuer, tournure
PŪR	guipure, impure, pure
SKŪR	obscure, skewer
VŪR	photogravure, gravure, autogravure, rotogravure

(See **OOR**)

UR

UR	*A* anterior, *B* borrower, burlier, *BL* blearier, *BR* breezier, brinier, *CH* cheerier, chillier, *D* dingier, dizzier, dowdier, doughtier, dustier, *DR* drearier, drowsier, *E* excelsior, exterior, emptier, er, 'er, err, Ur, earlier, eerier, easier, *F* filmier, filthier, foamier, funnier, fussier, *FL* fleecier, flimsier, flightier, *FR* friendlier, *G* giddier, guiltier, goutier, *GL* gloomier, glossier, *GR* greffier, grimier, *H* happier, hardanger, hardier, healthier, heavier, hillier, holier, homelier, huffier, hungrier, huskier, *HW* wheezier, *I* icier, inferior, inkier, interior, *J* jollier, journeyer, juicier,

K kindlier, kinglier, copier, costlier, cosier, curlier, *KL* cleanlier, *KR* creamier, creepier, *L* likelier, livelier, loftier, lowlier, lonelier, lovelier, *M* marrier, merrier, meteor, mightier, moldier, mossier, muskier, mustier, *N* narrower, knightlier, noisier, *P* pitier, portlier, posterior, pearlier, *PR* princelier, prosier, *R* rapier, rowdier, rosier, *S* seemlier, sightlier, sillier, soapier, sunnier, superior, surlier, *SH* shinier, shoddier, showier, *SK* skinnier, *SL* sleepier, slimier, *SP* spikier, spicier, spoonier, spongier, *SPR* springier, spritelier, *ST* steadier, stealthier, stingier, stormier, stuccoer, sturdier, *T* terrier, *TH* thirstier, thriftier, *TR* trustier, *U* ulterior, *V* valuer, *W* wealthier, wearier, widower, windier, wintrier

BLUR	blur
BRUR	br'er
BUR	birr, burr, butterbur, Excalibar, Excalibur, calaber, caliber, cocklebur, shillaber
CHUR	chirr, churr, calenture, *nightchurr,* ossiture, plicature
DUR	*A* ambassador, *H* highlander, horrider, *I* islander, *K* calendar, calender, colander, corridor, *L* lavender, lowlander, *PR* provender, *R* ruggeder, *S* cylinder, solider, *ST* stupider, *T* timider, *V* vivider
FLUR	fleur, persifleur, renifleur
FUR	*A* aquifer, artificer, *B* befur, bibliographer, biographer, *D* dapifer, defer, *F* philosopher, phonographer, photographer, fer, fir, fur, *furfur,* *FL* flammifer, *I* infer, *K* confer, conifer, *KR* chronopher, chronographer, crucifer, *L* lithographer, lucifer, Lucifer, *O* autobiographer, *P* pornographer, *PR* prefer,

	R refer, rotifer, *SH* chauffeur, *ST* stenographer, *T* typographer, topographer, *TR* transfer
HUR	Ben Hur, her
HWUR	whir, whirr
JUR	*A* armiger, astrologer, *BR* breviger, *CH* challenger, *D* derringer, disparager, dowager, *E* encourager, *F* philologer, forager, *H* harbinger, *I* integer, *K* cottager, *KL* claviger, *M* manager, messenger, mortgagor, *O* onager, *P* passenger, pillager, porringer, *R* ravager, *SK* scavenger, *T* tanager, teenager, *V* villager, vintager, voltigeur, voyager
KUR	incur, claqueur, coniaker, concur, cur, liqueur, massacre, occur, recur, sepulchre
KLUR	chronicler
LUR	*B* bachelor, *CH* chancellor, cheerfuller, chiseler, *DR* driveler, *E* enameler, *H* hoveler, *J* jeweler, *KR* crueler, *KW* quarreler, *L* labeler, leveler, libeler, loyaler, *M* mitrailleur, modeler, mournfuler, *O* odaler, *R* reveler, *SH* shoveler, *SK* skilfuler, *TR* traveler, *V* victualer, *W* wassailer, *Y* yodeler
MUR	*A* astronomer, *D* demur, dulcimer, *G* gossamer, *K* *costumer,* customer, *L* lissomer, lithesomer, lonesomer, lorimer, *M* myrrh, *R* ransomer, *W* winsomer
NUR	*A* almoner, *B* bargainer, burdener, *BL* blazoner, *CH* chastener, cheapener, *D* deepener, determiner, *E* examiner, executioner, emblazoner, enlightener, enlivener, easterner, evener, *F* fastener, fashioner, foreigner, *FL* flaneur, *G* gardener, governor, *H* hardener, hastener, *I* imprisoner, ironer, *K* commissioner, commoner, confectioner, coparcener, coroner, cozener, *KW* questioner,

quickener, *L* lengthener,
lessener, listener,
Londoner, loosener, *M*
mariner, milliner,
moistener, *N* northerner,
knur, *P* parishioner,
parcener, petitioner,
poisoner, *PR* practicioner,
prisoner, probationer, *R*
reasoner, reversioner,
revisioner, *S* seasoner,
sojourner, summoner,
summerer, southerner, *SH*
sharpener, shortener, *STR*
strengthener, *SW*
sweetener, *T* tobogganer,
THR threatener, *W*
wagoner, wakener,
weakener, westerner

PUR *D* developer, diaper, *E*
enveloper, *G* galloper,
gossiper, *H* hanaper, *J*
juniper, *K* caliper, *P* per,
purr, *W* walloper,
worshiper

RUR *A* adulterer, adventurer,
answerer, armorer, *B*
banterer, barterer, batterer,
bickerer, botherer, *BL*
blunderer, blusterer, *BR*
broiderer, *CH* chafferer,
chamferer, chatterer, *D*
deliverer, discoverer, *E*
embroiderer, emperor,
endeavorer, engenderer,
encounterer, *F* favorer,
fosterer, furtherer, *FL*
flatterer, flutterer, *FR*
franc-tireur, *G* gatherer, *H*
harborer, *HW* whimperer,
whisperer, *J* jabberer, *K*
capturer, caterer, cofferer,
conjecturer, conjurer,
conqueror, cornerer,
coverer, *KL* clamorer, *KW*
quaverer, *L* laborer,
lecturer, lingerer, loiterer,
M malingerer, maneuverer,
manufacturer, measurer,
murderer, murmurer,
mutterer, *N* naperer,
numberer, *O* offerer, *P*
palaverer, panderer,
pasturer, patterer,
pepperer, perjurer,
pesterer, pilferer,
poulterer, posturer,
pewterer, *PL* plasterer,
plunderer, *PR* profferer, *R*
roisterer, *S* saunterer,
sorcerer, sufferer,
succorer, *SH* shelterer, *SK*

scamperer, *SKW*
squanderer, *SL* slanderer,
slaughterer, slumberer, *SM*
smatterer, *SPL* splatterer,
splutterer, *ST* staggerer,
stammerer, stutterer, *SW*
swaggerer, *T* tamperer,
torturer, totterer, *TH*
thunderer, *TR* treasurer, *U*
upholsterer, utterer, usurer,
V verderer, *W* wagerer,
wanderer, waverer,
weatherer, wonderer

SHUR *A* admonisher, accoucheur,
assure, *B* banisher,
burnisher, *BL* blandisher,
BR Britisher, *CH*
cherisher, *D* demolisher, *E*
embellisher, embouchure,
ensure, establisher, *H*
hachure, *I* insure, *K*
cocksure, *L* languisher, *N*
nourisher, *P* polisher,
publisher, punisher, *R*
ravisher, reassure,
reinsure, relinquisher, *SH*
shirr, sure, cynosure, *SK*
skirmisher, *U* unsure, *V*
vanquisher

SLUR slur

SMUR smur, smurr

SPUR *hotspur, Hotspur,*
larkspur, spur

STUR *A* administer, apparitor,
astir, *B* baluster, banister,
bannister, barrister, bestir,
F forester, *H* harvester, *K*
canister, *M* maladminister,
minister, *P* Pasteur, *R*
restir, *ST* stir

SUR *A* affiancer, artificer, *F*
farceur, *H* harnesser, *K*
canvasser, connoisseur, *L*
licenser, *M* masseur, *O*
officer, *P* purchaser, *S*
silencer, sir, susurr, *SH*
chasseur, *TR* trespasser

TUR *A* accipiter, amateur,
amphitheater, *ancestor,*
arbiter, *archiater, B*
banqueter, barometer,
bucketer, *CH* chapiter,
chapter, D depositor,
deter, diameter, disinter,
distributor, *E* editor,
executor, expositor, *F*
forfeiter, *FR frankfurter, G*
guarantor, *H* harvester,
hexameter, hauteur, *I*
idolater, inheritor,
inquisitor, inter,
interlocutor, interpreter, *J*

janitor, Jupiter, *K*
carpenter, carpeter,
character, *colporteur,*
competitor, comforter,
compositor, conspirator,
contributor, *KR* creditor,
cricketer, *L* legator,
litterateur, *M* magister,
marketer, monitor, *O*
auditor, orator, auteur, *P*
pentameter, *PL* pleasanter,
PR presbyter,
primogenitor, progenitor,
proprietor, *R* register,
restaurateur, rioter, riveter,
S senator, servitor,
silenter, scimitar, sinister,
solicitor, sophister,
surfeiter, *SH* shamateur, *T*
tetrameter, *TH* theater,
theatre, thermometer, *TR*
traiteur, tregetour, trumpeter,
V visitor, *W* warranter

VUR Andover, aver, gilliver,
Gulliver, caliver, miniver,
Miniver, *passover,*
Passover, sandiver

WUR were

ZUR friseur

ZHUR melangeur, voltageur,
voyageur

(Add *-er* also to appropriate words not listed
here.)

URB

URB	herb, urb
BLURB	blurb
BURB	*suburb*
HURB	herb, *cowherb, potherb,* willowherb
JURB	gerb, gerbe
KURB	curb, uncurb
PURB	superb
SLURB	slurb
SURB	acerb, Serb
TURB	disturb, perturb, undisturb, unperturb
VURB	*adverb, proverb,* reverb, verb

URBD

(See **URB,** add *-ed* where appropriate.)

URCH

BURCH	birch, white birch, weeping birch (etc.)

CHURCH	church, unchurch
LURCH	lurch
PURCH	perch, *pikeperch*, reperch, *surfperch*, unperch
SMURCH	besmirch, smirch
SURCH	research, search

URCHT

(See **URCH**, add -ed where appropriate.)

ŪRD

(See **ŪR**, add -d where appropriate.)

URD

URD	urd
BURD	*B* bird, bowerbird, butcherbird, *BL blackbird, bluebird, D* diving bird, dollarbird, *F firebird, FR* friarbird, frigate bird, *G* gallows bird, *H* halberd, hedgebird, hummingbird, *HW* whirlybird, *J* jailbird, jarbird, *K* cardinal bird, *L* ladybird, *lyrebird, lovebird, M* myna bird, mockingbird, *N nightbird, P* pilotbird, *puffbird, R* rambird, redbird, *S* seabird, songbird, sunbird, *SN* snowbird, *ST* stormbird, *T* tailorbird, *TH* thunderbird, *W* wattlebird, weaverbird (etc.)
FURD	ferd, furred, fyrd
GURD	begird, engird, gird, undergird, ungird
HURD	*goatherd*, heard, herd, *cowherd*, overheard, *shepherd, swanherd, swineherd*, unheard
KURD	curd, Kurd, sepulchred, unsepulchred
MURD	immerd, mird
NURD	nerd
SHURD	*potsherd*
SNURD	Mortimer Snerd
SURD	absurd, surd
THURD	third
TURD	deterred, disinterred, interred, turd, undeterred
VURD	verd
WURD	*A* afterward, afterword, *B* byword, *F foreword, I* inward, *K* catchword, *KR* crossword, *L leeward, N* nonce word, *O* outward, overword, *P* password, *R* reword, *SW swearword, W watchword, wayward,* word

(See **UR,** add -red where appropriate.)

URF

URF	urf
KURF	kerf
NURF	nerf
SKURF	scurf
SURF	hippocerf, serf, surf
TURF	surf and turf, turf

URG

URG	erg
BURG	*B* berg, burg, burgh, *BR* Brandenburg, *G* Gettysburg, *H Hamburg, Hapsburg,* Harrisburg, Heidelberg, *homburg,* iceberg, *J* Johannesburg, *L* Lindbergh, *N* Nuremberg, *P* Pittsburgh, *S* Saint Petersburg, *STR Strasbourg, W* Williamsburg (etc.)
ZURG	exergue

URJ

URJ	demiurge, Demiurge, unurge, urge
DURJ	dirge
GURJ	gurge, regurge
MURJ	emerge, immerge, merge, submerge
PURJ	asperge, purge
SKURJ	scourge
SNURJ	snurge
SPLURJ	splurge
SPURJ	spurge
SURJ	resurge, serge, surge
TURJ	deterge, dramaturge, thaumaturge
VURJ	diverge, converge, verge

URJD

(See **URJ,** add -d where appropriate.)

URK

URK	erk, irk
BURK	berk, burke, *hauberk*

DURK	dirk
FURK	firk
GURK	gurk
JURK	jerk, jerque, soda jerk
KURK	*Dunkirk,* kirk
KLURK	clerk
KWURK	quirk
LURK	lurk
MURK	murk
PURK	perk
SHURK	shirk
SMURK	smirk
STURK	stirk
SURK	cirque
TURK	Turk
WURK	*A artwork, B beadwork, by-work, BR breastwork, brightwork, bridgework, brickwork, brushwork, E earthwork, F fancywork, farmwork, fieldwork, firework, falsework, footwork, FR framework, frostwork, H handiwork, housework, K casework, coachwork, KL clockwork, KR cribwork, L lattice work, legwork, M makework,* masterwork, *N needlework, network, O* overwork, outwork, *P patchwork, piecework, PR presswork, R roadwork, SL slopwork, SP spadework, ST stonework, T taskwork, teamwork, timework, U* underwork, *W waxwork, wirework,* waterwork, *woodwork,* wonderwork, work
YURK	yerk

URKT

(See **URK**, add -ed where appropriate.)

URL

URL	earl
BURL	birl, burl
CHURL	churl
FURL	furl, refurl, unfurl
GURL	girl, gurl, *callgirl, cowgirl,* papergirl, *playgirl, showgirl, switchgirl*
HURL	herl, herle, hurl
HWIRL	upwhirl, whirl, whorl
KURL	becurl, curl, uncurl, upcurl
KWURL	querl, quirl
MURL	merle
NURL	knurl

PURL   bepearl, impearl, culture
          pearl, mother-of-pearl,
          pearl, pirl, purl, *seedpearl*
SKURL skirl
SWURL swirl, upswirl
THURL thirl, thurl
TURL   tirl
TWURL twirl

URLD

WURLD afterworld, antiworld, new
           world, *old-world,* Third
           World, underworld, world

(See **URL,** add -*ed* where appropriate.)

URM

BURM   berm
CHURM   churm
DURM   blastoderm, derm,
            echtoderm, endoderm,
            phelloderm, mesoderm,
            pachyderm, periderm,
            xanthoderm
FURM   affirm, disaffirm, firm,
            infirm, confirm, reaffirm
JURM   germ
PURM   perm
SKWURM squirm
SPURM   endosperm, gymnosperm,
            sperm, zoosperm
THURM   isotherm, therm
TURM   *midterm,* misterm, term
WURM   angleworm, *blindworm,
            bookworm, earthworm,
            flatworm, glowworm,
            grubworm, inchworm,
            silkworm, pinworm, ring-
            worm, tapeworm,
            woodworm,* worm

URMD

(See **URM,** add *ed* where appropriate.)

URN

URN   earn, erne, inurn, lierne,
           urn
BURN   Berne, burn, *heartburn,
           Hepburn, ropeburn,
           sideburn, sunburn,
           Swinburne, windburn*
CHURN churn
DURN   dern, durn
FURN   fern, foehn
GURN   girn, intergern

HURN   hern, herne
JURN   adjourn, sojourn
KURN   kern
KWURN   quern
LURN   learn, unlearn
PURN   epergne, pirn
SPURN   spurn
STURN   astern, stern
SURN   discern, concern, lucern,
            lucerne, secern, unconcern
TURN   *A* attorn, *E* externe, eterne,
            G gittern, I intern, interne,
            N nocturne, O overturn, *R*
            return, *S Saturn,*
            sempitern, *cistern, cittern,*
            sauterne, *subaltern, T*
            taciturn, tern, terne, turn,
            U upturn
VURN   Jules Verne
YURN   yearn, yirn
ZURN   discern

URND

(See **URN,** add -*ed* where appropriate.)

URNT

URNT   earnt
BURNT   burnt, *mowburnt,
            sunburnt,* unburnt,
            windburnt
LURNT   learnt, unlearnt
WURNT   weren't

URNZ

BURNZ   *sideburns*

(See **URN,** add -*s* where appropriate.)

URP

BURP   burp
CHURP   chirp
LURP   lirp
SLURP   slurp
SURP   discerp
TURP   terp, turp
TWURP   twerp, twirp
WURP   *Antwerp*
ZURP   usurp

URPS

(See **URP,** add -*s* where appropriate.)

URPT

SURPT   excerpt

(See **URP,** add -*ed* where appropriate.)

URS

URS   Erse, coerce
BURS   birse, burse, disburse,
           imburse, reimburse
HURS   hearse, herse, inhearse,
           rehearse
KURS   accurse, excurse, curse,
           precurse
MURS   immerse, merse, submerse
NURS   dry nurse, *dry-nurse,* foster
           nurse, nurse, practical
           nurse, registered nurse,
           wet nurse, *wet-nurse*
PURS   asperse, disperse,
           cutpurse, perse, purse
SPURS intersperse
THURS thyrse
TURS   *sesterce,* terce, terse
VURS   *A* adverse, averse, *D*
           diverse, *I* inverse, *K*
           converse, *O* obverse, *P*
           perverse, *R* reverse, *S*
           subverse, *TR* transverse,
           traverse, *V* verse, *Y*
           universe
WURS   worse

URST

URST   erst
BURST   *airburst,* burst, *cloudburst,*
            outburst, *starburst,*
            sunburst
DURST   durst
FURST   first, feetfirst, headfirst
HURST   hearsed, Hearst, hurst,
            rehearsed, unrehearsed
KURST   accursed, accurst,
            becursed, becurst, cursed,
            curst
THURST athirst, thirst
VURST   reversed, unversed, versed,
            verst
WURST   *bratwurst,* liverwurst,
            knackwurst, wienerwurst,
            worst, wurst

(See **URS,** add -*d* where appropriate.)

URT

URT   inert
BLURT   blurt

CHURT	chert
DURT	dirt
FLURT	flirt
GURT	begirt, engirt, girt, gurt, *seagirt,* ungirt
HURT	hurt, unhurt
KURT	curt
KWURT	quirt
LURT	alert
NURT	inert
PURT	*expert, inexpert,* malapert, peart, pert
SHURT	*Blackshirt,* dress shirt, *nightshirt,* overshirt, *redshirt,* shirt, *T-shirt,* undershirt
SKURT	maxiskirt, midiskirt, microskirt, miniskirt, skirt
SKWURT	squirt
SPURT	spirt, spurt
SURT	assert, disconcert, exsert, insert, intersert, concert, navicert, *outsert,* preconcert, cert, syrt
VURT	*A* advert, ambivert, animadvert, avert, *D* divert, *E* extrovert, evert, *I* intervert, introvert, invert, *K* controvert, convert, *O* obvert, overt, *P* pervert, *R* reconvert, retrovert, revert, *S* subvert, *T* terreverte, *TR* transvert, *V* vert
WURT	*BL* bladderwort, *J* gipsywort, *L* liverwort, *lousewort, M* milkwort, moneywort, motherwort, *P* pennywort, *pipewort, R* ragwort, *SL* slipperwort, *ST* stonewort, *SW* sweetwort, *TH* thoroughwort, *W* woundwort
YURT	yurt
ZURT	desert, dessert, exert, indesert

URTS

ZURTS	xertz

(See **URT,** add *-s* where appropriate.)

URTH

URTH	earth, fuller's earth, inearth, mother earth, *night-earth,* unearth
BURTH	afterbirth, berth, birth, *childbirth,* rebirth, *stillbirth*

DURTH	dearth
FURTH	firth
GURTH	girth
MURTH	mirth
PURTH	Perth
WORTH	money's worth, pennyworth, unworth, worth

URV

DURV	derv, *hors d'oeuvre*
KURV	incurve, curve, *outcurve,* recurve
MURV	mirv
NURV	innerve, nerve, unnerve
PURV	perv
SURV	disserve, conserve, serve, subserve
SWURV	swerve
VURV	verve
ZURV	deserve, observe, preserve, reserve

URVD

ZURVD	ill-deserved, ill-preserved, preserved, undeserved, unpreserved, well-deserved, well-preserved

(See **URV,** add *-d* where appropriate.)

URVZ

DURVZ	*hors d'oeuvres*

(See **URV,** add *-s* where appropriate.)

URZ

URZ	rapiers
FURZ	furze

(See **UR,** add *-s* where appropriate.)

ŪS

ŪS	disuse, hard use, cayuse, misuse, use
BŪS	abuse, antabuse
DŪS	*A* adduce, *D* deduce, deuce, *E* educe, *I* induce, introduce, *K* conduce, *O* obduce, overproduce, *PR* produce, *R* reduce, reproduce, *S* seduce,

superinduce, *TR* traduce, *U* underproduce

FŪS	diffuse, profuse
KŪS	excuse
LŪS	luce
PŪS	catapuce, *prepuce,* puce
TŪS	obtuse

(See $\overline{\text{OOS}}$)

US

US	*A* abstemious, acrimonious, aculeus, aqueous, alimonious, alias, alluvious, amatorious, ambiguous, amphibious, anfractuous, arboreous, arduous, assiduous, Asclepius, Asmodeus, *B* Belisarius, bifarious, bilious, Boreas, bounteous, burglarious, beauteous, *BR* Briareus, *D* deciduous, deleterious, delirious, denarius, deciduous, devious, dichroous, Dionysius, dipnoous, discontinuous, discourteous, disingenuous, dubious, dulcifluous, duteous, *E* exiguous, expurgatorious, extemporaneous, extraneous, equilibrious, envious, erroneous, Aesculapius, ethereous, *F* farinaceous, fastidious, fatuous, felonious, ferreous, furious, *FL* flexuous, *FR* fructuous, *G* gaseous, *GL* glorious, *GR* gramineous, gregarious, griseous, *H* halituous, harmonious, herbaceous, heterogeneous, hideous, hilarious, homogeneous, homoousious, *I* igneous, ignis fatuus, ignominious, ileus, illustrious, impecunious, imperious, impervious, impetuous, impious, indubious, industrious, inglorious, inharmonious, ingenious, ingenuous, injurious, incongruous, inconspicuous, incurious, innocuous, inquisitorious, incendious, insensuous, incestuous, insidious,

instantaneous, invidious, *J*
genius, *K* caduceus,
calcaneus, calcareous,
calumnious, carious,
carneous, caseous,
Cassius, coleus,
commodious,
compendious, congruous,
consanguineous,
conspicuous,
contemporaneous,
contemptuous, contiguous,
continuous, contrarious,
contumelious, copious,
corneous, cupreous,
curious, courteous,
cutaneous, *KL*
chlamydeous, *KR*
cretaceous, *L* laborious,
lacteous, lascivious,
ligneous, litigious,
lugubrious, Lucretius,
luxurious, luteous, *M*
malleus, mellifluous,
melodious, menstruous,
meritorious,
miscellaneous, mysterious,
multifarious, multivious, *N*
nacreous, nefarious,
nectareous, nimious,
niveous, nocuous,
nauplius, nauseous,
notorious, nucleus, *O*
oblivious, obsequious,
obvious, odious,
Odysseus, opprobrious,
Orpheus, osseous, *P*
pancreas, parsimonious,
penurious, perfidious,
percutaneous, perspicuous,
pervious, Petronius,
pileous, piteous, Polybius,
punctilious, *PL* plenteous,
plumbeous, pluvious, *PR*
precarious, previous,
presumptuous,
promiscuous, Proteus, *R*
radius, *S* salubrious,
sanguineous,
sanctimonious, sardius,
censorious, sensuous,
ceremonious, Cereus,
serious, cernuous,
Sibelius, simultaneous,
cinereous, symphonious,
sinuous, circumfluous,
Sirius, citreous,
subaqueous, subcutaneous,
subterraneous, sumptuous,
superfluous, supercilious,
SK scabious, scarious, *SP*
spirituous, spontaneous,

spurious, *SPL* splenius, *ST*
stentorious, stibious,
studious, *STR* Stradivarius,
strenuous, struthious, *T*
tautoousious, tedious,
temerarious, tempestuous,
tenuous, Tiberius,
tortuous, tumultuous, *TH*
Theseus, thybius, *TR*
transpicuous, trapezius, *U*
euphonious, uxorious,
unctuous, unceremonious,
uproarious, us, usurious, *V*
vagarious, vacuous,
valetudinarious,
vainglorious, various,
Vesuvius, viduous,
vicarious, victorious,
viminious, viparious,
virtuous, vitreous,
voluptuous, *Y* euphonious,
usurious
tenebrous

BRUS
BUS *A* arquebus, *B* Barnabas,
bus, buss, *BL* blunderbuss,
E Erebus, *H* harquebus, *I*
incubus, *K* Colobus, *N*
kneeling bus, *O* omnibus,
autobus, *S* succubus,
syllabus, *Z* xerophobous

DUS hazardous, solidus
FUS fuss, Sisyphus
GUS *A* analagous,
androphagous, asparagus,
azygous, *E* esophagus, *G*
Galapagos, guss, *H*
heterologous, homologous,
homozygous, *I* isologous,
K carpophagous,
coprophagous, *KR*
creophagous, *M*
monophagous, *P*
pemphigus, polyphagous,
S saprophagous,
sarcophagus, *T*
tautologous, *TH*
theophagous, *Z*
xiphopagus, zoophagous
ludicrous

KRUS
KUS abacus, discuss, excuss,
cuss, *khuskhus*, Leviticus,
oligotokous, percuss,
posticus, repercuss,
succuss

LUS *A* abaculus, agriculous,
alkalous, altocumulus,
alveolus, amphibolous,
anemophilous, angulous,
angelus, Angelus,
anomalous, annulus,
arenicolous, acephalous,
asepalous, acidulous,

astragalus, *B* bibulous,
bipetalous, bicephalous,
Bucephalus, *D* Daedalus,
discobolus, *E* edentulous,
emulous, *F* fabulous,
famulus, photipholous,
funiculus, *FL* flocculous,
flocculus, *FR* frivolous, *G*
garrulous, *GL* gladiolus,
globulous, *GR* granulous,
H hamulus,
hydrocephalous,
homunculus, *I* incredulous,
K calculous, calculus,
canaliculus, carolus,
convolvulous,
convolvulus, cautelous,
cumulous, cumulus, *KR*
crapulous, credulous,
crepusculous, *KW*
querulous, *L* libelous,
limicolous, limulus, *M*
malleolus, marvelous,
meticulous, miraculous,
modiolus, modulus,
monoculous, musculus, *N*
nebulous, nidicolous,
nodulous, noctambulous,
nautilus, nucleolus, *O*
obolus, *P* patulous, *P*
pendulous, periculous,
perilous, petalous,
populace, populous, *R*
ranunculus, regulus,
ridiculous, Romulus, *S*
sabulous, saxicolous,
sedulous, cellulous,
sibilous, sympetalous,
scintillous, cirrocumulus,
surculus, *SK* scandalous,
scurrilous, *SKR* scrofulous,
scrupulous, *ST*
stercoricolous, stimulus,
STR stratocumulus,
stridulous, *T* tantalus,
Tantalus, temulous,
terricolous, tintinnabulous,
tuberculous, tubulus,
tumulus, *TR* tremulous, *U*
undulous, unscrupulous, *V*
variolus, ventricolus,
verisimilous, vernaculous,
volvulous, *Z* xerophilous

MUS *A* ́animus, anonymous, *B*
bigamous, *BL*
blasphemous, *D*
diatomous, didymous,
didymus, didynamous, *E*
enormous, eponymous, *F*
physostomous, *H*
heteronymous,
hippopotamus,

hypothalamus, *I* infamous, *J* ginglymus, *K* calamus, catadromous, *M* magnanimous, maximus, minimus, mittimus, monogamous, mumpsimus, muss, *O* onymous, autonymous, autonomous, *P* polygamous, polyonymous, posthumous, pusillanimous, *S* synonymous, pseudonymous, sumpsimus, *TR* tridynamous, *TH* thalamus, *V* venomous, *Y* unanimous, euonymus, *Z* xylotomous

NUS *A* albuminous, aluminous, amanous, androgenous, androgynous, acinous, acinus, athermanous, *B* bimanous, bituminous, *D* diaphanous, diginous, dichronous, diplostemonous, *E* endogenous, epiphanous, epigenous, erogenous, *F* ferruginous, foraminous, fortitudinous, phototonus, fuliginous, *FL* fluminous, *G* gangrenous, *GL* glutenous, glutinous, gluttonous, *H* hydrogenous, hypogenous, homophonous, homogenous, hircinous, *I* indigenous, *J* gelatinous, *K* cavernous, cacophonous, cartiliginous, consonous, contaminous, conterminous, coterminous, *KR* cretinous, criminous, *L* larcenous, leguminous, lentitudinous, libidinous, liminous, luminous, misogynous, *M* membranous, monotonous, mountainous, multitudinous, mucilaginous, mutinous, *N* nitrogenous, numinous, *O* oleaginous, ominous, autogenous, autochthonous, *P* pedimanous, perigynous, poisonous, polygonous, polygyonous, polygenous, putredinous, *PL* platinous, platitudinous, *R* ravenous, resinous, rubiginous,

ruinous, *S* sanguinous, synchronous, *SKR* scrutinous, *T* tendinous, terminus, terriginous, tetanus, tyrannous, torminous, *TR* treasonous, trigeminous, trigeminus, *V* valetudinous, velutinous, verminous, vertiginous, vicissitudinous, villainous, voluminous, voraginous, vortiginous, *Y* uranous, urinous, urogenous, *Z* xanthomelanous

PLUS nonplus, overplus, periplus, plus, *surplus*

PUS Oedipus, octopus, orthotropous, pithecanthropus, platypus, polypus, pus

RUS *A* adiaphorous, adulterous, adventurous, acarus, aliferous, aligerous, amorous, anserous, apiverous, apterous, arborous, armigerous, *B* balsamiferous, barbarous, boisterous, bulbiferous, *BL* blusterous, *D* dangerous, decorous, dexterous, dipterous, doloriferous, dolorous, *E* ephemerous, *F* fossiliferous, phosphorous, phosphorus, fulgurous, *FL* flavorous, *FR* frugivorous, fructivorous, *GL* glamorous, *GR* graminivorous, granivorous, *H* herbivorous, Hesperus, homopterous, horrorous, humorous, humerus, *I* Icarus, icterus, imponderous, imposturous, indecorous, inodorous, insectivorous, isomerous, *J* generous, *K* cadaverous, calciferous, cankerous, cancerous, coniferous, cantankerous, carboniferous, carnivorous, *KL* clamorous, *L* lactiferous, languorous, Lazarus, lecherous, *M* malodorous, mammiferous, melliferous, metalliferous, monomerous, multiparous, murderous, murmurous, *N* nectarous, nidorous, numerous, *O* obstreperous, odoriferous, odorous,

augurous, omnivorous, onerous, auriferous, oviparous, *P* perjurous, peripterous, pesterous, pestiferous, piscivorous, Pythagoras, polymerous, ponderous, pulverous, *PR* preposterous, prosperous, *R* rancorous, rapturous, rigorous, rhinoceros, roisterous, rhus, Russ, *S* sacchariferous, savorous, seminiferous, Cerberus, somniferous, sonorous, sudoriferous, sulphurous, *susurrous, susurrus, SH* chivalrous, *SK* scutiferous, *SL* slanderous, slaughterous, slumberous, *ST* stelliferous, stertorous, *T* tartarous, Tartarus, tetrapterous, timorous, torturous, tuberous, *TH* thunderous, *TR* traitorous, treacherous, *U* ulcerous, umbelliferous, ungenerous, unchivalrous, *V* valorous, vaporous, venturous, verdurous, vermivorous, vigorous, viperous, viviparous, vociferous, vulturous, *Y* uniparous, uriniferous, uterus, *Z* Zephyrus

STUS stuss

SUS Caucasus, Pegasus, megalonisus, suss, xeronisus

THUS antipathous, thus

TRUS idolatrous, sinistrous, truss, untruss

TUS *A* aditus, acclivitous, *D* Democritus, *E* edematous, eczematous, exitus, emeritus, *F* fatuitous, felicitous, fortuitous, *FR* fremitus, *GR* gratuitous, *H* halitus, Herodotus, Hypolitus, *I* impetus, infelicitous, iniquitous, *K* calamitous, covetous, *M* microstomatous, *N* necessitous, *P* pachydermatous, *PR* precipitous, propositous, *R* riotous, *S* circuitous, solicitous, *SKL* sclerodermatous, *SP* spiritous, *T* tuss, *TR* transitus, trinitous, *V* vagitous, velocitous, *Y* ubiquitous

VUS	atavus, mischievous, tritavus

ŪSH

(See OOSH)

USH

BLUSH	blush, outblush, unblush
BRUSH	*airbrush*, bottlebrush, brush, *hairbrush*, *clothesbrush*, *nailbrush*, *paintbrush*, *toothbrush*, underbrush
FLUSH	flush, outflush, unflush
FRUSH	frush
GUSH	gush
HUSH	hush
KRUSH	crush
KUSH	Cush, namaycush
LUSH	lush
MUSH	mush
PLUSH	plush
RUSH	*bullrush*, bum's rush, *inrush*, outrush, rush, *uprush*, *woodrush*
SLUSH	slush
THRUSH	hermit thrush, missal thrush, thrush
TUSH	tush

USK

BRUSK	brusque
BUSK	busk
DUSK	adusk, dusk
FUSK	fusc, subfusc
HUSK	dehusk, husk, *cornhusk*
KUSK	cusk
LUSK	lusk, *mollusk*
MUSK	musk
RUSK	rusk
TUSK	tusk

ŪST

PŪST	puist

(See OOST; see OOS and ŪS, add -*d* where appropriate.)

UST

BUST	bust, combust, robust
DUST	adust, angel dust, bedust, dost, dust, gold dust, *sawdust*, *stardust*

FUST	fussed, fust
GUST	august, disgust, gust
JUST	adjust, just, coadjust, misadjust, readjust, unjust
KRUST	encrust, crust, mumblecrust, *piecrust*
KUST	discussed, cussed
LUST	lust, wanderlust
MUST	mussed, must
NUST	venust
PLUST	*nonplussed*
RUST	rust
THRUST	overthrust, thrust, underthrust, upthrust
TRUST	betrust, blind trust, distrust, entrust, mistrust, self-distrust, trust, untrust
TUST	vetust

ŪT

BŪT	attribute, beaut, butte, Butte
FŪT	confute, refute
GŪT	argute
KŪT	acute, execute, electrocute, cute, persecute, prosecute, sub-acute
MŪT	*deafmute*, emeute, commute, Malemute, meute, mute, permute, transmute
NŪT	Canute, comminute, cornute, minute, newt
PŪT	depute, dispute, disrepute, impute, compute, suppute
SKŪT	scute
STŪT	astute, destitute, institute, constitute, prostitute, tute

(See OOT)

UT

BUT	abut, *blackbutt*, but, butt, *hagbut*, *hackbut*, halibut, rebut, *sackbut*, scuttlebutt, surrebut, water butt
FUT	phut, go phut
GLUT	englut, glut
GUT	*foregut*, gut, *hindgut*, catgut, midgut, rotgut
HUT	hut
JUT	jut
KUT	*haircut, clean-cut, clear-cut, crosscut*, cut, linocut, uncut, uppercut, *woodcut*
MUT	mutt
NUT	*B beechnut*, betelnut,

	bitternut, butternut, *BL* bladdernut, *BR* Brazil nut, *CH* chestnut, *D* doughnut, *G* gallnut, *GR* groundnut, *H* hazelnut, hickory nut, *K* candlenut, cashew nut, *cobnut*, coconut, macadamia nut, *N* nut, *P* peanut, *W* walnut
PUT	Lilliput, occiput, putt, putt-putt, sinciput
RUT	rut
SHUT	half-shut, outshut, shut, unshut
SKUT	scut
SLUT	slut
SMUT	besmut, smut
STRUT	astrut, strut
TUT	King Tut, tut, tut-tut

UT

(as in *put*)

(See OOT)

ŪTH

SMŪTH	smeuth

(See OOTH)

UTH

DUTH	doth
MUTH	*bismuth*, azimuth

UTS

KLUTS	klutz
PUTS	putz
STUTS	Stutz

(See **UT**, add -*s* where appropriate.)

ŪV

(See OOV)

UV

UV	hereof, whereof, of, thereof
BUV	above
DUV	dove, mourning dove, *ringdove*, rock dove, turtledove

GLUV   *foxglove,* glove, unglove
GUV   gov
LUV   ladylove, light-o'love,
           love, puppy love, self-
           love, *truelove*
SHUV   shove

ŪVD

(See **OOV**, add *-d* where appropriate.)

ŪZ

ŪZ   disuse, ill-use, misuse, use
BŪZ   abuse, disabuse
FŪZ   *BL* blow a fuse, *D* defuse,
          diffuse, *E* effuse, *F* fuse, *I*

infuse, interfuse, *K*
confuse, *P* percussion fuse,
perfuse, *R* refuse, *S*
suffuse, superinfuse, *TR*
transfuse
GŪZ   guze
HŪZ   hues
KŪZ   accuse, excuse, incuse,
           Syracuse
MŪZ   amuse, bemuse, meuse,
           mews, muse
NŪZ   news
SŪZ   sues (*danseuse, masseuse*
           are near-rhymes)
THŪZ   thews
TŪZ   contuse

(See **Ū**, add *-s* where appropriate.)

UZ

UZ   Uz
BUZ   abuzz, buzz, *humbuzz*
DUZ   does, doz
FUZ   fuzz, *peachfuzz*
KUZ   coz

ŪZD

(See **ŪZ**, **OOZ**, add *-d* where appropriate.)

ŪZH

(See **OOZH**)

DOUBLE RHYMES

(Words accented on the syllable before the last.
Also called *trochaic*, or *feminine*, rhymes.)

ĀA

FRĀA	Freya
HĀA	haya
LĀA	Himalaya
MĀA	Maya
ZĀA	Isaiah

ĀAL

BĀAL	Baal
FRĀAL	defrayal
GĀAL	gayal
TRĀAL	betrayal, portrayal
VĀAL	conveyal, purveyal, surveyal

ĀAM

FĀAM	faham
GRĀAM	graham
MĀAM	mayhem

ĀAN

GWĀAN	Paraguayan, Uruguayan
KĀAN	Biscayan
LĀAN	Malayan
MĀAN	Mayan
TĀAN	Altaian

ĀANS

BĀANS	abeyance
VĀANS	conveyance, purveyance, surveyance

ĀANT

BĀANT	abeyant
MĀANT	mayn't

ĀBA

FĀBA	faba
PĀBA	copaiba

ÄBA

ÄBA	aba
BÄBA	Addis Ababa, Ali Baba, baba, Cayubaba
DÄBA	indaba
KÄBA	kaaba, Kaaba
LÄBA	laaba
SÄBA	casaba, piassaba
TÄBA	aftaba

> *VISION SEEN THROUGH A HEADACHE*
>
> I love to watch the flocks
> Of Aspirin at play
> On Rheumatism Rocks
> Beside Placebo Bay.
> They frolic in the sun,
> They race along the shore;
> I hear them shout as one,
> "C O – H 8 – 0 4!"

ABARD

(See **ABERD**)

ĀBĒ

ĀBĒ	Abie
BĀBĒ	baby, big baby, bushbaby, crybaby
GĀBĒ	gaby
MĀBĒ	maybe

ABĒ

ABĒ	abbey
BABĒ	babby
BLABĒ	blabby
DABĒ	dabby
DRABĒ	drabby
FLABĒ	flabby
GABĒ	gabby
GRABĒ	grabby
KABĒ	cabby
KRABĒ	crabby
RABĒ	rabbi, kohlrabi
SABĒ	no sabe, sabe
SHABĒ	shabby
SKABĒ	scabby
SLABĒ	slabby
TABĒ	tabby
YABĒ	yabbi, yabby

ÄBĒ

DRÄBĒ	drabi
HÄBĒ	Wahabi
HWÄBĒ	whabby
JÄBĒ	Punjabi
RÄBĒ	rabi, kohlrabi
SKWÄBĒ	squabby
TÄBĒ	tabi
WÄBĒ	wabby, wabe

ABED

(See **ABID**)

ĀBER

GĀBER	Gheber
KĀBER	caber
LĀBER	belabor, labor
NĀBER	beggar-my-neighbor, good neighbor, neighbor
SĀBER	saber
TĀBER	tabor

ABER

BLABER	blabber
DABER	dabber
GABER	gabber
GRABER	grabber
JABER	jabber, gibber-jabber
KLABER	bonnyclabber, clabber
KRABER	crabber
NABER	knabber, nabber
SLABER	beslabber, slabber
STABER	stabber
YABER	yabber

ÄBER

(See **OBER**)

ĀBERD

(See **ĀBER**, add *-ed* where appropriate.)

ABERD

GABERD	gabbard
KLABERD	clapboard
SKABERD	scabbard
TABERD	tabard

(See **ABER**, add *-ed* where appropriate.)

ABET

(See **ABIT**)

ĀBĒZ

BĀBĒZ	babies
GĀBĒZ	gabies
RĀBĒZ	rabies
SKĀBĒZ	scabies
TĀBĒZ	tabes

ABID

KRABID	crabbed
RABID	rabid
TABID	tabid

ABIK

LABIK	asyllabic, bisyllabic, monosyllabic, multisyllabic, polysyllabic, trisyllabic
NABIK	cannabic
RABIK	rabik

ĀBIL

(See ĀBL)

ABIL

(See ABL)

ABIN

KABIN	cabin
SABIN	sabin

ABING

(See **AB**, add *-ing* where appropriate.)

ABIT

ABIT	abbot
BABIT	babbitt, Babbitt
DRABIT	drabbet
HABIT	habit, inhabit, cohabit
RABIT	jackrabbit, rabbet, rabbit
SABIT	sabot

ĀBL

ĀBL	able, Abel, disable, enable, unable
BĀBL	Babel
DWĀBL	dwaible
FĀBL	fable, fibble-fable
GĀBL	gable
JĀBL	jibble-jable
KĀBL	cable, pay cable
LĀBL	label, labile
NĀBL	nabel, nable
SĀBL	ensable, sable
STĀBL	stable, unstable

TĀBL	retable, Round Table, table, timetable, turntable, water table, worktable

ABL

(The adjective suffix *-able* in this category, when normally unstressed, provides only a forced and undesirable rhyme.)

ABL	*A* affiliable, amiable, *D* differentiable, dutiable, *E* expiable, enviable, *I* impermeable, imperviable, inexpiable, invaluable, invariable, irremediable, issuable, *J* justiciable, *L* leviable, *M* malleable, *P* permeable, perpetuable, pitiable, *R* remediable, renunciable, *S* semipermeable, *U* unenviable, *V* valuable, variable
BABL	babble, psychobabble
BRABL	brabble
DABL	bedabble, dabble, formidable, unformidable
DRABL	bedrabble, drabble
FABL	fibble-fabble
GABL	*G* gabble, gibble-gabble, *I* interrogable, irrigable, *M* mitigable, *N* navigable, *O* obligeable, *PR* propagable, *S* segregable, *U* unmitigable
GRABL	grabble
HABL	habile
JABL	acknowledgeable, challengeable, damageable, *dischargeable,* jabble, manageable, marriageable, knowledgeable, unchallengeable, unmanageable
KABL	*D* despicable, duplicable, *E*

educable, explicable, extricable, eradicable, *I* impracticable, inapplicable, inexplicable, *K* cabble, *M* manducable, masticable, *PR* practicable, prognosticable

KRABL	execrable
KWABL	*inequable*
LABL	incalculable, inoculable, inviolable, calculable, coagulable, regulable, violable
MABL	estimable, fathomable, inestimable, *reformable,* unfathomable
NABL	*D* disciplinable, *E* exceptionable, *F* fashionable, *I* imaginable, impassionable, impressionable, inalienable, interminable, *K* companionable, contaminable, *KW* questionable, *M* mentionable, *O* objectionable, *P* pardonable, pensionable, personable, poisonable, *PR* proportionable, *S* sanctionable, *U* unimaginable, unquestionable, unpardonable
PABL	developable, *exculpable,* undevelopable
RABL	*A* admirable, alterable, answerable, *D* deliverable, decipherable, dishonorable, discoverable, *E* exorable, *F* favorable, *I* immeasurable, immensurable, imponderable, inexorable, incommensurable, inconsiderable, innumerable, incensurable,

inseparable,
inseverable,
insufferable,
insuperable,
intolerable,
invulnerable,
irrecoverable, *K*
commemorable,
conquerable,
considerable, *M*
measurable,
memorable,
mensurable,
miserable, *N*
numerable, *O*
offerable, honorable,
P ponderable, *PL*
pleasurable, *PR*
preferable, *R* rabble,
recoverable,
rememberable,
renderable, ribble-
rabble, *S* censurable,
separable, cipherable,
sufferable, superable,
T temperable,
tolerable, *U*
undecipherable,
unalterable, *V*
venerable, vulnerable

SABL   balanceable,
disserviceable,
impassable,
noticeable,
purchasable,
serviceable,
unbalanceable,
unnoticeable,
unpurchasable,
unserviceable

SHABL   distinguishable,
extinguishable,
imperishable,
indistinguishable,
inextinguishable,
perishable,
publishable,
undistinguishable,
unextinguishable,
unpublishable

SKABL   scabble
SKRABL   scrabble, Scrabble
TABL   *A* attributable, *CH*
charitable, *D*
decapitable,
discreditable,
distributable,
dubitable, *E*
equitable, evitable, *F*
forgettable, H
habitable, heritable,
hospitable, *I*

illimitable,
indomitable,
indubitable,
inequitable,
inevitable,
inhabitable,
inhospitable,
inimitable,
interpretable,
irritable, *K*
comfortable,
covetable, *KR*
creditable, *L*
limitable, *PR*
precipitable,
profitable, *U*
uncharitable,
uncomfortable,
uninhabitable

TRABL   impenetrable
VABL   *unlivable, unlovable*

ÄBL

SKWÄBL   squabble
WÄBL   wabble, wobble

(See **OBL**)

ABLD

SMABLD   smabbled
SNABLD   snabbled

(See **ABL,** add *-d* where appropriate.)

ĀBLĒ

ĀBLĒ   ably
STĀBLĒ   stably

ABLĒ

BABLĒ   babbly
DABLĒ   dabbly
DRABLĒ   drably
GABLĒ   gabbly
SHABLĒ   Chablis
SKRABLĒ   scrabbly

ĀBLER

(See **ĀBL,** add *-r* where appropriate.)

ABLER

GABLER   gabbler, Hedda Gabler

(See **ABL,** add *-r* where appropriate.)

ABLET

KRABLET   crablet
TABLET   tablet

ABLISH

BABLISH   babblish
STABLISH   disestablish,
establish, reestablish,
stablish

ĀBŌ

VĀBŌ   lavabo
ZĀBŌ   gazabo, gazebo

ABŌ

ABŌ   babbo
SABŌ   sabot
ZHABŌ   jabot

ĀBOI

LĀBOI   layboy
PLĀBOI   playboy

ABOT

(See **ABIT**)

ÄBRA

ÄBRA   abra
DÄBRA   abracadabra
LÄBRA   candelabra

ĀBRAM

(See **ĀBRUM**)

ĀBRUM

ĀBRUM   Abram
FLĀBRUM   flabrum
LĀBRUM   labrum, candelabrum

ĀBRUS

ĀBRUS   Abrus
GLĀBRUS   glabrous
SKĀBRUS   scabrous

ACHĒ

BACHĒ	hibachi
KACHĒ	catchee, no catchee, seecatchie
MACHĒ	machi, matchy
PACHĒ	patchy
SKRACHĒ	scratchy
SNACHĒ	snatchy

ACHEL

HACHEL	hatchel
RACHEL	ratchel
SACHEL	satchel

ĀCHER

KĀCHER	*plicature*
KLĀCHER	nomenclature
LĀCHER	legislature
NĀCHER	denature, nature, unnature

ACHER

BACHER	bacher, batcher
KACHER	catcher, cony-catcher, *flycatcher*, birdcatcher, dogcatcher
SNACHER	bodysnatcher, snatcher

(See **ACH,** add *-er* where appropriate.)

ACHET

BRACHET	brachet
HACHET	hatchet
KRACHET	Bob Cratchet
LACHET	latchet
RACHET	ratchet
SMACHET	smatchet

ACHEZ

NACHEZ	Natchez

(See **ACH,** add *-es* where appropriate.)

ACHING

(See **ACH,** add *-ing* where appropriate.)

ACHLES

(See **ACH,** add *-less* where appropriate.)

ACHMENT

HACHMENT	hatchment
KACHMENT	catchment
PACHMENT	dispatchment
RACHMENT	ratchment
TACHMENT	attachment, detachment

ÄCHŌ

MÄCHŌ	macho
NÄCHŌ	nacho

ACHWERK

KACHWERK	catchwork
PACHWERK	patchwork

ĀDĀ

HĀDĀ	heyday
MĀDĀ	Mayday
PĀDĀ	payday
PLĀDĀ	playday

ĀDA

GRĀDA	digitigrada
KĀDA	cicada
MĀDA	armada
NĀDA	Granada, Grenada, panada
VĀDA	Veda

ADA

ADA	adda
DADA	dada
SADA	sadda

ÄDA

DÄDA	dada, Dada
GÄDA	Haggadah
KÄDA	cicada
LÄDA	big enchalada, enchalada, colada, mulada
MÄDA	armada
NÄDA	empanada, Granada, Grenada, journada, nada, panada
PÄDA	pratityasamutpada
SÄDA	pasada
SRÄDA	sraddha

STRÄDA	autostrada
TRÄDA	contrada
VÄDA	Nevada, Sierra Nevada
ZÄDA	shahzada

ĀDAL

TRĀDAL	tradal
VĀDAL	wedel

ADAM

ADAM	Adam
KADAM	macadam
MADAM	madam, queezmadam, prickmadam

ĀDANS

(See **ĀDENS**)

ĀDĒ

BRĀDĒ	braidy
FĀDĒ	fady
FRĀDĒ	'fraidy
GLĀDĒ	glady
JĀDĒ	jady
KĀDĒ	alcaide, cadi, cascady
LĀDĒ	bag lady, belady, charlady, forelady, cleaning lady, lady, landlady, milady
MĀDĒ	maidy
SHĀDĒ	shady
VĀDĒ	vade, vady

ADĒ

BADĒ	baddie, baddy
DADĒ	daddy, big daddy, sugar daddy
FADĒ	faddy
GADĒ	gaddi, Gaddi
GLADĒ	gladdie
HADĒ	haddie, finnan haddie
KADĒ	caddie, caddy
LADĒ	laddie, laddy
MADĒ	maddy
PADĒ	paddy
PLADĒ	plaidie

ÄDĒ

KÄDĒ	cadi, quadi
MÄDĒ	Mahdi

RĀDĒ	irade
SKWĀDĒ	squaddy
WĀDĒ	waddy, Wade, wadi

(See **ODĒ**)

ĀDED

(See **ĀD,** add *-ed* where appropriate.)

ADED

(see **AD,** add *-ed* where appropriate.)

ÄDED

(See **ĀD,** add-*ed* where appropriate.)

ĀDEN

ĀDEN	Aden
HĀDEN	menhaden
LĀDEN	heavy-laden, laden, overladen, underladen, unladen
MĀDEN	bower-maiden, dairy-maiden, flower-maiden, maiden, snow-maiden

ADEN

BADEN	Abaddon
GLADEN	engladden, gladden, regladden
MADEN	madden
SADEN	sadden

ĀDENS

| ĀDENS | aidance |
| KĀDENS | cadence, decadence |

ĀDENT

| ĀDENT | abraidant, aidant |
| KĀDENT | cadent, decadent |

ĀDER

| NĀDER | nadir |
| SÄDER | Seder |

(See **ĀD,** add *-er* where appropriate.)

ADER

ADER	adder
BADER	badder
BLADER	bladder
DADER	dadder
GADER	gadder
GLADER	gladder
LADER	ladder, stepladder
MADER	madder
NADER	nadder
SADER	sadr, sadder

(See **AD,** add *-er* where appropriate.)

ÄDER

| SÄDER | sadr |

(See **ÄD, OD,** add *-er* or *-der* where appropriate.)

ADEST

FADEST	faddist
GLADEST	gladdest
SADEST	saddest, sadist

ĀDĒZ

HĀDĒZ	Hades
KĀDĒZ	Cadiz
LĀDĒZ	ladies

ADĒZ

BADĒZ	baddies
DADĒZ	daddies
LADĒZ	laddies
PLADĒZ	plaidies

ADFUL

GLADFUL	gladful
MADFUL	madful
SADFUL	sadful

ADIK

ADIK	dyadic, triadic
GADIK	haggadic
KADIK	decadic, saccadic
KLADIK	Cycladic
LADIK	Helladic
MADIK	nomadic
NADIK	monadic, vanadic

RADIK	faradic, sporadic
TADIK	octadic, Sotadic
TRADIK	tetradic

ĀDING

(See **ĀD,** add *-ing* where appropriate.)

ADING

(See **AD,** add *-ing* where appropriate.)

ÄDING

(See **ÄD,** add *-ing,* **OD,** add *-ing,* where appropriate.)

ĀDISH

JĀDISH	jadish
MĀDISH	maidish, mermaidish, old-maidish
STĀDISH	staidish

ADISH

BADISH	baddish
FADISH	faddish
GLADISH	gladdish
KADISH	caddish, Kaddish
MADISH	maddish
PLADISH	plaidish
RADISH	horseradish, radish
SADISH	saddish

ADIST

(See **ADEST**)

ĀDL

DRĀDL	dreidel
GRĀDL	gradal
HĀDL	hadal
KRĀDL	encradle, cradle
TRADL	tradal
VĀDL	wedel

ADL

ADL	addle
DADL	daddle, skedaddle
FADL	faddle, fiddle-faddle
PADL	dogpaddle, paddle
RADL	raddle
SADL	packsaddle, saddle, sidesaddle, unsaddle, western saddle

SKADL	scaddle, skaddle
SPRADL	spraddle
STADL	staddle
STRADL	astraddle, bestraddle, straddle

ÄDL

KWÄDL	quaddle
SWÄDL	swaddle
TWÄDL	twaddle
WÄDL	waddle

(See **ODL**)

ĀDLD

KRĀDLD	encradled, cradled
WĀDLD	wedeled

ADLD

(See **ADL**, add -*d* where appropriate.)

ÄDLD

(See **ÄDL, ODL**, add -*d* where appropriate.)

ĀDLĒ

GRĀDLĒ	gradely, retrogradely
MĀDLĒ	dismayedly
STĀDLĒ	staidly

ADLĒ

BADLĒ	badly
GLADLĒ	gladly
MADLĒ	madly
SADLĒ	sadly

ÄDLĒ

TWÄDLĒ	twaddly
WÄDLĒ	waddly

(See **ODLĒ**)

ADLER

ADLER	Felix Adler, Mortimer Adler

(See **ADL**, add -*r* where appropriate.)

ÄDLER

(See **ÄDL, ODL**, add -*r* where appropriate.)

ĀDLES

ĀDLES	aidless

(See **ĀD**, add -*less* where appropriate.)

ĀDLING

KRĀDLING	encradling, cradling
MĀDLING	maidling
WĀDLING	wedeling

ADLING

(See **ADL**, add -*ing* where appropriate.)

ÄDLING

(See **ÄDL, ODL**, add -*ing* where appropriate.)

ĀDNES

FRĀDNES	afraidness, frayedness
STĀDNES	staidness, unstaidness

ADNES

BADNES	badness
GLADNES	gladness
MADNES	madness
PLADNES	plaidness
SADNES	sadness

ĀDŌ

BĀDŌ	gambado
DĀDŌ	dado
GĀDŌ	renegado
KĀDŌ	ambuscado, barricado, stoccado
KRĀDŌ	credo
LĀDŌ	scalado
MĀDŌ	fumado
NĀDŌ	bastinado, grenado, carbonado, tornado
PĀDŌ	strappado
RĀDŌ	desperado, Laredo
SĀDŌ	camisado, crusado
VĀDŌ	muscovado

ADŌ

RADŌ	Colorado
SHADŌ	foreshadow, overshadow, shadow

ÄDŌ

ÄDŌ	zapateado
DÄDŌ	dado
GÄDŌ	juzgado
KÄDŌ	avocado, imbrocado, incommunicado, Mikado, sticcado, stoccado
LÄDO	amontillado
MÄDŌ	quemado
NÄDŌ	aficionado, bastinado, carbonado
PÄDŌ	strappado
PRÄDŌ	Prado
RÄDŌ	amorado, desperado, dorado, El Dorado, Colorado
SÄDŌ	passado
TÄDŌ	pintado, remontado
VÄDŌ	bravado, muscovado

ÄDŌŌ

FÄDŌŌ	fado
SÄDOO	sadhu

ĀDŌS

BĀDŌS	Barbados
TRĀDŌS	extrados, intrados

ADSUM

GLADSUM	gladsome
MADSUM	madsome

ADUK

BADUK	baddock
HADUK	haddock
PADUK	paddock
SHADUK	shaddock

ĀDUS

GRĀDUS	gradus
KLĀDUS	cladus

ĀĒ

DĀĒ	Agnus Dei, Dei
HWĀĒ	wheyey
KLĀĒ	clayey
SPRĀĒ	sprayey

ÄĒ

BÄĒ	rubai
KÄĒ	kai, kai-kai
SÄĒ	sai
TÄĒ	Tai

ĀEM

ĀEM	A.M.

(See **ĀAM**)

ĀER

DĀER	doomsdayer
MĀER	mayor, mormaor
PLĀER	player, record player, video player
SĀER	assayer, doomsayer, nay-sayer, sayer, yea-sayer
VĀER	conveyor, kurveyor, purveyor, surveyor

(See **Ā,** add *-er* when appropriate.)

ĀFĀR

MĀFĀR	Mayfair
PLĀFĀR	play fair, Playfair

AFĒ

BAFĒ	baffy
CHAFĒ	chaffy
DAFĒ	daffy
DRAFĒ	draffy
FAFĒ	faffy
TAFĒ	taffy

ĀFER

CHĀFER	chafer, cockchafer
SĀFER	safer, vouchsafer
STRĀFER	strafer
WĀFER	wafer

AFER

CHAFER	chaffer
GAFER	gaffer, ghaffir
GRAFER	graffer
KAFER	Kaffir
KWAFER	quaffer
LAFER	laugher
PYAFER	piaffer
ZAFER	zaffer

ÄFER

KWÄFER	quaffer
LÄFER	laugher

(See **OFER**)

AFIK

DAFIK	edaphic
GRAFIK	*A* analyptographic, *B* bibliographic, biographic, *D* dactylographic, demographic, diagraphic, *E* engraphic, epigraphic, ethneographic, ethnographic, *F* phonographic, photographic, *G* galvanographic, *GL* glyptographic, *GR* graphic, *H* heliographic, heterographic, hydrographic, hierographic, hyetographic, histographic, historiographic, holographic, homographic, homolographic, horologiographic, *I* ideographic, idiographic, ichnographic, isographic, *J* geographic, *K* cacographic, calligraphic, cartographic, chirographic, choreographic, chorographic, cosmographic, *KL* clinographic, *KR* cryptographic, crystallographic, chromographic, chronographic, *L* lexigraphic, lexicographic, logographic, *M* macrographic, melographic, micrographic, monographic, *N* noematachographic, neurographic, *O* oleographic, orographic, orthographic, autobiographic, autographic, *P* paleographic, pantographic, paragraphic, pasigraphic, petrographic, pyrographic, polygraphic, pornographic, *S* selenographic, scenographic, sciagraphic, siderographic, cinematographic, seismographic, *SF* sphenographic, *ST* stenographic, stylographic, *STR* stratigraphic, stratographic, *T* tachygraphic, telegraphic, typographic, topographic, *Y* uranographic, *Z* xylographic, zincographic, zoographic
MAFIK	maffick
SAFIK	Sapphic
RAFIK	seraphic
TAFIK	epitaphic
TRAFIK	traffic

ĀFING

(See **ĀF,** add *-ing* where appropriate.)

AFING

(See **AF,** add *-ing* where appropriate.)

ÄFING

(See **ÄF,** add *-ing* where appropriate.)

AFIZM

SAFIZM	sapphism
SKAFIZM	scaphism

AFL

BAFL	baffle
DAFL	daffle
GAFL	gaffle
HAFL	haffle
MAFL	maffle
RAFL	raffle
SKRAFL	scraffle
SNAFL	snaffle
TAFL	taffle
YAFL	yaffle

ÄFL

FÄFL	faffel
WÄFL	waffle

(See OFL)

AFLD

SKAFLD	scaffold

(See AFL, add -d where appropriate.)

ÄFLD

FÄFLD	faffled
WÄFLD	waffled

AFLER

BAFLER	baffler
HAFLER	haffler
RAFLER	raffler
SKRAFLER	scraffler

AFLING

BAFLING	baffling
HAFLING	halfling
KAFLING	calfling
RAFLING	raffling
SKRAFLING	scraffling
SNAFLING	snaffling

ÄFLING

HÄFLING	halfling

KÄFLING	calfling
WÄFLING	waffling

AFTĒ

DRAFTĒ	drafty
GRAFTĒ	grafty
KRAFTĒ	crafty
RAFTĒ	rafty
WAFTĒ	wafty

AFTER

DAFTER	dafter
DRAFTER	drafter
GRAFTER	grafter
HAFTER	hafter
LAFTER	laughter
RAFTER	rafter
WAFTER	wafter

ÄFTER

ÄFTER	after, hereafter, hereinafter, whereafter, thereafter
DRÄFTER	drafter, draughter
LÄFTER	laughter
WÄFTER	wafter

AFTIJ

DRAFTIJ	draftage, draughtage
GRAFTIJ	graftage
WAFTIJ	waftage

ÄFTIJ

DRÄFTIJ	draftage, draughtage
WÄFTIJ	waftage

AFTING

(See AFT, add -ing where appropriate.)

AFTLES

(See AFT, add -less where appropriate.)

AFTSMAN

DRAFTSMAN	draftsman
KRAFTSMAN	craftsman, handicraftsman
RAFTSMAN	raftsman

ÄFTSMAN

DRAFTSMAN	draftsman
KRAFTSMAN	craftsman, handicraftsman
RAFTSMAN	raftsman

ĀFUL

NĀFUL	nayful
PLĀFUL	playful, unplayful
TRĀFUL	trayful
YĀFUL	yeaful

ĀGA

BĀGA	rutabaga
DĀGA	bodega, Onondaga
MĀGA	omega
PLĀGA	plaga
SĀGA	saga
STRĀGA	strega
VĀGA	vega, Vega

ÄGA

ÄGA	aga, agha
GÄGA	gaga
KWÄGA	quagga
MÄGA	maga
SÄGA	saga

ĀGAL

(See ĀGL)

AGAN

(See ĀGEN)

ÄGAR

(See ÄGER)

AGARD

(See AGERD)

AGART

(See AGERT)

AGAT

(See AGUT)

AGĒ

BAGĒ	baggie, baggy
BRAGĒ	braggy
DAGĒ	daggy
DRAGĒ	draggy
FAGĒ	faggy
FLAGĒ	flaggy
GAGĒ	gaggy
HAGĒ	haggy
JAGĒ	jaggy
KRAGĒ	craggy
KWAGĒ	quaggy
LAGĒ	laggy
NAGĒ	knaggy, naggy
RAGĒ	raggee, raggy, ragi
SAGĒ	saggy
SHAGĒ	shaggy
SKRAGĒ	scraggy
SLAGĒ	slaggy
SNAGĒ	snaggy
STAGĒ	staggy
SWAGĒ	swaggy
TAGĒ	taggy
WAGĒ	waggy

AGED

JAGED	jagged
KRAGED	cragged
RAGED	ragged
SKRAGED	scragged

ĀGEN

FĀGEN	fagin, Fagin
HĀGEN	Copenhagen
PĀGEN	pagan, upeygan
RĀGEN	Reagan
VĀGEN	Vegan

ĀGER

JĀGER	jager, jaeger
MĀGER	maigre
NĀGER	canaigre
PLĀGER	plaguer
VĀGER	vaguer
YĀGER	jaeger

AGER

AGER	agar, agar-agar
BAGER	bagger, carpetbagger, four-bagger, three-bagger, two-bagger, one-bagger

BRAGER	bragger
DAGER	dagger
DRAGER	dragger
FAGER	fagger
FLAGER	flagger
FRAGER	fragger
GAGER	gagger
JAGER	jagger
LAGER	lagger
MAGER	magger
NAGER	nagger
RAGER	ragger
SAGER	saggar, sagger
SHAGER	shagger
SNAGER	snagger
STAGER	stagger
SWAGER	swagger
TAGER	tagger
WAGER	wagger, wigwagger
ZAGER	zigzagger

ÄGER

ÄGER	agar, agar-agar
LÄGER	lager, laager

AGERD

BLAGERD	blackguard
BRAGERD	braggard
HAGERD	haggard
LAGERD	laggard
STAGERD	staggard, staggered
SWAGERD	swaggered

AGERT

BRAGERT	braggart
STAGERT	staggart

AGET

(See **AGUT**)

ĀGIN

(See **ĀGEN**)

AGING

FRAGING	fragging

(See **AG**, add -*ing* where appropriate.)

AGISH

BRAGISH	braggish
FLAGISH	flaggish

JAGISH	jaggish
LAGISH	laggish
NAGISH	naggish
WAGISH	waggish

ĀGL

BĀGL	bagel
HĀGL	Hegel
NĀGL	finagle
PĀGL	paigle
PLĀGL	plagal
VĀGL	vagal, inveigle

AGL

DAGL	bedaggle, daggle
DRAGL	bedraggle, draggle
GAGL	gaggle
HAGL	haggle
KWAGL	quaggle
PAGL	paggle
RAGL	raggle
STRAGL	straggle
TAGL	raggle-taggle
WAGL	waggel, waggle

ĀGLD

NĀGLD	finagled
VĀGLD	inveigled

AGLĒ

DRAGLĒ	draggly
HAGLĒ	haggly
STRAGLĒ	straggly
WAGLĒ	waggly

ĀGLER

NĀGLER	finagler
VĀGLER	inveigler

AGLER

DAGLER	daggler
DRAGLER	bedraggler, draggler
GAGLER	gaggler
HAGLER	haggler
STRAGLER	straggler
WAGLER	waggler

AGLING

DAGLING   boondaggling,
            daggling

(See **AGL,** add *-ing* where appropriate.)

AGMA

LAGMA   malagma
MAGMA   magma

AGMAN

BAGMAN   bagman
DRAGMAN   dragman
FLAGMAN   flagman
GAGMAN   gagman
RAGMAN   ragman

AGNĀT

AGNĀT   agnate
MAGNĀT   magnate
STAGNĀT   stagnate

AGNET

DRAGNET   dragnet
MAGNET   magnet

AGNUM

MAGNUM   magnum
SFAGNUM   sphagnum

AGNUS

MAGNUS   magnus
SFAGNUS   sphagnous

ĀGŌ

ĀGŌ   San Diego, pichiciago
BĀGŌ   lumbago, plumbago,
          sebago, Tobago
DĀGŌ   dago, solidago
FWĀGŌ   cacafuego, Tierra del
          Fuego
LĀGŌ   galago
MĀGŌ   archimago, imago
PĀGŌ   galapago
RĀGŌ   farrago, suffrago,
          virago, vorago
SĀGŌ   sago

ÄGŌ

ÄGŌ   Iago, Santiago
KÄGŌ   Chicago
LÄGŌ   salago
RÄGŌ   farrago

ĀGON

DĀGON   Dagon
SĀGON   Saigon

AGON

(See **AGUN**)

AGOT

(See **AGUT**)

ĀGRANS

FLĀGRANS   flagrance
FRĀGRANS   fragrance
VĀGRANS   vagrants

ĀGRANT

FLĀGRANT   flagrant
FRĀGRANT   fragrant, infragrant
VĀGRANT   vagrant

AGRIK

DAGRIK   podagric
RAGRIK   chiragric

AGUN

AGUN   agon
DRAGUN   dragon, pendragon,
          snapdragon
FLAGUN   flagon
WAGUN   chuckwagon, on the
          wagon, paddy wagon,
          wagon

ĀGUS

MĀGUS   archimagus, magus
PĀGUS   pagus
RĀGUS   choragus
TRĀGUS   tragus
VĀGUS   Las Vegas, vagus

AGUT

AGUT   agate
BAGUT   baggit
FAGUT   faggot, fagot
MAGUT   maggot, magot

ÄGWA

ÄGWA   agua
HÄGWA   majagua
JÄGWA   jagua
NÄGWA   Managua
RÄGWA   piragua
YÄGWA   yagua

AGZMAN

DRAGZMAN   dragsman
KRAGZMAN   cragsman
NAGZMAN   nagsman

ÄHA

ÄHA   aha, haha, taiaha
KÄHA   kaha
MÄHA   maha, maja
TÄHA   taha

ÄHOO

ÄHOO   Oahu
KÄHOO   kahu
MÄHOO   Mahu
SÄHOO   sahu
WÄHOO   wahoo
YÄHOO   yahoo, Yahoo

ĀIJ

DRĀIJ   drayage
PĀIJN   peage
WĀIJ   weighage

ĀIK

BRĀIK   algebraic,
          Alhambraic, Hebraic
DĀIK   Eddaic, Judaic, Chaldaic,
          sodaic, spondaic
KĀIK   Alcaic, archaic,
          Sadducaic, trochaic
LĀIK   formulaic, laic
MĀIK   Aramaic, Brahmaic,
          Romaic, Ptolemaic,
          stylagalmaic

NĀIK — Sinaic, Syrenaic
PĀIK — apotropaic, stenopaic
RĀIK — tesseraic
SĀIK — Pharisaic, Passaic
TĀIK — Altaic, deltaic, Jagataic, voltaic
ZĀIK — anti-Mosaic, mosaic, Mosaic, paradisaic, pre-Mosaic, prosaic, stanzaic

ĀIKS

TĀIKS — aretaics

(See **ĀIK,** add -s where appropriate.)

ĀIN

PRĀIN — pray-in
STĀIN — stay-in
WĀIN — weigh-in

ĀING

(See **Ā,** add -ing where appropriate.)

ĀIS

DĀIS — dais
LĀIS — Lais
NĀIS — nais
THĀIS — Thais

ĀISH

(See **Ā,** add -ish where appropriate.)

ĀIST

BRĀIST — algebraist
KĀIST — archaist
MĀIST — Ptolemaist
SĀIST — pharisaist
ZĀIST — prosaist

ĀIZM

DĀIZM — chaldaism
LĀIZM — Laism
ZĀIZM — Mosaism, prosaism

ĀJĒ

KĀJĒ — cagey
MĀJĒ — Meiji

RĀJĒ — ragy
SĀJĒ — sagy
STĀJĒ — stagy

AJĒ

HAJĒ — hadji
KAJĒ — cadgy
RAJĒ — karadji
WAJĒ — howadji

ĀJER

ĀJER — ager, golden-ager, teenager
GĀJER — disengager, engager, gager, gauger
KĀJER — cager
MĀJER — drum major, major, trumpet major
PĀJER — pager
RĀJER — enrager, rager
SĀJER — presager, sager
STĀJER — downstager, old-stager, stager, upstager
SWĀJER — assuager, swager
WĀJER — wager

AJER

AJER — agger
BAJER — badger
FAJER — fadger
KAJER — cadger

AJET

GAJET — gadget
WAJET — wadget

AJIK

FAJIK — androphagic, anthropophagic, lotophagic, omophagic, sarcophagic, theophagic
LAJIK — archipelagic, benthopelagic, ellagic, chimopelagic, pelagic
MAJIK — magic, theomagic
RAJIK — hemorrhagic, choragic
TRAJIK — antitragic, tragic

AJIL

AJIL — agile
FRAJIL — fragile

ĀJING

(See **ĀJ,** add -ing where appropriate.)

AJING

BAJING — badging
KAJING — cadging

ĀJLES

(See **ĀJ,** add -less where appropriate.)

ĀJMENT

GĀJMENT — disengagement, engagement, pre-engagement
KĀJMENT — encagement
RĀJMENT — enragement, curagement
SĀJMENT — presagement
SWĀJMENT — assuagement

ĀJUS

BĀJUS — ambagious
BRĀJUS — umbrageous
PĀJUS — rampageous
RĀJUS — harageous, courageous, oragious, outrageous
TĀJUS — advantageous, disadvantageous, contagious, noncontagious

ĀKA

ĀKA — cloaca, cueca
CHĀKA — Cheka
KĀKA — Macaca
LĀKA — kamalayka
MĀKA — Jamaica
RĀKA — bareca, raca
SHĀKA — abhiseka
WĀKA — weka

AKA

BAKA — bacca
DAKA — Dacca

FAKA	sifaka
LAKA	lacca, Malacca, polacca
PAKA	alpaca
RAKA	maraca

ÄKA

BÄKA	saltimbocca
DÄKA	medaca
HÄKA	Hakka
KÄKA	Titicaca, kaka
NÄKA	kanaka
PÄKA	paca
RÄKA	jararaca, karaka, raca
SÄKA	Osaka
TÄKA	pataca

AKAK

AKAK	ack-ack
KAKAK	kakkak

AKAL

(See **AKL**)

AKARD

PAKARD	Packard
PLAKARD	placard

ĀKĀT

PĀKĀT	opacate, pacate
PLĀKĀT	placate
VĀKĀT	vacate

AKĀT

BAKĀT	baccate
PLAKĀT	placate
SAKĀT	saccate

AKBRĀND

KRAKBRĀND	crackbrained
SLAKBRĀND	slackbrained

FORGETFULNESS

It was a lovely love affair . . .
One of those.
But who, or why, or when, or where,
God knows.

AKBUT

HAKBUT	hackbut
SAKBUT	sackbut

AKCHER

FAKCHER	facture, manufacture
FRAKCHER	fracture
PAKCHER	compacture
TRAKCHER	contracture

ĀKDOUN

BRĀKDOUN	breakdown
SHĀKDOUN	shakedown

AKDOUN

BAKDOUN	backdown
KRAKDOUN	crackdown

ĀKĒ

ĀKĒ	achy, headachy
BRĀKĒ	braky
FĀKĒ	faky
FLĀKĒ	flaky
KĀKĒ	caky
KWĀKĒ	quaky
LĀKĒ	laky
SHĀKĒ	shaky
SLĀKĒ	slaky
SNĀKĒ	snaky
TRĀKĒ	traiky

AKĒ

BLAKĒ	blackie, blacky
HAKĒ	hacky
HWAKĒ	whacky
KAKĒ	khaki
KRAKĒ	gimcracky, cracky
KWAKĒ	quacky
LAKĒ	lackey
MAKĒ	maki
NAKĒ	knacky
RAKĒ	raki
SAKĒ	Nagasaki, sake, saki
TAKĒ	tacky, ticky-tacky
WAKĒ	wacky

ÄKĒ

KÄKĒ	kaki, khaki, cocky
MÄKĒ	*theomachy*

RĀKĒ	Iraqi
SĀKĒ	Nagasaki, sake, saki
YĀKĒ	sukiyaki, teriyaki

(See **OK,** add *-y* where appropriate; also
see **OKĒ**.)

ĀKEN

BĀKEN	bacon
KRĀKEN	kraken
MĀKEN	Jamaican, Macon
SĀKEN	forsaken, Godforsaken, unforsaken
SHĀKEN	shaken, unshaken, wind-shaken
TĀKEN	mistaken, overtaken, taken, undertaken, untaken, uptaken
WĀKEN	awaken, reawaken, rewaken, waken

AKEN

BLAKEN	blacken
BRAKEN	bracken
KRAKEN	kraken
SLAKEN	slacken

ÄKEN

ÄKEN	Aachen
KRÄKEN	kraken
LÄKEN	Interlaken

ĀKER

ĀKER	acher, acre, fiacre stavesacre, wiseacre
BĀKER	baker
BRĀKER	backbreaker, braker, breaker, heartbreaker, housebreaker, icebreaker, jawbreaker, law-breaker, Sabbath-breaker, strikebreaker, tiebreaker, trucebreaker
FĀKER	faker, fakir
FLĀKER	flaker
KWĀKER	Quaker
LĀKER	laker, simulacre
MĀKER	boilermaker, bookmaker, dressmaker,

	haymaker,
	clockmaker,
	lawmaker, maker,
	matchmaker,
	pacemaker,
	peacemaker,
	shoemaker,
	troublemaker,
	watchmaker
NĀKER	nacre, naker
RĀKER	moonraker, raker
SĀKER	forsaker, saker
SHĀKER	boneshaker, shaker,
	Shaker
STĀKER	grubstaker, mistaker,
	painstaker, staker
TĀKER	caretaker, partaker,
	taker, undertaker
WĀKER	awaker, waker

AKER

AKER	coniaker
BAKER	backer
BLAKER	blacker
CHAKER	whinchacker
HAKER	hacker
HWAKER	bushwhacker, whacker
JAKER	hijacker
KLAKER	clacker
KRAKER	firecracker,
	clamcracker,
	corncracker, cracker,
	nutcracker
KWAKER	quacker
LAKER	lacker, lacquer,
	polacre
NAKER	knacker
PAKER	packer
RAKER	racker
SAKER	ransacker, sacker
SLAKER	slacker
SMAKER	smacker
SNAKER	snacker
STAKER	stacker
TAKER	attacker, tacker
THWAKER	thwacker
TRAKER	tracker
YAKER	yacker, yakker

AKET

BRAKET	bracket
FLAKET	flacket
HAKET	hurley-hacket
JAKET	bluejacket, jacket,
	leatherjacket,
	lumberjacket,
	redjacket, straitjacket,
	yellowjacket

KRAKET	cracket
NAKET	nacket
PAKET	packet
PLAKET	placket
RAKET	racket, rackett,
	racquet
SAKET	sacket
TAKET	tacket

ĀKIJ

BRĀKIJ	brakage, breakage
FLĀKIJ	flakage

AKIJ

PAKIJ	package
RAKIJ	wrackage
SAKIJ	sackage
STAKIJ	stackage
TRAKIJ	trackage

AKIK

AKIK	Noachic
BAKIK	bacchic
MAKIK	stomachic
SKAKIK	scacchic

ĀKING

(See **ĀK,** add -ing where appropriate.)

AKING

(See **AK,** add -ing where appropriate.)

ĀKISH

ĀKISH	achish
RĀKISH	rakish
SNĀKISH	snakish

AKISH

BLAKISH	blackish
BRAKISH	brackish
KWAKISH	quackish
NAKISH	knackish
SLAKISH	slackish

AKKLOTH

PAKKLOTH	packcloth
SAKKLOTH	sackcloth

AKL

AKL	*piacle*
BAKL	debacle
BRAKL	brackle
GRAKL	grackle
HAKL	hackle
JAKL	jackal
KAKL	cackle
KRAKL	crackle
KWAKL	quackle
MAKL	mackle, macle
NAKL	hibernacle, tabernacle
SHAKL	hamshackle,
	ramshackle, shackle,
	unshackle
SPAKL	spackle, Spackle
TAKL	tackle, retackle, untackle

AKLD

KAKLD	cackled

(See **AKL,** add -d where appropriate.)

AKLĒ

BLAKLĒ	blackly
KAKLĒ	cackly
KRAKLĒ	crackly
SHAKLĒ	ramshackly, shackly
SLAKLĒ	slackly
TAKLĒ	tackly

AKLER

HAKLER	hackler
KAKLER	cackler
KRAKLER	crackler
SHAKLER	hamshackler, shackler
TAKLER	tackler

ĀKLES

(See **ĀK,** add -less where appropriate.)

AKLES

(See **AK,** add -less where appropriate.)

AKLING

HAKLING	hackling
KAKLING	cackling
KRAKLING	crackling
SHAKLING	hamshackling,
	shackling
TAKLING	tackling

AKLOG

BAKLOG   backlog
HAKLOG   hacklog

AKMA

CHAKMA   chacma
DRAKMA   drachma, tetradrachma

ĀKMAN

BRĀKMAN   brakeman
KĀKMAN   cakeman

AKMAN

BLAKMAN   blackman
JAKMAN   jackman
PAKMAN   pac-man, packman

AKMĒ

AKMĒ   acme
LAKMĒ   Lakme
NAKMĒ   menacme

AKNĒ

AKNĒ   acne
HAKNĒ   hackney

AKNES

BLAKNES   blackness
SLAKNES   slackness

ĀKŌ

DRĀKŌ   Draco
KĀKŌ   macaco
MĀKŌ   mako
SHĀKŌ   shako
WĀKŌ   Waco

AKŌ

BAKŌ   tobacco
HWAKŌ   whacko
JAKŌ   jako
KAKŌ   icaco
RAKŌ   goracco
SHAKŌ   shako

SKWAKŌ   squacko
WAKŌ   wacko

ÄKŌ

CHÄKO   cheechako
GWÄKŌ   guaco
MÄKŌ   mako, makomako
NÄKŌ   guanaco
PÄKŌ   paco
TÄKŌ   taco, mataco

ĀKOF

RĀKOF   rakeoff
TĀKOF   takeoff

ĀKON

(See ĀKEN)

ĀKOUT

BRĀKOUT   breakout
SHĀKOUT   shakeout
STĀKOUT   stakeout
TĀKOUT   takeout

AKPOT

JAKPOT   jackpot
KRAKPOT   crackpot

ĀKRON

ĀKRON   Akron
DĀKRON   Dacron
MĀKRON   macron

ĀKRUM

LĀKRUM   simulacrum
SĀKRUM   sacrum, synsacrum

AKSĒ

BRAKSĒ   braxy
DAKSĒ   tachydidaxy
FLAKSĒ   flaxy
MAKSĒ   maxi
TAKSĒ   ataky, biotaxy, heterotaxy, homotaxy, geotaxy, taxi, eutaxy
WAKSĒ   waxy

AKSEN

AKSEN   axon, diaxon
DRAKSEN   dendraxon
FLAKSEN   flaxen
KAKSEN   caxon
KLAKSEN   klaxon
SAKSEN   Anglo-Saxon, Saxon
WAKSEN   waxen

AKSHUN

AKSHUN   *A* abreaction, action, affirmative action, *E* enaction, *I* inaction, interaction, *K* coaction, counteraction, covert action, *R* reaction, retroaction, *S* subaction, *TR* transaction
DAKSHUN   redaction
FAKSHUN   *B* benefaction, *D* dissatisfaction, *E* expergefaction, *F* faction, *K* calefaction, *L* labefaction, liquefaction, lubrifaction, *M* madefaction, malefaction, *P* petrifaction, putrefaction, *R* rarefaction, rubefaction, *S* satisfaction, *ST* stupefaction, *T* tabefaction, tepefaction, torrefaction, tumefaction
FRAKSHUN   diffraction, fraction, infraction, refraction
PAKSHUN   compaction, paction
STRAKSHUN   abstraction
TAKSHUN   contaction, taction
TRAKSHUN   attraction, detraction, distraction, extraction, contraction, counterattraction, protraction, retraction, subtraction, traction
ZAKSHUN   exaction

AKSHUS

FAKSHUS   factious
FRAKSHUS   fractious

AKSIS

AKSIS	axis
DAKSIS	pseudaxis
LAKSIS	anaphylaxis, prophylaxis
NAKSIS	synaxis
PRAKSIS	ideopraxis, chiropraxis, parapraxis, praxis, radiopraxis
STAKSIS	epistaxis, staxis
TAKSIS	phototaxis, hypotaxis, geotaxis, parataxis, taxis, thermotaxis

AKSMAN

KRAKSMAN	cracksman
TAKSMAN	tacksman

AKSON

(See **AKSEN**)

AKSTĀ

BAKSTĀ	backstay
JAKSTĀ	jackstay

AKTA

AKTA	acta
FAKTA	facta

AKTĀT

LAKTĀT	ablactate, lactate
TRAKTĀT	tractate

AKTED

(See **AKT,** add *-ed* where appropriate.)

AKTER

AKTER	acter, actor, bad actor, enacter, reenacter, reactor, transactor
BAKTER	abactor
DAKTER	redactor
FAKTER	benefactor, factor, malefactor, calefactor, olfactor
FRAKTER	diffractor, infractor, refractor
LAKTER	pylacter
MAKTER	climacter
PAKTER	compacter
PRAKTER	chiropractor
RAKTER	varactor
STRAKTER	abstractor
TAKTER	contactor, tactor
TRAKTER	attractor, distracter, extracter, extractor, contracter, contractor, protractor, retractor, subtracter, tractor, subcontractor
ZAKTER	exacter, exactor

AKTIK

DAKTIK	didactic
FRAKTIK	emphractic
LAKTIK	anaphylactic, extragalactic, phylactic, galactic, hylactic, catallactic, lactic, malactic, parallactic, prophylactic, circumgalactic
MAKTIK	anticlimactic, climactic
NAKTIK	synactic
PRAKTIK	chiropractic, practic
RAKTIK	ataractic
TAKTIK	atactic, heliotactic, protactic, syntactic, tactic

AKTIL

DAKTIL	adactyl, dactyl, didactyl, syndactyl, pterodactyl
FRAKTIL	fractile
TAKTIL	tactile
TRAKTIL	contractile, protractile, tractile

AKTING

(See **AKT,** add *-ing* where appropriate.)

AKTIV

AKTIV	active, enactive, photoactive, hyperactive, inactive, interactive, coactive, counteractive, overactive, radioactive, reactive, retroactive
FAKTIV	factive, calefactive, olfactive, petrifactive, putrefactive, rarefactive, satisfactive, stupefactive
FRAKTIV	diffractive, refractive
STRAKTIV	abstractive
TRAKTIV	attractive, detractive, distractive, extractive, contractive, protractive, retractive, subtractive, tractive, unattractive

AKTLĒ

BAKTLĒ	humpbackedly, hunchbackedly, stoopbackedly
FAKTLĒ	matter-of-factly
PAKTLĒ	compactly
STRAKTLĒ	abstractly
TAKTLĒ	intactly
ZAKTLĒ	exactly

AKTRES

AKTRES	actress
FAKTRES	benefactress, malefactress
ZAKTRES	exactress

AKTUM

AKTUM	actum
FAKTUM	factum

AKTŪR

(See **AKCHER**)

AKTUS

AKTUS	actus
KAKTUS	cactus
TAKTUS	tactus

ĀKUP

BRĀKUP	breakup
MĀKUP	makeup
WĀKUP	wake-up

AKUP

BAKUP	back-up

HWAKUP whack-up
KRAKUP crack-up

AKUS

BAKUS Bacchus
FLAKUS Flaccus
JAKUS jacchus

AKWĀ

BAKWĀ backway
PAKWĀ packway
TRAKWĀ trackway

AKWA

AKWA aqua
MAKWA namaqua
NAKWA anaqua

AKWERD

AKWERD bass-ackward
BAKWERD backward,
ass-backward

ĀLA

ĀLA ala, Venezuela
GĀLA gala
CHĀLA chela
KĀLA chela
LĀLA shillalah, shillelagh
MĀLA kamala, mala
NĀLA panela
SĀLA osela
ZWĀLA zarzuela

ÄLA

ÄLA Allah, koala
BÄLA gaballa, cabala,
kabala, quabbalah
GÄLA fala
HÄLA hala
KÄLA kala
MÄLA Guatemala, kamala
PÄLA impala
SÄLA Marsala
TÄLA patala, tala
WÄLA chuckwalla, owala,
pozzy-wallah, wallah,
walla-walla

ALAD

BALAD ballad
KALAD calid
PALAD impallid, pallid
SALAD salad
VALAD invalid, valid

ALANS

(See **ALENS**)

ĀLANT

(See **ĀLENT**)

ALAS

(See **ALUS**)

ALBA

ALBA alba
BALBA xibalba
GALBA galba

ALA

ALA alla, Allah, boobyalla
BALA cabala
GALA emagalla, gala, Galla
HALA Valhalla
KALA calla
PALA palla, pallah
SHALA inshala, mashalla
VALA cavalla

ÄLA

ÄLA Allah, koala
BÄLA gaballa, cabala,
kabala, quabbalah
GÄLA gala
HÄLA hala
KÄLA kala
MÄLA Guatemala, kamala
PÄLA impala
SÄLA Marsala

ALĀT

KALAĀT cal'late
VALĀT obvallate

ĀLĒ

ĀLĒ aly
BĀLĒ bailey, bailie, Bali,
Old Bailey

ĀLĒ

CHĀLĒ tjaele
DĀLĒ daily
FRĀLĒ frailly
GĀLĒ gaily
GRĀLĒ grayly
HĀLĒ halely
KĀLĒ cellidh
KWĀLĒ quaily, quale
LĀLĒ pasilaly, shillala,
shillelagh, ukulele
PĀLĒ palely, pali, paly
RĀLĒ Disraeli, Israeli, jus
naturalae
SHĀLĒ shaly
SKĀLĒ scaly
SNĀLĒ snaily
STĀLĒ stalely
TĀLĒ taily
TRĀLĒ traily
VĀLĒ vale
WĀLĒ waily
YĀLĒ Yalie

ALĒ

ALĒ alley, bially
BALĒ Bali, bally
DALĒ dally, dillydally
GALĒ Bengali, galley,
gally, Svengali
HALĒ Halley
KALĒ Kali, Mexicali,
teocalli
LALĒ soapolallie
MALĒ tamale, tomalley
PALĒ pally
RALĒ rally
SALĒ sallee, sally
SHALĒ challis, chally, shilly-
shally
TALĒ tally
VALĒ travale, trevally,
valley
WALĒ peelie-wally, wally

ÄLĒ

ÄLĒ Ali
BÄLĒ Bali, bally
DÄLĒ Dali
GÄLĒ Bengali, galee, gali,
galley, gally, gregale
HÄLĒ ahali, tahali
KÄLĒ Kali, Mexicali,
triticale
MÄLĒ hot tamale, Somali,
tamale
NÄLĒ finale
PÄLĒ pali, Pali
RÄLĒ pastorale

TÄLĒ   tali
VÄLĒ   vali, Vali

(See OLĒ)

ALĒD

DALĒD   dallied, dillydallied
RALĒD   rallied
SALĒD   sallied
SHALĒD   shilly-shallied
TALĒD   tallied

ĀLENS

SĀLENS   assailance
VĀLENS   *ambivalence,*
            bivalence,
            polyvalence,
            pronovalence,
            stasivalence,
            supinovalence,
            surveillance,
            trivalence,
            uxoravalence,
            uxorovalence, valence

ALENS

BALENS   balance,
            counterbalance,
            outbalance,
            overbalance,
            unbalance
VALENS   pronovalence,
            stasivalence,
            supinovalence,
            uxoravalence,
            uxorovalence, valance

ĀLENT

HĀLENT   exhalant, inhalant
KĀLENT   intranscalent,
            transcalent
SĀLENT   assailant
VĀLENT   *ambivalent,* bivalent,
            divalent, monovalent,
            polyvalent,
            pronovalent,
            stasivalent,
            supinovalent,
            surveillant, trivalent,
            uxoravalent,
            uxorovalent, valent,
            univalent

ALENT

GALENT   gallant, stoopgallant,
            topgallant, ungallant
TALENT   talent
VALENT   polyvalent,
            pronovalent,
            stasivalent,
            supinovalent,
            uxoravalent,
            uxorovalent

ĀLER

ĀLER   alar
BĀLER   bailer, bailor, baler
HĀLER   hailer, inhaler,
            loud-hailer
HWĀLER   whaler
KĀLER   *intercalar*
MĀLER   mailer, Mailer, malar
SĀLER   wholesaler, sailor
SKĀLER   scalar, scaler
SKWĀLER   squalor
TĀLER   retailer, tailor, talar
TRĀLER   housetrailer, trailer
WĀLER   waler, Waler

(See ĀL, add -er where appropriate.)

ALER

PALER   pallor
VALER   potvalor, valor

ÄLER

DÄLER   daler
HÄLER   haler
SKÄLER   scalar
TÄLER   taler
THÄLER   thaler
SKWÄLER   squalor

(See OLER)

ĀLES

(See Ā, ĀL, add -less where appropriate.)

ALET

BALET   ballot
GALET   gallet
KALET   callet
MALET   mallet
PALET   palate, palette, pallet

SALET   sallet
TALET   tallet
VALET   valet

ÄLET

SWÄLET   swallet
WÄLET   wallet

ALĒZ

VALĒZ   sherryvallies

(See ALĒ, change -y or -i to -ies where
appropriate.)

ALFA

ALFA   alfa, alpha
FALFA   alfalfa
TALFA   pentalpha

ĀLFUL

ĀLFUL   ailful
BĀLFUL   baleful
PĀLFUL   pailful, paleful
TĀLFUL   taleful
WĀLFUL   wailful

ALID

(See ALAD)

ĀLIF

ĀLIF   alef, aleph
BĀLIF   bailiff, bumbailiff
KĀLIF   calif, caliph

ĀLIJ

BĀLIJ   bailage
HĀLIJ   haylage
SĀLIJ   sailage
SKĀLIJ   scalage
TĀLIJ   entailage, curtailage,
            retailage
TRĀLIJ   treillage

ĀLIK

GĀLIK   Gaelic
MĀLIK   malic
SĀLIK   salic

ALIK

ALIK	smart-alec, wise-alec
BALIK	cabalic
DALIK	medallic, vandalic
FALIK	*A* acrocephalic, *BR* brachistocephalic, *D* dolichocephalic, *E* encephalic, *F* phallic, *I* ithyphallic, *M* macrencephalic, macrocephalic, mesophalic, microcephalic, *P* pacycephalic, *PL* platycephalic, *S* cephalic, *Y* eurycephalic
GALIK	Gallic, misogallic
GRALIK	grallic
KALIK	alkalic, intervocalic, prevocalic, vocalic
MALIK	malic
PALIK	rhopalic
RALIK	Uralic
SALIK	oxalic, salic
TALIK	bimetallic, italic, genitalic, metallic, monometallic, nonmetallic, tantalic
THALIK	thallic
VALIK	intervallic

ĀLIKS

KĀLIKS	epicalyx, calix, calyx
SALIKS	salix

ĀLING

(See **ĀL,** add *-ing* where appropriate.)

ALING

BALING	caballing
PALING	palling

ALIS

ALIS	allice, Alice
CHALIS	chalice
MALIS	malice
PALIS	palace
TALIS	digitalis

(See **ALUS**)

ĀLISH

FRĀLISH	frailish

PĀLISH	palish
SHĀLISH	shalish
STĀLISH	stalish

ALJA

(See **AL'JI.A**)

ALJĒ

ALJĒ	algae
LALJĒ	cephalalgy
RALJĒ	neuralgy
TALJĒ	nostalgy, odontalgy

ALJIK

ALJIK	algic
FALJIK	cephalgic
RALJIK	neuralgic
TALJIK	antalgic, nostalgic, odontalgic
TRALJIK	gastralgic

ĀLKÄR

MĀLKÄR	mail-car
RĀLKÄR	rail-car

ALMA

ALMA	alma, Alma
GALMA	agalma
HALMA	halma

ĀLMENT

ĀLMENT	ailment
BĀLMENT	bailment
GĀLMENT	regalement
HĀLMENT	exhalement, inhalement
PĀLMENT	impalement
RĀLMENT	derailment
SĀLMENT	assailment
TĀLMENT	entailment, curtailment
VĀLMENT	availment, prevailment
WĀLMENT	bewailment

ALMUD

ALMUD	almud
TALMUD	Talmud

ĀLNES

FRĀLNES	frailness
MĀLNES	femaleness, maleness
PĀLNES	paleness
STĀLNES	staleness

ĀLŌ

HĀLŌ	halo
NĀLŌ	canelo, Canelo

ALŌ

ALŌ	aloe
FALŌ	fallow
GALŌ	gallow
HALŌ	Allhallow, dishallow, hallow, unhallow
KALŌ	callow, mackalow
MALŌ	mallow, marshmallow
SALŌ	sallow
SHALŌ	shallow
TALŌ	tallow, talo

ÄLŌ

KÄLŌ	calo
LÄLŌ	lalo
MÄLŌ	malo
PÄLŌ	palo
SWÄLŌ	swallow
TÄLŌ	talo
WÄLŌ	hogwallow, wallow

(See **OLŌ**)

ALON

(See **ALUN**)

ALOP

(See **ALUP**)

ALPIN

ALPIN	Alpine
SPALPIN	Spalpeen

ALPING

PALPING	palping
SKALPING	scalping

ALSA

BALSA	balsa
SALSA	salsa

ALTŌ

ALTŌ	alto, Rialto
PALTŌ	paletot
TRALTŌ	contralto

ALUM

ALUM	alum
RALUM	chloralum
TALUM	catallum
VALUM	vallum

ALUN

GALUN	gallon
KALUN	kalon
SALUN	salon
TALUN	talon

ALUP

GALUP	gallop, galop
JALUP	jalap
SALUP	salep
SHALUP	shallop
SKALUP	escallop, scallop

ALUS

BALUS	aryballus, balas
DALUS	Dallas
FALUS	phallus
KALUS	callous, callus
PALUS	palace, Pallas
THALUS	thallous, thallus

(See **ALIS**)

ĀLYA

DĀLYA	dahlia, vedalia
FĀLYA	Westphalia
GĀLYA	galea, regalia
KĀLYA	cacalia
LĀLYA	barbaralalia, barylalia, echolalia, embolalia, eschrolalia, glossolalia, idiolalia, coprolalia, tachylalia
MĀLYA	mammalia
NĀLYA	Bacchanalia, marginalia, paraphernalia, saturnalia, terminalia
RĀLYA	psoralia
TĀLYA	genitalia, castalia
TRĀLYA	Australia, Centralia, penetralia
ZĀLYA	azalea

ĀLYAN

ĀLYAN	alien, marsupalian
DĀLYAN	Daedalian, hippomonstrosesqui-edalian, septipedalian, sesquipedalian
GĀLYAN	Phigalian, regalian
KĀLYAN	Deucalion
MĀLYAN	phantasmalian, mammalian, Pygmalion, tatterdemalion
NĀLYAN	bacchanalian, saturnalian, tenaillon, tobacconalian
PĀLYAN	episcopalian, Episcopalian
RĀLYAN	paralian
SĀLYAN	Messalian, universalian
THĀLYAN	thalian
TRĀLYAN	Australian, Centralian

(See **Ā'LI.AN**)

ĀLYÄRD

JĀLYÄRD	gaolyard, jailyard
KĀLYÄRD	kailyard

ĀLYŌ

RĀLYŌ	seraglio
TĀLYŌ	intaglio

ÄLYŌ

BÄLYŌ	caballo
RÄLYŌ	seraglio
TÄLYŌ	intaglio

ĀLYUN

(See **ĀLYAN, ĀL'LI.AN**)

ALYUN

DALYUN	medallion
PALYUN	rampallion
SKALYUN	rapscallion, scallion
STALYUN	stallion
TALYUN	battalion, Italian, rantallion

ĀLZMAN

DĀLZMAN	dalesman
HWĀLZMAN	whalesman
SĀLZMAN	salesman
TĀLZMAN	talesman

ĀMA

BRĀMA	Brahma
DĀMA	Aceldama
FĀMA	Fama
HĀMA	Bahama
KRĀMA	krama
LĀMA	lama
SKWĀMA	squama

AMA

AMA	amma
BAMA	Alabama
CHAMA	chamma
DRAMA	drama, docudrama, duodrama, melodrama, monodrama, psychodrama
GAMA	digamma, gamma
JAMA	pajama, pyjama
RAMA	D diorama, J georama, K cosmorama, M myriorama, N neorama, P panorama, panstereorama, polyorama, R Rama, ramarama, S cyclorama, cinerama

ÄMA

ÄMA	ama, amah
BÄMA	Alabama
BRÄMA	Brahma
DRÄMA	drama, duodrama, melodrama, monodrama, psychodrama

GRÄMA	grama
HÄMA	Bahama, Yokohama
JÄMA	jama, pajama, pyjama
KÄMA	caama, kaama, Kama
LÄMA	Dalai Lama, lama, llama, palama
MÄMA	mama, mamma
RÄMA	D diorama, J georama, K cosmorama, M myriorama, N neorama, P panorama, panstereorama, polyorama, R Rama, ramarama, S cyclorama, cinerama
SHÄMA	shama
YÄMA	Fujiyama, pranayama, Yama

ĀMAN

DĀMAN	dayman
DRĀMAN	drayman
HĀMAN	Haman, hayman
KĀMAN	caiman, cayman
LĀMAN	layman
SHĀMAN	shaman
WĀMAN	highwayman, railwayman

(See ĀMEN)

AMAN

(See AMUN)

ÄMAN

ÄMAN	*Amen*
BRÄMAN	Brahman, Parabrahman
SÄMAN	saman, zaman
SHÄMAN	shaman

ĀMANT

(See ĀMENT)

ĀMĀT

DĀMĀT	daymate
HĀMĀT	hamate
KWÄMĀT	desquamate, esquamate
PLĀMĀT	playmate
RĀMĀT	ramate
SKWÄMĀT	esquamate, squamate

AMBA

RAMBA	caramba
SAMBA	samba

AMBER

AMBER	amber, grisamber, liquidamber
KAMBER	camber
KLAMBER	clamber
SAMBER	sambar
TAMBER	tambour

AMBIK

AMBIK	elegiambic, galliambic, iambic, choliambic, choriambic, pythiambic
RAMBIK	dithyrambic

AMBIST

AMBIST	iambist
GAMBIST	gambist
KAMBIST	cambist

AMBIT

AMBIT	ambit
GAMBIT	gambit

AMBL

AMBL	amble, preamble
BRAMBL	bramble
FAMBL	famble
GAMBL	gamble, gambol
HAMBL	hamble
RAMBL	ramble
SHAMBL	shamble
SKAMBL	scamble, skimble-skamble
SKRAMBL	scramble, scrimble-scramble, unscramble
WAMBL	wamble

AMBLER

AMBLER	ambler
GAMBLER	gambler
RAMBLER	rambler
SHAMBLER	shambler
SKRAMBLER	scrambler
WAMBLER	wambler

AMBŌ

AMBŌ	ambo
FLAMBŌ	flambeau
JAMBŌ	jambeau
KRAMBŌ	crambo
MAMBŌ	mambo
SAMBŌ	sambo
ZAMBŌ	zambo

AMBUS

AMBUS	iambus
RAMBUS	dithyrambus

ĀMĒ

FLĀMĒ	flamy
GĀMĒ	gamy
MĀMĒ	cockamamy, cockamamie
RĀMĒ	rami
SĀMĒ	zemi

AMĒ

AMĒ	Miami
DAMĒ	damme
GAMĒ	gammy
HAMĒ	hammy
HWAMĒ	double-whammy, whammy
JAMĒ	jammy
KLAMĒ	clammy
MAMĒ	mammy
NAMĒ	bonami
RAMĒ	ramie, rammy
SAMĒ	sammy
SHAMĒ	chamois, shammy
TAMĒ	tamis, tammy
TRAMĒ	trammie

ÄMĒ

BÄMĒ	balmy
GÄMĒ	krigami, origami
JÄMĒ	jami
KÄMĒ	calmy, kami
KWÄMĒ	qualmy
LÄMĒ	palame, salami
MÄMĒ	malmy
NÄMĒ	tsunami
PÄMĒ	pahmi, palmy

| SWÄMĒ | swami |
| TRÄMĒ | pastrami |

(See OMĒ)

AMEL

KAMEL	camel
MAMEL	mammal
NAMEL	enamel
SKAMEL	scamell, scammel
STAMEL	stammel
TAMEL	Tamil
TRAMEL	entrammel, trammel

AMELD

(See AMEL, add -ed.)

ĀMEN

ĀMEN	amen
BRĀMEN	Bremen
DĀMEN	daimen, daimon
FLĀMEN	flamen
LĀMEN	laymen, velamen
NĀMEN	clinamen
RĀMEN	duramen, foramen
STĀMEN	stamen
TĀMEN	putamen
VĀMEN	gravamen
ZĀMEN	examen

(See ĀMAN)

ÄMEN

(See ĀMAN)

ĀMENT

ĀMENT	ament
FRĀMENT	defrayment
HĀMENT	adhamant
KLĀMENT	claimant, clamant, reclaimant
LĀMENT	allayment
PĀMENT	pament, payment, repayment
RĀMENT	raiment
TRĀMENT	betrayment

ĀMER

ĀMER	aimer, amor
BLĀMER	blamer
FĀMER	defamer, disfamer
FLĀMER	inflamer
FRĀMER	framer
GĀMER	gamer
KLĀMER	acclaimer, declaimer, disclaimer, exclaimer, claimer, proclaimer, reclaimer
LĀMER	lamer
MĀMER	maimer
NĀMER	misnamer, namer, nicknamer
SHĀMER	shamer
TĀMER	horsetamer, liontamer, tamer, testamur

AMER

DAMER	dammar, dammer, damner
DRAMER	mellerdrammer
GAMER	gammer
GLAMER	glamor, glamour
GRAMER	grammar, grammer, programmer
HAMER	hammer, jackhammer, ninny-hammer, sledgehammer, yellowhammer
JAMER	jammer, windjammer
KLAMER	clamor
KRAMER	crammer
LAMER	lamber, lammer
NAMER	enamor
RAMER	rammer
SHAMER	shammer
SKRAMER	scrammer
SLAMER	slammer
STAMER	stammer
YAMER	yammer

ÄMER

BÄMER	balmer, embalmer
KÄMER	calmer
PÄMER	palmer

AMFER

| CHAMFER | chamfer |
| KAMFER | camphor |

AMIJ

| DAMIJ | damage |
| RAMIJ | ramage |

AMIK

DAMIK	Adamic, pre-Adamic
GAMIK	agamic, epigamic, phanerogamic, gamic, homogamic, isogamic, monogamic, polygamic, syngamic
GRAMIK	engrammic, cryptogrammic, monogrammic, parallelogrammic, telegrammic, trigrammic
HAMIK	Abrahamic
LAMIK	epithalamic, Islamic, olamic
NAMIK	adynamic, aerodynamic, biodynamic, dynamic, electrodynamic, hydrodynamic, hyperdynamic, isodynamic, autodynamic, cinnamic, thermodynamic
RAMIK	dioramic, cosmoramic, panoramic, ceramic, cycloramic
SAMIK	balsamic
TAMIK	potamic

AMIKS

| NAMIKS | zoodynamics |

(See AMIK, add -s where appropriate.)

AMIL

| AMIL | amyl |
| TAMIL | tamil |

AMIN

AMIN	amin, amine
FAMIN	famine
GAMIN	gamin
LAMIN	lamin, prolamine
STAMIN	stamin
ZAMIN	examine, cross-examine, reexamine

ĀMING

(See ĀM, add -ing where appropriate.)

AMING

(See **AM,** add *-ming* where appropriate.)

ÄMING

BÄMING	embalming
KÄMING	calming
PÄMING	palming
WÄMING	walming

AMIS

AMIS	amice
KLAMIS	chlamys
NAMIS	dynamis
TAMIS	tamis

ĀMISH

LĀMISH	lamish
SĀMISH	Samish, samish
TĀMISH	tamish

AMISH

AMISH	Amish
FAMISH	affamish, enfamish, famish
KLAMISH	clammish
LAMISH	lambish
RAMISH	rammish

ÄMIST

BÄMIST	embalmist
PÄMIST	palmist
SÄMIST	psalmist

AML

(See **AMEL**)

ĀMLĒ

GĀMLĒ	gamely
LĀMLĒ	lamely
NĀMLĒ	namely
SĀMLĒ	samely
TĀMLĒ	tamely

ĀMLES

(See **ĀM,** add *-less* where appropriate.)

AMLES

(See **AM,** add *-less* where appropriate.)

ÄMLES

(See **AM,** add *-less* where appropriate.)

AMLET

HAMLET	hamlet, Hamlet
KAMLET	camlet
SAMLET	samlet

ÄMMENT

BÄMMENT	embalmment
KÄMMENT	becalmment

ĀMNES

GĀMNES	gameness
LĀMNES	lameness
SĀMNES	sameness
TĀMNES	tameness

AMOK

(See **AMUK**)

AMON

(See **AMUN**)

AMPA

GRAMPA	grampa
PAMPA	pampa
TAMPA	Tampa

FOOTNOTE TO THE SINKING OF ATLANTIS

When the praying mantis
Learned that Atlantis
   Was about to go down,
Not waiting for scanties
Or even for panties
   She hopped out of town.

AMPAN

JAMPAN	jampan
SAMPAN	sampan
TAMPAN	tampan

AMPAS

LAMPAS	lampas
PAMPAS	pampas

(See **AMPUS**)

AMPĒ

DAMPĒ	dampy
KRAMPĒ	crampy
SKAMPĒ	scampi
VAMPĒ	vampy

ÄMPĒ

(See **OMPĒ**)

AMPER

CHAMPER	champer
DAMPER	damper
HAMPER	hamper
KAMPER	camper
KLAMPER	clamper
KRAMPER	cramper
PAMPER	pamper, pampre
RAMPER	ramper
SKAMPER	scamper
STAMPER	stamper
TAMPER	tamper
TRAMPER	tramper
VAMPER	vamper

AMPERD

HAMPERD	hampered, unhampered
PAMPERD	pampered, unpampered
TAMPERD	tampered

AMPING

(See **AMP,** add *-ing* where appropriate.)

AMPISH

(See **AMP,** add *-ish* where appropriate.)

AMPL

AMPL	ample
SAMPL	ensample, sample
TRAMPL	trample
ZAMPL	example

AMPLD

SAMPLD	sampled
TRAMPLD	trampled
ZAMPLD	exampled

AMPLĒ

AMPLĒ	amply
DAMPLĒ	damply

AMPLER

(See **AMPL,** add -r where appropriate.)

AMPLING

SAMPLING	ensampling, sampling
TRAMPLING	trampling
ZAMPLING	exampling

AMPUS

GRAMPUS	grampus
KAMPUS	hippocampus, campus

(See **AMPAS**)

ÄMPUS

(See **OMPUS**)

AMSEN

DAMSEN	damson
KAMSEN	khamsin
RAMSEN	ramson
SAMSEN	Samson

(See **AMZUN**)

AMUK

HAMUK	hammock
DRAMUK	drammock
KAMUK	cammock
MAMUK	mammock

AMUN

AMUN	Ammon
DAMUN	daman
GAMUN	backgammon, gammon
MAMUN	mammon
SAMUN	salmon
SHAMUN	shaman

ĀMUS

DĀMUS	mandamus
FĀMUS	famous
HĀMUS	hamus
RĀMUS	biramous, ignoramus, ramous, ramus, uniramous
SHĀMUS	shamus
SKWĀMUS	squamous

AMUT

GAMUT	gamut
MAMUT	Mammut

AMZEL

AMZEL	amsel
DAMZEL	damsel
MAMZEL	ma'mselle

AMZUN

DAMZUN	damson
RAMZUN	ramson

(See **AMSEN**)

ĀNA

ĀNA	ana, fistiana, Jeffersoniana, Johnsoniana (etc.) nicotiana, omniana, poinciana
JĀNA	Cartagena
KĀNA	Americana (etc.), arcana, Cana
LĀNA	cantilena, Magdalena
MĀNA	vox humana
NĀNA	anana
PĀNA	campana
PLĀNA	geoplana
RĀNA	rena
SHĀNA	scena
TĀNA	Curtana, lantana

ANA

ANA	*A* ana, anna, Anna, *D* Diana, dulciana, *F* fistiana, *G* Guiana, goanna, *I* Indiana, ipecacuanha, *J* Georgiana, Jeffersoniana, Johnsoniana, *N* nicotiana, *L* liana, Louisiana, *O* Australiana, *P* poinciana, Pollyanna, *R* ruana, *T* tertiana, *SH* Shakespeariana, Victoriana (etc.)
BANA	Urbana
DANA	bandana, bandanna
HANA	Susquehanna
KANA	Americana, canna, Texarkana
LANA	alannah
MANA	manna
NANA	banana, nanna
TANA	lantana, Montana, sultana
VANA	Havana, savanna, Savannah
ZANA	hosanna

ÄNA

ÄNA	damiana, dulciana, fistiana, Guiana, Jeffersoniana, Georgiana, Johnsoniana, liana, Australiana, Shakespeariana, Victoriana
BÄNA	bana, Bana, ikebana
BWÄNA	bwana
DÄNA	apadana
GÄNA	Ghana, hagana, hiragana, nagana
GWÄNA	iguana
HWÄNA	marijuana
KÄNA	Americana (etc.), gymkhana, kana, katakana
LÄNA	pozzuolana
MÄNA	mana, manna, vox humana
NÄNA	anana, banana, cassabanana, zenana
PRÄNA	prana
RÄNA	kerana, piranha, purana, rana
SHÄNA	Rosh Hashanah
TÄNA	Curtana, lantana, Montana, sultana, Tana, tramontana
THÄNA	thana
VÄNA	Nirvana
WÄNA	marijuana, Tia Juana, Tijuana
YÄNA	dhyana, Guyana, Hinayane, Mahayna, mañana

ĀNAL

ĀNAL	anal
BĂNAL	banal

KĀNAL	decanal	**ANDA**		**ANDĒD**	
MĀNAL	bimanal, manal, septimanal			**BRANDĒD**	brandied
VĀNAL	interveinal, veinal	**GANDA**	propaganda, Uganda	**KANDĒD**	discandied, candied
		PANDA	panda		
		RANDA	jacaranda, memoranda, veranda		

ĀNĀT

LĀNĀT	lanate	**TANDA**	notanda
PĀNĀT	impanate	**VANDA**	observanda, vanda, Vanda

ANĀT

KANĀT	khanate
TANĀT	tannate

ANDĀD

BANDĀD	Band-Aid
HANDĀD	hand-aid

ANDED

KANDED	candid

(See **AND,** add *-ed* where appropriate.)

ANCHĒ

BRANCHĒ	branchy
MANCHĒ	Comanche
RANCHĒ	ranchy

ANDAL

(see **ANDL**)

ANDENT

KANDENT	candent
SKANDENT	scandent

ĀNCHĒ

(See **ÔNCHĒ**)

ANDBAG

HANDBAG	handbag
SANDBAG	sandbag

ĀNDER

MĀNDER	remainder
TĀNDER	attainder, detainder

ANCHER

(See **ANCH,** add *-er* where appropriate.)

ANDBOI

BANDBOI	bandboy
SANDBOI	sandboy

ANDER

ANDER	coriander, Leander, meander, oleander
BANDER	bander, disbander
BLANDER	blander
BRANDER	brander
DANDER	dander
GANDER	gander, goosey-gander
GLANDER	glander
GRANDER	grander
HANDER	backhander, forehander, hander, left-hander, right-hander
KANDER	Africander, candor
KLANDER	esclandre
LANDER	philander, Greenlander, Icelander, inlander, lander, Newfoundlander, outlander, solander, Uitlander
MANDER	demander, germander, gerrymander, calamander, commander, pomander, remander, reprimander, salamander, scamander
PANDER	expander, pandar, pander
RANDER	rander

ĀNCHER

LĀNCHER	launcher
STĀNCHER	stancher, stauncher

ANDBOKS

BANDBOKS	bandbox
SANDBOKS	sandbox

ANCHET

MANCHET	manchet
PLANCHET	planchet

ANDĒ

BANDĒ	bandy, bandy-bandy, onus probandi
BRANDĒ	brandy
DANDĒ	dandy, handy-dandy, jack-a-dandy, jim-dandy
GANDĒ	Ghandi
GLANDĒ	glandy
GRANDĒ	Rio Grande
HANDĒ	handy, unhandy
KANDĒ	discandy, candy, sugar-candy
PANDĒ	pandy
RANDĒ	jaborandi, randy
SANDĒ	sandy, sandhi
SHANDĒ	shandy, Shandy

ANCHING

(See **ANCH,** add *-ing* where appropriate.)

ĀNCHING

LĀNCHING	launching
STĀNCHING	stanching, staunching

ANCHLES

(See **ANCH,** add *-less* where appropriate.)

ĀNCHLES

(See **ĀNCH,** add *-less* where appropriate.)

ÄNDĒ

GÄNDĒ	Ghandi
GRÄNDĒ	Rio Grande

SANDER	Alexander, goosander, Isander, sander
SLANDER	slander
STANDER	bystander, outstander, stander, understander, withstander
STRANDER	strander
TANDER	dittander
ZANDER	Alexander, zander

ÄNDER

LÄNDER	Jutlander, uitlander
SKWÄNDER	squander
WÄNDER	wander

(See ONDER)

ANDERD

(See ANDER, add -ed where appropriate.)

ANDERZ

| FLANDERZ | Flanders |
| GLANDERZ | glanders |

(See ANDER, add -s where appropriate.)

ANDĒZ

| ANDĒZ | Andes |
| NANDĒZ | Hernandes |

(See ANDĒ, change -y to -ies where appropriate.)

ANDIJ

BANDIJ	bandage
GLANDIJ	glandage
STANDIJ	standage

ANDIK

GANDIK	propagandic
LANDIK	Icelandic
SANDIK	sandik

ANDING

| SPANDING | expanding, mind-expanding |
| STANDING | notwithstanding, withstanding |

(See AND, add -ing where appropriate.)

ANDISH

BLANDISH	blandish
BRANDISH	brandish
LANDISH	outlandish
STANDISH	standish

(See AND, add -ish where appropriate.)

ANDIST

| BANDIST | contrabandist |
| GANDIST | propagandist |

ANDIT

| BANDIT | bandit |
| PANDIT | Pandit |

ANDL

DANDL	dandle
HANDL	Handel, handle, manhandle, mishandle, panhandle
KANDL	candle
PANDL	pandal, pandle
SANDL	sandal
SKANDL	scandal, scandle
VANDL	vandal

ĀNDLĒ

| BRĀNDLĒ | bird-brainedly |
| STRĀNDLE | restrainedly |

(See ĀND, add -ly where appropriate.)

ANDLĒ

| BLANDLĒ | blandly |
| GRANDLĒ | grandly |

ANDLER

CHANDLER	chandler
DANDLER	dandler
HANDLER	handler, manhandler, panhandler
KANDLER	candler

ANDLES

(See AND, add -less where appropriate.)

ANDLING

BRANDLING	brandling
HANDLING	handling, manhandling, mishandling
KANDLING	candling

ANDMENT

| BANDMENT | disbandment |
| MANDMENT | commandment, remandment |

ANDNES

| BLANDNES | blandness |
| GRANDNES | grandness |

ANDŌ

BANDŌ	bandeau
LANDŌ	landau
MANDŌ	commando

ÄNDO

DÄNDŌ	ritardando
LÄNDŌ	calando
MÄNDŌ	declamando, lacrimando
TÄNDŌ	allentando, lentando, recitando, ritando
TSÄNDŌ	scherzando

ANDON

(See ANDUN)

ANDRA

| MANDRA | mandra |
| SANDRA | Cassandra |

ANDRĒ

ANDRĒ	polyandry
DANDRĒ	pseudandry
MANDRĒ	commandry
SHANDRĒ	shandry

ANDRIN

| MANDRIN | salamandrine |
| ZANDRIN | Alexandrine |

ANDSTAND

BANDSTAND	bandstand
GRANDSTAND	grandstand
HANDSTAND	handstand

ANDUM

LANDUM	manipulandum
MANDUM	mandom
RANDUM	memorandum, nil desperandum, random
TANDUM	notandum, tandem
VANDUM	observandum
ZANDUM	avizandum

ANDUN

BANDUN	abandon
LANDUN	Alf Landon

ANDZMAN

BANDZMAN	bandsman
LANDZMAN	landsman

ĀNĒ

BRĀNĒ	brainy
GĀNĒ	Allegheny
GRĀNĒ	grainy
KĀNĒ	cany
LĀNĒ	castellany, miscellany
MĀNĒ	Khomeini, meinie
RĀNĒ	Ranee, rainy
SĀNĒ	Dunsany
VĀNĒ	veiny
ZĀNĒ	zany

ANĒ

BRANĒ	branny
GANĒ	Afghani
GRANĒ	granny
KANĒ	canny, kokanee, uncanny
KLANĒ	clanny
KRANĒ	cranny
MANĒ	mannie
NANĒ	hootenanny, nanny
PANĒ	frangipanni, tin-panny
SHANĒ	shanny

ÄNĒ

ÄNĒ	ani
DÄNĒ	jamdani

PRÄNĒ	soprani
RÄNĒ	guarani, Guarani, Maharanee, Maharani, ranee, rani
STÄNĒ	Hindustani, Pakistani
SWÄNĒ	Suwanee, Swanee, swanny

(See **ONĒ**)

ANEL

ANEL	annal
BRANEL	branle
CHANEL	channel
FLANEL	flannel, outing flannel, winter flannel
KANEL	cannel
PANEL	empanel, impanel, panel, unpanel
SKRANEL	scrannel
STANEL	stannel

ĀNER

MĀNER	mainour

(See **ĀN,** add *-er* where appropriate.)

ANER

MANER	manner, manor
SKANER	photoscanner, scanner
VANER	caravanner

(See **AN,** add *-er* where appropriate.)

ANERD

BANER	banner
BANERD	bannered, unbannered
MANERD	ill-mannered, mannered, unmannered, well-mannered

ĀNES

DĀNES	everydayness

(See **Ā,** add *-ness* where appropriate.)

ANET

GANET	gannet
GRANET	granite, pomegranate

KANET	cannet
KWANET	quannet
MANET	manit
PLANET	planet
VANET	vannet

(See **ANIT**)

ĀNFUL

BĀNFUL	baneful
DĀNFUL	disdainful, undisdainful
GĀNFUL	gainful, ungainful
PĀNFUL	painful, unpainful
PLĀNFUL	complainful, uncomplainful

ANGĒ

BANGĒ	bangy
FANGĒ	fangy
HWANGĒ	whangy
KLANGĒ	clangy
SHANGĒ	collieshangie
SLANGĒ	slangy
TANGĒ	tangy
TWANGĒ	twangy

ANGER

BANGER	banger
FRANGER	franger
GANGER	doppelganger, ganger
HANGER	hangar, hanger, cliffhanger, paperhanger, straphanger
HWANGER	whanger, slang-whanger
KLANGER	clanger, clangor
LANGER	languor

ANGGER

ANGGER	anger, angor
BANGGER	Bangor
KLANGGER	clangor
LANGGER	languor

ANGGL

ANGGL	angle, leeangle, sexangle, triangle
BANGGL	bangle
BRANGGL	brangle, embrangle
DANGGL	dangle, fandangle

FANGGL	fangle, newfangle
GANGGL	gangle
JANGGL	interjangle, jangle, jingle-jangle
KRANGGL	cringle-crangle
LANGGL	phalangal
MANGGL	bemangle, mangle, mingle-mangle
RANGGL	quadrangle, wrangle
SPANGGL	bespangle, spangle
SPRANGGL	sprangle
STRANGGL	strangle
TANGGL	disentangle, entangle, intertangle, tangle, untangle, pentangle, rectangle, septangle
TWANGGL	twangle
WANGGL	wangle

ANGGLD

FANGGLD	newfangled

(See **ANGGL**, add -d where appropriate.)

ANGGLĒ

BANGGLĒ	bangly
DANGGLĒ	dangly
FRANGGLĒ	franglais
GANGGLĒ	gangly
JANGGLĒ	jangly
RANGGLĒ	wrangly
SPANGGLĒ	spangly
SPRANGGLĒ	sprangly
STRANGGLĒ	strangly
TANGGLĒ	tangly

ANGGLER

(See **ANGGL**, add -r where appropriate.)

ANGGLING

(See **ANGGL**, add -ing where appropriate.)

ANGGŌ

BANGGŌ	bango
DANGGŌ	fandango
KWANGGŌ	quango
MANGGŌ	mango
PANGGŌ	Pago Pago, Pango Pango
TANGGŌ	contango, tango

ANGGWIJ

LANGGWIJ	body language, language
SLANGGWIJ	slanguage

ANGGWIN

ANGGWIN	anguine
SANGGWIN	ensanguine, exsanguine, consanguine, sanguine, unsanguine

ANGGWISH

ANGGWISH	anguish
LANGGWISH	languish

ANGING

(See **ANG**, add -ing where appropriate.)

ANGKA

BLANGKA	Casablanca
FRANGKA	lingua franca
RANGKA	barranca
SANGKA	Sanka
TANGKA	tanka

ANGKĒ

ANGKĒ	ankee
BANGKĒ	banky
HANGKĒ	hankie
KLANGKĒ	clanky
KRANGKĒ	cranky
LANGKĒ	lanky
PANGKĒ	hanky-panky
PLANGKĒ	planky
PRANGKĒ	pranky
SWANGKĒ	swanky
TANGKĒ	tanky
THANGĒ	thank'ee
TRANGKĒ	tranky
YANGKĒ	Yankee

ANGKER

ANGKER	anchor, re-anchor, unanchor, up-anchor
BANGKER	banker
BLANGKER	blanker
DANGKER	danker
FLANGKER	flanker, outflanker
FRANGKER	franker
HANGKER	hanker
KANGKER	canker, encanker
KLANGKER	clanker
KRANGKER	cranker
LANGKER	lanker
PLANGKER	planker
RANGKER	rancor, ranker
SHANGKER	chancre, shanker
SPANGKER	spanker
TANGKER	tanker
THANGKER	thanker
YANGKER	yanker

ANGKERD

ANGKERD	anchored
BRANGKERD	brancard
TANGKERD	tankard

ANGKET

BANGKET	banket, *banquette*
BLANGKET	blanket

ANGKFUL

PRANGKFUL	prankful
TANGKFUL	tankful
THANGKFUL	thankful, unthankful

ANGKING

(See **ANGK**, add -ing where appropriate.)

ANGKISH

(See **ANGK**, add -ish where appropriate.)

ANGKL

ANGKL	ankle
HANGKL	hankle
KRANGKL	crankle
RANGKL	rankle
TANGKL	tankle

ANGKLĒ

BLANGKLĒ	blankly
DANGKLĒ	dankly
FRANGKLĒ	frankly
LANGKLĒ	lankly
RANGKLĒ	rankly

ANGKLER

(See **ANGKL**, add -er where appropriate.)

ANGKLES

(See **ANGK,** add *-less* where appropriate.)

ANGKLING

(See **ANGKL,** add *-ing* where appropriate.)

ANGKNES

(See **ANGK,** add *-ness* where appropriate.)

ANGKŌ

BANGKŌ	banco, saltimbanco, scaldabanco
MANGKŌ	calamanco

ANGKRUS

KANGKRUS	cancrous
SHANGKRUS	chancrous

ANGLES

(See **ANG,** add *-less* where appropriate.)

ANGMAN

GANGMAN	gangman
HANGMAN	hangman

ANGRAM

PANGRAM	pangram
TANGRAM	tangram

ANGSTER

ANGSTER	angster
BANGSTER	bangster
GANGSTER	gangster
HANGSTER	hangster
SLANGSTER	slangster

ANGUP

BANGUP	bang-up
HANGUP	hang-up

ĀNIJ

CHĀNIJ	chainage

DRĀNIJ	drainage
KRĀNIJ	cranage
TRĀNIJ	trainage

ANIJ

KRANIJ	crannage
MANIJ	manage, mismanage
PANIJ	pannage

ANIK

ANIK	*F* ferricyanic, *H* hydrocyanic, *I* interoceanic, *M* Messianic, *N* neanic, *O* opianic, oceanic, Ossianic, *S* cyanic, *TR* transoceanic, *V* valerianic
BANIK	Abanic
FANIK	Aristophanic, diaphanic, phanic, lexiphanic, theophanic
GANIK	exorganic, homorganic, inorganic, cosmorganic, organic, paganic
KANIK	aeromechanic, mechanic, automechanic, volcanic, vulcanic
LANIK	Magellanic, melanic
MANIK	Brahmanic, Germanic, Indo-Germanic, manic, Mussulmanic, aldermanic, Romanic, talismanic
PANIK	Hispanic, panic, tympanic
RANIK	Iranic, Koranic, ranic, transuranic, tyrannic, uranic
STANIK	stannic
TANIK	*B* botanic, *BR* Britannic, *KW* quercitannic, *M* montanic, *P* puritanic, *S* satanic, sultanic, *SH* charlatanic, *SP* Spartanic, *T* tannic, tetanic, titanic, Titanic
VANIK	galvanic

ANIKS

KANIKS	mechanics
MANIKS	humanics
PANIKS	panics

ĀNĪN

KĀNĪN	canine
RĀNĪN	ranine

ĀNING

(See **ĀN,** add *-ing* where appropriate.)

ANING

(See **AN,** add *-ing* where appropriate.)

ĀNISH

BĀNISH	urbanish
DĀNISH	Danish
SĀNISH	sanish
VĀNISH	vainish

ANISH

BANISH	banish
FANISH	fannish
KLANISH	clannish
MANISH	mannish, Mussulmanish
PLANISH	plannish
RANISH	Alcoranish
SPANISH	Spanish
VANISH	evanish, revanish, vanish

ÄNISH

SWÄNISH	swannish
WÄNISH	wannish

ANIST

ANIST	Orleanist, pianist
PRANIST	sopranist
RANIST	Alcoranist
TANIST	tanist

ANIT

(See **ANET**)

ĀNJĒ

MĀNJĒ	mangy
RĀNJĒ	rangy

ANJENT

FRANJENT	bifrangent, frangent, refrangent
PLANJENT	plangent
TANJENT	cotangent, subtangent, tangent

ĀNJER

| DĀNJER | danger |
| MĀNJER | manger |

(See ĀNJ, add -r where appropriate.)

ANJEZ

FLANJEZ	flanges
GANJEZ	Ganges
LANJEZ	phalanges
RANJEZ	*oranges*

ĀNJING

(See ĀNJ, add -ing where appropriate.)

ĀNJLES

(See ĀNJ, add -less where appropriate.)

ĀNJLING

| CHĀNJLING | changeling |
| STRĀNJLING | strangeling |

ĀNJMENT

CHĀNJMENT	changement, exchangement, interchangement
RĀNJMENT	arrangement, derangement, disarrangement, prearrangement, rearrangement
TRĀNJMENT	estrangement

ĀNLĒ

(See ĀN, add -ly where appropriate.)

ANLĒ

| MANLĒ | gentlemanly, manly, unmanly |
| SPANLĒ | spick-and-spanly |

ĀNLES

(See ĀN, add -less where appropriate.)

ANLES

(See AN, add -less where appropriate.)

ANLING

| MANLING | manling |
| TANLING | tanling |

ĀNMENT

CHĀNMENT	enchainment
DĀNMENT	ordainment, reordainment
GĀNMENT	regainment
RĀNMENT	arraignment
TĀNMENT	ascertainment, attainment, detainment, entertainment, containment, obtainment, retainment

ĀNNES

| DĀNNES | mundaneness |

(See ĀN, add -ness where appropriate.)

ĀNŌ

DRĀNŌ	Drano
KĀNŌ	hurricano, volcano
RĀNŌ	sereno
YĀNŌ	ripieno

ANŌ

| ANŌ | melopiano, piano, player piano |
| PRANŌ | mezzo-soprano, soprano |

ÄNŌ

ÄNŌ	anno, melopiano, piano, player piano, pudiano
GRÄNŌ	grano
GWÄNŌ	guano
KÄNŌ	Americano, Chicano, Meccano, Norte-Americano
LÄNŌ	solano
MÄNŌ	mano, Romano
PLÄNŌ	altiplano
PRÄNŌ	mezzo-soprano, soprano
RÄNŌ	marrano
SÄNŌ	Montesano
YÄNŌ	castellano, llano
ZÄNŌ	Cinzano

ANOK

(See ANUK)

ANON

ANON	Rhiannon
FANON	fanon
KANON	Buchanan, calecannon, cannon, canon, colcannon, water cannon
SHANON	Balleyshannon, Shannon

ANSĒ

ANSĒ	antsy, recreancy
CHANSĒ	chancy, mischancy, unchancy
DANSĒ	*accordancy*, dancy, *discordancy, mordancy, redundancy, verdancy*
FANSĒ	fancy, *infancy, sycophancy, unfancy*
GANSĒ	arrogancy, elegancy, extravagancy, termagancy
KANSĒ	insignificancy, mendicancy, significancy, supplicancy
LANSĒ	petulancy, sibilancy, vigilancy
MANSĒ	*A* aeromancy, axinomancy, aldermancy, alectromancy, alectryomancy, alphitomancy, aleuromancy, anthracomancy, anthropomancy, astragalomancy, *B* belomancy, bibliomancy, botanomancy, *D*

dactyliomancy,
diathermancy, *E*
oenomancy,
enoptromancy, *F*
phyllomancy, *FL*
floromancy, *G*
gastromancy, *H*
halomancy,
hieromancy,
hydromancy, *I*
ydromancy,
ichthyomancy, *J*
geomancy,
gyromancy, *K*
chalcomancy,
capnomancy,
captromancy,
chartomancy,
catoptromancy,
chiromancy,
coscinomancy, *KL*
cleromancy, *KR*
crithomancy,
crystallomancy, *L*
lampadomancy,
lecanomancy,
lithomancy,
logarithmancy,
logarithmomancy, *M*
mazomancy,
meteoromancy,
metopomancy,
myomancy,
molybdomancy, *N*
necromancy,
necyomancy,
knissomancy, *O*
ophiomancy,
onychomancy,
onymancy,
onomancy, oomancy,
ornithomancy,
austromancy, *P*
pedomancy,
pyromancy,
podomancy, *R*
rhabdomancy,
rhapsodomancy,
retromancy, *S*
cephalomancy,
psephomancy,
selenomancy,
ceromancy,
sideromancy,
psychomancy,
sycomancy,
sciomancy,
pseudomancy, *SK*
scapulomancy,
scatomancy, *SP*
spasmatomancy,
spatilomancy,

spatulamancy,
spodomancy, *ST*
stichomancy,
stiganomancy, *T*
tephromancy,
tyromancy,
topomancy, *TH*
theomancy,
theriomancy, *TR*
trochomancy, *U*
uromancy, *Z*
xenomancy,
zygomancy,
xylomancy

(For additional words ending in -*mancy,* see Appendix B)

NANSĒ   dissonancy,
                consonancy,
                lieutenancy,
                predominancy,
                pregnancy,
                stagnancy, tenancy
PANSĒ   *discrepancy,*
                occupancy
PRANSĒ   prancy
RANSĒ   *errancy,* exuberancy,
                preponderancy
STANSĒ   *inconstancy,*
                constancy
TANSĒ   *A accountancy,*
                assistancy, E
                exorbitancy,
                expectancy,
                exultancy, H
                habitancy, hesitancy,
                I inhabitancy,
                irritancy, *M*
                militancy, *O*
                oscitancy, *PR*
                precipitancy
TRANSĒ   recalcitrancy
VANSĒ   irrelevancy, relevancy
YANSĒ   *brilliancy*

ANSEL

CHANSEL   chancel
HANSEL   handsel, Hansel
KANSEL   cancel

ANSER

ANSER   answer
CHANSER   chancer
DANSER   ballet dancer, belly dancer, bubble dancer, dancer, exotic dancer, fan dancer, hula dancer, modern dancer, tap dancer
GANSER   merganser
GLANSER   glancer
HANSER   enhancer
KANSER   cancer
LANSER   lancer
MANSER   geomancer, chiromancer, necromancer, romancer
PRANSER   prancer
RANSER   rancer
TRANSER   entrancer
VANSER   advancer

ANSHAL

NANSHAL   financial, ganancial
STANSHAL   insubstantial, substantial, supersubstantial, circumstantial, transubstantial, unsubstantial

ANSHUN

MANSHUN   mansion
PANSHUN   expansion, panchion
SKANSHUN   scansion
STANSHUN   stanchion
ZANSHUN   Byzantian

ANSING

(See **ANS,** add -*ing* where appropriate.)

ANSIV

HANSIV   enhancive
PANSIV   expansive, inexpansive
VANSIV   advancive

ANSMENT

HANSMENT   enhancement
TRANSMENT   entrancement
VANSMENT   advancement, nonadvancement

ANSUM

HANSOM   handsome, hansom, unhandsome
RANSOM   ransom
TRANSOM   transom

ANTA

ANTA	anta
DANTA	danta, Vedanta
FANTA	Infanta
LANTA	Atlanta
MANTA	manta
PLANTA	planta
SANTA	Santa

ÄNTA

DÄNTA	danta
FÄNTA	Infanta

ANTAL

(See **ANTL**)

ANTAM

(See **ANTUM**)

ĀNTĒ

DĀNTĒ	dainty
FĀNTĒ	fainty, feinty
RĀNTĒ	suzerainty

ANTĒ

ANTĒ	ante, anti, auntie, aunty, Chianti
BANTĒ	banty
DANTĒ	andante, Dante
FANTĒ	infante
KANTĒ	bacchante, canty
LANTĒ	vigilante
MANTĒ	diamante
NANTĒ	Rosinante
PANTĒ	panty
RANTĒ	durante, ranty
SANTĒ	Santy
SHANTĒ	chanty, shanty
SKANTĒ	scanty
SLANTĒ	slanty
TANTĒ	dilettante, dilettanti, concertante, tanti
ZANTĒ	zante

ÄNTĒ

ÄNTĒ	aunty, Chianti
DÄNTĒ	andante, Dante

ĀNTED

(See **ĀNT**, add -*ed* where appropriate.)

ANTED

(See **ANT**, add -*ed* where appropriate.)

ANTEN

KANTEN	canton
PLANTEN	plantain
SANTEN	santon

ĀNTER

FĀNTER	fainter, feinter
KWĀNTER	acquainter, quainter
PĀNTER	painter
TĀNTER	attainter, tainter

ANTER

BANTER	banter, Brabanter
CHANTER	chanter, disenchanter, enchanter
GRANTER	granter, grantor
KANTER	almucantor, canter, cantor, decanter, descanter, recanter, trochanter
PANTER	panter
PLANTER	implanter, planter, supplanter, transplanter
RANTER	ranter
SKANTER	scanter
SLANTER	slanter
STANTER	instanter
VANTER	Levanter

ANTĒZ

ANTĒZ	antis, aunties
BANTĒZ	banties, corybantes
KANTĒZ	bacchantes
LANTĒZ	atlantes
PANTĒZ	panties
SHANTĒZ	chanties, shanties
SKANTĒZ	scanties
TANTĒZ	dilettantes

ANTHER

ANTHER	anther
PANTHER	panther

ANTHIK

NANTHIK	oenanthic
ZANTHIK	xanthic

ANTHIN

ANTHIN	anthine
KANTHIN	acanthin, acanthine, tragacanthin
MANTHIN	Rhadamanthine

ANTHUS

ANTHUS	amianthus, dianthus, helianthus, polyanthus, Strophanthus
KANTHUS	acanthous, acanthus, anacanthous, canthus, oxyacanthous
LANTHUS	ailanthus, galanthus
MANTHUS	haemanthus
NANTHUS	ananthous, monanthous, synanthous
PANTHUS	agapanthus, epanthous
RANTHUS	hysteranthous
SANTHUS	chrysanthous
ZANTHUS	xanthous

ANTIJ

PLANTIJ	plantage
SHANTIJ	chantage
VANTIJ	advantage, disadvantage, vantage

ANTIK

ANTIK	antic, antick, reboantic
BANTIK	corybantic
DANTIK	pedantic, Vedantic
FANTIK	elephantic, hierophantic, sycophantic
FRANTIK	frantic
GANTIK	gigantic
LANTIK	Atlantic, cisatlantic, transatlantic
MANTIK	*H* hydromantic, *J* geomantic, *K* chiromantic, *M* mantic, *N* necromantic, *O* onomantic, *P* pyromantic, *R* romantic, *S* semantic, *SP* spodomantic, *TH* theomantic
NANTIK	consonantic

ANTĪN

BANTĪN	Brabantine
FANTĪN	elephantine, chryselephantine
MANTĪN	adamantine
VANTĪN	Levantine
ZANTĪN	Byzantine

ĀNTING

FĀNTING	fainting, feinting
KWĀNTING	acquainting, reacquainting
PĀNTING	painting, repainting

ANTING

(See **ANT,** add *-ing* where appropriate.)

ANTIS

LANTIS	Atlantis
MANTIS	mantis, praying mantis

ĀNTISH

FĀNTISH	faintish
SĀNTISH	saintish

ANTIST

DANTIST	Vedantist
RANTIST	ignorantist, noncurantist
TANTIST	dilettantist

ÄNTIST

DÄNTIST	Vedantist
KÄNTIST	Kantist
RÄNTIST	Esperantist
TÄNTIST	dilettantist

ĀNTIV

PLĀNTIV	complaintive, plaintive
STRĀNTIV	constraintive

ANTIZM

KANTIZM	Kantism
RANTIZM	*ignorantism, obscurantism,* rantism
TANTIZM	dilettantism

ANTL

ANTL	antal
GANTL	gigantal
KANTL	cantle
LANTL	Atlantal
MANTL	dismantle, immantle, mantel, mantle, overmantle
NANTL	consonantal
RANTL	quadrantal

ANTLD

MANTLD	dismantled, mantled
SKANTLD	scantled

ĀNTLĒ

FĀNTLĒ	faintly, unfaintly
KWĀNTLĒ	quaintly, unquaintly
SĀNTLĒ	saintly, unsaintly

ANTLĒ

LANTLĒ	*gallantly*
SKANTLĒ	scantly
SLANTLĒ	aslantly, slantly

ANTLER

ANTLER	antler
MANTLER	dismantler, mantler
PANTLER	pantler

ANTLET

GANTLET	gantlet
KANTLET	cantlet
MANTLET	mantelet, mantlet
PLANTLET	plantlet

ANTLING

BANTLING	bantling
FRANTLING	frantling
MANTLING	mantling, dismantling
PLANTLING	plantling
SKANTLING	scantling

ĀNTNES

FĀNTNES	faintness
KWĀNTNES	quaintness

ANTŌ

KANTŌ	canto
MANTŌ	manteau, portmanteau
PANTŌ	panto
RANTŌ	Esperanto

ÄNTŌ

KÄNTŌ	canto
MÄNTŌ	portmanteau
RÄNTŌ	coranto, Esperanto
TÄNTŌ	allegro non tanto, pro tanto, tanto

ANTON

(See **ANTEN**)

ANTRĒ

CHANTRĒ	chantry
GANTRĒ	gantry
PANTRĒ	pantry

ANTRUM

ANTRUM	antrum
PANTRUM	hypantrum
TANTRUM	tantrum

ANTUM

ANTUM	Antum, adiantum
BANTUM	bantam
FANTUM	phantom

ĀNUM

KĀNUM	arcanum
LĀNUM	solanum

ANUK

BANUK	bannock
JANUK	jannock

ANUN

(See **ANON**)

ĀNUS

ĀNUS	anus
DĀNUS	pandanus

HĀNUS	heinous
JĀNUS	Janus
KĀNUS	incanous
LĀNUS	Coriolanus, parabolanus
MĀNUS	*bimanous*, *longimanous*, manus
VĀNUS	Silvanus, veinous

ĀNWURK

BRĀNWURK	brainwork
CHĀNWURK	chainwork
PLĀNWURK	plainwork

ANYAN

(See ANYUN)

ANYEL

| DANYEL | Daniel |
| SPANYEL | field spaniel, spaniel, springer spaniel, toy spaniel, water spaniel |

ANYERD

| LANYERD | lanyard |
| SPANYERD | Spaniard |

ANYUN

BANYUN	banian, banyan
FANYUN	fanion
FRANYUN	franion
KANYUN	cañon, canyon
PANYUN	companion

ANZA

ANZA	nyanza
GANZA	extravaganza, ganza, organza
GRANZA	granza
KWANZA	kwanza
NANZA	bonanza
STANZA	stanza
TANZA	matanza

ANZĒ

GANZĒ	ganzie
PANZĒ	chimpanzee, pansy
TANZĒ	tansy

ĀŌ

KĀŌ	cacao, K.O., kayo
MĀŌ	County Mayo, mayo
TRĀŌ	tetrao

ÄŌ

ÄŌ	ao
BÄŌ	carabao
DÄŌ	dao
KÄŌ	cacao, macao
LÄŌ	talao
NÄŌ	Mindanao
RÄŌ	karao, tarao
TÄŌ	tao

ĀON

KĀON	Lycaon
KRĀON	crayon
RĀON	rayon

ĀOR

(See ĀER)

ĀOS

KĀOS	chaos
LĀOS	Laos
NĀOS	epinaos, naos, pronaos
TĀOS	Taos

APA

| KAPA | kappa, Kappa |
| LAPA | lappa |

ÄPA

ÄPA	apa
HÄPA	jipijapa
KÄPA	capa, kapa, koppa
NÄPA	anapanapa
PÄPA	papa
TÄPA	tapa

APCHER

| KAPCHER | capture, manucapture, recapture |
| RAPCHER | enrapture, rapture |

ĀPĒ

GĀPĒ	gapy
KRĀPĒ	crapy, crepy
SKRĀPĒ	scrapy
TĀPĒ	red-tapy, tapy

APĒ

CHAPĒ	chappie, chappy
FLAPĒ	flappy
GAPĒ	gappy, gapy
HAPĒ	happy, slaphappy, unhappy
KAPĒ	cappy
KRAPĒ	crappie, crappy
MAPĒ	mappy
NAPĒ	knappy, nappy, shaganappi, shaganappy
PAPĒ	pappy
RAPĒ	serape
SAPĒ	sappy
SKRAPĒ	scrappy
SNAPĒ	snappy
TRAPĒ	trappy
YAPĒ	yappy

ÄPĒ

HÄPĒ	Hapi
KÄPĒ	okapi
RÄPĒ	serape

ĀPEN

| SHĀPEN | misshapen, shapen, unshapen |
| TĀPEN | tapen |

APEN

| HAPEN | happen |
| LAPEN | lapin |

ĀPER

ĀPER	aper
DRĀPER	draper, undraper
GĀPER	gaper
KĀPER	escaper, caper, nordcaper
PĀPER	endpaper, flypaper, newspaper, notepaper, paper, repaper, sandpaper, tarpaper, wallpaper

RĀPER	raper
SĀPER	sapor
SHĀPER	misshaper, reshaper, shaper
SKĀPER	landscaper
SKRĀPER	skyscraper, scraper
TĀPER	taper, tapir, red-taper
VĀPER	vapor

APER

CHAPER	chapper
DAPER	dapper, didapper
GAPER	gaper
KAPER	capper, handicapper
KLAPER	clapper, shoulderclapper
LAPER	lapper, overlapper
MAPER	mapper
NAPER	kidnapper, knapper, napper
RAPER	enwrapper, rapper, wrapper, unwrapper
SAPER	sapper
SKRAPER	scrapper
SLAPER	backslapper, slapper
SNAPER	whippersnapper, red snapper, snapper, snippersnapper
STRAPER	strapper, understrapper, unstrapper
TAPER	tapper, wiretapper
TRAPER	entrapper, trapper
YAPER	yapper
ZAPER	zapper

ÄPER

SWÄPER	swapper

(See **OPER**)

APET

LAPET	lappet
SKRAPET	scrappet
TAPET	tappet

APID

RAPID	rapid
SAPID	sapid
VAPID	vapid

APIJ

LAPIJ	lappage
RAPIJ	wrappage
SKRAPIJ	scrappage

APIN

(See **APEN**)

ĀPING

ĀPING	aping
DRĀPING	draping
GĀPING	gaping
KĀPING	escaping
PĀPING	Peiping
RĀPING	raping
SHĀPING	misshaping, reshaping, shaping
SKĀPING	landscaping
SKRĀPING	scraping, skyscraping
TĀPING	retaping, taping

ÄPING

(See **OP**, add -ing where appropriate.)

ĀPIS

ĀPIS	Apis, priapus
LĀPIS	lapis
NĀPIS	sinapis
TĀPIS	tapis

APIS

LAPIS	lapis
PAPIS	pappus
TAPIS	tapis
TRAPIS	trappous

ĀPISH

ĀPISH	apish
GĀPISH	gapish
PĀPISH	papish
TĀPISH	red-tapish, tapish

APISH

GAPISH	gappish
SNAPISH	snappish
YAPISH	yappish

ĀPIST

KĀPIST	escapist
PĀPIST	papist
RĀPIST	rapist
SKĀPIST	landscapist
TĀPIST	tapist, red-tapist

APIST

MAPIST	mappist
TRAPIST	Trappist

ĀPIZM

ĀPIZM	apism
KĀPIZM	escapism
PĀPIZM	papism
TĀPIZM	red-tapism

ĀPL

KĀPL	capel
MĀPL	maple
PĀPL	antipapal, nonpapal, papal, unpapal
STĀPL	staple, unstaple, woolstaple

APL

APL	apple, Big Apple, loveapple, crabapple, pineapple
CHAPL	antechapel, chapel, Whitechapel
DAPL	dapple
GRAPL	grapple
KAPL	capple
NAPL	knapple
SKAPL	scapple
SKRAPL	scrapple
THRAPL	thrapple

ĀPLES

(See **ĀP**, add -less where appropriate.)

APLES

(See **AP**, add -less where appropriate.)

ĀPLET

ĀPLET	apelet
GRĀPLET	grapelet
KĀPLET	capelet

APLET

CHAPLET	chaplet
STAPLET	staplet
STRAPLET	straplet
TAPLET	taplet

APLING

DAPLING	dappling
GRAPLING	grappling
LAPLING	lapling
SAPLING	sapling

ĀPLZ

MĀPLZ	maples
NĀPLZ	Naples
STĀPLZ	staples, woolstaples

APNEL

GRAPNEL	grapnel
SHRAPNEL	shrapnel

ÄPŌ

ÄPŌ	quiapo
GWÄPŌ	guapo
KÄPŌ	capo
SWÄPŌ	swapo

ĀPRUN

ĀPRUN	apron
NĀPRUN	napron

APSHUN

KAPSHUN	caption, manucaption, recaption, usucaption
LAPSHUN	elapsion, collapsion
TRAPSHUN	contraption

APTER

APTER	apter
CHAPTER	chapter
DAPTER	adapter
KAPTER	captor, manucaptor, recaptor
RAPTER	rapter, raptor

APTEST

APTEST	aptest, inaptest
BAPTEST	Anabaptist, Baptist

APTIV

DAPTIV	adaptive, unadaptive
KAPTIV	captive

APTLĒ

APTLĒ	aptly, inaptly
RAPTLĒ	raptly

APTNES

APTNES	aptness, inaptness, unaptness
RAPTNES	raptness

ĀPŬS

(See ĀPIS)

APUS

(See APIS)

ÂRA

ÂRA	Eire
BÂRA	capybara
DÂRA	madeira, caldera
HÂRA	Sahara
KÂRA	cascara, mascara
MÂRA	dulcamara, Mara, samara
PÂRA	para
RÂRA	siserara
VÂRA	vara

ÄRĀ

KÄRĀ	ricercaré
SWÄRĀ	soireé

ARA

ARA	tiara
KARA	cascara, mascara
KLARA	Santa Clara
PARA	*nullipara, primipara*
TARA	tantara, tarantara

ÄRA

ÄRA	tiara, ziara
BÄRA	capybara
DWÄRA	gurdwara
GÄRA	fugara
HÄRA	Guadelajara, Sahara, vihara
KÄRA	cara, caracara, sakkara
KLÄRA	Santa Clara
MÄRA	Gemara, Mara

NÄRA

NÄRA	kanara, carbonara, marinara, narra, sayonara
PÄRA	apara
RÄRA	Ferrara
TÄRA	chitarra, solfatara, tantara, tarantara, tuatara
VÄRA	vara

ARAB

ARAB	Arab
SKARAB	scarab

ARAK

ARAK	arrack
BARAK	barrack
KARAK	carack, carrack

ÂRANS

(See ÂRENS)

ARANT

ARANT	arrant
PARANT	apparent, nontransparent, parent, step-parent, transparent, unapparent

ARAS

ARAS	arras
BARAS	barras, debarrass, disembarrass, embarrass
HARAS	harass
NARAS	naras
PARAS	nonparous, Paris, parous

ÂRBEL

HÂRBEL	harebell
PRÂRBEL	prayerbell

ÄRBEL

BÄRBEL	barbel, barbell
KÄRBEL	carbell

ÄRBER

ÄRBER	arbor, Ann Arbor
BÄRBER	barber
HÄRBER	enharbor, harbor, unharbor

ÄRBERD

ÄRBERD	arbored
HÄRBERD	harbored
JÄRBERD	jarbird
KÄRBERD	carboard
LÄRBERD	larboard
STÄRBERD	starboard

ÄRBL

GÄRBL	garble
JÄRBL	jarble
MÄRBL	enmarble, marble

ÄRBLER

GÄRBLER	garbler
MÄRBLER	marbler

ÄRBLING

GÄRBLING	garbling
MÄRBLING	marbling

ÄRBON

KÄRBON	hydrocarbon, carbon
SHÄRBON	charbon

ÄRBOR

(See ÄRBER)

ÄRBORD

(See ÄRBERD)

ÄRCHĒ

ÄRCHĒ	archy
LÄRCHĒ	larchy
STÄRCHĒ	starchy

ÄRCHER

ÄRCHER	archer
MÄRCHER	marcher

PÄRCHER	parcher
STÄRCHER	starcher

ÄRCHING

(See ÄRCH, add -ing where appropriate.)

ÄRCHMENT

ÄRCHMENT	archment
PÄRCHMENT	parchment

ÄRDANT

(See ÄRDENT)

ÄRDĒ

BÄRDĒ	bardy
FÄRDĒ	Sephardi
HÄRDĒ	foolhardy, hardy
LÄRDĒ	lardy
TÄRDĒ	tardy

ÄRDED

(See ÄRD, add -ed where appropriate.)

ÄRDEL

BÄRDEL	bardel
FÄRDEL	fardel
KÄRDEL	cardel
SÄRDEL	sardel, sardelle

ÄRDEN

BÄRDEN	bombardon
GÄRDEN	garden, flower garden, vegetable garden
HÄRDEN	enharden, harden, caseharden, weather-harden
PÄRDEN	pardon

ÄRDEND

(See ÄRDEN, add -ed where appropriate.)

ÄRDENT

ÄRDENT	ardent, unardent
GÄRDENT	gardant, guardant, regardant
TÄRDENT	retardant

ÄRDER

ÄRDER	ardor
BÄRDER	bombarder
GÄRDER	disregarder, guarder, regarder
HÄRDER	harder
KÄRDER	discarder, false-carder, carder, wool carder
LÄRDER	larder
TÄRDER	retarder

ÄRDIK

BÄRDIK	bardic, Lombardic
KÄRDIK	anacardic, pericardic

ÄRDING

(See ÄRD, add -ing where appropriate.)

ÄRDLES

GÄRDLES	guardless, regardless
KÄRDLES	cardless
LÄRDLES	lardless
YÄRDLES	yardless

ÄRDMENT

BÄRDMENT	bombardment
TÄRDMENT	retardment

ÄRDNER

GÄRDNER	gardener
HÄRDNER	hardener
PÄRDNER	pardner, pardoner

ÄRDNING

GÄRDNING	gardening
HÄRDNING	hardening
PÄRDNING	pardoning

ÄRDON

(See ARDEN)

ÄRDSHIP

GÄRDSHIP	guardship
HÄRDSHIP	hardship

ÂRDUM

| ÂRDUM | heirdom |
| STÂRDUM | backstairdom |

ÄRDUN

(See ÄRDEN)

ÂRĒ

ÂRĒ   *A* accidentiary,
actuary, aerie, airy,
ary, eyrie, *B*
beneficiary, *E*
estuary, *F* February,
fiduciary, *I*
incendiary,
intermediary, *J*
January, *KW*
questuary, *M*
mortuary, *N* natuary,
noctuary, nucleary, *O*
obituary, ossuary,
ostiary, *P* pecuniary,
R residuary, retiary,
ruptuary, *S* sanctuary,
silentiary, subsidiary,
sumptuary, *SKR*
scriniary, *ST* statuary,
stipendiary, *T*
tertiary, topiary,
tumultuary, *V*
voluptuary

BÂRĒ	columbary, syllabary
BLÂRĒ	blary
CHÂRĒ	chary, unchary
DÂRĒ	dairy, dromedary, hebdomadary, *quandary*, lapidary, legendary, prebendary, secondary
FÂRĒ	airy-fairy, faerie, fairy
FLÂRĒ	flary
GÂRĒ	vagary
GLÂRĒ	glairy, glary
HÂRĒ	hairy, unhairy
KÂRĒ	apothecary, formicary, hypothecary, persicary
KLÂRĒ	clary
KWÂRĒ	antiquary, reliquary
LÂRĒ	*A* adminiculary, axillary, ancillary, *B* bacillary, *E* epistolary, *F* formulary, *K* capillary,

MÂRĒ   constabulary,
corollary, *L* lairy, *M*
maxillary,
mammillary,
medullary, *O* obolary,
P patibulary, *SK*
scapulary, *T* titulary,
tumulary, tutelary, *V*
vocabulary

NÂRĒ   accustomary, Ave
Mary, calamary,
customary,
lachrymary, mary,
rosemary
A ablutionary,
abolitionary,
additionary, *B*
bicentenary, *D*
dictionary,
disciplinary,
discretionary,
divisionary,
doctrinary, *E*
extraordinary,
eleemosynary,
elocutionary,
evolutionary, *F*
functionary, *G*
ganglionary, *I*
imaginary,
insurrectionary, *K*
canary,
confectionary,
confectionery,
consuetudinary,
coparcenery,
coronary, cautionary,
culinary, *KW*
questionary, *L*
latitudinary,
legionary, luminary,
M mercenary,
millinary, millinery,
missionary,
multitudinary, *N*
nary, *O* ordinary, *P*
parcenary,
passionary,
pensionary,
petitionary, popinary,
pulmonary, *PR*
precautionary,
preliminary,
probationary,
prolegomenary,
provisionary, *R*
reactionary,
reversionary,
revisionary,
revolutionary, *S*
sanguinary,
seditionary, seminary,

centenary, sublunary,
ST stationary,
stationery, *T*
tutionary, *TR*
traditionary, *V*
valetudinary,
veterinary, vicenary,
vicissitudinary,
visionary

PRÂRĒ	prairie
RÂRĒ	extemporary, itinerary, contemporary, literary, honorary, supernumerary, temporary, Tipperary, vulnerary
SÂRĒ	necessary, unnecessary
SKÂRĒ	scary
SNÂRĒ	snary
STÂRĒ	stary
TÂRĒ	*D* depositary, dietary, dignitary, distributary, *FR* fragmentary, *H* hereditary, *K* commentary, contributary, *M* military, momentary, monetary, *PL* planetary, *PR* proletary, proprietary, prothonotary, *S* salutary, sanitary, sedentary, secretary, circumplanetary, solitary, *TR* tributary, *U* ubiquitary, *V* voluntary
TRÂRĒ	arbitrary, contrary
VÂRĒ	salivary, vairy, vary
WÂRĒ	cassowary, unwary, wary

(See ERĒ)

ARĒ

GARĒ	gharry
HARĒ	harry
KARĒ	hari-kari, carry, miscarry
MARĒ	intermarry, marry, remarry, unmarry
PARĒ	pari, parry
TARĒ	tarry

ÄRĒ

| BÄRĒ | Bari, Karharbari |
| CHÄRĒ | charry |

HÄRĒ	mehari
KÄRĒ	harikari, uakari
LÄRĒ	lari
NÄRĒ	Carbonari
PÄRĒ	pari
RÄRĒ	curare
SÄRĒ	aracari
SKÄRĒ	scarry
STÄRĒ	starry
TÄRĒ	tarry
VÄRĒ	charivari

AREL

AREL	aril
BAREL	barrel, beer barrel, pork barrel
KAREL	carol, carrel
PAREL	apparel, disapparel, parral, parrel

ARELD

HARELD	Harold
BARELD	barreled, double-barreled

(See **AREL,** add -ed where appropriate.)

ÂREM

(See **ÂRUM**)

AREM

(See **ARUM**)

ÂRENS

BÂRENS	bearance, forbearance
PÂRENS	apparence, parents, transparence

ÂRENT

BÂRENT	forbearant
KLÂRENT	declarent
LÂRENT	celarent
PÂRENT	apparent, parent

ÂRER

ÂRER	airer
BÂRER	armor bearer, barer, bearer, forbearer, cupbearer, macebearer, overbearer, pallbearer, swordbearer, standard-bearer, tale-bearer
BLÂRER	blarer
DÂRER	darer, outdarer
FÂRER	fairer, farer, seafarer, unfairer, wayfarer
FLÂRER	flarer
KÂRER	carer, uncarer
KLÂRER	declarer
PÂRER	despairer, impairer, pairer, parer, preparer, repairer
RÂRER	rarer
SHÂRER	sharer
SKÂRER	scarer
SKWÂRER	squarer
SNÂRER	ensnarer, snarer
SPÂRER	sparer
STÂRER	starer
SWÂRER	swearer
TÂRER	tearer
WÂRER	awarer, wearer

(See ERER)

ARET

GARET	garret
KARET	carat, caret, carrot
KLARET	claret
PARET	parrot

ÂRĒZ

ÂRĒZ	Ares, Aries, Buenos Aires
KÂRĒZ	caries
LÂRĒZ	lares

(See **ÂRĒ,** add -s or change -y to -ies where appropriate.)

ÂRFĀST

BÂRFĀST	barefaced
FÂRFĀST	fair-faced

ÄRFISH

BÄRFISH	barfish
GÄRFISH	garfish, cigarfish
STÄRFISH	starfish
TÄRFISH	guitarfish

ÂRFUL

DÂRFUL	dareful
KÂRFUL	careful, uncareful
PÂRFUL	despairful
PRÂRFUL	prayerful, unprayerful

ÄRGL

ÄRGL	argal, argol, argle-bargle
GÄRGL	gargle

ÄRGŌ

ÄRGŌ	Argo, argot
BÄRGŌ	embargo
FÄRGŌ	Wells Fargo
KÄRGŌ	cargo, supercargo
LÄRGŌ	largo
PÄRGO	pargo
SÄRGO	sargo
TÄRGO	botargo

ÄRGON

ÄRGON	argon
JÄRGON	jargon

ARID

ARID	arid
LARID	Polarid

ARIF

HARIF	harif
TARIF	tariff

ARIJ

GARIJ	garage
KARIJ	carriage, miscarriage, undercarriage
MARIJ	intermarriage, marriage, remarriage
PARIJ	disparage

ARIK

ARIK	Balearic, stearic
BARIK	barbaric, baric, hyperbaric, isobaric, centrobaric, cinnabaric

DARIK	daric, Pindaric
GARIK	agaric, Bulgaric, margaric, Megaric
KARIK	saccharic
LARIK	polaric
MARIK	pimaric
TARIK	tartaric

ÂRING

(See ÂR, add -ing where appropriate.)

ÄRING

(See ÄR, add -ing where appropriate.)

ARINGKS

| FARINGKS | pharynx |
| LARINGKS | larynx |

ÂRIS

| LÂRIS | polaris |
| NÂRIS | naris |

ARIS

ARIS	arris
BARIS	baris
LARIS	phalaris, auricularis, polaris
PARIS	Paris

ÂRISH

BÂRISH	bearish
FÂRISH	fairish
GÂRISH	garish
MÂRISH	marish, nightmarish
PÂRISH	pairish
RÂRISH	rarish
SKWÂRISH	squarish

(See ERISH)

ÄRIST

TÄRIST	guitarist
TSÄRIST	tsarist
ZÄRIST	czarist

ÄRJENT

ÄRJENT	argent, minargent
MÄRJENT	margent
SÄRJENT	sergeant

ÄRJER

BÄRJER	barger
CHÄRJER	charger, discharger, turbocharger, overcharger, supercharger, surcharger, undercharger
LÄRJER	enlarger, larger
SPÄRJER	sparger

ÄRJIK

| LÄRJIC | pelargic |
| THÄRJIK | lethargic |

ÄRJING

(See ÄRJ, add -ing where appropriate.)

ÄRKA

CHÄRKA	charka, charkha
DÄRKA	bidarka
MÄRKA	markka
PÄRKA	parka
SÄRKA	anasarca

ÄRKAL

ÄRKAL	anarchal, matriarchal, patriarchal
GÄRKAL	oligarchal
NÄRKAL	monarchal
RÄRKAL	heterarchal, hierarchal, squirearchal

(See ÄRKL)

ÄRKĒ

ÄRKĒ	*anarchy,* arky, diarchy, hagiarchy, matriarchy, patriarchy, squirearchy, thearchy, triarchy
BÄRKĒ	barky
CHÄRKĒ	charqui
DÄRKĒ	bidarke, darky
GÄRKĒ	oligarchy
KÄRKĒ	carky
LÄRKĒ	larky, malarkey
MÄRKĒ	*nomarchy*
NÄRKĒ	*gynarchy,* menarche
PÄRKĒ	parky

RÄRKĒ	heterarchy, hetaerarchy, hierarchy
SHÄRKĒ	sharky
SPÄRKĒ	sparky
STÄRKĒ	starky
TÄRKĒ	*antarchy, heptarchy, cryptarchy, autarchy*

ÄRKEN

ÄRKEN	archon
BÄRKEN	barken
DÄRKEN	bedarken, darken, endarken
HÄRKEN	hearken
STÄRKEN	starken

ÄRKER

BÄRKER	barker, embarker
DÄRKER	darker
HÄRKER	harker
KÄRKER	carker
LÄRKER	larker, skylarker
MÄRKER	marker, markhor
PÄRKER	nosy-parker, parker
SHÄRKER	sharker
SPÄRKER	sparker
STÄRKER	starker

ÄRKERZ

| STÄRKERZ | starkers |

(See ÄRKER, add -s)

ÄRKĒZ

(See ÄRKĒ, change -y to -ies where appropriate.)

ÄRKIK

ÄRKIK	matriarchic, patriarchic
GÄRKIK	oligarchic
NÄRKIK	anarchic, antianarchic, monarchic, synarchic
RÄRKIK	hierarchic
TÄRKIK	heptarchic, climatarchic

I WAS PRODIGAL WITH TIME

I was prodigal with time—
　Spent it to my heart's content.
Now that I have passed my prime,
　Time remains, but I am spent.

ÄRKING

(See ÄRK, add -ing where appropriate.)

ÄRKISH

(See ÄRK, add -ish where appropriate.)

ÄRKIST

ÄRKIST	matriarchist, patriarchist
GÄRKIST	oligarchist
NÄRKIST	*anarchist, antianarchist, monarchist, synarchist*
RÄRKIST	hierarchist
TÄRKIST	*heptarchist*

ÄRKL

BÄRKL	barkle
DÄRKL	darkle
SÄRKL	sarcle
SPÄRKL	sparkle

(See ÄRKAL)

ÄRKLĒ

DÄRKLĒ	darkly
KLÄRKLĒ	clarkly, clerkly
STÄRKLĒ	starkly

ÄRKLET

PÄRKLET	parklet
SPÄRKLET	sparklet

ÄRKLING

DÄRKLING	darkling
LÄRKLING	larkling
SPÄRKLING	sparkling

ÄRKNER

DÄRKNER	darkener
HÄRKNER	hearkener

ÄRKNES

DÄRKNES	darkness
STÄRKNES	starkness

ÄRKTIK

ÄRKTIK	arctic, Arctic, Nearctic, Palearctic
BÄRKTIK	subarctic
LÄRKTIK	holarctic
TÄRKTIK	Antarctic

ÂRLĒ

BÂRLĒ	barely
FÂRLĒ	fairly, unfairly
NÂRLĒ	debonairly
RÂRLĒ	rarely
SKWÂRLĒ	squarely
WÂRLĒ	awarely
YÂRLĒ	yarely

ÄRLĒ

BÄRLĒ	barley
MÄRLĒ	marly
NÄRLĒ	gnarly
PÄRLĒ	parley
ZÄRLĒ	bizarrely

ÄRLER

JÄRLER	jarler
NÄRLER	gnarler
PÄRLER	parlor
SNÄRLER	snarler

ÂRLES

(See ÂR, add -less where appropriate.)

ÄRLES

PÄRLES	parlous

(See ÄR, add -less where appropriate.)

ÄRLET

HÄRLET	harlot
KÄRLET	carlet
MÄRLET	marlet
SKÄRLET	scarlet
STÄRLET	starlet
VÄRLET	varlet

ÄRLIK

GÄRLIK	garlic, pilgarlic
SÄRLIK	sarlyk

ÂRLĪN

ÂRLĪN	airline
HÂRLĪN	hairline

ÄRLIN

KÄRLIN	carlin, carline
MÄRLIN	marlin, marline

ÂRLĪND

HÂRLĪND	hairlined
KÂRLĪND	care-lined

ÄRLING

DÄRLING	darling
SNÄRLING	snarling
SPÄRLING	sparling
STÄRLING	starling

ÄRLĪT

KÄRLĪT	carlight
STÄRLĪT	starlight

ÄRLIT

FÄRLIT	farlit
KÄRLIT	carlit
STÄRLIT	starlit

ÄRLOK

CHÄRLOK	charlock
HÄRLOK	harlock
KÄRLOK	carlock
MÄRLOK	marlock

ÄRLOT

(See ÄRLET)

ÄRLOR

(See ÄRLER)

ÄRLUS

(See ARLES)

ÄRMA

DÄRMA	adharma, dharma
KÄRMA	karma

ÂRMAN

| ÂRMAN | airman |
| CHÂRMAN | chairman |

ÄRMĒ

ÄRMĒ	army
BÄRMĒ	barmy
FÄRMĒ	farmy
SMÄRMĒ	smarmy

ÄRMENT

BÄRMENT	debarment, disbarment
GÄRMENT	garment
SÄRMENT	sarment

ÄRMER

ÄRMER	armer, armor, disarmer, rearmer
CHÄRMER	charmer, snake-charmer
FÄRMER	dairy farmer, dirt farmer, farmer, subsistence farmer
HÄRMER	harmer
LÄRMER	alarmer

ÄRMFUL

ÄRMFUL	armful
CHÄRMFUL	charmful
HÄRMFUL	harmful, unharmful

ÄRMIK

| FÄRMIK | alexipharmic, pharmic, polypharmic |
| TÄRMIK | ptarmic |

ÄRMIN

| HÄRMIN | harmine |
| KÄRMIN | carmine, encarmine |

ÄRMING

(see ÄRM, add -ing where appropriate.)

ÄRMLES

(See ÄRM, add -less where appropriate.)

ÄRMLET

| ÄRMLET | armlet |
| CHÄRMLET | charmlet |

ÄRMOR

(see ARMER)

ÄRMOT

| KÄRMOT | carmot |
| MÄRMOT | marmot |

ÄRNA

ÄRNA	arna
DÄRNA	dharna
SÄRNA	sarna

ÄRNAL

(See ÄRNEL)

ÄRNARD

(see ÄRNERD)

ÄRNĒ

BÄRNĒ	barny
BLÄRNĒ	blarney
KÄRNĒ	carney, carny
LÄRNĒ	Killarney

ÄRNEL

CHÄRNEL	charnel
DÄRNEL	darnel
KÄRNEL	carnal, uncarnal

ÄRNER

DÄRNER	darner
GÄRNER	garner
YÄRNER	yarner

ÄRNERD

| BÄRNERD | Barnard |
| GÄRNERD | garnered |

ÂRNES

(See ÂR, add -ness where appropriate.)

ÄRNES

FÄRNES	farness
HÄRNES	harness, reharness, unharness
ZÄRNES	bizarreness

ÄRNING

DÄRNING	darning, goldarning, goshdarning
SÄRNING	consarning
YÄRNING	yarning

ÄRNISH

GÄRNISH	garnish
TÄRNISH	tarnish
VÄRNISH	varnish

ÄRNISHT

(See ÄRNISH, add -ed.)

ÂRŌ

FÂRŌ	faro
KÂRŌ	karo, Karo, vaquero
TÂRŌ	taro, tarot

(See ERŌ)

ARŌ

ARŌ	arrow
BARŌ	barrow, handbarrow, wheelbarrow
FARŌ	farrow
HARŌ	harrow, restharrow
KARŌ	carrow
MARŌ	marrow
NARŌ	narrow
SKARŌ	scarrow
SPARŌ	sparrow
TARŌ	tarot
YARŌ	yarrow

ÄRŌ

GÄRŌ	zingaro
GWÄRŌ	saguaro
JÄRŌ	Kilimanjaro
KÄRŌ	karo
KLÄRŌ	claro
NÄRŌ	denaro
SÄRŌ	Pissarro

TÄRŌ   cantaro, taro
ZÄRŌ   Pizarro

(See **ORŌ**)

AROL

(See **AREL**)

AROLD

(See **ARELD**)

ÂRON

HWÂRON   *whereon*
KÂRON   Charon
THÂRON   *thereon*

ARŌŌ

BARŌŌ   baru
MARŌŌ   maru

AROT

(See **ARET**)

ÄRPAL

(See **ÄRPL**)

ÄRPĒ

HÄRPĒ   harpy
KÄRPĒ   carpie, carpy
SHÄRPĒ   sharpie, sharpy

ÄRPER

HÄRPER   harper
KÄRPER   carper
SHÄRPER   cardsharper, sharper

ÄRPL

KÄRPL   carpal, intercarpal, metacarpal
PÄRPL   disparple

ÄRSEL

KÄRSEL   carcel
PÄRSEL   parcel
SÄRSEL   sarcel
TÄRSEL   metatarsal, tarsal

VÄRSEL   varsal
WÄRSEL   warsle

ÄRSER

KÄRSER   carcer
PÄRSER   parser
SÄRSER   Sarsar
SPÄRSER   sparser

ÄRSHA

GÄRSHA   Garcia
MÄRSHA   hamartia, Marcia

ÄRSHAL

MÄRSHAL   field marshal, immartial, marshal, martial, unmartial
PÄRSHAL   impartial, partial

ÄRSL

(See **ÄRSEL**)

ÄRSLĒ

PÄRSLĒ   parsley
SPÄRSLĒ   sparsely

ÄRSON

ÄRSON   arson
FÄRSON   mene mene tekel upharsin
PÄRSON   parson
SÄRSON   sarsen
SKWÄRSON   squarson

ÄRTA

KÄRTA   charta, Magna Charta
KWÄRTA   cuarta
SPÄRTA   Sparta

ÄRTAL

(See **ÄRTL**)

ÄRTAN

(See **ÄRTEN**)

ÄRTĒ

ÄRTĒ   arty
CHÄRTĒ   charty
DÄRTĒ   darty
HÄRTĒ   hearty
PÄRTĒ   ex parte, hen party, house party, nonparty, pajama party, party, stag party, tea party
SMÄRTĒ   smarty
STÄRTĒ   starty
TÄRTĒ   Astarte, tarty

ÄRTED

(See **ÄRT**, add *-ed* where appropriate.)

ÄRTEN

BÄRTEN   barton
GÄRTEN   kindergarten
HÄRTEN   dishearten, enhearten, hearten
KÄRTEN   carton
MÄRTEN   marten, martin
PÄRTEN   partan, parten
SMÄRTEN   smarten
SPÄRTEN   Spartan
TÄRTEN   tartan, tarten

ÄRTER

ÄRTER   arter
BÄRTER   barter
CHÄRTER   charter
DÄRTER   darter
GÄRTER   garter
MÄRTER   bemartyr, martyr, protomartyr, remartyr, unmartyr
PÄRTER   departer, imparter, parter
SÄRTER   sartor
SMÄRTER   smarter
STÄRTER   non-starter, restarter, self-starter, starter, upstarter
TÄRTER   cream-of-tartar, tartar, Tartar, tarter

ÄRTERD

(See **ÄRTER**, add *-ed* where appropriate.)

ÄRTING

(See **ART**, add *-ing* where appropriate.)

ÄRTIST

ÄRTIST	artist
CHÄRTIST	chartist, Chartist
PÄRTIST	Bonapartist

ÄRTL

DÄRTL	dartle
HÄRTL	hartal
PÄRTL	partle
STÄRTL	startle

ÄRTLĒ

PÄRTLĒ	partly
SMÄRTLĒ	smartly
TÄRTLĒ	tartly

ÄRTLES

(See ÄRT, add *-less* where appropriate.)

ÄRTLET

ÄRTLET	artlet
BÄRTLET	Bartlett
HÄRTLET	heartlet
MÄRTLET	martlet
PÄRTLET	partlet
TÄRTLET	tartlet

ÄRTLING

DÄRTLING	dartling
SPÄRTLING	spartling
STÄRTLING	startling

ÄRTNES

| SMÄRTNES | smartness |
| TÄRTNES | tartness |

ÄRTŌ

| GÄRTŌ | lagarto |
| PÄRTŌ | esparto |

ÄRTON

(See ÄRTEN)

ÄRTRIJ

| KÄRTRIJ | cartridge |
| PÄRTRIJ | partridge |

ÄRTWĀ

| KÄRTWĀ | cartway |
| PÄRTWĀ | partway |

A coffeemaker underneath a wood cabinet will send steam bellowing up, damaging the cabinet.
—FROM A LETTER TO ''DEAR HELOISE.''

Doth steam from coffeemaker bellow?
Did Minotaur in cavern billow?
It's confusing to a fellow,
Or maybe I should say a fillow.

ÂRUM

ÂRUM	arum
GÂRUM	garum
HÂRUM	harem
MÂRUM	marum
SKÂRUM	harum-scarum

ARUM

GARUM	garum
HARUM	harem
KARUM	carom
LARUM	alarum, larum
MARUM	marum

ÄRVEL

ÄRVEL	arval, Arval
BÄRVEL	barvel
KÄRVEL	carval, carvel
LÄRVEL	larval
MÄRVEL	marvel

ÄRVER

KÄRVER	carver
MÄRVER	marver
STÄRVER	starver

ÄRVEST

HÄRVEST	harvest
KÄRVEST	carvest
STÄRVEST	starvest

ÄRVING

| KÄRVING | carving |
| STÄRVING | starving |

ÄRVL

(See ARVEL)

ÄRVLING

| MÄRVLING | marveling |
| STÄRVLING | starveling |

ÂRWORN

| KÂRWORN | careworn |
| PRÂRWORN | prayer-worn |

ASA

DASA	Hadassah
DRASA	madrasah
KASA	casa
KWASA	oquassa
MASA	massa
NASA	NASA

ĀSAL

ĀSAL	oasal
BĀSAL	basal
KĀSAL	casal
VĀSAL	vasal

ASĀT

| KASĀT | cassate |
| KRASĀT | incrassate |

ĀSĒ

JĀSĒ	jasey, Jaycee
LĀSĒ	lacy
MĀSĒ	*contumacy*
PĀSĒ	pace
PRĀSĒ	précis
RĀSĒ	racy
SPĀSĒ	spacy

ASĒ

BRASĒ	brassie, brassy
CHASĒ	chassis
DASĒ	dassie
GASĒ	gassy, Malagasy
GLASĒ	glacé, glassy
GRASĒ	grassy
HASĒ	Tallahassee
KLASĒ	classy
LASĒ	Haile Selassie, lassie

MASĒ	massy
RASĒ	morassy, rasse
SASĒ	sassy
TASĒ	tassie

ASEL

(See ASIL)

ĀSEN

BĀSEN	basin, washbasin
CHĀSEN	chasten, enchasten, unchasten
HĀSEN	hasten
JĀSEN	Jason
KĀSEN	caisson
MĀSEN	freemason, mason, meson, stonemason
SĀSEN	sasin, sasine

ASEN

DASEN	spadassin
FASEN	fasten
SASEN	assassin

ĀSENS

BĀSENS	abaisance, obeisance
JĀSENS	adjacence, interjacence
NĀSENS	connascence, renascence
PLĀSENS	complacence, complaisance, uncomplacence, uncomplaisance

ĀSENT

BĀSENT	obeisant
JĀSENT	adjacent, interjacent, jacent, circumjacent, subjacent, superjacent
NĀSENT	enascent, connascent, naissant, nascent, renaissant, renascent
PLĀSENT	complacent, complaisant, uncomplacent, uncomplaisant
RĀSENT	indurascent

ĀSER

ĀSER	acer
BĀSER	abaser, baser, debaser
BRĀSER	bracer, embracer
CHĀSER	chaser, steeplechaser
FĀSER	defacer, effacer, facer
GRĀSER	begracer, disgracer, gracer
KĀSER	encaser, caser
KWĀSER	quasar
LĀSER	belacer, interlacer, lacer, laser, unlacer
MĀSER	grimacer, macer
PĀSER	outpacer, pacer
PLĀSER	displacer, misplacer, placer, replacer
RĀSER	eraser, footracer, horseracer, racer
SPĀSER	spacer
TRĀSER	tracer

ASER

GASER	gasser
HASER	hassar
KASER	antimacassar, macassar
MASER	amasser, masser
PASER	passer, surpasser
PLASER	placer
RASER	harasser

ĀSET

PLĀSET	placet
TĀSET	tacet

ASET

ASET	asset
BASET	basset
BRASET	brasset
FASET	facet, fascet
PLASET	placet
TASET	tacet, tacit, tasset

ĀSEZ

ĀSEZ	oases

(See ĀS, add -s where appropriate.)

ASEZ

GLASEZ	field glasses, glasses, granny glasses, opera glasses
LASEZ	molasses

(See AS, add -es where appropriate.)

ĀSHA

ĀSHA	Asia, Croatia
GĀSHA	Geisha
GRĀSHA	ex gratia
KĀSHA	acacia
LĀSHA	osteomalacia
MĀSHA	Dalmatia
RĀSHA	Eurasia

(See ĀZHA)

ĀSHAL

BĀSHAL	abbatial, basial
FĀSHAL	facial, craniofacial, unifacial
GLĀSHAL	glacial, postglacial, preglacial, subglacial
LĀSHAL	palatial, prelatial
MĀSHAL	primatial
RĀSHAL	interracial, multiracial, racial
SPĀSHAL	interspatial, spatial
TĀSHAL	mystacial

(See Ā'SHI.AL)

ASHBORD

DASHBORD	dashboard
SPLASHBORD	splashboard

ASHĒ

ASHĒ	ashy
BASHĒ	bashy
BRASHĒ	brashy
DASHĒ	dashy
FLASHĒ	flashy
HASHĒ	hashy
KLASHĒ	clashy
MASHĒ	mashie, mashy
PLASHĒ	plashy
SLASHĒ	slashy
SPLASHĒ	splashy
TRASHĒ	trashy

ĀSHENS

FĀSHENS	facience
PĀSHENS	impatience, patience, patients, outpatients

ĀSHENT

FĀSHENT	abortifacient, facient, calefacient,

liquefacient,
parturifacient,
rubefacient,somnifacient,
sorbefacient,
stupefacient,
tumefacient

PĀSHENT   impatient, inpatient,
outpatient, patient

ASHER

BASHER	abasher, basher
BRASHER	brasher
DASHER	dasher, haberdasher
FLASHER	flasher
GASHER	gasher
HASHER	hasher, rehasher
KASHER	casher
KLASHER	clasher
KRASHER	gate-crasher, crasher
LASHER	lasher
MASHER	masher
NASHER	gnasher
PASHER	pasher
RASHER	rasher
SLASHER	slasher
SMASHER	smasher
SPLASHER	splasher
STASHER	stasher
TASHER	tasher
THRASHER	thrasher
TRASHER	trasher

ÄSHER

KWÄSHER	quasher
SKWÄSHER	squasher
SWÄSHER	swasher
WÄSHER	dishwasher, whitewasher, washer

(See **OSHER**)

ASHEZ

MASHEZ	gamashes

(See **ASH**, add -es where appropriate.)

ASHFUL

BASHFUL	bashful, unbashful
GASHFUL	gashful
RASHFUL	rashful

ASHING

(See **ASH, OSH**, add -ing where appropriate.)

ÄSHING

(See **ÄSH, OSH**, add -ing where appropriate.)

ASHLĒ

FLASHLĒ	flashly
GASHLĒ	gashly
RASHLĒ	rashly

ASHMAN

ASHMAN	ashman
TRASHMAN	trashman

ĀSHUN

ĀSHUN   *A* abbreviation,
affiliation,
accentuation,
actuation,
acupunctuation,
alleviation, Alpha
radiation, allineation,
amelioration,
ampliation,
annunciation,
appreciation,
appropriation,
arcuation,
asphyxiation, Asian,
association,
attentuation, aviation,
B Beta radiation,
beneficiation,
boation, *D*
defoliation,
delineation,
denunciation,
depreciation,
despoliation,
devaluation,
deviation,
differentiation,
dimidiation,
disaffiliation,
discontinuation,
dissociation,
domiciliation, *E*
effectuation,
effoliation,
exfoliation,
excruciation,
expatiation,
expatriation,
expiation,
expoliation,
expropriation,
extenuation,
exuviation,
emaciation,
enunciation,
evacuation,
evaluation, *F*
fasciation, februation,
feriation, filiation,
foliation, *FL*
fluctuation, *FR*
friation, fructuation,
GL glaciation,
gloriation, *GR*
graduation, *H*
habituation,
humiliation, *I*
ideation, illaqueation,
inappreciation,
individuation,
inebriation,
infatuation,
infuriation,
ingratiation,
initiation, inchoation,
insinuation,
intercolumniation,
interlineation,
intermediation,
invultuation,
irradiation, *K*
calumniation,
caseation,
columniation,
confarreation,
conciliation,
consubstantiation,
continuation,
contumniation,
creation, Croatian, *L*
laniation, lixiviation,
lineation, licentiation,
laureation,
luxuriation, *M*
malleation,
maleficiation,
materiation,
mediation,
menstruation,
misappropriation,
mispronunciation, *N*
negotiation,
novitiation,
nucleation, *O*
obviation, officiation,
otiation, *P* palliation,
permeation,
perpetuation, piation,
punctuation, *PR*
procreation,
pronunciation,
propitiation, *R*
radiation,

reconciliation,
recreation,
remediation,
renunciation,
repatriation,
repudiation,
retaliation,
revaluation, *S*
satiation,
self-renunciation,
situation,
ciliation, sinuation,
circumstantiation,
sublineation,
substantiation,
superannuation, *SP*
spoliation, *STR*
striation, *SW*
suaviation, *T*
tumultuation, *TR*
trabeation,
transsubstantiation,
tripudiation, *V*
valuation, variation,
vindemiation,
vitiation

BĀSHUN *A* accubation,
approbation, *D*
decubation,
dealbation,
disapprobation, *E*
exacerbation, *H*
humicubation, *I*
incubation,
intubation, *J* jobation,
K conurbation,
cubation, *L* libation,
limbation, *M*
masturbation, *O*
orbation, *P*
perturbation, *PR*
probation, *R*
recubation,
reprobation, *S*
cibation, *T* titubation

BRĀSHUN *A* adumbration,
antilibration, *E*
equilibration, *K*
calibration, *L*
libration, lucubration,
P palpebration, *S*
celebration,
cerebration, *T*
terebration, *V*
vertebration, vibration

DĀSHUN *A* aggradation,
accommodation, *B*
backwardation, *D*
defedation,
defraudation,
degradation,
denudation,

deoxidation,
depredation,
desudation,
dilapidation, *E*
exudation,
exundation,
elapidation,
elucidation,
emendation, *F*
fecundation,
foundation, *FL*
fluoridation, *FR*
frondation, *GR*
gradation,
gravidation, *I*
infeudation,
ingravidation,
incommodation,
intimidation,
inundation,
invalidation, *K*
commendation,
consolidation,
cuspidation, *L*
lapidation,
liquidation, laudation,
N nodation, nudation,
O oxidation, *PR*
predacean, predation,
R recommendation,
recordation,
retardation,
retrogradation, *S*
sedation, secundation,
sudation, *TR*
transudation,
trepidation,
trucidation, *V*
validation

DRĀSHUN *D* dehydration, *H*
hydration

FĀSHUN philosophation
FLĀSHUN *A* afflation, *D*
deflation, *E* efflation,
exsufflation, *I*
inflation, insufflation,
K conflation, *P*
perflation, *R* reflation,
S sufflation, *SL*
slumpflation, *ST*
stagflation

GĀSHUN *A* abnegation,
abrogation,
aggregation,
allegation, alligation,
arrogation, avigation,
D delegation,
deligation,
denegation,
derogation,
desegregation,
divagation,

divulgation, *E*
expurgation,
elongation, evagation,
F fumigation,
fustigation, *H*
homologation, *I*
instigation,
interrogation,
investigation,
irrigation, *J* jugation,
K castigation,
compurgation,
congregation,
conjugation,
corrugation, *L*
legation, levigation,
ligation, litigation, *M*
mitigation, *N*
navigation, negation,
noctivigation,
nugation, *O*
objurgation,
obligation, *P*
purgation,
pervulgation, *PR*
profligation,
prolongation,
promulgation,
propagation,
prorogation, *R*
relegation,
renegation, rigation,
rogation, *S*
segregation,
subjugation,
subligation,
subrogation,
supererogation,
circumnavigation,
surrogation, *V*
variegation

GRĀSHUN *D* deflagration,
disintegration, *E*
emigration, *I*
immigration,
integration,
intermigration, *K*
conflagration, *M*
migration, *R*
redintegration,
reintegration,
remigration, *TR*
transmigration

HĀSHUN Haitian
KĀSHUN *A* abdication,
abjudication,
adjudication,
advocation,
albification,
albication,
alkalification,
allocation,

amplification,
Anglification,
application,
aerification,
acetification,
acidification,
asification,
averruncation,
avocation, *B*
basification,
beatification,
bifurcation,
beautification, *BR*
brutification, *D*
damnification,
dandification,
dedication,
defalcation,
defecation,
deification,
declassification,
deltafication,
demarcation,
demystification,
demulsification,
demarkation,
denazification,
deprecation,
desiccation,
detoxication,
detruncation,
dimication,
disbocation,
disembarkation,
disqualification,
dislocation,
divarication,
diversification,
domestication,
dulcinification,
duplication, *E*
edification, education,
exemplification,
excommunication,
explication,
exsiccation,
extrication,
equivocation,
electrification,
embarkation,
embourgeoisification,
embrocation,
emulsification,
emuscation,
eradication,
esterification,
evocation, *F*
fabrication, falcation,
falsification,
formication,
fornication,
fortification,

fossilification,
furcation, *FL*
floccinaucinihilipilification,
florification,
flossification, *FR*
franglification,
Frenchification,
frication,
fructification, *G*
gasification, *GL*
glorification, *GR*
granitification,
gratification, *H*
hypothecation,
horrification,
humidification, *I*
identification,
imbrication,
implication,
imprecation,
inapplication,
indemnification,
indication, infucation,
incarnification,
inculcation,
intensification,
intercommunication,
interlocation,
interlucation,
interstratification,
intoxication,
intrication,
invocation, *J*
jellification,
generification,
gentrification,
jollification,
justification, *K*
cacation,
calorification,
calcification,
carnification,
casefication,
codification,
cockneyfication,
collocation,
communication,
complication,
comprecation,
chondrification,
confiscation,
contraindication,
convocation,
cornification,
coruscation,
countrification, *KL*
clarification,
classification,
claudication, *KR*
crucification, *KW*
quadrification,
quadrifurcation,

quadruplication,
qualification,
quantification, *L*
ladyfication,
lactification,
liquefaction,
location, lorication,
lubrication,
ludification, *M*
magnification,
mastication,
matrification,
medification,
medication,
mendication,
metrification,
metrication, mication,
misapplication,
mystification,
modification,
mollification,
mortification,
multiplication,
mummification,
mundification, *N*
Nazification,
necation, nidification,
nigrification,
nimbification,
nitrification,
notification,
nudification,
nullification, *O*
obfuscation,
objectification,
occaecation,
altercation,
ossification,
authentication,
oversimplification,
ozonification, *P*
pacation, perfrication,
personification,
petrification,
piscation, publication,
purification,
putrefication, *PL*
placation,
plebification,
plication, *PR*
preachification,
predication,
presignification,
prevarication,
prettification,
prognostication,
prolification,
provocation, *R*
radication,
ramification,
rarefication,
ratification,

reduplication,
regentrification,
rectification,
renidification,
replication,
republication,
reciprocation,
rhetorication,
revivification,
revocation,
reunification,
rigidification,
rubefacation,
runcation, rustication,
S saccharification,
sacrification,
salification,
sanguification,
sanctification,
saponification,
certification,
sevocation,
signification,
siccation,
syllabification,
syllabication,
silication,
simplification,
citification,
sophistication,
solemnification,
solidification,
subjectification,
sublimification,
suffocation, sulcation,
supplication, SK
scarification,
scorification, SP
speechification,
specification,
spiflication, ST
stellification,
stultification,
stupefication, STR
stratification, T
telecommunication,
tepefication,
terrification,
testification,
typification,
toxication,
torrefication,
tumefication, TH
thurification, TR
translocation,
transmogrification,
triplication,
truncation, U
uglification, V
vacation, varication,
vellication,
verification,

KRĀSHUN

KWĀSHUN

LĀSHUN

versification,
vesication,
vilification,
vindication,
vinification,
vitrification,
vivification, vocation,
Y unification
D deconsecration,
desecration, E
execration, K
consecration, O
obsecration
adequation, equation,
inadequation,
inequation, liquation
A ablation,
adosculation,
adulation,
accumulation, alation,
alkylation,
ambulation,
angulation,
annihilation,
annulation,
appelation,
articulation,
assimilation,
assimulation,
avolation, B
bombilation, BL
blood relation, D de-
escalation,
decollation, delation,
demodulation,
denticulation,
dentilation,
deoppilation,
depeculation,
depilation,
depopulation,
desolation, dilation,
disconsolation,
dissimulation,
distillation, E
ejaculation, ejulation,
exhalation,
expostulation,
extrapolation,
exungulation, elation,
emasculation,
emulation,
entortillation,
escalation, etiolation,
evolation, F
phallation,
fasciculation,
fibrillation,
formulation, FL
flabellation,
flagellation,
floccilation, GL

glandulation, GR
granulation,
graticulation,
gratulation, H
halation, hariolation,
hyperventilation,
horripilation, I
illation,
immaculation,
immolation,
inarticulation,
infibulation,
inhalation,
inoculation,
inosculation,
insolation,
installation,
instillation,
insulation,
intercalation,
interpellation,
interpolation,
interrelation,
intertessellation,
invigilation, isolation,
J jaculation, gelation,
gemmulation,
geniculation,
gesticulation,
jubilation, jugulation,
K calculation,
cancellation,
cantillation,
capitulation,
carbunculation,
castellation,
coagulation,
collation,
colliculation,
compellation,
compilation,
confabulation,
conglobulation,
congratulation,
congelation,
consolation,
constellation,
contravallation,
contumulation,
copulation,
correlation,
cumulation,
cupellation, KR
crenellation,
crenulation, L
lallation, lamellation,
legislation, M
machicolation,
maculation,
malassimilation,
manipulation,
matriculation,

miscalculation,
modulation,
mutilation, *N*
nidulation,
noctambulation,
nummulation, *O*
oblation,
obnubilation,
orbiculation,
oscillation,
osculation, ovulation,
P pabulation,
pandiculation,
peculation,
pendiculation,
perambulation,
percolation,
pestillation,
pixillation,
poculation,
population,
postillation,
postulation,
pullulation,
pustulation, *PR*
prolation, *R*
refocillation,
regelation, regulation,
recapitulation,
relation, repopulation,
reticulation,
retrocopulation,
revelation, *S*
serrulation, sibilation,
simulation,
scintillation,
circulation,
surculation,
circumambulation,
circumvallation,
somnambulation,
sublation, suggilation,
SK scutellation, *SP*
spallation,
speculation,
sporulation, *ST*
stellation,
stimulation,
stipulation, *STR*
strangulation,
stridulation,
strigilation,
strobilation, *T*
tabulation,
tessellation,
tintinnabulation,
titillation, tubulation,
turbination, *TR*
translation,
tremulation,
triangulation,
tribulation, *U*

ululation, undulation,
ustulation, *V*
vacuolation,
vallation, vapulation,
variolation,
vacillation,
vexillation, velation,
ventilation,
vermiculation,
vibratiunculation,
vigilation, violation,
vitriolation,
vocabulation,
volation, *Y* ululation
A affirmation,
acclamation,
acclimation,
amalgamation,
animation,
approximation, *D*
Dalmatian,
defamation,
deformation,
declamation,
deplumation,
decimation,
desquamation,
disinformation, *E*
exhumation,
exclamation,
estimation, *F*
formation, *I*
inanimation,
inflammation,
information,
inhumation,
incremation,
intimation,
irrumation, *J*
gemmation, *K*
collimation,
commation,
confirmation,
conformation,
consummation, *KR*
cremation,
chrismation, *L*
lachrymation,
lacrimation,
legitimation,
limation, *M*
malformation,
malconfirmation,
misinformation, *O*
automation,
overestimation, *PR*
preformation,
proclamation, *R*
racemation,
reaffirmation,
reformation,
reclamation, *S*

MĀSHUN

NĀSHUN

sigmation,
sublimation,
summation, *SKW*
squammation,
T tetragrammation,
TR transanimation,
transformation, *U*
underestimation, *V*
vigesimation
A abalienation,
abacination,
abomination,
adnation, adornation,
agglutination,
agnomination,
accrimination,
acumination,
alienation,
alternation,
assassination,
assignation, *D*
damnation,
declination,
decontamination,
denomination,
deoxygenation,
desalination,
destination,
designation,
determination,
detonation,
devirgination,
dissemination,
disinclination,
discrimination,
divination,
doctrination,
domination, donation,
E eburnation,
effemination,
examination,
exornation,
explanation,
expugnation,
extermination,
elimination,
emanation, enation, *F*
fascination,
ferrumination,
fibrination,
phonation,
foreordination,
fulmination, *FR*
fraternation, *G*
gunation, *GL*
glutination, *H*
hallucination,
hibernation,
hydrogenation,
hyphenation, *I*
illumination,
imagination,

immanation,
impanation,
impersonation,
impregnation,
indetermination,
indignation,
indiscrimination,
indoctrination,
ingannation,
ingemination,
incarnation,
inclination,
incoordination,
incrimination,
inordination,
insemination,
insubordination,
intonation,
invagination, *J*
gelatination,
gemination,
germination, *K*
cachinnation,
calcination,
carbonation,
carnation, catenation,
cognation,
combination,
commination,
conation,
condemnation,
condonation,
concatenation,
consarcination,
consternation,
contamination,
coordination,
coronation,
culmination, *KL*
chlorination, *KR*
crenation,
crimination, cross-
examination, *L*
lamination,
lancination,
lumination, lunation,
M machination,
miscegenation, *N*
nation, nomination, *O*
obsignation,
obstination,
oxygenation,
alternation,
oppugnation,
ordination,
origination,
ozonation, *P*
pagination,
pectination,
peregrination,
perfectionation,
personation,

PASHUN

PLĀSHUN
PRĀSHUN

pollination, *PR*
predestination,
predetermination,
predomination,
preordination,
profanation,
procrastination,
pronation,
propination,
propugnation, *R*
ratiocination,
reincarnation,
rejuvenation,
reclination,
recombination,
recrimination,
remanation,
resupination,
resignation, ruination,
rumination, *S*
salination, semination,
sermocination,
cybernation,
signation,
subordination,
subornation,
subsannation,
supination,
sermocination, *ST*
stagnation, *T*
tarnation, turbination,
termination, *TR*
trutination, *V*
vaccination,
vaticination,
venation, venenation,
vermination,
vernation, *Y*
urination, *Z* zonation
A anticipation, *D*
dissipation,
disculpation, *E*
exculpation,
extirpation,
emancipation, *F*
forcipation, *I*
increpation,
inculpation, *K*
constipation, *KR*
crispation, *N*
nuncupation, *O*
obstipation,
occupation, *P*
palpation,
participation, *PR*
preoccupation, *S*
syncopation,
suppalpation, *Y*
usurpation
contemplation
manustupration,
stupration

RĀSHUN

A aberration,
abjuration, adjuration,
admiration, adoration,
agglomeration,
aggeration,
acceleration,
alliteration,
amelioration,
annumeration,
aration, asperation,
aspiration,
asseveration, *B*
botheration, *BL*
blusteration, *D*
defeneration,
defloration,
degeneration,
declaration,
decoration,
deliberation,
deliration,
depauperation,
deploration,
depuration,
deceleration,
desideration,
desperation,
deterioration,
deterration,
disfiguration,
discoloration,
disoperation,
disseveration,
duration, *E*
edulcoration,
ejuration,
exaggeration,
exasperation,
exhiliration,
exoneration,
expectoration,
expiration,
exploration,
elaboration,
enumeration,
epuration,
evaporation,
eviration,
evisceration, *F*
federation, feneration,
figuration,
fissiparation,
fulguration,
furfuration, *FL*
flusteration, *GL*
glomeration, *H*
Horatian, *I*
immoderation,
imploration,
induration,
incameration,
incarceration,

inclination,
inconsideration,
incorporation,
inauguration,
inauration,
incineration,
inspiration,
instauration,
insussuration,
inteneration,
intoleration,
invigoration,
irroration, iteration, *J*
generation, gyration,
K carburation,
carceration,
collaboration,
coloration,
commemoration,
commensuration,
commiseration,
comploration,
confederation,
configuration,
conglomeration,
conjuration,
concameration,
consideration,
contesseration,
cooperation,
corporation,
corroboration,
culturation, curation,
L laceration,
liberation, libration,
liration, literation, *M*
marmoration,
maceration,
maturation,
melioration,
mensuration,
moderation,
moration,
murmuration, *N*
narration,
noncooperation,
numeration,
neuration, *O*
obduration,
objuration,
obliteration,
obscuration,
auguration, alteration,
oneration, operation,
oration, *P* pejoration,
perforation,
peroration,
perseveration,
perspiration,
pignoration,
ponderation, *PR*
prefiguration,

preparation,
preponderation,
procuration,
proliferation,
protuberation, *R*
ration, refrigeration,
reiteration,
regeneration,
reconsideration,
recuperation,
remuneration,
reparation,
respiration,
restoration,
reverberation,
roboration, *S*
saburration,
saturation, separation,
cerration, serration,
sideration, cineration,
circumgyration,
subarrhation,
sulphuration,
suppuration,
suspiration,
sussuration, *SF*
spheration, *T*
temeration,
titteration, toleration,
TR tractoration,
transfiguration,
transculturation,
transliteration,
transpiration,
trilateration,
trituration, *U*
ulceration, *V*
vaporation,
veneration,
verberation,
verbigeration,
vituperation,
vociferation, *Y*
Eurasian

SĀSHUN

A adversation,
affixation,
aftersensation,
Alsatian, annexation,
D decussation,
dispensation,
dispersation, *E*
extravasation,
elixation,
endorsation, *F*
fixation, *FL* fluxation,
I incrassation,
inspissation,
intensation,
intravasation, *K*
cassation, coaxation,
compensation,
condensation,

conspissation,
conversation, *KW*
quassation, *L*
laxation, luxation, *M*
malversation, *O*
overcompensation, *P*
pulsation, *PR*
prefixation,
presensation, *R*
relaxation, rixation, *S*
sarmassation, sation,
sensation, cessation,
suffixation,
succusation,
suspensation, *T*
taxation,
tergiversation,
undercompensation, *V*
vexation

STĀSHUN outstation, station,
substation

TĀSHUN *A* ablactation,
absentation,
adaptation,
adhortation,
affectation, agitation,
acceptation,
accreditation,
alimentation,
amputation,
annotation,
argumentation,
argentation,
arrestation,
assentation,
attestation,
attrectation, *D*
debilitation,
deforestation,
degustation,
dehortation,
decantation,
decapitation,
decrepitation,
dextrorotation,
delactation,
delectation,
delimitation,
dementation,
denotation, dentation,
deportation,
depositation,
deputation,
detestation,
devastation,
digitation, dictation,
dilatation,
disputation,
dissentation,
dissertation, ditation,
documentation,
dotation, dubitation,

E exagitation,
exaltation,
exercitation,
exhortation,
expectation,
experimentation,
exploitation,
exportation,
excitation, exultation,
equitation, enatation,
eructation, *F*
facilitation,
felicitation,
fermentation,
fetation, foetation,
fomentation,
forestation, *FL*
flagitation, flirtation,
flotation, *FR*
fragmentation,
frequentation,
frumentation, *G*
gurgitation, gustation,
guttation, *GR*
gravitation, *H*
habitation,
hebetation, hesitation,
hortation,
humectation, *I*
illutation, imitation,
immutation,
implantation,
implementation,
importation,
imputation,
inaffectation,
indentation,
infestation,
ingurgitation,
inhabitation,
incantation,
incapacitation,
incrustation,
incitation,
instrumentation,
insultation,
integumentation,
interdigitation,
intermutation,
interpretation,
intestation, invitation,
irritation, *J* jactation,
jactitation, gestation,
jotation, *K* cantation,
capacitation,
capitation, captation,
castrametation,
cavitation, coaptation,
cohabitation,
cogitation,
commentation,
commutation,

compotation,
computation,
confrontation,
confutation,
connotation,
concertation,
constatation,
consultation,
contestation,
contrectation,
cooptation,
cunctation, curtation,
KR crepitation,
crustacean,
crustation, *KW*
quartation, quotation,
L lactation,
lamentation,
levitation,
levorotation,
limitation, licitation,
luctation, *M*
manifestation,
meditation,
mentation, militation,
misinterpretation,
misquotation,
misrepresentation,
molestation,
mussitation,
mutation, *N* natation,
nepotation,
necessitation,
nictation, nictitation,
nobilitation, notation,
nutation, *O*
obequitation,
augmentation,
occultation,
orientation,
ornamentation,
oscitation,
auscultation,
ostentation, *P*
palpitation, peltation,
perfectation,
periclitation,
permutation,
pernoctation,
perscrutation,
pigmentation,
pollicitation, potation,
putation, *PL*
plantation,
placentation, *PR*
premeditation,
precipitation,
prestidigitation,
presentation,
protestation, *R*
reforestation,
refutation,

regurgitation,
rehabilitation,
regimentation,
recantation,
reluctation,
representation,
reptation, reputation,
recitation,
resuscitation,
retractation, rotation,
ructation, *S* saltation,
salutation, sanitation,
sedimentation,
segmentation,
cementation,
septation,
circumnutation,
cetacean, citation,
solicitation,
subhastation,
superalimentation,
supplantation,
supplementation,
supportation,
sustentation, *SK*
scortation, *SKR*
scrutation, *SP*
sputation, *ST*
sternutation, *T*
temptation, tentation,
testamentation,
testacean, testation,
TR tractation,
transmutation,
transplantation,
transportation, *V*
vegetation,
vectitation, velitation,
venditation,
visitation, volitation,
votation

THRĀSHUN
TRĀSHUN

Thracian
A administration,
arbitration, *D*
defenestration,
demonstration, *E*
engastration, *F*
fenestration,
filtration, *FR*
frustration, *I*
illustration,
impenetration,
impetration,
infiltration,
interfenestration,
interpenetration, *K*
castration,
concentration, *L*
lustration, *M*
maladministration,
ministration,
monstration, *N*

nitration, *O*
oblatration,
orchestration, *P*
penetration,
perlustration,
perpetration, *PR*
prostration, *R*
registration,
recalcitration,
remonstration, *S* self-
concentration,
sequestration, *T*
titration

VĀSHUN *A* aggravation,
activation, acervation,
D decurvation,
depravation,
deprivation,
derivation, *E*
excavation, elevation,
enervation, estivation,
I innervation,
innovation, *K*
captivation,
conservation,
cultivation, curvation,
L lavation, *M*
motivation, *N*
nervation, nivation,
novation, *O*
observation, ovation,
PR preservation,
privation, *R*
renovation,
reservation, *S*
salivation, salvation,
self-preservation,
servation, solvation,
ST starvation, *T*
titivation

ZĀSHUN *A* aggrandization,
acclimatization,
accusation,
actualization,
alphabetization,
alcoholization,
alkalization,
allegorization,
Americanization,
amortization,
analyzation,
anathematization,
anaesthetization,
Anglicization,
animalization,
antagonization,
arborization,
arithmetization,
aromatization,
atomization, *BR*
brutalization, *CH*
chattelization, *D*

decriminalization,
demobilization,
demonetization,
demoralization,
denaturalization,
denationalization,
denization,
denuclearization,
deodorization,
deoxydization,
depauperization,
desensitization,
decentralization,
decimalization,
desulfurization,
detonization,
devocalization,
disorganization, *DR*
dramatization, *E*
economization,
extemporization,
externalization,
equalization,
electrization,
epitomization,
eternization,
etherealization,
evangelization, *F*
familiarization,
fertilization,
Finlandization,
focalization,
phoneticization,
phosphorization,
fossilization,
feudalization, *FR*
fraternization, *G*
galvanization, *H*
harmonization,
Hellenization,
hepatization,
Hibernization,
hybridization,
humanization, *I*
idealization,
idolization,
immortalization,
improvisation,
individualization,
intellectualization,
internationalization,
ionization, iridization,
J gelatinization,
generalization,
Judaization, *K*
canalization,
canonization,
capitalization,
characterization,
caramelization,
carbonization,
categorization,

catechization,
colonization,
columnization,
commercialization,
cauterization,
causation, *KR*
crystallization,
Christianization, *L*
Latinization,
legalization,
legitimization,
liberalization,
literalization,
localization,
magnetization,
macadamization,
maximization,
martyrization,
materialization,
mediatization,
mercerization,
mesmerization,
metallization,
methodization,
militarization,
minimization,
mobilization,
modernization,
monetization,
monopolization,
mortalization, *N*
naturalization,
nationalization,
nasalization,
mnemonization,
neologization,
normalization,
neutralization, *O*
oxidization,
organization,
ostracization,
authorization,
ozonization, *P*
palatalization,
paralyzation,
pasteurization,
patronization,
penalization,
polarization,
pollenization,
polymerization,
popularization,
pauperization,
porphyrization,
pausation,
pulverization, *PL*
pluralization, *PR*
proctorization, *R*
racialization,
realization,
recognization,
recusation,

remonetization,
reorganization,
revitalization, *S*
secularization,
self-actualization,
sensitization,
sensualization,
centralization,
syllogization,
symbolization,
synchronization,
systematization,
civilization,
solarization,
solemnization,
solmization,
subtilization,
sulphurization,
summarization, *SK*
scandalization, *SP*
specialization,
spiritualization, *ST*
stabilization,
standardization,
sterilization,
stigmatization, *T*
tabularization,
tantalization,
tartarization,
temporization,
totalization, *TH*
theorization, *TR*
tranquilization,
trullization, *U*
urbanization, *V*
valorization,
vandalization,
vaporization,
verbalization,
victimization,
vitalization,
vitriolization,
visualization,
vocalization,
volcanization,
vulcanization, *Y*
universalization,
utilization

ASHUN

ASHUN	ashen
FASHUN	disfashion, fashion, prefashion, refashion
KASHUN	Circassian
NASHUN	Parnassian
PASHUN	dispassion, impassion, compassion, passion, satispassion
RASHUN	deration, ration, unration

ASHUND

FASHUND	fashioned, new-fashioned, old-fashioned

(See **ASHUN,** add *-ed* where appropriate.)

ĀSHUNZ

(See **ĀSHUN,** add *-s* where appropriate.)

ĀSHUS

ĀSHUS	alliaceous, foliaceous, hordeaceous, coriaceous, liliaceous, oleaceous, scoriaceous, tileaceous
BĀSHUS	bibacious, bulbaceous, fabaceous, herbaceous, sabaceous, sebaceous
DĀSHUS	amaryllidaceous, audacious, bodacious, edacious, glandaceous, hamamelidaceous, iridaceous, mendacious, mordacious, orchidaceous, predacious, rudaceous
DRĀSHUS	cylindraceous
FĀSHUS	tophaceous, torfaceous
GĀSHUS	fugacious, fungacious, sagacious, saxifragaceous
GRĀSHUS	disgracious, gracious, misgracious, ungracious
GWĀSHUS	linguacious
KĀSHUS	efficacious, ericaceous, inefficacious, micaceous, perspicacious, pervicacious, procacious, salicaceous, urticaceous
KRĀSHUS	execratious
KWĀSHUS	loquacious, sequacious, somniloquacious
LĀSHUS	*A* amylaceous, argillaceous, *F* fallacious, ferulaceous, filaceous, *K* capillaceous, corallaceous, *L* lilaceous, *M* marlaceous, *P* palacious, perlaceous, polygalaceous, *R* ranunculaceous, *S* salacious, santalaceous, *SK* schorlaceous, *V* violaceous
MĀSHUS	fumacious, gemmaceous, contumacious, limaceous, palmaceous, pomaceous
NĀSHUS	*A* acanaceous, arenaceous, *E* erinaceous, *F* farinaceous, *G* gallinaceous, *K* carbonaceous, *M* minacious, *P* papillonaceous, pectinaceous, pertinacious, pugnacious, *R* resinaceous, *S* sanguinaceous, saponaceous, solanaceous, *T* tenacious, *V* vinaceous
PĀSHUS	incapacious, capacious, lappaceous, rampacious, rapacious, cepaceous
RĀSHUS	arboraceous, feracious, furacious, furfuraceous, hederaceous, camphoraceous, piperaceous, porraceous, pulveraceous, ceraceous, stercoraceous, veracious, voracious
SĀSHUS	vexatious
SPĀSHUS	spacious, unspacious
TĀSHUS	*D* disputatious, *FL* flirtatious, *FR* frumentaceous, *K* cactaceous, chartaceous, *KR* cretaceous, crustaceous, *O*

ostentatious, *P*
pultaceous, *R*
rutaceous, *S*
cetaceous, setaceous,
psittaceous, *T*
testaceous, *TR*
truttaceous
THĀSHUS acanthaceous
VĀSHUS curvaceous,
olivaceous, vivacious
ZĀSHUS quizzaceous,
rosaceous

ĀSĪD

BĀSĪD bayside
BRĀSĪD braeside
WĀSĪD wayside

ASID

ASID antacid, acid,
monoacid, nucleic
acid, oxyacid, triacid
(etc.)
BASID subacid
PLASID placid
TASID antacid

ASIJ

BRASIJ brassage
PASIJ passage

ĀSIK

BĀSIK basic, bibasic,
diabasic, polybasic,
tribasic
FĀSIK aphasic, monophasic,
phasic
PĀSIK carapasic
TĀSIK diastasic

ASIK

ASIK Liassic, Triassic
BASIK sebacic
KLASIK classic, neoclassic,
postclassic,
preclassic,
pseudoclassic
LASIK thalassic
RASIK boracic, Jurassic,
thoracic
TASIK potassic

ASIL

(See **ASL**)

ĀSIN

(See **ĀSEN**)

ASIN

(See **ASEN**)

ĀSING

(See **ĀS,** add -*ing* where appropriate.)

ASING

(See **AS,** add -*ing* where appropriate.)

ĀSIS

ĀSIS Acis, oasis
BĀSIS basis
FĀSIS phasis
FRĀSIS holophrasis
GLĀSIS glacis
KLĀSIS cataclasis
KRĀSIS crasis, krasis
STĀSIS hemostasis, stasis

ASIS

ASIS assis
CHASIS chassis
FASIS fascis
GLASIS glacis
KASIS *cassis*
NASIS Jackie Onassis
RASIS tarassis

ĀSIV

BRĀSIV abrasive
SWĀSIV assuasive, dissuasive,
persuasive, suasive
VĀSIV evasive, invasive,
pervasive

ASIV

MASIV massive
PASIV impassive, passive

ASKA

BASKA Athabasca

BRASKA Nebraska
LASKA Alaska
RASKA burrasca, marasca

ASKAL

MASKL mascle
PASKAL antepaschal, Pascal,
paschal
RASKAL rascal
TASKAL tascal

ASKER

ASKER asker
BASKER basker
FLASKER flasker
GASKER Madagascar
KASKER casker, casquer,
uncasker, uncasqer
LASKER Lascar
MASKER antimasker,
antimasquer, masker,
masquer, unmasker
TASKER tasker

ASKET

BASKET basket, breadbasket,
flower basket
FLASKET flasket
GASKET gasket
KASKET casket, casquet
LASKET lasket
TASKET taskit

ASKING

(See **ASK,** add -*ing* where appropriate.)

ASKL

(See **ASKAL**)

ASKŌ

ASKŌ fiasco
BASKŌ tabasco, verbasco
KASKŌ casco
TASKŌ tasco

ASKUS

ASKUS ascus
MASKUS Damascus

ASL

FASL	facile
GRASL	gracile
HASL	hassle
KASL	castle, forecastle, Newcastle
RASL	wrastle
TASL	entassel, tassel
VASL	envassal, vassal

ĀSLĒ

BĀSLĒ	basely
PLĀSLĒ	commonplacely

ĀSLES

(See ĀS, add -less where appropriate.)

ĀSLET

BRĀSLET	bracelet
HĀSLET	haslet
LĀSLET	lacelet

ASLET

HASLET	haslet
TASLET	taslet

ĀSLŌD

BĀSLŌD	baseload
KĀSLŌD	caseload

ASMAN

GASMAN	gasman
GLASMAN	glassman
GRASMAN	grassman
KLASMAN	classman, underclassman, upperclassman
PASMAN	passman

ĀSMENT

(See ĀS, add -ment where appropriate.)

ASMENT

MASMENT	amassment
RASMENT	harassment

ĀSNER

CHĀSNER	chastener
HĀSNER	hastener

ĀSŌ

PĀSŌ	peso
SĀSŌ	say-so

ASŌ

BASŌ	basso
GASŌ	Sargasso
LASŌ	lasso

ASOK

(See ASUK)

ĀSON

(See ĀSEN)

ASON

(See ASEN)

ASPER

ASPER	asper
GASPER	gasper
GRASPER	grasper
JASPER	jasper
KLASPER	enclasper, clasper, unclasper
RASPER	rasper

ASPING

(See ASP, add -ing where appropriate.)

ASTA

KASTA	shikasta
NASTA	canasta
SHASTA	Shasta
TASTA	catasta

ÄSTA

BÄSTA	basta
HÄSTA	hasta
PÄSTA	pasta

ASTARD

(See ASTERD)

ĀSTĒ

HĀSTĒ	hasty, unhasty
PĀSTĒ	pasty, unpasty
TĀSTĒ	tasty, untasty

ASTĒ

BLASTĒ	blasty
MASTĒ	masty
NASTĒ	photonasty, epinasty, hyponasty, nyctinasty, nasty
PLASTĒ	anaplasty, dermatoplasty, genioplasty, heteroplasty, keratoplasty, mammoplasty, neoplasty, autoplasty, rhinoplasty, cineplasty, zooplasty
RASTĒ	pederasty
TRASTĒ	contrasty
VASTĒ	vasty

ĀSTED

HĀSTED	hasted
PĀSTED	pasted
TĀSTED	distasted, foretasted, pretasted, tasted

ĀSTER

BĀSTER	baster
CHĀSTER	chaster
PĀSTER	paster
SLĀSTER	slaister
TĀSTER	foretaster, taster
WĀSTER	shirtwaister, waster

ASTER

ASTER	aster, China aster, geaster, oleaster, piaster, Zoroaster
BASTER	alabaster
BLASTER	blaster
DASTER	cadaster
FASTER	faster
GASTER	astrologaster, flabbergaster, gaster

KASTER	broadcaster, forecaster, grammaticaster, caster, castor, criticaster, medicaster
LASTER	interpilaster, opulaster, pilaster, stylaster
MASTER	*B* bandmaster, burgomaster, grandmaster, headmaster, housemaster, *K* concertmaster, cubmaster, *KW* choirmaster, quartermaster, *M* master, *O* overmaster, *P* past master, paymaster, postmaster, ringmaster, *SK* schoolmaster, scoutmaster, *ST* stationmaster, *T* taskmaster, toastmaster
NASTER	canaster, pinaster
PASTER	pastor
PLASTER	beplaster, court plaster, plaster, replaster, sticking plaster, unplaster
SASTER	disaster
TASTER	Latinitaster, poetaster
TRASTER	contraster
VASTER	vaster
ZASTER	disaster

ASTERD

BASTERD	bastard
DASTERD	dastard
LASTERD	pilastered
MASTERD	mastered, overmastered, unmastered
PLASTERD	beplastered, plastered, replastered, unplastered

ĀSTFUL

HĀSTFUL	hasteful
TĀSTFUL	distasteful, tasteful
WĀSTFUL	unwasteful, wasteful

ASTIK

ASTIK	ecclesiastic, encomiastic, enthusiastic, chiastic, chiliastic, autoschediastic, orgiastic, parasceuastic, scholiastic, unenthusiastic
BASTIK	bombastic
BLASTIK	amphiblastic
BRASTIK	Hudibrastic
DRASTIK	drastic
FRASTIK	antiphrastic, metaphrastic, paraphrastic, periphrastic
KASTIK	dichastic, hesychastic, sarcastic, stochastic
KLASTIK	anaclastic, anticlastic, iconoclastic, cataclastic, clastic, plagioclastic, synclastic
LASTIK	agelastic, elastic, inelastic, interscholastic, gelastic, scholastic
MASTIK	animastic, antonomastic, docimastic, gum mastic, mastic, onomastic, paronomastic
NASTIK	dynastic, gymnastic, monastic, pleonastic
PLASTIK	*A* anaplastic, aplastic, *B* bioplastic, *D* dentoplastic, *E* emplastic, esemplastic, *F* phelloplastic, *G* galvanoplastic, *N* neoplastic, *TH* thermoplastic, *THR* thromboplastic, *PL* plastic, *PR* proplastic, protoplastic, *S* ceroplastic, *Y* euplastic
RASTIK	pederastic, peirastic, pornerastic, rastik
SASTIK	doxastic
SPASTIK	epispastic, spastic
TASTIK	fantastic
TRASTIK	tetrastich

ĀSTING

(See **ĀST,** add -*ing* where appropriate.)

ASTING

| KASTING | broadcasting |
| LASTING | everlasting |

(See **AST,** add -*ing* where appropriate.)

ASTLĒ

FASTLĒ	steadfastly
GASTLĒ	ghastly
LASTLĒ	lastly
VASTLĒ	vastly

ASTMENT

| BLASTMENT | blastment |
| TRASTMENT | contrastment |

ASTNES

| FASTNES | fastness, *steadfastness* |
| VASTNES | vastness |

ASTON

| GASTON | Gaston |
| SPASTON | trispaston |

ASTOR

(See **ASTER**)

ASTRAL

ASTRAL	astral, subastral
DASTRAL	cadastral
KASTRAL	castral

ASTRON

| PASTRON | apastron |
| PLASTRON | plastron |

ASTRUM

ASTRUM	periastrum
BASTRUM	alabastrum
KASTRUM	castrum
PLASTRUM	plastrum

ASUK

| HASUK | hassock |
| KASUK | cassock |

ĀTA

ĀTA	eta
BĀTA	albata, beta
BRĀTA	invertebrata, vertebrata
DĀTA	data, caudata, chordata
LĀTA	postulata, relata
MĀTA	ultimata, squamata
RĀTA	desiderata, errata, pro rata, rata
SĀTA	peseta
STRĀTA	strata
TĀTA	dentata
THĀTA	theta
ZĀTA	zeta

ATA

ATA	atta
BATA	batta
GATA	regatta
MATA	matamata, paramatta
STRATA	strata

ÄTA

ÄTA	reata, riata
DÄTA	data
GÄTA	alpargata, regatta
HWÄTA	whata
KÄTA	imbrocata, stoccata, toccata
LÄTA	aballata
MÄTA	mata, matamata, paramatta
NÄTA	serenata, sonata
RÄTA	errata, inamorata, pro rata, rata
STRÄTA	strata
SÄTA	cassata
TÄTA	batata, cantata, patata

ĀTAL

DĀTAL	datal
FĀTAL	fatal
NĀTAL	antenatal, natal, neonatal, perinatal, postnatal, postneonatal, prenatal
RĀTAL	ratal, ratel
STĀTAL	statal
STRĀTAL	stratal, substratal

ĀTAN

(See ĀTEN)

ĀTANT

BLĀTANT	blatant
FLĀTANT	inflatant
LĀTANT	dilatant, latent
NĀTANT	natant, supernatant
PĀTANT	patent

ĀTĒ

ĀTĒ	Ate, eighty
HĀTĒ	Haiti, Hayti
LĀTĒ	Jubilate, Leyte
MĀTĒ	matey, maty
NĀTĒ	antenati
PLĀTĒ	platy
RĀTĒ	literati
SLĀTĒ	slaty
TĀTĒ	ex necessitate
WĀTĒ	weighty

ATĒ

BATĒ	batty
CHATĒ	chatty
FATĒ	fatty
KATĒ	catty
MATĒ	matty
NATĒ	gnatty, natty, Cincinnati
PATĒ	chapatty, patty
PLATĒ	platy
RATĒ	ratty
SKATĒ	scatty
TATĒ	tatty
YATĒ	yati

ÄTĒ

ÄTĒ	coati, piatti
LÄTĒ	Jubilate, oblati
MÄTĒ	Amati, mate
NÄTĒ	illuminati, Cincinnati
RÄTĒ	glitterati, karate, culturati, literati
SÄTĒ	Sati
SKWÄTĒ	squatty
SWÄTĒ	swatty
YÄTĒ	yachty
ZÄTĒ	zati

(See OTĒ)

ĀTED

ĀTED	superannuated
BĀTED	elumbated, surbated
KĀTED	indicated, contraindicated, spiflicated, vindicated
KWĀTED	torquated
LĀTED	etiolated, flammulated, mammilated, ocellated, stellated, tessellated
SĀTED	inspissated, spissated, sated, unsated

(See ĀT, add -ed where appropriate.)

ATED

ATED	caryatid

(See AT, add -ed.)

ĀTEN

DĀTEN	Dayton
PĀTEN	peyton
SĀTEN	Satan
STRĀTEN	straighten, straiten

ATEN

ATEN	Aten
BATEN	batten, Mountbatten
FATEN	fatten
FLATEN	flatten
GRATEN	au gratin, gratin, gratten
HATEN	Manhattan
LATEN	latten, Latin, pig Latin, Vulgar Latin
MATEN	*harmattan*, matin
PATEN	paten, patten, patin, patine
PLATEN	platan, platen
RATEN	rattan, ratten
SATEN	satin
STATEN	Staten

ĀTENT

(See ĀTANT)

ĀTER

ĀTER	*A* abbreviator, acutiator, annunciator, aviator, *D* delineator, *F* philiater, *GL* gladiator, *M* mediator, *N*

	negotiator, *K* caveator, *R* rabiator, radiator, *V* viator
BĀTER	abater, baiter, bater, debater, rebater
BLĀTER	ablator
BRĀTER	vibrator
DĀTER	dater, laudator
FRĀTER	frater, freighter, confrater
GĀTER	alligator, gaiter, 'gater, interrogator, investigator, corrugator, navigator, negator, propagator
GRĀTER	grater, greater
HĀTER	hater, manhater, womanhater
KĀTER	*A* adjudicator, allocator, applicator, *D* desiccator, divaricator, duplicator, *E* edificator, educator, *I* indicator, *J* judicator, *K* cater, comiconomenclator, *KL* classificator, *KW* qualificator, *L* lubricator, *M* modificator, multiplicator, *N* nomenclator, *P* pacificator, pontificator, purificator, *PL* placater, *S* significator, *SK* scarificator, *TR* trafficator, *V* vacater, vinificator
KRĀTER	crater
KWĀTER	equator, exequater
LĀTER	*A* ablator, accumulator, articulator, *D* defribillator, delator, dilator, *E* elater, *I* insulator, invigilator, *K* calculator, *L* later, *O* oscillator, *P* perambulator, pocket calculator, postulator, *R* regulator, relater, revelator, *S* simulator, scintillator, *SP* speculator, *ST* stimulator, *TR* translator, *V* ventilator
MĀTER	alma mater, dura mater, imprimatur, mater, Stabat Mater

NĀTER	*B* buccinator, *D* denominator, detonator, discriminator, *E* exterminator, *I* impersonator, *J* jejunator, *K* coordinator, *O* alternator, *PR* propugnator, *S* supinator, *T* terminator
PĀTER	Dis Pater, pater
PLĀTER	plaiter, plater
PRĀTER	prater
RĀTER	*A* accelerator, aspirator, *B* barrator, *D* decorator, *E* elaborator, *I* incinerator, *J* generator, *K* carburetor, collaborator, corporator, *L* liberator, literator, *M* moderator, *N* numerator, *O* operator, *R* refrigerator, recuperator, respirator, reverberator, *S* separator, cinerator, stellarator
SĀTER	malaxator, sater, satyr
SKĀTER	skater
TĀTER	agitator, annotater, illicitator, imitator, mutator, resuscitator, spectator, 'tater
TRĀTER	traitor
VĀTER	activator, elevator, innovator, conservator, cultivator, levator
WĀTER	dumbwaiter, waiter

ATER

ATER	attar
BATER	batter
BLATER	blatter
CHATER	chatter
FATER	fatter
FLATER	flatter
HATER	hatter, high-hatter, Mad Hatter
KATER	catter, quatre, wildcatter
KLATER	clatter, clitter-clatter
LATER	latter

MATER	antimatter, matter
NATER	natter
PATER	patter, pitter-patter
PLATER	platter
RATER	ratter
SATER	satyr
SHATER	shatter
SKATER	scatter
SMATER	smatter
SPATER	bespatter, spatter
SPLATER	splatter
SPRATER	spratter
TATER	tatter
VATER	vatter
YATER	yatter

ÄTER

MÄTER	alma mater, dura mater, mater, Stabat Mater
PÄTER	Dis Pater, pater
SKWÄTER	squatter
SWÄTER	swatter
YÄTER	yachter

(See **OTER**)

ATERN

PATERN	holding pattern, pattern
SATERN	Saturn
SLATERN	slattern

ĀTĒZ

ĀTĒZ	eighties
DĀTĒZ	Mithridates
FRĀTĒZ	Euphrates
KĀTĒZ	Achates
MĀTĒZ	mateys
NĀTĒZ	lares and penates, nates, penates
VĀTĒZ	vates

ATFOL

| **KATFOL** | catfall |
| **PRATFOL** | pratfall |

ĀTFUL

FĀTFUL	fateful
GRĀTFUL	grateful, ungrateful
HĀTFUL	hateful
PLĀTFUL	plateful

ATHED

| FATHED | fathead |
| FLATHED | flathead |

ĀTHER

(TH as in *then*)

BĀTHER	bather
LĀTHER	lather
SWĀTHER	swather

ATHER

(TH as in *then*)

BATHER	bather
BLATHER	blather
LATHER	lather

ÄTHER

(TH as in *then*)

| FÄTHER | father |
| SWÄTHER | swather |

(See **OTHER**)

ATHIK

(TH as in *thin*)

BATHIK	bathic, photobathic
MATHIK	philomathic, chrestomathic, polymathic
NATHIK	agnathic, gnathic, orthognathic, prognathic
PATHIK	*A* allopathic, antipathic, apathic, *E* electropathic, *H* heteropathic, hydropathic, homeopathic, *I* idiopathic, *K* cosmopathic, *N* naturopathic, neuropathic, *O* osteopathic, *P* pathic, *R* rectopathic, *S* psychopathic, *T* telepathic, *TH* theopathic
SPATHIK	feldspathic, spathic

ĀTHING

(TH as in *then*)

BĀTHING	bathing
LĀTHING	lathing
PLĀTHING	*plaything* (th as in thin)
SKĀTHING	scathing
SWĀTHING	swathing

ĀTHLES

(TH as in *thin*)

| FĀTHLES | faithless |
| SKĀTHLES | scatheless |

ATHLES

(TH as in *thin*)

BATHLES	bathless
MATHLES	mathless
PATHLES	pathless
RATHLES	wrathless

ATHLON

| KATHLON | decathlon |
| TATHLON | pentathlon |

ÄTHŌ

(th as in *then*)

(See **ÄDŌ**)

ĀTHOS

ĀTHŌS	Athos
BĀTHOS	bathos
NĀTHOS	*prognathous*
PĀTHOS	pathos

ATĪD

BATĪD	bat-eyed
KATĪD	cat-eyed
RATĪD	rat-eyed

ATIK

ATIK	*A* Adriatic, attic, Attic, aviatic, Asiatic, *D* diatic, *E* Eleatic, enneatic, *FL* fluviatic, *FR* phreatic, *H* halleluiatic, Hanseatic, *I* ischyatic, *K* caryatic, cuneatic, *KR* creatic, *M* mydriatic, muriatic, *O* opiatic, *P* pancreatic, *S* sciatic, *V* viatic
BATIK	acrobatic, adiabatic, anabatic, batic, ecbatic, hyperbatic, isodiabatic, catabatic, metabatic, sabbatic
FATIK	aliphatic, emphatic, phatic, phosphatic, lymphatic, sulphatic
KRATIK	*A* androcratic, aristocratic, arithmocratic, *B* bureaucratic, *D* democratic, Democratic, *F* pherecratic, physiocratic, *H* hagiocratic, harpocratic, Hippocratic, *I* idiocratic, idiosyncratic, isocratic, *J* gynocratic, *L* leuocecratic, *M* meritocratic, mesocratic, mobocratic, monocratic, *N* nomocratic, *O* ochlocratic, autocratic, *P* pancratic, pantisocratic, pornocratic, *PL* plutocratic, *S* Socratic, *SL* slavocratic, *SKW* squattocratic, *STR* stratocratic, *T* technocratic, timocratic, ptochocratic, *TH* theocratic
KWATIK	aquatic, subaquatic
LATIK	palatic, prelatic, villatic
MATIK	*A* aphorismatic, acousmatic, achromatic, acromonogrammatic, axiomatic, anagrammatic, anathematic, apophthegmatic, apochromatic, aposematic, aromatic, asymptomatic, astigmatic, athematic,

asthmatic, *D*
dalmatic,
diaphragmatic,
diagrammatic,
diastomatic,
dichromatic,
dilemmatic,
diplomatic, dogmatic,
DR dramatic, *E*
emblematic,
empyreumatic,
endermatic,
enigmatic,
epigrammatic,
episematic, *F*
phantomatic, *FL*
phlegmatic, *GR*
grammatic, gromatic,
H hematic,
hierogrammatic,
hypomnematic, *I*
idiomatic,
iconomatic,
isochromatic, *J*
judgmatic, *K*
charismatic,
categorematic,
cataclysmatic,
kinematic, komatik,
commatic, *KL*
climatic, *KR*
cryptogrammatic,
chromatic, *L*
lipogrammatic, *M*
magmatic,
macromatic,
mathematic,
melismatic,
melodramatic,
miasmatic,
micromatic,
monogrammatic,
monochromatic,
monomatic, *N*
noematic, pneumatic,
numismatic, *O*
onymatic, osmatic,
automatic, *P*
paradigmatic,
parallelogrammatic,
pathematic, pelmatic,
polygrammatic,
polychromatic,
porismatic, *PL*
plasmatic,
pleochromatic, *PR*
pragmatic, prismatic,
problematic,
programmatic,
proceleusmatic, *R*
rhematic, rheumatic,
S Sarmatic, sematic,

psychosomatic,
psymatic,
symptomatic,
synallagmatic,
cinematic, systematic,
schismatic, *SK*
schematic, *ST*
stigmatic, stomatic, *T*
termatic, *TH*
thematic,
theorematic, *TR*
traumatic,
trigrammatic,
trichromatic,
truismatic, *U*
unsystematic, *Z*
zygomatic, zeugmatic
agnatic, aplanatic,
enatic, fanatic,
morganatic, venatic
hepatic
platic
biquadratic, erratic,
hieratic, geratic,
quadratic, operatic,
piratic
A anastatic, antistatic,
apostatic, astatic, *D*
diastatic, *E* ecstatic,
electrostatic, *F*
photostatic, *H*
heliostatic,
hemostatic,
hydrostatic,
hypostatic, *I*
idiostatic, *J* geostatic,
gyrostatic, *K*
catastatic, *M*
majestatic, metastatic,
PR prostatic, *ST*
static, *TH*
thermostatic, *Y*
eustatic
protatic
magistratic
lavatic, sylvatic, vatic

NATIK

PATIK
PLATIK
RATIK

STATIK

TATIK
TRATIK
VATIK

(Add -*s* for noun form or plural where appropriate.)

ÄTIK

KWÄTIK	aquatic
YÄTIK	halleluiatic

(See **OTIK**)

ĀTĪM

DĀTĪM	daytime
MĀTĪM	Maytime

PĀTĪM	paytime
PLĀTĪM	playtime

ĀTIM

ĀTIM	seriatim
BĀTIM	verbatim
DĀTIM	gradatim
RĀTIM	literatim
TĀTIM	guttatim

ATIN

(See **ATEN**)

ĀTING

(See **ĀT,** add -*ing* where appropriate.)

ATING

(See **AT,** add -*ting* where appropriate.)

ÄTING

SKWÄTING	squatting
SWÄTING	swatting
YÄTING	yachting

(See **ÄT, OT,** add -*ing* where appropriate.)

ATIS

BRATIS	brattice
GRATIS	gratis
LATIS	lattice

ĀTISH

LĀTISH	latish
SLĀTISH	slatish
STRĀTISH	straightish

ATISH

BATISH	battish
BRATISH	brattish
FATISH	fattish
FLATISH	flattish
KATISH	cattish
SKATISH	scattish
RATISH	rattish

ĀTIV

ĀTIV	*A* alleviative, annunciative,

appreciative,
appropriative,
associative, *D*
denunciative,
depreciative,
dissociative, *E*
enunciative, *I*
inappreciative,
initiative, insinuative,
K conciliative,
continuative, *KR*
creative, *M*
mediative, *P*
palliative,
punctuative, *PR*
procreative,
pronunciative, *R*
radiative, recreative,
renunciative, *U*
unappreciative,
uncreative, *V*
variative

THE HARTEBEEST IS ON THE ENDANGERED
LIST.—*News report*

The hartebeest grows beastly, and his heart starts
  beating fast,
Whene'er a hartebeestess wanders innocently past.
The hartebeestess quickly of his longing gains an
  inkling;
The beestess is as beastly as the beest is in a twinkling.
So fast they shift, those hartebeests, from he's and
  she's to he-she's,
I find it hard to think of them as an endangered species.

BĀTIV   approbative,
            incubative,
            reprobative
DĀTIV   accommodative,
            dative, elucidative,
            consolidative
GĀTIV   abnegative,
            abrogative,
            aggregative,
            investigative,
            irrigative, mitigative,
            propagative,
            segregative
KĀTIV   *A* adjudicative, *D*
            dedicative,
            deprecative,
            desiccative,
            duplicative, *E*
            educative,
            excommunicative,
            explicative,
            exsiccative,
            eradicative, *I*
            imbricative,
            implicative,

incommunicative,
invocative, *J*
judicative, *K*
communicative,
complicative, *KW*
qualificative, *M*
medificative,
medicative,
modificative,
multiplicative, *P*
purificative, *PR*
prognosticative, *R*
replicative, *S*
significative,
suffocative,
supplicative, *U*
uncommunicative, *V*
vellicative,
verificative,
vindicative,
vivificative
nomenclative
execrative,
consecrative

KLĀTIV
KRĀTIV

LĀTIV   *A* accumulative,
            assimilative, *D*
            dilative, *E*
            expostulative, elative,
            emulative, illative, *J*
            jaculative,
            gesticulative, *K*
            calculative,
            coagulative, collative,
            congratulative,
            copulative,
            cumulative, *L*
            legislative, *M*
            manipulative,
            modulative, *O*
            oscillative, *PR*
            prolative, *R*
            regulative,
            recapitulative, *S*
            simulative,
            circulative, *SP*
            speculative, *ST*
            stimulative, *TR*
            translative, *U*
            undulative, *V*
            ventilative, violative

MĀTIV   animative,
            approximative,
            estimative

NĀTIV   *A* agglutinative, *D*
            denominative,
            determinative,
            designative,
            discriminative,
            disseminative,
            dominative, *E*
            emanative, *GL*
            glutinative, *I*

PĀTIV

PLĀTIV
RĀTIV

illuminative,
imaginative,
indiscriminative, *J*
geminative,
germinative, *K*
carminative,
combinative,
contaminative,
concionative,
coordinative, *KR*
criminative, *N* native,
nominative, non-
native, *O* opionative,
originative, *PR*
predestinative, *R*
ratiocinative,
recriminative,
ruminative, *S*
subordinative, *T*
terminative, *U*
unimaginative
anticipative,
participative
contemplative
A agglomerative,
accelerative,
alliterative,
ameliorative, *D*
degenerative,
decorative,
deliberative,
desiderative,
deteriorative, *E*
edulcorative,
exaggerative,
exhilarative,
exonerative,
elaborative,
enumerative,
evaporative, *F*
federative, figurative,
I incorporative,
inoperative,
invigorative, iterative,
J generative, *K*
commemorative,
commiserative,
confederative,
cooperative,
corporative,
corroborative, *L*
lacerative,
noncooperative, *O*
alterative, operative,
P perforative,
pignorative,
postoperative, *R*
refrigerative,
reiterative,
regenerative,
remunerative,
reverberative, *S*

TĀTIV
separative,
suppurative, *U*
ulcerative,
unremunerative, *V*
vituperative,
vulnerative
A agitative, *F*
facultative, *GR*
gravitative, *H*
hesitative, *I* imitative,
inhabitative,
incognitative,
interpretative,
irritative, *K*
cogitative,
commutative,
consultative, *KW*
qualitative,
quantitative, *L*
limitative, *M*
meditative, *N*
necessitative, *O*
authoritative, *PR*
premeditative, *R*
resuscitative, *V*
vegetative

TRĀTIV
administrative,
frustrative,
illustrative,
impenetrative,
ministrative,
penetrative

VĀTIV
innovative

ĀTL

(See **ĀTAL**)

ATL

ATL	Quetzalcoatl, Seattle
BATL	battel, battle, embattle
BRATL	brattle
CHATL	chattel
PRATL	prattle
RATL	death rattle, rattle
TATL	tattle, tittle-tattle

ÄTL

(See **OTL**)

ATLAS

ATLAS	atlas, Atlas

(See **AT**, add *-less* for approximate rhyme.)

ĀTLĒ

DĀTLĒ	sedately
GRĀTLĒ	greatly
LĀTLĒ	lately, oblately, prolately
NĀTLĒ	innately, ornately
STRĀTLĒ	straightly, straitly
STĀTLĒ	stately, unstately
TĀTLĒ	*dentately,* precipitately

(For words ending in *-ately* with the primary accent on an earlier syllable, see **ITLĒ**.)

ATLĒ

ATLĒ	atle
LATLĒ	philately

(See **AT**, add *-ly* where appropriate.)

ATLER

BATLER	battler
PRATLER	prattler
RATLER	rattler
TATLER	tattler, Tatler

ĀTLES

(See **ĀT**, add *-less* where appropriate.)

ATLES

(See **AT**, add *-less* where appropriate.)

ATLING

BATLING	batling, battling
FATLING	fatling
GATLING	gatling
KATLING	catling
PRATLING	prattling
RATLING	rattling
TATLING	tattling

ĀTMENT

BĀTMENT	abatement, rebatement
FRĀTMENT	affreightment
STĀTMENT	instatement, overstatement, reinstatement, statement, understatement

ĀTNES

DĀTNES	sedateness
GRĀTNES	greatness
LĀTNĒS	lateness, oblateness
NĀTNES	innateness, ornateness
RĀTNES	irateness
STRĀTNES	straightness, straitness

ATNES

FATNES	fatness
FLATNES	flatness
PATNES	patness

ĀTŌ

BĀTŌ	cabatoe
KĀTŌ	Cato
MĀTŌ	pomato, tomato
NĀTŌ	NATO
PLĀTŌ	Plato
TĀTŌ	potato

ATŌ

BATŌ	*bateau*
GATŌ	*gateau*
LATŌ	mulatto
PLATŌ	plateau
SHATŌ	*chateau*

ÄTŌ

BÄTŌ	rebato, rubato
BRÄTŌ	vibrato
DÄTŌ	dato, datto
GÄTŌ	arigato, fugato, legato, obbligato, sfogato
KÄTŌ	marcato, pizzicato, spiccato, staccato
LÄTŌ	isolato
MÄTŌ	pomato, sfumato, tomato
NÄTO	annatto, appassionato, ostinato, passionato
RÄTŌ	barato, disperato, enamorato, inamorato, literato, moderato
TÄTŌ	allentato
TRÄTŌ	castrato, ritratto
SHÄTŌ	*chateau*

(See **OTŌ**)

ĀTON

(See **ĀTEN**)

ĀTOR

(See ĀTER)

ÄTRA

MÄTRA   matra
NÄTRA   Sinatra

ĀTRES

RĀTRES   *oratress*
TĀTRES   dictatress, imitatress,
              spectatress
TRĀTRES   traitress
WĀTRES   waitress

ATRES

LATRES   mulattress
MATRES   mattress

ATRIK

ATRIK   physiatric, hippiatric,
              iatric, geriatric,
              kinesiatric, pediatric,
              psychiatric, theatric
MATRIK   matric
PATRIK   allopatric, St. Patrick,
              sympatric

ĀTRIKS

ĀTRIKS   aviatrix, bariatrics,
              physiatrix,
              impropriatrix
DĀTRIKS   fundatrix
KĀTRIKS   indicatrix, cicatrix
LĀTRIKS   Bellatrix, legislatrix,
              osculatrix
MĀTRIKS   matrix
NĀTRIKS   gubernatrix,
              nominatrix
PĀTRIKS   patrix
RĀTRIKS   generatrics,
              quadratrix, separatrix
SĀTRIKS   rixatrix
TĀTRIKS   dictatrix, imitatrix,
              spectatrix, testatrix
TRĀTRIKS   administratrix

ATRIKS

ATRIKS   bariatrics,
              phoniatrics,
              geriatrics, mediatrics,

pediatrics, cyniatrics,
theatrics, zoiatrics
MATRIKS   matrix
PATRIKS   St. Patrick's

ĀTSĒ

NĀTSĒ   Nazi
RĀTSĒ   paparazzi

(See OTSĒ)

ĀTRUN

MĀTRUN   matron
NĀTRUN   natron, salnatron
PĀTRUN   patron

ĀTUM

ĀTUM   seriatum
DĀTUM   datum
LĀTUM   mentholatum,
              petrolatum,
              postulatum, relatum
MĀTUM   pomatum, ultimatum
RĀTUM   ageratum,
              desideratum, erratum,
              quadratum
STRĀTUM   stratum, substratum,
              superstratum
TĀTUM   capitatum, testatum

ATUM

ATUM   atom
DATUM   datum
STRATUM   stratum

ĀTŪR

(See ĀCHER)

ĀTUS

ĀTUS   beatus, hiatus, meatus
FLĀTUS   afflatus, flatus,
              inflatus
LĀTUS   latus
NĀTUS   antenatus, conatus,
              postnatus, senatus
RĀTUS   apparatus, quadratus,
              literatus, saleratus
STĀTUS   status
STRĀTUS   altostratus,
              cumulostratus,
              nimbostratus,

cirrostratus, stratous,
stratus
TĀTUS   comitatus

ĀTWĀ

GĀTWĀ   gateway
STĀTWĀ   stateway
STRĀTWĀ   straightway

ĀUN

(See ĀAN)

ÄVA

BRÄVA   brava
GWÄVA   guava
JÄVA   Java
KÄVA   kava, kavakava
KLÄVA   balaclava
LÄVA   lava, lava-lava
SÄVA   cassava, piassava
TÄVA   ottava

ĀVĒ

ĀVĒ   ave, Ave
DĀVĒ   affidavy, Mahadevi
GĀVĒ   agave
GRĀVĒ   gravy
KĀVĒ   cave, cavie, cavy,
              peccavi
NĀVĒ   navy
PĀVĒ   pavy
SLĀVĒ   slavy
WĀVĒ   wavy

AVĒ

NAVĒ   navvy
SAVĒ   savvy

ÄVĒ

ÄVĒ   Ave
GRÄVĒ   grave
HÄVĒ   Mojave
KÄVĒ   Kavi, peccavi
TÄVĒ   Rikki-tiki-tavi

ĀVEL

ĀVEL   aval
GĀVEL   gavel
NĀVEL   naval, navel
TĀVEL   octaval

AVEL

GAVEL	gavel
GRAVEL	gravel
KAVEL	cavil
RAVEL	ravel, unravel
TAVEL	tavell
TRAVEL	travel

AVELD

(See **AVEL,** add -ed where appropriate.)

ĀVEN

ĀVEN	Avon
GRĀVEN	engraven, graven
HĀVEN	haven, New Haven
KRĀVEN	craven
MĀVEN	maven, mavin
RĀVEN	raven
SHĀVEN	cleanshaven, shaven

AVEN

RAVEN	raven
SPAVEN	spavin

AVEND

RAVEND	ravened
SPAVEND	spavined

AVENZ

AVENZ	avens
RAVENZ	ravens

ĀVER

BRĀVER	braver
DĀVER	cadaver
FĀVER	disfavor, favor
FLĀVER	flavor, overflavor, underflavor
GRĀVER	engraver, graver
HĀVER	haver
KLĀVER	claver, clishmaclaver
KRĀVER	craver
KWĀVER	demiquaver, demisemiquaver, hemidemisemiquaver, quasihemidemisemiquaver, quaver, semiquaver
LĀVER	laver, lavor
PĀVER	paver
PRĀVER	depraver
RĀVER	raver
SĀVER	lifesaver, saver, savor, timesaver
SHĀVER	shaver
SLĀVER	enslaver, slaver
SWĀVER	suaver
WĀVER	waiver, waver

AVER

DAVER	cadaver
HAVER	haver
KLAVER	claver
LAVER	palaver
SLAVER	beslaver, slaver

ÄVER

HÄVER	halver
KÄVER	calver
LÄVER	palaver
SÄVER	salver
SWÄVER	suaver

ĀVERD

FĀVERD	favored, ill-favored, well-favored
FLĀVERD	flavored, unflavored
KWĀVERD	quavered
SĀVERD	savored
WĀVERD	wavered

AVERN

KAVERN	cavern
TAVERN	tavern

AVID

AVID	avid
GRAVID	gravid
PAVID	impavid, pavid

AVIJ

LAVIJ	lavage
RAVIJ	ravage
SAVIJ	savage
SKAVIJ	scavage

AVIK

GRAVIK	gravic
SLAVIK	Slavic, panslavic, Yugoslavic
TAVIK	atavic

AVIN

SAVIN	savin
SPAVIN	spavin

ĀVING

(See **ĀV,** add -ing where appropriate.)

ĀVING

ĀVING	halving
KĀVING	calving
SĀVING	salving

ĀVIS

ĀVIS	rara avis
KLĀVIS	clavis
PĀVIS	pavis

ĀVISH

BRĀVISH	bravish
NĀVISH	knavish
SLĀVISH	slavish

I HAVE A LITTLE PHILTRUM

(The philtrum is the vertical groove in the middle of the upper lip, running to the nose.)

I have a little philtrum
    Wherein my spilltrum flows
When I am feeling illtrum
    And runny at the nose.

AVISH

LAVISH	lavish
RAVISH	enravish, ravish
SLAVISH	Slavish

ĀVIT

DĀVIT	affidavit, davit
KĀVIT	indicavit
SĀVIT	cessavit
TĀVIT	devastavit

ĀVLĒ

BRĀVLĒ	bravely
GRĀVLĒ	gravely
NĀVLĒ	knavely
SWĀVLĒ	suavely

ĀVLES

(See ĀV, add -less where appropriate.)

AVLIN

JAVLIN	javelin
RAVLIN	ravelin

AVLOK

GAVLOK	gavelock
HAVLOK	havelock

ĀVMENT

GRĀVMENT	engravement
LĀVMENT	lavement
PĀVMENT	pavement
PRĀVMENT	depravement
SLĀVMENT	enslavement

ĀVNES

BRĀVNES	braveness
GRĀVNES	graveness
SWĀVNES	suaveness

ĀVOR

(See ĀVER)

ĀVYER

GRĀVYER	photogravure, gravure, autogravure, pyrogravure
HĀVYER	behavior, havier, havior
KLĀVYER	clavier, klavier
PĀVYER	pavior
SĀVYER	savior

ĀWERD

BĀWERD	bayward
HĀWERD	hayward
WĀWERD	wayward

ĀWŌRN

DĀWŌRN	day-worn
SPRĀWŌRN	spray-worn
WĀWŌRN	wayworn

ĀYA

GLĀYA	Aglaia
NĀYA	naia
SĀYA	calisaya
ZĀYA	Isaiah

ÄYA

BÄYA	kabaya, Surabaya
LÄYA	jambalaya
MÄYA	Maia, maya, Maya
PÄYA	papaya
RÄYA	raya
SÄYA	saya

ĀYŌ

BLĀŌ	bleo
KĀYŌ	cacao, kayo, K.O.
MĀYŌ	mayo, Mayo

ÄZA

ÄZA	piazza
GÄZA	Gaza
KÄZA	caza
PLÄZA	plaza
RÄZA	tabula rasa

AZARD

(See AZERD)

ĀZĒ

BLĀZĒ	blazy
DĀZĒ	daisy, lack-a-daisy, upsy-daisy
FRĀZĒ	paraphrasy, phrasy
HĀZĒ	hazy
KRĀZĒ	crazy
LĀZĒ	lazy
MĀZĒ	mazy
PĀZĒ	Bel Paese
SLĀZĒ	sleazy
TĀZĒ	patesi

ĀZĒ

GĀZĒ	Bengasi, Benghazi, ghazi
NĀZĒ	Ashkenazi
WĀZĒ	ghawazi

AZEM

(See single A, AZM)

ĀZEN

BLĀZEN	blazon, emblazon
BRĀZEN	brazen
GLĀZEN	glazen
MĀZEN	malmaison, mezon
PĀZEN	diapason
RĀZEN	raisin

ĀZER

BLĀZER	blazer, trailblazer
FRĀZER	phraser, paraphraser
GĀZER	gazer, geyser, stargazer
GLĀZER	glazer
GRĀZER	grazer
HĀZER	hazer
KWĀZER	quasar
LĀZER	laser, lazer
MĀZER	maser, mazer
PRĀZER	appraiser, disappraiser, dispraiser, praiser
RĀZER	raiser, raser, razer, razor, upraiser

HAZERD

HAZERD	haphazard, hazard
MAZERD	mazard, mazzard

ĀZHA

ĀZHA	Asia
BĀZHA	abasia
FĀZHA	aphasia
FRĀZHA	paraphrasia
GĀZHA	ergasia
KRĀZHA	acrasia
LĀZHA	Australasia
MĀZHA	paronomasia
NĀZHA	gymnasia
PLĀZHA	aplasia
RĀZHA	Eurasia

TĀZHA Anastasia, astasia, fantasia

(See **ĀSHA**)

ĀZHAL

(See **Ā'ZI.AL**)

ĀZHER

ĀZHER   azure
BRĀZHER   brazier, embrasure
GLĀZHER   glazier
GRĀZHER   grazier
RĀZHER   erasure, razure

ÄZHING

FLÄZHING camouflaging, persiflaging
RÄZHING   barraging, garaging

ĀZHUN

ĀZHUN   Asian
BRĀZHUN   abrasion
KĀZHUN   Caucasian, occasion
KWĀZHUN   equation
PĀZHUN   upasian
RĀZHUN   erasion, Eurasian
SWĀZHUN   dissuasion, persuasion, suasion
VĀZHUN   evasion, invasion, pervasion

(See **Ā'ZI.AN**)

ĀZING

(See **ĀZ**, add -ing where appropriate.)

AZING

JAZING   jazzing
RAZING   razzing
TAZING   razzmatazzing

ĀZL

FRĀZL   frazil
HĀZL   hazel
NĀZL   nasal
PRĀZL   appraisal, reappraisal
ZĀZL   Azazel

AZL

BAZL   basil
DAZL   bedazzle, dazzle, razzledazzle
FRAZL   frazzle
GAZL   gazel

ĀZIN

(See **ĀZEN**)

ĀZING

(See **ĀZ**, add -ing where appropriate.)

ĀZLES

(See **ĀZ**, add -less where appropriate.)

AZMA

AZMA   asthma, miasma
FAZMA   phasma
PLAZMA   plasma, protoplasma
TAZMA   phantasma

AZMAL

AZMAL   miasmal
KAZMAL   chasmal
PLAZMAL   protoplasmal
TAZMAL   phantasmal

ĀZMENT

MĀZMENT   amazement
PRĀZMENT appraisement, praisement

AZMIK

AZMIK   miasmic
KAZMIK   chasmic
PLAZMIK   bioplasmic, plasmic, protoplasmic
RAZMIK   marasmic
SPAZMIK   spasmic
TAZMIK   phantasmic

ĀZON, ĀZUN

(See **ĀZEN**)

ĒA

ĒA   Aeaea
BĒA   dahabeah, obeah, rebia
CHĒA   Kampuchea
DĒA   badia, edea, idea, Judea, Chaldea, Medea
FĒA   kaffiyeh, ratafia
GRĒA   sangria
HĒA   Bahia, hia, ohia
JĒA   energia, Hygeia, eugea
KĒA   chia, quia-quia, latakia, pilikia
LĒA   abulia, dulia
MĒA   Crimea
NĒA   bromopnea, dyspnea, Dulcinea, eupnea hyperpnea
PĒA   pharmacopeia, Cassiopeia, melopoeia, onomatopoeia, pathopoeia, prosopopoeia, Tarpeia
RĒA   acoria, Ave Maria, diarrhea, galeria, gonorrhea, chorea, Korea, logorrhea, opisthoporeia, pyorrhea, rea, rhea, spirea, Spiraea
SĒA   Boadicea, Laodicea, panacea
TĒA   galatea, Galatea, callisteia, peripeteia, tortilla, zaptiah
THĒA   althea, barathea
TRĒA   aischrolatreia, Astraea
VĒA   tritavia, via
ZĒA   fantasia, Hosea, zea

ĒAL

DĒAL   beau ideal, ideal, unideal
FĒAL   feal, pheal
JĒAL   epigeal, pharyngeal, hypogeal, laryngeal, meningeal, perigeal
NĒAL   hymeneal
RĒAL   empyreal, correal, real, unreal

ĒAN

ĒAN   Aeaean, aeon, Behan, amoebean,

	antipodean,
	Jacobean, Caribbean,
	Maccabean,
	Niobean, plebeian,
	Sabaean, scarabaean
BLĒAN	Hyblaean
DĒAN	Andean, antipodean,
	Archimedean,
	Assidean, Hebridean,
	Judean, Chaldean,
	Pandean, Shandean
FĒAN	nymphean, Orphean,
	Sisyphean
JĒAN	Aegean, amphigean,
	apogean, Argean,
	epigean, phalangean,
	pharyngean,
	Hygeian, Augean,
	perigean
KĒAN	Achaean, ditrochean,
	Manichaean,
	trachean, trochean
KLĒAN	Sophoclean
LĒAN	Achillean, Antillean,
	Galilean, Herculean,
	leguleian, lien,
	mausolean,
	Mephistophelean,
	Ponce de Leon,
	spelean, Zoilean
MĒAN	Anomoean,
	Cadmean, Crimean,
	Nemean
NĒAN	Adonean, Etnean,
	Hasmonaean,
	hymenean, Linnaean,
	Pyrenean
PĒAN	Indo-European,
	paean, pampean,
	Parthenopean, peon,
	priapean, cyclopean,
	tempean, European
PRĒAN	Cyprean
RĒAN	Berean, empyrean,
	epicurean, *Iberian,*
	Korean, Pythagorean,
	terpsichorean
SĒAN	Pharisean, colossean,
	Laodicean, lyncean,
	Medicean, Odyssean,
	Sadducean, Circean,
	Tennesseean,
	theodicean
TĒAN	adamantean, antaean,
	Dantean, Atlantean,
	gigantean, protean
THĒAN	lethean, Pantheian,
	pantheon
TRĒAN	astraean, Eritrean,
	petrean

(See **ĒON**)

ĒAS

(See **ĒUS**)

ĒBA

ĒBA	iba
MĒBA	amoeba, entamoeba
PĒBA	peba
RĒBA	tireba, zareba
SHĒBA	Bathsheba, Sheba

ĒBAN

MĒBAN	amoeban
SHĒBAN	Sheban
THĒBAN	Theban

ĒBĒ

FĒBĒ	Phoebe
FRĒBĒ	freebie
HĒBĒ	Hebe
JĒBĒ	heebie-jeebie
SĒBĒ	Seabee

EBĒ

BLEBĒ	blebby
DEBĒ	debby
PLEBĒ	plebby
TEBĒ	Entebbe
WEBĒ	cobwebby, webby

EBER

EBER	ebber
WEBER	cobwebber, webber

EBING

EBING	ebbing, unebbing
WEBING	cobwebbing,
	webbing

EBISH

DEBISH	debbish
NEBISH	nebbish

EBL

DEBL	debile
PEBL	pebble

REBL	arch-rebel, rebel
TREBL	treble

EBLĒ

PEBLĒ	pebbly
TREBLĒ	trebly

ĒBŌ

ĒBŌ	Ibo, eboe
NĒBŌ	Nebo
SĒBŌ	placebo
ZĒBŌ	gazebo

ĒBŌRD

FRĒBŌRD	freeboard
KĒBORD	keyboard
SĒBŌRD	seaboard

ĒBÔRN

FRĒBÔRN	freeborn
SĒBÔRN	sea-born, sea-borne

ĒBRA

LĒBRA	cuba libra, libra
ZĒBRA	zebra

ĒBRAL

FĒBRAL	antifebrile, febrile
RĒBRAL	acerebral, cerebral

ĒBUS

FĒBUS	ephebus, Phoebus
GLĒBUS	glebous
RĒBUS	rebus

ĒCHĒ

BĒCHĒ	beachy, beechy
BLĒCHĒ	bleachy, bleechy
BRĒCHĒ	breachy
KWĒCHĒ	queachy
LĒCHĒ	leachy, leechy, litchi
MĒCHĒ	meechy
PĒCHĒ	campeche,
	campeachy, peachy
PRĒCHĒ	preachy
RĒCHĒ	reachy, reechy

SKRĒCHĒ	screechy
SLĒCHĒ	sleechy
SPĒCHĒ	speechy
TĒCHĒ	teachy
YĒCHĒ	yeechy

ECHĒ

FECHĒ	fetchy
SKECHĒ	sketchy
STRECHĒ	stretchy
TECHĒ	tetchy
VECHĒ	vetchy

ĒCHER

BĒCHER	beacher
BLĒCHER	bleacher
FĒCHER	defeature, feature
KRĒCHER	creature
LĒCHER	leacher, leecher
MĒCHER	meecher
PĒCHER	impeacher, peacher
PRĒCHER	preacher
RĒCHER	forereacher, overreacher, reacher
SĒCHER	beseecher
SKRĒCHER	screecher
SPĒCHER	free speecher
TĒCHER	gym teacher, schoolteacher, teacher

ECHER

ECHER	etcher
FECHER	fetcher
FLECHER	fletcher
KWECHER	quetcher
LECHER	lecher
SKECHER	sketcher
STRECHER	stretcher

ĒCHING

(See ĒCH, add -ing where appropriate.)

ECHING

(See ECH, add -ing where appropriate.)

ĒCHLES

(See ĒCH, add -less where appropriate.)

ĒCHMENT

PĒCHMENT	appeachment, impeachment
PRĒCHMENT	preachment
SĒCHMENT	beseechment

ĒDĀ

BĒDĀ	bidet
DĒDĀ	D-day
FĒDĀ	fee-day
VĒDĀ	V-day

ĒDA

ĒDA	Aida, Ouida
DRĒDA	olla-podrida
LĒDA	Leda
MĒDA	alameda, Alameda, Meda
SĒDA	kasida, quasida, reseda
VĒDA	Veda, vida

ĒDAL

(See ĒDL)

ĒDĒ

BĒDĒ	beady, bidet
DĒDĒ	deedy, indeedy
GRĒDĒ	greedy
HĒDĒ	heedy, unheedy
KRĒDĒ	creedy
MĒDĒ	mide, *Midi*
NĒDĒ	needy, unneedy
PĒDĒ	orthopedy
RĒDĒ	reedy
SĒDĒ	C.D., cedi, seedy, sidi
SPĒDĒ	speedy, unspeedy
TWĒDĒ	tweedy, untweedy
WĒDĒ	seaweedy, weedy

EDĒ

EDĒ	eddy
BEDĒ	beddy
BREDĒ	bready
HEDĒ	heady
LEDĒ	leady
NEDĒ	neddy
REDĒ	already, ready, reddy, unready
SHREDĒ	shreddy
STEDĒ	steady, unsteady
TEDĒ	teddy
THREDĒ	thready

ĒDED

(See ĒD, add -ed where appropriate.)

EDED

LEDED	leaded, non-leaded, unleaded

(See ED, add -ed or -ded where appropriate.)

ĒDEN

ĒDEN	Eden
RĒDEN	reeden
SWĒDEN	Sweden

EDEN

DEDEN	deaden
GEDEN	Armageddon
LEDEN	leaden
REDEN	redden
THREDEN	threaden

ĒDENS

KRĒDENS	credence
KWĒDENS	outrecuidance
PĒDENS	impedance
SĒDENS	antecedence, antecedents, intercedence, concedence, precedence, recedence, retrocedence, supersedence

ĒDENT

(See ĒDNT)

ĒDĒP

NĒDĒP	kneedeep
SĒDĒP	seadeep

ĒDER

BĒDER	beader
BLĒDER	bleeder
BRĒDER	breeder, cattlebreeder, stockbreeder

LĒDER

LĒDER	bandleader, cheerleader, leader ringleader
PLĒDER	interpleader, pleader
RĒDER	lipreader, reader, proofreader, scripture-reader
SĒDER	cedar, ceder, seeder

(See ĒD, add -er where appropriate.)

EDER

EDER	edder
BEDER	bedder, embedder
CHEDER	cheddar
DEDER	deader
DREDER	dreader
HEDER	beheader, doubleheader, header, triple-header
NEDER	nedder
REDER	redder
SHEDER	shedder
SHREDER	shredder
SLEDER	sledder
SPREADER	spreader
STEDER	homesteader
TEDER	tedder
THREDER	threader, unthreader
TREDER	retreader, treader
WEDER	wedder

ĒDFUL

DĒDFUL	deedful
HĒDFUL	heedful, unheedful
MĒDFUL	meadful, meedful
NĒDFUL	needful, unneedful
SĒDFUL	seedful
SPĒDFUL	speedful

ĒDGRŌN

RĒDGRŌN	reedgrown
SĒDGRŌN	seedgrown
WĒDGRŌN	weedgrown

EDHED

DEDHED	deadhead
REDHED	redhead

EDHĒT

DEDHĒT	dead-heat
REDHĒT	red-heat

EDĪ

DEDĪ	dead-eye
REDĪ	red-eye

ĒDIK

ĒDIK	logaoedic
MĒDIK	comedic
PĒDIK	encyclopedic, orthopedic, cyclopedic, talipedic
VĒDIK	Vedic

ĒDING

(See ĒD, add -ing where appropriate.)

EDING

(See ED, add -ing or -ding where appropriate.)

EDISH

EDISH	eddish
BEDISH	beddish
BREDISH	breadish
DEDISH	deadish
REDISH	reddish

EDIT

EDIT	edit, re-edit, sub-edit
KREDIT	accredit, disaccredit, discredit, credit, miscredit, Eurocredit

ĒDL

BĒDL	beadle
DĒDL	daedal, dedal
HWĒDL	wheedle
KWĒDL	conquedle
NĒDL	needle
PĒDAL	equipedal, millipedal, centipedal, solipedal
TWĒDL	tweedle

EDL

HEDL	heddle
MEDL	intermeddle, medal, meddle
PEDL	bipedal, semipedal

EDL (cont.)

REDL	reddle
TREDL	treadle
WEDL	wedel

EDLAND

HEDLAND	headland
ZEDLAND	zedland

EDLĒ

DEDLĒ	deadly
MEDLĒ	medley
REDLĒ	redly

ĒDLER

HWĒDLER	wheedler
NĒDLER	needler

EDLER

HEDLER	heddler
MEDLER	intermeddler, meddler, medlar
REDLER	reddler
TREDLER	treadler

ĒDLES

(See ĒD, add -less where appropriate.)

EDLES

(See ED, add -less where appropriate.)

EDLĪN

BREDLĪN	breadline
DEDLĪN	deadline
HEDLĪN	headline

ĒDLING

HWĒDLING	wheedling
NĒDLING	needling
RĒDLING	reedling
SĒDLING	seedling

EDLING

HEDLING	heddling
MEDLING	intermeddling, meddling
PEDLING	peddling

| REDLING | reddling |
| TREDLING | treadling |

EDLĪT

DEDLĪT	deadlight
HEDLĪT	headlight
REDLĪT	redlight

EDLOK

DEDLOK	deadlock
HEDLOK	headlock
KEDLOK	kedlock
WEDLOK	wedlock

ĒDMAN

| FRĒDMAN | freedman |
| SĒDMAN | seedman |

EDMAN

DEDMAN	deadman
HEDMAN	headman
REDMAN	redman

ĒDNT

KRĒDNT	credent
NĒDNT	needn't
SĒDNT	antecedent, decedent, intercedent, precedent, recedent, cedent

ĒDŌ

ĒDŌ	Aido, Ido
BĒDŌ	albedo, libido
KRĒDŌ	credo
LĒDŌ	Lido, Toledo
PĒDŌ	stampedo, torpedo
RĒDŌ	Laredo, teredo
VĒDŌ	gravedo

EDŌ

| EDŌ | eddo |
| MEDŌ | meadow |

EDON

| DEDON | dead-on |
| HEDON | head-on |

ĒDRA

| SĒDRA | exedra |
| THĒDRA | ex cathedra, cathedra |

ĒDRAL

| HĒDRAL | anhedral, decahedral, didocahedral, dihedral, hemihedral, orthotetrakal-dekahedral, polyhedral, rhombohedral, rhombicosidodedecah-edral, pseudorhombicuboctah-edral, trihedral |
| THĒDRAL | cathedral, procathedral |

EDREST

| BEDREST | bedrest |
| HEDREST | headrest |

ĒDRIK

| DĒDRIK | diedric |
| HĒDRIK | holohedric, polyhedric |

ĒDRON

| HĒDRON | dihedron, orthotetrakal-dekahedron, polyhedron, rhombohedron, rhombicosidodedeca-hedron, pseudorhombicubocta-hedron, trihedron |
| SĒDRON | cedron |

ĒDTĪM

| FĒDTĪM | feedtime |
| SĒDTĪM | seedtime |

ĒDUM

FRĒDUM	freedom
LĒDUM	ledum
PĒDUM	pedum

REFLECTION

The rich eat steak,
  The poor eat humbles;
That's the way
  The cooky crumbles.

EDWOOD

| DEDWOOD | deadwood |
| REDWOOD | redwood |

ĒDZMAN

| BĒDZMAN | beadsman, bedesman |
| SĒDZMAN | seedsman |

ĒER

FĒER	feer, fere
FLĒER	fleer
FRĒER	freer
GRĒER	agreer, disagreer
KRĒER	decreer
SĒER	*foreseer,* overseer, seer, sightseer

(See ÎR)

ĒFDUM

| CHĒFDUM | chiefdom |
| FĒFDUM | fiefdom |

ĒFE

BĒFĒ	beefy
LĒFĒ	leafy
RĒFĒ	reefy
SHĒFĒ	sheafy

ĒFER

BĒFER	beefer
BRĒFER	briefer
CHĒFER	chiefer
FĒFĒR	feoffer
LĒFER	leafer, liefer
RĒFER	reefer

EFER

DEFER	deafer
FEFER	feoffer, hasenpfeffer
HEFER	heifer
ZEFER	zephyr

EFIK

LEFIK	malefic
NEFIK	benefic
SEFIK	isopsephic
STREFIK	peristrephic

ĒFLĒ

BRĒFLĒ	briefly
CHĒFLĒ	chiefly

ĒFLES

(See **ĒF**, add -less where appropriate.)

ĒFOUL

PĒFOUL	peafowl
SĒFOUL	seafowl

EFTĒ

HEFTĒ	hefty
KEFTĒ	Kefti
LEFTĒ	lefty

EFTLĒ

DEFTLĒ	deftly
REFTLĒ	bereftly

ĒGA

DĒGA	bodega
MĒGA	omega
RĒGA	Riga
VĒGA	Vega
ZĒGA	ziega

ĒGAL

(See **ĒGL**)

EGĒ

EGĒ	eggy
DREGĒ	dreggy
KEGĒ	keggy
LEGĒ	leggy
PEGĒ	peggy
REGĒ	reggae
SEGĒ	seggy

ĒGER

ĒGER	eager, eagre, overeager
LĒGER	beleaguer, big-leaguer, leaguer, little-leaguer, major-leaguer, minor-leaguer
MĒGER	meager, meagre
TĒGER	fatiguer
TRĒGER	intriguer
ZĒGER	zieger

EGER

EGER	egger
BEGER	beggar, begger
LEGER	booklegger, bootlegger, legger
PEGER	pegger
SEGER	seggar, segger
SKEGER	skegger

EGERZ

PREGERZ	preggers

(See **EGER**, add -s where appropriate.)

ĒGING

LĒGING	enleaguing, leaguing
TĒGING	fatiguing
TRĒGING	intriguing

EGING

LEGING	bootlegging, legging

(See **EG**, add -ging where appropriate.)

ĒGL

ĒGL	bald eagle, double eagle, eagle, golden eagle, harpy eagle, sea eagle
BĒGL	beagle, porbeagle
GRĒGL	gregal
KLĒGL	kleagle
LĒGL	illegal, legal, paralegal
RĒGL	regal, vice-regal
SĒGL	seagull
TĒGL	teagle
VĒGL	inveigle

ĒGLER

BĒGLER	beagler
VĒGLER	inveigler

EGMEN

LEGMEN	legmen
TEGMEN	tegmen

EGNANT

PREGNANT	impregnant, pregnant
REGNANT	queen-regnant, regnant

ĒGŌ

ĒGŌ	ego, alter ego, superego
GRĒGŌ	grego
JĒGO	gigot
MĒGŌ	amigo
WĒGŌ	Oswego

ĒGRĒN

PĒGRĒN	pea-green
SĒGRĒN	sea-green

ĒGRES

ĒGRES	egress
NĒGRES	Negress
RĒGRES	regress

ĒHĒ

HĒHĒ	heehee
RĒHĒ	bahuvrihi
TĒHĒ	teehee

ĒHŌL

KĒHŌL	keyhole
NĒHŌL	kneehole

ĒIK

ĒIK	caffeic, choreic
LĒIK	oleic
PĒIK	mythopoeic, onomatopoeic, tropeic

RĒIK   diarrheic
SĒIK   caseic
TĒIK   proteic,
               xanthroproteic

ĒIN

DĒIN   codein
FĒIN   caffeine
ZĒIN   zein

ĒING

BĒING   being, inbeing,
               nonbeing, well-being
SĒING   farseeing, foreseeing,
               clear-seeing,
               overseeing, seeing,
               sightseeing,
               unforeseeing,
               unseeing

(See **Ē**, add -ing where appropriate.)

ĒIST

DĒIST   deist, ideist
KĒIST   Manicheist
THĒIST   antitheist, hylotheist,
               monotheist,
               polytheist, theist
ZĒIST   zeist

ĒIZM

DĒIZM   deism
KĒIZM   Manicheism
SĒIZM   Phariseeism,
               Parseeism,
               Sadduceeism
TĒIZM   absenteeism,
               Sutteeism
THĒIZM   A antitheism,
               atheism, F
               philotheism, H
               henotheism,
               hylotheism, K
               cosmotheism, M
               McCarthyism,
               misotheism, O
               autotheism, P
               polytheism, S
               schiotheism, TH
               theism
WĒIZM   we-ism

EJBURD

HEJBURD   hedgebird
SEJBURD   sedgebird

ĒJĒ

FĒJĒ   Fiji
JĒJĒ   Gigi
SKWĒJĒ   squeegee

EJĒ

EJĒ   edgy
HEJĒ   hedgy
KLEJĒ   cledgy
LEJĒ   ledgy
SEJĒ   sedgy
WEJĒ   wedgy

EJER

EJER   edger
DREJER   dredger
HEJER   hedger
KEJER   kedger
LEJER   alleger, ledger, leger
PLEJER   pledger, repledger
SLEJER   sledger

ĒJIK

PĒJIK   bibliopegic
PLĒJIK   hemiplegic,
               quadriplegic,
               paraplegic, cycoplegic
TĒJIK   strategic

EJING

(See **EJ**, add -ing where appropriate.)

ĒJIT

LĒJIT   college
MĒJIT   immediate

EJLING

FLEJLING   fledgling
HEJLING   hedgling

EJŌ

FEJŌ   solfeggio
PEJŌ   arpeggio

ĒJOO

ĒJOO   ejoo
BĒJOO   bijou

ĒJUN

LĒJUN   collegian, legion
RĒJUN   region, subregion,
               underregion
WĒJUN   Glaswegian,
               Norwegian,
               Sou'wegian

(See **Ē'JI.AN**)

ĒJUS

ĒJUS   aegis, egis
GRĒJUS   egregious
LĒJUS   sacrilegious

ĒKA

BĒKA   sabeca
KĒKA   quica
NĒKA   Dominica
PĒKA   Topeka
PRĒKA   paprika
RĒKA   Costa Rica, eureka,
               Eureka
SĒKA   sika
SPĒKA   spica, Spica
THĒKA   bibliotheca,
               endotheca,
               glyptotheca,
               lipsanotheca,
               pinacotheca, theca
WĒKA   weka
YĒKA   Tanganyika

EKA

EKA   Ecca, ekka
BEKA   Rebecca
MEKA   Mecca

ĒKAL

FĒKAL   faecal, fecal
KĒKAL   caecal
THĒKAL   bibliothecal,
               intrathecal, thecal
TRĒKAL   treacle

EKANT

(See **EKUNT**)

EKCHER

FEKCHER	confecture

ĒKĒ

FEKCHER	confecture
JEKCHER	dejecture, conjecture, projecture, subjecture
LEKCHER	belecture, lecture
TEKCHER	architecture

ĒKĒ

BĒKE	beaky
BLĒKĒ	bleaky
CHĒKĒ	cheeky, cheek-to-cheeky
FRĒKĒ	freaky
KLĒKĒ	cliquey
KRĒKĒ	creaky, creeky
LĒKĒ	cockaleeky, leaky, leeky
PĒKĒ	peaky, peeky
RĒKĒ	reeky
SĒKE	hide-and-seeky
SHĒKĒ	dashiki, sheiky
SHRĒKĒ	shrieky
SKWĒKĒ	squeaky
SLĒKĒ	sleeky
SNĒKE	sneaky
STRĒKĒ	streaky
TĒKĒ	batiky, teaky, tiki
VĒKĒ	Bolsheviki, Mensheviki
WĒKĒ	veni, vidi, vici

EKĒ

CHEKĒ	checky
FLEKĒ	flecky
KEKĒ	kecky
PEKĒ	pecky
REKĒ	wrecky, shipwrecky
SPEKĒ	specky

ĒKEN

BĒKEN	beacon
BLĒKEN	bleaken
DĒKEN	archdeacon, deacon
HĒKEN	Mohican
MĒKEN	meeken
SLĒKEN	sleeken
WĒKEN	weaken

EKEN

(See EKUN)

ĒKER

BĒKER	beaker
BLĒKER	bleaker
CHĒKER	cheeker
KRĒKER	creaker, krieker
LĒKER	leaker, obliquer
MĒKER	meeker
PĒKER	peeker
RĒKER	reeker
SĒKER	seeker, self-seeker
SHĒKER	chicer
SHRĒKER	shrieker
SKWĒKER	squeaker
SLĒKER	sleeker
SNĒKER	sneaker
SPĒKER	bespeaker, lipspeaker, speaker, stump-speaker
STRĒKER	streaker
TWĒKER	tweaker
WĒKER	weaker

EKER

CHEKER	checker, chequer, exchequer, rechecker
DEKER	bedecker, decker, double-decker, two-decker, three-decker
FLEKER	flecker
NEKER	necker, Dominecker
PEKER	henpecker, oxpecker, pecker, woodpecker
REKER	wrecker
SNEKER	snecker
TREKER	trekker, voortrekker

EKERD

CHEKERD	checkered
REKERD	record

EKERZ

CHEKERZ	checkers

(See EKER, add *s* where appropriate.)

ĒKĪD

LĒKĪD	oblique-eyed
MĒKĪD	meek-eyed
WĒKĪD	weak-eyed

ĒKING

(See ĒK, add *-ing* where appropriate.)

EKING

(See EK, add *-ing* where appropriate.)

ĒKISH

(See ĒK, add *-ish* where appropriate.)

ĒKL

(See ĒKAL)

EKL

DEKL	deckel, deckle
FREKL	befreckle, freckle
HEKL	heckle
JEKL	Jekyll
KEKL	keckle
SHEKL	shekel
SPEKL	bespeckle, kenspeckle, speckle

EKLD

(See EKL, add *-ed* where appropriate.)

ĒKLĒ

BLĒKLĒ	bleakly
LĒKLĒ	obliquely
MĒKLĒ	meekly
NĒKLĒ	uniquely
SLĒKLĒ	sleekly
TRĒKLĒ	treacly
WĒKLĒ	biweekly, semiweekly, triweekly, weakly, weekly

EKLĒ

FREKLĒ	freckly
SPEKLĒ	speckly

EKLER

FREKLER	freckler
HEKLER	heckler
SPEKLER	speckler

EKLES

(See EK, add *-less* where appropriate.)

EKLING

DEKLING	deckling
FREKLING	freckling

HEKLING   heckling
KEKLING   keckling
SPEKLING   speckling

EKMĀT

CHEKMĀT   checkmate
DEKMĀT   deckmate

ĒKNES

PRĒKNES   Preakness

(See ĒK, add -ness where appropriate.)

ĒKŌ

CHĒKŌ   chico, Chico
FĒKŌ   beccafico, fico
KLĒKŌ   Cliquot
MĒKŌ   mico
NĒKŌ   Nikko
PĒKŌ   pekoe, picot, Tampico
RĒKŌ   Puerto Rico
SĒKŌ   zortzico
TĒKŌ   matico

EKŌ

EKŌ   echo, re-echo
BEKŌ   bekko
DEKŌ   art deco, dekko
GEKŌ   gecko
GREKŌ   El Greco
SEKŌ   secco

ĒKOK

MĒKOK   meacock
PĒKOK   peacock
SĒKOK   sea-cock

ĒKON

(See ĒKEN)

EKON

(See EKUN)

ĒKOUT

FRĒKOUT   freakout
SPĒKOUT   speak-out

ĒKRAB

PĒKRAB   pea-crab
SĒKRAB   sea-crab
TRĒKRAB   tree-crab

EKSAL

NEKSAL   adnexal, annexal, nexal
PLEKSAL   plexal

EKSĒ

KEKSĒ   kexy
LEKSĒ   kyriolexy
PLEKSĒ   apoplexy, cataplexy
PREKSĒ   prexy
REKSĒ   pyrexy
SEKSĒ   sexy, unsexy

EKSER

DEKSER   indexer
FLEKSER   dorsiflexer, flexer, flexor
NEKSER   annexer
PLEKSER   perplexer, plexor
SEKSER   unsexer, unisexer
VEKSER   vexer

EKSHER

FLEKSHER   deflexure, flexure, inflexure, contraflexure
PLEKSHER   plexure

EKSHUN

EKSHUN   ebriection
FEKSHUN   A affection, D defection, disaffection, disinfection, E effection, I imperfection, infection, K confection, P perfection, PR profection, R refection, reinfection
FLEKSHUN   deflection, dorsiflection, flection, flexion, inflection, genuflection, reflection, retroflexion, circumflexion
JEKSHUN   A abjection, adjection, D dejection, E ejection, I injection, insubjection, interjection, introjection, O objection, PR projection, R rejection, S subjection, TR trajection
LEKSHUN   by-election, bolection, D dilection, E election, I intellection, K collection, L lection, PR predilection, pre-election, prelection, R reelection, recollection, S selection
NEKSHUN   disconnection, connection, reconnection
PLEKSHUN   complexion
REKSHUN   direction, erection, indirection, incorrection, insurrection, correction, misdirection, piloerection, redirection, rection, resurrection
SEKSHUN   B bisection, D dissection, E exsection, H half-section, I insection, intersection, KW quarter-section, M midsection, R resection, S section, subsection, TR trisection, V venesection, vivisection
SPEKSHUN   inspection, introspection, prospection, retrospection, circumspection
TEKSHUN   detection, overprotection, protection, underprotection
VEKSHUN   advection, evection, convection, provection, circumvection, vection

EKSHUR

(See **EKSHER**)

EKSHUS

FEKSHUS	infectious
LEKSHUS	selectious

LEKSIK

LEKSIK	lexic
REKSIK	anorexic

EKSĪL

EKSĪL	exile
FLEKSĪL	flexile

EKSING

EKSING	X-ing

(See **EKS,** add -ing where appropriate.)

EKSIS

LEKSIS	catalexis, lexes, lexis
PLEKSIS	epiplexis
REKSIS	orexis
TEKSIS	lymacatexis, syntexis, Texas
THEKSIS	cathexis

(See **EKSUS**)

EKSLĒ

PLEKSLĒ	complexly
VEKSLĒ	convexly

EKSTANT

EKSTANT	extant
SEKSTANT	sextant

EKSTIL

SEXTIL	bissextile, sextile
TEKSTIL	textile

EKSTRIN

DEKSTRIN	dextrin, dextrine
TEKSTRIN	textrine

EKSTRUS

DEKSTRUS	ambidextrous, dextrous
SEKSTRUS	ambisextrous

EKSUS

NEKSUS	connexus, nexus
PLEKSUS	amplexus, complexus, plexus, solar plexus

(See **EKSIS**)

EKTAL

EKTAL	ectal
LEKTAL	dialectal
REKTAL	rectal
TEKTAL	tectal

EKTANT

FEKTANT	disinfectant, infectant
FLEKTANT	reflectant
MEKTANT	humectant
NEKTANT	annectant
PEKTANT	aspectant, expectant, inexpectant, respectant, suspectant, unexpectant
PLEKTANT	amplectant

EKTED

PLEKTED	dark-complected, complected, light-complected

(See **EKT,** add -ed where appropriate.)

EKTENT

(See **EKTANT**)

EKTER

FEKTER	affecter, defector, disaffecter, disinfecter, effecter, infecter, perfecter
FLEKTER	deflecter, flector, inflecter, genuflector, nonreflector
GLEKTER	neglecter

HEKTER	hector, Hector
JEKTER	ejecter, injecter, interjecter, objector, projector, rejecter, subjecter
LEKTER	dialector, elector, lector, collector, prelector, recollecter, selecter
NEKTER	connector, nectar
PEKTER	expecter, suspecter
REKTER	director, erector, corrector, misdirecter, rector, resurrecter
SEKTER	bisector, dissecter, prosector, vivisecter
SPEKTER	disrespecter, expecter, inspector, prospector, respecter, specter, spectre
TEKTER	detector, protector
VEKTER	bivector, convector, odorivector, vector

EKTERD

HEKTERD	hectored
SPEKTERD	spectered

EKTEST

REKTEST	directist

(See **EKT,** add -est where appropriate.)

EKTFUL

GLEKTFUL	neglectful
SPEKTFUL	disrespectful, respectful, suspectful, unrespectful, unsuspectful

EKTIK

FEKTIK	ephectic
HEKTIK	hectic
KEKTIK	cachectic
KLEKTIK	eclectic
LEKTIK	acatalectic, analectic, bracycatalectic, dialectic, dyslectic, hypercatalectic, catalectic
NEKTIK	synectic
PEKTIK	isopectic, pectic
PLEKTIK	apoplectic, epiplectic

REKTIK

REKTIK	orectic
SMEKTIK	smectic
TEKTIK	orthotectic, syntectic, eutectic
THEKTIK	cathectic

EKTIL

JEKTIL	projectile
LEKTIL	supellectile
REKTIL	erectile
SEKTIL	insectile, sectile

EKTING

(See **EKT,** add *-ing* where appropriate.)

EKTIV

FEKTIV	affective, defective, effective, imperfective, ineffective, infective, perfective, refective
FLEKTIV	deflective, inflective, irreflective, reflective
GLEKTIV	neglective
JEKTIV	ejective, injective, conjective, objective, projective, rejective, subjective, unobjective
LEKTIV	elective, intellective, collective, recollective, selective, unselective
MEKTIV	humective
NEKTIV	disconnective, connective
REKTIV	directive, erective, corrective
SEKTIV	sective
SPEKTIV	inspective, introspective, irrespective, perspective, prospective, respective, retrospective, circumspective
TEKTIV	detective, protective
VEKTIV	invective

EKTIZM

KLEKTIZM	eclectism
SEKTIZM	sectism

EKTL

(See **EKTIL**)

EKTLĒ

(See **EKT,** add *-ly* where appropriate.)

EKTNES

JEKTNES	abjectness
LEKTNES	selectness
REKTNES	directness, erectness, indirectness, incorrectness, correctness
SPEKTNES	circumspectness

EKTOR

(See **EKTER**)

EKTORD

(See **EKTERD**)

EKTRES

LEKTRES	electress, lectress
REKTRES	directress, rectress
SPEKTRES	inspectress
TEKTRES	protectress

EKTRIKS

REKTRIKS	directrix, rectrix
SEKTRIKS	bisectrics, trisectrics
TEKTRIKS	tectrix

EKTRUM

LEKTRUM	electrum
PLEKTRUM	plectrum
SPEKTRUM	spectrum

EKTUS

FEKTUS	prefectus
LEKTUS	delectus
PEKTUS	pectous, pectus
REKTUS	rectus
SPEKTUS	conspectus, prospectus

ĒKUM

MĒKUM	vade mecum
SĒKUM	caecum, cecum

EKUN

BEKUN	beckon
FLEKUN	flecken
REKUN	reckon
SHNEKEN	schnecken

EKUND

FEKUND	fecund
REKUND	reckoned
SEKUND	femtosecond, nanosecond, picosecond, second

(See **EKUN,** add *-ed* where appropriate.)

EKUNT

PEKUNT	impeccant, peccant
SEKUNT	femtosecond, nanosecond, picosecond, second

ĒKWAL

ĒKWAL	equal, inequal, coequal, unequal
PRĒKWAL	prequel
SĒKWEL	sequel

ĒKWENS

FRĒKWENS	frequence, infrequence
SĒKWENS	sequence

ĒKWENT

FRĒKWENT	frequent, infrequent
SĒKWENT	sequent

ĒLA

ĒLA	Venezuela
BĒLA	belah
DĒLA	candela
GĒLA	narghile, nargile, Weigela
HĒLA	Gila
JĒLA	Weigel
KĒLA	chela, tequila
KWĒLA	sequela
LĒLA	palila
MĒLA	Philomela

SĒLA   selah
STĒLA   stela, stele
TĒLA   tela

ELA

ELA   paella
BELA   glabella, Isabella, clarabella, mabela, rubella, tabella
BRELA   umbrella
DELA   padella, predella
FELA   fellah
GELA   Shigella
MELA   columella, lamella
NELA   fifinella, fustanella, gentianella, justanella, canella, pimpinella, prunella, salmonella, citronella, villanella
PELA   a cappella, cappella, Capella
RELA   chlorella, corella, lirella, mozzarella, Cinderella, tiarella
SELA   agacella, bonsela, doncella, micella, navicella, osella, rosella, cella, sella, varicella, vorticella
TELA   fenestella, panatella, patella, scutella, tarantella
VELA   favela, favella, novella
ZELA   rosella

ĒLAND

ĒLAND   eland
ZĒLAND   New Zealand

ELANT

JELANT   flagellant
PELANT   appellant, expellant, expellent, impellant, interpellant, propellant, repellant
VELANT   divellent, revellent

ELAR

(See **ELER**)

ELAS

(See **ELUS**)

ELĀT

BELĀT   debellate, flabellate
PELĀT   appellate, interpellate, pellate
PRELĀT   prelate
SELĀT   ocellate, cellate, varicellate
STELĀT   *constellate,* stellate
TELĀT   patellate, scutellate

ELBA

ELBA   Elba
MELBA   peach melba

ELBORN

HELBORN   hell-born
WELBORN   well-born

ELBOUND

HELBOUND   hellbound
SPELBOUND   spellbound

ELCHER

BELCHER   belcher
SKWELCHER   squelcher
WELCHER   welcher

ELCHING

BELCHING   belching
SKWELCHING   squelching
WELCHING   welching

ĒLDĒ

WĒLDĒ   unwieldy, wieldy
YĒLDĒ   yieldy

ĒLDED

(See **ĒLD**, add *-ed* where appropriate.)

ELDED

GELDED   gelded
MELDED   melded
WELDED   welded

ĒLDER

FĒLDER   fielder, infielder, outfielder
SHĒLDER   shielder
WĒLDER   wielder
YĒLDER   non-yielder, yielder

ELDER

ELDER   elder
GELDER   gelder
MELDER   melder
SKELDER   skelder
WELDER   welder

ELDEST

ELDEST   eldest

(See **ELD**, add *-est* where appropriate.)

ĒLDING

(See **ĒLD**, add *-ing* where appropriate.)

ELDING

GELDING   gelding
MELDING   melding
WELDING   welding

ELDUM

SELDUM   seldom
SWELDUM   swelldom

ĒLĒ

ĒLĒ   eely, Ely
DĒLĒ   dele
FĒLĒ   feally, feelie, feely
FRĒLĒ   freely
GRĒLĒ   Greeley
HĒLĒ   Swahili
HWĒLĒ   wheely
LĒLĒ   Lely
MĒLĒ   mealie, mealy
NĒLĒ   campanili
PĒLĒ   peele, peelee, peely, pili
SĒLĒ   seely
SKWĒLĒ   squealy
STĒLĒ   steely, stele
TĒLĒ   genteelly
VĒLĒ   jus civile, vealy

ELĒ

BELĒ	belly, gorbelly, whitebelly, casus belli, Leadbelly, potbelly, redbelly, shadbelly, slowbelly, sowbelly, tenterbelly, underbelly, yellowbelly
CHELĒ	Botticelli, vermicelli
DELĒ	deli, Delhi
FELĒ	felly
HELĒ	helly, rakehelly
JELĒ	jelly
KELĒ	kelly
MELĒ	melee
NELĒ	Nelly, nice Nelly
SELĒ	cancelli, vermicelli
SHELĒ	Shelley, shelly
SKELĒ	skelly
SMELĒ	smelly
TELĒ	tagliatelli, telly

ELĒD

BELĒD	bellied
JELĒD	*gelid,* jellied

ĒLER

ĒLER	eeler
DĒLER	dealer, double-dealer, interdealer, misdealer, New Dealer, wheeler-dealer
FĒLER	feeler
HĒLER	healer, heeler, ward heeler
HWĒLER	four-wheeler, sidewheeler, three-wheeler, two-wheeler, wheeler
JĒLER	congealer
KĒLER	keeler
NĒLER	annealer, kneeler
PĒLER	appealer, pealer, peeler, repealer
RĒLER	reeler
SĒLER	concealer, sealer, seeler
SKWĒLER	squealer
SPĒLER	spieler
STĒLER	stealer, steeler, stelar
VĒLER	revealer, vealer, velar

ELER

BELER	beller, glabellar, rebeller
DWELER	apartment dweller, dweller, house dweller, cave dweller, country dweller, city dweller
FELER	feller, Rockefeller
HELER	heller
KELER	bierkeller, Helen Keller
KWELER	queller
MELER	lamellar
NELER	kneller
PELER	*A* appellor, *D* dispeller, *E* expeller, *I* impeller, *K* compeller, *KL* cloud-compeller, *PR* propeller, propellor, *R* repeller, *SK* screw propeller, *TW* twin propeller
SELER	exceller, salt cellar, cellar, sellar, seller, underseller, wine cellar
SHELER	sheller
SMELER	smeller
SPELER	speller
STELER	interstellar, nonstellar, circumstellar, stellar
SWELER	sweller
TELER	foreteller, fortune-teller, patellar, story-teller, tale-teller, teller
WELER	weller
YELER	yeller

ELET

PELET	pellet

(See **ELĀT**)

ELFIK

DELFIK	Delphic, diadelphic, monodelphic
GELFIK	Guelphic

ELFIN

ELFIN	elfin
DELFIN	delphin, Delphin, delphine

ELFISH

ELFISH	elfish
PELFISH	pelfish
SELFISH	selfish, unselfish
SHELFISH	shellfish

ELFRĒ

BELFRĒ	belfry
PELFRĒ	pelfry

ĒLFUL

ĒLFUL	eelful
SĒLFUL	seelful
WĒLFUL	wealful
ZĒLFUL	zealful

ĒLIJ

HWĒLIJ	wheelage
KĒLIJ	keelage
STĒLIJ	stealage

ELIK

BELIK	bellic
DELIK	infidelic, psychedelic
FELIK	fellic
HELIK	parhelic
JELIK	angelic, archangelic, evangelic, superangelic, unangelic
KELIK	nickelic
MELIK	melic
PELIK	sapropelic, scalpelic
RELIK	relic
SKELIK	skelic
TELIK	Aristotelic, philatelic, heterotelic, autotelic, Pentelic, telic

ĒLIN

BĒLIN	beeline
FĒLIN	feline
MĒLIN	meline
SĒLIN	sealine

ĒLING

SĒLING	ceiling
SHĒLING	shieling
SKĒLING	skeeling

(See **ĒL,** add *-ing* where appropriate.)

ELĪNG

(See **EL**, add *-ing* where appropriate.)

ELISH

BELISH	embellish
HELISH	hellish
RELISH	disrelish, relish
SWELISH	swellish
WELISH	wellish

ELIST

CHELIST	cellist
TRELIST	trellist

ELIT

BELIT	flabellate
PELIT	appellate
PRELIT	prelate

ĒLMENT

JĒLMENT	congealment
PĒLMENT	repealment
SĒLMENT	concealment
VĒLMENT	revealment

ELMET

HELMET	helmet
PELMET	pelmet
WELMET	well-met

ELMING

HELMING	dishelming, helming, unhelming
HWELMING	overwhelming, underwhelming, whelming

ĒLNES

LĒLNES	lealness
TĒLNES	genteelness

ELNES

FELNES	fellness
SWELNES	swellness
WELNES	unwellness, wellness

ELŌ

ELŌ	Aello, duello, niello
BELŌ	bellow, sgabello
CHELŌ	cello, Monticello, violoncello
DELŌ	bordello, Sordello
FELŌ	bedfellow, felloe, fellow, good fellow, playfellow, yokefellow
HELŌ	*hello*
JELŌ	bargello, Jell-O
MELŌ	mellow, unmellow
NELŌ	prunello, Punchinello, ritornello
PELŌ	cobra de capello
RELŌ	albarello, morello, saltarello
SELŌ	choralcelo
TELŌ	brocatello, martello
THELŌ	Othello
VELŌ	scrivello
YELŌ	yellow

OBEAH AND PARENESIS CAN ASK THEIR OWN PRICE

The kind of sorcerer folks call an obeah
Is not a man you'd want to hang around;
A word from him may fill you with a phobia,
Or cast a spell that lays you underground.

He shakes his spear and utters his parenesis
(A fancy way of saying 'exhortation').
Avoid him, for his voodoos are the genesis
Of babies' boils and dying men's damnation.

(Words ending *-phobia* arrive in batches,
With only *obeah* for rhyming mix;
There's no rhyme but *parenesis* that matches
Words ending *-genesis*—some twenty-six.)

ELŌD

BELŌD	bellowed
MELŌD	mellowed, unmellowed
YELŌD	yellowed

ELON

(See **ELUN**)

ELOT

HELOT	helot
ZELOT	zealot

ELPER

HELPER	helper, self-helper
HWELPER	whelper
KELPER	kelper
YELPER	yelper

ELPING

(See **ELP**, add *-ing* where appropriate.)

ELPLES

HELPLES	helpless
HWELPLES	whelpless
KELPLES	kelpless
YELPLES	yelpless

ĒLSKIN

ĒLSKIN	eelskin
SĒLSKIN	sealskin

ELTA

DELTA	delta
PELTA	pelta
SHELTA	shelta

ĒLTĒ

FĒLTĒ	fealty
RĒLTĒ	realty

ELTED

BELTED	belted
MELTED	melted
PELTED	pelted
SMELTED	smelted
WELTED	welted

ELTER

BELTER	belter
FELTER	felter
KELTER	kelter
MELTER	melter
PELTER	pelter
SHELTER	inshelter, shelter, tax shelter
SKELTER	helter-skelter, skelter
SMELTER	smelter
SPELTER	spelter
SWELTER	swelter
WELTER	welter

ELTERD

SHELTERED   sheltered

(See **ELTER,** add *-ed* where appropriate.)

ELTHĒ

HELTHĒ	healthy, unhealthy
STELTHĒ	stealthy
WELTHĒ	unwealthy, wealthy

ELTING

(See **ELT,** add *-ing* where appropriate.)

ELTLES

(See **ELT,** add *-less* where appropriate.)

ELTRĒ

PELTRĒ	peltry
SWELTRĒ	sweltry

ELUM

BELUM	antebellum, flabellum, cribellum, labellum, postbellum, prebellum, cerebellum
FELUM	phellum
GELUM	flagellum
PELUM	pelham, Pelham
SELUM	sacellum
TELUM	haustellum, clitellum, rostellum, scutellum
VELUM	vellum

ELUN

FELUN	enfelon, felon
MELUN	melon, mushmelon, muskmelon, watermelon

ELUS

HELUS	Hellas
JELUS	jealous
PELUS	pellas
SELUS	marcellus, nucellus, ocellus, procellas, procellous

TELUS	entellus, vitellus
VELUS	vellus
ZELUS	overzealous, zealous

ELVER

(See **ELV,** add *-r* where appropriate.)

ELVING

DELVING	delving
HELVING	helving
SHELVING	shelving

ĒLYA

DĒLYLA	seguidilla
BĒLYA	lobelia
FĒLYA	alcoholophilia, epistomophilia, coprophilia, chromatophilia, melcryptovesti- mentophilia, ophelia, Ophelia, scophophilia, spasmophilia
KĒLYA	Barranquilla
MĒLYA	amelia, iatramelia, camellia, cimelia

ĒLYUN

DĒLYUN	Mendelian
FĒLYUN	ephelion
HĒLYUN	helion, parhelion, perihelion
NĒLYUN	cornelian

ELYUN

ELYUN	perduellion
BELYUN	rebellion
HELYUN	hellion
KELYUN	kellion
SELYUN	selion
SKELYUN	tetraskelion

(See **EL'I.ON**)

ĒMA

ĒMA	empyema, seriema
BĒMA	bema, bimah
BLĒMA	emblema, epiblema
DĒMA	edema, myxedema
KĒMA	hyporchema

LĒMA	Lima
RĒMA	rhema, rima, sclerema, sorema, terza rima
SĒMA	emphysema
SHĒMA	Hiroshima
SKĒMA	schema
TĒMA	blastema, Fatima
THĒMA	enthema, erythema, thema
TMĒMA	tmema
ZĒMA	eczema

EMA

JEMA	gemma
LEMA	analemma, dilemma, lemma, neurilemma, polylemma, tetralemma, trilemma
NEMA	nema
REMA	maremma
STEMA	stemma
STREMA	stremma

ĒMAL

ĒMAL	hiemal
DĒMAL	demal
HĒMAL	hemal, pseudohemal
LĒMAL	lemel
TĒMAL	blastemel

ĒMAN

BĒMAN	beeman
DĒMAN	agathodemon, demon, cacodemon, endemon
FRĒMAN	freeman
JĒMAN	G-man
HĒMAN	he-man
LĒMAN	leman
SĒMAN	able seaman, merchant seaman, seaman, semen
TĒMAN	T-man, teaman

EMBER

EMBER	ember
MEMBER	dismember, disremember, member, nonmember, remember
SEMBER	December
TEMBER	September
VEMBER	November

EMBL

SEMBL	assemble, disassemble, dissemble, reassemble, semble
TREMBL	atremble, tremble
ZEMBL	resemble

EMBLANS

SEMBLANS	assemblance, dissemblance, semblance
ZEMBLANS	resemblance

EMBLANT

SEMBLANT	semblant
ZEMBLANT	resemblant

EMBLD

(See **EMBL,** add -d where appropriate.)

EMBLĒ

SEMBLĒ	assembly, disassembly, dissembly
TREMBLĒ	trembly

EMBLER

SEMBLER	assembler, disassembler, dissembler, reassembler, sembler
TEMBLER	temblor
TREMBLER	trembler
ZEMBLER	resembler

EMBLING

(See **EMBL,** add -ing where appropriate.)

EMBRAL

MEMBRAL	bimembral, membral, trimembral
SEMBRAL	Decembral
TEMBRAL	Septembral
VEMBRAL	Novembral

ĒMĒ

BĒMĒ	beamy
DRĒMĒ	day-dreamy, dreamy
GLĒMĒ	gleamy
KRĒMĒ	creamy
NĒMĒ	mneme
PRĒMĒ	preemie
SĒMĒ	monosemy, polysemy, seamy
SKRĒMĒ	screamy
STĒMĒ	steamie, steamy
STRĒMĒ	streamy
TĒMĒ	teamy, teemy

EMĒ

DEMĒ	demi
FLEMĒ	phlegmy
HEMĒ	hemi
JEMĒ	gemmy, jemmy
SEMĒ	semi
TREMĒ	tremie
ZEMĒ	zemmi

ĒMEL

(See **ĒMAL**)

ĒMENT

GRĒMENT	agreement, disagreement
KRĒMENT	decreement

ĒMER

ĒMER	emir
BĒMER	beamer
DĒMER	deemer, redeemer
DRĒMER	daydreamer, dreamer
FĒMER	blasphemer, femur
KRĒMER	creamer
LĒMER	lemur
PRĒMER	supremer
RĒMER	reamer
SĒMER	seamer
SKĒMER	schemer
SKRĒMER	screamer
STĒMER	steamer
STRĒMER	streamer
TĒMER	teemer
TRĒMER	extremer, tremor

EMER

EMER	emmer
DEMER	condemner

HEMER	hemmer
JEMER	begemmer
STEMER	stemmer
TEMER	contemner
TREMER	tremor

ĒMFUL

BĒMFUL	beamful
DRĒMFUL	dreamful
KRĒMFUL	creamful
RĒMFUL	reamful
SKĒMFUL	schemeful
STRĒMFUL	streamful
TĒMFUL	teemful

ĒMIK

FĒMIK	phemic
HĒMIK	hemic, polyhemic
NĒMIK	anemic, phonemic
RĒMIK	eremic
SĒMIK	racemic, semic, septicemic
SKĒMIK	schemic

EMIK

DEMIK	academic, edemic, ecdemic, endemic, epidemic, pandemic, polydemic
HEMIK	hemic, polyhemic
JEMIK	stratagemic
KEMIK	alchemic, ischemic
LEMIK	philopolemic, misopolemic, Moslemic, polemic
NEMIK	phonemic
REMIK	eremic, theoremic
SEMIK	semic
TEMIK	systemic, totemic

EMIKS

EMIKS	noemics

(See **EMIK,** add -s where appropriate.)

ĒMING

(See **ĒM,** add -ing where appropriate.)

EMING

(See **EM,** add -ing or -ming where appropriate.)

ĒMISH

(See ĒM, add -ish where appropriate.)

EMISH

BLEMISH	blemish, unblemish
FLEMISH	flemish, Flemish

ĒMIST

FĒMIST	blasphemist
PRĒMIST	supremist
SKĒMIST	schemist
TRĒMIST	extremist

ĒMLĒ

PRĒMLĒ	supremely
SĒMLĒ	seemly, unseemly
TRĒMLĒ	extremely

ĒMLES

YĒMLES	yemeless

(See ĒM, add -less where appropriate.)

EMLIN

GREMLIN	gremlin
KREMLIN	Kremlin

ĒMŌ

NĒMŌ	Little Nemo, Nemo
PRĒMŌ	primo, supremo

ĒMON

(See ĒMAN)

EMPER

SEMPER	semper, sic semper
TEMPER	attemper, distemper, temper, untemper

EMPL

STEMPL	stemple
TEMPL	temple

EMPLER

TEMPLER	templar
ZEMPLER	exemplar

EMPSHUN

EMPSHUN	exemption, emption, coemption, preemption
DEMPSHUN	ademption, redemption
REMPSHUN	diremption
ZEMPSHUN	exemption

EMPSTER

DEMPSTER	dempster
SEMPSTER	sempster

EMPTED

(See EMPT, add -ed where appropriate.)

EMPTER

EMPTER	empter, caveat emptor, coemptor, preemptor
KEMPTER	unkempter
TEMPTER	attempter, tempter
ZEMPTER	exempter

EMPTING

(See EMPT, add -ing where appropriate.)

EMPTIV

EMPTIV	preemptive
DEMPTIV	redemptive

ĒMSONG

DRĒMSONG	dream-song
THĒMSONG	theme song

ĒMSTER

DĒMSTER	deemster
SĒMSTER	seamster
TĒMSTER	teamster

ĒNA

ĒNA	hyena
BĒNA	amphisbaena, anabaena, verbena
CHĒNA	kachina
DĒNA	modena
FĒNA	saphena
GLĒNA	Euglena
HĒNA	tahina
JĒNA	gena, Cartagena
KĒNA	coquina, marikina
LĒNA	dolina, cantilena, galena, Catalina, salina, semolina
PĒNA	philopena, subpoena
RĒNA	arena, ballerina, farina, marina, tsarina, czarina
SĒNA	dracaena, encina, cassena, Messina, piscina, scena
TĒNA	Argentina, phlyctena, flutina, cantina, catena, cavatena, concertina, poltina, sestina, scarlatina, sonatina
THĒNA	Athena
VĒNA	avena, novena, vina
ZĒNA	maizena

ENA

ENA	duenna, sienna, Vienna
BENA	bena
HENA	Gehenna, henna
JENA	jenna
SENA	senna
TENA	antenna
VENA	Ravenna

ĒNAL

DĒNAL	duodenal
PĒNAL	penal
PLĒNAL	plenal
RĒNAL	adrenal, marinal, renal
SHĒNAL	machinal
VĒNAL	venal
WĒNAL	weanel

ENANS

PENANS	penance
TENANS	tenants

ENANT

| PENANT | pennant |
| TENANT | lieutenant, sublieutenant, tenant, tenent |

ENANTS

(See **ENANS**)

ENAS

(See **ENIS**)

ĒNĀT

| ĒNĀT | enate |
| KRĒNĀT | crenate |

ENĀT

PENĀT	brevipennate, impennate, latipennate, longipennate, pennate, tripennate
RENĀT	perennate
TENĀT	antennate

ENCHANT

(See **ENSHENT**)

ENCHER

BENCHER	backbencher, bencher, debenture
BLENCHER	blencher
DENCHER	denture, indenture, rudenture
DRENCHER	bedrencher, drencher
FLENCHER	flencher
KLENCHER	clencher, unclencher
KWENCHER	quencher
RENCHER	wrencher
TENCHER	tenture
TRENCHER	intrencher, trencher
VENCHER	adventure, maladventure, misadventure, peradventure, reventure, venture
WENCHER	wencher

ENCHING

(See **ENCH**, add -ing where appropriate.)

ENCHLES

(See **ENCH**, add -less where appropriate.)

ENCHMAN

| FRENCHMAN | Frenchman |
| HENCHMAN | henchman |

ENDA

ENDA	hacienda
BENDA	benda
DENDA	addenda, denda, credenda
JENDA	agenda, corrigenda, legenda
LENDA	delenda
RENDA	merenda, referenda

ENDAL

(See **ENDL**)

ENDANS

(See **ENDENS**)

ENDANT

(See **ENDENT**)

ENDĒ

BENDĒ	bendy
FENDĒ	effendi, fendi, fendy
TRENDĒ	trendy
VENDĒ	modus vivendi

ENDED

(See **END**, add -ed where appropriate.)

ENDENS

PENDENS	dependence, impendence, independence, interdependence
SENDENS	ascendance, descendence, condescendence, transcendence
SPLENDENS	resplendence
TENDENS	attendance, attendants, intendance, superintendence, superintendents, tendance

ENDENT

FENDENT	defendant
PENDENT	appendant, dependant, dependent, equipendent, impendent, independent, interdependent, pendant, pendent
SENDENT	ascendant, descendant, transcendent
SPLENDENT	resplendent, splendent, transplendent
TENDENT	attendant, intendant, contendant, superintendent

ENDER

ENDER	ender, tail-ender, weekender
BENDER	bender, fender-bender, mind-bender
BLENDER	blender, interblender
FENDER	defender, fender, offender
FLENDER	flender
HENDER	apprehender, comprehender, reprehender
JENDER	engender, gender
LENDER	lender, moneylender
MENDER	amender, emender, commender, mender, recommender
PENDER	depender, expender, perpender, suspender
PRENDER	prender
RENDER	render, surrender
SENDER	ascender, descender, sender
SLENDER	slender
SPENDER	spender
SPLENDER	splendor
TENDER	attender, bartender, extender, intender, contender, pretender
TRENDER	trender
VENDER	vender, vendor
WENDER	wender

ENDERD

JENDERD	engendered, gendered
RENDERD	rendered, surrendered
SPLENDERD	many-splendored

ENDING

RENDING	heart-rending

(See **END**, add *-ing* where appropriate.)

ENDL

BENDL	prebendal
SENDL	sendal, sendle
TRENDL	trendle

ENDLES

ENDLES	endless
BENDLES	bendless
FRENDLES	friendless
MENDLES	mendless
TRENDLES	trendless

ENDMENT

FRENDMENT	befriendment
MENDMENT	amendment, commendment
TENDMENT	intendment

ENDŌ

ENDŌ	diminuendo, innuendo
KENDŌ	kendo
SHENDŌ	crescendo

ENDOR

(See **ENDER**)

ENDUM

ENDUM	definiendum
DENDUM	addendum, dedendum, credendum
JENDUM	agendum, corrigendum
RENDUM	referendum

ENDUS

DENDUS	pudendous
MENDUS	tremendous
PENDUS	stupendous
RENDUS	horrendous

ĒNĒ

ĒNĒ	eeny
BĒNĒ	beanie, beany
BLĒNĒ	blini
CHĒNĒ	fantoccini, fettuccini
DĒNĒ	Houdini
GRĒNĒ	greeny
GWĒNĒ	linguine, linguini
HĒNĒ	Tahine, wahine
JĒNĒ	genie
KĒNĒ	bikini, Bikini, monokini, zucchini
KRĒNĒ	hippocrene
LĒNĒ	galeeny, lene, Mussolini, Selene, tortellini
MĒNĒ	meanie, meany, eeny-meeny
NĒNĒ	campanini, Toscanini
PĒNĒ	scaloppini
PLĒNĒ	pleny
SĒNĒ	grissini, Messene
SHĒNĒ	sheeny
SKĒNĒ	skene
SPLĒNĒ	spleeny
SWĒNĒ	sweeny
TĒNĒ	martini, teeny
VĒNĒ	visne
WĒNĒ	teeny-weeny, weeny, wieny
ZĒNĒ	tetrazzini

ENĒ

ENĒ	any
BENĒ	beni, benne, benny
BLENĒ	blenny
FENĒ	fenny
HENĒ	henny
JENĒ	jenny, spinning jenny
KENĒ	Kilkenny
MENĒ	many
PENĒ	half-penny, ha'penny, Henny-Penny, catchpenny, passpenny, penny, pinchpenny, sixpenny, tuppenny, twopenny
TENĒ	tenney, tenny
WENĒ	wenny

ENEK

(See **ENIK**)

ENEL

BENEL	bennel
FENEL	fennel
KENEL	kennel, rekennel, unkennel
KRENEL	crenel
VENEL	vennel

ENEM

DENEM	denim
MENEM	mennom
VENEM	envenom, venom

ĒNER

BĒNER	shebeener
GLĒNER	gleaner
GRĒNER	greener
KĒNER	keener
KLĒNER	cleaner, uncleaner, vacuum cleaner, window cleaner (etc.)
LĒNER	leaner, lienor
MĒNER	demeaner, demeanor, meaner, mesner, misdemeanor
PRĒNER	preener
RĒNER	serener, submariner
SĒNER	obscener
SHĒNER	machiner
SKRĒNER	screener
TĒNER	routiner, teener
TWĒNER	go-betweener
VĒNER	advener, convener, contravener, intervenor, supervenor
WĒNER	weaner, wiener
ZĒNER	magaziner

ENER

KENER	kenner
MENER	menhir
PENER	penner
TENER	contratenor, countertenor, tenner, tenor
YENER	yenner

ĒNES

(See **Ē**, add *-ness* where appropriate.)

ENET

BENET	bennett
DENET	dennet
JENET	genet, jennet
RENET	rennet
SENET	senate, sennet
TENET	tenet

ENGTHĒ

LENGTHĒ	lengthy
STRENGTHĒ	strengthy

ENGTHEN

LENGTHEN	lengthen
STRENGTHEN	strengthen

ĒNĪ

GRĒNĪ	green-eye
MĒNĪ	mean-eye
SĒNĪ	Iceni

ĒNĪD

GRĒNĪD	green-eyed
KĒNĪD	keen-eyed
MĒNĪD	mean-eyed

ĒNIJ

GRĒNIJ	greenage
RĒNIJ	careenage
TĒNIJ	teenage

ĒNIK

FĒNIK	phenic
SĒNIK	scenic
SPLĒNIK	splenic

ENIK

DENIK	Edenic
FENIK	alphenic, fennec, phenic
FRENIK	phrenic, hebrephrenic, cacophrenic, paraphrenic, schizophrenic
JENIK	*A* agnogenic, allogenic, anthropogenic, *D* deuterogenic, Diogenic, diplogenic, dysgenic, *E* embryogenic, enteropathogenic, *F* phosphorogenic, photogenic, *GL* glycogenic, *H* hallucinogenic, hepatogenic, hysterogenic, *I* iatrogenic, *J* gelogenic, genic, *KR* cryogenic, crystallogenic, chronogenic, *M* mediagenic, metagenic, mythogenic, *N* nitrogenic, *O* oxygenic, organogenic, *P* paragenic, parthenogenic, pathogenic, pyrogenic, pythogenic, polygenic, *PR* protogenic, *S* saprogenic, suicidogenic, *T* telegenic, typhogenic, *TH* thermogenic, *Y* eugenic, *Z* zoogenic
KENIK	lichenic
LENIK	philhellenic, galenic, Hellenic, geoselenic, Panhellenic, selenic
MENIK	ecumenic, poimenic
RENIK	irenic, sirenic
SENIK	Saracenic, acenic
SFENIK	sphenic
SPLENIK	splenic
STENIK	tungstenic
STHENIK	sthenic
TENIK	neotenic
THENIK	asthenic, Demosthenic, calisthenic, neurasthenic, parthenic

ENIKS

JENIKS	oligogenics, eugenics
THENIKS	euthenics

(See **ENIK,** add -*s* where appropriate.)

ENIM

(See **ENEM**)

ENIN

LENIN	Lenin
RENIN	rennin
VENIN	antivenin, venin

ĒNING

ĒNING	eaning
BĒNING	shebeening
DĒNING	deaning
GLĒNING	gleaning
GRĒNING	greening
KĒNING	keening
KLĒNING	cleaning
KWĒNING	queening
LĒNING	leaning, upleaning, trampolining
MĒNING	demeaning, double meaning, ill-meaning, meaning, unmeaning, well-meaning
PRĒNING	preening
RĒNING	careening
SĒNING	damascening, scening
SHĒNING	machining
SKRĒNING	screening
TĒNING	costeaning, quarantining
VĒNING	advening, intervening, contravening, convening, subvening, supervening
WĒNING	overweening, weaning, weening
YĒNING	yeaning

ENING

KENING	kenning
PENING	penning

ĒNIS

(See **ĒNUS**)

ENIS

MENIS	menace
TENIS	tenace, tennis
VENIS	Venice

ĒNISH

BĒNISH	beanish
GRĒNISH	greenish
KĒNISH	keenish
KLĒNISH	cleanish
KWĒNISH	queenish
LĒNISH	leanish
MĒNISH	meanish
SPLĒNISH	spleenish

ENISH

HENISH	hennish
PLENISH	deplenish, displenish, plenish, replenish
RENISH	Rhenish
WENISH	wennish

ĒNIST

PLĒNIST	plenist
SHĒNIST	machinist
TĒNIST	routinist
ZĒNIST	magazinist

ENIT

JENIT	jennet
SENIT	senate, sennet, sennit, sennight

ĒNLĒ

GRĒNLĒ	greenly
KĒNLĒ	keenly
KLĒNLĒ	cleanly
KWĒNLĒ	queenly
LĒNLĒ	leanly
MĒNLĒ	meanly
RĒNLĒ	serenely
SĒNLĒ	obscenely

ENLĪK

DENLĪK	denlike
FENLĪK	fenlike
HENLĪK	henlike
PENLĪK	penlike
RENLĪK	wrenlike

ĒNLING

ĒNLING	eanling
KWĒNLING	queenling
WĒNLING	weanling
YĒNLING	yeanling

ENMAN

FENMAN	fenman
PENMAN	penman

ĒNNES

(See ĒN, add -ness where appropriate.)

ĒNŌ

BĒNŌ	albino, bambino, beano, sabino, wabeno
CHĒNŌ	cappuccino, chino
DĒNŌ	ladino, San Bernardino, tondino
FĒNŌ	fino
KĒNŌ	baldachino, keno, maraschino, zecchino
LĒNŌ	leno
MĒNŌ	amino, camino, comino, Mino, palomino
NĒNŌ	pianino, spranino
PĒNŌ	Filipino
RĒNŌ	whiskerino, merino, peacherino, peperino, Reno, San Marino, sereno, solferino, vetturino
SĒNŌ	casino
TĒNŌ	andantino, batino, festino, concertino, Latino, Valentino
TRĒNŌ	neutrino
VĒNŌ	vino

ENOM

(See ENEM)

ENON

(See ENUN)

ĒNOR

(See ĒNER)

ENOR

(See ENER)

ENSAL

MENSAL	bimensal, commensal, mensal
RENSAL	forensal

(See ENSIL)

ENSĀT

DENSĀT	condensate
PENSĀT	compensate
SENSĀT	insensate, sensate
TENSĀT	intensate

ENSEN

ENSEN	ensign
DENSEN	densen
SENSEN	Sensen

ENSER

DENSER	denser, condenser
FENSER	fencer
FLENSER	flenser
HENSER	prehenser
MENSER	commencer, menser
PENSER	dispenser, recompenser
SENSER	censer, censor, incensor, senser, sensor
SPENSER	spencer, Spencer, Spenser
TENSER	extensor, intenser, tenser, tensor

ENSĒZ

ENSĒZ	amanuenses
JENSĒZ	Albigenses
MENSĒZ	menses

ENSFORTH

HENSFORTH	henceforth
HWENSFORTH	whenceforth
THENSFORTH	thenceforth

ENSHAL

ENSHAL	expediential, experiential, influential,

DENSHAL	incruential, obediential, sapiential, sciential *E* evidential, *J* jurisprudential, *K* confidential, *KR* credential, *PR* precedential, presidential, providential, prudential, *R* residential, rodential
JENSHAL	agential, bigential, indulgential, intelligential, tangential
KWENSHAL	inconsequential, consequential, sequential, subsequential
LENSHAL	pestilential, querulential
NENSHAL	exponential
RENSHAL	*D* deferential, differential, *I* inferential, irreverential, *K* conferential, *PR* preferential, *R* referential, reverential, *S* circumferential, *T* torrential, *TR* transferential, *U* unreverential
SENSHAL	essential, inessential, coessential, concupiscential, quintessential, nonessential, reminiscential, super-essential, unessential
TENSHAL	equipotential, existential, penitential, potential, sentential
VENSHAL	Provencial
ZENSHAL	omnipresential

ENSHENT

PENSHENT	penchant
SENSHENT	assentient, dissentient, insentient, consentient, presentient, sentient
TRENSHENT	trenchant

ĒNSHIP

DĒNSHIP	deanship
KWĒNSHIP	queenship

ENSHUN

DENSHUN	indention
HENSHUN	apprehension, deprehension, inapprehension, incomprehension, comprehension, misapprehension, preapprehension, prehension, reprehension
JENSHUN	gentian
KLENSHUN	declension
MENSHUN	dimension, mention
PENSHUN	pension, propension, repension, suspension
SENSHUN	accension, ascension, descension, dissension, incension, condescension, consension, presention, reascension, recension, uncondescension
STENSHUN	abstention
TENSHUN	*A* attention, *D* detention, distention, *E* extension, *H* hypertension, hypotension, hortensian, *I* inattention, inextension, intention, *K* co-extension, contention, *O* obtention, ostension, *P* portention, *PR* pretension, *R* retention, *T* tension, *TH* thermotension
VENSHUN	intervention, invention, contravention, convention, nonintervention, obvention, prevention, circumvention, subvention, supervention
ZENSHUN	presention

ENSHUND

MENSHUND	ill-mentioned, mentioned,

TENSHUND	unmentioned, well-mentioned ill-intentioned, intentioned, unintentioned, well-intentioned

ENSHUS

ENSHUS	conscientious
DENSHUS	tendentious
LENSHUS	pestilentious, silentious
SENSHUS	dissentious, licentious
TENSHUS	contentious, pretentious, sententious, uncontentious, unpretentious

ENSIL

HENSIL	prehensile
PENSIL	pensel, pencil, pensile
SENSIL	sensile
STENSIL	stencil
TENSIL	extensile, tensile, utensil

(See **ENSAL**)

ENSILD

PENSILD	pencilled
STENSILD	stencilled

ENSING

DENSING	condensing, uncondensing, evidencing
FENSING	fencing
FLENSING	flensing
MENSING	commencing, recommencing
PENSING	dispensing, prepensing, propensing, recompensing
RENSING	referencing, reverencing
SENSING	censing, incensing, sensing
TENSING	pretensing, tensing

ENSIV

ENSIV	influencive
DENSIV	condensive
FENSIV	defensive, indefensive, inoffensive, counteroffensive, offensive, self-defensive
HENSIV	apprehensive, inapprehensive, incomprehensive, comprehensive, prehensive, reprehensive, unapprehensive
PENSIV	expensive, inexpensive, pensive, recompensive, suspensive
SENSIV	ascensive, descensive, incensive, condescensive
TENSIV	distensive, extensive, energy-intensive, inextensive, intensive, coextensive, labor-intensive, ostensive, protensive, tensive

ENSL

(See **ENSAL, ENSIL**)

ENSLĒ

DENSLĒ	densely
MENSLĒ	immensely
PENSLĒ	propensely
TENSLĒ	intensely, tensely

ENSLES

FENSLES	defenseless, fenceless, offenseless
PENSLES	expenseless, recompenseless, penceless
SENSLES	senseless

ENSMENT

MENSMENT	commencement
SENSMENT	incensement

ENSNES

DENSNES	denseness
MENSNES	immenseness
PENSNES	propenseness
TENSNES	intenseness, tenseness

ENSOR

(See **ENSER**)

ENSUM

PENSUM	pensum
SENSUM	sensum

ENTA

JENTA	magenta
LENTA	polenta
MENTA	impedimenta, pedimenta, pimenta, rejectamenta
MYENTA	pimienta
NENTA	nenta
SENTA	placenta
YENTA	yenta

ENTAD

ENTAD	ectoentad, entad
PENTAD	pentad

ENTAL

ENTAL	ental, oriental
DENTAL	*A* accidental, antecedental, *B* bidental, dental, dentil, dentile, *E* edental, *I* incidental, interdental, *K* coincidental, *L* labiodental, linguadental, *O* occidental, *P* postdental, *TR* transcendental, tridental
JENTAL	argental, gentle, ungentle
LENTAL	Lental, lentil
MENTAL	*D* departmental, detrimental, developmental, documental, *E* excremental, experimental, elemental, environmental, *F* firmamental, fundamental, *FR* fragmental, *G* governmental, *I* impedimental, incremental, instrumental, *K* compartmental, complemental, complimental, condimental, *L* ligamental, *M* medicamental, mental, momental, monumental, *N* nutrimental, *O* ornamental, *P* parliamental, pedimental, pigmental, *PR* predicamental, *R* regimental, recremental, rudimental, *S* sacramental, sedimental, segmental, sentimental, submental, supplemental, *T* tegmental, tegumental, temperamental, tenemental, testamental, tournamental
NENTAL	intercontinental, componental, continental, transcontinental
RENTAL	biparental, grandparental, parental, rental
SENTAL	percental, placental, cental
TRENTAL	trental

ENTANS

PENTANS	repentance, unrepentance
SENTANS	sentence

ENTANT

PENTANT	repentant, unrepentant
ZENTANT	representant

ENTĀT

DENTĀT	bidentate, dentate, edentate, quadridentate, tridentate
MENTĀT	dementate, testamentate
RENTĀT	parentate

ENTĒ

ENTĒ	Agua Caliente, aguardiente, dolce far niente, niente
DENTĒ	al dente, presidente
LENTĒ	dolente, festina lente
MENTĒ	lentamente, tormenty
PENTĒ	diapente
PLENTĒ	aplenty, plenty
SHENTĒ	cognoscente, cognoscenti
TWENTĒ	twenty

ENTED

(See **ENT,** add *-ed* where appropriate.)

ENTENS

(See **ENTANS**)

ENTER

ENTER	enter, reenter, scienter
DENTER	denter, indenter
KWENTER	frequenter
LENTER	lentor, relenter
MENTER	*E* experimenter, *F* fermenter, fermentor, fomenter, *K* commenter, *L* lamenter, *M* mentor, *O* augmenter, ornamenter, *S* cementer, supplementer, *T* tormenter
PENTER	repenter
RENTER	renter
SENTER	*A* accentor, assenter, *B* barycenter, bucentaur, *D* dissenter, *E* epicenter, *H* hypocenter, *I* incentor, *K* concenter, consenter, *O* orthocenter, *PR* precentor, *S* center, centaur, succentor
SHLENTER	schlenter
STENTER	stentor
TENTER	contenter, retentor, tenter
VENTER	inventor, preventer, circumventor, venter
ZENTER	misrepresenter, presenter, representer, resenter

ENTERD

ENTERD	entered
SENTERD	centered

ENTFUL

MENTFUL	lamentful
SENTFUL	scentful
TENTFUL	contentful
VENTFUL	eventful, inventful, uneventful, uninventful
ZENTFUL	resentful, unresentful

ENTIJ

SENTIJ	percentage
VENTIJ	ventage

ENTIK

DENTIK	identic
JENTIK	argentic
SENTIK	crescentic
THENTIK	authentic

ENTĪL

JENTĪL	Gentile
SENTĪL	percentile, centile

ENTIN

DENTIN	dentin, dentine, Tridentine
KWENTIN	San Quentin
RENTIN	torrentine

ENTING

(See **ENT,** add *-ing* where appropriate.)

ENTIS

MENTIS	non compos mentis
PENTIS	appentice, pentice
PRENTIS	apprentice, prentice

ENTIST

DENTIST	dentist, irredentist
PRENTIST	apprenticed, prenticed
VENTIST	Adventist, preventist, Seventh Day Adventist

ENTIV

DENTIV	pendentive
MENTIV	lamentive
SENTIV	assentive, incentive
TENTIV	attentive, disincentive, detentive, inattentive, irretentive, retentive, unretentive
VENTIV	adventive, interventive, inventive, circumventive, preventive
ZENTIV	presentive, resentive

ENTL

(See **ENTAL**)

ENTLĒ

DENTLĒ	evidently, confidently
JENTLĒ	gently, ungently
LENTLĒ	excellently, insolently
NENTLĒ	eminently
SENTLĒ	innocently
TENTLĒ	impotently, intently

ENTLES

(See **ENT,** add *-less* where appropriate.)

ENTMENT

LENTMENT	relentment
TENTMENT	discontentment, contentment
ZENTMENT	presentment, representment, resentment

ENTŌ

ENTŌ	à bientôt
CHENTŌ	cinquecento, quattrocento
LENTŌ	lento
MENTŌ	divertimento, fomento, memento, pentimento, pimento, portamento, pronunciamento, rifacimento, Risorgimento, Sacramento
MYENTŌ	pimiento, repartimiento
RENTŌ	Sorrento
SENTŌ	cento

ENTOR

(See **ENTER**)

ENTRAL

SENTRAL	metacentral, paracentral, precentral, central, subcentral
VENTRAL	biventral, dorsiventral, ventral

ENTRĒ

ENTRĒ	entry
DENTRĒ	den-tree
JENTRĒ	gentry
SENTRĒ	sentry

ENTRES

MENTRES	tormentress
VENTRES	inventress

ENTRIK

SENTRIK	*A* anthropocentric, acentric, *B* barycentric, *E* egocentric, eccentric, ethnocentric, *H* haliocentric, homocentric, *J* geocentric, gyneocentric, *K* concentric, *M* metacentric, *P* paracentric, *S*

Saturnicentric
selenocentric

VENTRIK	ventric

ENTUM

GWENTUM	unguentum
MENTUM	*A* amentum, *F* fermentum, fundamentum, *M* momentum, *P* paludamentum, *R* ramentum, *S* sacramentum, sarmentum, cementum, *T* tegumentum, testamentum, tormentum, *V* velamentum
SENTUM	percentum

ENTŪR

(See **ENCHER**)

ENTUS

GWENTUS	unguentous
MENTUS	filamentous, immomentous, jumentous, ligamentous, momentous, pigmentous, sarmentous
TENTUS	pedententous, portentous

ENŪ

MENŪ	menu
VENŪ	change of venue, venue
ZHENŪ	*ingenue*

ĒNUM

DĒNUM	duodenum
FRĒNUM	frenum
PLĒNUM	plenum

ENUM

(See **ENEM**)

ENUN

MENUN	mennon, trimenon
PENUN	pennon
TENUN	tenon

(See **ENIN**)

ĒNUS

FĒNUS	saphenous
JĒNUS	genus
LĒNUS	scalenus, Silenus
PĒNUS	hemipenis, penis
SĒNUS	Maecenas
VĒNUS	intravenous, venous, Venus

ĒNYAL

JĒNYAL	homogeneal, genial, congenial, primigenial, primogenial, uncongenial
MĒNYAL	demesnial, menial
RĒNYAL	original
SPLĒNYAL	splenial
TĒNYAL	tenial
VĒNYAL	venial
ZĒNYAL	xenial

(See **Ē'NI.AL**)

ENYAL

(See **EN'I.AL**)

ĒNYENS

LĒNYENS	lenience
VĒNYENS	advenience, inconvenience, intervenience, introvenience, convenience, prevenience, supervenience

(See **Ē'NI.ENS**)

ĒNYENT

LĒNYENT	lenient, unlenient
VĒNYENT	advenient, inconvenient, intervenient, introvenient,

convenient,
prevenient,
supervenient

(See E'NI.ENT)

ĒNYER

| SĒNYER | Senior, signor, monsignor |

(See Ē'NI.ER)

ĒNYUS

| JĒNYUS | ingenious, genius |

(See Ē'NI.US)

ENZA

| ENZA | influenza, Spanish influenza |
| DENZA | cadenza, credenza |

ĒŌ

BRĒŌ	con brio
DĒŌ	deo
KLĒŌ	Clio
LĒŌ	Leo
NĒŌ	neo
PĒŌ	papiopio
RĒŌ	Rio, zorillo
TRĒŌ	trio

ĒŌL

| KRĒŌL | Creole |
| SHĒŌL | Sheol |

ĒON

ĒON	aeon
DĒON	odeon
KRĒON	Creon
LĒON	Ponce de Leon
NĒON	neon
PĒON	paeon, peon
PLĒON	pleon
THĒON	pantheon
THRĒON	thrion

(See ĒAN)

ĒPAL

(See ĒPL)

EPARD

(See EPERD)

ĒPĒ

CHĒPĒ	cheapy, cheepy
HĒPĒ	heapy
KĒPĒ	kepi
KRĒPĒ	creepy
LĒPĒ	Fra Lippo Lippi
PĒPĒ	pee-pee
SĒPĒ	seepy
SHĒPĒ	sheepy
SLĒPĒ	sleepy
STĒPĒ	steepy
TĒPĒ	tepee
WĒPĒ	weepy

EPĒ

KEPĒ	kepi
PEPĒ	Apepi, peppy
PREPĒ	preppy
STEPĒ	one-steppy, steppy, three-steppy, two-steppy
TEPĒ	tepee

ĒPEN

CHĒPEN	cheapen
DĒPEN	deepen
STĒPEN	steepen

ĒPER

ĒPER	Ypres
BĒPER	beeper
CHĒPER	cheaper, cheeper
DĒPER	deeper
HĒPER	heaper
KĒPER	barkeeper, beekeeper, bookkeeper, doorkeeper, gatekeeper, goalkeeper, hedge-keeper, housekeeper, innkeeper, keeper, shopkeeper, storekeeper, timekeeper, wicket-keeper
KRĒPER	creeper
LĒPER	leaper
NĒPER	Dnieper
PĒPER	peeper
RĒPER	Grim Reaper, reaper
SĒPER	seeper
SLĒPER	sleeper
STĒPER	steeper
SWĒPER	carpetsweeper, minesweeper, sweeper
TĒPER	tepor
WĒPER	weeper

EPER

HEPER	hepper
LEPER	leper
PEPER	pepper
STEPER	high-stepper, overstepper, stepper, three-stepper, two-stepper, one-stepper
STREPER	strepor
TEPER	tepor

EPERD

JEPERD	jeopard
LEPERD	leopard
PEPERD	peppered
SHEPERD	shepherd

EPID

LEPID	lepid
TEPID	tepid
TREPID	intrepid, trepid

ĒPIJ

| SĒPIJ | seepage |
| SWĒPIJ | sweepage |

EPIK

| EPIK | epic, orthoepic |
| NEPIK | monepic |

ĒPING

| KĒPING | beekeeping, bookkeeping, housekeeping, keeping, safekeeping, shopkeeping |
| SLĒPING | sleeping, unsleeping |

(See ĒP, add -ing where appropriate.)

ĒPISH

CHĒPISH	cheapish
DĒPISH	deepish
SHĒPISH	sheepish
STĒPISH	steepish

ĒPL

ĒPL	ipil
HWĒPL	wheeple
PĒPL	boat people, flower people, country people, peepul, people, repeople, townspeople, unpeople
STĒPL	church steeple, steeple
TĒPL	tepal

ĒPLĒ

CHĒPLĒ	cheaply
DĒPLĒ	deeply
STĒPLĒ	steeply

ĒPLES

BĒPLES	beepless
JĒPLES	jeepless
SHĒPLES	sheepless
SLĒPLES	sleepless

ĒPNES

CHĒPNES	cheapness
DĒPNES	deepness
STĒPNES	steepness

ĒPŌ

CHĒPŌ	cheapo
DĒPŌ	depot
RĒPŌ	repo

ĒPOI

SĒPOI	Sepoy
TĒPOI	teapoy, tepoy

EPOR

(See **EPER**)

EPSĒ

LEPSĒ	epilepsy, catalepsy, narcolepsy, nympholepsy, prosolepsy
PEPSĒ	apepsy, dyspepsy, Pepsi, eupepsy

EPSHUN

REPSHUN	direption, ereption, correption, obreption, proreption, subreption, surreption
SEPSHUN	*A* apperception, *D* deception, *E* exception, *I* imperception, inception, interception, introsusception, intussusception, *K* conception, contraception, *M* misconception, *P* perception, preception, *PR* preconception, preperception, *R* reception, *S* self-deception, susception

EPSIS

KEPSIS	omphaloskepsis
LEPSIS	analepsis, epanalepsis, metalepsis, narcolepsis, prolepsis, syllepsis
SEPSIS	antisepsis, asepsis

EPTANT

REPTANT	reptant
SEPTANT	acceptant, exceptant

EPTER

DEPTER	adepter
SEPTER	accepter, beneceptor, excepter, inceptor, interceptor, preceptor, receptor, scepter, sceptre, susceptor

EPTIK

KLEPTIK	kleptic
LEPTIK	acataleptic, analeptic, epanaleptic, epileptic, iatraleptic, cataleptic, metaleptic, narcoleptic, nympholeptic, organoleptic, proleptic, sylleptic
PEPTIK	apeptic, bradypeptic, dyspeptic, peptic, eupeptic
SEPTIK	antiseptic, aseptic, septic
SKEPTIK	sceptic, skeptic
THREPTIK	threptic
TREPTIK	protreptic

EPTĪL

REPTĪL	reptile
SEPTĪL	septile

EPTIL

REPTIL	reptile
SEPTIL	septile

EPTLĒ

EPTLĒ	eptly, ineptly
DEPTLĒ	adeptly

EPTNES

EPTNES	eptness, ineptness
DEPTNES	adeptness, unadeptness

EPTOR

(See **EPTER**)

ĒPWÔK

SHĒPWÔK	sheepwalk
SLĒPWÔK	sleepwalk

ĒRA

(See **ÎRA**)

ERA

| ERA | era, sierra |
| TERA | terra, Terra |

ERAF

(See **ERIF**)

ĒRAL

(See **ÎRAL**)

ĒRANS

(See **ÎRANS**)

ERALD

(See **ERILD**)

ERAZ

| ERAZ | eras, sierras |
| TERAZ | terras |

ĒRĒ

(See **ÎRĒ**)

ERĒ

| BERĒ | *B* bayberry, baneberry, barberry, beriberi, berry, bury, bilberry, bogberry, bumbleberry, burberry, *BL* blackberry, blueberry, *BR* brambleberry, breadberry, *CH* checkerberry, chinaberry, chokeberry, *D* dangleberry, dayberry, deerberry, dogberry, dewberry, *G* gooseberry, *GW* guavaberry, *H* hackberry, huckleberry, *HW* whortleberry, *I* inkberry, *J* Juneberry, *K* catberry, coffeeberry, *KR* cranberry, Christmasberry, crowberry, *L* |

loganberry, locustberry, lotusberry, *M* mossberry, mulberry, *N* naseberry, *O* orangeberry, *P* partridgeberry, pinkberry, *R* raspberry, redberry, rowanberry, *SH* shadberry, *SKW* squawberry, *SN* snowberry, *STR* strawberry, *T* tangleberry, *TH* thimbleberry, *W* wild strawberry, wineberry, winterberry, *U* unbury, *Y* youngberry

CHERĒ	cherry, chokecherry, Pondicherry
DERĒ	derry, Londonderry
FERĒ	ferry
FLERĒ	flerry
HWERĒ	wherry
JERĒ	jerry, Tom and Jerry
KERĒ	knobkerrie
KWERĒ	equerry
LERĒ	intercalary
MERĒ	mere, merry
NERĒ	matutinary, millinery, quatercentenary, stationary, stationery
PERĒ	perry
RERĒ	Miserere
SERĒ	lamasery, serry
SHERĒ	sherry
SKERĒ	skerry
TERĒ	phrontistery, lamastery, mesentery, monastery, presbytery, sedentary, cemetery, terry
VERĒ	very

(See **ÂRĒ**)

ĒRĒD

(See **ÎRĒD**)

ERĒD

| BERĒD | berried, buried, reburied, unburied |
| CHERĒD | cherried |

FERĒD	ferried
HWERĒD	wherried
SERĒD	serried, unserried

ĒRENS

(See **ÎRENS**)

ĒRENT

(See **ÎRENT**)

ĒRER

(See **ÎRER**)

ERER

| ERER | error |
| TERER | terror |

(See **ÂRER**)

ĒRES

(See **ÎRES**)

ERET

FERET	ferret
HERET	disherit, disinherit, inherit
HWERET	wherret
LERET	lerret
MERET	demerit, merit
SERET	serrate
TERET	terret

ĒRETH

(See **ÎRETH**)

ĒRĒZ

(See **ÎRĒZ**)

ERFOR

| HWERFOR | *wherefor,* wherefore |
| THERFOR | *therefor,* therefore |

ĒRĪD

(See **ÎRĪD**)

ERIF

| ERIF | eriff |

SERIF	sanserif, cerif, seraph, serif
SHERIF	sheriff

ĒRIJ

(See ÎRIJ)

ERIK

ERIK	eric, Eric
BERIK	suberic
DERIK	deric, derrick
FERIK	atmospheric, ferric, helispheric, hemispheric, chromospheric, peripheric, perispheric
KLERIK	cleric
LERIK	valeric
MERIK	alphanumeric, anisomeric, dimeric, Homeric, isomeric, chimeric, mesmeric, metameric, numeric, polymeric, poromeric
NERIK	dineric, generic
SERIK	ceric, glyceric
SFERIK	spheric
SKERIK	skerrick
STERIK	steric
TERIK	*A* alexiteric, amphoteric, *E* exoteric, ennaeteric, enteric, esoteric, *G* gastroenteric, *H* hysteric, *I* icteric, isoteric, *KL* climacteric, *N* neoteric, *P* penteteric, pteric, terek
THERIK	sciatheric

ERIKS

SFERIKS	atmospherics, spherics
TERIKS	hysterics

(See **ERIK,** add -*s* where appropriate.)

ERIL

BERIL	beryl, chrysoberyl
FERIL	ferrule, ferule
PERIL	imperil, peril
STERIL	sterile, unsterile

ERILD

HERILD	herald
PERILD	imperilled, perilled

ERIN

ERIN	Erin, errhyne
SERIN	serin, serine

ĒRING

(See ÎRING)

ERING

ERING	erring
BERING	Bering
HERING	herring

ERIS

DERIS	derris
FERIS	ferris
TERIS	terrace, terris

ERISH

CHERISH	cherish
PERISH	perish

(See ÂRISH)

ERIT

(See ERET)

ĒRLĒ

(See ÎRLĒ)

ĒRLES

(See ÎRLES)

ĒRLING

(See ÎRLING)

ĒRMENT

(See ÎRMENT)

ĒRNES

(See ÎRNES)

ĒRŌ

(See ÎRŌ)

ERŌ

BRERŌ	sombrero
CHERŌ	ranchero
DERŌ	escudero, hacendero, matadero
FERŌ	faro, Pharaoh
KERŌ	vaquero
LERŌ	bandalero, bolero, galero
MERŌ	primero
NERŌ	dinero, Rio de Janeiro, llanero
PERŌ	pampero
RERŌ	torero
TERŌ	montero, zapatero
YERŌ	banderillero, caballero
ZERŌ	cruzeiro

ĒRO͞OM

SĒRO͞OM	searoom
TĒRO͞OM	tearoom

EROR

(See ERER)

ERO͞OL

FERO͞OL	ferrule, ferule
PERO͞OL	perule
SFERO͞OL	spherule

ĒRSER

(See ÎRSER)

ĒRUS

(See ÎRUS)

ĒRZMAN

(See ÎRZMAN)

ESA

ESA	Duessa
DESA	Odessa
PESA	Marpessa
SESA	sessa

ESCHAL

BESCHAL	bestial
GRESCHAL	agrestial
LESCHAL	celestial, supercelestial

ESCHER

JESCHER	gesture
PRESCHER	purpresture
VESCHER	divesture, investure, revesture, vesture

ESCHUN

JESCHUN	digestion, indigestion, ingestion, congestion, suggestion
KWESCHUN	question, requestion

ESCHUND

JESCHUND	poorly digestioned, well-digestioned
KWESCHUND	questioned, requestioned, unquestioned

ĒSĒ

FLĒSĒ	fleecy
GRĒSĒ	greasy
KRĒSĒ	creasy
SĒSĒ	seesee

ESĒ

ESĒ	esse, esssse, in esse
DRESĒ	dressy, undressy
KRESĒ	Cressy
MESĒ	messy
TRESĒ	tressy

ĒSENS

BĒSENS	obeisance
DĒSENS	decence
RĒSENS	recence

ESENS

ESENS	acquiescence, essence, quiescence,
	nonacquiescence, requiescence
BESENS	albescence, erubescence, exacerbescence, contabescence, pubescence, rubescence, subescence
DESENS	frondescence, incandescence, iridescence, candescence, recrudescence, viridescence
GRESENS	nigrescence
JESENS	inturgescence, turgescence
KRESENS	accrescence, excrescence, concrescence, crescence, crescents, superexcrescence, supercrescence
KWESENS	deliquescence, liquescence
LESENS	A adolescence, D decalescence, E emollescence, H hyalescence, I incalescence, incoalescence, invalescence, K calescence, coalescence, convalescence, M mollescence, O obsolescence, opalescence, R recalescence, SP spinulescence, V virilescence
MESENS	detumescence, fremescence, intumescence, spumescence, tumescence
NESENS	evanescence, juvenescence, luminescence, rejuvenescence, senescence
PESENS	torpescence
RESENS	A arborescence, D deflorescence, E efflorescence, F phosphorescence, FL florescence, fluorescence, I inflorescence, K calorescence, R reflorescence,
	revirescence, S sonorescence, V vaporescence, virescence
SESENS	glaucescence
TESENS	delitescence, fructescence, frutescence, quintessence, lactescence, latescence, mutescence
TRESENS	petrescence, putrescence, vitrescence
VESENS	defervescence, effervescence, ineffervescence, ingravescence, noneffervescence

ĒSENT

BĒSENT	obeisant
DĒSENT	decent, indecent
RĒSENT	recent

ESENT

ESENT	acquiescent, quiescent, nonacquiescent, requiescent
BESENT	albescent, erubescent, herbescent, contabescent, pubescent, rubescent, tabescent
DESENT	frondescent, incandescent, iridescent, candescent, lapidescent, recrudescent, viridescent
FESENT	confessant, rufescent
GRESENT	nigrescent
GWESENT	languescent
JESENT	rigescent, surgescent, turgescent
KRESENT	accrescent, decrescent, excrescent, increscent, concrescent, crescent, superexcrescent, supercrescent
KWESENT	deliquescent, liquescent

LESENT
A adolescent, acaulescent, alkalescent, *D* decalescent, *E* emollescent, *I* incalescent, incoalescent, *K* calescent, coalescent, convalescent, *M* mollescent, *O* obsolescent, opalescent, *R* revalescent, *SP* spinulescent, *V* violescent, virilescent

MESENT
detumescent, fremescent, intumescent, spumescent, tumescent

NESENT
evanescent, gangrenescent, ignescent, juvenescent, canescent, luminescent, rejuvenescent, senescent, spinescent

PESENT
torpescent

PRESENT
antidepressant, depressant, compressant, oppressant, repressant, suppressant

RESENT
A arborescent, *D* deflorescent, *E* efflorescent, *FL* florescent, fluorescent, phosphorescent, *I* inflorescent, *K* calorescent, *M* maturescent, *S* cinerescent, sonorescent, *V* virescent

SESENT
acescent, glaucescent, incessant, marcescent, cessant

TESENT
delitescent, fructescent, frutescent, lactescent, latescent, lutescent, mutescent, obmutescent, suffrutescent

TRESENT
petrescent, putrescent, vitrescent

VESENT
effervescent, fervescent, flavescent, ineffervescent, ingravescent, uneffervescent

ĒSER

FLĒSER	fleecer
GRĒSER	greaser
KRĒSER	decreaser, increaser, creaser
LĒSER	leaser, releaser, subleaser
PĒSER	piecer

ESER

ESER	acquiescer, nonacquiescer
BLESER	blesser
DRESER	addresser, dresser, hairdresser, redresser, redressor, undresser
FESER	confessor, professor
GESER	guesser, second guesser
GRESER	aggressor, digressor, progressor, transgressor
LESER	lesser, lessor, sublessor
MESER	messer
PLESER	plesser
PRESER	depressor, impressor, clothes presser, oppressor, pants presser, presser, pressor, suit presser, suppressor
RESER	caresser
SESER	antecessor, assessor, intercessor, *microprocessor*, obsessor, predecessor, *processor*, cesser, successor, *word processor*
TRESER	distresser
ZESER	dispossesser, possessor

ĒSFUL

PĒSFUL	peaceful
PRĒSFUL	capriceful

ESFUL

SESFUL	nonsuccessful, successful, unsuccessful
TRESFUL	distressful, stressful, undistressful

ĒSHA

LĒSHA	silesia, Silesia
NĒSHA	magnesia, Polynesia
PĒSHA	alopecia
VĒSHA	Helvetia

(See **ĒZHA,** also **Ē'ZI.A.**)

ESHAL

(See **ESHL**)

ĒSHAN

(See **ĒSHUN**)

ĒSHĒ

MĒSHĒ	kamichi
SHĒSHĒ	chichi
VĒSHĒ	Vichy

ESHĒ

ESHĒ	esssse
FLESHĒ	fleshy
MESHĒ	meshy

ESHENS

(See **ESH'I.ENS**)

ESHENT

(See **ESH'I.ENT**)

ESHER

FLESHER	flesher
FRESHER	fresher, refresher
MESHER	mesher
PRESHER	high pressure, low pressure, nonpressure, pressure
THRESHER	grain-thresher, wheat-thresher, thresher
TRESHER	tressure

ESHING

FLESHING	fleshing
FRESHING	refreshing
MESHING	meshing
THRESHING	threshing

ESHL

DESHL	deasil
SPESHL	especial, special

ESHLĒ

FLESHLĒ	fleshly
FRESHLĒ	freshly

ESHMENT

FLESHMENT	enfleshment
FRESHMENT	refreshment
MESHMENT	enmeshment

ĒSHUN

GRĒSHUN	Grecian
KLĒSHUN	Diocletian
KRĒSHUN	accretion, excretion, incretion, concretion, secretion
LĒSHUN	deletion
NĒSHUN	internecion, magnesian, Polynesian, Venetian
PLĒSHUN	depletion, impletion, incompletion, completion, repletion
VĒSHUN	Helvetian

(See **Ē'SHI.AN**)

ESHUN

FESHUN	confession, profession
FRESHEN	enfreshen, freshen
GRESHUN	*A* aggression, *D* degression, digression, *E* egression, *I* ingression, introgression, *K* congression, *N* nonaggression, *PR* progression, *R* regression, retrogression, *S* subingression, *TR* transgression
HESHEN	Hessian
KRESHUN	discretion, indiscretion
PRESHUN	decompression, depression, expression, impression, intropression, compression, oppression, reimpression, repression, suppression
SESHUN	*A* accession, *I* insession, intercession, *J* jam session, *K* concession, *O* obsession, *PR* precession, procession, *R* recession, retrocession, *S* secession, cession, session, circumincession, succession, supersession
ZESHUN	dispossession, possession, prepossession, repossession, self-possession

ESHUNS

(See **ES'I.ENS**)

ĒSHUS

NĒSHUS	monoecious
SĒSHUS	facetious
SPĒSHUS	specious

ĒSĪD

KĒSĪD	quayside
LĒSĪD	leeside
SĒSĪD	seaside

ESIJ

MESIJ	message
PESIJ	pesage
PRESIJ	expressage, presage

ĒSIK

JĒSIK	algesic, analgesic
NĒSIK	gynesic, mnesic, polynesic

ESIK

DESIK	geodesic
NESIK	eugenesic
RESIK	xyresic

ESĪL

SESĪL	sessile
TRESĪL	tresayle

ESIL

(See **ESL**)

ĒSING

FLĒSING	fleecing
GRĒSING	greasing
KRĒSING	decreasing, increasing, creasing
LĒSING	leasing, policing, releasing
PĒSING	piecing
SĒSING	ceasing, surceasing, unceasing

ESING

ESING	acquiescing
BLESING	blessing, reblessing
DESING	dessing
DRESING	addressing, dressing, field dressing, readdressing, redressing, salad dressing, undressing, water dressing
FESING	fessing, confessing, professing
GESING	guessing
GRESING	digressing, progressing, regressing, retrogressing, transgressing
JESING	jessing, rejessing, unjessing
LESING	coalescing
MESING	messing
NESING	finessing

PRESING	depressing, expressing, impressing, compressing, oppressing, repressing, suppressing
RESING	caressing
SESING	assessing, excessing, processing, recessing
STRESING	stressing, restressing
TRESING	distressing, retressing, tressing, untressing
YESING	yessing
ZESING	dispossessing, possessing, prepossessing, repossessing, unprepossessing

ĒSIS

ĒSIS	acyesis, deëesis, diesis, hematopoiesis, noesis, poiesis, cyesis, pseudocyesis
JĒSIS	algesis, diegesis, exegesis, eisegesis, periegesis
KRĒSIS	antichresis, catachresis
LĒSIS	ochlesis
MĒSIS	koimesis, mimesis, necromimesis, neuromimesis, pathomimesis
NĒSIS	amnesis, anamnesis, phonesis, phronesis, kinesis
PĒSIS	aposiopesis
RĒSIS	aphaeresis, apocarteresis, diaphoresis, diaeresis, paresis, perichoresis, synderesis, synteresis
SĒSIS	amasesis, ascesis, execesis
SKĒSIS	schesis
TĒSIS	amniocentesis, erotesis, paracentesis, centesis
THĒSIS	anesthesis, anthesis, esthesis, hyperesthesis, mathesis, thesis
TMĒSIS	tmesis

ESIV

DRESIV	redressive
GRESIV	aggressive, digressive, ingressive, congressive, progressive, regressive, retrogressive, transgressive, unprogressive
KRESIV	concrescive, crescive
PRESIV	D depressive, E expressive, I impressive, inexpressive, K compressive, O oppressive, R repressive, S suppressive, U unexpressive, unimpressive, unoppressive
RESIV	caressive
SESIV	accessive, excessive, concessive, obsessive, recessive, successive, unexcessive
ZESIV	possessive, unpossessive

ESKĒ

DESKĒ	desky, Tedeschi
MESKĒ	kromeski
NESKĒ	Neskhi
PESKĒ	pesky

ESKLĒ

ESKLĒ	statuesquely
RESKLĒ	picturesquely
TESKLĒ	blottesquely, grotesquely

ESKNES

ESKNES	statuesqueness
RESKNES	picturesqueness
TESKNES	grotesqueness

ESKŌ

| DESKŌ | tedesco |
| FRESKŌ | al fresco, fresco |

ESKŪ

| FESKŪ | fescue |
| RESKŪ | rescue |

ESL

CHESL	chessel
DESL	deasil, decile, dessil
DRESL	redressal
KRESL	cresyl
NESL	nestle
PESL	pestle
RESL	wrestle
SESL	sessile
TRESL	trestle
VESL	vessel

ESLD

NESLD	nestled
PESLD	pestled
RESLD	wrestled

ESLER

NESLER	nestler
PESLER	pestler
RESLER	wrestler

ĒSLES

(See ĒS, add -less where appropriate.)

ESLING

ESLING	essling
NESLING	nestling
PESLING	pestling
RESLING	wrestling

ESMAN

CHESMAN	chessman
DESMAN	desman
PRESMAN	pressman
YESMAN	yes-man

ESMENT

DRESMENT	redressment
PRESMENT	impressment
SESMENT	assessment

ESOR

(See **ESER**)

ESPER

HESPER	Hesper
VESPER	vesper

ESTA

ESTA	fiesta, siesta
DESTA	podesta
JESTA	egesta, ingesta
KWESTA	cuesta
LESTA	celesta
SESTA	cesta
TESTA	testa
VESTA	Vesta, Zend-Avesta

ESTAL

FESTAL	festal
GRESTAL	agrestal
TESTAL	matripotestal, patripotestal
VESTAL	vestal

ESTANT

JESTANT	decongestant, digestant, gestant
RESTANT	restant
TESTANT	contestant

ĒSTĒ

BĒSTĒ	beastie, beasty, bheestie, bheesty
RĒSTĒ	reasty
SNĒSTĒ	sneasty
YĒSTĒ	yeasty

ESTĒ

CHESTĒ	chesty
FESTĒ	festy
KRESTĒ	cresty
PESTĒ	pesty
RESTĒ	resty
TESTĒ	teste, testy
WESTĒ	westy
ZESTĒ	zesty

ESTED

BESTED	bested
BRESTED	breasted, chicken-breasted, double-breasted, marble-breasted, pigeon-breasted, single-breasted, unbreasted
KRESTED	foam-crested, castle-crested, crested, uncrested

(See **EST,** add *-ed* where appropriate.)

ĒSTER

ĒSTER	down-easter, Easter, nor'easter, northeaster, sou'easter, southeaster
FĒSTER	feaster
KĒSTER	keister
NĒSTER	Dniester

ESTER

ESTER	ester
BESTER	bester
BRESTER	breaster, double-breaster, single-breaster
FESTER	fester, infester, manifester
JESTER	digester, jester, suggester
KWESTER	quaestor, quester, requester, sequester
LESTER	molester
MESTER	bimester, mid-semester, semester, trimester
NESTER	Dnester, nester, nestor, Nestor
PESTER	pester
PRESTER	prester
RESTER	arrester, rester, wrester
SESTER	*ancestor*
TESTER	attester, contester, protester, testar, tester
VESTER	divester, investor, vester
WESTER	far-wester, Midwester, nor'wester, sou'wester, wester
YESTER	yester
ZESTER	zester

ESTERD

FESTERD	festered
KWESTERD	sequestered, unsequestered
PESTERD	pestered

ESTERN

HESTERN	hestern
WESTERN	far-western, Midwestern, northwestern, southwestern, western
YESTERN	yestern

ESTFUL

BLESTFUL	blestful
JESTFUL	jestful
KWESTFUL	questful
RESTFUL	restful, unrestful
ZESTFUL	zestful

ESTIJ

PRESTIJ	prestige
VESTIJ	vestige

ESTIK

BESTIK	asbestic
GRESTIK	agrestic
HESTIK	alkahestic
JESTIK	gestic, majestic
KESTIK	orchestic
KRESTIK	catachrestic, polychrestic
LESTIK	telestic, telestich
MESTIK	domestic
NESTIK	amnestic, anamnestic
PESTIK	anapestic

ESTIN

BESTIN	asbestine
DESTIN	destine, clandestine, predestine
JESTIN	progestine
SESTIN	sestine
TESTIN	intestine

ĒSTING

ĒSTING	easting

BĒSTING	beasting, bee-sting
FĒSTING	feasting
KWĒSTING	queesting
YĒSTING	yeasting

ESTING

BESTING	besting
BREASTING	breasting
FESTING	infesting, manifesting
GESTING	guesting
JESTING	digesting, ingesting, jesting, congesting, predigesting, redigesting, suggesting, uncongesting
KRESTING	cresting
KWESTING	questing, requesting
LESTING	molesting
NESTING	nesting
RESTING	arresting, disinteresting, interesting, rearresting, resting, wresting, unarresting, uninteresting
TESTING	attesting, detesting, contesting, protesting, reattesting, reprotesting, retesting, unprotesting
VESTING	divesting, investing, reinvesting, vesting
WESTING	westing

ESTIS

(See **ESTUS**)

ESTIV

ESTIV	estive
FESTIV	festive, infestive, manifestive
JESTIV	digestive, congestive, suggestive
PESTIV	intempestive, tempestive
RESTIV	arrestive, restive
TESTIV	attestive

ĒSTLĒ

BĒSTLĒ	beastly
PRĒSTLĒ	priestly

ESTLES

(See **EST**, add *-less* where appropriate.)

ESTMENT

RESTMENT	arrestment
VESTMENT	divestment, investment, vestment

ESTŌ

FESTŌ	manifesto
PRESTŌ	presto

ĒSTŌN

FRĒSTŌN	freestone
KĒSTŌN	keystone

ESTRA

KESTRA	orchestra
LESTRA	palestra
NESTRA	fenestra

ESTRAL

KESTRAL	kestrel, orchestral
LESTRAL	palestral
MESTRAL	semestral, trimestral
NESTRAL	anoestral, fenestral
PESTRAL	campestral
SESTRAL	ancestral

ESTRĀT

KESTRĀT	*orchestrate*
KWESTRĀT	sequestrate
NESTRĀT	fenestrate

ESTRIK

KESTRIK	orchestric
LESTRIK	palestric

ESTŪR

(See **ESCHER**)

ESTUS

BESTUS	asbestos
RESTUS	restis
SESTUS	Alcestis, cestus

ĒSUS

(See **ĒSIS**)

ĒTA

ĒTA	eta, chaeta, paracoita
BĒTA	beta
CHĒTA	cheetah
DĒTA	dita, pandita
GĒTA	Bhagavad-Gita, geta
KĒTA	chiquita, keta, coquita
KRĒTA	excreta
LĒTA	Lolita, mulita, veleta
NĒTA	magneta, manzanita, planeta
PĒTA	pita
RĒTA	amorita, amrita, margarita, señorita
SĒTA	seta
TĒTA	partita, sortita
THĒTA	theta
VĒTA	chirivita, dolce vita, vita
WĒTA	vita
ZĒTA	granzita, zeta

ETA

ETA	arietta, comedietta
BETA	betta
BRETA	cabretta
DETA	codetta, vendetta
FETA	feta
LETA	burletta, caballetta, mantelletta, muleta, valetta, Valletta
META	animetta, lametta, meta
NETA	sinfonetta
RETA	biretta, moreta, operetta
VETA	anchovetta
ZETA	mozzetta, Rosetta

ĒTAL

(See **ĒTL**)

ĒTĒ

BĒTĒ	beety
FĒTĒ	graffiti
GLĒTĒ	gleety
JĒTĒ	jiti
MĒTĒ	meaty
PĒTĒ	peaty
RĒTĒ	pariti
SĒTĒ	spermaceti

SLĒTĒ sleety
SWĒTĒ sweety
TĒTĒ titi
TRĒTĒ entreaty, treaty

ETĒ

BETĒ Betty, brown betty
BRETĒ libretti
CHETĒ chetty, concetti
DETĒ vendetti
FETĒ confetti
FRETĒ fretty
GETĒ spaghetti
JETĒ jetty
NETĒ netty
PETĒ petit, petty
SETĒ spermaceti
SHETĒ machete
SWETĒ sweaty
YETĒ yeti
ZETĒ Rossetti, Sacco-Vanzetti

ĒTED

FĒTED fetid
LĒTED deleted, expletive deleted

(See ĒT, add -ed where appropriate.)

ETED

FETED feted, fetid

(See ET, add -ed where appropriate.)

ĒTEN

ĒTEN eaten, Eton, moth-eaten, overeaten, uneaten, worm-eaten
BĒTEN beaten, brow-beaten, storm-beaten, tempest-beaten, unbeaten, weather-beaten
HWĒTEN wheaten
JĒTEN zyzzogeton
KĒTEN Buster Keaton
KRĒTEN Cretan, cretin
PĒTEN piton
SĒTEN seton
SWĒTEN sweeten, unsweeten
TĒTEN Teton

ETEN

BRETEN Breton
FRETEN fretten
HWETEN whetten
THRETEN threaten

ĒTER

ĒTER A ant-eater, B beef-eater, D dirt-eater, dung-eater, E eater, F fire-eater, FL flesh-eater, FR frog-eater, GR grass-eater, H hay-eater, humble-pie eater, honey-eater, K cake-eater, KL clay-eater, KR crow-eater, L lotus-eater, M man-eater, O overeater, SM smoke-eater, T toad-eater, U undereater, W woman-eater
BĒTER beater, brow-beater, child-beater, drum-beater, eggbeater, goldbeater, jungle-beater, rug-beater, slave-beater, wife-beater
BLĒTER bleater
CHĒTER cheater, escheater, windcheater
FĒTER defeater, fetor
GRĒTER greeter
HĒTER heater, overheater, superheater, water heater
KRĒTER excreter, secreter
LĒTER decaliter, half liter, hectoliter, milliliter, liter, litre
MĒTER ammeter, Demeter, gas meter, kilometer, konimeter, meeter, meter, metre, nanometer, centimenter, taximeter, water meter

(See ETRIK, change -metric to -meter where appropriate.)

NĒTER neater
PĒTER competer, peter, repeater, St. Peter, saltpeter

PLĒTER depleter, completer, pleater, repleter
PRĒTER praetor, propraetor
RĒTER rhetor, uretor
SĒTER masseter, receptor, saeter, seater, two-seater, three-seater, unseater, one-seater
SKĒTER skeeter
SWĒTER sweeter
TĒTER teeter
TRĒTER entreater, ill-treater, maltreater, mistreater, retreater, treater
TWĒTER tweeter

ETER

BETER abetter, better, bettor
DETER debtor
FETER enfetter, fetter, unfetter
FRETER fretter
GETER begetter, forgetter, getter, go-getter
GRETER regretter
HWETER whetter
JETER jetter
LETER black letter, dead letter, letter, newsletter, red letter, scarlet letter
NETER netter
PETER petter
RETER carburetor, retter
SETER besetter, bonesetter, Irish setter, jetsetter, pacesetter, setter, somersetter, typesetter, upsetter
SWETER sweater, unsweater
TETER tetter
VETER curvetter
WETER wetter

ETERD

FETERD fettered, unfettered
LETERD lettered, unlettered
SWETERD sweatered, unsweatered

ĒTES

(See ĒTUS)

ETFUL

FRETFUL fretful, unfretful
GETFUL forgetful, unforgetful

| GRETFUL | regretful, unregretful |
| NETFUL | netful |

ĒTHAL

(TH as in *thin*)

ĒTHAL	ethal
KWĒTHAL	bequeathal
LĒTHAL	lethal

ĒTHĒ

(TH as in *thin*)

| HĒTHĒ | heathy |
| LĒTHĒ | philalethe, Lethe, prosopolethy |

ETHĒ

(TH as in *thin*)

| BRETHĒ | breathy |
| DETHĒ | deathy |

ETHEL

(TH as in *thin*)

ETHEL	ethal, ethel, Ethel, ethyl
BETHEL	Bethel
METHEL	methyl

ĒTHEN

(TH as in *then*)

| HĒTHEN | heathen |
| RĒTHEN | wreathen |

ĒTHER

(TH as in *then*)

ĒTHER	either
BRĒTHER	breather, lung-breather, mud-breather, water-breather
KWĒTHER	bequeather
NĒTHER	neither
RĒTHER	enwreather, wreather
SĒTHER	seether
SHĒTHER	sheather
TĒTHER	teether

ETHER

(TH as in *then*)

BLETHER	blether
FETHER	feather, white feather, pinfeather, tail-feather, unfeather
GETHER	altogether, together
HETHER	heather
HWETHER	whether
LETHER	boot-leather, hell-for-leather, whitleather, leather, patent leather, underspurleather
NETHER	nether
TETHER	tether, untether
WETHER	aweather, bellwether, weather, wether

ETHERD

(TH as in *then*)

BLETHERD	blethered
FETHERD	feathered, unfeathered
HETHERD	heathered
TETHERD	tethered, untethered
WETHERD	unweathered, weathered

ETHIL

(See ETHEL)

ĒTHING

(TH as in *then*)

BRĒTHING	breathing, inbreathing, incense-breathing, outbreathing
KWĒTHING	bequeathing
RĒTHING	enwreathing, wreathing
SĒTHING	seething
SHĒTHING	sheathing, ensheathing, unsheathing
SMĒTHING	smeething
TĒTHING	teething

ĒTHLES

(TH as in *thin*)

| RĒTHLES | wreathless |
| SHĒTHLES | sheathless |

ETHLES

(TH as in *thin*)

| BRETHLES | breathless |
| DETHLES | deathless |

ĒTHMENT

(TH as in *then*)

KWĒTHMENT	bequeathment
RĒTHMENT	enwreathment, wreathment
SHĒTHMENT	ensheathment

ĒTHRAL

| PĒTHRAL | hypaethral |
| RĒTHRAL | urethral |

ĒTIJ

ĒTIJ	eatage
CHĒTIJ	cheatage, escheatage
KLĒTIJ	cleatage
MĒTIJ	metage

ĒTIK

KRĒTIK	Cretic
RĒTIK	paretic
SĒTIK	acetic, cetic
THĒTIK	thetic

ETIK

ETIK	*A* abietic, aloetic, anoetic, *D* dianoetic, *G* galactopoietic, goetic, *H* hypnoetic, *M* mythopoetic, *N* noetic, nosopoetic, *O* onomatopoetic, *P* poetic, *R* robietic, *Z* zoetic
BETIK	alphabetic, diabetic, hebetic, quodlibetic, tabetic
DETIK	asyndetic, eidetic, geodetic, syndetic
FETIK	aphetic, Japhetic, prophetic
JETIK	*A* analgetic, apologetic, algetic, *E* energetic, exergetic, epexegetic, *G* Gangetic, *I* inergetic, *S* synergetic, syzygetic, *ST* strategetic

KETIK	catachetic		anchoretic, anoretic,
KRETIK	syncretic		antipyretic, apyretic,
LETIK	*A* amuletic, athletic,		*D* diaphoretic,
	B balletic, *BR*		diuretic, *E* emporetic,
	brachycataletic, *F*		*H* heuretic, *M*
	phyletic, *H*		Masoretic, *P* paretic,
	homiletic, *K* colletic,		pyretic, *PL*
	L Lettic, *O* ochletic,		plethoretic, *TH*
	auletic, *P*		theoretic, *Y* uretic
	polyphyletic, *Y* uletic	**SETIK**	ascetic, dipsetic,
METIK	arithmetic,		Docetic, copacetic,
	Baphometic, emetic,		quercetic, auxetic,
	epithymetic,		Ossetic
	gametic, hermetic,	**TETIK**	apatetic, dietetic,
	cosmetic,		erotetic, peripatetic,
	logarithmetic, metic,		synartetic, zetetic
	mimetic, seismetic	**THETIK**	*A* allopathic,
NETIK	*A* abiogenetic,		anesthetic,
	agamogenetic,		antipathetic,
	antimagnetic, *B*		antithetic, apathetic,
	biogenetic,		*B* bathetic, *D*
	biomagnetic, *D*		diathetic, *E* enthetic,
	diamagnetic,		epenthetic, epithetic,
	dianoetic, *E*		aesthetic, esthetic, *F*
	electromagnetic,		photosynthetic, *H*
	epigenetic, *F*		hyperesthetic,
	phylogenetic,		hypothetic, *I*
	phonetic, *FL*		idiopathetic, *K*
	phlognetic,		cosmothetic, *L*
	phlogogenetic, *FR*		ludicropathetic, *M*
	frenetic, *H*		mesothetic, *N*
	heterogenetic,		nomothetic, *P*
	histogenetic,		parathetic,
	homogenetic, *I*		parenthetic, pathetic,
	isomagnetic, *J*		polysynthetic, *PR*
	genetic,		prosthetic, prothetic,
	gyromagnetic, *K*		*S* sympathetic,
	kinetic, *L* limnetic,		synthetic, *TH*
	M magnetic,		theopathetic
	monogenetic,	**VETIK**	Helvetic
	morphogenetic, *O*		
	ontogenetic,		
	oogenetic,	**ETIKS**	
	autokinetic, *P*		
	paleogenetic,	**ETIKS**	poetics
	palingenetic,	**JETIKS**	apologetics,
	pangenetic,		exegetics, energetics
	parenetic,	**LETIKS**	athletics, homiletics,
	parthenogenetic,		signaletics
	pathogenetic,	**NETIKS**	aerodynetics
	pyrogenetic,		phonetics, genetics,
	polygenetic, *S*		kinetics, magnetics,
	cybernetic,		Mendelian genetics,
	psychogenetic, *SP*		molecular genetics,
	splenetic, *T*		cybernetics
	telekinetic, tonetic,	**RETIKS**	theoretics
	TH thermogenetic,	**TETIKS**	dietetics
	thermomagnetic,	**THETIKS**	anaesthetics,
	THR threnetic, *Y*		aesthetics, esthetics,
	eugenetic		prosthetics, synthetics
PETIK	flatulopetic		
RETIK	*A* alexipyretic,	(See **ETIK**, add *-s* where appropriate.)	

ĒTING

ĒTING	*B* beef-eating, *D* dirt-eating, dung-eating, *E* eating, *F* fire-eating, *FL* flesh-eating, *FR* frog-eating, *GR* grass-eating, *H* hay-eating, *KL* clay-eating, *KR* crow-eating, *M* man-eating, *O* overeating, *P* pork-eating, *S* smoke-eating, *T* toad-eating, *U* undereating, *V* vegetable-eating (etc.)
BĒTING	beating, brow-beating, child-beating, slave-beating, wife-beating (etc.)

(See **ĒT**, add *-ing* where appropriate.)

ETING

NETING	fish-netting, mosquito netting

(See **ET**, add *-ting* where appropriate.)

ĒTIS

(See **ĒTUS**)

ETISH

FETISH	fetish
KETISH	coquettish, croquettish
LETISH	Lettish
PETISH	pettish
WETISH	wettish

ĒTIST

FĒTIST	defeatist
KRĒTIST	accretist, decretist
SWĒTIST	honey-sweetest, sweetest

ETIST

ETIST	duettist
BRETIST	librettist
NETIST	clarinetist, cornetist

TETIST	motettist
YETIST	vignettist

ĒTIV

KRĒTIV	accretive, decretive, discretive, excretive, concretive, secretive
PLĒTIV	depletive, completive, repletive

ETIZM

BETIZM	alphabetism, analphabetism
SETIZM	concettism

ĒTL

ĒTL	hyetal
BĒTL	beetle, betel
FĒTL	fetal
HWĒTL	wheetle
KRĒTL	decretal
SĒTL	acetyl, setal
WĒTL	chalchihuitle

ETL

ETL	ettle
BETL	abettal
FETL	fettle, fine fettle
KETL	kettle
METL	Babbitt metal, gunmetal, white metal, metal, mettle, Monel metal, nonmetal, type metal
NETL	nettle, stinging nettle
PETL	petal, Popocatapetl, *centripetal*
SETL	resettle, settle, unsettle

ETLD

METLD	high-mettled

(See **ETL,** add -d or -ed where appropriate.)

ĒTLĒ

FĒTLĒ	featly
FLĒTLĒ	fleetly
KRĒTLĒ	discreetly, discretely, indiscreetly, concretely
LĒTLĒ	obsoletely
MĒTLĒ	meetly, unmeetly
NĒTLĒ	neatly, unneatly
PLĒTLĒ	incompletely, completely
SWĒTLĒ	sweetly

ETLES

DETLES	debtless
THRETLES	threatless
WETLES	wetless

ETLING

FETLING	fettling
NETLING	nettling
SETLING	resettling, settling, unsettling

ETMENT

BETMENT	abetment
DETMENT	indebtment
SETMENT	besetment
VETMENT	brevetment, revetment

ĒTNES

(See **ĒT,** add -ness where appropriate.)

ETNES

SETNES	setness
WETNES	wetness

ĒTŌ

FĒTŌ	graffito, sgraffito
KĒTŌ	keto, Quito, coquito, mosquito
LĒTŌ	angelito, Leto
NĒTŌ	bonito, incognito, magneto, sanbenito
RĒTŌ	burrito
TĒTŌ	Tito
VĒTŌ	veto

ĒTMENT

FĒTMENT	defeatment
TRĒTMENT	entreatment, ill-treatment, maltreatment, mistreatment, treatment

ETŌ

BRETŌ	libretto
CHETŌ	concetto
GETŌ	ghetto
GRETŌ	allegretto
KETŌ	punquetto, zucchetto
LETŌ	stiletto
METŌ	palmetto
NETŌ	giardinetto, sonnetto
PETŌ	in petto, rispetto
RETŌ	amaretto, amoretto, lazaretto, vaporetto
SETŌ	falsetto
STRETŌ	stretto
TRETŌ	neutretto
VETŌ	cavetto
ZETŌ	terzetto

ĒTON

(See **ĒTEN**)

ĒTOP

NĒTOP	netop
TRĒTOP	treetop

ETRAD

RETRAD	retrad
TETRAD	tetrad

ETRAL

METRAL	*diametral*
PETRAL	petrel, stormy petrel

ETRIK

METRIK	*A* accelerometric, actinometric, aerometric, algometric, alkalimetric, alcoholometric, allometric, altomometric, anisometric, anthropometric, astronometric, *B* barometric,

bathymetric,
bathometric,
biometric,
biosymmetric,
bolometric, *D*
densitometric,
decelerometric,
diametric,
dilatometric,
dimetric,
dynamometric, *E*
econometric,
electrometric, *F*
phonometric,
photometric, *FL*
fluorometric, *G*
galvanometric,
gasometric,
goniometric, *GR*
gravimetric, *H*
hexametric,
hydrometric,
hygrometric,
hypsometric, *I*
inclinometric,
interferometric,
iodometric,
isobarometric,
isometric, *J*
geometric, *K*
kilometric,
coulometric, *KL*
clinometric, *KR*
craniometric,
cryometric,
chronometric, *M*
magnetometric,
manometric, metric,
micrometric,
mileometric,
monometric, *N*
nitrometric, *O*
audiometric,
odometric,
optometric,
ozonometric, *P*
pedometric,
piezometric,
pycnometric,
pyrometric,
potentiometric, *PL*
planometric,
plastometric, *R*
radiometric,
refractometric,
rheometric, *S*
salinometric,
cephalometric,
sensitometric,
cyclometric,
psychometric,
sociometric, *SKL*

sclerometric, *SP*
speedometric,
spectrometric,
spirometric, *ST*
stereometric,
stoichiometric, *SW*
swingometric, *T*
tacheometric,
tachometric,
tellurometric,
tonometric, *TH*
thermometric, *TR*
trigonometric,
trimetric, *V*
viscometric,
volumetric, *Y*
eudiometric, *Z*
zoometric

TETRIK obstetric

ETRIKS

METRIKS econometrics,
  isometrics
STETRIKS obstetrics

(See **ETRIK,** add -*s* where appropriate.)

ETSAL

KWETSAL quetzal
PRETSAL pretzel

ĒTUM

BĒTUM zibetum
FRĒTUM fretum
NĒTUM pinetum
PĒTUM tapetum
RĒTUM arboretum
SĒTUM acetum, Equisetum
SWĒTUM sweetum

ĒTŪR

(See **ĒCHER**)

ĒTUS

ĒTUS coitus, quietus,
  paracoitus
BĒTUS diabetes
FĒTUS fetus, foetus
KĒTUS achaetous
LĒTUS boletus
SĒTUS acetous, Cetus
TĒTUS Epictetus
THĒTUS Thetis
TRĒTUS treatise

ETWERK

FRETWERK fretwork
NETWERK network

ĒUM

BĒUM amoebaeum
DĒUM odeum, stomodeum,
  te Deum
FĒUM trophaeum
JĒUM hypogeum, Geum
LĒUM mausoleum,
  propylaeum
MĒUM meum, tuum and
  meum
NĒUM atheneum, perineum,
  peritoneum,
  prytaneum
SĒUM gynaeceum,
  colosseum, lyceum,
  no-see'em
TĒUM bronteum, notaeum
ZĒUM museum

ĒUS

BĒUS *plumbeous,*
  scarabaeus
FĒUS coryphaeus
KĒUS Manichaeus
MĒUS Ptolemaeus
NĒUS Aeneas
PĒUS onomatopoeous
RĒUS choreus, piraeus,
  reus, uraeus
TĒUS aristaeus, gluteus

ĒVA

DĒVA diva, khedive,
  Mahadeva
JĒVA jivah
KĒVA kiva
NĒVA Geneva
SĒVA Siva
SHĒVA yeshiva
VĒVA viva

ĒVAL

ĒVAL evil, king's evil,
  coeval, medieval
HĒVAL upheaval
JĒVAL longeval
KWĒVAL equaeval
MĒVAL primeval
SHRĒVAL shrieval

THĒVAL	thival
TRĒVAL	retrieval
WĒVAL	boll weevil, weevil

ĒVANS

CHĒVANS	achievance
GRĒVANS	grievance
SĒVANS	perceivance
TRĒVANS	retrievance

ĒVĒ

ĒVĒ	evoe
PĒVĒ	peavey, peevy
SWĒVĒ	Suevi
TĒVĒ	TV

EVĒ

EVĒ	evoe
BEVĒ	bevvy, bevy
CHEVĒ	chevy
HEVĒ	heart-heavy, heavy, top-heavy
KLEVĒ	clevy
LEVĒ	levee, levy
NEVĒ	nevvy
PLEVĒ	replevy
SHEVĒ	Chevvy, chevy

EVEL

BEVEL	bevel
DEVEL	bedevil, daredevil, devil, red devil
KEVEL	kevel
LEVEL	level, on the level, sea level, spirit level, split level, water level
NEVEL	nevel
REVEL	revel
SHEVEL	dishevel, shevel

EVEN

DEVEN	Devon
HEVEN	heaven, midheaven
LEVEN	eleven, leaven, levin
PLEVEN	plevin, replevin
SEVEN	seven
SWEVEN	sweven

EVENTH

| LEVENTH | eleventh |
| SEVENTH | seventh |

ĒVER

ĒVER	naiver
BĒVER	beaver
CHĒVER	achiever, overachiever, underachiever
DĒVER	Danny Deever
FĒVER	enfever, fever, hay fever, jungle fever, sea fever, scarlet fever, spring fever, typhoid fever, yellow fever
GRĒVER	aggriever, griever
HĒVER	ballast heaver, heaver, coal heaver, upheaver
KĒVER	keever
LĒVER	*B* believer, *D* disbeliever, *I* interleaver, *K* cantilever, *L* leaver, lever, liever, livre, *M* make-believer, *R* reliever, *U* unbeliever
PĒVER	peever
PRĒVER	repriever
RĒVER	bereaver, reaver, reever, riever
SĒVER	deceiver, conceiver, misconceiver, perceiver, preconceiver, receiver, transceiver, undeceiver
SHĒVER	sheaver
TRĒVER	retriever
WĒVER	interweaver, weaver, weever

APPLESAUCE

The Apple which the Snake supplied
Arrived complete, with Worm inside.
Child, shun the Sequence of the Snake:
First Fruit, then Worm, then Belly-ache.

EVER

| EVER | *E* ever, *F* forever, *H* whoever, whomever, whomsoever, whosoever, however, howsoever, *HW* whatever, whatsoever, whencesoever, whenever, wherever, |

wheresoever, whichever, whichsoever, whithersoever

DEVER	endeavor
KLEVER	clever
LEVER	cantilever, lever
NEVER	never
SEVER	assever, dissever, sever, unsever

ĒVIJ

| KLĒVIJ | cleavage |
| LĒVIJ | leavage |

ĒVIL

(See ĒVAL)

EVIL

(See EVEL)

EVIN

(See EVEN)

ĒVING

(See ĒV, add -*ing* where appropriate.)

EVIS

BREVIS	brevis
CHEVIS	chevise
KLEVIS	clevis
KREVIS	crevis

ĒVISH

| PĒVISH | peevish |
| THĒVISH | thievish |

EVL

(See EVEL)

ĒVLESS

(See ĒV, add -*less* where appropriate.)

ĒVMENT

CHĒVMENT	achievement
RĒVMENT	bereavement
TRĒVMENT	retrievement

ĒVUS

GRĒVUS	grievous
JĒVUS	longevous
MĒVUS	primevous
NĒVUS	nevus

ĒWĀ

FRĒWĀ	freeway
LĒWĀ	leeway
SĒWĀ	seaway

ĒWERD

LĒWERD	leeward
SĒWERD	seaward

ĒWĒ

ĒWĒ	iiwi
KĒWĒ	kiwi
PĒWĒ	peewee
WĒWĒ	weewee

ĒYA

(See ĒA)

ĒYAN

(See ĒAN)

ĒZA

LĒZA	Mona Lisa
PĒZA	Pisa, tower of Pisa
VĒZA	visa, reentry visa

EZĀNS

(See EZENS)

EZANT

(See EZENT)

ĒZĒ

ĒZĒ	easy, free-and-easy, speakeasy, uneasy
BĒZĒ	Zambezi
BRĒZĒ	breezy
CHĒZĒ	cheesy, pachisi, parcheesi
FRĒZĒ	freezy

GRĒZĒ	greasy
HWĒZĒ	wheezy
KWĒZĒ	queasy
RĒZĒ	reasy
SLĒZĒ	sleasy
SNĒZĒ	sneezy

ĒZEL

(See ĒZL)

ĒZELZ

(See ĒZLZ)

EZENS

PLEZENS	pleasance
PREZENS	omnipresence, presence

EZENT

BEZENT	bezant
FEZENT	pheasant
PEZENT	peasant
PLEZENT	pleasant, unpleasant
PREZENT	present, omnipresent

EZENTS

(See EZENT, add -s where appropriate.)

ĒZER

ĒZER	easer
BĒZER	beezer
CHĒZER	cheeser
FĒZER	misfeasor
FRĒZER	freezer, friezer
GĒZER	geezer, geyser
GRĒZER	greaser
HWĒZER	wheezer
LĒZER	leaser
NĒZER	ebenezer
PĒZER	appeaser
PLĒZER	displeaser, pleaser
SĒZER	Caesar, seizer, seizor, disseizor
SKWĒZER	squeezer
SNĒZER	sneezer
TĒZER	teaser
TWĒZER	tweezer

ĒZHA

BĒZHA	frambesia, Zambesia
DĒZHA	Rhodesia

FRĒZHA	freesia, oxyosphresia
JĒZHA	analgesia, hyperthemalgesia
KLĒZHA	ecclesia
LĒZHA	silesia, Silesia
NĒZHA	amnesia, ecmnesia, hyperkinesia, Indonesia, magnesia, neomnesia, paleomnesia, paramnesia, Polynesia, telamnesia
PĒZHA	trapesia
RĒZHA	parrhesia
THĒZHA	anesthesia, esthesia, hyperesthesia, hypesthesia, hyposthesia, kinesthesia, cryptesthesia, oxyesthesia, radiesthesia, synesthesia, telesthesia, thermanerthesia, thermesthesia, zonesthesia

(This is also pronounced as a triple rhyme, Ē'ZI.A.)

ĒZHER

LĒZHER	leisure
SĒZHER	seizure

EZHER

LEZHER	leisure
MEZHER	admeasure, comeasure, countermeasure, measure, outmeasure
PLEZHER	displeasure, pleasure
TREZHER	entreasure, treasure

EZHERD

MEZHERD	admeasured, comeasured, measured, outmeasured
TREZHERD	entreasured, treasured

ĒZHUN

FĒZHUN	Ephesian

HĒZHUN   adhesion, inadhesion, inhesion, cohesion
KLĒZHUN   ecclesian
LĒZHUN   lesion, Milesian, Silesian
NĒZHUN   magnesian, Polynesian
PĒZHUN   trapezian
TĒZHUN   artesian, etesian, Cartesian

ĒZIKS

JĒZIKS   analgesics
SKĒZIKS   Sheezix

ĒZING

(See **ĒZ,** add *-ing* where appropriate.)

ĒZL

ĒZL   easel
DĒZL   diesel
TĒZL   teasel
WĒZL   weasel

ĒZLD

FĒZLD   ramfeezled
TĒZLD   teaseled
WĒZLD   weaseled

ĒZLZ

MĒZLZ   measles

(See **ĒZL,** add *-s* where appropriate.)

ĒZMENT

ĒZMENT   easement
PĒZMENT   appeasement

ĒZN

MĒZN   mezon
RĒZN   reason, unreason
SĒZN   season, seisin, seizin, reseason, unseason
TRĒZN   treason

ĒZON

(See **ĒZN**)

ĪA

ĪA   ayah
DĪA   dia
FĪA   asaphia, St. Sophia
KRĪA   chria
LĪA   dulia, hyperdulia, Thalia
MĪA   Jeremiah
NĪA   asthenia, gorgoneia, sthenia
PĪA   pia
PRĪA   praya
RĪA   Ave Maria, Black Maria, pariah
SĪA   messiah
STRĪA   stria
TĪA   aristeia, callisteia
TRĪA   aischrolatreia, latria
VĪA   via
ZĪA   jeziah

ĪAD

DĪAD   dyad
DRĪAD   dryad, hamadryad
MĪAD   jeremiad
NĪAD   naiad
PLĪAD   Pleiad

ĪAK

DĪAK   Dayak, Dyak
GĪAK   guiac
JĪAK   elegiac
KĪAK   kayak, kyack, kyak
NĪAK   Nyack
ZĪAK   phrenesiac

ĪAL

DĪAL   dial, moon dial, redial, sundial
FĪAL   phial, defial
HĪAL   basihyal
KRĪAL   decrial, descrial
MĪAL   myall
NĪAL   denial, genial, self-denial
PĪAL   espial, intrapial, pial
PLĪAL   supplial
RĪAL   rial
SĪAL   sial
SPĪAL   spial
STRĪAL   interstrial
TRĪAL   mistrial, trial, retrial
VĪAL   bass viol, vial, viol

(See **ĪL**)

ĪAM

LĪAM   lyam
PRĪAM   Priam
SĪAM   Siam

ĪAN

ĪAN   ion, zwitterion
BĪAN   bion
LĪAN   antlion, dandelion, lion, sea lion, thalian
NĪAN   anion, genian
RĪAN   Arion, Orion
SĪAN   Ixion, scion
STĪAN   styan
TĪAN   altaian
WĪAN   Hawaiian
ZĪAN   Zion

ĪANS

FĪANS   affiance, affiants, defiance
JĪANS   giants, supergiants
KLĪANS   clients
LĪANS   alliance, misalliance, reliance, self-reliance
PLĪANS   appliance, incompliance, compliance, noncompliance, pliance, repliance, suppliance
SĪANS   science

ĪANT

FĪANT   affiant, defiant, calorifient
HĪANT   hiant
JĪANT   Green Giant, giant, red giant
KLĪANT   client
LĪANT   alliant, reliant, self-reliant
PLĪANT   appliant, compliant, pliant, repliant, uncompliant
RĪANT   riant

ĪANTS

(See **ĪANS**)

ĪAR

(See **ĪER**)

ĪAS

ĪAS	eyas
BĪAS	bias, unbias
DRĪAS	drias, hamadryas
KĪAS	antibacchius, bacchius
LĪAS	lias
NĪAS	Ananias
PĪAS	pious, Pius
PRĪAS	nisi prius, prius
RĪAS	Darius, Zacharias

ĪAT

(See ĪET)

ĪBAK

BĪBAK	buyback
DĪBAK	dieback
FLĪBAK	flyback
HĪBAK	high-back
TĪBAK	tieback
SWĪBAK	zwieback

ĪBAL

(See ĪBL)

IBALD

(See IBLD)

IBĒ

FRIBĒ	fribby
JIBĒ	gibby, gibby-jibby
LIBĒ	libbie, women's libbie
NIBĒ	nibby, nibby-jibby
TIBĒ	tibby

ĪBEKS

ĪBEKS	ibex
VĪBEKS	vibex

ĪBER

BĪBER	imbiber
BRĪBER	briber
FĪBER	fiber
JĪBER	giber, jiber
KĪBER	kiber
LĪBER	liber, Liber
SKRĪBER	ascriber, describer, inscriber, prescriber, proscriber, circumscriber, scriber, subscriber, transcriber
TĪBER	Tiber

IBER

BIBER	bibber, winebibber
DIBER	dibber
FIBER	fibber
GLIBER	glibber
JIBER	flibber-gibber, gibber, jibber
KRIBER	cribber
LIBER	ad libber, gay libber, libber, women's libber
NIBER	knibber, nibber
RIBER	ribber
SKWIBER	squibber

IBET

HIBET	adhibit, inhibit, cohibit, prohibit
JIBET	flibbertigibbet, gibbet
LIBET	*quodlibet*, libbet
RIBET	ribbit
ZIBET	exhibit, zibet

ĪBĪ

BĪBĪ	bye-bye
FLĪBĪ	flyby

ĪBING

BĪBING	imbibing
BRĪBING	bribing
JĪBING	gibing, jibing
KĪBING	kibing
SCRĪBING	ascribing, describing, inscribing, prescribing, proscribing, circumscribing, scribing, subscribing, transcribing

IBING

BIBING	bibbing, wine-bibbing
FIBING	fibbing
JIBING	jibbing
KRIBING	cribbing
LIBING	ad libbing
RIBING	ribbing
SKWIBING	squibbing

IBIT

(See IBET)

ĪBL

BĪBL	Bible
LĪBL	libel
SĪBL	postcibal, precibal
SKĪBL	skybal
SKRĪBL	scribal
TRĪBL	intertribal, tribal

IBL

BIBL	bibble, ishkabibble
DIBL	dibble
DRIBL	dribble
FRIBL	fribble
GIBL	gibel
GRIBL	gribble
KIBL	kibble
KRIBL	cribble
KWIBL	quibble
NIBL	nibble
RIBL	ribble
SIBL	sibyl, Sybil, cibol
SKRIBL	scribble, rescribble, transcribble
STIBL	stibble
THRIBL	thribble
TRIBL	tribble

IBLD

RIBLD	ribald

(See IBL, add -d where appropriate.)

ANIMAL NOISE

The cry of a cat's a meow,
And an oink is the meow of a hog;
And a moo is the oink of a cow,
And a bark is the moo of a dog;

And a neigh is the bark of a horse,
And a trumpet's an elephant's neigh;
And the trumpets of lions are roars,
And the roar of a donkey's a bray;

And the bray of a duck is a quack,
And the quack of a snake is a hiss;
And if that doesn't take you aback,
You may be confounded by this:

The hiss of a sheep is a baa,
And a hyena's baa is a laugh;
And the laugh of a babe is a waa,
And the waa of a . . . say a . . . giraffe
  Is so small
   It is nothing
    Nothing at all.

IBLĒ

DRIBLĒ	dribbly
GLIBLĒ	glibly
KWIBLĒ	quibbly
NIBLĒ	nibbly
SKRIBLĒ	scribbly
THRIBLĒ	thribbly
TRIBLĒ	tribbly

IBLER

DIBLER	dibbler
DRIBLER	dribbler
FRIBLER	fribbler
KIBLER	kibbler
KRIBLER	cribbler
KWIBLER	quibbler
NIBLER	nibbler
SKRIBLER	scribbler, transcribbler

IBLET

DRIBLET	driblet
GIBLET	giblet
RIBLET	riblet
TRIBLET	triblet

IBLIK

BIBLIK	Biblic, philobiblic
NIBLIK	mashie-niblick, niblick

IBLING

KIBLING	kibbling
SIBLING	sibling

(See **IBL,** add -ing where appropriate.)

ĪBLŌ

BĪBLŌ	byblow
FLĪBLŌ	flyblow

ĪBÔL

ĪBÔL	eyeball
FLĪBÔL	flyball
HĪBÔL	highball
SKĪBÔL	skyball

ĪBÔLD

ĪBÔLD	eyeballed

| HĪBÔLD | highballed |
| PĪBÔLD | piebald |

IBON

(See **IBUN**)

ĪBÔRN

HĪBÔRN	high-born
SKĪBÔRN	sky-born

ĪBRĀT

LĪBRĀT	equilibrate, librate
VĪBRĀT	vibrate

ĪBRID

HĪBRID	hybrid, polyhybrid
LĪBRID	Librid

ĪBROU

ĪBROU	eyebrow
HĪBROU	highbrow

IBUN

GIBUN	gibbon
RIBUN	blue ribbon, white ribbon, red ribbon, ribbon, yellow ribbon (etc.)

IBUNZ

BIBUNZ	bibbons

(See **IBUN,** add -s.)

IBYA

LIBYA	Libya

(See **IB'I.A**)

ICHĒ

ICHĒ	itchy
BICHĒ	bitchy
FICHĒ	fitchy
HICHĒ	hitchy
KICHĒ	kitschy

PICHĒ	pitchy
STICHĒ	stitchy
SWICHĒ	switchy
TWICHĒ	twitchy
WICHĒ	witchy

ICHER

(See **ICH,** add -er where appropriate.)

ICHET

FICHET	fitchet
WICHET	witchet

ICHEZ

BRICHEZ	breeches, britches

(See **ICH,** add -es where appropriate.)

ICHING

(See **ICH,** add -ing where appropriate.)

ICHKOK

HICHKOK	Alfred Hitchcock
PICHKOK	pitchcock

ICHLES

(See **ICH,** add -less where appropriate.)

ICHMENT

RICHMENT	enrichment
WICHMENT	bewitchment

ĪDAL

(See **ĪDL**)

ĪDANS

BĪDANS	abidance
GĪDANS	guidance, misguidance
SĪDANS	subsidence

IDANS

BIDANS	biddance, forbiddance
RIDANS	good riddance, riddance

ĪDANT

(See ĪDENT)

ĪDAS

MĪDAS	Midas
NĪDAS	nidus

ĪDĒ

DĪDĒ	didy
FĪDĒ	bona fide
FRĪDĒ	Friday
KĪDĒ	alcaide
SĪDĒ	sidy
TĪDĒ	tidy, untidy
VĪDĒ	vide

IDĒ

BIDĒ	biddy, chickabiddy
DIDĒ	diddy
GIDĒ	giddy
KIDĒ	kiddy
MIDĒ	middy, midi
SKIDĒ	skiddy
STIDĒ	stiddy
TIDĒ	tiddy
WIDĒ	widdy

ĪDED

SĪDED	decided, coincided, many-sided, presided, sided, slab-sided, subsided, undecided, one-sided

(See ĪD, add -d where appropriate.)

IDED

HWIDED	whidded
KIDED	kidded
RIDED	ridded
SKIDED	skidded
THRIDED	thridded

ĪDEN

DRĪDEN	Dryden
GĪDEN	guidon
LĪDEN	Leyden
SĪDEN	Poseidon
WĪDEN	widen

IDEN

BIDEN	bidden, forbidden, God-forbidden, unbidden, unforbidden
CHIDEN	chidden
HIDEN	hidden, unhidden
MIDEN	kitchen midden, midden, muckmidden
RIDEN	B bed-ridden, beridden, CH child-ridden, F fever-ridden, H hag-ridden, O overriden, PL plague-ridden, PR priest-ridden, R ridden, U unridden, W wife-ridden
SLIDEN	slidden
STRIDEN	stridden

ĪDENT

BĪDENT	bident
GĪDENT	guidant
RĪDENT	rident
SĪDENT	subsident
STRĪDENT	strident
TRĪDENT	trident
VĪDENT	dividant

ĪDER

ĪDER	eider
BĪDER	abider, bider
CHĪDER	chider
FĪDER	confider
GĪDER	guider, misguider
GLĪDER	glider, hang-glider
HĪDER	hider
LĪDER	elider, collider
NĪDER	nidor
RĪDER	horseback rider, joyrider, nightrider, outrider, rider, Rough Rider
SĪDER	D decider, E East-sider, I insider, K coincider, N North-sider, O outsider, S cider, sider, South-sider, subsider, W West-sider
SLĪDER	backslider, slider
SPĪDER	spider
STRĪDER	bestrider, strider, stridor
VĪDER	divider, provider, subdivider
WĪDER	wider
ZĪDER	presider

IDER

BIDER	bidder, forbidder, outbidder, overbidder, rebidder, underbidder
KIDER	kidder
RIDER	ridder
SIDER	consider, reconsider, sidder, siddur
SKIDER	skidder
SLIDER	slidder
WIDER	widder

ĪDIJ

GĪDIJ	guidage
HĪDIJ	hidage
SĪDIJ	sideage

IDIK

IDIK	druidic
BIDIK	rubidic
KIDIK	arachidic
MIDIK	pyramidic
RIDIK	iridic, juridic
SIDIK	acidic
TIDIK	fatidic

ĪDING

(See ĪD, add -ing where appropriate.)

IDING

(See ID, add -ding where appropriate.)

ĪDINGZ

RĪDINGZ	ridings
TĪDINGZ	tidings

(See ĪD, add -ings where appropriate.)

ĪDĪV

HĪDĪV	highdive
SKĪDĪV	skydive

ĪDL

ĪDL	idle, idol, idyll
BRĪDL	bridal, bridle, rebridle, unbridle
SĪDL	B biocidal, F fungicidal, FR fratricidal, H

homicidal, *I*	
infanticidal,	
insecticidal, *L*	
liberticidal, *M*	
matricidal, *P*	
parricidal, patricidal,	
R regicidal, *S*	
septicidal, seidel,	
sidle, sororicidal,	
suicidal, *SP*	
spermicidal, *T*	
tyrannicidal, *U*	
uxoricidal, *V*	
vermicidal	
TĪDL	cotidal, tidal

IDL

DIDL	diddle, flumdiddle, flummadiddle, hey-diddle-diddle, condiddle, paradiddle, taradiddle
FIDL	fiddle
GRIDL	griddle
KIDL	kiddle
KWIDL	quiddle
MIDL	middle
PIDL	piddle
RIDL	riddle, unriddle
TIDL	rumtumtiddle, tiddle
TWIDL	twiddle
WIDL	widdle

ĪDLD

ĪDLD	idled
BRĪDLD	bridled, rebridled, unbridled
SĪDLD	sidled

IDLD

(See **IDL,** add -*d* where appropriate.)

ĪDLĒ

ĪDLĒ	idly
BRĪDLĒ	bridely
SĪDLĒ	sidly
WĪDLĒ	widely

ĪDLER

ĪDLER	idler
BRĪDLER	bridler
SĪDLER	sidler

IDLER

DIDLER	diddler
FIDLER	fiddler
GRIDLER	griddler
PIDLER	piddler
RIDLER	riddler
TWIDLER	twiddler
WIDLER	widdler

ĪDLĪN

GĪDLĪN	guideline
SĪDLĪN	sideline

ĪDLING

(See **ĪDL,** add -*ing* where appropriate.)

IDLING

(See **IDL,** add -*ing* where appropriate.)

IDNA

DIDNA	didna
KIDNA	echidna

IDNAP

KIDNAP	kidnap
MIDNAP	mid-nap

ĪDNES

PĪDNES	piedness
SNĪDNES	snideness
WĪDNES	wideness

ĪDŌ

DĪDŌ	dido, Dido
FĪDŌ	Fido

IDŌ

KIDŌ	aikido, kiddo
WIDŌ	widow

ĪDON

(See **ĪDEN**)

ĪDUS

(See **ĪDAS**)

ĪENS

(See **ĪANS**)

ĪENT

(See **ĪANT**)

ĪER

ĪER	eyer, evil-eyer
BĪER	buyer
BRĪER	briar, brier, green brier, sweetbrier
DĪER	dier, dyer, never-say-dier
DRĪER	blow dryer, dryer, hair dryer
FĪER	amplifier, dehumidifier, disqualifier, humidifier, intensifier, qualifier, quantifier, magnifier, pacifier, preamplifier, purifier
FLĪER	flier, flyer, heli-flier, highflyer, kiteflyer
FRĪER	friar, fryer
GĪER	lammergeier
HĪER	higher
KRĪER	crier, town crier
LĪER	inlier, liar, lier, lyre, outlier
NĪER	nigher
PĪER	occupier
PLĪER	photomultiplier, multiplier, plier, plyer, supplier
PRĪER	prior, pryer
RĪER	wryer
SLĪER	slyer
SPĪER	spyer
SPRĪER	spryer
TRĪER	trier, trior

(See **Ī,** add -*er* where appropriate; also see **ĪR**.)

ĪET

ĪET	eyot
DĪET	diet
FĪET	fiat
KWĪET	disquiet, inquiet, quiet, unquiet
PĪET	piet, piot
RĪET	riot, ryot
SĪET	Sciot

IFĒ

IFĒ	iffy
BIFĒ	biffy
HWIFĒ	whiffy
JIFĒ	jiffy
KLIFĒ	cliffy
SKWIFĒ	squiffy
SNIFĒ	sniffy
SPIFĒ	spiffy

ĪFEN

HĪFEN	hyphen
SĪFEN	siphon

IFEN

IFEN	if'n
BIFEN	biffin
GRIFEN	griffin, griffon
SHIFEN	chiffon
STIFEN	stiffen
STRIFEN	striffen
TIFEN	tiffin

ĪFER

BĪFER	bifer
FĪFER	fifer
LĪFER	lifer
NĪFER	knifer
RĪFER	rifer
SĪFER	decipher, encipher, cipher, sypher

IFER

DIFER	differ
HWIFER	whiffer
NIFER	niffer
SKWIFER	squiffer
SNIFER	sniffer
STIFER	stiffer

IFIK

IFIK	deific
BIFIK	morbific, orbific, rubific, tabific
BRIFIK	febrific, tenebrific
DIFIK	acidific, grandific, lapidific
GLIFIK	anaglyphic, dactyloglyphic, diaglyphic, phytoglyphic, photoglyphic, glyphic, hieroglyphic, geoglyphic, lithoglyphic, petroglyphic, triglyphic
JIFIK	algific
LIFIK	mellific, prolific
NIFIK	damnific, finific, cornific, magnific, nific, omnific, somnific, vulnific
RIFIK	*D* dolorific, *FR* frigorific, *H* horrific, humorific, *K* calorific, colorific, *M* mirific, *O* honorific, aurific, *S* sacrific, saporific, sonorific, soporific, sudorific, *T* terrific, torporific, *V* vaporific
SIFIK	*F* felicific, *K* calcific, conspecific, *KL* classific, *L* lucific, *M* mucific, *O* ossific, *P* pacific, Pacific, pulsific, *S* sensific, *SP* specific, *ST* stereospecific, *TR* transpacific
TIFIK	beatific, incoherentific, lactific, pontific, scientific, unscientific
TRIFIK	petrific
VIFIK	salvific, vivific

IFIN

(See **IFEN**)

IFING

HWIFING	whiffing
MIFING	miffing
SKIFING	skiffing
SNIFING	sniffing
TIFING	tiffing

IFISH

MIFISH	miffish
SKWIFISH	squiffish
SNIFISH	sniffish
STIFISH	stiffish
TIFISH	tiffish

ĪFL

ĪFL	Eiffel
NĪFL	nifle
RĪFL	rifle
STĪFL	stifle
TRĪFL	trifle

IFL

HWIFL	whiffle
NIFL	nifle
PIFL	piffle
RIFL	riffle
SNIFL	sniffle

ĪFLĒ

RĪFLĒ	rifely
WĪFLĒ	wifely

IFLĒ

SNIFLĒ	sniffly
STIFLĒ	stiffly

ĪFLER

RĪFLER	rifler
STĪFLER	stifler
TRĪFLER	trifler

IFLER

HWIFLER	whiffler
PIFLER	piffler
RIFLER	riffler
SNIFLER	sniffler

ĪFLES

(See **ĪF,** add -*less* where appropriate.)

ĪFLING

RĪFLING	rifling
STĪFLING	stifling
TRĪFLING	trifling

IFLING

HWIFLING	whiffling
PIFLING	piffling
RIFLING	riffling
SKIFLING	skiffling
SNIFLING	sniffling

IFTĒ

DRIFTĒ	drifty
FIFTĒ	fifty, fifty-fifty
KLIFTĒ	clifty
NIFTĒ	nifty
RIFTĒ	rifty
SHIFTĒ	shifty
SNIFTĒ	snifty
THRIFTĒ	thrifty

IFTED

(See IFT, add -ed where appropriate.)

IFTER

DRIFTER	drifter
LIFTER	lifter, shoplifter, uplifter, weight lifter
RIFTER	rifter
SHIFTER	scene-shifter, shifter
SNIFTER	snifter
SWIFTER	swifter

IFTIJ

DRIFTIJ	driftage
SHIFTIJ	shiftage
SIFTIJ	siftage

IFTING

DRIFTING	drifting
LIFTING	lifting, shoplifting, uplifting
RIFTING	rifting
SHIFTING	sceneshifting, shifting
SIFTING	sifting

IFTLES

(See IFT, add -less where appropriate.)

IFTHONG

DIFTHONG	diphthong
TRIFTHONG	triphthong

IFTNES

DRIFTNES	adriftness
MIFTINES	miffedness
SKWIFTNES	squiffedness
SWIFTNES	swiftness

ĪGA

BĪGA	biga
RĪGA	quadriga
SĪGA	saiga
STRĪGA	striga
TĪGA	taiga

ĪGAL

PĪGAL	dasypygal, pygal
ZĪGAL	zygal

IGAN

BRIGAN	balbriggan
PIGAN	piggin
WIGAN	wigan

ĪGĀT

LĪGĀT	ligate
STRĪGĀT	strigate

IGĒ

BIGĒ	biggy
PIGĒ	piggy
SIGĒ	ciggie
SPRIGĒ	spriggy
TWIGĒ	twiggy
WIGĒ	piggy-wiggywiggy

ĪGER

GĪGER	geiger
LĪGER	liger
NĪGER	Niger
TĪGER	tiger

IGER

BIGER	bigger
CHIGER	chigger
DIGER	digger, gold-digger, grave-digger
FIGER	figger, figure
GIGER	gigger
JIGER	bejigger, jigger
LIGER	ligger
NIGER	nigger, reneger
PRIGER	prigger
RIGER	market rigger, outrigger, rigger, rigor, thimble-rigger
SNIGER	snigger
SPRIGER	sprigger
SWIGER	swigger
TRIGER	trigger
TWIGER	twigger
VIGER	vigor

IGERD

FIGERD	figgered
JIGERD	bejiggered, jiggered
NIGERD	niggard
SNIGERD	sniggered
TRIGERD	triggered

IGET

(See IGOT)

IGIN

(See IGAN)

IGING

THIGING	thigging

(See IG, add -ing where appropriate.)

IGISH

HWIGISH	whiggish
JIGISH	jiggish
PIGISH	piggish
PRIGISH	priggish
RIGISH	riggish
WIGISH	wiggish

IGL

FRIGL	friggle
GIGL	giggle
HIGL	higgle
JIGL	jiggle
NIGL	niggle
RIGL	wriggle
SIGL	sigil
SKWIGL	squiggle
SNIGL	sniggle
STRIGL	striggle
SWIGL	swiggle
WIGL	porwigle, wiggle

ĪGLAS

ĪGLAS	eyeglass
SPĪGLAS	spyglass

IGLD

(See **IGL,** add -d where appropriate.)

IGLĒ

GIGLĒ	giggly
RIGLĒ	wriggly
WIGLĒ	Piggly Wiggly, Uncle Wiggly, wiggly

(See **IGL,** add -y where appropriate.)

IGLER

(See **IGL,** add -r where appropriate.)

IGLET

GIGLET	giglet
PIGLET	piglet
WIGLET	wiglet

ĪGLIF

DĪGLIF	diglyph
TRĪGLIF	monotriglyph, triglyph

IGLING

(See **IGL,** add -ing where appropriate.)

IGMA

NIGMA	enigma
RIGMA	kerygma, sterigma
SIGMA	sigma
STIGMA	hypostigma, stigma

IGMĒ

PIGMĒ	pygmy
RIGMĒ	borborygmy
STIGMĒ	stigme

IGMENT

FIGMENT	figment
PIGMENT	pigment

IGNAL

RIGNAL	orignal
SIGNAL	signal

IGNANT

DIGNANT	indignant
LIGNANT	malignant
NIGNANT	benignant

IGNUM

LIGNUM	lignum
RIGNUM	rignum
SIGNUM	ecce signum
TIGNUM	tignum

ĪGŌ

BĪGŌ	by-go
LĪGŌ	caligo, fuligo
PĪGŌ	serpigo
RĪGŌ	prurigo
SLĪGŌ	Sligo
TĪGŌ	impetigo, lentigo, tentigo, *vertigo*
TRĪGŌ	intertrigo

ĪGON

BĪGON	bygone
TRĪGON	trigon

IGOT

BIGOT	bigot
FRIGOT	frigate
JIGOT	gigot
RIGOT	riggot
SPIGOT	spigot

IGYER

FIGYER	disfigure, figure, configure, prefigure, refigure, transfigure
LIGYER	ligure

ĪĪD

DRĪĪD	dry-eyed
PĪĪD	pie-eyed
SLĪĪD	sly-eyed

ĪING

(See **Ī,** add -ing where appropriate.)

ĪISH

DRĪISH	dryish
SHĪISH	shyish
SLĪISH	slyish

ĪJAK

HĪJAK	highjack, hi-jack
SKĪJAK	skyjack

IJĒ

GIJĒ	gidgee
SKWIJĒ	squidgy

IJER

BRIJER	abridger, bridger
RIJER	ridger

IJEST

BLIJEST	disobligest, obligest
DIJEST	digest

IJET

DIJET	digit, double-digit, triple-digit
FIJET	fidget
MIJET	midget
NIJET	nidget
WIJET	widget

IJID

FRIJID	frigid, unfrigid
RIJID	nonrigid, rigid, semirigid, unrigid

IJIL

SIJIL	sigil
STRIJIL	strigil
VIJIL	vigil

IJING

BRIJING	abridging, bridging
FIJING	fidging
NIJING	nidging
RIJING	ridging

IJIT

(See **IJET**)

IJUN

LIJUN	irreligion, religion
PIJUN	gyropigeon, pidgin, pigeon
SMIJUN	smidgen
WIJUN	widgeon

IJUS

DIJUS	prodigious
LIJUS	irreligious, religious, sacrilegious
TIJUS	litigious, prestigious

ĪKA

GĪKA	nagaika
LĪKA	balalaika, kamalayka, Leica
MĪKA	formica, hydromica, mica, Micah
PĪKA	pica, pika
PLĪKA	plica
RĪKA	lorica, Myrica
SPĪKA	spica
STĪKA	styka

IKA

LIKA	licca
SIKA	sicca
TIKA	ticca, tikka

ĪKAL

(See **ĪKL**)

ĪKĀT

PLĪKĀT	plicate
SPĪKĀT	spicate

IKCHER

PIKCHER	depicture, impicture, picture, repicture, word picture
STRIKCHER	stricture

ĪKĒ

ĪKĒ	ikey, Ikey
DĪKĒ	dikey
KRĪKĒ	crikey, by crikey
NĪKĒ	Nike
PĪKĒ	piky
SĪKĒ	photopsyche, psyche, Psyche
TĪKĒ	Tyche

IKĒ

IKĒ	icky
BRIKĒ	bricky
CHIKĒ	chicky
DIKĒ	dickey, dicky
HIKĒ	doohickey, hickey
KWIKĒ	quicky
PIKĒ	picky
PRIKĒ	pricky
RIKĒ	gin rickey, jinriki, rickey
SIKĒ	sicky
STIKĒ	sticky
TIKĒ	Rikki-Tikki
TRIKĒ	tricky

IKEN

CHIKEN	chicken
QUIKEN	quicken
SIKEN	sicken
SLIKEN	slicken
STRIKEN	horror-stricken, stricken, terror-stricken, wonder-stricken
THIKEN	thicken

IKENZ

DIKENZ	dickens, Dickens

(See **IKEN**, add -s where appropriate.)

ĪKER

ĪKER	ichor
BĪKER	biker
DĪKER	diker, duiker
HĪKER	hiker, hitchhiker
LĪKER	liker, obliquer
PĪKER	piker
SPĪKER	spiker
STRĪKER	striker

IKER

IKER	icker
BIKER	bicker
DIKER	dicker
FLIKER	flicker
HWIKER	whicker
KIKER	high-kicker, kicker
KLIKER	clicker
KWIKER	quicker
LIKER	bootlicker, licker, liquor
NIKER	dominicker, knicker, nicker
PIKER	berrypicker, cherrypicker, fruitpicker, cottonpicker, (ect.), picker
PRIKER	pricker
RIKER	ricker
SHIKER	shicker
SIKER	sicker
SLIKER	slicker
SMIKER	smicker
SNIKER	snicker
STIKER	bumper sticker, pigsticker, spitsticker, sticker
THIKER	thicker
TIKER	ticker, tikker
TRIKER	tricker
VIKER	vicar
WIKER	wicker

IKERZ

NIKERZ	knickers

(See **IKER**, add -s where appropriate.)

IKET

KLIKET	clicket
KRIKET	cricket
PIKET	picket
PRIKET	pricket
SMIKET	smicket
SNIKET	snicket
SPIKET	spicket
THIKET	thicket
TIKET	ticket
WIKET	sticky wicket, wicket

IKETS

RIKETS	rickets

(See **IKET**, add -s where appropriate.)

IKIN

KIKIN	kick-in
NIKIN	nikin
SIKIN	sick-in

ĪKING

DĪKING	diking
HĪKING	hiking, hitch-hiking
LĪKING	disliking, liking
PĪKING	piking
SPĪKING	spiking
STRĪKING	striking
VĪKING	viking, Viking

IKING

LIKING	bootlicking, finger-licking, licking
PIKING	berry-picking, cherry-picking, cotton-picking (etc.), picking

(See **IK,** add -ing where appropriate.)

IKISH

(See **IK,** add -ish where appropriate.)

ĪKL

PĪKL	pical
PLĪKL	plical
SĪKL	epicycle, gigacycle, hemicycle, motorcycle, recycle, psychal, cycle, unicycle

IKL

BRIKL	brickle, bricole
CHIKL	chicle
FIKL	fickle, unfickle
MIKL	mickle
NIKL	cupronickel, nickel, nickle, plugged nickel, pumpernickel, wooden nickel
PIKL	pickle, picul, pikle
PRIKL	prickle
SIKL	bicycle, sickle, tricycle
STIKL	stickle
STRIKL	strickle
TIKL	tickle
TRIKL	trickle

IKLĒ

(See **IK,** add -ly where appropriate.)

IKLER

FIKLER	fickler
PIKLER	pickler
PRIKLER	prickler
SIKLER	bicycler, sickler
STIKLER	stickler
STRIKLER	strickler
TIKLER	tickler
TRIKLER	trickler

IKLET

CHIKLET	Chiclet
TRIKLET	tricklet

IKLING

CHIKLING	chickling
PIKLING	pickling
PRIKLING	prickling
SIKLING	sickling
STIKLING	stickling
STRIKLING	strickling
TIKLING	tickling
TRIKLING	trickling

IKLISH

PRIKLISH	pricklish
TIKLISH	ticklish
TRIKLISH	tricklish

IKNES

SIKNES	lovesickness, sickness, sleeping sickness

(See **IK,** add -ness where appropriate.)

IKNIK

PIKNIK	isopycnic, isopyknic, picnic, pyknic
STRIKNIK	strychnic

IKNING

(See **IK'EN.ING.**)

IKSCHER

FIKSCHER	affixture, fixture, transfixture
MIKSCHER	admixture, immixture, incommixture, intermixture, commixture, mixture

IKSĒ

DIKSĒ	dixie, Dixie
JIKSĒ	jixie
MIKSĒ	mixy
NIKSĒ	nixie, water nixie
PIKSĒ	pixie, pyxie
TRIKSĒ	tricksy

IKSEN

BIKSEN	bixin
MIKSEN	mixen
VIKSEN	vixen

IKSER

FIKSER	affixer, fixer, *prefixer*, transfixer
LIKSER	elixir
MIKSER	admixer, intermixer, mixer
NIKSER	nixer

IKSET

KWIKSET	quickset
THIKSET	thickset

IKSHUN

DIKSHUN	*A* addiction, *B* benediction, *D* diction, *I* indiction, interdiction, *J* jurisdiction, *K* contradiction, *M* malediction, *PR* prediction, *S* satisdiction, *V* valediction
FIKSHUN	affixion, fiction, crucifixion, nonfiction, prefixion, suffixion, transfiction
FLIKSHUN	affliction, infliction, confliction
FRIKSHUN	affriction, friction

LIKSHUN	dereliction, reliction
PIKSHUN	depiction
STRIKSHUN	abstriction, derestriction, constriction, obstriction, restriction, striction
VIKSHUN	eviction, conviction, preconviction

IKSHUS

DIKSHUS	contradictious
FIKSHUS	fictious

IKSING

FIKSING	affixing, fixing, prefixing, refixing, suffixing, transfixing
MIKSING	admixing, intermixing, overmixing
NIKSING	nixing

IKSTŪR

(See **IKSCHER**)

IKTĀT

DIKTĀT	dictate
NIKTĀT	nictate

IKTED

(See **IKT,** add -ed where appropriate.)

IKTER

DIKTER	interdictor, contradictor, predictor
FIKTER	fictor
FLIKTER	afflicter, inflicter, conflicter
LIKTER	lictor
PIKTER	depicter, Pictor
STRIKTER	boa constrictor, constrictor, stricter, vasoconstrictor
VIKTER	evictor, convictor, victor

IKTIK

IKTIK	ictic

DIKTIK	anapodictic, apodictic, dictic, endictic, epidictic
MIKTIK	amyctic

IKTING

(See **IKT,** add -ing where appropriate.)

IKTIV

DIKTIV	addictive, apodictic, benedictive, indictive, interdictive, jurisdictive, contradictive, predictive, vindictive
FIKTIV	fictive
FLIKTIV	afflictive, inflictive, conflictive
PIKTIV	depictive
STRIKTIV	astrictive, constrictive, nonrestrictive, restrictive, unrestrictive
VIKTIV	evictive, convictive

IKTLĒ

LIKTLĒ	derelictly
STRIKTLĒ	strictly

IKTUM

DIKTUM	dictum, obiter dictum
LIKTUM	delictum

IKTŪR

(See **IKCHER**)

IKTUS

IKTUS	ictus
DIKTUS	Benedictus
NIKTUS	acronyctous
RIKTUS	rictus
VIKTUS	Invictus

IKUP

DIKUP	dikkop
HIKUP	hiccup
KIKUP	kickup
PIKUP	pickup
STIKUP	stickup

ĪKUS

FĪKUS	ficus
LĪKUS	umbilicus
PĪKUS	Picus
SPĪKUS	spicous
TĪKUS	anticous, anticus, posticous, posticus

ULTIMATUM TO MY CONGRESSMAN, COMPOSED ON A MISERABLE DAY

Roads are muddy?
Make a study.

Day too warm?
Vote reform.

Feel a chill?
Draw a bill.

Morning raw?
Pass a law.

Snow and ice?
Pass it twice.

Storm and bluster?
Filibuster.

*Though the weather's not affected,
This will get you re-elected.*

ĪLA

ĪLA	Ila
BĪLA	strobila
HĪLA	hyla
LĪLA	Delilah
PĪLA	pyla

ILA

BILA	Sibylla
CHILA	chinchilla
DILA	granadilla, codilla, sabadilla, sapodilla, cedilla, seguidilla
GILA	megillah, Megillah
MILA	armilla, bismilla, camilla
NILA	anilla, granilla, manila, manilla, vanilla
RILA	barilla, gorilla, guerrilla, camarilla, cascarilla, sarsaparilla, sasparilla, spirilla, zorilla
SILA	axilla, maxilla, Scylla
SKWILA	squilla
TILA	flotilla, mantilla, scintilla
VILA	villa

ĪLAJ

(See ĪLIJ)

ĪLAKS

FĪLAKS	phylax
LĪLAKS	lilacs
SMĪLAKS	smilax

ILAN

(See ILIN)

ĪLAND

ĪLAND	island, Long Island, Rhode Island (etc.)
HĪLAND	highland
SKĪLAND	skyland
TĪLAND	Thailand

ĪLAR

(See ĪLER)

ĪLÄRK

FĪLÄRK	phylarch
SKĪLÄRK	skylark

ILCHER

FILCHER	filcher
MILCHER	milcher
PILCHER	pilcher

ILDA

HILDA	Brunhilde, Hilda
TILDA	tilde

ILDED

BILDED	builded
GILDED	begilded, gilded, guilded, unguilded

ĪLDER

MĪLDER	milder
WĪLDER	wilder

ILDER

BILDER	builder, home-builder, house-builder, castle-builder, rebuilder, shipbuilder, unbuilder
CHILDER	childer
GILDER	begilder, gilder, guilder
MILDER	milder
WILDER	bewilder, wilder

ĪLDING

CHĪLDING	childing
WĪLDING	wilding

ILDING

BILDING	building, housebuilding, homebuilding, castle-building, rebuilding, shipbuilding, unbuilding
GILDING	begilding, gilding, regilding, ungilding
HILDING	hilding

ĪLDISH

CHĪLDISH	childish
MĪLDISH	mildish
WĪLDISH	wildish

ĪLDLĒ

CHĪLDLĒ	childly
GĪLDLĒ	beguiledly
MĪLDLĒ	mildly
RĪLDLĒ	riledly
WĪLDLĒ	wildly

ĪLDLING

CHĪLDLING	childling
WĪLDLING	wildling

ĪLDNES

MĪLDNES	mildness
WĪLDNES	wildness

ĪLĒ

DĪLĒ	sedile
DRĪLĒ	drily
HĪLĒ	highly, hyle
KĪLĒ	kylie
RĪLĒ	wryly
SHĪLĒ	shyly
SĪLĒ	ancile
SLĪLĒ	slily, slyly
SMĪLĒ	smily
WĪLĒ	wily

ILĒ

ILĒ	illy
BILĒ	billy, Billy
CHILĒ	Chile, chili, chilly
DILĒ	daffy-down-dilly, daffodilly, dilly, Piccadilly
FILĒ	filly
FRILĒ	frilly
GILĒ	ghillie, gillie
GRILĒ	grilly
HILĒ	hilly
KILĒ	killy
KWILĒ	quilly
LILĒ	day lily, lily, meadow lily, piccalilli, pond lily, tiger lily, water lily, wood lily
NILĒ	willy-nilly
RILĒ	rilly
SHRILĒ	shrilly
SILĒ	silly
SKILĒ	skilly
STILĒ	stilly
THRILĒ	thrilly
TILĒ	tilly
TRILĒ	trilly
TWILĒ	twilly
WILĒ	nilly-willy, weary Willie, willy

ĪLEKS

ĪLEKS	ilex
SĪLEKS	silex

ĪLEM

(See ĪLUM)

ĪLER

ĪLER	defiler, filar, filer
GĪLER	beguiler
MĪLER	half-miler, quarter-miler, miler, two-miler (etc.)
PĪLER	compiler, pilar, piler, up-piler

RĪLER	riler
SĪLER	reconciler
SMĪLER	smiler
STĪLER	stylar, styler

ILER

ILER	iller
BILER	biller
CHILER	chiller
DILER	killer-diller
DRILER	driller
FILER	filler, fulfiller
FRILER	befriller, friller
GILER	giller
GRILER	griller
HILER	hiller
KILER	giant-killer, killer, lady-killer, man-killer, pain-killer, weed-killer (etc.)
KWILER	quiller
MILER	Joe Miller, miller
PILER	caterpillar, pillar
SHILER	schiller, shiller
SHRILER	shriller
SILER	maxillar, siller
SPILER	spiller
STILER	instiller, stiller
SWILER	swiller
THILER	thiller
THRILER	thriller
TILER	distiller, tiller
TRILER	pralltriller, triller
WILER	ill-willer, willer

ĪLES

ĪLES	eyeless

(See **Ī**, add -*less* where appropriate.)

ĪLET

ĪLET	eyelet, islet
PĪLET	co-pilot, Pilate, pilot, sky pilot
SMĪLET	smilet
STĪLET	stylet

ILET

BILET	billet
DRILET	drillet
FILET	fillet
KWILET	quillet
MILET	millet
PILET	pillet

RILET	rillet
SILET	penicillate, verticillate
SKILET	skillet
TILET	distillate
TRILET	trillet
WILET	pilwillet, willet

ILĒZ

KILĒZ	Achilles
WILĒZ	willies

(See **ILĒ**, add -*s* or change -*y* to -*ies* where appropriate.)

ĪLFUL

GĪLFUL	guileful
SMĪLFUL	smileful
WĪLFUL	wileful

ILFUL

SKILFUL	skillful
WILFUL	willful

ĪLIJ

MĪLIJ	mileage
SĪLIJ	silage
SMĪLIJ	smileage

ILIJ

GRILIJ	grillage
PILIJ	pillage
SPILIJ	spillage
STILIJ	stillage
TILIJ	tillage
VILIJ	global village, village

ILIK

DILIK	idyllic, odyllic
FILIK	*A* aelurophilic, Anglophilic, *B* bibliophilic, *D* discophilic, *E* ergophilic, *FR* Francophilic, *G* Gallophilic, gastrophilic, *H* halophilic, hemophilic, hydrophilic, *I* Italophilic, *J*

Japanophilic, Germanophilic, *KR* cryophilic, *L* lyophilic, lipophilic, *M* mesophilic, *N* necrophilic, Negrophilic, *P* pyrophilic, *R* rheophilic, Russophilic, *S* psychrophilic, *SL* Slavophilic, *T* typophilic, Turkophilic, *TH* theophilic, thermophilic, *Z* Zionophilic, zoophilic

KILIK	killick, trochilic
KRILIK	acrylic
MILIK	amylic
NILIK	vanillic
RILIK	Cyrillic
SILIK	bacillic, basilic, exilic, imbecilic, cresylic, salicylic
THILIK	ethylic, methylic
TILIK	dactylic, holodactylic, macrodactylic, zygodactylic
ZILIK	exilic

ILIN

VILIN	archvillain, villain, villein
ZILIN	hoitzitzillin

ĪLING

(See **ĪL**, add -*ing* where appropriate.)

ILING

(See **IL**, add -*ing* where appropriate.)

ILIS

RILIS	amaryllis
SILIS	cilice

ĪLĪT

DRĪLĪT	dry light
HĪLĪT	highlight
SKĪLĪT	skylight
STĪLĪT	stylite
TWĪLĪT	twilight
ZĪLĪT	xylite

ĪLIT

SILIT	penicillate
TILIT	distillate

IFEN

BIFEN	biffin
GRIFEN	griffin, griffon
SHIFEN	chiffon
STIFEN	stiffen
STRIFEN	striffen
TIFEN	tiffin

ILKĒ

MILKĒ	milky
SILKĒ	silky
WILKĒ	Wendell Willkie

ILKEN

MILKEN	milken
SILKEN	silken

ILKER

BILKER	bilker
MILKER	milker
SILKER	silker

ILKING

(See **ILK,** add -ing where appropriate.)

ĪLLES

BĪLLES	bileless
FĪLLES	fileless
GĪLLES	guileless
STĪLLES	styleless
TĪLLES	tileless
TRĪLLES	trialless
WĪLLES	wileless

ILMAN

BILMAN	billman
GRILMAN	grillman
HILMAN	hillman
MILMAN	millman
PILMAN	pillman

ĪLMENT

FĪLMENT	defilement
GĪLMENT	beguilement
PĪLMENT	compilement
SĪLMENT	domicilement, exilement, irreconcilement, reconcilement, resilement
VĪLMENT	revilement
ZĪLMENT	exilement

ILMENT

FILMENT	fulfillment
STILMENT	distillment, instillment

ĪLNES

NĪLNES	juvenileness
VĪLNES	vileness

ILNES

ILNES	illness
CHILNES	chillness
SHRILNES	shrillness
STILNES	stillness

ĪLŌ

BĪLŌ	bye-low
HĪLŌ	high-low
MĪLŌ	milo
SHĪLŌ	Shiloh
SĪLŌ	silo
STĪLŌ	stylo

ILŌ

BILŌ	billow, embillow
DILŌ	armadillo, grenadillo, peccadillo, tabardillo
FILŌ	phyllo
GRILŌ	Negrillo
KILŌ	killow, kilo
PILŌ	lapillo, pillow, unpillow
RILŌ	Murillo, cigarillo
VILŌ	pulvillo
WILŌ	weeping willow, willow

ILŌD

BILŌD	billowed
PILŌD	empillowed, pillowed, unpillowed

ĪLOID

STĪLOID	styloid
ZĪLOID	xyloid

ILOK

(See **ILUK**)

ĪLON

FĪLON	phylon
NĪLON	nylon
PĪLON	pylon
TRĪLON	trylon

ĪLŌS

FĪLŌS	filose
PĪLŌS	pilose

ĪLOT

(See **ĪLET**)

ILROOM

GRILROOM	grillroom
STILROOM	stillroom

ILSĪD

HILSĪD	hillside
RILSĪD	rillside

ILTĒ

GILTĒ	guilty
KILTĒ	kilty
KWILTĒ	quilty
LILTĒ	lilty
MILTĒ	milty
SILTĒ	silty
STILTĒ	stilty
TILTĒ	tilty
WILTĒ	wilty

ILTED

(See **ILT,** add -ed where appropriate.)

ILTER

FILTER	filter, philter, infilter, ultrafilter
JILTER	jilter
KILTER	kilter, out-of-kilter
KWILTER	quilter, crazy-quilter
LILTER	lilter
MILTER	milter
STILTER	stilter
TILTER	tilter
WILTER	wilter

ILTING

HILTING	hilting
JILTING	jilting
KILTING	kilting
KWILTING	quilting, crazy-quilting
LILTING	lilting
MILTING	milting
SILTING	silting
STILTING	stilting
TILTING	overtilting, tilting, tip-tilting, uptilting
WILTING	wilting

ILUK

FILUK	fillock
HILUK	hillock
SILUK	sillock

ĪLUM

FĪLUM	filum, phylum, subphylum
HĪLUM	hilum
HWĪLUM	whilom
SĪLUM	asylum
ZĪLUM	xylem

ILUM

FILUM	fillum
RILUM	spirillum

ĪLUS

HĪLUS	hilus
STĪLUS	monostylus, stylus

ILUS

BRILUS	*fibrillous*
FILUS	aphyllous, phyllous
GRILUS	grillos, gryllus, Grillus
JILUS	aspergillus, orgillous
KWILUS	quisquillous
MILUS	camillous
PILUS	lapillus
RILUS	arrilus
SILUS	bacillus
VILUS	favillous, pulvillus, villous, villus

ILYA

(See **IL'I.A**)

ILYAR

BILYAR	atrabiliar
MILYAR	familiar, overfamiliar, unfamiliar
SILYAR	domiciliar, conciliar
ZILYAR	auxiliar

(See **IL'I.AR**)

ILYARD

BILYARD	billiard
MILYARD	milliard

ILYARDZ

BILYARDZ	billiards
MILYARDZ	milliards

ILYENS

BRILYENS	brilliance
SILYENS	dissilience, consilience, transilience
ZILYENS	resilience

(See **IL'I.ENS**)

ILYENT

BRILYENT	brilliant
SILYENT	dissilient, consilient, transilient
ZILYENT	resilient

(See **IL'I.ENT**)

ILYUN

BILYUN	billion, tourbillion
DILYUN	mandillion, modillion
DRILYUN	drillion
JILYUN	gillion, jillion
KWILYUN	quisguillian
MILYUN	million, vermilion
NILYUN	nonillion, penillion
PILYUN	pillion
RILYUN	carillon, quadrillion
SILYUN	decillion
SKILYUN	skillion
STILYUN	stillion
TILYUN	dactylion, cotillion, quintillion, octillion, postillion, centillion, septillion, sextillion
TRILYUN	trillion
VILYUN	oyster villian, pavilion, civilian
ZILYUN	zillion

(See **IL'I.AN**)

ILYUS

BILYUS	atrabilious, bilious

(See **IL'I.US**)

ĪMA

FĪMA	phyma
LĪMA	lima, Lima, tellima
PĪMA	arapaima
RĪMA	rima
SĪMA	cyma, sima
TRĪMA	trima

IMAJ

(See **IMIJ**)

ĪMAKS

KLĪMAKS	climax
LĪMAKS	limax

ĪMAL

KĪMAL	isocheimal
KRĪMAL	isocrymal
PRĪMAL	primal
RĪMAL	rimal
SHTRĪMAL	shtreimel

IMAL

(See **IMEL**)

ĪMAN

(See **ĪMEN**)

ĪMĀT

(See ĪMIT)

IMBA

RIMBA	marimba
SIMBA	simba

IMBAL

(See IMBL)

IMBER

LIMBER	limber, unlimber
TIMBER	timber, timbre, retimber

IMBERD

LIMBERD	limbered, unlimbered
TIMBERD	timbered, untimbered

IMBL

BIMBL	bimbil
FIMBL	fimble
GIMBL	gimbal, gimble
NIMBL	nimble
SIMBL	cymbal, simbil, symbol, clavicymbal
THIMBL	thimble
THRIMBL	thrimble
TIMBL	tymbal, tymbale
WIMBL	wimble

IMBŌ

BIMBŌ	bimbo
KIMBŌ	akimbo, kimbo
LIMBŌ	limbo

IMBREL

HWIMBREL	whimbrel
TIMBREL	timbrel

IMBUS

LIMBUS	limbus, limbous
NIMBUS	nimbus, cumulo nimbus

ĪMĒ

BLĪMĒ	blimy, Gawblimy, cor blimy
GRĪMĒ	grimy
KRĪMĒ	crimy
LĪMĒ	limey, limy
PRĪMĒ	primy
RĪMĒ	rhymy, rimy
SLĪMĒ	beslimy, slimy
STĪMĒ	stymie
TĪMĒ	old-timey, thymy

IMĒ

IMĒ	immie
DIMĒ	dhimmie
GIMĒ	gimmie
HWIMĒ	whimmy
JIMĒ	jimmy
LIMĒ	limby
SHIMĒ	shimmy
SWIMĒ	swimmy
ZIMĒ	zimme, zimmy

ĪMEKS

SĪMEKS	cimex
TĪMEKS	Timex

ĪMEL

(See ĪMAL)

IMEL

GIMEL	gimel, gimmal
HIMEL	Himmel
KIMEL	kümmel

THE DANGEROUS YEARS

I'm aware a
Midlife crisis
Isn't rare a-
mong men's vices.
To defy a
Fading id-life
Some men try a
Mid-life mid-wife.

ĪMEN

HĪMEN	hymen, Hymen
LĪMEN	limen
SĪMEN	simple Simon
TĪMEN	timon, Timon

IMEN

SIMEN	persimmon
WIMEN	women

ĪMER

CHĪMER	chimer
DĪMER	dimer, nickel-and-dimer
GRĪMER	begrimer
KLĪMER	climber
LĪMER	sublimer, limer
MĪMER	mimer
PRĪMER	primer
RĪMER	rhymer, rimer
TĪMER	full-timer, old-timer, autotimer, part-timer, timer, timor, two-timer
TRĪMER	trimer

IMER

IMER	immer
BRIMER	brimmer
DIMER	dimmer
GIMER	gimmer
GLIMER	aglimmer, glimmer
GRIMER	grimmer
HIMER	hymner
KRIMER	krimmer
LIMER	limmer
NIMER	nimmer
PRIMER	primer, primmer
RIMER	rimmer
SHIMER	ashimmer, shimmer
SIMER	asimmer, simmer
SKIMER	hydroskimmer, skimmer
SLIMER	slimmer
SWIMER	nonswimmer, swimmer
TRIMER	trimmer

IMIJ

IMIJ	after-image, image
SKRIMIJ	scrimmage

ĪMIK

KĪMIK	isocheimic
RĪMIK	rhymic
THĪMIK	thymic
TĪMIK	hypothymic, catathymic, thymic
ZĪMIK	zymic

IMIK

BIMIK	cherubimic
GIMIK	gimmick
KIMIK	alchimic, cacochymic
MIMIK	mimic, pantomimic, zoömimic
NIMIK	acronymic, eponymic, homonymic, matronymic, metonymic, metronymic, patronymic, synonymic, pseudonymic, toponymic
THIMIK	lipothymic
TIMIK	etymic
ZIMIK	azymic, symic

IMIKS

(See **IMIK,** add -s where appropriate.)

ĪMING

CHĪMING	chiming
GRĪMING	begriming, griming
KLĪMING	climbing
MĪMING	miming
PRĪMING	priming, pump-priming
RĪMING	rhyming, riming
SLĪMING	sliming
TĪMING	timing, two-timing

IMING

BRIMING	brimming
DIMING	dimming
LIMING	limbing
SKIMING	skimming
SLIMING	slimming
SWIMING	swimming
TRIMING	retrimming, trimming

ĪMISH

CHĪMISH	chimish
RĪMISH	rhymish
TĪMISH	timish

IMISH

DIMISH	dimmish
GRIMISH	grimmish
PRIMISH	primmish
SLIMISH	slimmish
TRIMISH	trimmish

ĪMIST

RĪMIST	rhymist
TĪMIST	timist

(See **ĪM,** add -st where appropriate.)

ĪMIT

KLĪMIT	acclimate, climate
PRĪMIT	primate

ĪMLĒ

LĪMLĒ	sublimely
PRĪMLĒ	primely
TĪMLĒ	timely, untimely

IML

(See **IMEL.**)

IMLĒ

DIMLĒ	dimly
GRIMLĒ	grimly
PRIMLĒ	primly
SLIMLĒ	slimly
TRIMLĒ	trimly

ĪMLES

(See **ĪM,** add -less where appropriate.)

IMLES

(See **IM,** add -less where appropriate.)

IMNAL

HIMNAL	hymnal
SIMNAL	simnel

IMNER

HIMNER	hymner
LIMNER	limner

ĪMNES

LĪMNES	sublimeness
PRĪMNES	primeness

IMNES

DIMNES	dimness
GRIMNES	grimness
PRIMNES	primness
SLIMNES	slimness
TRIMNES	trimness

ĪMON

(See **ĪMAN**)

IMON

(See **IMEN**)

ĪMŌS

RIMŌS	rimose
SIMŌS	cymose

IMPĒ

IMPĒ	impi, impy
KRIMPĒ	crimpy
SHRIMPĒ	shrimpy
SKIMPĒ	skimpy
SKRIMPĒ	scrimpy
WIMPĒ	wimpy, Wimpy

IMPER

GIMPER	gimper
HWIMPER	whimper
KRIMPER	crimper
LIMPER	limper
SHRIMPER	shrimper
SIMPER	simper
SKIMPER	skimper
SKRIMPER	scrimper

IMPING

(See **IMP,** add -ing where appropriate.)

IMPISH

(See **IMP,** add -ish where appropriate.)

ĪMPIT

LĪMPIT	limepit
SLĪMPIT	slimepit

IMPL

DIMPL	dimple
KRIMPL	crimple

PIMPL	pimple
RIMPL	rimple
SIMPL	simple
WIMPL	bewimple, wimple

IMPLĒ

DIMPLĒ	dimply
KRIMPLĒ	crimply
LIMPLĒ	limply
PIMPLĒ	pimply
RIMPLĒ	rimply
SIMPLĒ	simply

IMPLEKS

IMPLEKS	implex
SIMPLEKS	simplex

IMPLER

(See **IMPL,** add *-er* where appropriate.)

IMPLING

DIMPLING	dimpling
KRIMPLING	crimpling
PIMPLING	pimpling
RIMPLING	rimpling

ĪMUS

PRĪMUS	primus
RĪMUS	rimous
SĪMUS	cymous, simous
THĪMUS	thymus
TĪMUS	timeous, untimeous

IMZĒ

FLIMZĒ	flimsy
HWIMZĒ	whimsy
MIMZĒ	mimsey
SLIMZĒ	slimsy

ĪNA

CHĪNA	China, Indochina
JĪNA	angina, vagina
KĪNA	trichina
LĪNA	Carolina, Catalina, North Carolina, salina, South Carolina
MĪNA	mina, myna, mynah
RĪNA	farina, globigerina, Catarrhina, casuarina, Platyrrhina
SĪNA	glucina, piscina

INA

BINA	binna
MINA	meminna
PINA	pinna

ĪNAKS

PĪNAKS	pinax
THRĪNAKS	Thrinax

ĪNAL

BĪNAL	binal
FĪNAL	final, quarterfinal, semifinal
JĪNAL	vaginal
KLĪNAL	acclinal, anticlinal, declinal, isoclinal, cataclinal, periclinal, synclinal
KRĪNAL	endocrinal, crinal
KWĪNAL	equinal
NĪNAL	caninal
RĪNAL	prorhinal, rhinal
SĪNAL	officinal, piscinal, sinal
SPĪNAL	cerebrospinal, spinal
TĪNAL	matutinal
TRĪNAL	trinal
VĪNAL	vinal, vinyl

ĪNĀT

BĪNĀT	binate
KWĪNĀT	quinate
SPĪNĀT	spinate

INĀT

INĀT	innate
PINĀT	pinnate

INCHER

PINCHER	penny-pincher, pincher

(See **INCH,** add *-er* where appropriate.)

INCHING

INCHING	inching
FLINCHING	flinching, unflinching
KLINCHING	clinching
LYNCHING	lynching

PINCHING	pinching, penny-pinching
SINCHING	cinching, uncinching

INCHPIN

LINCHPIN	linchpin
PINCHPIN	pinchpin

INDĒ

PINDĒ	pindy
SHINDĒ	shindy
SINDĒ	Sindhi
WINDĒ	windy

ĪNDED

BLĪNDED	blinded, self-blinded, snow-blinded
MĪNDED	*A* alike-minded, *B* bloody-minded, *D* double-minded, *E* earthly-minded, earthy-minded, even-minded, evil-minded, *F* fair-minded, feebleminded, *FL* fleshly-minded, *FR* free-minded, *H* high-minded, *K* carnal-minded, *L* like-minded, light-minded, lofty-minded, low-minded, *M* minded, *N* narrow-minded, *P* public-minded, *R* reminded, *S* simple-minded, single-minded, sober-minded, *ST* strong-minded, *TR* travel-minded, *W* weak-minded, worldly-minded
RĪNDED	rinded
WĪNDED	winded

INDED

BRINDED	brinded
SINDED	abscinded, exscinded, interscinded, rescinded, scinded, sinded
WINDED	long-winded, short-winded, winded

ĪNDER

BĪNDER	binder, bookbinder, spellbinder
BLĪNDER	blinder
FĪNDER	faultfinder, finder, pathfinder, rangefinder, viewfinder, waterfinder
GRĪNDER	grinder, organ-grinder
HĪNDER	hinder
KĪNDER	kinder, unkinder
MĪNDER	minder, reminder
WĪNDER	rewinder, sidewinder, stem-winder, winder

INDER

DINDER	dinder
FLINDER	flinder
HINDER	hinder
LINDER	linder
PINDER	pinder, Pindar
SINDER	rescinder, cinder
TINDER	tinder
WINDER	winder

INDIK

INDIK	indic
SINDIK	syndic

ĪNDING

BĪNDING	binding, bookbinding, inbinding, unbinding, upbinding

(See ĪND, add *-ing* where appropriate.)

INDL

BINDL	bindle
BRINDL	brindle
DINDL	dindle
DWINDL	dwindle
FINDL	findal
KINDL	enkindle, kindle, rekindle
RINDL	rindle
SPINDL	spindle
SWINDL	swindle

INDLD

(See **INDL**, add *-d* where appropriate.)

ĪNDLĒ

BLĪNDLĒ	blindly, purblindly
KĪNDLĒ	kindly, unkindly
BRINDLER	brindler
DWINDLER	dwindler
KINDLER	kindler
SPINDLER	spindler
SWINDLER	swindler

ĪNDLES

(See **ĪND,** add *-less* where appropriate.)

INDLING

(See **INDL,** add *-ing* where appropriate.)

ĪNDNES

BLĪNDNES	blindness, color blindness, night blindness, purblindness, sand-blindness, semiblindness, snow blindness
KĪNDNES	kindness, loving kindness, unkindness

INDŌ

LINDŌ	lindo
RINDŌ	tamarindo
WINDŌ	french window, shop window, window

INDRIFT

SPINDRIFT	spindrift
WINDRIFT	windrift

ĪNĒ

BRĪNĒ	briny
HĪNĒ	heinie
HWĪNĒ	whiney
LĪNĒ	liney, outliney
MĪNĒ	miny
PĪNĒ	piny
SHĪNĒ	moonshiny, shiny, sunshiny, starshiny
SĪNĒ	sine
SPĪNĒ	spiny
TĪNĒ	tiny
TWĪNĒ	twiny
VĪNĒ	viny
WĪNĒ	winy

INĒ

BLINĒ	blinny
BRINĒ	brinny
CHINĒ	chinny
FINĒ	finny
GINĒ	guinea, New Guinea
GRINĒ	grinny
HINĒ	hinny
HWINĒ	whinny
JINĒ	ginny, jinni
LINĒ	linhay
MINĒ	ignominy, mini
NINĒ	ninny, pickaninny
PINĒ	pinny
PLINĒ	Pliny
SHINĒ	shinny
SINĒ	cine
SKINĒ	skinny
SKWINĒ	squinny
SPINĒ	spinney
TINĒ	tinny
VINĒ	vinny

ĪNER

BĪNER	combiner
DĪNER	diner, condigner
FĪNER	definer, finer, confiner, refiner
HWĪNER	whiner
KLĪNER	incliner, recliner
LĪNER	A aquiliner, airliner, aligner, FR freightliner, H headliner, I eyeliner, J jetliner, L liner, M maligner, O outliner, P penny-a-liner, STR streamliner, Y underliner, W one-liner
MĪNER	miner, minor, underminer
NĪNER	benigner, forty-niner, saturniner
PĪNER	opiner, piner, repiner, supiner
SHĪNER	shiner
SHRĪNER	Shriner
SĪNER	assigner, designer, consigner, cosigner, countersigner, resigner, signer
TWĪNER	entwiner, twiner, intertwiner, untwiner
VĪNER	diviner, pulviner, viner
WĪNER	winer
ZĪNER	designer, resigner

INER

INER	inner
DINER	after-dinner, before-dinnner, dinner
FINER	finner
GINER	aginner, beginner
GRINER	grinner
JINER	ginner
PINER	pinner
SHINER	shinner
SINER	sinner
SKINER	muleskinner, skinner
SPINER	spinner
THINER	thinner
TINER	tinner
TWINER	twinner
WINER	breadwinner, winner

ĪNES

DRĪNES	dryness
FĪNES	finis
GĪNES	wise-guyness
HĪNES	highness
PĪNES	apple-pieness, humble-pieness
SHĪNES	shyness
SLĪNES	slyness
SPRĪNES	spryness

(See ĪNUS.)

INET

LINET	linnet
MINET	light-minute, minute
PINET	pinnet
SPINET	spinet

INFLIK

SINFLIK	sin-flick
SKINFLIK	skin-flick

INFUL

SINFUL	sinful
SKINFUL	skinful

INGBANG

BINGBANG	bingbang
JINGBANG	jingbang

INGBŌLT

KINGBŌLT	kingbolt
RINGBŌLT	ringbolt, wringbolt

INGĒ

BINGĒ	bingy
DINGĒ	dinghy
KLINGĒ	clinghy
PINGĒ	pingy
RINGĒ	ringy
SINGĒ	singy
SPRINGĒ	springy
STINGĒ	stingy
STRINGĒ	stringy
SWINGĒ	swingy
WINGĒ	wingy
ZINGĒ	zingy

INGER

BLINGER	blinger
BRINGER	bringer, fire bringer, news bringer
DINGER	dinger, humdinger
FLINGER	flinger
HWINGER	whinger
KLINGER	clinger
PINGER	pinger
RINGER	bell ringer, clothes-wringer, ringer, wringer
SINGER	ballad singer, blues singer, folksinger, jazz singer, choir singer, mastersinger, minnesinger, Meistersinger, opera singer, punk singer, rock singer, singer
SLINGER	gunslinger, hashslinger, ink-slinger, mudslinger, slinger, unslinger
SPRINGER	klipspringer, springer
STINGER	stinger
STRINGER	first-stringer, second-stringer, stringer
SWINGER	swinger
WINGER	left-winger, right-winger, winger
ZINGER	zinger

INGGA

HINGGA	anhinga
RINGGA	alcheringa, churinga
TINGGA	cotinga

INGGĒ

BINGGĒ	bingey, binghy, bingy
DINGGĒ	dinghy

INGGER

FINGGER	finger, fishfinger, forefinger, index finger, ladyfinger
LINGGER	linger, malinger

INGGERD

FINGGERD	fingered, light-fingered, rosy-fingered, web-fingered
LINGGERD	lingered, malingered

INGGL

INGGL	ingle
BINGGL	bingle
DINGGL	dingle, swing-dingle
JINGGL	jingal, jingle
KRINGGL	cringle, Kriss Kringle
LINGGL	lingel, lingle
MINGGL	immingle, intermingle, commingle, mingle
PINGGL	pingle
PRINGGL	pringle
SHINGGL	reshingle, shingle
SINGGL	single, surcingle
SPRINGGL	espringal, springal
SWINGGL	swingle
TINGGL	tingle
TRINGGL	tringle
TWINGGL	twingle

INGGLD

DINGGLD	dingled
JINGGLD	jingled
MINGGLD	immingled, intermingled, commingled, mingled
SHINGGLD	shingled
SINGGLD	singled
SWINGGLD	swingled
TINGGLD	tingled

INGGLĒ

DINGGLĒ	dingly
JINGGLĒ	jingly
MINGGLĒ	mingly

SHINGGLĒ	shingly
SINGGLĒ	singly
TINGGLĒ	tingly

INGGLER

JINGGLER	jingler
MINGGLER	intermingler, commingler, mingler
PINGGLER	pingler
SHINGGLER	shingler
TINGGLER	tingler

INGGLING

(See **INGGL,** drop -e and add -ing where appropriate.)

INGGLISH

| INGGLISH | English |
| TINGGLISH | tinglish |

INGGŌ

BINGGŌ	bingo
DINGGŌ	dingo, Mandingo
GRINGGŌ	gringo
JINGGŌ	jingo
LINGGŌ	lingo
MINGGŌ	flamingo, Santo Domingo
RINGGŌ	eryngo, Ringo
STINGGŌ	stingo

INGING

| SINGING | singing, scat-singing |

(See **ING,** add -ing where appropriate.)

INGKCHER

LINGKCHER	lincture, pollincture
SINGKCHER	encincture, cincture, uncincture
TINGKCHER	tincture, untincture

INGKCHERD

| SINGKCHERD | encinctured, cinctured, uncinctured |
| TINGCHERD | tinctured, untinctured |

INGKĒ

INGKĒ	inky
BLINGKĒ	blinky
CHINGKĒ	chinky
DINGKĒ	dinkey, dinky
KINGKĒ	kinky
LINGKĒ	linky
MINGKĒ	minky
PINGKĒ	pinky
SINGKĒ	Helsinki, sinky
SLINGKĒ	slinky
STINGKĒ	stinky
WINGKĒ	winky
ZINGKĒ	zinky

INGKER

INGKER	inker
BLINGKER	blinker
DRINGKER	drinker
KLINGKER	clinker
LINGKER	enlinker, linker
PINGKER	pinker
PRINGKER	prinker
RINGKER	rinker
SHRINGKER	headshrinker, shrinker
SINGKER	sinker
SKINGKER	skinker
SLINGKER	slinker
STINGKER	stinker
SWINGKER	swinker
THINGKER	bethinker, freethinker, thinker
TINGKER	tinker
WINGKER	hoodwinker, tiddledywinker, winker

INGKERD

| BLINGKERD | blinkard, blinkered |
| TINGKERD | tinkered |

INGKĪD

| BLINGKĪD | blink-eyed |
| PINGKĪD | pink-eyed |

INGKIJ

| LINGKIJ | linkage |
| SHRINGKIJ | shrinkage |

INGKING

(See **INGK,** add -ing where appropriate.)

INGKL

INGKL	inkle
KINGKL	kinkle
KRINGKL	crinkle
RINGKL	unwrinkle, wrinkle
SPRINGKL	besprinkle, sprinkle
STRINGKL	strinkle
TINGKL	tinkle
TWINGKL	twinkle
WINGKL	periwinkle, Rip Van Winkle, winkle

INGKLĒ

KRINGKLĒ	crinkly
PINGKLĒ	pinkly
RINGKLĒ	wrinkly
TINGKLĒ	tinkly
TWINGKLĒ	twinkly

INGKLER

INGKLER	inkler
RINGKLER	wrinkler
SPRINGKLER	sprinkler
STRINGKLER	strinkler
TINGKLER	tinkler
TWINGKLER	twinkler

CENTRIPETAL—CENTRIFUGAL

Centripetal force pulls an object toward the center of a circular path; centrifugal force pulls it away.

As planet gyres about its sun,
  Or cock about his hen,
'Round thee my revolutions run,
  And 'round and 'round again.

And yet as force centripetal
  Draws heart to waiting heart,
A counter-force centrifugal
  Keeps pulling us apart.

The push and pull go on and on,
  We never grasp the nettle.
I fear we two shall ne'er be one
  Centrifugalipetal.

INGKLING

(See **INGKL,** add -ing where appropriate.)

INGKŌ

CHINGKŌ	pachinko
GINGKŌ	gingko
PINGKŌ	pinko

INGTLĒ

SINGTLĒ   succinctly
TINGTLĒ   distinctly, indistinctly

INGKTNES

SINGTNES   succinctness
TINGTNES   distinctness,
                 indistinctness

INGKTŪR

(See INGKCHER)

INGKTŪRD

(See INGKCHERD)

INGKUS

RINGKUS   Ornithorhynchus,
                 ornithorhyncous,
                 Oxyrhynchus,
                 oxyrhyncous
SINGKUS   scincous
ZINGKUS   zincous

INGKWENS

LINGKWENS   delinquence,
                 relinquence
PINGKWENS   propinquence

INGKWENT

LINGKWENT   delinquent, relinquent
PINGKWENT   propinquent

INGKWISH

LINGKWISH   relinquish
VINGKWISH   vinquish

INGLĒ

(See ING, add -ly where appropriate.)

INGLES

(See ING, add -less where appropriate.)

INGLET

DINGLET   dinglet
KINGLET   kinglet

RINGLET   ringlet
SPRINGLET   springlet
WINGLET   winglet

INGLING

KINGLING   kingling
RINGLING   Ringling
WINGLING   wingling

INGTĪM

RINGTĪM   ringtime
SPRINGTĪM   springtime

ĪNIK

KĪNIK   kinic
PĪNIK   pinic
TĪNIK   neoteinic
VĪNIK   vinic

INIK

BINIK   albinic, Jacobinic,
                 rabbinic
DINIK   dinic, Odinic
FINIK   delphinic, finick,
                 Finnic
KINIK   kinic
KLINIK   aclinic,
                 apopemptoclinic,
                 isoclinic, clinic,
                 monoclinic,
                 polyclinic, triclinic
KRINIK   endocrinic, encrinic
KWINIK   quinic
LINIK   pollinic, porcelainic
MINIK   Brahminic, fulminic,
                 histaminic
PINIK   pinic
RINIK   mandarinic
SINIK   cynic, Sinic, succinic
TINIK   adiactinic, actinic,
                 diactinic, hematinic,
                 narcotinic, nicotinic,
                 platinic
VINIK   vinic

ĪNING

(See ĪN, add -ing where appropriate.)

INING

WINING   breadwinning,
                 winning

(See IN, add -ning where appropriate.)

INIS

FINIS   finis
PINIS   pinnace

INISH

FINISH   finish, Finnish,
                 refinish
MINISH   diminish
THINISH   thinnish
TINISH   tinnish

INIST

BINIST   Jacobinist
LINIST   violinist, zeppelinist

(See IN, add -est or -ist where
appropriate.)

ĪNĪT

FĪNĪT   finite
KRĪNĪT   crinite

INJĒ

DINJĒ   dingy
FRINJĒ   fringy
KRINJĒ   cringy
MINJĒ   mingy
STINJĒ   stingy
TWINJĒ   twingey

INJENS

PINJENS   impingence
STRINJENS   astringence, stringence
TINJENS   contingence

INJENT

FINJENT   fingent
FRINJENT   fringent, refringent
MINJENT   retromingent
PINJENT   impingent
RINJENT   ringent
STRINJENT   stringent
TINJENT   attingent, contingent,
                 tingent
TRINJENT   astringent,
                 constringent,
                 restringent

INJER

INJER	injure
FRINJER	fringer, infringer
HINJER	hinger
JINJER	ginger
KRINJER	cringer
PINJER	impinger
SINJER	singer
SPRINJER	springer
SWINJER	swinger
TINJER	tinger
TWINJER	twinger

INJING

(See **INJ,** add -ing where appropriate.)

INJLES

(See **INJ,** add -less where appropriate.)

INJMENT

FRINGJMENT	infringement
HINJMENT	hingement, unhingement
PINJMENT	impingement
STRINJMENT	perstringement
TRINJMENT	astringement

ĪNKLAD

PĪNKLAD	pine-clad
VĪNKLAD	vine-clad

ĪNKROUND

PĪNKROUND	pine-crowned
VĪNKROUND	vine-crowned

INLAND

INLAND	inland
FINLAND	Finland

ĪNLĒ

DĪNLĒ	condignly
FĪNLĒ	finely, superfinely
LĪNLĒ	aquilinely, malignly
NĪNLĒ	benignly, caninely, saturninely, unbenignly
PĪNLĒ	supinely
VĪNLĒ	divinely

INLĒ

INLĒ	inly
THINLĒ	thinly
TWINLĒ	twinly

ĪNLES

(See **ĪN,** add -less where appropriate.)

INLES

(See **IN,** add -less where appropriate.)

ĪNMENT

FĪNMENT	confinement, refinement
LĪNMENT	alignment, interlinement, malignment, realignment
SHRĪNMENT	enshrinement
SĪNMENT	assignment, consignment
TWĪNMENT	entwinement, intertwinement
ZĪNMENT	designment, resignment

ĪNNES

DĪNNES	condignness
FĪNNES	fineness, superfineness
LĪNNES	salineness
NĪNNES	benignness
PĪNNES	*supineness*
VĪNNES	divineness

INNES

INNES	inness, genuineness
KINNES	akinness
LINNES	masculineness
NINNES	feminineness
THINNES	thinness, withinness
TWINNES	twinness

ĪNŌ

BĪNŌ	albino, sabino
FĪNŌ	damfino
RĪNŌ	rhino
WĪNŌ	wino

INŌ

MINŌ	minnow, top minnow
WINŌ	winnow

INSER

MINSER	mincer
PINSER	pincer
RINSER	rinser
VINSER	convincer
WINSER	wincer

INSING

(See **INS,** add -ing where appropriate.)

INSKĒ

LINSKĒ	kolinsky
MINSKĒ	Minsky

INSTER

MINSTER	minster, Axminster, Westminster
SPINSTER	spinster

INTAJ

(See **INTIJ**)

INTAL

(See **INTL**)

INTĒ

FLINTĒ	flinty
GLINTĒ	glinty
LINTĒ	lintie, linty
MINTĒ	minty
SHINTĒ	shinty
SINTĒ	teosinte
SKWINTĒ	squinty
SPLINTĒ	splinty
TINTĒ	tinty

INTED

TINTED	rainbow-tinted, rosy-tinted, tinted

(See **INT,** add -ed where appropriate.)

INTER

INTER	*inter*
DINTER	dinter
FLINTER	flinter
GLINTER	glinter
HINTER	hinter
LINTER	linter
MINTER	minter
PINTER	Pinter
PRINTER	printer, imprinter, teleprinter
SINTER	sinter
SKWINTER	squinter
SPLINTER	splinter
SPRINTER	sprinter
STINTER	stinter
TINTER	aquatinter, mezzotinter, tinter
TWINTER	twinter
VINTER	vinter
WINTER	midwinter, overwinter, winter

INTHIK

RINTHIK	labyrinthic
SINTHIK	absinthic

INTHIN

BINTHIN	terebinthine
RINTHIN	labyrinthine
SINTHIN	absinthine, hyacinthine

INTĪD

FLINTĪD	flint-eyed
SKWINTĪD	squint-eyed

INTIJ

MINTIJ	mintage
SPLINTIJ	splintage
TINTIJ	tintage
VINTIJ	vintage

INTING

(See **INT,** add *-ing* where appropriate.)

INTL

JINTL	trigintal
KWINTAL	quintal
LINTL	lintel, lintle

PINTL	pintle
SINTL	scintle
SKINTL	skintle

INTŌ

PINTŌ	pinto
SHINTŌ	Shinto
TINTŌ	mezzotinto

INTRĒ

SPINTRĒ	spintry
VINTRĒ	vintry
WINTRĒ	wintry

(See **IN'TER.Ē**)

INŪ

FINŪ	finew
SINŪ	sinew, unsinew
TINŪ	discontinue, continue

INŪD

FINŪD	finewed
SINŪD	sinewed, unsinewed
TINŪD	discontinued, continued

ĪNUS

BĪNUS	binous
BRĪNUS	gambrinous
DĪNUS	dinus
FĪNUS	delphinus
KĪNUS	echinus, matroclinous, monoclinous
KLĪNUS	patroclinus
KWĪNUS	Aquinas
LĪNUS	botulinus, linous, salinous
MĪNUS	minus
PĪNUS	Pinus
RĪNUS	dirhinous, mesorhinous, platyrhinous
SĪNUS	sinus, incinus
SPĪNUS	spinous
TĪNUS	laurustinus
VĪNUS	pulvinus, vinous

(See **ĪNES**)

INYUN

JINYUN	Virginian
MINYUN	dominion, mignon, minion, minyan
PINYUN	opinion, pignon, pinion, pinyon

(See **IN'I.AN**)

INYUND

MINYUND	dominioned, minioned
PINYUND	opinioned, pinioned, self-opinioned

INZĒ

KWINZĒ	quinsy
LINZĒ	linsey

ĪŌ

ĪŌ	Io
HĪŌ	*heigh-ho,* Ohio
KLĪŌ	Clio

ĪOL

(See **ĪAL**)

ĪON

(See **ĪAN**)

ĪOR

(See **ĪER**)

ĪOT

(See **ĪET**)

ĪOUT

BĪOUT	buy-out
TRĪOUT	tryout

ĪPA

NĪPA	nipa
PĪPA	pipa
RĪPA	ripa
STĪPA	Stipa

IPAJ

(See **IPIJ**)

ĪPAL

(See ĪPL)

IPANT

FLIPANT	flippant
TRIPANT	trippant

ĪPĒ

GRĪPĒ	gripy
PĪPĒ	pipy
STRĪPĒ	stripy
SWĪPĒ	swipy
TĪPĒ	antitypy, daguerreotypy, phonotypy, chromotypy, polytypy

IPĒ

CHIPĒ	chippy
DIPĒ	dippy
DRIPĒ	drippy
GRIPĒ	grippy
HIPĒ	hippie, hippy
KLIPĒ	klippe
LIPĒ	lippy
NIPĒ	nippy, Aganippe
PIPĒ	pippy
SHIPĒ	shippy
SIPĒ	Mississippi
SLIPĒ	slippy
SNIPĒ	snippy
THIPĒ	Xanthippe
TIPĒ	tippy, Xanthippe
YIPĒ	yippee, yippie, yippy
ZIPĒ	zippy

ĪPED

BĪPED	biped
PĪPED	parallelepiped
STRĪPED	striped

ĪPEND

RĪPEND	ripened
STĪPEND	stipend

ĪPER

GRĪPER	griper
HĪPER	hyper
PĪPER	bagpiper, piper, sandpiper
RĪPER	riper
SNĪPER	sniper
STRĪPER	striper
SWĪPER	sideswiper, swiper
TĪPER	daguerreotyper, electrotyper, linotyper, monotyper, stereotyper, typer
VĪPER	Russell's viper, viper
WĪPER	windshield wiper, wiper, Ypres

IPER

CHIPER	chipper
DIPER	Big Dipper, dipper, hipper-dipper
DRIPER	dripper
FLIPER	flipper
FRIPER	fripper
GIPER	gipper
GRIPER	gripper
HIPER	hipper
HWIPER	horsewhipper, whipper
JIPER	gypper
KIPER	kipper, Yom Kippur
KLIPER	clipper
KWIPER	quipper
LIPER	lipper
NIPER	gallinipper, nipper
RIPER	Jack the Ripper, ripper
SHIPER	shipper
SIPER	sipper
SKIPER	mudskipper, skipper
SLIPER	lady's-slipper, slipper
SNIPER	snipper
STRIPER	outstripper, stripper
SWIPER	swipper
TIPER	tipper
TRIPER	daytripper, tripper
YIPER	yipper
ZIPER	zipper

IPERD

KIPERD	kippered
SKIPERD	skippered
SLIPERD	slippered

IPET

HWIPET	whippet
LIPET	microlipet
PIPET	pipit
RIPET	rippet
SIPET	sippet
SKIPET	skippet
SNIPET	snippet
TIPET	tippet
TRIPET	trippet

IPIJ

CHIPIJ	chippage
KIPIJ	kippage
KWIPIJ	equipage
SKRIPIJ	scrippage
SLIPIJ	slippage
STRIPIJ	strippage

IPIK

DIPIK	adipic
HIPIK	hippic
LIPIK	philippic
TIPIK	*A* atypic, *D* daguerreotypic, *E* electrotypic, *F* phonotypic, *H* heterotypic, homeotypic, homotypic, *I* idiotypic, *M* monotypic, *P* polytypic, *ST* stenotypic, stereotypic, *T* typic

ĪPING

PĪPING	Peiping

(See ĪP, add -*ing* where appropriate.)

IPING

(See IP, add -*ing* where appropriate.)

IPISH

GRIPISH	grippish
HIPISH	hippish
KWIPISH	quippish
SNIPISH	snippish

IPJAK

HWIPJAK	whipjack
SKIPJAK	skipjack

ĪPL

RĪPL	ripal
SĪPL	disciple
STĪPL	stipel
TĪPL	archetypal, ectypal, typal

IPL

FIPL	fipple
GRIPL	gripple
KRIPL	becripple, cripple
NIPL	nipple
PIPL	pipple
RIPL	ripple
SIPL	participle, sipple
STIPL	stipple
SWIPL	swiple, swipple
THRIPL	thripple
TIPL	tipple
TRIPL	triple

IPLĒ

KRIPLĒ	cripply
RIPLĒ	ripply
STIPLĒ	stipply
TRIPLĒ	triply

IPLER

(See **IPL,** add -r where appropriate.)

ĪPLES

(See **ĪP,** add -less where appropriate.)

IPLES

(See **IP,** add -less where appropriate.)

IPLET

CHIPLET	chiplet
LIPLET	liplet
RIPLET	ripplet
SIPLET	siplet
STRIPLET	striplet
TIPLET	tiplet
TRIPLET	triplet

IPLING

KIPLING	Kipling

(See **IPL,** add -ing where appropriate.)

IPMENT

GRIPMENT	gripment
KWIPMENT	equipment
SHIPMENT	shipment, transshipment

ĪPŌ

HĪPŌ	hypo
TĪPŌ	typo

IPŌ

HIPŌ	hippo
JIPŌ	gippo
LIPŌ	filippo
SHIPŌ	*shippo*

IPOF

RIPOF	ripoff
TIPOF	tipoff

IPON

JIPON	gipon
NIPON	Nippon
SHIPON	shippon
SLIPON	slip-on

IPSĒ

IPSĒ	ipse
DIPSĒ	dipsey, dipsie, dipsy
HIPSĒ	hipsy
JIPSĒ	gypsy
KIPSĒ	Poughkeepsie
TIPSĒ	tipsy

IPSHUN

JIPSHUN	Egyptian
NIPSHUN	conniption
KRIPSHUN	*A* ascription, *D* description, *I* inscription, *K* conscription, *PR* prescription, proscription, *R* rescription, *S* circumscription, subscription, superscription, *SK* scription, *T* teletranscription, *TR* transcription

IPSIS

KRIPSIS	krypsis
LIPSIS	ellipsis
STIPSIS	stypsis
TRIPSIS	tripsis

IPSTER

HWIPSTER	whipster
KWIPSTER	quipster
TIPSTER	tipster

IPSTIK

DIPSTIK	dipstick
LIPSTIK	lipstick

IPTIK

DIPTIK	diptych
GLIPTIK	anaglyptic, glyptic
KLIPTIK	ecliptic
KRIPTIK	holocryptic, cryptic, procryptic
LIPTIK	apocalyptic, elliptic, iatroliptic, polyptych
STIPTIK	hypostyptic, styptic
TRIPTIK	triptych

IPUS

HIPUS	Eohippus, Epihippus, hippus, Protohippus, Proterohippus
LIPUS	philippus

ĪRA

ĪRA	eyra
BĪRA	beira
DĪRA	daira
JĪRA	hegira, spirogyra
LĪRA	Lyra
MĪRA	almirah, palmyra
TĪRA	hetaera, tayra

ÎRA

ÎRA	era
DÎRA	Madeira
GÎRA	gerah
HÎRA	Hera
LÎRA	galera, lira
MÎRA	chimera
PÎRA	lempira
SHÎRA	asherah
SÎRA	phylloxera, sera
SKLÎRA	sclera
TÎRA	hetaera, rangatira

(See **IRA**)

IRA

LIRA	tirra-lira
SIRA	sirrah
WIRA	wirra

(See **ÎRA**)

ĪRAL

JĪRAL	gyral, polygyral
KĪRAL	allochiral, chiral
PĪRAL	papyral
SPĪRAL	spiral
STĪRAL	styryl
TĪRAL	retiral

ÎRAL

ÎRAL	eral
FÎRAL	feral, hemispheral
JÎRAL	vicegeral
SFÎRAL	spheral
SÎRAL	ceral
SKLÎRAL	scleral

ĪRANT

JĪRANT	gyrant
KWĪRANT	enquirent
PĪRANT	aspirant, expirant, conspirant, spirant
TĪRANT	archtyrant, tyrant
VĪRANT	sempivirent, virent

ĪRĀT

ĪRĀT	irate
JĪRĀT	agyrate, dextrogyrate, gyrate, sinistrogyrate, circumgyrate

ĪRĒ

ĪRĒ	eyrie, Dies Irae
DĪRĒ	dairi
KĪRĒ	kairi
KWĪRĒ	acquiry, enquiry, inquiry
MĪRĒ	miry
NĪRĒ	praemunire, venire
SKWĪRĒ	squiry
SPĪRĒ	expiree, expiry, perspiry, spiry
WĪRĒ	wiry

(See **I'ER.Ē**)

ÎRĒ

ÎRĒ	aerie, eerie, eery, Erie, eyrie
BÎRĒ	beery
BLÎRĒ	bleary
CHÎRĒ	cheery
DÎRĒ	dearie, deary
DRÎRĒ	dreary, Dundreary
JÎRĒ	jeery
KÎRĒ	bokmakierie, hara-kiri, keiri, kiri, kyrie
KWÎRĒ	query
LÎRĒ	whigmaleery, leary, leery
PÎRĒ	peri
RÎRĒ	miserere
SÎRĒ	seri, siri
SFÎRĒ	sphery
SMÎRĒ	smeary
SNÎRĒ	sneery
THÎRĒ	metatheory, theory
SPÎRĒ	speary
TÎRĒ	hetaerae, teary
VÎRĒ	veery
WÎRĒ	aweary, forweary, life-weary, overweary, weary, world-weary
YÎRĒ	cavaliere

ÎRĒD

KWÎRĒD	queried
WÎRĒD	unwearied, war-wearied, wearied, world-wearied

IREL

SKWIREL	squirrel
VIREL	virile

ĪRĒM

BĪRĒM	bireme
TRĪRĒM	trireme

ĪRĒN

ĪRĒN	irene, *Irene*
KĪRĒN	kairine, kyrine
PĪRĒN	pyrene
SKWĪRĒN	squireen
STĪRĒN	polystyrene, styrene

ĪREN

(See **ĪRUN**)

ÎRENS

FÎRENS	interference
HÎRENS	adherence, incoherence, inherence, coherence
KLÎRENS	clearance
PÎRENS	appearance, disappearance, non-appearance, reappearance
RÎRENS	arrearance
VÎRENS	perseverance

ĪRENT

(See **ĪRANT**)

ÎRENT

HÎRENT	adherent, inadherent, incoherent, inherent, coherent
JÎRENT	gerent, vicegerent
KWÎRENT	querent
VÎRENT	perseverant

ĪRER

(See **ĪR,** add -*er* where appropriate.)

ÎRER

(See **ÎR,** add -*er* where appropriate.)

ÎRES

PÎRES	peeress
SÎRES	seeress

ÎRĒZ

DÎRĒZ	dearies
DRÎRĒZ	dundrearies
HÎRĒZ	heres
QWÎRĒZ	queries
SÎRĒZ	Ceres, mini-series, series, World Series
WÎRĒZ	wearies

ĪRFUL

ĪRFUL	ireful
DÎRFUL	direful
ZĪRFUL	desireful

ÎRFUL

ÎRFUL	earful
CHÎRFUL	cheerful, uncheerful
FÎRFUL	fearful, unfearful
SNÎRFUL	sneerful
TÎRFUL	tearful

ĪRID

ĪRID	irid
MĪRID	mormyrid
VĪRID	sempervirid, virid
ZĪRID	xyrid

ÎRĪD

BLÎRĪD	blear-eyed
KLÎRĪD	clear-eyed
TÎRĪD	tear-eyed

IRID

IRID	irid
VIRID	virid

ÎRIJ

KLÎRIJ	clearage
PÎRIJ	peerage, pierage
RÎRIJ	arrearage
STÎRIJ	steerage

ĪRIK

NÎRIK	oneiric
PĪRIK	epeiric

IRIK

JIRIK	argyric, photogyric, gyric, panegyric
LIRIK	lyric
PIRIK	empiric, Pyrrhic, vampiric
TIRIK	butyric, satiric, satyric

IRIL

(See **IREL**)

ĪRING

(See **ĪR,** add -ing where appropriate.)

ÎRING

BÎRING	Bering

(See **ÎR,** add -ing where appropriate.)

ĪRIS

ĪRIS	iris
SĪRIS	Osiris, Cyrus

ĪRISH

ĪRISH	Irish
SKWĪRISH	squirish

ĪRIST

ĪRIST	irised
JĪRIST	gyrist
LĪRIST	lyrist

IRIST

JIRIST	panegyrist
LIRIST	lyrist

> **ON THE HERMIT CRAB**
>
> The hermit crab lives safely curled
> Inside the shell that is his world.
> If you expose him to the sky,
> He moans, ''I faint!''; he groans, ''I die!''
>
> Next day you'll find him doing well
> Inside some other hermit shell.
> (Come back, dear; I am frailer ab-
> solutely than the hermit crab.)

ĪRLĒ

DĪRLĒ	direly
SKWĪRLĒ	squirely
TĪRLĒ	entirely

ÎRLĒ

CHÎRLĒ	cheerly
DÎRLĒ	dearly
DRÎRLĒ	drearly
KLÎRLĒ	clearly
KWÎRLĒ	queerly
LÎRLĒ	cavalierly
MÎRLĒ	merely
NÎRLĒ	nearly

SÎRLĒ	insincerely, sincerely
TÎRLĒ	austerely
VÎRLĒ	severely
YÎRLĒ	yearly

ĪRLES

(See **ĪR,** add -less where appropriate.)

ÎRLES

(See **ÎR,** add -less where appropriate.)

ĪRLING

HĪRLING	hireling
SKWĪRLING	squireling

ÎRLING

SHÎRLING	shearling
STÎRLING	steerling
YÎRLING	yearling

ĪRMAN

FĪRMAN	fireman
NĪRMAN	venireman

ĪRMENT

KWĪRMENT	acquirement, requirement
MĪRMENT	bemirement
TĪRMENT	attirement, retirement

ÎRMENT

DÎRMENT	endearment
SÎRMENT	cerement

ĪRNES

DĪRNES	direness
TĪRNES	entireness

ÎRNES

DÎRNES	dearness
KLÎRNES	clearness
KWÎRNES	queerness
NÎRNES	nearness
SÎRNES	sincereness
TÎRNES	austereness
VÎRNES	severeness

ĪRŌ

JĪRŌ	giro, gyro, autogyro
KĪRŌ	Cairo, chirho
PĪRŌ	pyro
TĪRŌ	tyro

ÎRŌ

HÎRŌ	anti-hero, hero, superhero
KÎRŌ	chirho
LÎRŌ	lillibullero
NÎRŌ	Nero, Pinero, Rio de Janeiro
RÎRŌ	riroriro
SÎRŌ	cero
ZÎRŌ	absolute zero, above zero, below zero, subzero, zero

ĪRŌD

BĪRŌD	byroad
HĪRŌD	highroad

ÎROID

SFÎROID	spheroid
TÎROID	pteroid
THÎROID	theroid

IRŌS

JĪRŌS	gyrose
VĪRŌS	virose

ÎRSER

FÎRSER	fiercer
PÎRSER	ear-piercer, piercer

ĪRSUM

ĪRSUM	iresome
TĪRSUM	tiresome
ZĪRSUM	desiresome

ĪRUN

ĪRUN	iron
BĪRUN	Byron
KĪRUN	Chiron
SĪRUN	lepidosiren, siren
VĪRUN	environ, viron

IRUP

CHIRUP	chirrup
SIRUP	syrup
STIRUP	stirrup

ĪRUS

JĪRUS	gyrus
PĪRUS	apyrous, Epirus, papyrus
SĪRUS	Cyrus
SPĪRUS	spirous
VĪRUS	ultravirus, virous, virus

ÎRUS

SÎRUS	serous
SKLÎRUS	sclerous

IRUS

BIRUS	byrrus
SIRUS	cirrhous, cirrus
SKIRUS	scirrhus

ĪRWERKS

FĪRWERKS	fireworks
WĪRWERKS	wireworks

ÎRZMAN

STÎRZMAN	steersman
TÎRZMAN	frontiersman, privateersman

ĪSA

BĪSA	beisa
DĪSA	dhaisa
MĪSA	Meissa

ISA

BRISA	vibrissa
MISA	Missa
RISA	paterissa
SISA	abscissa
TISA	mantissa

ĪSAL

SKĪSAL	skysail
TRĪSAL	trysail

(See also **ĪSL**)

ĪSĒ

ĪSĒ	icy
DĪSĒ	dicey, dicy
NĪSĒ	Nisei, nisi
PRĪSĒ	pricey
RĪSĒ	ricy
SPĪSĒ	spicy
VĪSĒ	vice

ISĒ

HISĒ	hissy
KISĒ	kissy
MISĒ	missi, missy
NISĒ	nisse
PRISĒ	prissy
SISĒ	sissy

ISEN

(See **ISN**)

ISENS

HISENS	dehiscence, indehiscence
NISENS	reminiscence
PISENS	resipiscence
TISENS	fatiscence
VISENS	obliviscence, reviviscence

ISENT

HISENT	dehiscent, indehiscent
NISENT	reminiscent
PISENT	resipiscent
TISENT	fatiscent
VISENT	obliviscent, reviviscent

ĪSER

ĪSER	deicer, icer
DĪSER	dicer
FĪSER	sacrificer, self-sacrificer
GĪSER	geyser
NĪSER	nicer

PRĪSER   pricer
RĪSER   ricer
SĪSER   conciser, preciser,
             cicer, Cicer
SLĪSER   meat-slicer, potato-
             slicer, vegetable-
             slicer, slicer
SPĪSER   spicer
SPLĪSER resplicer, splicer
TĪSER   enticer

ISER

HISER   dehiscer, hisser
KISER   kissar, kisser
MISER   dismisser, misser,
             remisser
NISER   reminiscer
PISER   pisser

ISEZ

MISEZ   misses, missus, Mrs.

(See **IS,** add -s or -es where appropriate.)

ĪSFUL

LĪSFUL   lice-full
TĪSFUL   enticeful
RĪSFUL   rice-full
VĪSFUL   deviceful

ISFUL

BLISFUL blissful, unblissful
MISFUL   remissful

ISHA

LISHA   militia, euphelicia
MISHA   comitia
STISHA   interstitia

ISHAL

DISHAL   extrajudicial, judicial,
             nonjudicial,
             prejudicial, unjudicial
FISHAL   artificial, beneficial,
             edificial, official,
             sacrificial, superficial,
             unartificial, unofficial,
             veneficial
LISHAL   gentilitial, natalitial,
             policial

MISHAL   comitial, postcomitial
NISHAL   initial, tribunicial
STISHAL interstitial, solstitial
TISHAL   accrementitial,
             recrementitial, justicial
TRISHAL altricial
VISHAL   novitial
ZISHAL   exitial

ISHAN

(See **ISHUN**)

ISHĒ

DISHĒ   dishy
FISHĒ   fishy
RISHĒ   maharishi, rishi
SKWISHĒ squishy
SWISHĒ   swishy
VISHĒ   vichy, Vichy

ISHENS

FISHENS deficience, efficience,
             insufficience,
             maleficience,
             proficience, self-
             sufficience
NISHENS omniscience
SPISHENS perspicience,
             prospicience

ISHENT

FISHENT B beneficient, D
             deficient, E efficient, I
             indeficient, inefficient,
             insufficient, K
             calorificient,
             coefficient, M
             maleficient, P
             perficient, PR
             proficient, S self-
             sufficient, sufficient
JISHENT objicient
LISHENT volitient
NISHENT omniscient
VISHENT parviscient

ISHER

DISHER   disher
FISHER   fisher, fissure,
             kingfisher
SWISHER swisher
WISHER   ill-wisher, well-
             wisher, wisher

ISHFUL

DISHFUL dishful
WISHFUL wishful

ISHING

DISHING   dishing
FISHING   fishing
HWISHING whishing
SKWISHING squishing
SWISHING swishing
WISHING   ill-wishing, well-
              wishing, wishing

ISHOO̅

ISHOO̅   issue
FISHOO̅   fichu
TISHOO̅   tissue

ISHUN

ISHUN   exspuition, fruition,
             intuition, coition,
             circuition, tuition
BISHUN   adhibition, ambition,
             exhibition, imbibition,
             inhibition, prohibition,
             ratihabition,
             redhibition
BRISHUN Hebrician, rubrician
DISHUN   A addition, D
             dedition, deperdition,
             E edition, expedition,
             extradition, erudition,
             K condition, O
             audition, P perdition,
             PR precondition, R
             reddition, recondition,
             rendition, S sedition,
             subaudition, super-
             addition, TR tradition,
             V vendition
FISHUN   binary fission, fission,
             nuclear fission
JISHUN   logician, magician
LISHUN   abolition, demolition,
             ebullition, Galician,
             coalition, nolition,
             Paulician, rebullition,
             volition
MISHUN   A admission,
             academician, D
             demission, dismission,
             E expromission,
             emission, I immission,
             insubmission,
             intermission,

intromission,
irremission, *K*
commission, *M*
manumission,
mission, *O*
obdormition,
omission, *P*
permission, *R*
readmission,
remission, *S*
submission, *TR*
transmission, *V*
vomition

NISHUN   *A* abannition,
admonition, affinition,
agglutinition,
ammunition, *D*
definition, *E*
exinanition, epinicion,
F Phoenician, *I*
ignition, illinition,
inanition, inition, *K*
cognition, *KL*
clinician, *M*
mechanician,
monition, munition, *N*
neoplatonician, *P*
pyrotechnician, *PR*
precognition,
premonition,
premunition, *R*
recognition, reunition,
S submonition, *T*
technician, *TR*
tribunitian

PISHUN   suspicion
PRISHUN   Priscian
RISHUN   apparition, deperition,
futurition, ligurition,
micturition,
parturition, preterition,
rhetorician,
vomiturition

SISHUN   abscission, scission,
transition
STISHUN   superstition
TISHUN   *A* aglutition,
accrementition,
acoustician,
arithmetician, *B* bi-
partition, beautician,
D dedentition,
deglutition, dentition,
departition,
diagnostician,
dialectition, dietitian,
E equipartition,
esthetician, *GL*
glutition, *H*
hydrostatician, *K*
competition,
cosmetician, *L*

logistician, *M*
magnetition,
mathematician,
mortician, *O* optician,
P partition, petition,
politician, *PR*
practition, *R*
repartition, repetition,
S sortition, *ST*
statistician, *T*
tactician, Titian, *TH*
theoretician, *TR*
tralatition, tripartition

TRISHUN   attrition, detrition,
electrician,
geometrician,
geriatrician,
contrition,
malnutrition,
metrician, nutrition,
obstetrician, patrician,
pediatrician

ZISHUN   *A* acquisition,
apposition, *D*
deacquisition,
decomposition,
deposition,
disposition,
disquisition, *E*
exposition, *F*
physician, *I*
imposition,
indisposition,
inquisition,
interposition, *J*
juxtaposition, *K*
composition,
contraposition, *M*
malposition,
metaphysician,
missionary position,
musician, *O*
opposition, *P* position,
PR predisposition,
preposition,
presupposition,
proposition, *R*
requisition, reposition,
S superposition,
supposition, *TR*
transposition,
transition

(See **IS'I.AN**)

ISHUNZ

TISHUNZ   antiscians

(See **ISHUN,** add -*s* where appropriate.)

ISHUS

BISHUS   ambitious
BRISHUS   lubricious
DISHUS   expeditious, indicious,
injudicious, judicious,
seditious, spadiceous
FISHUS   beneficious,
inofficious, officious,
veneficious
JISHUS   flagitious
LISHUS   delicious, gentilitious,
malicious, mollitious,
natalitious, pulicious,
satellitious, cilicious,
siliceous
MISHUS   pumiceous,
vermicious
NISHUS   pernicious, puniceous
PISHUS   inauspicious,
auspicious, propitious,
suspicious,
unpropitious,
unsuspicious
PLISHUS   multiplicious
PRISHUS   capricious
RISHUS   avaricious, lateritious,
Mauritius, piperitious,
sericeous
STISHUS   superstitious
TISHUS   *A* addititious,
adjectitious,
adscititious,
adventitious,
arreptitious,
ascititious,
ascriptitious, *D*
deglutitious, *E*
exititious, *F* factitious,
fictitious, *I*
irreptitious, *O*
obreptitious, *PR*
profectitious, *R*
repetitious, *S*
secretitious,
subdititious,
supposititious,
surreptitious, *ST*
stillatitious, *TR*
tralatitious
TRISHUS   meretricious,
nutritious,
obstetricious
VISHUS   novitious, vicious
ZISHUS   supposititious

ISIK

LISIK   silicic
NISIK   anisic
TISIK   masticic

ISIL

(See **ISL**)

ĪSIN

LĪSIN	lysin
MĪSIN	tetramycin

ĪSING

ĪSING	icing
DĪSING	dicing
FĪSING	sacrificing, self-sacrificing, sufficing
PRĪSING	pricing
RĪSING	ricing
SLĪSING	slicing
SPISĪNG	spicing
SPLĪSING	splicing
TĪSING	enticing, ticing
VĪSING	vising

ISING

DISING	prejudicing
HISING	dehiscing, hissing
KISING	kissing
MISING	dismissing, missing
NISING	reminiscing
PISING	pissing

ĪSIS

ĪSIS	Isis
DĪSIS	misapodysis
FĪSIS	physis
KRĪSIS	energy crisis, epicrisis, identity crisis, crisis, midlife crisis
LĪSIS	lysis
NĪSIS	Dionysus, nisus
TĪSIS	phthisis

ISIT

LISIT	elicit, illicit, licit, solicit
PLISIT	explicit, implicit, inexplicit

ĪSIV

LĪSIV	collisive
RĪSIV	derisive

SĪSIV	decisive, indecisive, incisive
TRĪSIV	cicatrisive
VĪSIV	divisive

ISIV

FISIV	fissive
MISIV	*A* admissive, *D* demissive, dismissive, *E* emissive, *I* intermissive, irremissive, *K* commissive, *M* missive, *N* non-submissive, *O* omissive, *P* permissive, *PR* promissive, *R* remissive, *S* submissive, *TR* transmissive, *U* unsubmissive

ISKAL

DISKAL	discal
FISKAL	fiscal
FRISKAL	friscal
LISKAL	obeliscal

ISKĀT

FISKĀT	confiscate
PISKĀT	expiscate
VISKĀT	inviscate

ISKĒ

FRISKĒ	frisky
HWISKĒ	Bourbon whiskey, grain whiskey, whiskey, whisky, Irish whiskey, Canadian whiskey, malt whiskey, rye whiskey, Scotch whiskey
PISKĒ	pisky
RISKĒ	risky

ISKER

BRISKER	brisker
FRISKER	frisker
HWISKER	bewhisker, whisker
RISKER	risker

ISKET

BISKET	biscuit, dog biscuit
BRISKET	brisket
FRISKET	frisket
TISKET	tisket
WISKET	wisket

ISKFUL

FRISKFUL	friskful
RISKFUL	riskful

ISKIN

GRISKIN	griskin
HWISKIN	whiskin
SISKIN	siskin

ISKING

BRISKING	brisking
FRISKING	frisking
HWISKING	whisking
RISKING	risking

ISKIT

(See **ISKET**)

ISKŌ

BISKŌ	Nabisco
DISKŌ	disco
FRISKŌ	frisco, Frisco
SISKŌ	San Francisco, cisco

ISKUS

BISKUS	hibiscus
DISKUS	discous, discus
FISKUS	fiscus
KISKUS	trochiscus
KWISKUS	quiscos, quisquous
NISKUS	lemniscus, meniscus
SISKUS	abaciscus
THISKUS	calathiscus
TISKUS	lentiscus
VISKUS	viscous, viscus

ĪSL

DĪSL	paradisal
SKĪSL	skys'l
TRĪSL	trys'l

(See **ĪSĀL**)

ISL

BISL	abyssal
BRISL	bristle
FISL	fissile
GRISL	gristle
HWISL	whistle, penny whistle, police whistle, wolf whistle
KISL	kissel
MISL	dismissal, heat-seeking missile, cacomistle, cruise missile, missal, missile, mistle
NISL	Nissl
PISL	epistle
RISL	rissel, rissle
SISL	dickcissle, scissel, scissile, sisal, sistle
THISL	thistle

ĪSLĒ

NĪSLĒ	nicely, overnicely
SĪSLĒ	concisely, precisely

ISLĒ

BRISLĒ	bristly
GRISLĒ	gristly
THISLĒ	thistly

ĪSLES

(See **ĪS,** add -less where appropriate.)

ISLING

BRISLING	brisling, bristling
HWISLING	whistling

ĪSMAN

ĪSMAN	iceman
DĪSMAN	diceman
VĪSMAN	viceman, viseman

ĪSMENT

FĪSMENT	self-sufficement, sufficement
TĪSMENT	enticement

ISMUS

ISMUS	isthmus
KRISMUS	Christmas
TRISMUS	trismus

ISN

GLISN	glisten
KRISN	christen
LISN	lissen, listen
TISN	datiscin
VISN	viscin

ĪSNES

NĪSNES	niceness, overniceness
SĪSNES	conciseness, preciseness

ISNES

MISNES	remissness
THISNES	thisness

ISNING

GLISNING	glistening
KRISNING	christening
LISNING	listening

ISNZ

LISNZ	lissens, listens

(See **ISN,** add -s where appropriate.)

ISOM

(See **ISUM**)

ĪSON

BĪSON	bison
GRĪSON	grison
HĪSON	hyson
VĪSON	vison

ISPĒ

KRISPĒ	crispy
LISPĒ	lispy
WISPĒ	wispy

ISPER

HWISPER	stage whisper, whisper
KRISPER	crisper
LISPER	lisper
RISPER	risper
WISPER	wisper

ISPING

(See **ISP,** add -ing where appropriate.)

ISTA

KRISTA	crista
LISTA	ballista
NISTA	genista
RISTA	arista
VISTA	Buena Vista, vista

ISTAL

DISTAL	distal
KRISTAL	crystal
LISTAL	listel
MISTAL	mistal
PISTAL	pistil, pistol, pocket pistol, water pistol
SISTAL	cystal
VISTAL	vistal

ISTANS

DISTANS	distance, equidistance, outdistance
SISTANS	assistance, assistants, inconsistence, insistence, consistence, persistence, subsistence
ZISTANS	desistance, existence, inexistence, coexistence, nonexistence, nonresistance, persistence, pre-existence, resistance, unresistance

ISTANT

DISTANT	distant, equidistant
SISTANT	assistant, inconsistent, insistent, consistent, persistent, subsistent
ZISTANT	existent, inexistent, coexistent,

nonexistent,
nonresistant,
persistent, pre-
existent, resistant,
unresistant

ISTED

FISTED	fisted, hard-fisted, iron-fisted, close-fisted, tight-fisted, two-fisted
LISTED	blacklisted, enlisted, white-listed, listed, relisted, unlisted
MISTED	misted
RISTED	limp-wristed, strong-wristed, wristed, thick-wristed, thin-wristed, weak-wristed
SISTED	assisted, encysted, insisted, consisted, cysted, subsisted, unassisted
TRISTED	trysted
TWISTED	entwisted, intertwisted, twisted, untwisted
ZISTED	desisted, existed, persisted, pre-existed, resisted

ISTĒN

LISTĒN	Philistine
PRISTĒN	pristine
SISTĒN	Sistine
THISTĒN	amethystine

(Also **ISTĪN**)

ISTENS

(See **ISTANS**)

ISTENT

(See **ISTANT**)

ISTER

ISTER	Istar
BISTER	bister, bistre
BLISTER	blister, water blister
GLISTER	glister
JISTER	agistor, magister
KLISTER	clyster
LISTER	enlister, lister
MISTER	mister, Mr.

RISTER	limp-wrister
SISTER	assister, foster-sister, half-sister, insister, sister, sob-sister, subsister
TWISTER	intertwister, tongue-twister, twister, untwister
ZISTER	exister, nonresister, passive resister, persister, resister, xyster

ISTFUL

FISTFUL	fistful
LISTFUL	listful
MISTFUL	mistful
WISTFUL	wistful

ISTIK

ISTIK	*A* altruistic, atheistic, *D* deistic, *E* egoistic, epideistic, *H* Hebraistic, *J* jingoistic, Judaistic, *K* casuistic, *M* monotheistic, pantheistic, polytheistic, *T* Taoistic, *TH* theistic, *TR* tritheistic
BRISTIK	hubristic
DISTIK	aphrodistic, Buddhistic, distich, methodistic, sadistic, Talmudistic
FISTIK	philosophistic, fistic, sophistic
GWISTIK	linguistic
HISTIK	Elohistic
JISTIK	*A* aphlogistic, antiphlogistic, *B* bibliopegistic, *D* dialogistic, dyslogistic, *E* epilogistic, phlogistic, *L* logistic, *N* neologistic, *P* paleologistic, *S* syllogistic, synergistic, *SFR* sphragistic, *Y* eulogistic
KISTIK	anarchistic, ekistic, catechistic, masochistic, sadomasochistic
KRISTIK	paleocrystic

LISTIK	*A* annalistic, anomalistic, *B* ballistic, bibliopolistic, *D* dualistic, *E* electroballistic, evangelistic, *F* familistic, fatalistic, phenomenalistic, formalistic, feudalistic, *I* idealistic, imperialistic, individualistic, *J* journalistic, *K* cabalistic, cameralistic, cannibalistic, capitalistic, commercialistic, communalistic, curialistic, *L* liberalistic, *M* materialistic, monopolistic, moralistic, *N* nationalistic, naturalistic, nihilistic, nominalistic, novelistic, *P* parallelistic, pugilistic, *R* rationalistic, realistic, ritualistic, royalistic, *S* sensationalistic, sensualistic, symbolistic, sciolistic, socialistic, somnambulistic, surrealistic, *SP* spiritualistic, *ST* stylistic, *U* universalistic, *V* vitalistic
MISTIK	alchemistic, animistic, hemistich, intermistic, mystic, optimistic, pessimistic, euphemistic
NISTIK	*A* agonistic, achronistic, anachronistic, antagonistic, *F* feuillitonistic, *H* hedonistic, Hellenistic, humanistic, *I* illuministic, impressionistic, Impressionistic, *K* Calvinistic, canonistic, communistic, *L* Latinistic, *M*

mechanistic, modernistic, monistic, *P* post-impressionistic, *R* Romanistic, *S* synchronistic, *SH* chauvinistic, *Y* eudemonistic, unionistic

PISTIK philanthropistic, papistic, pistic

PLISTIK simplistic

RISTIK *A* adiaphoristic, aphoristic, allegoristic, aoristic, behavioristic, *E* eristic, *F* formularistic, futuristic, *FL* floristic, *H* humoristic, heuristic, *J* juristic, *K* characteristic, *M* meristic, *P* polaristic, poristic, puristic, *S* solaristic, *T* terroristic, touristic, *V* voyeuristic, *Y* euhemeristic, eucharistic

SHISTIK fetishistic, schistic

SISTIK cystic, solecistic

TISTIK *A* absolutistic, anabaptistic, artistic, *B* baptistic, *E* egotistic, *F* filiopietistic, *H* hypnotistic, *I* inartistic, *KR* chromatistic, *KW* quietistic, *O* autistic, *P* pietistic, *R* romanistic, *ST* statistic

TRISTIK belletristic, patristic, tristich

VISTIK atavistic, Jehovistic, relativistic

ISTIKS

JISTIKS sphragistics
KISTIKS ekistics

(See **ISTIK**, add -*s* where appropriate.)

ISTIKS

(See **ISTIK**, add -*s* where appropriate.)

ISTĪN

(See **ISTĒN**)

ISTL

(See **ISTAL**)

ISTLES

LISTLES listless
MISTLES mistless
TWISTLES twistless
ZISTLES resistless

ISTMENT

JISTMENT agistment
LISTMENT enlistment

ISTOID

HISTOID histoid
SISTOID cystoid

ISTOL

(See **ISTAL**)

ISTRAL

MISTRAL mistral
NISTRAL sinistral

ISTUS

HISTUS anhistous
SHISTUS schistous
SISTUS rock-cistus, cistus
THISTUS acathistus
ZISTUS xystus

ISŪ

(See **ISHOO**)

ISUM

BLISUM blissom
KRISUM crissum
LISUM alyssum, lissom, lissome
MISSUM fideicommissum

ĪSUS

(See **ĪSIS**)

ISUS

BISUS byssus
SISUS narcissus

ĪTA

LĪTA amalaita
RĪTA baryta
VĪTA vita

ITA

LITA lytta
PITA pitta
SHITA shittah
VITA vitta

ĪTAL

DĪTAL dital
FĪTAL microphytal
KWĪTAL requital
SĪTAL cital, parasital, recital
TĪTAL disentitle, entitle, mistitle, subtitle, title
TRĪTAL detrital
VĪTAL vital

ITAL

(See **ITL**)

ITANS

KWITANS acquittance, quittance
MITANS admittance, omittance, permittance, remittance, transmittance
PITANS pittance

ĪTĒ

BLĪTĒ blighty
DĪTĒ Aphrodite
FLĪTĒ flighty
HWĪTĒ whitey, whity
LĪTĒ pendente lite
MĪTĒ almighty, God almighty, mighty, mity
NĪTĒ nightie, Venite
RĪTĒ all righty
TRĪTĒ Amphitrite
VĪTĒ aqua vitae, arbor vitae, lignum vitae, vitae

ITĒ

BITĒ ambitty, bitty, itty-bitty

CHĬTĒ	chitty
DĬTĒ	banditti, ditty, poditti
FLĬTĒ	flitty
GRĬTĒ	gritty, nitty-gritty
KĬTĒ	kitty
MĬTĒ	committee, subcommittee, Walter Mitty
NĬTĒ	nitty
PĬTĒ	pity, self-pity
PRĬTĒ	pretty
SHĬTĒ	shitty
SĬTĒ	inner city, intercity, city
SKĬTĒ	skitty
SLĬTĒ	slitty
SMRĬTĒ	smriti
TĬTĒ	titty
TWĬTĒ	twitty
WĬTĒ	wittee, witty

ĪTED

BĪTED	bighted
BLĪTED	blighted
DĪTED	bedighted, dighted, dited, indicted, indited, undighted
FLĪTED	eagle-flighted
FRĪTED	affrighted, frighted, unaffrighted, unfrighted
HWĪTED	whited
KĪTED	kited
KWĪTED	requited, unrequited
LĪTED	alighted, delighted, candlelighted, lighted, relighted, unlighted
MĪTED	dynamited
NĪTED	beknighted, benighted, ignited, knighted, nighted, reunited, unbenighted, unknighted, united
PLĪTED	plighted, troth-plighted, unplighted
RĪTED	copyrighted, righted, unrighted
SĪTED	E eagle-sighted, excited, F farsighted, foresighted, I incited, KL clear-sighted, KW quick-sighted, L long-sighted, N nearsighted, O overexcited, oversighted, R recited, S second-sighted, cited, sighted, sited, SH sharpsighted, short-sighted, U unsighted

SLĪTED	slighted, unslighted
SPĪTED	despited, spited
TRĪTED	attrited, detrited
VĪTED	invited, reinvited, uninvited

ĬTĒD

DĬTĒD	dittied
PĬTĒD	pitied
SĬTĒD	citied, uncitied

ĬTED

BĬTED	bitted, rebitted, unbitted
FĬTED	befitted, fitted, misfitted, counterfeited, outfitted, refitted, unfitted
FLĬTED	flitted, reflitted
GRĬTED	gritted, regritted
KWĬTED	acquitted, quitted, reacquitted, requitted, unacquitted
MĬTED	admitted, demitted, emitted, committed, compromitted, manumitted, omitted, permitted, recommitted, remitted, transmitted, submitted
NĬTED	interknitted, knitted, reknitted, unknitted
PĬTED	pitted
TWĬTED	twitted, retwitted
WĬTED	A after-witted, BL blunt-witted, D dimwitted, dullwitted, F fat-witted, H half-witted, KW quick-witted, L lean-witted, N nimble-witted, O outwitted, R ready-witted, S subtle-witted, SH sharp-witted, short-witted, U under-witted, W witted

ĪTEM

ĪTEM	item
BLĪTEM	Blitum
NĪTEM	ad infinitum
SĪTEM	quaesitum

ĪTEN

BRĪTEN	brighten, Brighton
FRĪTEN	frighten
HĪTEN	heighten
HWĪTEN	whiten
KĬTEN	chitin, chiton
KRĬTON	Admirable Crichton
LĪTEN	enlighten, lighten, reenlighten
RĪTEN	righten
SĪTEN	cyton
TĪTEN	tighten, Titan
TRĪTEN	triton, Triton

ĬTEN

BĬTEN	bitten, flea-bitten, fly-bitten, frostbitten, hunger-bitten, weather-bitten
BRĬTEN	Britain, Briton, Great Britain
KĬTEN	kitten, sex kitten
LĬTEN	litten
MĬTEN	mitten
RĬTEN	handwritten, written, typewritten, underwritten, unwritten
SMĬTEN	heart-smitten, conscience-smitten, smitten, sun-smitten, terror-smitten, unsmitten
WĬTAN	witan

ĪTER

ĪTER	iter
BĪTER	backbiter, biter
BLĪTER	blighter
FĪTER	bullfighter, fighter, gunfighter, prizefighter
KĪTER	check kiter, kiter
LĪTER	gaslighter, Gauleiter, lamplighter, lighter, moonlighter
MĪTER	bemitre, miter, mitre, unmiter, unmitre
NĪTER	igniter, niter, all-nighter
RĪTER	ghostwriter, copywriter, writer, scriptwriter, songwriter, telewriter, typewriter, underwriter
SĪTER	exciter, excitor, sighter
TĪTER	titer

ITER

BITER	bitter, embitter
CHITER	chitter
FITER	befitter, benefitter, fitter, counterfeiter, outfitter, pipe fitter, refitter
FLITER	flitter
FRITER	fritter
GITER	go-gitter
GLITER	glitter
HITER	base-hitter, hitter, pinch-hitter
HWITER	whitter
JITER	jitter
KRITER	critter
KWITER	acquitter, quitter, quittor
LITER	litter
MITER	admitter, emitter, committer, manumitter, omitter, permitter, recommitter, remitter, transmitter
NITER	knitter
PITER	pitter
RITER	ritter
SITER	baby-sitter, house-sitter, outsitter, sitter
SKITER	skitter
SLITER	slitter
SPITER	spitter
SPLITER	lip-splitter, rail-splitter, splitter
TITER	titter
TWITER	atwitter, twitter
WITTER	outwitter

ITERN

BITERN	bittern
FLITERN	flittern
GITERN	gittern
SITERN	cittern

ĪTFUL

FRĪTFUL	frightful
LĪTFUL	delightful
MĪTFUL	mightful
RĪTFUL	rightful
SPĪTFUL	despiteful, spiteful
SPRĪTFUL	sprightful

ITFUL

FITFUL	fitful
WITFUL	witful

ĪTHĒ

(**TH** as in *then*)

LĪTHĒ	lithy
SLĪTHĒ	slithy

ITHĒ

(**TH** as in *thin*)

PITHĒ	pithy
PRITHĒ	prithee
SMITHĒ	smithy
STITHĒ	stithy
WITHĒ	twigwithy, withey, withy

ĪTHER

(**TH** as in *then*)

ĪTHER	either
BLĪTHER	blither
NĪTHER	neither
RĪTHER	writher
TĪTHER	tither

ITHER

(**TH** as in *then*)

BLITHER	blither
DITHER	dither
HITHER	behither, hither
HWITHER	anywhither, whither, nowhither, somewhither
LITHER	lither
NITHER	nither
SLITHER	slither
SWITHER	swither
THITHER	thither
TITHER	tither
WITHER	wither
ZITHER	zither

ITHERD

(See **ITHER,** add *-ed* where appropriate.)

ITHERZ

WITHERZ	withers

(See **ITHER,** add *-s* where appropriate.)

ĪTHFUL

(**TH** as in *thin*)

BLĪTHFUL	blitheful
LĪTHFUL	litheful

ITHIK

(**TH** as in *thin*)

LITHIK	archaeolithic, eolithic, lithic, megalithic, microlithic, monolithic, neolithic, Paleolithic, trilithic
MITHIK	mythic, polymythic
NITHIK	philornithic, ornithic

ĪTHING

(**TH** as in *then*)

NĪTHING	nithing
RĪTHING	writhing
SĪTHING	scything
TĪTHING	tithing
TRĪTHING	trithing

ĪTHLĒ

(**TH** as in *then*)

BLĪTHLĒ	blithely
LĪTHLĒ	lithely

ĪTHNES

(**TH** as in *then*)

BLĪTHNES	blitheness
LĪTHNES	litheness

ĪTHSUM

(**TH** as in *then*)

BLĪTHSUM	blithesome
LĪTHSUM	lithesome

ITIK

ITIK	Jesuitic, Sinaitic
BITIK	phlebitic, Jacobitic, cenobitic, trilobitic
DITIK	aphroditic, hermaphroditic, troglodytic
FITIK	anthropomorphitic, eophytic, epiphytic, graphitic, holophytic, mephitic, necrophytic, neophytic, xerophytic, zoophytic
FRITIK	nephritic

GRITIK	Negritic
JITIK	laryngitic, meningitic
KITIK	bronchitic, conchitic, rachitic, trachitic
KLITIK	anaclitic, enclitic, heteroclitic, proclitic, euclitic
KRITIK	diacritic, hypercritic, hypocritic, critic, oneirocritic
LITIK	*A* acrolitic, actinolitic, analytic, *B* bacteriolytic, biolytic, *D* dialytic, *E* electrolytic, *GR* granulitic, *H* hydrolytic, *I* Israelitic, *K* catalytic, *L* lytic, *N* nummulitic, *O* oolitic, *P* paralytic, *S* scialytic, syphilitic, sympatholytic, psychoanalytic, *SF* spherulitic, *T* tonsillitic, toxophillitic, *TH* theodolitic, thermolytic, *V* variolitic, *Z* zeolitic
MITIK	*A* Adamitic, anti-Semitic, *D* dynamitic, dolomitic, *E* eremitic, *H* Hamitic, *I* Islamitic, *P* palmitic, *PR* pre-Adamitic, protosemitic, *S* Semitic, *ST* stalagmitic
NITIK	aconitic, granitic, lenitic, lignitic, sagenitic, selenitic, syenitic, Sinitic, Titanitic, tympanitic, uranitic
RITIK	diphtheritic, phosphoritic, Cabiritic, margaritic, meteoritic, Nazaritic, neritic, pyritic, pleuritic, porphyritic, sybaritic

SHITIK	Cushitic
SITIK	anthracitic, erythrocitic, lymphocytic, parasitic, semiparasitic
SKRITIK	Sanskritic
THRITIK	arthritic, osteoarthritic
TITIK	hematitic, stalactitic, steatitic, strontitic
TRITIK	dentritic
VITIK	gingivitic, Levitic

ĪTING

BĪTING	backbiting, biting
RĪTING	handwriting

(See **ĪT,** add *-ing* where appropriate.)

ITING

FITING	fitting, pipefitting, steamfitting
HITING	hard-hitting, pinch-hitting
MITING	remitting, unremitting
SPLITING	hair-splitting, rail-splitting, splitting
WITING	unwitting, witting

(See **IT,** add *-ing* where appropriate.)

ĪTIS

ĪTIS	fasciitis, ileitis, ophryitis, osteitis, uveitis
BĪTIS	phlebitis
DĪTIS	endocarditis, carditis, mastoiditis, pericarditis, thyroiditis
FĪTIS	mephitis, typhitis
FRĪTIS	nephritis
JĪTIS	pharyngitis, laryngitis, meningitis, salpingitis
KĪTIS	bronchitis, rachitis, trachitis
LĪTIS	*D* diverticulitis, *E* encephalitis, *H* hyalitis, *K* colitis, *My* myelitis, *O* osteomyelitis, *P* pyelitis, poliomyelitis, *S* cellulitis, *SP* spondylitis, *T* tonsillitis, *V* valvulitis, *Y* utriculitis, uvulitis
MĪTIS	mitis, ophthalmitis
NĪTIS	adenitis, colonitis,

	pneumonitis, peritonitis, rhinitis, splenitis, vaginitis
RĪTIS	arteritis, blepharitis, enteritis, gastroenteritis, iritis, neuritis, ovaritis, scleritis
SĪTIS	appendicitis, bursitis, fibrositis, glossitis, sinusitis
THRĪTIS	arthritis, osteoarthritis, urethritis
TĪTIS	dermatitis, hepatitis, keratitis, mastitis, otitis, parotitis, prostatitis, cystitis
TRĪTIS	gastritis, metritis
VĪTIS	gingivitis, conjunctivitis, synovitis, vulvitis (etc.)

ĪTISH

(See **ĪT,** add *-ish* where appropriate.)

ITISH

BRITISH	British
SKITISH	skittish

(See **IT,** add *-ish* where appropriate.)

ĪTIV

DĪTIV	expeditive
SĪTIV	excitive
TĪTIV	appetitive
TRĪTIV	attritive

ĪTL

(See **ĪTAL**)

ITL

ITL	it'll
BRITL	brittle, peanut brittle
GRITL	grittle
HWITL	whittle
KITL	kittle
KWITL	acquittal
LITL	belittle, Chicken Little, little
MITL	committal, noncommittal, remittal, transmittal
NITL	knittle

SKITL	skittle
SPITL	lickspittle, spital, spittle
TITL	tittle
VITL	victual
WITL	wittol

ĪTLĒ

BRĪTLĒ	brightly
DĪTLĒ	eruditely
HWĪTLĒ	whitely
LĪTLĒ	impolitely, lightly, politely
NĪTLĒ	fortnightly, knightly, nightly, unknightly
RĪTLĒ	forthrightly, rightly, uprightly
SĪTLĒ	sightly, unsightly
SLĪTLĒ	slightly
SPRĪTLĒ	sprightly
TĪTLĒ	tightly
TRĪTLĒ	contritely, tritely

ITLĒ

(See **IT**, add -ly where appropriate.)

ITLER

BRITLER	brittler
HITLER	Hitler
HWITLER	whittler
SKITLER	skitler
LITLER	belittler, littler
TITLER	tittler
VITLER	victualler

ĪTLES

(See **ĪT**, add -less where appropriate.)

ITLES

(See **IT**, add -less where appropriate.)

ITLING

CHITLING	chitling
HWITLING	whittling
KITLING	kitling
LITLING	belittling
TITLING	titling, tittling
VITLING	victualing
WITLING	witling

ITLZ

SKITLZ	skittles
VITLZ	victuals

(See **ITL**, add -s where appropriate.)

ITMAN

HWITMAN	Whitman
PITMAN	pitman, Pitman
TITMAN	titman

ĪTMENT

DĪTMENT	indictment, reindictment
FRĪTMENT	affrightment, frightment
SĪTMENT	excitement, incitement
VĪTMENT	invitement

ITMENT

FITMENT	fitment, refitment
KWITMENT	acquitment
MITMENT	commitment, remitment

ĪTN

(See **ĪTEN**)

ITN

(See **ITEN**)

ITNĒ

HWITNĒ	Mount Whitney
JITNĒ	jitney
WITNĒ	witney

ĪTNER

BRĪTNER	brightener
FRĪTNER	frightener
HĪTNER	heightener
HWĪTNER	whitener
LĪTNER	enlightener, lightener

ĪTNES

(See **ĪT**, add -ness where appropriate.)

ITNES

FITNES	fitness, unfitness
WITNES	eyewitness, witness

ĪTNING

LĪTNING	chain lightning, enlightening, white lightning, lightening, lightning, sheet lightning, streak lightning

(See **ĪTEN**, add -ing where appropriate.)

ITOL

(See **ITL**)

ĪTON

(See **ĪTEN**)

ĪTRĀT

NĪTRĀT	nitrate
TĪTRĀT	titrate

ITRIK

SITRIK	citric
VITRIK	vitric

ITSĒ

BITSĒ	itsy bitsy
GLITSĒ	glitsy
RITSĒ	ritzy
SKITSĒ	schizzy

ĪTUM

(See **ĪTEM**)

ITUP

SITUP	sit-up
TITUP	tittup

ĪTUS

JĪTUS	vagitus
KLĪTUS	Heraclitus, Polyclitus
LĪTUS	litus

NĪTUS	tinnitus
RĪTUS	pruritus, ritus
SĪTUS	situs
TRĪTUS	attritus, detritus
VĪTUS	St. Vitus

ĪUN

(See ĪAN)

ĪUP

FRĪUP	fry-up
TĪUP	tieup

ĪUS

(See ĪAS)

ĪVA

ĪVA	iva
DĪVA	daiva, Godiva
LĪVA	saliva
TĪVA	conjunctiva
VĪVA	viva

ĪVAL

JĪVAL	ogival
KĪVAL	archival
LĪVAL	salival
NĪVAL	nival
PRĪVAL	deprival
RĪVAL	arrival, corrival, nonarrival, outrival, rival, unrival
THĪVAL	thivel
TĪVAL	adjectival, aestival, estival, imperatival, genitival, conjunctival, nominatival, relatival
VĪVAL	revival, survival

ĪVANS

NĪVANS	connivance
RĪVANS	arrivance
TRĪVANS	contrivance
VĪVANS	survivance

ĪVANT

NĪVANT	connivant
RĪVANT	arrivant
TRĪVANT	contrivant
VĪVANT	survivant

ĪVĒ

ĪVĒ	ivy, poison ivy
JĪVĒ	jivy
SKĪVĒ	skivie
STĪVĒ	stivy

IVĒ

BIVĒ	bivvy
CHIVĒ	chivvy
DIVĒ	dividivi, divvy
GIVĒ	givey
LIVĒ	Livy
PRIVĒ	privy
SIVĒ	civvy
SKIVĒ	skivvy
TIVĒ	tantivy, tivy

IVĒD

CHIVĒD	chivvied
DIVĒD	divvied

IVEL

DRIVEL	drivel
FRIVEL	frivol
RIVEL	rivel
SHRIVEL	shrivel
SIVEL	civil, uncivil
SNIVEL	snivel
SWIVEL	swivel

ĪVEN

ĪVEN	Ivan
DĪVEN	divan
LĪVEN	enliven, liven

IVEN

DRIVEN	driven, overdriven, rain-driven, snow-driven, storm-driven, underdriven, weather-driven, wind-driven
GIVEN	forgiven, given, unforgiven
RIVEN	riven
SHRIVEN	shriven, unshriven
SKRIVEN	scriven
STRIVEN	striven
THRIVEN	thriven

ĪVER

DĪVER	deep-sea diver, diver, helldiver, pearl diver, scuba diver
DRĪVER	driver, co-driver, screwdriver, slave driver
FĪVER	fiver
HĪVER	hiver
JĪVER	jiver
LĪVER	aliver, liver, livor
NĪVER	conniver
PRĪVER	depriver
RĪVER	arriver, deriver, river
SHRĪVER	shriver
SKĪVER	skiver
SLĪVER	sliver
STĪVER	stiver
STRĪVER	striver
THRĪVER	thriver
TRĪVER	contriver
VĪVER	reviver, survivor

IVER

FLIVER	flivver
GIVER	forgiver, giver, Indian giver, life-giver, lawgiver, misgiver
KWIVER	quiver
LIVER	deliver, free-liver, liver, outliver
RIVER	river
SHIVER	shiver
SIVER	siever
SKIVER	skiver
SLIVER	sliver
STIVER	stiver
TIVER	tiver
YIVER	yiver

IVERD

FLIVERD	flivvered
KWIVERD	quivered
LIVERD	delivered, white-livered, lily-livered, livered, pale-livered, undelivered, yellow-livered
SHIVERD	shivered
SKIVERD	skivered
SLIVERD	slivered

IVET

DIVET	divot
GRIVET	grivet

PIVET	pivot
PRIVET	privet
RIVET	rivet, unrivet
SIVET	civet
TRIVET	trivet

ĪVID

LIVID	livid
VIVID	vivid

IVIL

(See **IVEL**)

ĪVING

(See **ĪV**, add -ing where appropriate.)

IVING

GIVING	forgiving, giving, life-giving, law-giving, misgiving, thanksgiving, Thanksgiving, unforgiving
LIVING	everliving, living, outliving, reliving, unliving
SIVING	sieving

ĪVL

(See **ĪVAL**)

IVLING

(See **IVEL**, add -ing where appropriate.)

ĪVMENT

PRĪVMENT	deprivement
VĪVMENT	revivement

IVOL

(See **IVEL**)

IVOT

(See **IVET**)

ĪVUS

DĪVUS	divus
KLĪVUS	acclivous, declivous, clivus, proclivous
LĪVUS	salivous
VĪVUS	redivivus

IVYAL

(See **IV'I.AL**)

ĪWĀ

BĪWĀ	byway
FLĪWĀ	flyway
HĪWĀ	highway
SKĪWĀ	skyway

ĪZA

BĪZA	beisa
LĪZA	Eliza, Liza
RĪZA	coryza

ĪZAL

(See **ĪZL**)

IZARD

IZARD	izard, izzard, A to izzard
BLIZARD	blizzard
GIZARD	gizzard
LIZARD	lizard, lounge lizard, sofa lizard
SIZARD	scissored, sizzard
VIZARD	visored, vizard
WIZARD	wizard

IZBĒ

FRIZBĒ	Frisbee
THIZBĒ	Thisbe

IZĒ

BIZĒ	busy
DIZĒ	dizzy
FIZĒ	fizzy
FRIZĒ	frizzy
KWIZĒ	quizzy
LIZĒ	busy Lizzie, Lizzie, tin lizzie
MIZĒ	mizzy
NIZĒ	nizy
TIZĒ	tizzy

IZĒD

BIZĒD	busied, unbusied
DIZĒD	dizzied

IZEM

(See **IZM**)

ĪZEN

(See **ĪZON**)

IZEN

DIZEN	bedizen, dizen
HIZEN	his'n
JIZEN	jizzen
MIZEN	mizzen
PRIZEN	imprison, prison, reimprison
RIZEN	arisen, re-arisen, risen, unrisen
TIZEN	ptisan
WIZEN	wizen

ĪZER

DĪZER	aggrandizer, gormandizer, liquidizer
GĪZER	geyser, disguiser
JĪZER	apologizer, eulogizer
KĪZER	catechiser, Kaiser
LĪZER	A analyzer, BR Breathalyzer, D demoralizer, dialyser, E equalizer, elisor, F fertilizer, I idolizer, J generalizer, M monopolizer, moralizer, N neutralizer, P papalizer, paralyzer, S symbolizer, civilizer, ST stabilizer, sterilizer, T tantalizer, totalizer, TR tranquilizer, V vitalizer, vocalizer
MĪZER	atomizer, economizer, epitomizer, miser, remiser, surmiser
NĪZER	FR fraternizer, H harmonizer, humanizer, K canonizer, L lionizer, M modernizer, moisturizer, O organizer, P patronizer, S sermonizer, synchronizer, solemnizer, SK scrutinizer, W womanizer

RĪZER deodorizer, extemporizer, high-riser, cauterizer, mesmerizer, authorizer, pulverizer, riser, temporizer, terrorizer, theorizer
PRĪZER appriser, enterpriser, prizer, surpriser
SĪZER assiser, exerciser, exorciser, incisor, capsizer, synthesizer, sizar, sizer
THĪZER nonsympathizer, sympathizer
TĪZER advertiser, appetizer, baptizer, chastiser, magnetizer
VĪZER advisor, devisor, divisor, supervisor, visor

IZER

FIZER fizzer
FRIZER befrizzer, frizzer
HWIZER whizzer
KWIZER quizzer
SIZER scissor
VIZER visor

IZERD

(See **IZARD**)

IZHUN

FRIZHUN Frisian
LIZHUN allision, elision, Elysian, illision, collision, prodelision
PRIZHUN misprision
RIZHUN derision, irrision, Parisian, subrision
SIZHUN *A* abscission, *D* decision, *E* excision, *I* imprecision, indecision, incision, *K* concision, *O* occision, *PR* precisian, precision, *R* recision, rescission, *S* circumcision, scission
VIZHUN *D* division, *E* envision, *O* audiovision, *PR* prevision, provision, *R* revision, *S* subdivision, supervision, *ST*

stereovision, *T* television, tunnel vision, *V* vision, *X* x-ray vision, *Y* Eurovision

(See **IZ'I.AN**)

IZIK

DIZIK paradisic
FIZIK biophysic, physic, hydrophysic, geophysic, metaphysic, zoophysic
JIZIK jizzick
TIZIK phthisic

IZIKS

FIZIKS physics, metaphysics, paraphysics

(See **IZIK**, add -s where appropriate.)

ĪZING

(See **ĪZ**, add -ing where appropriate.)

IZING

FRIZING frizzing
KWIZING quizzing
ZIZING zizzing

IZIT

KWIZIT exquisite
VIZIT revisit, visit

ĪZL

ĪZL izle
DĪZL paradisal
MĪZL surmisal
PRĪZAL appraisal, apprizal, comprisal, reprisal, surprisal
RĪZL arrhizal
SĪZL insizal, capsizal, sisal, sizal
VĪZL advisal, revisal

IZL

CHIZL chisel, enchisel
DRIZL drizzle

FIZL fizzle
FRIZL frizzle
GRIZL grizzle
KRIZL crizzle
MIZL mizzle
PIZL pizzle
SIZL sizzle
SWIZL rumswizzle, swizzle
TWIZL twizzle

IZLD

(See **IZL**, add -d or ed where appropriate.)

IZLĒ

CHIZLĒ chiselly
DRIZLĒ drizzly
FRIZLĒ frizzly
GRIZLĒ grisly, grizzly
MIZLĒ misly, mizzly
SIZLĒ sizzly

IZLER

CHIZLER chiseler
FRIZLER frizzler
GRIZLER grizzler

IZLING

KWIZLING quisling

(See **IZL**, add -ing where appropriate.)

IZMA

LIZMA melisma
RIZMA charisma

IZMAL

BIZMAL abysmal, Pepto-Bismol, strabysmal
DIZMAL dismal
KIZMAL catechismal
KLIZMAL cataclysmal
KRIZMAL chrismal
LIZMAL embolismal
PRIZMAL prismal
RIZMAL aneurismal
SIZMAL paroxysmal
TIZMAL baptismal, rheumatismal

ĪZMAN

PRĪZMAN	prizeman
SĪZMAN	exciseman

ĪZMENT

CHĪZMENT	*disenfranchisement, disfranchisement, enfranchisement, franchisement*
DĪZMENT	aggrandizement
PRĪZMENT	apprizement
SĪZMENT	assizement
TĪZMENT	advertisement, baptizement
VĪZMENT	advisement

IZMIK

KLIZMIK	cataclysmic, clysmic
LIZMIK	embolismic
RIZMIK	aphorismic, algorismic
SIZMIK	paroxysmic
TRIZMIK	trismic

IZMUS

BIZMUS	strabismus
NIZMUS	vaginismus
SIZMUS	accismus, hircismus
TIZMUS	tarantismus
TRIZMUS	trismus

ĪZŌ

RĪZŌ	Valparaiso
VĪZŌ	aviso, improviso, proviso

ĪZON

BĪZON	bison
DĪZON	bedizen, dizen
GRĪZON	greisen, grison
LĪZON	Kyrie eleison, spiegeleisen
PĪZON	pizen
RĪZON	horizon

ĪZOR

(See ĪZER)

ŌA

ŌA	*Iowa*
BŌA	balboa, Balboa, boa, jerboa
DŌA	Shenandoah
GŌA	goa, Goa
LŌA	aloha, loa, Kanaloa
MŌA	moa, Samoa
NŌA	anoa, *Genoa, quinoa,* Noah
PŌA	leipoa
PRŌA	proa
STŌA	stoa
TŌA	Krakatoa, toatoa
ZŌA	Anthozoa, entozoa, epizoa, Hydrozoa, Metazoa, microzoa, protozoa, spermatozoa, Sporozoa

ŌAJ

(See ŌIJ)

ŌAN

ŌAN	eoan
KŌAN	cowan
LŌAN	lowan
MŌAN	Samoan
NŌAN	*dipnoan,* Minoan
RŌAN	rowan
ZŌAN	bryozoan, hydrozoan, protozoan

ŌBA

DŌBA	*cordoba*
GŌBA	*dagoba*
HŌBA	jojoba, cohoba
KŌBA	koba
RŌBA	algarroba, araroba, arroba, bona roba
TŌBA	Manitoba

ŌBAL

(See ŌBL)

ŌBĀT

GLŌBĀT	globate, conglobate
KRŌBĀT	crowbait
LŌBĀT	bilobate, lobate, trilobate
PRŌBĀT	probate

ŌBĒ

ŌBĒ	obi
BÔBĒ	bawby
DŌBĒ	adobe, dhobi, dobee, dobie
GLŌBĒ	globy
GŌBĒ	Gobi, goby
RŌBĒ	Nairobi
TŌBĒ	toby, Toby

ÔBĒ

DÔBĒ	dauby
GÔBĒ	gauby

OBĒ

BLOBĒ	blobby
BOBĒ	bobby
DOBĒ	dobby
GLOBĒ	globby
GOBĒ	gobby
HOBĒ	hobby
KOBĒ	cobby
LOBĒ	lobby
MOBĒ	mobby
NOBĒ	knobby, nobby
POBĒ	pobby
SKOBĒ	scobby
SNOBĒ	snobby

ŌBER

LŌBER	lobar
MŌBER	amobyr
PRŌBER	prober
RŌBER	disrober, enrober, rober, robur
SŌBER	sober
TŌBER	October

ÔBER

DÔBER	bedauber, dauber
KÔBER	Micawber

OBER

BLOBER	blobber
JOBER	jobber, stockjobber
KLOBER	clobber
KOBER	cobber
LOBER	lobber
NOBER	knobber
ROBER	robber
SLOBER	beslobber, slobber

SNOBER	snobber
SOBER	sobber
SWOBER	swabber
THROBER	throbber

OBET

GOBET	gobbet
HOBET	hobbit

ŌBIK

ŌBIK	niobic
FŌBIK	aerophobic, agorophobic, acrophobic, phobic, phobophobic, photophobic, hydrophobic, claustrophobic, necrophobic, xenophobic (For more words ending in -phobic, see FŌ'BI.A and change -a to -ic.)
KRŌBIK	microbic
RŌBIK	aerobic
STRŌBIK	strobic

OBIK

OBIK	niobic
STROBIK	strobic

ŌBIKS

RŌBIKS	aerobics

(See ŌBIK, add -s where appropriate.)

ŌBIL

(See ŌBL)

OBIN

BOBIN	bobbin
DOBIN	dobbin
ROBIN	cock robin, ragged robin, robbin, robin, round robin, wake robin

ŌBING

GLŌBING	englobing, globing

RŌBING	disrobing, enrobing, robing, unrobing
PRŌBING	probing

OBING

BOBING	bobbing
JOBING	jobbing
KOBING	cobbing
LOBING	lobbing
MOBING	mobbing
NOBING	hobnobbing
ROBING	robbing
SNOBING	snobbing
SOBING	sobbing
THROBING	throbbing

OBISH

BOBISH	bobbish
MOBISH	mobbish
NOBISH	nobbish
SKWOBISH	squabbish
SNOBISH	snobbish

ŌBL

GLŌBL	global
KŌBL	coble
KRŌBL	microbal
LŌBL	lobal
MŌBL	mobile, upwardly mobile, upward-mobile
NŌBL	ennoble, Grenoble, ignoble, noble, unnoble
PRŌBL	probal
TŌBL	Cristobal

ÔBL

BÔBL	bauble

(See OBL)

OBL

GOBL	gobble
HOBL	hobble
KOBL	cobble, coble
NOBL	nobble
SKWOBL	squabble
WOBL	wabble, wobble

(See ÄBL)

OBLĒ

OBLĒ	obley
GOBLĒ	gobbly
HOBLĒ	hobbly
SKWOBLĒ	squabbly
WOBLĒ	wabbly, wobbly, Wobbly

OBLER

GOBLER	gobbler, turkey gobbler
KOBLER	blackberry cobbler, cobbler, peach cobbler

(See OBL, add -r where appropriate.)

OBLING

(See OBL, add -ing where appropriate.)

ŌBŌ

ŌBŌ	oboe
BŌBŌ	bobo
DŌBŌ	adobo
HŌBŌ	hobo
KŌBŌ	kobo
LŌBŌ	lobo
ZŌBŌ	zobo

ŌBOI

ŌBOI	hautboy
DŌBOI	doughboy
HŌBOI	hautboy

ÔBŌNZ

JÔBŌNZ	jawbones
SÔBŌNZ	sawbones

ŌBRA

DŌBRA	dobra
KŌBRA	cobra

OBSON

DOBSON	dobson
JOBSON	hobson-jobson

OBSTER

LOBSTER	lobster
MOBSTER	mobster

OBŪL

GLOBŪL	globule
LOBŪL	lobule

ŌBUS

ŌBUS	obus
GLŌBUS	globous
KŌBUS	jacobus

ŌCHĒ

LŌCHĒ	veloce
VŌCHĒ	sotto voce, viva voce

OCHĒ

BLOCHĒ	blotchy
BOCHĒ	botchy
KROCHĒ	crotchy
NOCHĒ	notchy
SKOCHĒ	Scotchy
SPLOCHĒ	splotchy
VOCHĒ	sotto voce, viva voce

ŌCHER

BRŌCHER	broacher
KLŌCHER	cloture
KŌCHER	coacher, stage-coacher
KRŌCHER	encroacher
PŌCHER	poacher
PRŌCHER	approacher, reproacher

ÔCHER

BÔCHER	debaucher
WÔCHER	night watcher, watcher

OCHER

BLOCHER	blotcher
BOCHER	botcher
NOCHER	notcher, top-notcher
SKOCHER	hopscotcher
SPLOCHER	splotcher

SWOCHER	swatcher
WOCHER	bird-watcher, weight-watcher, watcher

OCHET

KROCHET	crotchet
KLOCHET	*clochette*
ROCHET	rochet

ŌCHING

(See **ŌCH,** add *-ing* where appropriate.)

ÔCHING

BÔCHING	debauching
WÔCHING	watching

OCHING

BLOCHING	blotching
BOCHING	botching
HOCHING	hotching
KROCHING	crotching
NOCHING	notching
POCHING	hotchpotching

OCHMAN

SKOCHMAN	Scotchman
WOCHMAN	watchman

ŌCHMENT

KRŌCHMENT	encroachment
PRŌCHMENT	approachment

ŌDA

ŌDA	oda
GŌDA	pagoda
KŌDA	coda
SŌDA	baking soda, bourbon and soda, brandy and soda, whiskey and soda, ice-cream soda, scotch and soda (etc.), salsoda, soda

ŌDAL

(See **ŌDL**)

ÔDAL

(See **ŌDL**)

ODAL

(See **ODL**)

ŌDĒ

ŌDĒ	O.D.
BŌDĒ	bodhi
GŌDĒ	wally-gowdy
LŌDĒ	petalody
NŌDĒ	staminody
PŌDĒ	polypody
TŌDĒ	toady, tody
WŌDĒ	woady

ÔDĒ

BÔDĒ	bawdy
DÔDĒ	dawdy
GÔDĒ	gaudy
LÔDĒ	cum laude, Lawdy, magna cum laude, summa cum laude

ODĒ

BODĒ	afterbody, antibody, body, busybody, disembody, dogsbody, embody, anybody, everybody, nobody, somebody, underbody, wide-body
DODĒ	hoddy-doddy
HODĒ	hoddy
KLODĒ	cloddy
NODĒ	noddy, tomnoddy
PODĒ	poddy
RODĒ	roddy
SHODĒ	shoddy
SKWODĒ	squaddy
SODĒ	soddy
TODĒ	toddy
WODĒ	Irrawaddy, waddy, wadi

(See **ÄDĒ**)

ŌDED

(See **ŌD,** add *-d* or *-ed* where appropriate.)

ODĒD

BODĒD	able-bodied, bodied, disembodied,

	embodied, unbodied, unembodied
TODĒD	toddied, well-toddied

ÔDED

FRÔDED	defrauded
LÔDED	belauded, lauded, unlauded
PLÔDED	applauded, unapplauded
RÔDED	marauded

ODED

(See OD, add -ed where appropriate.)

ŌDEL

(See ŌDL)

ŌDEN

ŌDEN	Odin
BŌDEN	boden, foreboden
WŌDEN	Wodin

ODEN

HODEN	hodden
SODEN	sodden, water-sodden
TRODEN	downtrodden, trodden, untrodden

ŌDENT

| PLŌDENT | explodent |
| RŌDENT | corrodent, erodent, rodent |

ŌDER

ŌDER	malodor, Oder, odor
BŌDER	boder, foreboder
GŌDER	goader
KŌDER	decoder, coder, uncoder
LŌDER	loader, muzzle-loader, reloader, unloader
PLŌDER	exploder
RŌDER	eroder, corroder, roader
WŌDER	woader

ÔDER

BRÔDER	broader
FRÔDER	defrauder
LÔDER	belauder, lauder
PLÔDER	applauder
RÔDER	marauder
SÔDER	sawder, soft sawder

ODER

ODER	odder
DODER	dodder
FODER	fodder, cannon fodder
KODER	Cape Codder, codder
NODER	nodder
PLODER	plodder
PODER	podder
PRODER	prodder
SODER	sodder, solder

ODERD

DODERD	doddard
FODERD	foddered
SODERD	soldered

ODES

| BODES | bodice |
| GODES | demigoddess, goddess |

ODEST

ODEST	oddest
BODEST	bodiced
MODEST	immodest, modest

ŌDIK

| ŌDIK | odic |
| NŌDIK | palinodic |

ODIK

ODIK	antiperiodic, aperiodic, hydriodic, iodic, geodic, odic, periodic, euodic
KODIK	sarcodic
LODIK	melodic
MODIK	antispasmodic, psalmodic, spasmodic
NODIK	anodic, hellanodic, palinodic, synodic, threnodic

PODIK	epodic
RODIK	parodic
SODIK	episodic, exodic, kinesodic, rhapsodic
THODIK	methodic

ŌDING

(See ŌD, add -ing where appropriate.)

ÔDING

FRÔDING	defrauding
LÔDING	belauding, lauding, relauding
PLÔDING	applauding, reapplauding

ODING

| NODING | nid-nodding, nodding |
| PLODING | plodding |

ODIS

(See ODES)

ŌDISH

| MŌDISH | modish |
| TŌDISH | toadish |

ODISH

ODISH	oddish
GODISH	goddish
KLODISH	cloddish
KODISH	coddish
PODISH	poddish

ŌDIST

ŌDIST	odist
KŌDIST	codist
MŌDIST	modist
NŌDIST	palinodist

ÔDIT

| ÔDIT | audit |
| PLÔDIT | plaudit |

ŌDL

| ŌDL | odal |
| MŌDL | modal |

NŌDL	binodal, internodal, nodal, trinodal
YŌDL	yodel

ÔDL

DÔDL	dawdle
KÔDL	bicaudal, caudal, caudle, longicaudal

ODL

BRODL	broddle
DODL	doddle
KODL	coddle, mollycoddle
MODL	model, remodel, role model
NODL	niddle-noddle, noddle
TODL	toddle
WODL	waddle

(See ÄDL)

ODLĒ

ODLĒ	oddly
GODLĒ	godly, ungodly
TODLĒ	toddly, untoddly

(See ÄDLĒ)

ODLER

KODLER	coddler, mollycoddler
MODLER	modeler
TODLER	toddler

(See ÄDL, ODL, add -r where appropriate.)

ODLING

GODLING	godling
KODLING	coddling, codling, mollycoddling
TODLING	toddling

ODMAN

ODMAN	oddman
DODMAN	dodman
HODMAN	hodman

ŌDŌ

DŌDŌ	dodo
MŌDŌ	Quasimodo, quomodo

ŌDOR

(See ŌDER)

ŌDOUN

GŌDOUN	godown
HŌDOUN	hoedown
LŌDOUN	lowdown
SHŌDOUN	showdown
SLŌDOUN	slowdown
STŌDOUN	stowdown

ÔDRĒ

BÔDRĒ	bawdry
NÔDRĒ	minauderie
TÔDRĒ	tawdry

ŌDSTER

GŌDSTER	goadster
RŌDSTER	roadster

ŌDSTŌN

LŌDSTŌN	loadstone, lodestone
TŌDSTŌN	toadstone

ODŪL

MODŪL	module
NODŪL	nodule

ŌDUS

MŌDUS	modus
NŌDUS	nodous, nodus

ŌĒ

BŌĒ	bowie, Bowie
BLŌĒ	blowy

MOSES INFANTI

She took for him an ark of bulrushes, and daubed it with slime and with pitch, and put the child therein; and she laid it in the flags by the river's brink.

—Exodus 2:3

Among the flags did Moses lie,
Cradled in akaakai,
While a hippopotamus
Made a borborygmic fuss.

DŌĒ	doughy
GLŌĒ	glowy
HŌĒ	pahoehoe
PŌĒ	poë, poi
RŌĒ	rowy
SHŌĒ	showy
SNŌĒ	snowy
TŌĒ	towy
VŌĒ	evoe, evohe

ÔĒ

FLÔĒ	flawy
JÔĒ	jawy
STRÔĒ	strawy
THÔĒ	thawy
YÔĒ	yawy

(See OI)

ŌEM

BŌEM	jeroboam
FLŌEM	phloem
PŌEM	mythopoem, poem
PRŌEM	proem

ŌER

ŌER	o'er, ower
BLŌER	blower, glass blower, whistle-blower, snow blower
GLŌER	glower
GŌER	churchgoer, foregoer, goer, concertgoer, moviegoer, outgoer, playgoer, racegoer, undergoer
GRŌER	flower grower, grower, wine grower (etc.)
HŌER	hoer
KRŌER	cockcrower, crower
LŌER	lower
MŌER	lawn mower, mower
NŌER	foreknower, knower
RŌER	rower
SHŌER	foreshower, shower
SLŌER	slower
SŌER	sewer, sower
STŌER	bestower, stower
THRŌER	overthrower, thrower
TŌER	tower

ÔER

ÔER	awer, overawer
DRÔER	drawer, wire drawer, withdrawer

FÔER   guffawer
JÔER   jawer
KLÔER   clawer
KÔER   cawer
NÔER   gnawer
PÔER   pawer
RÔER   rawer
SÔER   sawer
TÔER   tawer

ŌERD

FRŌERD   froward
LŌERD   lowered
TŌERD   toward, untoward

ÔFAL

(See **ÔFL**)

ŌFĒ

ŌFĒ   oafy
STRŌFĒ   monostrophe, strophe
TRŌFĒ   trophy

OFĒ

KOFĒ   coffee
SPOFĒ   spoffy
TOFĒ   toffee

OFEN

(See **OFN**)

ŌFER

ŌFER   Ophir
GŌFER   gaufre, gofer, gopher
LŌFER   loafer, penny-loafer
SHŌFER   chauffeur

OFER

OFER   offer
DOFER   doffer
GOFER   goffer
KOFER   coffer, cougher
PROFER   proffer
SKOFER   scoffer

OFET

PROFET   archprophet, profit, prophet, weather prophet
SOFET   soffit

OFIK

OFIK   ophic
SOFIK   philosophic, theophilosophic, theosophic
STROFIK   anostrophic, antistrophic, apostrophic, geostrophic, catastrophic, strophic
TROFIK   atrophic, hypertrophic, heterotrophic, oligotrophic, autotrophic, protrophic, trophic, eutrophic

ÔFIN

(See **ÔFN**)

OFING

OFING   offing
DOFING   doffing
GOFING   golfing
KOFING   coughing
SKOFING   scoffing

ŌFISH

ŌFISH   oafish
BLŌFISH   blowfish

ÔFISH

KRÔFISH   crawfish
SÔFISH   sawfish
SKWÔFISH   squawfish

OFISH

OFISH   offish, standoffish
SPOFISH   spoffish

OFIT

(See **OFET**)

ÔFL

ÔFL   awful, offal
LÔFL   lawful, unlawful

OFL

KOFL   coffle
TOFL   pantoffle
WOFL   waffle

(See **ÄFL**)

ÔFN

DÔFN   dauphin

(See **OFN**)

OFN

OFN   often
KOFN   encoffin, coffin
SOFN   soften

(See **ÔFN**)

OFNER

OFNER   oftener
SOFNER   softener

(See **OF'EN.ER**)

ŌFOOT

KRŌFOOT   crowfoot
SLŌFOOT   slow-foot

OFTĒ

LOFTĒ   lofty, toplofty
SOFTĒ   softy

OFTER

KROFTER   crofter
LOFTER   lofter
SOFTER   softer

ŌFUL

BLŌFUL   blowful
DŌFUL   doughful
RŌFUL   roeful
WŌFUL   woeful

ÔFUL

(See **ÔFL**)

ŌGA

ŌGA	Tioga
RŌGA	daroga, Ticonderoga
SNŌGA	snoga
TŌGA	conestoga, Saratoga, toga
YŌGA	yoga

ŌGAN

BRŌGAN	brogan
HŌGAN	hogan
LŌGAN	logan
MŌGAN	Hogen-Mogen
RŌGAN	rogan
SLŌGAN	slogan

OGAN

BOGAN	toboggan
GOGAN	goggan
LOGAN	loggin
MOGAN	moggan, pogamoggan
NOGAN	noggin

OGBOUND

FOGBOUND	fogbound
SMOGBOUND	smogbound

ŌGĒ

BŌGĒ	bogey, bogie
DŌGĒ	dogie, judogi
FŌGĒ	fogey, old fogey
HŌGĒ	hoagie, hoagy
LŌGĒ	killogie, logy
PŌGĒ	pogy
STŌGĒ	stogie, stogy
VŌGĒ	voguey
YŌGĒ	yogi

OGĒ

BOGĒ	boggy
DOGĒ	doggy
FOGĒ	foggy
FROGĒ	froggy
GOGĒ	demagogy, pedagogy
SOGĒ	soggy

(See **OG,** add -y where appropriate.)

OGEN

(See **OGAN**)

ŌGER

(See **ŌGR**)

ÔGER

ÔGER	auger, augur
MÔGER	mauger
NÔGER	inaugur
SÔGER	sauger

OGER

DOGER	dogger
FLOGER	flogger
FOGER	befogger, pettifogger
HOGER	hogger, whole-hogger, road-hogger
JOGER	jogger
KLOGER	clogger
KOGER	cogger
LOGER	dialoguer, epiloguer, cataloguer, logger, monologuer, epiloguer
SLOGER	slogger
TOGER	togger

OGIN

(See **OGAN**)

OGING

(See **OG,** add -ing where appropriate.)

ŌGISH

RŌGISH	roguish
VŌGISH	voguish

OGISH

DOGISH	doggish
FROGISH	froggish
HOGISH	hoggish
WOGISH	woggish

ŌGL

ŌGL	ogle
BŌGL	bogle
FŌGL	fogle
MŌGL	mogul

OGL

BOGL	boggle
DOGL	boondoggle
GOGL	goggle, jargoggle
JOGL	joggle
KOGL	coggle
SWOGL	hornswoggle
TOGL	toggle
WOGL	woggle

OGLER

BOGLER	boggler
DOGLER	boondoggler
GOGLER	goggler
JOGLER	joggler
SWOGLER	hornswoggler

OGLING

(See **OGL,** add -ing where appropriate.)

ŌGŌ

GŌGŌ	a-go-go, go-go
LŌGŌ	logo, Logo
MŌGŌ	mogo
NŌGŌ	no-go
PŌGŌ	pogo, Pogo
TŌGŌ	Togo
ZŌGŌ	zogo

ŌGR

ŌGR	ogre
DRŌGR	drogher

ŌGRAM

FŌGRAM	fogram
PRŌGRAM	deprogram, program

ŌGRES

ŌGRES	ogress
PRŌGRES	progress

OGTROT

DOGTROT	dogtrot
HOGTROT	hogtrot
JOGTROT	jogtrot

OGWOOD

BOGWOOD	bogwood
DOGWOOD	dogwood
LOGWOOD	logwood

ŌHŌ

ŌHŌ	oho
KŌHŌ	coho
MŌHŌ	moho, mojo
RŌHŌ	coroho
SŌHŌ	Soho

OIA

GOIA	Goya
HOIA	hoya
KWOIA	Sequoia
NOIA	dianoia, palinoia, paranoia
SOIA	soya

OIAL

LOIAL	disloyal, loyal
ROIAL	chapel royal, penny-royal, royal, surroyal, viceroyal

OIANS

BOIANS	buoyance, flamboyance
JOIANS	joyance
NOIANS	annoyance
TOIANS	chatoyance
VOIANS	clairvoyance, prevoyance

OIANT

OIANT	buoyant, flamboyant
DOIANT	ondoyant
MOIANT	larmoyant
NOIANT	annoyant
TOIANT	chatoyant
BOIANT	clairvoyant, prevoyant

OICHER

PLOICHER	exploiture
VOICHER	voiture

OIDAL

(See **OID,** add *-al* where appropriate.)

OIDER

BROIDER	broider, embroider
MOIDER	moider
VOIDER	avoider, voider

OIDIK

PLOIDIK	diploidic
ROIDIK	spheroidic

OIEM

GOIEM	goyim
TNOIEM	tnoyim

OIER

OIER	oyer
BOIER	boyar, boyer
FOIER	foyer
JOIER	enjoyer
KOIER	decoyer, coir, coyer
LOIER	caloyer
NOIER	annoyer
PLOIER	deployer, employer, self-employer
STROIER	destroyer, self-destroyer
TOIER	toyer

(See **ÔYER**)

OIIJ

BOIIJ	buoyage
LOIIJ	alloyage
VOIIJ	voyage

ŌING

FRŌING	to-and-froing

(See **Ō,** add *-ing* where appropriate.)

OIING

BOIING	buoying
JOIING	joying, enjoying
KLOIING	cloying
KOIING	coying, decoying
LOIING	alloying
NOIING	annoying
PLOIING	deploying, employing, ploying, self-employing
STROIING	destroying
TOIING	toying
VOIING	envoying, convoying

OIISH

BOIISH	boyish
JOIISH	joyish
KOIISH	coyish
TOIISH	toyish

ŌIJ

FLŌIJ	flowage
STŌIJ	stowage
TŌIJ	towage

ŌIK

KŌIK	anechoic, echoic
KRŌIK	amphicroic, dichroic, melanochroic, pleochroic, xanthochroic
NŌIK	dipnoic
PLŌIK	diploic
RŌIK	heroic, mock-heroic, unheroic
STŌIK	stoic
TRŌIK	Troic
ZŌIK	*A* azoic, *B* benzoic, *E* entozoic, Eozoic, epizoic, *H* hylozoic, hypnozoic, holozoic, *KR* cryptozoic, *M* Mesozoic, *N* Neozoic, *P* Paleozoic, polyzoic, *PR* protozoic, *S* saprozoic, Cenozoic

ŌIKS

RŌIKS	heroics
ZŌIKS	phthisozoics

(See **ŌIK,** add *-s* where appropriate.)

OILĒ

OILĒ	oily
DOILĒ	doily
KOILĒ	coyly

| NOILĒ | noily |
| ROILĒ | roily |

OILER

OILER	oiler
BOILER	boiler
BROILER	broiler, embroiler
FOILER	foiler, tin-foiler
KOILER	coiler, recoiler, uncoiler
MOILER	moiler
ROILER	roiler
SOILER	soiler
SPOILER	despoiler, spoiler
TOILER	toiler

OILET

| OILET | oillet |
| TOILET | toilet |

OILING

(See **OIL,** add *-ing* where appropriate.)

OILMENT

BROILMENT	embroilment
KOILMENT	recoilment
SPOILMENT	despoilment
TOILMENT	entoilment

OILSUM

| ROILSUM | roilsome |
| TOILSUM | toilsome |

OIMAN

HOIMAN	hoyman
KOIMAN	decoyman
TOIMAN	toyman

OIMENT

JOIMENT	enjoyment
KLOIMENT	cloyment
PLOIMENT	deployment, employment, ployment, unemployment

OINDER

| JOINDER | joinder, misjoinder, nonjoinder, rejoinder |
| POINDER | poinder |

OINER

GOINER	zigeuner
JOINER	enjoiner, joiner, conjoiner, rejoiner
KOINER	coiner
LOINER	purloiner

ŌING

ŌING	ohing, owing
BLŌING	blowing, mind-blowing
GŌING	easygoing, going, sea-going, thoroughgoing

(See **Ō,** add *-ing* where appropriate.)

ÔING

| SHÔING | wappenschawing |

(See **Ô,** add *-ing* where appropriate.)

OINING

(See **OIN,** add *-ing* where appropriate.)

OINTED

(See **OINT,** add *-ed* where appropriate.)

OINTER

JOINTER	disjointer, jointer
NOINTER	anointer
POINTER	appointer, disappointer, pointer

OINTING

(See **OINT,** add *-ing* where appropriate.)

OINTLES

| JOINTLES | jointless |
| POINTLES | pointless |

OINTMENT

OINTMENT	ointment
JOINTMENT	disjointment
NOINTMENT	anointment
POINTMENT	appointment, disappointment, reappointment

OISER

CHOISER	choicer
JOISER	rejoicer
VOISER	invoicer, voicer

ŌISH

(See **Ō,** add *-ish* where appropriate.)

OISING

| JOISING | rejoicing, unrejoicing |
| VOISING | invoicing, unvoicing, voicing |

OISLES

(See **OIS,** add *-less* where appropriate.)

OISTĒ

| FOISTĒ | foisty |
| MOISTĒ | moisty |

OISTER

OISTER	oyster, pearl oyster
DOISTER	Ralph Roister Doister
FOISTER	foister
HOISTER	hoister
KLOISTER	encloister, cloister, uncloister
MOISTER	moister
ROISTER	roister

OISTING

FOISTING	foisting
HOISTING	hoisting
JOISTING	joisting

OISTREL

| KOISTREL | coistrel, coystrel |
| KLOISTREL | cloistral |

OISUM

KLOISUM	cloysome
NOISUM	noisome
TOISUM	toysome

ŌIT

KŌIT	inchoate
PŌIT	poet

OITĒ

KOITĒ	dacoity
OITĒ	hoity-toity

OITED

DOITED	doited
KWOITED	quoited
PLOITED	exploited, unexploited

OITER

DROITER	adroiter
GOITER	goiter
KWOITER	quoiter
LOITER	loiter
NOITER	reconnoiter, reconnoitre
PLOITER	exploiter

OITRER

LOITRER	loiterer
NOITRER	reconnoitrer

(See **OIT'ER.ER**)

OITRING

LOITRING	loitering
NOITRING	reconnoitering

(See **OIT'ER.ING**)

OITŪR

(See **OICHER**)

OIUS

JOIUS	joyous
NOIUS	annoyous

OIZER

HOIZER	Tannhäuser
NOIZER	noiser
POIZER	poiser

OIZING

NOIZING	noising
POIZING	poising

OIZUN

FOIZUN	foison
POIZUN	empoison, poison
TOIZUN	toison

ŌJĒ

ŌJĒ	ogee
GŌJĒ	agoge, anagoge, androgogy, apagoge, epagoge, isagoge, paragoge, pedagogy, xenagogy
SHŌJĒ	shoji

OJĒ

DOJĒ	dodgy
GOJĒ	androgogy, demagogy, pedagogy
POJĒ	podgy
STOJĒ	stodgy

OJER

BOJER	bodger
DOJER	dodger
KOJER	codger
LOJER	dislodger, lodger
POJER	podger
ROJER	roger, Roger
STOJER	stodger

ŌJEZ

(See **ŌJ**, add -es where appropriate.)

OJIK

GOJIK	*A* agogic, anagogic, apagogic, *D* demagogic, *E* epagogic, *H* hypnagogic, *I* isagogic, *My* mystagogic, *P* paragogic, pedagogic, *S* sialagogic, psychagogic
LOJIK	*A* aerologic, agrologic, acrologic, anthropologic, archaeologic, astrologic, *CH* choplogic, dialogic, *E* entomologic, epilogic, ethnologic, ethologic, etymologic, *F* philologic, physiologic, phytologic, phonologic, photologic, *FR* phraseologic, *H* hagiologic, hydrologic, hierologic, hypnologic, histologic, homologic, horologic, *I* ideologic, icthyologic, *J* geologic, *K* catalogic, cosmologic, curiologic, *KR* chronologic, *L* lexicologic, lithologic, logic, *M* martyrologic, metalogic, meteorologic, mycologic, micrologic, mineralogic, myologic, mythologic, morphologic, *N* necrologic, neologic, gnomologic, *O* ophiologic, ontologic, *P* paralogic, pathologic, penologic, *S* sarcologic, psychologic, cytologic, sociologic, *T* toxicologic, tautologic, *TH* theologic, *TR* tropologic, *U* eulogic, *Z* zymologic, zoologic

OJING

DOJING	dodging
LOJING	dislodging, lodging

ŌJŌ

DŌJŌ	do-jo
JŌJŌ	Jo-jo
MŌJŌ	mojo

ŌJOB

BLŌJOB	blow-job
SNŌJOB	snow-job

OJŌŌL

(See **ODŪL**)

ŌJUN

TRŌJUN	Trojan
YŌJUN	yojan

ŌKĀ

ŌKĀ	O. K., okay
KRŌKĀ	croquet
RŌKĀ	roquet
TŌKĀ	Tokay

ŌKA

ŌKA	oca, oka, Oka, carioca, tapioca
BŌKA	boca, curiboca
CHŌKA	choca
FŌKA	phoca
KŌKA	coca, jocoque
LŌKA	loka
MŌKA	mocha
PŌKA	polka, mishpocheh
SLŌKA	sloka
STŌKA	stocah
TRŌKA	troca, trocha

OKA

BOKA	bocca
CHOKA	choca
KWOKA	quokka
ROKA	rocca

ŌKĀK

HŌKĀK	hoecake
NŌKĀK	nocake

ŌKAL

LŌKAL	lo-cal
NŌKAL	no-cal

(See **ŌKL**)

ŌKĒ

ŌKĒ	oaky, Okie
CHŌKĒ	choky
DŌKĒ	okey-dokey
HŌKĒ	hokey
JŌKĒ	joky
KŌKĒ	jocoqui, coky
KRŌKĒ	croaky
LŌKĒ	Loki, loci
MŌKĒ	moki, Moki, moky, Moqui
PŌKĒ	hokey-pokey, poky, slowpoky
RŌKĒ	roky
SŌKĒ	soaky
TRŌKĒ	ditrochee, troche, trochee
SMŌKĒ	smoky
YŌKĒ	yoky, yolky

ÔKĒ

BÔKĒ	balky
CHÔKĒ	chalky
GÔKĒ	gawky
HÔKĒ	hawky
PÔKĒ	pawky
SKWÔKĒ	squawky
STÔKĒ	stalky
TÔKĒ	talkie, talky, walky-talky
WÔKĒ	Milwaukee, walkie

OKĒ

BLOKĒ	blocky
FLOKĒ	flocky
HOKĒ	field hockey, hockey, ice hockey
JOKĒ	disc jockey, jockey, outjockey
KOKĒ	cocky
KROKĒ	crocky
LOKĒ	lochy, locky
POKĒ	pocky
ROKĒ	rocky
SHLOKĒ	schlocky
STOKĒ	stocky
WOKĒ	Jabberwocky

(See **ÄKĒ**)

ŌKEN

ŌKEN	oaken, ryokan
BŌKEN	Hoboken
BRŌKEN	broken, heartbroken, housebroken, unbroken
SŌKEN	soaken
SPŌKEN	B bespoken, F fair-spoken, fine-spoken, forespoken, FR free-spoken, O outspoken, PL plainspoken, S soft-spoken, SH short-spoken, SM smooth-spoken, SP spoken, TR true-spoken, U unspoken, W well-spoken
TŌKEN	betoken, foretoken, token
WŌKEN	awoken, woken

ŌKER

ŌKER	mediocre, ochre
BRŌKER	broker, pawnbroker, power broker, stockbroker
CHŌKER	choker
HŌKER	hoker
JŌKER	joker
KLŌKER	cloaker, uncloaker
KŌKER	coker
KRŌKER	croaker
PŌKER	poker
RŌKER	roker
SMŌKER	nonsmoker, smoker
SŌKER	soaker
STŌKER	stoker
STRŌKER	stroker
VŌKER	evoker, invoker, convoker, provoker, revoker
YŌKER	yoker

ÔKER

BÔKER	balker
CHÔKER	chalker
GÔKER	gawker
HÔKER	hawker, jayhawker, tomahawker
KÔKER	calker, cawker, caulker
SKWÔKER	squawker
STÔKER	deer-stalker, stalker
TÔKER	talker
WÔKER	floorwalker, jaywalker, nightwalker, shopwalker, sleepwalker, streetwalker, walker

OKER

OKER	ocker
BLOKER	beta-blocker, blocker
CHOKER	chocker
DOKER	docker
FLOKER	flocker
FOKER	focker, Fokker
HOKER	hocker, hougher
JOKER	jocker
KLOKER	clocker
KOKER	cocker
LOKER	locker
MOKER	mocker
NOKER	knocker
ROKER	patent rocker, rocker
SHOKER	penny shocker, shilling shocker, shocker
SMOKER	smocker
SOKER	soccer, socker
STOKER	stocker

OKERZ

BOKERZ	knickerbockers

(See **OKER,** add -s where appropriate.)

OKET

BROKET	brocket
DOCKET	docket
KOKET	cocket
KROKET	crocket, Davy Crockett
LOKET	locket
POKET	air pocket, hip-pocket, impocket, pickpocket, pocket, vest-pocket, watch-pocket
ROKET	retrorocket, rocket, skyrocket, space-rocket
SOKET	socket
SPROKET	sprocket

OKHED

BLOKHED	blockhead
SHOKHED	shockhead

ŌKIJ

BRŌKIJ	brokage
CHŌKIJ	chokage
KLŌKIJ	cloakage
SŌKIJ	soakage

OKIJ

DOKIJ	dockage
LOKIJ	lockage
SOKIJ	socage

ŌKING

(See **ŌK,** add -ing where appropriate.)

ÔKING

(See **ÔK,** add -ing where appropriate.)

OKING

BOKING	bocking
STOKING	bluestocking, stocking

(See **OK,** add -ing where appropriate.)

ÔKISH

BÔKISH	balkish
CHÔKISH	chalkish
HÔKISH	hawkish
MÔKISH	mawkish

OKISH

BLOKISH	blockish
KOKISH	cockish, peacockish
MOKISH	mockish
STOKISH	stockish

ŌKL

BŌKL	bocal
DŌKL	okle-dokle
FŌKL	bifocal, focal, phocal, hyperfocal
LŌKL	collocal, local, matrilocal, neolocal, patrilocal, uxorilocal
SŌKL	socle
TRŌKL	trochal
VŌKL	bivocal, equivocal, multivocal, vocal
YŌKL	jokul, yokel

OKL

BROKL	brockle
KOKL	cockle
SOKL	socle
STROKL	strockle

ŌKLES

(See **ŌK,** add -less where appropriate.)

OKLET

FLOKLET	flocklet
LOKLET	locklet
SOKLET	socklet

OKLING

FLOKLING	flockling
KOKLING	cockling
ROKLING	rockling

OKNĒ

KOKNĒ	cockney
LOKNĒ	lock-knee
PROKNĒ	Procne

ŌKŌ

ŌKŌ	con fuoco
FŌKŌ	loco-foco
GŌKŌ	ngoko
KŌKŌ	barococo, cocoa, cocoa, koko, rococo
LŌKŌ	loco, Popoloco
MŌKŌ	moko, moko-moko
NŌKŌ	Orinoco
PŌKŌ	poco, poco-a-poco
RŌKŌ	baroco
SMŌKŌ	smoko
SŌKŌ	soco
TŌKŌ	toco
TRŌKŌ	troco

OKŌ

JOKŌ	Jocko
ROKŌ	Morocco, sirocco
SOKŌ	socko
YOKŌ	yocco

OKOUT

LOKOUT	lockout
NOKOUT	knockout

OKSA

DOKSA	chionodoxa
KOKSA	coxa
MOKSA	moxa

NOKSA   noxa
TOKSA   toxa

OKSAL

DOKSAL   paradoxal
KOKSAL   coxal
NOKSAL   noxal

OKSĒ

BOKSĒ   boxy
DOKSĒ   doxy, heterodoxy, cacodoxy, orthodoxy, paradoxy
DROKSĒ   hydroxy
FOKSĒ   foxy
LOKSĒ   Biloxi
MOKSĒ   moxie, Moxie
POKSĒ   poxy
PROKSĒ   proxy
ROKSĒ   roxy, Roxy

OKSEN

(See **OKSN**)

ŌKSER

HŌKSER   hoaxer
KŌKSER   coaxer

OKSER

OKSER   oxer
BOKSER   boxer
DOKSER   philodoxer, paradoxer
FOKSER   foxer
SOKSER   bobbysoxer

OKSĪD

OKSĪD   ox-eyed, oxide, peroxide
FOKSĪD   fox-eyed

OKSIK

KOKSIK   streptococcic, gonococcic
POKSIK   hypoxic
TOKSIK   nontoxic, radiotoxic, toxic

OKSIKS

KOKSIKS   coccix
TOKSIKS   antitoxics, toxics

OKSIN

(See **OKSN**)

ŌKSING

HŌKSING   hoaxing
KŌKSING   coaxing

OKSING

BOKSING   boxing, shadowboxing
FOKSING   foxing

ŌKSMAN

SPŌKSMAN   spokesman
STRŌKSMAN   strokesman

OKSN

OKSN   oxen, dioxin, myoxine
KOKSN   coxswain
TOKSN   antitoxin, tocsin, toxin

ŌKSTER

FŌKSTER   folkster
JŌKSTER   jokester

OKTER

DOKTER   doctor
KOKTER   decocter, concocter
PROKTER   proctor

OKTIL

OKTIL   trioctile
KOKTIL   coctile

OKTIV

OKTIV   octave
KOKTIV   decoctive, concoctive

ŌKUM

ŌKUM   oakum
HŌKUM   hokum
LŌKUM   locum
KŌKUM   kokam, kokum
SLŌKUM   slowcome

OKUP

KOKUP   cockup
LOKUP   lockup
MOKUP   mock-up

ŌKUS

FŌKUS   focus, unfocus
HŌKUS   hocus, Hohokus
KRŌKUS   crocus
LŌKUS   locus
PŌKUS   hocus-pocus
TŌKUS   tokis, tokus

ÔKUS

BÔKUS   Baucis
GLÔKUS   glaucous
KÔKUS   caucus
RÔKUS   raucous

OKUS

FLOKUS   floccus
KOKUS   echinococcus, pneumococcus, staphylococcus, streptococcus
LOKUS   lochus

ŌKUST

FŌKUST   focussed, unfocussed
LŌKUST   honey locust, locust, seven-year locust, sweet locust
PŌKUST   hocus-pocussed

ŌLA

ŌLA   gayola, gladiola, crayola, payola, scagliola, viola
BŌLA   bola, bowla, carambola
DŌLA   gondola, mandola
FŌLA   boffola

GŌLA	Angola, drugola, gola, plugola
KŌLA	Coca-Cola, cola, Cola, kola, Pensacola, Pepsi-cola
MŌLA	Mola, pimola
NŌLA	granola, pianola
RŌLA	pyrola, Savonarola
SKŌLA	schola
SŌLA	sola
STŌLA	stola
TŌLA	ayatollah, tola
TRŌLA	Victrola
YŌLA	scagliola
ZŌLA	Gorgonzola, Mazola, shnozzola, Zola

OLA

OLA	olla
HOLA	holla
ROLA	corolla
TOLA	ayatollah
WOLA	chuckwalla, wallah, walla-walla, Walla Walla

ŌLAND

LŌLAND	lowland
RŌLAND	Roland

ŌLAR

(See ŌLER)

OLARD

BOLARD	bollard
HOLARD	hollered
KOLARD	collard, collared
LOLARD	Lollard
POLARD	pollard
SKOLARD	scholared

ÔLBOI

BÔLBOI	ballboy
HÔLBOI	hallboy
KÔLBOI	callboy
TÔLBOI	tallboy

ŌLDĒ

ŌLDĒ	oldy, golden-oldy
FŌLDĒ	foldy
GŌLDĒ	goldy
MŌLDĒ	moldy

ŌLDED

(See **OLD,** add *-ed* where appropriate.)

ŌLDEN

ŌLDEN	olden
BŌLDEN	embolden
GŌLDEN	golden
HŌLDEN	beholden, holden, misbeholden, withholden
SŌLDEN	soldan

ŌLDER

ŌLDER	older
BŌLDER	bolder, boulder
FŌLDER	bill folder, enfolder, folder, infolder, interfolder, manifolder, refolder, unfolder
HŌLDER	*B* beholder, bond-holder, bottle-holder, *FR* freeholder, *G* gas-holder, *H* hand-holder, holder, householder, *K* candleholder, copyholder, *L* landholder, leaseholder, *SH* shareholder, *SL* slaveholder, *SM* smallholder, *ST* stadholder, stockholder, *T* ticket holder, *U* upholder, *W* withholder
KŌLDER	colder
MŌLDER	molder, moulder
PŌLDER	polder
SHŌLDER	cold-shoulder, shoulder
SKŌLDER	scolder
SMŌLDER	smolder, smoulder

ÔLDER

ÔLDER	alder
BÔLDER	balder, Balder
SKÔLDER	scalder

ŌLDERD

BŌLDERD	bouldered
MŌLDERD	moldered, mouldered

SHŌLDERD	broad-shouldered, narrow-shouldered, round-shouldered, square-shouldered, shouldered, stoop-shouldered, wide-shouldered
SMŌLDERD	smoldered, smouldered

ŌLDING

FŌLDING	enfolding, folding, interfolding
HŌLDING	*B* beholding, bond-holding, bottle-holding, *FR* freeholding, *H* hand-holding, holding, *L* landholding, leaseholding, *SH* shareholding, *SL* slave-holding, *ST* stock-holding, *U* upholding, *W* withholding
MŌLDING	molding
SKŌLDING	scolding

ÔLDING

BÔLDING	balding
SKÔLDING	scalding

ŌLDISH

ŌLDISH	oldish
BŌLDISH	boldish
KŌLDISH	coldish
MŌLDISH	moldish

ŌLDLĒ

ŌLDLĒ	oldly
BŌLDLĒ	boldly
KŌLDLĒ	coldly

ŌLDMENT

FŌLDMENT	enfoldment
HŌLDMENT	withholdment

ŌLDNES

BŌLDNES	boldness
KŌLDNESS	coldness, stone-coldness

RÔLDNES	enrolledness, unenrolledness
SÔLDNES	low-souledness, high-souledness
TRÔLDNES	controlledness, uncontrolledness

ÔLDRUN

| KÔLDRUN | cauldron |
| PÔLDRUN | pauldron |

ŌLĒ

ŌLĒ	aioli, Ole, ravioli
BŌLĒ	Stromboli, bolly, bowly
DRŌLĒ	drolly
FŌLĒ	foaly
GŌLĒ	goalie
HŌLĒ	holey, holy, wholly, maholi, unholy
KŌLĒ	caracoli, choli, coaly, coley, coly
LŌLĒ	lowly
MŌLĒ	guacamole, molely, moly
NŌLĒ	anole, cannoli, knolly, pinole
PŌLĒ	poly, rolypoly
RŌLĒ	rolly
SHŌLĒ	shoaly, sho'ly
SKRŌLĒ	scrolly
SLŌLĒ	slowly
SŌLĒ	posole, rissole, solely, soli
STRŌLĒ	strolly

ÔLĒ

ÔLĒ	awly
DRÔLĒ	drawly
GÔLĒ	gally
HWÔLĒ	whally
KÔLĒ	Macaulay
KRÔLĒ	crawly
MÔLĒ	mauley
RÔLĒ	rawly
SKRÔLĒ	scrawly
SKWÔLĒ	squally
SPRÔLĒ	sprawly

OLĒ

BOLĒ	Bali
DOLĒ	Dali, dolly
FOLĒ	folly
GOLĒ	golly
HOLĒ	holly
JOLĒ	jolly
KOLĒ	collie, colly, melancholy
LOLĒ	loblolly, trollylolly
MOLĒ	molle
POLĒ	poly
ROLĒ	rolley
TROLĒ	Toonerville trolley, trolley
VOLĒ	volley

(See ÄLĒ)

OLĒD

DOLĒD	dollied
JOLĒD	jollied
KOLĒD	collied
VOLĒD	volleyed, vollied

ŌLEM

DŌLEM	idolum
GŌLEM	golem
SŌLEM	solum

OLEM

| KOLEM | column |
| SOLEM | solemn |

ŌLEN

DŌLEN	eidolon
KŌLEN	colon, semicolon
SŌLEN	solen, solon, Solon
STŌLEN	stolen, stollen, stolon
SWŌLEN	swollen, unswollen

ÔLEN

(See ÔLIN)

ŌLENT

ŌLENT	olent
DŌLENT	dolent, condolent
VŌLENT	non-volent, volent

ŌLER

ŌLER	olor
BŌLER	bolar, bowler
DŌLER	doler, dolor, condoler
DRŌLER	droller
FŌLER	foaler
GŌLER	goaler, two-goaler, one-goaler
HŌLER	holer, wholer, potholer
JŌLER	cajoler
KŌLER	coaler
MŌLER	molar, premolar
NŌLER	knoller
PŌLER	multipolar, polar, poler, poller, circumpolar, transpolar, unipolar
RŌLER	enroller, high-roller, Holy Roller, lush-roller, pill-roller, roadroller, roller, steamroller, unroller, uproller
SHŌLER	shoaler
SKRŌLER	scroller
SŌLER	consoler, lunisolar, solar, soler
STRŌLER	stroller
TŌLER	extoller, toller

IDYL FOR MY IDLE IDOL

My idol!—your idle
  Tears drown my poor heart;
Why bridle, when bridal
  Delights I'd impart?
Think not from your side'll
  I side, my pet;
This idyl that died'll
  Abide a bit yet.
All loving is tidal;
  The tide'll go slack—
Yet after you've cried, 'll
  Come billowing back.

| TRŌLER | comptroller, controller, patroller, troller |
| VŌLER | volar |

ÔLER

BÔLER	baseballer, basketballer, baller, bawler, footballer, highballer, volleyballer
BRÔLER	brawler
DRÔLER	drawler
FÔLER	faller
HÔLER	hauler, overhauler
KÔLER	hog caller, caller, train caller
KRÔLER	crawler, pub-crawler
MÔLER	bemauler, mauler

SKRÔLER scrawler
SKWÔLER squaller
SMÔLER smaller
SPRÔLER sprawler
STÔLER forestaller, staller
THRÔLER enthraller
TÔLER taller
TRÔLER trawler
WÔLER caterwauler, potwaller
YÔLER yawler

OLER

DOLER dollar, dolor, petrodollar, rix-dollar, Eurodollar
HOLER holler
KOLER choler
LOLER loller
SKOLER scholar
SKWOLER squalor
SOLER soller
TOLER extoller

OLERD

(See **OLARD**)

ÔLES

ÔLES aweless
FLÔLES flawless
JÔLES jawless
KLÔLES clawless
KÔLES cawless
LÔLES lawless
MÔLES mawless
PÔLES pawless
SÔLES sawless
STRÔLES strawless

OLET

KOLET collet
SWOLET swallet
WOLET wallet

(See **ĀLET**)

OLĒZ

FOLĒZ follies
JOLĒZ jollies

(See **OLĒ**, change -y to -ies where appropriate.)

ŌLFUL

BŌLFUL bowlful
DŌLFUL doleful
SŌLFUL soulful

ŌLHOUS

PŌLHOUS pollhouse
TŌLHOUS tollhouse

OLID

OLID olid
SKWOLID squalid
SOLID semi-solid, solid
STOLID stolid

ŌLĪF

LŌLĪF low-life
PRŌLĪF pro-life

ÔLIJ

HÔLIJ hallage, haulage
NÔLIJ naulage
STÔLIJ stallage

OLIJ

KOLIJ college, community college, state college
NOLIJ acknowledge, foreknowledge, knowledge, self-knowledge

ÔLIK

ÔLIK aulic, interaulic
DRÔLIK hydraulic
GÔLIK Gaulic

OLIK

OLIK Aeolic, Eolic, variolic, vitriolic
BOLIK anabolic, diabolic, embolic, hyperbolic, carbolic, catabolic, metabolic, parabolic, symbolic
FROLIK frolic
GOLIK hypergolic, Mongolic

HOLIK alcoholic, workaholic
KOLIC bucolic, echolic, colic, melancholic, retrocollic
POLIK bibliopolic, epipolic
ROLIK rollick
TOLIK apostolic, diastolic, epistolic, systolic, vicar-apostolic
TROLIK petrolic

ÔLIN

ÔLIN all-in
FÔLIN downfallen, fallen, crestfallen, fall-in
KÔLIN cauline, call-in
PÔLIN Pauline, tarpaulin

ŌLING

(See **ŌL**, add -ing where appropriate.)

ÔLING

(See **ÔL**, add -ing where appropriate.)

OLING

DOLING baby-dolling
KOLING caracolling, colling
LOLING loblolling, lolling

OLIS

FOLIS follis
KOLIS torticollis
POLIS polis
SOLIS solace
WOLIS Cornwallis

ŌLISH

DRŌLISH drollish
PŌLISH Polish
SŌLISH soulish
TRŌLISH trollish

ÔLISH

GÔLISH Gaulish
SKWÔLISH squallish
SMÔLISH smallish
TÔLISH tallish

OLISH

BOLISH	abolish
DOLISH	dollish
LOLISH	lollish
MOLISH	demolish, mollish
POLISH	polish

OLISHT

BOLISHT	abolished, reabolished, unabolished
MOLISHT	demolished, redemolished, undemolished
POLISHT	polished, repolished, silver-polished, unpolished

ÔLKAN

BÔLKAN	Balkan
FÔLKAN	falcon

ÔLLES

(See **ÔL,** add -less where appropriate.)

ŌLMAN

KŌLMAN	coalman
TŌLMAN	tollman

ŌLMENT

DŌLMENT	condolement
JŌLMENT	cajolement
RŌLMENT	enrollment
TRŌLMENT	controlment

ÔLMENT

PÔLMENT	appallment, epaulement
STÔLMENT	installment
THRÔLMENT	disenthrallment, enthrallment

ŌLNES

DRŌLNES	drollness
HŌLNES	wholeness
SŌLNES	soleness

ÔLNES

ÔLNES	allness
SMÔLNES	smallness
TÔLNES	tallness

ŌLŌ

ŌLŌ	criollo
BŌLŌ	bolo, bolo-bolo
CHŌLŌ	cholo
GŌLŌ	golo
KŌLŌ	kolo, yakolo
LŌLŌ	palolo
PŌLŌ	Marco Polo, polo
RŌLŌ	barolo
SŌLŌ	solo
STŌLŌ	stolo

OLŌ

FOLŌ	follow
HOLŌ	hollo, hollow
POLŌ	Apollo
SWOLŌ	swallow
WOLŌ	wallow, hogwallow

(See **ÂLŌ**)

ŌLOK

MŌLOK	Moloch
RŌLOK	rowlock

OLOK

(See **OLUK**)

ŌLON

(See **ŌLEN**)

OLOP

(See **OLUP**)

ŌLOR

(See **ŌLER**)

ÔLSER

FÔLSER	falser
WÔLSER	waltzer

ŌLSTER

BŌLSTER	bolster
HŌLSTER	holster, reholster, reupholster, unholster, upholster

ŌLSUM

DŌLSUM	dolesome
HŌLSUM	wholesome, unwholesome

ÔLTA

MÔLTA	Malta
VÔLTA	Volta
YÔLTA	Yalta

ÔLTĒ

FÔLTĒ	faulty
MÔLTĒ	malty
SÔLTĒ	salty
VÔLTĒ	vaulty

ŌLTED

(See **ŌLT,** add -ed where appropriate.)

ÔLTED

(See **ÔLT,** add -ed where appropriate.)

ŌLTER

BŌLTER	bolter, unbolter
JŌLTER	jolter
KŌLTER	colter
MŌLTER	molter
VŌLTER	revolter

ÔLTER

ÔLTER	altar, alter, unalter
BRÔLTER	Gibraltar
FÔLTER	defaulter, falter, faulter, foot-faulter
HÔLTER	halter, unhalter, waghalter
MÔLTER	malter
PÔLTER	palter
SMÔLTER	smalter
SÔLTER	assaulter, psalter, salter
VÔLTER	vaulter
ZÔLTER	exalter

ÔLTERN

ÔLTERN	altern, subaltern
SÔLTERN	saltern

ŌLTIJ

BŌLTIJ	boltage
VŌLTIJ	voltage

ÔLTIJ

FÔLTIJ	faultage
MÔLTIJ	maltage
VÔLTIJ	vaultage

ÔLTIK

BÔLTIK	Baltic, cobaltic
FÔLTIK	asphaltic
SÔLTIK	basaltic
STŌLTIK	peristaltic
TÔLTIK	cystaltic

ŌLTING

BŌLTING	bolting, unbolting
JŌLTING	jolting
KŌLTING	colting
MŌLTING	molting
VŌLTING	revolting

ÔLTING

FÔLTING	defaulting, faulting
HÔLTING	halting
MÔLTING	malting
SÔLTING	assaulting, salting
VÔLTING	vaulting
ZÔLTING	exalting

ŌLTISH

DŌLTISH	doltish
KŌLTISH	coltish

ÔLTLES

FÔLTLES	faultless
MÔLTLES	maltless
SÔLTLES	saltless

ÔLTSER

(See ÔLSER)

OLUK

LOLUK	lollock
POLUK	pollack, pollock

ŌLUM

(See ŌLEM)

OLUP

DOLUP	dollop
GOLUP	gollop
JOLUP	jollop
KOLUP	collop
LOLUP	lollop
SKOLUP	escallop, escalop, scallop, scollop
TROLUP	trollop
WOLUP	codswallop, wallop

OLUPT

(See OLUP, add -ed where appropriate.)

ŌLUS

ŌLUS	gladiolus
BŌLUS	bolus, holus-bolus
DŌLUS	dolous, dolus, *subdolous*
SŌLUS	solus

OLVENT

SOLVENT	insolvent, solvent, absolvent
VOLVENT	evolvent
ZOLVENT	dissolvent, resolvent

OLVER

SOLVER	absolver, solver
VOLVER	devolver, evolver, involver, revolver
ZOLVER	dissolver, resolver

OLVING

SOLVING	absolving, dissolving, resolving, solving
VOLVING	devolving, evolving, intervolving, involving, obvolving, revolving, circumvolving
ZOLVING	dissolving, exolving, resolving

ÔLWĀ

HÔLWĀ	hallway
KRÔLWĀ	crawlway

ÔLWĀZ

ÔLWĀZ	always
HÔLWĀZ	hallways
KRÔLWĀZ	crawlways

OLYUM

KOLYUM	colyum
VOLYUM	volume

ŌMA

ŌMA	angioma, glioma, myoma, osteoma
BŌMA	aboma
BRŌMA	broma, firbroma, theobroma
GŌMA	agoma, zygoma
HŌMA	Oklahoma
KŌMA	glaucoma, coma, sarcoma, Tacoma, trachoma
LŌMA	aloma, encephaloma, condyloma, loma, myeloma, papilloma, Point Loma, spiloma
NGOMA	ngoma
NŌMA	adenoma, carcinoma, noma
PLŌMA	diploma
PŌMA	lipoma
RŌMA	aroma, atheroma, Roma, scleroma
SŌMA	prosoma, soma
STŌMA	stoma
STRŌMA	stroma
THŌMA	xanthoma
TŌMA	phytoma, hematoma, scotoma
ZŌMA	rhizoma

ÔMA

KÔMA	cauma
TRÔMA	trauma

OMA

KOMA	comma
MOMA	mama, mamma, momma
SOMA	zyxomma

ŌMAL

BRŌMAL	bromal
DŌMAL	domal
SŌMAL	prosomal, somal
STRŌMAL	stromal

ŌMAN

BŌMAN	bowman
FŌMAN	foeman
RŌMAN	Roman
SHŌMAN	showman
YŌMAN	yeoman

OMBĀ

BOMBĀ	Bombay
POMBĀ	pombe

OMBA

BOMBA	zambomba
DOMBA	domba
LOMBA	calomba
POMBA	pombe
TROMBA	tromba

OMBAT

KOMBAT	combat
WOMBAT	wombat

OMBĒ

DOMBĒ	Dombey
ZOMBĒ	zombie

OMBER

OMBER	omber, ombre
SKOMBER	scomber
SOMBER	somber

ŌMĒ

ŌMĒ	Cleome
DŌMĒ	domy
FŌMĒ	foamy
HŌMĒ	homey, homy
KRŌMĒ	photochromy, heliochromy, metallochromy, monochromy, polychromy, stereochromy

LŌMĒ	loamy, lomi-lomi, Salome
RŌMĒ	roamy

OMĒ

KOMĒ	Commie
MOMĒ	mommy
POMĒ	pommy
TOMĒ	tommy

(See ÄMĒ)

OMEL

POMEL	pommel
TROMEL	trommel

ŌMEN

ŌMEN	omen
BŌMEN	bowmen
DŌMEN	abdomen
FŌMEN	foemen
LŌMEN	lowmen
NŌMEN	agnomen, cognomen, gnomon, nomen, praenomen
YŌMEN	yeomen

ŌMENT

FŌMENT	foment
LŌMENT	loment
MŌMENT	moment
STŌMENT	bestowment

ŌMER

ŌMER	Omar, omer
GŌMER	gomer, Gomer
HŌMER	homer, Homer
KŌMER	beachcomber, comber, wool comber
NŌMER	misnomer
RŌMER	roamer
VŌMER	vomer

OMET

DOMET	domett
GROMET	grommet
HOMET	Mahomet
KOMET	comet
VOMET	vomit

OMIJ

HOMIJ	homage
POMIJ	pommage

ŌMIK

ŌMIK	ohmic
BRŌMIK	bromic, hydrobromic, theobromic
DŌMIK	domic
KRŌMIK	achromic, bathochromic, dichromic, heliochromic, hypsochromic, chromic, monochromic, polychromic, stereochromic
NŌMIK	gnomic

OMIK

OMIK	Suomic
BROMIK	antibromic, hydrobromic, theobromic
DOMIK	oecodomic
DROMIK	dromic, exodromic, hippodromic, loxodromic, orthodromic, palindromic, paradromic, syndromic
KOMIK	acersecomic, encomic, heroicomic, comic, quasi-comic, seriocomic, tragicomic
KROMIK	achromic, bathochromic, dichromic, heliochromic, hypsochromic, monochromic, polychromic, stereochromic, xanthochromic
MOMIK	cinnamomic
NOMIK	A agronomic, astronomic, B bionomic, D dinomic, Deuteronomic, E economic, ennomic, F physiognomic, phoronomic, G gastronomic, I isonomic, K

chironomic, *M*
metronomic, *N*
gnomic, nomic, *O*
autonomic, *P*
pathognomic,
pyrognomic, *PL*
plutonomic, *S*
socioeconomic, *T*
taxonomic, *U*
uneconomic

PROMIK promic
SOMIK acersomic
TOMIK *A* anatomic, atomic,
D dermatomic,
diatomic, dystomic, *E*
entomic, epitomic, *F*
phantomic, *I*
interatomic, intra-
atomic, *M* microtomic,
monatomic, *O*
orthatomic, *P*
pentomic, *S* subatomic,
ST stereotomic, *T*
tesseratomic, *TR*
triatomic
VOMIK vomic

OMIKS

KOMIKS comics
NOMIKS agronomics,
bionomics,
economics,
Nixonomics,
Reaganomics

(See **OMIK,** add -*s* where appropriate.)

ŌMING

ŌMING Wyoming
DŌMING doming
FŌMING foaming
GLŌMING gloaming
HŌMING homing
KŌMING beachcombing,
haircombing,
honeycombing,
coxcombing,
coaming, combing,
wool combing
KRŌMING chroming
LŌMING loaming
RŌMING roaming

OMIS

PROMIS promise
TOMIS doubting Thomas

ŌMISH

DŌMISH domish
FŌMISH foamish
LŌMISH loamish
NŌMISH gnomish
RŌMISH Romish
TŌMISH tomish

ŌMLES

(See **ŌM,** add -*less* where appropriate.)

ŌMLET

DŌMLET domelet
HŌMLET homelet
TŌMLET tomelet

ŌMŌ

DŌMŌ majordomo
DWŌMŌ duomo
HŌMŌ ecce homo, homo
KŌMŌ Lake Como
KRŌMŌ chromo
MŌMŌ momo
PRŌMŌ promo

OMPĒ

POMPĒ Pompey
ROMPĒ rompy
SKOMPĒ scampi
SWOMPĒ swampy

OMPISH

ROMPISH rompish
SWOMPISH swampish

OMPUS

POMPUS pompous
WOMPUS gallywampus,
catawampus, wampus

ŌMUS

DŌMUS domus
KRŌMUS chromous
MŌMUS momus
SŌMUS disomus

ŌNA

ŌNA ona
BŌNA bona, carbona
DRŌNA madrona
JŌNA Jonah
KŌNA kona, cinchona
KRŌNA krona
LŌNA Barcelona, Bellona,
bologna
MŌNA Desdemona, kimono,
mona, Pomona
NŌNA annona
RŌNA corona, Verona
SŌNA persona
TŌNA Daytona
TRŌNA trona
ZŌNA Arizona, canzona, zona

ÔNA

FÔNA avifauna, fauna,
piscifauna
SÔNA sauna

ŌNAD

GŌNAD gonad
MŌNAD monad

ŌNAL

BŌNAL subumbonal
FÔNAL phonal
KRÔNAL chronal
RŌNAL coronal
THRŌNAL thronal
TŌNAL atonal, tonal
ZŌNAL polyzonal, zonal

ŌNANT

(See **ŌNENT**)

ŌNĀT

DŌNĀT donate
FŌNĀT phonate
PRŌNĀT pronate
ZŌNĀT zonate

ÔNCHĒ

HÔNCHĒ haunchy
KRÔNCHĒ craunchy
PÔNCHĒ paunchy
RÔNCHĒ raunchy

ÔNCHEZ

(See **ÔNCH,** add -es where appropriate.)

ÔNCHING

HÔNCHING	haunching
KRÔNCHING	craunching
LÔNCHING	launching
STÔNCHING	staunching

ONCHŌ

HONCHŌ	honcho
PONCHŌ	poncho

ONDA

FONDA	Fonda
HONDA	honda, Honda
KONDA	anaconda, *La Gioconda*, Golconda
NONDA	nonda
ZONDA	zonda

ONDED

BONDED	bonded, unbonded
SKONDED	absconded
SPONDED	desponded, corresponded, responded

ŌNDEF

STŌNDEF	stone-deaf
TŌNDEF	tone-deaf

ONDEL

(See **ONDL**)

ONDENS

SKONDENS	abscondence
SPONDENS	despondence, correspondence, respondence

ONDENT

FRONDENT	frondent
SPONDENT	despondent, corespondent, correspondent, respondent

ÔNDER

LÔNDER	launder
MÔNDER	maunder

ONDER

BLONDER	blonder
BONDER	bonder
FONDER	fonder
KONDER	hypochonder, condor
PONDER	ponder
SKONDER	absconder
SKWONDER	squander
SPONDER	desponder, coresponder, corresponder, responder
WONDER	wander
YONDER	yonder

(See **ÄNDER**)

ONDIJ

BONDIJ	bondage, vagabondage
FRONDIJ	frondage

ONDING

ONDING	onding
BONDING	bonding, female-bonding, male-bonding, pair-bonding
SKONDING	absconding
SPONDING	desponding, corresponding, responding

ONDL

FONDL	fondle
RONDL	rondel, rondle

ONDLĒ

BLONDLĒ	blondly
FONDLĒ	fondly, overfondly

ONDNES

BLONDNES	blondness, blondeness
FONDNES	fondness

ONDŌ

HONDŌ	Hondo
KONDŌ	condo
RONDŌ	rondeau, rondo
TONDŌ	tondo

ŌNĒ

BŌNĒ	bony
DŌNĒ	Bodoni, chalcedony
DRŌNĒ	drony, padrone
FŌNĒ	phony, lamprophony, *euphony*
GŌNĒ	gony, kongoni
KŌNĒ	cony, Marconi
KRŌNĒ	crony
LŌNĒ	abalone, baloney, bologna, globaloney, cannelloni, polony
MŌNĒ	agrimony, acrimony, alimony, antimony, querimony, matrimony, palimony, parsimony, patrimony, sanctimony, ceremony, spumone, testimony
PŌNĒ	compony, pony
RŌNĒ	chitarrone, lazzaroni, macaroni, cicerone
SHŌNĒ	Shoshone
STŌNĒ	stony
STRŌNĒ	minestrone
TŌNĒ	panettone, tony, tortoni
YŌNĒ	yoni, zabaglione
ZŌNĒ	calzone, canzone

ÔNĒ

ÔNĒ	awny
BRÔNĒ	brawny
DÔNĒ	dawny
FÔNĒ	fawny
LÔNĒ	lawny
PÔNĒ	pawnee
PRÔNĒ	prawny
SKRÔNĒ	scrawny
SÔNĒ	sawney
SWÔNĒ	Suwanee, Swanee
TÔNĒ	mulligatawny, orange-tawny, Punxsutawney, tawny
YÔNĒ	yawny

ONĒ

BONĒ	bonnie, bonny
GONĒ	paizogony

RONĒ   gironny, gyronny
SWONĒ   Swanee, swanny
WONĒ   Sewanee
YONĒ   yonnie
ZONĒ   mezonny

(See ÄNE)

ŌNENT

PŌNENT   deponent, exponent, imponent, interponent, component, opponent, ponent, proponent
SŌNENT   intersonant, rhonisonant, sonant, supersonant
TŌNENT   tonant

ŌNER

ŌNER   landowner, co-owner, non-owner, owner, part-owner, shipowner
BŌNER   boner
DŌNER   donor, condoner
DRŌNER   droner
FŌNER   phoner, telephoner
GRŌNER   groaner, grunt-and-groaner
HŌNER   honer
LŌNER   loaner, loner
MŌNER   bemoaner, moaner
PŌNER   postponer
STŌNER   stoner
THRŌNER   dethroner, enthroner
TŌNER   atoner, intoner, toner

ÔNER

ÔNER   awner
BRÔNER   brawner
FÔNER   fawner
GÔNER   goner
PÔNER   pawner
SPÔNER   spawner
YÔNER   yawner

ONER

ONER   dishonor, honor, Scout's honor, Your Honor
KONER   aleconner, conner

ONERD

ONERD   honored
DONERD   donnered

ŌNES

LŌNES   lowness
SLŌNES   slowness

ONET

BONET   bluebonnet, bonnet, graybonnet, unbonnet
SONET   sonnet

ONGER

LONGER   longer, prolonger
PRONGER   pronger
RONGER   wronger
STRONGER   stronger
TONGER   tonger

ONGFUL

RONGFUL   wrongful
SONGFUL   songful
THRONGFUL   throngful

ONGGA

BONGGA   bonga
DONGGA   donga
KONGGA   conga
TONGGA   Batonga, tonga, Tonga
WONGGA   wonga, wonga-wonga

ONGGER

KONGGER   conger
LONGGER   longer
STRONGGER   stronger

ONGING

DONGING   ding-donging, donging
FONGING   underfonging
LONGING   belonging, longing, prolonging
PONGING   ponging
RONGING   wronging
THRONGING   thronging

ONGISH

LONGISH   longish
RONGISH   wrongish
STRONGISH   strongish

ONGKĒ

DONGKĒ   donkey
HONGKĒ   honkie, honky
KONGKĒ   conky
TONGKĒ   honkytonky
WONGKĒ   wonky

ONGKER

HONGKER   honker
KONGKER   conker, conquer, reconquer

ONGKERS

BONGKERZ   bonkers
HONKERZ   honkers
YONKERZ   Yonkers

ONGKUS

BRONGKUS   bronchus
RONGKUS   rhonchus

ONGLĒ

LONGLĒ   longly
RONGLĒ   wrongly
STRONGLĒ   strongly

ONGNES

LONGNES   longness
RONGNES   wrongness

ŌNIJ

DRŌNIJ   dronage
NŌNIJ   nonage
RŌNIJ   chaperonage
TRŌNIJ   tronage

ONIK

ONIK   *A* amphictyonic, avionic, *B* bionic, *E* embryonic, *F*

Pharaonic, *G* gallionic, ganglionic, *H* histrionic, *I* interganglionic, ionic, *K* chameleonic, *N* Napoleonic, nucleonic, *O* Olympionic, *P* paeonic, pantheonic, *T* talionic, *TH* thermionic, thionic, *Z* zoonic

BONIK   bubonic, carbonic, Sorbonic

BRONIK   vibronic

DONIK   Adonic, algedonic, hedonic, Chalcedonic, chelidonic, sardonic

FONIK   *A* antiphonic, aphonic, *B* baryphonic, *D* diaphonic, dodecaphonic, *F* phonic, photophonic, *H* homophonic, *K* cacophonic, cataphonic, colophonic, *KW* quadraphonic, *M* megaphonic, megalophonic, microphonic, monophonic, *P* polyphonic, *R* radiophonic, *S* psaphonic, saxophonic, siphonic, symphonic, *ST* stentorophonic, stereophonic, *T* telephonic, typhonic, *U* euphonic, *Z* xylophonic

GONIK   agonic, glottogonic, isogonic, jargonic, geogonic, cosmogonic, polygonic, theogonic, trigonic

KLONIK   anticyclonic, cyclonic, clonic

KONIK   aconic, aniconic, draconic, iconic, conic, laconic, obconic, polyconic, Tychonic, zirconic

KRONIK   acronic, anachronic, diachronic, chronic, monochronic, synchronic

LONIK   Babylonic, colonic

MONIK   *A* ammonic, anharmonic, *B* daemonic, demonic, *E* enharmonic, etymonic, *F* philharmonic, *H* harmonic, hegemonic, *N* mnemonic, gnomonic, nonharmonic, pneumonic, *P* pathognomonic, pulmonic, *S* sermonic, cinnamonic, Solomonic, *U* eudaemonic

NONIK   canonic, nonic

PONIK   hydroponic, Japonic, geoponic

RONIK   Byronic, ironic, macaronic, moronic, Neronic, Pyrrhonic, stentoronic

SONIK   freemasonic, imsonic, infrasonic, masonic, parsonic, subsonic, supersonic, transonic, ultrasonic

THONIK   benthonic, Brythonic, gnathonic, pythonic, chthonic

TONIK   *A* architectonic, atonic, *D* diatonic, *E* electrotonic, epitonic, *F* phototonic, *H* hematonic, hypertonic, hypotonic, Housatonic, *I* isotonic, *KR* crotonic, *M* Metonic, Miltonic, monotonic, *N* neoplatonic, neuratonic, *O* orthotonic, *P* paratonic, pentatonic, polytonic, *PL* planktonic, platonic, plutonic, *PR* protonic, *S* semitonic, syntonic, subtonic, supertonic, *STR* stratonic, *T* tectonic, tonic, Teutonic

TRONIK   electronic, microelectronic, technetronic

VONIK   Slavonic

YONIK   yonic

ZONIK   ozonic, zonic

ONIKS

ONIKS	avionics, bionics, histrionics, cryonics, nucleonics, onyx, thermionics
DONIKS	hedonics, chalcedonyx, sardonyx
FONIKS	phonics, quadraphonics
KONIKS	conics
LONIKS	Megalonyx
MONIKS	harmonics, mnemonics, gnomonics, eudaemonics
PONIKS	hydroponics, geoponics
SONIKS	supersonics, ultrasonics
TONIKS	tectonics
TRONIKS	electronics, microelectronics

(See **ONIK,** add -*s* where appropriate.)

ŌNING

BŌNING	boning, jawboning

(See **ŌN,** add -*ing* where appropriate.)

ÔNING

ÔNING	awning
DÔNING	dawning
FÔNING	fawning
PÔNING	pawning
SPÔNING	spawning
YÔNING	yawning

ONING

DONING	donning
KONING	conning

ŌNISH

DRŌNISH	dronish
KŌNISH	conish
LŌNISH	Babylonish
STŌNISH	stonish

ONISH

DONISH	donnish
MONISH	admonish, monish, premonish

STONISH   stonish
TONISH   astonish, tonish, tonnish
WONISH   wannish

ONJĒ

KONJĒ   congee
PONJĒ   pongee

ŌNLĒ

ŌNLĒ   eyes-only, only, one-and-only
LŌNLĒ   alonely, lonely
PRŌNLĒ   pronely

ŌNLES

(See ŌN, add -less where appropriate.)

ŌNMENT

ŌNMENT   disownment
DŌNMENT   condonement
PŌNMENT   postponement
THRŌNMENT   dethronement, enthronement
TŌNMENT   atonement, intonement

ŌNNES

ŌNNES   ownness
LŌNNES   aloneness, loneness
NŌNNES   knownness, unknownness
PRŌNNES   proneness

ŌNŌ

FŌNŌ   fono, phono
MŌNŌ   kakemono, kimono, makimono
NŌNŌ   no-no

ONSL

KONSL   consul, proconsul, vice-consul
SPONSL   responsal, sponsal
TONSL   tonsil

ONSOR

SPONSOR   sponsor
TONSOR   chirotonsor, tonsor

ONTAL

ONTAL   ontal
DONTAL   periodontal
FONTAL   fontal
FRONTAL   frontal
KWONTAL   quantal
PONTAL   pontal
RONTAL   gerontal
ZONTAL   horizontal

ÔNTĒ

FLÔNTĒ   flaunty
HÔNTĒ   haunty
JÔNTĒ   jaunty
VÔNTĒ   vaunty

ÔNTED

DÔNTED   daunted, undaunted
FLÔNTED   flaunted
HÔNTED   haunted
JÔNTED   jaunted
TÔNTED   taunted
VÔNTED   vaunted
WÔNTED   help wanted, unwanted, wanted

ÔNTER

(See ÔNT, add -er where appropriate.)

ONTIF

PONTIF   pontiff
YONTIF   yontif

ONTIJ

PONTIJ   pontage
WONTIJ   wantage

ONTIK

ONTIK   Anacreontic
DONTIK   mastodontic, odontic, orthodontic, periodontic
KONTIK   archontic
KWONTIK   quantic
PONTIK   pontic
RONTIK   gerontic

ONTĪN

KONTĪN   dracontine

PONTĪN   Hellespontine, pontine, cispontine, transpontine

ONTIN

KONTIN   dracontine
PONTIN   Hellespontine, pontine, cispontine, transpontine
TONTIN   tontine

ÔNTING

DÔNTING   daunting, undaunting
FLÔNTING   flaunting
JÔNTING   jaunting
TÔNTING   taunting
VÔNTING   vaunting
WÔNTING   wanting

ÔNTLES

DÔNTLES   dauntless
WÔNTLES   wantless

ONTŌ

KONTŌ   conto
PRONTŌ   pronto
RONTŌ   Toronto
TONTŌ   Tonto

ONTON

FRONTON   fronton
WONTON   wanton, wonton

ONTUS

DONTUS   microdontous
HONTUS   Pocahontas

ŌNUS

ŌNUS   onus
BŌNUS   bonus
LŌNUS   colonus
KŌNUS   conus
TŌNUS   tonus

ONZŌ

BONZŌ   Bonzo
GONZŌ   gonzo

OͫOA

HOͫOA	lehua
LOͫOA	ulua

(See ŪA)

OͫOAL

(See OͫOEL, ŪAL)

OOAN

(See OͫOIN)

OͫOANS

CHOͫOANS	eschewance

(See ŪANS)

OͫOANT

(See OͫOENT)

OͫOBA

JOͫOBA	juba
POͫOBA	pooh-bah
ROͫOBA	Aruba, Simarouba
SKOͫOBA	scuba
SOͫOBA	subah, tsuba
TOͫOBA	saxtuba, tuba

(See ŪBA)

OͫOBÂL

SKROͫOBÂL	screwball

(See ŪBÂL)

OͫOBAL

JOͫOBAL	Jubal

(See ŪBAL)

OͫOBĒ

BOͫOBĒ	booby
DOͫOBĒ	do-bee
JOͫOBĒ	jube
LOͫOBĒ	looby
ROͫOBĒ	ruby

(See ŪBĒ)

OͫOBER

GOͫOBER	goober
KOͫOBER	Khubur
ZOͫOBER	zubr

(See ŪBER)

OͫOBĒZ

BOͫOBĒZ	boobies
LOͫOBĒZ	loobies
ROͫOBĒZ	rubies

(See ŪBĒZ)

OͫOBIK

ROͫOBIK	cherubic, Rubic

(See ŪBIK)

OͫOBING

LOͫOBING	lubing

(See ŪBING)

OͫOBIT

TOͫOBIT	two-bit

(See ŪBIT)

OͫOBL

JOͫOBL	Jubal
ROͫOBL	ruble
TOͫOBL	tubal

(See ŪBL)

OͫOBRIK

ROͫOBRIK	rubric
LOͫOBRIK	lubric

OͫOCHĒ

DOͫOCHĒ	Il Duce
KOͫOCHĒ	hootchy-kootchy
LOͫOCHĒ	Baluchi
MOͫOCHĒ	mamamouchi
NOͫOCHĒ	penuche, penuchi
POͫOCHĒ	poochy, Vespucci
SMOͫOCHĒ	smoochy

OͫOCHER

MOͫOCHER	moocher
SMOͫOCHER	smoocher
SPOͫOCHER	spoucher

(See ŪCHER)

OͫODA

BOͫODA	Buddha
JOͫODA	Judah
KOͫODA	barracuda, picuda
MOͫODA	remuda

(See ŪDA)

OͫODAL

(See OͫODL)

OͫODĒ

BOͫODĒ	boodie
BROͫODĒ	broody
GOͫODE	wally-goudy
HOͫODĒ	yehudi, Yehudi
MOͫODĒ	almude, moody

(See ŪDĒ)

OODĒ

GOODĒ	goody, goody-goody
HOODĒ	hoody
WOODĒ	woody

OͫODED

(See OͫOD, ŪD, add -ed where appropriate.)

OODED

HOODED	hooded
WOODED	dense-wooded, green-wooded, copse-wooded, red-wooded, thick-wooded, well-wooded (etc.), wooded

OͫODENS

PROͫODENS	jurisprudence, prudence

(See OͫODENT, ŪDENT, add -s or change -t to -ce where appropriate.)

O͞ODENT

KLO͞ODENT	concludent, occludent
PRO͞ODENT	imprudent, jurisprudent, prudent
STO͞ODENT	student

(See Ū̄DENT)

O͞ODER

BRO͞ODER	brooder
KLO͞ODER	excluder, includer, concluder
KRO͞ODER	cruder
RO͞ODER	ruder
SHRO͞ODER	shrewder
TO͞ODER	two-door, Tudor
TRO͞ODER	detruder, extruder, intruder, protruder

OODER

| GOODER | do-gooder |
| HOODER | hooder |

O͞ODIK

(See Ū̄DIK)

O͞ODING

BRO͞ODING	brooding
KLO͞ODING	excluding, including, concluding, occluding, precluding, secluding
LO͞ODING	alluding, deluding, eluding, colluding
TRO͞ODING	detruding, extruding, intruding, protruding, retruding, subtruding
ZO͞ODING	exuding

(See Ū̄DER)

OODING

GOODING	do-gooding
HOODING	hooding
POODING	Indian pudding, pudding

O͞ODISH

MO͞ODISH	moodish
PRO͞ODISH	prudish
RO͞ODISH	rudish

(See Ū̄DISH)

OODISH

GOODISH	goodish
HOODISH	hoodish
WOODISH	woodish

O͞ODIST

| BO͞ODIST | Buddhist |
| PRO͞ODIST | prudist |

(See Ū̄DIST)

O͞ODL

BO͞ODL	boodle, caboodle
DO͞ODL	doodle, flapdoodle, fopdoodle, whangdoodle, cadoodle, wingdoodle, Yankee Doodle
KO͞ODL	coodle
KRO͞ODL	croodle
LO͞ODL	paludal
NO͞ODL	canoodle, noodle
PO͞ODL	poodle
RO͞ODL	roodle
SO͞ODL	soodle
STRO͞ODL	strudel

(See Ū̄DL)

O͞ODLĒ

KRO͞ODLĒ	crudely
PRO͞ODLĒ	prudely
RO͞ODLĒ	rudely
SHRO͞ODLĒ	shrewdly

(See Ū̄DLĒ)

O͞ODLZ

| O͞ODLZ | oodles |

(See O͞ODL, add -s where appropriate.)

OODMAN

GOODMAN	goodman
HOODMAN	hoodman
WOODMAN	woodman

O͞ODNES

KRO͞ODNES	crudeness
LO͞ODNES	lewdness
RO͞ODNES	rudeness
SHRO͞ODNES	shrewdness

(See Ū̄DNES)

O͞ODŌ

BO͞ODŌ	barbudo, budo
KO͞ODŌ	picudo
SKO͞ODŌ	escudo, scudo

(See Ū̄DŌ)

O͞ODO͞O

HO͞ODO͞O	hoodoo
PO͞ODO͞O	pudu
TO͞ODO͞O	to-do
VO͞ODO͞O	voodoo

O͞OĒ

BLO͞OĒ	blooie, bluey
BO͞OĒ	bambui, bowie, buoy, Drambuie
CHO͞OĒ	chewy
FLO͞OĒ	flooey, fluey
FO͞OĒ	fooey, pfui, phooey
GLO͞OĒ	gluey
GO͞OĒ	gooey
HO͞OĒ	hooey, hui
KO͞OĒ	cooee
SKRO͞OĒ	screwy
SO͞OĒ	chop suey
TO͞OĒ	ratatouille, tattooey, tui

(See Ū̄Ē)

O͞OEL

CHO͞OEL	eschewal
DO͞OEL	dual, duel
GRO͞OEL	gruel
JO͞OEL	bejewel, jewel
KRO͞OEL	crewel, cruel
SHO͞OEL	shewel

(See Ū̄AL)

O͞OEN

(See O͞OIN)

O͞OENT

| FLO͞OENT | fluent, confluent, perfluent |

LOOENT — eluent
SOOENT — pursuant, suant
TROOENT — truant

OOER

BLOOER — bluer
BROOER — brewer
CHOOER — chewer, eschewer
DOOER — doer, evildoer, misdoer, outdoer, overdoer, wrongdoer, undoer
GLOOER — gluer, ungluer
KOOER — cooer
KROOER — cruer
NOOER — canoer, revenuer
POOER — pooh-pooher, shampooer
ROOER — ruer
SHOOER — shoer
SOOER — pursuer, sewer, suer
SKROOER — screwer
STROOER — strewer
TOOER — tattooer
TROOER — truer
WOOER — wooer

(See ÜER)

OOERD

LOOERD — leeward

(See ÜERD)

OOET

BLOOET — bluet
CHOOET — chewet
KROOET — cruet
MOOET — Moet
SOOET — suet
TOOET — intuit

OOF

BLOOF — blow-off
FLOOF — flow-off
SHOOF — show-off

OOFA

BOOFA — buffa
CHOOFA — chufa
GOOFA — gufa
LOOFA — catalufa, loofa

STOOFA — stufa
TOOFA — tufa

OOFE

OOFE — oofy
GOOFE — goofy
ROOFE — roofy
SPOOFE — spoofy
WOOFE — woofy

OOFER

GOOFER — goofer
LOOFER — aloofer
ROOFER — roofer
SPOOFER — spoofer
TOOFER — twofer
WOOFER — woofer

OOFING

GOOFING — goofing
PROOFING — bulletproofing, waterproofing, weatherproofing
ROOFING — composition roofing, roofing, cedar roofing, shake roofing, shingle roofing
SPOOFING — spoofing
WOOFING — woofing

OOFLES

GOOFLES — goofless
HOOFLES — hoofless
PROOFLES — proofless
ROOFLES — roofless
SPOOFLES — spoofless
WOOFLES — woofless

OOFUS

GOOFUS — goofus
ROOFUS — hirsutorufous, rufous

OOGA

FOOGA — fuga
LOOGA — beluga
MOOGA — mooga
NOOGA — Chattanooga
ROOGA — ruga
YOOGA — yuga

OOGAL

(See OOGL)

OOGE

BOOGE — boogey
POOGE — poogye
WOOGE — boogie-woogie

OOGER

KOOGER — cougar
LOOGER — Luger
SNOOGER — snooger

OOGER

BOOGER — booger
SHOOGER — beet sugar, brown sugar, cane sugar, maple sugar, spun sugar, sugar

OOGL

FROOGL — frugal, unfrugal
GOOGL — Barney Google
JOOGL — jugal, *conjugal*

(See ÜGL)

OOID

BLOOID — blue-eyed
TROOID — true-eyed

(See ÜID)

OOID

DROOID — druid
FLOOID — fluid, semifluid, superfluid

OOIJ

BROOIJ — brewage
SOOIJ — sewage

See ÜIJ)

OOIK

LOOIK — toluic

(See ÜIK)

OOIN

BROOIN	Bruin
LOOIN	punaluan
SOOIN	auruin, ruin
SOOIN	sewen

(See OOAN)

OOING

(See OO, Ū, add -ing where appropriate.)

OOISH

BLOOISH	blueish
GLOOISH	glueish
JOOISH	Jewish

There is a Greek word *synathroesmus* which means "the piling up of adjectives." This is the way it works:

THE SYNATHROESMIC CAT

O mangy cat, O scruffy cat,
O one-eyed, bobtailed, toughy cat—
You're fleas and meows from foot to head,
You mouse-destructive quadruped!

At times you are a lazy sort,
A dozing, lackadaisy sort,
A sleep-all-day-upon-the-bed-
With-paws-upended quadruped;

A give-the-sofa-leg-a-swipe,
Rub-up-against-the-pantleg type;
But still, dear cat, when all is said,
A worth-the-bother quadruped.

SHROOISH	shrewish
TROOISH	trueish

(See ŪISH)

OOIST

NOOIST	canoeist

(See ŪIST)

OOJĒ

BOOJĒ	bougie
FOOJĒ	fugie, fuji, Mt. Fuji
ROOJĒ	rougy, rugae
SOOJĒ	suji

OOKA

BOOKA	cambuca, sambouka
FOOKA	Juan de Fuca
LOOKA	felucca, melaleuca, noctiluca, palooka
NOOKA	manuka, nucha
ROOKA	farruca, garookuh, verruca
TOOKA	festuca, fistuca, katuka
ZOOKA	bazooka

(See ŪKA)

OOKA

HOOKA	hookah
LOOKA	felucca

OOKAL

KOOKAL	coucal

(See ŪKAL)

OOKAN

TOOKAN	toucan

(See ŪKAN)

OOKĒ

BOOKĒ	kabuki
FLOOKĒ	fluky
KOOKĒ	kooky
ROOKĒ	rouky
SNOOKĒ	snooky
SOOKĒ	sookie
SPOOKĒ	spooky
ZOOKĒ	bouzouki

OOKĒ

BOOKĒ	bookie, booky
BROOKĒ	brooky
HOOKĒ	hookey, hooky
KOOKĒ	cookie, cooky, sugar cooky
LOOKĒ	looky
NOOKĒ	nooky
ROOKĒ	rookie, rooky

OOKER

FLOOKER	fluker
LOOKER	involucre, lucre
SNOOKER	snooker

(See ŪKER)

OOKER

BOOKER	booker
HOOKER	hooker
CHOOKER	chukar
KOOKER	electric cooker, fireless cooker, cooker, pressure cooker
LOOKER	bad-looker, good-looker, landlooker, looker, onlooker, overlooker
ROOKER	rooker
STOOKER	stooker

OOKING

BOOKING	booking, overbooking, rebooking, underbooking
BROOKING	brooking
HOOKING	hooking, unhooking
KOOKING	cooking, overcooking, undercooking
LOOKING	bad-looking, good-looking, ill-looking, looking, onlooking, overlooking, well-looking

OOKISH

BOOKISH	bookish
HOOKISH	hookish
KOOKISH	cookish
KROOKISH	crookish
NOOKISH	nookish
ROOKISH	rookish

OOKLET

BOOKLET	booklet
BROOKLET	brooklet
NOOKLET	nooklet

OOKOO

KOOKOO	kavakuku, coocoo, kuku
POOKOO	seppuku
TOOKOO	kotukuku

OOKUS

(See ŪKUS)

OOKT

(See **OOK,** add *-ed*)

ŌŌLA

BŌŌLA	Ashtabula, bamboula, boola, boola-boola
BRŌŌLA	zebrula
GŌŌLA	goolah
HŌŌLA	hula-hula
JŌŌLA	joola
KŌŌLA	Bellacoola
MŌŌLA	moola
SŌŌLA	Missoula

ŌŌLĒ

ŌŌLĒ	oolly
BLŌŌLĒ	bluely
BŌŌLĒ	booly
CHŌŌLĒ	patchouli
DRŌŌLĒ	drooly
HŌŌLĒ	gilhooley
KŌŌLĒ	douroucouli, Grand Coolee, coulee, coolie, coolly
RŌŌLĒ	unruly
SKŌŌLĒ	high-schooly, schoolie, schooly
THŌŌLĒ	Thule
TŌŌLĒ	Thule
TRŌŌLĒ	truly, untruly, yours truly
YŌŌLĒ	guayule

(See **ŪLĒ**)

OOLĒ

BOOLĒ	bully
CHOOLĒ	patchouli
FOOLĒ	fully
MOOLĒ	mulley
POOLĒ	puli, pulley
WOOLĒ	woolly

OOLĒD

| BOOLĒD | bullied |
| POOLĒD | pullied |

ŌŌLER

DRŌŌLER	drooler
FŌŌLER	fooler
KŌŌLER	cooler, water cooler, wine cooler
PŌŌLER	pooler
RŌŌLER	ruler
SPŌŌLER	spooler
TŌŌLER	retooler, tooler

(See **ŪLER**)

OOLER

BOOLER	buller
FOOLER	fuller
POOLER	puller, wire puller

ŌŌLES

JŌŌLES	Jewless
KLŌŌLES	clueless
SKRŌŌLES	screwless

(See **Ū, ŌŌ,** add *-less* where appropriate.)

OOLET

BOOLET	bullet, magic bullet
KOOLET	culett
POOLET	pullet

ŌŌLING

DRŌŌLING	drooling
FŌŌLING	fooling
KŌŌLING	cooling, recooling
PŌŌLING	pooling
RŌŌLING	misruling, overruling, ruling
SKŌŌLING	schooling
STŌŌLING	stooling
SPŌŌLING	spooling
TŌŌLING	retooling, tooling

(See **ŪLING**)

OOLING

| BOOLING | bulling |
| POOLING | pulling, wire-pulling |

ŌŌLIP

| JŌŌLIP | julep, mint julep |
| TŌŌLIP | tulip |

(See **ŪLIP**)

ŌŌLISH

FŌŌLISH	foolish, pound-foolish, tomfoolish
GŌŌLISH	ghoulish
KŌŌLISH	coolish
SKŌŌLISH	schoolish

(See **ŪLISH**)

OOLISH

BOOLISH	bullish
FOOLISH	fullish
WOOLISH	woolish

ŌŌLLES

(See **ŌŌL,** add *-less* where appropriate.)

ŌŌLŌŌ

| ŌŌLŌŌ | ulu |
| HŌŌLŌŌ | hulu |

WHY THINKING IS ITS OWN WORST ENEMY

How dangerous it is to *think*!
 To think too much may make you *know;*
To know too much may make you *drink;*
 To drink too much may make you *throw*
All thought of thinking down the sink.
 How dangerous it is to think!

LŌŌLŌŌ	Honolulu, Lulu, lulu
SŌŌLŌŌ	Sulu
ZŌŌLŌŌ	Zulu

ŌŌMA

DŌŌMA	Duma
RŌŌMA	empyreuma
SŌŌMA	satsuma
ZŌŌMA	mazuma, Montezuma

(See **ŪMA**)

ŌŌMAL

| BRŌŌMAL | brumal |
| TŌŌMAL | tombal |

ŌŌMĒ

| BLŌŌMĒ | bloomy |
| BŌŌMĒ | boomy |

BROOME broomy
GLOOME gloomy
GROOME groomy
PLOOME plumy
ROOME rheumy, roomy

(See ŪMĒ)

OOMEN

FLOOMEN flumen
KROOMEN crewmen
NOOMEN numen
ROOMEN rumen, cerumen

(See ŪMEN)

OOMENT

BROOMENT imbruement
CHOOMENT eschewment
KROOMENT accruement

(See ŪMENT)

OOMER

BLOOMER bloomer, late-bloomer
BOOMER baby-boomer, boomer, schuss-boomer
DOOMER doomer
GROOMER animal groomer, dog groomer, groomer, hair groomer, cat groomer
PLOOMER plumer
ROOMER roomer, rumor
STOOMER stumor
TOOMER entomber, tumor

(See ŪMER)

OOMERD

BLOOMERD bloomered
ROOMERD rumored

(See ŪMERD)

OOMIJ

DOOMIJ doomage
PLOOMIJ plumage
ROOMIJ roomage

(See ŪMIJ)

OOMIK

TOOMIK tombic

(See ŪMIK)

OOMING

(See OOM, ŪM, add -ing where appropriate.)

OOMKĒ

KOOMKĒ koomkie
ROOMKĒ room key

OOMLES

(See OOM, ŪM, add -less where appropriate.)

OOMOO

OOMOO umu
MOOMOO muumuu, mumu

OOMUS

BROOMUS brumous
GROOMUS grumous
PLOOMUS plumous

(See ŪMUS)

OOMZMAN

DOOMZMAN doomsman
GROOMZMAN groomsman

OONA

GOONA guna
HOONA kahuna
KOONA lacuna, vicuna
LOONA luna, Luna
POONA puna
ROONA koruna
TOONA tuna

(See ŪNA)

OONAL

GOONAL lagoonal

(See ŪNAL)

OONĒ

KLOONĒ Cluny
LOONĒ loony
MOONĒ Moonie, moony, Sakyamuni
SPOONĒ spoony
SWOONĒ swoony
TOONĒ festoony

(See ŪNĒ)

OONER

GOONER dragooner
KROONER crooner
LOONER ballooner, extralunar, interlunar, lunar, novilunar, plenilunar, semilunar, circumlunar, cislunar, sublunar, translunar
MOONER honeymooner, mooner
POONER harpooner, lampooner
PROONER pruner
ROONER marooner, runer
SKOONER schooner
SOONER sooner
SPOONER spooner
SWOONER swooner

(See ŪNER)

OONES

BLOONES blueness
TROONES trueness

(See ŪNES)

OONĒZ

BOONĒZ boonies
LOONĒZ loonies
MOONĒZ Moonies

OONFUL

LOONFUL balloonful
ROONFUL runeful
SPOONFUL spoonful, tablespoonful, teaspoonful
TOONFUL tuneful

(See ŪNFUL)

O͞ONIK

RO͞ONIK	runic
TO͞ONIK	tunic

(See ŪNIK)

O͞ONING

KRO͞ONING	crooning
LO͞ONING	ballooning
MO͞ONING	mooning
NO͞ONING	nooning
PO͞ONING	harpooning, lampooning
PRO͞ONING	pruning
SO͞ONING	bassooning
SPO͞ONING	spooning
SWO͞ONING	swooning
TO͞ONING	cartooning, tuning

(See ŪNING)

O͞ONISH

(See O͞ON, ŪN, add -ish where appropriate.)

O͞ONIST

DO͞ONIST	rigadoonist
JO͞ONIST	jejunest
LO͞ONIST	balloonist
PO͞ONIST	harpoonist
SO͞ONIST	bassoonist
TO͞ONIST	cartoonist, opportunist

(See ŪNIST)

O͞ONIZM

FO͞ONIZM	buffoonism
TRO͞ONIZM	poltroonism

(See ŪNIZM)

O͞ONLES

BLO͞ONLES	doubloonless
BO͞ONLES	baboonless, boonless
DO͞ONLES	bridoonless, doonless, rigadoonless
DRO͞ONLES	gadroonless, quadroonless
FO͞ONLES	buffoonless, typhoonless
GO͞ONLES	dragoonless, goonless, lagoonless
JO͞ONLES	Juneless
KO͞ONLES	barracoonless, cacoonless, cocoonless, coonless, raccoonless, rockoonless, tycoonless
LO͞ONLES	balloonless, galloonless, pantaloonless, saloonless, shalloonless, Walloonless
MO͞ONLES	honeymoonless, moonless
NO͞ONLES	noonless
PO͞ONLES	harpoonless, lampoonless, poonless
RO͞ONLES	floroonless, macaroonless, octoroonless, runeless, seroonless, vinegarroonless
SHO͞ONLES	shoonless
SKO͞ONLES	sconless
SO͞ONLES	bassoonless, gossoonless, monsoonless
SPO͞ONLES	spoonless, tablespoonless, teaspoonless
TO͞ONLES	altunless, frigatoonless, cartoonless, coquetoonless, musketoonless, pontoonless, platoonless, ratoonless, spittoonless, spontoonless, toonless
TRO͞ONLES	quintroonless, patroonless, poltroonless

(See ŪNLES)

O͞ONLĪT

MO͞ONLĪT	moonlight
NO͞ONLĪT	noonlight

O͞ONLIT

MO͞ONLIT	moonlit
NO͞ONLIT	noonlit

O͞ONNES

JO͞ONNES	jejuneness, Juneness

(See ŪNNES)

O͞ONŌ

O͞ONŌ	Numero Uno, uno
JO͞ONŌ	Juneau, Juno

(See ŪNŌ)

O͞ONUM

O͞ONUM	e pluribus unum
JO͞ONUM	jejunum

O͞OPA

RO͞OPA	rupa, kamarupa
SO͞OPA	supa
STO͞OPA	stupa
TO͞OPA	ketupa

(See ŪPA)

O͞OPĒ

DRO͞OPĒ	droopy
GRO͞OPĒ	groupie
HWO͞OPĒ	whoopy
LO͞OPĒ	loopy
KRO͞OPĒ	croupy
LO͞OPĒ	Guadalupe
RO͞OPĒ	rupee
SKO͞OPĒ	scoopy
SNO͞OPĒ	snoopy
SO͞OPĒ	soupy
STO͞OPĒ	stoopy
SWO͞OPĒ	swoopy

(See ŪPĒ)

O͞OPER

BLO͞OPER	blooper
DO͞OPER	super-duper
DRO͞OPER	drooper
GRO͞OPER	grouper
HO͞OPER	hooper
HWO͞OPER	whooper
KO͞OPER	cooper, recouper
KRO͞OPER	crouper
LO͞OPER	looper, loop-the-looper

SK͞O͞OPER   pooper-scooper, scooper
SN͞O͞OPER   snooper
S͞O͞OPER   peasouper, souper, super
ST͞O͞OPER   stooper, stupor
SW͞O͞OPER   swooper
TR͞O͞OPER   mosstrooper, paratrooper, stormtrooper, trooper, trouper

(See ŪPER)

O͞OPING

(See O͞OP, ŪP, add *-ing* where appropriate.)

O͞OPISH

DR͞O͞OPISH   droopish
GR͞O͞OPISH   groupish
KR͞O͞OPISH   croupish
L͞O͞OPISH   loopish
SK͞O͞OPISH   scoopish
SN͞O͞OPISH   snoopish
ST͞O͞OPISH   stoopish
SW͞O͞OPISH   swoopish

O͞OPL

D͞O͞OPL   duple, subduple
DR͞O͞OPL   drupel, quadruple
SKR͞O͞OPL   scruple
T͞O͞OPL   quintuple, octuple, centuple, septuple, sextuple

(See ŪPL)

O͞OPLET

DR͞O͞OPLET   drupelet, quadruplet
H͞O͞OPLET   hooplet
L͞O͞OPLET   looplet
T͞O͞OPLET   quintuplet, octuplet, septuplet, sextuplet

O͞OPMENT

GR͞O͞OPMENT   aggroupment, groupment, regroupment
K͞O͞OPMENT   recoupment

O͞OPON

J͞O͞OPON   jupon

K͞O͞OPON   coupon
Y͞O͞OPON   yupon

(See ŪPON)

O͞ORA

B͞O͞ORA   tamboura
J͞O͞ORA   jura
K͞O͞ORA   cura
L͞O͞ORA   lura
R͞O͞ORA   tambaroora
SH͞O͞ORA   fissura, flexura
T͞O͞ORA   acciaccatura, appoggiatura, coloratura, scordatura, tarsiatura, territura, velatura, vettura, villegiatura

(See ŪRA)

OORA

DOORA   madura
JOORA   Jura
PLOORA   pleura
SOORA   asura, sura, surra, surrah

OORAL

JOORAL   jural
KROORAL   bicrural, crural
PLOORAL   pleural, plural
ROORAL   rural
SHOORAL   commisural

O͞ORANS

(See ŪRANS)

OORAT

JOORAT   jurat
SOORAT   surat

O͞ORĒ

BR͞O͞ORĒ   brewery
D͞O͞ORĒ   tandoori
H͞O͞ORĒ   houri
J͞O͞ORĒ   Jewry
P͞O͞ORE   potpourri

(See ŪRĒ)

OORĒ

FLOORĒ   fleury, counterfleury
JOORĒ   de jure, grand jury, jury, petit jury
LOORĒ   lurry
MOORĒ   moory
POORĒ   potpourri
ZOORĒ   Missouri

(See URĒ)

OORENS

(See URENS)

OORENT

JOORENT   adjurant, jurant
SHOORENT   assurant, insurant, reassurant

(See URENT)

OORER

MOORER   moorer, unmoorer
POORER   poorer
TOORER   detourer, tourer

(See URER)

OOREST

(See OORIST)

O͞ORING

CH͞O͞ORING   maturing
D͞O͞ORING   enduring, perenduring, perduring
L͞O͞ORING   alluring

(See ŪRING)

OORING

CHOORING   caricaturing, maturing
MOORING   mooring, unmooring
TOORING   detouring, maturing, touring

(See URING)

O͞ORISH

CH͞O͞ORISH   amateurish

(See ŪRISH)

OORISH

BOORISH	boorish
CHOORISH	maturish
DOORISH	dourish
MOORISH	Moorish

(See **URISH**)

OORISHT

(See **URISHT**)

OORIST

CHOORIST	caricaturist
DOORIST	dourest
JOORIST	jurist
POORIST	poorest
TOORIST	Intourist, tourist

OORLĒ

DOORLĒ	dourly
CHOORLĒ	maturely
POORLĒ	poorly
SHOORLĒ	surely

(See **URLĒ**)

OORMENT

JOORMENT	abjurement, conjurement
LOORMENT	allurement
NOORMENT	manurement

(See **URMENT**)

OORNES

DOORNES	dourness
POORNES	poorness
SHOORNES	cocksureness

OORŌ

DOORŌ	duro, maduro
SKOORŌ	chiaroscuro
TROORŌ	Truro

(See **URŌ**)

OORTĒ

SHOORTĒ	cocksurety, surety

(See **SHUR'E.TĒ**)

OORUP

STURUP	stirrup
YOORUP	Europe

(See **URUP**)

OORUS

DOORUS	Honduras
KROORUS	macrurous

(See **URUS**)

OOSA

DOOSA	medusa, Medusa
LOOSA	lallapaloosa, Tuscaloosa
POOSA	Tallapoosa
ROOSA	babirusa
SOOSA	Sousa
THOOSA	arethusa, Arethusa
TOOSA	tuza

(See **USA**)

OOSAL

KLOOSAL	occlusal
NOOSAL	hypotenusal

(See **USL**)

OOSĒ

DOOSĒ	Duce, Il Duce
GOOSĒ	goosy
JOOSĒ	juicy
MOOSĒ	moosey
SLOOSĒ	sluicy

(See **USĒ**)

OOSENS

(See **USENS**)

OOSENT

(See **USENT**)

OOSER

GOOSER	gooser
JOOSER	juicer
LOOSER	looser
SLOOSER	sluicer
SPROOSER	sprucer
STROOSER	abstruser

(See **USER**)

OOSFUL

GOOSFUL	gooseful
JOOSFUL	juiceful
SNOOSFUL	snooseful

(See **USFUL**)

OOSHAL

DOOSHAL	fiducial
KROOSHAL	crucial

(See **USHAL**)

OOSHED

GOOSHED	goosehead
JOOSHED	juicehead
MOOSHED	moosehead

OOSHER

BOOSHER	busher
POOSHER	drug-pusher, pedal-pusher, pen-pusher, pusher

OOSHING

DOOSHING	douching
ROOSHING	rouching, ruching

OOSHUN

DOOSHUN	caducean
FOOSHUN	Confucian
KROOSHUN	crucian, Rosicrucian
LOOSHUN	*A* ablution, absolution, Aleutian, *D* devolution, dilution, dissolution, *E* evolution, *I* involution, irresolution, *K* convolution, counterrevolution, *O* obvolution, *P* pollution, *R* resolution, revolution,

S self-pollution, circumvolution, solution, *T* Tuscaloosian, *TH* thermopollution, *V* volution

RŌŌSHUN Rooshan
TŌŌSHUN destitution, institution, constitution, prostitution, restitution, substitution

(See ŪSHUN)

ŌŌSIK

GLŌŌSIK glucic

(See ŪSIK)

ŌŌSING

LŌŌSING loosing, unloosing
SPRŌŌSING sprucing

(See ŪS, ŌŌS, add *-ing* where appropriate.)

ŌŌSIS

KRŌŌSIS anacrusis

(See ŪSIS)

ŌŌSIV

KLŌŌSIV exclusive, inclusive, inconclusive, conclusive, reclusive, seclusive
LŌŌSIV allusive, delusive, elusive, illusive, collusive
TRŌŌSIV inobtrusive, intrusive, obtrusive, unobtrusive

(See ŪSIV)

ŌŌSLĒ

LŌŌSLĒ loosely
STRŌŌSLĒ abstrusely

(See ŪSLĒ)

ŌŌSLES

GŌŌSLES gooseless
JŌŌSLES juiceless
MŌŌSLES mooseless
SLŌŌSLES sluiceless

(See ŪSLES)

ŌŌSNES

KLŌŌSNES recluseness
LŌŌSNES looseness
SPRŌŌSNES spruceness
STRŌŌSNES abstruseness

(See ŪSNES)

ŌŌSŌ

HŌŌSŌ whoso
KRŌŌSŌ Robinson Crusoe
RŌŌSŌ Caruso, Rousseau
TRŌŌSŌ trousseau

ŌŌSTER

BŌŌSTER booster
BRŌŌSTER brewster
JŌŌSTER jouster
RŌŌSTER rooster

ŌŌSUM

GRŌŌSUM gruesome
TŌŌSUM twosome

ŌŌTA

KŌŌTA barracouta, macuta
LŌŌTA valuta
TŌŌTA battuta

(See ŪTA)

ŌŌTANT

LŌŌTANT pollutant

(See ŪTANT)

ŌŌTĒ

BŌŌTĒ bootee, booty, Djibouti, freebooty
FLŌŌTĒ fluty
FRŌŌTĒ fruity, tutti-frutti
GŌŌTĒ agouti
KŌŌTĒ cootie
MŌŌTĒ gomuti
PŌŌTĒ pampootee, putti
RŌŌTĒ rooty
SŌŌTĒ sooty
SNŌŌTĒ snooty
TŌŌTĒ sweet patootie, tutti

(See ŪTĒ)

ŌŌTED

BŌŌTED jackbooted

(See ŪT, ŌŌT, add *-ed* where appropriate.)

ŌŌTED

FŌŌTED *B* barefooted, big-footed, *D* dog-footed, duck-footed, *F* footed, four-footed, *FL* flat-footed, *K* cat-footed, *KL* claw-footed, cloven-footed, club-footed, *L* lame-footed, left-footed, light-footed, *N* nimble-footed, *P* pussyfooted, *S* six-footed, *SH* sure-footed, *SPL* splay-footed, *SW* swift-footed, *T* two-footed, *W* web-footed, wing-footed, one-footed (etc.)
SŌŌTED sooted

ŌŌTEN
(See ŌŌTN)

ŌŌTER

BŌŌTER booter, freebooter
BRŌŌTER bruiter
FLŌŌTER fluter
FŌŌTER fouter, foutre
FRŌŌTER fruiter
HŌŌTER hooter
JŌŌTER coadjutor
KŌŌTER accoutre, cooter
KRŌŌTER recruiter
LŌŌTER diluter, looter, luter, polluter, saluter

MŌŌTER	mooter
NŌŌTER	neuter
RŌŌTER	rooter, router, uprooter
SHŌŌTER	beanshooter, deershooter, duckshooter, crapshooter, parachuter, peashooter, sharpshooter, shooter, chuter, skeetshooter, troubleshooter
SKŌŌTER	scooter
SŌŌTER	cloak-and-suiter, souter, suiter, suitor
TŌŌTER	astutor, institutor, constitutor, prostitutor, protutor, restitutor, ring-tailed tooter, substitutor, tooter, tutor

(See ŪTER)

OOTER

FOOTER	first-footer, footer, four-footer, pussyfooter, six-footer, two-footer, web-footer (etc.)
POOTER	down-putter, putter, shotputter

ŌŌTHER

(TH as in *then*)

SŌŌTHER	soother
SMŌŌTHER	smoother

ŌŌTHER

(TH as in *thin*)

KŌŌTHER	couther, uncouther
LŌŌTHER	Luther

ŌŌTHFUL

(TH as in *thin*)

RŌŌTHFUL	ruthful
TŌŌTHFUL	toothful
TRŌŌTHFUL	truthful, untruthful
YŌŌTHFUL	youthful

ŌŌTHING

(TH as in *then*)

SMŌŌTHING	smoothing
SŌŌTHING	soothing
TŌŌTHING	toothing

ŌŌTHLES

(TH as in *thin*)

RŌŌTHLES	ruthless
SŌŌTHLES	soothless
TŌŌTHLES	toothless
TRŌŌTHLES	truthless
YŌŌTHLES	youthless

ŌŌTHSUM

TŌŌTHSUM	toothsome
YŌŌTHSUM	youthsome

ŌŌTIJ

FRŌŌTIJ	fruitage
RŌŌTIJ	rootage

(See ŪTIJ)

ŌŌTIK

LŌŌTIK	probouleutic
NŌŌTIK	digoneutic, hermeneutic, ichneutic
RŌŌTIK	toreutic

(See ŪTIK)

ŌŌTING

LŌŌTING	highfaluting

(See ŌŌT, add *-ing* where appropriate.)

OOTING

FOOTING	footing, pussyfooting
POOTING	putting, shot-putting
SOOTING	sooting

ŌŌTISH

BRŌŌTISH	brutish
JŌŌTISH	Jutish
SŌŌTISH	sootish

ŌŌTIST

FLŌŌTIST	flutist
FRŌŌTIST	fruitist
LŌŌTIST	absolutist, lutist
SHŌŌTIST	parachutist
SŌŌTIST	pharmaceutist

(See ŪTIST)

ŌŌTIV

FRŌŌTIV	fruitive
JŌŌTIV	coadjutive

(See ŪTIV)

ŌŌTIZM

BRŌŌTIZM	brutism
LŌŌTIZM	absolutism

(See ŪTIZM)

ŌŌTL

BRŌŌTL	brutal
FŌŌTL	footle
KRŌŌTL	recruital
RŌŌTL	rootle, rutile
TŌŌTL	tootle

(See ŪTL)

ŌŌTLĒ

BRŌŌTLĒ	brutely
KŌŌTLĒ	Xiuhtecutli
LŌŌTLĒ	absolutely, dissolutely, convolutely, posilutely, resolutely

(See ŪTLĒ)

ŌŌTLES

BŌŌTLES	bootless
FRŌŌTLES	fruitless
RŌŌTLES	rootless

(See ŪTLES)

ŌŌTLING

FŌŌTLING	footling
TŌŌTLING	tootling

O͞OTMENT

BRO͞OTMENT	imbrutement
KRO͞OTMENT	recruitment

(See ŪTMENT)

O͞OTN

GLO͞OTN	gluten, glutin
LO͞OTN	highfalutin'
RO͞OTN	rutin
TO͞OTN	rootin'-tootin'

(See ŪTN, O͞OTON)

O͞OTNES

BRO͞OTNES	bruteness
LO͞OTNES	absoluteness, dissoluteness

(See ŪTNES)

O͞OTO͞

O͞OTO͞	prosciutto
BO͞OTO͞	marabuto
LO͞OTO͞	assoluto, risoluto
NO͞OTO͞	ritenuto, sostenuto, tenuto
PLO͞OTO͞	Pluto
SKRO͞OTO͞	scruto
TO͞OTO͞	tutto

O͞OTON

BO͞OTON	bouton
KRO͞OTON	crouton
MO͞OTON	mouton

(See O͞OTN, ŪTN)

O͞OTSE

WO͞OTSE	tootsy-wootsy

(See O͞OTSĒ)

O͞OTSĒ

FO͞OTSĒ	footsie
WO͞OTSĒ	tootsie-wootsie

O͞OTUM

RO͞OTUM	verutum

(See ŪTUM)

O͞OTUP

SHO͞OTUP	shoot-up
SO͞OTUP	suit-up

O͞OTUS

BRO͞OTUS	Brutus

(See ŪTUS)

O͞OVAL

MO͞OVAL	removal
PRO͞OVAL	approval, disapproval, disproval, reproval

O͞OVĒ

GRO͞OVĒ	groovy
MO͞OVĒ	movie

O͞OVEN

HO͞OVEN	hooven
PRO͞OVEN	disproven, proven, unproven

O͞OVER

GRO͞OVER	groover
HO͞OVER	Hoover, hoover
KO͞OVER	Vancouver
LO͞OVER	louver, louvre, Louvre
MO͞OVER	mover, people mover, remover
NO͞OVER	maneuver
PRO͞OVER	approver, disapprover, disprover, improver, prover, reprover

O͞OVING

(See O͞OV, add -ing where appropriate.)

O͞OVMENT

MO͞OVMENT	movement, women's movement

PRO͞OVMENT	approvement, disprovement, improvement

O͞OYA

HO͞OYA	Huia
LO͞OYA	alleluia, hallelujah

O͞OZA

LO͞OZA	lallapalooza
SO͞OZA	Sousa
THO͞OZA	arethusa
TO͞OZA	tuza

O͞OZĒ

O͞OZĒ	oozy
BLO͞OZĒ	bluesy
BO͞OZĒ	boozy, bousy
CHO͞OZĒ	choosy
DO͞OZĒ	doozy
DRO͞OZĒ	drusy
FLO͞OZĒ	floozy
NO͞OZĒ	newsy
SNO͞OZĒ	snoozy
TO͞OZĒ	Watusi
WO͞OZĒ	woozy

O͞OZEL

(See O͞OZL)

O͞OZER

O͞OZER	oozer
BO͞OZER	boozer
BRO͞OZER	bruiser
CHO͞OZER	chooser
KRO͞OZER	cruiser
LO͞OZER	loser, palouser
SNO͞OZER	snoozer
RO͞OZER	peruser

(See ŪZER)

O͞OZHUN

KLO͞OZHUN	exclusion, inclusion, interclusion, conclusion, malocclusion, occlusion, preclusion, reinclusion, reclusion, reocclusion, seclusion
LO͞OZHUN	allusion, delusion,

	disillusion, elusion, illusion, collusion, prolusion, self-delusion	KŌPĒ	pericope	DOPER	dopper, Dopper
		MŌPĒ	mopy	DROPER	dropper, eavesdropper, eye-dropper
		RŌPĒ	ropy		
		SLŌPĒ	slopy		
STROO͞ZHUN	abstrusion	SŌPĒ	soapy	FLOPER	flip-flopper, flippety-flopper, flopper
THOO͞ZHUN	Malthusian	TŌPĒ	topee, topi		
TOO͞ZHUN	pertusion			HOPER	froghopper, grasshopper, hedge-hopper, hopper, clodhopper, table-hopper, treehopper
TROO͞ZHUN	detrusion, extrusion, intrusion, obtrusion, protrusion, retrusion, trusian	**OPĒ**			
		CHOPĒ	choppy	HWOPER	whopper
		DROPĒ	droppy	KLOPER	clip-clopper, clippety-clopper, clopper
(See ŪZHUN)		FLOPĒ	flippety-floppy, flip-floppy, floppy		
				KOPER	copper
OO͞ZL		HOPĒ	hoppy	KROPER	come a cropper, cropper, sharecropper
		KLOPĒ	clip-cloppy, clippety-cloppy, cloppy		
OO͞ZL	ouzel			LOPER	lopper
BOO͞ZL	bamboozle	KOPĒ	copy, phenocopy, photocopy, microcopy, recopy	MOPER	mopper
FOO͞ZL	foozle, gumfoozle			PLOPER	plopper
ROO͞ZL	perusal			POPER	finger-popper, corn-popper, popper
		KROPĒ	croppy		
		LOPĒ	loppy, jalopy	PROPER	improper, proper, propper
(See ŪZAL)		MOPĒ	moppy		
		PLOPĒ	ploppy	SHOPER	shopper, window-shopper
OO͞ZLER		POPĒ	poppy, prosopopy		
		SHOPĒ	shoppe, shoppy		
BOO͞ZLER	bamboozler	SLOPĒ	sloppy	SLOPER	slopper
FOO͞ZLER	foozler	SOPĒ	soppy	SOPER	sopper
GOO͞ZLER	gougoozler	STROPĒ	stroppy	STOPER	stopper
				STROPER	stropper
				SWOPER	swapper
OO͞ZMAN		**ŌPER**		TOPER	overtopper, tiptopper, topper
TROO͞ZMAN	trewsman	DŌPER	doper		
		GRŌPER	groper		
		HŌPER	hoper	**OPET**	
(See ŪZMAN)		KŌPER	coper		
		LŌPER	eloper, interloper, landloper, loper	LOPET	loppet
ŌPA				MOPET	moppet
		MŌPER	moper	POPET	poppet
ŌPA	opah	RŌPER	jump-roper, roper		
CHŌPA	chopa	SLŌPER	sloper		
DŌPA	L-dopa, Ropa Dopa, methyldopa	SŌPER	soft-soaper, soaper, sopor	**OPHED**	
				HOPHED	hophead
KŌPA	Bacopa, copa	STŌPER	stoper	MOPHED	mophead
RŌPA	Europa	TŌPER	toper		
SKŌPA	scopa				
		ÔPER		**OPIJ**	
OPA					
(See ÄPA)		PÔPER	pauper	MOPIJ	moppage
		SKÔPER	scauper	PROPIJ	proppage
		YÔPER	yawper	STOPIJ	estoppage, stoppage
ŌPAL					
(See ŌPL)		**OPER**		**OPIK**	
ŌPĒ		BOPER	bopper, teeny-bopper, weeny-bopper	OPIK	boöpic, Ethiopic, myopic, presbyopic
DŌPĒ	dopey	CHOPER	chopper, meat-chopper, vegetable chopper	DROPIK	hydropic
HŌPĒ	hopi			KLOPIK	cyclopic
				KOPIK	acopic, syncopic

LOPIK	nyctalopic
NOPIK	canopic, sinopic
SKOPIK	*A* aeroscopic,
	aposcopic,
	arthoscopic, *D*
	dichroscopic,
	deuteroscopic, *E*
	electroscopic, *F*
	photoscopic, *FL*
	fluoroscopic, *G*
	galvanoscopic, *H*
	hagioscopic,
	helioscopic,
	hydroscopic,
	hygroscopic,
	horoscopic, *J*
	geoscopic,
	gyroscopic, *K*
	kaleidoscopic, *L*
	laryngoscopic,
	lychnoscopic, *M*
	macroscopic,
	metoscopic,
	microscopic, *N*
	necroscopic,
	noöscopic, *O*
	orthoscopic,
	autoscopic, *P*
	pantascopic,
	periscopic,
	polyscopic,
	poroscopic, *R*
	rheoscopic, *SK*
	scopic, *SP*
	spectroscopic, *ST*
	stereoscopic,
	stethoscopic, *STR*
	stroboscopic, *T*
	telescopic, *TH*
	thermoscopic
SOPIK	Aesopic,
	dolichroprosopic,
	prosopic
THROPIK	anthropic,
	philanthropic,
	lycanthropic,
	misanthropic,
	neoanthropic,
	paleanthropic,
	psilanthropic,
	theanthropic,
	theophilanthropic,
	therianthropic
TOPIK	atopic, ectopic,
	entopic, heterotopic,
	isotopic, metopic,
	polytopic,
	radioisotopic, topic
TROPIK	*A* allotropic,
	aerotropic, atropic, *D*
	dexiotropic, diatropic,
	E exotropic, *F*

	phototropic, *H*
	heliotropic,
	heterotropic,
	hydrotropic, *I*
	idiotropic, inotropic,
	isentropic, isotropic,
	J geotropic, *M*
	monotropic, *N*
	nyctitropic,
	neurotropic, *O*
	orthotropic,
	autotropic, *P*
	polytropic, *S*
	syntropic, subtropic,
	ST stenotropic, *TH*
	thixotropic, *TR*
	tropic, *V* vagotropic,
	Y eurytropic

ŌPING

ŌPING	oping, reoping
DŌPING	doping
GRŌPING	groping
HŌPING	hoping
KŌPING	coping
LŌPING	eloping, interloping, loping
MŌPING	moping
PŌPING	dispoping, poping, unpoping
RŌPING	roping
SLŌPING	sloping
SŌPING	soft-soaping, soaping

OPING

(See **OP,** add *-ping* where appropriate.)

ŌPISH

MŌPISH	mopish
PŌPISH	popish
TŌPISH	taupish

OPISH

FOPISH	foppish
POPISH	poppish, soda poppish
SHOPISH	shoppish

ŌPL

ŌPL	opal, periople
KŌPL	copal
NŌPL	Adrianople, Constantinople, nopal, *sinople*

OPL

HOPL	hopple
KOPL	copple
POPL	popple
STOPL	estoppel, stopple
THROPL	thropple
TOPL	overtopple, topple

ŌPLES

(See **ŌP,** add *-less* where appropriate.)

OPLIN

JOPLIN	Joplin
POPLIN	poplin

OPLING

FOPLING	fopling
HOPLING	hoppling
STOPLING	stoppling
TOPLING	overtoppling, toppling

OPLĪT

HOPLĪT	hoplite
STOPLĪT	stop light

OPOUT

DROPOUT	dropout
KOPOUT	cop-out
POPOUT	pop-out

OPSĒ

DROPSĒ	dropsy
FLOPSĒ	Flopsy
LOPSĒ	lopsy
MOPSĒ	Mopsy
POPSĒ	popsy
TOPSĒ	Topsy

OPSHUN

OPSHUN	option
DOPSHUN	adoption, readoption

OPSIS

OPSIS	caryopsis, coreopsis, stereopsis
KOPSIS	lycopsis

LOPSIS	ampelopsis
NOPSIS	synopsis
TOPSIS	thanatopsis

OPTED

OPTED	co-opted, opted
DOPTED	adopted, readopted, unadopted

OPTER

OPTER	diopter, co-opter, opter
DOPTER	adopter
KOPTER	phenicopter, helicopter, copter
THOPTER	ornithopter, orthopter

OPTIK

OPTIK	optic
KOPTIK	Coptic
NOPTIK	synoptic
THOPTIK	orthoptic
TOPTIK	autoptic

OPTIV

OPTIV	co-optive, optive
DOPTIV	adoptive

ŌPUS

ŌPUS	opus
GŌPUS	lagopous, Lagopus
MŌPUS	mopus
NŌPUS	Canopus
RŌPUS	pyropus

ŌRĀ

KŌRĀ	kore
LŌRĀ	con dolore
MŌRĀ	con amore, Moray
NYŌRĀ	signore
TORĀ	improvisatore, cacciatore

ORĀ

FORĀ	foray
MORĀ	Moray

ŌRA

ŌRA	ora
BŌRA	bombora, bora, Bora Bora, rasbora
DŌRA	Andorra, dumb Dora, fedora, Floradora, Pandora, rhodora
FLŌRA	flora, Passiflora
GŌRA	angora
HŌRA	hora
KŌRA	kora
MŌRA	mora
NŌRA	menorah
NYŌRA	señora, signora
RŌRA	aurora, Tuscarora
SŌRA	Masora, sora
TŌRA	tora, torah, totora
YŌRA	señora, signora

ÔRA

ÔRA	aura
SÔRA	chamaesaura

ORA

ORA	orra
DORA	Andorra
GORA	begorra
MORA	Gomorra, gomorrah
SORA	sorra

ŌRAKS

BŌRAKS	borax
STŌRAKS	storax
THŌRAKS	thorax

ŌRAL

ŌRAL	aboral, oral
FLŌRAL	floral, trifloral
GŌRAL	goral
HŌRAL	horal
KLŌRAL	chloral
KŌRAL	choral, coral
PŌRAL	poral
RŌRAL	auroral, peroral, roral, sororal
THŌRAL	thoral

ÔRAL

ÔRAL	binaural, monaural, aural
LÔRAL	laurel
SÔRAL	saurel

ORAL

FORAL	forel
KWORAL	quarrel
MORAL	amoral, Balmoral, immoral, moral, unmoral
SORAL	sorrel

ORAN

LORAN	loran
SPORAN	sporran

(See **OREN**)

ŌRANT

SŌRANT	soarant
VŌRANT	devorant, vorant

ORANT

(See **ORENT**)

ŌRĀT

ŌRĀT	orate
BŌRĀT	borate
FLŌRĀT	biflorate, deflorate, florate
FŌRĀT	biforate
KLŌRĀT	chlorate, perchlorate

ÔRĀT

ÔRĀT	inaurate
STÔRĀT	instaurate

ÔRBĒ

ÔRBĒ	orby
KÔRBĒ	corby

ÔRBEL

ÔRBEL	orbell
KÔRBEL	corbel

(See **ÔRBL**)

ÔRBING

ÔRBING	orbing

SÔRBING absorbing, reabsorbing, resorbing

ÔRBL

WÔRBL warble

(See ÔRBEL)

ÔRCHER

SKÔRCHER scorcher
TÔRCHER torcher, torture

ÔRCHERD

ORCHERD orchard
TORCHERD tortured, retortured, untortured

ÔRCHING

SKÔRCHING scorching
TÔRCHING torching

ÔRCHUN

FÔRCHUN bad fortune, befortune, enfortune, fortune, good fortune, misfortune
PÔRCHUN importune

ÔRDAN

(See ÔRDEN)

ÔRDANT

KÔRDANT accordant, disaccordant, discordant, inaccordant, concordant
MÔRDANT mordant, mordent

ŌRDED

BÔRDED boarded
FŌRDED afforded, forded
HŌRDED hoarded
SÔRDED sworded

ÔRDED

KÔRDED accorded, chorded, corded, recorded, unrecorded
LÔRDED belorded, lorded, unlorded
SÔRDED sordid, sworded
SWÔRDED swarded
WÔRDED awarded, rewarded, unrewarded, warded

ÔRDEN

JÔRDEN Jordan
KÔRDEN cordon
WÔRDEN game warden, prison warden, warden

ÔRDENT

(See ÔRDANT)

ŌRDER

BŌRDER bed-and-boarder, boarder, star boarder
FŌRDER afforder, forder
HŌRDER hoarder
SŌRDER sworder

ÔRDER

ÔRDER disorder, law and order, money order, order, overorder, reorder, short order, suborder, tall order, underorder, unorder
BÔRDER border, emborder
KÔRDER accorder, chorder, corder, recorder
SÔRDER sordor
WÔRDER awarder, rewarder, warder

ÔRDERD

ÔRDERD ordered, overordered, reordered, short-ordered, unordered
BÔRDERD bordered, embordered

ÔRDFUL

KÔRDFUL discordful
WÔRDFUL awardful

ÔRDIJ

BÔRDIJ boardage, bordage
KÔRDIJ cordage
WÔRDIJ wardage

ŌRDING

BŌRDING beaver-boarding, boarding, weatherboarding
FŌRDING affording, fording
HŌRDING hoarding
SŌRDING swording

(See ÔRDING)

ÔRDING

KÔRDING according, cording, chording, recording
LÔRDING lording, milording, overlording
WÔRDING awarding, rewarding, unrewarding, warding

(See ŌRDING)

ÔRDSHIP

LÔRDSHIP lordship
WÔRDSHIP wardship

ŌRĒ

ŌRĒ a fortiori, a posteriori, a priori, maggiore, oary, ory
BŌRĒ mbori
DŌRĒ dory, hunky-dory
FLŌRĒ flory, counterflory
GLŌRĒ glory, Old Glory, vainglory
GŌRĒ allegory, amphigory, phantasmagory, gory, category, tautegory
HŌRĒ hoary, whory
KŌRĒ kore, kori
LŌRĒ lory, pilori
MŌRĒ con amore, memento mori, more, pro patria mori, viola d'amore
NYŌRĒ signore
PŌRĒ pory
RŌRĒ furore
SHŌRĒ shory
SNŌRĒ snory
SŌRĒ dimissory,

Montessori,
promissory

SPŌRĒ apospory
STŌRĒ basement story,
blindstory, clerestory,
multistory, short
story, sob story, story

TŌRĒ *A* abbreviatory,
abjuratory,
absolutory, additory,
adhortatory,
adjuratory,
admonitory,
adulatory,
advocatory,
affirmatory,
acclamatory,
acceleratory,
accusatory, aleatory,
alleviatory, amatory,
ambagitory,
ambulatory,
amendatory,
annotatory,
annunciatory,
anticipatory,
appellatory,
applicatory,
appreciatory,
approbatory, aratory,
articulatory,
aspiratory,
asseveratory,
assimilatory, *B*
bibitory, *D*
damnatory,
deambulatory,
dedicatory,
defamatory,
dehortatory,
declamatory,
declaratory,
decretory, deletory,
delineatory,
demonstratory,
denunciatory,
depilatory,
depository,
deprecatory,
depreciatory,
depredatory,
derogatory,
desquatory, desultory,
designatory,
dictatory, dilatory,
disapprobatory,
discriminatory,
dispensatory,
distillatory,
divinatory, donatory,
dormitory, *E*
edificatory,

educatory,
exaggeratory,
exhibitory,
exhortatory,
ejaculatory,
execratory,
executory,
exclamatory,
excretory,
exculpatory,
excusatory, expiatory,
expiratory,
explanatory,
expletory,
explicatory,
exploratory,
expository,
expostulatory,
expurgatory,
excitatory,
extenuatory,
exterminatory,
equivocatory,
elucidatory,
emancipatory,
emasculatory,
emendatory,
emigratory,
emulatory,
enunciatory, *F*
feretory, flagellatory,
phonatory, feudatory,
fulminatory,
fumatory, fumitory,
funambulatory, *FR*
frigeratory, *G*
gustatory, *GL*
gladiatory, *GR*
gradatory, grallatory,
gratulatory, *H*
habilitory,
hallucinatory,
hortatory, *I*
Il Trovatore,
immigratory,
imperatory,
imprecatory,
improvisatory,
improvvisatore,
indicatory,
inflammatory,
informatory,
inhibitory, initiatory,
incantatory,
incriminatory,
incubatory,
inculpatory,
inspiratory,
interlocutory,
interrogatory,
inventory,
investigatory,

invitatory,
invocatory,
involutory, *J*
jaculatory, gestatory,
gesticulatory,
gyratory, judicatory,
juratory, *K*
cachinnatory,
calculatory,
calumniatory,
castigatory,
commandatory,
commendatory,
comminatory,
communicatory,
compellatory,
compensatory,
competitory,
compulsatory,
condemnatory,
condolatory,
confabulatory,
confirmatory,
confiscatory,
congratulatory,
consecratory,
conservatory,
conciliatory,
consolatory,
constellatory,
consultatory,
contributory,
corroboratory,
cosignatory,
cubatory, culpatory,
curatory, *KR*
crematory,
criminatory, crinitory,
chrismatory, *L*
laboratory,
lachrymatory,
lacrimatory, lavatory,
libatory, liberatory,
libratory, laudatory,
lucubratory, *M*
mandatory,
manducatory,
manipulatory,
masticatory,
mediatory, migratory,
minatory, monitory,
mundatory, mutatory,
N narratory, natatory,
negatory, negotiatory,
nugatory, *O*
objurgatory,
obligatory,
observatory, auditory,
offertory, auxiliatory,
olitory, oratory,
oscillatory,
osculatory,

auscultatory, *P*
palliatory, parlatory,
pacificatory, pellitory,
perambulatory,
peremptory,
perfumatory,
perspiratory,
piscatory,
postulatory, potatory,
pulsatory, punitory,
purgatory,
purificatory, *PL*
placatory, plauditory,
PR preambulatory,
predatory,
predicatory,
prefatory,
premonitory,
preparatory,
preservatory,
probatory,
profanatory,
prohibitory,
proclamatory,
procrastinatory,
procuratory,
promonitory,
pronunciatory,
propitiatory, *R*
radiatory, raspatory,
reformatory,
refrigeratory,
refutatory, regulatory,
regeneratory,
recognitory,
recommendatory,
reconciliatory,
recriminatory,
requisitory,
remuneratory,
remourtratory,
repertory, repository,
reprobatory,
reptatory,
reciprocatory,
respiratory,
restoratory,
retaliatory,
retardatory,
retributory,
revelatory,
reverberatory,
revocatory, rogatory,
rotatory, *S*
sacrificatory,
saltatory, salutatory,
salvatory, sanatory,
sensificatory,
certificatory,
sibilitory, signatory,
significatory,
simulatory,

circulatory,
circumambulatory,
circumgyratory,
circumlocutory,
circumrotatory,
citatory, sublimatory,
sudatory,
supererogatory,
suppletory,
supplicatory,
suppository,
sussultatory, *SP*
speculatory, *ST*
statutory,
sternutatory, storey,
story, *T* terminatory,
territory, tory, *TR*
transitory,
transmigratory,
transpiratory,
transudatory, *U*
undulatory,
usurpatory, *V*
vacillatory,
viaggiatory,
vehiculatory,
vesicatory, vibratory,
vindicatory, vomitory

| YŌRĒ | signore |
| ZŌRĒ | zori |

ÔRĒ

LÔRĒ	Annie Laurie, outlawry
SKÔRĒ	scaurie
SÔRĒ	saury
TÔRĒ	Alpha Centauri, centaury

ORĒ

KORĒ	corrie
KWORĒ	quarry
LORĒ	lorry
SORĒ	sorry

ÔREL

(See ÔRAL)

OREL

(See ORAL)

OREN

| FLOREN | florin |
| FOREN | foreign |

| SPOREN | sporran |
| WOREN | rabbit warren, warren |

ÔRENS

| HÔRENS | abhorrence |
| LÔRENS | St. Lawrence |

(See ORENS)

ORENS

FLORENS	Florence
TORENS	torrents
WORENS	warrants

(See ÔRENS)

ORENT

HORENT	abhorrent
TORENT	torrent
WORENT	death warrant, search warrant, warrantk

ŌRER

BŌRER	borer, woodborer
DŌRER	adorer
FLŌRER	floorer
GŌRER	gorer
HŌRER	horror
KŌRER	decorer, encorer, corer
NŌRER	ignorer
PLŌRER	deplorer, explorer, implorer
PŌRER	outpourer, porer, pourer
SHNŌRER	schnorrer
SHŌRER	shorer
SKŌRER	scorer
SNŌRER	snorer
SŌRER	outsoarer, soarer, sorer
STŌRER	restorer, storer

(See ÔRER)

ÔRER

| HÔRER | abhorrer |
| WÔRER | warrer |

(See ŌRER)

OREST

FOREST	afforest, deforest, enforest, forest
KOREST	choused
SOREST	sorest

(See **ŌR,** add *-est* where appropriate.)

ŌRĒZ

MŌRĒZ	mores

(See **ŌRĒ,** add *-s* or change *-y* to *-ies* where appropriate.)

ÔRFIK

ÔRFIK	Orphic
MÔRFIK	*A* allomorphic, amorphic, anthropomorphic, *B* biomorphic, *D* dimorphic, deuteromorphic, *E* ephemeromorphic, exomorphic, ectomorphic, endomorphic, *H* heteromorphic, holomorphic, *I* idiomorphic, ichthyomorphic, isomorphic, *J* geomorphic, *M* mesomorphic, metamorphic, mnemomorphic, monomorphic, morphic, *O* ophiomorphic, automorphic, *P* pantamorphic, paramorphic, polymorphic, *PR* protomorphic, *S* pseudomorphic, *T* tauromorphic, *TH* theomorphic, theriomorphic, theromorphic, *TR* trimorphic, *Z* zygomorphic, zoomorphic

ÔRFING

DWÔRFING	dwarfing
HWÔRFING	wharfing

ÔRFIST

HWÔRFIST	wharfist
MÔRFIST	anthropomorphist

(Substitute *-ist* for concluding *-ic* in appropriate words under **ÔRFIK.**)

ÔRFIZM

(Substitute *-ism* for concluding *-ic* in appropriate words under **ORFIK.**)

ÔRGAN

ÔRGAN	barrel organ, biorgan, idorgan, organ
DÔRGAN	idorgan
GÔRGAN	Demogorgon, gorgon, Gorgon
MÔRGAN	morgan, morgen

ŌRHOUS

HŌRHOUS	whorehouse
STŌRHOUS	storehouse

ŌRĪD

BŌRĪD	boride
FŌRĪD	four-eyed
KLŌRĪD	bichloride, dichloride, hydrochloride, chloride, perchloride, tetrachloride, trichloride
SŌRĪD	sore-eyed

ÔRID

SÔRID	labrosaurid, mosasaurid
TÔRID	centaurid, Taurid

(See **ORID**)

ORID

FLORID	florid
FORID	forehead
HORID	horrid
TORID	torrid

(See **ÔRID**)

ŌRIJ

ŌRIJ	oarage
BŌRIJ	borage
FŌRIJ	forage
PŌRIJ	porridge
SHŌRIJ	shorage
STŌRIJ	storage

(See **ORIJ**)

ORIJ

KORIJ	corrige
PORIJ	porridge

(See **ŌRIJ**)

ÔRIK

ÔRIK	auric
TÔRIK	androtauric, tauric

ŌRIK

BŌRIK	boric
DŌRIK	elydoric
KL;ŌRIK	chloric
LŌRIK	folkloric, peloric
RŌRIK	roric

(See **ORIK**)

ORIK

ORIK	fluoric, meteoric, theoric
DORIK	Doric, elydoric, sudoric
FORIK	amphoric, epiphoric, phosphoric, camphoric, cataphoric, metaphoric, pyrophoric, prophoric, semaphoric, symphoric, euphoric, zoophoric
GORIK	allegoric, amphigoric, phantasmagoric, goric, categoric, paregoric, Pythagoric
KLORIK	chloric, hydrochloric, perchloric
KORIK	enchoric, choric
LORIK	caloric, peloric, pyloric

MORIK Armoric, sophomoric
SPORIK zoosporic
THORIK plethoric, thelyphthoric
TORIK aleatoric, diatoric, historic, oratoric, pictoric, prehistoric, *rhetoric*, toric, unhistoric
YORIK Yorick

(See ŌRIK)

ŌRIKS

ŌRIKS oryx

(See ŌRIK, add -*s* where appropriate.)

ORIKS

ORIKS oryx

(See ORIK, add -*s* where appropriate.)

ORIN

(See OREN)

ŌRING

ŌRING oaring
BŌRING boring
DŌRING adoring
FLŌRING flooring
GŌRING goring
HŌRING whoring
KŌRING decoring, encoring, coring
NŌRING ignoring
PLŌRING deploring, exploring, imploring
RŌRING roaring
SHNŌRING schnorring
SHŌRING shoring
SKŌRING scoring
SNŌRING snoring
SŌRING outsoaring, soaring
STŌRING restoring, storing

ÔRING

HÔRING abhorring
WÔRING warring

ŌRIS

KLŌRIS chloris

LŌRIS loris
TŌRIS cantoris

(See ORIS, ŌRUS, ÔRUS)

ORIS

ORIS orris
DORIS doch-an-dorris
HORIS Horace

(See ŌRIS, ŌRUS, ÔRUS)

ORIST

FLORIST florist
FORIST afforest, deforest, disafforest, forest, reafforest, reinforest
KORIST chorist

ÔRJAL

KÔRJAL cordial

(See ÔR'DI.AL)

ÔRJĒ

ÔRJĒ orgy
KÔRJĒ corgi
PÔRJĒ Georgy Porgy
STÔRJĒ storge

ÔRJER

ÔRJER ordure
FÔRJER forger
GÔRJER gorger, disgorger

ÔRJING

FÔRJING forging
GÔRJING gorging, disgorging

ÔRKĒ

(See ÔRK, add -*y* where appropriate.)

ÔRKER

ÔRKER kwashiorkor
FÔRKER forker
KÔRKER corker
PÔRKER porker
YÔRKER New Yorker, yorker

ÔRKING

FÔRKING forking
KÔRKING corking, uncorking
YÔRKING yorking

ÔRKUS

ÔRKUS orchis
NÔRKUS anorchous

ÔRLĒ

SHÔRLĒ schorly
WÔRLĒ warly

ÔRLES

(See ÔR, add -*less* where appropriate.)

ŌRLOK

ŌRLOK oarlock
FŌRLOK forelock

(See ÔRLOK)

ÔRLOK

WÔRLOK warlock

(See ŌRLOK)

ÔRMAL

FÔRMAL formal, informal, conformal, uniformal
KÔRMAL cormel
NÔRMAL abnormal, anormal, normal, paranormal, subnormal, supernormal

ŌRMAN

(See ŌRMEN)

ÔRMANS

(See ÔRMENS)

ÔRMANT

DÔRMANT dormant

FÔRMANT   formant, informant, conformant, performant

(See **ŌRMENT**)

ŌRMAT

DŌRMAT   doormat
FLŌRMAT   floormat

ÔRMAT

DÔRMAT   doormat
FLÔRMAT   floormat
FÔRMAT   format

ÔRMĒ

DÔRMĒ   dormie, dormy
FÔRMĒ   forme, formy, conformy, uniformy
HÔRMĒ   horme
STÔRMĒ   stormy
SWÔRMĒ   swarmy
WÔRMĒ   warmy

ŌRMEN

DŌRMEN   doorman, doormen
FLŌRMEN   floorman, floormen
FŌRMEN   foreman, foremen
KŌRMEN   corpsman, corpsmen
MŌRMEN   Mormon
SHŌRMEN   longshoreman, longshoremen
STŌRMAN   storeman, storemen

ÔRMENS

DÔRMENS   dormance
FÔRMENS   conformance, performance

ŌRMENT

DŌRMENT   adorement
NŌRMENT   ignorement
PLŌRMENT   deplorement, explorement, implorement
STŌRMENT   restorement

(See **ÔRMANT**)

ÔRMER

ÔRMER   ormer
WÔRMER   bedwarmer, benchwarmer, footwarmer, warmer

(See **ÔRM**, add -er where appropriate.)

ÔRMING

(See **ÔRM**, add -ing where appropriate.)

ÔRMIST

FÔRMIST   conformist, nonconformist, reformist, uniformist
WÔRMIST   lukewarmest, warmest

ÔRML

(See **ÔRMAL**)

ÔRMLĒ

FÔRMLĒ   uniformly
WÔRMLĒ   warmly

ÔRMLES

(See **ÔRM**, add -less where appropriate.)

ÔRMOUTH

SÔRMOUTH   sore-mouth
WÔRMOUTH   warmouth

ÔRMUS

FÔRMUS   multiformous
KÔRMUS   cormous, cormus
NÔRMUS   abnormous, enormous

ÔRNĒ

HÔRNĒ   horny
KÔRNĒ   corny
SKÔRNĒ   scorny
THÔRNĒ   thorny

ÔRNER

BÔRNER   suborner
DÔRNER   adorner

HÔRNER   horner, Little Jack Horner
KÔRNER   chimney corner, catercorner, cattycorner, kittycorner, corner
MÔRNER   mourner
SKÔRNER   bescorner, scorner
SÔRNER   sorner
WÔRNER   forewarner, warner

ÔRNET

HÔRNET   hornet
KÔRNET   cornet

ÔRNFUL

MÔRNFUL   mournful
SKÔRNFUL   scornful

ÔRNING

BÔRNING   aborning

(See **ÔRN**, add -ing where appropriate.)

ÔRNIS

ÔRNIS   Aepyornis, Archaeornis, ornis, Heliornis, Ichthyornis
KÔRNIS   cornice
NÔRNIS   Dinornis
TÔRNIS   Gastornis, Notornis

ÔRNISH

HÔRNISH   hornish
KÔRNISH   Cornish
THÔRNISH   thornish

ÔRNLES

(See **ÔRN**, add -less where appropriate.)

ŌRŌ

ŌRŌ   oro
BŌRŌ   Boro
LŌRŌ   loro
MŌRŌ   moro, Moro
PŌRŌ   Poro
SŌRŌ   aposoro
TŌRŌ   toro, torotoro

ORŌ

BORŌ	borrow
MORŌ	amorrow, good morrow, morro, morrow, tomorrow
SORŌ	seeksorrow, sorrow, Zorro

ŌRON

BŎRON	boron
MŌRON	moron

ÔRŌS

PÔRŌS	porose
TÔRŌS	torose

ÔRPER

SKÔRPER	scorper
TÔRPER	torpor
WÔRPER	warper

ÔRSĒ

GÔRSĒ	gorsy
HÔRSĒ	horsy

ÔRSEL

(See **ÔRSL**)

ŌRSEN

HÔRSEN	hoarsen, whoreson
KÔRSEN	coarsen

ŌRSER

HÔRSER	hoarser
KÔRSER	coarser, courser, discourser

ÔRSER

DÔRSER	endorser
FÔRSER	enforcer, forcer, reinforcer
HÔRSER	horser, unhorser
VÔRSER	divorcer

ŌRSFUL

ZŌRSFUL	resourceful, unresourceful

(See **ÔRSFUL**)

ÔRSFUL

FÔRSFUL	forceful, unforceful
MÔRSFUL	remorseful, unremorseful

(See **ÔRSFUL**)

ÔRSHUN

BÔRSHUN	abortion, anti-abortion, pro-abortion
PÔRSHUN	apportion, disproportion, portion, proportion
SÔRSHUN	consortion
TÔRSHUN	contortion, detortion, distortion, extorsion, extortion, intorsion, retorsion, torsion

ÔRSING

(See **ÔRS**, add -ing where appropriate.)

ŌRSIV

KÔRSIV	discoursive

(See **ÔRSIV**)

ÔRSIV

FÔRSIV	enforcive
TÔRSIV	extorsive, contorsive, torsive

(See **ŌRSIV**)

HOW ABOUT YOU AND ME ALLITERATING?

''Alliteration's artful aid''—
That is what the poet said:
''Sing a song of silliness'';
''King and queen and court caress'';
''Babes blow bubbles in a box'';
''Seagulls sing when sewing socks'';
''Down the drain the donkeys dive'';
''Lions leap on lambs alive.''
See? You needn't be a great
Genius to alliterate.

ÔRSL

DÔRSL	dorsal
MÔRSL	morsel
NÔRSL	norsel
SÔRSL	ensorcell, ensorcel
TÔRSL	torcel, torsal
TRÔRSL	dextrorsal, sinistrorsal

ŌRSLĒ

HÔRSLĒ	hoarsely
KÔRSLĒ	coarsely

ÔRSLES

(See **ÔRS**, add -less where appropriate.)

ÔRSMAN

HÔRSMAN	horseman, light-horseman
NÔRSMAN	Norseman

ÔRSMENT

DÔRSMENT	endorsement
FÔRSMENT	deforcement, enforcement, forcement, reinforcement
VÔRSMENT	divorcement

ÔRSMĒT

FÔRSMĒT	forcemeat
HÔRSMĒT	horsemeat

ŌRSNES

HÔRSNES	hoarseness
KÔRSNES	coarseness

ÔRSŌ

DÔRSŌ	dorso
KÔRSŌ	corso
TÔRSŌ	torso

ŌRSUM

FŌRSUM	foursome

(See **ÔRSUM**)

ÔRSUM

DÔRSUM	dorsum

(See **ŌRSUM**)

ÔRTA

ÔRTA	aorta
KWÔRTA	sesquiquarta
TÔRTA	torta

ÔRTAL

(See **ÔRTL**)

ÔRTANS

(See **ÔRTENS**)

ÔRTĒ

DÔRTĒ	dorty
FÔRTĒ	forte, forty, pianoforte
PÔRTĒ	porty
SHÔRTĒ	shorty
SNÔRTĒ	snorty
SÔRTĒ	sortie, resorty
SPÔRTĒ	sporty
SWÔRTĒ	swarty
WÔRTĒ	warty

ÔRTED

(See **ÔRT**, add *-ed*)

ÔRTEKS

KÔRTEKS	cortex
VÔRTEKS	vortex

ÔRTEN

CHÔRTEN	chorten
KWÔRTEN	quartan
SHÔRTEN	foreshorten, shorten

ÔRTENS

PÔRTENS	importance, comportance, transportance, supportance
SÔRTENS	sortance

ÔRTER

BÔRTER	aborter
HÔRTER	dehorter
KÔRTER	escorter, courter
KWÔRTER	forequarter, hindquarter, quarter, last quarter, weather-quarter
MÔRTER	mortar
PÔRTER	disporter, exporter, importer, colporteur, porter, reporter, supporter, transporter
SHÔRTER	shorter
SNÔRTER	ripsnorter, snorter
SÔRTER	assorter, kicksorter, consorter, resorter, sorter, wool sorter (etc.)
SPÔRTER	sporter
SWÔRTER	swarter
THWÔRTER	thwarter
TÔRTER	detorter, distorter, extorter, contorter, retorter
ZÔRTER	exhorter

ÔRTERZ

KWÔRTERZ	fall quarters, headquarters, quarters, spring quarters, summer quarters, winter quarters

(See **ÔRTER**, add *-s* where appropriate.)

ŌRTGĪD

PŌRTGĪD	port guide

(See **ÔRTGĪD**)

ÔRTGĪD

KÔRTGĪD	court guide

(See **ŌRTGĪD**)

ŌRTIJ

PŌRTIJ	portage

(See **ÔRTIJ**)

ÔRTIJ

SHÔRTIJ	shortage

(See **ŌRTIJ**)

ÔRTING

(See **ÔRT**, add *-ing* where appropriate.)

ÔRTIS

FÔRTIS	fortis
MÔRTIS	mortice, mortise
TÔRTIS	tortoise

ÔRTIV

ÔRTIV	ortive
BÔRTIV	abortive
PÔRTIV	nonsupportive, supportive, transportive, unsupportive
SPÔRTIV	disportive, sportive, transportive
TÔRTIV	distortive, extortive, contortive, retortive, tortive

ÔRTL

ÔRTL	aortal
CHÔRTL	chortle
HWÔRTL	whortle
MÔRTL	immortal, mortal
PÔRTL	portal, transportal
SÔRTL	sortal

ŌRTLĒ

KÔRTLĒ	courtly, uncourtly
PÔRTLĒ	portly

(See **ÔRTLĒ**)

ÔRTLĒ

SHÔRTLĒ	shortly

(See **ŌRTLĒ**)

ÔRTLING

CHÔRTLING	chortling
MÔRTLING	mortling

ÔRTMENT

KÔRTMENT	escortment
PÔRTMENT	deportment, disportment, comportment, transportment
SÔRTMENT	assortment, consortment, sortment

ÔRTNES

SWÔRTNES	swartness
THWÔRTNES	thwartness

ÔRTRES

FÔRTRES	fortress
MÔRTRES	mortress

ÔRTŪRD

(See **ÔRCHERD**)

ŌRUM

ŌRUM	variorum
FŌRUM	forum
JŌRUM	jorum
KŌRUM	decorum, indecorum
KWŌRUM	quorum
LŌRUM	ad valorem, cockalorum
NŌRUM	pons asinorum
SNŌRUM	snipsnapsnorum
SPŌRUM	Pittosporum
TŌRUM	sanctum sanctorum, schola cantorum

ÔRUM

ÔRUM	aurum

(See **ŌRUM**)

ŌRUS

FLŌRUS	tubuliflorous
HŌRUS	Horus
KLŌRUS	chlorous
KŌRUS	decorous, indecorous, corous, chorus
LŌRUS	pelorus, pylorus
NŌRUS	canorous, sonorous
PŌRUS	imporous, porous
SŌRUS	sorus
TŌRUS	torus

(See **ŌRIS, ORIS, ÔRUS**)

ÔRUS

ÔRUS	aurous
LÔRUS	laurus
SKÔRUS	scaurous
SÔRUS	*B* Brontosaurus, *D* Dolichosaurus, *H* Hadrosaurus, *I* Ichthyosaurus, *L* Labrosaurus, *M* Megalosaurus, Mixosaurus, Mosasaurus, *PL* Plesiosaurus, *PR* protorosaurus, *T* Teleosaurus, Tyrannosaurus, *TH* thesaurus
TÔRUS	Centaurus, Taurus

(See **ŌRIS, ORIS, ŌRUS**)

ÔRWERD

FÔRWERD	forward, henceforward, straightforward, thenceforward
NÔRWERD	nor'ward

ŌSA

DŌSA	dosa
KŌSA	mucosa
MŌSA	Formosa, mimosa
PŌSA	mariposa
RŌSA	Via Dolorosa, serosa
VŌSA	anorexia nervosa

OSA

OSA	Ossa
FOSA	fossa
GLOSA	glossa
GOSA	Saragossa
ROSA	Barbarossa

OSAL

(See **OSL**)

OSBAK

HOSBAK	hossback
MOSBAK	mossback
TOSBAK	tossback

ÔSĒ

GÔSĒ	gawsie
SÔSĒ	saucy

OSĒ

BOSĒ	bossy
DROSĒ	drossy
FLOSĒ	flossy
GLOSĒ	glossy
LOSĒ	lossy
MOSĒ	mossie, mossy
POSĒ	in posse, posse
PROSĒ	prossie
TOSĒ	tossy

ŌSENT

DŌSENT	docent
NŌSENT	nocent

ŌSER

DŌSER	doser
GRŌSER	engrosser, greengrocer, grocer
KLŌSER	closer
KŌSER	jocoser
RŌSER	moroser

ÔSER

CHÔSER	Chaucer
HÔSER	hawser
SÔSER	saucer

(See **OSER**)

OSER

BOSER	bosser, embosser
DOSER	dosser
GLOSER	glosser
JOSER	josser
KROSER	crosser
ROSER	rosser
TOSER	tosser

(See **ÔSER**)

OSET

BOSET	bosset
KOSET	cosset
POSET	posset, sack posset
TOSET	tossut

ŌSHA

| ŌSHA | Beotia, OSHA |
| SKŌSHA | Nova Scotia, Scotia |

OSHĒ

JOSHĒ	joshy
SKWOSHĒ	squashy
SLOSHĒ	sloshy
SWOSHĒ	swashy
TOSHĒ	toshy
WOSHĒ	washy, wishy-washy

ŌSHER

GŌSHER	gaucher
KLŌSHER	clocher
KŌSHER	kosher

OSHER

BOSHER	bosher
JOSHER	josher
KOSHER	cosher
POSHER	posher
SKWOSHER	squasher
SLOSHER	slosher
SWOSHER	swasher
TOSHER	tosher
WOSHER	dishwasher, whitewasher, washer

OSHING

| WOSHING | dishwashing, whitewashing, washing |

(See **OSH,** add *-ing* where appropriate.)

ŌSHUN

ŌSHUN	Boeotion, ocean
DŌSHUN	braggadocian
GŌSHUN	Goshen
GRŌSHUN	groschen
KŌSHUN	nicotian
LŌSHUN	lotion
MŌSHUN	Brownian motion, demotion, emotion, commotion, locomotion, motion, promotion, remotion, notion, prenotion
NŌSHUN	notion, prenotion
PŌSHUN	potion
VŌSHUN	devotion, indevotion, self-devotion

ÔSHUN

| KÔSHUN | caution |

(See **OSHUN**)

OSHUN

| FOSHUN | defossion |

(See **ÔSHUN**)

ŌSHUS

DŌSHUS	supercalifragilistic-expialidocious
KŌSHUS	precocious
PŌSHUS	nepotious
RŌSHUS	ferocious
STŌSHUS	stotious
TRŌSHUS	atrocious

ÔSIJ

| GÔSIJ | gaussage |
| SÔSIJ | sausage |

(See **OSIJ**)

OSIJ

| BOSIJ | bossage |
| FOSIJ | fossage |

(See **ÔSIJ**)

OSIK

FOSIK	fossick
GLOSIK	glossic
LOSIK	molossic

(See **ÔSIK**)

ÔSIK

| NOSIK | banausic |

(See **OSIK**)

OSIL

(See **OSL**)

ŌSING

| DŌSING | dosing |
| GRŌSING | engrossing, grossing |

OSING

| KROSING | children crossing, deer crossing, grade crossing, cattle crossing, crossing, railroad crossing |

(See **OS,** add *-ing* where appropriate.)

ŌSIS

ŌSIS	*A* abiosis, anabiosis, anastomosis, antibiosis, apotheosis, *B* biosis, *E* enantiosis, endometriosis, *H* heliosis, *I* ichthyosis, *K* coccideosis, *M* meiosis, miosis, mononucleosis, *N* pneumonoultra-microscopicsilico-volcanoconiosis, *N* necrobiosis, pneumoconiosis, *O* orthobiosis, *P* parabiosis, pyosis, poliosis, *S* semiosis, symbiosis, *SK* scoliosis
BŌSIS	thrombosis
DŌSIS	lordosis
DRŌSIS	ischidrosis, cacidrosis, kakidrosis, maschalephildrosis, podobromhydrosis
FŌSIS	anamorphosis, gomphosis, morphosis
FRŌSIS	nephrosis
GŌSIS	rhigosis, zygosis
KŌSIS	metempsychosis, narcosis, sarcosis, psittacosis, psychosis
KRŌSIS	phalacrosis, necrosis
LŌSIS	ankylosis, dacrygelosis, diverticulosis, furunculosis, helosis, melosis, pediculosis, psilosis, tuberculosis
MŌSIS	endosmosis, exosmosis, cagamosis, limosis,

	osmosis, patharmosis, zymosis
NŌSIS	*A* asteriognosis, avitaminosis, *D* diagnosis, *H* hallucinosis, hypervitaminosis, hypnosis, hyssinosis, *J* geognosis, *K* kenosis, *L* lagnosis, loganamnosis, *K* carcinosis, *P* pollinosis, *N* gnosis, *S* cyanosis, *ST* stenosis, stereognosis, *T* telegnosis, *TR* trichinosis
PLŌSIS	anadiplosis, epanadiplosis
PŌSIS	adiposis, hypotyposis
RŌSIS	*A* amaurosis, arteriosclerosis, atherosclerosis, *FL* phlabosclerosis, *H* heterosis, *K* chorosis, *M* morosis, *N* neurosis, *P* pyrosis, *S* cirrhosis, scirrhosis, sorosis, *SK* sclerosis, *T* tephrosis, *Z* xerosis
THŌSIS	diorthosis, epanorthosis
TŌSIS	*D* dermatosis, *E* epidermophytosis, *H* halitosis, hematosis, *J* gestosis, *K* kinetosis, *M* metasomatosis, metemptosis, metensomatosis, myxomatosis, *O* otosis, *PR* proemptosis, *S* cittosis, *T* teratosis, ptosis

ŌSIV

PLŌSIV	explosive, implosive, inexplosive, plosive
RŌSIV	erosive, corrosive

OSL

OSL	ossal
DOSL	docile, dosel, dossal, dossil
FOSL	fossil
GLOSL	glossal, hypoglossal
JOSL	jostle
LOSL	colossal

POSL	apostle
THROSL	throstle
TOSL	tossel
WOSL	wassail

ŌSLĒ

BŌSLĒ	verbosely
GRŌSLĒ	grossly
KLŌSLĒ	closely
KŌSLĒ	bellicosely, jocosely
RŌSLĒ	morosely

OSLER

OSLER	ostler
HOSLER	hostler
JOSLER	jostler

ŌSNES

BŌSNES	verboseness
GRŌSNES	grossness
KLŌSNES	closeness
KŌSNES	bellicoseness, jocoseness
RŌSNES	moroseness
TŌSNES	ventoseness

ŌSŌ

ŌSŌ	arioso, furioso, grandioso, gracioso, capriccioso, curioso, Mafioso, virtuoso
LŌSŌ	tremoloso
MŌSŌ	animoso, lacrimoso, mosso
PŌSŌ	pomposo
RŌSŌ	amoroso, doloroso, corozo, oloroso, penseroso
SŌSŌ	soso, so-so
TŌSŌ	maestoso, strepitoso
TRŌSŌ	nitroso

OSTA

HOSTA	Hosta
KOSTA	costa, subcosta

ŌSTAL

KŌSTAL	intercoastal, intracoastal, coastal
PŌSTAL	postal

OSTAL

(See **OSTEL**)

OSTĀT

KOSTĀT	costate, quadricostate, laticostate
POSTĀT	apostate
PROSTĀT	prostate

OSTĒ

FROSTĒ	frosty
PROSTĒ	prostie

ŌSTED

BŌSTED	boasted
GŌSTED	ghosted
HŌSTED	hosted
KŌSTED	coasted
PŌSTED	*composted*, posted, riposted, unposted
RŌSTED	roasted, unroasted
TŌSTED	toasted, untoasted

ÔSTED

ZÔSTED	exhausted

(See **OSTED**)

OSTED

FROSTED	defrosted, frosted
KOSTED	accosted

(See **ÔSTED**)

OSTEL

HOSTEL	hostel, hostile
KOSTEL	infracostal, intercostal, costal, Pentacostal, supracostal
POSTEL	postil
ROSTEL	rostel

OSTEN

BOSTEN	Boston
KOSTEN	costean

ŌSTER

BŌSTER	boaster
GŌSTER	ghoster
KŌSTER	coaster, roller coaster
PŌSTER	four-poster, poster, riposter, wall poster
RŌSTER	roaster
THRŌSTER	throwster
TŌSTER	toaster

ÔSTER

ZÔSTER	exhauster

(See **OSTER**)

OSTER

FOSTER	foster
FROSTER	defroster, froster
GLOSTER	Gloucester
GOSTER	snollygoster
KOSTER	accoster, coster, pentecoster
NOSTER	paternoster, Pater Noster
POSTER	imposter
ROSTER	roster
ZOSTER	zoster

(See **ÔSTER**)

OSTERD

FOSTERD	fostered
KOSTERD	costard

ŌSTHOUS

ŌSTHOUS	oasthouse
GŌSTHOUS	ghosthouse
PŌSTHOUS	posthouse

ÔSTIK

KÔSTIK	encaustic, diacaustic, catacaustic, caustic
LÔSTIK	apolaustic

OSTIK

OSTIK	eteostic
KOSTIK	pentacostic
KROSTIK	acrostic, paracrostic, pentacrostic

NOSTIK	agnostic, diagnostic, geognostic, metagnostic, gnostic, prognostic

OSTIL

(See **OSTEL**)

ŌSTING

BŌSTING	boasting
GŌSTING	ghosting
HŌSTING	hosting
KŌSTING	coasting
PŌSTING	posting, riposting
RŌSTING	roasting
TŌSTING	toasting

ÔSTING

ZÔSTING	exhausting

(See **OSTING**)

OSTING

FROSTING	defrosting, frosting
KOSTING	accosting, costing

(See **ÔSTING**)

ÔSTIV, OSTIV

KOSTIV	costive
ZÔSTIV	exhaustive, inexhaustive

ŌSTLĒ

GŌSTLĒ	ghostly
MŌSTLĒ	mostly

ÔSTRAL

ÔSTRAL	austral
KLÔSTRAL	claustral
PLÔSTRAL	plaustral

OSTRAL

KOSTRAL	costrel
NOSTRAL	nostril
ROSTRAL	lamellirostral, longirostral, rostral

OSTRĀT

PROSTRĀT	prostrate
ROSTRĀT	brevirostrate, erostrate, hemirostrate, rostrate

OSTRUM

LOSTRUM	colostrum
NOSTRUM	nostrum
ROSTRUM	rostrum

OSUM

BLOSUM	apple blossom, blossom, cherry blossom, emblossom, fruit blossom, quince blossom, orange blossom, peach blossom, pear blossom (etc.), reblossom
GLOSUM	odontoglossum
POSUM	opossum, possum, water opossum

OSUS

LOSUS	colossus, molossus
NOSUS	Knossos

(See **OS,** add *-es* for imperfect rhyme where appropriate.)

ŌTA

ŌTA	iota, biota
BŌTA	bota
FLŌTA	flota
KŌTA	Dakota, North Dakota, South Dakota
KWŌTA	quota, non-quota
LŌTA	lota, lotah, pelota
PŌTA	sapota
RŌTA	rota
SŌTA	Minnesota
TŌTA	tota

OTA

GOTA	gotta
KOTA	cotta, ricotta, terra-cotta
KROTA	chrotta
POTA	pottah

ŌTAL

(See ŌTL)

OTAL

(See OTL)

ŌTANT

FLŌTANT	flotant
PŌTANT	*impotent*, counterpotent, potent, prepotent

ŌTĀT

NŌTĀT	*annotate*, denotate, notate
RŌTĀT	rotate

ŌTĒ

ŌTĒ	oaty
BLŌTĒ	bloaty
DŌTĒ	dhoti, doty
FLŌTĒ	floaty
GŌTĒ	goaty
HŌTĒ	Don Quixote
LŌTĒ	melote
RŌTĒ	roti
THRŌTĒ	throaty
YŌTĒ	coyote, peyote

ÔTĒ

HÔTĒ	haughty
LÔTĒ	philauty
NÔTĒ	naughty

OTĒ

BLOTĒ	blotty
DOTĒ	dotty
GROTĒ	grotty
HOTĒ	hottie
KLOTĒ	clotty
KOTĒ	cotty, manicotti
NOTĒ	Menotti, knotty
PLOTĒ	plotty
POTĒ	potty
SHOTĒ	shotty
SKOTĒ	Scottie, Scotty
SNOTĒ	snotty
SPOTĒ	spotty
TOTĒ	totty
ZLOTĒ	zloty

(See ÄTĒ)

ŌTED

ŌTED	oated
BLŌTED	bloated
BŌTED	boated, sailboated, steamboated
DŌTED	doted, anecdoted
FLŌTED	floated, refloated
GLŌTED	gloated
GŌTED	goated
KŌTED	frock-coated, coated, morning-coated, party-coated, petticoated, sugar-coated
KWŌTED	quoted, misquoted
MŌTED	demoted, moated, moted, promoted
NŌTED	denoted, connoted, noted, unnoted
THRŌTED	deep-throated, dry-throated, full-throated, honey-throated, red-throated, ruby-throated, swan-throated, throated, yellow-throated
TŌTED	toted
VŌTED	devoted, self-devoted, undevoted, voted

ÔTED

NÔTED	juggernauted
THÔTED	merry-thoughted, sad-thoughted

OTED

OTED	cheviotted
BLOTED	blotted, reblotted, unblotted
DOTED	dotted, redotted, undotted
JOTED	jotted, rejotted, unjotted
KLOTED	clotted, reclotted, unclotted
LOTED	alotted, misalloted, realotted, unalotted
NOTED	knotted, reknotted, unknotted
PLOTED	plotted, replotted, unplotted
POTED	potted, repotted, unpotted
ROTED	carotid, parotid, rotted

SKWOTED	squatted, resquatted
SLOTED	slotted, reslotted, unslotted
SNOTED	resnotted, unsnotted
SOTED	besotted, sotted, unsotted
SPOTED	respotted, spotted, unspotted
STOTED	stotted
SWOTED	reswatted, swatted, unswatted
TOTED	retotted, totted, untotted
TROTED	dogtrotted, foxtrotted, jogtrotted, trotted, turkey-trotted
VOTED	gavotted
YOTED	yachted

ŌTEN

(See ŌTN)

OTEN

GOTEN	*B* begotten, *F* first-begotten, forgotten, *G* gotten, *H* hard-gotten, *I* ill-gotten, *M* misbegotten, misgotten, *U* unbegotten, unforgotten, ungotten
GROTEN	Groton
KOTEN	guncotton, cotton
ROTEN	rotten
SHOTEN	shotten

ŌTENT

(See ŌTANT)

ŌTER

MŌTER	*B* bimotor, *D* demoter, *H* hydromotor, *L* locomotor, *M* magnetomotor, motor, *P* pulmotor, *PR* promoter, *R* remoter, rotomotor, *TR* trimotor, *V* vasomotor
RŌTER	rotor

(See ŌT, add -*er* where appropriate.)

ÔTER

ÔTER	oughter
DÔTER	daughter, goddaughter, granddaughter, stepdaughter
KÔTER	cauter
SLÔTER	manslaughter, slaughter
WÔTER	backwater, breakwater, dishwater, firewater, fizzwater, fresh water, giggle water, limewater, milk-and-water, rosewater, soda water, salt water, shearwater, water, zimmenwater

OTER

OTER	otter
BLOTER	blotter
DOTER	dotter
HOTER	hotter
JOTER	jotter
KLOTER	clotter
KOTER	cotter
NOTER	knotter, unknotter
PLOTER	complotter, plotter, underplotter, unplotter
POTER	potter
ROTER	garotter, rotter
SHOTER	shotter
SKWOTER	squatter
SPOTER	spotter
STOTER	stotter
SWOTER	swatter
TOTER	totter
TROTER	bogtrotter, globetrotter, prom-trotter, trotter
YOTER	yachter

(See **ÄTER**)

ŌTERD

DŌTERD	dotard
GŌTERD	goatherd
MŌTERD	motored

ŌTEST

| MŌTEST | remotest |
| PRŌTEST | protest |

OTHĒ

(TH as in *thin*)

BOTHĒ	bothy
FROTHĒ	frothy
MOTHĒ	mothy
SWOTHĒ	swathy

ÔTHER

(TH as in *thin*)

| ÔTHER | author |

(See **OTHER**, TH as in *thin*)

OTHER

(TH as in *thin*)

| FROTHER | frother |
| MOTHER | mother |

(See **ÔTHER**, TH as in *thin*)

OTHER

(TH as in *then*)

BOTHER	bother
FOTHER	fother
POTHER	pother

(See **ÄTHER**)

ŌTHING

(TH as in *then*)

CLŌTHING	clothing
LŌTHING	loathing
TRŌTHING	betrothing

OTID

(See **OTED**)

ŌTIJ

BŌTIJ	boatage
DŌTIJ	anecdotage, dotage, sacerdotage
FLŌTIJ	floatage, flotage

OTIJ

KLOTIJ	clottage
KOTIJ	cottage
PLOTIJ	plottage

| POTIJ | pottage |
| WOTIJ | wattage |

ŌTIK

ŌTIK	otic
FŌTIK	aphotic, photic, dysphotic
LŌTIK	lotic
RŌTIK	parotic

ÔTIK

| NÔTIK | astronautic, cosmonautic |

(See **OTIK**)

OTIK

OTIK	*A* abiotic, alleotic, amphibiotic, amniotic, antibiotic, antipatriotic, *B* biotic, *E* enzootic, epizootic, *H* halobiotic, *I* idiotic, ichthyotic, iscariotic, *K* chaotic, catabiotic, *M* macrobiotic, microbiotic, meiotic, *N* nebulochaotic, *O* otic, *P* patriotic, periotic, *S* semiotic, symbiotic, *Z* zootic, zoosemiotic
BOTIK	robotic, sybotic, thrombotic
DOTIK	anecdotic, lordotic
DROTIK	hidrotic
FOTIK	kyphotic, morphotic
GLOTIK	diglottic, epiglottic, glottic, polyglottic
GOTIK	argotic, dizygotic, indigotic, legotic, zygotic
KOTIK	dichotic, helcotic, mycotic, narcotic, postpsychotic, prepsychotic, psychotic
KROTIK	acrotic, anacrotic, dicrotic, catacrotic, monocrotic, necrotic, polycrotic, tricrotic
KWOTIK	aquatic
LOTIK	ankylotic, epulotic, culottic, Nilotic, sans-culottic, psilottic

MOTIK	demotic, endosmotic, exosmotic, enzymotic, osmotic, thermotic, seismotic, zymotic
NOTIK	*A* agrypnotic, acapnotic, *B* binotic, *H* henotic, hypnotic, *K* kenotic, *M* melanotic, monotic, *N* neurohypnotic, *O* autohypnotic, *P* pycnotic, posthypnotic, *S* cyanotic, *ST* stenotic
POTIK	despotic, nepotic, thalpotic
ROTIK	*A* amphierotic, *E* erotic, *KL* chlorotic, *N* neurotic, *O* oneirotic, *P* parotic, pyrotic, porotic, *R* rhinocerotic, *S* cerotic, psychoneurotic, *SK* sclerotic, *Z* xerotic
SOTIK	exotic, creosotic, quixotic, loxotic
THOTIK	orthotic, xanthotic
TOTIK	anaptotic, aptotic, asymptotic, entotic
ZOTIK	azotic, exotic, rhizotic

OTIKS

| BOTIKS | robotics |

(See **OTIK,** add *-s* where appropriate.)

ŌTING

BLŌTING	bloating
BŌTING	boating, sail-boating
DŌTING	doting
FLŌTING	floating, refloating
GLŌTING	gloating
KŌTING	coating, sugar-coating
KWŌTING	quoting, misquoting
MŌTING	demoting, promoting
NŌTING	denoting, connoting, noting
TŌTING	toting
VŌTING	devoting, voting

ŌTISH

| ŌTISH | oatish |

BŌTISH	boatish
DŌTISH	dotish
GŌTISH	goatish

OTISH

HOTISH	hottish
SHOTISH	schottische
SKOTISH	Scottish
SOTISH	sottish

ŌTIST

DŌTIST	anecdotist
NŌTIST	noticed, unnoticed
PRŌTIST	protist
SKŌTIST	Scotist
VŌTIST	votist

ŌTIV

FLŌTIV	floative
MŌTIV	electromotive, emotive, locomotive, motive, promotive
NŌTIV	denotive, connotive
VŌTIV	votive

ŌTL

DŌTL	anecdotal, antidotal, dotal, extradotal, sacerdotal
FŌTL	faustenil
NŌTL	notal
RŌTL	rotal, sclerotal
TŌTL	grand total, subtotal, sumtotal, teetotal, total

OTL

OTL	Quetzalcoatl
BOTL	bluebottle, bottle, greenbottle
DOTL	dottle
GLOTL	epiglottal, glottal
HWOTL	Nahuatl
KOTL	acocotl
KROTL	crottle
LOTL	axolotl
MOTL	mottle
POTL	pottle
ROTL	rotl
THROTL	throttle
TOTL	Aristotle, tottle
TWOTL	twattle
WOTL	wattle

OTLĒ

| HOTLĒ | hotly |
| MOTLĒ | motley |

OTLER

BOTLER	bottler
MOTLER	mottler
THROTLER	throttler
TOTLER	tottler
TWOTLER	twattler
WOTLER	wattler

ŌTLES

(See **ŌT,** add *-less* where appropriate.)

ÔTLES

NÔTLES	aeronautless, argonautless, astronautless, dreadnoughtless, hydronautless, juggernautless, cosmonautless
SLÔTLES	onslaughtless
THÔTLES	thoughtless

OTLES

(See **OT,** add *-less* where appropriate.)

OTLING

(See **OTL,** add *-ing* where appropriate.)

ŌTMAN

| BŌTMAN | boatman |
| GŌTMAN | goatman |

ŌTMENT

MŌTMENT	demotement, promotement
NŌTMENT	denotement
VŌTMENT	devotement

OTMENT

| LOTMENT | allotment |
| SOTMENT | besotment |

ŌTN

ŌTN	oaten
KRŌTN	crotin, croton
PRŌTN	proton

ŌTŌ

FŌTŌ	photo, telephoto
KŌTŌ	koto
MŌTŌ	con moto, Mr. Moto
RŌTŌ	roto
TŌTŌ	in toto
VŌTŌ	divoto, ex voto

OTŌ

OTŌ	otto, Otto
BLOTŌ	blotto
DOTŌ	ridotto
GOTŌ	fagotto
JOTŌ	jotto
KOTŌ	staccato
LOTŌ	lotto
MOTŌ	motto
POTŌ	potto
SOTŌ	risotto
WOTŌ	Watteau

(See ÄTŌ)

ŌTON

(See ŌTN)

ŌTSĒ

NOTSĒ	Nazi
ROTSĒ	paparazzi, ROTC
TOTSĒ	hotsy-totsy

OTSMAN

| SKOTSMAN | Scotsman |
| YOTSMAN | yachtsman |

ŌTUM

KWŌTUM	quotum
NŌTUM	notum, pronotum
SKRŌTUM	scrotum
TŌTUM	factotum, teetotum, totem, totum

ŌTUS

BRŌTUS	brotus
KRŌTUS	macrotous
LŌTUS	lotus
MŌTUS	amotus
NŌTUS	gymnotus, Notus
SKŌTUS	Duns Scotus

OUAN

| GOUAN | gowan |
| ROUAN | rowan, rowen |

OUANS

| LOUANS | allowance, disallowance |
| VOUANS | avowance, disavowance |

OUARD

| KOUARD | coward |

(See **OUER,** add *-ed* where appropriate.)

OUCHĒ

GROUCHĒ	grouchy
KROUCHĒ	crouchy
POUCHĒ	pouchy
SLOUCHĒ	slouchy

OUCHER

GROUCHER	groucher
KOUCHER	coucher
KROUCHER	croucher
POUCHER	poucher
SLOUCHER	sloucher
VOUCHER	avoucher, voucher

OUCHING

(See **OUCH,** add *-ing* where appropriate.)

OUDA

| GOUDA | gouda |
| HOUDA | howdah |

OUDĒ

DOUDĒ	apple-pan dowdy, dowdy, pandowdy, rowdy-dowdy
GOUDĒ	Goudy
HOUDĒ	howdie, howdy
KLOUDĒ	cloudy, uncloudy
KROUDĒ	crowdy
LOUDĒ	cum laude, magna cum laude, summa cum laude
PROUDĒ	proudy
ROUDĒ	rowdy
SHROUDĒ	shroudy
TOUDĒ	towdy

OUDED

KLOUDED	beclouded, enclouded, interclouded, clouded, overclouded, reclouded, thunderclouded, unclouded
KROUDED	crowded, overcrowded
SHROUDED	beshrouded, disenshrouded, enshrouded, reshrouded, shrouded, unshrouded

OUDER

CHOUDER	clam chowder, chowder
KROUDER	crowder
LOUDER	louder
POUDER	baking powder, bepowder, face powder, gunpowder, powder, Seidlitz powder
PROUDER	prouder

OUDING

KLOUDING	beclouding, clouding, unclouding
KROUDING	crowding, overcrowding
SHROUDING	enshrouding, shrouding
STROUDING	strouding

OUDISH

LOUDISH	loudish
PROUDISH	proudish

OUDLĒ

LOUDLĒ	loudly
PROUDLĒ	proudly

OUDNES

LOUDNES	loudness
PROUDNES	proudness

OUĒ

DOUĒ	dowie
KOUĒ	cowy
WOUĒ	wowie
ZOUĒ	zowy

OUEL

BOUEL	bowel, disembowel, embowel
DOUEL	dowel
HOUEL	howel
KOUEL	cowal
NOUEL	nowel
ROUEL	rowel
TOUEL	towel
TROUEL	trowel

MAY I INTRODUCE ALISTOR CHANCELLAIR?

When announcers announce
John Chancellor,
Why do they pronounce
The name they announce
As if it rhymed with *or?*
I'd think he'd prefer
Ur.

They don't rhyme Alistair
Cooke with *air.*
Alistair, sir,
They end with *ur,*
And I should say
He likes it that way.

Now if Chancellor
Were spelled Chancellair,
And if Alistair
Were spelled Alistor,
Which would rhyme with *ur,*
And which with *or?*
Or would one rhyme with *air?*
You say you don't care?

Well, just you try to stand up in a crowd
And say this verse right—off the cuff—out loud.

VOUEL	avowal, disavowal, semivowel, vowel

(See **OUL**)

OUER

BOUER	bower, embower, imbower
DOUER	dower, endower
FLOUER	*B* beflower, bloodflower, *D* dayflower, deflower, *E* enflower, *F* fameflower, fanflower, flower, *G* gillyflower, *GR* grapeflower, *K* cauliflower, coneflower, cornflower, lampflower, *M* Mayflower, mistflower, moonflower, *P* passion flower, *S* safflower, sunflower, *SH* shoeflower, *T* tongueflower, *W* wallflower, windflower (etc.)
GLOUER	glower
KOUER	cower
LOUER	allower, lower
PLOUER	plougher, plower
POUER	empower, electric power, flower power, horsepower, candlepower, manpower, overpower, power, steam power, student power, superpower, waterpower
ROUER	rower
SHOUER	shower, thundershower
TOUER	beacontower, churchtower, fire tower, overtower, tower, watchtower
VOUER	avower, disavower, vower
WOUER	wower

(See **OUR**)

OUHAND

KOUHAND	cowhand
PLOUHAND	plowhand

OUHOUS

BOUHOUS	Bauhaus
CHOUHOUS	chowhouse

OUING

WOUING	bowwowing
YOUING	meowing

(See **OU,** add *-ing* where appropriate.)

OULĒ

OULĒ	owly
GROULĒ	growly
HOULĒ	haole
SKOULĒ	scowly

OULER

OULER	owler
FOULER	fouler, fowler
GROULER	growler
HOULER	howler
PROULER	prowler
SKOULER	scowler
YOULER	yowler

OULET

OULET	owlet
HOULET	howlet
ROULET	rowlet

OULING

OULING	owling
FOULING	befouling, fouling, fowling
GROULING	growling
HOULING	howling
KOULING	cowling
PROULING	prowling
SKOULING	scowling

OULISH

OULISH	owlish
FOULISH	foulish
GROULISH	growlish

OUMENT

DOUMENT	endowment

LOUMENT allowment, disallowment
VOUMENT avowment, disavowment

OUNDED

(See **OUND,** add *-ed* where appropriate.)

OUNDER

BOUNDER bounder, rebounder
FLOUNDER flounder
FOUNDER dumfounder, founder, iron founder, confounder, profounder, type founder
HOUNDER hounder
POUNDER expounder, four-pounder, hundred-pounder (etc.), impounder, compounder, pounder, propounder
ROUNDER rounder, surrounder
SOUNDER sounder
STOUNDER astounder
ZOUNDER resounder

OUNDIJ

GROUNDIJ groundage
POUNDIJ impoundage, poundage
SOUNDIJ soundage

OUNDING

BOUNDING abounding, bounding
SOUNDING big-sounding, deep-sounding, evil-sounding, high-sounding, low-sounding (etc.), sounding

(See **OUND,** add *-ing* where appropriate.)

OUNDLĒ

FOUNDLĒ profoundly
ROUNDLĒ roundly
SOUNDLĒ soundly, unsoundly

OUNDLES

BOUNDLES boundless

GROUNDLES groundless
SOUNDLES soundless

OUNDLING

FOUNDLING foundling
GROUNDLING groundling

OUNDMĒL

GROUNDMĒL groundmeal
STOUNDMĒL stoundmeal

OUNDNES

FOUNDNES profoundness
ROUNDNES roundness
SOUNDNES soundness, unsoundness

OUNĒ

BROUNĒ brownie, browny
DOUNĒ downy
FROUNĒ frowny
KLOUNĒ clowny
TOUNĒ towny

OUNER

BROUNER browner
DOUNER downer, sundowner
DROUNER drowner
FROUNER frowner
KROUNER crowner
TOUNER downtowner, out-of-tower, towner, uptowner

OUNING

BROUNING browning, Browning
DOUNING downing
DROUNING drowning
FROUNING frowning
GOUNING gowning
KLOUNING clowning
KROUNING crowning, encrowning

OUNISH

(See **OUN,** add *-ish* where appropriate.)

OUNJER

LOUNJER lounger
SKROUNJER scrounger

OUNJING

LOUNJING lounging
SKROUNJING scrounging

OUNLES

DOUNLES downless
GOUNLES gownless
KLOUNLES clownless
KROUNLES crownless
TOUNLES townless

OUNSER

BOUNSER bouncer
FLOUNSER flouncer
NOUNSER announcer, denouncer, pronouncer, renouncer
POUNSER pouncer
TROUNSER trouncer

OUNSING

(See **OUNS,** add *-ing* where appropriate.)

OUNTĒ

BOUNTĒ bounty
KOUNTĒ county, viscounty
MOUNTĒ Mountie

OUNTED

(See **OUNT,** add *-ed* where appropriate.)

OUNTER

KOUNTER accounter, discounter, encounter, counter, reencounter, recounter
MOUNTER mounter, remounter, surmounter

OUNTIN

FOUNTIN fountain
MOUNTIN catamountain, cat o' mountain, man-mountain, mountain

OUNTING

KOUNTING	accounting, discounting, counting, miscounting, recounting
MOUNTING	amounting, dismounting, mounting, remounting, surmounting

OUNWERD

DOUNWERD	downward
TOUNWERD	townward

OUNZMAN

GOUNZMAN	gownsman
TOUNZMAN	townsman

OURĒ

CHOURĒ	chowry
DOURĒ	dowry
FLOURĒ	floury, flowery
HOURĒ	houri
KOURĒ	kauri, cowrie, cowry
LOURĒ	loury, lowery
MOURĒ	Maori
VOURĒ	avowry

OURER

FLOURER	deflowerer
LOURER	lourer, lowerer
SKOURER	scourer
SOURER	sourer
VOURER	devourer

(See **OUER,** add *-er* where appropriate.)

OURING

SKOURING	bescouring, off-scouring, scouring

(See **OUR, OUER,** add *-ing* where appropriate.)

OURLĒ

OURLĒ	half-hourly, quarter-hourly, hourly

DOURLĒ	dourly
SOURLĒ	sourly

OURNES

DOURNES	dourness
SOURNES	sourness

OUSBRĒCH

HOUSBRĒCH	housebreach
SPOUSBRĒCH	spousebreach

OUSING

BLOUSING	blousing
DOUSING	dousing
MOUSING	mousing
SOUSING	sousing

OUSTED

OUSTED	ousted
JOUSTED	jousted
ROUSTED	rousted

OUSTER

OUSTER	ouster
JOUSTER	jouster
ROUSTER	rouster

OUSTING

(See **OUST,** add *-ing* where appropriate.)

OUTĒ

DOUTĒ	doughty
DROUTĒ	droughty
GOUTĒ	gouty
GROUTĒ	grouty
LOUTĒ	louty
POUTĒ	pouty
SNOUTĒ	snouty
SPOUTĒ	spouty
TOUTĒ	touty
TROUTĒ	trouty

OUTED

DOUTED	doubted
FLOUTED	flouted
GROUTED	grouted
KLOUTED	clouted

NOUTED	knouted
POUTED	pouted
ROUTED	derouted, routed
SHOUTED	shouted
SKOUTED	scouted
SMOUTED	smouted
SNOUTED	snouted
SPOUTED	spouted
SPROUTED	resprouted, sprouted
TOUTED	touted

OUTER

OUTER	down-and-outer, far-outer, in-and-outer, out-and-outer, outer
BOUTER	bouter
DOUTER	doubter, nondoubter
FLOUTER	flouter
GROUTER	grouter
JOUTER	jowter
KLOUTER	clouter
KROUTER	sauerkrauter
NOUTER	knouter
POUTER	pouter
ROUTER	router
SHOUTER	shouter
SKOUTER	scouter
SPOUTER	spouter
SPROUTER	sprouter
STOUTER	stouter
TOUTER	touter
TROUTER	trouter
VOUTER	devouter

OUTING

(See **OUT,** add *-ing* where appropriate.)

OUTISH

OUTISH	outish
LOUTISH	loutish
STOUTISH	stoutish

OUTLĒ

STOUTLĒ	stoutly
VOUTLĒ	devoutly

OUTNES

STOUTNES	stoutness
VOUTNES	devoutness

OUWOU

BOUWOU	bowwow

POUWOU	powwow
WOUWOU	wou-wou, wow-wow

OUZAL

(See **OUZL**)

OUZĒ

BLOUZĒ	blousy, blowzy
BOUZĒ	bousy
DROUZĒ	drowsy
FROUZĒ	frowsy, frowzy
GROUZĒ	grousy
HOUZĒ	housy
LOUZĒ	lousy
MOUZĒ	mousy
SPOUZĒ	spousy

OUZEL

(See **OUZL**)

OUZER

BOUZER	bouser, bowser
BROUZER	browser
DOUZER	douser, dowser
HOUZER	houser
MOUZER	Mauser, mouser
ROUZER	arouser, carouser, rouser
POUZER	espouser
SHNOUZER	schnauzer
TOUZER	towser
TROUZER	trouser
WOUZER	wowser
YOUZER	yowzer

OUZERZ

TROUZERZ	trousers

(See **OUZER**, add -s where appropriate.)

OUZIJ

HOUZIJ	housage
SPOUZIJ	espousage, spousage

OUZING

(See **OUZ**, add -ing where appropriate.)

OUZL

OUZL	ousel, ouzel
HOUZL	housal, housel

POUZL	espousal
SPOUZL	spousal
ROUZL	arousal, carousal
TOUZL	tousle

OUZLD

HOUZLD	houselled, unhouselled
TOUZLD	tousled, untousled

ŌVA

ŌVA	ova
HŌVA	Jehovah
KŌVA	Markova
LŌVA	Pavlova
NŌVA	ars nova, bossa nova, Casanova, nova, supernova, Villanova
RŌVA	korova

ŌVĒ

CHŌVĒ	anchovy
GRŌVĒ	grovy

OVEL

GROVEL	grovel
HOVEL	hovel
NOVEL	novel

(See **UVEL**)

ŌVEN

HŌVEN	hoven
KLŌVEN	cloven, uncloven
WŌVEN	interwoven, inwoven, rewoven, woven

ŌVER

ŌVER	CH changeover, FL flashover, flyover, flopover, H half-seas-over, hangover, KR crossover, L leftover, M moreover, O over, P Passover, pullover, pushover, R wrapover, runover, SL sleepover, slipover, ST stopover, T turnover, W walkover

DŌVER	Andover, Dover
DRŌVER	drover
KLŌVER	four-leaf clover, in clover, clover, sweet clover
NŌVER	Hanover
PLŌVER	plover
RŌVER	rover, sea rover
STŌVER	stover
TRŌVER	trover

ŌVERZ

TŌVERZ	estovers, leftovers

(See **ŌVER**, add -s where appropriate.)

ŌVĪN

ŌVĪN	ovine
BŌVĪN	bovine

ŌVING

KŌVING	coving
RŌVING	roving
SHRŌVING	shroving
STŌVING	stoving

ŌVŌ

ŌVŌ	ab ovo
NŌVŌ	de novo
PRŌVŌ	provost

ŌYER

ŌYER	oyer
BŌYER	bowyer

ÔYER

BÔYER	buoyer
LÔYER	lawyer, delawyer
SÔYER	sawyer, topsawyer

(See **OIER**)

ŌZA

NŌZA	Spinoza
PŌZA	Mariposa

ŌZAL

(See **ŌZEL**)

ÔZAL

KLÔZAL	clausal
KÔZAL	causal
PÔZAL	pausal

ŌZAL

PŌZAL	deposal, disposal, interposal, opposal, presupposal, reposal, supposal, transposal
RŌZAL	rosal

ŌZĒ

DŌZĒ	dozy
FŌZĒ	fozy
KŌZĒ	egg cozy, cosy, cozy, tea cozy
MŌZĒ	mozey
NŌZĒ	nosy
PŌZĒ	posy
PRŌZĒ	prosy
RŌZĒ	rosy
TŌZĒ	tosy, tozee, tozie

ÔZĒ

GÔZĒ	gauzy
KÔZĒ	causey
LÔZĒ	lawsie

ŌZĒD

PŌZĒD	posied
RŌZĒD	rosied

ŌZEL

LÔZEL	losel
PŌZEL	deposal, disposal, opposal, proposal, supposal, transposal

ŌZEN

CHŌZEN	chosen, forechosen
FRŌZEN	frozen
HŌZEN	hosen
RŌZEN	rosen
SKWŌZEN	squozen

ŌZER

DŌZER	bulldozer, dozer
GLŌZER	glozer
HŌZER	hoser
KLŌZER	discloser, encloser, forecloser, incloser, closer, uncloser
NŌZER	noser
PŌZER	D decomposer, deposer, disposer, E exposer, I imposer, interposer, J juxtaposer, K composer, O opposer, P poser, PR predisposer, presupposer, proposer, R reimposer, reposer, S superimposer, supposer, TR transposer
PRŌZER	proser
RŌZER	roser

ÔZER

HÔZER	hawser
KÔZER	first causer, causer
PÔZER	pauser

OZET

(See OZIT)

ŌZHA

BRŌZHA	ambrosia
MŌZHA	afrormosia

ŌZHER

ŌZHER	osier
HŌZHER	hosier
KLŌZHER	disclosure, enclosure, foreclosure, inclosure, closure
KRŌZHER	crosier
PŌZHER	discomposure, disposure, exposure, composure, superimposure

(See Ō'ZI.ER)

ŌZHUN

KLŌZHUN	eclosion
KŌZHUN	icosian
PLŌZHUN	applosion, explosion, implosion, plosion
RŌZHUN	erosion, corrosion

ŌZING

(See ŌZ, add -ing where appropriate.)

ÔZING

KÔZING	causing
PÔZING	pausing

OZIT

KLOZIT	closet
POZIT	deposit, interposit, juxtaposit, composite, oviposit, posit, reposit

OZL

NOZL	nozzle
SHNOZL	schnozzle
SNOZL	snozzle
SOZL	sozzle

OZMIK

OZMIK	aosmic, osmic
DOZMIK	endosmic
KOZMIK	cosmic, macrocosmic, microcosmic, neocosmic

ŌZŪR

(See ŌZHER)

ŪA

SKŪA	skua
SŪA	Apologia Pro Vita Sua
TŪA	atua

(See O͞OA)

ŪAL

DŪAL	dual, duel, subdual
FŪAL	fuel, refuel, synfuel
HŪAL	hwyl
NŪAL	newel, renewal, urban renewal
SŪAL	pursual
TŪAL	tewel
VŪAL	reviewal

(See O͞OEL)

ŪANS

NŪANS   renewance, nuance
SŪANS   pursuance

(See $\overline{OO}$ANS)

ŪANT

FLŪANT   fluent, perfluent
SŪANT   pursuant, suant

(See $\overline{OO}$ANT)

ŪARD

(See $\overline{OO}$ARD)

ŪBA

JŪBA   Juba, jubbah
KŪBA   Cuba
SŪBA   subah, tsuba
TŪBA   saxtuba, tuba

(See $\overline{OO}$BA)

ŪBÂL

KŪBÂL   cue ball

(See $\overline{OO}$BÂL)

ŪBAL

KŪBAL   cubal
TŪBAL   tubal

(See $\overline{OO}$BAL)

ŪBĒ

KŪBĒ   cuby

(See $\overline{OO}$BĒ)

UBĒ

BUBĒ   bubby
CHUBĒ   chubby
FUBĒ   fubby
GRUBĒ   grubby
HUBĒ   hubby
KLUBĒ   clubby
KUBĒ   cubby
NUBĒ   knubby, nubby

RUBĒ   Rabi, Rubbee
SHRUBĒ   shrubby
SKRUBĒ   scrubby
SLUBĒ   slubby
STUBĒ   stubby
TUBĒ   tubby

ŪBER

KŪBER   Khubur, cuber
SŪBER   suber
TŪBER   tubar, tuber

(See $\overline{OO}$BER)

UBER

BLUBER   blubber
DRUBER   drubber
DUBER   dubber, redubber
FLUBER   flubber
GLUBER   glubber
GRUBER   grubber, money-
                grubber
HUBER   hubber
KLUBER   clubber
LUBER   *landlubber,* lubber
RUBER   India rubber, rubber
SKRUBER   scrubber
SLUBER   slubber
SNUBER   snubber
STUBER   stubber
TUBER   tubber

UBERD

BLUBERD   blubbered
HUBERD   Mother Hubbard
KUBERD   cupboard
RUBERD   rubbered

ŪBĒZ

PŪBĒZ   pubes

(See $\overline{OO}$BĒZ)

ŪBIJ

KŪBIJ   cubage
TŪBIJ   tubage

ŪBIK

KŪBIK   cubic
PŪBIK   pubic

(See $\overline{OO}$BIK)

UBIN

DUBIN   dubbin
NUBIN   nubbin

ŪBING

KŪBING   cubing
TŪBING   tubing

(See $\overline{OO}$BING)

UBING

(See **UB,** add *-ing* where appropriate.)

UBISH

GRUBISH   grubbish
KLUBISH   clubbish
KUBISH   cubbish
RUBISH   rubbish
SHRUBISH   shrubbish
SNUBISH   snubbish

ŪBIT

KŪBIT   cubit

(See $\overline{OO}$BIT)

ŪBL

KŪBL   cubal
TŪBL   tubal

(See $\overline{OO}$BL)

UBL

BUBL   bubble, hubble-bubble
DUBL   daily double, double,
                redouble, subdouble
HUBL   hubble
NUBL   nubble
RUBL   rubble
STUBL   stubble
TRUBL   trouble

UBLD

BUBLD   bubbled
DUBLD   doubled, redoubled
STUBLD   stubbled
TRUBLD   troubled

UBLĒ

BUBLĒ	bubbly
DUBLĒ	doubly
HUBLĒ	hubbly
NUBLĒ	knubbly, nubbly
RUBLĒ	rubbly
STRUBLĒ	strubbly
STUBLĒ	stubbly

ŪBLET

KŪBLET	cubelet
TŪBLET	tubelet

UBLER

RUBLER	rubbler

(See **UBL,** add *-r* where appropriate.)

UBLET

DUBLET	doublet
KUBLET	cublet
SUBLET	sublet

UBLING

(See **UBL,** add *-ing* where appropriate.)

UBLZ

FUBLZ	mubble-fubbles

(See **UBL,** add *-s* where appropriate.)

ŪBRIK

(See **OOBRIK**)

UBSTĀK

GRUBSTĀK	grubstake
KLUBSTĀK	club steak

ŪCHĒ

(See **OOCHĒ**)

UCHĒ

DUCHĒ	archduchy, duchy
KLUCHĒ	clutchy
SMUCHĒ	smutchy
TUCHĒ	touchy

ŪCHER

BLŪCHER	blucher
FŪCHER	future
PŪCHER	puture
SŪCHER	suture

(See **OOCHER**)

UCHER

DUCHER	Dutcher
HUCHER	hutcher
KLUCHER	clutcher
RUCHER	rutcher
SKUCHER	scutcher
SMUCHER	smutcher
TUCHER	retoucher, toucher

UCHING

(See **UCH,** add *-ing* where appropriate.)

ŪDA

MŪDA	Bermuda

(See **OODA**)

ŪDAL

(See **ŪDL, OODL**)

ŪDĒ

FŪDĒ	feudee, feudy
MŪDĒ	almude
NŪDĒ	nudie

(See **OODĒ**)

UDĒ

BLUDĒ	bloody
BUDĒ	buddy, anybody, everybody, nobody, somebody
DUDĒ	fuddy-duddy
KRUDĒ	cruddy
KUDĒ	cuddy
MUDĒ	muddy
NUDĒ	nuddy
PUDĒ	puddy
RUDĒ	ruddy
SKUDĒ	scuddy
STUDĒ	brown study, microstudy, overstudy, studdy, study, understudy
SUDĒ	soapsuddy

ŪDED

(See **ŪD, OOD,** add *-d, -ed* where appropriate.)

UDĒD

BLUDĒD	bloodied
MUDĒD	muddied
RUDĒD	ruddied
STUDĒD	overstudied, studied, understudied, unstudied

UDED

STUDED	star-studded

(See **UD,** add *-ed* where appropriate.)

ŪDENS

(See **OODENS**)

ŪDENT

STŪDENT	student

(See **OODENT**)

ŪDER

LŪDER	alluder, deluder, eluder, lewder
NŪDER	denuder, nuder
SŪDER	sudor
TŪDER	Tudor

(See **OODER**)

UDER

UDER	udder
CHUDER	chudder
DUDER	dudder
FLUDER	flooder
JUDER	judder
MUDER	mudder
PUDER	pudder
RUDER	rudder
SHUDER	shudder
SKUDER	scudder
SUDER	sudder

UDIJ

BUDIJ	buddage
FLUDIJ	floodage

ŪDIK

LŪDIK	paludic
PŪDIK	antipudic, pudic

ŪDING

FŪDING	feuding
NŪDING	denuding
SŪDING	exuding, transuding
ZŪDING	exuding

(See ŌŌD, add -ing where appropriate.)

UDING

BLUDING	blooding
BUDING	budding
FLUDING	flooding
KUDING	cudding
MUDING	mudding
RUDING	rudding
SKUDING	scudding
SPUDING	spudding
STUDING	bestudding, studding, unstudding
SUDING	sudding
THUDING	thudding

ŪDISH

DŪDISH	dudish
NŪDISH	nudish

(See ŌŌDISH)

ŪDIST

FŪDIST	feudist
NŪDIST	nudist

(See ŌŌDIST)

ŪDL

ŪDL	udal, kiyoodle
FŪDL	feudal
LŪDL	paludal

(See ŌŌDL)

UDL

BUDL	buddle
FUDL	befuddle, fuddle
HUDL	huddle
KUDL	cuddle
MUDL	bemuddle, muddle
NUDL	nuddle
PUDL	puddle
RUDL	ruddle
SKUDL	scuddle
STUDL	studdle

UDLD

(See UDL, add -ed where appropriate.)

ŪDLĒ

LŪDLĒ	lewdly
NŪDLĒ	nudely

(See ŌŌDLĒ)

UDLĒ

FUDLĒ	fuddly
KUDLĒ	cuddly
PUDLĒ	puddly

UDLER

FUDLER	befuddler, fuddler
HUDLER	huddler
KUDLER	cuddler
MUDLER	muddler
PUDLER	puddler

UDLING

(See UDL, add -ing where appropriate.)

ŪDNES

LŪDNES	lewdness
NŪDNES	nudeness

(See ŌŌDNES)

ŪDŌ

SŪDŌ	pseudo
TŪDŌ	testudo, consuetudo

(See ŌŌDŌ)

ŪDŌŌ

(See ŌŌDŌŌ)

UDUK

PUDUK	puddock
RUDUK	ruddock

Ū Ē

DŪĒ	bedewy, dewy, Dewey, mildewy
STŪĒ	stewy
THŪĒ	thewy

(See ŌŌĒ)

ŪEL

(See ŪAL, ŌŌEL)

ŪER

ŪER	ewer
DŪER	subduer
FŪER	fewer
HŪER	hewer
NŪER	newer, renewer
SŪER	ensuer, pursuer, sewer, suer
VŪER	interviewer, viewer

(See ŌŌER)

ŪERD

SŪERD	sewered
SKŪERD	skewered
STŪERD	steward

(See ŌŌERD)

ŪET

(See ŌŌET)

ŪFA

(See ŌŌFA)

ŪFĒ

(See ŌŌFĒ)

UFĒ

BLUFĒ	bluffy
BUFĒ	buffy

CHUFĒ	chuffy
FLUFĒ	fluffy
FUFĒ	fuffy
GUFĒ	guffy
HUFĒ	huffy
KUFĒ	cuffy
PLUFĒ	pluffy
PUFĒ	puffy
RUFĒ	roughie, ruffy
SKRUFĒ	scruffy
SLUFĒ	sloughy
SNUFĒ	snuffy
STUFĒ	stuffy
TUFĒ	toughy

UFEN

(See **UFIN**)

ŪFER

(See **OOFER**)

UFER

BLUFER	bluffer
BUFER	buffer
CHUFER	chuffer
DUFER	duffer
FLUFER	fluffer
GRUFER	gruffer
GUFER	guffer
HUFER	huffer
KUFER	cuffer
LUFER	luffer
MUFER	muffer
PLUFER	pluffer
PUFER	puffer
RUFER	rougher, ruffer
SKUFER	scuffer
SLUFER	slougher, sluffer
SNUFER	snuffer
STUFER	stocking-stuffer, stuffer
SUFER	suffer
TUFER	tougher

UFET

BUFET	buffet
FUFET	fuffit
MUFET	Little Miss Muffet
TUFET	tuffet

UFIN

BUFEN	buffin
GUFEN	guffin
MUFEN	muffin, ragamuffin

PUFEN	puffin
RUFEN	mumruffin, roughen
TUFEN	toughen

ŪFING

(See **OOFING**)

UFING

(See **UF,** add *-ing* where appropriate.)

UFISH

(See **UF,** add *-ish* where appropriate.)

UFIT

(See **UFET**)

UFL

BUFL	buffle
DUFL	duffle
FUFL	fuffle, kerfuffle
HWUFL	whuffle
MUFL	bemuffle, muffle, unmuffle
RUFL	ruffle, unruffle
SHUFL	double shuffle, reshuffle, shuffle
SKUFL	scuffle
SNUFL	snuffle
TRUFL	truffle

UFLD

(See **UFL,** add *-d* where appropriate.)

UFLĒ

BLUFLĒ	bluffly
GRUFLĒ	gruffly
MUFLĒ	muffly
RUFLĒ	roughly, ruffly
SKUFLĒ	scuffly
SNUFLĒ	snuffly
TRUFLĒ	truffly
TUFLĒ	toughly

UFLER

MUFLER	muffler
RUFLER	ruffler
SHUFLER	shuffler
SKUFLER	scuffler
SNUFLER	snuffler

UFLING

(See **UFL,** add *-ing* where appropriate.)

UFNES

(See **UF,** add *-ness* where appropriate.)

UFTĒ

MUFTĒ	mufti
TUFTĒ	tufty

ŪFUS

(See **OOFUS**)

ŪGA

(See **OOGA**)

ŪGAL

(See **ŪGL**)

ŪGAR

(See **OOGER**)

ŪGĒ

(See **OOGĒ**)

UGĒ

BUGĒ	buggy
DRUGĒ	druggie
FUGĒ	fuggy
LUGĒ	luggie, luggy
MUGĒ	muggy
PLUGĒ	pluggy
PUGĒ	puggi, puggy
RUGĒ	ruggy
SHUGĒ	shuggy
SLUGĒ	sluggy
THUGĒ	thuggee
VUGĒ	vuggy

ŪGER

(See **OOGER**)

UGER

BUGER	bugger
CHUGER	chugger
DRUGER	drugger
HUGER	hugger
LUGER	luggar, lugger

MUGER huggermugger,
cuggermugger,
mugger
NUGER nugger
PLUGER plugger
PUGER pugger
RUGER rugger
SHRUGER shrugger
SLUGER slugger
SMUGER smugger
SNUGER snugger
TUGER tugger

UGET

DRUGET drugget
MUGET mugget
NUGET nugget

UGING

(See **UG,** add -ing where appropriate.)

UGISH

(See **UG,** add -ish where appropriate.)

ŪGL

BŪGL bugle
FŪGL febrifugal, fugal,
fugle, vermifugal

(See **OOGL**)

UGL

GUGL guggle
JUGL juggle
PUGL puggle
SMUGL smuggle
SNUGL snuggle
STRUGL death struggle,
struggle

UGLĒ

UGLĒ plug-ugly, ugli, ugly
GUGLĒ guggly
JUGLĒ juggly
SMUGLĒ smugly
SNUGLĒ snugly
STRUGLĒ struggly

ŪGLER

BŪGLER bugler
FŪGLER fugler

UGLER

JUGLER juggler
SMUGLER smuggler
SNUGLER snuggler
STRUGLER struggler

UGLING

(See **UGL,** add -ing where appropriate.)

UGNES

SMUGNES smugness
SNUGNES snugness

ŪĪD

SKŪĪD skew-eyed

(See **OOĪD**)

ŪĪJ

SŪĪJ sewage

(See **OOĪJ**)

ŪĪK

BŪĪK Buick

(See **OOĪK**)

ŪĪNG

(See **Ū, OO,** add -ing where appropriate.)

ŪĪSH

NŪĪSH newish

(See **OOĪSH**)

ŪĪST

VŪĪST revuist, reviewist

(See **OOĪST**)

ŪJĒ

(See **OOJĒ**)

UJĒ

FUJĒ fudgy
PUJĒ pudgy
SLUJĒ sludgy
SMUJĒ smudgy

UJER

BUJER budger
DRUJER drudger
FUJER fudger
GRUJER begrudger, grudger
JUJER adjudger, forejudger,
judger, misjudger,
prejudger, rejudger
NUJER nudger
SLUJER sludger
SMUJER smudger
TRUJER trudger

UJING

(See **UJ,** add -ing where appropriate.)

UJUN

BLUJUN bludgeon
DUJUN dudgeon,
humdudgeon
GUJUN gudgeon
MUJUN curmudgeon
TRUJUN trudgeon

ŪKA

(See **OOKA**)

UKA

BUKA bucca
LUKA felucca
PUKA pucka, pukka
YUKA yuca, yucca

ŪKAL

DŪKAL archducal, ducal
LŪKAL noctilucal
NŪKAL nucal, nuchal
TŪKAL pentateuchal

(See **OOKAL**)

ŪKAN

LŪKAN antelucan

(See **OOKAN**)

ŪKĒ

(See $\overline{OO}$KĒ)

UKĒ

BUKĒ	buckie, bucky
DUKĒ	ducky
KLUKĒ	clucky
LUKĒ	lucky, unlucky
MUKĒ	mucky
PLUKĒ	plucky
TRUKĒ	truckie
TUKĒ	Kentucky, tucky
YUKĒ	yucky

ŪKER

ŪKER	euchre
BŪKER	rebuker
PŪKER	puker

(See $\overline{OO}$KER)

UKER

BUKER	bucker
CHUKER	chucker, chukker
DUKER	ducker
KLUKER	clucker
MUKER	mucker
PLUKER	plucker
PUKER	pucker
SHUKER	clam-shucker, oyster-shucker, shucker
SUKER	bloodsucker, goatsucker, honeysucker, all-day sucker, sapsucker, seersucker, windsucker, succor, sucker
TRUKER	trucker
TUKER	tucker

UKET

BUKET	bucket, gutbucket, milk bucket, water bucket
MUKET	mucket
TUKET	Nantucket, Pawtucket, tucket

UKIJ

PLUKIJ	pluckage
SUKIJ	suckage
TRUKIJ	truckage

ŪKING

BŪKING	rebuking
PŪKING	puking

UKING

(See **UK,** add -ing where appropriate.)

UKISH

BUKISH	buckish
MUKISH	muckish
PUKISH	puckish

UKL

BRUKL	bruckle
BUKL	buccal, buckle, parbuckle, swashbuckle, turnbuckle, unbuckle
CHUKL	chuckle
HUKL	huckle
MUKL	muckle
NUKL	knuckle
SUKL	honeysuckle, suckle
TRUKL	truckle
YUKL	yukkel

HOBSON'S CHOICE

Feeling sick?
Take your pick:
   Anemia—
   Leukemia—
   Toxemia—
   Uremia—
All ways of dying
Worth trying.

UKLD

BUKLD	buckled, swashbuckled, unbuckled
CHUKLD	chuckled
KUKLD	cuckold
NUKLD	knuckled
SUKLD	suckled
TRUKLD	truckled

UKLER

BUKLER	buckler, swashbuckler
CHUKLER	chuckler
NUKLER	knuckler
SUKLER	suckler
TRUKLER	truckler

UKLES

(See **UK,** add -less)

UKLING

DUKLING	duckling, ugly duckling
SUKLING	suckling

(See **UKL,** change -e to -ing where appropriate.)

UKOLD

(See **UKLD**)

UKSĒ

DRUKSĒ	druxy
LUKSĒ	Biloxi
MUKSĒ	mucksy
PUKSĒ	pucksy, puxy

UKSHUN

DUKSHUN	*A* abduction, adduction, *D* deduction, duction, *E* eduction, eroduction, *I* induction, introduction, *K* conduction, *L* lavoduction, *M* manuduction, mass production, *N* nonconduction, *O* obduction, overproduction, *PR* production, *R* reduction, reproduction, *S* seduction, subduction, superinduction, *TR* traduction, transduction, *U* underproduction
FLUKSHUN	affluxion, defluxion, effluxion, fluxion, influxion, solifluction
RUKSHUN	ruction
STRUKSHUN	destruction, instruction, construction, misconstruction, obstruction, reconstruction, self-destruction, substruction, superstruction
SUKSHUN	suction

UKSUM

BUKSUM	buxom
LUKSUM	lucksome

UKTANS

DUKTANS	inductance, conductance
LUKTANS	reluctance

UKTER

DUKTER	abducter, adductor, ductor, eductor, inductor, introductor, conductor, manuductor, nonconductor, producer, semiconductor
STRUKTER	destructor, instructor, constructor, obstructor, reconstructor

UKTED

(See **UKT,** add *-ed* where appropriate.)

UKTING

(See **UKT,** add *-ing* where appropriate.)

UKTIV

DUKTIV	*A* adductive, *D* deductive, *I* inductive, introductive, *K* conductive, counterproductive, *M* manuductive, *N* nonconductive, *O* overproductive, *PR* productive, *R* reductive, reconductive, reproductive, *S* seductive, superinductive, *TR* traductive, *U* underproductive
STRUKTIV	destructive, instructive, constructive, obstructive, reconstructive, self-destructive, superstructive

UKTOR

(See **UKTER**)

UKTRES

DUKTRES	abductress, introductress, conductress, seductress
STRUKTRES	instructress

ŪKUS

DŪKUS	caducous
FŪKUS	fucous, fucus
LŪKUS	leucous, noctilucous
MŪKUS	mucous, mucus

UKUS

MUKUS	mukkus
RUKUS	ruckus
SUKUS	exsuccus, succus

ŪLA

ŪLA	ula
GŪLA	gula

(See $\overline{\text{OOLA}}$)

ULA

DULA	medulla
GULA	Gullah
KULA	cuculla
MULA	mullah
NULA	nullah, nullanulla
PULA	ampulla
SULA	sulla, Sulla

ULCHER

KULCHER	*A* agriculture, aquaculture, apiculture, arboriculture, aviculture, *B* boviculture, domiculture, *FL* floriculture, *H* horticulture, *I* inculture, *K* counterculture, culture, *M* mariculture, monoculture, *P* pisciculture, pomiculture, puericulture, *S* self-culture, sericulture, sylviculture, *ST* stirpiculture, *T* terraculture, *V* vegeculture, viniculture, viticulture
MULCHER	mulcher, multure
PULCHER	sepulture
VULCHER	vulture

ŪLĒ

DŪLĒ	duly, iconoduly, unduly
GŪLĒ	guly
MŪLĒ	muley
NŪLĒ	newly
THŪLĒ	Thule, Ultima Thule

(See $\overline{\text{OOLĒ}}$)

ULĒ

DULĒ	dully
GULĒ	gully, hully-gully
HULĒ	hully
KULĒ	cully
MULĒ	mulley
SKULĒ	skully
SULĒ	sully

ULĒD

GULĒD	gullied
SULĒD	sullied, unsullied

ULEN

MULEN	mullein, mullen
SULEN	sullen

ŪLER

KŪLER	ridiculer
MŪLER	mewler
PŪLER	puler

(See $\overline{\text{OOLER}}$)

ULER

DULER	duller, medullar
GULER	guller

HULER	dehuller, huller
KRULER	cruller
KULER	discolor, color, culler, miscolor, multicolor, recolor, rose-color, Technicolor, tricolor, versicolor, watercolor
LULER	luller
MULER	muller
NULER	annuller
PULER	ampuller
SKULER	sculler

ULERD

DULERD	dullard
KULERD	*D* discolored, *E* every-colored, *H* high-colored, *K* colored, *M* many-colored, multicolored, *O* overcolored, *P* particolored, party-colored, peach-colored, *R* recolored, rosy-colored, *SK* sky-colored, *U* uncolored, *W* wine-colored (etc.)

ŪLES

(See **Ū**, $\overline{OO}$, **ŪL**, $\overline{OOL}$, add *-less* where appropriate.)

ULET

GULET	gullet
KULET	cullet
MULET	mullet, surmullet

ULGAR

(See **ULGER**)

ULGĀT

ULGĀT	promulgate
VULGĀT	divulgate, evulgate, pervulgate, vulgate

ULGER

BULGER	Bulgar
FULGER	fulgor
VULGER	vulgar

ULIJ

ULIJ	ullage
GULIJ	gullage
KULIJ	cullage
SULIJ	sullage

ŪLING

FŪLING	fueling
KŪLING	ridiculing
MŪLING	mewling, muling
PŪLING	puling

(See $\overline{OO}$LING)

ULING

(See **UL**, add *-ing* where appropriate.)

ŪLIP

TŪLIP	tulip

(See $\overline{OO}$LIP)

ŪLISH

MŪLISH	mulish
PŪLISH	pulish

(See $\overline{OO}$LISH)

ULISH

DULISH	dullish
GULISH	gullish

ULJENS

DULJENS	indulgence, self-indulgence
FULJENS	affulgence, effulgence, refulgence
VULJENS	divulgence

ULJENT

DULJENT	indulgent, self-indulgent
FULJENT	effulgent, fulgent, profulgent, refulgent, circumfulgent
MULJENT	emulgent

ULJER

BULJER	bulger
DULJER	indulger
MULJER	promulger
VULJER	divulger

ULJMENT

DULJMENT	indulgement
VULJMENT	divulgement

ULKĀT

KULKĀT	inculcate
SULKĀT	sulcate, trisulcate

ULKĒ

BULKĒ	bulky
HULKĒ	hulky
SKULKĒ	skulky
SULKĒ	sulky

ULKER

BULKER	bulker
HULKER	hulker
SKULKER	skulker
SULKER	sulker

ULKING

(See **ULK**, add *-ing* where appropriate.)

ULŌ

HULŌ	hullo
NULŌ	nullo

ULPĒ

GULPĒ	gulpy
PULPĒ	pulpy

ULPER

GULPER	gulper
PULPER	pulper
SKULPER	sculper

ULSER

ULSER	ulcer

| PULSER | expulser, pulsar, repulser |
| | |

ULSHUN

ULSHUN	ultion
MULSHUN	demulsion, emulsion
PULSHUN	appulsion, expulsion, impulsion, compulsion, lateropulsion, propulsion, pulsion, repulsion
VULSHUN	avulsion, divulsion, evulsion, convulsion, revulsion

ULSING

| PULSING | expulsing, pulsing, repulsing |
| VULSING | convulsing |

ULSIV

MULSIV	emulsive
PULSIV	appulsive, expulsive, impulsive, compulsive, propulsive, pulsive, repulsive
VULSIV	divulsive, convulsive, revulsive

ULSTER

| ULSTER | Ulster |
| HULSTER | hulster |

ULTANT

| SULTANT | insultant, consultant |
| ZULTANT | exultant, resultant |

ULTED

KULTED	occulted
PULTED	catapulted
SULTED	insulted, consulted
ZULTED	exulted, resulted

ULTER

(See **ULT,** add -er where appropriate.)

ULTING

KULTING	occulting
PULTING	catapulting
SULTING	insulting, consulting
ZULTING	exulting, resulting

ULTIV

KULTIV	occultive
SULTIV	consultive
ZULTIV	exultive, resultive

ULTNES

| DULTNES | adultness |
| KULTNES | occultness |

ULTŪR

(See **ULCHER**.)

ŪLŪ

(See $\overline{OO}\overline{LOO}$.)

ULVER

| HULVER | hulver |
| KULVER | culver |

ULYUN

GULYUN	slubberdegullion, slumgullion
KULYUN	cullion
MULYUN	mullion
RULYUN	rullion
SKULYUN	scullion

ŪMA

ŪMA	Yuma
NŪMA	pneuma
PŪMA	puma

(See $\overline{OO}MA$.)

ŪMAL

(See $\overline{OO}MAL$.)

ŪMAN

(See **ŪMEN**.)

ŪMĀT

| HŪMĀT | exhumate, inhumate |
| PŪMĀT | despumate |

UMBA

BLUMBA	blumba
DUMBA	dumba
LUMBA	calumba, Columba
RUMBA	rumba

UMBEL

(See **UMBL**)

UMBER

UMBER	umber
KLUMBER	clumber
KUMBER	disencumber, encumber, cucumber, cumber, unencumber
LUMBER	lumbar, lumber
NUMBER	number, outnumber, renumber
SLUMBER	slumber

UMBERD

(See **UMBER,** add -ed where appropriate.)

UMBIK

| LUMBIK | columbic |
| PLUMBIK | plumbic |

UMBL

UMBL	umbel, umble
BUMBL	bumble
DRUMBL	drumble
FUMBL	fumble
GRUMBL	grumble
HUMBL	humble
JUMBL	bejumble, jumble
KRUMBL	crumble
MUMBL	mumble
NUMBL	numble
RUMBL	rumble
SKUMBL	scumble
STUMBL	stumble
TUMBL	tumble

UMBLD

(See **UMBL,** add -d where appropriate.)

UMBLĒ

(See **UMBL,** change *-e* to *-y* where appropriate.)

UMBLER

(See **UMBL,** add *-r* where appropriate.)

UMBLING

BUMBLING	bumbling
DRUMBLING	drumbling
FUMBLING	fumbling
GRUMBLING	grumbling
HUMBLING	humbling
JUMBLING	jumbling
KRUMBLING	crumbling
MUMBLING	mumbling
RUMBLING	rumbling
SKUMBLING	scumbling
STUMBLING	stumbling
TUMBLING	tumbling

UMBLZ

UMBLZ	umbles
NUMBLZ	numbles

(See **UMBL,** add *-s* where appropriate.)

UMBŌ

DUMBŌ	Dumbo
GUMBŌ	gumbo
JUMBŌ	jumbo, Jumbo, mumbo-jumbo
LUMBŌ	columbo
PUMBŌ	pumbo

UMBRA

UMBRA	umbra
NUMBRA	penumbra

UMBRAL

UMBRAL	umbral
DUMBRAL	adumbral
NUMBRAL	penumbral
TUMBRAL	tumbrel

UMBRĀT

UMBRĀT	inumbrate, obumbrate
DUMBRĀT	adumbrate

UMBREL

UMBREL	umbral
DUMBREL	adumbral
NUMBREL	penumbral
TUMBREL	tumbrel

UMBRUS

UMBRUS	umbrous
KUMBRUS	cumbrous
NUMBRUS	penumbrous
SLUMBRUS	slumbrous

UMBUS

PLUMBUS	plumbous
LUMBUS	Columbus

ŪMĒ

FŪMĒ	fumy, perfumy
SPŪMĒ	spumy

(See $\overline{OO}$MĒ)

UMĒ

CHUMĒ	chummy
DUMĒ	double dummy, dummy
GLUMĒ	glummy
GUMĒ	gummy
KRUMĒ	crumby, crummie
LUMĒ	Lord lumme, lummy
MUMĒ	mummy
PLUMĒ	plummy
RUMĒ	auction rummy, English rummy, four-hand rummy, Java rummy, gin rummy, Michigan rummy, rummy, Word Rummy
SKRUMĒ	scrummy
SKUMĒ	scummy
SLUMĒ	slummy
THRUMĒ	thrummy
THUMĒ	thumby
TUMĒ	tummy
YUMĒ	yummy

UMEL

GRUMEL	grummel
HUMEL	hummel

PUMEL	bepummel, pommel, pummel
TRUMEL	trummel

ŪMEN

BŪMEN	albumen, albumin
GŪMEN	energumen, hegumen, legumen, legumin, *tegumen*
HŪMEN	human, inhuman, nonhuman, preterhuman, protohuman, superhuman, ultrahuman
KŪMEN	acumen, catechumen
NŪMEN	ichneumon, numen
TŪMEN	bitumen

(See $\overline{OO}$MEN)

ŪMENT

BŪMENT	imbuement
DŪMENT	induement, subduement
NŪMENT	renewment

(See $\overline{OO}$MENT)

ŪMER

FŪMER	fumer, perfumer
HŪMER	bad humor, black humor, good humor, humor, ill-humor, sick humor
LŪMER	illumer
SŪMER	assumer, consumer
TŪMER	costumer
ZŪMER	presumer, resumer

(See $\overline{OO}$MER)

UMER

BUMER	bummer
DRUMER	drummer
DUMER	dumber
GLUMER	glummer
GRUMER	grummer
GUMER	gummer
HUMER	hummer
KUMER	incomer, comer, cummer, late-comer, newcomer, succumber
MUMER	mummer

NUMER	number
PLUMER	plumber, plummer
RUMER	rummer
SKRUMER	scrummer
SKUMER	scummer
SLUMER	slummer
STRUMER	banjo-strummer, strummer
SUMER	midsummer, summer
THRUMER	thrummer
THUMER	thumber

ŪMERD

HŪMERD	bad-humored, foul-humored, good-humored, humored, ill-humored
TŪMERD	tumored

(See OOMERD)

UMET

GRUMET	grummet
PLUMET	plummet
SUMET	consummate, summit

ŪMID

FŪMID	fumid
HŪMID	humid
TŪMID	tumid

ŪMIJ

FŪMIJ	fumage

(See OOMIJ)

UMIJ

CHUMIJ	chummage
PLUMIJ	plumbage
RUMIJ	rummage
SKRUMIJ	scrummage
SUMIJ	summage

ŪMIK

HŪMIK	humic
KŪMIK	cumic
TŪMIK	costumic

(See OOMIK)

UMING

FRUMING	to-and-froming

(See UM, add -ing where appropriate.)

UMKWÄT

KUMKWÄT	cumquat
PLUMKWÄT	plumquat

UMLĒ

CHUMLĒ	Cholmondesley
DUMLĒ	dumbly
GLUMLĒ	glumly
KUMLĒ	comely, uncomely
MUMLĒ	mumly
NUMLĒ	numbly
PLUMLĒ	plumbly
RUMLĒ	rumly
SUMLĒ	frolicsomely, humorsomely, cumbersomely, troublesomely

ŪMLES

FŪMLES	fumeless, perfumeless
GŪMLES	legumeless
NŪMLES	neumeless
SPŪMLES	spumeless

UMNAL

LUMNAL	columnal
TUMNAL	autumnal

UMNES

(See UM, add -ness where appropriate.)

UMOK

(See UMUK)

UMOKS

(See UMUKS)

ŪMOR

(See ŪMER)

UMPAS

(See UMPUS)

UMPĒ

BUMPĒ	bumpy
CHUMPĒ	chumpy
DUMPĒ	dumpy
FRUMPĒ	frumpy
GRUMPĒ	grumpy
HUMPĒ	humpy
JUMPĒ	jumpy
KLUMPĒ	clumpy
KRUMPĒ	crumpy
LUMPĒ	lumpy
MUMPĒ	mumpy
PLUMPĒ	plumpy
RUMPĒ	rumpy
SKRUMPĒ	scrumpy
SLUMPĒ	slumpy
STUMPĒ	stumpy
THUMPĒ	thumpy
YUMPĒ	Yumpy

UMPER

BUMPER	bumper
DUMPER	dumper
FLUMPER	flumper
FRUMPER	frumper
GLUMPER	glumper
GRUMPER	grumper
HUMPER	humper
JUMPER	broad-jumper, high-jumper, jumper, counter-jumper
KLUMPER	clumper
KRUMPER	crumper
LUMPER	lumper
MUMPER	mumper
PLUMPER	plumper
PUMPER	pumper
RUMPER	rumper, Rumper
SLUMPER	slumper
STUMPER	stumper
SUMPER	sumper
THUMPER	bethumper, Bible thumper, thumper, tub-thumper
TRUMPER	no-trumper, over-trumper, trumper
TUMPER	tumper

UMPERZ

PLUMPERZ	plumpers

(See UMPER, add -s where appropriate.)

UMPET

KRUMPET	crumpet

STRUMPET	strumpet
TRUMPET	trumpet

UMPIJ

PUMPIJ	pumpage
STUMPIJ	stumpage

UMPING

THUMPING	tub-thumping

(See **UMP,** add -ing)

UMPISH

(See **UMP,** add -ish where appropriate.)

UMPKIN

BUMPKIN	bumpkin
LUMPKIN	lumpkin
PUMPKIN	pumpkin

UMPL

KRUMPL	crumple
RUMPL	rumple, unrumple

UMPLING

DUMPLING	dumpling
KRUMPLING	crumpling
RUMPLING	rumpling, unrumpling

UMPSHUN

GUMPSHUN	gumption, rumgumption
SUMPSHUN	assumption, consumption, presumption, resumption, subsumption, transumption

UMPSHUS

BUMPSHUS	bumptious
GUMPSHUS	gumptious
SKRUMPSHUS	scrumptious

UMPTIV

SUMPTIV	assumptive, consumptive, subsumptive
ZUMPTIV	presumptive, resumptive

UMPUS

KUMPUS	astrocompass, encompass, gyrocompass, compass
RUMPUS	rumpus

UMUK

DRUMUK	drummock
HUMUK	hummock
STUMUK	stomach

UMUKS

FLUMUKS	flummox
GLUMUKS	glommox
HUMUKS	hummocks
LUMUKS	lummox
STUMUKS	stomachs

ŪMUS

DŪMUS	dumous
FŪMUS	fumous
HŪMUS	humous, humus, posthumous
SPŪMUS	spumous

(See $\overline{OO}$MUS)

UMZĒ

KLUMZĒ	clumsy
MUMZĒ	mummsy, mumsie

ŪNA

ŪNA	Una
KŪNA	lacuna
PŪNA	puna
TŪNA	Fortuna, tuna

(See $\overline{OO}$NA)

ŪNAL

BŪNAL	tribunal
DŪNAL	dunal
KŪNAL	lacunal
MŪNAL	communal

(See $\overline{OO}$NAL)

UNCHĒ

BUNCHĒ	bunchy
HUNCHĒ	hunchy
KRUNCHĒ	crunchy
MUNCHĒ	munchy
PUNCHĒ	punchy
SKRUNCHĒ	scrunchy

UNCHER

PUNCHER	cowpuncher, puncher

(See **UNCH,** add -er where appropriate.)

UNCHĒZ

KRUNCHĒZ	Crunchies
MUNCHĒZ	Munchies

UNCHING

BRUNCHING	brunching
BUNCHING	bunching
HUNCHING	hunching
KRUNCHING	crunching
LUNCHING	lunching
MUNCHING	munching
SKRUNCHING	scrunching

UNCHUN

BRUNCHUN	bruncheon
LUNCHUN	luncheon
NUNCHUN	nuncheon
PUNCHUN	puncheon
SKUNCHUN	scuncheon
TRUNCHUN	truncheon

UNDA

BUNDA	floribunda
MUNDA	barramunda, osmunda
TUNDA	rotunda

UNDANS

BUNDANS	abundance, overabundance, superabundance
DUNDANS	redundance

UNDANT

BUNDANT	abundant, overabundant, superabundant
DUNDANT	redundant

UNDĒ

UNDĒ	aliunde, undy
BUNDĒ	bundy
FUNDĒ	fundi, Fundy
GRUNDĒ	Mrs. Grundy
GUNDĒ	gundi, salmagundi, Salmagundi
MUNDĒ	Monday
RUNDĒ	jaguarundi
SUNDĒ	Whitsunday, Sunday

UNDED

UNDED	undead
BUNDED	bunded
FUNDED	funded, refunded
TUNDED	retunded, rotunded

UNDER

UNDER	down-under, hereunder, thereunder, under
BLUNDER	blunder
BUNDER	bunder
CHUNDER	chunder
DUNDER	dunder
FUNDER	funder, refunder
PLUNDER	plunder
SUNDER	asunder, sunder
THUNDER	enthunder, thunder
TUNDER	rotunder
WUNDER	wonder

UNDL

BUNDL	bundle, unbundle
MUNDL	mundil, mundle
RUNDL	rundle
TRUNDL	trundle

UNDLD

BUNDLD	bundled, unbundled
TRUNDLD	trundled

UNDLER

BUNDLER	bundler
TRUNDLER	trundler

UNDLING

BUNDLING	bundling, unbundling
TRUNDLING	trundling

UNDŌ

FUNDŌ	basso profundo
KUNDŌ	secundo

UNDRUS

THUNDRUS	thundrous
WUNDRUS	wondrous

ŪNĒ

ŪNĒ	uni
DŪNĒ	duny
PŪNĒ	puisne, puny
TŪNĒ	tuny

(See OŌNĒ)

UNĒ

BUNĒ	bunny
DUNĒ	dunny
FUNĒ	do-funny, funny
GUNĒ	gunny
HUNĒ	honey, wild honey
KUNĒ	cunny
MUNĒ	agrimony, acrimony, alimony, antimony, baldmoney, front money, matrimony, money, parsimony, patrimony, sanctimony, ceremony, testimony
PUNĒ	punny
RUNĒ	runny
SUNĒ	sonny, Sunni, sunny, unsunny
TUNĒ	tunny

UNĒD

HUNĒD	honeyed
MUNĒD	monied

UNEL

FUNEL	funnel
GUNEL	gun'l, gunnel, gunwale
RUNEL	runnel
TRUNEL	trunnel
TUNEL	tunnel

ŪNER

KŪNER	lacunar
MŪNER	communer, cassumunar
PŪNER	expugner, impugner
TŪNER	attuner, importuner, piano tuner, tuner

(See OŌNER)

UNER

DUNER	dunner
GUNER	gunner
KUNER	cunner
PUNER	punner
RUNER	forerunner, frontrunner, gunrunner, outrunner, overrunner, roadrunner, rumrunner, runner
SHUNER	shunner
SKUNER	scunner
STUNER	stunner
TUNER	tonner, tunner, two-tonner, one-tonner (etc.)
WUNER	oner

ŪNES

FŪNES	fewness
NŪNES	newness

(See OŌNES)

UNET

PUNET	punnet
RUNET	runnet

ŪNFUL

TŪNFUL tuneful

(See O͞ONFUL)

UNGER

BUNGER bunger
LUNGER lunger
TUNGER tonguer

UNGGER

HUNGGER enhunger, hunger
MUNGGER *B* balladmonger, barbermonger, boroughmonger, *F* fashionmonger, fellmonger, fishmonger, *G* gossipmonger, *H* whoremonger, *I* ironmonger, *K* costermonger, *M* meritmonger, monger, *SK* scandalmonger, scaremonger, *W* witmonger, warmonger
YUNGGER younger

UNGGL

BUNGGL bungle
JUNGGL jungle
PUNGGL pungle

UNGGUS

DUNGGUS mundungus
FUNGGUS fungus, smellfungus
MUNGGUS humongous

UNGKARD

(See UNGKERD)

UNGKĀT

RUNGKĀT averruncate
TRUNGKĀT detruncate, truncate

UNGKCHER

JUNKCHER juncture, conjuncture

PUNKCHER

acupuncture, quackupuncture, puncture

UNGKĒ

CHUNGKĒ chunky
FLUNGKĒ flunky
FUNGKĒ funky
HUNGKĒ hunky
JUNGKĒ junkie, junky
MUNGKĒ grease monkey, monkey, powder monkey, spider monkey (etc.)
PUNGKĒ morpunkee, punkie, punky
SKUNGKĒ skunky
SPUNGKĒ spunky

UNGKEN

DRUNGKEN drunken
PUNGKEN punkin
SHRUNGKEN shrunken
SUNGKEN sunken

UNGKER

BLUNGKER blunker
BUNGKER Archie Bunker, bunker, kennebunker, mossbunker
DRUNGKER drunker
DUNGKER dunker
FLUNGKER flunker
FUNGKER funker
HUNGKER hunker
JUNGKER junker
KLUNGKER clunker
PUNGKER punker
TUNGKER tunker
YUNGKER younker, Junker

UNGKERD

BLUNGKERD blunkered
BUNGKERD bunkered
DRUNGKERD drunkard
DUNGKERD Dunkard
HUNGKERD hunkered

UNGKET

JUNGKET junket
TUNGKET tunket

UNGKISH

DRUNGKISH drunkish
LUNGKISH lunkish
MUNGKISH monkish
PUNGKISH punkish
SKUNGKISH skunkish
SPUNGKISH spunkish

UNGKL

UNGKL septiuncle, uncle
BUNGKL carbuncle
DUNGKL peduncle
MUNGKL homuncle, sermuncle
NUNGKL nuncle
RUNGKL furuncle, caruncle
TRUNGKL truncal

UNGKŌ

UNGKŌ unco
BUNGKŌ bunko
JUNGKŌ junko
PUNGKŌ punko

UNGKUS

DUNGKUS aduncous
HUNGKUS dohunkus
JUNGKUS juncous

UNGKSHUN

UNGKSHUN extreme unction, inunction, unction
FUNGKSHUN defunction, dysfunction, function, malfunction
JUNGKSHUN adjunction, disjunction, injunction, interjunction, junction, conjunction, rejunction, sejunction, subjunction
PUNGKSHUN expunction, interpunction, compunction, punction

UNGKSHUS

UNGKSHUS unctious
BUNGKSHUS rambunctious
PUNGKSHUS compunctious

UNGKTIV

| JUNGKTIV | abjunctive, adjunctive, disjunctive, conjunctive, subjunctive |
| PUNGKTIV | compunctive |

UNGKTŪR

(See UNGKCHER)

UNGSTER

| TUNGSTER | tonguester |
| YUNGSTER | youngster |

UNIJ

DUNIJ	dunnage
GUNIJ	gunnage
PUNIJ	punnage
TUNIJ	tonnage

ŪNIK

MŪNIK	Munich
PŪNIK	Punic
TŪNIK	tunic

(See ŌŌNIK)

ŪNING

| MŪNING | communing |
| TŪNING | attuning, importuning, retuning, tuning |

(See ŌŌNING)

UNING

DUNING	dunning
FUNING	funning
GUNING	gunning
KUNING	cunning
PUNING	punning
RUNING	gunrunning, outrunning, overrunning, rumrunning, running
SHUNING	shunning
STUNING	stunning
SUNING	sunning
TUNING	tunning

UNISH

BUNISH	bunnish
HUNISH	hunnish, Hunnish
NUNISH	nunnish
PUNISH	punish, punnish

ŪNIST

| TŪNIST | opportunist |

(See ŌŌNIST)

ŪNIZM

| TUNIZM | opportunism |

(See ŌŌNIZM)

UNJĒ

GRUNJĒ	grungy
PLUNJĒ	plungy
SPUNJĒ	spongy

UNJER

BLUNJER	blunger
KUNJER	conjure
LUNJER	lunger
PLUNJER	plunger
SPUNJER	expunger, sponger

UNJING

BLUNJING	blunging
LUNJING	lunging
PLUNJING	plunging
SPUNJING	expunging, sponging

ŪNLES

| TŪNLES | tuneless |

(See ŌŌNLES)

UNLES

PUNLES	punless
RUNLES	runless
SUNLES	sonless, sunless

ŪNLĪT

(See ŌŌNLĪT)

ŪNLIT

(See ŌŌNLIT)

ŪNNES

| TŪNNES | inopportuneness, opportuneness |

(See ŌŌNNES)

ŪNŌ

| ŪNŌ | unau, you-know, UNO |

(See ŌŌNŌ)

UNSHAL

| UNSHAL | uncial |
| NUNSHAL | internuncial, pronuncial |

UNSTER

| GUNSTER | gunster |
| PUNSTER | punster |

UNTA

BUNTA	marabunta
JUNTA	junta
PUNTA	punta

UNTAL

(See UNTL)

UNTĒ

PUNTĒ	punty
RUNTĒ	runty
STUNTĒ	stunty
WUNTĒ	wuntee

UNTED

| WUNTED | unwonted, wonted |

(See UNT, add -ed where appropriate.)

UNTER

| BLUNTER | blunter |
| BUNTER | bunter |

FRUNTER	affronter, fronter, confronter
GRUNTER	grunter
HUNTER	fortune hunter, headhunter, hunter, lion hunter, scalp hunter (etc.)
PUNTER	punter
SHUNTER	shunter
STUNTER	stunter

UNTING

BLUNTING	blunting
BUNTING	bunting, red bunting, snow bunting, yellow bunting
FRUNTING	affronting, fronting, confronting
GRUNTING	grunting
HUNTING	brush-hunting, fortune hunting, head-hunting, hunting, lion-hunting, scalp-hunting
PUNTING	punting
SHUNTING	shunting
STUNTING	stunting

UNTL

BUNTL	balibuntal, buntal
FRUNTL	frontal, full-frontal, confrontal, prefrontal
GRUNTL	disgruntle, gruntle
PUNTL	contrapuntal, puntal

UNTLES

(See **UNT,** add *-less* where appropriate.)

ŪNUM

(See $\overline{OO}$NUM)

ŪNYUN

ŪNYUN	disunion, labor union, company union, nonunion, reunion, trade union, union
MŪNYUN	excommunion, intercommunion, communion

UNYUN

UNYUN	onion, wild onion
BUNYUN	bunion, John Bunyan

RUNYUN	ronion, ronyon
TRUNYUN	trunnion

ŪPA

PŪPA	pupa
STŪPA	stupa

(See $\overline{OO}$PA)

UPANS

UPANS	come-uppance
THRUPANS	thruppence

ŪPĒ

KŪPĒ	kewpy

(See $\overline{OO}$PĒ)

UPĒ

GUPĒ	guppy
KUPĒ	hiccoughy, hiccupy, cuppy
PUPĒ	bumblepuppy, hushpuppy, puppy
YUPĒ	Yuppy

ŪPER

DŪPER	duper, super-duper
STŪPER	stupor
SŪPER	super

(See $\overline{OO}$PER)

UPER

UPER	upper
KRUPER	crupper
KUPER	cupper, kupper
SKUPER	scupper
SUPER	supper

UPET

MUPET	muppet
PUPET	puppet
SKUPET	scuppet

ŪPID

KŪPID	cupid

LŪPID	Lupid
STŪPID	stupid

UPING

UPING	swan-upping
KUPING	hiccoughing, hiccuping, cupping
SUPPING	supping
TUPPING	tupping

ŪPISH

(See $\overline{OO}$PISH)

UPISH

UPISH	uppish
KUPISH	cuppish
PUPISH	puppish

ŪPL

KŪPL	cupel
PŪPL	pupil

(See $\overline{OO}$PL)

UPL

KUPL	decouple, couple, recouple, uncouple
SUPL	supple

UPLER

KUPLER	coupler, recoupler, uncoupler
SUPLER	suppler

UPLET

KUPLET	couplet, cuplet
RUPLET	*quadruplet*
TUPLET	*quintuplet, sextuplet, septuplet*

ŪPMENT

(See $\overline{OO}$PMENT)

ŪPON

ŪPON	yupon

(See $\overline{OO}$PON)

ŪRA

LŪRA	lura
SKŪRA	camera obscura
TŪRA	coloratura
VŪRA	bravura
ZŪRA	caesura

(See OŌRA)

ŪRAL

ŪRAL	Ural
DŪRAL	dural, subdural
KŪRAL	sinecural
LŪRAL	lural, tellural
MŪRAL	antemural, extramural, intermural, intramural, mural
NŪRAL	adneural, interneural, neural
PŪRAL	hypural
SŪRAL	sural

URAL

(See OORAL)

ŪRANS

ŪRANS	durance, endurance, perdurance
KŪRANS	procurance
LŪRANS	allurance

ŪRANT

DŪRANT	durant, endurant, perdurant
KŪRANT	procurant
LŪRANT	allurant
SKŪRANT	obscurant

URANT

(See URENT)

ŪRĀT

KŪRĀT	curate
PŪRĀT	*purpurate*

URBAL

(See URBL)

URBAN

(See URBN)

URBĀT

SURBĀT	acerbate
TURBĀT	*perturbate*

URBĒ

URBĒ	herby
BLURBĒ	blurby
DURBĒ	derby, Derby
HURBĒ	herby
VURBĒ	verby

URBER

BLURBER	blurber
BURBER	Berber
KURBER	curber
PURBER	superber
TURBER	disturber, perturber

URBET

BURBOT	burbot
SHURBOT	sherbet
TURBOT	turbit, turbot

URBING

URBING	herbing
BLURBING	blurbing
HURBING	herbing
KURBING	curbing
TURBING	disturbing
VURBING	verbing

URBĪT

(See URBET)

URBL

URBL	herbal
BURBL	burble
HURBL	herbal
JURBL	gerbil, jirble
VURBL	biverbal, nonverbal, verbal

URBN

URBN	interurban, urban

BURBN	Bourbon, suburban
TURBN	turban, turbine

URBOT

(See URBET)

URCHANT

MURCHANT	merchant
PURCHANT	perchant

URCHĒ

BURCHĒ	birchy
CHURCHĒ	churchy
LURCHĒ	lurchy
SMURCHĒ	smirchy

URCHEN

URCHEN	urchin
BURCHEN	birchen

URCHER

BURCHER	bircher
CHURCHER	churcher
LURCHER	lurcher
NURCHER	nurture
PURCHER	percher
SMURCHER	besmircher, smircher
SURCHER	researcher, searcher

URCHING

(See URCH, add *-ing* where appropriate.)

URCHLES

(See URCH, add *-less* where appropriate.)

URDBOOK

BURDBOOK	bird book
HURDBOOK	herdbook
WURDBOOK	wordbook

URDĒ

BURDĒ	birdy
GURDĒ	hurdy-gurdy
KURDĒ	curdy
PURDĒ	purdy
STURDĒ	sturdy
WURDĒ	wordy

URDED

(See **URD,** add *-ed* where appropriate.)

URDEN

BURDEN	burden, disburden, overburden, reburden, unburden
GURDEN	guerdon
LURDEN	lurdan

URDER

BURDER	birder
GURDER	engirder, girder
HURDER	goat-herder, herder, sheep-herder
MURDER	murder, first-degree murder (etc.), self-murder
SURDER	absurder
THURDER	thirder
WURDER	worder

URDING

BURDING	birding
GURDING	engirding, girding
HURDING	herding
WURDING	miswording, rewording, wording

URDL

FURDL	furdel, furdle
GURDL	begirdle, engirdle, girdle
HURDL	hurdle
KURDL	curdle

URDLĒ

KURDLĒ	curdly
SURDLĒ	absurdly
THURDLĒ	thirdly

URDZMAN

HURDZMAN	herdsman
WURDZMAN	wordsman

ŪRĒ

FŪRĒ	fury
KŪRĒ	curie, Curie

(See **OŌRĒ**)

URĒ

BLURĒ	blurry
BURĒ	burry
DURĒ	durrie, durry
FLURĒ	flurry, snow flurry
FURĒ	firry, furry
GURĒ	ghurry, gurry
HURĒ	hurry
HWURĒ	whirry
KURĒ	curry
LURĒ	lurry
MURĒ	murrey
PURĒ	purry
SKURĒ	hurry-scurry, scurry
SLURĒ	slurry
SPURĒ	spurry
SURĒ	surrey
WURĒ	worry

URĒD

FLURĒD	flurried, unflurried
HURĒD	hurried, unhurried
KURĒD	curried, uncurried
SKURĒD	scurried
WURĒD	unworried, worried

UREL

BUREL	burrel
FUREL	deferral, referral
MUREL	demurral
SKWUREL	squirrel
STUREL	bestirral

URENS

FURENS	transference
KURENS	incurrence, intercurrence, concurrence, nonconcurrence, occurrence, recurrence
SHURENS	assurance, health insurance, insurance, life insurance (etc.), reassurance, reinsurance
TURENS	deterrence, nondeterrence

URENT

KURENT	decurrent, intercurrent, concurrent, crosscurrent, currant, current, recurrent, undercurrent
MURENT	demurrent
SURENT	susurrant
TURENT	deterrent

ŪRER

ŪRER	inurer
DŪRER	Dürer, durer, endurer
FŪRER	Fuehrer, furor
KŪRER	curer
MŪRER	immurer
NŪRER	manurer
PŪRER	purer
SKŪRER	obscurer
TŪRER	immaturer, maturer

URER

BLURER	blurrer
FURER	deferrer, inferrer, conferrer, preferrer, transferrer
JURER	abjurer, adjurer, grand juror, juror, petty juror, trial juror
KURER	incurrer, concurrer
LURER	allurer, lurer
MURER	demurrer
PURER	purrer
SHURER	assurer, ensurer, insurer, reassurer, reinsurer, shirrer, surer
SLURER	slurrer
SPURER	spurrer
STURER	bestirrer, stirrer
TURER	deterrer, interrer
VURER	averrer

(See **OORER**)

URFĒ

MURFĒ	murphy
SKURFĒ	scurfy
SURFĒ	surfy

URFING

SKURFING	skurfing
SURFING	surfing, windsurfing

URGAL

(See **URGL**)

URGĀT

JURGĀT	objurgate
PURGĀT	expurgate
VURGĀT	virgate

URGL

URGL	ergal
BURGL	burgle
GURGL	gurgle
TURGL	tergal
VURGL	virgal

URGLER

BURGLER	burglar
GURGLER	gurgler

URGŌ

URGŌ	ergo
VURGŌ	Virgo

URGUS

URGUS	demiurgus
PURGUS	Walpurgis
TURGUS	thaumaturgus

URIJ

KURIJ	discourage, encourage, courage
MURIJ	demurrage
STURIJ	stirrage

ŪRIK

FŪRIK	hydrosulphuric, sulphuric
KŪRIK	mercuric
LŪRIK	hydrotelluric, telluric
NŪRIK	aneuric, neuric
PŪRIK	purpuric
SŪRIK	caesuric
ZŪRIK	caesuric

URIK

PLURIK	pleuric

(See **ŪRIK**)

ŪRIN

ŪRIN	urine
FŪRIN	furan
NŪRIN	neurine

ŪRING

ŪRING	inuring
DŪRING	during, enduring, perduring, perenduring
FŪRING	coiffuring
KŪRING	curing, manicuring, pedicuring, procuring, securing
LŪRING	alluring, luring
MŪRING	immuring, muring
NŪRING	manuring
SKŪRING	obscuring
TŪRING	caricaturing, maturing

(See **OORING, OORING**)

URING

BLURING	blurring
BURING	birring, burring
CHURING	chirring, churring
FURING	befurring, furring, inferring, conferring, preferring, referring, transferring
HWURING	whirring
JURING	abjuring, adjuring, conjuring
KURING	incurring, concurring, occurring, recurring, sepulchering
MURING	demurring
NURING	manuring
SHURING	assuring, insuring, reinsuring, shirring
SLURING	slurring
SMURING	smurring
SPURING	spurring
STURING	administering, bestirring, restirring, stirring, unstirring
SURING	sirring
TURING	deterring, disinterring, interring
VURING	averring

ŪRISH

MŪRISH	demurish
PŪRISH	purish
SKŪRISH	obscurish
TŪRISH	amateurish, maturish

URISH

BURISH	burrish
FLURISH	flourish
KURISH	currish
NURISH	nourish, overnourish, undernourish
PURISH	poorish, purrish
TURISH	amateurish, maturish

(See **OORISH**)

URISHT

FLURISHT	flourished
NURISHT	nourished, overnourished, undernourished

ŪRIST

KŪRIST	manicurist
PŪRIST	purist
TŪRIST	caricaturist

ŪRIZM

PŪRIZM	purism

(See **URIZM**)

URIZM

TURIZM	

(See **ŪRIZM**)

URJĒ

URJĒ	aciurgy, periergy, theurgy
DURJĒ	dirgie, dirgy
KLURJĒ	clergy
KRURJĒ	micrurgy
LURJĒ	metallurgy
MURJĒ	chemurgy, zymurgy
SURJĒ	surgy
TURJĒ	dramaturgy, thaumaturgy

URJENS

URJENS	urgence
MURJENS	emergence, mergence, submergence
SURJENS	insurgence, resurgence

TURJENS

TURJENS	detergence
VURJENS	divergence, convergence, vergence

URJENT

URJENT	urgent
MURJENT	emergent, mergent, submergent
SPLURJENT	splurgent
STURJENT	abstergent
SURJENT	assurgent, insurgent, resurgent
TURJENT	detergent
VURJENT	divergent, convergent, vergent

URJER

URJER	urger
BURJER	berger
MURJER	emerger, merger, submerger
PURJER	perjure, purger
SKURJER	scourger
SPLURJER	splurger
VURJER	diverger, converger, verdure, verger

URJIK

URJIK	demiurgic, exoergic, endoergic, theurgic
LURJIK	allergic, metallurgic
NURJIK	adrenurgic, anergic, cholinergic
RURJIK	chirurgic
SURJIK	lysurgic
TURJIK	dramaturgic, liturgic, thaumaturgic

URJING

(See **URJ,** add *-ing* where appropriate.)

URJIST

LURJIST	metallurgist
TURJIST	dramaturgist, thaumaturgist

URJMENT

MURJMENT	submergement
VURJMENT	divergement, convergement

URJUN

BURJUN	burgeon
GURJUN	gurjun
STURJUN	sturgeon
SURJUN	neurosurgeon, surgeon
VURJUN	virgin

URKA

BURKA	burka
CHURKA	charkha
FURKA	furca
GURKA	Gurkha
MURKA	amurca
SURKA	circa
ZURKA	mazurka

URKAL

(See **URKL**)

URKĒ

JURKĒ	jerky
KURKĒ	Albuquerque
KWURKĒ	quirky
LURKĒ	lurky, Turkey-lurkey
MURKĒ	murky
PURKĒ	perky
SHURKĒ	shirky
SMURKĒ	smirky
TURKĒ	turkey, Turkey

URKER

BURKER	burker
JURKER	jerker, jerquer, soda jerker, tearjerker
KURKER	kirker
LURKER	lurker
PURKER	coffee-perker, perker
SHURKER	shirker
SMURKER	smirker
WURKER	guessworker, hard worker, migrant worker, nonworker, outworker, pieceworker, wonder worker, worker

URKIN

FURKIN	firkin
GURKIN	gherkin
JURKIN	jerkin
MURKIN	merkin
PURKIN	perkin

URKING

WURKING	guessworking, hardworking, nonworking, pieceworking, wonder working, working

(See **URK,** add *-ing*)

URKISH

JURKISH	jerkish
KLURKISH	clerkish
KWURKISH	quirkish
PURKISH	perkish
TURKISH	Turkish

URKL

SURKL	encircle, excircle, heterocercal, homocercal, inner circle, semicircle, cercle, circle
TURKL	turkle
VURKL	novercal

URKLĒ

BURKLĒ	Berkeley
KLURKLĒ	clerkly
SURKLĒ	circly

URKMAN

TURKMAN	Turkman
WURKMAN	workman

URKSUM

URKSUM	irksome
KWURKSUM	quirksome
MURKSUM	murksome

URKUS

FURKUS	bifurcous
MURKUS	amurcous
SURKUS	circus

ŪRLĒ

KŪRLĒ	securely
MŪRLĒ	demurely

PŪRLĒ	impurely, purely
SKŪRLĒ	obscurely
TŪRLĒ	immaturely, maturely, prematurely

URLĒ

URLĒ	early
BURLĒ	burley, burly, hurly-burly
CHURLĒ	churly
DURLĒ	dourly
FURLĒ	ferly
GURLĒ	girlie, girly, gurly
HURLĒ	hurley
HWURLĒ	whirly
KURLĒ	curly
MURLĒ	murly
NURLĒ	knurly
PURLĒ	pearly, pirlie, poorly
SHURLĒ	surely
SURLĒ	surly
SWURLĒ	swirly
TWURLĒ	twirly
WURLĒ	wurley

(See OORLĒ)

URLER

BURLER	birler, burler
FURLER	furler
HURLER	hurler
HWURLER	whirler
KURLER	curler
PURLER	pearler, purler
SKURLER	skirler
SWURLER	swirler
TWURLER	twirler

URLET

BURLET	burlet
PURLET	pearlet
SPURLET	spurlet
STURLET	sterlet

URLIN

KURLIN	carline
MURLIN	merlin, Merlin, murlin
PURLIN	pearlin, purlin

URLING

BURLING	birling, burling
FURLING	furling
HWURLING	whirling
KURLING	hair-curling, curling
PURLING	pearling, purling
SKURLING	skirling
SPURLING	sperling
SWURLING	swirling
TWURLING	twirling

URLISH

CHURLISH	churlish
GURLISH	girlish
PURLISH	pearlish

URLOIN

| PURLOIN | purloin |
| SURLOIN | sirloin |

URLŪ

| KURLŪ | curlew |
| PURLŪ | purlieu |

URMA

BURMA	Burma
DURMA	derma, pachyderma, xeroderma
FURMA	terra firma
SURMA	syrma

URMAL

| DURMAL | dermal, epidermal, hypodermal, pachydermal, taxidermal |
| THURMAL | diathermal, hydrothermal, isogeothermal, isothermal, geothermal, synthermal, thermal |

URMAN

URMAN	ermine
FURMAN	firman
JURMAN	german, German, germon, cousin-german
MURMAN	merman, mermen
SURMAN	sermon
TURMAN	determine, redetermine, termen, termin, termon

URMĒ

DURMĒ	taxidermy
FURMĒ	Fermi
JURMĒ	germy
SKWURMĒ	squirmy
SPURMĒ	spermy
THURMĒ	aluminothermy, diathermy, radiothermy
WURMĒ	wormy

URMEN

(See URMAN)

ŪRMENT

ŪRMENT	inurement
KŪRMENT	procurement, securement
LŪRMENT	allurement
MŪRMENT	immurement
SKŪRMENT	obscurement

URMENT

RURMENT	affirmant, deferment, ferment, preferment, referment
TURMENT	determent, disinterment, interment
VURMENT	averment

(See OORMENT)

URMER

FURMER	affirmer, firmer, infirmer, confirmer
MURMER	bemurmur, murmur
SKWURMER	squirmer
TURMER	first-termer, second-termer (etc.), termer, termor
WURMER	wormer

URMĒZ

| HURMĒZ | Hermes |
| KURMĒZ | kermes |

URMIK

| DURMIK | dermic, endermic, epidermic, |

SPURMIK	spermic
THURMIK	adiathermic, diathermic, exothermic, endothermic, photothermic, isogeothermic, geothermic, thermic, euthermic

hydrodermic, hypodermic, clerodermic, pachydermic, taxidermic

URMIN

(See **URMAN**)

URMIND

URMIND	ermined
TURMIND	determined, undetermined
VURMIND	vermined

URMING

FURMING	affirming, firming, confirming
JURMING	germing
SKWURMING	squirming
TURMING	terming
WURMING	worming

URMIS

(See **URMUS**)

URMISH

| SKURMISH | skirmish |
| WURMISH | wormish |

URMIT

| HURMIT | hermit |
| PURMIT | permit |

URMLĒ

| FURMLĒ | firmly, infirmly |
| TURMLĒ | termly |

URMON

(See **URMAN**)

URMUS

DURMUS	dermis, exodermis, endodermis, epidermis, hypodermis, malacodermous
HURMUS	hirmos
KURMUS	kermes, kermis
NURMUS	inermous
SPURMUS	spermous
THURMUS	thermos
VURMUS	vermis

URNA

BURNA	taberna
DURNA	Dharna
FURNA	parapherna
SMURNA	Smyrna
STURNA	Sterna

URNAL

URNAL	diurnal, hodiernal, semidiurnal, terdiurnal, urnal
BURNAL	hibernal
FURNAL	infernal, paraphernal
JURNAL	journal
KURNAL	colonel, kernel
PURNAL	supernal
STURNAL	asternal, sternal
THURNAL	cothurnal
TURNAL	D diuturnal, E eternal, external, FR fraternal, H hesternal, I internal, K coeternal, M maternal, N nocturnal, P paternal, S sempiternal
VURNAL	cavernal, vernal

URNĒ

URNĒ	enurny
BURNĒ	byrnie, burny, burny-burny
FURNĒ	ferny
GURNĒ	gurney
JURNĒ	journey
PURNĒ	pirnie
TURNĒ	attorney, tourney

URNENT

SURNENT	secernent
TURNENT	alternant
VURNENT	vernant

URNER

URNER	earner
BURNER	back burner, bookburner, bra burner, burner, four-burner, front burner, gas-burner, hay-burner, oil-burner, two-burner
CHURNER	churner
JURNER	adjourner
LURNER	learner
PURNER	pirner
SPURNER	spurner
STURNER	sterner
SURNER	discerner
TURNER	overturner, returner, turner
YURNER	yearner
ZURNER	discerner

ŪRNES

KŪRNES	insecureness, secureness
MŪRNES	demureness
SKŪRNES	obscureness

URNES

CHURNES	matureness
FURNES	furnace
PURNES	poorness
SHURNES	cocksurness, sureness
THURNES	cothurnus

(See **URNNES**)

URNEST

| URNEST | earnest |

(See **URN**, add -est)

URNING

| URNING | earning |
| LURNING | book-learning, learning |

(See **URN**, add -ing where appropriate.)

URNISH

| BURNISH | burnish, reburnish |
| FURNISH | furnish, refurnish |

URNISHT

(See **URNISH**, add *-ed* where appropriate.)

URNIT

TURNIT	*alternate,* biternate, quaternate, *subalternate,* ternate
THURNIT	cothurnate

URNMENT

JURNMENT	adjournment, sojournment
SURNMENT	discernment, concernment, secernment
TURNMENT	attornment, internment
ZURNMENT	discernment

URNNES

STURNNES	sternness
TURNNES	taciturnness

(See **URNES**)

URNŌ

FURNŌ	inferno
JURNŌ	journo
LURNŌ	Salerno
PURNŌ	Pernod
STURNŌ	sterno, Sterno

URNUM

BURNUM	alburnum, laburnum, viburnum
STURNUM	episternum, sternum, xiphisternum

URNUS

THURNUS	cothurnus
VURNUS	Avernus

ŪRŌ

BŪRŌ	bureau, Politbureo
SKŪRO	chiarascuro

URŌ

BURŌ	borough, burro, interborough, rotten borough
FURŌ	furrow
THURŌ	thorough, unthorough

(See **OORŌ**)

UROR

(See **URER**)

URPĒ

URPĒ	irpe
BURPĒ	Burpee, burpy
CHURPĒ	chirpy
SLURPĒ	slurpy

URPER

BURPER	burper
CHURPER	chirper
PURPER	hyperper
SLURPER	slurper
SURPER	usurper
ZURPER	usurper

URPĒZ

BURPĒZ	Burpee's
HURPĒZ	herpes
STURPĒZ	per stirpes, stirpes

URPING

(See **URP**, add *-ing* where appropriate.)

URPL

HURPL	hirple
KURPL	curple
PURPL	purple

URSA

URSA	ursa
BURSA	bursa
JURSA	djersa
VURSA	vice-versa

URSAL

(See **URSL**)

URSANT

KURSANT	recursant
VURSANT	aversant, conversant, multiversant, versant

URSĒ

BURSĒ	bersy
HURSĒ	hirci
MURSĒ	gramercy, mercy
NURSĒ	nursy
PURSĒ	pursy
SURSĒ	Circe
VURSĒ	arsey-versey, controversy

URSER

URSER	coercer
BURSER	bursar, disburser, reimburser
HURSER	hearser, rehearser
KURSER	accurser, antecursor, curser, cursor, precursor
MURSER	amercer, immerser, commercer, mercer
NURSER	nurser
PURSER	disperser, purser
SPURSER	intersperser
VURSER	converser, perverser, reverser, traverser, verser, versor
WURSER	worser

> *"CLUCK, CLUCK!" SAID THE CHICKENS*
>
> Charles Dickens was caught by the Devil
>   Stealing the Devil's chickens.
> "What the dickens!" said the Devil.
>   "What the Devil!" said Charles Dickens.

URSET

TURSET	tercet
VURSET	verset

URSHA

URSHA	inertia
PURSHA	Persia
TURSHA	sesquitertia, tertia

URSHAL

URSHAL	inertial
MURSHAL	commercial, noncommercial, uncommercial
TURSHAL	sesquitertial, tertial
VURSHAL	controversial

URSHUN

URSHUN	coercion
KURSHUN	discursion, excursion, incursion, recursion
MURSHUN	emersion, immersion, mersion, submersion
PURSHUN	apertion, aspersion, dispersion, Persian
SPURSHUN	aspersion, inspersion, interspersion
STURSHUN	abstertion
SURSHUN	assertion, disconcertion, insertion, intersertion, concertion, lacertian, self-assertion
TURSHUN	extension, nasturtion, sesquitertian, Cistercian, tersion, tertian
VURSHUN	A animadversion, aversion, B bioconversion, D diversion, E extroversion, eversion, I introversion, inversion, K contraversion, controversion, conversion, O obversion, P perversion, R retroversion, reversion, S circumversion, subversion, V version
ZURSHUN	desertion, exertion

URSĪN

| URSĪN | urçine |
| HURSĪN | hircine |

URSING

(See **URS,** add -ing where appropriate.)

URSIV

URSIV	coercive
KURSIV	decursive, discursive, excursive, incursive, cursive, precursive, recursive
MURSIV	immersive
PURSIV	aspersive, dispersive
STURSIV	abstersive
VURSIV	aversive, perversive, subversive

URSL

URSL	ursal
BURSL	birsle, bursal
HURSL	hirsel, rehearsal
KURSL	cursal, succursal
MURSL	demersal
NURSL	nursle
PURSL	aspersal, dispersal
SPURSL	interspersal
TURSL	tercel
VURSL	quaquaversal, partiversal, reversal, transversal, versal, universal

URSLĒ

| TURSLĒ | tersely |
| VURSLĒ | adversely, aversely, diversely, inversely, conversely, obversely, perversely, reversely, transversely |

URSMENT

| BURSMENT | disbursement, imbursement, reimbursement |
| MURSMENT | amercement |

URSN

| URSN | urson |
| PURSN | chairperson, mediaperson, nonperson, newsperson, person, spokesperson, unperson |

URSNES

| TURSNES | terseness |

| VURSNES | adverseness, averseness, diverseness, inverseness, converseness, obverseness, perverseness, transverseness |

URSŌ

| KURSŌ | concurso |
| VURSŌ | reverso, verso |

URSON

(See **URSN**)

URSTED

BURSTED	bursted
THURSTED	thirsted
WURSTED	worsted

URSTER

BURSTER	burster
FURSTER	America Firster, firster
THURSTER	thirster
WURSTER	worster

URSTING

BURSTING	bursting
THURSTING	thirsting
WURSTING	worsting

URSUS

URSUS	ursus
KURSUS	excursus, concursus, cursus
LURSUS	melursus
THURSUS	thyrsus
VURSUS	adversus, conversus, transversus, versus

URTAL

(See **URTL**)

URTAN

(See **URTN**)

URTĒ

CHURTĒ	cherty
DURTĒ	dirty, down and dirty
FLURTĒ	flirty
MURTĒ	Trimurti
PURTĒ	purty
SHURTĒ	shirty
SKWURTĒ	squirty
SPURTĒ	spurty
SURTĒ	certie
THURTĒ	thirty

URTED

SHURTED	blackshirted, brownshirted, shirted, unshirted

(See **URT**, add *-ed* where appropriate.)

URTER

FLURTER	flirter
FURTER	frankfurter
HURTER	hurter
KURTER	curter
PURTER	perter
SHURTER	blackshirter, brownshirter (etc.)
SKURTER	skirter
SKWURTER	squirter
SPURTER	spurter
STURTER	stertor
SURTER	asserter, disconcerter, inserter, concerter, preconcerter
VURTER	adverter, animadverter, averter, diverter, everter, evertor, inverter, converter, perverter, reverter, subverter
ZURTER	deserter, exerter

URTHĒ

(**TH** as in *thin*)

URTHĒ	earthy
BURTHĒ	birthy

(See **URTHĒ, TH** as in then.)

URTHĒ

(**TH** as in *then*)

WURTHĒ	noteworthy, praiseworthy, seaworthy, trustworthy, worthy, unworthy

(See **URTHĒ, TH** as in thin.)

URTHEN

(**TH** as in *thin*)

URTHEN	earthen
BURTHEN	burthen, disburthen, unburthen

URTHFUL

(**TH** as in *thin*)

MURTHFUL	mirthful
WURTHFUL	worthful

URTHLES

URTHLES	earthless
BURTHLES	birthless
GURTHLES	girthless
MURTHLES	mirthless
WURTHLES	worthless

URTIN

(See **URTN**)

URTING

(See **URT**, add *-ing* where appropriate.)

URTIV

FURTIV	furtive
SURTIV	assertive, insertive, self-assertive
VURTIV	divertive, extrovertive, introvertive, invertive, convertive, revertive
ZURTIV	exertive

URTL

FURTL	fertile, infertile
HURTL	hurtle
HWURTL	whortle
KURTL	kirtle, curtal
MURTL	myrtle
SPURTL	spurtle
SURTL	consertal
TURTL	turtle

URTLĒ

URTLĒ	inertly
KURTLĒ	curtly
LURTLĒ	alertly
PURTLĒ	*expertly, inexpertly,* pertly
TURTLĒ	turtly

URTLES

SHURTLES	shirtless
SKURTLES	skirtless
SKWURTLES	squirtless
SPURTLES	spurtless

URTN

BURTN	burton
KURTN	encurtain, iron curtain, curtain
SURTN	certain, uncertain

URTNES

URTNES	inertness
KURTNES	curtness
LURTNES	alertness
PURTNES	*expertness, inexpertness,* peartness, pertness
PYURTNES	peartness

URTUM

FURTUM	furtum
SURTUM	assertum, sertum

URUP

CHURUP	chirrup
STURUP	stirrup
YURUP	Europe

(See **OORUP**)

URUS

CHURUS	churrus
DURUS	Honduras
KURUS	dolichurus, mercurous
NURUS	anurous, coenurus
SURUS	susurrous
TURUS	Arcturus
WURUS	wurrus
YURUS	anurous, urus

(See **OORUS**)

URVA

URVA	urva
FURVA	conferva
NURVA	Minerva, Nerva
YURVA	contrayerva

URVAL

(See **URVL**)

URVĀT

KURVĀT	incurvate, curvate, curvet, recurvate
NURVĀT	enervate, innervate, trinervate
SURVĀT	acervate

URVĒ

KURVĒ	curvy
NURVĒ	nervy
SKURVĒ	scurvy
TURVĒ	topsy-turvy

URVENS

FURVENS	fervence
SURVENS	inobservance, observance, servants, unobservance

URVENT

FURVENT	fervent
KURVENT	curvant, recurvant
SURVENT	bondservant, conservant, maidservant, manservant, servant
ZURVENT	inobservant, observant, unobservant

URVER

FURVER	fervor
NURVER	nerver, unnerver
SURVER	conserver, server, time-server
SWURVER	swerver
ZURVER	deserver, game preserver, life preserver, observer, preserver, reserver

URVET

KURVET	curvet
VURVET	vervet

URVIL

(See **URVL**)

URVĪN

NURVĪN	nervine
SURVĪN	cervine

URVIN

NURVIN	nervine
SURVIN	cervine

URVING

KURVING	*incurving,* curving, *outcurving*
NURVING	nerving, unnerving
SURVING	conserving, serving, time-serving
SWURVING	swerving, unswerving
ZURVING	deserving, observing, preserving, reserving, undeserving, unobserving

URVL

CHURVL	chervil
FURVL	conferval
NURVL	adnerval, nerval
SURVL	acerval, serval, servile
VURVL	vervel

URVLES

DURVLES	hors d'oeuvreless
KURVLES	curveless
NURVLES	nerveless
VURVLES	verveless

URVUS

FURVUS	confervous
KURVUS	curvous, recurvous
NURVUS	nervous, unnervous

URZĒ

FURZĒ	furzy
JURZĒ	jersey, Jersey, New Jersey
KURZĒ	kersey

URZHUN

KURZHUN	discursion, excursion, incursion
PURZHUN	Persian
SPURZHUN	aspersion, interspersion, dispersion
TURZHUN	extersion
VURZHUN	*A* animadversion, aversion, *D* deorsumversion, diversion, *E* extroversion, eversion, *I* introversion, inversion, *K* conversion, *O* obversion, *P* perversion, *R* retroversion, *V* version

ŪSA

DŪSA	medusa, Medusa
FŪSA	subsemifusa
MŪSA	Musa

(See **OOSA**)

ŪSAL

(See **OOSAL**)

USCHUN

USCHUN	inustion, ustion
BUSCHUN	combustion, moxibustion
DUSCHUN	adustion
FUSCHUN	fustian

ŪSĒ

BŪSĒ	Debussy
DŪSĒ	acey-deucy

(See **OOSĒ**)

USĒ

FUSĒ	fussy, overfussy
GUSĒ	gussie
HUSĒ	henhussy, hussy
MUSĒ	mussy
PUSĒ	pussy

ŪSENS

LŪSENS	lucence, noctilucence, tralucence, translucence
NŪSENS	nuisance

ŪSENT

DŪSENT	abducent, adducent, conducent, producent, reducent, traducent
LŪSENT	interlucent, lucent, noctilucent, nonlucent, radiolucent, relucent, tralucent, translucent, unlucent

ŪSER

DŪSER	adducer, deducer, inducer, introducer, conducer, producer, reducer, reproducer, seducer, traducer

(See **OŌSER**)

USER

BUSER	busser
FUSER	fusser
KUSER	cusser, discusser, percussor
MUSER	musser
PLUSER	nonplusser
TRUSER	trusser

USET

GUSET	gusset
RUSET	russet

ŪSFUL

ŪSFUL	unuseful, useful

(See **OŌSFUL**)

USHA

PRUSHA	Prussia
RUSHA	Russia

ŪSHAL

DŪSHAL	fiducial
NŪSHAL	minutial

(See **OŌSHAL**)

USHĒ

BLUSHĒ	blushy
BRUSHĒ	brushy
GUSHĒ	gushy
LUSHĒ	lushy
MUSHĒ	mushy
PLUSHĒ	plushy
RUSHĒ	rushy
SLUSHĒ	slushy
THRUSHĒ	thrushy
TUSHĒ	tushy

USHER

USHER	usher
BLUSHER	blusher
BRUSHER	brusher
FLUSHER	flusher, four-flusher
GUSHER	gusher
HUSHER	husher
KRUSHER	crusher
LUSHER	lusher
MUSHER	musher
PLUSHER	plusher
RUSHER	rusher
SHUSHER	shusher

USHING

FLUSHING	flushing, four-flushing
RUSHING	onrushing, rushing

(See **USH,** add -ing where appropriate.)

ŪSHUN

BŪSHUN	attribution, distribution, contribution, redistribution, retribution
FŪSHUN	Confucian
GŪSHUN	redargution
KŪSHUN	*A* allocution, *E* execution, electrocution, elocution, *I* insecution, interlocution, *K* collocation, *L* locution, *P* persecution, *PR* prosecution, *S* circumlocution, *V* ventrilocution
NŪSHUN	diminution, imminution, comminution
PŪSHUN	Lilliputian
TŪSHUN	destitution, institution, constitution, prostitution, restitution, substitution

(See **OŌSHUN**)

USHUN

HUSHUN	hushion
KUSHUN	discussion, incussion, concussion, percussion, recussion, repercussion, succusian
PRUSHUN	prushun, Prussian
RUSHUN	Russian

ŪSID

DŪSID	deuced
LŪSID	lucid, pellucid, translucid
MŪSID	mucid

ŪSIJ

ŪSIJ	disusage, misusage, usage
BŪSIJ	abusage

ŪSIK

FŪSIK	fucic
JŪSIK	ageusic, parageusic
KŪSIK	anacusic
MŪSIK	mucic

(See **OŌSIK**)

ŪSING

(See ŪS, OOS, add -ing where appropriate.)

USING

BUSING	busing, bussing
FUSING	fussing
KUSING	discussing, concussing, cussing, percussing
MUSING	mussing
PLUSING	nonplussing
TRUSING	trussing, untrussing

ŪSIS

NŪSIS	prosneusis
PŪSIS	therapeusis
TŪSIS	pertusis

(See OOSIS)

ŪSIV

BŪSIV	abusive
DŪSIV	deducive, educive, inconducive, inducive, conducive, seducive
FŪSIV	diffusive, effusive, infusive, confusive, perfusive, transfusive
LŪSIV	allusive, delusive, elusive, illusive, collusive
TŪSIV	contusive

(See OOSIV)

USIV

JUSIV	jussive
KUSIV	discussive, concussive, percussive, repercussive, succussive
TUSIV	antitussive, tussive

USKAN

BUSKAN	buskin
DUSKAN	dusken
LUSKAN	molluscan
RUSKAN	ruskin, Ruskin
TRUSKAN	Etruscan
TUSKAN	Tuscan

USKĀT

FUSKĀT	infuscate, obfuscate
RUSKĀT	coruscate

USKĒ

BUSKĒ	busky
DUSKĒ	dusky
HUSKĒ	husky
MUSKĒ	musky
RUSKĒ	rusky, Rusky

USKER

BUSKER	busker
HUSKER	husker, cornhusker
TUSKER	tusker

USKET

BUSKET	busket
MUSKET	musket

USKIN

(See USKAN)

USKING

BUSKING	busking
DUSKING	dusking
HUSKING	husking, cornhusking
TUSKING	tusking

USKŪL

JUSKŪL	majuscule
KUSKŪL	ulcuscule
NUSKŪL	minuscule
PUSKŪL	crepuscule, opuscule

USKUS

FUSKUS	fuscous
KUSKUS	khuskhus
MUSKUS	muscous

ŪSL

DŪSL	medusal
NŪSL	hypotenusal

(See OOSAL)

USL

BUSL	arbuscle, bustle
DUSL	duscle
HUSL	hustle
JUSL	jussel, justle
KUSL	ulcuscle
MUSL	muscle, mussel
PUSL	corpuscle, crepuscle, opuscle
RUSL	rustle
TRUSL	trusseil
TUSL	pertussal, tussal, tussle

ŪSLĒ

FŪSLĒ	diffusely, profusely

(See OOSLĒ)

USLĒ

MUSLĒ	muscley
RUSLĒ	rustly
THUSLĒ	thusly

USLER

BUSLER	bustler
HUSLER	hustler
RUSLER	rustler
TUSLER	tussler

ŪSLES

ŪSLES	useless

(See OOSLES)

USLING

(See USL, add -ing where appropriate.)

ŪSNES

FŪSNES	diffuseness, profuseness
TŪSNES	obtuseness

(See OOSNES)

ŪSŌ

(See OOSŌ)

USTA

GUSTA	Augusta
HUSTA	hasta
KRUSTA	lincrusta

USTARD

(See USTERD)

USTĒ

BUSTĒ	busty
DUSTĒ	dusty
FUSTĒ	fusty
GUSTĒ	gusty
KRUSTĒ	crusty
LUSTĒ	lusty
MUSTĒ	mustee, musty
RUSTĒ	rusty
TRUSTĒ	trusty, trustee

USTED

BUSTED	busted, combusted
DUSTED	bedusted, dusted
GUSTED	disgusted, gusted
JUSTED	adjusted, coadjusted, misadjusted, readjusted
LUSTED	lusted
RUSTED	rusted
TRUSTED	distrusted, entrusted, mistrusted, trusted

(See OOSTER)

USTER

BLUSTER	bluster
BUSTER	blockbuster, broncobuster, buster, filibuster, combustor, robuster, trustbuster
DUSTER	duster, knuckleduster
FLUSTER	fluster
JUSTER	adjuster, juster, coadjuster, readjuster
KLUSTER	cluster
LUSTER	lackluster, luster
MUSTER	muster
RUSTER	ruster, rustre
THRUSTER	thruster
TRUSTER	distruster, mistruster, truster

USTERD

BLUSTERD	blustered
BUSTERD	bustard
FLUSTERD	beflustered, flustered
KLUSTERD	clustered, unclustered
KUSTERD	custard
LUSTERD	lustered
MUSTERD	mustard, mustered
RUSTERD	rustred

USTFUL

GUSTFUL	disgustful, gustful
LUSTFUL	lustful
RUSTFUL	rustful
TRUSTFUL	distrustful, mistrustful, trustful

USTIK

BUSTIK	bustic
FUSTIK	fustic
KRUSTIK	anacrustic
RUSTIK	rustic

USTING

BUSTING	busting
DUSTING	dusting
GUSTING	disgusting, gusting
JUSTING	adjusting, coadjusting, maladjusting, readjusting
KRUSTING	encrusting, crusting
LUSTING	lusting
RUSTING	rusting
THRUSTING	thrusting
TRUSTING	distrusting, entrusting, mistrusting, trusting

USTINGZ

| HUSTINGZ | hustings |

(See USTING, add -s where appropriate.)

USTIS

| GUSTIS | Augustus |
| JUSTIS | justice, Justus |

USTIV

| BUSTIV | combustive |
| JUSTIV | adjustive |

USTLĒ

BUSTLĒ	robustly
GUSTLĒ	augustly
JUSTLĒ	justly

USTMENT

JUSTMENT	adjustment, maladjustment, readjustment
KRUSTMENT	encrustment
TRUSTMENT	entrustment

USTNES

BUSTNES	robustness
GUSTNES	augustness
JUSTNES	justness, unjustness

USTŌ

| BUSTŌ | basso robusto, robusto |
| GUSTŌ | gusto |

USTRAL

| KUSTRAL | lacustral |
| LUSTRAL | lustral, palustral |

USTRĀT

| FRUSTRĀT | frustrate |
| LUSTRĀT | illustrate, lustrate, perlustrate |

USTRIN

| KUSTRIN | interlacustrine, lacustrine |
| LUSTRIN | palustrine |

USTRUM

| FLUSTRUM | flustrum |
| LUSTRUM | lustrum |

USTRUS

| BLUSTRUS | blustrous |
| LUSTRUS | illustrous, lacklustrous, lustrous |

USTUS

(See USTIS)

ŪSUM

(See OOSUM)

ŪTA

LŪTA   aluta

(See OOTA)

UTA

GUTA   gutta
KUTA   Calcutta

ŪTANT

MŪTANT   commutant, mutant
NŪTANT   nutant
PŪTANT   disputant

(See OOTANT)

ŪTAL

(See ŪTL)

UTAL

(See UTL)

ŪTĀT

MŪTĀT   immutate, mutate
NŪTĀT   circumnutate, nutate
SKŪTĀT   scutate

ŪTĒ

BŪTĒ   beauty
DŪTĒ   duty
KŪTĒ   cutie

(See OOTĒ)

UTĒ

BUTĒ   butty
CHUTĒ   chuttie
GUTĒ   gutty
JUTĒ   jutty
KUTĒ   cutty

NUTĒ   nutty
PUTĒ   puttee, putty
RUTĒ   rutty
SKUTĒ   scutty
SMUTĒ   smutty
SUTĒ   suttee
TUTĒ   tutty
YUTĒ   yati

ŪTED

FŪTED   confuted, refuted
KŪTED   electrocuted,
              executed, persecuted,
              prosecuted
LŪTED   diluted, convoluted,
              polluted, revoluted,
              saluted, voluted
MŪTED   commuted, muted,
              permuted, transmuted
NŪTED   comminuted, cornuted
PŪTED   deputed, disputed,
              imputed, computed,
              putid, supputed

(See OOT, add -ed where appropriate.)

UTED

(See UT, add -ed or -ted where appropriate.)

ŪTEN

(See ŪTN)

UTEN

(See UTN)

ŪTER

FŪTER   confuter, refuter
KŪTER   acuter, executor,
              electrocuter,
              collucutor, cuter,
              persecutor, prosecutor
MŪTER   commuter, muter,
              permuter, transmuter
NŪTER   minuter, neuter
PŪTER   deputer, digital

ONLY ONE DRINK AT A TIME, PLEASE

A nimiety of gin
Sows ebriety and sin;
In respectable society
This is viewed as impropriety;
The man of sagacity
Refrains from bibacity.

---

              computer, disputer,
              imputer, computer,
              microcomputer,
              pewter

(See OOTER)

UTER

UTER   utter
BUTER   abutter, bread-and-
              butter, butter, peanut
              butter, rebutter,
              surrebutter
FLUTER   flutter
GLUTER   glutter
GUTER   gutter
HWUTER   whutter
KLUTER   clutter
KUTER   daisycutter, cutter,
              leafcutter, meatcutter,
              pilot cutter,
              stonecutter,
              woodcutter
MUTER   mutter
NUTER   nutter
PUTER   putter
RUTER   rutter, swartrutter
SHUTER   shutter
SKUTER   scutter
SPLUTER   splutter
SPUTER   sputter
STRUTER   strutter
STUTER   stutter
SUTER   sutter

ŪTERD

NŪTERD   neutered
TŪTERD   tutored

UTERD

(See UTER, add -ed where appropriate.)

ŪTHER

(See OOTHER)

UTHER

(TH as in then)

UTHER   other
BRUTHER   brother, charter
              brother, foster
              brother, half brother,
              lodge brother,
              stepbrother

MUTHER   den mother,
                   foremother, foster
                   mother, godmother,
                   grandmother, mother,
                   stepmother
NUTHER   another, one another
SMUTHER   smother
TUTHER   t'other
WUTHER   wuther

UTHERZ

DRUTHERZ   druthers

(See **UTHERZ,** add *-s* where appropriate.)

ŪTHFUL

(See $\overline{\text{OO}}$THFUL)

ŪTHING

(See $\overline{\text{OO}}$THING)

ŪTHLES

(See $\overline{\text{OO}}$THLES)

ŪTHSUM

(See $\overline{\text{OO}}$THSUM)

ŪTIJ

MŪTIJ   mutage
PŪTIJ   putage
SKŪTIJ   scutage

(See $\overline{\text{OO}}$TIJ)

ŪTIK

ŪTIK   halieutic, maieutic
BŪTIK   antiscorbutic,
                   scorbutic
DŪTIK   paideutic,
                   propaedeutic
LŪTIK   probouleutic
MŪTIK   mutic
NŪTIK   digoneutic,
                   hermeneutic,
                   ichneutic
PŪTIK   radiotherapeutic,
                   therapeutic
SŪTIK   pharmaceutic
TŪTIK   emphyteutic
ZŪTIK   diazeutic

(See $\overline{\text{OO}}$TIK)

ŪTIKS

(See **ŪTIK,** add *-s* where appropriate.)

ŪTIL

(See **ŪTL**)

ŪTING

(See **ŪT,** $\overline{\text{OO}}$**T,** add *-ing* where appropriate.)

ŪTISH

(See $\overline{\text{OO}}$TISH)

UTISH

NUTISH   nuttish
RUTISH   ruttish
SLUTISH   sluttish

ŪTIST

NŪTIST   hermeneutist
PŪTIST   therapeutist
SŪTIST   pharmaceutist

(See $\overline{\text{OO}}$TIST)

ŪTIV

BŪTIV   *retributive*
KŪTIV   persecutive
LŪTIV   evolutive,
                   convolutive,
                   resolutive
TŪTIV   constitutive,
                   restitutive,
                   substitutive

(See $\overline{\text{OO}}$TIV)

ŪTIZM

MŪTIZM   mutism

(See $\overline{\text{OO}}$TIZM)

ŪTL

ŪTL   utile, inutile
FŪTL   futile, refutal
SŪTL   sutile

(See $\overline{\text{OO}}$TL)

UTL

BUTL   abuttal, buttle,
                   rebuttal, surrebuttal
GUTL   guttle
KUTL   cuttle
RUTL   ruttle
SHUTL   shuttle, space shuttle
SKUTL   scuttle
SUTL   subtle, suttle, unsubtle

ŪTLĒ

KŪTLĒ   acutely, cutely
MŪTLĒ   mutely
NŪTLĒ   minutely
TŪTLĒ   astutely

(See $\overline{\text{OO}}$TLĒ)

UTLER

BUTLER   butler
KUTLER   cutler, cuttler
SKUTLER   scuttler
SUTLER   subtler, sutler

ŪTLES

PŪTLES   reputeless

(See $\overline{\text{OO}}$TLES)

UTLET

KUTLET   cutlet
NUTLET   nutlet

ŪTLING

(See $\overline{\text{OO}}$TLING)

UTLING

BUTLING   buttling
GUTLING   gutling, guttling
SKUTLING   scuttling
SUTLING   sutling

ŪTMENT

FŪTMENT   confutement

(See $\overline{\text{OO}}$TMENT)

ŪTN

KŪTN	cutin
TŪTN	Teuton

(See OŌTN, OŌTON)

UTN

UTN	ughten
BUTN	bachelor button, belly button, bluebutton, button, unbutton
GLUTN	glutton
MUTN	mutton

ŪTNES

KŪTNES	acuteness, cuteness
MŪTNES	muteness
NŪTNES	minuteness
SŪTNES	hirsuteness
TŪTNES	astuteness

(See OŌTNES)

UTNING

BUTNING	buttoning
HUTNING	huttoning

ŪTŌ

(See OŌTŌ)

ŪTRIKS

KŪTRIKS	persecutrix
TŪTRIKS	tutrix

ŪTSĒ

KŪTSĒ	cutesie

(See OŌTSĒ)

UTUK

BUTUK	buttock, quakebuttock
FUTUK	futtock

ŪTUM

SKŪTUM	scutum
SPŪTUM	sputum

(See OŌTUM)

ŪTŪR

(See ŪCHER)

ŪTUS

KŪTUS	gyascutus

(See OŌTUS)

ŪVAL

(See OŌVAL)

ŪVĒ

(See OŌVĒ)

UVĒ

DUVĒ	dovey, lovey-dovey
KUVĒ	covey
LUVĒ	lovey

UVEL

GRUVEL	grovel
HUVEL	hovel
SHUVEL	shovel
SKUVEL	scovel

(See OVEL)

ŪVEN

(See OŌVEN)

UVEN

UVEN	oven
KUVEN	coven
SLUVEN	sloven

ŪVER

(See OŌVER)

UVER

GLUVER	glover
HUVER	hover, windhover
KUVER	discover, cover, recover, rediscover, tablecover, undercover, uncover
LUVER	lover, animal lover (etc.)

PLUVER	plover
SHUVER	shover

ŪVING

(See OŌV, add -ing where appropriate.)

UVING

GLUVING	gloving, ungloving
LUVING	loving, animal loving (etc.)
SHUVING	shoving

ŪVMENT

(See OŌVMENT)

ŪYA

(See OŌYA)

ŪZA

MŪZA	musa
TŪZA	tuza

(See OŌZA)

ŪZAL

FŪZAL	fusel, refusal, rumtifusel
KŪZAL	accusal
MŪZAL	musal

(See OŌZL)

ŪZANS

ŪZANS	misusance, usance
KŪZANS	recusance

UZARD

UZARD	uzzard
BUZARD	buzzard
HUZARD	huzzard

ŪZĒ

(See OŌZĒ)

UZĒ

BUZĒ	buzzy
FUZĒ	fuzzy

GUZĒ	fuzzy-guzzy
HUZĒ	hussy
MUZĒ	muzzy, tuzzymuzzy
SKUZĒ	skuzzy
WUZĒ	fuzzy-wuzzy, Fuzzy-Wuzzy, wuzzy

UZEN

DUZEN	dozen
KUZEN	cousin

UZENS

DUZENZ	dozens
KUZENZ	cousins

ŪZER

ŪZER	misuser, nonuser, user
BŪZER	abuser
FŪZER	diffuser, fuser, infuser, interfuser, confuser, refuser, suffuser, transfuser
KŪZER	accuser, excuser
MŪZER	amuser, muser

(See $\overline{OO}$ZER)

UZER

BUZER	buzzer
FUZER	fuzzer
NUZER	nuzzer

ŪZHUN

BŪZHUN	abusion
FŪZHUN	A affusion, D diffusion, E effusion, F fusion, I infusion, interfusion, K confusion, P perfusion, PR profusion, R refusal, S circumfusion, suffusion, TR transfusion
TŪZHUN	extusion, contusion, pertusion

(See $\overline{OO}$ZHUN)

ŪZING

(See **Ū̄Z**, $\overline{OO}$**Z**, add -ing where appropriate.)

UZING

BUZING	buzzing
FUZING	fuzzing
MUZING	muzzing

ŪZIV

KŪZIV	accusive
MŪZIV	amusive, unamusive

ŪZL

(See $\overline{OO}$ZL, ŪZAL)

UZL

BUZL	buzzle
FUZL	fuzzle
GUZL	guzzle
MUZL	bemuzzle, muzzle, unmuzzle
NUZL	nuzzle
PUZL	Chinese puzzle, jigsaw puzzle, crossword puzzle, monkey puzzle, puzzle, word puzzle

UZLĒ

(See **UZL**, add -y where appropriate.)

ŪZLER

(See $\overline{OO}$ZLER)

UZLER

GUZLER	gas guzzler, guzzler
MUZLER	muzzler
NUZLER	nuzzler
PUZLER	puzzler, word puzzler

UZLING

(See **UZL**, add -ing where appropriate.)

ŪZMAN

NŪZMAN	newsman

(See $\overline{OO}$ZMAN)

ŪZMENT

KŪZMENT	accusement
MŪZMENT	amusement

UZN

DUZN	dozen
KUZN	catercousin, quatercousin, cousin, cozen

UZNT

DUZNT	doesn't
WUZNT	wasn't

TRIPLE RHYMES

(Words accented on the syllable before the next-to-the-last syllable, or, in a few cases, on one or more syllables before *that*. They are also called dactylic rhymes.)

Ā′A.BL

FRĀ′A.BL	defrayable
PĀ′A.BL	impayable, payable, prepayable, repayable, unpayable
PLĀ′A.BL	playable, unplayable
PRĀ′A.BL	prayable, unprayable
SĀ′A.BL	sayable, unsayable
SLĀ′A.BL	slayable
SPĀ′A.BL	spayable
SWĀ′A.BL	swayable, unswayable
TRĀ′A.BL	portrayable, unportrayable
VĀ′A.BL	conveyable, surveyable, unconveyable, unsurveyable
WĀ′A.BL	weighable, unweighable

AB′A.RET

KAB′A.RET	cabaret
TAB′A.RET	tabaret

AB′A.BL

GRAB′A.BL	grabbable
JAB′A.BL	jabbable
NAB′A.BL	nabbable
STAB′A.BL	stabbable
TAB′A.BL	tabbable

AB′A.SIS

NAB′A.SIS	anabasis
RAB′A.SIS	parabasis
TAB′A.SIS	catabasis, metabasis

Ā′BER.ING

LĀ′BER.ING	belaboring, laboring
NĀ′BER.ING	neighboring
TĀ′BER.ING	taboring

Ā′BER.ER

LĀ′BER.ER	laborer
TĀ′BER.ER	taberer

Ā′BI.A

LĀ′BI.A	labia
RĀ′BI.A	Arabia, Bessarabia
SWĀ′BI.A	Swabia
TRĀ′BI.A	trabea

Ā′BI.AN

FĀ′BI.AN	Fabian
GĀ′BI.AN	gabion
RĀ′BI.AN	Arabian, Sorabian
SĀ′BI.AN	Sabian
SWĀ′BI.AN	Swabian

AB′ID.NES

RAB′ID.NES	rabidness
TAB′ID.NES	tabidness

AB′I.ER

BLAB′I.ER	blabbier
FLAB′I.ER	flabbier
GAB′I.ER	gabbier
GRAB′I.ER	grabbier
KRAB′I.ER	crabbier
SHAB′I.ER	shabbier
SKAB′I.ER	scabbier

Ā′BI.ĒZ

Ā′BI.ĒZ	abies
RĀ′BI.ĒZ	rabies
SKĀ′BI.ĒZ	scabies

AB′I.FĪ

LAB′I.FĪ	dissyllabify, labefy, syllabify
TAB′I.FĪ	tabefy

AB′I.KAL

LAB′I.KAL	monosyllabical, multisyllabical, polysyllabical, syllabical
RAB′I.KAL	Arabical

AB′I.LĒ

BLAB′I.LĒ	blabbily
FLAB′I.LĒ	flabbily
GAB′I.LĒ	gabbily
KRAB′I.LĒ	crabbily
LAB′I.LĒ	ballabile
SKAB′I.LĒ	scabbily

AB′I.NES

(See AB′Ē, add -ness where appropriate.)

AB′IT.Ē

BAB′IT.Ē	babbitty
RAB′IT.Ē	rabbity

AB′IT.ING

BAB′IT.ING	babbitting
HAB′IT.ING	habiting, inhabiting, cohabiting
RAB′IT.ING	rabbiting

AB′I.TŪD

HAB′I.TŪD	habitude
TAB′I.TŪD	tabitude

AB′L.MENT

BAB′L.MENT	babblement
BRAB′L.MENT	brabblement
DAB′L.MENT	dabblement
DRAB′L.MENT	drabblement
GAB′L.MENT	gabblement
GRAB′L.MENT	grabblement
RAB′L.MENT	rabblement
SKAB′L.MENT	scabblement
SKRAB′L.MENT	scrabblement

Ā′BL.NES

Ā′BL.NES	ableness
SĀ′BL.NES	sableness
STĀ′BL.NES	stableness, unstableness

AB′LI.ER

(See ABLĒ, change -y and add -er where appropriate.)

AB′O.LA

RAB′O.LA	parabola, sporabala
TAB′O.LA	Metabola

AB′O.LĪZ

RAB′O.LĪZ	parabolize
TAB′O.LĪZ	metabolize

AB′O.LIZM

AB′O.LIZM	diabolism
NAB′O.LIZM	anabolism
TAB′O.LIZM	catabolism, metabolism

AB′Ū.LA

FAB′Ū.LA	fabula
NAB′Ū.LA	incunabula
TAB′Ū.LA	tabula

AB′Ū.LAR

FAB′Ū.LAR	fabular, confabular
NAB′Ū.LAR	incunabular, cunabular, tintinnabular
PAB′Ū.LAR	pabular
TAB′Ū.LAR	acetabular, tabular

AB′Ū.LĀT

FAB′Ū.LĀT	fabulate, confabulate
NAB′Ū.LĀT	tintinnabulate
TAB′Ū.LĀT	tabulate

AB′Ū.LIST

FAB′Ū.LIST	fabulist
KAB′Ū.LIST	vocabulist
NAB′Ū.LIST	incunabulist, tintinnabulist

AB′Ū.LUM

NAB′Ū.LUM	incunabulum, tintinnabulum
PAB′Ū.LUM	pabulum
TAB′Ū.LUM	acetabulum

AB′Ū.LUS

FAB′Ū.LUS	fabulous
NAB′Ū.LUS	tintinnabulous
PAB′Ū.LUS	pabulous
SAB′Ū.LUS	sabulous
TAB′Ū.LUS	fantabulous

ACH′A.BL

BACH′A.BL	batchable
HACH′A.BL	hatchable, crosshatchable, unhatchable
KACH′A.BL	catchable, uncatchable
LACH′A.BL	latchable, unlatchable
MACH′A.BL	immatchable, matchable, rematchable, unmatchable
PACH′A.BL	dispatchable, patchable, repatchable, unpatchable
SKRACH′A.BL	scratchable, unscratchable
SNACH′A.BL	snatchable, unsnatchable
THACH′A.BL	thatchable, unthatchable

ACH′E.LA

MACH′E.LA	comatula
SKACH′E.LA	scatula
SPACH′E.LA	spatula

ACH′ER.Ē

HACH′ER.Ē	hatchery
PACH′ER.Ē	patchery

ACH′I.NES

(See **ACH,** add *-iness* where appropriate.)

ACH′OO.LĀT

GRACH′OO.LĀT	gratulate, congratulate
SPACH′OO.LĀT	spatulate

ACH′OOR.ĀT

MACH′OOR.ĀT	maturate
SACH′OOR.ĀT	polyunsaturate, saturate, supersaturate

Ā′DA.BL

BRĀ′DA.BL	braidable, unbraidable, upbraidable
GRĀ′DA.BL	biodegradable, degradable, gradable, undegradable, ungradable
SHĀ′DA.BL	shadable, unshadable
SWĀ′DA.BL	dissuadable, persuadable, undissuadable, unpersuadable
TRĀ′DA.BL	retradable, tradable, untradable
VĀ′DA.BL	evadable, invadable
WĀ′DA.BL	unwadable, wadable

Ā′DED.LĒ

FĀ′DED.LĒ	fadedly
GRĀ′DED.LĒ	degradedly
JĀ′DED.LĒ	jadedly

Ā′DED.NES

(See **ĀD,** add *-edness* where appropriate.)

Ā′DI.A

KĀ′DI.A	Acadia, Arcadia
LĀ′DI.A	Palladia
STĀ′DI.A	stadia

Ā′DI.AL

RĀ′DI.AL	multiradial, radial, uniradial
STĀ′DI.AL	interstadial, stadial

Ā′DI.AN

BĀ′DI.AN	Barbadian
KĀ′DI.AN	Acadian, Arcadian, Orcadian, circadian
LĀ′DI.AN	palladian
MĀ′DI.AN	gammadion, nomadian
NĀ′DI.AN	Canadian, Grenadian
RĀ′DI.AN	radian, steradian

Ā′DI.ANT

GRĀ′DI.ANT	gradient
RĀ′DI.ANT	irradiant, radiant

Ā′DING.LĒ

FĀ′DING.LĒ	fadingly
GRĀ′DING.LĒ	degradingly
VĀ′DING.LĒ	pervadingly

AD'ISH.NES

BAD'ISH.NES	baddishness
FAD'ISH.NES	faddishness
KAD'ISH.NES	caddishness
MAD'ISH.NES	maddishness
SAD'ISH.NES	saddishness

AD'I.TIV

AD'I.TIV	additive
TRAD'I.TIV	traditive

Ā'DI.UM

LĀ'DI.UM	caladium, palladium
NĀ'DI.UM	vanadium
RĀ'DI.UM	radium
STĀ'DI.UM	stadium
VĀ'DI.UM	vadium

Ā'DI.US

GLĀ'DI.US	gladius
RĀ'DI.US	adradius, hyporadius, radius

AF'I.A

GRAF'I.A	agraphia, dysgraphia, mogigraphia, paragraphia, strephographia
MAF'I.A	maffia, mafia
RAF'I.A	raffia
SAF'I.A	asaphia
TAF'I.A	tafia

AF'I.KAL

GRAF'I.KAL	*A* anthropographical, *B* bibliographical, biographical, biogeographical, *D* diagraphical, *E* electrocardiographical, epigraphical, ethnographical, *F* physiographical, phytographical, photographical, *GL* glossographical, *GR* graphical, *J* geographical, *K* calligraphical, cartographical, cosmographical, *L* lexigraphical, lexicographical, *O* autobiographical, autographical, orthographical, *P* paleographical, paleontographical, paragraphical, pornographical, *T* pterylographical, telegraphical, typographical, topographical *Z* zoographical, zoogeographical
RAF'I.KAL	seraphical
TAF'I.KAL	epitaphical

AF'L.MENT

BAF'L.MENT	bafflement
RAF'L.MENT	rafflement
SKRAF'L.MENT	scrafflement
SNAF'L.MENT	snafflement

AFT'A.BL

(See **AFT**, add *-able* where appropriate.)

AF'TI.LĒ

DRAF'TI.LĒ	draftily, draughtily
KRAF'TI.LĒ	craftily

AFT'LES.LĒ

DRAFT'LES.LĒ	draftlessly
GRAFT'LES.LĒ	graftlessly
KRAFT'LES.LĒ	craftlessly
SHAFT'LES.LĒ	shaftlessly

AG'A.BL

BAG'A.BL	baggable
DRAG'A.BL	draggable
FLAG'A.BL	flaggable
FRAG'A.BL	irrefragable
GAG'A.BL	gaggable
JAG'A.BL	jaggable
NAG'A.BL	naggable
RAG'A.BL	raggable
SAG'A.BL	saggable
SHAG'A.BL	shaggable
SKAG'A.BL	scaggable
SNAG'A.BL	snaggable
TAG'A.BL	taggable
WAG'A.BL	waggable

AG'ED.LĒ

JAG'ED.LĒ	jaggedly
RAG'ED.LĒ	raggedly
SKRAG'ED.LĒ	scraggedly

AG'ED.NES

JAG'ED.NES	jaggedness
KRAG'ED.NES	craggedness
RAG'ED.NES	raggedness
SKRAG'ED.NES	scraggedness

AG'ER.Ē

FAG'ER.Ē	faggery
JAG'ER.Ē	jaggery
LAG'ER.Ē	inlagary
RAG'ER.Ē	raggery
STAG'ER.Ē	staggery
SWAG'ER.Ē	swaggery
WAG'ER.Ē	waggery
ZAG'ER.Ē	zig-zaggery

AG'ER.ER

STAG'ER.ER	staggerer
SWAG'ER.ER	swaggerer

AG'ER.ING

STAG'ER.ING	staggering
SWAG'ER.ING	swaggering

AG'I.LĒ

BAG'I.LĒ	baggily
KRAG'I.LĒ	craggily
NAG'I.LĒ	naggily
RAG'I.LĒ	raggily
SHAG'I.LĒ	shaggily
SKRAG'I.LĒ	scraggily

AG'I.NES

BAG'I.NES	bagginess
BRAG'I.NES	bragginess
FLAG'I.NES	flagginess
KRAG'I.NES	cragginess
NAG'I.NES	knagginess, nagginess
SHAG'I.NES	shagginess
SKRAG'I.NES	scragginess

AG'ISH.LĒ

BRAG'ISH.LĒ	braggishly
HAG'ISH.LĒ	haggishly
NAG'ISH.LĒ	naggishly
WAG'ISH.LĒ	waggishly

AG'ON.AL

AG'ON.AL	agonal, diagonal, preagonal, triagonal
SAG'ON.AL	hexagonal
TAG'ON.AL	heptagonal, octagonal, pentagonal
TRAG'ON.AL	tetragonal

AG'O.NIST

AG'O.NIST	agonist, deuteragonist
TAG'O.NIST	antagonist, protagonist, tritagonist

AG'O.NĪZ

AG'O.NĪZ	agonize
TAG'O.NĪZ	antagonize

AG'O.TĒ

FAG'O.TĒ	faggoty, fagoty
MAG'O.TĒ	maggoty

Ā'GRAN.SĒ

FLĀ'GRAN.SĒ	flagrancy
FRĀ'GRAN.SĒ	fragrancy
VĀ'GRAN.SĒ	vagrancy

Ā'I.KAL

BRĀ'I.KAL	algebraical, Hebraical
DĀ'I.KAL	Judaical
KĀ'I.KAL	alcaical, archaical, trochaical
LĀ'I.KAL	formulaical, laical
MĀ'I.KAL	Aramaical, Ptolemaical
PĀ'I.KAL	apotropaical
ZĀ'I.KAL	pharisaical, Mosaical, paradisaical

Ä'ING.LĒ

Ä'ING.LĒ	ahingly, oh-and-ahingly
BÄ'ING.LĒ	baaingly, bahingly
BLÄ'ING.LĒ	blahingly, blah-blahingly

Ā'I.TĒ

GĀ'I.TĒ	gaiety
LĀ'I.TĒ	laity

Ā'JA.BL

GĀ'JA.BL	engageable, gaugeable
STĀ'JA.BL	stageable, unstageable
SWĀ'JA.BL	assuageable

AJ'ER.Ē

NAJ'ER.Ē	menagerie
TAJ'ER.Ē	potagerie

Ā'JI.A

FĀ'JI.A	aphagia, aerophagia, dysphagia, gamophagia, kreatophagia, omophagia, autophagia, pagophagia, polyphagia, chthonophagia
HĀ'JI.A	hagia
NĀ'JI.A	Panagia
RĀ'JI.A	menorrhagia, metrorrhagia

Ā'JI.AN

LĀ'JI.AN	archipelagian, pelagian
MĀ'JI.AN	magian

AJ'I.KAL

MAJ'I.KAL	magical, theomagical
TRAJ'I.KAL	tragical

Ā'JI.LĒ

KĀ'JI.LĒ	cagily
STĀ'JI.LĒ	stagily

AJ'IL.NES

AJ'IL.NES	agileness
FRAJ'IL.NES	fragileness

AJ'I.NAL

MAJ'I.NAL	imaginal
PAJ'I.NAL	paginal
VAJ'I.NAL	vaginal

AJ'I.NĀT

MAJ'I.NĀT	imaginate
PAJ'I.NĀT	paginate
SAJ'I.NĀT	saginate
VAJ'I.NĀT	evaginate, invaginate, vaginate

AJ'I.NUS

AJ'I.NUS	oleaginous
BAJ'I.NUS	lumbaginous
LAJ'I.NUS	cartilaginous, mucilaginous
RAJ'I.NUS	farraginous, voraginous
VAJ'I.NUS	favaginous

AJ'I.Ō

AJ'I.Ō	agio
DAJ'I.Ō	adagio

AJ'I.TĀT

AJ'I.TĀT	agitate
SAJ'I.TĀT	sagittate

Ā'JUS.LĒ

BRĀ'JUS.LĒ	umbrageously
PĀ'JUS.LĒ	rampageously
RĀ'JUS.LĒ	courageously, outrageously
TĀ'JUS.LĒ	advantageously, disadvantageously, contagiously

Ā'KA.BL

Ā'KA.BL	acheable
BRĀ'KA.BL	breakable, unbreakable
PĀ'KA.BL	impacable, pacable

PLĀ′KA.BL implacable, placable
SHĀ′KA.BL shakable, unshakable
SLĀ′KA.BL slakable, unslakable
TĀ′KA.BL mistakable, takable,
undertakable,
unmistakable
WĀ′KA.BL awakable, wakable

AK′A.NAL

AK′A.NAL diaconal
BAK′A.NAL bacchanal

Ā′KĀ.TED

PLĀ′KĀ.TED placated, unplacated
VĀ′KĀ.TED revacated,
unvacated, vacated

AK′A.TŌ.RĒ

NAK′A.TŌ.RĒ kincknackatory
PLAK′A.TŌ.RĒ placatory

Ā′KA.WĀ

BRĀ′KA.WĀ breakaway
TĀ′KA.WĀ takeaway

AK′CHER.ING

FAK′CHER.ING manufacturing
FRAK′CHER.ING fracturing,
refracturing

AK′CHŌŌ.AL

AK′CHŌŌ.AL actual
FAK′CHŌŌ.AL factual
PAK′CHŌŌ.AL impactual
TAK′CHŌŌ.AL contactual, tactual
TRAK′CHŌŌ.AL contractual

AK′EN.ING

BLAK′EN.ING blackening
SLAK′EN.ING slackening

Ā′KER.Ē

BĀ′KER.Ē bakery
FĀ′KER.Ē fakery, fakiry
KWĀ′KER.Ē quakery, Quakery
RĀ′KER.Ē rakery

SNĀ′KER.Ē snakery
TĀ′KER.Ē undertakery

AK′ER.Ē

HAK′ER.Ē hackery
JAK′ER.Ē hijackery
KRAK′ER.Ē jimcrackery
KWAK′ER.Ē quackery
NAK′ER.Ē knackery, knick-
knackery
SNAK′ER.Ē snackery
THAK′ER.Ē Thackeray

AK′ER.EL

KAK′ER.EL cackerel
MAK′ER.EL mackerel

Ā′KER.IZM

FĀ′KER.IZM fakirism
KWĀ′KER.IZM Quakerism
SHĀ′KER.IZM Shakerism

AK′ER.ŌŌ

JAK′ER.ŌŌ Jackaroo, jackeroo
SMAK′ER.ŌŌ smackeroo

AK′ET.ED

BRAK′ET.ED bracketed
JAK′ET.ED jacketed
PAK′ET.ED packeted
PLAK′ET.ED placketed
RAK′ET.ED racketed

AK′ET.ING

(See **AKET,** add -ing where appropriate.)

Ā′KI.A

MĀ′KI.A naumachia
TRĀ′KI.A Batrachia, trachea

Ā′KI.AL

BRĀ′KI.AL brachial
RĀ′KI.AL rachial
TRĀ′KI.AL trachial

Ā′KI.AN

Ā′KI.AN Noachian
LĀ′KI.AN selachian
MĀ′KI.AN tauromachian
STĀ′KI.AN eustachian
TRĀ′KI.AN batrachian, trachean

AK′I.NĀT

KAK′I.NĀT cacchinate
MAK′I.NĀT machinate

Ā′KI.NES

FĀ′KI.NES fakiness
FLĀ′KI.NES flakiness
KWĀ′KI.NES quakiness
SHĀ′KI.NES shakiness
SNĀ′KI.NES snakiness

AK′I.NES

HAK′I.NES hackiness
HWAK′I.NES whackiness
KRAK′I.NES gimcrackiness
TAK′I.NES tackiness
WAK′I.NES wackiness

IN CASE ANYONE SHOULD ESK YOU

A stomach pump's required to rescue
A sheep that's eaten too much fescue.

AK′ISH.NES

BLAK′ISH.NES blackishness
BRAK′ISH.NES brackishness
KWAK′ISH.NES quackishness
NAK′ISH.NES knackishness
SLAK′ISH.NES slackishness

AK′Ō.NĪT

AK′Ō.NĪT aconite
TAK′Ō.NĪT taconite

AK′RI.TĒ

AK′RI.TĒ acrity
LAK′RI.TĒ alacrity

AK′RŌ.DONT

AK′RŌ.DONT acrodont
MAK′RO.DONT macrodont

AK'RO.NIZM

NAK'RO.NIZM	anachronism
RAK'RO.NIZM	parachronism
TAK'RO.NIZM	metachronism

AK'SA.BL

LAK'SA.BL	relaxable, unrelaxable
TAK'SA.BL	taxable, untaxable

AK'SHUN.AL

(See **AK'SHUN**, add -al where appropriate.)

AK'SA.BL

AK'SA.BL	axable
TAK'SA.BL	taxable

AK'SHUS.NES

FAK'SHUS.NES	factiousness
FRAK'SHUS.NES	fractiousness

AK'SI.A

PRAK'SI.A	apraxia, echopraxia
RAK'SI.A	ataraxia
TAK'SI.A	ataxia

AK'SI.AL

AK'SI.AL	axial, biaxial, coaxial
BAK'SI.AL	abaxial

AK'TA.BL

AK'TA.BL	actable, enactable, reactable, transactable
DAK'TA.BL	redactable
FAK'TA.BL	olfactible
FRAK'TA.BL	infractible, irrefractable, refractable
PAK'TA.BL	impactable, compactible
STRAK'TA.BL	abstractable, distractible
TAK'TA.BL	intactable, contactable, tactable
TRAK'TA.BL	abstractable, attractable, detractible, distractible, extractible, intractable, contractable, protractable, retractable, tractable

AK'TED.NES

PAK'TED.NES	impactedness
STRAK'TED.NES	abstractedness
TRAK'TED.NES	distractedness, contractedness, protractedness

AK'TER.Ē

AK'TER.Ē	enactory
FAK'TER.Ē	benefactory, dissatisfactory, factory, calefactory, malefactory, manufactory, olfactory, satisfactory, unsatisfactory
FRAK'TER.Ē	refractory
LAK'TER.Ē	lactary, phylactery
TRAK'TER.Ē	detractory, tractory

AK'TI.AL

BRAK'TI.AL	bracteal
LAK'TI.AL	lacteal

AK'TI.KAL

DAK'TI.KAL	didactical
LAK'TI.KAL	stalactical
PRAK'TI.KAL	impractical, practical, unpractical
TAK'TI.KAL	syntactical, tactical

AK'TIV.NES

(See **AK'TIV**, add -ness.)

AK'TŪ.AL

(See **AK'CHOO.AL**)

AK'TŪR.ING

(See **AK'CHER.ING**)

AK'Ū.ĀT

AK'Ū.ĀT	acuate
VAK'Ū.ĀT	evacuate

AK'Ū.LA

BAK'Ū.LA	bacula
DRAK'Ū.LA	Dracula
FAK'Ū.LA	facula
MAK'Ū.LA	macula
TAK'Ū.LA	tentacula

AK'Ū.LAR

AK'Ū.LAR	piacular
NAK'Ū.LAR	supernacular, tabernacular, vernacular
RAK'Ū.LAR	oracular
TAK'Ū.LAR	ante-jentacular, jentacular, post-jentacular, spectacular, sustentacular, tentacular

AK'Ū.LĀT

JAK'Ū.LĀT	ejaculate, interjaculate, jaculate
MAK'Ū.LĀT	bimaculate, immaculate, maculate
SAK'Ū.LĀT	sacculate
TAK'Ū.LĀT	tentaculate

AK'Ū.LUM

AK'Ū.LUM	biaculum
BAK'Ū.LUM	baculum
NAK'Ū.LUM	hibernaculum
TAK'Ū.LUM	tentaculum

AK'Ū.LUS

BAK'Ū.LUS	abaculus, baculus
NAK'Ū.LUS	vernaculous
RAK'Ū.LUS	meraculous, miraculous, oraculous
SAK'Ū.LUS	sacculus

AK'Ū.PUNGK'CHER

AK'Ū.PUNGK.CHER	*acupuncture*

KWAK'Ū.PUNGK.CHER
quackupuncture

AK'WI.US

AK'WI.US	aqueous
BAK'WI.US	subaqueous
RAK'WI.US	terraqueous

Ā'LA.BL

BĀ'LA.BL	bailable
HĀ'LA.BL	exhalable, inhalable
JĀ'LA.BL	jailable, unjailable
MĀ'LA.BL	mailable, unmailable
NĀ'LA.BL	nailable, unnailable
SĀ'LA.BL	assailable, wholesalable, sailable, salable, unassailable, unsalable, unsailable
SKĀ'LA.BL	scaleable, unscaleable
TĀ'LA.BL	retailable
TRĀ'LA.BL	trailable, untrailable
VĀ'LA.BL	available, unavailable

Ā'LER.Ē

Ā'LER.Ē	alary, subalary
NĀ'LER.Ē	nailery
RĀ'LER.Ē	raillery

AL'ER.Ē

AL'ER.Ē	alary, subalary, subalary
GAL'ER.Ē	gallery
KAL'ER.Ē	intercalary, calorie, kilocalorie
SAL'ER.Ē	salary
VAL'ER.Ē	vallary

AL'ER.JĒ

AL'ER.JĒ	allergy
TAL'ER.JĒ	metallurgy

AL'ET.ED

BAL'ET.ED	balloted
VAL'ET.ED	valeted

Ā'LI.A

Ā'LI.A	marsupialia
DĀ'LI.A	dahlia, idalia, vedalia
FĀ'LI.A	Westphalia
GĀ'LI.A	galea, regalia
KĀ'LI.A	Lupercalia
LĀ'LI.A	echolalia, eschrolalia, glossolalia, copralalia, mogilalia, palilalia, paralalia, pseudolalia
MĀ'LI.A	mammalia
NĀ'LI.A	bacchanalia, marginalia, paraphernalia, saturnalia, terminalia
PĀ'LI.A	palea
RĀ'LI.A	Psoralea
SĀ'LI.A	sponsalia
SKĀ'LI.A	tragomaschalia
TĀ'LI.A	Arctalia, genitalia
TRĀ'LI.A	Australia, penetralia, Centralia
ZĀ'LI.A	azalea

(See ĀL'YA)

Ā'LI.AN

Ā'LI.AN	alien, marsupialian
DĀ'LI.AN	Daedalian, hippopotomonstro-sesquipedalian, sesquipedalian
GĀ'LI.AN	Phigalian, regalian
KĀ'LI.AN	Deucalion
MĀ'LI.AN	phantasmalian, mammalian, Pygmalion, tatterdemalion
NĀ'LI.AN	bacchanalian, saturnalian, tenaillon, tobacconalian
PĀ'LI.AN	episcopalian, Episcopalian, saranapalian
RĀ'LI.AN	paralian
SĀ'LI.AN	Messalian, universalian
TRĀ'LI.AN	Australian, Centralian

(See ĀL'YAN)

AL'I.ANS

DAL'I.ANS	dalliance
RAL'I.ANS	ralliance
VAL'I.ANS	valiance
ZAL'I.ANS	mesalliance

Ā'LI.AS

Ā'LI.AS	alias
BĀ'LI.AS	Sibelius

AL'IAS

GAL'IAS	galleass
PAL'IAS	palliasse

AL'I.ĀT

GAL'I.ĀT	galeate
MAL'I.ĀT	maleate, malleate
PAL'I.ĀT	palliate
TAL'I.ĀT	retaliate, talliate

AL'I.A.TŌ'RĒ

AL'I.A.TŌ'RĒ	aleatory
TAL'I.A.TŌ'RĒ	retaliatory

AL'ID.LĒ

KAL'ID.LĒ	callidly
PAL'ID.LĒ	pallidly
VAL'ID.LĒ	invalidly, validly

AL'ID.NES

KAL'ID.NES	callidness
PAL'ID.NES	impallidness, pallidness
VAL'ID.NES	invalidness, validness

AL'I.ER

DAL'I.ER	dallier
RAL'I.ER	rallier
SAL'I.ER	sallier
TAL'I.ER	tallier

AL'I.FĪ

KAL'I.FĪ	alkalify, calefy
SAL'I.FĪ	salify

AL'I.ING

DAL'I.ING	dallying
RAL'I.ING	rallying
SAL'I.ING	sallying
TAL'I.ING	tallying

AL'IK.LĒ

GAL'IK.LĒ	Gallicly
KAL'IK.LĒ	vocalicly
TAL'IK.LĒ	metallicly, smart-alecly

AL'I.MŌ.NĒ

AL'I.MŌ.NĒ	alimony
PAL'I.MŌ.NĒ	palimony

Ā'LI.NES

Ā'LI.NES	ailiness
DĀ'LI.NES	dailiness
SKĀ'LI.NES	scaliness
WĀ'LI.NES	wailiness

AL'I.PED

AL'I.PED	aliped
TAL'I.PED	taliped

AL'I.POT

GAL'I.POT	galipot, gallipot
TAL'I.POT	talipot

AL'I.SIS

AL'I.SIS	dialysis, electrodialysis, hemodialysis
NAL'I.SIS	analysis, electroanalysis, phyloanalysis, cryptanalysis, metanalysis, microanalysis, psychoanalysis, urinalysis
RAL'I.SIS	paralysis
TAL'I.SIS	catalysis

AL'I.SUN

AL'I.SUN	alison
MAL'I.SUN	malison

AL'I.TĒ

AL'I.TĒ	*A* actuality, artificiality, *B* bestiality, *D* duality, *E* effectuality, exterritoriality, extraterritoriality, essentiality, ethereality, eventuality, *F* filiality, *GR* graduality, *H* heterosexuality, hypersexuality, hyposexuality, *I* ideality, immateriality, impartiality, individuality, ineffectuality, inconsequentiality, intellectuality, *J* geniality, joviality, *K* collegiality, colloquiality, commerciality, confidentiality, congeniality, connubiality, consequentiality, conceptuality, consubstantiality, conviviality, cordiality, corporeality, curiality, *L* lineality, *M* materiality, mutuality, *O* officiality, *P* parochiality, partiality, perenniality, potentiality, punctuality, *PR* primordiality, proverbiality, provinciality, prudentiality, *R* reality, *S* sexuality, sequentiality, sensuality, seriality, circumstantiality, sociality, substantiality, pseudomutuality, superficiality, *SP* spatiality, speciality, spirituality, *T* territoriality, *TR* triality, triviality, *U* unreality, unusuality, *V* veniality, virtuality, visuality
BAL'I.TĒ	verbality
DAL'I.TĒ	àlàmodality, bipedality, feudality, modality, pedality, sesquipedality, sodality
GAL'I.TĒ	egality, frugality, illegality, conjugality, legality, prodigality, regality
GRAL'I.TĒ	integrality
KAL'I.TĒ	*B* Biblicality, *F* fantasticality, farcicality, *HW* whimsicality, *I* illogicality, impracticality, inimicality, intrinsicality, *K* comicality, cosmicality, *KL* classicality, clericality, *L* laicality, logicality, locality, *N* nonsensicality, *PR* pragmaticality, practicality, *R* radicality, rascality, reciprocality, *T* technicality, topicality, *TH* theatricality, theoreticality, *V* verticality, vocality
LAL'I.TĒ	molality
MAL'I.TĒ	abnormality, animality, formality, informality, normality, subnormality
NAL'I.TĒ	*A* atonality, *B* banality, *D* devotionality, *E* exceptionality, externality, *F* feminality, finality, *I* impersonality, intentionality, internality, irrationality, *K* carnality, commonality, conditionality, constitutionality, conventionality, *KR* criminality, *M* meridionality, mesnality, *N* nationality,

notionality, *O*
originality, *P*
penality, personality,
polytonality, *PR*
proportionality, *R*
rationality, *S*
sectionality,
septentrionality,
signality, *T* tonality,
TR traditionality, *U*
unconventionality, *V*
venality, vernality, *Z*
zonality

PAL'I.TĒ   municipality,
                principality
RAL'I.TĒ   *A* amorality, *E*
                ephemerality, *G*
                gutturality, *I*
                immorality, *J*
                generality, *K*
                collaterality,
                conjecturality,
                corporality, *L*
                laterality, liberality,
                literality, *M*
                morality, *N*
                naturality, *P*
                pastorality, *PL*
                plurality, *PR*
                preternaturality, *R*
                rurality, *S* severality,
                supernaturality, *SP*
                spirality, *T*
                temporality

SAL'I.TĒ   commensality,
                orthodoxality,
                universality

TAL'I.TĒ   *A* accidentality, *BR*
                brutality, *E*
                elementality, *F*
                fatality,
                fundamentality, *FR*
                frontality, *H*
                horizontality,
                hospitality, *I*
                immortality,
                inhospitality,
                instrumentality, *M*
                mentality, mortality,
                N natality, *O*
                occidentality,
                orientality, *S*
                sentimentality, *T*
                totality, *TR*
                transcendentality, *V*
                vegetality, vitality

THAL'I.TĒ   lethality
TRAL'I.TĒ   dextrality, magistrality,
                neutrality, centrality,
                spectrality
VAL'I.TĒ   coevality, rivality
ZAL'I.TĒ   causality, nasality

Ā'LI.UM

GĀ'LI.UM	Galium
KĀ'LI.UM	kalium
TRĀ'LI.UM	penetralium

AL'I.UM

AL'I.UM	allium
BAL'I.UM	ecballium
GAL'I.UM	gallium
PAL'I.UM	pallium
THAL'I.UM	thallium
VAL'I.UM	valium

Ā'LI.US

(See **Ā'LI.AS**)

AL'JI.A

AL'JI.A	analgia, hemialgia, cardialgia, myalgia
FAL'JI.A	cephalgia
FRAL'JI.A	nephralgia
KAL'JI.A	psychalgia
LAL'JI.A	cephalalgia
RAL'JI.A	neuralgia
SAL'JI.A	coxalgia, ombrosalgia
TAL'JI.A	dentalgia, nostalgia, odontalgia, otalgia, proctalgia, rectalgia
THRAL'JI.A	arthralgia
TRAL'JI.A	gastralgia, metralgia
ZAL'JI.A	causalgia

AL'MI.A

KAL'MI.A	kalmia
THAL'MI.A	ophthalmia, xerothalmia

AL'O.ER

FAL'O.ER	fallower
HAL'O.ER	hallower
KAL'O.ER	callower
SHAL'O.ER	shallower
TAL'O.ER	tallower

ÄL'O.ER

SWÄL'O.ER	swallower
WÄL'O.ER	wallower

(See **OL'O.ER**)

AL'O.ING

(See **AL'Ō**, add *-ing* where appropriate.)

ÄL'O.ING

SWÄL'O.ING	swallowing
WÄL'O.ING	wallowing

(See **OL'O.ING**)

AL'O.ISH

FAL'O.ISH	fallowish
SAL'O.ISH	sallowish
SHAL'O.ISH	shallowish
TAL'O.ISH	tallowish

AL'O.JĒ

AL'O.JĒ	genealogy, genethlialogy, nealogy
BAL'O.JĒ	pyroballogy
DAL'O.JĒ	dontepedalogy
MAL'O.JĒ	mammalogy
NAL'O.JĒ	analogy
RAL'O.JĒ	mineralogy, oralogy, paralogy
TAL'O.JĒ	crustalogy
TRAL'O.JĒ	tetralogy

AL'O.JIST

AL'O.JIST	dialogist, genealogist
KAL'O.JIST	Decalogist
MAL'O.JIST	mammalogist
NAL'O.JIST	analogist
RAL'O.JIST	mineralogist, paralogist

AL'O.JĪZ

AL'O.JĪZ	dialogize, genealogize
NAL'O.JĪZ	analogize
RAL'O.JĪZ	mineralogize, paralogize

AL'O.JIZM

AL'O.JIZM	alogism, dialogism
NAL'O.JIZM	analogism
RAL'O.JIZM	paralogism

AL'O.NES

(See **AL'Ō**, add *-ness* where appropriate.)

AL'UP.ER

GAL'UP.ER	galloper
KAL'UP.ER	escalloper
SKAL'UP.ER	scalloper

ÄL'UP.ER

(See OLUP, add -er)

AL'UP.ING

GAL'UP.ING	galloping
KAL'UP.ING	escalloping
SKAL'UP.ING	scalloping

Ē'VAL'Ū.ĀT

Ē'VAL'Ū.ĀT	evaluate
DĒ'VAL'Ū.ĀT	devaluate
RĒ'VAL'Ū.ĀT	revaluate

ĀL'YEN.IZM

ĀL'YEN.IZM	alienism
DĀL'YEN.IZM	sesquipedalianism
NĀL'YEN.IZM	bacchanalianism, saturnalianism
PĀL'YEN.IZM	episcopalianism
SĀL'YEN.IZM	universalianism

AL'YUN.ISH

DAL'YUN.ISH	medallionish
SKAL'YUN.ISH	rapscallionish, scallionish
STAL'YUN.ISH	stallionish

Ā'MA.BL

BLĀ'MA.BL	blamable, unblamable
FRĀ'MA.BL	framable, unframable
KLĀ'MA.BL	claimable, irreclaimable, reclaimable, unreclaimable
NĀ'MA.BL	namable, unnamable
TĀ'MA.BL	tamable, untamable

AM'A.NĒ

SKAM'A.NĒ	scammony
TAM'A.NĒ	Tammany

AM'ER.Ē

GRAM'ER.Ē	gramarye
MAM'ER.Ē	mammary
YAM'ER.Ē	yammery

AM'A.TIST

DRAM'A.TIST	dramatist, melodramatist
GRAM'A.TIST	anagrammatist, diagrammatist, epigrammatist, grammatist, hierogrammatist, lipogrammatist

AM'A.TIV

AM'A.TIV	amative
KLAM'A.TIV	exclamative

AM'A.TĪZ

DRAM'A.TĪZ	dramatize
GRAM'A.TĪZ	anagrammatize, diagrammatize, epigrammatize

AM'A.TŌ'RĒ

AM'A.TŌ'RĒ	amatory
FAM'A.TŌ'RĒ	defamatory
FLAM'A.TŌ'RĒ	inflammatory
KLAM'A.TŌ'RĒ	declamatory, exclamatory, proclamatory

AM'BŪ.LANT

AM'BŪ.LANT	ambulant, deambulant, circumambulent
NAM'BŪ.LANT	funambulant, somnambulant
RAM'BŪ.LANT	perambulant
TAM'BŪ.LANT	noctambulant

AM'BŪ.LĀT

AM'BŪ.LĀT	ambulate, deambulate
MAM'BŪ.LĀT	circumambulate
NAM'BŪ.LĀT	funambulate, somnambulate
RAM'BŪ.LĀT	perambulate
TAM'BŪ.LĀT	noctambulate

AM'BŪ.LIST

AM'BŪ.LIST	ambulist, deambulist, circumambulist, perambulist
NAM'BŪ.LIST	funambulist, somnambulist
TAM'BŪ.LIST	noctambulist

AM'BŪ.LIZM

AM'BŪ.LIZM	ambulism, deambulism, perambulism, circumambulism
NAM'BŪ.LIZM	funambulism, somnambulism
TAM'BŪ.LIZM	noctambulism

AM'ER.AL

KAM'ER.AL	bicameral, decameral, cameral, unicameral
SAM'ER.AL	hexameral
TAM'ER.AL	pentameral

AM'ER.ER

HAM'ER.ER	hammerer
KLAM'ER.ER	clamorer
STAM'ER.ER	stammerer
YAM'ER.ER	yammerer

AM'ER.ING

(See AM'ER.ER, change -er to -ing.)

AM'ER.UN

KAM'ER.UN	decameron
SAM'ER.UN	hexameron
TAM'ER.UN	heptameron

AM'ER.US

AM'ER.US	amorous
GLAM'ER.US	glamorous, unglamorous
KAM'ER.US	decamerous
KLAM'ER.US	clamorous
MAM'ER.US	nummamorous
SAM'ER.US	hexamerous
TAM'ER.US	heptamerous
TRAM'ER.US	tetramerous

ĀM′FUL.NES

ĀM′FUL.NES	aimfulness
BLĀM′FUL.NES	blamefulness
GĀM′FUL.NES	gamefulness
SHĀM′FUL.NES	shamefulness

Ā′MI.A

DĀ′MI.A	macadamia
LĀ′MI.A	lamia
NĀ′MI.A	adynamia
TĀ′MI.A	Mesopotamia
ZĀ′MI.A	zamia, Zamia

AM′I.KAL

AM′I.KAL	amical
NAM′I.KAL	dynamical
SAM′I.KAL	balsamical

ÄM′I.LĒ

| BÄM′I.LĒ | balmily |
| PÄM′I.LĒ | palmily |

AM′I.NA

LAM′I.NA	lamina
RAM′I.NA	foramina
STAM′I.NA	stamina

AM′I.NĀT

AM′I.NĀT	aminate, deaminate
LAM′I.NĀT	delaminate, interlaminate, laminate
RAM′I.NĀT	foraminate
STAM′I.NĀT	staminate
TAM′I.NĀT	decontaminate, contaminate

AM′I.NES

HAM′I.NES	hamminess
JAM′I.NES	jamminess
KLAM′I.NES	clamminess

ÄM′ISH.LĒ

| KÄM′ISH.LĒ | calmishly |
| KWÄM′ISH.LĒ | qualmishly |

ÄM′IS.TRĒ

| PÄM′IS.TRĒ | palmistry |
| SÄM′IS.TRĒ | psalmistry |

AM′I.TĒ

| AM′I.TĒ | amity |
| LAM′I.TĒ | calamity |

AM′I.TER

AM′I.TER	diameter, pluviameter, viameter
NAM′I.TER	dynameter
RAM′I.TER	parameter, peirameter
SAM′I.TER	hexameter
TAM′I.TER	heptameter, octameter, pentameter, voltameter
TRAM′I.TER	tetrameter

ĀM′LES.NES

(See ĀM, add -lessness where appropriate.)

AM′O.NĒ

(See DM′A.NĒ)

AM′O.NIZM

| MAM′O.NIZM | mammonism |
| SHAM′O.NIZM | shamanism |

AM′OR.US

(See AM′ER.US)

AM′PER.ER

HAM′PER.ER	hamperer
PAM′PER.ER	pamperer
SKAM′PER.ER	scamperer
TAM′PER.ER	tamperer

AM′PER.ING

HAM′PER.ING	hampering
PAM′PER.ING	pampering
SKAM′PER.ING	scampering
TAM′PER.ING	tampering

AM′PI.LĒ

| KRAM′PI.LĒ | crampily |
| VAM′PI.LĒ | vampily |

AM′PI.UN

CHAM′PI.UN	champion
KAM′PI.UN	campion
LAM′PI.UN	lampion
TAM′PI.UN	tampion

AM′Ū.LUS

FAM′Ū.LUS	famulus
HAM′Ū.LUS	hamulus
RAM′Ū.LUS	ramulous, ramulus

Ā′NA.BL

(See ĀN, add -able where appropriate.)

Ā′NA.BLĒ

(See ĀN, add -ably where appropriate.)

AN′A.BL

BAN′A.BL	bannable
HAN′A.BL	Hannibal
KAN′A.BL	cannable, cannibal
MAN′A.BL	mannable
PAN′A.BL	pannable
SAN′A.BL	insanable, sanable
TAN′A.BL	tannable

AN′A.KL

(See AN′I.KL)

AN′A.LĪZ

AN′A.LĪZ	analyze
CHAN′A.LĪZ	channelize
KAN′A.LĪZ	canalize

AN′BER.Ē

| BAN′BER.Ē | Banbury |
| KRAN′BER.Ē | cranberry |

AN′DA.BL

| MAN′DA.BL | mandible |

(See AND, add -able where appropriate.)

AN'DA.LĬZ

SKAN'DA.LĬZ	scandalize
VAN'DA.LĬZ	vandalize

AN'DED.LĒ

HAN'DED.LĒ	backhandedly, highhandedly, openhandedly, underhandedly
KAN'DED.LĒ	candidly

AN'DED.NES

BAN'DED.NES	bandedness
BRAN'DED.NES	brandedness
HAN'DED.NES	left-handedness, off-handedness, right-handedness, underhandedness
KAN'DED.NES	candidness
LAN'DED.NES	landedness

AN'DER.ER

AN'DER.ER	meanderer
LAN'DER.ER	philanderer
PAN'DER.ER	panderer
SLAN'DER.ER	slanderer

ÄN'DER.ER

SKWÄN'DER.ER	squanderer
WÄN'DER.ER	wanderer

(See **ON'DER.ER**)

AN'DER.ING

AN'DER.ING	meandering
LAN'DER.ING	philandering
PAN'DER.ING	pandering
SLAN'DER.ING	slandering

ÄN'DER.ING

SKWÄN'DER.ING	squandering
WÄN'DER.ING	wandering

(See **ON'DER.ING**)

AN'DER.US

PAN'DER.US	panderous
SLAN'DER.US	slanderous

AN'DI.ER

BAN'DI.ER	bandier
DAN'DI.ER	dandier
HAN'DI.ER	handier, unhandier
RAN'DI.ER	randier
SAN'DI.ER	sandier

AN'DI.FĪ

DAN'DI.FĪ	dandify
KAN'DI.FĪ	candify

AN'DI.IZM

DAN'DI.IZM	dandyism
RAN'DI.IZM	randyism
SHAN'DI.IZM	Tristram Shandyism

AN'DI.LĒ

BAN'DI.LĒ	bandily
DAN'DI.LĒ	dandily
HAN'DI.LĒ	handily, unhandily
RAN'DI.LĒ	randily
SAN'DI.LĒ	sandily

AN'DI.NES

(See **AN'DĒ**, add -*ness* where appropriate.)

AN'DING.LĒ

MAN'DING.LĒ	demandingly, commandingly
STAN'DING.LĒ	outstandingly, understandingly

AN'DING.NES

MAN'DING.NES	demandingness, commandingness
STAN'DING.NES	outstandingness, understandingness

AN'DISH.ING

BLAN'DISH.ING	blandishing
BRAN'DISH.ING	brandishing

AN'DISH.MENT

BLAN'DISH.MENT	blandishment
BRAN'DISH.MENT	brandishment

AN'EL.ING

CHAN'EL.ING	channeling
FLAN'EL.ING	flanneling
PAN'EL.ING	paneling

AN'EL.ĪZ

(See **AN'AL.ĪZ**)

Ā'NER.Ē

GRĀ'NER.Ē	granary
KĀ'NER.Ē	chicanery

AN'ER.Ē

CHAN'ER.Ē	channery
GRAN'ER.Ē	granary
KAN'ER.Ē	cannery
PAN'ER.Ē	panary
STAN'ER.Ē	stannary
TAN'ER.Ē	charlatanery, tannery

AN'ER.ET

BAN'ER.ET	banneret
LAN'ER.ET	lanneret

AN'E.TER'Ē

(See **AN'I.TER'Ē**)

ĀN'FUL.Ē

BĀN'FUL.Ē	banefully
DĀN'FUL.Ē	disdainfully
GĀN'FUL.Ē	gainfully, ungainfully
PĀN'FUL.Ē	painfully

ĀN'FUL.NES

DĀN'FUL.NES	disdainfulness
GĀN'FUL.NES	gainfulness, ungainfulness
PĀN'FUL.NES	painfulness

ANG'GLING.LĒ

(See **ANGGL**, add -*ingly* where appropriate.)

ANG'GL.SUM

ANG'GL.SUM	anglesome
DANG'GL.SUM	danglesome

JANG'GL.SUM	janglesome
RANG'GL.SUM	wranglesome
TANG'GL.SUM	tanglesome

ANG'GŪ.LAR

ANG'GŪ.LAR	angular, triangular
RANG'GŪ.LAR	quadrangular
SLANG'GŪ.LAR	slangular
TANG'GŪ.LAR	octangular, pentangular, rectangular

ANG'GŪ.LĀT

| ANG'GŪ.LĀT | angulate, triangulate |
| STRANG'GŪ.LĀT | strangulate |

ANG'I.LĒ

BANG'I.LĒ	bangily
KLANG'I.LĒ	clangily
SLANG'I.LĒ	slangily
TANG'I.LĒ	tangily
TWANG'I.LĒ	twangily

ANG'ING.LĒ

(See ANG, add -ingly where appropriate.)

ANG'KER.ER

| ANG'KER.ER | anchorer, reanchorer |
| HANG'KER.ER | hankerer |

ANG'KER.ING

ANG'KER.ING	anchoring, reanchoring
HANG'KER.ING	hankering
KANG'KER.ING	cankering

ANG'KER.US

HANG'KER.US	hankerous
KANG'KER.US	cankerous
TANG'KER.US	cantankerous

Ā'NI.A

Ā'NI.A	Lithuania, euania
BĀ'NI.A	Albania
DĀ'NI.A	succedanea
FĀ'NI.A	menophania
KĀ'NI.A	misocainia

KRĀ'NI.A	Ukrainia
LĀ'NI.A	miscellanea
MĀ'NI.A	*A* ablutomania, amania, andromania,, Anglomania, *B* Beatlemania, bibliomania, *BR* bruxomania, *D* dacnomania, decalcomania, demomania, dinomania, dipsomania, discomania, doromania, *DR* drapetomania, dromomania, *E* egomania, ecomania, eleutheromania, empleomania, entheomania, erotographomania, erotomania, *F* phagomania, phaneromania, *FL* florimania, *FR* Francomania, *G* Gallomania, gamomania, *H* habromania, hydromania, hippomania, *I* Italomania, *J* Germanomania, *K* callomania, catapedamania, choreomania, *KL* kleptomania, clinomania, *L* logomania, *M* mania, megalomania, melomania, metromania, misomania, mythomania, monomania, *N* nymphomania, nosomania, nostomania, nothosomania, *O* oniomania, onomatomania, opsomania, orchestromania, *P* pyromania, potichomania, potomania, *PL* planomania, *R* Rumania, Russomania, *S* sebastomania,

sophomania, pseudomania, *T* Tasmania, tomomania, *TH* theomania, thanatomania, *TR* trichotillomania, *Z* xenomania

(See Appendix D for additional words ending in -*mania*.)

RĀ'NI.A	Pomerania, Urania
SĀ'NI.A	dysania
TĀ'NI.A	Aquitania, castanea, collectanea, Lusitania, Mauretania, Ruritania, Titania, Tripolitania
VĀ'NI.A	Pennsylvania, Sylvania, Transylvania

AN ACYROLOGIC TREATISE ON GRAMMAR

Don't tell *me* no grammatic rules:
    Hey, man, I get on good enough.
    I don't talk like no powder puff,
But ladies looks at me and drools,
And feels my chest in swimming pools—
    Talk ain't no match for he-man stuff.
Don't tell *me* no grammatic rules;
    Hey, man, I get on good enough.

Man, when did junk you learns in schools
    Help anyone when times gets tough?
    I thumbs my nose; I calls your bluff.
I leaves that sissy stuff to fools.
Don't tell *me* no grammatic rules.

Ā'NI.AL

KRĀ'NI.AL	acranial, intracranial, cranial
MĀ'NI.AL	domanial, demesnial
RĀ'NI.AL	geranial, subterraneal
TĀ'NI.AL	cutaneal, subcutaneal

Ā'NI.AN

Ā'NI.AN	Lithuanian, cyanean
BĀ'NI.AN	Albanian
DĀ'NI.AN	Jordanian
KĀ'NI.AN	volcanian, vulcanian
KRĀ'NI.AN	Ukrainian
MĀ'NI.AN	Alemanian, Panamanian, Rumanian, Tasmanian
RĀ'NI.AN	extemporanean, Iranian, contemporanean,

TĀ'NI.AN	Mediterranean, Pomeranian, circumforanean, subterranean, terranean, Turanian, Uranian castanean, castanian
VĀ'NI.AN	Pennsylvanian, Transylvanian

AN'I.EST

KAN'I.EST	canniest, uncanniest
KLAN'I.EST	clanniest

AN'I.FĪ

MAN'I.FĪ	humanify
SAN'I.FĪ	insanify, sanify

AN'I.KIN

KAN'I.KIN	cannikin
MAN'I.KIN	manikin, mannequin
PAN'I.KIN	pannikin

AN'I.KL

GAN'I.KL	organical
KAN'I.KL	mechanical
MAN'I.KL	Brahmanical, manacle
PAN'I.KL	panicle
RAN'I.KL	tyrannical
SAN'I.KL	sanicle
TAN'I.KL	botanical, charlatanical, puritanical
VAN'I.KL	galvanical

AN'I.MUS

AN'I.MUS	animus, exanimous, flexanimous
LAN'I.MUS	pusillanimous
NAN'I.MUS	magnanimous, unanimous
TAN'I.MUS	multanimous

Ā'NI.NES

BRĀ'NI.NES	braininess
GRĀ'NI.NES	graininess
RĀ'NI.NES	raininess
VĀ'NI.NES	veininess

AN'I.NES

KAN'I.NES	canniness
KLAN'I.NES	clanniness

Ā'NING.LĒ

PLĀ'NING.LĒ	complainingly, uncomplainingly
TĀ'NING.LĒ	entertainingly

AN'ISH.ING

BAN'ISH.ING	banishing
PLAN'ISH.ING	planishing
VAN'ISH.ING	vanishing

AN'ISH.MENT

BAN'ISH.MENT	banishment
VAN'ISH.MENT	evanishment, vanishment

AN'IS.TER

BAN'IS.TER	banister, bannister
GAN'IS.TER	ganister
KAN'IS.TER	canister

AN'I.TĒ

AN'I.TĒ	Christianity, inanity
BAN'I.TĒ	inurbanity, urbanity
DAN'I.TĒ	mundanity
FAN'I.TĒ	profanity
GAN'I.TĒ	inorganity, organity, paganity
KAN'I.TĒ	volcanity
MAN'I.TĒ	aldermanity, gigmanity, humanity, immanity, inhumanity, yahoomanity
RAN'I.TĒ	subterranity
SAN'I.TĒ	insanity, sanity
VAN'I.TĒ	vanity

AN'I.TER.Ē

PLAN'I.TER.Ē	planetary
SAN'I.TER.Ē	sanitary

Ā'NI.UM

DĀ'NI.UM	succedaneum, suppedaneum

KRĀ'NI.UM	endocranium, cranium, pericranium
LĀ'NI.UM	Herculaneum
MĀ'NI.UM	germanium
RĀ'NI.UM	actinouranium, geranium, uranium
TĀ'NI.UM	titanium

Ā'NI.US

Ā'NI.US	cyaneous
BRĀ'NI.US	membraneous
DĀ'NI.US	antecedaneous, succedaneous
KĀ'NI.US	calcaneus, siccaneous, supervacaneous
LĀ'NI.US	miscellaneous, porcellaneous, subtegulaneous
RĀ'NI.US	A araneous, E extemporaneous, exterraneous, extraforaneous, F foraneous, K contemporaneous, M Mediterraneous, S circumforaneous, subterraneous, T temporaneous, terraneous
TĀ'NI.US	D dissentaneous, I instantaneous, K castaneous, coetaneous, consectaneous, consentaneous, cutaneous, M momentaneous, P percutaneous, PR proletaneous, S simultaneous, subcutaneous, SP spontaneous
TRĀ'NI.US	extraneous, frustraneous

ĀN'JA.BL

CHĀN'JA.BL	changeable, exchangeable, interchangeable, unchangeable
RĀN'JA.BL	arrangeable, derangeable, rearrangeable

AN'JEN.SĒ

PLAN'JEN.SĒ	plangency
TAN'JEN.SĒ	tangency

AN'JI.A

DRAN'JI.A	hydrangea
KAN'JI.A	cangia
SPRAN'JI.A	sprangia

AN'JI.BL

FRAN'JI.BL	frangible, infrangible, irrefrangible, refrangible
TAN'JI.BL	intangible, tangible

ĀN'JI.NES

MĂN'JI.NES	manginess
RĂN'JI.NES	ranginess

AN'O.GRAF

AN'O.GRAF	pianograph
KAN'O.GRAF	mechanograph
VAN'O.GRAF	galvanograph

AN'O.SKŌP

FAN'O.SKŌP	diaphanoscope
VAN'O.SKŌP	galvanoscope

AN'SI.LĒ

CHAN'SI.LĒ	chancily
DAN'SI.LĒ	dancily .
FAN'SI.LĒ	fancily
PRAN'SI.LĒ	prancily

AN'SING.LĒ

DAN'SING.LĒ	dancingly
GLAN'SING.LĒ	glancingly
PRAN'SING.LĒ	prancingly
TRAN'SING.LĒ	entrancingly, trancingly

AN'SIV.NES

PAN'SIV.NES	expansiveness, inexpansiveness
VAN'SIV.NES	advanciveness

AN'SUM.ER

HAN'SUM.ER	handsomer
RAN'SUM.ER	ransomer

AN'SUM.EST

HAN'SUM.EST	handsomest
RAN'SUM.EST	ransomest

ĀN'TA.BL

KWĂN'TA.BL	acquaintable
PĂN'TA.BL	paintable
TĂN'TA.BL	taintable

AN'TA.BL

CHAN'TA.BL	chantable, disenchantable, enchantable, unchantable, unenchantable
GRAN'TA.BL	grantable, ungrantable
KAN'TA.BL	decantable, cantable, recantable, undecantable, uncantable, unrecantable
PLAN'TA.BL	implantable, plantable, supplantable, transplantable, unplantable, untransplantable
SLAN'TA.BL	slantable, unslantable

AN'TE.LŌP

AN'TE.LŌP	antelope
KAN'TE.LŌP	cantaloupe

AN'TER.ER

BAN'TER.ER	banterer
KAN'TER.ER	canterer

AN'TER.ING

BAN'TER.ING	bantering
KAN'TER.ING	cantering

AN'THRO.PĒ

AN'THRO.PĒ	boanthropy, physianthropy, galeanthropy, theanthropy, zoanthropy
KAN'THRO.PĒ	lycanthropy

LAN'THRO.PĒ	aphilanthropy, philanthropy, psilanthropy, theophilanthropy
PAN'THRO.PĒ	apanthropy
SAN'THRO.PĒ	misanthropy
ZAN'THRO.PĒ	misanthropy

AN'THRO.PIST

AN'THRO.PIST	theanthropist
LAN'THRO.PIST	philanthropist, psilanthropist, theophilanthropist
SAN'THRO.PIST	misanthropist
ZAN'THRO.PIST	misanthropist

(See **AN'THRO.PĒ**, change -y to -ist where appropriate.)

AN'THRO.PIZM

AN'THRO.PIZM	physianthropism, theantropism, zoanthropism
KAN'THRO.PIZM	lycanthropism
LAN'THRO.PIZM	aphilanthropism, philanthropism, psilanthropism, theophilanthropism
SAN'THRO.PIZM	misanthropism
ZAN'THRO.PIZM	misanthropism

AN'TIK.LĒ

AN'TIK.LĒ	anticly
DAN'TIK.LĒ	pedantically
FRAN'TIK.LĒ	frantically
GAN'TIK.LĒ	gigantically
MAN'TIK.LĒ	romanticly

AN'TIK.NES

AN'TIK.NES	anticness
DAN'TIK.NES	pedanticness
FRAN'TIK.NES	franticness
MAN'TIK.NES	romanticness

AN'TI.LĒ

BAN'TI.LĒ	bantily
RAN'TI.LĒ	rantily
SKAN'TI.LĒ	scantily
SLAN'TI.LĒ	slantily

AN'TING.LĒ

CHAN'TING.LĒ	enchantingly
KAN'TING.LĒ	cantingly
PAN'TING.LĒ	pantingly
RAN'TING.LĒ	rantingly
SLAN'TING.LĒ	slantingly

AN'TI.SĪD

FAN'TI.SĪD	infanticide
GAN'TI.SĪD	giganticide

AN'Ū.AL

AN'Ū.AL	annual, biannual, semiannual
MAN'Ū.AL	manual

AN'Ū.LA

GRAN'Ū.LA	granula
KAN'Ū.LA	cannula
PAN'Ū.LA	campanula
PLAN'Ū.LA	planula
RAN'Ū.LA	ranula

AN'Ū.LAR

AN'Ū.LAR	annular, penannular
GRAN'Ū.LAR	granular
KAN'Ū.LAR	cannular
PAN'Ū.LAR	campanular
RAN'Ū.LAR	ranular

AN'Ū.LĀT

AN'Ū.LĀT	annulate
GRAN'Ū.LĀT	granulate
KAN'Ū.LĀT	cannulate
PAN'Ū.LĀT	campanulate

AN'Ū.LET

AN'Ū.LET	annulet
GRAN'Ū.LET	granulet

Ā'PA.BL

DRĀ'PA.BL	drapable
KĀ'PA.BL	escapable, incapable, inescapable, capable, unescapable, uncapable
PĀ'PA.BL	papable
RĀ'PA.BL	rapable
SHĀ'PA.BL	reshapable, shapable
SKRĀ'PA.BL	scrapable
TĀ'PA.BL	tapable

AP'A.BL

FLAP'A.BL	flappable, unflappable
MAP'A.BL	mappable, unmappable
RAP'A.BL	rappable, wrappable, unrappable, unwrappable
SAP'A.BL	sappable, unsappable
SNAP'A.BL	snappable, unsnappable
STRAP'A.BL	strappable, unstrappable
TAP'A.BL	tappable, untappable
TRAP'A.BL	trappable, untrappable
ZAP'A.BL	zappable, unzappable

AP'A.THĒ

AP'A.THĒ	apathy
PRAP'A.THĒ	naprapathy

AP'CHER.ING

KAP'CHER.ING	capturing, recapturing
RAP'CHER.ING	enrapturing, rapturing

Ā'PER.Ē

Ā'PER.Ē	apery
DRĀ'PER.Ē	drapery
GRĀ'PER.Ē	grapery
JĀ'PER.Ē	japery
KĀ'PER.Ē	capery
NĀ'PER.Ē	napery
PĀ'PER.Ē	papery
VĀ'PER.Ē	vapory

Ā'PER.ER

KĀ'PER.ER	caperer
NĀ'PER.ER	naperer
PĀ'PER.ER	paperer
TĀ'PER.ER	taperer
VĀ'PER.ER	vaporer

Ā'PER.ING

KĀ'PER.ING	capering
PĀ'PER.ING	papering
TĀ'PER.ING	tapering
VĀ'PER.ING	vaporing

AP'ID.LĒ

RAP'ID.LĒ	rapidly
SAP'ID.LĒ	sapidly
VAP'ID.LĒ	vapidly

AP'ID.NES

RAP'ID.NES	rapidness
SAP'ID.NES	sapidness
VAP'ID.NES	vapidness

AP'I.DUS

AP'I.DUS	sciapodous
LAP'I.DUS	lapidous

Ā'PI.ER

NĀ'PI.ER	Napier
RĀ'PI.ER	rapier

AP'I.ER

GAP'I.ER	gappier
HAP'I.ER	happier, unhappier
KRAP'I.ER	crappier
NAP'I.ER	nappier
SAP'I.ER	sappier
SKRAP'I.ER	scrappier
SNAP'I.ER	snappier

AP'I.LĒ

GAP'I.LĒ	gappily
HAP'I.LĒ	happily
KRAP'I.LĒ	crappily
SAP'I.LĒ	sappily
SKRAP'I.LĒ	scrappily
SNAP'I.LĒ	snappily

AP'I.NES

(See APĒ, add -ness where appropriate.)

ÄP'I.TĒ

(See OP'I.TĒ)

AP'O.LIS

AP'O.LIS	Minneapolis

NAP'O.LIS	Annapolis, Indianapolis
TAP'O.LIS	pentapolis
TRAP'O.LIS	tetrapolis

ÂR'A.BL

ÂR'A.BL	airable, unairable
BÂR'A.BL	bearable, unbearable
DÂR'A.BL	darable, undarable
KLÂR'A.BL	declarable, undeclarable
PÂR'A.BL	pairable, repairable, unpairable, unparable, unrepairable
SHÂR'A.BL	sharable, unsharable
SKÂR'A.BL	scarable, unscarable
SKWÂR'A.BL	squarable, unsquarable
SPÂR'A.BL	sparable, unsparable
SWÂR'A.BL	swearable
TÂR'A.BL	tearable, untearable
WÂR'A.BL	unwearable, wearable

(See ER'I.BL)

AR'A.BL

AR'A.BL	arable
NAR'A.BL	inennarable
PAR'A.BL	parable
SPAR'A.BL	sparable

AR'A.GON

AR'A.GON	Aragon
PAR'A.GON	paragon
TAR'A.GON	tarragon

AR'A.GRAF

| BAR'A.GRAF | barograph |
| PAR'A.GRAF | paragraph |

AR'ANT.LĒ

| AR'ANT.LĒ | arrantly |
| PAR'ANT.LĒ | apparently, transparently |

AR'AS.ING

| BAR'AS.ING | disembarrassing, embarrassing |
| HAR'AS.ING | harassing |

AR'AS.MENT

| BAR'AS.MENT | embarrassment, disembarrassment |
| HAR'AS.MENT | harassment |

AR'A.TIV

KLAR'A.TIV	declarative
NAR'A.TIV	narrative
PAR'A.TIV	comparative, preparative, reparative

AR'A.TŌ.RĒ

| KLAR'A.TŌ.RĒ | declaratory |
| PAR'A.TŌ.RĒ | preparatory |

ÄR'BER.ING

| BÄR'BER.ING | barbering |
| HÄR'BER.ING | harboring |

ÄR'DEN.ING

GÄR'DEN.ING	gardening
HÄR'DEN.ING	hardening
PÄR'DEN.ING	pardoning

ÄR'DI.A

GÄR'DI.A	LaGuardia
KÄR'DI.A	bradycardia, megalocardia, tachycardia
LÄR'DI.A	gaillardia

ÄR'DI.AN

GÄR'DI.AN	guardian
KÄR'DI.AN	pericardian
WÄR'DI.AN	Edwardian

ÄR'DI.LĒ

| HÄR'DI.LĒ | foolhardily, hardily |
| TÄR'DI.LĒ | tardily |

ÄR'DI.NES

| HÄR'DI.NES | foolhardiness, hardiness |
| TÄR'DI.NES | tardiness |

AR'EL.ING

BAR'EL.ING	barreling, pork-barreling, caroling
KAR'EL.ING	caroling
PAR'EL.ING	appareling

AR'E.NĪT

| AR'E.NĪT | arenite |
| MAR'E.NĪT | Maronite |

AR'ENT.LĒ

(See AR'ANT.LĒ)

ÂR'FUL.Ē

DÂR'FUL.Ē	darefully
KÂR'FUL.Ē	carefully, uncarefully
SPÂR'FUL.Ē	despairfully
PRÂR'FUL.Ē	prayerfully, unprayerfully

ÂR'FUL.NES

KÂR'FUL.NES	carefulness, uncarefulness
PRÂR'FUL.NES	prayerfulness
SPÂR'FUL.NES	sparefulness
WÂR'FUL.NES	awarefulness, wa.efulness

ÂR'I.A

ÂR'I.A	area, aria, miliaria, topiaria
BÂR'I.A	herbaria
GÂR'I.A	Bulgaria
KÂR'I.A	araucaria, Icaria, persicaria, cercaria, urticaria
KWÂR'I.A	aquaria
LÂR'I.A	adularia, alfilaria, filaria, Hilaria, malaria, solaria, talaria
MÂR'I.A	Samaria
NÂR'I.A	laminaria, ranaria, sanguinaria
PÂR'I.A	pariah
RÂR'I.A	honoraria, cineraria
SÂR'I.A	adversaria
TÂR'I.A	dataria, digitaria, cataria, planetaria, wistaria
VÂR'I.A	Bavaria, varia

ÂR'I.AL

ÂR'I.AL	actuarial, aerial, areal, Ariel, diarial, estuarial
DÂR'I.AL	calendarial
KÂR'I.AL	vicarial
LÂR'I.AL	antimalarial, malarial
NÂR'I.AL	narial
PÂR'I.AL	puparial, riparial
SÂR'I.AL	adversarial, bursarial, glossarial, commissarial
TÂR'I.AL	nectarial, notarial, secretarial, sectarial
VÂR'I.AL	ovarial

ÂR'I.AN

ÂR'I.AN	apiarian, Arian, Aryan, Briarean, diarian, estuarian, sententiarian
BÂR'I.AN	barbarian
BRÂR'I.AN	librarian
DÂR'I.AN	abecedarian, Abecedarian, Darien, lapidarian, cnidarian, stipendarian, ultracrepidarian
FÂR'I.AN	Rastafarian
GÂR'I.AN	Bulgarian, gregarian, Hungarian, vulgarian
GRÂR'I.AN	agrarian
KÂR'I.AN	Icarian, sicarian, suburbicarian
KWÂR'I.AN	antiquarian, aquarian, ubiquarian
LÂR'I.AN	atrabilarian, aularian, sertularian, telarian
MÂR'I.AN	grammarian
NÂR'I.AN	*A* adessenarian, altitudinarian, Apollinarian, attitudinarian, *D* disciplinarian, doctrinarian, *KW* quadragenarian, quinquagenarian, *L* latitudinarian, lunarian, lupanarian, *M* millenarian, miscellenarian, *N* nonagenarian, *O* octogenarian, *P* pornogenarian, *PL* planarian, platitudinarian, plenitudinarian, *PR* predestinarian, *S* seminarian, centenarian, sexagenarian, septimanarian, septuagenarian, superseptuagenarian, *V* valetudinarian, veterinarian
PÂR'I.AN	Parian, riparian
RÂR'I.AN	orarian
SÂR'I.AN	infralapsarian, necessarian, janissarian, supralapsarian
TÂR'I.AN	*A* alphabetarian, anecdotarian, antidisestablishmentarian, antisabbitarian, antitrinitarian, *D* dietarian, *E* egalitarian, experimentarian, equalitarian, *F* futilitarian, *FR* fruitarian, *H* humanitarian, *K* communitarian, *L* libertarian, limitarian, *N* necessitarian, nectarian, noli-mi-tangerietarian, nonsectarian, *O* authoritarian, *P* parliamentarian, *PR* proletarian, *R* Rotarian, *S* sabbatarian, sacramentarian, sanitarian, sectarian, societarian, *T* totalitarian, *TR* tractarian, trinitarian, *V* vegetarian, *Y* ubiquitarian, unitarian, utilitarian
VÂR'I.AN	Bavarian, ovarian
ZÂR'I.AN	janizarian, rosarian, Caesarian

ÂR'I.ANT

(See ÂR'I.ENT)

ÂR'I.ĀT

KÂR'I.ĀT	vicariate
VÂR'I.ĀT	variate

ÂR'I.AT

CHÂR'I.AT	chariot
KÂR'I.AT	Iscariot
LÂR'I.AT	lariat, salariat
SÂR'I.AT	commissariat
TÂR'I.AT	proletariat, prothonotariat, secretariat

ÂR'I.ENT

PÂR'I.ENT	omniparient
TRÂR'I.ENT	contrarient
VÂR'I.ENT	bivariant, invariant, covariant, variant

ÂR'I.ER

ÂR'I.ER	airier
CHÂR'I.ER	charier
GLÂR'I.ER	glarier
HÂR'I.ER	hairier
SKÂR'I.ER	scarier
VÂR'I.ER	varier
WÂR'I.ER	warier

AR'I.ER

BAR'I.ER	barrier
FAR'I.ER	farrier
HAR'I.ER	harrier
KAR'I.ER	carrier, miscarrier
MAR'I.ER	intermarrier, marrier, remarrier
PAR'I.ER	parrier
TAR'I.ER	tarrier

ÂR'I.EST

(See ÂRĒ, change -*y* to -*iest* where appropriate.)

ÂR'I.ĒZ

ÂR'I.ĒZ	Aries
KÂR'I.ĒZ	caries
PÂR'I.ĒZ	paries

ÂR'I.FĪ

ÂR'I.FĪ	aerify

(See ER'I.FĪ)

AR'I.FĪ

KAR'I.FĪ	saccharify
KLAR'I.FĪ	clarify
SKAR'I.FĪ	scarify

ÂR'I.FÔRM

ÂR'I.FÔRM	aeriform, scalariform
NÂR'I.FÔRM	nariform
VÂR'I.FÔRM	variform

AR'I.ING

HAR'I.ING	harrying
KAR'I.ING	carrying, miscarrying
MAR'I.ING	intermarrying, marrying
PAR'I.ING	parrying
TAR'I.ING	tarrying

ÂR'I.LĒ

ÂR'I.LĒ	airily
CHÂR'I.LĒ	charily
HÂR'I.LĒ	hairily
NÂR'I.LĒ	sanguinarily
RÂR'I.LĒ	temporarily
SKÂR'I.LĒ	scarily
STÂR'I.LĒ	starily
TÂR'I.LĒ	momentarily, salutarily, sedentarily, solitarily, voluntarily
WÂR'I.LĒ	warily

(See ER'I.LĒ)

AR'I.NĀT

KAR'I.NĀT	carinate
MAR'I.NĀT	marinate

ÂR'I.NES

ÂR'I.NES	airiness, tumultuariness
CHÂR'I.NES	chariness
GLÂR'I.NES	glariness
HÂR'I.NES	hairiness
NÂR'I.NES	sanguinariness
RÂR'I.NES	temporariness
TÂR'I.NES	momentariness, salutariness, sedentariness, solitariness, ubiquitariness, voluntariness
TRÂR'I.NES	arbitrariness, contrariness
WÂR'I.NES	wariness

ÄR'I.NES

STÄR'I.NES	starriness
TÄR'I.NES	tarriness

ÂR'ING.LĒ

BÂR'ING.LĒ	forbearingly
BLÂR'ING.LĒ	blaringly
DÂR'ING.LĒ	daringly
FLÂR'ING.LĒ	flaringly
GLÂR'ING.LĒ	glaringly
KÂR'ING.LĒ	caringly
SPÂR'ING.LĒ	sparingly
STÂR'ING.LĒ	staringly
TÂR'ING.LĒ	tearingly
WÂR'ING.LĒ	wearingly

ÂR'I.Ō

NÂR'I.Ō	scenario
SÂR'I.Ō	impresario
THÂR'I.Ō	lothario, Lothario

ÂR'I.ON

FÂR'I.ON	orpharion
MÂR'I.ON	Marion

AR'I.ON

KAR'I.ON	carrion
KLAR'I.ON	clarion
MAR'I.ON	Marion

ÂR'I.OT

(See ÂR'I.AT)

ÂR'ISH.LĒ

BÂR'ISH.LĒ	bearishly
GÂR'ISH.LĒ	garishly

ÂR'ISH.NES

BÂR'ISH.NES	bearishness
GÂR'ISH.NES	garishness

AR'I.SUN

GAR'I.SUN	garrison
PAR'I.SUN	caparison, comparison, parison
WAR'I.SUN	warison

ÂR'I.TĒ

NÂR'I.TĒ	debonairity
RÂR'I.TĒ	rarity

(See ER'I.TĒ)

AR'I.TĒ

AR'I.TĒ	familiarity, curvilinearity, multicollinearity, peculiarity, rectilinearity, unfamiliarity
BAR'I.TĒ	barbarity
CHAR'I.TĒ	charity, uncharity
DAR'I.TĒ	solidarity
GAR'I.TĒ	vagarity, vulgarity
KLAR'I.TĒ	clarity
LAR'I.TĒ	A angularity, D dissimilarity, GL glandularity, globularity, GR granularity, H hilarity, I insularity, irregularity, J jocularity, K capillarity, consularity, L lunularity, M modularity, molarity, molecularity, muscularity, N nodularity, O orbicularity, P particularity, perpendicularity, piacularity, polarity, popularity, pupilarity, R regularity, rectangularity, S secularity, similarity, singularity, circularity, SP spatularity, ST stellularity, T titularity, TR triangularity, U unpopularity, V vascularity, vernacularity
PAR'I.TĒ	disparity, fissiparity, imparity, gemniparity, multiparity, omniparity, oviparity, parity, viviparity
PLAR'I.TĒ	exemplarity

(See ER'I.TĒ)

AR'I.TŌ.RĒ

KLAR'I.TŌ.RĒ	declaratory
PAR'I.TŌ.RĒ	preparatory

ÂR'I.UM

ÂR'I.UM	glaciarium, polyzoarium
BÂR'I.UM	barium, herbarium, columbarium, verbarium
DÂR'I.UM	caldarium, sudarium, tepidarium, viridarium
KRÂR'I.UM	sacrarium
KWÂR'I.UM	aquarium
LÂR'I.UM	solarium, velarium
MÂR'I.UM	fumarium, samarium
NÂR'I.UM	oceanarium, ranarium, sabbulonarium
PÂR'I.UM	puparium
RÂR'I.UM	honorarium, cinerarium, terrarium
SÂR'I.UM	leprosarium
TÂR'I.UM	armamentarium, insectarium, cometarium, lactarium, planetarium, sanitarium, termitarium
VÂR'I.UM	aquivarium, vivarium
ZÂR'I.UM	rosarium

AR'I.UN

(See AR'I.ON)

ÂR'I.US

ÂR'I.US	Briareus
BÂR'I.US	cibarious
FÂR'I.US	bifarious, multifarious, nefarious, omnifarious
GÂR'I.US	gregarious, vagarious
KÂR'I.US	Icarius, calcareous, carious, precarious, sicarious, vicarious
KWÂR'I.US	Aquarius
LÂR'I.US	atribilarious, hilarious, malarious
MÂR'I.US	Marius
NÂR'I.US	arenarious, denarius, quadragenarious, senarius, testudinarious, valetudinarious
PÂR'I.US	riparious, viparious
RÂR'I.US	honorarious, temerarious
SÂR'I.US	confessarius

SKÂR'I.US	scarious
TÂR'I.US	acetarious, fimetarious, frumentarious, lutarious, nectarious, octarius, Sagittarius, setarious, tartareous
TRÂR'I.US	arbitrarious, contrarious
VÂR'I.US	various, Stradivarius

ÄR'KĀ.IST

ÄR'KĀ.IST	archaist
PÄR'KĀ.IST	parquatist

ÄR'KET.RĒ

MÄR'KET.RĒ	marketry
PÄR'KET.RĒ	parquetry

ÄR'KI.AN

RÄR'KI.AN	Petrarchian
TÄR'KI.AN	aristarchian

ÄR'KI.KAL

ÄR'KI.KAL	anarchical, archical
NÄR'KI.KAL	monarchical
RÄR'KI.KAL	hierarchical, tetrarchical

ÄR'LA.TAN

SHÄR'LA.TAN	charlatan
TÄR'LA.TAN	tarlatan

ÄR'MA.BL

ÄR'MA.BL	armable, forearmable, disarmable, rearmable, unarmable
CHÄR'MA.BL	charmable, uncharmable
FÄR'MA.BL	farmable, unfarmable
HÄR'MA.BL	harmable, unharmable
LÄR'MA.BL	alarmable, unalarmable

ÄR'MER.Ē

ÄR'MER.Ē	armory
DÄR'MER.Ē	gendarmerie

ÄR'MING.LĒ

ÄR'MING.LĒ	disarmingly
CHÄR'MING.LĒ	charmingly
HÄR'MING.LĒ	harmingly
LÄR'MING.LĒ	alarmingly

ÄR'MOR.Ē

(See ÄR'MER.Ē)

ÄR'NISH.ER

GÄR'NISH.ER	garnisher
TÄR'NISH.ER	tarnisher
VÄR'NISH.ER	varnisher

ÄR'NISH.ING

GÄR'NISH.ING	garnishing
TÄR'NISH.ING	tarnishing
VÄR'NISH.ING	varnishing

AR'O.Ē

AR'O.Ē	arrowy
BAR'O.Ē	barrowy
MAR'O.Ē	marrowy
SPAR'O.Ē	sparrowy
YAR'O.Ē	yarrowy

AR'O.ER

BAR'O.ER	barrower, wheelbarrower
FAR'O.ER	farrower
HAR'O.ER	harrower
NAR'O.ER	narrower

AR'O.GRAF

(See AR'A.GRAF)

AR'O.ING

AR'O.ING	arrowing
BAR'O.ING	barrowing, wheelbarrowing
FAR'O.ING	farrowing
HAR'O.ING	harrowing
NAR'O.ING	narrowing

AR'O.NĪT

(See AR'E.NĪT)

AR'OT.ING

GAR'OT.ING	garroting
PAR'OT.ING	parroting

ÄR'SE.NĒ

LÄR'SE.NĒ	larceny
PÄR'SE.NĒ	coparceny

ÄR'SE.NER

LÄR'SE.NER	larcener
PÄR'SE.NER	coparcener, parcener

ÄR'SHAL.IZM

MÄR'SHAL.IZM	martialism
PÄR'SHAL.IZM	partialism

ÄR'TED.NES

HÄR'TED.NES	BL blackheartedness, F falseheartedness, fickle-heartedness, frank-heartedness, free-heartedness, H hard-heartedness, K kind-heartedness, L light-heartedness, O open-heartedness, S soft-heartedness, T tender-heartedness, W warm-heartedness
PÄR'TED.NES	departedness, partedness

ÄR'TER.Ē

ÄR'TER.Ē	artery
BÄR'TER.Ē	bartery
MÄR'TER.Ē	martyry

ÄR'TER.ER

BÄR'TER.ER	barterer
CHÄR'TER.ER	charterer

ÄR'TER.ING

BÄR'TER.ING	bartering
CHÄR'TER.ING	chartering
GÄR'TER.ING	garter-ring
MÄR'TER.ING	martyring

ÄR'TI.KL

ÄR'TI.KL	article
PÄR'TI.KL	particle

ÄR'TI.ZAN

ÄR'TI.ZAN	artisan
BÄR'TI.ZAN	bartizan
PÄR'TI.ZAN	bipartisan, partisan

ÄRT'LES.LĒ

ÄRT'LES.LĒ	artlessly
HÄRT'LES.LĒ	heartlessly

ÄRT'LES.NES

ÄRT'LES.NES	artlessness
HÄRT'LES.NES	heartlessness

ĀS'A.BL

BĀS'A.BL	abasable, basable, debasable
CHĀS'A.BL	chasable
FĀS'A.BL	defaceable, effaceable, faceable, ineffaceable
GRĀS'A.BL	disgraceable
LĀS'A.BL	enlaceable, laceable
PĀS'A.BL	paceable
PLĀS'A.BL	displaceable, emplaceable, irreplaceable, misplaceable, placeable, replaceable
RĀS'A.BL	erasable, unerasable
SPĀS'A.BL	spaceable
SWĀS'A.BL	persuasible, suasible, unpersuasible
TRĀS'A.BL	retraceable, traceable, untraceable
VĀS'A.BL	evasible

AS'A.BL

KLAS'A.BL	declassable, classable, outclassable
MAS'A.BL	amassable, massable
NAS'A.BL	innascible, renascible
PAS'A.BL	bypassable, impassable, passable, passible, surpassable, unsurpassable
RAS'A.BL	irascible
SAS'A.BL	sassable, unsassable

AS'A.BLĒ

KLAS'A.BLĒ	classably, unclassably
PAS'A.BLĒ	passably, impassably, surpassably, unpassably, unsurpassably
RAS'A.BLĒ	irascibly

AS'E.LĀT

SFAS'E.LĀT	sphacelate
VAS'E.LĀT	vacillate

Ā'SEN.SĒ

JĀ'SEN.SĒ	adjacency, interjacency
PLĀ'SEN.SĒ	complacency

AS'E.RĀT

AS'E.RĀT	acerate
LAS'E.RĀT	lacerate
MAS'E.RĀT	emacerate, macerate

Ā'SE.RĒ

BRĀ'SE.RĒ	bracery, embracery
TRĀ'SE.RĒ	tracery

Ā'SHAL.Ē

FĀ'SHAL.Ē	facially
GLĀ'SHAL.Ē	glacially
RĀ'SHAL.Ē	racially

ASH'E.RĒ

ASH'E.RĒ	ashery
DASH'E.RĒ	haberdashery
FASH'E.RĒ	fashery
HASH'E.RĒ	hashery
SASH'E.RĒ	sashery
TRASH'E.RĒ	trashery

Ā′SHI.A

Ā′SHI.A	Asia
BĀ′SHI.A	sabbatia
GRĀ′SHI.A	ex gratia
KĀ′SHI.A	acacia
LĀ′SHI.A	Galatia, osteomalacia, solatia
MĀ′SHI.A	Dalmatia
RĀ′SHI.A	Eurasia, Laurasia
SĀ′SHI.A	Alsatia
TĀ′SHI.A	cetacea, crustacea

(See Ā′SHA, Ā′ZHA)

ASH′I.A

FASH′I.A	fascia
KASH′I.A	cassia, Circassia
NAS′I.A	Parnassia

Ā′SHI.AL

BĀ′SHI.AL	abbatial
FĀ′SHI.AL	facial
GLĀ′SHI.AL	glacial, postglacial, preglacial, subglacial
LĀ′SHI.AL	palatial
MĀ′SHI.AL	primatial
RĀ′SHI.AL	multiracial, racial
SPĀ′SHI.AL	interspatial, spatial
TĀ′SHI.AL	mystacial

(See Ā′SHAL)

Ā′SHI.AN

Ā′SHI.AN	Asian, Australasian
HĀ′SHI.AN	Haitian
LĀ′SHI.AN	Galatian
NĀ′SHI.AN	Athanasian
RĀ′SHI.AN	Eurasian
SĀ′SHI.AN	Alsatian
STĀ′SHI.AN	Eustachian
THRĀ′SHI.AN	Thracian

(See Ā′ZI.AN, also Ā′SHUN, Ā′ZHUN)

ASH′I.AN

KASH′I.AN	Circassian
NASH′I.AN	Parnassian

(See ASH′UN)

Ā′SHI.ĀT

GĀ′SHI.ĀT	sagatiate
GLĀ′SHI.ĀT	glaciate
GRĀ′SHI.ĀT	ingratiate
MĀ′SHI.ĀT	emaciate
PĀ′SHI.ĀT	expatiate
SĀ′SHI.ĀT	insatiate, satiate
SPĀ′SHI.ĀT	spaciate

(See Ā′SI.ĀT)

ASH′I.ER

ASH′I.ER	ashier
DASH′I.ER	dashier
FLASH′I.ER	flashier
HASH′I.ER	hashier
PLASH′I.ER	plashier
SPLASH′I.ER	splashier
TRASH′I.ER	trashier

Ā′SHI.Ō

LĀ′SHI.Ō	fellatio, Nova Constellatio
RĀ′SHI.Ō	Horatio, ratio

Ā′SHUN.AL

Ā′SHUN.AL	associational, aviational, ideational, creational, mediational, radiational, recreational, transubstantiational, variational
BĀ′SHUN.AL	incubational, probational
BRĀ′SHUN.AL	vibrational
DĀ′SHUN.AL	gradational
GĀ′SHUN.AL	interrogational, congregational, conjugational
GRĀ′SHUN.AL	emigrational, immigrational
KĀ′SHUN.AL	educational, convocational, vocational
KWĀ′SHUN.AL	equational
LĀ′SHUN.AL	relational, revelational, translational
MĀ′SHUN.AL	informational
NĀ′SHUN.AL	denominational, inclinational, combinational, terminational
PĀ′SHUN.AL	occupational
RĀ′SHUN.AL	inspirational, gyrational, commemorational, operational, respirational
SĀ′SHUN.AL	compensational, condensational, conversational, sensational
STĀ′SHUN.AL	stational
TĀ′SHUN.AL	deputational, dissertational, gravitational, imitational, quotational, presentational, representational, rotational, salutational
VĀ′SHUN.AL	amotivational, derivational, conservational, motivational, observational

(See ĀSHUN, add -al where appropriate.)

ASH′UN.AL

NASH′UN.AL	international, multinational, national, supranational
PASH′UN.AL	passional
RASH′UN.AL	irrational, rational

ASH′UN.AL.IST

NASH′UN.AL.IST	nationalist
RASH′UN.AL.IST	rationalist

ASH′UN.AL.ĪZ

NASH′UN.AL.ĪZ	denationalize, internationalize, nationalize
RASH′UN.AL.ĪZ	rationalize

Ā′SHUN.ER

BĀ′SHUN.ER	probationer, reprobationer
DĀ′SHUN.ER	foundationer
KĀ′SHUN.ER	summer vacationer, vacationer, winter vacationer
LĀ′SHUN.ER	oblationer
RĀ′SHUN.ER	rationer, restorationer
STĀ′SHUN.ER	stationer

Ā'SHUN.ING

(See ĀSHUN, add -ing where appropriate.)

ASH'UN.ING

FASH'UN.ING	fashioning, refashioning
PASH'UN.ING	compassioning

Ā'SHUN.IST

Ā'SHUN.IST	irradiationist, creationist, rationist, re-creationist, repudiationist
DĀ'SHUN.IST	foundationist
FLĀ'SHUN.IST	deflationist, inflationist
GRĀ'SHUN.IST	emigrationist, immigrationist
KĀ'SHUN.IST	educationist, convocationist, vacationist
LĀ'SHUN.IST	annihilationist, isolationist, neoisolationist
MĀ'SHUN.IST	cremationist
PĀ'SHUN.IST	emancipationist
RĀ'SHUN.IST	degenerationist, federationist, inspirationist, moderationist, reparationist, restorationist, tolerationist
SĀ'SHUN.IST	annexationist, conversationist
TĀ'SHUN.IST	annotationist, imitationist, transmutationist
VĀ'SHUN.IST	innovationist, salvationist
ZĀ'SHUN.IST	causationist, colonizationist

(See Ā'SHUN, add -ist where appropriate.)

Ā'SHUN.LES

(See Ā'SHUN, add -less where appropriate.)

Ā'SHUS.LĒ

DĀ'SHUS.LĒ	audaciously, edaciously, mendaciously, mordaciously, predaciously
GĀ'SHUS.LĒ	fugaciously, sagaciously
GRĀ'SHUS.LĒ	graciously, ungraciously
KĀ'SHUS.LĒ	efficaciously, inefficaciously, perspicaciously
KWĀ'SHUS.LĒ	loquaciously
LĀ'SHUS.LĒ	fallaciously, salaciously
MĀ'SHUS.LĒ	contumaciously
NĀ'SHUS.LĒ	minaciously, pertinaciously, pugnaciously, tenaciously
PĀ'SHUS.LĒ	capaciously, rapaciously
RĀ'SHUS.LĒ	veraciously, voraciously
SĀ'SHUS.LĒ	vexatiously
SPĀ'SHUS.LĒ	spaciously
TĀ'SHUS.LĒ	disputatiously, flirtatiously, ostentatiously
VĀ'SHUS.LĒ	curvaceously, vivaciously

(See ĀSHUS, add -ly where appropriate.)

Ā'SHUS.NES

(See Ā'SHUS, add -ness where appropriate.)

Ā'SI.ĀT

KĀ'SI.ĀT	caseate

(See Ā'SHI.ĀT)

AS'I.FĪ

GAS'I.FĪ	gasify
KLAS'I.FĪ	declassify, classify, reclassify
PAS'I.FĪ	pacify, repacify

AS'I.KL

FAS'I.KL	fascicle
KLAS'I.KL	classical, neoclassical, nonclassical

AS'I.LĀT

(See AS'E.LĀT)

AS'I.NĀT

BAS'I.NĀT	abacinate
FAS'I.NĀT	fascinate
RAS'I.NĀT	deracinate
SAS'I.NĀT	assassinate

Ā'SI.NES

LĀ'SI.NES	laciness
RĀ'SI.NES	raciness
SPĀ'SI.NES	spaciness

AS'I.NES

BRAS'I.NES	brassiness
GAS'I.NES	gassiness
GLAS'I.NES	glassiness
GRAS'I.NES	grassiness
KLAS'I.NES	classiness
MAS'I.NES	massiness
SAS'I.NES	sassiness

AS'I.TĒ

BAS'I.TĒ	bibacity, urbacity
DAS'I.TĒ	audacity, edacity, mendacity, mordacity
GAS'I.TĒ	fugacity, sagacity
KAS'I.TĒ	dicacity, perspicacity, pervicacity, procacity
KWAS'I.TĒ	loquacity, sequacity
LAS'I.TĒ	bellacity, salacity
MAS'I.TĒ	emacity, contumacity
NAS'I.TĒ	minacity, pertinacity, pugnacity, saponacity, tenacity
PAS'I.TĒ	incapacity, capacity, opacity, rapacity
RAS'I.TĒ	feracity, veracity, voracity
VAS'I.TĒ	vivacity

AS'I.TUS

AS'I.TUS	acetus
TAS'I.TUS	Tacitus

AS'IV.LĒ

MAS'IV.LĒ	massively
PAS'IV.LĒ	impassively, passively

Ā'SIV.NES

BRĀ'SIV.NES	abrasiveness
SWĀ'SIV.NES	assuasiveness, dissuasiveness, persuasiveness, suasiveness
VĀ'SIV.NES	evasiveness, invasiveness, pervasiveness

AS'IV.NES

MAS'IV.NES	massiveness
PAS'IV.NES	impassiveness, passiveness

AS'PE.RĀT

AS'PE.RĀT	asperate, aspirate
ZAS'PE.RĀT	exasperate

AS'PING.LĒ

GAS'PING.LĒ	gaspingly
GRAS'PING.LĒ	graspingly
RAS'PING.LĒ	raspingly

AS'TAR.DĒ

BAS'TAR.DĒ	bastardy
DAS'TAR.DĒ	dastardy

AS'TA.SIS

AS'TA.SIS	diastasis
TAS'TA.SIS	metastasis

AS'TER.Ē

KAS'TER.Ē	dicastery
MAS'TER.Ē	mastery, self-mastery

AS'TER.ING

FAS'TER.ING	philophastering
MAS'TER.ING	mastering, overmastering
PAS'TER.ING	pastoring
PLAS'TER.ING	beplastering, plastering
TAS'TER.ING	poetastering

AS'TER.SHIP

MAS'TER.SHIP	mastership
PAS'TER.SHIP	pastorship

ĀST'FUL.Ē

TĀST'FUL.Ē	distastefully, tastefully
WĀST'FUL.Ē	wastefully

AS'TI.GĀT

FAS'TI.GĀT	fastigate
KAS'TI.GĀT	castigate

AS'TI.KAL

AS'TI.KAL	ecclesiastical, encomiastical, enthusiastical
LAS'TI.KAL	elastical
NAS'TI.KAL	gymnastical, monastical
TAS'TI.KAL	fantastical

AS'TI.KĀT

LAS'TI.KĀT	elasticate, scholasticate
MAS'TI.KĀT	masticate

AS'TIK.LĒ

AS'TIK.LĒ	ecclesiastic'ly, encomiastic'ly, enthusiastic'ly
BAS'TIK.LĒ	bombastic'ly
DRAS'TIK.LĒ	drastic'ly
KAS'TIK.LĒ	sarcastic'ly
LAS'TIK.LĒ	elastic'ly, scholastic'ly
NAS'TIK.LĒ	gymnastic'ly, monastic'ly
PLAS'TIK.LĒ	plasticly
TAS'TIK.LĒ	fantasticly

ĀS'TI.LĒ

HĀS'TI.LĒ	hastily
PĀS'TI.LĒ	pastily
TĀS'TI.LĒ	tastily

AS'TI.LĒ

GAS'TI.LĒ	ghastily
NAS'TI.LĒ	nastily

AS'TI.SIZM

AS'TI.SIZM	ecclesiasticism, orgiasticism
BRAS'TI.SIZM	Hudibrasticism
KLAS'TI.SIZM	iconoclasticism
LAS'TI.SIZM	scholasticism
NAS'TI.SIZM	monasticism
PLAS'TI.SIZM	plasticism
TAS'TI.SIZM	fantasticism

AS'TRI.AN

AS'TRI.AN	Zoroastrian
BAS'TRI.AN	alabastrian

AS'TRO.FĒ

AS'TRO.FĒ	diastrophe
NAS'TRO.FĒ	anastrophe, epanastrophe
TAS'TRO.FĒ	catastrophe

Ā'TA.BL

Ā'TA.BL	abbreviatable

(See ĀT, add *-able* where appropriate.)

AT'A.BL

AT'A.BL	get-at-able, come-at-able, unget-at-able, uncome-at-able
BAT'A.BL	battable, combatable, unbattable, uncombatable

FOR PLANETS FORSAKEN

For planets forsaken;
   For galaxies lorn;
For youth from me taken—
   Forever I mourn.

For sin unforgiven;
   For passion forborne;
For heart from me riven—
   Forever I mourn.

For life without leaven;
   For duty forsworn;
For forfeiting heaven—
   Forever I mourn.

HAT'A.BL	hattable, unhattable
MAT'A.BL	mattable, unmattable
PAT'A.BL	biocompatible, impatible, incompatible, compatible, patible, pattable, unpattable
RAT'A.BL	rattable
VAT'A.BL	vattable

Ā'TAL.Ē

FĀ'TAL.Ē	fatally
NĀ'TAL.Ē	natally, postnatally, prenatally

AT'E.LĪT

MAT'E.LĪT	stromatalite
SAT'E.LĪT	satellite

AT'EN.ING

BAT'EN.ING	battening
FAT'EN.ING	fattening, unfattening
FLAT'EN.ING	flattening

KAT'E.NĀT

(See KAT'I.NĀT)

Ā'TEN.SĒ

LĀ'TEN.SĒ	latency
PĀ'TEN.SĒ	patency

AT'ER.AN

KAT'ER.AN	cateran
LAT'ER.AN	Lateran

AT'E.RĒ

BAT'E.RĒ	battery
CHAT'E.RĒ	chattery
FLAT'E.RĒ	flattery
HAT'E.RĒ	hattery
KAT'E.RĒ	cattery
SHAT'E.RĒ	shattery
SKAT'E.RĒ	scattery
SLAT'E.RĒ	slattery
TAT'E.RĒ	tattery

AT'ER.ER

BAT'ER.ER	batterer
BLAT'ER.ER	blatterer

CHAT'ER.ER	chatterer
FLAT'ER.ER	flatterer
KLAT'ER.ER	clatterer
PAT'ER.ER	patterer
SHAT'ER.ER	shatterer
SKAT'ER.ER	scatterer
SMAT'ER.ER	smatterer
SPAT'ER.ER	bespatterer, spatterer
SPLAT'ER.ER	splatterer

AT'ER.ĒZ

FRAT'ER.ĒZ	frateries

(See AT'ER.Ē, change -y to -ies where appropriate.)

Ā'TER.FA.MĒL.YUS

MĀ'TER.FA.MĒL.YUS	*materfamilias*
PĀ'TER.FA.MĒL.YUS	*paterfamilias*

AT'ER.ING

(See AT'ER, add -ing where appropriate.)

AT'FOOT.ED

FAT'FOOT.ED	fat-footed
FLAT'FOOT.ED	flat-footed
KAT'FOOT.ED	cat-footed
RAT'FOOT.ED	rat-footed

ĀT'FUL.Ē

FĀT'FUL.Ē	fatefully
GRĀT'FUL.Ē	gratefully, ungratefully
HĀT'FUL.Ē	hatefully

ATH'ER.ER

(TH as in *then*)

BLATH'ER.ER	blatherer
GATH'ER.ER	forgatherer, gatherer, ingatherer, tax gatherer, toll gatherer, upgatherer, woolgatherer
LATH'ER.ER	lather
SLATH'ER.ER	slatherer

ATH'ER.ING

(TH as in *then*)

BLATH'ER.ING	blathering
GATH'ER.ING	forgathering, gathering, ingathering, woolgathering
LATH'ER.ING	lathering
SLATH'ER.ING	slathering

ATH'E.SIS

(TH as in *thin*)

ATH'E.SIS	diathesis
RATH'E.SIS	parathesis
TATH'E.SIS	metathesis

ATH'I.KAL

(TH as in *thin*)

MATH'I.KAL	philomathical, chrestomathical
PATH'I.KAL	anthropopathical, idiopathical

AT'I.BL

(See AT'A.BL)

ÄT'I.ER

SKWÄT'I.ER	squattier
SWÄT'I.ER	swattier
YÄT'I.ER	yachtier

(See OT'I.ER)

AT'I.FĪ

AT'I.FĪ	beatify
GRAT'I.FĪ	gratify
RAT'I.FĪ	ratify
STRAT'I.FĪ	interstratify, stratify

AT'I.KA

AT'I.KA	Attica, sciatica
JAT'I.KA	Jataka
MAT'I.KA	dalmatica
PAT'I.KA	hepatica

(See ÄTIKA)

Ä'TI.KA

JÄ'TI.KA	Jatika

(See AT'I.KA)

AT'I.KAL

AT'I.KAL	sciatical
BAT'I.KAL	abbatical, acrobatical, sabbatical
FAT'I.KAL	emphatical
KRAT'I.KAL	aristocratical, bureaucratical, democratical, idiosyncratical, autocratical, Socratical
KWAT'I.KAL	aquatical, semiaquatical, subaquatical
MAT'I.KAL	*A* acroamatical, axiomatical, anagrammatical, anathematical, anidiomatical, apophthegmatical, asthmatical, *D* diplomatical, dogmatical, *DR* dramatical, *E* emblematical, enigmatical, epigrammatical, *F* phantasmatical, *GR* grammatical, *H* hebdomatical, *I* idiomatical, *KL* climatical, *M* mathematical, *N* numismatical, *O* automatical, *PR* pragmatical, primatical, prismatical, problematical, *S* schismatical, symptomatical, systematical, somatical, *SP* spasmatical, *U* ungrammatical, unsystematical
NAT'I.KAL	fanatical
RAT'I.KAL	erratical, hieratical, leviratical, operatical, piratical, separatical
STAT'I.KAL	aerostatical, apostatical, ecstatical, hydrostatical, hypostatical, statical
VAT'I.KAL	vatical

(See AT'IK, add -al where appropriate.)

AT'I.NA

PAT'I.NA	patina
PLAT'I.NA	platina

AT'I.NĀT

KAT'I.NĀT	catenate, concatenate
LAT'I.NĀT	gelatinate, Latinate, Palatinate
PAT'I.NĀT	patinate

Ā'TI.NES

SLĀ'TI.NES	slatiness
WĀ'TI.NES	weightiness

AT'I.NES

BAT'I.NES	battiness
CHAT'I.NES	chattiness
FAT'I.NES	fattiness
KAT'I.NES	cattiness
NAT'I.NES	nattiness
RAT'I.NES	rattiness

ÄT'I.NES

SKWÄT'I.NES	squattiness
SWÄT'I.NES	swattiness
YÄT'I.NES	yachtiness

(See OT'I.NES)

Ā'TING.LĒ

(See ĀT, add -ingly where appropriate.)

AT'IN.ĪZ

LAT'IN.ĪZ	gelatinize, Latinize
PLAT'IN.ĪZ	platinize
RAT'IN.ĪZ	keratinize

AT'I.NUS

LAT'I.NUS	gelatinous
PLAT'I.NUS	platinous

AT'I.SĪZ

AT'I.SĪZ	Atticize
MAT'I.SĪZ	emblematicize, grammaticize
NAT'I.SĪZ	fanaticize

AT'I.SIZM

AT'I.SIZM	Asiaticism
MAT'I.SIZM	grammaticism, pragmaticism
NAT'I.SIZM	fanaticism

AT'I.TŪD

AT'I.TŪD	attitude, beatitude
GRAT'I.TŪD	gratitude, ingratitude
LAT'I.TŪD	latitude
PLAT'I.TŪD	platitude

AT'I.TŪ'DI.NĪZ

AT'I.TŪ'DI.NĪZ	attitudinize
PLAT'I.TŪ'DI.NĪZ	platitudinize

Ā'TIV.LĒ

Ā'TIV.LĒ	insinuatively, creatively, uncreatively
KĀ'TIV.LĒ	implicatively, incommunicatively, multiplicatively, predicatively, significatively
LĀ'TIV.LĒ	accumulatively, emulatively, gesticulatively, cumulatively, legislatively, manipulatively
NĀ'TIV.LĒ	determinatively, imaginatively, germinatively, natively, opinionatively, terminatively
PĀ'TIV.LĒ	anticipatively, participatively
RĀ'TIV.LĒ	alliteratively, decoratively, invigoratively, commemoratively, commiseratively, cooperatively, corroboratively, operatively, reiteratively, vituperatively
TĀ'TIV.LĒ	dubitatively, hesitatively, imitatively, indubitatively,

cogitatively,
qualitatively,
quantitatively,
meditatively,
authoritatively
TRĀ′TIV.LĒ   administratively

(See **ĀTIV,** add *-ly* where appropriate.)

Ā′TIV.NES

(See **Ā′TIV,** add *-ness* where appropriate.)

AT′L.MENT

BAT′L.MENT   battlement,
                   embattlement
PRAT′L.MENT   prattlement
TAT′L.MENT   tattlement

AT′O.MĒ

AT′O.MĒ   atomy
NAT′O.MĒ   anatomy
RAT′O.MĒ   tesseratomy

AT′O.MIST

AT′O.MIST   atomist, diatomist
NAT′O.MIST   anatomist

AT′O.MĪZ

AT′O.MĪZ   atomize
NAT′O.MĪZ   anatomize

AT′O.MIZM

AT′O.MIZM   atomism
NAT′O.MIZM   anatomism

AT′O.MUS

AT′O.MUS   diatomous
RAT′O.MUS   paratomous

Ā′TO.RĒ

KRĀ′TO.RĒ   obsecratory
LĀ′TO.RĒ   *recapitulatory*
NĀ′TO.RĒ   *ratiocinatory*

Ā′TRI.AL

Ā′TRI.AL   atrial
PĀ′TRI.AL   patrial

AT′RI.KAL

AT′RI.KAL   iatrical,
                   psychiatrical,
                   theatrical
LAT′RI.KAL   idolatrical
MAT′RI.KAL   matrical

AT′RI.MŌ.NĒ

MAT′RI.MŌ.NĒ   matrimony
PAT′RI.MŌ.NĔ   patrimony

AT′RI.SĪD

FRAT′RI.SĪD   fratricide
MAT′RI.SĪD   matricide
PAT′RI.SĪD   patricide

Ā′TRON.AL

MĀ′TRON.AL   matronal
PĀ′TRON.AL   patronal

Ā′TRON.IJ

MĀ′TRON.IJ   matronage
PĀ′TRON.IJ   patronage

Ā′TRO.NĪZ

MĀ′TRO.NĪZ   matronize
PĀ′TRO.NĪZ   patronize

AT′Ū.LĀT

(See **ACH′OO.LĀT**)

AT′Ū.RĀT

(See **ACH′OO.RĀT**)

Ā′VA.BL

LĀ′VA.BL   lavable
PĀ′VA.BL   pavable, repavable,
                   unpavable
SĀ′VA.BL   savable, unsavable
SHĀ′VA.BL   shavable, unshavable

WĀ′VA.BL   unwaivable,
                   unwavable,
                   waivable, wavable

AV′A.JER

(See **AV′I.JER**)

AV′EL.ER

GAV′EL.ER   gaveler
GRAV′EL.ER   graveler
KAV′EL.ER   caviler
RAV′EL.ER   raveler, unraveler
TRAV′EL.ER   traveler

AV′E.LIN

JAV′E.LIN   javelin
RAV′E.LIN   ravelin

AV′EL.ING

(See **AVEL,** add *-ing* where appropriate.)

AV′E.LINZ

NAV′E.LINZ   manavelins

(See **AV′E.LIN,** add *-s* where appropriate.)

AV′EN.DER

CHAV′EN.DER   chavender
LAV′EN.DER   lavender

Ā′VE.RĒ

BRĀ′VE.RĒ   bravery
FLĀ′VE.RĒ   flavory
GRĀ′VE.RĒ   gravery
KWĀ′VE.RĒ   quavery
NĀ′VE.RĒ   knavery
SĀ′VE.RĒ   savory, unsavory
SLĀ′VE.RĒ   anti-slavery, pro-
                   slavery, slavery
WĀ′VE.RĒ   wavery

Ā′VER.ER

FĀ′VER.ER   favorer
FLĀ′VER.ER   flavorer
HĀ′VER.ER   haverer
KWĀ′VER.ER   quaverer
LĀ′VER.ER   laverer

SĀ'VER.ER   savorer
WĀ'VER.ER   waverer

Ā'VER.ING

(See Ā'VER.ER, change -er to -ing.)

AV'ER.ING

HAV'ER.ING   havering
KLAV'ER.ING   clavering
LAV'ER.ING   palavering

Ā'VER.US

FĀ'VER.US   favorous
FLĀ'VER.US   flavorous
KWĀ'VER.US   quaverous
SĀ'VER.US   savorous

AV'ER.US

DAV'ER.US   cadaverous
PAV'ER.US   papaverous

Ā'VI.A

GRĀ'VI.A   Belgravia
NĀ'VI.A   ignavia, Scandinavia
RĀ'VI.A   Moravia
TĀ'VI.A   Batavia, Octavia

Ā'VI.AL

GĀ'VI.AL   gavial
KLĀ'VI.AL   clavial

Ā'VI.AN

Ā'VI.AN   avian
GRĀ'VI.AN   Belgravian
KLĀ'VI.AN   subclavian
NĀ'VI.AN   Scandinavian
RĀ'VI.AN   Moravian
SHĀ'VI.AN   Shavian
TĀ'VI.AN   Batavian, Octavian

Ā'VI.ER

KLĀ'VI.ER   clavier
WĀ'VI.ER   wavier

AV'I.JER

KLAV'I.JER   claviger
RAV'I.JER   ravager

SAV'I.JER   savager
SKAV'I.JER   scavager

AV'IJ.ING

RAV'IJ.ING   ravaging
SAV'IJ.ING   savaging
SKAV'IJ.ING   scavaging

AV'ISH.ER

LAV'ISH.ER   lavisher
RAV'ISH.ER   enravisher, ravisher

AV'ISH.ING

LAV'ISH.ING   lavishing
RAV'ISH.ING   enravishing, ravishing

AV'ISH.MENT

LAV'ISH.MENT   lavishment
RAV'ISH.MENT   enravishment, ravishment

Ā'VISH.NES

NĀ'VISH.NES   knavishness
SLĀ'VISH.NES   slavishness

AV'ISH.NES

LAV'ISH.NES   lavishness
SLAV'ISH.NES   Slavishness

AV'I.TĒ

GRAV'I.TĒ   gravity
KAV'I.TĒ   cavity, concavity
PRAV'I.TĒ   depravity, pravity
SWAV'I.TĒ   suavity

Ā'ZA.BL

FRĀ'ZA.BL   phrasable, unphrasable
GRĀ'ZA.BL   grazable, ungrazable
PRĀ'ZA.BL   appraisable, praisable, unappraisable, unpraisable
RĀ'ZA.BL   raisable, unraisable
SWĀ'ZA.BL   persuasible, suasible, unpersuasible

AZ'A.RĒN

MAZ'A.RĒN   mazarine
NAZ'A.RĒN   Nazarene

Ā'ZI.A

Ā'ZI.A   Asia
BĀ'ZI.A   abasia
FĀ'ZI.A   aphasia, paraphasia
FRĀ'ZI.A   paraphrasia, tachyphrasia
GĀ'ZI.A   ergasia
KĀ'ZI.A   Caucasia, sicchasia
KRĀ'ZI.A   dyscrasia
LĀ'ZI.A   onlochalasia, Australasia
MĀ'ZI.A   paronomasia, prosonomasia
NĀ'ZI.A   athanasia, gymnasia, euthanasia
PĀ'ZI.A   Aspasia
PLĀ'ZI.A   aplasia
RĀ'ZI.A   Laurasia, Eurasia
STĀ'ZI.A   Anastasia, astasia, hemostasia
TĀ'ZI.A   fantasia

(See ĀSHA, ĀZHA)

Ā'ZI.AL

BĀ'ZI.AL   basial
NĀ'ZI.AL   gymnasial

Ā'ZI.AN

Ā'ZI.AN   Asian
KĀ'ZI.AN   Caucasian
LĀ'ZI.AN   Australasian, Rabelasian
NĀ'ZI.AN   Athanasian
RĀ'ZI.AN   Eurasian

(See Ā'SHUN, Ā'ZHUN, Ā'SHI.AN)

Ā'ZI.LĒ

HĀ'ZI.LĒ   hazily
KRĀ'ZI.LĒ   crazily
LĀ'ZI.LĒ   lazily

Ā'ZI.NES

HĀ'ZI.NES   haziness
KRĀ'ZI.NES   craziness
LĀ'ZI.NES   laziness
MĀ'ZI.NES   maziness

Ā′ZING.LĒ

BLĀ′ZING.LĒ	blazingly
DĀ′ZING.LĒ	dazingly
GĀ′ZING.LĒ	gazingly
MĀ′ZING.LĒ	amazingly

AZ′L.MENT

DAZ′L.MENT	bedazzlement, dazzlement
FRAZ′L.MENT	frazzlement

AZ′Ū.RĪT

AZ′Ū.RĪT	azurite
LAZ′Ū.RĪT	lazurite

Ē′A.BL

FĒ′A.BL	feeable
FLĒ′A.BL	fleeable
FRĒ′A.BL	freeable
GRĒ′A.BL	agreeable, disagreeable
KRĒ′A.BL	decreeable, undecreeable
MĒ′A.BL	irremeable, meable, remeable
RĒ′A.BL	reable
SĒ′A.BL	seeable, unseeable
SKĒ′A.BL	skiable, unskiable
TRĒ′A.BL	treeable

Ē′A.LĒ

DĒ′A.LĒ	ideally
LĒ′A.LĒ	leally
RĒ′A.LĒ	really

Ē′A.LIST

DĒ′A.LIST	idealist
RĒ′A.LIST	realist, surrealist

Ē′A.LĪZ

DĒ′A.LĪZ	idealize
RĒ′A.LĪZ	realize

Ē′A.LIZM

DĒ′A.LIZM	idealism
RĒ′A.LIZM	realism, surrealism

Ē′AL.TĒ

FĒ′AL.TĒ	fealty
LĒ′AL.TĒ	lealty
RĒ′AL.TĒ	realty

Ē′A.NIZM

BĒ′A.NIZM	plebeianism
KĒ′A.NIZM	Manicheanism
PĒ′A.NIZM	paeanism
RĒ′A.NIZM	epicureanism, Pythagoreanism
SĒ′A.NIZM	Laodiceanism

EB′I.ER

BLEB′I.ER	blebbier
NEB′I.ER	nebbier
WEB′I.ER	cobwebbier, webbier

EB′I.EST

BLEB′I.EST	blebbiest
NEB′I.EST	nebbiest
WEB′I.EST	cobwebbiest, webbiest

EB′RI.TĒ

EB′RI.TĒ	muliebrity
LEB′RI.TĒ	celebrity
NEB′RI.TĒ	tenebrity

Ē′BRI.US

Ē′BRI.US	ebrious, inebrious
NĒ′BRI.US	funebrious, tenebrious

Ē′CHA.BL

BLĒ′CHA.BL	bleachable
PĒ′CHA.BL	impeachable, unimpeachable
PRĒ′CHA.BL	preachable, unpreachable
RĒ′CHA.BL	reachable, unreachable
TĒ′CHA.BL	teachable, unteachable

ECH′A.BL

ECH′A.BL	etchable, unetchable

FECH′A.BL

FECH′A.BL	fetchable, unfetchable
SKECH′A.BL	sketchable, unsketchable
STRECH′A.BL	stretchable, unstretchable

ECH′E.RĒ

LECH′E.RĒ	lechery
TRECH′E.RĒ	treachery

ECH′ER.US

LECH′ER.US	lecherous
TRECH′ER.US	treacherous

ĒCH′I.FĪ

PRĒCH′I.FĪ	preachify
SPĒCH′I.FĪ	speechify

Ē′CHI.NES

PĒ′CHI.NES	peachiness
PRĒ′CHI.NES	preachiness
SKRĒ′CHI.NES	screechiness

ECH′I.NES

SKECH′I.NES	sketchiness
STRECH′I.NES	stretchiness
TECH′I.NES	tetchiness

Ē′DA.BL

DĒ′DA.BL	deedable
FĒ′DA.BL	feedable
HĒ′DA.BL	heedable
LĒ′DA.BL	leadable, unleadable
NĒ′DA.BL	kneadable, unkneadable
PĒ′DA.BL	impedible
PLĒ′DA.BL	pleadable, unpleadable
RĒ′DA.BL	readable, unreadable
SĒ′DA.BL	exceedable, seedable, supersedable, unexceedable, unseedable
WĒ′DA.BL	unweedable, weedable

ED′A.BL

(See ED′I.BL)

ED'A.LĒ

(See ED'I.LĒ)

ED'EN.ING

DED'EN.ING	deadening
LED'EN.ING	leadening
RED'EN.ING	reddening

Ē'DER.SHIP

LĒ'DER.SHIP	leadership
RĒ'DER.SHIP	readership

ĒD'FUL.Ē

HĒD'FUL.Ē	heedfully, unheedfully
NĒD'FUL.Ē	needfully, unneedfully

ĒD'FUL.NES

HĒD'FUL.NES	heedfulness, unheedfulness
NĒD'FUL.NES	needfulness, unneedfulness

Ē'DI.A

MĒ'DI.A	intermedia, comedia, media, print media, multimedia
PĒ'DI.A	encyclopedia, pharmacopedia, fissipedia, hypnopedia, lassipedia, misopedia, cyclopedia
SĒ'DI.A	acedia, epicedia

Ē'DI.AL

MĒ'DI.AL	admedial, intermedial, irremedial, comedial, medial, remedial
PĒ'DI.AL	pedial
PRĒ'DI.AL	praedial
SĒ'DI.AL	epicedial

Ē'DI.AN

JĒ'DI.AN	tragedian
MĒ'DI.AN	Archimedean, comedian, median, picedian
SĒ'DI.AN	encyclopedian
PĒ'DI.AN	

Ē'DI.A

MĒ'DI.A	media, multimedia
PĒ'DI.A	encyclopedia, hypnopedia, cyclopedia
SĒ'DI.A	acedia

ED'I.BL

ED'I.BL	edible, inedible
BED'I.BL	beddable, unbeddable
DRED'I.BL	dreadable
KRED'I.BL	incredible, credible
PED'I.BL	impedible

Ē'DI.ENS

BĒ'DI.ENS	disobedience, obedience
GRĒ'DI.ENS	ingredients
PĒ'DI.ENS	expedience, expedients, inexpedience

Ē'DI.ENT

BĒ'DI.ENT	disobedient, obedient
GRĒ'DI.ENT	digredient, ingredient
MĒ'DI.ENT	mediant, submediant
PĒ'DI.ENT	expedient, impedient, inexpedient

Ē'DI.ER

BĒ'DI.ER	beadier
GRĒ'DI.ER	greedier
NĒ'DI.ER	needier
RĒ'DI.ER	reedier
SĒ'DI.ER	seedier
SPĒ'DI.ER	speedier
WĒ'DI.ER	weedier

ED'I.ER

BRED'I.ER	breadier
HED'I.ER	headier
RED'I.ER	readier, unreadier
SHRED'I.ER	shreddier
SPRED'I.ER	spreadier
STED'I.ER	steadier, unsteadier
THRED'I.ER	threadier

ED'I.ING

ED'I.ING	eddying
RED'I.ING	readying
STED'I.ING	steadying

ED'I.KAL

(See ED'I.KL)

ED'I.KANT

DED'I.KANT	dedicant
MED'I.KANT	medicant
PRED'I.KANT	predicant

ED'I.KĀT

DED'I.KĀT	dedicate, rededicate
MED'I.KĀT	medicate, remedicate
PRED'I.KĀT	predicate, depredicate

ED'I.KL

MED'I.KL	medical, pre-medical
PED'I.KL	pedicle

Ē'DI.LĒ

BĒ'DI.LĒ	beadily
GRĒ'DI.LĒ	greedily
NĒ'DI.LĒ	needily
RĒ'DI.LĒ	reedily
SĒ'DI.LĒ	seedily
SPĒ'DI.LĒ	speedily
WĒ'DI.LĒ	weedily

ED'I.LĒ

DED'I.LĒ	logodaedaly
HED'I.LĒ	headily
RED'I.LĒ	readily, unreadily
STED'I.LĒ	steadily, unsteadily

ED'I.MENT

| PED'I.MENT | impediment, pediment |
| SED'I.MENT | sediment |

Ē'DI.NES

(See ĒDĒ, add -ness where appropriate.)

ED'I.NES

| SED'I.NES | mucediness |

(See EDĒ, add -ness where appropriate.)

Ē'DING.LĒ

HĒ'DING.LĒ	heedingly, unheedingly
LĒ'DING.LĒ	leadingly, misleadingly
PLĒ'DING.LĒ	pleadingly
SĒ'DING.LĒ	exceedingly

ED'I.NUS

BED'I.NUS	rubedinous
GWED'I.NUS	pinguedinous
SED'I.NUS	mucediness
TRED'I.NUS	putredinous

ED'I.TĒ

| BED'I.TĒ | rubedity |
| RED'I.TĒ | heredity |

ED'I.TED

| ED'I.TED | edited, unedited |
| KRED'I.TED | accredited, discredited, credited, miscredited, unaccredited, undiscredited |

ED'I.TER

| ED'I.TER | editor, executive editor, managing editor, city editor, subeditor (etc.) |
| KRED'I.TER | creditor |

ED'I.TING

| ED'I.TING | editing |
| KRED'I.TING | accrediting, discrediting, crediting, miscrediting |

ED'I.TIV

KRED'I.TIV	creditive
PED'I.TIV	impeditive
RED'I.TIV	redditive
SED'I.TIV	sedative

ED'I.TOR

(See ED'I.TER)

Ē'DI.UM

MĒ'DI.UM	intermedium, medium
PĒ'DI.UM	cypripedium, Cypripedium
RĒ'DI.UM	soredium, uredium
SĒ'DI.UM	epicedium
TĒ'DI.UM	tedium

Ē'DI.US

| MĒ'DI.US | gluteus medius, intermedious, medious |
| TĒ'DI.US | tedious |

ĒD'LES.LĒ

| HĒD'LES.LĒ | heedlessly |
| NĒD'LES.LĒ | needlessly |

ĒD'LES.NES

| HĒD'LES.NES | heedlessness |
| NĒD'LES.NES | needlessness |

ED'Ū.LUS

| KRED'Ū.LUS | incredulous, credulous |
| SED'Ū.LUS | sedulous, unsedulous |

EF'ER.ENS

DEF'ER.ENS	deference
PREF'ER.ENS	preference
REF'ER.ENS	cross-reference, reference

EF'ER.ENT

EF'ER.ENT	efferent
DEF'ER.ENT	deferent
PREF'ER.ENT	preferent
REF'ER.ENT	referent

Ē'FI.NES

BĒ'FI.NES	beefiness
LĒ'FI.NES	leafiness
RĒ'FI.NES	reefiness

EF'I.SENS

| LEF'I.SENS | maleficence |
| NEF'I.SENS | beneficence |

EF'I.SENT

| LEF'I.SENT | maleficent |
| NEF'I.SENT | beneficent |

EG'A.BL

| BEG'A.BL | beggable |
| PEG'A.BL | peggable |

Ē'GAL.Ē

| LĒ'GAL.Ē | illegally, legally |
| RĒ'GAL.Ē | regally |

EG'A.LITH

| MEG'A.LITH | megalith |
| REG'A.LITH | regolith |

Ē'GA.LIZM

| LĒ'GA.LIZM | legalism |
| RĒ'GA.LIZM | regalism |

Ē'GAL.NES

| LĒ'GAL.NES | legalness, illegalness |
| RĒ'GAL.NES | regalness |

EG′E.RĒ

EG′E.RĒ	eggery
BEG′E.RĒ	beggary

Ē′GER.LĒ

Ē′GER.LĒ	eagerly, overeagerly, uneagerly
MĒ′GER.LĒ	meagerly

Ē′GER.NES

Ē′GER.NES	eagerness, overeagerness, uneagerness
MĒ′GER.NES	meagerness

EG′I.NES

EG′I.NES	egginess
DREG′I.NES	dregginess
LEG′I.NES	legginess

EG′NAN.SĒ

PREG′NAN.SĒ	pregnancy
REG′NAN.SĒ	regnancy

EG′Ū.LAR

REG′Ū.LAR	irregular, regular
TEG′Ū.LAR	tegular

Ē′I.FĪ

DĒ′I.FĪ	deify
RĒ′I.FĪ	reify

Ē′I.TĒ

BĒ′I.TĒ	plebeity
BLĒ′I.TĒ	tableity
DĒ′I.TĒ	deity, hermaphrodeity
LĒ′I.TĒ	velleity
NĒ′I.TĒ	D diathermaneity, E extraneity, erogeneity, F femineity, H heterogeneity, homogeneity, I instantaneity, K contemporaneity, M

	momentaneity, O omneity, P personeity, S simultaneity, SP spontaneity
RĒ′I.TĒ	incorporeity, corporeity
SĒ′I.TĒ	aseity, gaseity, haecceity, ipseity, perseity, seity
TĒ′I.TĒ	multeity

Ē′IZ.EM

(See ĒIZM)

EJ′A.BL

EJ′A.BL	edgeable, unedgeable
DREJ′A.BL	dredgeable, undredgeable
HEJ′A.BL	hedgeable, unhedgeable
KEJ′A.BL	kedgeable, unkedgeable
LEJ′A.BL	allegeable, illegible, legible
PLEJ′A.BL	pledgeable, unpledgeable
WEJ′A.BL	unwedgeable, wedgeable

Ē′JI.A

LĒ′JI.A	aquilegia
PLĒ′JI.A	diplegia, hemiplegia, quadriplegia, cycloplegia
RĒ′JI.A	aqua regia

Ē′JI.AN

FWĒ′JI.AN	Fuegian
LĒ′JI.AN	collegian
WĒ′JI.AN	Norwegian, sou'wegian

(See EJUN)

EJ′I.O

FEJ′I.O	solfeggio
PEJ′I.O	arpeggio

Ē′JUS.LĒ

GRĒ′JUS.LĒ	egregiously
LĒ′JUS.LĒ	sacrilegiously

Ē′JUS.NES

GRĒ′JUS.NES	egregiousness
LĒ′JUS.NES	sacrilegiousness

Ē′KA.BL

LĒ′KA.BL	leakable, unleakable
SPĒ′KA.BL	speakable, unspeakable

EK′A.BL

CHEK′A.BL	checkable, uncheckable
PEK′A.BL	impeccable, peccable
SEK′A.BL	inseccable

EK′A.NAL

DEK′A.NAL	decanal
SEK′A.NAL	Seconal

EK′CHER.AL

JEK′CHER.AL	conjectural
TEK′CHER.AL	architectural

EK′CHER.ER

JEK′CHER.ER	conjecturer
LEK′CHER.ER	lecturer

EK′CHŌŌ.AL

FEK′CHŌŌ.AL	effectual, ineffectual, prefectual
LEK′CHŌŌ.AL	anti-intellectual, intellectual, lectual, nonintellectual, unintellectual
PEK′CHŌŌ.AL	aspectual

Ē′KI.LĒ

BĒ′KI.LĒ	beakily
CHĒ′KI.LĒ	cheekily
KRĒ′KI.LĒ	creakily
LĒ′KI.LĒ	leakily
SKWĒ′KI.LĒ	squeakily
SLĒ′KI.LĒ	sleekily
SNĒ′KI.LĒ	sneakily

Ē'KI.NES

(See ĒKĒ, add -ness where appropriate.)

Ē'KISH.NES

FRĒ'KISH.NES	freakishness
SNĒ'KISH.NES	sneakishness

(See ĒK, add -ishness where appropriate.)

EK'LI.NĀT

DEK'LI.NĀT	declinate
REK'LI.NĀT	reclinate

EK'OND.LĒ

(See EK'UND.LĒ)

EK'ON.ING

(See EK'UN.ING)

EK'RE.MENT

DEK'RE.MENT	decrement
REK'RE.MENT	recrement

EK'SA.BL

(See EK'SI.BL)

EK'SA.GON

FLEK'SA.GON	flexagon
HEK'SA.GON	hexagon

EK'SED.LĒ

PLEK'SED.LĒ	perplexedly
VEK'SED.LĒ	convexedly, vexedly

EK'SHUN.AL

FEK'SHUN.AL	affectional
FLEK'SHUN.AL	flectional, inflectional, reflectional, reflexional
JEK'SHUN.AL	interjectional, objectional, projectional
LEK'SHUN.AL	collectional
NEK'SHUN.AL	connectional
PLEK'SHUN.AL	complexional
REK'SHUN.AL	directional, insurrectional, correctional, resurrectional
SEK'SHUN.AL	bisectional, dissectional, intersectional, resectional, sectional, vivisectional
TEK'SHUN.AL	protectional
VEK'SHUN.AL	convectional

EK'SHUN.ER

FEK'SHUN.ER	confectioner, perfectioner
JEK'SHUN.ER	interjectioner, objectioner, projectioner
REK'SHUN.ER	correctioner

EK'SHUN.IST

FEK'SHUN.IST	perfectionist
JEK'SHUN.IST	projectionist
REK'SHUN.IST	insurrectionist, resurrectionist
SEK'SHUN.IST	antivivisectionist, vivisectionist
TEK'SHUN.IST	antiprotectionist, protectionist

EK'SHU.NĪZ

REK'SHU.NĪZ	insurrectionize, resurrectionize
SEK'SHU.NĪZ	sectionize

EK'SI.A

KEK'SI.A	cachexia
LEK'SI.A	alexia
NEK'SI.A	pleonexia
REK'SI.A	anorexia, parorexia
SEK'SI.A	aprosexia

EK'SI.BL

FLEK'SI.BL	flexible, inflexible, reflexible
NEK'SI.BL	annexable
VEK'SI.BL	vexable

EK'SI.KAL

DEK'SI.KAL	indexical
LEK'SI.KAL	lexical
REK'SI.KAL	pyrexical

EK'SI.TĒ

FLEK'SI.TĒ	reflexity
PLEK'SI.TĒ	duplexity, intercomplexity, complexity, perplexity
VEK'SI.TĒ	convexity

EK'SIV.NES

FLEK'SIV.NES	reflexiveness
PLEK'SIV.NES	perplexiveness

EK'TA.BL

(See EK'TI.BL)

EK'TA.SIS

EK'TA.SIS	bronchiectasis
LEK'TA.SIS	atalectasis

EK'TED.LĒ

FEK'TED.LĒ	affectedly, disaffectedly, infectedly, unaffectedly
FLEK'TED.LĒ	reflectedly
GLEK'TED.LĒ	neglectedly
LEK'TED.LĒ	electedly, collectedly, recollectedly, selectedly
NEK'TED.LĒ	disconnectedly, connectedly
SPEK'TED.LĒ	expectedly, respectedly, suspectedly, unexpectedly, unsuspectedly
TEK'TED.LĒ	protectedly, unprotectedly

EK'TED.NES

(See EKT, add -edness where appropriate.)

EK'TE.RAL

FEK'TE.RAL	prefectoral
LEK'TE.RAL	electoral
PEK'TE.RAL	pectoral
REK'TE.RAL	directoral, rectoral
SEK'TE.RAL	sectoral
SPEK'TE.RAL	inspectoral
TEK'TE.RAL	protectoral

EK'TER.ĀT

PEK'TER.ĀT	expectorate

(See EK'TER.IT)

EK'TE.RĒ

FEK'TE.RĒ	refectory, confectory
JEK'TE.RĒ	interjectory, trajectory
NEK'TE.RĒ	nectary
REK'TE.RĒ	directory, correctory, rectory
SEK'TE.RĒ	sectary
TEK'TE.RĒ	protectory

EK'TER.IT

LEK'TER.IT	electorate
REK'TER.IT	directorate, rectorate
SPEK'TER.IT	inspectorate
TEK'TER.IT	protectorate

(See EK'TER.ĀT)

EKT'FUL.Ē

GLEKT'FUL.Ē	neglectfully
SPEKT'FUL.Ē	disrespectfully, respectfully, unrespectfully

EKT'FUL.NES

GLEKT'FUL.NES	neglectfulness
SPEKT'FUL.NES	disrespectfulness, respectfulness, suspectfulness, unrespectfulness, unsuspectfulness

EK'TI.BL

FEK'TI.BL	affectible, defectible, effectible, indefectible, infectible, perfectible, unaffectible
FLEK'TI.BL	deflectible, reflectible
JEK'TI.BL	objectable, rejectable, subjectable, unrejectable
LEK'TI.BL	delectable, indelectable, collectable, uncollectable
NEK'TI.BL	connectible, unconnectible
SPEK'TI.BL	expectable, respectable, suspectible, unrespectable, unsusceptible
SEK'TI.BL	dissectible, undissectible
TEK'TI.BL	detectable, undetectable

EK'TI.FĪ

JEK'TI.FĪ	objectify, subjectify
REK'TI.FĪ	rectify

EK'TI.KL

LEK'TI.KL	dialectical
PLEK'TI.KL	apoplectical
SPEK'TI.KL	spectacle

EK'TING.LĒ

FEK'TING.LĒ	affectingly
FLEK'TING.LĒ	reflectingly
JEK'TING.LĒ	objectingly

EK'TI.TOOD

NEK'TI.TOOD	senectitude
REK'TI.TOOD	rectitude

EK'TI.VIST

JEK'TI.VIST	objectivist
LEK'TI.VIST	collectivist

EK'TIV.LĒ

(See EKTIV, add -ly where appropriate.)

EK'TIV.NES

(See EKTIV, add -ness where appropriate.)

EK'TO.MĒ

DEK'TO.MĒ	appendectomy, omphalectomy, orchidectomy
LEK'TO.MĒ	tonsillectomy, umbilectomy
PEK'TO.MĒ	lipectomy, lumpectomy
REK'TO.MĒ	hysterectomy, laparohysteroal- pingooophorectomy
SEK'TO.MĒ	vasectomy
TEK'TO.MĒ	mastectomy

EK'TO.RĒ

(See EK'TE.RĒ)

EK'TŪ.AL

(See EK'CHOO.AL)

EK'TUR.ER

(See EK'CHER.ER)

EK'Ū.LAR

LEK'Ū.LAR	molecular, vallecular
PEK'Ū.LAR	vulpecular
SEK'Ū.LAR	secular
SPEK'Ū.LAR	specular

EK'Ū.LĀT

PEK'Ū.LĀT	peculate
SPEK'Ū.LĀT	speculate

EK'Ū.LUM

SEK'Ū.LUM	seculum
SPEK'Ū.LUM	speculum

EK'UND.LĒ

FEK'UND.LĒ	fecundly
SEK'UND.LĒ	secondly

EK'UN.ING

BEK'UN.ING	beckoning
REK'UN.ING	dead-reckoning, reckoning

EK'Ū.TIV

SEK'Ū.TIV	consecutive, subsecutive, unconsecutive
ZEK'Ū.TIV	executive

Ē'KWEN.SĒ

FRĒ'KWEN.SĒ	frequency, infrequency
SĒ'KWEN.SĒ	sequency

ĒL'A.BL

DĒL'A.BL	dealable, undealable
FĒL'A.BL	feelable, unfeelable
HĒL'A.BL	healable, unhealable
JĒL'A.BL	congealable, uncongealable
NĒL'A.BL	annealable
PĒL'A.BL	appealable, pealable, peelable, repealable, unpeelable, unrepealable
RĒL'A.BL	reelable
SĒL'A.BL	concealable, sealable, unconcealable, unsealable

EL'A.BL

BEL'A.BL	bellable
DEL'A.BL	delible, indelible
FEL'A.BL	fellable
JEL'A.BL	ingelable, gelable, jellable, unjellable
KWEL'A.BL	quellable, unquellable
PEL'A.BL	expellable, compellable
SPEL'A.BL	spellable, unspellable
TEL'A.BL	foretellable, tellable, untellable

EL'AN.US

FEL'A.NUS	felonous

MEL'A.NUS	leucomelanous, melanous, xanthomelanous

EL'A.TIN

JEL'A.TIN	gelatin
SKEL'A.TIN	skeleton

EL'A.TIV

PEL'A.TIV	appellative, compellative
REL'A.TIV	irrelative, correlative, relative

EL'E.GĀT

DEL'E.GĀT	delegate
REL'E.GĀT	relegate, religate

ĒL'ER.Ē

SĒL'ER.Ē	sealery
TWĒ'LER.Ē	Tuileries

EL'ER.Ē

HEL'ER.Ē	hellery
SEL'ER.Ē	celery, cellary
STEL'ER.Ē	stellary

EL'ET.Ē

DEL'ET.Ē	fidelity, infidelity
PEL'ET.Ē	pellety

EL'FISH.LĒ

EL'FISH.LĒ	elfishly
SEL'FISH.LĒ	selfishly, unselfishly

EL'FISH.NES

EL'FISH.NES	elfishness
SEL'FISH.NES	selfishness, unselfishness

Ē'LI.A

Ē'LI.A	syringomyelia
BĒ'LI.A	lobelia
DĒ'LI.A	grindelia, Cordelia

MĒ'LI.A	phocomelia, camellia

Ē'LI.AN

Ē'LI.AN	Ismailian
DĒ'LI.AN	Delian
FĒ'LI.AN	aphelion, Mephistophelian
HĒ'LI.AN	anthelion, parhelion, perihelion
MĒ'LI.AN	chameleon
NĒ'LI.AN	carnelian
PĒ'LI.AN	Pelion
SĒ'LI.AN	Caelian
TĒ'LI.AN	Aristotelian
THĒ'LI.AN	anthelion

EL'I.AN

EL'I.AN	Pantagruelian, pantagruelion
JEL'I.AN	evangelian
SKEL'I.AN	tetraskelion
VEL'I.AN	Machiavelian, Machiavellian
WEL'I.AN	Boswellian, Cromwellian

(See **ELYUN**)

EL'I.BL

(See **EL'A.BL**)

EL'I.FÔRM

KEL'I.FÔRM	cheliform
STEL'I.FÔRM	stelliform

EL'I.ING

BEL'I.ING	bellying
JEL'I.ING	jellying

EL'I.KAL

BEL'I.KAL	bellical
HEL'I.KAL	helical
JEL'I.KAL	angelical, evangelical
PEL'I.KAL	pellicle

EL'ING.LĒ

KWEL'ING.LĒ	quellingly
PEL'ING.LĒ	compellingly

TEL'ING.LĒ   tellingly
WEL'ING.LĒ   wellingly

Ē'LI.ON

DĒ'LI.ON   Mendelian
HĒ'LI.ON   Helion, perihelion

(See ĒL'YUN)

EL'ISH.ING

BEL'ISH.ING   embellishing
REL'ISH.ING   relishing

EL'ISH.MENT

2BEL'ISH.MENT   embellishment
REL'ISH.MENT   relishment

Ē'LI.US

BĒ'LI.US   Sibelius
HĒ'LI.US   Helios
MĒ'LI.US   contumelious
RĒ'LI.US   Aurelius

EL'O.DĒ

JEL'O.DĒ   hypogelody
MEL'O.DĒ   melody

EL'O.Ē

BEL'O.Ē   bellowy
MEL'O.Ē   mellowy
YEL'O.Ē   yellowy

EL'O.ER

BEL'O.ER   bellower
CHEL'O.ER   celloer
MEL'O.ER   mellower
YEL'O.ER   yellower

EL'O.ING

(See ELŌ, add -ing where appropriate.)

EL'O.NĒ

FEL'O.NĒ   felony
MEL'O.NĒ   melony

EL'O.NUS

FEL'O.NUS   felonous
MEL'O.NUS   leucomelanous, melanous, xanthomelanous

EL'TER.Ē

SHEL'TER.Ē   sheltery
SMEL'TER.Ē   smeltery
SWEL'TER.Ē   sweltery

EL'TER.ER

SHEL'TER.ER   shelterer
SMEL'TER.ER   smelterer
SWEL'TER.ER   swelterer
WEL'TER.ER   welterer

EL'TER.ING

SHEL'TER.ING   sheltering
SWEL'TER.ING   sweltering
WEL'TER.ING   weltering

EL'THI.ER

HEL'THI.ER   healthier
STEL'THI.ER   stealthier
WEL'THI.ER   wealthier

EL'THI.EST

HEL'THI.EST   healthiest
STEL'THI.EST   stealthiest
WEL'THI.EST   wealthiest

EL'THI.LĒ

HEL'THI.LĒ   healthily
STEL'THI.LĒ   stealthily
WEL'THI.LĒ   wealthily

EL'Ū.LAR

SEL'Ū.LAR   intercellular, cellular, unicellular
STEL'Ū.LAR   interstellular, stellular

EL'US.LĒ

JEL'US.LĒ   jealously, unjealously

ZEL'US.LĒ   overzealously, unzealously, zealously

Ē'MA.BL

(See ĒM, add -able where appropriate.)

EM'A.NĒ

(See EM'O.NĒ)

Ē'MA.TIST

SKĒ'MA.TIST   schematist
THĒ'MA.TIST   thematist

EM'A.TIST

BLEM'A.TIST   emblematist
REM'A.TIST   theorematist

EM'BER.ISH

EM'BER.ISH   emberish
SEM'BER.ISH   Decemberish
TEM'BER.ISH   Septemberish
VEM'BER.ISH   Novemberish

EM'ER.A

FEM'ER.A   ephemera
REM'ER.A   remora

EM'ER.AL

FEM'ER.AL   ephemeral, femerell, femoral
HEM'ER.AL   hemeral, trihemeral
NEM'ER.AL   nemoral

ĒM'ER.E

DRĒM'ER.Ē   dreamery
KRĒM'ER.Ē   creamery

EM'ER.Ē

EM'ER.Ē   emery
JEM'ER.Ē   gemmery
MEM'ER.Ē   memory

EM'E.SIS

| EM'E.SIS | emesis |
| NEM'E.SIS | nemesis |

Ē'MI.A

Ē'MI.A	pyemia
DĒ'MI.A	academia
HĒ'MI.A	Bohemia
FĒ'MI.A	coprophemia
KĒ'MI.A	ischemia, leukemia
LĒ'MI.A	paraphilemia
NĒ'MI.A	anemia
PRĒ'MI.A	sapremia
RĒ'MI.A	bacteremia, diarhemia, paroemia, uremia
SĒ'MI.A	anoxemia, hyperglycemia, hypoglycemia, septicemia, toxemia
THĒ'MI.A	schizothemia

Ē'MI.AL

Ē'MI.AL	proemial
DĒ'MI.AL	academial, endemial, vindemial
GRĒ'MI.AL	gremial
NĒ'MI.AL	cnemial
PRĒ'MI.AL	premial
RĒ'MI.AL	paroemial, uremial

Ē'MI.AN

| DĒ'MI.AN | academian |
| HĒ'MI.AN | Bohemian |

Ē'MI.ER

BĒ'MI.ER	beamier
DRĒ'MI.ER	dreamier
GLĒ'MI.ER	gleamier
KRĒ'MI.ER	creamier
PRĒ'MI.ER	premier
STĒ'MI.ER	steamier

EM'I.KAL

DEM'I.KAL	academical, endemical, epidemical, pandemical
KEM'I.KAL	alchemical, electrochemical, photochemical, chemical
LEM'I.KAL	polemical

Ē'MI.LĒ

BĒ'MI.LĒ	beamily
DRĒ'MI.LĒ	dreamily
GLĒ'MI.LĒ	gleamily
KRĒ'MI.LĒ	creamily
STĒ'MI.LĒ	steamily

EM'I.NAL

FEM'I.NAL	feminal
JEM'I.NAL	bigeminal, geminal, tergeminal
SEM'I.NAL	seminal

EM'I.NĀT

FEM'I.NĀT	effeminate, feminate
JEM'I.NĀT	ingeminate, geminate, tergeminate
SEM'I.NĀT	disseminate, inseminate, seminate

Ē'MI.NES

(See ĒMĒ, add -ness where appropriate.)

Ē'MING.LĒ

(See ĒM, add -ingly where appropriate.)

EM'I.PED

| REM'I.PED | remiped |
| SEM'I.PED | semiped |

EM'I.TĒ

| SEM'I.TĒ | Yosemite |
| TREM'I.TĒ | extremity |

Ē'MI.UM

| PRĒ'MI.UM | premium, proemium |
| SĒ'MI.UM | gelsemium |

EM'NI.FĪ

| DEM'NI.FĪ | indemnify |
| LEM'NI.FĪ | solemnify |

EM'NI.TĒ

| DEM'NI.TĒ | indemnity |
| LEM'NI.TĒ | solemnity |

EM'O.NĒ

JEM'O.NĒ	hegemony
LEM'O.NĒ	lemony
NEM'O.NĒ	anemone, pantanemone
SEM'O.NĒ	Gethsemane

EM'ON.STRĀT

| DEM'ON.STRĀT | demonstrate |
| REM'ON.STRĀT | *remonstrate* |

EM'PE.RĒ

EM'PE.RĒ	empery
STEM'PE.RĒ	extempore
TEM'PE.RĒ	tempery, tempore

EM'PER.ER

| EM'PER.ER | emperor |
| TEM'PER.ER | temperer |

EMP'TE.RĒ

| DEMP'TE.RĒ | redemptory |
| REMP'TE.RĒ | peremptory |

EM'Ū.LENT

EM'Ū.LENT	emulant
TEM'Ū.LENT	temulent
TREM'Ū.LENT	tremulant, tremulent

EM'Ū.LUS

| EM'Ū.LUS | emulous |
| TREM'Ū.LUS | tremulous |

Ē'NA.BL

GLĒ'NA.BL	gleanable, ungleanable
LĒ'NA.BL	leanable
MĒ'NA.BL	amenable, meanable, unamenable
VĒ'NA.BL	convenable, unconvenable

EN'A.BL

| MEN'A.BL | amenable |
| PEN'A.BL | pennable |

REN′A.BL renable
TEN′A.BL tenable, untenable

EN′A.RĒ

(See EN′E.RĒ)

EN′A.TER

JEN′A.TER genitor, primogenitor, progenitor
SEN′A.TER senator

EN′CHOO.AL

SEN′CHOO.AL accentual, percentual
VEN′CHOO.AL adventual, eventual, conventual

EN′CHOO.ĀT

SEN′CHOO.ĀT accentuate
VEN′CHOO.ĀT eventuate

EN′DA.BL

EN′DA.BL endable
BEN′DA.BL bendable, unbendable
FEN′DA.BL defendable, undefendable
HEN′DA.BL comprehendible
LEN′DA.BL lendable, unlendable
MEN′DA.BL amendable, emendable, commendable, mendable, recommendable, unamendable, unemendable, uncommendable, unmendable, unrecommendable
PEN′DA.BL appendable, dependable, impendable, pendable, suspendable
REN′DA.BL rendable
SEN′DA.BL accendible, ascendible
TEN′DA.BL extendable
VEN′DA.BL vendible, invendible

EN′DEN.SĒ

PEN′DEN.SĒ appendency, dependency, impendency, independency, interdependency, pendency
SEN′DEN.SĒ ascendancy, transcendency
SPLEN′DEN.SĒ resplendency, splendency
TEN′DEN.SĒ ambitendency, attendency, intendency, countertendency, superintendency, tendency

EN′DER.ER

JEN′DER.ER engenderer, genderer
REN′DER.ER renderer, surrenderer
SLEN′DER.ER slenderer
TEN′DER.ER tenderer

EN′DER.EST

SLEN′DER.EST slenderest
TEN′DER.EST tenderest

E3′DER.ING

JEN′DER.ING engendering, gendering
REN′DER.ING rendering, surrendering

EN′DER.LĒ

SLEN′DER.LĒ slenderly
TEN′DER.LĒ tenderly

EN′DER.NES

SLEN′DER.NES slenderness
TEN′DER.NES tenderness

EN′DI.US

PEN′DI.US dispendious, compendious
SEN′DI.US incendious

END′LES.LĒ

END′LES.LĒ endlessly
BEND′LES.LĒ bendlessly
BLEND′LES.LĒ blendlessly
FREND′LES.LĒ friendlessly

END′LES.NES

(See END, add -lessness where appropriate.)

EN′DUS.LĒ

MEN′DUS.LĒ tremendously
PEN′DUS.LĒ stupendously
REN′DUS.LĒ horrendously

EN′DUS.NES

MEN′DUS.NES tremendousness
PEN′DUS.NES stupendousness
REN′DUS.NES horrendousness

EN′ER.Ā.SHUN

JEN′ER.Ā.SHUN ingeneration, generation, progeneration, regeneration
TEN′ER.Ā.SHUN inteneration
VEN′ER.Ā.SHUN veneration

EN′E.RĀT

JEN′E.RĀT degenerate, ingenerate, generate, progenerate, regenerate
TEN′E.RĀT intenerate
VEN′E.RĀT venerate

Ē′NE.RĒ

BĒ′NE.RĒ beanery
DĒ′NE.RĒ deanery, denary, duodenary
GRĒ′NE.RĒ greenery
PLĒ′NE.RĒ plenary
SĒ′NE.RĒ scenery, senary
SHĒ′NE.RĒ machinery
TĒ′NE.RĒ bicentenary, quatercentenary, quincentenary, centenary

EN′ER.Ē

DEN′ER.Ē denary
HEN′ER.Ē hennery

PLEN'ER.Ē — plenary
SEN'ER.Ē — decenary, decennary, senery
TEN'ER.Ē — quatercentenary, centenary, septennary
VEN'ER.Ē — venery

EN'ER.IS

JEN'ER.IS — sui generis
VEN'ER.IS — mons veneris

EN'E.SIS

JEN'E.SIS — *A* abiogenesis, agenesis, anthropogenesis, *B* biogenesis, *E* ectogenesis, epigenesis, *F* phylogenesis, photogenesis, *H* hematogenesis, heterogenesis, hylogenesis, histogenesis, homogenesis, *I* iatrogenesis, *J* genesis, *K* catagenesis, *M* metagenesis, monogenesis, morphogenesis, *N* neogenesis, *O* ontogenesis, oogenesis, organogenesis, osteogenesis, *P* palingenesis, pangenesis, paragenesis, parthenogenesis, pathogenesis, pyrogenesis, polygenesis, *R* regenesis, *S* psychogenesis, *SP* spermatogenesis, sporogenesis, *Y* eugenesis, *Z* xenogenesis, zoogenesis
REN'E.SIS — parenesis

EN'E.TING

JEN'E.TING — jenneting
REN'E.TING — renneting

ENG'THEN.ING

LENG'THEN.ING — lengthening
STRENG'THEN.ING — strengthening

Ē'NI.A

DĒ'NI.A — gardenia
DRĒ'NI.A — hypoadrenia
FRĒ'NI.A — *A* aphilophrenia, azygophrenia, *H* hebephrenia, *K* castrophrenia, *L* lypophrenia, *M* malneirophrenia, *N* nosocomephrenia, *O* oligophrenia, *PR* presbyophrenia, *SK* schizophrenia, *ST* strataphrenia, *Y* euniophrenia
MĒ'NI.A — Armenia, catamenia, neomenia
PĒ'NI.A — leucopenia
SĒ'NI.A — sarracenia
STHĒ'NI.A — sthenia
TĒ'NI.A — taenia
THĒ'NI.A — asthenia, phonasthenia, myasthenia, neurasthenia, Parthenia, psychasthenia
VĒ'NI.A — Slovenia
ZĒ'NI.A — xenia

EN'I.A

DREN'I.A — quadrennia
LEN'I.A — millennia
SEN'I.A — decennia

Ē'NI.AL

JĒ'NI.AL — homogeneal, genial, congenial, primigenial, primogenial, uncongenial
MĒ'NI.AL — demesnial, menial
SPLĒ'NI.AL — splenial
TĒ'NI.AL — taenial
VĒ'NI.AL — venial
ZĒ'NI.AL — xenial

(See ĒNYAL)

EN'I.AL

EN'I.AL — biennial, triennial
KWEN'I.AL — quinquennial
LEN'I.AL — millennial
REN'I.AL — perennial, plurennial, quadrennial
SEN'I.AL — decennial, duodecennial, quindecennial, tricennial, vicennial
TEN'I.AL — bicentennial, quincentennial, quotennial, octennial, centennial, septennial, tercentennial, tricentennial
VEN'I.AL — novennial

(See ENYAL)

Ē'NI.AN

FĒ'NI.AN — Fenian
LĒ'NI.AN — Hellenian, selenian
MĒ'NI.AN — Armenian, neomenian
RĒ'NI.AN — sirenian, Cyrenian
THĒ'NI.AN — Athenian, Ruthenian

Ē'NI.ENS

LĒ'NI.ENS — lenience
VĒ'NI.ENS — advenience, inconvenience, intervenience, introvenience, convenience, prevenience, supervenience

(See ĒNYENS)

Ē'NI.ENT

LĒ'NI.ENT — lenient, unlenient
VĒ'NI.ENT — advenient, inconvenient, intervenient, introvenient, convenient, prevenient

(See ĒNYENT)

Ē'NI.ER

PLĒ'NI.ER	plenier
SHĒ'NI.ER	sheenier
SPLĒ'NI.ER	spleenier
TĒ'NI.ER	teenier
WĒ'NI.ER	teeny-weenier, weenier

(See ĒN'YER)

EN'I.FORM

PEN'I.FORM	bipenniform, penniform
TEN'I.FORM	antenniform

EN'I.KAL

EN'I.KAL	hygienical
LEN'I.KAL	galenical
MEN'I.KAL	ecumenical, catechumenical
REN'I.KAL	sirenical
SEN'I.KAL	arsenical, scenical

EN'I.TĒ

LEN'I.TĒ	lenity
MEN'I.TĒ	amenity
REN'I.TĒ	serenity, terrenity
SEN'I.TĒ	obscenity

EN'I.TEN.SĒ

PEN'I.TEN.SĒ	penitency
REN'I.TEN.SĒ	renitency

EN'I.TENT

PEN'I.TENT	penitent
REN'I.TENT	renitent

EN'I.TIV

JEN'I.TIV	genitive, primogenitive, progenitive
LEN'I.TIV	lenitive
SPLEN'I.TIV	splenitive

EN'I.TŪD

LEN'I.TŪD	lenitude
PLEN'I.TŪD	plenitude
REN'I.TŪD	serenitude

Ē'NI.UM

LĒ'NI.UM	selenium, solenium
MĒ'NI.UM	hymenium
RĒ'NI.UM	rhenium
SĒ'NI.UM	postscenium, proscenium
THĒ'NI.UM	calisthenium, ruthenium
ZĒ'NI.UM	xenium

EN'I.UM

EN'I.UM	biennium, triennium
KWEN'I.UM	quinquennium
LEN'I.UM	millennium
REN'I.UM	quadrennium
SEN'I.UM	decennium, sexennium
TEN'I.UM	septennium

Ē'NI.US

Ē'NI.US	aeneous
JĒ'NI.US	extrageneous, heterogeneous, homogeneous, genius, nitrogeneous, primigeneous
LĒ'NI.US	selenious
MĒ'NI.US	pergameneous
SĒ'NI.US	arsenious
SPLĒ'NI.US	splenius

(See ĒNYUS)

EN'I.ZEN

BEN'I.ZEN	benison
DEN'I.ZEN	denizen, endenizen
VEN'I.ZEN	venison

Ē'NO.KRIST

FĒ'NO.KRIST	phenocryst
ZĒ'NO.KRIST	xenocryst

Ē'NO.TĪP

FĒ'NO.TĪP	phenotype
JĒ'NO.TĪP	genotype

EN'SA.BL

DEN'SA.BL	incondensable, condensable

FEN'SA.BL	defensible, indefensible
HEN'SA.BL	apprehensible, deprehensible, incomprehensible, irreprehensible, comprehensible, reprehensible
PEN'SA.BL	dispensable, indispensable, suspensible
SEN'SA.BL	insensible, sensible, subsensible
TEN'SA.BL	distensible, extensible, inostensible, ostensible, tensible

---

COMPARATIVE AFFECTION

A Quad, I'm told, is a quadril-
lion British Thermal Units, each
Of which is equal to ten mil-
lion Ergs. To use poetic speech,
I put my love for you above a Quad,
And yours for me below an Erg, by God.

EN'SA.TIV

(See EN'SI.TIV)

EN'SE.RĒ

DEN'SE.RĒ	condensery
FEN'SE.RĒ	defensory
HEN'SE.RĒ	prehensory, reprehensory
PEN'SE.RĒ	dispensary, suspensory
SEN'SE.RĒ	extrasensory, incensory, sensory, somatosensory
TEN'SE.RĒ	ostensory

EN'SHE.RĒ

EN'SHE.RĒ	obedientiary
DEN'SHE.RĒ	redentiary, residentiary
LEN'SHE.RĒ	silentiary
TEN'SHE.RĒ	penitentiary, plenipotentiary, sententiary

EN'SHI.ĀT

REN'SHI.ĀT	differentiate
SEN'SHI.ĀT	essentiate, licentiate
TEN'SHI.ĀT	potentiate

EN'SHOO.AL

MEN'SHOO.AL	mensual, trimensual
SEN'SHOO.AL	consensual, censual, sensual

EN'SHUN.A.BL

MEN'SHUN.A.BL	mentionable, unmentionalbe
PEN'SHUN.A.BL	pensionable, unpensionable

EN'SHUN.AL

MEN'SHUN.AL	dimensional, hypertridimensional
SEN'SHUN.AL	ascensional, descensional
STEN'SHUN.AL	extensional
TEN'SHUN.AL	attentional, intentional, contentional, unintentional
VEN'SHUN.AL	conventional, preventional, unconventional

EN'SHUN.ER

MEN'SHUN.ER	mentioner
PEN'SHUN.ER	pensioner
VEN'SHUN.ER	conventioner

EN'SHUN.ING

MEN'SHUN.ING	mentioning
PEN'SHUN.ING	pensioning
TEN'SHUN.ING	tensioning

EN'SHUN.IST

SEN'SHUN.IST	ascenscionist, descenscionist, recensionist
TEN'SHUN.IST	extensionist
VEN'SHUN.IST	conventionist, preventionist

EN'SHUS.NES

(See ENSHUS, add -ness.)

EN'SI.BL

(See EN'SA.BL)

EN'SI.BLĒ

FEN'SI.BLĒ	defensibly
HEN'SI.BLĒ	incomprehensibly, comprehensibly, reprehensibly
SEN'SI.BLĒ	insensibly, sensibly
STEN'SI.BLĒ	ostensibly

EN'SI.FĪ

DEN'SI.FĪ	densify
SEN'SI.FĪ	sensify
TEN'SI.FĪ	intensify

EN'SI.KAL

REN'SI.KAL	forensical
SEN'SI.KAL	nonsensical

EN'SI.TĒ

DEN'SI.TĒ	density, condensity
MEN'SI.TĒ	immensity
PEN'SI.TĒ	propensity
TEN'SI.TĒ	attensity, intensity, tensity

EN'SI.TIV

DEN'SI.TIV	condensative
PEN'SI.TIV	dispensative, compensative, pensative
SEN'SI.TIV	photosensitive, hypersensitive, insensitive, radiosensitive, sensitive
TEN'SI.TIV	intensative

EN'SIV.LĒ

(See ENSIV, add -ly.)

EN'SIV.NES

(See ENSIV, add -ness.)

ENS'LES.LĒ

FENS'LES.LĒ	defenselessly, indefenselessly, inoffenselessly, offenselessly
SENS'LES.LĒ	senselessly
TENS'LES.LĒ	tenselessly

ENS'LES.NES

(See ENSLES, add -ness.)

EN'SO.RĒ

(See EN'SE.RĒ)

EN'TA.BL

KWEN'TA.BL	frequentable
MEN'TA.BL	fermentable, *lamentable*
PEN'TA.BL	repentable
REN'TA.BL	rentable
TEN'TA.BL	contentable, tentable
VEN'TA.BL	inventible, preventable, unpreventable
ZEN'TA.BL	presentable, representable, unpresentable

EN'TA.BLĒ

(See EN'TA.BL, change -e to -y.)

EN'TA.KL

DEN'TA.KL	dentical, denticle, identical
PEN'TA.KL	pentacle
TEN'TA.KL	tentacle
THEN'TA.KL	authentical
VEN'TA.KL	conventical, conventicle

EN'TAL.Ē

EN'TAL.Ē	orientally
DEN'TAL.Ē	accidentally, incidentally, occidentally, transcendentally
MEN'TAL.Ē	*A* alimentally, *D* detrimentally, developmentally, *E* experimentally, elementally, *F* fundamentally, *FR* fragmentally, *G* governmentally, *I* instrumentally, *K* complimentally, *M* mentally, momentally, monumentally, *O* ornamentally, *P* pigmentally, *R*

regimentally, *D*
segmentally,
sentimentally,
supplementally, *T*
temperamentally

NEN'TAL.Ē continentally
REN'TAL.Ē parentally

EN'TAL.IST

EN'TAL.IST Orientalist
DEN'TAL.IST Occidentalist,
transcendentalist
MEN'TAL.IST experimentalist,
environmentalist,
fundamentalist,
instrumentalist,
mentalist,
sentimentalist

EN'TAL.ĬZ

EN'TAL.ĬZ orientalize
DEN'TAL.ĬZ occidentalize
MEN'TAL.ĬZ departmentalize,
compartmentalize,
experimentalize,
mentalize,
sentimentalize
NEN'TAL.ĬZ continentalize

EN'TAL.IZM

EN'TAL.IZM Orientalism
DEN'TAL.IZM accidentalism,
Occidentalism,
transcendentalism
MEN'TAL.IZM elementalism,
environmentalism,
fundamentalism,
mentalism,
sentimentalism

EN'TAL.NES

(See **ENTAL**, add *-ness* where appropriate.)

EN'TA.TIV

(See **ENT**, add *-ative* where appropriate.)

EN'TED.LĒ

DEN'TED.LĒ unprecedentedly
KWEN'TED.LĒ frequentedly,
unfrequentedly

MEN'TED.LĒ dementedly,
lamentedly,
tormentedly,
unlamentedly

EN'TED.NES

(See **ENT**, add *-edness* where appropriate.)

EN'TER.ĀT

LEN'TER.ĀT coelenterate
TEN'TER.ĀT extenterate

EN'TER.ING

EN'TER.ING entering, re-entering
SEN'TER.ING centering, recentering,
self-centering

EN'TER.Ē

DEN'TER.Ē accidentary, dentary
MEN'TER.Ē *A* alimentary, *D*
documentary, *E*
elementary,
emolumentary, *F*
filamentary, *FR*
fragmentary, I
instrumentary,
integumentary, *K*
complementary,
complimentary, *P*
parliamentary,
pigmentary, R
rudimentary, *S*
sacramentary,
sedimentary,
segmentary,
supplementary, *T*
tegumentary,
testamentary, *U*
uncomplimentary,
unparliamentary
SEN'TER.Ē placentary

EN'TER.ON

EN'TER.ON enteron
SEN'TER.ON mesenteron

ENT'FUL.Ē

VENT'FUL.Ē eventfully,
inventfully,
uneventfully

ZENT'FUL.Ē resentfully,
unresentfully

ENT'FUL.NES

(See **ENTFUL**, add *-ness*)

EN'THE.SIS

PEN'THE.SIS epenthesis
REN'THE.SIS parenthesis

EN'TI.KL

(See **EN'TA.KL**)

EN'TI.KŪL

DEN'TI.KŪL denticule
LEN'TI.KŪL lenticule

EN'TI.MENT

SEN'TI.MENT sentiment
ZEN'TI.MENT presentiment

EN'TI.NAL

DEN'TI.NAL dentinal
SEN'TI.NAL sentinel

EN'TING.LĒ

LEN'TING.LĒ relentingly,
unrelentingly
MEN'TING.LĒ augmentingly,
tormentingly
PEN'TING.LĒ repentingly,
unrepentingly
SEN'TING.LĒ assentingly,
dissentingly,
consentingly

EN'TI.TĒ

EN'TI.TĒ entity, nonentity
DEN'TI.TĒ identity

EN'TIV.LĒ

TEN'TIV.LĒ attentively,
retentively
VEN'TIV.LĒ inventively,
preventively
ZEN'TIV.LĒ presentively

EN'TIV.NES

(See **ENTIV,** add *-ness* where appropriate.)

EN'TL.NES

(See **ENTAL,** add *-ness* where appropriate.)

EN'TRAL.Ē

SEN'TRAL.Ē	centrally, subcentrally
VEN'TRAL.Ē	dorsoventrally, ventrally

EN'TRI.KL

SEN'TRI.KL	eccentrical, concentrical, centrical
VEN'TRI.KL	ventricle

EN'TŪ.AL

(See **EN'CHOO.AL**)

EN'TŪ.ĀT

(See **EN'CHOO.ĀT**)

EN'TUS.LĒ

MEN'TUS.LĒ	momentously
TEN'TUS.LĒ	portentously

EN'TUS.NES

MEN'TUS.NES	momentousness
TEN'TUS.NES	portentousness

Ē'NUN.SI.ĀT

Ē'NUN.SI.ĀT	*enunciate*
DĒ'NUN.SI.ĀT	*denunciate*

EN'Ū.US

JEN'Ū.US	disingenuous, ingenuous
STREN'Ū.US	strenuous
TEN'Ū.US	tenuous

ĒN'YEN.SĒ

LĒN'YEN.SĒ	leniency
VĒN'YEN.SĒ	adveniency, inconveniency, interveniency, introveniency, conveniency, superveniency

ĒN'YENT.LĒ

(See **ĒNYENT,** add *-ly* where appropriate.)

Ē'O.FĪT

JĒ'O.FĪT	geophyte
NĒ'O.FĪT	neophyte

Ē'O.KRAT

RĒ'O.KRAT	rheocrat
THĒ'O.KRAT	theocrat

Ē'O.LA

BĒ'O.LA	rubeola
RĒ'O.LA	areola
VĒ'O.LA	alveola, foveola
ZĒ'O.LA	roseola

Ē'O.LUS

LĒ'O.LUS	malleolus, nucleolus
VĒ'O.LUS	alveolus

EP'A.RĀT

REP'A.RĀT	reparate
SEP'A.RĀT	separate

EP'ER.US

LEP'ER.US	leperous
STREP'ER.US	obstreperous, streperous

EP'I.DŌT

EP'I.DŌT	epidote
LEP'I.DŌT	lepidote

Ē'PI.LĒ

KRĒ'PI.LĒ	creepily
SLĒ'PI.LĒ	sleepily
WĒ'PI.LĒ	weepily

Ē'PI.NES

KRĒ'PI.NES	creepiness
SLĒ'PI.NES	sleepiness
WĒ'PI.NESS	weepiness

EP'I.TANT

KREP'I.TANT	crepitant
STREP'I.TANT	strepitant

EP'SI.A

BLEP'SI.A	ablepsia, chionablepsia, monoblepsia, opsablepsia
PEP'SI.A	apepsia, dyspepsia, eupepsia

EP'TI.KL

LEP'TI.KL	sylleptical
SEP'TI.KL	antiseptical, aseptical, conceptacle, receptacle, septical
SKEP'TI.KL	skeptical, unskeptical

ER'A.FIM

SER'A.FIM	seraphim
TER'A.FIM	teraphim

ER'A.KLĒZ

ER'A.KLĒZ	Heracles
PER'A.KLĒZ	Pericles

ER'AN.SĒ

ER'AN.SĒ	errancy, inerrancy
BER'AN.SĒ	aberrancy

ER'E.MŌ.NĒ

KWER'E.MŌ.NĒ	querimony
SER'E.MŌ.NĒ	ceremony

ER′ET.ED

FER′ET.ED	ferreted
HER′ET.ED	disherited, disinherited, inherited, uninherited
HWER′ET.ED	wherreted
MER′ET.ED	demerited, emerited, merited

ER′ET.ER

(See **ERET**, add *-er* where appropriate.)

ER′ET.ING

(See **ERET**, add *-ing* where appropriate.)

ĒR′I.A

(See **ÎR′I.A**)

ER′I.A

NER′I.A	spaneria
STER′I.A	hysteria

ĒR′I.AD

(See **ÎR′I.AD**)

ĒR′I.AL

(See **ÎR′I.AL**)

ĒR′I.A.LIST

(See **ÎR′I.A.LIST**)

ĒR′I.A.LIZM

(See **ÎR′I.A.LIZM**)

ĒR′I.AN

(See **ÎR′I.AN**)

ER′I.BL

ER′I.BL	errable, inerrable
TER′I.BL	terrible

(See **ÂR′A.BL**)

ĒR′I.ER

(See **ÎR′I.ER**)

ER′I.ER

BER′I.ER	berrier, burier
FER′I.ER	ferrier
MER′I.ER	merrier
TER′I.ER	terrier

ER′I.FĪ

SFER′I.FĪ	spherify
TER′I.FĪ	esterify, terrify
VER′I.FĪ	verify

(See **ÂR′I.FĪ**)

ER′I.ING

BER′I.ING	berrying, burying, blackberrying, blueberrying, huckleberrying, cranberrying, strawberrying (etc.)
FER′I.ING	ferrying
HWER′I.ING	wherrying
SER′I.ING	serrying

ER′I.KA

ER′I.KA	erica
MER′I.KA	America

ER′I.KAL

FER′I.KAL	atmospherical
KLER′I.KAL	anticlerical, clerical, pro-clerical
MER′I.KAL	Homerical, chimerical, mesmerical, numerical
NER′I.KAL	generical
SER′I.KAL	rhinocerical
SFER′I.KAL	heliospherical, hemispherical, spherical, sphericle
TER′I.KAL	exoterical, esoterical, phylacterical, hysterical, climacterical

ER′I.KAN

JER′I.KAN	jerrican
MER′I.KAN	American

ĒR′I.LĒ

(See **ÎR′I.LĒ**)

ER′I.LĒ

MER′I.LĒ	merrily
VER′I.LĒ	verily

(See **ÂR′I.LĒ**)

ER′I.MAN

FER′I.MAN	ferryman
HWER′I.MAN	wherryman
MER′I.MAN	merryman

ER′I.MENT

MER′I.MENT	merriment
PER′I.MENT	experiment

ĒR′I.NES

(See **ÎRĒ**, add *-ness* where appropriate.)

ĒR′ING.LĒ

(See **ÎR′ING.LĒ**)

ĒR′I.Ō

(See **ÎR′I.Ō**)

ER′ISH.ING

CHER′ISH.ING	cherishing
PER′ISH.ING	perishing, unperishing

ER′I.TA.BL

HER′I.TA.BL	heritable, inheritable
VER′I.TA.BL	veritable

ER′I.TĒ

FER′I.TĒ	ferity
JER′I.TĒ	legerity
LER′I.TĒ	celerity
MER′I.TĒ	temerity
PER′I.TĒ	asperity, prosperity
SER′I.TĒ	insincerity, procerity, sincerity
TER′I.TĒ	alterity, ambidexterity,

VER'I.TĒ   dexterity, indexterity, austerity, posterity severity, verity

(See ÂR'I.TĒ)

ER'IT.ED

(See ER'ET.ED)

ER'I.TIV

PER'I.TIV   aperitive, imperative
TER'I.TIV   preteritive

ER'I.TŌ.RĒ

FER'I.TŌR.Ē   feretory
TER'I.TŌR.Ē   territory

ĒR'I.UM

(See ÎR'I.UM)

ĒR'I.US

(See ÎR'I.US)

ĒR'LES.NES

(See ÎR'LES.NES)

ER'O.GĀT

DER'O.GĀT   derogate
RER'O.GĀT   supererogate
TER'O.GĀT   interrogate

ER'O.POD

TER'O.POD   pteropod
THER'O.POD   theropod

ER'UP.ON

HWER'UP.ON   whereupon
THER'UP.ON   thereupon

Ē'SA.BL

(See ĒS, add -able where appropriate.)

ES'A.BL

(See ES'I.BL)

ES'CHER.AL

JES'CHER.AL   gestural
VES'CHER.AL   vestural

ES'CHOO.US

ES'CHOO.US   estuous
PES'CHOO.US   tempestuous
SES'CHOO.US   incestuous

Ē'SEN.SĒ

DĒ'SEN.SĒ   decency, indecency
RĒ'SEN.SĒ   recency

ES'EN.SĒ

ES'EN.SĒ   acquiescency, quiescency
BES'EN.SĒ   erubescency, pubescency
DES'EN.SĒ   incandescency, recrudescency
JES'EN.SĒ   turgescency
KRES'EN.SĒ   excrescency
KWES'EN.SĒ   liquescency
LES'EN.SĒ   adolescency, alkalescency, incalescency, convalescency
RES'EN.SĒ   efflorescency
SES'EN.SĒ   acescency
TES'EN.SĒ   delitescency
VES'EN.SĒ   defervescency, effervescency

Ē'SENT.LĒ

DĒ'SENT.LĒ   decently, indecently
RĒ'SENT.LĒ   recently

ES'ER.Ē

FES'ER.Ē   confessary, professory
PES'ER.Ē   pessary
SES'ER.Ē   accessory, intercessory, concessory, successary
ZES'ER.Ē   possessory

ES'FUL.Ē

BLES'FUL.Ē   blessfully

STRES'FUL.Ē   distressfully, stressfully
SES'FUL.Ē   successfully, unsuccessfully

ESH'EN.ER

FRESH'EN.ER   freshener
SESH'EN.ER   accessioner

Ē'SHI.A

LĒ'SHI.A   silesia, Silesia, kerdomeletia
NĒ'SHI.A   magnesia, Polynesia
PĒ'SHI.A   alopecia
VĒ'SHI.A   Helvetia

(See ĒSHA, ĒZHA)

Ē'SHI.AN

GRĒ'SHI.AN   Grecian
LĒ'SHI.AN   Silesian
NĒ'SHI.AN   internecian, Pelopennesian, Venetian
TĒ'SHI.AN   Epictetian
VĒ'SHI.AN   Helvetian

(See ĒSHUN)

ESH'I.ENS

(See ESHENS)

ESH'I.ENT

NESH'I.ENT   nescient
PRESH'I.ENT   prescient

(See ESHENT)

ESH'I.NES

FLESH'I.NES   fleshiness
MESH'I.NES   meshiness

Ē'SHI.UM

DRĒ'SHI.UM   androecium
NĒ'SHI.UM   gynoecium, technetium
TĒ'SHI.UM   lutecium, lutetium

ESH'UN.AL

FESH'UN.AL	confessional, professional, semiprofessional, unprofessional
GRESH'UN.AL	digressional, congressional, progressional, transgressional
KRESH'UN.AL	discretional
PRESH'UN.AL	expressional, impressional, compressional
SESH'UN.AL	accessional, intercessional, processional, recessional, retrocessional, sessional, successional
ZESH'UN.AL	possessional

ESH'UN.IST

FESH'UN.IST	confessionist
GRESH'UN.IST	progressionist, retrogressionist
PRESH'UN.IST	expressionist, impressionist, Impressionist
SESH'UN.IST	concessionist, processionist, retrocessionist, secessionist
ZESH'UN.IST	possessionist

Ē'SHUS.NES

SĒ'SHUS.NES	facetiousness
SPĒ'SHUS.NES	speciousness

ES'I.BL

DES'I.BL	decibel
DRES'I.BL	dressable, redressible, undressable, unredressible
GES'I.BL	guessable, unguessable
GRES'I.BL	gressible, transgressible
KRES'I.BL	concrescible
PRES'I.BL	*D* depressible, *E* expressible, *I* impressible, incompressible, inexpressible, insuppressible, irrepressible, *K* compressible, *PR* pressable, *R* repressable, *S* suppressible
SES'I.BL	accessible, assessable, immarcescible, inaccessible, incessable, concessible, marcescible, unassessable
TES'I.BL	fermentescible
TRES'I.BL	imputrescible, putrescible, vitrescible
VES'I.BL	effervescible, ineffervescible
ZES'I.BL	possessable, unpossessable

(See **ES,** add *-able* or *-ible* where appropriate.)

ES'I.BLĒ

(See **ES'I.BL,** replace *-e* with *-y;* see **ES,** add *-ably* or *-ibly* where appropriate.)

Ē'SI.ER

FLĒ'SI.ER	fleecier
GRĒ'SI.ER	greasier
KRĒ'SI.ER	creasier

ES'I.KA

JES'I.KA	Jessica
VES'I.KA	vesica

ES'I.KANT

DES'I.KANT	desiccant
VES'I.KANT	vesicant

ES'I.KĀT

DES'I.KĀT	desiccate
VES'I.KĀT	vesicate

ES'I.MAL

DES'I.MAL	decimal, duodecimal, hexadecimal
JES'I.MAL	quadragesimal, quinquagesimal, nonagesimal, septuagesimal, sexagesimal, trigesimal, vigesimal
LES'I.MAL	millesimal
TES'I.MAL	infinitesimal, centesimal

ES'I.MEN

DES'I.MEN	quartodeciman
SPES'I.MEN	specimen

Ē'SING.LĒ

KRĒ'SING.LĒ	decreasingly, increasingly
SĒ'SING.LĒ	unceasingly

ES'ING.LĒ

PRES'ING.LĒ	depressingly, pressingly
RES'ING.LĒ	caressingly
TRES'ING.LĒ	distressingly
ZES'ING.LĒ	prepossessingly

ES'I.TĒ

BES'I.TĒ	obesity
SES'I.TĒ	necessity, cecity

ES'IV.LĒ

GRES'IV.LĒ	aggressively, digressively, progressively, regressively, transgressively
PRES'IV.LĒ	depressively, expressively, impressively, oppressively, repressively
SES'IV.LĒ	excessively, successively
ZES'IV.LĒ	possessively

ES'IV.NES

(See **ESIV,** add *-ness* where appropriate.)

ES'TA.BL

(See **ES'TI.BL**)

ES'TA.MENT

TES'TA.MENT	testament
VES'TA.MENT	vestiment

ES'TER.ING

FES'TER.ING	festering
KWES'TER.ING	sequestering
PES'TER.ING	pestering
WES'TER.ING	westering

EST'FUL.Ē

KWEST'FUL.Ē	questfully
REST'FUL.Ē	restfully
ZEST'FUL.Ē	zestfully

ES'TI.AL

(See ESCHAL)

ES'TI.BL

JES'TI.BL	digestible, indigestible, congestible, suggestible
MES'TI.BL	comestible
TES'TI.BL	detestable, incontestable, intestable, contestable, testable, untestable
VES'TI.BL	divestible

ES'TI.KL

JES'TI.KL	majestical
KRES'TI.KL	catachrestical
PES'TI.KL	anapestical
TES'TI.KL	testicle

ES'TI.MĀT

ES'TI.MĀT	estimate, overestimate, underestimate
GES'TI.MĀT	guesstimate

ES'TI.NAL

DES'TI.NAL	destinal, predestinal
TES'TI.NAL	intestinal

ES'TI.NĀT

DES'TI.NĀT	predestinate
FES'TI.NĀT	festinate

ĒS'TI.NES

RĒS'TI.NES	reastiness
YĒS'TI.NES	yeastiness

ES'TI.NES

RES'TI.NES	restiness
TES'TI.NES	testiness

ES'TING.LĒ

JES'TING.LĒ	jestingly
RES'TING.LĒ	interestingly, uninterestingly
TES'TING.LĒ	protestingly, testingly

ES'TIV.LĒ

FES'TIV.LĒ	festively
JES'TIV.LĒ	suggestively
RES'TIV.LĒ	restively

ES'TIV.NES

FES'TIV.NES	festiveness
JES'TIV.NES	suggestiveness
RES'TIV.NES	restiveness

ĒST'LI.NES

BĒST'LI.NES	beastliness
PRĒST'LI.NES	priestliness

EST'Ō.VERZ

EST'Ō.VERZ	estovers
REST'Ō.VERZ	rest-overs

ES'TRI.AL

DES'TRI.AL	pedestrial
MES'TRI.AL	bimestrial, decimestrial, trimestrial
RES'TRI.AL	extraterrestrial, superterrestrial, terrestrial

ES'TRI.AN

DES'TRI.AN	pedestrian
KWES'TRI.AN	equestrian
LES'TRI.AN	palestrian
PES'TRI.AN	campestrian, rupestrian
VES'TRI.AN	sylvestrian

ES'TRI.US

DES'TRI.US	pedestrious
RES'TRI.US	terrestrious

ES'TŪ.RAL

(See ES'CHER.AL)

ES'TŪ.US

(See ES'CHŌŌ.US)

ĒT'A.BL

ĒT'A.BL	eatable, uneatable
BĒT'A.BL	beatable, unbeatable
CHĒT'A.BL	cheatable, escheatable, uncheatable
FĒT'A.BL	defeatable, undefeatable
HĒT'A.BL	heatable, preheatable, reheatable, unheatable
LĒT'A.BL	deletable, undeletable
PĒT'A.BL	repeatable, unrepeatable
SĒT'A.BL	seatable, unseatable
TRĒT'A.BL	entreatable, treatable, unentreatable, untreatable

ET'A.BL

GET'A.BL	begettable, forgettable, gettable, unforgettable, ungettable
HWET'A.BL	whettable
LET'A.BL	lettable
NET'A.BL	bayonettable, nettable
PET'A.BL	pettable
SET'A.BL	settable, unsettable, unupsettable, upsettable

ET'A.BLĒ

GET'A.BLĒ	forgettably, unforgettably
GRET'A.BLĒ	regrettably

ET'A.LĪN

(also -LIN)

MET'A.LĪN	metalline
PET'A.LĪN	petaline

ET'AL.IZM

MET'AL.IZM	bimetallism, monometallism
PET'AL.IZM	petalism

ET'A.LOID

MET'A.LOID	metalloid
PET'A.LOID	petaloid

ET'A.NĒ

BET'A.NĒ	betony
TET'A.NĒ	tetany

ĒT'ED.LE

FĒT'ED.LĒ	defeatedly, undefeatedly
HĒT'ED.LĒ	heatedly
PĒT'ED.LĒ	repeatedly

ET'ER.Ē

KRET'ER.Ē	secretory
PLET'ER.Ē	depletory, completory, repletory

Ē'TER.ING

MĒ'TER.ING	metering
PĒ'TER.ING	petering

ET'ER.ING

BET'ER.ING	bettering
FET'ER.ING	fettering
LET'ER.ING	lettering

ET'ER.IT

PRET'ER.IT	preterit, preterite
VET'ER.IT	inveterate

ET'FUL.Ē

FRET'FUL.Ē	fretfully
GET'FUL.Ē	forgetfully
GRET'FUL.Ē	regretfully

ET'FUL.NES

FRET'FUL.NES	fretfulness
GET'FUL.NES	forgetfulness
GRET'FUL.NES	regretfulness

ETH'A.NOL

ETH'A.NOL	ethanol
METH'A.NOL	methanol

ETH'ER.Ē

(TH as in *then*)

FETH'ER.Ē	feathery
HETH'ER.Ē	heathery
LETH'ER.Ē	leathery
TETH'ER.Ē	tethery
WETH'ER.Ē	weathery

ETH'ER.ING

(TH as in *then*)

FETH'ER.ING	feathering
LETH'ER.ING	leathering
TETH'ER.ING	tethering, untethering
WETH'ER.ING	weathering

ETH'I.KAL

ETH'I.KAL	ethical, non-ethical, unethical
LETH'I.KAL	alethical

ETH'I.LĀT

ETH'I.LĀT	ethylate
METH'I.LĀT	methylate

ETH'LES.LĒ

(TH as in *thin*)

BRETH'LES.LĒ	breathlessly
DETH'LES.LĒ	deathlessly

ETH'LES.NES

(TH as in *thin*)

BRETH'LES.NES	breathlessness
DETH'LES.NES	deathlessness

ET'I.KAL

ET'I.KAL	dianoetical, noetical, poetical, unpoetical
BET'I.KAL	alphabetical, analphabetical, diabetical
DET'I.KAL	syndetical
FET'I.KAL	prophetical
JET'I.KAL	apologetical, exegetical, energetical
KET'I.KAL	catachetical
KRET'I.KAL	syncretical
LET'I.KAL	athletical, homiletical
MET'I.KAL	arithmetical, emetical, hermetical, cosmetical, mismetical
NET'I.KAL	antimagnetical, isomagnetical, genetical, magnetical, planetical, thermomagnetical, threnetical
RET'I.KAL	anchoretical, diaphoretical, diuretical, emporetical, heretical, theoretical
SET'I.KAL	ascetical
TET'I.KAL	dietetical, peripatetical
THET'I.KAL	*A* antipathetical, antithetical, apathetical, *E* aesthetical, epithetical, *F* photosynthetical, *H* hyperthetical, hypothetical, *M* metathetical, *N* nomothetical, *P* parenthetical, pathetical, polysynthetical, *S* synthetical, *TH* thetical

ET'I.KŪL

ET'I.KŪL	poeticule
RET'I.KŪL	reticule

ĒT′I.NES

MĒT′I.NES	meatiness
PĒT′I.NES	peatiness
SLĒT′I.NES	sleetiness

ET′I.NES

JET′I.NES	jettiness
PET′I.NES	pettiness
SWET′I.NES	sweatiness

ET′IN.Ū

DET′IN.Ū	detinue
RET′IN.Ū	retinue

ET′ISH.LĒ

KET′ISH.LĒ	coquettishly
PET′ISH.LĒ	pettishly

ET′ISH.NES

KET′ISH.NES	coquettishness
PET′ISH.NES	pettishness

ET′I.SIZM

LET′I.SIZM	athleticism
NET′I.SIZM	phoneticism
SET′I.SIZM	asceticism
TET′I.SIZM	peripateticism
THET′I.SIZM	aestheticism

ET′I.TIV

PET′I.TIV	competitive, noncompetitive, repetitive, uncompetitive
VET′I.TIV	vetitive

ET′L.SUM

MET′L.SUM	mettlesome
NET′L.SUM	nettlesome

ET′RI.FĪ

MET′RI.FĪ	metrify
PET′RI.FĪ	petrify

ET′RI.KAL

MET′RI.KAL	*A* alkalimetrical, asymmetrical, *B* barometrical, bisymmetrical, *D* diametrical, dynametrical, *GR* graphometrical, *H* hexametrical, heptometrical, horometrical, *I* isometrical, isoperimetrical, *J* geometrical, *K* kilometrical, *KL* clinometrical, *KR* craniometrical, chronometrical, *M* metrical, *P* pedometrical, perimetrical, *PL* planimetrical, pluviometrical, *S* symmetrical, *ST* stichometrical, *TR* trigonometrical, *U* unsymmetrical
STET′RI.KAL	obstetrical

ĒV′A.BL

CHĒV′A.BL	achievable, unachievable
GRĒV′A.BL	grievable
HĒV′A.BL	heavable, unheavable
KLĒV′A.BL	cleavable, uncleavable
LĒV′A.BL	believable, relievable, unbelievable, unrelievable
SĒV′A.BL	deceivable, imperceivable, inconceivable, conceivable, perceivable, receivable, undeceivable

ĒV′A.BLĒ

(See **ĒV′A.BL**, add -y where appropriate.)

EV′A.LIN

EV′A.LIN	Evalyn
SHEV′A.LIN	chevaline

EV′EL.ER

BEV′EL.ER	beveler
DEV′EL.ER	bedeviler, deviler
LEV′EL.ER	leveler
REV′EL.ER	reveler
SHEV′EL.ER	disheveler, sheveler

EV′EL.ING

(See **EVEL**, add -*ing* where appropriate.)

EV′EL.IZM

DEV′EL.IZM	devilism
LEV′EL.IZM	levelism

EV′EL.MENT

DEV′EL.MENT	bedevilment, devilment
SHEV′EL.MENT	dishevelment, shevelment
REV′EL.MENT	revelment

EV′EL.RĒ

DEV′EL.RĒ	devilry
REV′EL.RĒ	revelry

EV′ER.ĀT

LEV′ER.ĀT	levirate
SEV′ER.ĀT	asseverate

EV′ER.Ē

EV′ER.Ē	every
REV′ER.Ē	reverie

EV′ER.ENS

REV′ER.ENS	irreverence, reverence
SEV′ER.ENS	disseverance, severance

EV′ER.ER

DEV′ER.ER	endeavorer
KLEV′ER.ER	cleverer
LEV′ER.ER	leverer
SEV′ER.ER	severer

EV′ER.EST

EV′ER.EST	Everest
KLEV′ER.EST	cleverest

(See **EVER,** add *-est* where appropriate for archaic verbs.)

EV′ER.IJ

BEV′ER.IJ	beverage
LEV′ER.IJ	leverage

EV′ER.ING

DEV′ER.ING	endeavoring
LEV′ER.ING	levering
SEV′ER.ING	severing

EV′ER.MŌR

EV′ER.MŌR	evermore
NEV′ER.MŌR	nevermore

Ē′VI.ĀT

BRĒ′VI.ĀT	abbreviate
DĒ′VI.ĀT	deviate
LĒ′VI.ĀT	alleviate

Ē′VISH.LĒ

PĒ′VISH.LĒ	peevishly
THĒ′VISH.LĒ	thievishly

Ē′VISH.NES

PĒ′VISH.NES	peevishness
THĒ′VISH.NES	thievishness

EV′I.TĒ

BREV′I.TĒ	brevity
JEV′I.TĒ	longevity
LEV′I.TĒ	levity

Ē′VI.US

DĒ′VI.US	devious
PRĒ′VI.US	previous

EV′O.LENS

LEV′O.LENS	malevolence
NEV′O.LENS	benevolence
PREV′O.LENS	prevalence

EV′O.LENT

LEV′O.LENT	malevolent
NEV′O.LENT	benevolent
PREV′O.LENT	prevalent

EV′O.LUS

LEV′O.LUS	malevolous
NEV′O.LUS	benevolous

EV′O.LŪT

EV′O.LŪT	evolute
DEV′O.LŪT	devolute
REV′O.LŪT	revolute

Ē′ZA.BL

FĒ′ZA.BL	defeasible, feasible, indefeasible, infeasible
FRĒ′ZA.BL	freezable
HĒ′ZA.BL	cohesible
PĒ′ZA.BL	appeasible, inappeasable, unappeasable
SĒ′ZA.BL	seizable
SKWĒ′ZA.BL	squeezable

EZ′AN.TRĒ

FEZ′AN.TRĒ	pheasantry
PEZ′AN.TRĒ	peasantry
PLEZ′AN.TRĒ	pleasantry

EZH′ER.ER

MEZH′ER.ER	measurer
PLEZH′ER.ER	pleasurer
TREZH′ER.ER	treasurer

EZH′ER.ING

MEZH′ER.ING	measuring
PLEZH′ER.ING	pleasuring
TREZH′ER.ING	treasuring

EZH′ER.LES

MEZH′ER.LES	measureless
PLEZH′ER.LES	pleasureless
TREZH′ER.LES	treasureless

Ē′ZHI.A

(See **Ē′ZI.A**)

Ē′ZHI.AN

(See **ĒZHUN**)

Ē′ZI.A

BĒ′ZI.A	framboesia, Zambesia
DĒ′ZI.A	Rhodesia
FRĒ′ZI.A	freesia, oxyosphresia
JĒ′ZI.A	analgesia, hyperthermalgesia
KLĒ′ZI.A	ecclesia
LĒ′ZI.A	silesia, Silesia
MĒ′ZI.A	iatromisia
NĒ′ZI.A	amnesia, hyperkinesia, hypermnesia, Indonesia, magnesia, neomnesia, paleomnesia, paramnesia, pseudomnesia, Tunisia
PĒ′ZI.A	trapezia
RĒ′ZI.A	parrhesia
THĒ′ZI.A	anesthesia, esthesia, hyperesthesia, hypesthesia, kinesthesia, cryptesthesia, oxyesthesia, radiesthesia, synesthesia, telesthesia, thermanesthesia, thermesthesia, zonesthesia

(See **ĒZHA**)

Ē′ZI.AN

FĒ′ZI.AN	Ephesian
KLĒ′ZI.AN	ecclesian
PĒ′ZI.AN	trapezian
TĒ′ZI.AN	Artesian, etesian, Cartesian

(See **ĒZHUN**)

Ē′ZI.BL

(See Ē′ZA.BL)

EZ′I.DENT

PREZ′I.DENT	president, vice-president
REZ′I.DENT	resident, non-resident

Ē′ZI.ER

Ē′ZI.ER	easier, uneasier
BRĒ′ZI.ER	breezier
CHĒ′ZI.ER	cheesier
GRĒ′ZI.ER	greasier
HWĒ′ZI.ER	wheezier
KWĒ′ZI.ER	queasier
SLĒ′ZI.ER	sleazier
SNĒ′ZI.ER	sneezier

Ē′ZI.LĒ

Ē′ZI.LĒ	easily, uneasily
BRĒ′ZI.LĒ	breezily
CHĒ′ZI.LĒ	cheesily
GRĒ′ZI.LĒ	greasily
HWĒ′ZI.LĒ	wheezily
KWĒ′ZI.LĒ	queasily
SLĒ′ZI.LĒ	sleazily
SNĒ′ZI.LĒ	sneezily

Ē′ZI.NES

(See ĒZĒ, add -ness where appropriate.)

ĒZ′ING.LĒ

FRĒZ′ING.LĒ	freezingly
HWĒZ′ING.LĒ	wheezingly
PĒZ′ING.LĒ	appeasingly
PLĒZ′ING.LĒ	displeasingly, pleasingly
SNĒZ′ING.LĒ	sneezingly
TĒZ′ING.LĒ	teasingly

Ē′ZUN.A.BL

RĒ′ZUN.A.BL	reasonable, unreasonable
SĒ′ZUN.A.BL	seasonable, unseasonable
TRĒ′ZUN.A.BL	treasonable, untreasonable

Ē′ZUN.ER

RĒ′ZUN.ER	reasoner
SĒ′ZUN.ER	seasoner

Ē′ZUN.ING

RĒ′ZUN.ING	reasoning, unreasoning
SĒ′ZUN.ING	seasoning

Ī′A.BL

Ī′A.BL	eyeable
FĪ′A.BL	*A* acidifiable, *D* diversifiable, *E* electrifiable, exemplifiable, *F* falsifiable, fortifiable, *I* identifiable, *J* justifiable, *KL* classifiable, *KW* qualifiable, *L* liquefiable, *M* magnifiable, modifiable, *P* pacifiable, petrifiable, *R* rarefiable, rectifiable, *S* sanctifiable, saponifiable, satisfiable, solidifiable, *U* unidentifiable, unjustifiable, *V* verifiable, vitrifiable
FRĪ′A.BL	friable
LĪ′A.BL	liable, reliable, unreliable
NĪ′A.BL	deniable, undeniable
PLĪ′A.BL	appliable, impliable, compliable, multipliable, pliable
TRĪ′A.BL	triable
VĪ′A.BL	viable

Ī′A.BLĒ

FĪ′A.BLĒ	justifiably, unjustifiably
LĪ′A.BLĒ	liably, reliably, unreliably
NĪ′A.BLĒ	deniably, undeniably
PLĪ′A.BLĒ	appliably, compliably, pliably

Ī′A.DĒZ

DRĪ′A.DĒZ	dryades, hamadryades
HĪ′A.DĒZ	Hyades
NĪ′A.DĒZ	naiades
PLĪ′A.DĒZ	Pleiades

Ī′A.GRAM

DĪ′A.GRAM	diagram
SKĪ′A.GRAM	skiagram
VĪ′A.GRAM	viagram

Ī′A.KAL

DĪ′A.KAL	dandiacal, encyclopediacal, cardiacal, prosodiacal, zodiacal
DRĪ′A.KAL	hypochondriacal
JĪ′A.KAL	elegiacal
LĪ′A.KAL	heliacal
NĪ′A.KAL	bibliomaniacal, demoniacal, dipsomaniacal, kleptomaniacal, maniacal, pyromaniacal, simoniacal
RĪ′A.KAL	theriacal
ZĪ′A.KAL	paradisiacal

Ī′A.LIN

HĪ′A.LIN	hyaline
TĪ′A.LIN	ptyalin
VĪ′A.LIN	violin

Ī′A.LĪT

HĪ′A.LĪT	hyalite
KRĪ′A.LĪT	cryolite
RĪ′A.LĪT	rhyolite

Ī′A.LIZM

MĪ′A.LIZM	myalism
TĪ′A.LIZM	ptyalism

Ī′A.LOID

HĪ′A.LOID	hyaloid
STĪ′A.LOID	styaloid

Ī'AN.SĒ

KLĪ'AN.SĒ	cliency
PLĪ'AN.SĒ	compliancy, pliancy
RĪ'AN.SĒ	riancy

Ī'ANT.LĒ

FĪ'ANT.LĒ	defiantly
LĪ'ANT.LĒ	reliantly
PLĪ'ANT.LĒ	compliantly, pliantly, uncompliantly

Ī'A.RĒ

(See Ī'E.RĒ)

Ī'A.RIST

| DĪ'A.RIST | diarist |
| PĪ'A.RIST | Piarist |

Ī'ÄR.KĒ

DĪ'ÄR.KĒ	diarchy
JĪ'ÄR.KĒ	hagiarchy
TRĪ'ÄR.KĒ	triarchy

Ī'A.SIS

BĪ'A.SIS	amoebiasis
DĪ'A.SIS	archdiocese, diocese
DRĪ'A.SIS	hypochondriasis, mydriasis
FĪ'A.SIS	gomphiasis
KĪ'A.SIS	psychiasis, trichiasis
MĪ'A.SIS	myasis, schistosomiasis, trypanosomiasis
NĪ'A.SIS	leishmaniasis, pogoniasis, teniasis
RĪ'A.SIS	acariasis, ascariasis, filariasis, satyriasis, psoriasis
THĪ'A.SIS	lithiasis
TĪ'A.SIS	elephantiasis, odontiasis
ZĪ'A.SIS	bilharziasis

Ī'A.SIZM

| DRĪ'A.SIZM | hypochondriacism |
| NĪ'A.SIZM | demoniacism |

Ī'A.SKŌP

BĪ'A.SKŌP	bioscope
DĪ'A.SKŌP	diascope, apidiascope
SKĪ'A.SKŌP	skiascope

Ī'A.TER

| KĪ'A.TER | archiater, psychiater |
| PĪ'A.TER | hippiater |

Ī'A.TRĒ

DĪ'A.TRĒ	podiatry
KĪ'A.TRĒ	antipsychiatry, neuropsychiatry, psychiatry
NĪ'A.TRĒ	phoniatry
PĪ'A.TRĒ	hippiatry

Ī'A.TRIST

DĪ'A.TRIST	podiatrist
KĪ'A.TRIST	psychiatrist
PĪ'A.TRIST	hippiatrist

ĪB'A.BL

| BRĪB'A.BL | bribable, unbribable |
| SKRĪB'A.BL | A ascribable, D describable, I indescribable, inscribable, P postscribable, PR prescribable, S circumscribable, subscribable, SK scribable, U undescribable, uninscribable, unscribable |

IB'ET.ED

(See IBET, add -ed where appropriate.)

IB'ET.ING

(See IBET, add -ing where appropriate.)

IB'ET.IV

(See IBET, add -ive where appropriate.)

IB'I.A

| FIB'I.A | amphibia |
| TIB'I.A | tibia |

(See IBYA)

IB'I.AL

FIB'I.AL	amphibial
STIB'I.AL	stibial
TIB'I.AL	tibial

IB'I.AN

FIB'I.AN	amphibian
LIB'I.AN	Lybian
THIB'I.AN	bathybian

IB'ING.LĒ

BIB'ING.LĒ	bibbingly
FIB'ING.LĒ	fibbingly
JIB'ING.LĒ	jibbingly
KRIB'ING.LĒ	cribbingly
LIB'ING.LĒ	ad libbingly
RIB'ING.LĒ	ribbingly
SKWIB'ING.LĒ	squibbingly

IB'IT.ER

| HIB'IT.ER | inhibiter, inhibitor, cohibitor, noninhibitor, prohibiter, prohibitor |
| ZIB'IT.ER | exhibitor, nonexhibitor |

IB'I.US

FIB'I.US	amphibious, triphibious
LIB'I.US	Polybius
STIB'I.US	stibious
THIB'I.US	bathybius

IB'Ū.LAR

DIB'Ū.LAR	infundibular, mandibular
FIB'Ū.LAR	fibular
STIB'Ū.LAR	vestibular

ICH'E.RĀT

BICH'E.RĀT	barbiturate
LICH'E.RĀT	liturate
TRICH'E.RĀT	triturate

ICH'E.RĒ

BICH'E.RĒ	bitchery
FICH'E.RĒ	fitchery
MICH'E.RĒ	michery
PICH'ER.Ē	pituri
STICH'E.RĒ	stitchery
WICH'E.RĒ	bewitchery, witchery

ICH'E.TĒ

TWICH'E.TĒ	twitchety
WICH'E.TĒ	witchetty

ICH'ING.LĒ

ICH'ING.LĒ	itchingly
PICH'ING.LĒ	pitchingly
RICH'ING.LĒ	enrichingly
SWICH'ING.LĒ	switchingly
TWICH'ING.LĒ	twitchingly
WICH'ING.LĒ	bewitchingly, witchingly

ICH'I.NES

(See **ICHĒ,** add -ness)

ICH'OO.AL

BICH'OO.AL	habitual, obitual, unhabitual
RICH'OO.AL	ritual
SICH'OO.AL	situal

ICH'OO.ĀT

BICH'OO.ĀT	habituate
SICH'OO.ĀT	situate

ICH'OO.LER

PICH'OO.LER	capitular
MICH'OO.LER	amitular
TICH'OO.LER	titular

ĪD'A.BL

GĪD'A.BL	guidable, unguidable
HĪD'A.BL	hidable
LĪD'A.BL	elidable
RĪD'A.BL	ridable, unridable
SĪD'A.BL	decidable, undecidable
STRĪD'A.BL	bestridable
VĪD'A.BL	dividable, providable, undividable, unprovidable

ID'A.BL

BID'A.BL	biddable, forbiddable, rebiddable, unbiddable, unforbiddable
KID'A.BL	kiddable, unkiddable

Ī'DED.LĒ

(See **ĪD,** add -edly where appropriate.)

ID'EN.NES

BID'EN.NES	forbiddenness
HID'EN.NES	hiddenness

ID'I.AL

SID'I.AL	presidial
TID'I.AL	noctidial

ID'I.AN

FID'I.AN	nullifidian, ophidian, solifidian, ultrafidian
GID'I.AN	Gideon
KID'I.AN	rachidian
KLID'I.AN	Euclidean
LID'I.AN	Lydian
MID'I.AN	Numidian
NID'I.AN	anidian
PID'I.AN	taxaspidean
RID'I.AN	antemeridian, enchiridion, meridian, post-meridian, viridian
SID'I.AN	ascidian, obsidian, proboscidean
TID'I.AN	quotidian
VID'I.AN	Dravidian, Ovidian

ID'I.ĀT

MID'I.ĀT	dimidiate
SID'I.ĀT	insidiate

ID'I.FĪ

ID'I.FĪ	fluidify
JID'I.FĪ	rigidify
LID'I.FĪ	solidify
MID'I.FĪ	humidify, dehumidify
NID'I.FĪ	nidify
PID'I.FĪ	lapidify
SID'I.FĪ	acidify, rancidify

ID'I.KAL

ID'I.KAL	druidical
MID'I.KAL	pyramidical
RID'I.KAL	juridical, veridical
SID'I.KAL	spurcidical
ZID'I.KAL	causidical

ĪD'ING.LĒ

BĪD'ING.LĒ	abidingly
CHĪD'ING.LĒ	chidingly, unchidingly
FĪD'ING.LĒ	confidingly
GĪD'ING.LĒ	guidingly, misguidingly
GLĪD'ING.LĒ	glidingly
HĪD'ING.LĒ	hidingly, unhidingly
SĪD'ING.LĒ	sidingly
SLĪD'ING.LĒ	slidingly
STRĪD'ING.LĒ	stridingly

ID'I.NUS

BID'I.NUS	libidinous
GWID'I.NUS	pinguidinous

ID'I.OM

(See **ID'I.UM**)

ID'I.TĒ

ID'I.TĒ	fluidity, superfluidity
BID'I.TĒ	morbidity, rabidity, turbidity
BRID'I.TĒ	hybridity
GWID'I.TĒ	pinguidity
JID'I.TĒ	algidity, frigidity, rigidity, turgidity

KRID'I.TĒ	acridity	**HID'I.US**	hideous	**NĪ'E.TĒ**	omniety
KWID'I.TĒ	quiddity, liquidity	**MID'I.US**	chlamydeous	**PĪ'E.TĒ**	impiety, piety
LID'I.TĒ	insolidity,	**PID'I.US**	lapideous	**PRĪ'E.TĒ**	impropriety,
	invalidity, gelidity,	**SID'I.US**	insidious,		propriety
	calidity, pallidity,		parricidious,	**RĪ'E.TĒ**	contrariety,
	solidity, squalidity,		stillicidious		luxuriety, notoriety,
	stolidity, validity	**TID'I.US**	fastidious		variety
MID'I.TĒ	humidity, timidity,	**VID'I.US**	invidious	**SĪ'E.TĒ**	society
	tumidity			**TĪ'E.TĒ**	satiety
PID'I.TĒ	*H* hispidity, *I*			**ZĪ'E.TĒ**	anxiety

ID'Ū.AL

(See **IJ'OO.AL**)

PID'I.TĒ	*H* hispidity, *I* insipidity, intrepidity, *K* cupidity, *L* limpidity, *R* rapidity, *S* sapidity, *ST* stupidity, *T* tepidity, torpidity, *TR* trepidity, *V* vapidity

ID'Ū.ĀT

(See **IJ'OO.ĀT**)

ID'Ū.LĀT

(See **IJ'OO.LĀT**)

RID'I.TĒ	aridity, floridity, torridity, viridity
SID'I.TĒ	acidity, flaccidity, hyperacidity, hypoacidity, lucidity, marcidity, pellucidity, placidity, rancidity, translucidity, viscidity
TID'I.TĒ	putidity
TRID'I.TĒ	putridity
VID'I.TĒ	avidity, gravidity, lividity, pavidity, vividity

ID'Ū.LUS

(See **IJ'OO.LUS**)

ID'U.US

(See **IJ'OO.US**)

Ī'EN.SĒ

(See **Ī'AN.SĒ**)   Ī'E.RĒ

Ī'ET.ED

DĪ'ET.ED	dieted
KWĪ'ET.ED	disquieted, quieted, unquieted
RĪ'ET.ED	rioted

Ī'ET.ER

DĪ'ET.ER	dieter
KWĪ'ET.ER	disquieter, quieter
PRĪ'ET.ER	proprietor
RĪ'ET.ER	rioter

Ī'ET.ING

DĪ'ET.ING	dieting
KWĪ'ET.ING	disquieting, quieting
RĪ'ET.ING	rioting

ID'I.UM

ID'I.UM	idiom, oïdium, Oïdium
BID'I.UM	rubidium
FRID'I.UM	nephridium
KID'I.UM	glochidium
NID'I.UM	gonidium, conidium, ctenidium
RID'I.UM	ante meridiem, antheridium, hesperidium, iridium, osmiridium, peridium, post meridiem
SID'I.UM	basidium, miracidium, presidium, psidium, cecidium
TRID'I.UM	clostridium

Ī'EN.SĒ — (continued)

BRĪ'E.RĒ	briary, briery
DĪ'E.RĒ	diary
FĪ'E.RĒ	fiery
FRĪ'E.RĒ	friary
LĪ'E.RĒ	lyery
PRĪ'E.RĒ	priory

(See **ĪRĒ**)

Ī'E.TAL

DĪ'E.TAL	dietal
HĪ'E.TAL	hyetal, isohyetal
RĪ'E.TAL	parietal, varietal
SĪ'E.TAL	societal

Ī'E.TĒ

BĪ'E.TĒ	dubiety, nullibiety, ubiety
BRĪ'E.TĒ	ebriety, inebriety, insobriety, sobriety
DĪ'E.TĒ	mediety
LĪ'E.TĒ	filiety
MĪ'E.TĒ	nimiety

Ī'E.TIST

PĪ'E.TIST	pietist
PRĪ'E.TIST	proprietist
RĪ'E.TIST	varietist
ZĪ'E.TIST	anxietist

Ī'E.TIZM

KWĪ'E.TIZM	quietism
PĪ'E.TIZM	pietism
RĪ'E.TIZM	varietism

Ī'FE.NĀT

HĪ'FE.NĀT	hyphenate
SĪ'FE.NĀT	siphonate

IF'E.NĒ

LIF'E.NĒ	polyphony
PIF'E.NĒ	epiphany
SIF'E.NĒ	oxyphony

ID'I.US

DID'I.US	splendidious
FID'I.US	ophidious, perfidious, Phidias

TIF′E.NĒ	antiphony, tiffany, Tiffany
TRIF′E.NĒ	triphony

IF′ER.ĀT

LIF′ER.ĀT	proliferate
SIF′ER.ĀT	vociferate

IF′ER.US

IF′ER.US	oleiferous
BIF′ER.US	bulbiferous, herbiferous, limbiferous, morbiferous, nimbiferous, nubiferous, plumbiferous
BRIF′ER.US	umbriferous
DIF′ER.US	acidiferous, diamondiferous, frondiferous, glandiferous, geodiferous, splendiferous
GWIF′ER.US	sanguiferous
JIF′ER.US	frugiferous, tergiferous
KIF′ER.US	branchiferous, conchiferous, zinciferous
KRIF′ER.US	lucriferous
KWIF′ER.US	aquiferous
LIF′ER.US	*A* aliferous, *F* favilliferous, filiferous, foliferous, fossiliferous, *GL* glanduliferous, *GR* granuliferous, *K* cheliferous, cauliferous, coraliferous, *L* lameliferous, *M* maculiferous, maliferous, mammaliferous, melliferous, metalliferous, *N* nickeliferous, *P* papilliferous, papuliferous, petroliferous, piliferous, pistilliferous, *PR* proliferous, *R* ramuliferous, *S* saliferous, celliferous, soboliferous, *ST*

	stelliferous, *T* tentaculiferous, *U* umbelliferous, umbraculiferous, *V* vasculiferous, veliferous
MIF′ER.US	*A* armiferous, atomiferous, *B* balsamiferous, *F* fumiferous, *FL* flammiferous, *J* gemmiferous, *K* coniferous, *M* mammiferous, *P* palmiferous, pomiferous, *R* ramiferous, racemiferous
NIF′ER.US	*A* aluminiferous, antenniferous, *B* balaniferous, *GR* graniferous, *I* igniferous, *K* carboniferous, coniferous, *L* laniferous, ligniferous, luminiferous, *M* membraniferous, *O* omniferous, ozoniferous, *P* penniferous, pulmoniferous, *PL* platiniferous, *PR* pruniferous, *R* resiniferous, *S* saliniferous, somniferous, soniferous, *ST* stanniferous, stoloniferous, *V* veneniferous
PIF′ER.US	polypiferous, scopiferous
RIF′ER.US	*D* doloriferous, *F* ferriferous, *FL* floriferous, *H* hederiferous, *K* calcariferous, cupriferous, *L* lauriferous, *N* nectariferous, *O* odoriferous, auriferous, *P* poriferous, *R* roriferous, *S* sacchariferous, ceriferous, cirriferous, soporiferous, sudoriferous, *T* tuberiferous, *TH*

	thuriferous, *V* vaporiferous
SIF′ER.US	*B* bacciferous, boraciferous, *F* furciferous, *J* gypsiferous, *K* calciferous, calyciferous, corticiferous, *KR* cruciferous, *KW* quartziferous, *L* lanciferous, laticiferous, luciferous, *M* muciferous, *N* nuciferous, *O* ossiferous, *S* sensiferous, siliciferous, succiferous, *SP* spiciferous, *V* vociferous, *Z* zucciferous
STRIF′ER.US	monstriferous, rostriferous
THIF′ER.US	lethiferous
TIF′ER.US	*A* ammonitiferous, argentiferous, *D* diamantiferous, *E* estiferous, *F* fatiferous, *FL* fluctiferous, *FR* fructiferous, *K* chaetiferous, *L* lactiferous, lignitiferous, luctiferous, *M* magnetiferous, margaritiferous, mortiferous, multiferous, *N* noctiferous, *O* oölitiferous, *P* pestiferous, *S* salutiferous, setiferous, *SK* scutiferous
TRIF′ER.US	astriferous, nitriferous, ostriferous
VIF′ER.US	oviferous, valviferous

IF′I.KAL

NIF′I.KAL	magnifical
RIF′I.KAL	mirifical, saporifical
SIF′I.KAL	pacifical, specifical
TIF′I.KAL	beatifical, lactifical, pontifical
VIF′I.KAL	vivifical

IF'I.KANT

DIF'I.KANT	mundificant, nidificant
NIF'I.KANT	insignificant, significant
RIF'I.KANT	sacrificant

IF'I.KĀT

DIF'I.KĀT	nidificate
LIF'I.KĀT	improlificate, prolificate
SIF'I.KĀT	pacificate
TIF'I.KĀT	pontificate, certificate
TRIF'I.KĀT	nostrificate

ĪF'LING.LĒ

TRĪF'LING.LĒ	triflingly
STĪF'LING.LĒ	stiflingly

IF'LOO.US

GWIF'LOO.US	sanguifluous
LIF'LOO.US	fellifluous, mellifluous

IF'O.NĒ

(See **IF'A.NĒ**)

IFT'A.BL

LIFT'A.BL	liftable
SHIFT'A.BL	shiftable
SIFT'A.BL	siftable

IF'TI.LĒ

NIF'TI.LĒ	niftily
SHIF'TI.LĒ	shiftily
THRIF'TI.LĒ	thriftily

IF'TI.NES

NIF'TI.NES	niftiness
SHIF'TI.NES	shiftiness
THRIF'TI.NES	thriftiness

IFT'LES.LĒ

SHIFT'LES.LĒ	shiftlessly
SHRIFT'LES.LĒ	shriftlessly
THRIFT'LES.LĒ	thriftlessly

IF'Ū.GAL

BRIF'Ū.GAL	febrifugal
MIF'Ū.GAL	vermifugal
TRIF'Ū.GAL	centrifugal

IF'Ū.GUS

DIF'Ū.GUS	nidifugous
MIF'Ū.GUS	vermifugous
NIF'Ū.GUS	somnifugous
SIF'Ū.GUS	lucifugous

IG'A.MĒ

BIG'A.MĒ	bigamy
DIG'A.MĒ	digamy
LIG'A.MĒ	polygamy
SIG'A.MĒ	opsigamy
TRIG'A.MĒ	trigamy

IG'A.MIST

BIG'A.MIST	bigamist
DIG'A.MIST	digamist
LIG'A.MIST	polygamist
RIG'A.MIST	quadrigamist
TRIG'A.MIST	trigamist

IG'A.MUS

BIG'A.MUS	bigamous
DIG'A.MUS	digamous, myriadigamous
LIG'A.MUS	polygamous
TRIG'A.MUS	trigamous

IG'ER.Ē

HWIG'ER.Ē	whiggery, Whiggery
PIG'ER.Ē	piggery
TRIG'ER.Ē	triggery
WIG'ER.Ē	wiggery

IG'ER.US

RIG'ER.US	rigorous
VIG'ER.US	vigorous

IG'ET.Ē

BIG'ET.Ē	biggety
SPIG'ET.Ē	spigotty

IG'HED'ED.NES

BIG'HED'ED.NES	bigheadedness
PIG'HED'ED.NES	pigheadedness

IG'MA.TIST

NIG'MA.TIST	enigmatist
STIG'MA.TIST	stigmatist

IG'MA.TĪZ

DIG'MA.TĪZ	paradigmatize
NIG'MA.TĪZ	enigmatize
STIG'MA.TĪZ	stigmatize

IG'NAN.SĒ

DIG'NAN.SĒ	indignancy
LIG'NAN.SĒ	malignancy
NIG'NAN.SĒ	benignancy

IG'NANT.LĒ

DIG'NANT.LĒ	indignantly
LIG'NANT.LĒ	malignantly
NIG'NANT.LĒ	benignantly

IG'NI.FĪ

IG'NI.FĪ	ignify
DIG'NI.FĪ	dignify, condignify, undignify
LIG'NI.FĪ	lignify, malignify
SIG'NI.FĪ	presignify, signify

IG'NI.TĒ

DIG'NI.TĒ	dignity, indignity, condignity
LIG'NI.TĒ	malignity
NIG'NI.TĒ	benignity

IG'NI.US

IG'NI.US	igneous
LIG'NI.US	ligneous, pyroligneous
SIG'NI.US	cygneous

IG'O.NAL

LIG'O.NAL	polygonal
TRIG'O.NAL	ditrigonal, trigonal

IG'OR.US

(See **IG'ER.US**)

IG'RA.FĒ

KIG'RA.FĒ	tachygraphy
LIG'RA.FĒ	calligraphy, polygraphy
PIG'RA.FĒ	epigraphy, pseudepigraphy
SIG'RA.FĒ	lexigraphy, pasigraphy
TIG'RA.FĒ	stratigraphy

IG'Ū.LĀT

FIG'Ū.LĀT	figulate
LIG'Ū.LĀT	ligulate

IG'Ū.US

BIG'Ū.US	ambiguous
RIG'Ū.US	irriguous
TIG'Ū.US	contiguous
ZIG'Ū.US	exiguous

Ī'ING.LĒ

Ī'ING.LĒ	eyeingly
FĪ'ING.LĒ	defyingly, gratifyingly, mystifyingly, satisfyingly
FLĪ'ING.LĒ	flyingly
LĪ'ING.LĒ	lyingly
PRĪ'ING.LĒ	pryingly
SĪ'ING.LĒ	sighingly
VĪ'ING.LĒ	vyingly

IJ'E.NUS

BIJ'E.NUS	ambigenous, nubigenous, rubigenous
DIJ'E.NUS	digenous, indigenous
GWIJ'E.NUS	sanguigenous
LIJ'E.NUS	alkaligenous, fuliginous, caliginous, cauligenous, coralligenous, melligenous, nepheligenous, polygenous, uliginous
NIJ'E.NUS	ignigenous, omnigenous, unigenous
PIJ'E.NUS	epigenous
RIJ'E.NUS	marigenous, pruriginous, rurigenous, terrigenous
SIJ'E.NUS	oxygenous
TIJ'E.NUS	gelatigenous, lentigenous, montigenous, tentiginous, vertigenous, vortigenous

IJ'E.RĀT

BIJ'E.RĀT	verbigerate
FRIJ'E.RĀT	refrigerate
LIJ'E.RĀT	belligerate
RIJ'E.RĀT	hederigerate

IJ'ER.ENT

FRIJ'ER.ENT	refrigerant
LIJ'ER.ENT	belligerent
RIJ'ER.ENT	hederigerent

IJ'ER.US

DIJ'ER.US	pedigerous
LIJ'ER.US	aligerous, belligerous, coraligerous, peligerous, veligerous
MIJ'ER.US	armigerous, plumigerous
NIJ'ER.US	cornigerous, lanigerous, linigerous, pennigerous, spinigerous
PIJ'ER.US	palpigerous
RIJ'ER.US	immorigerous, morigerous, cirrigerous
SIJ'ER.US	disciger ous, crucigerous
TIJ'ER.US	dentigerous, setigerous
VIJ'ER.US	navigerous, ovigerous

IJ'I.A

BRIJ'I.A	Cantabrigia
FLIJ'I.A	oenophilygia
FRIJ'I.A	Phrygia
JIJ'I.A	Ogygia
PIJ'I.A	pygia, steatopygia
TIJ'I.A	fastigia

IJ'I.AN

BRIJ'I.AN	Cantabrigian
FRIJ'I.AN	Phrygian
JIJ'I.AN	Ogygian
PIJ'I.AN	Callipygian, steatopygian
RIJ'I.AN	acanthopterygian, crossopterygian, malacopterygian
STIJ'I.AN	Stygian
TIJ'I.AN	vestigian

IJ'ID.LĒ

FRIJ'ID.LĒ	frigidly
RIJ'ID.LĒ	rigidly

IJ'ID.NES

FRIJ'ID.NES	frigidness
RIJ'ID.NES	rigidness

IJ'I.TĒ

DIJ'I.TĒ	digiti
FIJ'I.TĒ	fidgety
MIJ'I.TĒ	midgety

IJ'IT.ER

FIJ'IT.ER	fidgeter
LIJ'I.TER	subintelligitur

IJ'I.UM

FRIJ'I.UM	phrygium
PIJ'I.UM	uropygium
RIJ'I.UM	pterygium
TIJ'I.UM	fastigium
ZIJ'I.UM	syzygium

IJ'OO.AL

VIJ'OO.AL	individual, dividual
ZIJ'OO.AL	residual

IJ'OO.ĀT

SIJ'OO.ĀT	assiduate
VIJ'OO.ĀT	individuate

IJ'OO.LĀT

NIJ'OO.LĀT	nidulate
SIJ'OO.LĀT	acidulate
STRIJ'OO.LĀT	stridulate

IJ'OO.LUS

SIJ'OO.LUS	acidulous
STRIJ'OO.LUS	stridulous

IJ'OO.US

IJ'OO.US	druiduous
BIJ'OO.US	biduous
SIJ'OO.US	assiduous, deciduous, occiduous, prociduous, succiduous
VIJ'OO.US	viduous
ZIJ'OO.US	residuous

IJ'US.LĒ

DIJ'US.LĒ	prodigiously
LIJ'US.LĒ	irreligiously, religiously
TIJ'US.LĒ	litigiously

IJ'US.NES

DIJ'US.NES	prodigiousness
LIJ'US.NES	religiousness
TIJ'US.NES	litigiousness, prestigiousness

ĪK'A.BL

LĪK'A.BL	dislikable, likable, unlikable
SPĪK'A.BL	spikable, unspikable

ED'IK'A.MENT

MED'IK'A.MENT	*medicament*
PRED'IK'A.MENT	*predicament*

IK'A.TIV

DIK'A.TIV	abdicative, *applicative,* indicative, *judicative,* predicative, vindicative
FRIK'A.TIV	affricative, fricative
NIK'A.TIV	*communicative*
PLIK'A.TIV	explicative, *multiplicative,* plicative
SIK'A.TIV	desiccative, exsiccative, siccative

IK'A.TRIS

FRIK'A.TRIS	fricatrice
SIK'A.TRIS	cicatrice

IK'EN.ER

KWIK'EN.ER	quickener
THIK'EN.ER	thickener

IK'EN.ING

KWIK'EN.ING	quickening
SIK'EN.ING	sickening
THIK'EN.ING	thickening

IK'ER.Ē

IK'ER.Ē	ikary
CHIK'E.RĒ	chicory
HIK'E.RĒ	hickory
LIK'E.RĒ	lickery, liquory
MIK'E.RĒ	mickery
SIK'E.RĒ	terpsichore
TRIK'E.RĒ	trickery

IK'ER.ING

BIK'ER.ING	bickering
DIK'ER.ING	dickering
FLIK'ER.ING	flickering
SNIK'ER.ING	snickering

IK'ET.Ē

KRIK'ET.Ē	crickety
NIK'ET.Ē	pernickety
RIK'ET.Ē	rickety
SNIK'ET.Ē	persnickety
THIK'ET.Ē	thickety

IK'ET.ER

KRIK'ET.ER	cricketer
PIK'ET.ER	picketer, picqueter
TIK'ET.ER	ticketer

IK'ET.ING

KRIK'ET.ING	cricketing
PIK'ET.ING	picketing
TIK'ET.ING	ticketing

IK'I.LĒ

STIK'I.LĒ	stickily
TRIK'I.LĒ	trickily

IK'I.NES

STIK'I.NES	stickiness
TRIK'I.NES	trickiness

IK'LI.NES

PRIK'LI.NES	prickliness
SIK'LI.NES	sickliness

IK'O.LIST

BIK'O.LIST	plebicolist
NIK'O.LIST	ignicolist
RIK'O.LIST	agricolist

IK'O.LUS

BIK'O.LUS	plebicolous, urbicolous
DIK'O.LUS	nidicolous
MIK'O.LUS	fimicolous, limicolous
NIK'O.LUS	arenicolous, Father Nicholas, sphagnicolous, stagnicolous
PIK'O.LUS	sepicolous
RIK'O.LUS	agricolous, maricolous, stercoricolous, terricolous
SIK'O.LUS	saxicolous
VIK'O.LUS	silvicolous

IK'O.MUS

RIK'O.MUS	auricomous
VIK'O.MUS	flavicomous

IK′O.PĒ

RIK′O.PĒ	pericope
WIK′O.PĒ	wicopy

IK′O.RĒ

(See IK′ER.Ē)

Ī′KRO.MAT.IK

BĪ′KRO.MAT.IK	*bichromatic*
DĪ′KRO.MAT.IK	*dichromatic*

IK′SA.BL

FIK′SA.BL	fixable, unfixable
MIK′SA.BL	immixable, mixable, unmixable

IK′SED.LĒ

FIK′SED.LĒ	fixedly
MIK′SED.LĒ	mixedly

IK′SHUN.AL

DIK′SHUN.AL	benedictional, jurisdictional, contradictional, maledictional
FIK′SHUN.AL	fictional, nonfictional
FRIK′SHUN.AL	frictional
VIK′SHUN.AL	convictional

IK′SI.TĒ

FIK′SI.TĒ	fixity
LIK′SI.TĒ	prolixity
NIK′SI.TĒ	phoenixity
SIK′SI.TĒ	siccity

IK′TA.BL

DIK′TA.BL	contradictable, predictable, unpredictable
STRIK′TA.BL	restrictable, unrestrictable
VIK′TA.BL	convictable, unconvictable

IK′TIV.LĒ

DIK′TIV.LĒ	predictively, vindictively
FIK′TIV.LĒ	fictively
FLIK′TIV.LĒ	conflictively
STRIK′TIV.LĒ	constrictively, nonrestrictively, restrictively

IK′TIV.NES

DIK′TIV.NES	predictiveness, vindictiveness
FIK′TIV.NES	fictiveness
FLIK′TIV.NES	conflictiveness
STRIK′TIV.NES	constrictiveness, nonrestrictiveness, restrictiveness

IK′TER.Ē

DIK′TER.Ē	benedictory, interdictory, contradictory, maledictory, valedictory
RIK′TER.Ē	serictery
VIK′TER.Ē	victory

IK′Ū.LA

BIK′Ū.LA	corbicula
DIK′Ū.LA	fidicula
NIK′Ū.LA	canicula, cunicula
RIK′Ū.LA	curricula, auricula
SIK′Ū.LA	acicula
TIK′Ū.LA	cuticula, reticula, zeticula

IK′Ū.LANT

TIK′Ū.LANT	articulant
TRIK′Ū.LANT	matriculant

IK′Ū.LAR

BIK′Ū.LAR	cubicular, orbicular, scobicular
DIK′Ū.LAR	appendicular, pedicular, perpendicular, radicular
HIK′Ū.LAR	extravehicular, vehicular
LIK′Ū.LAR	follicular, calycular, pellicular
MIK′Ū.LAR	vermicular
NIK′Ū.LAR	adminicular, funicular, canicular, cunicular
PIK′Ū.LAR	apicular
RIK′Ū.LAR	extracurricular, curricular, auricular
SIK′Ū.LAR	acicular, fascicular, versicular, vesicular
SPIK′Ū.LAR	spicular
TIK′Ū.LAR	articular, denticular, cuticular, quinquarticular, lenticular, particular, reticular, subcuticular
TRIK′Ū.LAR	matricular, ventricular
VIK′Ū.LAR	clavicular, navicular, ovicular

IK′Ū.LĀT

BIK′Ū.LĀT	orbiculate, scrobiculate
DIK′Ū.LĀT	pediculate
GWIK′Ū.LĀT	unguiculate
MIK′Ū.LĀT	vermiculate
NIK′Ū.LĀT	geniculate, corniculate, paniculate
RIK′Ū.LĀT	auriculate
SIK′Ū.LĀT	aciculate, fasciculate, vesiculate
SPIK′Ū.LĀT	spiculate
TIK′Ū.LĀT	articulate, disarticulate, gesticulate, particulate, reticulate
TRIK′Ū.LĀT	matriculate

IK′Ū.LIT

BIK′Ū.LIT	orbiculate, scrobiculate
DIK′Ū.LIT	appendiculate, pediculate
FIK′Ū.LIT	forficualte
GWIK′Ū.LIT	unguiculate
LIK′Ū.LIT	folliculate, caniculate
MIK′Ū.LIT	vermiculate
NIK′Ū.LIT	funiculate, geniculate, corniculate, paniculate
PIK′Ū.LIT	apiculate
RIK′Ū.LIT	auriculate, turriculate

SIK'Ū.LIT	aciculate, fasciculate, vesicualte
SPIK'Ū.LIT	spiculate
TIK'Ū.LIT	articualte, denticulate, inarticulate, monticulate, particulate, reticulate, straticulate

IK'Ū.LUM

BIK'Ū.LUM	cubiculum
NIK'Ū.LUM	Janiculum, geniculum
RIK'Ū.LUM	curriculum, periculum
SIK'Ū.LUM	aciculum
SPIK'Ū.LUM	spiculum
TIK'Ū.LUM	reticulum

IK'Ū.LUS

DIK'Ū.LUS	pediculous, pediculus, ridiculous
DRIK'Ū.LUS	dendriculous
LIK'Ū.LUS	folliculous, calyculous, canaliculus, cauliculous
MIK'Ū.LUS	vermiculous
NIK'Ū.LUS	funiculus, cuniculous, panniculous
SIK'Ū.LUS	fasciculus, vesiculous
TIK'Ū.LUS	denticulous, meticulous
TRIK'Ū.LUS	ventriculous

IK'Ū.US

| IK'Ū.US | proficuous |
| SPIK'Ū.US | inconspicuous, conspicuous, perspicuous, transpicuous |

IK'WI.TĒ

BIK'WI.TĒ	ubiquity
LIK'WI.TĒ	obliquity
NIK'WI.TĒ	iniquity
TIK'WI.TĒ	antiquity

IK'WI.TUS

BIK'WI.TUS	ubiquitous
NIK'WI.TUS	iniquitous
LIK'WI.TUS	obliquitous

ĪL'A.BL

FĪL'A.BL	defilable, filable
GĪL'A.BL	beguilable
HĪL'A.BL	heilable
NĪL'A.BL	enislable
PĪL'A.BL	compilable, pilable, recompilable, repilable, unpilable
RĪL'A.BL	rilable
SĪL'A.BL	domicilable, ensilable, exilable, reconcilable, irreconcilable
SPĪL'A.BL	spilable
STĪL'A.BL	stylable
TĪL'A.BL	tilable
VĪL'A.BL	revilable
ZĪL'A.BL	exilable

IL'A.BL

| SIL'A.BL | henedecasyllable, monosyllable, multisyllable, polysyllable, syllable |

(See **IL**, add *-able* where appropriate.)

IL'A.BUB

| SIL'A.BUB | sillabub |
| TRIL'A.BUB | trillibub |

IL'A.JER

(See **IL'I.JER**)

Ī'LAN.DER

Ī'LAN.DER	islander
HĪ'LAN.DER	highlander
SKĪ'LAN.DER	skylander
TĪ'LAN.DER	Thailander

Ī'LAT.ER.AL

| BĪ'LAT.ER.AL | *bilateral* |
| TRĪ'LAT.ER.AL | *trilateral* |

IL'A.TŌ.RĒ

| DIL'A.TŌ.RĒ | dilatory |
| PIL'A.TŌ.RĒ | depilatory |

IL'E.GRAM

KIL'E.GRAM	kilogram
MIL'E.GRAM	milligram
TIL'E.GRAM	dactylogram

IL'E.JENT

(See **IL'I.JENT**)

Ī'LER.Ē

GĪL'ER.Ē	guilery
PĪ'LER.Ē	pilary
TĪ'LER.Ē	tilery

IL'ER.Ē

FIL'ER.Ē	phyllary
FRIL'ER.Ē	frillery
MIL'ER.Ē	armillary
PIL'ER.Ē	capillary, pillery, pillory
SIL'ER.Ē	ancillary, axillary, codicillary, cilery, submaxillary
TIL'ER.Ē	artillery, distillery, fritillary

IL'ET.ED

| BIL'ET.ED | billeted, unbilleted |
| FIL'ET.ED | filleted, unfilleted |

IL'ET.ING

| BIL'ET.ING | billeting |
| FIL'ET.ING | filleting |

ĪL'FUL.Ē

| GĪL'FUL.Ē | beguilefully, guilefully |
| WĪL'FUL.Ē | wilefully |

IL'FUL.Ē

| SKIL'FUL.Ē | skilfully, unskilfully |
| WIL'FUL.Ē | wilfully, unwilfully |

ĪL'FUL.NES

GĪL'FUL.NES	guilefulness
WĪL'FUL.NES	wilefulness

IL'FUL.NES

SKIL'FUL.NES	skillfulness, unskillfulness
WIL'FUL.NES	willfulness

IL'I.A

IL'I.A	ilia
BIL'I.A	imponderabilia, memorabilia, mirabilia, notabilia, sensibilia
DIL'I.A	sedilia
FIL'I.A	*A* ailurophilia, alcoholophilia, androphilia, Anglophilia, anophilia, *B* bibliophilia, *F* phallophilia, *FR* Francophilia, *G* gamophilia, *H* hemophilia, *J* Germanophilia, *K* coprophilia, *L* lygophilia, *M* melcryptovestiment- aphilia, *N* necrophilia, *O* osphresiophilia, *P* pedophilia, *R* Russophilia, *SP* spasmophilia, *T* taphophilia, *U* urinophilia, *V* vulvophilia, *Z* zoophilia (etc.)
MIL'I.A	familia
NIL'I.A	juvenilia
SIL'I.A	Brasilia, cilia
TIL'I.A	adactylia, dactylia

IL'I.AD

IL'I.AD	Iliad
GIL'I.AD	Gilead
KIL'I.AD	chiliad
MIL'I.AD	milliad

IL'I.AL

IL'I.AL	ilial

FIL'I.AL	filial, grandfilial, unfilial
MIL'I.AL	familial

IL'I.AN

BIL'I.AN	perfectabilian
CHIL'I.AN	Chilean
DIL'I.AN	crocodilian
JIL'I.AN	Virgilian
MIL'I.AN	Maximilian
PIL'I.AN	epyllion
SIL'I.AN	caecilian, Sicilian
SKIL'I.AN	skillion
TIL'I.AN	Castilian, lacertilian, reptilian, vespertilian
VIL'I.AN	civilian
ZIL'I.AN	Brazilian

(See ILYUN)

IL'I.AR

BIL'I.AR	atrabiliar
MIL'I.AR	familiar, unfamiliar
SIL'I.AR	domiciliar, conciliar
ZIL'I.AR	auxiliar

(See ILYAR)

IL'I.ARDZ

(See ILYARDZ)

IL'I.ER.Ē

(See IL'YER.Ē)

IL'I.ĀT

FIL'I.ĀT	affiliate, disaffiliate, filiate
MIL'I.ĀT	forisfamiliate, humiliate
PIL'I.ĀT	pileate
SIL'I.ĀT	comiciliate, conciliate, reconciliate, ciliate

IL'I.ENS

BRIL'I.ENS	brilliance
SIL'I.ENS	dissilience, consilience, transilience
ZIL'I.ENS	resilience

(See ILYENS)

IL'I.ENT

BRIL'I.ENT	brilliant
SIL'I.ENT	dissilient, intersillient, consilient, transilient
ZIL'I.ENT	resilient

(See ILYENT)

IL'I.ER

CHIL'I.ER	chillier
FRIL'I.ER	frillier
HIL'I.ER	hillier
KWIL'I.ER	quillier
RIL'I.ER	rillier
SIL'I.ER	sillier
STIL'I.ER	stillier
THRIL'I.ER	thrillier
TIL'I.ER	tillier
TRIL'I.ER	trillier
TWIL'I.ER	twillier

(See IL'YAR)

IL'I.EST

(See IL'I.ER; change -r to -st.)

IL'I.FĪ

BIL'I.FĪ	nobilify, stabilify
HIL'I.FĪ	nihilify
SIL'I.FĪ	fossilify
VIL'I.FĪ	vilify

IL'I.FÔRM

FIL'I.FÔRM	filiform, phylliform
LIL'I.FÔRM	liliform
NIL'I.FÔRM	moniliform
PIL'I.FÔRM	papilliform
SIL'I.FÔRM	ypsiliform
STIL'I.FÔRM	stilliform

IL'I.JENT

DIL'I.JENT	diligent
NIL'I.JENT	omniligent

IL'I.JER

PIL'I.JER	pillager
VIL'I.JER	villager

IL'I.KAL

BIL'I.KAL umbilical
FIL'I.KAL filical
SIL'I.KAL basilical, silicle

IL'I.KIN

BIL'I.KIN billikin
SIL'I.KIN basilican
SPIL'I.KIN spilikin, spillikin

IL'I.NES

CHIL'I.NES chilliness
FIL'I.NES dilliness
HIL'I.NES hilliness
SIL'I.NES silliness

Ī'LING.LĒ

GĪ'LING.LĒ beguilingly
SMĪ'LING.LĒ smilingly,
unsmilingly

IL'ING.LĒ

CHIL'ING.LĒ chillingly
FIL'ING.LĒ fillingly
KIL'ING.LĒ killingly
THRIL'ING.LĒ thrillingly
TRIL'ING.LĒ trillingly
WIL'ING.LĒ unwillingly,
willingly

IL'I.Ō

BIL'I.Ō billyo
TIL'I.Ō punctilio
VIL'I.Ō pulvilio

IL'I.SĪD

SIL'I.SĪD silicide
STIL'I.SĪD stillicide

IL'I.TĀT

BIL'I.TĀT abilitate, debilitate,
habilitate,
impossibilitate,
nobilitate,
rehabilitate,
stabilitate
MIL'I.TĀT militate

SIL'I.TĀT facilitate,
imbecilitate

IL'I.TĒ

BIL'I.TĒ *A* ability,
absorbability,
adaptability,
addability,
adjustability,
admirability,
admissibility,
adoptability,
adorability,
advisability,
affectibility,
agreeability,
accendibility,
acceptability,
accessibility,
accountability,
acquirability,
alienability,
amability,
amenability,
amiability,
amicability,
admissibility,
answerability,
appetibility,
applicability,
approachability,
ascendability,
assimilability,
associability,
attainability,
attemptability,
attractability,
availability,
avoidability, *B*
biodegradability, *BR*
bribability, *CH*
changeability,
chargeability, *D*
damnability,
debility,
deceptibility,
deductibility,
defectibility,
defensibility,
defeatibility,
delectability,
demisability,
demonstrability,
deplorability,
descendibility,
describability,
despicability,
destructibility,
determinability,
detestability,

desirability,
diffusibility,
digestibility,
dilatability,
dirigibility,
disability,
dispensability,
dissolubility,
dissolvability,
disputability,
distensibility,
divisibility,
docibility,
durability, *E*
edibility,
educability,
effectibility,
effervescibility,
exchangeability,
excitability,
exhaustibility,
existibility,
exorability,
expansibility,
expressibility,
extensibility,
equability,
eligibility,
endurability,
enunciability,
errability, *F*
fallibility,
feasibility,
fermentability,
formidability,
fusibility, *FL*
flammability,
flexibility,
fluxibility,
fluctuability, *FR*
frangibility,
friability, *G*
gullibility,
governability, *H*
habitability,
hereditability,
hyperirritability, *I*
ignobility, illability,
illegibility,
illimitability,
imitability,
immeability,
immeasurability,
immiscibility,
immobility,
immovability,
immutability,
impalpability,
impartibility,
impassibility,
impeccability,
impenetrability,

imperdibility,
imperfectibility,
imperishability,
impermeability,
imperceptibility,
imperturbability,
imperviability,
implacability,
imponderability,
impossibility,
impracticability,
impregnability,
impressibility,
impressionability,
imprescriptibility,
improbability,
improvability,
imputability,
inability,
inadmissibility,
inaccessibility,
indefatigability,
indefeasibility,
indefectibility,
indefensibility,
indelibility,
indemonstrability,
indescribability,
indestructibility,
indigestibility,
indiscernibility,
indiscerptibility,
indescribability,
indispensability,
indissolubility,
indisputability,
indestructability,
indivisibility,
indocibility,
inducibility,
inedibility,
ineffability,
ineffervescibility,
inexcusability,
inexhaustibility,
inexorability,
inexplicability,
inexpressibility,
ineligibility,
ineradicability,
inerrability,
inevitability,
infallibility,
infeasibility,
inflexibility,
influencibility,
infrangibility,
infusibility,
inhability,
inhabitability,
inheritability,
inimitability,

incalculability,
incapability,
incognitability,
incognizability,
incognoscibility,
incogitability,
incombustibility,
incommensurability,
incommeasurability,
incommunicability,
incommutability,
incomparability,
incompatibility,
incomprehensibility,
incompressibility,
incondensability,
inconceivability,
incontestability,
incontrovertibility,
inconvertibility,
incorrigibility,
incorruptibility,
incredibility,
inoperability,
innumerability,
inaudibility,
insanability,
insatiability,
insensibility,
inseparability,
insurability,
inscrutability,
insolubility,
insociability,
instability,
insuperability,
insurmountability,
insusceptibility,
intangibility,
intelligibility,
interchangeability,
intractability,
invariability,
invendibility,
invincibility,
inviolability,
invisibility,
invulnerability,
irascibility,
irredeemability,
irredressibility,
irreductibility,
irreducibility,
irreformability,
irrefragability,
irrefutability,
irremissibility,
irremovability,
irreparability,
irrepressibility,
irreproachability,
irresponsibility,

irretrievability,
irreversibility,
irrevocability,
irritability,
irresistibility,
irresolvability, *J*
generability,
justifiability, *K*
calculability,
capability,
coagulability,
cognizability,
cognoscibility,
cohesibility,
collapsibility,
combustibility,
commensurability,
communicability,
commutability,
comparability,
compatibility,
comprehensibility,
compressibility,
computability,
condensability,
conductability,
conformability,
confusability,
conceivability,
contemptibility,
contractibility,
convertibility,
convincibility,
corrigibility,
corrodibility,
corrosibility,
corruptibility,
culpability,
curability, *KR*
credibility,
creditability, *KW*
questionability,
quotability, *L*
lability,
laminability,
legibility, liability,
laudability, *M*
malleability,
manageability,
manipulability,
marketability,
masticability,
meliorability,
memorability,
mensurability,
mentionability,
measurability,
miscibility,
mobility,
modifiability,
modificability,
movability,

mutability, *N*
namability,
navigability,
negotiability,
nobility, notability,
knowability,
nubility, nullibility,
O audibility,
alterability,
opposability,
organizability,
ostensibility, *P*
palpability,
partibility,
passibility,
peccability,
penetrability,
perdurability,
perfectibility,
perishability,
permeability,
permissibility,
perceptibility,
persuasibility,
perturbability,
ponderability,
portability,
possibility,
potability,
punishability, *PR*
practicability,
predictability,
preferability,
precipitability,
prescriptibility,
preventability,
probability,
producibility,
provability, *R*
ratability,
readability,
redeemability,
redressibility,
reductibility,
reducibility,
reflectibility,
reformability,
refragability,
refrangibility,
refutability,
recognizability,
reconcilability,
relatability,
reliability,
remissibility,
removability,
remunerability,
renewability,
reparability,
repealability,
receivability,
receptibility,

responsibility,
retractability,
retrievability,
reversibility,
revocability,
resistibility,
resolvability,
writability, risibility,
S salability,
salvability,
sanability,
seducibility,
secability,
sensibility,
censurability,
separability,
solubility,
solvability,
sociability,
suability,
suggestibility,
susceptibility,
suspensibility,
suitability, *SKW*
squeezability, *SP*
sportability, *ST*
stability, *SW*
swayability, *T*
taxability,
tamability,
tangibility,
temptability,
tenability,
tensibility,
tolerability,
torsibility, *TR*
tractability,
transferability,
translatability,
transmissibility,
transmutability,
transportability,
traceability, *U*
unaccountability,
unbelievability,
undesirability,
unreliability,
unsuitability,
untranslatability,
unutterability,
utterability, *V*
vaporability,
variability,
vegetability,
vendibility,
venerability,
versability, viability,
vindicability,
vincibility,
violability,
visibility, vocability,
volubility,

	vulnerability, *W*
	wearability,
	workability
BRIL'I.TĒ	febrility
DIL'I.TĒ	crocodility
HIL'I.TĒ	nihility
JIL'I.TĒ	agility, fragility
KWIL'I.TĒ	tranquillity
MIL'I.TĒ	humility,
	verisimility
NIL'I.TĒ	anility, feminility,
	juvenility, senility,
	vernility
RIL'I.TĒ	febrility, neurility,
	puerility, scurrility,
	sterility, virility
SIL'I.TĒ	*D* docility, *E* exility,
	F facility, fossility,
	FL flexility, *GR*
	gracility, *I*
	imbecility,
	indocility, *P*
	pensility, *PR*
	prehensility, *T*
	tensility
TIL'I.TĒ	*B* beautility, *D*
	ductility, *F* fertility,
	fictility, futility, *H*
	hostility, *I*
	inductility,
	infantility,
	infertility, inutility,
	J gentility, *K*
	contractility, *M*
	motility, *R*
	retractility, *T*
	tactility, tortility, *TR*
	tractility, *V*
	versatility,
	vibratility, volatility,
	Y utility
VIL'I.TĒ	incivility, servility,
	civility

IL'I.UM

IL'I.UM	ileum, ilium, Ilium,
	illium
LIL'I.UM	Liliom, Lilium
MIL'I.UM	millium
PIL'I.UM	pileum
RIL'I.UM	beryllium
SIL'I.UM	concilium,
	penicillium, cillium
TRIL'I.UM	trillium
ZIL'I.UM	auxilium

IL'I.US

| **BIL'I.US** | atrabilious, bilious |

SIL'I.US supercilious
TIL'I.US punctilious

(See **ILYUS**)

IL'KI.ER

MIL'KI.ER milkier
SIL'KI.ER silkier

IL'KI.EST

MIL'KI.EST milkiest
SIL'KI.EST silkiest

Ī'LO.BĀT

STĪ'LO.BĀT stylobate
TRĪ'LO.BĀT trilobate

IL'O.Ē

BIL'O.Ē billowy
PIL'O.Ē pillowy
WIL'O.Ē willowy

Ī'LO.GRAF

STĪ'LO.GRAF stilograph
ZĪ'LO.GRAF xylograph

IL'O.ING

BIL'O.ING billowing
PIL'O.ING pillowing
WIL'O.ING willowing

IL'O.JĒ

DIL'O.JĒ dilogy
KIL'O.JĒ brachylogy
LIL'O.JĒ palilogy, polilogy
SIL'O.JĒ fossilogy, sylloge
TIL'O.JĒ antilogy, festilogy
TRIL'O.JĒ trilogy

IL'O.JĪZ

PIL'O.JĪZ epilogize
SIL'O.JĪZ syllogize

IL'O.JIZM

FIL'O.JIZM amphilogism
PIL'O.JIZM epilogism
SIL'O.JIZM episyllogism, pseudosyllogism, syllogism

IL'O.KWĒ

DIL'O.KWĒ blandiloquy, grandiloquy
JIL'O.KWĒ longiloquy
LIL'O.KWĒ melliloquy, soliloquy
NIL'O.KWĒ inaniloquy, magniloquy, pleniloquy, somniloquy, vaniloquy
RIL'O.KWĒ pectoriloquy, veriloquy
SIL'O.KWĒ dulciloquy, flexiloquy, mendaciloquy, pauciloquy
TIL'O.KWĒ antiloquy, dentiloquy, multiloquy, sanctiloquy, stultiloquy, tolutiloquy, tristiloquy
TRIL'O.KWĒ gastriloquy, ventriloquy
VIL'O.KWĒ breviloquy, suaviloquy

IL'O.KWENS

(See **IL'O.KWĒ,** change concluding -y to -ence.)

IL'O.KWENT

(See **IL'O.KWĒ,** change concluding -y to -ent.)

IL'O.KWIST

(See **IL'O.KWĒ,** change concluding -y to -ist.)

IL'O.KWĪZ

(See **IL'O.KWĒ,** change concluding -y to -ize.)

IL'O.KWIZM

(See **IL'O.KWĒ,** change concluding -y to -ism.)

IL'O.KWUS

(See **IL'O.KWĒ,** change concluding -y to -ous.)

IL'YEN.SĒ

BRIL'YEN.SĒ brilliancy
SIL'YEN.SĒ transiliency
ZIL'YEN.SĒ resiliency

IL'YER.Ē

BIL'YER.Ē atrabiliary, biliary, nobiliary
MIL'YER.Ē miliary
SIL'YER.Ē domiciliary, superciliary
ZIL'YER.Ē auxiliary

IM'A.NUS

DIM'A.NUS pedimanous
JIM'A.NUS longimanous

IM'A.THĒ

SIM'A.THĒ opsimathy
TIM'A.THĒ timothy, Timothy

IM'BRI.KĪT

IM'BRI.KĪT imbricate
FIM'BRI.KĪT fimbricate

Ī'ME.NĒ

KRĪ'ME.NĒ crimeny
SĪ'ME.NĒ simony

IM'E.NĒ

JIM'E.NĒ jiminy
SIM'E.NĒ simony
TIM'E.NĒ antimony

Ī'MER.Ē

PRĪ'MER.Ē primary
RĪ'MER.Ē rhymery

IM'ER.Ē

GLIM'ER.Ē	glimmery
SHIM'ER.Ē	shimmery
SIM'ER.Ē	simmery

IM'ER.ING

GLIM'ER.ING	glimmering
SHIM'ER.ING	shimmering
SIM'ER.ING	simmering

IM'ER.US

DIM'ER.US	dimerous
GLIM'ER.US	glimmerous
LIM'ER.US	polymerous
TRIM'ER.US	trimerous

IM'E.TER

DIM'E.TER	acidimeter, dimeter
LIM'E.TER	alkalimeter, delimiter, limiter, polymeter, salimeter
NIM'E.TER	planimeter
RIM'E.TER	calorimeter, colorimeter, perimeter, polarimeter, saccharimeter, solarimeter, vaporimeter
SIM'E.TER	dasymeter, dousimeter, dosimeter, focimeter, licimeter, pulsimeter, rhysimeter, scimitar, tasimeter, velocimeter, zymosimeter
TIM'E.TER	altimeter, *centimeter*, voltimeter
TRIM'E.TER	trimeter
VIM'E.TER	gravimeter, pelvimeter

IM'E.TRĒ

DIM'E.TRĒ	acidimetry, oxidimetry
LIM'E.TRĒ	alkalimetry
NIM'E.TRĒ	planimetry
RIM'E.TRĒ	dolorimetry, calorimetry, perimetry, polarimetry

SIM'E.TRĒ	asymmetry, dyssemetry, symmetry
THIM'E.TRĒ	bathymetry
TIM'E.TRĒ	altimetry

IM'I.A

LIM'I.A	bulimia
MIM'I.A	hypermimia, paramimia
SIM'I.A	Simia
THIM'I.A	parathymia, pikithymia

IM'I.AN

DIM'I.AN	Endymion
PIM'I.AN	opimian
SIM'I.AN	prosimian, simian

IM'I.KAL

KIM'I.KAL	alchymical
MIM'I.KAL	mimical, pantomimical
NIM'I.KAL	anonymical, homonymical, inimical, metonymical, patronymical, toponymical

IM'IK.RĒ

GIM'IK.RĒ	gimmickry
MIM'IK.RĒ	mimicry, theriomimicry

IM'I.NAL

BIM'I.NAL	bimanal
JIM'I.NAL	regiminal
KRIM'I.NAL	criminal
LIM'I.NAL	liminal, subliminal
VIM'I.NAL	viminal, Viminal

IM'I.NĀT

KRIM'I.NĀT	discriminate, incriminate, indiscriminate, criminate, recriminate
LIM'I.NĀT	eliminate

IM'I.NĒ

BIM'I.NĒ	Bimini
JIM'I.NĒ	jiminy
KRIM'I.NĒ	criminy
LIM'I.NĒ	postliminy
PIM'I.NĒ	nimini-pimini

Ī'MI.NES

GRĪ'MI.NES	griminess
LĪ'MI.NES	liminess
RĪ'MI.NES	riminess
SLĪ'MI.NES	sliminess

IM'I.NUS

KRIM'I.NUS	criminous
LIM'I.NUS	moliminous

IM'I.ON

(See **IM'I.AN**)

IM'I.TĀT

IM'I.TĀT	imitate
LIM'I.TĀT	delimitate, limitate

IM'I.TĒ

DIM'I.TĒ	dimity
LIM'I.TĒ	limity, ophelimity, sublimity
NIM'I.TĒ	anonymity, equanimity, longanimity, magnanimity, parvanimity, pusillanimity, sanctanimity, pseudonymity, synonymity, unanimity
SIM'I.TĒ	proximity, simity

IM'I.TER

(See **IM'E.TER**)

IM'I.TRĒ

(See **IM'E.TRĒ**)

IM'PER.ER

HWIM'PER.ER	whimperer
SIM'PER.ER	simperer

IM'PER.ING

HWIM'PER.ING whimpering
SIM'PER.ING simpering

IM'Ū.LANT

SIM'Ū.LANT simulant
STIM'Ū.LANT stimulant

IM'Ū.LĀT

SIM'Ū.LĀT assimulate, dissimulate, simulate
STIM'Ū.LĀT stimulate, restimulate

IM'Ū.LUS

LIM'Ū.LUS limulus
STIM'Ū.LUS stimulus

ĪN'A.BL

BĪN'A.BL combinable, uncombinable
FĪN'A.BL definable, finable, indefinable, refinable, unfinable, unrefinable
KLĪN'A.BL declinable, inclinable, indeclinable
LĪN'A.BL linable
MĪN'A.BL minable, unminable
PĪN'A.BL opinable
SĪN'A.BL assignable, consignable, signable
TWĪN'A.BL intertwinable, twinable, untwinable
VĪN'A.BL divinable, undivinable
ZĪN'A.BL designable

IN'A.BL

HIN'A.BL hinnible
PIN'A.BL pinnable
SKIN'A.BL skinnable
WIN'A.BL winnable

ĪN'A.BLĒ

KLĪN'A.BLĒ declinably
FĪN'A.BLĒ definably, undefinably

SĪN'A.BLĒ assignably, unassignably

IN'A.KL

BIN'A.KL binnacle, binocle, rabbinical
FIN'A.KL finical
KLIN'A.KL clinical, synclinical
MIN'A.KL adminicle, Brahmnical, dominical, cominical, flaminical
PIN'A.KL pinnacle
SIN'A.KL Sinical, cynical

Ī'NA.LĒ

FĪ'NA.LĒ finally
SPĪ'NA.LĒ spinally

Ī'NA.RĒ

(See Ī'NE.RĒ)

IN'A.TIV

(See IN'I.TIV)

IN'CHING.LĒ

(See INCH, add -ingly where appropriate.)

ĪN'DE.RĒ

BĪN'DE.RĒ bindery
GRĪN'DE.RĒ grindery

IN'DER.Ē

SIN'DER.Ē cindery
TIN'DER.Ē tindery

IN'DI.KĀT

IN'DI.KĀT indicate, contraindicate
SIN'DI.KĀT syndicate
VIN'DI.KĀT vindicate

IN'E.MA

(See IN'I.MA)

IN'E.RĀT

SIN'E.RĀT incinerate
TIN'E.RĀT itinerate

Ī'NE.RĒ

BĪ'NE.RĒ binary
FĪ'NE.RĒ finery, refinery
KWĪ'NE.RĒ quinary
MĪ'NE.RĒ minery
PĪ'NE.RĒ alpinery, pinery
SWĪ'NE.RĒ swinery
VĪ'NE.RĒ vinery
WĪ'NE.RĒ winery

ING'GER.ER

FING'GER.ER fingerer
LING'GER.ER lingerer, malingerer

ING'GER.ING

FING'GER.ING fingering
LING'GER.ING lingering, malingering

ING'GŪ.LĀT

LING'GŪ.LĀT lingulate
SING'GŪ.LĀT cingulate

INGK'A.BL

DRINGK'A.BL drinkable, undrinkable
LINGK'A.BL linkable, unlinkable
SHRINGK'A.BL shrinkable, unshrinkable
SINGK'A.BL sinkable, unsinkable
THINGK'A.BL thinkable, unthinkable
WINGK'A.BL winkable

INGK'I.NES

INGK'I.NES inkiness
KINGK'I.NES kinkiness
PINGK'I.NES pinkiness
SLINGK'I.NES slinkiness

INGK'ING.LĒ

(See INGK, add -ingly where appropriate.)

INGK'WI.TĒ

JINGK'WI.TĒ	longinquity
PINGK'WI.TĒ	propinquity

IN'I.A

IN'I.A	inia
BIN'I.A	robinia
DIN'I.A	anodynia, oneirodynia, pleurodynia, Sardinia
HIN'I.A	bauhinia
JIN'I.A	albuginea, discalloginia, Virginia
LIN'I.A	linea
SIN'I.A	Abyssinia, dosinia, Dulcinia, gloxinia, lacinia, vaccinia
TIN'I.A	actinia, Nemertinea, tinea
VIN'I.A	vinea
ZIN'I.A	zinnia

IN'I.AL

IN'I.AL	inial
FIN'I.AL	finial
GWIN'I.AL	consanguineal, sanguineal
LIN'I.AL	interlineal, lineal, matrilineal, patrilineal
MIN'I.AL	dominial, gramineal, stamineal
PIN'I.AL	pineal
TIN'I.AL	pectineal, tineal
VIN'I.AL	vineal

IN'I.AN

DIN'I.AN	Sardinian
FIN'I.AN	Delphinian
JIN'I.AN	anthropophaginian, Carthaginian, viraginian, Virginian
LIN'I.AN	Carolinian, sterquilinian
MIN'I.AN	Arminian, Flaminian
RIN'I.AN	leptorrhinian, czarinian
SIN'I.AN	Abyssinian
TIN'I.AN	Augustinian, Justinian, Palestinean, serpentinean
WIN'I.AN	Darwinian

(See **INYUN**)

IN'I.ĀT

LIN'I.ĀT	delineate, lineate
MIN'I.ĀT	miniate
SIN'I.ĀT	laciniate

Ī'NI.ER

BRĪ'NI.ER	brinier
SHĪ'NI.ER	shinier
SPĪ'NI.ER	spinier
TĪ'NI.ER	tinier
WĪ'NI.ER	winier

IN'I.ER

DRIN'I.ER	Fourdrinier
FIN'I.ER	finnier
LIN'I.ER	colinear, bilinear, interlinear, curvilinear, linear, rectilinear, trilinear
SKIN'I.ER	skinnier
TIN'I.ER	tinnier

IN'I.FÔRM

MIN'I.FÔRM	aluminiform
SIN'I.FÔRM	laciniform
TIN'I.FÔRM	actiniform

IN'I.KIN

FIN'I.KIN	finikin
MIN'I.KIN	minikin

IN'I.KL

(See **IN'A.KL**)

IN'I.MA

MIN'I.MA	minima
SIN'I.MA	cinema

IN'I.MENT

LIN'I.MENT	liniment
MIN'I.MENT	miniment

IN'ISH.ER

FIN'ISH.ER	finisher
MIN'ISH.ER	diminisher

IN'ISH.ING

FIN'ISH.ING	finishing, refinishing
MIN'ISH.ING	diminishing, undiminishing

IN'IS.TER

MIN'IS.TER	administer, minister
SIN'IS.TER	ambisinister, sinister

IN'IS.TRAL

MIN'IS.TRAL	ministral
SIN'IS.TRAL	dextrosinistral, sinistral

IN'I.TĒ

FIN'I.TĒ	affinity, diffinity, finity, infinity, confinity
GRIN'I.TĒ	peregrinity
GWIN'I.TĒ	exsanguinity, consanguinity, sanguinity
JIN'I.TĒ	viraginity, virginity
LIN'I.TĒ	alkalinity, felinity, masculinity, salinity
NIN'I.TĒ	asininity, caninity, femininity
SIN'I.TĒ	inconcinnity, concinnity, vicinity
TIN'I.TĒ	Latinity, satinity
TRIN'I.TĒ	trinity
VIN'I.TĒ	divinity, patavinity

IN'I.TIV

BIN'I.TIV	combinative
FIN'I.TIV	affinitive, definitive, finitive, infinitive
MIN'I.TIV	carminitive

JOGGER, JOG!

Jogger, jog, and runner, run!
How I envy you your fun!
Agony distorts your face;
Yet I know some hidden grace—
Some ebullient, inner leaven—
Raises you to joggers' heaven.

Jogger, gasping by the road,
Easing lungs of overload,
May I have your name, old scout?
If the leaven should run out—
If you jog off to your Maker—
I will call the undertaker.

IN'I.UM

FIN'I.UM	delphinium
JIN'I.UM	virginium
KLIN'I.UM	androclinium, triclinium
LIN'I.UM	gadolinium, illinium
MIN'I.UM	aluminium, dominium, condominium, minium, postliminium
RIN'I.UM	perineum
SIN'I.UM	tirocinium
TIN'I.UM	actinium, protactinium

IN'I.US

BIN'I.US	rubineous
DIN'I.US	testudineous
GWIN'I.US	consanguineous, sanguineous
JIN'I.US	cartilagineous
MIN'I.US	flamineous, fulmineous, gramineous, ignominious, stamineous, stramineous, vimineous

IN'JEN.SĒ

FRIN'JEN.SĒ	refringency
STRIN'JEN.SĒ	astringency, constringency, stringency
TIN'JEN.SĒ	contingency

IN'JI.LĒ

DIN'JI.LĒ	dingily
STIN'JI.LĒ	stingily

IN'JI.NES

DIN'JI.NES	dinginess
STIN'JI.NES	stinginess

IN'LAN.DER

IN'LAN.DER	inlander
FIN'LAN.DER	Finlander

IN'O.LIN

KRIN'O.LIN	crinoline
KWIN'O.LIN	quinoline

Ī'NŌ.MI.AL

BĪ'NŌ.MI.AL	binomial
TRI'NŌ.MI.AL	trinomial

IN'SING.LĒ

MIN'SING.LĒ	mincingly
VIN'SING.LĒ	convincingly

IN'TE.GRĀT

IN'TE.GRĀT	integrate, reintegrate
DIN'TE.GRĀT	redintegrate
SIN'TE.GRĀT	disintegrate

IN'TER.Ē

PRIN'TER.Ē	printery
SPLIN'TER.Ē	splintery
WIN'TER.Ē	wintery

(See INTRĒ)

IN'TER.ING

SPLIN'TER.ING	splintering
WIN'TER.ING	wintering

IN'THI.AN

RIN'THI.AN	Corinthian, labyrinthian
SIN'THI.AN	absinthian, hyacinthian

IN'Ū.ĀT

SIN'Ū.ĀT	insinuate, sinuate
TIN'Ū.ĀT	continuate

IN'Ū.IT

IN'Ū.IT	Innuit
SIN'Ū.IT	sinuate

IN'Ū.US

SIN'Ū.US	sinuous

TIN'Ū.US	discontinuous, continuous

Ī'O.FĪT

BRĪ'O.FĪT	bryophite
KRĪ'O.FĪT	cryophite

Ī'O.JEN

BĪ'O.JEN	biogen
KRĪ'O.JEN	cryogen

Ī'O.LA

RĪ'O.LA	variola
VĪ'O.LA	viola, Viola

Ī'O.LET

STRĪ'O.LET	striolet
TRĪ'O.LET	triolet
VĪ'O.LET	violet

Ī'O.LIN

(See I'A.LIN)

Ī'O.LIST

SĪ'O.LIST	sciolist
VĪ'O.LIST	violist

Ī'O.LĪT

(See I'A.LĪT)

Ī'O.LUS

DĪ'O.LUS	gladiolus, modiolus, Modiolus
RĪ'O.LUS	variolous
SĪ'O.LUS	sciolous

Ī'O.NĪZ

Ī'O.NĪZ	ionize
KĪ'O.NĪZ	kyanize
LĪ'O.NĪZ	lionize

Ī'O.PĒ

BĪ'O.PĒ	presbyopy
LĪ'O.PĒ	calliope
MĪ'O.PĒ	myopy

Ī'O.SĒN

MĪ'O.SĒN	Miocene, post-Miocene
PLĪ'O.SĒN	Pliocene, post-Pliocene

Ī'O.SIS

(See **Ī'A.SIS**)

Ī'O.SKŌP

(See **Ī'A.SKŌP**)

IP'A.BL

CHIP'A.BL	chippable
DIP'A.BL	dippable
KLIP'A.BL	clippable
NIP'A.BL	nippable
PIP'A.BL	pippable
RIP'A.BL	rippable
SHIP'A.BL	shippable
TIP'A.BL	tippable

IP'A.RA

(See **IP'A.RUS**, change -ous to -a.)

Ī'PÄR'TĪT

BĪ'PÄR'TĪT	bipartite
TRĪ'PÄR'TĪT	tripartite

IP'AR.US

IP'AR.US	deiparous
BIP'AR.US	ambiparous, biparous
DIP'AR.US	frondiparous
LIP'AR.US	gemelliparous, nulliparous, polyparous
MIP'AR.US	gemmiparous, primiparous, vermiparous
NIP'AR.US	criniparous, omniparous, uniparous
PIP'AR.US	opiparous
RIP'AR.US	floriparous, pluriparous, sudoriparous
SIP'AR.US	fissiparous
TIP'AR.US	dentiparous, fructiparous, multiparous, sextiparous
VIP'AR.US	larviparous, oviparous, ovoviparous, viviparous

IP'A.THĒ

NIP'A.THĒ	somnipathy
TIP'A.THĒ	antipathy

IP'A.THIST

NIP'A.THIST	somnipathist
TIP'A.THIST	antipathist

IP'ER.Ē

FLIP'ER.Ē	flippery
FRIP'ER.Ē	frippery
SLIP'ER.Ē	slippery

IP'E.TAL

(See **IP'I.TAL**)

IP'I.ENT

PIP'I.ENT	pipient
SIP'I.ENT	appercipient, desipient, incipient, insipient, percipient, recipient

IP'I.NES

(See **IPĒ**, add -ness)

ĪP'ING.LĒ

GRĪP'ING.LĒ	gripingly
PĪP'ING.LĒ	pipingly

IP'I.TAL

SIP'I.TAL	ancipital, bicipital, occipital
TRIP'I.TAL	centripetal

IP'I.TUS

DIP'I.TUS	serendipitous
KRIP'I.TUS	lucripetous
SIP'I.TUS	precipitous

IP'LI.KĀT

KWIP'LI.KĀT	sesquiplicate
TRIP'LI.KĀT	triplicate

IP'I.TAL

SIP'I.TAL	ancipetal, basipetal, bicipital, occipital, sincipital
TRIP'I.TAL	centripetal

IP'O.DĒ

DIP'O.DĒ	dipody
TRIP'O.DĒ	tripody

IP'O.DĒZ

DIP'O.DĒZ	dipodies, Pheidippides
RIP'O.DĒZ	Euripides
TIP'O.DĒZ	antipodes

IP'O.LĒ

LIP'O.LĒ	Gallipoli
TRIP'O.LĒ	Tripoli

IP'O.TENS

MIP'O.TENS	armipotence
NIP'O.TENS	ignipotence, omnipotence, plenipotence

IP'O.TENT

IP'O.TENT	deipotent
LIP'O.TENT	bellipotent
MIP'O.TENT	armipotent
NIP'O.TENT	ignipotent, omnipotent, plenipotent
RIP'O.TENT	viripotent
TIP'O.TENT	cunctipotent, multipotent, noctipotent
TRIP'O.TENT	ventripotent

IP'TER.AL

DIP'TER.AL	dipteral
MIP'TER.AL	hemipteral
RIP'TER.AL	peripteral

IP'TER.US

DIP'TER.US	dipterous
RIP'TER.US	peripterous
TRIP'TER.US	tripterous

IP'TI.KAL

GLIP'TI.KAL	glyptical
KLIP'TI.KAL	ecliptical
KRIP'TI.KAL	cryptical, procryptical
LIP'TI.KAL	apocalyptical, elliptical

IP'Ū.LAR

NIP'Ū.LAR	manipular
STIP'Ū.LAR	stipular

IP'Ū.LĀT

DIP'Ū.LĀT	pedipulate
NIP'Ū.LĀT	manipulate
STIP'Ū.LĀT	astipulate, stipulate

ĪR'A.BL

(See ĪR, add -able where appropriate.)

IR'A.KL

(See IR'I.KL)

Ī'RA.SĒ

PĪ'RA.SĒ	piracy
TĪ'RA.SĒ	retiracy

IR'A.SĒ

LIR'A.SĒ	deliracy
SPIR'A.SĒ	conspiracy

Ī'RĀT.ED

JĪ'RĀT.ED	gyrated
SPĪ'RĀT.ED	spirated

ÎR'FUL.Ē

CHÎR'FUL.Ē	cheerfully
FÎR'FUL.Ē	fearfully
TÎR'FUL.Ē	tearfully

ÎR'FUL.NES

ÎR'FUL.NES	irefulness
DÎR'FUL.NES	direfulness
ZÎR'FUL.NES	desirefulness

ÎR'FUL.NES

(See ÎRFUL, add -ness where appropriate.)

ÎR'I.A

ÎR'I.A	eria
BÎR'I.A	Iberia, Liberia, Siberia
FÎR'I.A	feria
JÎR'I.A	Algeria, Egeria, Nigeria
MÎR'I.A	krameria, cryptomeria, latimeria
PÎR'I.A	Hesperia
SÎR'I.A	ceria
SKLÎR'I.A	scleria
THÎR'I.A	diphtheria, gaulthiria
TÎR'I.A	acroteria, asteria, bacteria, hysteria, cafeteria, criteria, nitrobacteria, wisteria, washateria
VÎR'I.A	echeveria, sanseveria

(See IR'I.A)

IR'I.A

FIR'I.A	porphyria
KIR'I.A	Valkyria
LIR'I.A	Elyria, Illyria
SIR'I.A	Assyria, Syria
STIR'I.A	Styria

(See ÎR'I.A)

ÎR'I.AD

PÎR'I.AD	period
TÎR'I.AD	anteriad, posteriad

(See IR'I.AD)

IR'I.AD

MIR'I.AD	myriad

(See ÎR'I.AD)

ÎR'I.AL

ÎR'I.AL	aerial
DÎR'I.AL	intersiderial, siderial
FÎR'I.AL	ferial
JÎR'I.AL	managerial
NÎR'I.AL	funereal, manereal, venereal
PÎR'I.AL	imperial
SÎR'I.AL	biserial, rhinocerial, cereal, serial
THÎR'I.AL	diphtherial, ethereal, therial
TÎR'I.AL	arterial, asterial, bacterial, immaterial, magisterial, material, ministerial, monasterial, presbyterial
ZÎR'I.AL	vizerial

ÎR'I.A.LIST

PÎR'I.A.LIST	imperialist
THÎR'I.A.LIST	etherealist
TÎR'I.A.LIST	immaterialist, materialist

ÎR'I.A.LĪZ

SÎR'I.A.LĪZ	serialize
TÎR'I.A.LĪZ	arterialize, dematerialize, immaterialize, materialize
THÎR'I.A.LĪZ	etherealize

ÎR'I.A.LIZM

PÎR'I.A.LIZM	imperialism
THÎR'I.A.LIZM	etherealism
TÎR'I.A.LIZM	immaterialism, materialism

ÎR'I.AN

ÎR'I.AN	aerian, Erian, Pierian
BÎR'I.AN	Iberian, Liberian, Siberian
FÎR'I.AN	Luciferian
JÎR'I.AN	Algerian
LÎR'I.AN	allerion, Keplerian, valerian
MÎR'I.AN	Cimmerian, Sumerian
NÎR'I.AN	Wagnerian

PÎR'I.AN   Hesperian,
                Hyperion,
                Shakespearean
SÎR'I.AN   Chaucerian,
                Spencerian,
                Spenserian, tricerion
STÎR'I.AN   phalansterian
TÎR'I.AN   criterion,
                Presbyterian,
                psalterian
THÎR'I.AN   philotherian,
                metatherian,
                prototherian,
                eutherian
VÎR'I.AN   Hanoverian
ZÎR'I.AN   mezereon

(See **IR'I.AN**)

IR'I.AN

KIR'I.AN   Valkyrian
SIR'I.AN   Assyrian, Syrian

(See **ÎR'I.AN**)

ÎR'I.ER

ÎR'I.ER   eerier
BÎR'I.ER   beerier
BLÎR'I.ER   blearier
CHÎR'I.ER   cheerier
DRÎR'I.ER   drearier
FÎR'I.ER   inferior
PÎR'I.ER   superior
TÎR'I.ER   anterior, exterior,
                interior, posterior,
                tearier, ulterior
WÎR'I.ER   wearier

ÎR'I.FÔRM

PÎR'I.FÔRM   viperiform
SFÎR'I.FÔRM   spheriform
SÎR'I.FÔRM   seriform

IR'I.KL

JIR'I.KL   panegyrical
LIR'I.KL   lyrical
MIR'I.KL   miracle
PIR'I.KL   empirical,
                metempirical
SPIR'I.KL   spiracle
TIR'I.KL   satirical, satyrical

ÎR'I.LĒ

ÎR'I.LĒ   eerily
BÎR'I.LĒ   beerily
BLÎR'I.LĒ   blearily
CHÎR'I.LĒ   cheerily
DRÎR'I.LĒ   drearily
TÎR'I.LĒ   tearily
WÎR'I.LĒ   wearily

ÎR'I.NES

(See **ÎRĒ**, change -y to -iness where appropriate.)

ĪR'ING.LĒ

KWĪR'ING.LĒ   inquiringly
MĪR'ING.LĒ   admiringly
SPĪR'ING.LĒ   aspiringly,
                  inspiringly,
                  conspiringly
TĪR'ING.LĒ   retiringly, tiringly
ZĪR'ING.LĒ   desiringly

ÎR'ING.LĒ

CHÎR'ING.LĒ   cheeringly
DÎR'ING.LĒ   endearingly
FÎR'ING.LĒ   fearingly,
                  unfearingly
JÎR'ING.LĒ   jeeringly
NÎR'ING.LĒ   domineeringly
PÎR'ING.LĒ   peeringly

ÎR'I.Ō

CHÎR'I.Ō   cheerio
DÎR'I.Ō   deario
SÎR'I.Ō   serio

ÎR'I.OR

(See **ÎR'I.ER**)

IR'I.SIST

LIR'I.SIST   lyricist
PIR'I.SIST   empiricist

IR'I.SIZM

LIR'I.SIZM   lyricism
PIR'I.SIZM   empiricism

ÎR'I.UM

DÎR'I.UM   desiderium
FÎR'I.UM   atmospherium
PÎR'I.UM   imperium,
                puerperium
SÎR'I.UM   cerium
TÎR'I.UM   acroterium,
                apodyterium,
                bacterium,
                deuterium,
                elaterium,
                magisterium,
                ministerium,
                psalterium
THÎR'I.UM   Dinotherium,
                Megatherium,
                Nototherium,
                Paleotherium,
                Titanotherium
ZÎR'I.UM   mezereum

(See **IR'I.UM**)

IR'I.UM

LIR'I.UM   delirium, collyrium

(See **ÎR'I.UM**)

ÎR'I.US

BÎR'I.US   Tiberius
DÎR'I.US   siderious
NÎR'I.US   cinerious
PÎR'I.US   imperious,
                suspirious
SÎR'I.US   jocoserious,
                ludicroserious,
                cereous, cereus,
                serious
STÎR'I.US   stirious
THÎR'I.US   ethereous
TÎR'I.US   deleterious,
                mysterious

(See **IR'I.US**)

IR'I.US

LIR'I.US   delirious
SIR'I.US   Sirius

(See **ÎR'I.US**)

ÎR'LES.NES

BÎR'LES.NES   beerlessness
CHÎR'LES.NES   cheerlessness

FÎR′LES.NES   fearlessness
PÎR′LES.NES   peerlessness

Ī′RO.NĒ

Ī′RO.NĒ   irony
JĪ′RO.NĒ   gyrony
SĪ′RO.NĒ   sireny

ĪS′A.BL

PRĪS′A.BL   priceable, unpriceable
SLĪS′A.BL   sliceable, unsliceable
SPĪS′A.BL   spiceable, unspiceable
RĪS′A.BL   riceable, unriceable
TĪS′A.BL   enticeable, unenticeable

IS′A.BL

(See **IS′I.BL**)

IS′A.BLĒ

(See **IS′I.BLĒ**)

IS′CHOO.LA

FIS′CHOO.LA   fistula
VIS′CHOO.LA   Vistula

IS′EN.ER

KRIS′EN.ER   christener
LIS′EN.ER   listener

IS′EN.ING

GLIS′EN.ING   glistening
KRIS′EN.ING   christening
LIS′EN.ING   listening

IS′ER.ĀT

VIS′ER.ĀT   eviscerate, viscerate

(See **IS′ER.IT**)

IS′ER.IT

LIS′ER.IT   chelicerate

(See **IS′ER.ĀT**)

Ī′SE.RĒ

RĪ′SE.RĒ   derisory, irrisory
SĪ′SE.RĒ   decisory, incisory
SPĪ′SE.RĒ   spicery

(See **Ī′ZER.Ē**)

IS′ER.Ē

MIS′ER.Ē   admissory, dimissory, dismissory, emissory, remissory
SIS′ER.Ē   rescissory

ISH′AL.Ē

(See **ISHAL**, add -ly.)

ISH′AL.IZM

DISH′AL.IZM   judicialism
FISH′AL.IZM   officialism

ISH′EN.SĒ

FISH′EN.SĒ   beneficiency, deficiency, efficiency, inefficiency, insufficiency, proficiency, self-sufficiency, sufficiency
LISH′EN.SĒ   alliciency

ISH′ENT.LĒ

(See **ISHENT**, add -ly where appropriate.)

ISH′ER.Ē

DISH′ER.Ē   judiciary
FISH′ER.Ē   beneficiary, officiary
TISH′ER.Ē   justiciary

ISH′I.A

DISH′I.A   indicia
LISH′I.A   Galicia
MISH′I.A   comitia
NISH′I.A   Phoenicia, Tunisia
SISH′I.A   apositia, asitia, syssitia
TISH′I.A   adventitia, noticia

ISH′I.ĀT

FISH′I.ĀT   maleficiate, officiate
NISH′I.ĀT   initiate
PISH′I.ĀT   propitiate

(See **ISH′I.IT**)

ISH′I.ENS

(See **ISHENS**)

ISH′I.ENT

(See **ISHENT**)

ISH′I.IT

NISH′I.IT   initiate
TRISH′I.IT   patriciate
VISH′I.IT   novitiate, vitiate

(See **ISH′I.ĀT**)

ISH′UN.AL

ISH′UN.AL   intuitional, tuitional
BISH′UN.AL   exhibitional
DISH′UN.AL   additional, conditional, preconditional, traditional, unconditional
LISH′UN.AL   salicional, volitional
MISH′UN.AL   commissional, missional
NISH′UN.AL   definitional, recognitional
SISH′UN.AL   transitional
TISH′UN.AL   petitional, repetitional
TRISH′UN.AL   nutritional
ZISH′UN.AL   *D* depositional, disquisitional, dispositional, *E* expositional, *I* impositional, inquisitional, *K* compositional, *P* positional, *PR* prepositional, propositional, *S* suppositional, *TR* transitional, transpositional

ISH′UN.ER

BISH′UN.ER   exhibitioner
DISH′UN.ER   conditioner, traditioner

LISH'UN.ER	coalitioner
MISH'UN.ER	commissioner, missioner
NISH'UN.ER	admonitioner
RISH'UN.ER	parishioner
TISH'UN.ER	partitioner, petitioner, practitioner

ISH'UN.ING

DISH'UN.ING	conditioning, auditioning, reconditioning, traditioning
FISH'UN.ING	fissioning, refissioning
MISH'UN.ING	commissioning, missioning
PISH'UN.ING	suspicioning
TISH'UN.ING	partitioning, petitioning, repetitioning
ZISH'UN.ING	positioning, repositioning

ISH'UN.IST

BISH'UN.IST	exhibitionist, prohibitionist
DISH'UN.IST	traditionist
LISH'UN.IST	abolitionist, coalitionist
ZISH'UN.IST	oppositionist, requisitionist

ISH'US.LĒ

(See **ISHUS,** add *-ly* where appropriate.)

ISH'US.NES

(See **ISHUS,** add *-ness* where appropriate.)

IS'I.BL

KIS'I.BL	kissable, unkissable
MIS'I.BL	*A* admissible, amissible, *D* dismissible, *I* immiscible, incommiscible, irremissable, *M* miscible, missable, *O* omissible, *P* permiscible, permissible, *R* remissable, *TR*

	transmissible, *U* unpermissable, untransmissible
SIS'I.BL	scissible
VIS'I.BL	obliviscible

IS'I.BLĒ

KIS'I.BLĒ	kissably
MIS'I.BLĒ	admissibly, permissibly
SIS'I.BLĒ	scissibly
VIS'I.BLĒ	obliviscibly

Ī'SI.ER

Ī'SI.ER	icier
SPĪ'SI.ER	spicier

IS'I.ER

KIS'I.ER	kissier
PRIS'I.ER	prissier
SIS'I.ER	sissier

Ī'SI.KL

Ī'SI.KL	icicle
BĪ'SI.KL	bicycle
TRĪ'SI.KL	tricycle

Ī'SI.LĒ

Ī'SI.LĒ	icily
SPĪ'SI.LĒ	spicily

IS'I.LĒ

PRIS'I.LĒ	prissily
SIS'I.LĒ	Sicily, sissily

IS'I.MŌ

CHIS'I.MŌ	dolcissimo
LIS'I.MŌ	generalissimo
NIS'I.MŌ	pianissimo
TIS'I.MŌ	altissimo, fortissimo, prestissimo
VIS'I.MŌ	bravissimo

IS'I.NAL

DIS'I.NAL	fidicinal, medicinal
FIS'I.NAL	officinal

PIS'I.NAL	piscinal
TIS'I.NAL	vaticinal
VIS'I.NAL	vicinal

Ī'SI.NES

Ī'SI.NES	iciness
RĪ'SI.NES	riceyness
SPĪ'SI.NES	spiciness

IS'I.PĀT

DIS'I.PĀT	dissipate
TIS'I.PĀT	anticipate, participate

IS'I.TĒ

IS'I.TĒ	stoicity
BIS'I.TĒ	cubicity, nullibicity
BRIS'I.TĒ	lubricity, rubricity
DIS'I.TĒ	benedicity, immundicity, impudicity, mendicity, periodicity, pudicity, spheroidicity
LIS'I.TĒ	alcoholicity, evangelicity, felicity, helicity, infelicity, catholicity, Catholicity, publicity, triplicity
MIS'I.TĒ	atomicity, endemicity
NIS'I.TĒ	atonicity, electronicity, canonicity, conicity, tonicity, volcanicity, vulcanicity, unicity
PIS'I.TĒ	hygroscopicity
PLIS'I.TĒ	accomplicity, duplicity, complicity, quadruplicity, multiplicity, simplicity, triplicity
RIS'I.TĒ	historicity, caloricity, sphericity
SIS'I.TĒ	basicity, toxicity
TIS'I.TĒ	*A* achromaticity, *D* domesticity, *E* elasticity, ellipticity, ensynopticity, *H* heteroscedasticity, homoscedasticity, *I* inelasticity, *K*

causticity, *KR*
chromaticity, *M*
mysticity, *O*
authenticity,
autopticity, *P*
pepticity, *PL*
plasticity, *R*
rusticity, *S* septicity,
SP spasticity, *ST*
stypticity, *V*
verticity, vorticity, *Y*
eupepticity
egocentricity,
eccentricity,
electricity,
photoelectricity,
hydroelectricity,
concentricity,
centricity, tetricity,
thermoelectricity

TRIS'I.TĒ

IS'IT.LĒ

LIS'IT.LĒ   illicitly, licitly
PLIS'IT.LĒ   explicitly, implicitly

IS'IT.NES

LIS'IT.NES   illicitness, licitness
PLIS'IT.NES   explicitness,
     implicitness

IS'I.TŪD

LIS'I.TŪD   solicitude
SIS'I.TŪD   vicissitude
SPIS'I.TŪD   spissitude

Ī'SIV.LĒ

RĪ'SIV.LĒ   derisively
SĪ'SIV.LĒ   decisively,
     incisively,
     indecisively

Ī'SIV.NES

RĪ'SIV.NES   derisiveness
SĪ'SIV.NES   decisiveness,
     indecisiveness,
     incisiveness

IS'KI.ER

FRIS'KI.ER   friskier
RIS'KI.ER   riskier

ISK'I.LĒ

FRISK'I.LĒ   friskily
RISK'I.LĒ   riskily

IS'Ō.NUS

NIS'Ō.NUS   unisonous
TIS'Ō.NUS   fluctisonous

IS'OR.Ē

(See **IS'ER.Ē**)

IS'TEN.SĒ

DIS'TEN.SĒ   distancy
SIS'TEN.SĒ   inconsistency,
     insistency,
     consistency,
     persistency,
     subsistency
ZIS'TEN.SĒ   existency,
     pre-existency

IS'TENT.LĒ

DIS'TENT.LĒ   distantly
SIS'TENT.LĒ   inconsistently,
     insistently, consistently,
     persistently,
     subsistently
ZIS'TENT.LĒ   existently,
     pre-existently

IS'TER.Ē

BIS'TER.Ē   bistoury
BLIS'TER.Ē   blistery
DIS'TER.Ē   faldistory
HIS'TER.Ē   history, prehistory,
     protohistory,
     psychohistory
MIS'TER.Ē   mystery
SIS'TER.Ē   consistory
TIS'TER.Ē   baptistery

IST'FUL.Ē

LIST'FUL.Ē   listfully
WIST'FUL.Ē   wistfully

IS'TI.KAL

IS'TI.KAL   atheistical, deistical,
     egoistical,

casuistical,
pantheistical,
theistical,
euphuistical
DIS'TI.KAL   methodistical
FIS'TI.KAL   paragraphistical,
     sophistical,
     theosophistical
GWIS'TI.KAL   linguistical
JIS'TI.KAL   dialogistical,
     logistical,
     synergistical,
     eulogistical
KIS'TI.KAL   anarchistical,
     antanarchistical,
     catechistical
LIS'TI.KAL   anomalistical,
     cabalistical
MIS'TI.KAL   alchemistical,
     hemistichal,
     chemistical,
     mystical,
     euphemistical
NIS'TI.KAL   agonistical,
     antagonistical,
     Calvinistical,
     canonistical,
     synchronistical
PIS'TI.KAL   papistical
RIS'TI.KAL   aoristical,
     aphoristical,
     eristical,
     hypocoristical,
     juristical,
     characteristical,
     puristical,
     eucharistical
TIS'TI.KAL   artistical, egotistical,
     pietistical,
     statistical,
     syncretistical
THIS'TI.KAL   apathistical
TRIS'TI.KAL   patristical

IS'TI.KĀT

FIS'TI.KĀT   sophisticate
JIS'TI.KĀT   dephlogisticate,
     phlogisticate

IS'TI.KUS

DIS'TI.KUS   distichous
TRIS'TI.KUS   tristichous

IST'LES.NES

LIST'LES.NES   listlessness
ZIST'LES.NES   resistlessness

IS′TOR.Ē

(See IS′TER.Ē)

IS′TŪ.LA

(See IS′CHOO.LA)

Ī′SUL.FĪD

BĪ′SUL.FĪD	*bisulphide*
DĪ′SUL.FĪD	*disulfide*

ĪT′A.BL

DĪT′A.BL	extraditable, indictable, inditable, unindictable, uninditable
KWĪT′A.BL	requitable, unrequitable
LĪT′A.BL	lightable, unlightable
NĪT′A.BL	ignitable, reunitable, unignitable, unitable, ununitable
RĪT′A.BL	writable, unwritable
SĪT′A.BL	excitable, incitable, recitable, citable, sightable, unexcitable, unincitable, uncitable, unsightable

IT′A.BL

FIT′A.BL	fittable, unfittable
HIT′A.BL	hittable, Mehitable, unhittable
KWIT′A.BL	acquittable, quittable, unacquittable
MIT′A.BL	admittable, committable, omittable, permittable, submittable, transmittable, unadmittable, unremittable, unsubmittable
NIT′A.BL	knittable, unknittable
PIT′A.BL	pittable

Ī′TA.BLĒ

DĪ′TA.BLĒ	indictably

NĪ′TA.BLĒ	unitably
SĪ′TA.BLĒ	excitably, unexcitably

IT′A.LĒ

(See IT′I.LĒ)

IT′AN.Ē

BRIT′AN.Ē	Brittany
DIT′AN.Ē	dittany
KIT′AN.Ē	kitteny
LIT′AN.Ē	litany

Ī′TA.TIV

KWĪ′TA.TIV	requitative
RĪ′TA.TIV	writative
SĪ′TA.TIV	excitative, incitative, recitative

ĪT′EN.ER

BRĪT′EN.ER	brightener
FRĪT′EN.ER	frightener
HĪT′EN.ER	heightener
HWĪT′EN.ER	whitener
LĪT′EN.ER	enlightener, lightener

(See ÎTNER)

Ī′TEN.ING

(See ÎTEN, add *-ing* where appropriate.)

IT′ER.AL

BIT′ER.AL	presbyteral
LIT′ER.AL	adlittoral, alliteral, biliteral, illiteral, literal, littoral, triliteral

IT′ER.ĀT

IT′ER.ĀT	iterate, reiterate
LIT′ER.ĀT	alliterate, obliterate, transliterate

(See IT′ER.IT)

IT′ER.Ē

GLIT′ER.Ē	glittery
JIT′ER.Ē	jittery

LIT′ER.Ē	littery
TIT′ER.Ē	tittery
TWIT′ER.Ē	twittery

IT′ER.ER

(See ITER, add *-er* where appropriate.)

IT′ER.ING

(See ITER, add *-ing* where appropriate.)

IT′ER.IT

BIT′ER.IT	Presbyterate
LIT′ER.IT	illiterate, literate

(See IT′ER.ĀT)

ĪT′FUL.Ē

FRĪT′FUL.Ē	frightfully
LĪT′FUL.Ē	delightfully
RĪT′FUL.Ē	rightfully
SPĪT′FUL.Ē	spitefully
SPRĪT′FUL.Ē	sprightfully

ITH′ER.Ē

DITH′ER.Ē	dithery
SMITH′ER.Ē	smithery
WITH′ER.Ē	withery

ITH′ER.ING

BLITH′ER.ING	blithering
DITH′ER.ING	dithering
WITH′ER.ING	withering

ITH′I.A

LITH′I.A	lithia
SITH′I.A	forsythia
TITH′I.A	hamartithia

ITH′I.SIS

PITH′I.SIS	epithesis
TITH′I.SIS	antithesis

ĪTH′SUM.LĒ

(TH as in *then*)

BLĪTH′SUM.LĒ	blithesomely
LĪTH′SUM.LĒ	lithesomely

ĪTH′SUM.NES

(TH as in *them*)

BLĪTH′SUM.NES	blithesomeness
LĪTH′SUM.NES	lithesomeness

Ī′TI.ER

FLĪ′TI.ER	flightier
MĪ′TI.ER	almightier, mightier

IT′I.ER

FLIT′I.ER	flittier
GRIT′I.ER	grittier
HWIT′I.ER	Whittier
PRIT′I.ER	prettier
WIT′I.ER	wittier

IT′I.GĀT

LIT′I.GĀT	litigate, vitilitigate
MIT′I.GĀT	mitigate

IT′I.KAL

IT′I.KAL	Jesuitical
KRIT′I.KAL	acritical, diacritical, hypercritical, hypocritical, critical, oneirocritical
LIT′I.KAL	analytical, apolitical, cosmopolitical, metropolitical, political
MIT′I.KAL	eremitical, hermitical, stalagmitical
RIT′I.KAL	soritical
SIT′I.KAL	parasitical, thersitical
TIT′I.KAL	stalactitical
TRIT′I.KAL	tritical
VIT′I.KAL	Levitical

Ī′TI.LĒ

FLĪ′TI.LĒ	flightily
MĪ′TI.LĒ	almightily, mightily
SPRĪ′TI.LĒ	sprightily

IT′I.LĒ

IT′I.LĒ	Italy
GRIT′I.LĒ	grittily

PRIT′I.LĒ	prettily
WIT′I.LĒ	wittily

ĪT′I.NES

(See ĪTĒ, add -ness)

IT′I.NES

(See ITĒ, add -ness)

ĪT′ING.LĒ

BĪT′ING.LĒ	bitingly
BLĪT′ING.LĒ	blightingly
SĪT′ING.LĒ	sightingly
SLĪT′ING.LĒ	slightingly
VĪT′ING.LĒ	invitingly

IT′ING.LĒ

(See IT; ITING; add *-ingly* or *-ly* where appropriate.)

IT′I.SĪD

MIT′I.SĪD	miticide
RIT′I.SĪD	pariticide

IT′I.SĪZ

KRIT′I.SĪZ	criticize
LIT′I.SĪZ	depoliticize, politicize

IT′I.SIZM

BRIT′I.SIZM	Briticism
KRIT′I.SIZM	criticism
WIT′I.SIZM	witticism

ĪT′LI.NES

NĪT′LI.NES	knightliness
SĪT′LI.NES	sightliness
SPRĪT′LI.NES	sprightliness

IT′L.NES

BRIT′L.NES	brittleness
LIT′L.NES	littleness

IT′RI.FĪ

NIT′RI.FĪ	nitrify
VIT′RI.FĪ	vitrify

IT′RI.KA

FIT′RI.KA	amphitrica
RIT′RI.KA	peritricha

IT′Ū.AL

(See ICH′OO.AL)

IT′Ū.LER

(See ICH′OO.LER)

IT′Ū.RĀT

(See ICH′E.RĀT)

ĪV′A.BL

DRĪV′A.BL	drivable, undrivable
PRĪV′A.BL	deprivable
RĪV′A.BL	derivable, underivable
TRĪV′A.BL	contrivable, uncontrivable
VĪV′A.BL	revivable, survivable, unrevivable, unsurvivable

IV′A.BL

GIV′A.BL	forgivable, givable, unforgivable, ungivable
LIV′A.BL	livable, unlivable

IV′A.LENT

BIV′A.LENT	ambivalent, bivalent
DIV′A.LENT	divalent
KWIV′A.LENT	equivalent, quinquivalent
LIV′A.LENT	polyvalent
NIV′A.LENT	omnivalent, univalent
SIV′A.LENT	diversivolent
TIV′A.LENT	multivalent, multivolent
TRIV′A.LENT	trivalent

ĪV′AN.SĒ

NĪV′AN.SĒ	connivancy
TRĪV′AN.SĒ	contrivancy
VĪV′AN.SĒ	survivancy

IV'A.TIV

PRIV'A.TIV	deprivative, privative
RIV'A.TIV	derivative

IV'EL.ER

DRIV'EL.ER	driveller
SIV'EL.ER	civiller
SNIV'EL.ER	sniveller

Ī'VE.RĒ

Ī'VE.RĒ	ivory
VĪ'VE.RĒ	vivary

IV'ER.Ē

KWIV'ER.Ē	quivery
LIV'ER.Ē	delivery, livery
RIV'ER.Ē	rivery
SHIV'ER.Ē	shivery
SLIV'ER.Ē	slivery

IV'ER.ER

LIV'ER.ER	deliverer
KWIV'ER.ER	quiverer
SHIV'ER.ER	shiverer
SLIV'ER.ER	sliverer

IV'ER.ING

(See **IVER,** add -ing where appropriate.)

IV'ER.US

BIV'ER.US	herbivorous
DIV'ER.US	frondivorous
FIV'ER.US	amphivorous
GWIV'ER.US	sanguivorous
JIV'ER.US	frugivorous
KWIV'ER.US	equivorous
LIV'ER.US	mellivorous
MIV'ER.US	limivorous, pomivorous, vermivorous
NIV'ER.US	graminivorous, granivorous, carnivorous, omnivorous, panivorous, ranivorous, sanguinivorous
PIV'ER.US	apivorous, cepivorous
SIV'ER.US	baccivorous, fucivorous, mucivorous, nucivorous, ossivorous, piscivorous, succivorous
TIV'ER.US	fructivorous, phytivorous, photivorous, insectivorous, vegetivorous
VIV'ER.US	ovivorous
ZIV'ER.US	oryzivorous

IV'I.A

LIV'I.A	Bolivia, Olivia
TRIV'I.A	trivia

IV'I.AL

DRIV'I.AL	quadrivial
LIV'I.AL	oblivial
SIV'I.AL	lixivial
TRIV'I.AL	trivial
VIV'I.AL	convivial

IV'ID.LĒ

LIV'ID.LĒ	lividly
VIV'ID.LĒ	vividly

IV'ID.NES

LIV'ID.NES	lividness
VIV'ID.NES	vividness

IV'IL.Ē

SIV'IL.Ē	civilly, uncivilly
SNIV'IL.Ē	snivelly

ĪV'ING.LĒ

(See **ĪV,** add -ingly where appropriate.)

IV'ING.LĒ

(See **IVING,** add -ly where appropriate.)

IV'I.TĒ

KLIV'I.TĒ	acclivity, declivity, proclivity
PRIV'I.TĒ	privity
SIV'I.TĒ	expressivity, emissivity, impassivity, compassivity, passivity
TIV'I.TĒ	A absorptivity, activity, F festivity, hyperactivity, I inactivity, inductivity, incogitativity, instinctivity, K captivity, cogitativity, collectivity, conductivity, connectivity, correlativity, causativity, KR creativity, M motivity, N nativity, negativity, O objectivity, alternativity, P permittivity, perceptivity, positivity, PR productivity, R radioactivity, reactivity, reflectivity, relativity, reproductivity, receptivity, retroactivity, resistivity S selectivity, sensitivity, subjectivity, susceptivity

IV'I.UM

DRIV'I.UM	quadrivium
SIV'I.UM	lixivium
TRIV'I.UM	trivium

IV'I.US

BIV'I.US	bivious
BLIV'I.US	oblivious
NIV'I.US	niveous
SIV'I.US	lascivious, lixivious
TIV'I.US	multivious

IV'O.KAL

KWIV'O.KAL	equivocal, unequivocal
NIV'O.KAL	univocal

IV'O.LĒ

RIV'O.LĒ	Rivoli
TIV'O.LĒ	Tivoli

Ī'VO.RĒ

(See Ī'VE.RĒ)

IV'OR.US

(See IV'ER.US)

ĪZ'A.BL

NĪZ'A.BL	cognizable

(See ĪZ, add -ABL)

IZ'A.BL

KWIZ'A.BL	acquisible, quizzable, unquizzable
RIZ'A.BL	derisible, risible
VIZ'A.BL	divisible, indivisible, invisible, undivisible, visible

ĪZ'A.BLĒ

SĪZ'A.BLĒ	sizably
VĪZ'A.BLĒ	advisably, inadvisably

ĪZ'ED.LĒ

MĪZ'ED.LĒ	surmisedly
VĪZ'ED.LĒ	advisedly, improvisedly, provisedly, unadvisedly

Ī'ZER.Ē

RĪ'ZER.Ē	derisory, irrisory
VĪ'ZER.Ē	advisory, provisory, revisory, supervisory

IZ'ER.Ē

KWIZ'ER.Ē	quizzery
MIZ'ER.Ē	misery

IZH'UN.AL

SIZH'UN.AL	transitional, precisional
VIZH'UN.AL	divisional, previsional, provisional, revisional, visional

IZ'I.AK

DIZ'I.AK	aphrodisiac
NIZ'I.AK	Dionysiac

IZ'I.AN

DIZ'I.AN	aphrodisian, paradisian
FRIZ'I.AN	Frisian
LIZ'I.AN	Elysian
RIZ'I.AN	Parisian

(See IZHUN)

IZ'I.BL

(See IZ'A.BL)

IZ'I.ER

BIZ'I.ER	busier
DIZ'I.ER	dizzier
FIZ'I.ER	fizzier
FRIZ'I.ER	frizzier

IZ'I.EST

(See IZĒ, change -y to -iest.)

IZ'I.KAL

DIZ'I.KAL	paradisical
FIZ'I.KAL	biophysical, physical, geophysical, cataphysical, metaphysical, psychophysical, zoophysical
KWIZ'I.KAL	quizzical
TIZ'I.KAL	phthisical

IZ'I.LĒ

BIZ'I.LĒ	busily
DIZ'I.LĒ	dizzily
FIZ'I.LĒ	fizzily

IZ'I.NES

BIZ'I.NES	busyness
DIZ'I.NES	dizziness
FIZ'I.NES	fizziness

ĪZ'ING.LĒ

LĪZ'ING.LĒ	tantalizingly
NĪZ'ING.LĒ	agonizingly, scrutinizingly
PRĪZ'ING.LĒ	apprisingly, enterprisingly, surprisingly, unsurprisingly
SPĪZ'ING.LĒ	despisingly
TĪZ'ING.LĒ	appetizingly

IZ'ING.LĒ

HWIZ'ING.LĒ	whizzingly
KWIZ'ING.LĒ	quizzingly

IZ'I.TOR

KWIZ'I.TOR	acquisitor, disquisitor, inquisitor, requisitor
VIZ'I.TOR	visitor

Ī'ZO.RĒ

(See Ī'ZE.RĒ)

Ō'A.BL

Ō'A.BL	owable
BLŌ'A.BL	blowable
MŌ'A.BL	mowable
NŌ'A.BL	knowable, unknowable
RŌ'A.BL	rowable
SHŌ'A.BL	showable
SLŌ'A.BL	slowable
SŌ'A.BL	sewable, sowable, unsewable, unsowable
STŌ'A.BL	bestowable, stowable
THRŌ'A.BL	overthrowable, throwable
TRŌ'A.BL	trowable, untrowable

OB'A.BL

PROB'A.BL	improbable, probable

ROB'A.BL robbable,
unrobbable

Ō'BER.Ē

KRŌ'BER.Ē crowberry
SNŌ'BER.Ē snowberry

ÔB'ER.Ē

DÔB'ER.Ē dauberie
STRÔB'ER.Ē strawberry

OB'ER.Ē

BOB'ER.Ē bobbery
JOB'ER.Ē jobbery,
stock-jobbery
KLOB'ER.Ē clobbery
NOB'ER.Ē hobnobbery
ROB'ER.Ē corroboree, robbery
SLOB'ER.Ē slobbery
SNOB'ER.Ē snobbery

OB'ER.ING

KLOB'ER.ING clobbering
SLOB'ER.ING slobbering

Ō'BI.A

Ō'BI.A obeah
FŌ'BI.A *A* aerophobia,
agoraphobia,
airphobia,
acarophobia,
acousticophobia,
acrophobia,
algophobia,
amathophobia,
amaxophobia,
androphobia,
Anglophobia,
anthropophobia,
anuptaphobia,
arachibutyrophobia,
astrophobia,
atychiphobia, *B*
bacteriophobia,
ballistrophobia,
basophobia,
batophobia,
batrachophobia,
blennophobia, *BR*
bromidrosiphobia,
brontophobia, *D*
dextrophobia,

demonphobia,
dermatophobia,
dikephobia,
dysmorphobia,
dystychiphobia,
domatophobia,
doraphobia, *DR*
dromophobia, *E*
ecophobia,
enissophobia,
enosiophobia,
eosophobia,
eremophobia,
ergasophobia,
ergophobia,
erythrophobia,
erotophobia, *F*
pharmacophobia,
fibriphobia,
philophobia, phobia,
phobophobia,
phonophobia,
photophobia, *FR*
Francophobia, *G*
Galliphobia,
gamophobia, *H*
hagiophobia,
hamartiophobia,
harpaxophobia,
helminthophobia,
heresyphobia,
hydrophobia,
hydrophobophobia,
hygrophobia,
hyophobia,
hypengyophobia,
hypnophobia,
hodophobia,
homichlophobia,
homophobia, *I*
iatrophobia,
ichthyophobia, *J*
gephyrophobia,
geniophobia,
jentaculophobia,
gerascophobia,
gymnophobia,
gynekophobia, *K*
kakorrhaphiophobia,
catageophobia,
kathisophobia,
kenophobia,
cherophobia,
kinesophobia,
kokophobia, *KL*
climacophobia,
clinophobia,
claustrophobia, *KR*
chrematophobia,
cremnophobia,
chronophobia, *L*
lallophobia,

levophobia,
lygophobia,
lilapsophobia,
linonophobia,
lyssophobia, *M*
maieusiophobia,
macrophobia,
maniaphobia,
mastigophobia,
mechanophobia,
megalophobia,
melissophobia,
melophobia,
metrophobia,
myophobia,
mysophobia,
mytrophobia,
molysmophobia,
monophobia,
muriphobia, *N*
nebulaphobia,
negrophobia,
nyctophobia,
nosophobia,
noysnophobia,
novercaphobia,
numerophobia, *O*
odynophobia,
ophidiophobia,
ophthalmophobia,
ochlophobia,
ombrophobia,
onomatophobia,
optophobia,
osmophobia, *P*
paralilipophobia,
parthenophobia,
pathophobia,
pediculophobia,
paedophobia,
pediophobia,
peccatiphobia,
peniaphobia,
pentheraphobia,
pyrophobia,
pogonophobia,
ponophobia,
porphyrophobia,
pornophobia, *PL*
placophobia,
pluviophobia *PR*
prosophobia, *R*
rhabdophobia,
rhyophobia,
rhytiphobia,
Russophobia, *S*
selenophobia,
cenophobia,
sciaphobia,
cibophobia,
siderodromophobia,
syphiliphobia,

syngenosophobia,
cynophobia,
sitophobia,
soceraphobia,
sociophobia, *SK*
scoleciphobia,
scopophobia,
Scotophobia, *SP*
spectrophobia, *ST*
stasibasiphobia,
stasiphobia,
stenophobia,
stygiophobia,
staurophobia, *T*
taphephobia,
tapinophobia,
technophobia,
teleophobia,
teratophobia,
tobaccophobia,
tocophobia,
tonitrophobia,
topophobia,
teutophobia, *TH*
thalassophobia,
thanatophobia,
theophobia,
phthiriophobia, *TR*
traumatophobia,
triskaidekaphobia,
tropophobia, *V*
verbophobia,
verminophobia, *Y*
euphobia,
uranophobia,
urethrophobia, *Z*
xanthophobia,
zelophobia,
xenophobia,
zoophobia*

KŌ'BI.A   cobia

Ō'BI.AN

GRŌ'BI.AN	grobian
KRŌ'BI.AN	macrobian, microbian
NŌ'BI.AN	cenobean

OB'I.NET

BOB'I.NET	bobbinet
ROB'I.NET	robinet

(*For still more phobias, see Appendix
D. How many phobias we do have—and
to rhyme with them all, just two little
words: *obeah,* ''a religious belief of
African origin involving witchcraft''; and
cobia—the sergeant fish!

Ō'BI.UM

Ō'BI.UM	niobium
RŌ'BI.UM	aerobium
ZŌ'BI.UM	rhizobium

OB'O.LUS

OB'O.LUS	obolus
KOB'O.LUS	discobolus

OB'Ū.LAR

GLOB'Ū.LAR	globular
LOB'Ū.LAR	lobular

ŌCH'A.BL

PŌCH'A.BL	poachable
PRŌCH'A.BL	approachable, irreproachable, reproachable, unapproachable

Ô'DA.BL

Ô'DA.BL	audible, inaudible
LÔ'DA.BL	laudable, unlaudable
PLÔ'DA.BL	applaudable, plaudable

Ō'DA.LER

Ō'DA.LER	odaller
YŌ'DA'.LER	yodeler

OD'ER.ER

DOD'ER.ER	dodderer
FOD'ER.ER	fodderer
SOD'ER.ER	solderer

OD'ER.ING

DOD'ER.ING	doddering
FOD'ER.ING	foddering
SOD'ER.ING	soldering

Ō'DI.AK

KŌ'DI.AK	Kodiak
NŌ'DI.AK	nodiak
ZŌ'DI.AK	zodiac

Ō'DI.AL

LŌ'DI.AL	allodial
NŌ'DI.AL	palinodial, threnodial
PŌ'DI.AL	podial
SŌ'DI.AL	episodial, prosodial
TŌ'DI.AL	custodial

Ō'DI.AN

Ō'DI.AN	triodion
BŌ'DI.AN	Cambodian
LŌ'DI.AN	collodion, melodeon, nickelodeon
RŌ'DI.AN	Rhodian
SŌ'DI.AN	prosodian
TŌ'DI.AN	custodian

Ô'DI.BL

(See Ô'DA.BL)

OD'I.FĪ

KOD'I.FĪ	codify
MOD'I.FĪ	modify

OD'I.KAL

OD'I.KAL	periodical
KOD'I.KAL	codical
MOD'I.KAL	spasmodical
NOD'I.KAL	monodical, nodical, synodical
SOD'I.KAL	episodical, prosodical, rhapsodical
THOD'I.KAL	methodical, unmethodical

ÔD'I.NES

BÔD'I.NES	bawdiness
GÔD'I.NES	gaudiness

Ō'DI.ON

(See Ō'DI.AN)

OD'I.TĒ

OD'I.TĒ	oddity
KWOD'I.TĒ	quoddity
MOD'I.TĒ	discommodity, incommodity, commodity

Ô'DI.TER

Ô'DI.TER	auditor
PLÔ'DI.TER	plauditor

Ō'DI.UM

Ō'DI.UM	odeum, odium, triodium
LŌ'DI.UM	allodium
MŌ'DI.UM	plasmodium
PŌ'DI.UM	lycopodium, monopodium, parapodium, podium, sympodium
RŌ'DI.UM	rhodium
SŌ'DI.UM	sodium, taxodium

Ō'DI.US

Ō'DI.US	odious
LŌ'DI.US	melodious, unmelodious
MŌ'DI.US	Asmodeus, discommodious, incommodious, commodious, uncommodious

OD'Ū.LAR

MOD'Ū.LAR	modular
NOD'Ū.LAR	nodular

OF'A.GA

OF'A.GA	zoöphaga
KOF'A.GA	sarcophaga

OF'A.GAL

OF'A.GAL	zoöphagal
KOF'A.GAL	sarcophagal

OF'A.GAN

OF'A.GAN	ichthyophagan, geophagan, ophiophagan, theophagan, zoophagan
DROF'A.GAN	androphagan
KOF'A.GAN	batrachophagan, sarcophagan
KROF'A.GAN	necrophagan
LOF'A.GAN	hylophagan, xylophagan
POF'A.GAN	hippophagan
PROF'A.GAN	saprophagan
THOF'A.GAN	lithophagan
THROF'A.GAN	anthrophagan

OF'A.GUS

OF'A.GUS	ichthyophagous, geophagous, creophagous, ophiophagous, theophagous, zoophagous
DROF'A.GUS	androphagous
GOF'A.GUS	oligophagous
KOF'A.GUS	batrachophagous, sarcophagous, sarcophagus, scolecophagous
KROF'A.GUS	necrophagous
LOF'A.GUS	hylophagous, xylophagous
POF'A.GUS	hippophagous
PROF'A.GUS	saprophagous
SOF'A.GUS	esophagus
THOF'A.GUS	lithophagous
THROF'A.GUS	anthrophagous
TOF'A.GUS	phytophagous, galactophygous, harpactophagous, pantophagous, scatophagous

OF'A.JĒ

OF'A.JĒ	ichthyophagy, geophagy, ophiophagy, ostreophagy, theophagy, zoophagy
DOF'A.JĒ	cardophagy
DROF'A.JĒ	androphagy
KOF'A.JĒ	batrachophagy, mycophagy, onychophagy, sarcophagy
KROF'A.JĒ	necrophagy
LOF'A.JĒ	hylophagy, xylophagy
MOF'A.JĒ	omophagy, psomophagy
POF'A.JĒ	anthropophagy, hippophagy
PROF'A.JĒ	saprophagy
ROF'A.JĒ	Heterophagi, xerophagy
SOF'A.JĒ	exophagy, opsophagy

THOF'A.JĒ	lithophagy
TOF'A.JĒ	phytophagy, galactophagy, Lotophagi, pantophagy, poltophagy

OF'A.JIK

(See OF'A.JĒ, replace -y with -ic)

OF'A.JIST

(See OF'A.JĒ, replace -y with -ist)

O'FA.NĒ

(See O'FO.NĒ)

OF'EN.ER

OF'EN.ER	oftener
KOF'EN.ER	encoffiner, coffiner
SOF'EN.ER	softener

(See OF'TEN.ER)

OF'ER.ER

OF'ER.ER	offerer
GOF'ER.ER	gofferer
KOF'ER.ER	cofferer
PROF'ER.ER	profferer

OF'ER.ING

OF'ER.ING	burnt offering, offering, peace offering
GOF'ER.ING	goffering
KOF'ER.ING	coffering
PROF'ER.ING	proffering

OF'E.RUS

OF'E.RUS	zoophorous, zoophorus
GOF'E.RUS	mastigophorous
LOF'E.RUS	phyllophorous
NOF'E.RUS	adenophorous
ROF'E.RUS	pyrophorous
SOF'E.RUS	isophorous
TOF'E.RUS	galactophorous, chaetophorous
TROF'E.RUS	electrophorous, loutrophoros

OF'I.KAL

SOF'I.KAL	philosophical, sophical, theosophical
TROF'I.KAL	trophical

OF'I.LIST

OF'I.LIST	bibliophilist, zoophilist
KOF'I.LIST	Francophilist
NOF'I.LIST	oenophilist
ROF'I.LIST	peristerophilist

OF'I.LIZM

OF'I.LIZM	bibliophilism, biophilism
KOF'I.LIZM	Francophilism
KROF'I.LIZM	necrophilism

OF'I.LUS

OF'I.LUS	heliophilous, Theophilus, zoophilous
BROF'I.LUS	ombrophilous
DOF'I.LUS	acidophilus
DROF'I.LUS	dendrophilous, hydrophilous
GROF'I.LUS	hygrophelous
KOF'I.LUS	sarcophilous
LOF'I.LUS	xylophilous
MOF'I.LUS	anemophilous, chasmophilous, nemophilous, potamophilous
NOF'I.LUS	limnophilous
POF'I.LUS	tropophilous
PROF'I.LUS	coprophilous, saprophilous
ROF'I.LUS	xerophilous
THOF'I.LUS	ornithophilous
ZOF'I.LUS	mazophilous

OF'O.LIST

NOF'O.LIST	cacophonophilist, canopholist
SOF'O.LIST	chrysopholist

OF'O.NĒ

OF'O.NĒ	radiophany, stereophany, theophany

JOF'O.NĒ	laryngophony
KOF'O.NĒ	cacophony
KROF'O.NĒ	microphony
LOF'O.NĒ	colophony, xylophony
MOF'O.NĒ	homophony
NOF'O.NĒ	monophany, satanophany
PROF'O.NĒ	lamprophony
ROF'O.NĒ	heterophony
THOF'O.NĒ	orthophony
TOF'O.NĒ	photophony, Christophony, tautophony

OF'O.NIST

(See **OF'O.NĒ**, change -y to -ist where appropriate.)

OF'O.NUS

DROF'O.NUS	hydrophanous
GROF'O.NUS	hygrophanous
KOF'O.NUS	cacophonous
LOF'O.NUS	megalophonous
MOF'O.NUS	homophonous
NOF'O.NUS	monophonous
ROF'O.NUS	pyrophanous, pyrophonous, stentorophonous

OF'O.RUS

(See **OF'ER.US**)

OF'TEN.ER

OF'TEN.ER	oftener
SOF'TEN.ER	softener

(See **OF'EN.ER**)

Ô'FUL.Ē

Ô'FUL.Ē	awfully
LÔ'FUL.Ē	lawfully, unlawfully

Ô'FUL.NES

Ô'FUL.NES	awfulness
LÔ'FUL.NES	lawfulness, unlawfulness

OG'A.MĒ

OG'A.MĒ	oögamy
DOG'A.MĒ	endogamy

FOG'A.MĒ	adelphogamy
KOG'A.MĒ	dichogamy
MOG'A.MĒ	homogamy
NOG'A.MĒ	monogamy
ROG'A.MĒ	deuterogamy, heterogamy
SOG'A.MĒ	anisogamy, exogamy, isogamy, mixogamy, misogamy
TOG'A.MĒ	autogamy

OG'A.MIST

DOG'A.MIST	endogamist
NOG'A.MIST	monogamist
ROG'A.MIST	deuterogamist
SOG'A.MIST	exogamist, misogamist
TOG'A.MIST	cryptogamist

OG'A.MUS

DOG'A.MUS	endogamous
MOG'A.MUS	homogamous
NOG'A.MUS	monogamous
ROG'A.MUS	phanerogamous, heterogamus
SOG'A.MUS	exogamous
TOG'A.MUS	cryptogamous

OG'ER.Ē

DOG'ER.Ē	doggery
FOG'ER.Ē	pettifoggery
FROG'ER.Ē	froggery
GOG'ER.Ē	demagoguery
GROG'ER.Ē	groggery
HOG'ER.Ē	hoggery
TOG'ER.Ē	toggery

OG'ER.EL

DOG'ER.EL	doggerel
HOG'ER.EL	hoggerel

Ō'GI.IZM

BŌ'GI.IZM	bogeyism
FŌ'GI.IZM	fogeyism

OG'NO.MĒ

OG'NO.MĒ	physiognomy, craniognomy
ROG'NO.MĒ	chirognomy
THOG'NO.MĒ	pathognomy

OG'NO.SĒ

OG'NO.SĒ	geognosy
KOG'NO.SĒ	pharmacognosy

OG'O.NĒ

OG'O.NĒ	bibliogony, physiogony, heroögony, geogony, theogony
HOG'O.NĒ	mahogany
MOG'O.NĒ	homogony, cosmogony
NOG'O.NĒ	monogony
ROG'O.NĒ	heterogony
THOG'O.NĒ	mythogony, pathogony

OG'O.NIST

OG'O.NIST	theogonist
MOG'O.NIST	cosmogonist

OG'RA.FĒ

OG'RA.FĒ *A* areography, archaeography, *B* balneography, bibliography, biography, biogeography, *BR* brachyography, *D* dactyliography, *E* ecclesiography, electrocardiography, *F* phythogeography, physiography, *H* hagiography, haliography, heliography, heresiography, historiography, horography, horologiography, *I* ideography *J* geography, *K* cacography, cardiography, choreography, *M* myography, *N* neography, *O* ophiography, oreography, osteography, autobiography, *P* paleography, paramiography, *R* radiography, *S* semeiography, symbolaeography, sciography, *ST* stereography, *T* tacheography, *Z* zoogeography, zoography

DOG'RA.FĒ celidography, pseudography

DROG'RA.FĒ dendrography, hydrography

FOG'RA.FĒ glyphography, morphography

GOG'RA.FĒ logography

KOG'RA.FĒ discography, pharmacography, phycography, cacography, calcography, chalcography, lexicography, zincography

KROG'RA.FĒ macrography, micrography

LOG'RA.FĒ *D* dactylography, *E* encephalography, epistolography, *H* haplography, hyalography, holography, *KR* crystallography, chromoxylography, *M* metallography, *P* pyelography, *S* sigillography, sillography, *ST* stelography, stylography, *T* pterylography, *Z* xylography

MOG'RA.FĒ *A* anemography, *D* demography, *F* phantasmography, filmography, *H* homography, *K* cosmography, *M* mammography, microcosmography, mimography, *N* nomography, pneumography, *S* psalmography, seismography, *T* tomography, *TH* thermography

NOG'RA.FĒ *E* ethnography, *F* phonography, *G* galvanography, *H* hymnography, *I* ichnography, iconography, *KR* Christianography,

chronography, *L* lichenography, lipsanography, *M* mechanography, monography, *O* organography, oceanography, *P* paleethnography, pornography, *PL* planography, *S* scenography, *SF* sphenography, *ST* stenography, *T* technography, *Y* uranography, *Z* zenography

POG'RA.FĒ anthropography, phototypography, lipography, prosopography, stereotypography, topography, typography

PROG'RA.FĒ reprography

ROG'RA.FĒ *H* heterography, hierography, horography, *K* chirography, chorography, *M* macrography, *N* neurography, *O* orography, *P* papyrography, petrography, pyrography, *R* rhyparography, *S* cerography, siderography, *T* pterography, xerography, xylopyrography

SOG'RA.FĒ doxography, hypsography, isography, gypsography, nosography, thalassography

THOG'RA.FĒ anthography, ethography, photolithography, chromolithography, lithography, mythography, orthography

TOG'RA.FĒ *A* astrophotography, *D* dittography, *F* phantasmatography, phytography, photography, *GL* glyptography, *H* hematography, hyetography,

histography, *K* cartography,
chartography,
cometography, *KL* climatography, *KR* cryptography,
chromatography,
chromophotography,
N numismatography,
pneumatography, *O* odontography,
ontography,
autography, *P* paleontography,
pantography,
perspectography, *PL* plastography, *S* sematography,
cinematography, *SK* skeletography,
scotography, *STR* stratography, *T* telephotography,
toreumatography,
TH thanatography

TROG'RA.FĒ   petrography

OG'RA.FER

(See **OG'RA.FĒ,** change -*y* to -*er* where appropriate.)

OG'RA.FIST

(See **OG'RA.FĒ,** change -*y* to -*ist* where appropriate.)

OI'A.BL

BOI'A.BL	buoyable
JOI'A.BL	enjoyable
KLOI'A.BL	cloyable
KOI'A.BL	decoyable
PLOI'A.BL	deployable, employable
TOI'A.BL	toyable
VOI'A.BL	convoyable

OI'AL.Ē

LOI'AL.Ē	disloyally, loyally
ROI'AL.Ē	royally

OI'A.LIST

LOI'A.LIST	loyalist
ROI'A.LIST	royalist

OI'A.LIZM

LOI'A.LIZM	loyalism
ROI'A.LIZM	royalism

OI'AL.TĒ

LOI'AL.TĒ	disloyalty, loyalty
ROI'AL.TĒ	royalty, vice-royalty

OI'AN.SĒ

BOI'AN.SĒ	buoyancy, flamboyancy
TOI'AN.SĒ	chatoyancy
VOI'AN.SĒ	clairvoyancy

OI'ANT.LĒ

BOI'ANT.LĒ	buoyantly, flamboyantly
VOI'ANT.LĒ	clairvoyantly

OI'ING.LĒ

KLOI'ING.LĒ	cloyingly
NOI'ING.LĒ	annoyingly
TOI'ING.LĒ	toyingly

Ō'I.KAL

GŌ'I.KAL	egoical
RŌ'I.KAL	heroical
STŌ'I.KAL	stoical

Ō'IL.Ē

BLŌ'IL.Ē	blowily
SHŌ'IL.Ē	showily
SNŌ'IL.Ē	snowily

OIL'ING.LĒ

(See **OIL,** add -*ingly* where appropriate.)

OIN'A.BL

JOIN'A.BL	disjoinable, joinable
KOIN'A.BL	coinable, uncoinable

Ō'ING.LE

FLŌ'ING.LĒ	flowingly
GLŌ'ING.LĒ	glowingly

KRŌ'ING.LĒ	crowingly
NŌ'ING.LĒ	knowingly, unknowingly

OIN'TED.LĒ

JOIN'TED.LĒ	disjointedly, jointedly
POIN'TED.LĒ	pointedly

OIS'TER.ER

KLOIS'TER.ER	cloisterer
ROIS'TER.ER	roisterer

OIS'TER.ING

KLOIS'TER.ING	cloistering
ROIS'TER.ING	roistering

OIS'TER.US

BOIS'TER.US	boisterous
ROIS'TER.US	roisterous

OI'SUM.LĒ

KLOI'SUM.LĒ	cloysomely
NOI'SUM.LĒ	noisomely
TOI'SUM.LĒ	toysomely

OI'TER.ER

LOI'TER.ER	loiterer
NOI'TER.ER	reconnoiterer

(See **OITRER**)

OI'TER.ING

LOI'TER.ING	loitering
NOI'TER.ING	reconnoitering

(See **OITRING**)

OJ'E.NĒ

OJ'E.NĒ	abiogeny, biogeny, embryogeny, geogeny, cryogeny, ontogeny, oögeny, ostogeny, zoögeny
DOJ'E.NĒ	pseudogyny
DROJ'E.NĒ	androgeny, androgyny

LOJ′E.NĒ	philogeny, philogyny, metallogeny
MOJ′E.NĒ	homogeny, nomogeny
NOJ′E.NĒ	ethnogeny, hymenogeny, monogeny, monogyny, spanogyny
POJ′E.NĒ	anthropogeny
PROJ′E.NĒ	progeny
ROJ′E.NĒ	epeirogeny, erogeny, heterogeny, orogeny
SOJ′E.NĒ	misogyny
THOJ′E.NĒ	pathogeny
TOJ′E.NĒ	autogeny, photogeny, histogeny, odontogeny, ontogeny, autogeny, protogyny

OJ′E.NIST

OJ′E.NIST	abiogenist, biogenist
LOJ′E.NIST	philogynist
NOJ′E.NIST	monogenist, monogynist
ROJ′E.NIST	heterogynist
SOJ′E.NIST	misogynist

OJ′E.NĪZ

MOJ′E.NĪZ	homogenize
TROJ′E.NĪZ	nitrogenize

(See **OJ′E.NĒ,** change *-y* to *-ize* where appropriate.)

OJ′E.NUS

OJ′E.NUS	biogenous, ideogenous, idiogenous, geogenous
DOJ′E.NUS	endogenous, kedogenous, spodogenous
DROJ′E.NUS	androgenous, androgynous, hydrogenous
LOJ′E.NUS	philogynous
MOJ′E.NUS	homogenous, primogenous, thermogenous
NOJ′E.NUS	monogenous, monogynous

POJ′E.NUS	hypogenous
ROJ′E.NUS	heterogenous, pyrogenous
SOJ′E.NUS	exogenous, isogenous, misogynous
THOJ′E.NUS	lithogenous
TROJ′E.NUS	nitrogenous

Ō′JI.A

BŌ′JI.A	cambogia
LŌ′JI.A	apologia

Ō′JI.AN

BŌ′JI.AN	gambogian
LŌ′JI.AN	archaelogian, astrologian, philologian, geologian, mythologian, neologian, theologian

OJ′I.KAL

GOJ′I.KAL	anagogical, apagogical, demagogical, synagogical

(See **OL′O.JĒ,** change *-y* to *-ical* where appropriate; see **OJIK,** add *-al* where appropriate.)

OJ′I.NĒ

(See **OJ′E.NĒ**)

OJ′I.NUS

(See **OJ′E.NUS**)

Ō′KA.BL

PŌ′KA.BL	pokable
SMŌ′KA.BL	smokable, unsmokable
VŌ′KA.BL	invocable, revokable, vocable
YŌ′KA.BL	unyokable, yokable

Ō′KAL.Ē

FŌ′KAL.Ē	focally
LŌ′KAL.Ē	locally
VŌ′KAL.Ē	vocally

Ō′KA.LIST

LŌ′KA.LIST	philocalist, localist
VŌ′KA.LIST	vocalist

Ō′KA.LĪZ

FŌ′KA.LĪZ	focalize
LŌ′KA.LĪZ	localize
VŌ′KA.LĪZ	vocalize

Ō′KA.LIZM

LŌ′KA.LIZM	localism
VŌ′KA.LIZM	vocalism

ÔK′A.TIV

TÔK′A.TIV	talkative

(See **OK′A.TIV**)

OK′A.TIV

LOK′A.TIV	locative
VOK′A.TIV	invocative, provocative, vocative

(See **ÔK′A.TIV**)

Ō′KEN.LĒ

BRŌ′KEN.LĒ	brokenly
SPŌ′KEN.LĒ	outspokenly

OK′ER.Ē

KROK′ER.Ē	crockery
MOK′ER.Ē	mockery
ROK′ER.Ē	rockery
STOK′ER.Ē	Comstockery

Ō′KI.ER

Ō′KI.ER	oakier
CHŌ′KI.ER	chokier
KRŌ′KI.ER	croakier
PŌ′KI.ER	pokier
SMŌ′KI.ER	smokier
SŌ′KI.ER	soakier
YŌ′KI.ER	yolkier

OK'I.LĒ

| KOK'I.LĒ | cockily |
| STOK'I.LĒ | stockily |

ÔK'I.LĒ

CHÔK'I.LĒ	chalkily
GÔK'I.LĒ	gawkily
PÔK'I.LĒ	pawkily
SKWÔK'I.LĒ	squawkily
STÔK'I.LĒ	stalkily

Ō'KI.NES

(See ŌKĒ, add -ness where appropriate.)

ÔK'I.NES

CHÔK'I.NES	chalkiness
GÔK'I.NES	gawkiness
PÔK'I.NES	pawkiness
SKWÔK'I.NES	squawkiness
STÔK'I.NES	stalkiness
TÔK'I.NES	talkiness

(See OK'I.NES)

OK'I.NES

KOK'I.NES	cockiness
ROK'I.NES	rockiness
STOK'I.NES	stockiness

(See ÔK'I.NES)

Ō'KING.LĒ

CHŌ'KING.LĒ	chokingly
JŌ'KING.LĒ	jokingly
KRŌ'KING.LĒ	croakingly
STRŌ'KING.LĒ	strokingly
VŌ'KING.LĒ	provokingly, unprovokingly

OK'ING.LĒ

| MOK'ING.LĒ | mockingly |
| SHOK'ING.LĒ | shockingly |

OK'LI.A

| KOK'LI.A | cochlea |
| TROK'LI.A | trochlea |

OK'RA.SĒ

OK'RA.SĒ	hagiocracy, idiocracy, neocracy, plousiocracy, theocracy, theocrasy
BOK'RA.SĒ	mobocracy, snobocracy
DOK'RA.SĒ	landocracy
DROK'RA.SĒ	androcracy
GOK'RA.SĒ	logocracy
HOK'RA.SĒ	adhocracy
KLOK'RA.SĒ	ochlocracy
KOK'RA.SĒ	gynecocracy, ptococracy
LOK'RA.SĒ	doulocracy, ochlocracy
MOK'RA.SĒ	arithmocracy, democracy, cosmocracy, nomocracy, timocracy
NOK'RA.SĒ	ethnocracy, juvenocracy, cottonocracy, millionocracy, monocracy, pornocracy, technocracy
POK'RA.SĒ	hypocrisy, shopocrasy
ROK'RA.SĒ	bureaucracy, hierocracy
SOK'RA.SĒ	isocracy, chrysocracy, pantisocracy, thalassocracy
TOK'RA.SĒ	A aristocracy, D despotocracy, E ergatocracy, J gerontocracy, K kakistocracy, KL kleptocracy, M meritocracy, O autocracy, P pedantocracy, PL plantocracy, plutocracy, SKW squattocracy, STR stratocracy, T ptochocracy
VOK'RA.SĒ	slavocracy

OK'RA.TIZM

OK'RA.TIZM	theocratism
MOK'RA.TIZM	democratism
ROK'RA.TIZM	bureaucratism
SOK'RA.TIZM	Socratism

(See OK'RA.SĒ, change -cy to -tism where appropriate.)

OK'RO.NUS

NOK'RO.NUS	monochronous
SOK'RO.NUS	isochronous
TOK'RO.NUS	tautochronous

OK'SI.KAL

DOK'SI.KAL	orthodoxical, paradoxical
POK'SI.KAL	hypoxical
TOK'SI.KAL	radiotoxical, toxical

ŌK'SING.LĒ

| HŌK'SING.LĒ | hoaxingly |
| KŌK'SING.LĒ | coaxingly |

OK'TOR.SHIP

| DOK'TOR.SHIP | doctorship |
| PROK'TOR.SHIP | proctorship |

OK'Ū.LAR

OK'Ū.LAR	ocular
JOK'Ū.LAR	jocular
LOK'Ū.LAR	locular
NOK'Ū.LAR	binocular, monocular, senocular
VOK'Ū.LAR	vocular

OK'Ū.LĀT

OK'Ū.LĀT	exoculate, oculate
FLOK'Ū.LĀT	flocculate
NOK'Ū.LĀT	binoculate, inoculate

OK'Ū.LUS

OK'Ū.LUS	oculus
FLOK'Ū.LUS	flocculus
LOK'Ū.LUS	loculus
NOK'Ū.LUS	monoculous, monoculus

Ō'KUS.ING

| FŌ'KUS.ING | focusing, focussing |
| HŌ'KUS.ING | hocusing, hocussing |

ŌL′A.BL

BŌL′A.BL	bowlable, unbowlable
GŌL′A.BL	goalable
HŌL′A.BL	holable, unholable
JŌL′A.BL	cajolable, uncajolable
PŌL′A.BL	pollable, unpollable
RŌL′A.BL	enrollable, rollable, unenrollable, unrollable
SŌL′A.BL	inconsolable, consolable, unconsolable
TŌL′A.BL	extollable, tollable
TRŌL′A.BL	controllable, uncontrollable

ÔL′A.BL

KÔL′A.BL	callable, recallable, uncallable, unrecallable
THRÔL′A.BL	enthrallable, unenthrallable

ŌL′A.BLĒ

(See **ŌL′A.BL,** add -y where appropriate.)

ŌL′AR.Ē

(See **ŌL′ER.Ē**)

Ō′LA.RĪZ

PŌ′LA.RĪZ	depolarize, polarize
SŌ′LA.RĪZ	solarize

OL′A.TER

(See **OL′A.TRĒ,** change concluding -ry to -er where appropriate.)

OL′A.TRĒ

OL′A.TRĒ	A angeolatry, archaeolatry, B babyolatry, bibliolatry, E ecclesiolatry, F physiolatry, H hagiolatry, heliolatry, hygiolatry, I idiolatry, ichthyolatry, J

geolatry, geniolatry, gynaeolatry, M Mariolatry, O orphiolatry, P patriolatry, TH theolatry, Z zoolatry

BOL′A.TRĒ	mobolatry
DOL′A.TRĒ	bardolatry, idolatry, lordolatry
KROL′A.TRĒ	necrolatry
LOL′A.TRĒ	angelolatry, symbololatry
MOL′A.TRĒ	cosmolatry
NOL′A.TRĒ	demonolatry, iconolatry, monolatry, onolatry, parthenolatry, cynolatry, thenolatry, uranolatry
POL′A.TRĒ	anthropolatry, topolatry
ROL′A.TRĒ	arborolatry, hierolatry, pyrolatry, staurolatry
THOL′A.TRĒ	litholatry
TOL′A.TRĒ	grammatolatry, Christolatry, autolatry, plutolatry, thaumatolatry
TROL′A.TRĒ	astrolatry

OL′A.TRUS

(See **OL′A-TRĒ,** change concluding -y to -ous where appropriate.)

ŌL′DA.BL

FŌL′DA.BL	foldable, unfoldable
MŌL′DA.BL	moldable, unmoldable
SKŌL′DA.BL	scoldable, unscoldable

ŌL′ER.E

BŌL′ER.Ē	bolary
DRŌL′ER.Ē	drollery
JŌL′ER.Ē	cajolery
MŌL′ER.Ē	molary
PŌL′ER.Ē	polary
RŌL′ER.Ē	rigamarolery
SŌL′ER.Ē	solary
VŌL′ER.Ē	volary

ŌL′FUL.Ē

DŌL′FUL.Ē	dolefully
SŌL′FUL.Ē	soulfully

Ō′LI.A

BŌ′LI.A	strephyosymbolia
GŌ′LI.A	Mongolia
KŌ′LI.A	melancholia
NŌ′LI.A	magnolia
SKŌ′LI.A	scholia
TŌ′LI.A	Aetolia, Anatolia

Ō′LI.AN

Ō′LI.AN	Aeolian, Creolian
BŌ′LI.AN	metabolian
GŌ′LI.AN	Mongolian
KŌ′LI.AN	melancholian
MŌ′LI.AN	simoleon
PŌ′LI.AN	Napoleon
TŌ′LI.AN	Aetolian, Anatolian, capitolian

Ō′LI.Ā′SHUN

FŌ′LI.Ā′SHUN	defoliation, foliation
SPŌ′ Ā′SHUN	despolition, spoliation

Ō′LI.ĀT

Ō′LI.ĀT	oleate
FŌ′LI.ĀT	bifoliate, defoliate, exfoliate, foliate, infoliate
SPŌ′LI.ĀT	spoliate

OL′ID.LĒ

SKWOL′ID.LĒ	squalidly
SOL′ID.LĒ	solidly
STOL′ID.LĒ	stolidly

OL′ID.NES

SKWOL′ID.NES	squalidness
SOL′ID.NES	solidness
STOL′ID.NES	stolidness

OL′I.DUS

OL′I.DUS	olidous
SOL′I.DUS	solidous

Ō′LI.ER

FŌ′LI.ER	foliar
GRŌ′LI.ER	Grolier

HŌ'LI.ER   holier, unholier
LŌ'LI.ER   lowlier

OL'I.FĪ

DOL'I.FĪ   idolify
JOL'I.FĪ   jollify
KWOL'I.FĪ   disqualify, qualify, unqualify
MOL'I.FĪ   mollify

OL'I.FĪD

(See **OL'I.FĪ**, change -y to -ied)

ÔL'I.FÔRM

KÔL'I.FÔRM   cauliform

(See **OL'I.FÔRM**)

OL'I.FÔRM

BOL'I.FÔRM   emboliform
KOL'I.FÔRM   colliform

(See **ÔL'I.FÔRM**)

Ô'LI.KL

KÔ'LI.KL   caulicle

(See **OL'I.KL**)

OL'I.KL

BOL'I.KL   diabolical, hyperbolical, parabolical, symbolical
FOL'I.KL   follicle
POL'I.KL   bibliopolical
STOL'I.KL   apostolical, diastolical, systolical
THOL'I.KL   catholical

(See **Ô'LI.KL**)

OL'IK.SUM

FROL'IK.SUM   frolicsome
ROL'IK.SUM   rollicksome

Ō'LI.NES

HŌ'LI.NES   holiness, unholiness
LŌ'LI.NES   lowliness
SHŌ'LI.NES   shoaliness

ŌL'ING.LĒ

DŌL'ING.LĒ   condolingly
JŌL'ING.LĒ   cajolingly
SŌL'ING.LĒ   consolingly
TŌL'ING.LĒ   extollingly

ÔL'ING.LĒ

DRÔL'ING.LĒ   drawlingly
KRÔL'ING.LĒ   crawlingly
PÔL'ING.LĒ   appallingly
THRÔL'ING.LĒ   enthrallingly

Ō'LI.Ō

Ō'LI.Ō   oleo, olio
BRŌ'LI.Ō   imbroglio
FŌ'LI.Ō   folio, portfolio
PŌ'LI.Ō   polio
RŌ'LI.Ō   roleo
VŌ'LI.Ō   Malvolio

OL'ISH.ER

BOL'ISH.ER   abolisher
MOL'ISH.ER   demolisher
POL'ISH.ER   polisher

OL'ISH.ING

BOL'ISH.ING   abolishing
MOL'ISH.ING   demolishing
POL'ISH.ING   polishing

OL'I.SIS

OL'I.SIS   bacteriolysis, biolysis
DROL'I.SIS   hydrolysis
KOL'I.SIS   glycolysis
MOL'I.SIS   hemolysis, thermolysis
ROL'I.SIS   catarolysis, neurolysis
TOL'I.SIS   autolysis, histolysis, pneumatolysis, cytolysis
TROL'I.SIS   electrolysis

OL'I.TĒ

JOL'I.TĒ   jollity
KWOL'I.TĒ   equality, inequality, coequality, quality

POL'I.TĒ   interpolity, isopolity, polity
VOL'I.TĒ   frivolity

Ō'LI.UM

Ō'LI.UM   oleum
FŌ'LI.UM   folium, trifolium
NŌ'LI.UM   linoleum
SKŌ'LI.UM   scholium
TŌ'LI.UM   crystoleum
TRŌ'LI.UM   petroleum

OL'I.WOG

GOL'I.WOG   golliwog
POL'I.WOG   polliwog

ÔL'KA.NĪZ

BÔL'KA.NĪZ   Balkanize

(See **OL'KA.NĪZ**)

OL'KA.NĪZ

VOL'KA.NĪZ   volcanize

(See **ÔL'KA.NĪZ**)

OL'O.ER

FOL'O.ER   follower
HOL'O.ER   holloer, hollower

(See **ÄL'D.ER**)

OL'O.GUS

MOL'O.GUS   homologous
ROL'O.GUS   heterologous
SOL'O.GUS   isologous
TOL'O.GUS   tautologous

OL'Ō.ING

FOL'Ō.ING   following
HOL'Ō.ING   holloing, hollowing

(See **ÄL'O.ING**)

Ō'LO.IST

PŌ'LO.IST   poloist
SŌ'LO.IST   soloist

OL'O.JĒ

OL'O.JĒ *A* abiology, agriology, agrobiology, acryology, axiology, alethiology, algriology, amphibiology, areology, archaeology, arteriology, astrogeology, astrotheology, atheology, *B* bacteriology, balneology, bibliology, biology, *BR* bryology, bromatology, *D* dactyliology, deltiology, dicaeology, dysteleology, *E* ecclesiology, exobiology, electrobiology, electrophysiology, embryology, endemiology, entozoology, epidemiology, aesthiology, etiology, *F* phytophysiology, phytosociology, physiology, *FR* phraseology, *GL* glaciology, *H* hagiology, hamartiology, heliology, heresiology, heroölogy, hygiology, historiology, *I* ideology, ichthyology, *J* geology, *K* caliology, chaology, cardiology, conchiology, koniology, choreology, *KR* craniology, cryobiology, *L* liturgiology, *M* Mariology, microbiology, microgeology, myology, mommiology,

museology, *N* naology, neology, noölogy, gnosiology, *O* audiology, ophiology, ology, oölogy, osteology, *P* palaeology, palaetiology, palaeozoology, pantheology, paroemiology, *PR* praxiology, protozoology, *R* radiobiology, radiology, rheology, *S* semasiology, semeiology, semiology, psychobiology, sophiology, sociobiology, sociology, soteriology, *SP* speleology, *ST* stoichiology, storiology, *T* teleology, testaceology, *TH* theology, thereology, *TS* tsiology, *V* venereology, vermeology, *Z* zoölogy

BOL'O.JĒ amphibology, phlebology, symbology

BROL'O.JĒ ambrology, ombrology, timbrology

DOL'O.JĒ acidology, methodology, monadology, odology, orchidology, paedology, pedology, periodology, podology, pseudology, pteridology, tidology

DROL'O.JĒ dendrology, hydrology

FOL'O.JĒ edaphology, graphology, geomorphology, metamorphology, morphology, nephology, psephology, trophology, ufology

FROL'O.JĒ nephrology
GOL'O.JĒ algology, bugology, ergology, pharyngology, fungology, laryngology, logology, otolaryngology, spongology

GROL'O.JĒ agrology, hygrology
KOL'O.JĒ *A* acology, archology, *E* ecology, *F* pharmacology, phycology, filicology, *I* idiopsychology, *J* gynecology, *K* cacology, codicology, conchology, *L* lexicology, *M* malacology, metapsychology, mycology, myrmecology, muscology, musicology, *O* oikology, oncology, autecology, *P* paleopsychology, parapsychology, *S* sarcology, psychology, synecology, *T* ptochology, tocology, toxicology, *TR* trichology, *Y* euchology

KROL'O.JĒ macrology, micrology, necrology

LOL'O.JĒ *A* angelology, *D* dactylology, diabolology, *F* philology, *H* haplology, hylology, hoplology, *K* callology, kalology, *P* pelology, *S* syphilology, psylology, *T* typhlology, *V* vexilology, *Z* xylology

MOL'O.JĒ *A* anemology, atomology, *D* desmology, docimology, *E* entomology, enzymology,

epistemology,
etymology, *H*
hebephalmology,
homology, *J*
gemmology, *K*
cosmology, *KR*
chresmology, *M*
miasmology, *N*
gnomology,
nomology,
pneumology, *O*
ophthalmology,
orismology, *P*
paromology,
polemology,
pomology,
potamology, *S*
syndesmology,
seismology, *SF*
sphygmology, *SP*
spasmology,
spermology, *TH*
thermology, *Z*
zymology

NOL'O.JĒ *A* aphnology,
agnology,
actinology,
arachnology,
asthenology, *B*
biocenology,
botanology, *D*
demonology,
dendrochronology,
E eccrinology,
emmenology,
endochrinology,
enology, oenology,
ethnology, *F*
phenology,
phenomenology,
phonology, *FR*
phrenology, *G*
galvanology, *H*
hymenology,
hymnology,
hypnology, *I*
ichnolithnology,
ichnology,
iconology,
immunology, *J*
geochronology, *K*
campanology,
carpology,
carcinology,
kinology, *KR*
criminology,
chronology, *KW*
quinology, *L*
lichenology,
limnology, *M*
maternology,
mechanology,

meconology,
menology,
menonology,
monology, *N*
gnomonology,
noseconology,
neurypnology, *O*
organology,
oceanology, *P*
palaeoethnology,
palynology,
parthenology,
penology,
pogonology,
punnology, *R*
rhinology,
roentgenology,
runology, *S*
selenology,
synchronology,
Sinology, cynology,
SPL splanchnology,
splenology, *T*
technology,
terminology,
termonology,
tonology, *V*
volcanology,
vulcanology, *Y*
uranology,
urinology

POL'O.JĒ antapology,
anthropology,
apology,
escapology,
hippology,
carpology,
kompology,
paleanthropology,
typology, topology,
tropology

ROL'O.JĒ *A* aerology,
acarology,
arthrology,
acyrology,
astrometeorology, *B*
barology, *D*
dolorology, *E*
enterology, *F*
pharology,
futurology, *G*
gastroenterology, *H*
heterology,
hierology,
hysterology,
horology, *I*
ichorology, *K*
chirology,
coprology,
chorology, *M*
martyrology,
meteorology,

morology, *N*
necrology,
numerology,
neurology, *O*
oneirology, orology,
P papyrology,
pyrology,
ponerology, *S*
serology, *T*
pterology, *TH*
therology, *V*
virology, *Y* urology

SOL'O.JĒ *D* doxology,
dosology, *GL*
glossology, *J*
gypsology, *KR*
chrysology, *M*
misology, *N*
neossology,
nosology, *O*
auxology,
osmonosology, *P*
paradoxology,
parisology,
posology, *S*
sexology,
psychonosology, *T*
taxology, *THR*
threpsology, *Y*
universology

STROL'O.JĒ astrology,
gastrology

THOL'O.JĒ *A* agathology,
anthology, *E*
ethology, *F*
phytolithology,
phytopathology,
helminthology, *L*
lithology, *M*
mythology, *N*
neuropathology, *O*
ornithology,
orthology, *P*
pathology, *S*
sexology,
psychopathology,
TH theomythology

THROL'O.JĒ arthrology

TOL'O.JĒ *A* agmatology,
agrostology,
aretology,
aristology, *B*
battology, *BR*
bromatology,
brontology, *CH*
chartology, *D*
deontology,
dermatology,
dialectology,
dittology, *E*
Egyptology,
emblematology,

emetology,
enigmatology,
environmentology,
erotology,
eschatology,
aesthematology,
esthetology, *F*
fetology,
philematology,
phytology,
photology, *GL*
glottology, *GR*
grammatology, *H*
heartology,
hematology,
herpetology,
hyetology,
histology, *I*
insectology, *J*
geratology,
gerontology,
gigantology, *K*
cartology,
kymatology, *KL*
climatology, *KR*
cryptology,
Christology,
chromatology, *L*
leptology, *M*
mantology,
melittology,
microclimatology,
micropalaeontology,
N neontology,
nostology,
pneumatology,
numismatology, *O*
odontology,
olfactology,
onomatology,
ontology,
oryctology, otology,
P palaeophytology,
palaeoclimatology,
palaeontology,
pantology,
parasitology,
patronomatology,
pestology,
pyritology,
pistology, *PL*
planktology,
plutology, *PR*
primatology,
proctology,
protophytology, *R*
rhematology,
rheumatology, *S*
semantology,
sematology,
cetology,
scientology,

psicatology,
symptomatology,
systematology,
cytology, sitology,
somatology,
Sovietology, *SK*
scatology,
skeletology, *SP*
spermatology, *ST*
statistology,
stomatology, *STR*
stromatology, *T*
tantology,
telematology,
teratology,
ctetology, typtology,
tautology, *TH*
thanatology,
thermatology,
thaumatology, *THR*
thremmatology, *Z*
zoophytology

THROL'O.JĒ arthrology
TROL'O.JĒ astrology,
electrology,
gastrology,
iatrology,
metrology,
patrology, petrology

OL'O.JER

DOL'O.JER   sockdolager

(See **OL'O.JĒ**; drop *-y*, add *-er* where appropriate.)

OL'O.JIST

ROL'O.JIST   moirologist

(See **OL'O.JĒ**; drop *-y*, add *-ist* where appropriate.)

OL'O.JĪZ

THOL'O.JĪZ   demythologize

(See **OL'O.JĒ**; drop *-y*, add *ize* where appropriate.)

OL'OP.ER

(See **OLUP**, add *-er* where appropriate.)

OL'OP.ING

(See **OLUP**, add *-ing* where appropriate.)

OL'O.TĪP

HOL'O.TĪP	holotype
KOL'O.TĪP	collotype

ŌL'STER.ER

BŌL'STER.ER	bolsterer
HŌL'STER.ER	upholsterer

ÔL'TER.ER

ÔL'TER.ER	alterer
FÔL'TER.ER	falterer
HÔL'TER.ER	halterer, unhalterer
PÔL'TER.ER	palterer
SÔL'TER.ER	psalterer

ÔL'TER.ING

ÔL'TER.ING	altering, unaltering
FÔL'TER.ING	faltering, unfaltering
HÔL'TER.ING	haltering, unhaltering
PÔL'TERING	paltering

ÔL'TI.NES

FÔL'TI.NES	faultiness
MÔL'TI.NES	maltiness
SÔL'TI.NES	saltiness

OL'Ū.BL

SOL'Ū.BL	indissoluble, insoluble, soluble
VOL'Ū.BL	voluble

OL'Ū.BLĒ

SOL'Ū.BLĒ	indissolubly, insolubly, solubly
VOL'Ū.BLĒ	volubly

OL'Ū.TIV

SOL'Ū.TIV	solutive
VOL'Ū.TIV	supervolutive, volutive

OL'VA.BL

SOL'VA.BL	absolvable, insolvable, solvable

ZOL'VA.BL   dissolvable, indissolvable, resolvable, unresolvable

OL'VEN.SĒ

SOL'VEN.SĒ   insolvency, solvency
VOL'VEN.SĒ   revolvency

OM'A.KĒ

OM'A.KĒ   alectryomachy, batrachomyomachy, duomachy, hieromachy, sciomachy, theomachy
GOM'A.KĒ   logomachy
KOM'A.KĒ   psychomachy
NOM'A.KĒ   iconomachy, monomachy, naumachy
ROM'A.KĒ   pyromachy, centauromachy, tauromachy
TOM'A.KĒ   giantomachy
WOM'A.KĒ   wommacky

OM'A.THĒ

KOM'A.THĒ   pharmacomathy
LOM'A.THĒ   philomathy
SOM'A.THĒ   misomathy
TOM'A.THĒ   chrestomathy

Ō'MA.TIZM

KRŌ'MA.TIZM   achromatism, chromatism
PLŌ'MA.TIZM   diplomatism

OM'E.NA

GOM'E.NA   antilegomena, prolegomena
NOM'E.NA   phenomena
POM'E.NA   paralipomena

OM'E.NAL

(See **OM'I.NAL**)

OM'E.NON

(See **OM'I.NUN**)

OM'E.TER

OM'E.TER   *A* absorptiometer, aerometer, areometer, *B* biometer, *FL* fluviometer, *G* goniometer, *H* heliometer, *J* geometer, *K* cardiometer, *KR* craniometer, cryometer, *M* mileometer, *O* audiometer, oleometer, oömeter, *P* potentiometer, *PL* pluviometer, *R* radiometer, *ST* stereometer, *SW* swingometer, *T* tacheometer, tensionometer, *V* variometer, *Y* eudiometer

BOM'E.TER   tribometer
BROM'E.TER   ombrometer, vibrometer
DOM'E.TER   odometer, pedometer, speedometer, udometer
DROM'E.TER   dendrometer, hydrometer
FOM'E.TER   graphometer
GOM'E.TER   algometer, ergometer, logometer
GROM'E.TER   hygrometer
KLOM'E.TER   cyclometer
KOM'E.TER   echometer, oncometer, psychometer, tachometer, trochometer, viscometer
KROM'E.TER   macrometer, micrometer, psychrometer
LOM'E.TER   alcoholometer, bolometer, kilometer, coulometer, oscillometer, cephalometer, sillometer, silometer, scintillometer, psycholometer, stylometer
MOM'E.TER   *A* anemometer, arithmometer, atmometer, *D* dermometer, dynamometer, *E* endosmometer, *J* geothermometer, *KR* chromometer, *O* osmometer, *P* pulmometer, *S* cymometer, seismometer, *TH* thermometer, *TR* tromometer, *V* volumometer, *Z* zymometer

NOM'E.TER   *A* actionometer, actinometer, *D* declinometer, diaphanometer, *F* phonometer, *G* galvanometer, *H* harmonometer, horizonometer, *I* inclinometer, *KL* clinometer, *KR* chronometer, *M* manometer, micronometer, monometer, *N* nanometer, *O* ozonometer, *P* passionometer, pycnometer, *PL* planometer, *S* salinometer, sonometer, *SF* sphygmomanometer, *T* tannometer, tonometer, *TR* trigonometer, *V* vinometer, volumenometer

POM'E.TER   hippometer, nauropometer, tropometer
ROM'E.TER   *A* accelerometer, aerometer, *B* barometer, *FL* fluorometer, *H* horometer, *I* interferometer, *O* orometer, *P* pyrometer, *R* respirometer, *S* saccharometer, *SF* spherometer, *SKL* sclerometer, *SP* spirometer, *T* tellurometer
SOM'E.TER   drosometer, gasometer, hypsometer, opisometer,

	passometer, pulsometer, thalassometer
THOM'E.TER	bathometer, stethometer
TOM'E.TER	*A* altometer, *CH* chartometer, *F* photometer, *H* haptometer, hectometer, *K* chartometer, comptometer, *KL* climatometer, *KR* chromatometer, *L* lactometer, leptometer, *M* magnetometer, *N* pneumatometer, *O* olfactometer, optometer, *P* pantometer, *PL* platometer, *R* refractometer, *S* sensitometer, cyrtometer, *ST* stactometer, *STR* stratometer, *TH* thanatometer
TROM'E.TER	astrometer, electrometer, nitrometer, spectrometer
ZOM'E.TER	applauseometer, horizometer, piezometer

OM'E.TRĒ

OM'E.TRĒ	biometry, historiometry, geometry, craniometry, osteometry, sociometry, stereometry, stoichiometry, tacheometry, zoometry
DOM'E.TRĒ	iodometry
FOM'E.TRĒ	morphometry
HOM'E.TRĒ	Mahometry
KOM'E.TRĒ	psychometry, stichometry
LOM'E.TRĒ	allometry, colometry
MOM'E.TRĒ	anemometry, anthropomometry, dynamometry, pneumometry
NOM'E.TRĒ	chronometry, ozonometry, trigonometry, uranometry

POM'E.TRĒ	anthropometry, typometry
ROM'E.TRĒ	gyrometry, chorometry
SOM'E.TRĒ	hypsometry, isometry
TOM'E.TRĒ	photometry, optometry
THOM'E.TRĒ	orthometry
TROM'E.TRĒ	astrometry

(See **OM'E.TER,** change *-er* to *-ry* where appropriate.)

Ō'MI.A

KŌ'MI.A	acomia, encomia
NŌ'MI.A	lethonomia
TŌ'MI.A	ozostomia

Ō'MI.AL

NŌ'MI.AL	binomial, monomial, nomial
TŌ'MI.AL	tomial

Ō'MI.ER

DŌ'MI.ER	domier
FŌ'MI.ER	foamier
HŌ'MI.ER	homier
KRŌ'MI.ER	chromier
LŌ'MI.ER	loamier

OM'I.KAL

DOM'I.KAL	domical
KOM'I.KAL	comical, coxcombical, tragicomical
NOM'I.KAL	agronomical, astronomical, economical, gastronomical, iconomachal, metronomical, uneconomical
TOM'I.KAL	anatomical, atomical, phantomical, zoötomical

OM'I.NAL

DOM'I.NAL	abdominal
NOM'I.NAL	adnominal, binominal, phenomenal, cognominal, nominal, prenominal, pronominal, surnominal

OM'I.NANS

DOM'I.NANS	dominance, predominance, subdominance
PROM'I.NANS	prominence

OM'I.NANT

DOM'I.NANT	dominant, predominant, subdominant, superdominant
PROM'I.NANT	prominent

OM'I.NĀT

OM'I.NĀT	preominate
BOM'I.NĀT	abominate
DOM'I.NĀT	dominate, predominate
KOM'I.NĀT	comminate
NOM'I.NĀT	agnominate, denominate, nominate, prenominate, renominate

OM'I.NĒ

DOM'I.NĒ	dominie
HOM'I.NĒ	Chicahominy, hominy
NOM'I.NĒ	nominee, nominy
ROM'I.NĒ	Romany

Ō'MI.NES

DŌ'MI.NES	dominess
FŌ'MI.NES	foaminess
HŌ'MI.NES	hominess
KRŌ'MI.NES	chrominess
LŌ'MI.NES	loaminess

ŌM'ING.LĒ

FŌM'ING.LĒ	foamingly
GLŌM'ING.LĒ	gloamingly
HŌ'MING.LĒ	homingly
RŌ'MING.LĒ	roamingly

OM'I.NA

(See OM'E.NA)

OM'I.NAL

DOM'I.NAL	abdominal
GOM'I.NAL	antilegomenal, prolegomenal
NOM'I.NAL	adnominal, binominal, phenomenal, nominal, prenominal
POM'I.NAL	paralipomenal

OM'I.NĀ'SHUN

BOM'I.NĀ'SHUN	abomination
DOM'I.NĀ'SHUN	domination, predomination
KOM'I.NĀ'SHUN	commination denomination,
NOM'I.NĀ'SHUN	nomination

OM'I.NUN

GOM'I.NUN	antilegomenon, prolegomenon
NOM'I.NUN	phenomenon
POM'I.NUN	paralipomenon

OM'I.NUS

OM'I.NUS	ominous
DOM'I.NUS	abdominous, Dominus
GOM'I.NUS	prolegomenous
NOM'I.NUS	binominous

Ō'MI.UM

KŌ'MI.UM	encomium, gerontocomium, nosocomium
KRŌ'MI.UM	ferrochromium, chromium
TŌ'MI.UM	prostomium, tomium

ŌN'A.BL

ŌN'A.BL	ownable
BŌN'A.BL	bonable
DŌN'A.BL	condonable
FŌN'A.BL	phonable
HŌN'A.BL	honable, unhonable
LŌN'A.BL	loanable, unloanable

PŌN'A.BL	exponible, unexponable
TŌN'A.BL	atonable, tonable, unatonable
ZŌN'A.BL	unzonable, zonable

ON'A.KAL

(See ON'I.KAL)

ÔN'DER.ER

LÔN'DER.ER	launderer
MÔN'DER.ER	maunderer

ON'DER.ER

PON'DER.ER	ponderer

(See ÄN'DER.ER)

ÔN'DER.ING

LÔN'DER.ING	laundering
MÔN'DER.ING	maundering

ON'DER.ING

PON'DER.ING	pondering

(See ÄN'DER.ING)

ON'ER.US

ON'ER.US	onerous
SON'ER.US	sonorous

Ō'NI.A

Ō'NI.A	bryonia, Ionia
DŌ'NI.A	anhedonia, hyperhedonia, Caledonia, Macedonia, nikhedonia
FŌ'NI.A	aphonia, dysphonia, heraphonia, rhinophonia
GŌ'NI.A	begonia, Patagonia, pogonia, tecnogonia
HŌ'NI.A	mahonia
KŌ'NI.A	aniseikonia, Laconia, zirconia
LŌ'NI.A	Babylonia, escalonia, Catalonia, paulownia, cephalonia, valonia

MŌ'NI.A	ammonia, bronchopneumonia, harmonia, pleuropneumonia, pneumonia, eudemonia
NŌ'NI.A	bignonia
RŌ'NI.A	boronia
SŌ'NI.A	asonia
TŌ'NI.A	boltonia, houstonia, catatonia, claytonia, myotonia
VŌ'NI.A	Livonia, Slavonia

Ō'NI.AL

KŌ'NI.AL	aconeal
LŌ'NI.AL	colonial, intercolonial
MŌ'NI.AL	demonial, harmonial, matrimonial, monial, patrimonial, sanctimonial, testimonial
RŌ'NI.AL	baronial

Ō'NI.AN

Ō'NI.AN	aeonian, eonian, halcyonian, Ionian
DŌ'NI.AN	Aberdonian, Caledonian, Macedonian, Myrmidonian
FŌ'NI.AN	colophonian
GŌ'NI.AN	gonion, gorgonian, Oregonian, Patagonian
KŌ'NI.AN	Baconian, draconian, Franconian, Laconian, shaconian
LŌ'NI.AN	Apollonian, Babylonian, Catalonian, chelonian, Thessalonian
MŌ'NI.AN	demonian, Lacedaemonian
PŌ'NI.AN	Lapponian
RŌ'NI.AN	Pyrrhonian, Ciceronian
SHŌ'NI.AN	Shoshonean
SŌ'NI.AN	Jeffersonian, Johnsonian, Oxonian, Smithsonian
THŌ'NI.AN	chthonian

TŌ′NI.AN

	Estonian, Etonian, Hambletonian, catachtonian, Miltonian, Newtonian, Plutonian, Washingtonian
VŌ′NI.AN	Devonian, favonian, pavonian, Slavonian
ZŌ′NI.AN	Amazonian, bezonian

Ō′NI.ER

BŌ′NI.ER	bonier
DRŌ′NI.ER	dronier
PHŌ′NI.ER	phonier
STŌ′NI.ER	stonier
TŌ′NI.ER	tonier

ÔN′I.ER

BRÔN′I.ER	brawnier
TÔN′I.ER	tawnier

ÔN′I.EST

BRÔN′I.EST	brawniest
TÔN′I.EST	tawniest

ON′I.FĪ

BON′I.FĪ	bonify
PON′I.FĪ	saponify
SON′I.FĪ	personify
ZON′I.FĪ	ozonify

ON′I.KA

MON′I.KA	harmonica, Santa Monica
PON′I.KA	japonica
RON′I.KA	veronica
TON′I.KA	santonica

ON′I.KAL

ON′I.KAL	histrionical
BON′I.KAL	Sorbonical
FON′I.KAL	antiphonical, diaphonical, tautophonical, euphonical
GON′I.KAL	cosmogonical
KON′I.KAL	aconical, conical, iconical

KRON′I.KAL	acronical, acronycal, antichronical, diachronical, chronicle, synchronical
LON′I.KAL	Babylonical
MON′I.KAL	harmonical, monachal, monocle, mnemonical
NON′I.KAL	canonical, uncanonical
PON′I.KAL	geoponical
RON′I.KAL	ironical
SON′I.KAL	thrasonical
TON′I.KAL	architectonical, tonical

(See **ONIK**, add -al where appropriate.)

ON′I.KON

KRON′I.KON	chronicon
MON′I.KON	harmonicon

ON′I.MĒ

LON′I.MĒ	poecilonymy
MON′I.MĒ	homonymy
NON′I.MĒ	synonymy, teknonymy
PON′I.MĒ	eponymy, toponymy
TON′I.MĒ	metonymy
TRON′I.MĒ	patronymy

(See **ON′O.MĒ**)

ON′I.MIST

(See **ON′O.MIST**)

ON′I.KL

(See **ON′I.KAL**)

ON′I.MUS

ON′I.MUS	onymous, polyonymous, euonymous
DON′I.MUS	pseudonymous
LON′I.MUS	allonymous
MON′I.MUS	homonymous
NON′I.MUS	anonymous, synonymous
PON′I.MUS	eponymous
RON′I.MUS	heteronymous, Hieronymus, paronymous
TON′I.MUS	autonymous

(See **ON′O.MUS**)

ÔN′ING.LĒ

FÔN′ING.LĒ	fawningly
YÔN′ING.LĒ	yawningly

ON′ISH.ING

MON′ISH.ING	admonishing, monishing, premonishing
STON′ISH.ING	astonishing

ON′ISH.MENT

MON′ISH.MENT	admonishment, premonishment
STON′ISH.MENT	astonishment

ON′I.SIZM

ON′I.SIZM	histrionicism
DON′I.SIZM	sardonicism
KON′I.SIZM	laconicism
TON′I.SIZM	Teutonicism

Ō′NI.UM

FŌ′NI.UM	euphonium
GŌ′NI.UM	agonium, ascogonium, carpogonium, pelargonium, spermogonium, sporogonium
KŌ′NI.UM	conium, meconium, synconium, zirconium
LŌ′NI.UM	polonium
MŌ′NI.UM	ammonium, harmonium, pandemonium, stramonium, testimonium
SŌ′NI.UM	opsonium
TŌ′NI.UM	plutonium
TRŌ′NI.UM	positronium

Ō′NI.US

DŌ′NI.US	ideoneous
FŌ′NI.US	symphonious, euphonious
LŌ′NI.US	felonious, Polonius
MŌ′NI.US	A acrimonious, alimonious, H harmonious, I inharmonious, KW

	querimonious, *M* matrimonious, *P* parsimonious, *S* sanctimonious, ceremonious, *U* unceremonious, unsanctimonious
RŌ'NI.US	erroneous
TRŌ'NI.US	Petronius, ultroneous

ŌN'O.GRAF

FŌN'O.GRAF	phonograph
RŌN'O.GRAF	coronograph
TŌN'O.GRAF	tonograph

ON'O.GRAF

KRON'O.GRAF	chronograph
MON'O.GRAF	monograph
TON'O.GRAF	tonograf

Ō'NO.GRAM

FŌ'NO.GRAM	phonogram
TŌ'NO.GRAM	tonogram

ON'O.GRAM

KRON'O.GRAM	chronogram
MON'O.GRAM	monogram
SON'O.GRAM	sonogram
TON'O.GRAM	tonogram

ON'O.MĒ

ON'O.MĒ	polyonomy, theonomy
BON'O.MĒ	bonhommie
FON'O.MĒ	morphonomy
GRON'O.MĒ	agronomy
KON'O.MĒ	economy
LON'O.MĒ	dactylonomy
MON'O.MĒ	homonomy
NON'O.MĒ	synonomy
PON'O.MĒ	antroponomy
RON'O.MĒ	aeronomy, Deuteronomy
SON'O.MĒ	isonomy, nosonomy, cytotaxonomy, taxonomy
TON'O.MĒ	autonomy
TRON'O.MĒ	astronomy, gastronomy, metronomy

(See **ON'I.MĒ**)

ON'O.MER

MON'O.MER	monomer
STRON'O.MER	astronomer
TRON'O.MER	gastronomer

ON'O.MIST

ON'O.MIST	polyonomist
GRON'O.MIST	agronomist
KON'O.MIST	economist
NON'O.MIST	synonymist
PON'O.MIST	eponymist
TON'O.MIST	autonomist, plutonomist
TRON'O.MIST	gastronomist

ON'O.MĪZ

KON'O.MĪZ	economize
STRON'O.MĪZ	astronomize
TON'O.MĪZ	autonomize
TRON'O.MĪZ	gastronomize

ON'O.MUS

ON'O.MUS	polyonomous
RON'O.MUS	heteronomous
SON'O.MUS	isonomous, taxonomous
TON'O.MUS	autonomous
TRON'O.MUS	gastronomous

(See **ON'I.MUS**)

ÔNT'ING.LĒ

DÔNT'ING.LĒ	dauntingly
HÔNT'ING.LĒ	hauntingly
TÔNT'ING.LĒ	tauntingly
VÔNT'ING.LĒ	vauntingly
WÔNT'ING.LĒ	wantingly

ŌN'WOR.THĒ

GRŌN'WUR.THĒ	groanworthy
LŌN'WUR.THĒ	loanworthy
MŌN'WUR.THĒ	moanworthy

OO'A.BL

DŌŌ'A.BL	doable, subduable, undoable
NŌŌ'A.BL	renewable, unrenewable
SHŌŌ'A.BL	shoeable, shooable, unshoeable, unshooable
SŌŌ'A.BL	pursuable, suable, unpursuable, unsuable
STŌŌ'A.BL	stewable, unstewable
STRŌŌ'A.BL	construable, strewable, unconstruable, unstrewable

(See **Ū'A.BL**)

OO'ANT.LĒ

FLŌŌ'ANT.LĒ	fluently, confluently
SŌŌ'ANT.LĒ	pursuantly
TRŌŌ'ANT.LĒ	truantly

OO'BER.ANS

TŌŌ'BER.ANS	protuberance
ZŌŌ'BER.ANS	exuberance

OO'BER.ANT

TŌŌ'BER.ANT	protuberant
ZŌŌ'BER.ANT	exuberant

OO'BER.Ē

BLŌŌ'BER.Ē	blueberry

(See **Ū'BER.Ē**)

OO'BER.US

TŌŌ'BER.US	protuberous, tuberous
ZŌŌ'BER.US	exuberous

(See **Ū'BER.US**)

OO'BI.A

NŌŌ'BI.A	Nubia
RŌŌ'BI.A	rubia

OO'BI.KL

RŌŌ'BI.KL	cherubical

(See **Ū'BI.KL**)

OO'BI.LĀT

JOO'BI.LĀT	jubilate

(See Ū'BI.LĀT)

OO'BI.US

DOO'BI.US	dubious
ROO'BI.US	rubious

(See Ū'BI.US)

OO'BRI.KĀT

LOO'BRI.KĀT	lubricate
ROO'BRI.KĀT	rubricate

OO'BRI.US

GOO'BRI.US	lugubrious
LOO'BRI.US	insalubrious, salubrious

(See Ū'BRI.US)

OOD'A.BL

KLOOD'A.BL	includable, includible, concludable, precludable
LOOD'A.BL	eludible, ineludible

OO'DEN.SĒ

KLOO'DEN.SĒ	concludency
KROO'DEN.SĒ	recrudency

(See Ū'DEN.SĒ)

OO'DI.A

(See Ū'DI.A)

OO'DI.NAL

LOO'DI.NAL	paludinal
TOO'DI.NAL	altitudinal, aptitudinal, attitudinal, desuetudinal, consuetudinal, latitudinal, longitudinal, testitudinal

(See ŪDI.NAL)

OO'DI.NES

BROO'DI.NES	broodiness
MOO'DI.NES	moodiness

OOD'I.NES

GOOD'I.NES	goodiness, goody-goodiness
WOOD'I.NES	woodiness

AT'I.TOO'DI.NĪZ

AT'I.TOO'DI.NĪZ *attitudinize*
PLAT'I.TOO'DI.NIZ
       platitudinize

(See AT'I.TÜ.DI.NĪZ)

OO'DI.NUS

LOO'DI.NUS	paludinous
TOO'DI.NUS	fortitudinous, latitudinous, longitudinous, multitudinous, platitudinous, solicitudinous, vicissitudinous

(See Ū'DI.NUS)

OO'DI.Ō

LOO'DI.Ō	preludio
STOO'DI.Ō	studio

(See Ū'DI.Ō)

OO'DI.TĒ

KROO'DI.TĒ	crudity
NOO'DI.TĒ	nudity
ROO'DI.TĒ	rudity

(See Ū'DI.TĒ)

OO'DI.UM

LOO'DI.UM	postludium, preludium
STOO'DI.UM	studium

(See Ū'DI.UM)

OO'DI.US

LOO'DI.US	preludious
STOO'DI.US	studious

OO'EL.ER

DOO'EL.ER	dueler
GROO'EL.ER	grueler
JOO'EL.ER	jeweler
KROO'EL.ER	creweler, crueler

(See Ū'EL.ER)

OO'EL.ING

DOO'EL.ING	dueling
GROO'EL.ING	grueling
JOO'EL.ING	bejewelling, jewelling

(See Ū'EL.ING)

OO'EL.IST

DOO'EL.IST	duelist
KROO'EL.IST	crewelist, cruelest

OO'EN.SĒ

FLOO'EN.SĒ	fluency
TROO'EN.SĒ	truancy

OO'ER.Ē

BROO'ER.E	brewery

(See Ū'ER.Ē)

OO'I.NES

DOO'I.NES	dewiness
GLOO'I.NES	glueyness
GOO'I.NES	gooiness
SKROO'I.NES	screwiness

OO'I.NUS

BROO'I.NUS	bruinous
PROO'I.NUS	pruinous
ROO'I.NUS	ruinous

OO'ISH.NES

JOO'ISH.NES	Jewishness

NŌŌ'ISH.NES   newishness
SHRŌŌ'ISH.NES shrewishness

$\overline{OO}'$I.TĒ

DŌŌ'I.TĒ   assiduity
FLŌŌ'I.TĒ   superfluity
GRŌŌ'I.TĒ   incongruity,
             congruity
KRŌŌ'I.TĒ   cruety
NŌŌ'I.TĒ   annuity,
             discontinuity,
             ingenuity,
             continuity, tenuity
SŌŌ'I.TĒ   suety
TŌŌ'I.TĒ   fatuity, fortuity,
             gratuity, perpetuity

(See $\bar{U}'$I.TĒ)

$\overline{OO}'$I.TIV

FRŌŌ'I.TIV   fruitive

(See $\bar{U}'$I.TIV)

$\overline{OO}'$I.TUS

(See $\bar{U}'$I.TUS)

$\overline{OO}'$JI.NUS

NŌŌ'JI.NUS   lanuginous
RŌŌ'JI.NUS   aeruginous,
             ferruginous
SŌŌ'JI.NUS   salsuginous

$\overline{OO}'$KER.Ē

DŌŌ'KER.Ē   dukery, caducary
JŌŌ'KER.Ē   jookerie
SPŌŌ'KER.Ē   spookery

OOK'ER.Ē

BOOK'ER.Ē   bookery
KOOK'ER.Ē   cookery
NOOK'ER.Ē   nookery
ROOK'ER.Ē   rookery

$\overline{OO}'$LI.A

BŌŌ'LI.A   abulia, dysbulia,
             hyperbulia, parabulia,
             sthenobulia
THŌŌ'LI.A   thulia

$\overline{OO}'$LI.AN

JŌŌ'LI.AN   joulean, Julian
RŌŌ'LI.AN   cerulean

(See $\bar{U}'$LI.AN)

$\overline{OO}'$LI.FÔRM

(See $\bar{U}'$LI.FÔRM)

OOL'I.NES

BOOL'I.NES   bulliness
WOOL'I.NES   wooliness

$\overline{OO}'$LISH.LĒ

FŌŌ'LISH.LĒ   foolishly
GŌŌ'LISH.LĒ   ghoulishly
KŌŌ'LISH.LĒ   coolishly

(See $\bar{U}'$LISH.LĒ)

$\overline{OO}'$LISH.NES

FŌŌ'LISH.NES   foolishness
GŌŌ'LISH.NES   ghoulishness
KŌŌ'LISH.NES   coolishness

(See $\bar{U}'$LISH.NES)

OOL'ISH.NES

BOOL'ISH.NES   bullishness
FOOL'ISH.NES   fullishness
WOOL'ISH.NES   woolishness

Ō'Ö.LĪT

Ō'Ö.LĪT   oölite
ZŌ'Ö.LĪT   zoölite

$\overline{OO}'$LI.TĒ

DŌŌ'LI.TĒ   incredulity,
             credulity, sedulity
RŌŌ'LI.TĒ   garrulity

$\overline{OO}$M'A.BL

(See $\overline{OO}$M, add -*able* where appropriate.)

$\overline{OO}'$ME.NAL

(See $\overline{OO}'$MI.NAL)

$\overline{OO}'$MER.AL

NŌŌ'MER.AL   numeral

(See $\bar{U}'$MER.AL)

$\overline{OO}'$MERD.LĒ

RŌŌ'MERD.LĒ   rumoredly

(See $\bar{U}'$MERD.LĒ)

OO'MER.Ē

BLŌŌ'MER.Ē   bloomery
PLŌŌ'MER.Ē   plumery
TŌŌ'MER.Ē   costumery

(See $\bar{U}'$MER.Ē)

$\overline{OO}'$MER.US

NŌŌMER.US   numerous,
            innumerous
RŌŌ'MER.US   rumorous
TŌŌ'MER.US   tumerous

(See $\bar{U}'$MER.US)

$\overline{OO}'$MI.LĒ

BŌŌ'MI.LĒ   boomily
GLŌŌ'MI.LĒ   gloomily
RŌŌ'MI.LĒ   rheumily, roomily

(See $\bar{U}'$MI.LĒ)

$\overline{OO}'$MI.NA

LŌŌ'MI.NA   alumina, lumina
NŌŌ'MI.NA   numina

$\overline{OO}'$MI.NAL

LŌŌ'MI.NAL   luminal, voluminal
NŌŌ'MI.NAL   noumenal
RŌŌ'MI.NAL   ruminal

(See $\bar{U}'$MI.NAL)

$\overline{OO}'$MI.NANT

LŌŌ'MI.NANT   illuminant, luminant
RŌŌ'MI.NANT   nonruminant,
              ruminant

OO'MI.NĀ'SHUN

LOOMI.NĀ'SHUN illumination
ROO'MI.NĀ'SHUN
                rumination

OO'MI.NĀT

LOO'MI.NĀT   illuminate, luminate
ROO'MI.NĀT   ferruminate,
             ruminate

(See Ū'MI.NĀT)

OO'MI.NES

BLOO'MI.NES   bloominess
GLOO'MI.NES   gloominess
PLOO'MI.NES   pluminess
ROO'MI.NES   rheuminess,
             roominess

(See Ū'MI.NES)

OO'MING.LĒ

(See OOM, ŪM, add *-ingly* where appropriate.)

OO'MI.NĪZ

LOO'MĬ.NĪZ   aluminize
TOO'MI.NĪZ   bituminize

(See U'MI.NĪZ)

OO'MI.NUS

BOO'MI.NUS   albuminous
FLOO'MI.NUS   fluminous
GOO'MI.NUS   leguminous
LOO'MI.NUS   aluminous,
             luminous,
             voluminous
NOO'MI.NUS   numinous
TOO'MI.NUS   bituminous

(See Ū'MI.NUS)

OO'MŪ.LĀT

TOO'MŬ.LĀT   intumulate, tumulate

(See Ū'MŪ.LĀT)

OON'ER.Ē

FOON'ER.Ē   buffoonery
KOON'ER.Ē   cocoonery
LOON'ER.Ē   lunary,
             pantalooneery,
             plenilunary,
             sublunary
TOON'ER.Ē   festoonery
TROON'ER.Ē   poltroonery

OO'NI.FORM

LOO'NI.FORM   luniform
ROO'NI.FORM   runiform

(See Ū'NI.FORM)

OO'NI.KL

(See Ū'NI.KL)

OO'NI.LĒ

LOO'NI.LĒ   loonily
MOO'NI.LĒ   moonily
SPOO'NI.LĒ   spoonily
SWOO'NI.LĒ   swoonily

OO'NISH.LĒ

FOO'NISH.LĒ   buffoonishly
TROO'NISH.LĒ   poltroonishly

OO'NI.TĒ

JOO'NI.TĒ   jejunity
(See Ū'NI.TĒ)

OO'PA.BL

KOO'PA.BL   recoupable,
             unrecoupable

(See Ū'PA.BL)

OO'PE.RĀT

KOO'PE.RĀT   recuperate
TOO'PE.RĀT   vituperate

OO'PER.Ē

DOO'PER.Ē   dupery
KOO'PER.Ē   coopery

OO'PI.AL

ROO'PI.AL   rupial
SOO'PI.AL   marsupial
TROO'PI.AL   troopial, troupial

OO'PI.ER

DROO'PI.ER   droopier
KROO'PI.ER   croupier
LOO'PI.ER   loopier
SOO'PI.ER   soupier

OOP'ING.LĒ

DROOP'ING.LĒ   droopingly
HWOOP'ING.LĒ   whoopingly
LOOP'ING.LĒ   loopingly
SKOOP'ING.LĒ   scoopingly
SNOOP'ING.LĒ   snoopingly
STOOP'ING.LĒ   stoopingly
SWOOP'ING.LĒ   swoopingly
TROOP'ING.LĒ   troopingly

OOP'LI.KĀT

DOOP'LI.KĀT   duplicate,
             reduplicate
DROOP'LI.KĀT   quadruplicate
TOOP'LI.KĀT   contortuplicate,
             centuplicate

(See Ū'PLI.KĀT)

OO'PŪ.LUS

LOO'PŪ.LUS   lupulus
SKROO'PŪ.LUS   scrupulous,
             unscrupulous

OOR'A.BLĒ

DOOR'A.BLĒ   durably, endurably,
             unendurably

(See UR'A.BLĒ)

OOR'A.LĒ

PLOOR'A.LĒ   plurally
MYOOR'A.LĒ   murally
ROOR'A.LĒ   rurally

OOR'A.LIST

PLOOR'A.LIST	pluralist
ROOR'A.LIST	ruralist

(See Ū'RA.LIST)

OOR'A.LĬZ

PLOOR'A.LĬZ	pluralize
ROOR'A.LĬZ	ruralize

OOR'A.LIZM

PLOOR'A.LIZM	pluralism
ROOR'A.LIZM	ruralism

OOR'A.TIV

DOOR'A.TIV	durative, indurative
TOOR'A.TIV	maturative

(See ŪR'A.TIV)

OOR'I.A

CHOOR'I.A	Manchuria
NOOR'I.A	anuria
TROOR'I.A	Etruria

OOR'I.AL

OOR'I.AL	oorial, urial

(See Ū'RI.AL)

OOR'I.AN

CHOOR'I.AN	Manchurian
DOOR'I.AN	Durian
GOOR'I.AN	Ben-Gurion, pagurian
KOOR'I.AN	decurion
LOOR'I.AN	Silurian, tellurian, tellurion
MOOR'I.AN	lemurian
THOOR'I.AN	Arthurian, holothurian
TOOR'I.AN	centurion, turion
TROOR'I.AN	Etrurian
ZOOR'I.AN	Missourian

OOR'I.ĀT

(See UR'I.ĀT)

OOR'I.ENS

(See UR'I.ENS)

OOR'I.ENT

(See UR'I.ENT)

OOR'ING.LĒ

LOOR'ING.LĒ	alluringly

(See UR'ING.LĒ)

OOR'I.TĒ

SHOOR'I.TĒ	cocksurety, surety

(See Ū'RI.TĒ)

OOR'I.US

JOOR'I.US	injurious, perjurious
ZHOOR'I.US	luxurious, usurious

(See Ū'RI.US)

OOS'A.BL

DOOS'A.BL	adducible, deducible, educible, inducible, irreducible, conducible, produceable, seducible, traducible, unproduceable, unseducible, untraducible
KROOS'A.BL	crucible
LOOS'A.BL	loosable, unloosable

OO'SE.RĒ

KLOO'SE.RĒ	exclusory, conclusory, reclusory
LOO'SE.RĒ	delusory, elusory, illusory, collusory, lusory, prelusory, prolusory
TROO'SE.RĒ	extrusory

(See Ū'SER.Ē)

OO'SHI.A

FOO'SHI.A	fuchsia
NOO'SHI.A	minutia

OO'SHI.AL

(See OOSHAL)

OO'SHUN.AL

LOO'SHUN.AL	evolutional, revolutional
TOO'SHUN.AL	institutional, constitutional, substitutional

(See Ū'SHUN.AL)

OO'SHUN.ER

LOO'SHUN.ER	ablutioner, resolutioner, revolutioner

(See Ū'SHUN.ER)

OO'SHUN.IST

LOO'SHUN.IST	evolutionist, revolutionist, resolutionist
TOO'SHUN.IST	constitutionist

(See Ū'SHUN.IST)

OO'SI.AN

(See OOSHUN, ŪSHUN)

OO'SI.BL

(See OO'SA.BL)

OO'SID.LĒ

DOO'SID.LĒ	deucedly
LOO'SID.LĒ	lucidly, pellucidly

(See Ū'SID.LĒ)

OO'SI.FER

KROO'SI.FER	crucifer
LOO'SI.FER	Lucifer

OO'SI.FÔRM

KROO'SI.FÔRM   cruciform
LOO'SI.FÔRM   luciform
NOO'SI.FÔRM   nuciform

OO'SIV.LĒ

KLOO'SIV.LĒ   exclusively,
   inclusively,
   inconclusively,
   conclusively
LOO'SIV.LĒ   allusively,
   delusively,
   elusively, illusively,
   collusively
TROO'SIV.LĒ   inobtrusively,
   intrusively,
   obtrusively,
   protrusively

(See Ū'SIV.LĒ)

OO'SIV.NES

DOO'SIV.NES   conduciveness
KLOO'SIV.NES   exclusiveness,
   inclusiveness,
   inconclusiveness,
   conclusiveness
LOO'SIV.NES   allusiveness,
   delusiveness,
   elusiveness,
   illusiveness,
   collusiveness
TROO'SIV.NES   inobtrusiveness,
   intrusiveness,
   obtrusiveness,
   protrusiveness

(See Ū'SIV.NES)

OO'SO.RĒ

(See OO'SE.RĒ)

OO'TA.BL

LOO'TA.BL   lootable, unlootable
MOO'TA.BL   mootable
SOO'TA.BL   suitable, unsuitable
SKROO'TA.BL   inscrutable,
   scrutable
TOO'TA.BL   tootable

(See Ū'TA.BL)

OO'TA.BLĒ

(See OO'TA.BL, Ū'TA.BL, change -e to
-y where appropriate.)

OO'TER.Ē

BOO'TER.Ē   bootery, free-
   bootery
FROO'TER.Ē   fruitery
ROO'TER.Ē   rootery
ZHOO'TER.Ē   bijouterie

(See Ū'TER.Ē)

OOTH'FUL.Ē

ROOTH'FUL.Ē   ruthfully
TROOTH'FUL.Ē   truthfully

(See ŪTH'FUL.Ē)

OOTH'FUL.NES

ROOTH'FUL.NES ruthfulness
TROOTH'FUL.NES
   truthfulness

(See ŪTH'FUL.NES)

OO'TI.AL

GLOO'TI.AL   gluteal
LOO'TI.AL   luteal

(See Ū'TI.AL)

OO'TI.FĪ

BROO'TI.FĪ   brutify

(See Ū'TI.FĪ)

OO'TI.FUL

DOO'TI.FUL   dutiful, undutiful

(See Ū'TI.FUL)

OO'TI.KL

SOO'TI.KL   pharmaceutical
TROO'TI.KL   latreutical

(See Ū'TI.KL)

OO'TI.LĪZ

BROO'TI.LĪZ   brutalize

(See Ū'TI.LĪZ)

OO'TI.NĀT

GLOO'TI.NĀT   agglutinate
SKROO'TI.NĀT   scrutinate
TROO'TI.NĀT   trutinate

OO'TI.NĒ

SKROO'TI.NĒ   scrutiny

(See Ū'TI.NĒ)

OO'TI.NES

FROO'TI.NES   fruitiness
SNOO'TI.NES   snootiness
SOO'TI.NES   sootiness

OO'TI.NÎR

BOO'TI.NÎR   boutonniere
SKROO'TI.NÎR   scrutineer

(See Ū'TI.NÎR)

OO'TI.NUS

GLOO'TI.NUS   glutinous
LOO'TI.NUS   velutinous
SKROO'TI.NUS   scrutinous

(See Ū'TI.NUS)

OO'TI.US

DOO'TI.US   duteous
GLOO'TI.US   gluteous
LOO'TI.US   luteous

(See Ū'TI.US)

OO'VA.BL

MOO'VA.BL   immovable,
   irremovable,
   movable,
   removable

PROO'VA.BL   approvable, improvable, provable, reprovable, unprovable, unimprovable

OO'VI.AL

FLOO'VI.AL   effluvial, fluvial
LOO'VI.AL   alluvial, antediluvial, diluvial, colluvial, post-diluvial
PLOO'VI.AL   pluvial
ZOO'VI.AL   exuvial

(See Ū'VI.AL)

OO'VI.AN

HOO'VI.AN   Scandihoovian
LOO'VI.AN   alluvian, antediluvian, diluvian, post-diluvian
ROO'VI.AN   Peruvian
SOO'VI.AN   Vesuvian

OO'VI.ĂT

LOO'VI.ĂT   alluviate
SOO'VI.ĂT   exuviate

OO'VING.LE

MOO'VING.LĒ   movingly
PROO'VING.LĒ   approvingly, reprovingly

OO'VI.UM

FLOO'VI.UM   effluvium
LOO'VI.UM   alluvium, diluvium, eluvium, colluvium, pediluvium
PLOO'VI.UM   impluvium, compluvium

OO'VI.US

GLOO'VI.US   ingluvious
PLOO'VI.US   Jupiter Pluvius, pluvious
SOO'VI.US   Vesuvius

OO'ZA.BL

LOO'ZA.BL   losable, unlosable
ROO'ZA.BL   perusable
TROO'ZA.BL   protrusible

(See Ū'ZA.BL)

OO'ZHUN.IST

LOO'ZHUN.IST   delusionist, illusionist
KLOO'ZHUN.IST   exclusionist

OP'A.THĒ

OP'A.THĒ   homeopathy, ideopathy, osteopathy, theopathy
DROP'A.THĒ   hydropathy
KOP'A.THĒ   psychopathy
LOP'A.THĒ   allopathy
NOP'A.THĒ   somnopathy
ROP'A.THĒ   deuteropathy, heteropathy, naturopathy, neuropathy
SOP'A.THĒ   isopathy
TOP'A.THĒ   autopathy

OP'A.THIST

OP'A.THIST   homeopathist, osteopathist
DROP'A.THIST   hydropathist
KOP'A.THIST   psychopathist
LOP'A.THIST   allopathist, hylopathist
NOP'A.THIST   somnopathist
ROP'A.THIST   neuropathist

Ō'PE.RĒ

DŌ'PE.RĒ   dopery
MŌ'PE.RĒ   mopery
PŌ'PE.RĒ   popery
RŌ'PE.RĒ   ropery

OP'ER.Ē

OP'ER.Ē   opery, zoöpery
FOP'ER.Ē   foppery
KOP'ER.Ē   coppery

OP'E.TĒ

HOP'E.TĒ   hippety-hoppety, hoppety
KLOP'E.TĒ   clippety-cloppety, cloppety
WOP'E.TĒ   wapiti

Ō'PI.A

Ō'PI.A   amblyopia, Ethiopia, myopia, presbyopia
KŌ'PI.A   cornucopia
LŌ'PI.A   hemeralopia, nyctalopia
NŌ'PI.A   asthenopia, protanopia, tritanopia
PLŌ'PI.A   diplopia
SKŌ'PI.A   keraunoscopia, rhytiscopia
TŌ'PI.A   dystopia, ectopia, photopia, heterotopia, scotopia, topia, Utopia

Ō'PI.AN

Ō'PI.AN   Ethiopian
KŌ'PI.AN   cornucopian
LŌ'PI.AN   Fallopian
SŌ'PI.AN   Aesopian
TŌ'PI.AN   Utopian

Ō'PI.ER

DŌ'PI.ER   dopier
MŌ'PI.ER   mopier
SLŌ'PI.ER   slopier
SŌ'PI.ER   soapier

OP'I.ER

CHOP'I.ER   choppier
FLOP'I.ER   floppier
HOP'I.ER   hoppier
KOP'I.ER   copier
SLOP'I.ER   sloppier
SOP'I.ER   soppier

OP'I.KAL

SKOP'I.KAL   metoscopical, microscopical

THROP'I.KAL philanthropical, misanthropical
TOP'I.KAL topical
TROP'I.KAL allotropical, subtropical, tropical

Ō'PI.NES

DŌ'PI.NES dopiness
MŌ'PI.NES mopiness
RŌ'PI.NES ropiness
SLŌ'PI.NES slopiness
SŌ'PI.NES soapiness

Ō'PISH.NES

DŌ'PISH.NES dopishness
MŌ'PISH.NES mopishness
PŌ'PISH.NES popishness

OP'I.TĒ

(See OP'E.TĒ)

OP'O.LIS

OP'O.LIS Heliopolis
BOP'O.LIS boobopolis
KROP'O.LIS acropolis, necropolis
LOP'O.LIS megalopolis
MOP'O.LIS cosmopolis
PROP'O.LIS propolis
TROP'O.LIS metropolis

OP'O.LIST

OP'O.LIST bibliopolist
KOP'O.LIST pharmacopolist
NOP'O.LIST monopolist

OP'O.LĪT

MOP'O.LĪT cosmopolite
TROP'O.LĪT metropolite

OP'SI.KL

DROP'SI.KL dropsical
MOP'SI.KL mopsical
POP'SI.KL popsicle
TOP'SI.KL nimptopsical

OP'TER.AN

ROP'TER.AN chiropteran
THOP'TER.AN orthopteran

OP'TER.US

DOP'TER.US lepidopterous
KROP'TER.US macropterous
THOP'TER.US orthopterous

OP'TI.KAL

OP'TI.KAL optical
NOP'TI.KAL synoptical
TOP'TI.KAL autoptical

OP'Ū.LĀT

KOP'Ū.LĀT copulate
POP'Ū.LĀT depopulate, populate

OP'Ū.LUS

OP'Ū.LUS opulous
POP'Ū.LUS populous, unpopulous

ÔR'A.BL

DÔR'A.BL adorable
HÔR'A.BL abhorrable, horrible
PLÔR'A.BL deplorable, explorable, unexplorable
SÔR'A.BL soarable
STÔR'A.BL restorable, storable, unrestorable, unstorable

ÔR'A.BLĒ

DÔR'A.BLĒ adorably
HÔR'A.BLĒ abhorrably, horribly
PLÔR'A.BLĒ deplorably

ÔR'A.KL

ÔR'A.KL meteorical, auricle, oracle
FÔR'A.KL anaphorical, metaphorical
GÔR'A.KL allegorical, categorical, tautegorical
KÔR'A.KL coracle
TÔR'A.KL historical, mythihistorical, oratorical, pictorical, rhetorical

Ō'RAL.Ē

Ō'RAL.Ē orally
GŌR'A.LE gorily
FLŌ'RAL.Ē florally
MŌ'RAL.Ē morally

Ō'RAL.IST

Ō'RAL.IST oralist
MŌ'RAL.IST moralist

Ō'RAL.ĬZ

FLŌ'RAL.ĬZ floralize
MŌ'RAL.ĬZ moralize

OR'A.TŌ.RĒ

OR'A.TŌ.RĒ oratory
BOR'A.TŌ.RĒ laboratory
PLOR'A.TŌ.RĒ exploratory

ÔR'A.TIV

JÔR'A.TIV pejorative
PLÔR'A.TIV explorative
STÔR'A.TIV restorative
VÔR'A.TIV devorative

ÔR'CHE.NIT

FÔR'CHE.NIT fortunate
PÔR'CHE.NIT importunate

ÔR'DER.ING

ÔR'DER.ING ordering
BÔR'DER.ING bordering, embordering

ÔR'DI.AL

MÔR'DI.AL primordial
SÔR'DI.AL exordial

(See ÔR'JAL)

ÔR'DI.AN

GÔR'DI.AN Gordian
KÔR'DI.AN accordion
WÔR'DI.AN Edwardian

ÔR'DI.NĀT

ÔR'DI.NĀT	foreordinate, coordinate, ordinate
BÔR'DI.NĀT	subordinate

ÔR'DI.NIT

ÔR'DI.NIT	inordinate, coordinate, ordinate, uncoordinate
BÔR'DI.NIT	insubordinate, subordinate

ÔR'DI.ON

(See ÔR'DI.AN)

ÔR'FIZ.M

(Subsitute -ism for concluding -ic in words under ÔRFIK.)

ÔR'GA.NĪZ

ÔR'GA.NĪZ	disorganize, organize, reorganize
GÔR'GA.NĪZ	gorgonize
MÔR'GA.NĪZ	morganize

ŌR'I.A

Ō'RI.A	Peoria, theoria
FŌ'RI.A	dysphoria, haptodysphoria, euphoria
GLŌ'RI.A	Gloria
GŌ'RI.A	phantasmagoria, oligoria
LŌ'RI.A	peloria
MŌ'RI.A	memoria
NŌ'RI.A	noria
PŌ'RI.A	aporia, emporia
SKŌ'RI.A	scoria
SŌ'RI.A	infusoria
STŌ'RI.A	Astoria, Waldorf Astoria, Castoria
THŌ'RI.A	thoria
TŌ'RI.A	littoria, moratoria, Pretoria, Victoria

Ō'RI.AL

Ō'RI.AL	oriel
BŌ'RI.AL	arboreal, boreal, subboreal
DŌ'RI.AL	ambassadorial

FŌ'RI.AL	phosphoreal
GŌ'RI.AL	phantasmagorial
KŌ'RI.AL	enchorial, correal
KWŌ'RI.AL	aequorial
MŌ'RI.AL	armorial, immemorial, marmoreal, memorial
NŌ'RI.AL	manorial, seignorial
PŌ'RI.AL	corporeal, emporial, incorporeal
SKŌ'RI.AL	Escorial
SŌ'RI.AL	A accessorial, assessorial, D dismissorial, F fossorial, GR gressorial, I infusorial, insessorial, intercessorial, K compromissorial, cursorial, PR professorial, R rasorial, responsorial, risorial, S censorial, sensorial, SK scansorial, SP sponsorial, T tonsorial, U uxorial
THŌ'RI.AL TŌ'RI.AL	authorial A adaptorial, admonitorial, accusatorial, amatorial, ancestorial, assertorial, D dedicatorial, dictatorial, directorial, disquisitorial, doctorial, E editorial, executorial, expurgatorial, exterritorial, extraterritorial, equatorial, electorial, F factorial, G gubernatorial, GL gladiatorial, GR grallatorial, I inquisitorial, J gestatorial, K cantorial, commentatorial, compurgatorial, consistorial, conspiratorial, curatorial, KL clamatorial, L legislatorial, M mediatorial, mentorial, monitorial, motorial, multifactorial, N natatorial, O observatorial, auditorial, auctorial, oratorial, P pictorial, piscatorial, purgatorial, PR praetorial, prefatorial, prefectorial, preceptorial, proctorial, procuratorial, proprietorial, protectorial, R raptorial, rectorial, repertorial, reportorial, reptatorial, S salatorial, sartorial, sectorial, senatorial, suctorial, sutorial, SK scriptorial, SP spectatorial, speculatorial, T tectorial, textorial, territorial, tinctorial, tutorial, V vectorial, victorial, visitatorial
ZŌ'RI.AL	rasorial, rosorial

ÔR'I.A.LĪZ

MÔR'I.LĪZ	memorialize
TÔR'I.A.LĪZ	editorialize, territorialize

Ō'RI.AN

BŌ'RI.AN	brimborion, hyperborean, roborean
DŌ'RI.AN	Dorian
GŌ'RI.AN	Gregorian
MŌ'RI.AN	marmorean
RŌ'RI.AN	aurorean
SŌ'RI.AN	censorian

(See Ô'RI.AN)

TŌRI.AN

TŌR'I.AN	A amatorian, D dictatorian, GL gladiatorian, H

historian, *K*
consistorian, *N*
Nestorian, *O*
oratorian, *P*
purgatorian, *PR*
praetorian, *S*
salutatorian,
senatorian, *ST*
stentorian, *V*
valedictorian,
Victorian

Ô'RI.AN

SÔ'RI.AN   dinosaurian,
morosaurian, saurian
TÔ'RI.AN   centaurian, taurian

(See Ō'RI.AN)

Ō'RI.AT

FLŌ'RI.ĀT   floriate
KŌ'RI.ĀT   excoriate
SŌ'RI.ĀT   professoriate
STŌ'RI.ĀT   storiate

ÔR'I.BL

(See ÔR'A.BL)

OR'ID.LĒ

FLOR'ID.LĒ   floridly
HOR'ID.LĒ   horridly
TOR'ID.LĒ   torridly

ÔR'I.ENT

ÔR'I.ENT   orient
MÔR'I.ENT   commorient

ÔR'I.ER

KWÔR'I.ER   quarrier
SÔR'I.ER   sorrier
WÔR'I.ER   warrior

(See OR'I.ER)

Ō'RI.FĪ

GLŌ'RI.FĪ   glorify
LŌ'RI.FĪ   calorify
SKŌ'RI.FĪ   scorify
STŌ'RI.FĪ   historify, storify

(See OR'I.FĪ)

OR'I.FĪ

HOR'I.FĪ   horrify
TOR'I.FĪ   torrefy

(See Ō'RI.FĪ)

Ō'RI.FÔRM

PŌ'RI.FORM   poriform

(See OR'I.FORM)

OR'I.FÔRM

BOR'I.FÔRM   arboriform
FLOR'I.FÔRM   floriform
MOR'I.FÔRM   moriform

ÔR'I.IT

ÔR'I.IT   aureate
LÔR'I.IT   baccalaureate,
laureate, poet
laureate

ÔR'I.KL

(See ÔR'A.KL)

Ō'RI.NES

GŌ'RI.NES   goriness
HŌ'RI.NES   hoariness, whoriness
PŌ'RI.NES   poriness
TŌ'RI.NES   desultoriness,
dilatoriness,
peremptoriness

Ō'RI.ŌL

Ō'RI.ŌL   oriole
GLŌ'RI.ŌL   gloriole

ÔR'I.ŌL

ÔR'I.ŌL   aureole, oriole
LÔR'I.ŌL   laureole

OR'I.TĒ

OR'I.TĒ   anteriority,
deteriority,
exteriority,
inferiority,
interiority, meliority,
posteriority,
priority, superiority
JOR'I.TĒ   majority
NOR'I.TĒ   minority, sonority
ROR'I.TĒ   sorority
THOR'I.TĒ   authority
YOR'I.TĒ   juniority, seniority

Ō'RI.UM

BŌ'RI.UM   ciborium
FŌ'RI.UM   triforium
KŌ'RI.UM   corium
MŌ'RI.UM   in memoriam
NŌ'RI.UM   anticlinorium,
synclinorium
PŌ'RI.UM   emporium
SŌ'RI.UM   aspersorium,
sensorium, uxorium
THŌ'RI.UM   thorium
TŌ'RI.UM   *D* digitorium, *F*
fumatorium, *H*
haustorium, *I*
inclinatorium, *KR*
crematorium, *M*
moratorium, *N*
natatorium, *O*
auditorium, *P*
pastorium, *PR*
praetorium,
prospectorium, *S*
sanatorium,
sudatorium, *SK*
scriptorium, *Y*
eupatorium

Ō'RI.US

BŌ'RI.US   arboreous, Boreas,
laborious
GLŌ'RI.US   glorious, inglorious,
vainglorious
RŌ'RI.US   uproarious
SKŌ'RI.US   scorious
SŌ'RI.US   accessorious,
censorious,
subderisorious,
uxorious
TŌ'RI.US   notatorious,
notorious,
proditorious,
sartorius

Ô'RI.US

Ô'RI.US   aureous

(See Ō'RI.US)

ÔR'MA.BL

FÔR'MA.BL	formable, informable, conformable, performable, transformable
STÔR'MA.BL	stormable
WÔR'MA.BL	warmable

ÔR'MA.LĪZ

| FÔR'MA.LĪZ | formalize, informalize |
| NÔR'MA.LĪZ | normalize |

ÔR'MA.TIV

| DÔR'MA.TIV | dormative |
| FÔR'MA.TIV | afformative, deformative, formative, informative, reformative, transformative |

ÔR'MI.TĒ

| FÔR'MI.TĒ | deformity, inconformity, conformity, multiformity, nonconformity, uniformity |
| NÔR'MI.TĒ | abnormity, enormity |

ÔR'NI.A

| FÔR'NI.A | California |
| KÔR'NI.A | cornea, salicornia |

OR'O.ER

| BOR'O.ER | borrower |
| SOR'O.ER | sorrower |

OR'O.ING

BOR'O.ING	borrowing
MOR'O.ING	morrowing, tomorrowing
SOR'O.ING	sorrowing

Ô'RO.SKŌP

| HOR'O.SKŌP | horoscope |
| STÔ'RO.SKŌP | stauroscope |

ÔRS'A.BL

DÔRS'A.BL	endorsable
FÔRS'A.BL	enforceable, forcible
VÔRS'A.BL	divorceable

ÔR'SHUN.AL

| BÔR'SHUN.AL | abortional |
| TÔR'SHUN.AL | distortional, contortional, torsional |

ÔR'SHUN.IST

| BÔR'SHUN.IST | abortionist, antiabortionist, pro-abortionist |
| TÔR'SHUN.IST | extortionist, contortionist |

ÔRT'A.BL

KÔRT'A.BL	courtable, uncourtable
PÔRT'A.BL	deportable, exportable, importable, insupportable, portable, reportable, transportable
SÔR'TA.BL	sortable, unsortable
TÔR'TA.BL	distortable

ÔR'TA.TIV

HÔR'TA.TIV	hortative
POR'TA.TIV	portative
ZÔR'TA.TIV	exhortative

ÔR'TER.IJ

| KWÔR'TER.IJ | quarterage |
| PÔR'TER.IJ | porterage |

ÔR'TI.FĪ

| FÔR'TI.FĪ | fortify |
| MÔR'TI.FĪ | mortify |

ÔR'TI.KL

| KÔR'TI.KL | cortical |
| VÔR'TI.KL | vortical |

ŌRT'LI.NES

| KŌRT'LI.NES | courtliness |
| PŌRT'LI.NES | portliness |

Ō'RUS.LĒ

KŌ'RUS.LĒ	decorously
NŌ'RUS.LĒ	sonorously
PŌ'RUS.LĒ	porously

Ō.RI.US.LĒ

BŌ.RI.US.LĒ	laboriously
GLŌ'RI.US.LĒ	gloriously, ingloriously, vaingloriously
RŌ'RI.US.LĒ	uproariously
SŌ'RI.US.LĒ	censoriously, uxoriously
TŌ'RI.US.LĒ	meritoriously, notoriously, stentoriously, stertoriously, victoriously

OS'FO.RUS

| BOS'FO.RUS | Bosphorus |
| FOS'FO.RUS | phosphorous, phosphorus |

Ō'SHA.BL

| GŌ'SHA.BL | negotiable, non-negotiable, unnegotiable |
| SŌ'SHA.BL | dissociable, sociable, unsociable |

Ō'SHI.A

KŌ'SHI.A	nicotia
KRŌ'SHI.A	macrotia, microtia
NŌ'SHI.A	anotia
RŌ'SHI.A	miserotia

Ō'SHI.AN

(See ŌSHUN)

Ō'SHI.ANT

Ō'SHI.ANT	otiant
GŌ'SHI.ANT	negotiant
SŌ'SHI.ANT	dissociant

Ō'SHI.ĀT

GŌ'SHI.ĀT	negotiate
SŌ'SHI.ĀT	associate, dissociate, consociate

Ō'SHUN.AL

MŌ'SHUN.AL	emotional, commotional, motional, promotional, unemotional
NŌ'SHUN.AL	notional
VŌ'SHUN.AL	devotional

Ō'SHUS.LĒ

KŌ'SHUS.LĒ	precociously
RŌ'SHUS.LĒ	ferociously
TRŌ'SHUS.LĒ	atrociously

Ō'SHUS.NES

KŌ'SHUS.NES	precociousness
RŌ'SHUS.NES	ferociousness
TRŌ'SHUS.NES	atrociousness

Ō'SI.ĀT

(See **Ō'SHI.ĀT**)

OS'I.BL

DOS'I.BL	docible, indocible
POS'I.BL	impossible, possible

OS'I.NĀT

OS'I.NĀT	ratiocinate
TROS'I.NĀT	patrocinate

ÔS'I.ER

BÔS'I.ER	bossier
FLÔS'I.ER	flossier
GLÔS'I.ER	glossier
MÔS'I.ER	mossier
SÔS'I.ER	saucier

ÔS'I.NES

BÔS'I.NES	bossiness
DRÔS'I.NES	drossiness
FLÔS'I.NES	flossiness
GLÔS'I.NES	glossiness
MÔS'I.NES	mossiness
SÔS'I.NES	sauciness

ÔS'I.TĒ

PÔS'I.TĒ	paucity
RÔS'I.TĒ	raucity

(See **OS'I.TĒ**)

OS'I.TĒ

OS'I.TĒ	*A* actuosity, anfractuosity, *D* dubiosity, *E* ebriosity, *F* foliosity, furiosity, *FL* flexuosity, *FR* fructuosity, *GR* grandiosity, graciosity, *H* hideosity, *I* impecuniosity, impetuosity, *I* infractuosity, ingeniosity, incuriosity, *K* curiosity, *O* otiosity, *PR* preciosity, *R* religiosity, *S* sensuosity, seriosity, sinuosity, *SP* speciosity, *ST* strenuosity, *T* tortuosity, *U* unctuosity, *V* viciosity, virtuosity, vitiosity, vitreosity
BOS'I.TĒ	gibbosity, globosity, verbosity
BROS'I.TĒ	tenebrosity
DOS'I.TĒ	docity, nodosity
GOS'I.TĒ	fungosity, rugosity
KOS'I.TĒ	bellicosity, hircosity, jocosity, mucosity, uscosity, precocity, spicosity, varicosity, viscosity
KWOS'I.TĒ	aquosity
LOS'I.TĒ	*A* ampollosity, angulosity, *F* fabulosity, filosity, *G* gulosity, *GL* glandulosity, *K* callosity, *M* meticulosity, musculosity, *N* nebulosity, *P* pilosity, *R* ridiculosity, rugulosity, *S* sabulosity, *SKR* scrupulosity, *T* tumulosity, *V* velocity, villosity
MOS'I.TĒ	animosity, anonymosity, fumosity, gemmosity, gummosity, plumosity, rimosity
NOS'I.TĒ	*A* arenosity, *F* fuliginosity, *GL* glutinosity, *K* caliginosity, carnosity, *L* libidinosity, luminosity, *SP* spinosity, *V* venosity, vinosity, voluminosity
POS'I.TĒ	pomposity
PROS'I.TĒ	reciprocity
ROS'I.TĒ	*F* ferocity, *J* generosity, *N* neurocity, *P* ponderosity, porosity, *S* saporosity, scirrhosity, serosity, *T* torosity, tuberosity, *V* vaporosity, vociferosity
STROS'I.TĒ	monstrosity
TOS'I.TĒ	schistosity
TROS'I.TĒ	atrocity
VOS'I.TĒ	nervosity, nivosity

(See **ÔS'I.TĒ**)

Ō'SIV.LĒ

PLŌ'SIV.LĒ	explosively, implosively
RŌ'SIV.LĒ	erosively, corrosively

Ō'SIV.NES

PLŌ'SIV.NES	explosiveness, implosiveness
RŌ'SIV.NES	erosiveness, corrosiveness

ÔS'KO.PĒ

NÔS'KO.PĒ nauscopy

(See OS'KO.PĒ)

OS'KO.PĒ

OS'KO.PĒ bioscopy, geoscopy, cranioscopy, cryoscopy, radioscopy, stereoscopy
DOS'KO.PĒ endoscopy
KROS'KO.PĒ microscopy, necroscopy
LOS'KO.PĒ dactyloscopy, geloscopy
MOS'KO.PĒ ophthalmoscopy
NOS'KO.PĒ lecanoscopy, organoscopy, retinoscopy, rhinoscopy, ceraunoscopy, uranoscopy
POS'KO.PĒ metoposcopy
ROS'KO.PĒ deuteroscopy, fluoroscopy, hieroscopy, horoscopy, meteoroscopy, uroscopy
SOS'KO.PĒ mixoscopy, misoscopy
THOS'KO.PĒ ornithoscopy, stethoscopy
TOS'KO.PĒ autoscopy, brontoscopy, omoplatoscopy, teratoscopy
TROS'KO.PĒ gastroscopy, spectroscopy

(See ÔS'KO.PĒ)

OS'KO.PIST

(See OS'KO.PĒ, drop concluding -y and add -ist where appropriate.)

OS'O.FĒ

OS'O.FĒ theosophy
LOS'O.FĒ philosophy, psilosophy
NOS'O.FĒ gymnosophy
POS'O.FĒ anthroposophy
ROS'O.FĒ chirosophy
SOS'O.FĒ misosophy

OS'O.FER

OS'O.FER theosopher
LOS'O.FER philosopher, psilosopher
SOS'O.FER misosopher

OS'O.FIST

OS'O.FIST theosophist
LOS'O.FIST philosophist
NOS'O.FIST deipnosophist, gymnosophist
POS'O.FIST anthroposophist
ROS'O.FIST chirosophist
SOS'O.FIST misosophist

OS'O.FĪZ

OS'O.FĪZ theosophize
LOS'O.FĪZ philosophize

OS'TA.SĒ

POS'TA.SĒ apostosy
SOS'TA.SĒ isostasy

OS'TER.OL

OS'TER.OL zoösterol
GOS'TER.OL ergosterol
TOS'TER.OL sitosterol

OS'TE.RŌN

DOS'TE.RŌN aldosterone
DROS'TE.RŌN androsterone
STOS'TER.ŌN testosterone

OS'TI.KAL

KROS'TI.KAL acrostical
NOS'TI.KAL agnostical, gnostical

ŌS'TING.LĒ

BŌS'TING.LĒ boastingly
KŌS'TING.LĒ coastingly
RŌS'TING.LĒ roastingly
TŌS'TING.LĒ toastingly

OS'TI.SIZM

KROS'TI.SIZM acrosticism

NOS'TI.SIZM agnosticism, Gnosticism

ŌST'LI.NES

GŌST'LI.NES ghostliness
HŌST'LI.NES hostliness

OS'TRO.FĒ

NOS'TRO.FĒ monostrophe
POS'TRO.FĒ apostrophe

Ō'TA.BL

FLŌ'TA.BL floatable
KWŌ'TA.BL quotable, unquotable
NŌ'TA.BL denotable, notable, unnotable
PŌ'TA.BL potable, unpotable
VŌ'TA.BL votable, unvotable

Ō'TA.BLĒ

KWŌ'TA.BLĒ quotably
NŌ'TA.BLĒ notably

Ō'TA.LIZM

DŌ'TA.LIZM sacerdotalism
TŌ'TA.LIZM teetotalism

OT'A.NĒ

(See OT'O.NĒ)

Ō'TA.RĒ

KŌ'TA.RĒ coterie
NŌ'TA.RĒ notary
RŌ'TA.RĒ rotary
VŌ'TA.RĒ votary

Ō'TA.TIV

FLŌ'TA.TIV flotative
NŌ'TA.TIV connotative, denotative
RŌ'TA.TIV rotative

Ō'TED.LĒ

BLŌ'TED.LĒ bloatedly
NŌ'TED.LĒ notedly

THRŌT'ED.LĒ	deep-throatedly, sweet-throatedly
VŌ'TED.LĒ	devotedly

Ō'TE.RĒ

(See Ō'TA.RĒ)

ÔT'E.RĒ

KÔT'ER.Ē	cautery
WÔT'ER.E	watery

OT'E.RĒ

LOT'ER.Ē	lottery
POT'ER.Ē	pottery
TOT'ER.Ē	tottery

ÔT'ER.ER

SLÔT'ER.ER	slaughterer
WÔT'ER.ER	waterer

OT'ER.ER

POT'ER.ER	potterer
TOT'ER.ER	totterer

ÔT'ER.ING

SLÔT'ER.ING	slaughtering
WÔT'ER.ING	watering

OT'ER.ING

POT'ER.ING	pottering
TOT'ER.ING	tottering

Ō'TER.ĬZ

MŌ'TER.ĬZ	motorize
NŌ'TER.ĬZ	notarize

Ô'TER.MAN

SLÔ'TER.MAN	slaughterman
WÔ'TER.MAN	waterman

OTH'E.SIS

POTH'E.SIS	apothesis, hypothesis
PROTH'E.SIS	prothesis

ÔT'I.ER

HÔT'I.ER	haughtier
NÔT'I.ER	naughtier

OT'I.ER

BLOT'I.ER	blottier
DOT'I.ER	dottier
KLOT'I.ER	clottier
POT'I.ER	pottier
SKWOT'I.ER	squattier
SPOT'I.ER	spottier

(See ÄT'I.ER)

OT'I.KA

ROT'I.KA	erotica
ZOT'I.KA	exotica

OT'I.KAL

OT'I.KAL	biotical, idiotical
DOT'I.KAL	anecdotical
GOT'I.KAL	bigotical
LOT'I.KAL	zealotical
POT'I.KAL	despotical
ROT'I.KAL	erotical
ZOT'I.KAL	exotical

OT'I.LĒ

DOT'I.LĒ	dottily
SNOT'I.LĒ	snottily
SPOT'I.LĒ	spottily

ÔT'I.LĒ

HÔT'I.LĒ	haughtily
NÔT'I.LĒ	naughtily

ÔT'I.LUS

KÔT'I.LUS	cautilous
NÔT'I.LUS	nautilus

ÔT'I.NES

HÔT'I.NES	haughtiness
NÔT'I.NES	naughtiness

OT'I.NES

DOT'I.NES	dottiness
NOT'I.NES	knottiness
SKWOT'I.NES	squattiness
SNOT'I.NES	snottiness
SPOT'I.NES	spottiness

(See ÄT'I.NES)

Ō'TING.LĒ

BLŌ'TING.LĒ	bloatingly
DŌ'TING.LĒ	dotingly
GLŌ'TING.LĒ	gloatingly
KWŌ'TING.LĒ	quotingly

OT'I.SIZM

ROT'I.SIZM	eroticism, neuroticism
ZOT'I.SIZM	exoticism

Ō'TIV.LĒ

MŌ'TIV.LĒ	emotively
VŌ'TIV.LĒ	votively

OT'O.MĒ

OT'O.MĒ	episiotomy, herniotomy, ichthyotomy, cardiotomy, craniotomy, osteotomy, Otomi, ovariotomy, peotomy, stereotomy, tracheotomy, zootomy
BOT'O.MĒ	bottomy, phlebotomy, lobotomy, strabotomy
FROT'O.MĒ	nephrotomy
GOT'O.MĒ	pharyngotomy, laryngotomy
KLOT'O.MĒ	cyclotomy
KOT'O.MĒ	bronchotomy, dichotomy, leucotomy, thoracotomy, trichotomy, varicotomy
KROT'O.MĒ	microtomy, necrotomy

LOT'O.MĒ	encephalotomy, helotomy, colotomy, tonsillotomy
MOT'O.MĒ	dermotomy
NOT'O.MĒ	pogonotomy, tenotomy
PLOT'O.MĒ	aplotomy
POT'O.MĒ	anthropotomy, apotome, hippopotamy
ROT'O.MĒ	enterotomy, hysterotomy, laparotomy, neurotomy, Caesarotomy, sclerotomy
SKOT'O.MĒ	scotomy
SOT'O.MĒ	loxotomy
THOT'O.MĒ	lithotomy
TOT'O.MĒ	phytotomy, autotomy, cystotomy
TROT'O.MĒ	gastrotomy

OT'O.MIST

(See **OT'O.MĒ,** change -y to -ist where appropriate.)

OT'O.MĪZ

(See **OT'O.MĒ,** change -y to -ize where appropriate.)

OT'O.NĒ

OT'O.NĒ	neoteny
BOT'O.NĒ	astrobotany, botany, paleobotany
KOT'O.NĒ	cottony
MOT'O.NĒ	homotony
NOT'O.NĒ	monotony
ROT'O.NĒ	chirotony

Ō'TO.TĪP

| FŌ'TO.TĪP | phototype |
| PRŌ'TO.TĪP | prototype |

OT'RI.KUS

OT'RIK.KUS	leiotrichous
LOT'RI.KUS	ulotrichous
SOT'RI.KUS	lissotrichous

OU'A.BL

| PLOU'A.BL | plowable, unplowable |

DOU'A.BL	endowable
LOU'A.BL	allowable, disallowable
VOU'A.BL	avowable, unavowable, vowable

OU'A.BLĒ

| LOU'A.BLĒ | allowably, unallowably |
| VOU'A.BLĒ | avowably |

OUD'ED.NES

| KLOUD'ED.NES | becloudedness, cloudedness |
| KROUD'ED.NES | crowdedness, overcrowdedness, uncrowdedness |

OU'DI.IZM

| DOU'DI.IZM | dowdyism |
| ROU'DI.IZM | rowdyism |

OU'DI.LĒ

DOU'DI.LĒ	dowdily
KLOU'DI.LĒ	cloudily
ROU'DI.LĒ	rowdily

OU'DI.NES

DOU'DI.NES	dowdiness
KLOU'DI.NES	cloudiness
ROU'DI.NES	rowdiness

OU'ER.Ē

BOU'ER.Ē	bowery
DOU'ER.Ē	dowery
FLOU'ER.Ē	flowery
GLOU'ER.Ē	glowery
LOU'ER.Ē	lowery
SHOU'ER.Ē	showery
TOU'ER.Ē	towery

OU'ER.ING

(See **OUER,** add -ing where appropriate.)

OU'ER.LES

| DOU'ER.LES | dowerless |

| FLOU'ER.LES | flowerless, flourless |
| POU'ER.LES | powerless |

OUL'ER.Ē

OUL'ER.Ē	owlery
FOUL'ER.Ē	fowlery
PROUL'ER.Ē	prowlery

OUN'DA.BL

BOUN'DA.BL	boundable, unboundable
FOUN'DA.BL	dumfoundable, confoundable, unconfoundable
GROUN'DA.BL	groundable
POUN'DA.BL	impoundable, compoundable
ROUN'DA.BL	roundable
SOUN'DA.BL	resoundable, soundable, unsoundable
STOUN'DA.BL	astoundable
ZOUN'DA.BL	resoundable

OUN'DED.LĒ

BOUN'DED.LĒ	unboundedly
FOUN'DED.LĒ	dumbfoundedly, confoundedly, unconfoundedly
TOUN'DED.LĒ	astoundedly

OUN'DED.NES

(See **OUND,** add -edness where appropriate.)

OUN'DING.LĒ

(See **OUND,** add -ingly where appropriate.)

OUND'LES.LĒ

BOUND'LES.LĒ	boundlessly
GROUND'LES.LĒ	groundlessly
SOUND'LES.LĒ	soundlessly

OUN'TA.BL

| KOUN'TA.BL | accountable, discountable, countable, unaccountable, uncountable |

MOUN'TA.BL insurmountable,
mountable,
surmountable,
unmountable

OUN'TA.BLĒ

KOUN'TA.BLĒ accountably,
unaccountably
MOUN'TA.BLĒ insurmountably

OU'TI.NES

DOU'TI.NES doughtiness
DROU'TI.NES droughtiness
GOU'TI.NES goutiness
SPOU'TI.NES spoutiness

OU'ZI.LĒ

DROU'ZI.LĒ drowsily
FROU'ZI.LĒ frowsily

OU'ZI.NES

DROU'ZI.NES drowsiness
FROU'ZI.NES frowsiness
LOU'ZI.NES lousiness

OU'ZING.LĒ

BROU'ZING.LĒ browsingly
ROU'ZING.LĒ carousingly,
rousingly

OV'EL.ER

GROV'EL.ER groveler
HOV'EL.ER hoveler

OV'EL.ING

GROV'EL.ING groveling
HOV'EL.ING hoveling

Ō'VEN.LĒ

KLŌ'VEN.LĒ clovenly
WŌ'VEN.LĒ interwovenly,
wovenly

Ō'VI.A

FŌ'VI.A fovea

GŌ'VI.A Segovia
NŌ'VI.A synovia
RŌ'VI.A Monrovia

Ō'VI.AL

FŌ'VI.AL foveal
JŌ'VI.AL jovial
NŌ'VI.AL synovial

Ō'ZA.BL

KLŌ'ZA.BL closable, reclosable,
unclosable
PŌ'ZA.BL decomposable,
deposable,
disposable, imposable,
indisposable,
opposable, supposable,
transposable,
undisposable,
untransposable

ÔZ'A.BL

KÔZ'A.BL causable
PLÔZ'A.BL implausible,
plausible

Ō'ZE.RĒ

DŌ'ZER.Ē dozery
PŌ'ZER.Ē composery
RŌ'ZER.Ē rosary

Ō'ZHE.RĒ

Ō'ZHE.RĒ osiery
HŌ'ZHE.RĒ hosiery

Ō'ZI.A

BRŌ'ZI.A ambrosia
PŌ'ZI.A symposia

Ō'ZI.AL

BRŌ'ZI.AL ambrosial
RŌ'ZI.AL roseal

Ō'ZI.ER

KŌ'ZI.ER cozier
MŌ'ZI.ER moseyer

NŌ'ZI.ER nosier
PRŌ'ZI.ER prosier
RŌ'ZI.ER rosier

(See ŌZHER)

Ō'ZI.LĒ

KŌ'ZI.LĒ cozily
NŌ'ZI.LĒ nosily
PRŌ'ZI.LĒ prosily
RŌ'ZI.LĒ rosily

Ō'ZI.NES

DŌ'ZI.NES doziness
FŌ'ZI.NES foziness
KŌ'ZI.NES coziness
NŌ'ZI.NES nosiness
PRŌ'ZI.NES prosiness
RŌ'ZI.NES rosiness

ÔZ'I.TIV

KÔZ'I.TIV causative

(See OZ'I.TIV)

OZ'I.TIV

POZ'I.TIV appositive,
depositive,
expositive,
compositive,
positive,
prepositive,
postpositive,
suppositive,
transpositive

(See ÔZ'I.TIV)

Ū'A.BL

NŪ'A.BL renewable,
unrenewable
STŪ'A.BL stewable,
unstewable
VŪ'A.BL reviewable,
unreviewable,
unviewable,
viewable

(See OO'A.BL)

Ū'ANT.LĒ

(See OO'ANT.LĒ)

UB'A.BL

KLUB'A.BL	clubbable
RUB'A.BL	rubbable
SKRUB'A.BL	scrubbable
TUB'A.BL	tubbable

Ū'BER.ANS

TŪ'BER.ANS	protuberance

(See OO'BER.ANS)

Ū'BER.ANT

TŪ'BER.ANT	protuberant

(See OO'BER.ANT)

Ū'BER.Ē

NŪ'BER.Ē	Newbury

(See OO'BER.Ē)

UB'ER.Ē

BLUB'ER.Ē	blubbery
RUB'ER.Ē	rubbery
SHRUB'ER.Ē	shrubbery
SKRUB'ER.Ē	scrubbery

Ū'BER.TĒ

Ū.BER.TĒ	uberty
PŪ'BER.TĒ	puberty

Ū'BER.US

Ū'BER.US	uberous
SŪ'BER.US	suberous
TŪ'BER.US	protuberous, tuberous

(See OO'BER.US)

Ū'BI.A

(See OO'BI.A)

UB'I.ER

CHUB'I.ER	chubbier
GRUB'I.ER	grubbier
SHRUB'I.ER	shrubbier
SKRUB'I.ER	scrubbier
TUB'I.ER	tubbier

Ū'BI.KL

BŪ'BI.KL	bubukle
KŪ'BI.KL	cubicle

(See OO'BI.KL)

Ū'BI.LĀT

LŪ'BI.LĀT	volubilate
NŪ'BI.LĀT	nubilate, obnubilate

(See OO'BI.LĀT)

UB'I.LĒ

CHUB'I.LĒ	chubbily
GRUB'I.LĒ	grubbily
SHRUB'I.LĒ	shrubbily
SKRUB'I.LĒ	scrubbily
STUB'I.LĒ	stubbily
TUB'I.LĒ	tubbily

UB'I.NES

(See UBĒ, add -ness where appropriate.)

Ū'BI.US

DŪ'BI.US	dubious

(See OO'BI.US)

Ū'BRI.KĀT

(See OO'BRI.KĀT)

Ū'BRI.US

(See OO'BRI.US)

Ū'DA.BL

(See OO'DA.BL)

Ū'DEN.SĒ

PŪ'DEN.SĒ	pudency

(See OO'DEN.SĒ)

UD'ER.Ē

UD'ER.Ē	uddery
DUD'ER.Ē	duddery
SHUD'ER.Ē	shuddery
STUD'ER.Ē	studdery

Ū'DI.A

NŪ'DI.A	iatronudia
STŪ'DI.A	studia

UD'I.ER

BLUD'I.ER	bloodier
MUD'I.ER	muddier
RUD'I.ER	ruddier

UD'I.LĒ

BLUD'I.LĒ	bloodily
DUD'I.LĒ	fuddy-duddily
MUD'I.LĒ	muddily
RUD'I.LĒ	ruddily

Ū'DI.NAL

TŪ'DI.NAL	altitudinal, aptitudinal, attitudinal, desuetudinal, consuetudinal, latitudinal, longitudinal, testitudinal

(See OO'DI.NAL)

Ū'DI.NES

(See OO'DI.NES)

UD'I.NES

BLUD'I.NES	bloodiness
MUD'I.NES	muddiness
RUD'I.NES	ruddiness

Ū'DI.NUS

TŪ'DI.NUS	fortitudinous, latitudinous, longitudinous, multitudinous, solicitudinous,

testudinous,
vicissitudinous

(See OO'DI.NUS)

Ū'DI.Ō

LŪ'DI.Ō	preludio
STŪ'DI.Ō	studio

(See OO'DI.Ō)

Ū'DI.TĒ

NŪ'DI.TĒ	nudity, seminudity

(See OO'DI.TĒ)

Ū'DI.UM

LŪ'DI.UM	postludium, preludium
STŪ'DI.UM	studium

(See OO'DI.UM)

Ū'DI.US

LŪ'DI.US	preludious
STŪ'DI.US	studious

(See OO'DI.US)

Ū'EL.ER

DŪ'EL.ER	dueler, dueller
FŪ'EL.ER	fueler, fueller

(See OO'EL.ER)

Ū'EL.ING

DŪ'EL.ING	dueling, duelling
FŪ'EL.ING	fueling, fuelling, refueling, refuelling

(See OO'EL.ING)

Ū'ER.Ē

Ū'ER.Ē	ewery

(See OO'ER.Ē)

UF'A.BL

BLUF'A.BL	bluffable
BUF'A.BL	buffable
RUF'A.BL	ruffable, unruffable

UF'I.ER

FLUF'I.ER	fluffier
HUF'I.ER	huffier
PUF'I.ER	puffier
SNUF'I.ER	snuffier
STUF'I.ER	stuffier

UF'I.LĒ

FLUF'I.LĒ	fluffily
HUF'I.LĒ	huffily
PUF'I.LĒ	puffily
SNUF'I.LĒ	snuffily
STUF'I.LĒ	stuffily

UF'I.NES

(See UFĒ, add *-ness* where appropriate.)

UF'ING.LĒ

(See UF, add *-ingly* where appropriate.)

UG'A.BL

HUG'A.BL	huggable
PLUG'A.BL	pluggable

UG'ER.Ē

BUG'ER.Ē	buggery
DRUG'ER.Ē	druggery
DUG'ER.Ē	skullduggery
PUG'ER.Ē	puggaree
SNUG'ER.Ē	snuggery
THUG'ER.Ē	thuggery

UG'ER.MUG'ER

HUG'ER.MUG'ER	huggermugger
KUG'ER.MUG'ER	cuggermugger

UG'I.NES

BUG'I.NES	bugginess
HUG'I.NES	hugginess
MUG'I.NES	mugginess
PUG'I.NES	pugginess
SLUG'I.NES	slugginess

Ū'GL.MAN

BŪ'GL.MAN	bugleman
EŪ'GL.MAN	fugleman

Ū'I.NES

DŪ'I.NES	dewiness

(See OO'I.NES)

Ū'I.NUS

(See OO'I.NUS)

Ū'ISH.NES

(See OO'ISH.NES)

Ū'I.TĒ

DŪ'I.TĒ	assiduity
GŪ'I.TĒ	ambiguity, exiguity, contiguity
KŪ'I.TĒ	acuity, innocuity, conspicuity, perspicuity, promiscuity, circuity, vacuity
NŪ'I.TĒ	annuity, discontinuity, ingenuity, continuity, tenuity
SŪ'I.TĒ	suety
TŪ'I.TĒ	fatuity, fortuity, gratuity, perpetuity

(See OO'I.TĒ)

Ū'I.TIV

TŪ'I.TIV	intuitive, tuitive

(See OO'I.TIV)

Ū'I.TUS

KŪ'I.TUS	circuitous
TŪ'I.TUS	fatuitous, fortuitous, gratuitous, pituitous

UJ'ER.Ē

BUJ'ER.Ē	budgeree
DRUJ'ER.Ē	drudgery
GRUJ'ER.Ē	grudgery

Ū'JI.NUS

(See OO'JI.NUS)

Ū'KER.Ē

(See OO'KER.Ē)

UK'ER.ING

PUK'ER.ING   puckering
SUK'ER.ING   succoring, suckering

UK'I.LĒ

LUK'I.LĒ   luckily
PLUK'I.LĒ   pluckily

ŪK'I.NES

Ū'KI.NES   yeukiness
PŪ'KI.NES   pukiness

UK'SHUN.AL

DUK'SHUN.AL   deductional,
                    inductional,
                    conductional,
                    productional,
                    reductional
FLUK'SHUN.AL   fluxional
SUK'SHUN.AL   suctional
STRUK'SHUN.AL   destructional,
                    instructional,
                    constructional,
                    obstructional

UK'SHUN.IST

(See UKSHUN, add -ist)

UK'TI.BL

DUK'TI.BL   abductible,
                    deductible,
                    inductible,
                    conductible,
                    productible,
                    seductible,
                    reductible,
                    unproductible
LUK'TI.BL   eluctable,
                    ineluctable
STRUK'TI.BL   destructible,
                    indestructible,
                    instructible,
                    constructible,
                    obstructible,
                    reconstructible,
                    unreconstructible

UK'TIV.LĒ

(See UKTIV, add -ly where appropriate.)

UK'TIV.NES

(See UKTIV, add -ness where
appropriate.)

UK'Ū.LENS

SUK'Ū.LENS   succulence
TRUK'Ū.LENS   truculence

Ū'KŪ.LENT

LŪ'KŪ.LENT   luculent
MŪ'KŪ.LENT   muculent

UK'Ū.LENT

SUK'Ū.LENT   succulent
TRUK'Ū.LENT   truculent

UL'CHER.AL

KUL'CHER.AL   agricultural,
                    apicultural,
                    floricultural,
                    horticultural,
                    cultural
VUL'CHER.AL   vultural

UL'CHER.IZM

KUL'CHER.IZM   agriculturism
VUL'CHER.IZM   vulturism

UL'ER.Ē

DUL'ER.Ē   medullery
GUL'ER.Ē   gullery
KUL'ER.Ē   colory
SKUL'ER.Ē   scullery, skullery
TRUL'ER.Ē   trullery

Ū'LI.A

(See OO'LI.A)

Ū'LI.AN

KŪ'LI.AN   Herculean

(See OO'LI.AN)

Ū'LI.FÔRM

KŪ'LI.FÔRM   baculiform,
                    cuculiform
MŪ'LI.FÔRM   cumuliform

Ū'LING.LĒ

KŪ'LING.LĒ   ridiculingly
MŪ'LING.LĒ   mewlingly
PŪ'LING.LĒ   pulingly

(See OOL, ŪL add -ingly where
appropriate.)

Ū'LISH.LĒ

MŪ'LISH.LĒ   mulishly

(See OO'LISH.LĒ)

Ū'LISH.NES

MŪ'LISH.NES   mulishness

(See OO'LISH.NES)

UL'ISH.NES

DUL'ISH.NES   dullishness
GUL'ISH.NES   gullishness

Ū'LI.TĒ

(See OO'LI.TĒ)

Ū'LI.UM

BŪ'LI.UM   nebulium
KŪ'LI.UM   peculium
THŪ'LI.UM   thulium

UL'KI.NES

BUL'KI.NES   bulkiness
HUL'KI.NES   hulkiness
SUL'KI.NES   sulkiness

UL'MI.NANT

FUL'MI.NANT   fulminant
KUL'MI.NANT   culminant

UL'PA.BL

GUL'PA.BL   gulpable
KUL'PA.BL   inculpable, culpable

UL'MI.NĀT

FUL'MI.NĀT   fulminate
KUL'MI.NĀT   culminate

UL'SI.FĪ

DUL'SI.FĪ   dulcify
MUL'SI.FĪ   demulsify, emulsify

UL'SIV.LĒ

PUL'SIV.LĒ   impulsively, compulsively, repulsively
VUL'SIV.LĒ   convulsively, revulsively

UL'SIV.NES

PUL'SIV.NES   impulsiveness, compulsiveness, repulsiveness
VUL'SIV.NES   convulsiveness, revulsiveness

UL'TER.Ē

DUL'TER.Ē   adultery
SUL'TER.Ē   consultary

UL'TI.MIT

UL'TI.MIT   ultimate
NUL'TI.MIT   penultimate

UL'TING.LĒ

SUL'TING.LĒ   insultingly
ZUL'TING.LĒ   exultingly, resultingly

UL'TŪR.IZM

(See UL'CHER.IZM)

UL'VER.IN

KUL'VER.IN   culverin
PUL'VER.IN   pulverin

Ū'MA.BL

(See OOM, ŪM, add -able where appropriate.)

UM'A.JER

RUM'A.JER   rummager
SKRUM'A.JER   scrummager

UM'BER.Ē

UM'BER.Ē   umbery
SLUM'BER.Ē   slumbery

UM'BER.ER

(See UMBER, add -er where appropriate.)

UM'BER.ING

KUM'BER.ING   disencumbering, encumbering, cumbering
LUM'BER.ING   lumbering
NUM'BER.ING   numbering, outnumbering
SLUM'BER.ING   slumbering

UM'BER.US

NUM'BER.US   numberous
SLUM'BER.US   slumberous

UM'BLING.LĒ

RUM'BLING.LĒ   rumblingly
STUM'BLING.LĒ   stumblingly
TUM'BLING.LĒ   tumblingly

Ū'ME.NAL

KŪ'ME.NAL   cacuminal, catechumenal

(See OO'M.NAL)

Ū'MER.AL

HŪ'MER.AL   humeral
NŪ'MER.AL   numeral

(See OO'MER.AL)

Ū'MERD.LĒ

HŪ'MERD.LĒ   bad-humoredly, good-humoredly, ill-humoredly

(See OO'MERD.LĒ)

Ū'MER.Ē

FŪ'MER.Ē   perfumery
TŪ'MER.Ē   costumery

(See OO'MER.Ē)

UM'ER.Ē

CHUM'ER.Ē   chummery
FLUM'ER.Ē   flummery
MUM'ER.Ē   mummery
NUM'ER.Ē   nummary
PLUM'ER.Ē   plumbery
SUM'ER.Ē   summary, summery

Ū'MER.US

HŪ'MER.US   humerus, humorous, unhumorous
TŪ'MER.US   tumerous

(See OO'MER.US)

Ū'MI.FĪ

HŪ'MI.FĪ   humify
TŪ'MI.FĪ   tumefy

Ū'MI.LĒ

FŪ'MI.LĒ   fumily

(See OO'MI.LĒ)

Ū'MI.NAL

KŪ'MI.NAL   cacuminal, catechumenal

(See OO'MI.NAL)

Ū'MI.NANT

(See OO'MI.NANT)

Ū'MI.NĀ.SHUN

(See OO'MI.NĀ.SHUN)

Ū'MI.NĀT

KŪ'MI.NĀT   acuminate,
cacuminate,
catechumenate

(See OO'MI.NĀT)

Ū'MI.NES

FŪ'MI.NES   fuminess

(See OO'MI.NES)

Ū'MING.LĒ

FŪ'MING.LĒ   fumingly

(See OOM, add -ingly where appropriate.)

UM'ING.LĒ

HUM'ING.LĒ   hummingly
KUM'ING.LĒ   becomingly, unbecomingly
NUM'ING.LĒ   benumbingly, numbingly
STRUM'ING.LĒ   strummingly

Ū'MI.NĪZ

HŪ'MI.NĪZ   dehumanize, humanize

(See OO'MI.NĪZ)

Ū'MI.NUS

BŪ'MI.NUS   albuminous
GŪ'MI.NUS   leguminous
KŪ'MI.NUS   acuminous
NŪ'MI.NUS   numinous

UMP'CHOO.US

SUMP'CHOO.US   sumptuous
ZUMP'CHOO.US   presumptuous

UMP'ER.Ē

FRUMP'ER.Ē   frumpery
TRUMP'ER.Ē   trumpery

UM'PI.NES

DUM'PI.NES   dumpiness
FRUM'PI.NES   frumpiness
HUM'PI.NES   humpiness
GRUM'PI.NES   grumpiness
JUM'PI.NES   jumpiness
LUM'PI.NES   lumpiness
STUM'PI.NES   stumpiness

UM'PISH.NES

(See UMP, add -ishness where appropriate.)

UMP'SHUS.LĒ

BUMP'SHUS.LĒ   bumptiously
SKRUMP'SHUS.LĒ   scrumptiously

UMP'SI.MUS

MUMP'SI.MUS   mumpsimus
SUMP'SI.MUS   sumpsimus

UMP'TŪ.US

(See UMP'CHOO.US)

Ū'MŪ.LĀT

KŪ'MŪ.LĀT   accumulate, cumulate

(See OOM'Ū.LĀT)

Ū'MŪ.LUS

KŪ'MŪ.LUS   cumulus
TŪ'MŪ.LUS   tumulus

UN'A.BL

PUN'A.BL   punnable
RUN'A.BL   runnable
SHUN'A.BL   shunnable

UNCH'A.BL

(See UNCH, add -able where appropriate.)

UN'DANT.LĒ

BUN'DANT.LĒ   abundantly, superabundantly
DUN'DANT.LĒ   redundantly

UN'DER.ER

BLUN'DER.ER   blunderer
PLUN'DER.ER   plunderer
SUN'DER.ER   sunderer
THUN'DER.ER   thunderer
WUN'DER.ER   wonderer

UN'DER.ING

BLUN'DER.ING   blundering
PLUN'DER.ING   plundering
SUN'DER.ING   sundering
THUN'DER.ING   thundering
WUN'DER.ING   wondering

UN'DER.US

BLUN'DER.US   blunderous
CHUN'DER.US   chunderous
PLUN'DER.US   plunderous
THUN'DER.US   thunderous
WUN'DER.US   wonderous

(See UN'DRUS)

UN'DI.TĒ

BUN'DI.TĒ   moribundity
FUN'DI.TĒ   profundity
KUN'DI.TĒ   fecundity, infecundity, jocundity, jucundity, rubicundity
MUN'DI.TĒ   immundity
TUN'DI.TĒ   obtundity, orotundity, rotundity

Ū'NER.Ē

(See OON'ER.Ē)

UN'ER.Ē

GUN'ER.Ē   gunnery
NUN'ER.Ē   nunnery

UNG'GER.ING

HUNG'GER.ING   hungering

MUNG'GER.ING   fishmongering, whoremongering, ironmongering, costermongering, mongering, newsmongering, scandalmongering, scaremongering, warmongering, wordmongering

UNGK'SHUN.AL

UNGK'SHUN.AL   unctional
FUNGK'SHUN.AL   functional
JUNGK'SHUN.AL   junctional, conjunctional

UNGK'TER.Ē

FUNGK'TER.Ē   perfunctory
MUNGK'TER.Ē   emunctory

UNG'KŪ.LAR

UNG'KŪ.LAR   uncular
BUNG'KŪ.LAR   carbuncular
DUNG'KŪ.LAR   peduncular
RUNG'KŪ.LAR   caruncular
VUNG'KŪ.LAR   avuncular

UNG'KŪ.LĀT

DUNG'KŪ.LĀT   pedunculate
VUNG'KŪ.LĀT   avunculate

UNG'KŪ.LUS

MUNG'KŪ.LUS   homunculus
RUNG'KŪ.LUS   ranunculus

Ū'NI.FÔRM

Ū'NI.FÔRM   uniform
FŪ'NI.FÔRM   funiform
KŪ'NI.FÔRM   cuneiform

(See **OO'NI.FÔRM**)

Ū'NI.KĀT

MŪ'NI.KĀT   excommunicate, communicate
TŪ'NI.KĀT   tunicate

Ū'NI.KL

FŪ'NI.KL   funicle
TŪ'NI.KL   tunicle

UN'I.LĒ

FUN'I.LĒ   funnily
SUN'I.LĒ   sunnily

Ū'NING.LĒ

TŪ'NING.LĒ   tuningly

(See **OONING, ŪNING**, add -ly where appropriate.)

Ū'NI.TĒ

Ū'NI.TĒ   unity, triunity
MŪ'NI.TĒ   immunity, intercommunity, community, munity
PŪ'NI.TĒ   impunity
TŪ'NI.TĒ   importunity, inopportunity, opportunity

(See **OO'NI.TĒ**)

Ū'NI.TIV

Ū'NI.TIV   unitive
MŪ'NI.TIV   communitive
PŪ'NI.TIV   punitive

UN'JI.BL

FUN'JI.BL   fungible
PUN'JI.BL   expungible, inexpungible

UN'SI.NĀT

UN'SI.NĀT   uncinate
RUN'SI.NĀT   runcinate

UN'SI.Ō

MUN'SI.Ō   homuncio
NUN'SI.Ō   nuncio

UN'STA.BL

DUN'STA.BL   dunstable
KUN'STA.BL   constable

UN'TED.LĒ

FRUN'TED.LĒ   affrontedly
HUN'TED.LĒ   huntedly
STUN'TED.LĒ   stuntedly
WUN'TED.LĒ   unwontedly, wontedly

UN'TI.NES

RUN'TI.NES   runtiness
STUN'TI.NES   stuntiness

UN'TING.LĒ

BUN'TING.LĒ   buntingly
GRUN'TING.LĒ   gruntingly
HUN'TING.LĒ   huntingly
STUN'TING.LĒ   stuntingly

ŪN'YUN.IST

ŪN'YUN.IST   nonunionist, reunionist, unionist
MŪN'YUN.IST   communionist

Ū'PA.BL

DŪ'PA.BL   dupable, undupable
(See **OO'PA.BL**)

Ū'PE.RĀT
(See **OO'PE.RĀT**)

Ū'PER.Ē
(See **OO'PER.Ē**)

Ū'PI.AL
(See **OO'PI.AL**)

Ū'PING.LĒ
(See **OO'PING.LĒ**)

Ū'PLI.KĀT
(See **OOP'LI.KĀT**)

Ū'PŪ.LUS

(See ŌŌ'PŪ.LUS)

Ū'RA.BL

DŪ'RA.BL	durable, endurable, undurable, unendurable
KŪ'RA.BL	incurable, curable, procurable, securable

UR'A.BL

FUR'A.BL	inferable, conferable, referable, transferable
MUR'A.BL	demurrable
SHUR'A.BL	assurable, insurable, unassurable, uninsurable
STUR'A.BL	stirrable

Ū'RA.BLĒ

DŪ'RA.BLĒ	durably, endurably, unendurably
KŪ'RA.BLĒ	curably, incurably

Ū'RA.LIST

MŪ'RA.LIST	muralist

(See OOR'A.LIST)

Ū'RA.LIZM

(See ŌŌR'A.LIZM)

ŪR'A.TIV

DŪR'A.TIV	durative, indurative
KŪR'A.TIV	curative
PŪR'A.TIV	depurative
TŪR'A.TIV	maturative

UR'BA.BL

BLUR'BA.BL	blurbable
KUR'BA.BL	curbable, uncurbable
TUR'BA.BL	disturbable, imperturbable, perturbable, undisturbable

UR'BAL.IST

UR'BAL.IST	herbalist
HUR'BAL.IST	herbalist
VUR'BAL.IST	verbalist

UR'BA.LĪZ

PUR'BA.LĪZ	hyperbolize
VUR'BA.LĪZ	verbalize

UR'BAL.IZM

HUR'BAL.IZM	herbalism
VUR'BAL.IZM	verbalism

UR'BI.A

BUR'BI.A	suburbia
SUR'BI.A	Serbia
TUR'BI.A	ytterbia

UR'BI.AL

BUR'BI.AL	suburbial
VUR'BI.AL	adverbial, proverbial

UR'BI.SĪD

HUR'BI.SĪD	herbicide
VUR'BI.SĪD	verbicide

UR'BI.UM

UR'BI.UM	erbium
TUR'BI.UM	terbium

UR'BŪ.LENT

HUR'BŪ.LENT	herbulent
TUR'BŪ.LENT	turbulent

UR'DER.ER

MUR'DER.ER	murderer
VUR'DER.ER	verderer

UR'DI.LĒ

STUR'DI.LĒ	sturdily
WUR'DI.LĒ	wordily

UR'DI.NES

KUR'DI.NES	curdiness
STUR'DI.NES	sturdiness
WUR'DI.NES	wordiness

UR'EN.SĒ

FUR'EN.SĒ	conferrency, transferency
KUR'EN.SĒ	concurrency, currency, recurrency

UR'FLŌŌ.US

PUR'FLŌŌ.US	superfluous
TUR'FLŌŌ.US	subterfluous

Ū'RI.A

Ū'RI.A	polyuria, thiourea, urea
KŪ'RI.A	decuria, curia
NŪ'RI.A	albuminuria, anuria, phenylketonuria, hemoglobinuria, ketonuria
SŪ'RI.A	glycosuria
TŪ'RI.A	hematuria

(See OOR'I.A)

UR'I.A

(See OOR'I.A)

Ū'RI.AL

GŪ'RI.AL	augurial, figurial
KŪ'RI.AL	curial, mercurial
NŪ'RI.AL	seigneurial
PŪ'RI.AL	purpureal
TŪ'RI.AL	centureal

(See ŌŌ'RI.AL)

UR'I.AN

(See OOR'I.AN)

Ū'RI.ĀT

FŪ'RI.ĀT	infuriate
MŪ'RI.ĀT	muriate
TŪ'RI.ĀT	centuriate, parturiate
ZHŪ'RI.ĀT	luxuriate

UR'ID.LĒ

FLUR'ID.LĒ	flurriedly
HUR'ID.LĒ	hurriedly
WUR'ID.LĒ	worriedly

UR'I.ENS

PRUR'I.ENS	prurience
SUR'I.ENS	esurience
TUR'I.ENS	parturience, scripturience
ZHUR'I.ENS	luxuriance

UR'I.ENT

PRUR'I.ENT	prurient
SUR'I.ENT	esurient
TUR'I.ENT	parturient, scaturient, scripturient
ZHUR'I.ENT	luxuriant

UR'I.ER

BUR'I.ER	burrier
FLUR'I.ER	flurrier
FUR'I.ER	furrier
HUR'I.ER	hurrier
KUR'I.ER	courier, currier, vancourier
PUR'I.ER	purrier
SKUR'I.ER	scurrier
SPUR'I.ER	spurrier
WUR'I.ER	worrier

UR'I.ER.Ē

FUR'I.ER.Ē	furriery
KUR'I.ER.Ē	curriery

Ū'RI.FĪ

PŪ'RI.FĪ	purify
THŪ'RI.FĪ	thurify

UR'I.ING

FLUR'I.ING	flurrying
HUR'I.ING	hurrying
KUR'I.ING	currying

Ū'RI.KĀT

SŪ'RI.KĀT	suricate

(See Ū'RI.KIT)

Ū'RI.KIT

MŪ'RI.KIT	muricate

(See Ū'RI.KĀT)

UR'I.MENT

FLUR'I.MENT	flurriment
WUR'I.MENT	worriment

UR'ING.LĒ

UR'ING.LĒ	erringly, inerringly
BLUR'ING.LĒ	blurringly
DUR'ING.LĒ	enduringly
FUR'ING.LĒ	deferringly, inferringly, conferringly
HWUR'ING.LĒ	whirringly
LUR'ING.LE	alluringly
MUR'ING.LĒ	demurringly
KUR'ING.LĒ	concurringly, nonconcurringly, recurringly
SHUR'ING.LĒ	assuringly, reassuringly
PUR'ING.LĒ	purringly
SLUR'ING.LĒ	slurringly
STUR'ING.LĒ	stirringly
VUR'ING.LĒ	averringly

Ū'RI.Ō

DŪ'RI.Ō	durio
KŪ'RI.Ō	curio

UR'ISH.ING

FLUR'ISH.ING	flourishing
NUR'ISH.ING	nourishing

UR'ISH.LĒ

BUR'ISH.LĒ	boorishly
KUR'ISH.LĒ	currishly
PUR'ISH.LĒ	poorishly
TUR'ISH.LĒ	amateurishly

Ū'RI.TĒ

KŪ'RI.TĒ	insecurity, security, Social Security
MŪ'RI.TĒ	demurity
PŪ'RI.TĒ	impurity, purity
SKŪ'RI.TĒ	obscurity
TŪ'RI.TĒ	futurity, immaturity, maturity, prematurity

(See OOR'I.TĒ)

ŪRI.US

FŪRI.US	furious, sulphureous
GŪRI.US	strangurious
KŪRI.US	incurious, curious
NŪRI.US	penurious
SPŪRI.US	spurious

UR'JEN.SĒ

UR'JEN.SĒ	urgency
MUR'JEN.SĒ	emergency
SUR'JEN.SĒ	assurgency, insurgency, resurgency
TUR'JEN.SĒ	detergency
VUR'JEN.SĒ	divergency, convergency, vergency

UR'JER.Ē

PUR'JER.Ē	perjury, purgery
RUR'JER.Ē	chirurgery
SUR'JER.Ē	electrosurgery, cryosurgery, neurosurgery, psychosurgery, surgery
VUR'JER.Ē	vergery

UR'JI.KAL

UR'JI.KAL	demiurgical, theurgical
KLUR'JI.KAL	clergical
LUR'JI.KAL	metallurgical
NUR'JI.KAL	energical, synergical
RUR'JI.KAL	chirurgical
SUR'JI.KAL	electrosurgical, cryosurgical, neurosurgical, psychosurgical, surgical
TUR'JI.KAL	dramaturgical, liturgical, thaumaturgical

UR'KA.LĀT

PUR'KA.LĀT	percolate
TUR'KA.LĀT	intercalate

UR'KI.LĒ

JUR'KI.LĒ	jerkily
MUR'KI.LĒ	murkily
PUR'KI.LĒ	perkily

UR'KŪ.LAR

BUR'KŪ.LAR	tubercular
FUR'KŪ.LAR	furcular
PUR'KŪ.LAR	opercular
SUR'KŪ.LAR	semicircular, circular

UR'KŪ.LĀT

BUR'KŪ.LĀT	tuberculate
PUR'KŪ.LĀT	operculate
SUR'KŪ.LĀT	recirculate, circulate

UR'KŪ.LUM

BUR'KŪ.LUM	tuberculum
FUR'KŪ.LUM	furculum
PUR'KŪ.LUM	operculum

UR'KŪ.LUS

BUR'KŪ.LUS	tuberculous
SUR'KŪ.LUS	surculous, surculus

UR'LI.ER

UR'LI.ER	earlier
BUR'LI.ER	burlier
CHUR'LI.ER	churlier
KUR'LI.ER	curlier
PUR'LI.ER	pearlier
SUR'LI.ER	surlier

UR'LI.NES

(See **URLĒ**, add -ness where appropriate.)

UR'LISH.LĒ

CHUR'LISH.LĒ	churlishly
GUR'LISH.LĒ	girlishly

UR'LISH.NES

CHUR'LISH.NES	churlishness
GUR'LISH.NES	girlishness

UR'MA.NĒ

JUR'MA.NĒ	Germany
VUR'MA.NĒ	verminy

UR'MA.NĪZ

JUR'MA.NĪZ	Germanize
SUR'MA.NĪZ	sermonize

UR'MA.RĒ

FUR'MA.RĒ	infirmary
SPUR'MA.RĒ	spermary

UR'MI.NAL

JUR'MI.NAL	germinal
TUR'MI.NAL	adterminal, conterminal, terminal

UR'MI.NANT

JUR'MI.NANT	germinant
TUR'MI.NANT	determinant, interminant, terminant

UR'MI.NĀT

JUR'MI.NĀT	germinate
TUR'MI.NĀT	determinate, exterminate, indeterminate, interminate, predeterminate, terminate

UR'MI.NUS

TUR'MI.NUS	coterminous, terminous
VUR'MI.NUS	verminous

UR'MI.SĪD

JUR'MI.SĪD	germicide
SPUR'MI.SĪD	spermicide
VUR'MI.SĪD	vermicide

UR'MO.FĪL

SPUR'MO.FĪL	spermophile
THUR'MO.FĪL	thermophile

UR'NA.BL

BUR'NA.BL	burnable, unburnable
LUR'NA.BL	learnable, unlearnable
SUR'NA.BL	discernible, indiscernible
TUR'NA.BL	nonreturnable, overturnable, returnable, turnable, unreturnable, unturnable

UR'NA.LĒ

FUR'NA.LĒ	infernally
TUR'NA.LĒ	externally, eternally, internally
VUR'NA.LĒ	vernally

UR'NA.LIST

JUR'NA.LIST	journalist
TUR'NA.LIST	eternalist, externalist, internalist

UR'NA.LĪZ

JUR'NA.LĪZ	journalize
FUR'NA.LĪZ	infernalize
TUR'NA.LĪZ	externalize, eternalize, internalize
VUR'NA.LĪZ	vernalize

UR'NA.LIZM

FUR'NA.LIZM	infernalism
JUR'NA.LIZM	journalism
TUR'NA.LIZM	externalism, eternalism

UR'NED.LĒ

LUR'NED.LĒ	learnedly
SUR'NED.LĒ	concernedly, unconcernedly

UR'NER.Ē

FUR'NER.Ē	fernery
TUR'NER.Ē	ternery, turnery

UR′NI.A

BUR′NI.A	Hibernia
HUR′NI.A	hernia
TUR′NI.A	Saturnia
VUR′NI.A	evernia

UR′NI.AN

BUR′NI.AN	eburnean, Hibernian
TUR′NI.AN	quaternion, Saturnian
VUR′NI.AN	Avernian

UR′NI.CHER

FUR′NI.CHER	furniture
SUR′NI.CHER	cerniture

UR′NISH.ER

BUR′NISH.ER	burnisher
FUR′NISH.ER	furnisher, refurnisher

UR′NISH.ING

BUR′NISH.ING	burnishing
FUR′NISH.ING	furnishing, refurnishing

UR′NI.TĒ

DUR′NI.TĒ	modernity
TUR′NI.TĒ	alternity, diuturnity, eternity, fraternity, coeternity, maternity, paternity, sempiternity, taciturnity

UR′NI.TŪR

(See UR′NI.CHER)

UR′O.ER

BUR′O.ER	burrower
FUR′O.ER	furrower

UR′PEN.TĬN

SUR′PEN.TĬN	serpentine
TUR′PEN.TĬN	turpentine

UR′PI.ER

BUR′PI.ER	burpier
CHUR′PI.ER	chirpier
SLUR′PI.ER	slurpier

UR′PI.LĒ

BUR′PI.LĒ	burpily
CHUR′PI.LĒ	chirpily
SLUR′PI.LĒ	slurpily

UR′PI.NES

(See URPĒ, add -ness where appropriate.)

UR′SA.BL

(See UR′SI.BL)

UR′SA.RĒ

BUR′SA.RĒ	bursary
KUR′SA.RĒ	discursory, cursory, precursory
NUR′SA.RĒ	nursery
SPUR′SA.RĒ	aspersory
VUR′SA.RĒ	anniversary, controversary

UR′SHI.A

(See URSHA)

UR′SHI.AL

(See URSHAL)

UR′SHI.AN

(See URSHUN)

UR′SHI.UM

KWUR′SHI.UM	quinquertium
TUR′SHI.UM	nasturtium

UR′SI.BL

UR′SI.BL	coercible, incoercible
BUR′SI.BL	reimbursable
MUR′SI.BL	amerceable, immersible, submersible
VUR′SI.BL	introversible, irreversible, conversable, reversible, traversable

UR′SI.FÔRM

UR′SI.FÔRM	ursiform
BUR′SI.FÔRM	bursiform
FUR′SI.FÔRM	furciform
VUR′SI.FÔRM	diversiform, versiform

UR′SIV.LĒ

UR′SIV.LĒ	coercively, uncoercively
KUR′SIV.LĒ	decursively, discursively, excursively
SPUR′SIV.LĒ	aspersively, dispersively
TUR′SIV.LĒ	detersively

UR′SIV.NES

UR′SIV.NES	coerciveness
KUR′SIV.NES	decursiveness, discursiveness, excursiveness
SPUR′SIV.NES	aspersiveness, dispersiveness

URTH′LES.NES

MURTH′LES.NES	mirthlessness
WURTH′LES.NES	worthlessness

UR′TI.BL

HUR′TI.BL	hurtable
SUR′TI.BL	insertable
VUR′TI.BL	avertible, divertible, incontrovertible, inconvertible, invertible, controvertible, convertible

UR′TI.TŪD

UR′TI.TŪD	inertitude
SUR′TI.TŪD	incertitude, certitude

UR′VA.BL

KUR′VA.BL	curvable

SUR'VA.BL	conservable, observable, preservable, reservable, servable
SWUR'VA.BL	swervable, unswervable
ZUR'VA.BL	reservable

UR'VA.TIV

KUR'VA.TIV	curvative
NUR'VA.TIV	enervative
SUR'VA.TIV	conservative, neoconservative
ZUR'VA.TIV	observative, preservative, reservative

UR'VED.LĒ

| FUR'VED.LĒ | fervidly |
| ZUR'VED.LĒ | deservedly, observedly, reservedly, undeservedly, unreservedly |

UR'VEN.SĒ

FUR'VEN.SĒ	fervency
SUR'VEN.SĒ	conservancy
ZUR'VEN.SĒ	observancy

UR'VI.LĒ

KUR'VI.LĒ	curvily
NUR'VI.LĒ	nervily
SWUR'VI.LĒ	swervily
TUR'VI.LĒ	topsy-turvily

UR'ZHUN.AL

| KUR'ZHUN.AL | excursional |
| VUR'ZHUN.AL | aversional, conversional, reversional, versional |

UR'ZHUN.IST

KUR'ZHUN.IST	excursionist
MUR'ZHUN.IST	immersionist, total-immersionist
VUR'ZHUN.IST	aversionist, conversionist, reversionist, versionist

ŪS'A.BL

(See OOS'A.BL)

US'A.BL

BUS'A.BL	busable, bussable
KUS'A.BL	discussable, cussable, undiscussable, uncussable
MUS'A.BL	mussable, unmussable

UR'NER.Ē

| FUR'NER.Ē | fernery |
| TUR'NER.Ē | quaternary, ternary, turnery |

UR'ZHI.AN

(See URZHUN)

US'CHOO.LIT

| US'CHOO.LIT | ustulate |
| PUS'CHOO.LIT | pustulate |

Ū'SED.LĒ

(See Ū.SID.LĒ)

Ū'SE.LIS

(See Ū'SI.LIS)

Ū'SER.Ē

| Ū'SER.Ē | usury |

(See OO'SE.RĒ)

USH'A.BL

BRUSH'A.BL	brushable
FLUSH'A.BL	flushable
HUSH'A.BL	hushable
KRUSH'A.BL	crushable, uncrushable

Ū'SHI.A

(See OO'SHI.A)

Ū'SHI.AL

| DŪ'SHI.AL | fiducial |

(See OO'SHI.AL)

USH'I.LĒ

| GUSH'I.LĒ | gushily |
| MUSH'I.LĒ | mushily |

USH'ING.LĒ

BLUSH'ING.LĒ	blushingly
GUSH'ING.LĒ	gushingly
KRUSH'ING.LĒ	crushingly
RUSH'ING.LĒ	rushingly

Ū'SHUN.AL

| KŪ'SHUN.AL | elocutional, circumlocutional |

(See OO'SHUN.AL)

Ū'SHUN.ER

| KŪ'SHUN.ER | executioner, elocutioner |

(See OO'SHUN.ER)

Ū'SHUN.IST

| KŪ'SHUN.IST | elocutionist, executionist, perpilocutionist |

(See OO'SHUN.IST)

Ū'SI.AN

(See OOSHUN, ŪSHUN)

Ū'SI.BL

(See OO'SA.BL)

Ū'SID.LĒ

DŪ'SID.LĒ	deucedly
LŪ'SID.LĒ	lucidly, pellucidly, translucidly
MŪ'SID.LĒ	mucidly

(See OO'SID.LĒ)

Ū'SI.FER

(See OO'SI.FER)

Ū'SI.FÔRM

| LŪ'SI.FÔRM | luciform |
| NŪ'SI.FÔRM | nuciform |

(See $\overline{OO}$'SI.FÔRM)

Ū'SI.LIJ

FŪ'SI.LIG	fuselage
MŪ'SI.LIJ	mucilage
PŪSI.LIJ	pucelage

Ū'SIV.LĒ

BŪ'SIV.LĒ	abusively
DŪ'SIV.LĒ	conducively
FŪ'SIV.LĒ	diffusively, effusively

(See $\overline{OO}$'SIV.LĒ)

Ū'SIV.NES

BŪ'SIV.NES	abusiveness
DŪ'SIV.NES	conduciveness
FŪ'SIV.NES	diffusiveness, effusiveness

(See $\overline{OO}$'SIV.NES)

US'KI.LĒ

DUS'KI.LĒ	duskily
HUS'KI.LĒ	huskily
MUS'KI.LĒ	muskily

US'KI.NES

DUS'KI.NES	duskiness
HUS'KI.NES	huskiness
MUS'KI.NES	muskiness
TUS'KI.NES	tuskiness

US'KŪ.LAR

JUS'KŪ.LAR	majuscular
KUS'KŪ.LAR	lacuscular
MUS'KŪ.LAR	bimuscular, muscular, neuromuscular, unmuscular
NUS'KŪ.LAR	minuscular

| PUS'KŪ.LAR | corpuscular, crepuscular, opuscular |

US'KŪ.LUS

| MUS'KŪ.LUS | musculus |
| PUS'KŪ.LUS | corpusculous, crepusculous |

US'TA.BL

BUS'TA.BL	bustable, incombustible, combustible
DUS'TA.BL	dustable
GUS'TA.BL	gustable, ingustable
JUS'TA.BL	adjustable, inadjustable
RUS'TA.BL	rustable
THRUS'TA.BL	thrustable
TRUS'TA.BL	trustable

US'TER.Ē

BLUS'TER.Ē	blustery
FLUS'TER.Ē	flustery
KLUS'TER.Ē	clustery

US'TER.ER

BLUS'TER.ER	blusterer
FLUS'TER.ER	flusterer
KLUS'TER.ER	clusterer
MUS'TER.ER	musterer

US'TER.ING

(See USTER, add -ing where appropriate.)

UST'FUL.Ē

GUST'FUL.Ē	disgustfully, gustfully
LUST'FUL.Ē	lustfully
TRUST'FUL.Ē	distrustfully, mistrustfully, trustfully

US'TI.BL

(See US'TA.BL)

US'TI.ER

DUS'TI.ER	dustier
FUS'TI.ER	fustier
GUS'TI.ER	gustier
KRUS'TI.ER	crustier
LUS'TI.ER	lustier
MUS'TI.ER	mustier
RUS'TI.ER	rustier
TRUS'TI.ER	trustier

US'TI.LĒ

(See USTĒ, add -ly where appropriate.)

US'TI.NES

(See USTĒ, add -ness where appropriate.)

US'TRI.US

| DUS'TRI.US | industrious |
| LUS'TRI.US | illustrious |

ŪT'A.BL

FŪT'A.BL	irrefutable, confutable, refutable, unconfutable
KŪT'A.BL	executable, prosecutable
MŪT'A.BL	immutable, incommutable, commutable, mutable, permutable, transmutable
PŪT'A.BL	disputable, imputable, indisputable, computable, uncomputable
SŪT'A.BL	suitable, unsuitable

(See $\overline{OOT}$'A.BL)

Ū'TA.BLĒ

(See Ū'TA.BL, $\overline{OO}$'TA.BL, change -e to -y where appropriate.)

Ū'TA.TIV

| FŪ'TA.TIV | confutative, refutative |
| MŪ'TA.TIV | commutative, mutative, transmutative |

NŪ'TA.TIV   sternutative
PŪ'TA.TIV   disputative,
                       imputative, putative,
                       reputative

Ū'TED.LĒ

MŪ'TED.LĒ   mutedly
PŪ'TED.LĒ   reputedly

Ū'TER.Ē

PŪ'TER.Ē   pewtery

(See $\overline{OO}$'TER.Ē)

UT'ER.Ē

BUT'ER.Ē   buttery
FLUT'ER.Ē   fluttery
GUT'ER.Ē   guttery
MUT'ER.Ē   muttery
PUT'ER.Ē   puttery
SPLUT'ER.Ē   spluttery
SPUT'ER.Ē   sputtery
STUT'ER.Ē   stuttery

UT'ER.ER

(See **UTER,** add *-er* where appropriate.)

UT'ER.ING

(See **UTER,** add *-ing* where appropriate.)

UTH'ER.Ē

(TH as in *then*)

MUTH'ER.Ē   mothery
SMUTH'ER.Ē   smothery

UTH'ER.ER

(TH as in *then*)
BRUTH'ER.ER   brotherer
MUTH'ER.ER   motherer
SMUTH'ER.ER   smotherer

UTH'ER.ING

(TH as in *then*)
BRUTH'ER.ING   brothering
MUTH'ER.ING   mothering
SMUTH'ER.ING   smothering
SUTH'ER.ING   southering
WUTH'ER.ING   wuthering

UTH'ER.LĒ

(TH as in *then*)
BRUTH'ER.LĒ   brotherly,
                       unbrotherly
MUTH'ER.LĒ   motherly,
                       unmotherly
SUTH'ER.LĒ   southerly

ŪTH'FUL.Ē

ŪTH'FUL.Ē   youthfully

(See $\overline{OO}$TH'FUL.Ē)

ŪTH'FUL.NES

ŪTH'FUL.NES   youthfulness

(See $\overline{OO}$TH'FUL.NES)

Ū'TI.AL

PŪ'TI.AL   puteal

(See $\overline{OO}$'TI.AL)

Ū'TI.FĪ

BŪ'TI.FĪ   beautify

(See $\overline{OO}$'TI.FĪ)

Ū'TI.FUL

BŪ'TI.FUL   beautiful
DŪ'TI.FUL   dutiful, undutiful

(See $\overline{OO}$'TI.FUL)

Ū'TI.KL

BŪ'TI.KAL   antiscorbutical,
                       scorbutical
DŪ'TI.KAL   propaedeutical
KŪ'TI.KL   cuticle
NŪ'TI.KL   hermaneutical
PŪ'TI.KL   therapeutical

(See $\overline{OO}$'TI.KL)

Ū'TI.LĪZ

Ū'TI.LĪZ   utilize

(See $\overline{OO}$'TI.LĪZ)

Ū'TI.NĒ

MŪ'TI.NĒ   mutiny

(See $\overline{OO}$'TI.NĒ)

UT'ING.LĒ

JUT'ING.LĒ   juttingly
KUT'ING.LĒ   cuttingly
STRUT'ING.LĒ   struttingly

Ū'TI.NÎR

MŪ'TI.NÎR   mutineer
(See $\overline{OO}$'TI.NÎR)

Ū'TI.NUS

MŪ'TI.NUS   mutinous
(See $\overline{OO}$'TI.NUS)

Ū'TI.US

BŪ'TI.US   beauteous
DŪ'TI.US   duteous

(See $\overline{OO}$'TI.US)

UT'LER.Ē

BUT'LER.Ē   butlery
KUT'LER.Ē   cutlery
SUT'LER.Ē   sutlery

UT'ON.Ē

BUT'ON.Ē   buttony
GLUT'ON.Ē   gluttony
MUT'ON.Ē   muttony

Ū'VA.BL

(See $\overline{OO}$'VA.BL)

UV'A.BL

LUV'A.BL   lovable, unlovable
SHUV'A.BL   shovable

UV'EL.ER

HUV'EL.ER   hoveler
SHUV'EL.ER   shoveler

UV'ER.Ē

KUV'ER.Ē	discovery, recovery
PLUV'ER.Ē	plovery

UV'ER.ER

HUV'ER.ER	hoverer
KUV'ER.ER	discoverer, coverer, recoverer, uncoverer

UV'ER.ING

HUV'ER.ING	hovering
KUV'ER.ING	discovering, covering, recovering, uncovering

UV'ER.LĒ

KUV'ER.LĒ	deCoverley
LUV'ER.LĒ	loverly

Ū'VI.AL

Ū'VI.AL	uveal

(See $\overline{\text{OO}}$'VI.AL)

Ū'VI.AN

(See $\overline{\text{OO}}$'VI.AN)

Ū'VING.LĒ

(See $\overline{\text{OO}}$'VING.LĒ)

Ū'VI.UM

(See $\overline{\text{OO}}$'VI.UM)

Ū'VI.US

(See $\overline{\text{OO}}$'VI.US)

ŪZ'A.BL

ŪZ'A.BL	usable

FŪZ'A.BL	diffusible, fusible, infusible, confusible, transfusible

(See $\overline{\text{OO}}$'ZA.BL)

Ū'ZHUN.IST

(See $\overline{\text{OO}}$'ZHUN.IST)

UZ'I.LĒ

FUZ'I.LĒ	fuzzily
MUZ'I.LĒ	muzzily
WUZ'I.LĒ	wuzzily

UZ'I.NES

BUZ'I.NES	buzziness
FUZ'I.NES	fuzziness
MUZ'I.NES	muzziness
WUZ'I.NES	wuzziness

THE GLOSSARY

CAUTION Of the manifold defects of commisson and omission in this glossary, two humble me particularly.

First, I became so entranced by odd meanings that I quite *forgot to check whether all the words rhymed*. By the time the oversight occurred to me, the section was already in page proofs. I have thrown out the interlopers I could find in haste; but I am by no means sure that I found them all. It is some small comfort that if non-rhyming words do remain, they should not bother you much, since you will generally be going from the rhyming list to the glossary, not the other way around.

Second, my original purpose was to define all the rhyming words I had that do not appear in most college-level dictionaries. But after I had adopted or adapted dictionary definitions for perhaps 9,000 of these—all there was room for—others continued to appear; I would guess that the rhyming list contains at least 25,000 such uncommon words, of which 16,000 remain undefined.

Oh well—some day the publisher may let me publish the missing meanings in a companion volume. And even now, you do have a fighting chance—say one in three—of finding the definition you want. You don't get as good odds as that with a lottery ticket.

W.R.E.

How Dreka's Blotting-Case Fathered a Glossary

About seventy-five years ago a young man named Cecil Jefferson Espy, soon to become my uncle, either bought, borrowed, found, or was given—I am sure he did not steal—a Dreka's Blotting-Case. This was, as the name indicates, a container for blotters, and a handsome one, bound in genuine simulated leather.

Uncle Cecil, not being one to let a good thing slip away from him, still had Dreka's Blotting-Case in his desk drawer when he died not long ago at the age of ninety-three; and his daughter Barbara kindly gave it to me as a keepsake. Besides several ink-smudged blotters, the case contains a twenty-four-page word list, printed in type too small to be read without a magnifying glass.

Mr. Dreka introduced the list with these remarks:

"This word book, being an addition to the ordinary Blotting-Case, renders it of the greatest assistance to the letter-writer, with but a trifling addition to its bulk or cost, and comprehending the whole of the English language in general use. The absence of definitions will not diminish its utility to the letter-writer, for whom alone it is intended; it is not he, but the *reader* (Mr. Dreka's italics) who seeks them."

Mr. Dreka's definition of the purpose of his word list could not have been more fitting for my own project of the moment—this book.

Or, indeed, for any current rhyming dictionary of my acquaintance. Their authors seem to be in agreement that poets—as Mr. Dreka said about letter writers—need not bother to understand (much less explain) the words in their verses—let the readers worry about the meanings. Rhyming dictionaries and Mr. Dreka's word book have at least this in common: they both dispense with definitions.

So I decided to call my book not a dictionary but simply *Words to Rhyme With*.

But if only for my own satisfaction I did want to know the meanings of the words I was listing. If I could not find them in a college, unabridged, or specialized dictionary, I left them out. If they were not in a college-level dictionary but were in one of the others, I recorded the words with their definitions on filing cards.

The time came when my file defined 9,000 unfamiliar words, and I faced the fact that it would be unfair not to share their meanings with my readers. Dreka's Blotting-Case had fathered a glossary.

Not a comprehensive one, to be sure, as you are aware from the cautionary note a few pages back. But enough is enough; I am through.

I am also through rechecking the rhyming list as well. With each new look another word pops up, waving its letters about as an octopus waves its arms, and insisting that it too deserves a place in the glossary. I would have caught more of them, and corrected more errors, too, were it not that I tend to doze off while reviewing word lists, particularly when in the midst of interminable rhyme categories like ĀSHUN and OLOJĒ. If you find misspellings, or words that show up neither in your desk dictionary nor in my glossary, or that show up in both places, I apologize.

To be eligible for the glossary, a word had not only to rhyme, bit to be too rarefied for most college-level dictionaries. Countless words that tickled my fancy could not be defined here because they did not meet one or the other requirement. Take, for instance, the variety of lovely names of just one field flower, names that nod their sun-colored heads in this anthological quatrain:

INSTRUCTIONS FOR MY FLORIST

Send my dear a cowslip; send my dear an oxlip.
  Send my dear a cuckooflower; a stitchwort send her.
Send my dear a crowfoot, ragged robin, paigle,
  Wood sorrel, primrose . . . tender for the tender.

Of all those delightful names, only *paigle*—defined in Webster's Second and so here as ''The cowslip, or the oxlip; the cuckooflower; the stitchwort; any of several crow-foots''—is entered in the following pages. *Cowslip* and *oxlip* are out because they have no rhyming matches.* The others do (though you have to puff a little on the last syllable of *stitchwort* and *crowfoot* to blow them into the ring)—but they are ineligible for the glossary because they appear in most college dictionaries.

A number of words that deal with acids, chemicals, minerals, and the like did make the glossary. I could work up little interest in them. But who knows? For you they may be just what the muse ordered.

Some words improve on acquaintance. There may seem little, for instance, to be made in rhyme of geometrical terms such as *rhombicosidecahedron* or *pseudorhombicuboc-*

---

*This is not quite correct. They would have plenty of matches if I listed them in italics to indicate they were to be accented (illegitimately) on the last syllable. But I did not.

tahedronal; but they are willing to cooperate—certainly for jingles, or nominies, or amphigories, if not for Poetry. Jingles and nominies have their place in the tolerant world of rhyme; if I did not believe so, I would not be rhyming. Alexander the Great was permitted to slice the Gordian knot in two with his sword; surely one may be permitted to slice a knotty word like *rhombicosidecahedron* into manageable sections:

ANN, BECKY, AND CLEO:

TRAGEDY OF A CRYSTAL, A PRISM, AND A SOLID

> A Crystal and a Prism
> Spoke nasty criticism
>   Of the profile of a Solid in the street.
> This resulted in a squalid
> Altercation; for the Solid
>   Considered her appearance rather neat.
>
>   So Ann, Beck, and Cleo
>   Debated, *con brio*
>   And static,
>   Which one of the trio
>   Was really most Pleo-
>   chromatic.
>
> A honey was Rebecca!—
> A Rhombicosideca-
>   hedron, and sexangled to attract!
> Ann's lure was more back-homey—
> A little Pseudorhombi-
>   cuboctrahedronal, in point of fact.
>
> And Cleo!—her Hexagonal
> Was *blatantly* Sexagonal!
>   She barely tried to hide her Dodecants.
> In angles as in features
> All three were charming creatures,
>   Configured for Euclidean romance.
>
> They vied for top position
> In a beauty competition,
>   Each feeling prettiest of all the pretty.
> But a Parallelepiped
> Is a Prism, not a biped;
>   They weren't considered at Atlantic City.
>
>   A tragical blow!
>   No way to show
>   They were pretty!
>   Poor, rhombidec
>   Ann, Cleo, Beck!
>   What a pity!
>   What a pity!

Easy-come-easy-go verses, no better and no worse than the foregoing, are scattered throughout the glossary to show unfamiliar words at play.

If the glossary had been around in Mr. Dreka's time, he might have used it to prepare the Dreka word list. But of course he would have left out the definitions.

To Use the Glossary Effectively, Remember That . . .

• The pronunciation guide below explains the symbols used to show the pronunciation of words.

• Appendix A explains the numerals that accompany some definitions. The number 9, for instance, stands for *archaic;* 44D for *Scotland and dialectal;* 58 for *humorous.*

• Appendices B, C, and D define, respectively, words ending in -mancy, -mania, and -phobia that are not included in the rhyming list.

*Words forming triple rhymes may be used to match single rhymes by adding stress to the last syllable. Double rhymes may sometimes be made into single rhymes in the same way, though the result is likely to be awkward.

KEY TO PRONUNCIATIONS IN THE GLOSSARY

This key explains the system used in the glossary to approximate the pronunciation of the words defined. There are differences between the scheme used here and the one for identifying rhyme categories in the list of rhymes. Here, for instance, the sound of long e followed by r in a stressed syllable is shown as ĒR: **fearful:** (fēr′ful). In the rhyming list, the same sound is given as ÎR: **FÎRFUL** (fearful). The sound of a long unstressed e making up the last syllable of a word is shown in the glossary as i: **only** (ōn′li), but in the rhyming list as Ē: **ŌNLĒ.**

A′ following a syllable indicates stress:

ectal (ek′tal):

A. following a syllable indicates lack of stress:

mistetch (mis.tech′):

A syllable with little or no stress at the end of a word has no accent mark:

poimenics (poi.men′iks)
abaculus (a.bak′ū.lus)
pretty (prit′i)

If a word of several syllables has one major stress and one or more minor stresses, the minor stresses are occasionally but not always shown:

chimopelagic (kī′mo.pi.laj′ik)
chimopelagic (kī.mo.pi.laj′ik)

Phonetic marking		*Sounds as in*
ā	in stressed syllables	**weight** (wāt)
		retainer (ri.tā′ner)
		matelassé (mat′la.sā)
	in unstressed syllables	**chaotic** (kā.ot′ik)
âr	only in stressed syllables	**air** (âr)
		octarius (ok.târ′i.us)

a	in stressed syllables	**battery** (batʹer.i)
	in unstressed and indeterminate syllables	**phalacrosis** (falʹa.krōʹsis) **tetrao** (tetʹra.ō)
ä	only in stressed syllables	**alala** (äʹla.lä) **majagua** (ma.häʹgwa) **father** (fäʹther) **Lakme** (läkʹmi)
är	in both stressed and unstressed syllables	**archaist** (ärʹkā.ist) **archiater** (är.kīʹa.ter)
ar	in stressed syllables	**carriage** (karʹij)
ē	only in stressed syllables	**compete** (kum.pēt) **feeling** (fēʹling)
e	in stressed syllables	**bet** (bet) **bellow** (belʹō)
e	in unstressed syllables	**escudo** (es.kūʹdo, -koōʹdō)
er	in stressed syllables	**berry** (berʹi)
	in unstressed syllables	**quaver** (kwāʹver) **pervade** (per.vādʹ) **circuitous** (ser.kūʹi.tus)
ī	in stressed syllables	**fiery** (fīʹer.i) **alight** (a.lītʹ)
	in unstressed syllables	**iambic** (ī.amʹbik)
i	in stressed syllables in unstressed syllables, the sound of long unstressed e or of -y	**middle** (midʹl) **depart** (di.pärtʹ) **lonely** (lōnʹli) **archaeology** (ärʹki.olʹo.ji)
	in unstressed -ate or -age ending a word, the sound of i in it; or ij	**intemperate** (in.temʹper.it) **immaculate** (i.makʹu.lit) **courage** (kurʹij) **carnage** (kärʹnij)
ō	in stressed syllables	**goat** (gōt) **revolt** (ri.vōltʹ)
	in unstressed syllables, at the end of a word	**hollow** (holʹō) **faro** (fârʹō)
ô	in stressed or unstressed syllables	**exaugurate** (eg.zôgʹū.rāt) **gorbelly** (gôrʹbel.i) **musquashroot** (musʹkwôsh.roōt)

o	in stressed syllables	**got** (got)
		bottle (bot′l)
		Hottentot (hot′n.tot)
	in unstressed syllables (when not the last sound in the word)	**orthodoxy** (ôr′tho.dok′si)
		plutocrat (pl$\overline{oo}$′to.krat)
$\overline{oo}$	in stressed and unstressed syllables	**canoodle** (ka.n$\overline{oo}$′dl)
		catalufa (kat′a.l$\overline{oo}$′fa)
oo	in stressed and unstressed syllables	**foot** (foot)
		carucage (kar′oo.kij)
ou	in stressed syllables	**allowed** (a.loud′)
ū	in stressed syllables	**acute** (a.kūt′)
		pituitary (pi.tū′i.ter′i)
	in unstressed syllables	**utility** (ū.til′i.ti)
		diminuendo (di.min′ū.en′dō)
u	in stressed and unstressed syllables	**butter** (but′er)
		datum (dā′tum)
		compare (kum.pâr)
ur	in stressed and some unstressed syllables	**courage** (kur′ij)
		courageous (ku.rā′jus)

There are no phonetic keys for the pronunciation of consonants, except in two cases:

- N indicates the French nasal sound.
        malentendu: mal′äN.täN.dū
- K indicates the sound of -ch in Scottish *loch* or German *ich*.

                    loch: loK
                    ich: iK

KEY TO ABBREVIATIONS IN THE GLOSSARY

cap.	capitalized	**n. pl.**	noun plural
dial.	dialectal	**obs.**	obsolete
eccl.	ecclesiastical	**orig.**	originally
Eng.	English	**part.**	particularly
equiv.	equivalent	**pert.**	pertaining
esp.	especially	**pl.**	plural
fem.	feminine	**prob.**	probably
fig.	figuratively	**specif.**	specifically
hist.	historically	**usu.**	usually
incl., inc.	including	**v.**	verb
n.	noun	**var.**	variant

A

aar (är): in South Africa, an underground stream.

abacinate (a.bas'i.nāt): to blind by means of a red-hot metal plate held before the eyes. 52.

abaciscus (ab'a.sis'kus): an abaculus.

abactor (ab.ak'ter): one that steals cattle.

abaculus (a.bak'ū.lus): a mosaic tile; a tessera.

abalienation (ab.āl'yen.ā'shun): the transference of a legal title.

aband (a.band'): forsake, abandon. 1.

abannition (ab'a.nish'un): a curse.

abasia (a.bā'zhi.a): inability to coordinate muscular actions properly in walking.

abatis (ab'a.tis, a.bat'i): a defensive obstacle of felled trees, with their butts toward the place defended and their sharpened points toward the enemy.

abatize (ab'a.tīz): to make an abatis.

abaton (ab'a.ton): among the ancient Greeks, a sacred place forbidden to unauthorized visitors.

abducent (ab.dū'sent): carrying or drawing away; abducting.

abecedism (ā'bi.si.dizm): a word created from the initials of a word in a phrase; an acronym.

aberdevine (ab'er.di.vīn): the European siskin, a kind of finch.

abiotic (ā'bī.ot'ik): characterized by the absence of life.

abishag (ab'i.shag): per Mrs. Byrne, the child of a woman and a married man not her husband.

ablactate (ab.lak'tāt): to wean.

ablegate (ab'li.gāt): a papal envoy on a special mission.

ablepsia (ab.lep'si.a): blindness.

ablutomania (a.bloo'to.mā'ni.a): a mania for washing oneself.

abnormous (ab.nôr'mus): abnormal, irregular. 9.

aboma (a.bō'ma): any of several large South American constrictor snakes.

abra (ä'bra): a narrow pass or defile. 35A.

abraxis (a.brak'sis): a word that creates a powerful charm if carved into wood or stone.

abreaction (ab.ri.ak'shun): the release of repressed ideas or emotions during psychoanalysis.

Abrus (ābrus): a genus of tropical vines incl. the Indian licorice.

abscinder (ab.sind'er): one that cuts (something) off.

absinthiate (ab.sin'thi.āt): to impregnate with wormwood.

absinthium (ab.sin'thi.um): the common wormwood, or its dried leaves and tops, used as a bitter stomachic and tonic.

abstergent (ab.stur'jent): a substance used in cleansing; a detergent.

abstersion (ab.stur'shun): the process of cleansing, esp. by wiping.

abstersive (ab.stur'siv): abstergent. 1.

acanaceous (ak'a.nā'shus): prickly.

acanthine (a.kan'thīn, -thin): pert. to or resembling the acanthus plant or its leaves.

acara (a.kä'ra): a South American fish that builds nests and guards its young.

acapnotic (a.kap.not'ik): a nonsmoker.

acarophobia (ak'a.ro.fō'bi.a): fear of itching, or of insects causing itching.

acarpous (a.kär'pus): fruitless, sterile.

acataleptic (a.kat.a.lep'tik): one who suspends judgment, believing certainty is impossible.

acathistus (ak.a.this'tus): a Lenten hymn of the Eastern Orthodox Church.

acceptilation (ak.sep'ti.lā'shun): the settlement of a debt without payment.

accidentary (ak.si.den'ta.ri): fortuitous; also, nonessential. 1.

accidentiary (ak.si.den'shi.âr.i): pert. to the accidence, an elementary book of (esp. Latin) grammar; hence, rudiments.

accipient (ak.sip'i.ent): one who receives. 1.

accipitrine (ak.sip'i.trīn): hawklike, raptorial.

accismus (ak.siz'mus): in rhetoric, a feigned refusal.

accite (ak.sīt): to cite; summon. 1.

accolent (ak'o.lent): neighboring.

accresce (a.kres'): to accrue. 1.

accrescence (a.kres'ens): continuous growth; accretion.

accubitum (a.kū'bi.tum): a Roman couch of crescent shape, accommodating five persons at a meal.

acersecomic (a.ser.si.com'ic): one whose hair has never been cut.

acervuline (a.sur'vū.-līn, -lin): resembling small heaps.

acescency (a.ses'en.si): the condition of turning sour.

achaetous (a.kē'tus): hairless.

aciniform (a.sin'i.form): shaped like a grape cluster.

aciurgy (as'i.ur.ji): operative surgery.

aclinal (a.klī'nal): not sloping; horizontal.

acocotl (ak'o.kot'l): the clarin, a trumpetlike wind instrument used by the aborigines in Mexico.

acomia (a.kō'mi.a): baldness; *alopecia*.

acopic (a.kop'ik): in medicine, relieving weariness.

acousticophobia (a.koos'ti.ko.fō'bi.a): fear of noise.

acquent (a.kwent'): acquainted. 11.

acquest (a.kwest'): acquisition. 9. (cap) Property acquired through means other than inheritance.

acrity (ak'ri.ti): sharpness, keenness. 1.

acrolith (ak'ro.lith): a statue with a trunk of wood, usu. covered with metal or drapery, and with extremities of stone.

acronic (a.kron'ik), acronyctous (a.kro.nik'tus): occurring at nightfall, or sunset—said of the rising or setting of a star.

acronyx (ak'ro.niks): in medicine, an ingrowing nail.

acroterium (ak.ro.tē'ri.um): on a classical building, one of the angles of a pediment. A statue or ornament placed at one of these angles.

acrotic (a.krot'ik): in medicine, pert. to or affecting the surface.

actinograph (ak.tin'o.graf): an instrument for calculating exposure time in photography.

actinolitic (ak'tin.o.lit'ik): pert. to actinolite, a bright green or grayish green variety of amphibole.

actuosity(ak'tū.os'i.ti): great activity.1.

actus (ak'tus): an act or thing done, specif. a mental or spiritual act.

acutate (a.kū'tāt): in botany, slightly sharpened.

acutiator (a.kū'shi.ā'ter): in medieval times, a sharpener of weapons.

acyesis (as'i.ē'sis): female sterility.

acyrology (as.i.rol'o.ji): poor diction.

adactyl (a.dak'til): congenitally lacking fingers or toes.

adactylia (a.dak.til'i.a): congenital lack of fingers and toes.

adapic (ad'a.pik), adapid (ad'a.pid): pert. to a genus of crested fossil lemurs from the Eocene of Europe.

adda (ad'a): the common Egyptian skink.

adelophogamy (ad.el.o.fog'a.mi): marriage in which brothers share wives.

Adessenarian (ad.es'i.när'i.an): one believing in the real presence of Christ's body in the Eucharist, but not by transsubstantiation.

adhamant (ad.hā'mant): clinging as if by hooks—used esp. of the feet of certain birds, as the swift.

adharma (a.där'ma): in Hindu religion, unrighteousness—opposed to *dharma*, religious law or gospel.

adhibit (ad.hib'it): to let in (as a person), bring in. To affix (a label). To use, administer.

adiantum (ad'i.an'tum): a genus of plants comprising the maidenhair fern.

adiaphoristic (ad'i.af'o.ris'tik), adiaphorous (ad'i.af'o.rus): indifferent concerning religious or theological matters.

adipate (ad'i.pāt): a salt of edipic acid.

adipogenesis (ad'i.po.jen'e.sis): the formation of fat or fatty tissue.

aditus (ad'i.tus): a passage or opening for entrance.

adjag (aj'ag): a wild dog found in Java.

adject (a.jekt'): to add or annex; to join.

adlittoral (ad.lit'o.ral): pert. to the shallow water near the shore.

admedial (ad.mē'di.al): in biology, near the median plane.

adminicle (ad.min'i.kl): in law, a help or support; an auxiliary. Corroborative or explanatory proof.

adminiculary (ad.mi.nik'ū.lar.i): one who supplies help.

adnerval (ad.nur'val): in physiology, toward a nerve—said of electrical impulses passing toward the nerve through a muscle fiber.

adneural (ad.nū'ral): adjacent to a nerve.

adonean (ad'o.nē'an): pert. to Adonis.

adosculation (ad.os'kū.lā'shun): fertilization by external contact only.

adradius (ad.rā'di.us): in corals, sea anemones, jellyfishes, etc., one of the imaginary radial lines dividing the body into similar parts.

adrogation (ad'ro.gā'shun): adoption of a boy under 14 or a girl under 12.

adterminal (ad.tur'mi.nal): passing toward the end of a muscle—said in physiology of electrical impulses.

adulterine (a.dul'ter.īn): an illegitimate child.

aduncous (a.dung'kus): curved inward; hooked.

adustion (a.dus'chun): a burning or parching.

advenience (ad.vēn'yens): result of outward causes.

adversus (ad.vur'sus): against; toward in a hostile sense.

advesperate (ad.ves'pe.rāt): to draw toward evening.

advowee (ad'vou.ē'): one with the right of presenting a nominee to a vacant ecclesiastical benefice.

adynamia (a.dī.nā'mi.a): in medicine, lack or loss of the vital powers, caused by disease.

Aello (a.el'ō): a harpy.

aelurophile (i.lōō'ro.fīl): a cat lover.

aeneous (a.ē'ni.us): brassy; brasslike.

Aepyornis (ē'pi.ôr'nis): a genus of gigantic ratite birds known from remains found in Madagascar and believed to be the source of legends about the roc. They laid eggs fourteen inches long.

aequorial (i.kwôr'i.al): marine; oceanic. 52.

aeration (ā'er.ā'shun): aerating; exposure to air. Also, a process for eliminating undesirable flavors in milk or cream.

aerolite (ā.er.o.līt), aerolith (ā'er.o.lith): a stony meteorite.

aerophane (ā'er.o.fān): a thin, transparent crepe material.

aerophobia (ā'er.o.fō'bi.a): abnormal fear of flying.

aerotropic (ā'er.o.trop'ik): in plants, responding by changes in direction of growth of roots to changes in oxygen tension.

aesthematology, esthematology (es.-thē'ma.tol.o.ji): formerly, the science of the senses and the sense organs.

aesthesiology, esthesiology (es.thē'zi.ol.o.ji): the science of sensations.

Aetolian (i.tō'li.an): pert. to Aetolia, a district of Greece, or its inhabitants.

affiche (a.fēsh'): a placard posted in a public place.

affidavy (af'i.dā'vi): affidavit.

afflatus (a.flā'tus): an artistic inspiration.

aftaba (af.tä'ba): in Persia, a metal water vessel with a handle and long spout.

agacella (ag.a.sel'a): in heraldry, an antelope somewhat resembling a tiger, but with horns and hoofs.

agal (a.gal', äg'al): a cord of goats' hair, worn by Bedouins to hold down the neckerchief.

agalma (a.gal'ma): a memorial; specif., a primitive Greek statue of a god.

ABERDEVINE

This yellow bird, who loves to frisk in
	The umbrage of the pine,
Describes himself as Piny Siskin,
	Or else Aberdevine.
But caught off guard, or in a pinch,
He's just an ordinary Finch.

Agapemone (ag'a.pem'o.ni): a communistic establishment, founded about 1849 at Spaxton, England, that had a reputation for immoral behavior; hence any institution practicing free love.

agathism (ag'a.thizm): the concept that all is for the better.

agathokakological (ag'a.tho.kak'o.loj'i.kal): composed of both good and evil.

agathology (ag'a.thol.o.ji): the science or doctrine of the good.

agee (a.jē'): off the straight line; awry. 11.

agerasia (aj'e.rā'zi.a): youthful appearance in an older person.

ageusic (a.gū'sik): in medicine, relating to the absence or impairment of the sense of taste.

agger (aj'er): a double tide; high, with two maxima, and low, with two minima. Also, a Roman earthwork or road.

aggeration (aj.er.ā'shun): an accumulation.

aggerose (aj'er.ōs): in heaps; filled with heaps.

agistment (a.jist'ment): the taking in of livestock for feeding at a specified rate; the opening of a forest to livestock for a specified period; prices paid in these connections.

agmatology (ag'ma.tol'o.ji): the branch of surgery that treats of fractures.

agnathic (ag.nath'ik): jawless.

agnogenic (ag.no.jen'ik): of unknown cause.

agnology (ag.nol'o.ji): the study of ignorance.

agon (ag'ōn, -on): a struggle or contest in ancient Greece, as in sports, literature, or music, or the dramatic conflict between the chief characters in a play.

agonistic (ag'o.nis'tik): combative.

agonium (a.gō'ni.um): any of the four Roman festivals celebrated yearly on January 9, March 17, May 21, and December 11.

agricere (ag'ri.sēr): a waxy coating on soil particles.

agroof (a.grōōf'): flat on one's face. 44.

agrypnotic (a.grip.not'ik): anything that induces wakefulness, as strong tea or coffee.

agyrate (a.jī'rāt): in botany, without whorls.

ahemeral (a.hem'er.al): not constituting a full day.

aikido (a.kī'dō): a Japanese method of self-defense involving powerful concentration and harmonious movements.

ailette (e.let'): in medieval armor, a plate of forged iron or steel worn over the coat of mail to protect the shoulder.

aischrolatreia (īs'kro.la.trī'a): the worship of filth.

ait (āt): an islet.

alabastrum (al'a.bas'trum): an ancient Greek or Roman jar for oils, ointments, or perfumes.

alala (ä'la.lä): a war cry of the ancient Greeks.

albarello (al'ba.rel'ō): a majolica jar with concave sides, used esp. to contain drugs.

albata (al.bā'ta): a kind of German silver.

albicant (al'bi.kant): becoming white.

Alceste (al.sest'): the hero of Molière's *Le Misanthrope*, a man outraged by the duplicity of society.

alchimic, alchymic (al.kim'ik): var. of alchemic.

aleconner (āl'kon'er): an English town official formerly charged with tasting and testing beer and ale.

alectryomancy (a.lek'tri.o.man'si): divination by means of a cock encircled by grains of corn placed on letters of the alphabet, which are then put together in the order in which the cock ate the grain.

alef, aleph (ā′lef, ä′lef): the first letter of the Hebrew alphabet, or the corresponding letter of other Semitic alphabets.

alethical (a.leth′i.kal): pert. to truth.

alette (a.let′): the pilasterlike abutment of an arch.

aleuromancy (a.lōō′ro.man′si): divination by means of flour.

alexia (a.lek′si.a): inability to read.

alexiteric (a.lek′si.ter′ik): resisting poison. An antidote against poison.

algedonic (al.je.don′ik): pert. to pain, esp. as associated with pleasure.

algesis (al.jē′sis): sensitiveness to pain.

algetic (al.jet′ik): sensitive to pain.

algophobia (al′go.fō′bi.a): fear of pain.

algriology (al.gri.ol′o.ji): the study of the customs of savages.

aliferous (a.lif′er.us), aligerous (a.lij′er.us): winged.

aliped (al′i.ped): wing-footed, as the bat.

alk (alk): resin of Chian turpentine.

alkahest (al′ka.hest): the universal solvent vainly sought by alchemists.

alla (äl′la): according to; in the manner or style of (as Italians say it).

Allemanian (al′e.mā′ni.an): the group of dialects of German spoken in Alsace, Switzerland, and southwestern Germany.

allerion (a.lēr′i.on): in heraldry, an eagle without beak or feet, and with extended wings.

allice (al′is): a European shad of the Severn and other rivers.

alliciency (a.lish′en.si): attractiveness.

alligation (al.i.gā′shun): the act of attaching or the state of being attached.

allineation (a.lin′i.ā′shun): alignment.

allochiral (al′o.kī′ral): symmetrically alike, but reversed in arrangement as to right and left, as one's hands.

allocochick (al′o.ko.chik): Indian shell money of northern California.

allogenic (al.o.jen′ik): genetically different.

allograft (al′o.graft): a tissue graft from the body of another person.

allograph (al′o.graf): a signature made for someone else.

allonymous (a.lon′i.mus): ghosted; ghostwritten.

allotheism (al′o.thē.izm): worship of strange gods.

allotriphagy (al′o.trif′a.ji): a craving for unlikely food.

allumette (a.lū.met′): a match for lighting.

almagest (al′ma.jest): a treatise on astronomy.

almirah (al.mī′ra): an Anglo-Indian cabinet, wardrobe.

almoign, almoin (al.moin′, al′moin): alms; an alms chest. *Frankalmoign.* 1.

almud, almude (al.mōōd′, -mōō′di): any of various old Portuguese and Spanish units of measure.

alogism (al′o.jizm): something contrary to or regardless of logic; an irrational statement or piece of reasoning.

aloma (a.lō′ma): light brown to yellowish brown.

alopecia (al′o.pē′shi.a): baldness.

alopecoid (a.lop.e.koid): foxlike, foxy.

alose (a.lōs): any fish of the genus Alosa, esp. the common European shad. To praise; commend. 1.

alpeen (al.pēn′): a cudgel. 50.

alphenic (al.fen′ik): the crystallized juice of the sugar cane; sugar candy.

alphitomancy (al.fit′o.man′si): divination by means of barley flour and honey loaves. 1.

alpigene (al′pi.jēn): growing in alpine regions.

altaian, altaic (al.tā′an, al.tā′ik): pert. to the Altai mountains of central Asia, or to the Altai people or language family (Turkic, Tungusic, and Mongolic).

alterity (al.ter′i.ti): otherness.

altrigenderism (al′tri.jen′der.izm): the point of development at which one becomes attracted to persons of the opposite sex.

altun (al.tōōn′): gold. Specif., a gold piece first issued by Mohammed II in the 15th century.

aluta (a.lōō′ta): a soft tanned leather.

aly (āl′i): of or like ale.

amalaita (ä′ma.lī′ta): in South Africa, native criminals or hooligans.

amalgamize (a.mal′ga.mīz): to amalgamate.

amania (a.mā′ni.a): a gold coin of Afghanistan.

amaranthine (am′a.ran′thīn): everlasting, unfading. Reddish purple in color.

amasesis (am′a.sē′sis): the inability to chew.

amathophobia (a.math′o.fō′bi.a): fear of dust.

amaxophobia (a.mak′so.fō′bi.a): fear of riding in an automobile.

ambagitory (am.baj′i.tō′ri): circumlocutory; circuitous.

ambassade (am′ba.sād): embassy.

ambigenous (am.bij′i.nus): of two kinds. Among plants, having the outer series of floral leaves differing from the inner.

ambiparous (am.bip′a.rus): pert. to buds that contain both flowers and leaves.

ambrology (am.brol′o.ji): the natural history of amber.

ambrosialize (am.brō′zhi.a.līz): to turn into ambrosia.

ambulophobia (am′bū.lo.fō′bi.a): fear of walking.

ambuscado (am′bus.kā′do): ambuscade. 9.

ameen, amin (a.mēn): in India, a confidential agent.

amelia (a.mēl′ya): a limbless monster. Congenital absence of the arms or legs.

amercement (a.murs′ment): the infliction of a penalty at the discretion of the court.

ametropic (am′i.trop′ik): pert. to an abnormal condition of the eye in which visual images do not come to a focus.

amidin (am′i.din): a hydrochloride.

amissible (a.mis′i.bl): liable to be lost. 52.

amma (am′a): an abbess or spiritual mother.

amobyr (a.mō′ber): in Welsh law, a fee formerly payable for a woman to the lord of the manor upon her marriage.

amoebaeum (am′i.bē′um): a kind of poem by Vergil involving alternate speakers. Also, a member of an order of rhyopods, incl. the common soil and water amoebas.

amort (a.môrt′): in Shakespeare, as if dead; spiritless.

amotus (a.mō′tus): not touching the ground; elevated—said of the hind toe of some birds. 52.

amourette (am′oor.et): a trifling love affair.

ampelite (am′pe.līt): a black earth abounding in pyrites, used by the ancients to kill insects on vines.

amphiblastic (am′fi.blas′tik): in embryology, segmenting unequally—said of certain eggs.

amphierotic (am′fi.e.rot′ik): capable of erotic reaction toward either sex.

amphigaean, amphigean (am.fi.jē′an): occurring in both hemispheres.

amphigory (am′fi.gō′ri): nonsense verse or composition.

amphilogism (am.fil′o.jizm): ambiguity of speech; equivocation.

amphivorous (am.fiv′o.rus): eating both animal and vegetable food.

amplectant, amplectic (am.plek′tant, -tik): pert. to the mating embrace of the frog or toad, during which eggs are shed into the water and there fertilized.

ampliate (am′pli.āt): with a prominent outer edge, as the wings of certain insects.

ampollosity (am′po.los′i.ti): bombast.

amsel (am′sel): the ring ouzel. The European blackbird.

amurca (a.mur′ka): lees of olive oil.

amurcous (a.mur′kus): full of dregs; foul. 52.

amyctic (a.mik′tik): irritating; abrasive.

amyous (a.mī'us): without strength.

anacardic (an'a.kär'dik): relating to the cashew and other tropical American trees having kidney-shaped fruit.

anaclastic (an'a.klas'tik): capable of springing back.

"ABATIS: A DEFENSIVE OBSTACLE OF FELLED TREES"

I felled my words as trees fall . . . fanned their stout
Rough trunks before me in an abatis,
The butt ends in, the sharp ends pointing out,
Pretending to defend against your kiss.
(Of course you knew I really had in mind
Piling a screen of words to kiss behind.)

---

anacrotic (an'a.krot'ik): pert. to an abnormality of the blood circulation shown by a sphygmographic tracing.

anacrusis (an'a.kroo'sis): in music, an upbeat.

anacusic (an'a.kū'sik): pert. to absolute deafness.

anaglyphy (a.nag'li.fi): the art of carving, chasing, or embossing in relief.

anagnost (an'ag.nost): a cleric in the first of the minor orders of the Eastern church.

analect (an'a.lekt): a literary fragment, short saying.

analeptic (an'a.lep'tik): a restorative; tonic.

analgic (an.al'jik): analgesic.

analysand (a.nal'i.zand): a person undergoing analysis, esp. psychoanalysis.

ananas (a.nä'nas): a pineapple or pinguin.

ananym (an'a.nim): a name written backward.

anapanapa (a.nä'pa.nä'pa): a widely distributed tropical shrub. The bark is used as soap. 38.

anapodeictic (an.ap'o.dīk'tik): undemonstrable.

anaptotic (an'ap.tot'ik): of a language, characterized by deterioration and deficiency of declensional forms, as English.

anaqua (a.nä'kwa): a shade tree of southern Texas and Mexico.

anarchal (an.ärk'al): pert. to or tending toward anarchy.

anastatic (an'a.stat'ik): pert. to a process of printing from a zinc plate that leaves a transferred design in relief.

anastrophic (an'a.strof'ik): pert. to the inversion of the usual syntactical order of words for rhetorical effect.

anatheme (an'a.thēm): anathema. Also, a votive offering.

anatine (an'a.tīn): ducklike.

anatron (an'a.tron): native soda carbonate; nitron.

ancile (an.sī'li): any of the 12 sacred shields of the ancient Romans that were thought to guarantee the preservation of the city.

ancipital (an.sip'i.tal): having two edges.

anconeal (an.kō'ni.al): pert. to the elbow.

androcentrism (an'dro.sen'trizm): emphasis on maleness.

androcratic (an'dro.krat'ik): pert. to the political and social supremacy of men—contrasted with *gynecocratic*.

androgeny (an.droj'i.ni): a condition in which the chromosomes of the embryo come only from the father.

androgyny (an.droj'i.ni): effeminacy; hermaphroditism.

andromania (an.dro.mā'ni.a): nymphomania.

androphagan, androphagic, androphagous (an.drof'a.gan, -a.jik, -a.gus): man-eating.

androphobia (an.dro.fō'bi.a): dread of men; repugnance to the male sex.

anenst (a.nenst'): anent. 1.

angekok (ang'ge.kok): an Eskimo medicine man.

angor (ang'gor): great anxiety accompanied by painful constriction at the upper part of the belly.

angster (ang'ster): a Swiss minor coin of copper coined from the 15th to the 19th centuries.

angulous (ang'gū.lus): angular.

angusticlave (ang.gus'ti.klāv): a narrow purple stripe worn on each side of the head as a mark of rank by minor Roman aristocrats.

anhedonia (an'hi.dō'ni.a): the inability to be happy.

anhistous (an.his'tus): not differentiated into tissues; noncellular.

anidian (a.nid'i.an): shapeless.

anility (a.nil'i.ti): state of being an old woman.

animastic (an'i.mas'tik): spiritual.

animetta (an'i.met'a): the cover for the cloth in the Eucharist.

animoso (an'i.mō'sō): animated—a direction in music.

anisomeric (an'i.so.mer'ik): tending to become differentiated; not having the same elements in the same proportions; not isomeric.

ankee (ang'ki): barn grass. The Mohaves grind its seed into flour.

annectant, annectent (a.nek'tent): connecting, linking. Used esp. of a species or group having characters intermediate between those of two other species or groups.

annona (a.nō'na): in ancient Rome, the agricultural product of a year. (cap) A genus of trees and shrubs with leathery leaves, solitary nodding flowers, and compound fruit, incl. the custard apple and the soursop.

annulose (an'ū.lōs): ringed, as the *Annulosa*, a genus of worms with a body composed of ringlike segments.

annumerate (a.nū'mer.āt): to add on; count in.

anoetic (an'o.et'ik): unthinkable. 52.

anomoean (an'o.mē'an): one who believes that since the son of God is a created being, he is unlike God in essence.

anorchous (an.ôr'kus): without testicles.

anoretic (an'o.ret'ik), anorexic (an.o.rek'sik): suffering lack of appetite, esp. from emotional distress.

anotia (a.nō'shi.a): absence of the ears.

anserous (an'ser.us): gooselike; stupid.

antaean (an.tē'an): pert. to Antaeus, a legendary wrestler who was invincible as long as he was touching the earth.

antapology (an'ta.pol'o.ji): an answer to an apology.

antecedaneous (an'ti.si.dā'ni.us): antecedent; preceding in time.

antecessor (an'ti.ses'er): a previous incumbent or owner; predecessor.

antecibal (an'ti.sī'bal): happening before meals.

antecursor (an'ti.kur'ser): forerunner; preceder. 1.

antelucan (an'ti.loo'kan): before dawn. 9.

antenati (an'ti.nä'ti): persons born before a certain date or event, esp. with regard to political rights.

antepaschal (an'ti.pas'kal): before Passover or Easter.

anteriad (an.tēr'i.ad): toward the front part of the body.

anthine (an'thīn, an'thin): belonging to a genus of singing birds, the typical pipits.

anthracomancy (an'thra.ko.man'si): divination using burning coal.

anthropographical (an'thro.po.graf'i.kal): pert. to the branch of anthropology that treats of the human race in its different divisions.

anthropolith (an'thro.po.lith): a petrified human body.

anthroponymy (an'thro.pon'i.mi): the science of the study of personal names.

anthropophagan (an.thro.pof'a.gan): anthropophagous.

anthropophobia (an'thro.po.fō'bi.a): fear of meeting strangers.

antibacchius (an'ti.ba.kī'us): in prosody, a metrical foot of three syllables of differing stresses.

antibromic (an'ti.brō'mik): a deodorant.

antichresis (an'ti.krē'sis): a mortgage contract by which the mortgagee takes possession of the property and has its fruits or profits in lieu of interest.

anticlinal (an′ti.klī′nal): inclining in opposite directions.

anticous (an.tī′kus): in botany, turned away from the axis, facing anteriorly.

anticus (an.tī′kus): anterior.

antilegomena (an′ti.li.gom′e.na): those books of the New Testament whose canonicity was for a time in dispute.

antilogy (an.til′o.ji): a contradiction in terms of ideas.

antiloquy (an.til′o.kwi): contradiction. 1.

antinomian (an′ti.nō′mi.an): one who holds that faith alone is sufficient for salvation.

antipathic (an′ti.path′ik), antipathous (an.tip′a.thus): antipathetic; contrarious. 1.

antiperiodic (an′ti.pēr′i.od′ik): preventing periodic returns of paroxysms or exacerbations of disease. An antiperiodic remedy.

antiphrastic (an′ti.fras′tik): referring to the use of words in senses opposite to the generally accepted meanings, usu. for humorous or ironic purposes.

antipudic (an′ti.pū′dik): worn to conceal the genitals.

antiscians (an.tish′anz): people living on the same meridian, but on different sides of the equator, so that at noon they cast shadows in opposite directions.

antispast (an′ti.spast): in prosody, a foot of four syllables.

Antum (an′tum): in the Babylonian religion, the consort of Anu, the god of heaven.

anuptaphobia (a.nup′ta.fō′bi.a): fear of remaining single.

ao (ä′ō): among the Maoris and Polynesians, the personification of light and of the upper world of the living.

aosmic (a.oz′mik): odorless.

apa (ä′pa): the wallaba tree.

apadana (a′pa.dä′na): the great hall in ancient Persian palaces.

apagoge (a′pa.gō′ji): abduction. Also, argument by the reductio ad absurdum.

apagogic (ap′a.goj′ik): in rhetoric, proceeding by the method of disproving the proposition that contradicts the one to be established.

apar, apara (a.pär′, -pä′ra): the three-banded armadillo of South America.

apanthropy (a.pan′thro.pi): love of solitude.

apastron (ap.ast′ron): the point in the orbit of one star of a binary when it is farthest from the other.

apathic (a.path′ik): having no sensation.

apathistical (a.pa.this′ti.kal): devoid of feeling or emotion.

apepsy (a.pep′si): var. of apepsia, indigestion.

apeptic (a.pep′tik): suffering from indigestion.

aphilanthropy (af′i.lan′thro.pi): distaste for social intercourse.

aphlophrenia (a.fil′o.frē′ni.a): a feeling that one is unloved or unwanted.

aphlogistic (a′flo.jis′tik): flameless.

aphnology (af.nol′o.ji): the science of wealth.

apiole, apiol (ā′pi.ōl, ap′i.ōl, -ol): a colorless crystalline ether.

aplotomy (a.plot′o.mi): in surgery, a simple incision.

apocarteresis (ap′o.kär′te.rē′sis): suicide by starvation.

apodictic (ap′o.dik′tik): clearly true.

apodysophilia (ap′o.dis′o.fil′ya): a feverish desire to undress.

apodyterium (ap′o.di.tē′ri.um): an undressing room in an ancient Greek or Roman bath or gymnasium.

apojove (ap′o.jōv): that point farthest from the planet Jupiter of each of its satellites.

apolaustic (ap′o.lôs′tik): fond of pleasure; self-indulgent.

apologue (ap′o.log): a fable with a moral.

apopemptoclinic (a.po.pemp′to.klin′ik): inclined toward divorce.

apositia (a.po.sish′i.a): aversion to food.

aposoro (ap′o.sō′ro): one of the African lemurs, esp. the potto of West Africa, which resembles the loris in its nocturnal, arboreal, and slow-moving habits.

apothesis (a.poth′i.sis): in early churches, a place on the south side of the chancel for books, vestments, etc. A dressing room at a public bath. The setting of a fractured or dislocated limb.

apotome (a.pot′o.mi): an interval in Greek music. A variety of the mineral celestite.

apotropaic (ap′o.tro.pā′ik): designed to avert or turn aside evil.

appeach (a.pēch′): to impeach; accuse. To cast aspersions on. 1.

appentice (a.pen′tis): a penthouse. 1.

appetant (ap′e.tant): pert. to desire. In phonetics, a gliding sound.

applosion (a.plō′zhun): in phonetics, the interruption and compression of a breath.

appulsion (a.pul′shun): the act of striking against. A bringing to land. 1. The near approach of one celestial body to another. In civil law, the process by which land is visibly torn away from one part of the banks of a stream and added to another part.

apricate (ap′ri.kāt): to bask in or expose to the sun.

aprosexia (ap′ro.sek′si.a): inability to concentrate.

aptote (ap′tōt): an indeclinable noun.

aptotic (ap.tot′ik): (of a language) lack-

ing denominational inflections, as Chinese.

apyrous (a.pī′rus): noncombustible.

aracari (är′a.sä′ri): any of several brilliantly colored South American toucans.

arachibutyrophobia (a.rak′i.bū.tī′ro.fō′bi.a): fear of peanut butter sticking to the roof of the mouth.

arachidic (ar′a.kid′ik): caused by or pert. to peanuts.

araneous (a.rā′ni.us): arachnoid.

arara (a.rä′ra): a macaw. The palm cockatoo of Australia. (cap) An Indian of a Cariban tribe in Brazil.

aratory (ar′a.tō′ri): contributing to tillage. 52.

arbuscle (är′bus′l): a dwarf tree or tree-like shrub.

archaist (är′kā.ist): an antiquary. One who uses archaisms.

archiater (är.kī′a.ter): a chief physician of the court of a Hellenistic king or a Roman emperor. Later, a leading local physician, publicly employed.

archical (är′ki.kl): governmental; primary, primordial. 1.

archimagus (är′ki.mā′gus): a great wizard, magician, or enchanter.

archology (är.kol′o.ji): the doctrine of origins. The science of government.

archtoid (ärk′toid): like a bear.

Arctalia (ärk.tāl′ya): a marine realm including all northern seas as far south as floating ice occurs.

arefy (ar′e.fī): to dry. 1.

arenosity (ar′i.nos′i.ti): sandiness.

areometer (ar′i.om′e.ter): a hydrometer.

aretaics (ar′i.tā′iks): the study of virtue.

arethusa (ar′i.thōō′za): any of several orchids having a solitary rose-purple flower fringed with yellow. (cap) In mythology, a wood nymph who, pursued by the river god Alpheus, was changed by Artemis into a stream.

aretological (ar′i.to.loj′i.kal): pert. to moral philosophy. 1.

argh (ärg): timid, cowardly. 2.

argillaceous (ar′ji.lā′shus): clayey; containing clay.

argute (är.gūt′): sharp, shrill; acute, sagacious.

arigato (ar′i.gä′to): ''thank you'' in Japanese.

ariole (ar′i.ōl): a soothsayer. 1.

Aristaeus (ar′is.tē′us): in Greek mythology, a beneficent hero, usu. said to have been the son of Apollo and the nymph Cyrene.

armilla (är.mil′a): the annular ligament of the wrist. Also, a stole like the ecclesiastical stole used in the British coronation ceremony.

armitage (är′mi.tij): hermitage. 1.

armscye (ärm′sī): the armhole or opening in a garment for the attaching of a sleeve.

arna (är′na): a wild water buffalo.

arrect (a.rekt′): to make erect. To direct. 1. Erect; attentive.

arreptitious (ar.ep.tish′us): snatched away; possessed, as a demoniac; raving; mad. 1.

Arretine (ar′e.tīn): pert. to ancient Arretium, now Arezzo, Italy, where the red terracotta ware called Arretine was made in ancient times.

arrhizal (a.rī′zal): destitute of a true root, as a parasitic plant.

arride (a.rīd′): to smile or laugh at. To please, delight. 1.

arriviste (a′ri′vēst): an opportunist; one who uses any means to attain success.

arter (är′ter): var. of *after*.

arthrology (är.throl′o.ji): the science that treats of joints.

arva (är′va): mistaken spelling of *′ava* (kava) in Herman Melville's *Typee*.

arval (är′val): a funeral feast. (cap) Relating to a body of ancient Roman priests who presided over an annual May fertility rite.

arvicole (är′vi.kōl): a water vole.

ary (âr′i): any. 11.

aryballos, aryballus (ar′i.bal′os, -us): a short-necked flask or bottle having a single handle, small orifice, and globular body, used for holding oils or ointments.

asaphia (a.sä′fi.a): indistinct utterance, as that due to cleft palate.

ascesis (a.sē′sis): rigorous training, self-discipline, or self-restraint.

ascian (ash′i.an, ash′un): one without a shadow, as an inhabitant of the torrid zone, where for a few days each year the sun is vertical at noon.

aseity (a.sē′i.ti): the quality or state of being self-derived or self-originated; God in his eternal and independent being.

asherah (a.shē′ra): a sacred wooden post that stood near the altar in Canaanite high places and symbolized the goddess Asherah.

asitia (a.sish′i.a): want of appetite; loathing of food.

asonia (a.sō′ni.a): deafness to certain tones or pitches.

aspectant (as.pek′tant): looking at; beholding. 1.

asperge (as.purj′): to sprinkle.

assart (a.särt′): act of grubbing, as bushes; land so cleared.

assertum (a.sur′tum): something that is asserted.

assidean (a.si.dē′an), hasidean (ha.si.dē′an): pert. to the Hasidim, a Jewish sect devoted to mysticism and strict ritual observance.

assiduate (a.sid′ū.it): assiduous; diligent. 1.

assis (a.sē′, as′is): sitting down; used of animals in heraldry.

assise (a.sēz′): a succession of paleontological zones bearing fossils of the same genera.

assoluto (äs′so.lo͞o′tō): in music, absolute; one voice alone.

assuetude (as′wi.to͞od): custom; habit. In medicine, accustomedness to disturbing influences. 1.

astasia (as.tä′zhi.a): inability to sit or stand erect.

asteism (as′ti.izm): genteel irony; polite and ingenious derision.

astereognosis (as.tēr′i.og.nō′sis): loss of ability to recognize the shapes of objects by touch.

asteria (as.tē′ri.a): in Greek antiquity, a gem reflecting light in six rays, suggesting a star—perhaps the star sapphire.

asthenia (as.thē′ni.a): loss of strength.

asthenology (as′thi.nol′o.ji): the scientific study of disease due to debility.

astorgia (as.stôr′ji.a): lack of interest in one's children.

astragalomancy (as.trag′a.lo.man′si): divination by means of small bones or dice.

astrologaster (as.trol′o.gas′ter): a charlatan astrologer.

Astrophel (as′tro.fel): the name used for himself by Sir Philip Sidney in his sonnet sequence *Astrophel and Stella* (1591).

astrophobia (as′tro.fō′bi.a): fear of outer space.

asura (a.so͞o′ra): in the oldest parts of the Rig-Veda, a god or spirit; later, a demon; an enemy of the gods.

ataunt (a.tônt′): of a sailing vessel, fully rigged; shipshape.

atavus (at′a.vus): an ancestor or ancestral type, from which a character is assumed to be inherited. Spec., a grandfather.

ate (ā′ti): blind impulse, reckless ambition, or excessive folly that drives men to ruin. (cap) A Greek goddess of infatuation.

Aten (ä′ten, at′en): the sun as god, which Amenhotep of Egypt (d. about 1358 B.C.) sought to make the supreme cult of the people.

athanasia (ath′a.nä′zhi.a): deathlessness; immortality.

athetize (ath′i.tīz): to spurn, reject.

atis (a.tēs′): a poisonous herb of the monkshood family, found in the Himalayas.

atle (at′li): the tamarask salt tree of western Asia and India.

atmospherium (at.mos.fē′ri.um): a room for simulating atmospheric or meteorological phenomena.

atocia (a.tō′shi.a): female sterility.

atopic (a.top′ik): not in the usual place—said by physicians of an organ in the body.

atrabilarian (at′ra.bi.lâr′i.an): a hypochondriac.

atrabile (at′ra.bīl): black bile; melancholy. 1.

atrichia (a.trik′i.a): baldness.

atropic (a.trop′ik): pert. to atropine, a bitter, poisonous alkaloid.

atry (a.trī′): (a ship) kept bow to the sea by a balance of sails.

Atta (at′a): a New World genus of leaf-eating, chiefly tropical ants, often very destructive to plants. (not cap) In India, the sweetsop tree; also, unsorted wheaten flour or meal.

attensity (a.ten′si.ti): sensory clearness; differentiation between a sensation that is the focus of attention and one that is not.

attent (a.tent′): attentive; heedful.

attingent (a.tin′jent): touching; in contact. 1.

attornment (a.turn′ment): an assignment. In law, the acknowledgment by a tenant that he holds his property on behalf of a new landlord.

attrahent (at′ra.hent): an attractant, as a magnet.

attrectation (a.trek.tā′shun): handling or touching. 1.

atua (a.to͞o′a): in Polynesia and esp. among the Maoris, a supernatural being; a god or demon.

atychiphobia (a.tik′i.fō′bi.a): fear of failure.

aube (ōb): archaic form of *alb, albe,* a liturgical vestment.

aubergiste (ō′ber.zhēst): an innkeeper.

auctorial (ôk.tō′ri.al): like an author.

aularian (ô.lâr′i.an): pert. to a hall.

aum (ôm): alum. 44.

auricomous (ô.rik′o.mus): golden-haired.

auricularis (ô.rik′ū.lä′ris): any of three muscles attached to the cartilage of the external ear.

aurify (ô′ri.fī): to turn into gold.

auriscalp (ô.ri.skalp): an earpick.

auscultate (ôs′kul.tāt): to examine by listening, as with a stethoscope.

austral (ôs′tral): southern.

autodidact (ô′to.di.dakt): one self-taught.

autogeny (ô.toj′e.ni): self-generation.

autognosis (ô.tog.nō′sis): self-awareness.

automysophobia (ô′to.mī′so.fōbi.a): fear of being dirty.

autophagia (ô.to.fā′ji.a): the feeding of the body by the consumption of its own tissues, as in fasting. Also, biting oneself.

autoptic (ô.top′tik): based on personal observation.

autoschediastic (ô.to.skē′di.as.tik): impromptu.

autotomy (ô.tot′o.mi): self-mutilation.

autotype (ô′to.tīp): a picture made by a carbon process.

auxilium (ôg.zil′i.um): a military ambulance wagon. In old English law, an extraordinary yearly tax.

Avena (a.vē′na): a genus of widely distributed grasses, incl. the oats.

averruncate (av′e.rung′kāt): to avert; ward off; also, erroneously, ro root up.

aviatic (ā′vi.at′ik): pert. to flight.

avizandum (av′i.zan′dum): in Scots law, private consideration.

awk (ôk): done in the wrong way; clumsy. 1.

awless (ô′les): var. of aweless.

awn (ôn): in grasses, one of the slender bristles that terminate the scales of the spikelet. Among reptiles, one of the barbs on the hemipenis.

axinomancy (ak.sin′o.man′si): divination by means of an ax placed on a post.

azarole (az′a.rōl): a shrub of southern Europe, or its edible and pleasant-flavored fruit.

azurine (az′ū.rīn, -rin): azure.

B

babby (bab′i): dial. var. of *baby*.

babyolatry (bā′bi.ol′a.tri): baby worship.

bacca (bak′a): tobacco. 21.

bacchius (ba.kī′us): in prosody, a metrical foot of three syllables of varying stresses.

bacillary (bas′i.ler′i): rod-shaped. Pert. to bacilli.

Bacopa (ba.kō′pa): a genus of chiefly tropical herbs, inc. the water hyssop, with opposite leaves and small solitary flowers.

bacula (bak′ū.la): in astronomy, strips or streamers of nebulous matter.

baculus (bak′ū.lus): a staff or rod, esp. one symbolizing authority, as the pastoral staff of a bishop.

badderlocks (bad′er.loks): a large black seaweed often eaten as a vegetable in Europe.

baddock (bad′uk): the pollack, or coalfish. 44.

badia (ba.dē′a): in Italy, a monastery or abbey.

baffy (baf′i): a short wooden golf club with a deeply lofted face.

baggitt (bag′it): a recently spawned salmon, or a female just before or after spawning. 41.

baira, beira (bī′ra): a small gazelle-like antelope of Somaliland that is purplish black and brightly marked with yellowish fawn.

bal (bal): a mine. 41A.

balaniferous (bal′a.nif′er.us): bearing acorns.

balanoid (bal′a.noid): acorn-shaped.

balatron (bal′a.tron): a buffoon.

baldicoot (bôl′di.koot): the bald coot. A monk.

Bali (bä′li): a king of the monkeys in the Sanskrit epic *Ramayana*.

balisaur (bal′i.sôr): the hog-nosed badger of India.

ballabile (ba.lä′bi.lā): in classical ballet, a dance performed by the corps de ballet with or without the principal dancers.

ballistrophobia (ba.lis′tro.fō′bi.a): fear of missiles, or of being shot.

bamboula (bam.boo′la): a primitive drum used in voodoo ceremonies and incantations, or the dance performed to its beat.

bambuk (bam.book′), bambui (bam.boo′i): butter from the seeds of the shea, an African tree.

Bana (bä′na): in Hindu mythology, a thousand-armed giant.

banausic (ba.nô′sik): smacking of the workshop.

bandoline (ban′do.lin): a glutinous pomade for dressing the hair.

banig (ba.nēg′): in the Philippines, a mat or matting made of dried palm leaves or grass.

banket (bang′ket): the auriferous conglomerate rock of the Transvaal.

A PERPLEXITY OF PISCINITY

It's written in each piscine part, it's stamped upon the whole fish:
A pollack is a baddock, and a baddock is a coalfish.
Yet coalfish-pollack-baddock isn't haddock—which is odd,
Since coalfish-pollack-baddock
Is just the same as haddock
In being quite inferior-tasting cod.

Baphometic (baf′o.met′ik): pert. to Baphomet, an idol that the Templars were accused of using in their mysterious rites.

barbaralalia (bär′ber.a.lāl′ya): a speech impairment manifested when speaking a foreign language.

barble (bär′bl): barbarian.

bardel, bardell (bär.del′): a packsaddle. 1.

bardolatry (bär.dol′a.tri): Shakespeare-worship.

bareca, bareka (ba.rä′ka): on ships, a small cask; a breaker.

baric (bar′ik): pert. to barium.

baris (bar′is): a Balinese spear dance or warriors' dance depicting a sham battle. A flat-bottomed rowboat used for freight on the Nile.

barken (bär′ken): made of bark.

barkle (bär′kl): to encrust, cake. 13.

barley-bree, barley-broo (bär′li.bri, bär′li.broo): liquor made from barley. Whiskey; also, strong ale. 44.

barmecide (bär′mi.sīd): a false benefactor.

barolo (ba.rō′lō): a red wine of Piedmont, Italy.

barracan (bar′a.kan): a fabric of the Levant. A mantle or wrap of such fabric.

barracouta (bar′a.koo′ta): a large food fish found along the coasts of Australia, New Zealand, and southern Africa; barracuda.

barras (bar′as): galpot, a crude turpentine formed from the pine tree. Also, a kind of coarse linen.

barricado (bar′i.kä′dō): barricade.

barton (bär′ton): a large farm. A farmyard or the outbuildings behind a farmhouse. A poultry yard or hen coop. 13.

barvel, barvell (bär′vel): a fisherman's large leather apron. 28A.

barylalia (bar′i.lāl′ya): indistinctly articulated speech.

baryphonic (bar′i.fon′ik): pert. to difficulty of speech.

baryta (ba.rī′ta): any of several compounds of barium; esp., barium monoxide.

basial (bā′zi.al): kissing; osculatory.

basiate (bā′zi-āt): to kiss. 52.

basihyal (bā′si.hī′al): pert. to a bone at the ventral point of the arch that forms the hyoid bone at the base of the human tongue.

basilect (bas′i.lekt): to speakers of a language, the variety or dialect with least prestige.

basilicon (ba.sil′i.kon): an ointment composed of rosin, yellow wax, and lard.

basophobia (bā′so.fō′bi.a): inability to stand caused by fear of falling.

basta (bas′ta): the third-highest trump (queen of spades) in omber, solo, and other card games.

batata (ba.tä′ta): sweet potato.

batch (bach): a bachelor. 26.

batcher (bach′er): one who operates the machine that weighs the material for batches of concrete; the machine itself.

bathetic (ba.thet′ik): falsely sentimental.

bathic (bath′ik): pert. to depth, esp. the depth of the sea.

bathybian (ba.thib′i.an): pert. to or living in the deepest parts of the sea.

batino (ba.tē′nō): a Philippine tree that yields a moderately valuable timber.

batophobia (bat′o.fō.bi.a): fear of being close to high buildings.

batrachomyomachy (bat′ra.ko.mi.om′a.ki): the battle between the frogs and the mice—a Greek parody of the *Iliad*.

batrachophobia (bat′ra.ko.fō′bi.a): terror of frogs and toads.

batta (bat′a): in India, subsistence money (as for a witness or prisoner); maintenance or traveling expenses of an employee. Also, extra pay.

battologize (ba.tol′o.jīz): to repeat needlessly; to iterate.

battue (ba.tōō′): a hunt where the game is driven into the arms of the hunters; the game so driven; any mass slaughter of the unresisting.

battuta (bat.tōōt′a): the beat of a musical composition. A measure.

bawbee (bô′bi): an old Scottish coin. An English halfpenny.

beal (bēl): a mouth or narrow pass, as of a river or valley. 44. To bellow; roar. 1. To come to a head, as a pimple. 2.

beatus (bi.ā′tus): in the Roman Catholic Church, a man or boy who has been beatified.

bedaggle (bi.dag′l): daggle. To clog with mud and mire. 1.

beele (bēl): the crossbar of a yoke. 1. A pickax with both ends sharp, used to pick out ore from rocks. 2.

beeve (bēv): beef; a "beef creature," per Washington Irving.

beezer (bē′zer): nose. 21.

beisa (bī′sa): an antelope found in northeastern Africa.

beken (bi.ken′): to make known; deliver; commend; entreat. 1.

bekko (bek′ō): in Japan, articles made from tortoise shell.

belah (bē′la): a beefwood of Australia. A tall forest tree of Queensland.

Bellatrix (be.lāt′riks): a bright star in Orion.

belletristic (bel′le.tris′tik): pert. to belles lettres.

bellic (bel′ik): martial. 1.

bellipotent (be.lip′o.tent): strong in war.

belomancy (bel′o.man′si): divination by drawing arrows at random from a container.

belton (bel′tun): a combination of blue and lemon colors, as in the coats of certain collies and setters. A dog with a coat of these two tones.

benda (ben′da): a measure of weight in Guinea.

beneceptor (ben′i.sep′ter): any sense organ that is responsive to beneficial stimulus.

beneficious (ben′i.fish′us): pert. to a benefice.

benet (bi.net′): to catch with a net; to ensnare.

benn (ben): a colored silk sash. 44.

bennel (ben′el): the ditch reed. 13.

benthonic (ben.thon′ik): occurring on the bottom underlying a body of water.

benthopelagic (ben.thop′i.laj′ik): inhabiting the depths of the ocean.

beray (bi.rā′): to make foul; to soil.

Berean (bi.rē′an): a native or inhabitant of the ancient city Beroea, in either Macedonia or Syria.

bever (bē′ver): a drink, a between-meals snack. 1. To tremble. 13.

bhang (bang): an intoxicant made from Indian hemp; hashish, cannabis.

bheestie, bheesty (bēs′ti): in India, a water carrier of a household or regiment.

bibacious (bī.bā′shus, bi-): addicted to drinking; bibulous.

bibasic (bī.bā′sik): in chemistry, containing two replaceable hydrogen atoms; dibasic.

bibble (bib′l): to drink often, much, or noisily. 11.

bibbons (bib′uns): a nonsense word used and prob. coined by Edward Lear to supplement *ribbons* in his poem *The Quangle Wangle's Hat*.

biblioclasm (bib′li.o.klazm): destruction of the Bible, or of books generally.

bibliognost (bib′li.og.nost): one knowledgeable about books and bibliography.

bibliomancy (bib′li.o.man′si): divination by picking Bible passages at random.

bibliopegic (bib′li.o.pej′ik), bibliopegistic (bib′li.o.pe.jis′tik): pert. to bookbinding.

bibliotaph (bib′li.o.taf): one who hoards or hides books.

bicaudal (bī.kô′dal): having or terminating in two tails.

bicephalous (bī.sef′a.lus): two-headed.

bicrural (bī.kroor′al): having two legs.

biduous (bid′ū.us): lasting, or remaining open, two days, as some flowers.

bifer (bī′fer): a plant that bears fruit twice a year.

biflex (bī′fleks): bent in two directions.

bifronted (bī.frun′ted): having two fronts.

biga (bī′ga): a two-horse chariot of ancient Mediterranean countries.

bigential (bī.jen′shal): including two tribes or races.

biggin (big′in): house, outbuilding. 13. A coffee percolator used early in the 19th century. A child's cap; nightcap.

Billiken (bil′i.ken): a squat, smiling, comic figure used as a mascot.

billikin (bil′i.kin): a billy or billycan. 53.

billingsgate (bil′ingz.gāt): coarse or abusive talk.

billman (bil′man): a soldier or watchman armed with a bill (a kind of pike).

billot (bil′ut): firewood. 1. Bullion, in the bar or mass.

bim (bim): a woman, esp. one of loose morals. 21. Nickname for an inhabitant of Barbados.

bimaculate (bī.mak′ū.lit): marked with two blotches.

bimanal (bim′a.nal, bī.mā′nal), bimanous (bim′a.nus): having two hands.

bimbil (bim′bil): the Australian eucalypt, whose flowers yield a good honey.

bimester (bī.mes′ter): two months.

binghi (bing.gi): aborigine. 23A.

binna (bin′a): unless; be not. 44.

binocle (bin′o.kl): a binocular telescope, field glass, or opera glass.

binotic (bī.not′ik): pert. to both ears.

binous (bī′nus): double; binate.

bint (bint): a daughter; girl; woman. 53.

biocompatible (bī′o.kom.pat′i.bl): not causing rejection—said of certain transplanted tissues.

biome (bī.ōm′): a community of living organisms of a single major ecological region.

bion (bī′on): in biology, the physiological individual, as opposed to the morphological, or structural individual.

biophilism (bī.of′i.lizm): the belief that animals have rights that humans should respect.

bioplasmic (bī′o.plaz′mik): *bioplastic*.

bioplastic (bī′o.plas′tik): pert. to the bioplast, or cell.

biorgan (bī′ôr′gan): a physiological organ—distinguished from *idorgan*.

bioscopy (bī.os′ko.pi): examination of a body to discover whether life is present.

biotaxy (bī′o.tak′si): taxonomy.

bipenniform (bī.pen′i.fôrm): resembling a feather barbed on both sides—said of certain muscles.

biretta (bi.ret′a): the hat of a Catholic priest (black), bishop (purple), or cardinal (red).

birse (burs): a bristle or bristles. Temper or irritation. To scorch or toast; to broil. 43.

bise (bīz): a cold, dry north wind of southern France, Switzerland, and Italy. Hence, any cold wind; fig., winter.

bisectric (bī.sek′trik): having a straight line that bisects an angle or a line segment.

bisectrix (bī.sek′triks): a line bisecting the angle between the optic axes of a biaxial crystal.

biserial (bī.sēr′i.al): arranged in two rows or series.

bismarine (bis′ma.rēn′): between two seas.

bissextile (bi.seks′til): leap year.

biternate (bī.tur′nit): double trifoliate, as when each division of a three-part leaf is also tripartite.

bivector (bī.vek′ter): a quantity in mathematics.

biverbal (bī.vur′bal): pert. to two words; punning.

bixin (bik′sin): a dark-red crystalline compound, the chief coloring principle of the dyestuff annatto.

blad (blad): a slap; also, a blotting pad. 44.

blandiloquence (blan.dil′o.kwens): smooth speech; flattering talk. 52.

blas (blas): an emanation from the stars. 1.

bleb (bleb): a blister or bubble, as in water or glass; to bubble, cover with bubbles.

bleery (blēr′i): a firebrand. 44. A kind of thin gruel. 11.

blennophobia (blen′o.fō′bi.a): horror of slime.

bleo (blā′o): a tropical American shrubby cactus used for hedges; also, its edible fruit.

blepharospasm (blef′a.ro.spazm): uncontrollable winking.

blet (blet): internal decay in fruit.

blinger (bling′er): a superlative example of its kind. 21.

blissom (blis′um): in heat. To copulate with a ewe.

Blitum (blī′tum): a genus of two species of herbs of the goosefoot family, the blites.

blottesque (blot.esk′): painted with heavy touches or blotlike brushwork.

bluet (blōō′et): a delicate plant of the U.S. with four-parted bluish flowers and tufted stems; called also *innocence, quaker-ladies.* A small Texas plant with a single blue flower. A light to moderate blue.

blumba (blum′ba): a certifying tag attached to kosher meat.

blunge (blunj): to amalgamate and blend; to beat up or mix (as clay) in water. *(Plunge + blend.)*

bly (blī): look, aspect; species, character. 2.

blype (blīp): a piece or shred, as of skin. 44.

SONG FOR A SLOW DANCE

Swing and sway with me, my dear,
In our band of biosphere.
As we circle we shall pass
Other clumps of biomass,
All biota, each with home
In some suitable biome,
Heeling, toeing, to the fiddle
Of a biologic riddle.

---

boanthropy (bo.an′thro.pi): a type of insanity in which one thinks oneself an ox.

boation (bo.ā′shun): a loud noise; bellowing, roaring. 1.

bobo (bō′bō): the owala tree. Also, a mullet of the rivers and cataracts of Mexico and Central America.

boca (bō′ka): a river mouth; a harbor entrance (as of a South American seaport).

bocal (bō′kal): the mouthpiece of a brass wind instrument.

bocardo (bo.kär′dō): a prison—originally, that in the north gate in Oxford. In logic, a figure: "some M is not P; all M is S; hence some S is not P."

bocca (bok′a): the mouth of a glass furnace. A vent on the side or near the base of an active volcano from which lava issues.

boce (bōs): a brightly colored European fish of the Spiradae family.

bocking (bok′ing): the red herring.

bodega (bo.dē′ga): a small grocery or liquor store.

boden (bō′den): equipped, provided. 44A.

bodger (boj′er): one who botches (something). 11. A woodcarver or woodturner, esp. a turner of beechwood chairs.

bodhi (bō′di): in Buddhism, the state of enlightenment attained by one who has practiced the Eight-fold Path and achieved salvation.

bodikin (bod′i.kin): a tiny body; an atom. 1.

bogle (bō′gl): a Scottish bogy, or boggart. Hide-and-seek. 44A.

bogue (bōg): in sailing, to fall away to leeward. Also, a creek. 40.

bolar, bolary (bō′ler, -ler.i): pert. to bole or clay; clayey.

bolo-bolo (bō′lo.bō′lō): a West African tree and its fiber, resembling jute.

bombilation (bom′bi.lā′shun): a buzzing, droning sound.

bona (bō′na): property—used in Roman and civil law of real and personal property.

bonga (bong′ga): in the Philippines, the betel palm; the betel nut.

bonhomie (bon′o.mi): cheerfulness.

bonify (bon′i.fī): to convert into, or render, good.

bonnibel (bon′i.bel): a handsome girl. 9.

boobopolis (bōō.bop′o.lis): an imaginary hick town.

boodie (bōō′di): hobgoblin. 44.

boof (bōōf): a scare. 28. Peach brandy. 39.

booger (boog′er): boogerman. 12. A piece of dried nasal mucus. 11. A head louse. 41B. To take fright, shy. To startle (an animal).

booly (bōō′li): a temporary enclosure for the shelter of cattle or their keepers. A company of herdsmen wandering with their cattle. 50.

boondaggling (boon′dag.ling): var. of *boondoggling.*

boöpis (bo.op′is): ox-eyed; applied to certain Greek goddesses.

borachio (bo.rä′ki.ō): a large leather bottle for holding liquor; hence, a drunkard. (cap) A drunken follower of Don John in Shakespeare's *Much Ado About Nothing.*

boracite (bō′ra.sīt): a mineral, pyroelectric borate and chloride of magnesium.

borassic (bo.ras′ik): pert. to the Borassus, a genus of sugar palms of Africa naturalized throughout the tropics.

borborygm (bôr.bô.rim′), borborygmy (bor.bô.rig.mi): the noise made by gas in the bowels, or leaving them; a fart. 1.

boro (bō′rō): in India, rice harvested in the spring. (cap) A people of southeastern Colombia, northeastern Peru, and adjacent areas in Brazil.

bosch, bosh (bosh): butterine. 41.

bosset (bos′et): the rudimentary antler of a young male red deer.

bot, bott (bot): the larva of the botfly, esp. the species infesting the horse.

botargo (bo.tär′gō): a relish of salted mullet or tunny roes.

bothy (both′i): a rude dwelling. A hut, as a shepherd's shelter or quarters for unmarried laborers. 44A.

bourn, bourne (bōrn, bôrn): boundary; domain. To limit or bound. 52.

bousy (bōō′zi, bou′zi): drunken; sotted; boozy.

bovarysm (bō′va.rizm): one's romantic conception of oneself.

bovver (bov′er): street fighting. 23.

bowla (bō′la): a tart of sugar, apple, and bread. 41.

boyar (bo.yär′, boi′er): a member of a Russian aristocratic order that was next in rank to the ruling princes.

boyer (boi′er): a small Flemish sailing boat.

brab (brab): the palmyra palm.

brabblement (brab′l.ment): quarreling; the noise of discord. 2.

brabypeptic (brab′i.pep′tik): slow in digestion; sluggish in temperament.

brach, brachet (brach, brak, brach′et): a bitch hound.

brachiation (brā′ki.ā′shun, brak′i.ā′shun): locomotion by swinging from hold to hold by the arms.

brachistocephalic (bra.kis′to.si.fal′ik): in craniology, short-headed or broad-headed with a cephalic index of over 85.

brachycataletic (brak′i.kat′a.let′ik): in prosody, characterized by the omission of two syllables at the end of a verse.

brachyography (brak′i.og′raf.i): stenography

bradypeptic (brad′i.pep′tik): *brabypeptic.*

braggard (brag′ard): var. of *braggart.*

brancard (brang′kerd): a horse litter.

brangle (brang′gl): a squabble, wrangle, set-to. 13.

brank (brangk): a sort of bridle with wooden sidepieces.

branks (brangks): an iron frame used for correcting a scolding woman, surrounding the head and having a triangular piece entering the mouth. Also, the mumps. 44.

brassage (bras′ij): a charge made to an individual under a system of free coinage for the minting of any gold or silver brought to the mint.

brasset (bras′et): archaic var. of *brassard, brassart*—armor for the upper arm.

brawner (brôn′er): a boar killed for the table.

braxy (brak′si): a malignant edema of sheep. A sheep dead from natural causes; also, mutton from its carcass.

bree (brē): an eyelid, eyelash, eyebrow. 1. Liquor or broth. 44. To scare. 1.

brek (brek): outcry. 1.

bret (bret): a kind of flatfish, the brill. Also, the turbot.

bretelle (bre.tel′): an ornamental shoulder strap like a suspender.

breviloquence (bre.vil′o.kwens): brevity of speech.

breviped (brev′i.ped): having short legs. A short-legged bird.

brevipennate (brev′i.pen′āt): short-winged—said of birds having such short wings that they cannot fly.

brevirostrate (brev′i.ros′trāt): having a short nose.

bricole (bri.kōl′): a catapult. Also, an apparatus with hooks and rings to drag guns. In court tennis, the rebound of a ball from the wall. In billiards, a shot in which the cue ball strikes the cushion after hitting the object ball and before hitting the carom ball.

brigue (brēg): a cabal, intrigue, quarrel. To beguile; to intrigue. 1.

brimborion (brim.bō′ri.on): a charm—used derisively. Something nonsensical or useless.

brinded (brin′ded): brindled. 9.

britch (brich): breech. 1.

brockle (brok′l): of weather, variable; of cattle, apt to break fence. Rubbish; fragments. 2.

broderie (brôd.rē′): a style of pottery decoration resembling embroidery.

brog (brog): a pointed instrument, as an awl; a branch or stick, as a pole or goad. 17.

broma (brō′ma): aliment; food. Also, a form of cocoa from which the oil has been thoroughly extracted.

bromal (brō′mal): an oily, colorless fluid related to bromoform as chloral is to chloroform.

bromatology (brō′ma.tol′o.ji): the science of nutrition.

bromidrosiphobia (brō′mi.dro.si.fō′bi.a): fear of body odors.

bromopnea (brō′mop.nē′a): bad breath.

brontophobia (bron′to.fō′bi.a): fear of thunderstorms.

broo (brōō): broth; juice; water. Good opinion; inclination. 45.

brool (brōōl): a low roar; a deep murmur or humming.

brose (brōz): a dish made by pouring boiling liquid on meal (esp. oatmeal). 44.

brotus (brō′tus): an extra measure without charge, as a baker's dozen.

browst (broust, brōōst): a brewing, as of malt; hence, the consequences of one's conduct. 43.

THEY WOULD HAVE CALLED HIM BILLY HIRPLE IF HE'D LIMPED

The Scots may have some moral taint,
But sycophants is what they ain't.
I prove this by the dreadful things
They used to call their English kings.

Take one whom they detested lots
(Though he had only slain some Scots).
He had a flower named for him.
The Scottish view of this was dim.

Sweet William was its English name;
The Scots forgathered to proclaim
This inappropriate and silly,
And called the blossom Stinky Billy.

Though William grew up in the purple,
Those vulgar Scots, alas,
Remember him as Billy Curple
(That's ''Billy, horse's ass.'')

---

bruckle (bruk′l): to dirty, begrime. 1. Breakable, brittle. 44C.

brumous (brōō′mus): foggy.

bruxomania (bruk′so.mā′ni.a): the habit of unconsciously grinding one's teeth.

bubukle (bū′buk.l): a red pimple.

bucca (buk′a): in insects, the cheek or part of the head next to the mouth.

buccinator (buk′si.nā′ter): a thin broad muscle forming the wall of the cheek.

bucentaur (bū.sen′tôr): a fabulous monster, half man, half ox; a centaur with a bull's body. Also, the state barge of Venice, used by the doge in the ceremony of the marriage of the Adriatic.

buckeen (buk.ēn′): in Ireland, a young man of the poorer gentry, aping the style of the rich; a shabby genteel idler. 51. In Guiana, an Indian woman.

budgeree (buj′er.i): good; fine; handsome or pretty—a bush word. 54.

budgereegah (buj′er.i.gä′): the zebra parakeet. 53.

buffa (bōōf′fa): a woman singer of comic roles in opera.

buffin (buf′in): a coarse woolen fabric used for clothing in England during the 16th and 17th centuries. 1.

buffle (buf′l): a buffalo. A fool; a bufflehead. 1.

bulse (buls): a purse or bag in which to carry or measure valuables. Broadly, a packet of jewels.

Bumbledom (bum′bl.dum): the pomposity of petty officials; beadledom—after Bumble, a parish beadle in *Oliver Twist.*

bummalo (bum′a.lō): a small Asiatic fish, the Bombay duck.

bunce (buns): money; a bonus. 21.

bunder (bun′der): a Netherlands measure of land area equal to about 2½ acres. In the East, a landing place; pier.

bundy (bun′di): a timeclock. 53.

burletta (bur.let′a): a kind of musical comic opera popular in England in the latter half of the 18th century.

burrasca (bur.as′ka): a musical passage that imitates a storm.

burrel (bur′el): a sort of pear.

busket (bus′ket): a small bush. 1.

bustic (bus′tik): a hardwood tree of Florida and the West Indies having shining lanceolate leaves and white flowers.

butterine (but′er.ēn): artificial butter or oleomargarine, esp. if made with the addition of butter.

buzzle (buz′l): a buzzing sound.

bwana (bwä′na): in Africa, master, boss.

byrrus (bir′us): a heavy woolen cape worn by the ancient Romans, and in the Middle Ages by the lower orders.

byte (bīt): a group of adjacent binary digits processed as a unit by a computer.

C

caama (käm′a): a South American fox. In Africa, a hartebeest.

caballetta (kab′a.let′a): a melody imitating a horse's gallop; the last, fast strains of an aria.

caballine (kab′a.līn): pert. to horses; equine.

cabane (ka.ban′): a framework supporting the wings of an airplane at the fuselage.

cabble (kab′l): to break up, as from bars or slabs, into pieces suitable for forming fagots.

Cabiritic (kab′i.rit′ik): pert. to the Cabiri, ancient Greek deities whose cult was connected with the mysteries of Samothrace.

caboceer (kab′o.sēr): a west African native chief.

Cacalia (ka.kāl′i.a): any plant of the genus *Emilia,* as the tassel flower.

cacation (ka.kā′shun): excretion.

cacestogenous (kak′es.toj′e.nus): caused by unfavorable home environment.

cacidrosis (kak′i.drō′sis): smelly sweat.

cackerel (kak′er.el): a small Mediterranean fish.

cacodoxy (kak.o.dok′si): departure from orthodoxy; heterodoxy.

cacology (ka.kol′o.ji): poor pronunciation or diction.

cacophemism (ka.kof′i.mizm): an unfairly harsh word or description.

cacophrenic (kak′o.fren′ik): pert. to an inferior intellect.

cacozeal (kak′o.zēl): faulty imitation or affectation in literary composition. Perverted or misdirected zeal. 1.

cactolith (kak′to.lith): according to the *Glossary of Geology and Related Sciences,* a quasi-horizontal chonolith composed of anastomising ductoliths, whose distal ends curl like a harpolith, thin like a sphenolith, or bulge discordantly like an akmolith or ethmolith.

cadi (kä.di, kā′di): a low-ranking magistrate or judge among the Mohammedans.

caducary (ka.dū′ka.ri): in law, pert. to, or transferred by, escheat, lapse, or forfeiture.

caecal, cecal (sē′kal): pert. to the *caecum.*

caecum, cecum (sē′kum): a bodily cavity open at one end; esp. the blind gut of the large intestine.

cag (kag): offend, insult. 2.

cagamosis (kag′a.mō′sis): an unhappy marriage.

calaber (kal.a.ber): in commerce, the gray fur of a Siberian squirrel.

calamary (kal′a.mer′i): a squid.

calcite (kal′sīt): calcium carbonate crystallized in hexagonal form.

calcographer (kal.kog′ra.fer): one who draws with chalks or pastels.

calcuminate (kal.kū′min.āt): to make sharp or pointed.

calecannon (kăl.kan′on): var. of *colcannon.*

calefactory (kal′i.fak′to.ri): producing or communicating heat.

calefy (kal′i.fī): to warm; to become warm.

calescence (ka.les′ens): heat.

calid (kal′id): warm; hot; burning.

caliology (kal′i.ol′o.ji): the study of birds' nests.

calistheneum (kal′is.thē′ni.um): a gymnasium for calisthenics.

callet (kal′et): a prostitute; scold; virago. To rail, scold, gossip. 2.

callidly (kal′id.li): cunningly; craftily. 52.

callisteia (kal′is.tē′a): prizes for beauty, awarded in competition among the ancient Greeks.

callomania (kal′o.mā′ni.a): the delusion that one is beautiful.

calology (ca.lol′o.ji): the study of beauty.

calomba (ka.lom′ba): an Australian cloverlike plant with yellow flowers and fragrant foliage, valued as forage.

calor (kal′er, kal′ôr): heat. 1.

calumba (ka.lum′ba), columba (ko.lum′ba): the root of an African plant. It contains the bitter principle columbin, and is used as a tonic.

calx (kalks): the friable residue of a burned or calcinated metal.

cambuca (kam.bōō′ka): a bishop's staff or crook.

camino (ka.mē′nō): a road.

cammock (kam′uk): a curved or crooked stick, esp. a field hockey stick. 5. A European woody herb (restharrow) with pink flowers; also, loosely, tansy ragwort, etc.

campeachy, campeche (kam.pē′chi): logwood.

canaster (ka.nas′ter): a kind of tobacco, formerly imported from South America in rush baskets.

cancelli (kan.sel′i): latticework; a latticed wall or screen, as between the chancel and nave of a church. In anatomy, the intersecting plates and bars of which spongy bone is composed.

canella (ka.nel′a): the cinnamon, or any of several related trees. Its highly aromatic inner bark.

canelo (ka.nā′lo): the Winter's bark of Chile. (cap) An Indian people of central Ecuador.

cangia (kan′ji.a): a kind of long light sailboat used on the Nile.

cannabic (ka.nab′ik, kan′a.bik): pert. to hemp; derived from hemp.

cannet (kan′et): in heraldry, a representation of a duck without feet or bill.

canoodle (ka.nōōd′l): to caress. 21.

canopholist (ka.nof′o.list): a dog lover.

cantatrice (kan′ta.trē′chi): a woman singer, esp. an opera singer.

cantilena (kan′ti.lē′na): in music, graceful; legato.

cantlet (kant′let): a small cantle; a piece; a fragment.

cantoris (kan.tō′ris): relating to the north side of the choir of a cathedral or church; cantorial. Also, pert. to a cantor.

capa (kä′pa): a mantle or cloak.

capel (kä′pel): a rock composed of quartz, tourmaline, and hornblende, occurring in the walls of some tin and copper lodes. 41A.

capillose (kap′i.lōs): hairy.

capitatum (kap′i.tā′tum): the largest bone of the wrist.

capnomancy (kap′no.man′si): divination by smoke.

capple (kap′l): having a white face with reddish or brown spots, said of a cow. Of a person, pale and sickly looking. 13.

capripede (kap′ri.pēd): a satyr.

caprylic (ka.pril′ik): pert. to the strong smell of an animal, esp. a goat.

captation (kap.tā′shun): a reaching after something, as favor or applause, esp. by flattery.

cara (kä′ra): dear. (cap) An Indian of an extinct Barbacoan tribe, traditionally from Ecuador.

caracoli (kar′a.kō′li): an alloy of gold, silver, and copper, used in making jewelry. A timber tree of northern South America used for dugout canoes.

carambola (kar′am.bō′la): an East Indian tree. Its green to yellow, usu. acid fruit is much used in Chinese cooking.

carambole (kar′am.bōl): a carom. Also, a shot in billiards in which the cue ball strikes more than one cushion before completing the carom. 1.

carbona (kär.bō′na): in mining, an irregular deposit of tin ore consisting of a network of veinlets; a stockwork. 41A.

carcel (kär′sel): a light standard much used in France, with illuminating power from 8.9 to 9.6 British standard candles.

carcer (kär′ser): a prison. Also, one of the stalls at the starting point of the race course of a Roman circus.

carcinomorphic (kär′si.no.môr′fik): crablike.

cardophagy (kär.dof′a.ji): the eating of thistles.

carinate (kar′i.nāt): shaped like the keel or bow of a ship. Also, one of the carinates, an old classification for the principal group of birds.

carker (kär′ker): one who loads or burdens (others), as with a worry. One who is anxious, troubled. 1.

carky (kär′ki): troubled, anxious.

carlin (kär′lin): a small silver coin first struck by Charles II, king of Naples and Sicily at the end of the 13th century.

carline (kär′lin, kur′lin): a woman, esp. an old one; often used contemptuously, as of a witch. 44A. A variety of pool, called also *Russian pool.* 47 E.

carmagnole (kär′ma.nyōl): a lively song popular during the French Revolution. A street dance to the tune of this song.

carnificial (kär′ni.fish′al): pert. to a public executioner or a butcher.

carrow (kar′ō): an itinerant gambler. 50.

carval (kär′val): a hymn formerly sung in church on Christmas Eve. 55.

casal (kā′sal): in grammar, pert. to case. Also, a hamlet, as in Italy or Malta.

casco (kas′kō): a ship's hull. A barge or lighter, sometimes with sails, used in the Philippines.

caseic (ka.sē′ik): cheeselike.

casquer (kas′ker): one who provides or wears a casque.

casquet (kas′ket): a helmet-shaped hat; a light, open headpiece. Also, var. of casket.

casquette (kas.ket′): a cap with a visor.

cassabanana (kas.a.ba.nä′na): an ornamental tropical vine, called also musk cucumber.

cassena (ka.sē′na): a species of holly, the *yaupon*.

cassolette (kas′o.let): a box or vase in which perfumes may be kept or burned.

cassonade (kas.on.ād′): unrefined or raw sugar.

cassumunar (kas′oo.mū′ner): the pungent root of an East Indian plant, resembling ginger.

Castalia (kas.tā′li.a): a spring sacred to the Muses at Delphi; hence, a source of poetic inspiration.

castanean, castanian (kas.tā′ni.an): of or belonging to the genus *Castanea*, the chestnuts.

castaneous (kas.tā′ni.us): of chestnut color.

castoreum (kas′tō.ri.um): castor.

castral (kas′tral): pert. to a camp.

castrametation (kas.tra.mi.tā′shun): the act or art of military encampment.

castrophrenia (kas′tro.frē′ni.a): the belief that one's thoughts are being stolen by enemies.

castrum (kas′trum), pl. castra (kas′tra): a Roman encampment.

catabasis (ka.tab′a.sis): the stage of decline of a disease.

catabatic (kat′a.bat′ik): declining by degrees, as a fever.

catabiotic (kat′a.bī.ot′ik): pert. to the degenerative changes accompanying cellular senescence.

catachthonian (kat′ak.thō′ni.an): underground.

cataclastic (kat′a.klas′tik): pert. to a granular fragmental texture induced in rocks by mechanical crushing.

catacrotic (kat′a.krot′ik): in physiology, pert. to a particular form of pulse tracing.

catagenesis (kat′a.jen′e.sis): retrogressive evolution.

catageophobia (kat′a.jē′o.fō′bi.a): fear of being ridiculed.

catalexis (kat′a.lek′sis): in prosody, incompleteness of the last foot of a verse, or, loosely, any foot.

catallactic (kat′a.lak′tik): pert. to exchange.

catallum (ka.tal′um): in law, orig., capital wealth, property of all kinds; in the feudal system, movable property; a chattel.

catalufa (kat′a.loo′fa): any of various brightly colored marine percoid fishes of tropical seas.

catamenia (kat′a.mē′ni.a): menstruation.

catapedamania (kat′a.pē′da.mā′ni.a): an impulse to jump from high places.

cataplexy (kat′a.plek′si): the motionless, rigid, and supposedly insensible condition of an animal feigning death; catalepsy.

catarolysis (kat′a.rol′i.sis): the relief of one's emotions by cursing.

catasta (ka.tas′ta): a scaffold or stage, as where slaves were sold or criminals tortured. The stocks. 1.

catasterism (ka.tas′ter.izm): the use of mythological names for constellations.

catathymic (kat′a.thī′mik): resulting from an emotional complex.

catechetical (kat′a.ket′i.kal): consisting of questions and answers.

catenoid (kat′i.noid): chain-shaped, referring esp. to the colonies of certain protozoans.

cateran (kat′er.an): an irregular soldier or marauder of the Scottish Highlands. A freebooter; brigand.

catercousin (kā′ter.kuz′n, kat′er.kuz′n): a distant relative, esp. a cousin. An intimate friend.

cathisophobia (kath′is.o.fō′bi.a): fear of sitting.

catoptromancy (ka.top′tro.man′si): the use of mirrors for divination.

catter (kat′er): one who flogs with a cat-o′-nine-tails. To fish for catfish. 27. To vomit. 23.

cauline (kô′līn, -lin): belonging to or growing on the upper part of a stem.

cauma (kô′ma): great heat, as in fever.

cauponize (kô′po.nīz): to mix and adulterate for profit.

cautelous (kô′te.lus): crafty; wily; cautious.

cauter (kô′ter): an iron for cauterizing.

cavaliere (ka′va.lyâr′i): a cavalier; knight; cavalier servente, a gallant attentive to a married lady.

cavatina (käv′a.tē′na): orig. a melody of simpler form than the aria; now, almost any kind of musical composition.

cawk (kôk): to utter a cawk, as a crow.

caxon (kak′sun): a wig, esp. one much worn. 1.

caza (kä.za): in Turkey, a subdivision of a vilayet, or administrative district.

cebil (sā.bēl′): a South American tree that yields angico gum, used in tanning.

cecidium (si.si′di.um): a gall or swelling of plant tissue due to parasites.

cecity (ses′i.ti): blindness.

cedron (sē′drun): the fruit of a tropical American tree, used against snakebite and hydrophobia.

celarent (si.lâr′ent): in logic, the proposition "No M is P; all S is M; hence, no S is P."

celidography (sel′i.dog′ra.fi): the description of the markings on the disk of the sun or on the planets.

cellate (sel′āt): in zoology, formed as, divided into, or furnished with a cell or cells. Cellated.

cellidh (kā′li): a visit; a private conversation; an evening's musical entertainment. 44, 51.

cenobian (si.nō′bi.an): pert. to a cenoby, a religious community. Monkish, monastic.

cenophobia (sen′o.fō′bi.a): fear of empty spaces.

centesis (sen.tē′sis): in surgery, a puncture, as of a cavity or tumor.

centillion (sen.til′yun): the number denoted by a unit with 303 zeros annexed (in French and American notation) or with 600 (in British and German).

cepaceous (si.pā′shus): like an onion.

cephalocide (sef′al.o.sīd): the murder of intellectuals as a group.

cephaloid (sef′a.loid): in botany, abruptly enlarged; headshaped. Capitate.

cephalonamancy (sef′a.lo.na.man′si): divination by boiling an ass's head.

cepivorous (si.piv′o.rus): onion-eating. 60.

ceraunograph (si.rô′no.graf): an instrument that records thunder and lightning.

ceraunoscopy (ser′ô.nos′ko.pi): the observance of thunder as an omen.

cereous (sēr′i.us): waxen.

ceriferous (si.rif′er.us): producing wax.

cerniture (sur′ni.cher): in Roman law, a formal acceptance of an inheritance.

cerography (si.rog′ra.fi): the art of making designs in wax.

ceromancy (sēr′o.man′si): the use of melted wax, dropped in water, for divination.

cerulean (si.roo′li.an): azure; sky blue.

cervicide (sur′vi.sīd): deer-killing.

cessavit (se.sā′vit): a writ given by Edward I to recover lands upon the tenants' failure to meet the conditions of tenure.

cessed (sest): assessed; taxed. 41.

cesser (ses′er): in law, failure of a tenant to perform due services. Also, a ceasing of liability.

chaetiferous (ki.tif′er.us): having bristles.

chamade (sha.mäd): the drumbeat or trumpet blast announcing a surrender.

Chamaesaura (kam'i.sô'ra): a genus of African snakelike lizards, limbless or with scaly vestigial limbs.

chamma (cham'ma): the chief garment of the Abyssinians, a wide cotton scarf wrapped around the body leaving one arm free.

chandoo (chan.doo'): a preparation of opium smoked in China.

chank (changk): a large spiral shell found near the coasts of the East Indies.

chaology (kā.ol'o.ji): the study of chaos.

chapatty (cha.pat'i): a thin griddlecake of unleavened bread, used in northern India.

charbon (shär'bon): a small black spot remaining in the cavity of the corner tooth of a horse after the large spot has been obliterated.

charientism (kar'i.en.tizm): a gracefully veiled insult.

chartomancy (kär'to.man'si): divination by maps.

charuk (cha.rook): a sandal with up-turned tips, used in Anatolia from remote antiquity.

chasmophilous (kaz.mof'i.lus): fond of nooks, crannies, chasms.

chatoyant (sha.toi'ant): having a changeable luster marked by an undulating narrow band of white light, as a cat's eye in the dark.

chavender (chav'en.der): the chevin (the chub fish).

cheechako (chi.chä'kō): a tenderfoot.

cheet (chēt): to cheep. 11. To call a cat. 44.

cheimaphilic (kī'ma.fil'ik): fond of cold.

chelidonic (kē'li.don.ik): a kind of crystalline acid.

cheliferous (ki.lif'er.us): bearing a pincerlike organ or claw.

Chen (chen): the genus of the snow goose.

cherophobia (kēr'o.fō'bi.a): fear of gaiety.

chessel (ches'el): a cheese vat.

chetty (chet'i): a caste of Tamil merchants in southern India and Ceylon.

chevaline (shev'a.lin): horselike. Horseflesh.

cheve (shēv): to turn out (well, ill, etc.); hence, to prosper. 1.

chevrette (shev.ret'): a thin kind of goatskin.

chewet (choo'et): a small European bird of the crow family; a chough; hence a chatterer. A pie of minced meat or fish, with fruits, spices, etc. 1.

chia (chē'a): a tea-like beverage. 1. Any of several species of the herb Salvia of Mexico and the southwestern U.S.; its seeds make a beverage or oil.

chicago (shi.kä'gō): in Algonquian, fields of wild onions—of a particularly odoriferous sort, according to John Chancellor. (cap) The largest city in the Middle West.

chichevache (shēsh'vash): a fabulous monster that ate only patient (some say faithful) wives, and was therefore very lean.

Chickahominy (chik.a.hom'i.ni): an Indian of an Algonquin tribe in eastern Virginia.

chiel (chēl): fellow, lad, child. 44A.

chil (chil): a small hawk of India. The chir pine.

chimb (chim): (var. of chime) to ring chimes with bells.

chimopelagic (kī.mop.i.laj'ik): pert. to certain deep-sea organisms that surface only in winter.

chinquapin (ching'ka.pin): the dwarf chestnut of the U.S. or related trees. The sweet edible nut of this tree.

chinse (chins): to calk temporarily, as a boat.

chionablepsia (kī.o.no.blep'si.a): snow blindness.

chiragric (kī.rag'rik): affected with gout in the hand.

chiral (kī'ral): pert. to the hand.

chirognomy (kī.rog'no.mi): palmistry.

chirology (kī.rol'o.ji): study of the hands.

chiropraxis (kī'ro.prak'sis): chiropractic.

chirospasm (kī'ro.spazm): writer's cramp.

chirotony (kī.rot'o.ni): an election or appointment by show of hands. Ecclesiastically, the extension of hands in blessing, etc.

chitarra (ki.tär'a): a guitar in Italy.

chittak (chi.täk'): in India, a measure of weight ranging from about half an ounce to about three ounces.

chloralism (klō'ral.izm): a morbid condition resulting from habitual use of chloral.

chloralum (klōr.al'um): an aqueous solution of aluminum chloride, used as an antiseptic.

Chloris (klō.ris): a genus of grass including finger grass and crabgrass.

choca (chok'a): a beverage of coffee and chocolate.

choliamb (kō'li.amb), choliambic (kō'li.am'bik): in prosody, an iambic trimeter having a spondee or trochee in the last foot.

Cholo (chō'lō): in Spanish America, a civilized Indian. (not cap) A lower-class Mexican or person of Mexican ancestry—often used disparagingly. A person of mixed Spanish and Indian blood.

chopa (chō'pa): any of several rudder-fishes, said to accompany ships.

choralcelo (kō'ral.sel'ō): an electric piano.

choreomania (kō'ri.o.mā'ni.a): mania for dancing, sometimes occurring in epidemics.

choreus (ko.rē'us): a trochee.

chorten (chôr'ten): a Lamaist shrine or monument.

chouse (chous): a chiaus—a Turkish messenger. A cheat, swindler. One easily cheated; a gull, dupe. 1. A trick, sham, imposition.

chowry (chou'ri): an East Indian fly swatter made from a yak's tail.

chrematophobia (kri.mat.o.fō'bi.a): fear of money.

chresmology (kres.mol.o.ji): in ancient Greek religion, the utterance of oracular prophecies.

chria (krī'a): in rhetoric, a quotation or aphoristic saying developed according to a prescribed scheme into a short essay.

Christophany (kris.tof'a.ni): an appearance of Christ after resurrection, esp. as recorded in the Gospels.

chromophobia (krō'mo.fō'bi.a): fear of colors.

chromoxylography(krō'mo.zī.log'ra.fi): printing in colors from wooden blocks.

chronicon (kron'i.kon): a chronicle or chronology. 6.

chronogram (kron'o.gram): an inscription in which certain letters taken in order express a particular date or epoch.

chronophobia (kron'o.fō'bi.a): fear of the passage of time.

chrotta (krot'a): a crwth or crowd, an ancient Celtic musical instrument. A small medieval harp.

chrysopholist (kri'sof'o.list): a lover of gold.

chthonic (thon'ik): designating gods or spirits of the underworld.

chthonophagia (thon'o.fā'ji.a): the eating of dirt.

chummage (chum'ij): a fee demanded from a new prisoner by old prisoners. 25. The quartering of persons together as chums.

churrus (chur.us): in India, a device for drawing water from deep wells, consisting of a leather bag hung on a rope running over a pulley and drawn by oxen. Var. of charas, a narcotic and intoxicating resin that exudes from hemp; a smoking mixture containing it.

cibarious (si.bâr'i.us): pert. to food; edible.

cibation (si.bā'shun): in alchemy, the process of feeding the crucible with fresh material. The act of taking food. 1.

cibol (sib'ul): the Welsh onion. A shallot.

cibophobia (sī'bo.fō'bi.a): fear of food.

cicer (sī'ser): the chick-pea. 1. (cap) A genus of herbs of the pea family.

ciconine (sik′o.nīn, -nin): storklike.

cilery (sil′er.i): in architecture, the carved foliage, etc., ornamenting the head of a column; a volute. 9.

cilicious (si.lish′us): made of haircloth. 1.

cimelia (si.mē′lya): treasure; esp. in the 17th and 18th centuries, heirlooms or church treasures.

cincinnate (sin′si.nāt): curled in ringlets.

cineplasty (sin′i.plas′ti): surgical fitting of a muscle to a prosthetic device to be operated by muscle contractions.

cinerescent (sin′er.es′ent): ashen, grayish.

circumduct (sur′kum.dukt): to turn about an axis; revolve. In law, to put a limit or end to; to abrogate, annul.

circumforaneous (sur′kum.fo.rā′ni.us): wandering from market to market, or place to place.

circumfulgent (sur′kum.ful′jent): shining around or about.

circumincession (sur′kum.in.sesh′un): the doctrine of the reciprocal existence in each other of the three persons of the Trinity.

cirrigerous (si.rij′er.us): forming curls or ringlets.

cismarine (sis′ma.rēn): on the near side of the sea.

Cistus (sis′tus): a genus of shrubs, the rockroses.

cital (sī′tal): citation. 1.

citole (sit′ōl, si.tōl′): a small flat-backed lute of medieval times.

cittosis (si.tō′sis): abnormal desire for strange foods.

cladus (klā′dus): a branch of one of the branching spicules that support the soft tissues of sponges and some other invertebrates.

clapperclaw (klap′er.klô), clappermaclaw (klap′er.ma.klô): to claw and scratch; to scold. 10.

claribel (klar′i.bel): brightly fair.

clart (klärt): a clot or daub of mud or other sticky substance. 11.

clavial (klā′vi.al): an upright piano of the sostinenta pianoforte type.

clavicin (klav.i.sin): the harpsichord. Also, the keys by which a bell ringer plays a carillon.

clavicymbal (klav′i.sim′bl): an old name of the harpsichord.

clavicytherium (klav′i.si.thēr′i.um): a harpsichord-like musical instrument.

claviger (klav′i.jer): one who keeps the keys; a custodian, warden.

clavis (klā′vus): a key; a glossary to aid interpretation.

cleck (klek): to hatch. 44A.

cledge (klej): clay or clayey soil.

cledonism (klē′do.nizm): the use of euphemisms to avert misfortune.

clem (klem): to suffer or cause to suffer from hunger, thirst, or cold. 2. A fight or brawl between circus or carnival workers and the local townspeople. 21.

DIRGE IN C

When my craft first set to sea,
Never chopa swam by me,
Showing me the way to go.
  No;
I was frequently adrift,
  Squiffed,
Or at tropic isle ashore;
  For
Capripede I made my role—
Chose to dance the carmignole;
With the great-eyed maidens croodled,
Sighed and trembled and canoodled.
Now, where once sang gay conquecle,
Digs the sexton, prays the beadle;
Now, where hair sprang fair and flaxen,
Sits askew the stringy caxon;
Cheek, once redder than an apple,
  Now capple;
Eyes, once eager, twinkly-sparky,
  Carky;
Voice, once honey in its talk,
  Cawk.
Grudgingly I face my culp,
  And gulp.

---

clematite (klem′a.tīt): the European birthwort.

cletch (klech): a brood or hatching; a clutch. Contemptuously, a family or clique. 13.

cleve (klēv): a cliff; also, a brae. 2.

clevy (klev′i): var. of *clevis*, a U-shaped device used on the end of the tongue of a wagon, etc., to attach it to the whiffletree, etc.

clifty (klif′ti): clifty.

climacophobia (klī.ma.ko.fō.bi.a): fear of falling downstairs.

climacter (klī.mak′ter): a climacteric period. 1.

clinamen (klī.nā′men): a turn; bias; twist.

clinomania (klī′no.mā.ni.a): excessive desire to stay in bed.

clinophobia (klī′no.fōbi.a): fear of going to bed.

clishmaclaver (klish′ma.klav′er): foolish gossip. 43.

clive (klīv): a plant of the genus *Agrimonia*, inc. the common burdock. 13.

clocher (klō′sher): a bell tower.

clochette (klo.shet′): in the arts, any small bell-shaped ornament; also, a bell-shaped cover, as for dishes.

cloff (klof): a cleft or fork, as of legs, branches, or hills. 43. An allowance formerly given on certain goods to cover small losses in retailing.

clonic (klon′ik): spastic.

cloop (klo͞op): the sound made when a cork is drawn from a bottle, or any such sound.

cloot (klo͞ot): a cleft hoof, or one of its divisions, as in the ox. (usu. cap & pl.) A devil. 44A.

Clootie (klo͞ot′i): cloot.

clough (kluf): gully.

clunch (klunch): a clump or lump. A lout. Lumpy, stiff, as clay. 2.

cnemial (nē′mi.al): pert. to the shin or shinbone.

coak (kōk): a projection connecting the notched face of a timber with the similarly notched face of another timber. A dowel set into timbers to unite them or keep them from slipping. To join by the aid of coaks.

coaptation (ko.ap.tā′shun): the mutual adaptation of broken parts to each other, as the edges of a wound.

coarb (ko′ärb): in early Irish and Scottish churches, the incumbent of an abbey or bishopric as successor to the patron saint.

cobby (kob′i): hearty, lively. Headstrong. 13. Like a cob horse in shape, with a deep strong body and relatively short sturdy legs.

cobra de capello (kō′bra dē ka.pel′ō): a variety of venomous Asiatic and African snakes.

cockawee (kok′a.wi): the old-squaw, a common sea duck of the far northern latitudes—called also *old injun, oldwife*.

coctile (kok′til, -til): made by baking or exposure to heat (as a brick).

codetta (ko.det′a.): in music, a short coda.

codilla (ko.dil′a): the shorter fibers produced in scutching flax.

coemption (ko.emp′shun): purchase of the whole supply of commodities in the market, as for purposes of monopoly.

coggle (kog′l): to repair roughly, cobble (used with *up*). 11. A ceramics tool used to make indentations or grooves in the outer edges of plates.

cogman (kog′man): one who erects mine cogs; a cogger. A roller in charge of the first set of rolls in a steelworks.

cohibit (ko.hib′it): to restrain or restrict.

cohoba (ko.hō′ba): a narcotic snuff made from the leaves of a tropical American tree, *Piptadena peregrinia*.

coign (koin), quoin (kwoin): an angle; corner. A wedge.

coistrel, coystrel (kois′trel): a groom employed to care for a knight's horses. A mean fellow.

Colada (ko.lä′da): the gold-hilted sword which the Cid took from Ramon Berenger.

colcannon (kol.kan′un, kol′kan.un): a

stew made mostly from potatoes and greens. 50.

colletic (ko.let′ik): made of glue.

colliculation (ko.lik′ū.lā′shun): a low hill.

collieshangie (kol′i.shang′i): a noisy or confused fight. 44.

colliform (kol′i.fôrm): neckshaped.

colling (kol′ing): embracing, petting. 13.

collocution (kol′o.kū′shun): a speaking together.

colobin (kol′o.bin): a long-tailed African monkey.

colometry (ko.lom′i.tri): in prosody, measurement of verses by cola, which are smaller and less independent than a sentence but larger and less dependent than a phrase.

colonus (ko.lō′nus): a freeborn serf or tenant farmer in the later Roman empire.

colossean (kol′o.sē′an): colossal.

columbic (ko.lum′bik): pert. to or containing columbium.

columbo (ko.lum′bō): var. of *columba,* a root used in medicine as a stomachic and tonic.

comino (ko.mē′nō): a path or trail; also, a journey.

comitatus (kom′i.tā′tus): a body of wellborn men attached to a king or chieftain by the duty of military service.

commandry (kom.man′dri): var. of *commandery.*

commasculation (ko.mas′kū.lā′shun): sexuality between men.

commatic (ko.mat′ik): divided into short clauses or verses, as a hymn. Pert. to a minute difference in pitch.

commentitious (kom′en.tish′us): imaginary.

commorient (ko.mō′ri.ent): dying together.

comoid (kō′moid): resembling a tress or tuft of hair.

comosce (kō′mōs): hairy, tufted.

compend (kom.pend′): a compendium, epitome.

compere (kom.pēr′): a master of ceremonies, esp. on radio or television. To act as a compere.

compesce (kom.pes′): to restrain.

comploration (kom.plôr.ā′shun): wailing and weeping together.

complot (kom′plot): a plot, conspiracy. To plot together, conspire. 9.

comprecation (kom′pri.kā′shun): a prayer meeting.

compt (kompt): neat; spruce; polished. 1.

compursion (kom.pur′shun): the wrinkling of one's face.

concameration (kon.kam′er.ā′shun): vaulting; a vaulted roof or ceiling.

concent (kon.sent′): a concert of voices, concord of sounds. Accordance; consistency. 9.

concetto (kon.chet′tō) pl. concetti (kon.chet.i): a witty turn of thought or expression; quip, conceit.

conchitic (kong.kit′ik): composed of shells.

concilium (kon.sil′i.um): council.

concitation (kon.si.tā′shun): the act of exciting or stirring up.

concursus (kon.kur′sus): influence of divine causation upon secondary causes; esp. the doctrine that before the fall man was preserved from sin by the aid of God.

condensary (kon.den′sa.ri): a factory for condensing, as of milk.

condylure (kon′di.lōōr): the star-nosed mole.

confarreation (kon.far.i.ā′shun): in Roman law, a ceremony of patrician marriage that conferred upon the husband absolute control of the wife.

confirmand (kon′fer.mand): a candidate for ecclesiastical confirmation.

confix (kon.fiks′): to fasten together.

confrater (kon.frā′ter): an honorary guest member of a monastery.

conglaciate (kon.glā′shi.āt): to freeze.

conglobulation (kon.glob′ū.lā′shun): the act or result of gathering (something) into a global mass.

congreet (kon.grēt′): to greet mutually.

congroid (kon′groid): pert. to the conger eels.

coniaker (ko.nī′a.ker): a coin counterfeiter.

conject (kon.jekt′): to prognosticate. To throw, or throw together. Connection; plan, plot. 1.

connascence (ko.nas′ens): the state of being born together, united at birth. 52.

connex (ko.neks′): a bond, tie. A connected incident or property. A conditional proposition in logic. 1.

conoid (kō′noid): shaped like a cone.

conquedle (kon.kwē′dl): the bobolink. 12.

consarcination (kon.sär.si.nā′shun): the act of patching.

conscribe (kon.skrīb′): to limit, circumscribe. To enlist by force; conscript.

consectaneous (kon.sek.tā′ni.us): relating to a logical consequence.

consertal (kon.sur′tal): designating texture of igneous rocks in which the irregularly shaped crystals interlock.

consilience (kon.sil′i.ens): concurrence in inferential results.

consortion (kon.sôr′shun): association, alliance.

conspissation (kon′spi.sā′shun): thickness; the act of thickening. 1.

conspue (kon.spū′): to spurn contemptuously.

conspurcate (kon′sper.kāt): to pollute, defile.

constuprate (kon′stū.prāt): to violate, debauch.

contabescence (kon′ta.bes′ens): a wasting away.

contect (kon.tekt′): to cover or cover up.

contesseration (kon.tes′er.ā′shun): the act of making friends. 1.

contortuplicate (kon′tor.tōōp′li.kāt): twisted back upon itself.

contrada (kon.trä.da): a street or way; also, a quarter or ward.

contrahent (kon′tra.hent): a contracting party. Entering into a contract.

contraplex (kon′tra.pleks): capable of sending two telegraphed messages in opposite directions at the same time.

contrectation (kon.trek.tā′shun): touching, handling. In psychology, the first of two stages of the sexual act.

contumulation (con.tū.mū.lā′shun): burial in the same tomb with another.

Conus (kō′nus): a genus of tropical marine snails comprising the cones and incl., among many beautiful and harmless forms, some that inject a paralytic venom.

conversus (kon.vur′sus): a lay brother—orig. applied to one who entered a monastery to do penance. An administrator of episcopal or monastic property.

convive (kon.vīv′): a comrade at table. To feast together. 1.

coodle (kōō′dl): a terrapin. 35.

coomb (kōōm): four bushels.

copa (kō′pa): a gum-yielding tree of Panama, called also *yaya.*

copple (kop′l): a crest on a bird's head; also, a hill or knoll of land. 2.

coprolalia (kop′ro.lāl′ya): the use of words relating to dirt and excrement.

coprophemia (kop′ro.fē′mi.a): obscene language.

corallite (kor′a.līt): the skeleton formed by a single coral polyp.

corb (kôrb), corf (kôrf): a truck, tub, or basket used in a mine.

corbie, corby (kôr′bi): the raven; the carrion crow.

cordel (kôr.del′): name of certain old coins of Cuba, Paraguay, and Spain.

corella (ko.rel′a): a parrot of the genus *Trichoglossus,* as the Australian crested parakeet; also, any of certain cockatoos.

corge (kôrj): a score; twenty. 51A.

corke, corcir (kôrk, -kir): any of the colors imparted by the dye archil, varying from moderate red to dark purplish red.

corm (kôrm): a short, bulblike, fleshy stem, bearing buds at the summit, as in the corcus and gladiolus.

cormel (kôr′mel): a small or secondary corm produced by an old corm.

cormus (kôr′mus): the plant body in the higher plants, with segmentation into stem and leaf units. The entire body or colony of a compound animal.

cornific (kôr.nif′ik): producing horns; forming horn.

coronach (kôr′o.nak): a dirge played on bagpipes.

coronoid (kôr′o.noid): resembling the beak of a crow.

corozo (ko.rō′sō): any of several American palms, incl. the ivory palm and the cohune palm.

correal (kor′i.al): pert. in civil law to a joint obligation or right that may be enforced against any one of several joint debtors or by any one of several joint creditors against a single debtor.

correption (ko.rep′shun): a shortening in pronunciation. Also, chiding; reproof; reproach. 1.

cosmopathic (koz′mo.path′ik): receiving impressions from the universe by other means than through the senses.

cosmorama (koz′mo.rä′ma): an exhibition of views made to appear natural by mirrors, lenses, illumination, etc.

cosmorganic (koz′môr.gan′ik): pert. to an organic cosmos.

cosmothetic (koz′mo.thet′ik): pert. to a doctrine that affirms the real existence of the external world.

costean (kos.tēn′, kos′ten): to dig trenches or pits into rock so as to determine the course of a mineral deposit.

coucal (koo′kal): any of various large long-tailed, brown-and-black cuckoos of Africa, southern Asia, and Australia, pheasant-like in plumage, pattern, and habits.

couchee (koo′shā, koo.shā′): bedtime; a bedtime visitor; hist., a reception held at the time of going to bed.

coumb (koom): a comb. 1.

coutil (koo.til′): a close-woven cotton fabric used for mattresses, corsets, etc.

cowal (kou′al): a depression or channel, similar to a billabong. 31A.

cowan (kou′an): one who is not a Freemason; esp., one who would pretend to Freemasonry or intrude upon its secrets. Also, a dry-stone diker; one not a regular mason.

cowle (koul): in India, an engagement in writing, esp. of safe conduct or amnesty.

cowy (kou′i): suggestive of a cow.

coze (kōz): friendly chat.

cran (kran): the common swift. Also, a measure for quantity of fresh herring, amounting to 45 gallons. 41.

craniofacial (krā′ni.o.fā′shal): both cranial and facial.

crannage (kran′ij): in herring fishing, the total catch in *crans*.

crapaudine (krap′o.dēn): swinging on top and bottom pivots like a door. The socket for such a pivot.

crassitude (kras′i.tūd): thickness, as of a solid body. 1. Grossness, or an instance of it.

cratch (krach): a crib or rack, esp. for fodder. 11.

craunch (krônch, kränch): crunch. 26.

creatic (kri.at′ik): pert. to, or caused by, flesh or animal food.

cremnophobia (krem′no.fō′bi.a): fear of cliffs.

crenelle (kre.nel′): an indentation in a parapet from which projectiles are launched upon the enemy.

creophagous (kri.of′a.gus): carnivorous.

crescive (kres′iv): increasing; growing.

cribble (krib′l): in engraving, to make a pattern of small round punctures in a block or plate. A sieve. Coarse flour or meal. To sift. 1.

criblé (krē′blā): in engraving, having a background of small white dots produced by cribbling the plate.

crig (krig): a bruising blow.

crimply (krim′pli): curly, wavy.

crin (krin): a heavy silk.

crinal (krī′nal): pert. to the hair.

crine (krīn): hair; head of hair. To shrink; shrivel. 44.

criniparous (krin.ip′er.us): producing hair.

crith (krith): the weight of a liter of hydrogen at 0°C and 760 mm pressure.

crithomancy (krith′o.man′si): divination by the dough in the cakes offered in ancient sacrifices.

cro (krō): among the ancient Celts, the compensation made for the slaying of a man, according to his rank.

croche (krōch): a little knob at the top of a deer's antler. A pastoral staff; a crozier. 1.

cronk (krongk): the croak of a raven or honk of a wild goose. Discordant, harsh. Sick or unsound, physically or financially. 23B.

croodle (kroo′dl): to cling to; to nestle together.

crore (krōr): a sum of money equal to 10 million rupees, or 100 lacs. Ten million.

crossette (kros.et′): a projection at the corner of an arch or a door or window casing.

crotaline (krot.a.līn, -lin; krō′ta.līn, -lin): pert. to rattlesnakes.

crotin (krō′tin): a mixture of poisonous proteins found in the seeds of a small Asiatic tree related to the spurges.

crottle (krot′l): any of several lichens from which dyes are made.

croupade (kroo.päd′): a curvet (of a horse) with the hind legs well under the belly.

cruor (kroo′ôr): clotted blood.

crurophilous (kroo.rof′il.us): liking legs.

crustation (krus.tā′shun): an incrustation.

crwth (krooth): an ancient Celtic musical instrument with a shallow body and a varying number of strings. (Called also *chrotta, crowd*.)

cryobiology (krī′o.bī.ol′o.ji): the study of the effects of freezing on living things.

cryptarchy (krip′tär.ki): rule by a secret authority.

ctetology (ti.tol′o.ji): the study of acquired characteristics.

cuarta (kwär′ta): a measure of quantity or of distance in Brazil, Paraguay, Spain, and Guatemala.

cubatory (kū′ba.tō′ri): reclining; resting.

cuck (kuk): to void. To be punished by the cucking stool, in which an offender was fastened, to be pelted and hooted at by the mob. 1. To utter the call of the cuckoo. 13.

cuculine, cuculoid (kū′kū.līn, -lin, -loid): pert. to the cuckoos.

cuculla (kū.kul′a): a loose sleeveless garment put on over the head and used esp. to protect other garments; specif., the sleeveless outer part of a monk's habit.

cueca (kwā′ka): a dance of Peruvian origin, popular in South American countries.

cuggermugger (kug′er.mug′er): whispered gossip. 50.

cullion (kul′yun): a testicle.

culottic (kū.lot′ik): wearing breeches; respectable.

culp (kulp): sin; guilt. 1.

cumic (kū′mik): pert. to or designating a certain white crystalline acid.

cummer (kum′er): a godmother; a midwife; also, a witch. An intimate female companion. A woman or girl; a lass. 44A.

cunabula (kū.nab′ū.la): cradle; earliest abode.

cunctipotent (kungk′tip′o.tent): omnipotent.

cuniculus (kū.nik′ū.lus): an underground passage, as a mine or rabbit burrow.

cunny (kun′i): the cony.

cuproid (kū′proid): a solid related to a tetrahedron and having 12 equal triangular faces.

cupronickel (kū′pro.nik′el): an alloy of copper and nickel.

curiboca (koo′ri.bō′ka): a dark-complexioned Brazilian of mixed white and Indian or Indian and black blood.

curple (kur′pl): the cruppers, rump, posterior. 44.

cursal (kur′sal): pert. to a course or series of studies.

cursus (kur′sus): a course, as for racing. A course of study. Movement or flow (of style).

Curtana (ker.tä′na): the pointless sword carried by British monarchs at their coronation, and emblematically considered the sword of mercy.

cush (kush): in India, sorghum. (cap) In the Bible, the eldest son of Ham. Bread or crackers boiled and seasoned. 35. A cow. 11. Money. 22.

cushlamochree (koosh′la.ma.kri): darling. 50.

custodee (kus′to.di): one to whom custody is given.

cuticula (kū.tik′ū.la): cuticle; specif., the outer body wall of an insect, secreted by the hypodermis.

cuttle (kut′l): a swaggerer or ruffian; a cutler. 1.

cyanean (sī′a.nē′an): of a genus of jellyfish; also, the dark blue color of certain jellyfish.

cycloplegic (sī′klo.plej′ik): producing paralysis of the ciliary muscle of the eye.

cyclotomy (sī.klot′o.mi): in mathematics, the theory of the division of the circle into equal parts. In surgery, an incision or division of the ciliary body of the eyeball.

cyanthropy (sī.an′thro.pi): insanity in which one fancies oneself a dog.

cyniatrics (sin′i.at′riks): that branch of veterinary medicine that treats of diseases of the dog.

cynoid (sī′noid, sin-): doglike. Pert. to the dog family.

cynolatry (sī.nol′a.tri, sin.ol′-): dog worship.

cynophobia (sī′no.fō′bi.a): fear of dogs.

cyrtometer (ser.tom′i.ter): in medicine, an instrument for determining the dimensions and movements of curved surfaces, esp. of the chest.

cyton (sī′ton): a cell, esp. a nerve cell.

D

dacnomania (dak′no.mā′ni.a): a mania for killing.

dacrygelosis (dak′ri.ji.lō′sis): the condition of alternately laughing and crying.

dactyliography (dak.til′i.og′ra.fi): the history or art of gem engraving. 52.

dactylion (dak.til′i.on): the tip of the middle finger. Also, an obsolete device for developing the fingers of a piano player.

dactylology (dak′ti.lol′o.ji): the art of communicating ideas by signs made with the fingers, as in the manual alphabets of deaf-mutes.

dactyloscopy (dak′ti.los′ko.pi): identification by or classification of fingerprints.

dadder (dad′er): to shiver, tremble. 4.

daff (daf): a numbskull; a coward. 2. To act foolishly. 42. To thrust aside. 1.

daffle (daf′l): to be mentally senile. 13.

daggle (dag′l): to clog or befoul with mud or mire. To draggle.

daggly (dag′li): wet; drizzly. 11.

daggy (dag′i): having daglocks—said of sheep. Drizzling; misty. 15A.

Dagon (dā′gon): the principal deity of the Philistines, first a fish god, later a god of agriculture. (not cap) A piece, as of a blanket. 1.

dahabeah (dä′ha.bē′a): a long, light-draft houseboat, lateen-rigged but often propelled by engines, used on the Nile.

Daikoku (dī.kō′koo): in Japanese mythology, one of the seven gods of happiness.

daimen (dā′min): occasional. 44A.

daint (dānt): dainty.

daira (da.ē′ra): formerly, any of several valuable estates of the Egyptian khedive or his family.

dak (dak): in India, transport by relay of men or horses; hence, post; mail.

dal (däl): a kind of yellow split pea.

daler (dä′ler): obs. var. of *dollar*. Also, a Spanish or Swedish dollar.

Damara (da.mä′ra): a native of Damaraland, southwest Africa.

damascene (dam′a.sēn): damask. 1. Pert. to damask. The damson plum. The color damson. (cap) Pert. to Damascus.

damassin (dam′a.sin): a kind of damask or brocade made with gold and silver floral ornamentation.

damiana (dam′i.an.a): a dried leaf used as a tonic and aphrodisiac. Any other drug prepared from plants of the family Carduaceae.

dand (dand): a dandy.

dandiacal (dan.dī′a.kal): characterized by dandyism.

dao (dä′ō): a very large Philippine tree having edible fruit and fibrous bark used for cordage.

dapifer (dap′i.fer): one who brings meat to the table; hence, the steward of a king's or nobleman's household.

daroga (da.rō′ga): in India, a chief officer; partic. the head of a police, customs, or excise station.

darnel (där′nel, -nl): an annual grass found as a weed in cultivated grounds.

darrein (dar′ān): in old law, "last," as in "darrein resort."

dasymeter (da.sim′e.ter): formerly, a thin glass globe weighed in gases to measure their density.

dataria, datary (dā.tä′ri.a, dā′ta.ri): an office of the Roman Curia charged with investigating the fitness of candidates for benefices.

datil (dä′til): any of several plants and

their fibers from Mexico or Central or South America used for baskets or hats.

dauw (dou): the Burchell zebra, having a striped body and plain legs.

dawdy (dô′di): dowdy. 13.

dawk (dôk): var. of *dak*.

dealbation (dē′al.bā′shun): hair bleaching.

deambulant, deambulatory (di.am′bu.lant, -bu.latō.ri): going about from place to place; wandering.

deasil, dessil (desh′l): right-handwise; clockwise; sunwise. Also, a charm performed by going three times about the object, following the course of the sun.

debarrass (di.bar′as): to disembarrass, relieve.

debellate (di.bel′āt): to conquer.

debitum (deb′i.tum): in law, a debt.

deblaterate (di.blat′er.āt): to babble.

debulliate (di.bul′i.āt): to boil over.

decadic (di.kad′ik): pert. to the decimal system of counting.

decaliter (dek′a.lē′ter): a metric measure of volume containing 10 liters.

Decalogist (de.kal′o.jist): an expounder of the Ten Commandments.

decameral (di.kam′er.al): in mathematics, divided into ten parts.

Decameron (di.kam′er.on): a collection of 100 stories written by Boccaccio in the 14th century.

decile (des′il): in statistics, any of 9 numbers in a series dividing the distribution of the individuals in the series into 10 groups of equal frequency. One of these groups.

declamando (dā′kla.män′do): in declamatory style.

decourt (di.kôrt): to banish from court. 1.

decurtate (di.kur′tat): curtailed. 1.

decurvation (dē′kur.vā′shun): the attribute of being curved or bent downward.

dedal, daedal (dē′dal): ingenious, highly skilled; intricate; varied.

dedendum (di.den′dum): in mechanics, the root of a gear tooth.

dedentition (dē′den.tish′un): the loss of teeth.

dedition (di.dish′un): surrender.

deesis (di.ē′sis): a tripartite icon of the Eastern Orthodox Church showing Christ usu. enthroned between the Virgin Mary and St. John the Baptist.

defeneration (di.fen′er.ā′shun): usury.

defervescency (dē′fer.ves′en.si): in medicine, a loss of heat; cooling. The subsidence of a fever.

deflex (di.fleks′): to bend or curve downward.

defluxion (di.fluk′shun): in medicine, a flowing down of fluid matter, as a copious discharge from the nose in catarrh.

Inflammation. Formerly, sudden loss of hair.

defoedation (dē.fi.dā′shun): the act of polluting.

defossion (di.fosh′un): live burial.

defunction (di.fungk′shun): death. 52.

dehort (di.hôrt′): to urge to abstain or refrain; to dissuade. 52.

deil (dēl): the Devil. 44.

deiparous (di.ip′a.rus): giving birth to a god—said of the Virgin Mary, hence called Deipara.

deipnosophist (dīp.nos′o.fist): one adept in table talk.

dejecture (di.jek′cher): excrement.

dekko (dek′ō): look, peep. 21.

delate (di.lāt): to make public, report.

delator (di.lā′ter): an accuser; esp. a common informer.

delectus (di.lek′tus): a book of selected passages, esp. for learners of Latin or Greek.

delenda (di.len′da): things to be deleted.

delf (delf): an excavation, usu. a mine or quarry. A pond; also, a drain, ditch. 13.

delictum (di.lik′tum): an offense or transgression against law; a delict.

deligation (del′i.gā′shun): bandaging.

deliquium (di.lik′wi.um): deliquescence. 1.

delitescent (del′i.tes′ent): lying hid; inactive.

delphin (del′fin): classics prepared for the use of the dauphin in the reign of King Louis XIV of France. A dolphin. 1.

delphine (del′fin, -fīn): pert. to the dolphins.

demal (dē′mal): in physical chemistry, having a concentration of one gram equivalent per cubic centimeter.

demersal (di.mur′sal): tending to sink, as certain fish eggs.

demesnial (di.mān′i.al, di.mēn′-): pert. to or belonging to a demesne.

demi (dem′i): a half. 1.

demijambe (dem′i.jam): a piece of armor for the front of the leg.

demiquaver (dem′i.kwā′ver): a semiquaver.

Demogorgon (dē′mo.gôr′gun): in mythology, a mysterious, terrible, and evil divinity, commanding the spirits of the lower world.

demology (di.mol′o.ji): the science of collective human activities.

demophil (dem′o.fil): a friend of the people.

dempster (demp′ster): in old Scots law, an officer whose duty it was to pronounce the doom of the court.

demulsion (di.mul′shun): the act of soothing. That which soothes.

NO RANKS OF INALIENABLE LAW FOR DEMOGORGON
(with the barest of nods to George Meredith)

Great Demogorgon[1], on a daggly[2] day,
Uprose diversivolent[3] to the light.
Dasypygal,[4] disomous[5] too he lay
Until a tender virgin hove in sight—
A dryad, toothsome and devorative[6],
Who, puzzled, paused and gave the fiend the eye.
''No roots . . . no leaves.'' She murmured, ''As I live,
Here is an object hard to classify.''

She was dendrophilous[7]—a lass who weened
All strangers to be variants of trees.
Some doty dotterel[8], she thought the fiend;
She figured she could chop him down with ease.

But he proceeded to dilaniate[9] her,
    And ate her.

[1] a terrible divinity, commanding the spirits of the lower world.
[2] drizzly, if you insist on plain speaking.
[3] looking for trouble.
[4] hairy-assed.
[5] having two joined bodies.
[6] he could swallow her in one bite.
[7] living in trees, and loving it.
[8] a decaying tree, or an old fool. The *doty* is redundant.
[9] rend to bits.

---

denary (den′a.ri): tenfold; based on tens. The number ten; a tithing; a group of ten. A gold coin of the ancient Romans—a denarius. 1.

denda (den′da): a measure of length in ancient India.

dendraxon (den.drak′son): in anatomy, a nerve cell whose axis cylinder divides into terminal filaments soon after leaving the cell.

dendrochronology (den′dro.kro.nol′o.ji): the computation of time by counting tree rings.

dendrophilous (den.drof′i.lus): treeloving; living in or on trees.

dene (dēn): a sandy tract by the sea; a dune. 41.

dennet (den′et): a light, open, twowheeled, one-horse carriage popular around 1825; a gig.

dentata (den.tā′ta): part of the second vertebra of the neck of higher vertebrates.

dentelle (den.tel′): lace; lacework. A lacy style of bookcover decoration.

dentiloquy (den.til′o.kwi): the practice of speaking through the teeth.

dentoplastic (den′to.plas′tik): a plastic used in dentistry.

den-tree (den′tri): the popular box, widely used for hedges, etc. 53.

Deo (dē′ō): God.

deodand (dē′o.dand): a thing forfeited or given to God because it was the immediate cause of a death.

---

deontology (dē′on.tol′o.ji): the study of morality or ethics.

deoppilation (di.op′i.lā′shun): the act of freeing from or removing obstruction.

deorsumversion (di.ôr′sum.vur′zhun): a turning downward.

deosculate (di.os′kū.lāt): to kiss affectionately. 1.

depeculation (di.pek′ū.lā′shun): the embezzlement of public funds.

deperition (dep′er.ish′un): a destructive process.

dephlogisticate (dē′flo.jis′ti.kāt): to make fireproof.

depone (di.pōn): to testify under oath. To depose.

depredicate (di.pred′i.kāt): to proclaim aloud; call out; celebrate.

deprehensible (dep′ri.hen′si.bl): able to be seized, detected, apprehended. 1.

depucelate (di.pū′si.lāt): to deflower. 1.

deraign (di.rān′): in old law, a combat to settle a claim or dispute. To fight for this purpose.

deric (der′ik): pert. to the skin.

derm (durm): skin; cuticle; dermis.

dermophyte (dur′mo.fīt): an organism living on or in the skin.

desecate (des′i.kāt): to cut off.

desiderium (des′i.dē′ri.um): an ardent desire or longing; a feeling of grievous loss.

desidious (di.sid′i.us): slothful.

desipient (di.sip′i.ent): foolish.

desmology (des.mol′o.ji): the science treating of the ligaments. The art of bandaging.

desparple (des.pär′pl): to scatter, become scattered.

despumate (des′pū.māt): to skim.

dess (des): a layer or pile, as of stones or hay. To arrange in layers. 43.

detenebrate (di.ten′i.brāt): to lighten.

detorter (di.tôr′ter): one that twists, detorts, perverts. 9.

detrition (di.trish′un): erosion by friction.

detruncate (di.trung′kāt): to shorten by cutting; lop off; decapitate.

deuteragonist (dū′ter.ag′o.nist): in Greek drama, an actor taking the parts of second importance.

deuterogamist (dū′ter.og′a.mist): a widower or widow who remarries.

deuteroscopy (dū′ter.os′ko.pi): hidden meaning or second sight.

devall (di.vôl′): cessation; pause. To leave off, cease. 44.

devast (di.vast′): to devastate.

devastavit (dev′as.tā′vit): a common-law writ against an executor or administrator for mismanagement. Such mismanagement.

devorative (di.vôr′a.tiv): capable of being swallowed whole.

dexiotropic (dek′si.o.trop′ik): turning to the right, dextral—said of certain shells.

dextrogyrate (dek′stro.ji′rāt): turning toward the right hand, or clockwise.

dextrophobia (dek′stro.fō′bi.a): fear of anything on the right.

dextrosinistral (dek′stro.sin′is.tral): in anatomy, extending in a right and left direction. Naturally left-handed but trained to use the right hand in writing.

dghaisa (dī′sa): in Malta, a small boat resembling a gondola.

dhabb (dab): the dried flesh of the skink, used as a medicine.

dharna (dur′na): in India, a way of collecting debts by sitting on the debtor's doorstep.

dhimmi (dim′i): a person living in a region overrun by Moslem conquest who was accorded a special status and allowed to retain his original faith.

dhobi, dobee, dobie (dō′bi): a member of a low caste in India once employed to wash; a washerman or washerwoman.

dhyana (dyä′na): in Hinduism and Buddhism, religious meditation.

dia (dī′a): a medical or pharmaceutical preparation. 1.

diacope (dī.ak′o.pi): the separation of a word by the insertion of another, as *dis-horrible-gusting;* tmesis. In surgery, a deep incised wound or cut.

diaglyphic (dī′a.glif′ik): pert. to sculpture, engraving, etc., formed by depressions in the surface, as in intaglio.

diagraphical (dī′a.graf′i.kal): pert. to graphic representation, esp. drawing. 52.

diapente (dī′a.pen′ti): in ancient music, the interval or consonance of the fifth. In pharmacy, a composition of five ingredients. 1.

diaphane (dī′a.fān): a diaphanous substance, as a woven silk scarf with transparent figures.

diaphanic (dī′a.fan′ik): diaphanous. 1.

diarhemia (dī′a.rē′mi.a): an abnormally watery state of the blood often occurring in animals heavily infested with parasites.

diarian (dī′âr′i.an): the writer of a diary; formerly, a journalist.

diastomatic (dī′as.to.mat′ik): through the pores. Also, gap-toothed.

diathesis (dī.ath′i.sis): an inherited tendency toward certain diseases.

diatoric (dī′a.tôr′ik): having a recess in the base for attachment to the dental plate—used of an artificial tooth.

diaxon (dī.ak′son): a nerve cell with two axons.

diazeuctic (dī′a.zōōk′tik), diazeutic (dī′a.zōō′tik): in ancient music, disjointed; applies to two tetrachords so placed as to have a tone between them, or to the resultant tone.

dibber (dib′er): a pointed gardening tool used to make holes; a dibble.

dicacity (di.kas′i.ti): raillery; sauciness. 1.

dicaeology (di′si.ol.o.ji): in rhetoric, defense by urging justification.

dichastasis (dī.kas′ta.sis): spontaneous subdivision.

dichroous (dī′kro.us): presenting different colors by transmitted light, when viewed in two different directions.

didactyl (dī.dak′til): said of animals having only two digits on each extremity.

diddy (did′i): nipple; teat; breast milk. 11.

didelf (di′delf): one of a group of mammals comprising the marsupials, as the opossums, kangaroos, etc.

didgeridoo (dij′er.i.doo′): a large bamboo musical pipe of the Australian aborigines.

didodecahedral (dī′do.dek′a.hē′dral): pert. to a diploid, an isometric crystal form that has 24 similar quadrilateral faces arranged in pairs.

dieb (dēb): a jackal of North Africa.

diegesis (dī′i.jē′sis): a recitation or narration.

diffluent (dif′lōō.ent): readily dissolving; deliquescent.

diffugient (di.fū′ji.ent): scattering.

digamous (dig′a.mus): married a second time.

digenesis (dī.jen′i.sis): reproduction that is alternately sexual and asexual.

digenous (dij′i.nus): bisexual.

Digitigrada (dij.i.ti.grā′da): a group of animals consisting of the digitigrade carnivora, in which only the digits bear on the ground.

digitorium (dij′i.tō′ri.um): a silent machine for piano practice.

diglot (dī′glot): bilingual. A diglot edition, as of a book.

diglyph (dī′glif): in a Doric frieze, a projecting face like the triglyph, but having only two grooves.

digoneutic (dig′o.nyū′tik): reproducing twice a year.

digredient (dī.grē′di.ent): in mathematics, subject to different linear transformations—opposed to *cogredient.*

dikephobia (dī′ke.fō′bi.a): fear of police, courts, and jails.

dikkop (dik′kop): in South Africa, the thick-knee; stone curlew.

dilaniate (di.lā′ni.āt): to rend or tear to pieces.

dilection (di.lek′shun): love; also, one's choice.

dilogical (dī.loj′i.kal): ambiguous; having more than one interpretation.

dilogy (dil′o.ji): an ambiguous speech or remark, as in the young couple's statement: "We are telling people we are married."

dimication (dim′i.kā′shun): a contest.

dimidiation (di.mid′i.ā′shun): the state of being halved; halving.

dimplement (dim′pl.ment): the state of being dimpled. 52.

dinge (dinj): a dent made by a blow; a surface depression. To bruise. To make dingy. Dinginess. A black—usu. used disparagingly. 21.

dingle (ding′gl): a dell, esp. a secluded ravine. A tinkle. Also, a storm door or weather shed at the entrance of a camp or house. A roofed-over passageway between the cooking and sleeping areas of a logging camp. 33A.

dinic (din′ik): pert. to dizziness.

dink (dingk): trim; neat. To dress elegantly. 44. A drop shot in tennis. A small boat, esp. one used in duck shooting. The beanie traditionally worn by college freshmen.

dinomania (din′o.mā′ni.a): a mania for dancing.

dinomic (dī.nom′ik): belonging to two divisions of the globe.

Dinornis (dī.nôr′nis): a genus of ratite birds inc. the extinct flightless moas of New Zealand, which reached 12 feet in height.

dinus (dī′nus): vertigo.

diorthosis (dī.ôr′tho.sis): a straightening out. The reshaping of deformed limbs.

dipleidoscope (dip.lī′do.skōp): an instrument for determining the time of apparent noon.

dipnoous (dip′no.us): having both lungs and gills.

dipsetic (dip′set′ik): a thirst-provoker. Thirst-provoking.

diptote (dip′tōt): a noun that has only two cases.

diremption (di.remp′shun): a tearing apart. Specif., the utter separation of a man and wife, as by death. 52.

direption (di.rep′shun): in history, sack or pillage.

dirgie, dirgy (dur′ji): a funeral feast. 44.

dis (dēs): in Norse mythology, a generic title for any of several kinds of superhuman female beings such as Valkyries and Norns. (cap) An underworld Roman god identical with the Greek Pluto.

disbocation (dis.bo.kā′shun): deforestation.

discal (dis′kal): like, or pert. to, a disk.

discalceate (dis.kal′si.āt): to take off one's shoes.

discalogynia (dis.cal.o.jīn′i.a): dislike of beautiful women.

discerp (di.surp′): to tear; to rend.

discinct (di.singkt): without a belt; ungirdled; loosely dressed.

disembogue (dis′em.bōg): to pass through the mouth of a stream in a sea; to flow into; to emerge.

disgregate (dis′gre.gāt): to separate; disperse.

disomus (dī.sō′mus): in zoology, a two-bodied monster.

Dis pater (dis pā′ter): (also Dis), an underworld god of the Romans, identical with the Greek Pluto.

dispondee (di.spon′di): in prosody, a foot having two long syllables.

dispope (dis.pōp′): to remove from popehood.

diss (dis): a reedlike Mediterranean grass, utilized in basketry and for making cordage, etc.

dissentaneous (dis′en.tā′ni.us): disagreeable; negative.

dissilient (di.sil′i.ent): bursting apart.

distent (dis.tent′): distended. Breadth, distention. 1.

dita (dē′ta): a forest tree of eastern Asia and the Philippines, called *devil′s tree* in India. Also, its bark, used as a tonic and antiperiodic.

dital (dī′tal): a key by which the pitch is raised a half step in a harp guitar.

ditation (dī.tā′shun): the act of making rich. 1.

ditrigonal (dī.trig′o.nal): designating a six-sided crystal whose alternate interfacial angles only are equal.

ditrochean, ditrochic (dī.tro.kē′an, dī.trō′kik): in prosody, relating to a double trochee.

dittamy, dittany (dit′a.mi, dit′a.ni): an aromatic plant of Crete, once famous for its supposed medical virtues.

dittander (di.tan′der): a fern, the European pepperwort.

diuturnal (dī′ū.tur′nal): of long continuance; lasting.

div (div): to do. 43.

divel (di.vel′): to rend asunder. 9, 52.

divellent (di.vel′ent): drawing asunder. 52.

diversivolent (di.vur′si.vō′lent): looking for trouble.

dividual (di.vid′ū.al): separate, distinct. Fragmentary; divisible. Divided or shared.

divoto (di.vō′tō): with religious emotion—a direction in music.

divus (dī′vus): divine, or of godlike nature—an epithet applied by the Romans to deceased emperors.

dobby (dob′i): a silly person; dolt. A brownie or sprite. 13. A loom or loom attachment for weaving small figures; a fabric made with a *dobby*.

dobra (dō′bra): any of various former Portuguese coins.

doch-an-dorrach, doch-an-dorris (dok′an.dôr.ak, -is): a stirrup cup; a nightcap. 44.

docible (dos.i.bl): easily taught or managed. Impartable by teaching. 52.

docimastic (dos′i.mas′tik): relating to proof by experiments or tests. 9.

docity (dos′i.ti): teachability. 11.

doddard (dod′ard): a branchless tree stump. Also, a dotard. 1.

dodecant (dō′de.kant): any of the 12 parts about the center of a hexagonal crystal.

dodman (dod′man): a snail. 2.

doit (doit): a trifle. To go about stupidly; to confuse. 43.

doited (doit′ed): declining into dotage; confused. 44A.

dolabriform (do.lab′ri.fôrm): shaped like an ax head.

dolent (dō′lent): sad.

dolente (do.len′ti): in music, plaintive—a direction indicating mood.

dolichopodous (dol.i.kop′o.dus): having long feet.

dolichoprosopic (dol.i.ko.pro.sop′ik): having a disproportionately long face.

Dolichosaurus (dol.i.ko.sô′rus): a genus of small long-necked aquatic fossil lizards from the Upper Cretaceous of England.

dolichurus (dol′i.kōōr′us): in Greek and Latin prosody, a dactylic hexameter with an actual or apparent redundant syllable in the last foot.

dollyman (dol′i.man): a laborer who works with a dolly.

dolorifuge (do.lôr′i.fūj): something that relieves sadness or pain.

dolorology (dō′lo.rol′o.ji): the scientific study of pain. 32.

dolus (dō′lus): in Roman, civil, and Scots law, the doing of anything that is contrary to good conscience.

dom (dom): a member of one of the lowest castes of India.

domatophobia (dō′ma.to.fō′bi.a): loathing of housekeeping.

domba (dom′ba): the *poon.*

domet, domett (dom′et, -it): a cotton or wool flannel; outing flannel.

domiculture (dom′i.kul.cher): home economics.

domn (dom): lord. The official title of the ruler of Rumania, Prince Carol I, from 1866 to 1881, when he was proclaimed king.

domus (dō′mus): a dwelling of ancient Roman or medieval times.

doncella (don.sel′a): any of several wrasse-like fishes of the West Indies and Florida; specif., the *puddingwife,* slippery eel, and related species.

donnered (don′erd): stupefied; stunned; dazed. 43.

dontepedalogy (don′ti.pi.dal′o.ji): a propensity for putting one′s foot in one′s mouth.

doob (dōōb): the Bermuda grass of India.

doodlebug (dōō′dl.bug): the larva of the ant lion.

doodlesack (dōō′dl.sak): a bagpipe. 17A.

doon (dōōn): a large Ceylonese tree yielding durable wood and a colorless varnish resin.

dop (dop): a brandy of South Africa. Also, a cup in which a diamond is held while being cut. To dive; to duck or curtsey. 1.

doramania (dôr′a.mā′ni.a): a passion for the possession of furs.

doraphobia (dôr′a.fō′bi.a): dread of touching the fur or skin of an animal.

dorn (dôrn): the thornback ray. 30.

dorp (dôrp): a village, esp. in the Netherlands. 1. A village or township in South Africa.

dorsiflexor (dôr′si.flek′ser): a muscle causing flexion in a dorsal direction.

dorso (dôr′sō): an endorsement on the outside or reverse of a manuscript record.

dorsum (dôr′sum): the back part of the tongue.

dorty (dôr′ti): peevish; sulky. 44.

dosa (dō′sa): in Buddhism, a ceremonial ride by the sheik of the Sa′di dervishes over the prostrate bodies of his followers. Also, hatred.

Dosinia (do.sin′i.a): a genus of bivalve mollusks having a flattened round shell.

dossil (dos′il): a spigot. 4. In surgery, a small roll of lint, for keeping a sore, wound, etc., open.

dotation (do.tā′shun): an endowment or bestowal.

doty (dōt′i): of timber, affected by incipient or partial decay. Weak-minded; having the mentality impaired in old age. 35.

doulocracy (dōō.lok′ra.si), dulocracy (dū.lok′ra.si): government by slaves.

doum (dōōm): the doom palm, also called *dome palm.*

dowie, dowy (dou′i. dō′i): doleful; dispirited; dull and oppressive. 44A.

doxastic (dok.sas′tik): pert. to opinion.

doxography (dok.sog′ra.fi): a compilation of extracts from the ancient Greek philosophers.

drabbet (drab′et): a coarse drab linen fabric, or duck, used for smocks, etc. 41.

dracontine (dra.kon′tīn, -tin): dragonlike; belonging to a dragon.

draffy (draf′i): dreggy; waste; worthless.

dragade (dra.gād´): to break up (glass) by pouring (it) molten into water.

dragman (drag´man): one who drags something, as a fisherman who uses a dragnet.

dragonnade (drag´o.nād): the persecution of Protestants under Louis XIV by dragoons; hence, any rapid and devastating incursion.

drammock (dram´uk): a mixture, gen. raw, of meal and water. 45.

drap (drap): var. of *drop*. 15A.

drapetomania (drap´i.to.mā´ni.a): an overwhelming desire to run away from home.

dree (drē): suffering. To undergo, suffer. Tedious, dreary, stingy. 43A.

dreidel (drā´dl): a 4-sided toy that revolves like a top, used esp. during the Hanukkah festival. A game of chance played with the dreidel.

drek (drek): filth. 21.

dreng, drengh (dreng): a free tenant, esp. in pre-Norman Northumbria.

drepanoid (drep´a.noid): shaped like a scythe or sickle.

drias (drī´as): the deadly carrot, a large European herb with an emetic and cathartic root.

drillet (dril´et): a commercial product formed of the acorn cups of the valonia oak, used for tanning and dyeing.

drogh (drōg): a hooped canvas bag towed at the stern of a boat to prevent it from turning broadside to the waves. A contrivance attached to the end of a harpoon line to check the movements of a whale.

drogher (drō´ger): a sailing barge used in the West Indian trade. A clumsy cargo boat. A carrier, porter.

dromic (drō´mik): pert. to the shape of a racecourse. Having a long and narrow ground plan.

dromomania (drō´mo.mā´ni.a): a compulsion to travel.

dromophobia (drō´mo.fō´bi.a): fear of running.

drumble (drum´bl): a sluggish person or animal; to be sluggish or lazy; to be confused; to mumble. 2. To disturb; to render turbid. 43.

drummock (drum´uk): var. of *drammock*.

drury (drōō´ri): short for the Drury Lane theater.

druxy (druk´si): having decayed spots in the heartwood—applied to timber.

dryades (drī´a.dēz) (pl. of *dryas*): in Greek mythology, wood nymphs whose life is bound to that of their trees.

Duat (dōō´at): in Egyptian mythology, one of the abodes of the dead.

duction (duk´shun): the act of leading.

ductor (duk´ter): one that leads.

dudder (dud´er): to shiver; tremble. 2. To confuse with noise, bewilder. 44C.

duddyfunk (dud´i.fungk): a pie made of beef, lamb, or venison, and salt pork and ground cloves. 37A.

dulcamara (dul´ka.mā´ra): the bittersweet, or deadly nightshade, a sprawling, poisonous Old World plant that in America is a weed.

dulce (duls): sweet; sweetness; to sweeten. 1.

dulcifluous (dul.sif´lōō.us): sweet-flowing. 52.

dulciloquy (dul.sil´o.kwi): a soft manner of speaking. 1.

dulcorate (dul´ko.rāt): to sweeten. 1.

dulia (dū.lī´a): lesser kind of veneration or worship, given to the angels and saints as the servants and friends of God.

dumba (dum´ba): a fat-tailed sheep of Bukhara and the Kirghiz steppe, which furnishes astrakhan.

dumbledor (dum´bl.dôr): a dorbeetle or bumblebee.

dumose, dumous (dū´mōs, -mus): bushy.

duomachy (dū.om´a.ki): single combat.

dup (dup): to open. 1.

duplify (dū´pli.fī): to make double.

dynamis (dī´na.mis): in Aristotelianism, a state not yet fully realized; potentiality.

dynamitard (dī´na.mi.tärd): a dynamiter.

Dyophysite (dī.of´i.sīt): one who maintains that Christ was at once fully divine and fully human.

dysania (di.sā´ni.a): difficulty in waking up.

dysbulia (dis.bōō´li.a): loss of will-power.

dysgenics (dis.jen´iks): the science dealing with hereditary deterioration.

PERHAPS HE PREFERS FISHES

A Fish dreamed the sea had turned dry as the shore,
And rendered his species extinct.
A Man dreamed he'd entered his office discinct,
And his trousers had dropped to the floor.

So they prayed. If one prays just as hard as one can,
God is certain to answer one's wish.
With lungs He augmented the gills of the Fish—
With suspenders, the belt of the Man.

Two splendid advances! Why then did He plan
Fame for one—and t'other one squish? . . .
For we all know the Fish is the Dipnoous Fish,
But who knows the name of the Man?

---

dyslogistic (dis´lo.jis´tik): unfavorable—opposed to *eulogistic*.

dysmorphophobia (dis´môr.fo.fō´bi.a): dread of misshapenness.

dyspathy (dis´pa.thi): the opposite of sympathy; antipathy.

dysphemism (dis´fi.mizm): the substi-

tution of an offensive for an inoffensive word—opposed to *euphemism*.

dysthymic (dis.thim´ik): chronically sad or depressed.

dystomic (dis.tom´ik): difficult to split, as certain rocks.

dystopia (dis.tō´pi.a): the disagreeable opposite of utopia.

dystychiphobia (dis.tik.i.fō´bi.a): fear of accidents.

dzo (dzō): a hybrid between the yak and the domestic cow.

E

ean (ēn): to give birth; *yean*.

eanling (ēn´ling): a young lamb or kid.

ebenezer (eb.en.ē´zer): a memorial stone. A dissenting chapel.

eboe (ē´bō): a Central American tree, the roots of which yield eboe oil.

ebriection (eb´ri.ek´shun): a breakdown from overdrink.

ebrious (ē´bri.us): tending to overimbibe; slightly drunk.

ebullism (eb´ul.izm): the bubbling of body fluids, resulting from a sudden reduction of air pressure.

eburnean (i.bur´ni.an): resembling ivory in color.

ecbactic (ek.bak´tik): in grammar, denoting a mere result or consequence, as distinguished from *telic*, denoting intention or purpose.

ecballium (ek.bal´i.um): the squirting cucumber.

ecce (ek´si, ek´i): (Latin *see, behold*); used to call attention, often to one persecuted unjustly, as in *Ecce Homo*.

ecdemic (ek.dem´ik): not endemic; of a foreign cause.

echinidan (e.kin´i.dan): a sea urchin.

echopraxia (ek´o.prak´si.a): a habit of repeating the actions of other people.

ecmnesia (ek.nē´zhi.a): loss of the memory of a recent period, with retention of earlier memories.

ecofreak (ē´ko.frēk): a fervent conservationist or environmentalist. 21.

ecomania (ē´ko.mā´ni.a): humility toward superiors combined with arrogance toward one's own family.

ecophobia (ē´ko.fō´bi.a): fear of home.

ectal (ek´tal): exterior; outer.

ectoentad (ek´to.en´tad): from without inward.

ectogenesis (ek´to.jen´i.sis): development outside the body, esp. of a mammalian embryo in an artificial environment.

ectophyte (ek´to.fīt): a vegetable parasite that lives on the exterior of animals.

edaphology (ed´a.fol´o.ji): the science of soils.

Eddaic, Eddic (e.dā′ik, ed′ik): referring to the Old Norse Edda, a 13th century collection of mythology and heroic and gnomic songs.

eddish (ed′ish): aftermath, stubble. 13.

edea (e.dē′a): the external genitals.

edentulous (i.den′tū.lus): toothless.

edipol (ed′i.pōl): a mild oath; any common asseveration.

educt (ē′dukt): something which is educed, as by analysis. In chemistry, a substance separated from material in which it has already existed.

edulcoration (i.dul′ko.rā′shun): the act of sweetening.

efflation (e.flā′shun): an emanation; a puff; blowing or puffing. 52.

effleurage (ef′ler.äzh): a gentle stroking movement used in massage and lovemaking.

effulge (e.fulj′): to shine forth, radiate.

egotheism (ē′go.thi.izm): self-deification.

egredouce (eg′re.dōōs): a sweet-and-sour sauce. Formerly, a rabbit curry.

eidograph (ī′do.graf): a kind of pantograph.

eigne (ān): the firstborn, eldest, heir-apparent.

Eir (âr): in Norse religion, the goddess of healing.

eirenicon (ī.ren′i.kon): *irenicon*.

eisegesis (ī′se.jē′sis): misinterpretation of a text by reading into it one's own ideas.

ejoo (i.jōō′): the Malay *gomuti*, also a feather palm; also its wiry fiber.

ejulation (ej.ū.lā′shun): lamentation. 1.

ejuration (ej.ū.rā′shun): renunciation, repudiation.

ekka (ek′a): in India, a native one-horse carriage.

elapid, elapine (el′a.pid, el′a.pīn, -pin): pert. to a family of front-fanged venomous snakes inc. the cobras, mambas, and coral snakes.

elaterium (el′a.tēr′i.um): a purgative substance precipitated as a fine powder from the juice of the squirting cucumber.

eld (eld): age; old age. Old times; antiquity; an old person. 9.

electicism (e.lek′ti.sizm): eclecticism. 52.

electropathic (i.lek′tro.path′ik): electrotherapeutic.

elegiambic (el′e.ji.am′bik): pert. to a type of verse in classical Greek and Latin poetry.

eleutheromania (i.lū′ther.o.mā′ni.a): frantic zeal for freedom.

ellagic (e.laj′ik): pert. to or designating a crystallinic acid found in beozar stones, oak galls, etc.

elogy (el′o.ji): an inscription, esp. on a tombstone; a funeral oration. 1. A characterization or biographical sketch, esp. in praise. 9.

elusory (i.lōō′so.ri): pert. to an attempt to elude.

elute (i.lūt): to wash out.

elydoric (el′i.dō′rik): pert. to painting that combines oil and watercolor.

embolalia (em′bo.lā′li.a): habitual utterance of nonsense.

embracery (em.brās′er.i): in law, an attempt to influence a court, jury, etc., corruptly, by promises, money, threats, entertainments, etc.

eme (ēm): an uncle. Also, a friend; a gossip. 11.

emerods (em′er.odz): hemorrhoids. 9.

emgalla (em.gal′a): the South American warthog.

emmenology (em′i.nol′o.ji): the branch of medical science that deals with menstruation.

empasm (em.pazm′): deodorant powder.

emphractic (em.frak′tik): closing the pores of the skin. In medicine, an emphractic agent.

emphyteutic (em′fi.tū′tik): in civil law, relating to a land grant made subject to keeping up the land, paying annual rent, or other conditions.

emplastic (em.plas′tik): adhesive; also, costive.

empleomania (em.plē′o.mā′ni.a): a violent desire to hold public office.

emporetical (em′po.ret′i.kal): pert. to trade or merchandise; emporeutic. Also, merchandise.

emporeutic (em′po.rōō′tik): pert. to trade or merchandising.

emption (emp′shun): in law, a buying; purchase.

emptor (emp′tôr): a purchaser or buyer.

empyreumatic (em′pi.rōō.mat′ik): having the peculiar smell of organic substances burned in close vessels.

emuscation (i.mus.kā′shun): the act of freeing from moss. 1.

enantiosis (en.an′ti.ō′sis): in rhetoric, a negative statement of what is to be understood affirmatively, or vice versa.

enatation (en′a.tā′shun): escape by swimming.

enation (i.nā′shun): kinship on the mother's side.

encephaloid (en.sef′a.loid): like the brain in form or structure. An encephaloid cancer.

encrinic (en.krin′ik): pert. to, or made up of enclinites, as certain limestones; encrinal.

endocoele (en′do.sēl): the primitive digestive sac of certain embryos.

endogamy (en.dog′a.mi): marriage within the tribe, caste, or social group; inbreeding.

endogen (en′do.jen): a plant that grows from the inside out.

endometric (en′do.met′rik): pert. to the measurement of the interior of a cavity.

endothecal (en′do.thē′kal): pert. to the interior tissue of the interseptal chambers of most stony corals.

enew (e.nū′): to plunge (a fowl) into water. 1.

engastration (en.gas.trā′shun): the art of stuffing one fowl inside another.

VIRTUE TRIUMPHS AGAIN

A fair entellus in a banyan swung,
By tail secured, and by her faith in Brahma.
(Entellesus are sacred beasts among
The simple folk out there in Sutra Khama.)
That she was lissom, virtuous, and young
Made her estiverous for blissom male
Entelluses who ogled as she hung,
And called her to descend, to no avail.

Those rammish males, their dreams epithymastic,
Their hips extorsive, pranced, and cried ''Evoe!''
Till, whelmed by exundation orgiastic,
They fell afaint beneath the banyan tree,
And lay unmoving after all that ruckus—
If not exanimous, at least exsuccous.

---

engastrimyth (en.gas′tri.mith): a ventriloquist. 1.

enissophobia (en.is′o.fō′bi.a): fear of being reproached.

enneaeteric (en.i.a.ter′ik): occurring every eighth or ninth year, depending on how you count.

enneatic (en′i.at′ik): occurring once in every nine times; every ninth.

ennomic (en.nom′ik): lawful.

enoptromancy (en.op′tro.man′si): divination by means of a mirror.

enosiophobia (en.o′si.o.fō′bi.a): fear of having committed an unpardonable sin.

enquete (en.ket′): in France, an inquiry, investigation.

ens, ense (ens): else. 44.

ensky (en.skī′): to make immortal.

ensynopticity (en′sin.op.tis.i.ti): the capacity to take a general view.

entad (en′tad): inward; toward the center.

ental (en′tal): inner; opposed to *ectal*.

entellus (en.tel′us): an East Indian long-tailed monkey regarded as sacred by the natives.

enteropathogenic (en′ter.o.path′o.jen.-ik): producing intestinal disease.

entheomania (en′thi.o.mā′ni.a): the unfounded conviction that one is divinely inspired.

entomoid (en′to.moid): resembling an insect. 52.

entomolite (en.tom′o.līt): a fossil insect-like animal.

entopic (en.top′ik): in anatomy, occurring in the usual place.

entortillation (en.tôr′ti.lā′shun): turning in a circle.

entotic (en.tō′tik): pert. to the interior of the ear.

enurny (en.ur′ni): in heraldry, a bordure charged with beasts.

eoan (i.ō′an): pert. to the dawn or the east.

eonism (ē′on.izm): the tendency to adopt the mental attitudes, habits, and costume of the other sex.

eosophobia (i.os′o.fō′bi.a): the fear of dawn.

Eozoic (ē′o.zō′ik): in geology, pre-Cambrian, Proterozoic, or Algonkin.

epagoge (ep′a.gog): logical induction from all the particulars implied under the inferred generalization. Induction by simple enumeration.

epanadiplosis (ep.an′a.di.plō′sis): in rhetoric, use of a word both at the beginning and the end of a sentence.

epanalepsis (ep.an′a.lep′sis): in rhetoric, a repetition; echo.

epanorthosis (ep.an′ôr.thō′sis): the substitution of a more emphatic word or phrase for one just preceding it.

epanthous (ep.an′thus): growing on flowers; said of certain fungi.

ephectic (ef.ek′tik): given to suspension of judgment.

ephemeromorph (i.fem′er.o.môrf): a low form of life intermediate between an animal and a plant.

epiblema (ep′i.blē′ma): among the ancient Greeks, an outer garment; shawl.

epicede (ep′i.sēd): a funeral song or ode. A dirge; elegy.

epideictic (ep′i.dīk′tik): designed primarily for rhetorical effect.

epidermophytosis (ep′i.dur′mo.fī.tō′sis): athlete's foot.

epigamic (ep′i.gam′ik): tending to attract the opposite sex during the breeding season, as the *epigamic* coloration of a bird.

epigean (ep′i.jē′an): living close to the ground, as some insects.

epilate (ep′i.lāt): to remove hair.

epimyth (ep′i.mith): the moral of a story.

epinaos (ep′i.nā′os): a room or vestibule in the rear of a Greek temple.

epinician (ep′i.nish′un): celebrating victory; as, an *epinician* ode.

epiphoric (ep′i.fôr′ik): relating to the watering of the eyes.

epiphytic (ep′i.fit′ik): pert. to or like an epiphyte, a plant that grows upon others, but is not parasitic.

epiplexis (ep′i.plek′sis): in rhetoric, an upbraiding.

epipolic (ep′i.pol′ik): in optics, fluorescent.

episematic (ep′i.se.mat′ik): designating certain markings that assist individ-

uals of the same species in recognizing each other.

epistemophilia (i.pis′ti.mo.fil′i.a): obsession with knowledge.

epitaxis, epitaxy (ep′i.tak′sis, -si): the oriented growth of one crystalline substance on a substrate of a different crystalline substance.

epithymetic (ep′i.thi.met′ik): pert. to desire; sensual.

epitonic (ep′i.ton′ik): overstrained.

epulotic (ep′ū.lot′ik): having healing power.

epuration (ep′ū.rā′shun): the act of purifying.

equaeval (i.kwē′val): of equal age.

equipendent (ek′wi.pen′dent): hanging in equipoise. 1.

equivorous (i.kwiv′o.rus): eating horseflesh.

eral (ēr′al): pert. to an era. 52.

eremic (i.rē′mik): pert. to desert or sandy regions.

eremophobia (er′e.mo.fō′bi.a): fear of loneliness.

ereption (i.rep′shun): a snatching away.

ergal (ur′gal): in physics, potential energy.

ergasiophobia (er.gas′i.o.fō′bi.a): fear of work; ergophobia.

ergatocracy (ur′ga.tok′ra.si): government by workers.

ergophile (ur′go.fīl): one who loves work.

ergophobia (ur′go.fō′bi.a): a strong aversion to work. *Ergasiophobia.*

eria (ā′ri.a, ē′ri.a): the Assam silkworm, which feeds on the castor-oil plant.

eric (er′ik): in old Irish law, a blood fine.

Erica (er′i.ka): a genus of low evergreen shrubs, the true heaths. (not cap) A plant of this genus.

erinaceous (er′i.nā′shus): pert. to the hedgehog.

erminois (ur′mi.noiz): in heraldry, spots of black ermine fur on a golden field.

eroduction (ē′ro.duk′shun): a pornographic motion picture.

erostrate (i.ros′trāt): beakless.

eroteme (er′o.tēm): a mark indicating a question, as (?).

erotesis (er′o.tē′sis): interrogation for rhetorical effect.

erotographomania (i.rō′to.graf′o.mā′-ni.a): an irresistible impulse to write love letters.

erotology (ē′ro.tol′o.ji): the study of love.

errabund (er′a.bund): wandering; erratic.

erugate (er′ū.gāt): without wrinkles; smooth.

Eryngium (i.rin′ji.um): a genus of

coarse bristly herbs having white or blue flowers in dense heads.

erythrophobia (i.rith′ro.fō′bi.a): fear of redness or blushing.

eschrolalia (es′kro.lā′li.a): dirty language.

esclandre (es.klän′dr): notoriety; a disgraceful occurrence or scene.

esclavage (es′kla.väzh): a necklace resembling 18th-century slave chains.

escribe (i.skrīb′, es.krīb′): to copy out. 1. To draw (a circle) touching one side of a triangle externally and the other two sides internally.

escrime (es.krēm): fencing.

escudero (es′kōō.thā′rō): a shield-bearer.

esemplastic (es′em.plas′tik): unifying.

esquamate (es.kwā′māt): having no scales.

esquisse (es.kēs′): a preliminary sketch or model.

essling (es′ling): a young salmon. 13.

essoin (e.soin′): an excuse for not appearing in court. To excuse (one) for nonappearance.

esssse (esh′i): ashes. 1.

estafette (es′ta.fet): a mounted courier.

estiferous (es.tif′er.us): producing heat.

estive (es′tiv): pert. to summer; hot. 1.

estoile (es.toil′, -twäl): a star conventionally represented in heraldry, usu. with six wavy points.

estrade (es.träd′, -trād′): a dais.

estrapade (es′tra.pād): the attempt of a horse to get rid of its rider by rearing, plunging, etc.

estuous (es′tū.us): excited, passionate, agitated.

et (et): dial. past tense and past participle of *eat.*

eteostic (et′i.os′tik): a chronogram. 1.

ethal (eth′al, ē′thal): cetyl alcohol.

ethel (eth′el): ancestral land. 6. The *atle.*

ettle (et′l): to plan, try, design. 11. Nettle. 11. An intent; chance. 44.

euania (ū.ā′ni.a): ease of waking up in the morning.

eugenesis (ū.jen′i.sis): fertility between hybrids.

euhemeristic (ū.hem′er.is′tik): pert. to the interpretation of myths as traditional accounts of historical personages and events.

eumorphous (u.môr′fus): well-formed.

euneirophrenia (ū.nī′ro.frē′ni.a): peace of mind after a pleasant dream.

euodic (ū.od′ik): aromatic.

euphelicia (ū.fe.lis′i.a): well-being resulting from having all one's wishes granted.

euphobia (ū.fō′bi.a): fear and hatred of what is good.

euphon (ū′fon): euphonic.

euphone (ū′fōn): a free-reed organ stop, giving a soft expressive tone.

eurethrophobia (ū.rē′thro.fō′bi.a): fear of blushing.

euripize (ū.ri.pīz): to fluctuate.

Euroclydon (ū.rok′li.don): a strong cold northeast wind of the Mediterranean.

eurycephalic (ū′ri.si.fal′ik): brachycephalic with a cephalic index from .80 to .84.

euthermic (ū.thur′mik): inducing warmth.

eutrophied (ū′tro.fid): polluted.

evagation (ē′va.ga′shun, ev′a.-): mental wandering; digression.

evasé (ā′va.zā): enlarging gradually, as a chimney, funnel, etc.

Evernia (i.vur′ni.a): a genus of lichens. (not cap) Any lichen of this genus.

evertor (i.vur′ter): a muscle that rotates a part outward.

eviration (ē′vi.rā′shun): castration. 1.

evoe (e.vē′, i.vē′): an exclamation expressing exhilaration; the cry of bacchanals.

evolation (ev.o.lā′shun): a flying out or up. 1.

evulgate (i.vul′gāt): to publish, divulge.

ewery (ū.er.i): a room for pitchers, basins, towels, etc.

exagitation (ek.saj′i.tā′shun): a stirring up; agitation; harassment. 1.

exanimous (eg.zan′i.mus): lifeless.

exaugurate (eg.zôg′ū.rāt): to unhallow; desecrate.

excalceate (eks.kal′si.āt): to unshoe. 52.

excerebrose (ek.ser′i.brōs): brainless.

excide (ek′sīd′): to cut out, excise.

excircle (eks.sur′kl): in mathematics, an enscribed circle.

excogitation (eks.koj′i.tā′shun): a contrivance; the act of inventing or contriving.

excursus (eks.kur′sus): an appendix to a work, containing a more extended exposition of some point or topic. A digression; an incidental discussion.

excuss (eks.kus′): to shake off or out; discard. To investigate. 1. In civil law, to proceed against (a principal debtor) before falling back on a surety.

exergue (eg.zurg′, ek′surg): on a coin or medal, the segment beneath the base line of the subject, often with the date, place, or engraver's name.

exfodiate (eks.fō′di.āt): to dig out.

exheredate (eks.her′i.dāt): to disinherit.

exinanition (eg.zin′a.nish′un): an emptying, enfeeblement, humiliation, abasement.

exobiology (ek′so.bī.ol′o.ji): the study of life outside the earth.

exoculate (eg.zok′ū.lāt): to blind; to deprive of eyes.

exodic (eg.zod′ik): in physiology, conveying outward, or discharging; efferent.

exodromic (ek′so.drom′ik): relating to the movement of exchange between two countries designed to stabilize or fix the rates.

exogen (ek′so.jen): a plant that grows from the outside in.

exolve (eg.zolv): to slacken, diminish. 1.

exophagy (eg.zof′a.ji): cannibalism outside the tribe.

exorganic (eks′ôr.gan′ik): having lost organic character.

exornation (ek′sôr.nā′shun): an ornament, decoration.

exotropic (ek′so.trop′ik): curved away from the main axis.

expergefaction (eks.pur′ji.fak′shun): an awakening; the state of being awakened.

experientialism (eks.pēr′i.en′shal.izm): the doctrine that experience is the source of all knowledge.

expiscate (eks.pis′kāt): to search out; to investigate skillfully.

expromission (eks′pro.mish′un): in law, the act of binding oneself for another's debt.

expurger (eks.pur′jer): one that expurges; expurgater.

exsect (ek.sekt′): to cut out.

exsiccant (ek′si.kant): drying up; causing to dry up.

exspuition (eks′pū.ish′un): the act of spitting. 52.

exsuccous (eks.suk′us): dry, sapless.

extersion (eks.tur′shun): the act of wiping or rubbing out. 1.

extorsion (eks.tôr′shun): outward rotation (as of a body part) about an axis or fixed part.

extraforaneous (eks′tra.fo.rā′ni.us): outdoor.

extravagate (eks.trav′a.gāt): to rove; to exceed normal limits; to elaborate.

extusion (eks.tū′zhun): the act of beating or forcing (something) out. 52.

exuberous (eg.zū′ber.us): exuberant.

exundation (eks′un.dā′shun): an overflowing. 52.

eyot (ī′ut, āt): an islet.

F

faba (fā′ba): a genus of leguminous plants comprising the broad bean.

fabaceous (fa.bā′shus): of the nature of, or like, a bean.

fabular (fab′ū.lar): pert. to a fable.

fabulate (fab′ū.lāt): to fable. 1.

facette (fa.set′): facetious; witty. 9. Polished; elegant. 1.

facient (fā′shent): one that does something; a doer, agent.

factive (fak′tiv): making; having power to make. 1.

factum (fak′tum): in law, a man's own act and deed. The due execution of a will; a fact; event.

facundity (fa.kun′di.ti): eloquence.

fadge (faj): wheaten or barley flat cake. 45. A round thick loaf of bread. 44A. Potato cake or bread. 50A. A heavy package of wool. 53.

fadger (faj′er): one who or that which thrives or succeeds by fitting to surroundings. 9.

faff (faf): to blow in puffs. 44.

faffle (faf′l): to stammer; to mumble; to saunter; to fumble; (of a sail) to flap lazily. 2.

faffy (faf′i): blowing in puffs; puffy. 43.

fagin (fā′gin): a teacher of crime.

fagotto (fa.got′ō): a bassoon. An eight-foot pipe-organ stop of the same general quality as a bassoon.

faham (fä′am, fā′am): the leaves of an orchid used (in France) as a substitute for Chinese tea; also, the plant.

fainague, finagle (fi.nāg′, fi.nā′gl): to revoke at cards; hence, to shrink, to cheat.

falcade (fal.kād′): in equitation, the action of a horse in throwing itself on its haunches two or three times, bending in quick curvets.

faldistory (fal.dis′tō.ri): the throne or seat of a bishop within the chancel.

fallowchat (fal′o.chat): a wheatear.

falx (falks): a fold of the inner surface enveloping the brain.

Fama (fā′ma): rumor, personified.

famble (fam′bl): to stutter. 2.

familistere (fa.mē′li.stâr): a house for communal living.

famulus (fam′ū.lus): the servant of a medieval scholar or magician.

fangle (fang′gl): a silly or foolish contrivance; a gewgaw. 1.

fanion (fan′yun): a small flag orig. used by horse brigades, now by soldiers and surveyors to mark positions.

fantoccini (fan′to.chē′ni): puppets moved by machinery, or the shows in which they are used.

fantocine (fan′to.sēn): a puppet.

fard (färd): paint; to paint, as with cosmetics. Also, a kind of date tree.

fardh (färd): a commercial variety of date.

farkleberry (fär′kl.ber′i): a multi-seeded blackberry bush.

farraginous (fa.raj′i.nus): formed of various materials; mixed; hotchpotch. 52.

CARPING NOTE TO A THOUGHTFUL MAN

You whose joy is intellect 'll
Stare when I admit I'm ectal—
Must consider one inferior
Who's confined to his exterior,
Stretching, yawning, dozing, laughing,
Singing, dancing, kissing, quaffing,
Doing push-ups—quite neglecting
The rewards of intellecting.

You are used to comrades ental,
Grave or gay, but ever mental.
Come a joke, they measure it
Less by humor than by wit—
Expiscating and explaining,
Probing, judging—ever braining.

Brain and bowel are entopic
(One on-top-ic, one more drop-ic);
Yet together they decay,
Mind and matter the same way.
When I hold no lover close,
You will be excerebrose.

Maybe you are right to trust
That the dream defies the dust—
Books are all about to show it.
But the dust will never know it.

---

farruca (fa.rōōk′a): a Spanish gypsy dance having sudden changes of mood and tempo.

fascine (fa.sēn′): a long bundle of sticks, used for filling ditches, etc. To cover or strengthen with fascines.

fascis (fas′is): a bundle.

fash (fash): to vex; annoy. 43A.

fasset (fas′et): in glass manufacturing, a tool used to carry bottles to the annealing furnace.

fastigate (fas′ti.gāt): pointed.

fastigium (fas.tij′i.um): apex; summit; specif., the ridge of a house.

fatiferous (fa.tif′er.us): destructive; deadly.

fatiscent (fa.tis′ent): chinky. 52.

favaginous (fa.vaj′i.nus): like a honeycomb.

favilliferous (fav′il.if′er.us): producing lava.

favillous (fa.vil′us): of or resembling ashes.

feak (fēk): a lock of hair. 1. To twitch, fidget. 11. In falconry, to wipe (the hawk's beak) after feeding.

feal (fēl): faithful; loyal. 9.

februation (feb′rōō.ā′shun): exorcism; religious purification.

feck (fek): efficacy; force; value. 43. Amount; quantity. 44D.

feeze (fēz): to drive, impel, drive away, put to flight; to disturb, worry; to beat; rush; rub; a short run before a jump. 2. Fretful excitement or alarm. 27. To turn, as a screw. 44C. A heavy impact. 57.

feil (fēl): neat and cozy; comfortable. 44A.

feldspathic, felspathic (feld.spath′ik, fel.spath′ik): containing feldspar.

fellic (fel′ik): pert. to a crystalline acid present in human bile.

fellifluous (fe.lif′lōō′us): flowing with gall. 52.

fellness (fel′nes): destructive cruelty.

felloe, felly (fel′ō, -i): the exterior rim of a wheel, or part of it.

femcee (fem.sē′): a female emcee.

femerell (fem′er.el): a small open structure on a roof (as of a medieval kitchen) for ventilation or escape of smoke. 9.

feminate (fem′i.nāt): feminine; effeminate. 1.

fendy (fen′di): clever in providing; thrifty. 11.

feneration (fen′er.ā′shun): lending on interest. 1.

fenestella (fen′es.tel′a): a small window.

fenestral (fi.nes′tral): a window sash closed with cloth or translucent paper instead of glass. 9. Windowlike.

fent (fent): a remnant of cloth; an imperfect piece of goods. A slit or opening in a garment, esp. a neck opening. 13.

fenting (fen′ting): a type of Chinese porcelain with a soft-looking white glaze.

feracious (fi.rā′shus): fruitful; fertile.

feratory (fer′a.tō′ri): a bier. 52. A generally ornate bier for the relics of saints.

ferd (furd): an army; a large number; fear. 1.

fere (fēr): a mate, companion. 10. A peer. 1. To accompany; mate. 1. Sympathetic; companionable. 11. Able; healthy. 5.

feriation (fēr′i.ā′shun): the keeping of a holiday, esp. by not working.

ferly (fur′li): a sudden, surprising, or unusual sight; a marvel; an eccentricity, foible. 2. To amaze; wonder. 2.

fermentor (fer.men′ter): an apparatus for fermenting.

ferrumination (fe.rōō′mi.nā′shun): the act of soldering or uniting, as metals.

ferulaceous (fer′ōō.lā′shus): reedlike.

fervescent (fer.ves′ent): growing hot or feverish.

festilogy (fes.til′o.ji): historically, a treatise on church festivals.

festinate (fes′ti.nāt): to hasten. In a hurry. 52.

festine, festino (fes.tēn′, -tē′nō): a feast; entertainment.

festspiel (fest′shpēl): a festival play.

festuca (fes.tōō′ka): a large genus of grasses, the fescues. Among the Franks, a rod or staff given as a symbol to bind a contract.

fet (fet): to fetch. 11.

feu (fū): in Scots law, a fee; a tenure where the return is made in grain or money. Land so held. To grant (land) upon feu.

feudee (fū.dē′): a feudal tenant. 52.

fibble-fabble, fibble-fable (fib′l.fab′l, -fā′bl): nonsense. 11.

fibriphobia (fib′ri.fō′bi.a): fear of fever.

ficelle (fi.sel′): a device, trick. 21. Thread-colored. 2.

fiche (fēsh): a card; ticket; label.

fico (fē′kō): a fig. Also, a sign of contempt made by the fingers, signifying "a fig for you." 1.

fictor (fik′ter. -tor): one who fashions or shapes, esp. an artist. 1.

fiddleback (fid′l.bak): anything conceived of as shaped like a fiddle.

fideicommissum (fī′di.ko.mis′um): a bequest in which a decedent asks his heir to turn over a portion of the estate to another.

fidge (fij): an uneasy or restless motion or person. 44B. To fidget, esp. in eagerness or anxiety. 11.

fidicinal (fi.dis′i.nal): pert. to stringed instruments.

fidicula (fi.dik′ū.la): a small lyre-like stringed instrument; a lute.

fifinella (fif.i.nel′a): a female gremlin.

figulate (fig′ū.lat): made or molded of potter's clay. 52.

fike (fīk): to fidget; fuss; flirt. 45. To trouble; vex. 44. A whimsey; trifle. 43.

filaceous (fi.lā′shus): composed of threads. 52.

filicology (fil.i.kol′o.ji): *pteriodology*.

filiopietistic (fil′i.o.pī′e.tis′tik): pert. to ancestor worship.

filippo (fi.lip′po): a silver scudo struck at Milan by the Spanish under Philips II, III, and IV (1556–1665).

fillock (fil′uk): a wanton girl. 1.

fimble (fim′bl): the male hemp plant; its fiber. Also, to feel with the fingers moving lightly over (anything). 11.

fimbricate (fim′bri.kāt): fringed.

fimetarious (fim′i.târ′i.us): growing or living in excrement.

finewed (fin′ūd): moldy.

fingent (fin′jent): fashioning; molding.

finick (fin′ik): to mince; put on airs; dawdle.

finific (fi.nif′ik): to Coleridge, a limiting element or quality.

finitive (fin′i.tiv): in grammar, terminative.

fioritura (fyō.ri.tōō′ra): in music, an embellishment (usu. in pl., *fioriture*).

firk (furk): a freak; trick; a smart stroke, lash; to help, drive; to hasten, be frisky. 1. To beat; conquer. 9. To move jerkily; fidget. 14.

fiscus (fis′kus): the public treasury of Rome; esp. the branch that was most under imperial control.

fishgarth (fish′gärth): a dam or weir for keeping or taking fish.

Fissipedia (fis′i.pē′di.a): a suborder of Carnivora, including the land carnivores, as the dogs, cats, and bears.

fistiana (fis′ti.an′a): pugilistic anecdotes, records, etc.

fistuca (fis.tōō′ka): an instrument used by the ancients in driving piles.

fitchery (fich′er.i): (in mining) obstructive; containing an obstacle, or itself constituting one—said of ground in which a drill sticks.

fitchet (fich′et): the polecat of Europe.

flabrum (flā′brum): a fan; flabellum.

flacket (flak′et): a barrel-shaped bottle; flagon. 5.

flaminical (fla.min′i.kal): in Roman religion, pert. to a flamen—a priest devoted to the service of a particular god.

flammifer (flam′i.fer): something producing flame.

flammulated (flam′ū.lāt.ed): rusty, reddish.

flanch (flanch): a flange, esp. of a wheel. 41.

flanconnade (flang′ko.nād): in fencing, a maneuver ending in a thrust under the adversary's arm.

flatulopetic (flat′ū.lo.pet′ik): pert. to flatulence.

flaught (flôt): a flake; a flash of fire; a bit of wool or hair; turf. 44D. Flight; flutter; lying flat, with outstretched arms, eagerly. 44.

flavicomous (fla.vik′o.mus): having yellow hair.

fleam (flēm): a sharp lancet used for bloodletting. A stream, esp. a millstream.

---

*FLAVICOMOUS, AURICOMOUS
BY ANY OTHER NAME . . .*

Her lambent gaze came up, a full moon rising;
   And venturing the path of light it shed,
He touched and held her. (This is not surprising—
   Less moon drew Oceanus from his bed.)

Yet not of love triumphant is my story;
   I speak that other lovers may beware
Of giving to a woman's crowning glory
   A name that she has never heard for hair.

I know 'twas but the color he referred to,
   The while his fingers ran in worship through it;
But I suspect he really used the word to
   Impress her by displaying that he knew it.

He whispered that her tresser were *flavicomous* . . .
   She shuddered, and the moon grew sick and wan.
Then tenderly he labelled them *auricomous* . . .
   Down went the moon. She ordered him begone.

The moral of this sad account, young fellow,
   Is, *women like to ken what they are told.*
Why didn't he just say her hair was *yellow?*—
   Or (oh, she would have loved to hear it) *gold?*

---

flect (flekt): in heraldry, short for *flected*, bent-bowed.

fleech (flēch): coaxing; flattery. 44.

fleed, flead (flēd): the inside fat of a hog before it is melted into lard.

flench, flense (flench, flens): to strip the skin or blubber from (as a whale or seal).

flender (flen′der): to go fast. 35.

flerry (fler′i): to split—said of slate.

flet (flet): made from skimmed milk. 13. A plaited straw mat to protect the back of a packhorse. 44.

fleur (flur): the fleur-de-lys. An ornamental flower. A patterned woolen stuff like a Brussels carpet.

flexanimous (fleks.an′i.mus): mentally flexible.

flexiloquy (fleks.il′o.kwi): ambiguity of speech.

flittern (flit′ern): a young oak. 11.

floccilation (flok′si.lā′shun): an aimless semiconscious plucking at the bedclothes.

floccose (flok′ōs, flō.kōs′): woolly, flocculent. Of plants, having tufts of soft, woolly, often deciduous hairs.

flong (flong): a sheet of specially prepared paper used for making a matrix or mold.

flōta (flō′ta): a fleet of Spanish ships that sailed every year from Cadiz to Vera Cruz in Mexico to obtain the products of the Spanish colonies for Spain.

fluminous (flōō′mi.nus): pert. to rivers; also, abounding in rivers and streams.

flump (flump): to set, move, or fall suddenly and heavily.

flustrum (flus′trum): fluster. 52.

flutina (flōō.tē′na): a small musical instrument resembling the accordion.

fnast (fnast): breath; to pant. 1.

fnese (fnēz): to breathe heavily, snore. 1.

fogle (fō′gl): a silk handkerchief or neckerchief.

foliole (fō′li.ōl): a plant leaflet. In zoology, a small leaf-shaped organ or part.

follis (fol′is): a silver-coated Roman coin of the late Empire. A large bronze Byzantine coin of the 6th century.

fomento (fo.men′tō): patronage; encouragement.

fono (fō′nō): a Samoan council, the central political structure of a village, district, or island.

foozle (fōō′zl): a bungler. To bungle, as a golf shot. 26.

fopdoodle (fop′dōō.dl): a fool, an insignificant wretch. 1.

foraminous (fo.ram′i.nus): having small openings; porous.

foraneous (fo.rā′ni.us): pert. to a law court or a market.

forel, forrel (for′el): a sheath, a case. 4. A book jacket.

forisfamiliate (fō′ris.fa.mil′i.āt): to disinherit; to shed parental authority.

forlie (for.lī′): to deflower, to commit fornication or adultery. 1.

forme (fôr′me): first; former. 1. A form of heraldic crown.

formeret (fôr′mer.et): a wall rib in a roof vaulted with ribs.

fornent, fornenst (fôr.nent′, -nenst′): in front of; opposite. Near to; alongside. 11A.

forset (for.set′): to beset; invest; waylay. 2.

forslack (for.slak′): to hinder or delay by laziness; to be remiss. 1.

forslug (for.slug′): to lose by sluggishness. 1.

fortalice (fôr′ta.lis): a small fort, or an outwork of a fortification.

fossette (fo.set′): a little hollow; a dimple.

fou (foo): var. of *foul, full.* 15A. A bushel. 44.

foud (foud): a magistrate, sheriff, or bailie in the Orkney, Shetland, and Faroe islands.

fouter, foutre (fōō′ter): a fig (a word of contempt). Something of little value. 9. A chap, fellow; an objectionable or tedious person; a worthless or bungling person. 44A.

foveola (fo.vē′o.la): a very small pit. In botany and embryology, a small depression.

fozy (fō′zi): of a vegetable, overgrown. Of a person, obese; also, fatheaded. 44A.

foziness (fō.zi.nes): sponginess; flabbiness; fat-wittedness; mugginess (of weather). 44D.

frab (frab): to scold, nag. 13.

fractile (frak′tīl, -til): fragile; also, of or pert. to fracture.

francisc (fran.sisk′): a battle-ax or hatchet used by the Franks, often as a missile.

franion (fran′yun): a paramour; a gay, idle fellow; a loose woman. 1.

frankalmoign (frangk′al.moin): a tenure in which a religious organization holds land on condition of praying for the souls of the donors.

frateries (frā′ter.iz): dining halls in monasteries.

frazil (fra.zil′, fraz′l, frā′zl): ice crystals within a body of water.

fream (frēm): to roar, as a boar in rut.

fremd (fremd): alien, strange, unfriendly. 2.

fremescence (fri.mes′ens): the state of being murmurous, or noisy. 52.

frescade (fres.kād′, -käd): a cool or shady place.

frett (fret): to prepare (materials for glass) by heat; to fuse partially.

frette (fret): a hoop of wrought iron or

steel, shrunk on a cast-iron gun to strengthen it.

fretum (frē′tum): a narrow waterway or canal.

friation (frī.ā′shun): act of breaking up or pulverizing.

fribby (frib′i): small; short—said of locks of wool.

fricandel (frik′an.del): a fried or boiled ball of minced meat mixed with bread crumbs, seasoning, and egg.

fricatrice (frik′a.tris): a lewd woman; a harlot. 52.

friggle (frig′l): to fuss. 13.

frim (frim): flourishing; thriving; juicy. 2.

fringent (frin′jent): (of uncertain meaning, used by Emerson in "a shower of meteors—lit by *fringent* air." Perh., as O.E.D. interprets, "exercising friction.")

fripper (frip′er): one who deals in frippery or old clothes. 1.

frist (frist): a delay. To grant a delay; to postpone. 1.

froise (froiz): a large, thick pancake, often with bacon in it. 2.

frondesce (fron.des′): to unfold leaves.

fronton (fron.ton′): a court or building for the game of jai alai or pelota.

frounce (frouns): curl, frizzle. 9. A disease of hawks, in which white spittle gathers about the bill. A disease of horses, marked by small warts on the palate.

fructescent (fruk.tes′ent): beginning to bear fruit. 52.

frugivore (fōō′ji.vôr): an animal, esp. a primate, that feeds on fruits.

frush (frush): the frog of a horse's hoof; the discharge from it. Thrush. Decayed to the point of brittleness; of soil, friable and mellow. 13. A din; a clash of weapons. 5. To rush. 1.

frustraneous (frus′trā′ni.us): vain, useless. 1.

fub (fub): a plump child. (var. of *fob*), to cheat. 1.

fubby, fubsy (fub′i, -si): plump; chubby: short and stuffy; as a *fubsy* sofa. 25A.

fucic (fū′sik): a gelatinous acid found in the fucoids and other algae.

fucivorous (fū.siv′o.rus): eating seaweeds.

fucous (fū′kus): pert. to the fucoids, a kind of seaweed.

fud (fud, food): the buttocks; the tail of a hare, rabbit, etc; woolen waste, for mixing with mungo and shoddy. 43.

fuff (fuf): puff; whiff; sputter. 43.

fuffit (fuf′it): the long-tailed titmouse.

fuffle (fuf′l): to be, or put, in disorder. 44.

fug (fug): reek. 21.

fugara (fōō.gä′ra): in music, a labial

organ stop of 8-foot or 4-foot pitch and of string quality.

fulgor (ful′ger): dazzling brightness; splendor.

fuligo (fū.lī′go): soot. Also, a widely distributed genus of slime molds.

fumacious (fū.mā′shus): smoky; hence, fond of smoking or addicted to tobacco.

fumado (fū.mā′dō): a salted and smoked pilchard.

fumage (fū′mij): hearth money. 6.

fumet, fumette (fū′met, fū.met′): a concentrated essence of game or fish, herbs, and spices used in flavoring a sauce.

fumid (fū′mid): smoky; vaporous. 1.

fumiduct (fū′mi.dukt): an outlet for smoke.

funambulist (fū.nam′bū.list): a tightrope walker.

fundatrix (fun.dāt′riks): a female aphid that founds a new colony.

fundi (fun′di): a tropical African grass cultivated for its millet-like seed.

AN INGLE IS AN INSIDE ANGLE

Seek out the Elbow Ingle,
Ye bride and benedick;
Ye lovers, wed or single,
Seek out the Elbow Ingle,
The tender of the Tingle,
The turner of the Wick—
The ready Elbow Ingle,
Where nerve and vein commingle . . .
Seek out the Elbow Ingle—
A touch will do the trick.

---

funebrious, funebrous (fū.nē′bri.us, -nē′brus): funereal. 1.

funest (fū.nest′): portending death or evil; fatal, dire, doleful.

funiform (fū′ni.fôrm): resembling a cord or rope.

furacious (fū.rā′shus): thievish.

furca (fur′ka): a fork; yoke; instrument of torture. Any forked structure in an insect.

furibund (fū′ri.bund): furious, frenzied.

furole (fū.rōl′): St. Elmo's fire. 52. Also, furfural, a colorless oily liquid.

furtum (fur′tum): in Latin, theft.

fusarole (fū′za.rōl): a rounded molding placed beneath the capital of a Doric, Ionic, or Corinthian column.

fusc (fusk): of dusky or somber hue. 52.

fust (fust): mustiness; to taste or smell moldy or stale. 13. The shaft of a column or pilaster. A wine cask. 1. Dial. var. of *first*.

fustanella (fus′ta.nel′a): a short full skirt of stiffened white linen or cotton worn by men in some Balkan countries.

fyrd (furd, fērd): prior to the Norman conquest, the English armed forces; the duty of serving in them.

G

ga (gä): Scottish var. of *gall*. Also, an obsolete system of denoting the tones of a musical scale.

gabelle (ga.bel′): a tax. Specif., an impost on salt, levied in France for several centuries prior to the French Revolution.

gaddi (gad′i): in India, a cushion, esp. for a throne; hence, a throne. (cap) One of a low-caste people of Kashmir, mostly shepherds.

gaffle (gaf′l): a steel lever to bend a crossbow. A musket fork or rest. 6.

gair (gâr): a corner section of unplowed ground. Sharp, eager, greedy. 43.

galactophogy (gal′ak.tof′o.ji): milkdrinking.

galactophygous (gal.′ak.tof′i.gus): arresting the secretion of milk.

Galanthus (ga.lan′thus): a small genus of European bulbous herbs, the snowdrops.

galapago (ga.lä′pa.gō): one of the huge land tortoises of the Galapagos islands. Also a short cape.

galba (gal′ba): corruption of *calaba*, an evergreen tropical American tree.

galea (gā′li.a): in ancient Rome, a helmet. In zoology, a helmetlike structure of certain birds; part of the membrane enveloping a fetus, etc. In botany, any helmet-shaped part of a calyx or corolla.

galeanthropy (gal′i.an′thro.pi): the delusion that one has become a cat.

galee (gal′i): in India, abuse.

galeeny (ga.lē′ni): a guinea fowl. 13.

galenic (ga.len′ik): pert. to galena, or lead sulphide. (cap) Pert. to Galen, a noted physician of ancient Rome.

galera (ga.lē′ra): the tayra, a long-tailed mammal of South and Central America, related to the weasel.

galericulate (gal.er.ik′u.lät): covered, as with a hat or cap.

galette (ga.let′): a flat, round pastry, usu. sweet. Also, a sea biscuit.

galipot (gal′i.pot): a crude turpentine formed by exudation upon the bark of the cluster pine in southern Europe.

Galium (gā′li.um): a genus of usu. trailing herbs, such as cleavers and wild licorice.

gallet (gal′et): a chip of stone; a spall. To fill in the fresh mortar joints of (rubble masonry) with gallets.

galliambic (gal′i.am′bik): in prosody, consisting of two iambic dimeters cataletic of which the last lacks the final syllable.

galliardise (gal′yer.diz): great merriment.

gallionic (gal′i.on′ik): indifferent; careless; irresponsible.

gallium (gal′i.um): a rare bluish white metallic element, obtained usu. as a byproduct in the extraction of aluminum from bauxite or of zinc from zinc ores.

gally (gôl′i): like gall; bitter as gall.

galp (gälp): a gaping. To yawn; to gape; to belch. 1.

galvanoplastic (gal′van.o.plas′tik, gal. van′o.-): employing the science of electroforming; something so formed.

gamashes (ga.mash′ez, gam′ash.-): leggings worn for protection by horsemen.

gambade (gam.bād′): a spring of a horse.

gamdeboo (gam′de.bōō): a South African tree having tough wood.

gambist (gam′bist): a performer on the viola da gamba.

gambrinous (gam.brī′nus): full of beer.

gambroon (ga.n.broon′): a twilled cloth of linen, of linen and wool, or wool alone.

gammacism (gam′a.sizm): difficulty in pronouncing gutturals *(g, k)*. Childish talk.

gammadion (ga.mā′di.on): a cross resembling the swastika, made of four capital gammas.

gamophagia (gam′o.fā′ji.a): the destruction of one gamete by the other during fertilization.

gamophobia (gam′o.fō′bi.a): fear of sexual union.

ganancial (ga.nan′shal): relating to the Spanish system of law, which controls the title and disposition of property acquired during marriage by the husband or wife.

ganch (ganch): to execute by impaling on stakes or hooks.

gange (ganj): to fasten a fishhook to a line; to protect the line nearest the fishhook by winding it with fine wire.

ganza (gan′za): one of the birds that (in a romance by Bp. F. Godwin) bore Domingo Gonsales to the moon. 52.

ganzie (gan′zi): waste cotton cloth used as a wiping material around machinery or as rags for making paper.

gapo (ga.pō′): a forest that borders a river and is inundated in rainy seasons.

garce (gärs): a measure of capacity or weight in India.

garden (gär.dēn′): guardian. 1.

gardyloo (gär′di.lōō): a warning cry used in Scotland when it was customary to throw household slops from upstairs windows.

gare (gâr): coarse wool on the legs of a sheep. A depot. Beware!—take care! Violent excitement. 1. Keen, esp. covetous. 44.

garookuh (ga.rōō′ku): a shallow-keeled fishing boat used in the Persian Gulf.

garum (gā′rum, gâr′um): a fish sauce of the ancient Greeks, prob. a sort of caviar.

gasogene, gazogene (gas′o.jēn, gaz-): an apparatus that produces a combustible gas for motor fuel by burning charcoal or wood.

gaster (gas′ter): in ants, the enlarged part of the abdomen behind the pedicel.

Gastornis (gas.tôr′nis): a genus of large extinct birds from the Eocene formations of the Paris basin, perhaps allied to the goose.

gastralgia (gas.tral′ji.a): pain in the stomach or epigastrium, esp. of a neuralgic type.

gastriloquy (gas.tril′o.kwi): ventriloquy.

gastromancy (gas′tro.man′si): divination by ventriloquism or crystal gazing.

gastropholite (gas.trof′o.līt): one fond of pampering the stomach. 52.

gateau (ga.tō′): cake, esp. a rich or fancy cake.

gaub (gôb): an East Indian persimmon tree; its fruit, which has strong astringent qualities.

gaud (gôd): a trick or fraud; a trinket; to make merry. 1.

gault (gôlt): a heavy clay; to cover (soil) with clay from the subsoil. 13. (cap) a series of Lower Cretaceous beds of clay and marl in southern England.

gavelock (gav′e.lok): a spear or dart; an iron crowbar or lever. 10.

gaw (gô): a drain; trench. 44A. To gape. 1. Var. of *gall.* 44C.

gawsie (gô′si): large and jolly; lusty. 43.

gazel, ghazel (gā′zel): a type of Arabic lyric, usu. erotic. An Arabian melody characterized by the frequent recurrence of a short refrain.

geck (gek): a dupe, object of scorn. 5. To scorn, cheat, trick. 45.

geegee (jē′ji): a horse. 26.

geest (gēst): alluvial matter of considerable age on the surface of the land. Loose earth or soil formed by decay of rocks.

gelastic (ji.las′tik): disposed to laugh.

gelogenic (jel′o.jen′ik): laughter-provoking.

geloscopy (ji.los′ko.pi): divination by interpretation of laughter.

Gelsemium (jel.sē′mi.um): a genus of woody vines incl. the yellow jasmine.

gemellipara (jem′e.lip′a.ra): a woman who has given birth to twins.

gena (jē′na): the cheek or lateral part of the head.

genappe (ji.nap′): a yarn used with silk in braids, fringes, etc.

genethlialogy (je.neth′li.al′o.ji): the art of casting nativities in astrology. Also, a theory of the lineage of the gods.

geniculum (ji.nik′ū.lum): a small knee-shaped anatomical structure.

geniophobia (jen′i.o.fō′bi.a): fear of chins.

genioplasty (jen′i.o.plas′ti): plastic surgery of the chin.

Genista (ji.nis′ta): an Old World genus of often spiny shrubs of the pea family, inc. the woodwaxen. (not cap) Any plant of this genus. The Canary broom.

gentianella (jen′shan.el′la): a blue color. Any of several large gentians having large blue flowers.

TEMPEST IN A FUFFIT NEST

There's scandal out in Birdland. One morning Mr. Fuffit

Was overseen delivering a mighty fuffit buffet

On little Mrs. Fuffit; he declared that she was dottle

For always building birdnests in the fashion of a bottle.

He faffed and drabbed and friggled, and he called her wicked words;

He said that she was fuffled, and her nests were for the birds.

A fallowchat said, ''Dearie, what your husband really means

Is, you are on the wait-list for a two-room nest in Queens.''

The bird was right, and (I suspect this won't be news to you)

The two-room nest in Queens is shaped much like a bottle too.

The Fuffits, though, are happy there, and gaily gibble-gabble;

They'll hear no talk of quarrels—they would call it fibble-fabble.

---

gentilitial (jen′ti.lish′al): pert. to a family or a people; national. Of gentle birth.

genuflex (jen′ū.fleks): to genuflect. 52.

geodic (ji.od′ik): pert. to a geode, a nodule of stone having a cavity lined with crystals or mineral matter.

geogenous (ji.oj′e.nus): growing in or on the ground.

geognost (jē′og.nost): one knowledgeable about the materials of the earth and its general exterior and interior constitution.

geogony (ji.og′o.ni): the science of the formation of the earth.

georama (jē′o.ram′a): a hollow globe on the inner surface of which is a map of the world, to be examined by one inside.

geoselenic (jē′o.si.len′ik): pert. to earth and moon.

geostatic (jē′o.stat′ik): in civil engineering, pert. to pressure exerted by the earth.

geotaxis, geotaxy (jē′o.tak′sis, -tak′si): a response to a stimulation in which the force of gravitation is the directive factor.

gephyrophobia (ji.fī′ro.fō′bi.a): fear of crossing bridges.

gerascophobia (jer.as′ko.fō′bi.a): fear of growing old.

geratic (je.rat′ik): pert. to old age; geriatric.

gerb, gerbe (jurb): a sheaf, as of wheat. A firework throwing a shower of sparks.

germon (jur′mun): albacore.

geromorphism (jer′o.môr′fizm): the condition of appearing older than one is.

gerontocomium (ji.ron′to.kō′mi.um): an institution for the care of the aged.

geysir (gī′ser): var. of *geyser.*

ghafir (ga.fēr): in Egypt, a native guard or watchman.

gharri, gharry (gar′i): in India, a wheeled cart or carriage, often one for hire.

ghawazi (ga.wä′zi): Egyptian female dancers, who call themselves *Baramika* and do not marry outside of their tribe.

ghoom (gōōm): to hunt in the dark, in India.

ghurry (gur′i): a waterclock or other timepiece of India. A period of twenty-four minutes among Hindus; among Anglo-Indians, an hour.

giardinetto (ji.är′di.net′ō): precious stones arranged into a spray of flowers for a ring or brooch.

gibbed (jibd): castrated, as a cat.

gibby (gib′i): a walking stick with a crook; a similar stick of candy. 30.

gibel (gib′l): the crucian carp of Europe.

giglet (gig′let): a wanton; a lascivious woman. 9.

gigmanity (gig.man′i.ti): the worship of smug respectability as the great object in life; philistinism.

gillaroo (gil′a.rōō): an Irish trout with thickened gizzard-like inner walls for crushing the shells of freshwater mollusks.

gilliver (jil′i.ver): the common wallflower of Europe.

gillygaloo (gil′i.ga.lōō): a mythical bird that lays square eggs. 21.

gilravage (gil.rav′ij): a noisy celebration. To frolic in a disorderly fashion.

gimble (gim′bl): to make a wry face, grimace. 11.

gime (gīm): a hole made when water pours through a leak in an embankment.

gimmal (gim′l): joined work (as clockwork) whose parts move within each other. Made or consisting of gimmals.

gipon (ji.pon′, jip′on): a tight-fitting garment like a shirt often worn under medieval armor; a jupon.

gippo (jip′ō): a short tunic or cassock; also, a scullion, varlet. 1.

Gir (jir): a breed of medium-sized Indian cattle of dairy type, having a distinctive dull red or brown speckling on a white background. An animal of this breed.

girn (gurn): to snarl, whine, bare the teeth in rage. 2, 44C.

gish (gish): in Moroccan public domain, land subject to usufructuary rights.

gittern (git′ern): a medieval wire-strung musical instrument like a guitar, played with a plectrum.

givy (givy): relaxed. 32.

gizz (giz): a wig. 43.

gladius (glā′di.us): the internal shell of a cuttlefish or squid.

glandaceous (glan.dā′shus): acorn-colored.

Glaswegian (glas.wē′jan): a native or inhabitant of Glasgow, Scotland; pert. to Glasgow.

glaucescent (glô.ses′ent): having a somewhat glaucous appearance; becoming glaucous.

glebous (glē′bus): full of clods; like a clod; earthy. 52.

gleek (glēk): a gibe, jest, practical joke; a flirtatious glance. 2. To gain an advantage (as by trickery). 9. An old three-handed card game.

glenoid (glē′noid): in anatomy, having the form of a smooth shallow depression, as the cavity of the scapula.

gliff (glif): a fleeting glance, faint sound, brief moment, or sudden shock. To frighten. 5A.

glin (glin): haze on the horizon at sea, signaling an approaching storm.

glink (glingk): to look at slyly, sideways. 43.

glist (glist): mica. A gleam. To glisten. 1.

globaloney (glōb′a.lō.ni): softheaded world politics, as described by Clare Booth Luce.

gloff (glof): a shock; a scare. To feel a shock. 44.

glom (glom): to take, steal, swipe. 21.

glome (glōm): a ball or clue, as of thread. 1.

glommox (glom′uks): a conglomeration; muss. 12.

glose (glōz): var. of *gloze.*

glot (glot): Alistair Reid's word for a person who cannot bear to waste anything.

glottonogonic (glo.ton′o.gon′ik): pert. to the origin of language.

glucic (glōō′sik): referring to an acid obtained as a viscid syrup by the action of lime or baryta on glucose.

glucina (gloo.sī′na): beryllia.

gluck, gluck-gluck (gluk, gluk′gluk): a gulping sound.

glutenous (glōō′ti.nus): resembling or containing gluten.

glutition (glōō.tish′un): the act of swallowing.

glycolimia (glī′ko.lim′i.a): a craving for sweets.

glyphography (glī.fog′ra.fi): a process for making relief printing plates, first engraving the design on a wax-covered matrix.

Glyptodon (glip′to.don): a genus of large extinct mammals related to the armadillos.

glyptotheca (glip.to.thē′ka): a building or room devoted to works of sculpture.

gnathonic, gnathonical (na.thon′ik, -ik.al): flattering, deceitful.

gnoff (nof): a lout, boor. 1.

gnomonics (no.mon′iks): the art or science of constructing dials, esp. sundials.

gnosiology (nō′si.ol′o.ji): the theory of the origin, nature, and validity of knowledge; epistemology.

goaf (gōf): a mow or rick of grain or hay, stored in a born; a bay of a barn. 13.

gobby (gob′i): rough or uneven; lumpy; in gobs; also, viscous. 11A.

gobemouche (gōb′mōōsh′): a gullible person; lit., a fly-swallower.

goff (gof): a silly clown; a foolish fellow. 11.

goggan (gog′an): a small wooden or metal dish or noggin; a game played with such vessels. 13.

gola (gō′la): a warehouse for grain in India. (cap.) An Indian caste, chiefly engaged in preparing rice and salt.

Golo (gō′lō): one of a Nilotic tribe in eastern Sudan.

gombeen (gom.bēn′): usury. 50.

gombroon (gom.brōōn′): a kind of white semiporcelain.

gomer (gō′mer): a conical chamber at the breech of the bore in old smoothbore ordnance. (cap) A northern people from the Armenian highlands; also, wife of the prophet Hosea.

gomphiasis (gom.fī′a.sis): looseness of the teeth.

gomuti (go.mōō′ti): a Malayan feather palm, yielding sweet sap from which palm wine is made.

gonemous (gō′ni.mus): bearing many children.

gonfalon, gonfanon (gon′fa.lon, -non): the small pennant attached to a knight's lance. A lance that flies a pennant.

gony, goney (gō′ni): a booby; dunce. 2. Any of several large seabirds, esp. the black-footed albatross and the young of the black-tailed albatross.

gool (gōol): a ditch or sluice. A breach in a bank or seawall; a fissure. 13.

goolah (gōo′la): in India, an earthen water vessel.

goozle (gōo′zl): guzzle. 11.

goracco (go.rak′ō): a tobacco paste smoked in hookahs.

gorbelly (gôr′bel.i): a prominent belly; a big-bellied person. 2.

goric (gor′ik): in Breton folklore, one of a class of malevolent spirits supposed to dance about monoliths.

gork (gôrk): one who has lost mental function from senility, stroke, etc.

gorp (gôrp): a mixture of dried fruits and nuts, seeds, and the like. 32.

gotch (goch): a bulging jug or pitcher. 13.

gradatim (grā.dā′tim): step by step; gradually.

graffer (graf.er): a notary or scrivener. 1.

graip (grāp): a pitchfork or dungfork. 45.

graith (grāth): readiness. 1. Furniture, apparel. 5. Material, also soapy water. 44A. Ready; prepared. 1. To build. 1. To furnish, adorn. 44C.

grallatorial, grallatory (gral′a.tō′ri.al, -tō′ri): pert. to the Grallatores, or wading birds.

grallic (gral′ik): grallatorial.

grammaticaster (gra.mat′i.kas′ter): a petty grammarian; a grammatical pedant.

grammatolatry (gra.ma.tol′a.tri): the worship of letters or words.

granadillo (gran′a.dil′ō): the granadilla tree. Any of various tropical American passion flowers, or their oblong fruit.

grandgousier (grän′gōo.zyā): a glutton.

granza (gran′za): mercury ore in pieces over an inch in diameter.

graphospasm (graf′o.spazm): writer's cramp.

gratten (grat′en): stubble. 11.

gravedo (gra.vē′dō): a head cold.

gravic (grav′ik): pert. to gravitation. 52.

gravimeter (gra.vim′i.ter): an instrument to measure weight or density.

grece (grēs): a flight of steps; also, a step in a flight. 2.

greenth (grēnth): green growth; verdure.

greffier (gref′i.er): a register or recorder.

gregal (grē′gal): pert. to a flock. 9. Gregarious. 1.

gregale (grā.gä′le): a dry, cold northeast wind over Malta.

grege, greige (grāzh): a textile in an early stage of preparation.

grego (grē′gō, grā′gō): a short hooded jacket or cloak of thick, coarse cloth, worn in the Levant and formerly by seamen.

gremial (grē′mi.al): pert. to the lap or bosom; specif., eccl., pert. to an apron used by a bishop when seated at Mass or when anointing during ordination ceremonies. The apron itself. Intimate, ''bosom''; hence, in history, having a full or resident membership in a society or university. 6. A bosom friend. 1.

grenado (gri.nä′dō): a grenade. 9.

gressible (gres′i.bl): able to walk.

grice (grīs): a young pig. 9, 17A.

griffe (grif): the offspring of a black and a mulatto. A person of mixed black and American Indian blood (also *griff*). In architecture, an ornament resembling a claw that projects from the round base of a column.

griffonage (grif.o.näzh): careless handwriting; an illegible scribble.

grike (grīk): a crevice; chink; ravine. 13. A narrow opening in a fence that allows people but not farm animals to get through.

grimme (grim): a small West African antelope, colored deep bay.

griph (grif): a puzzle; enigma. A vulture. 1.

gripple (grip′l): a drain; ditch. 10.

grisamber (grēs′am′ber): ambergris. 1.

griskin (gris′kin): the spine of a hog; the lean part of a pork loin; a small piece of meat for roasting. 41.

grivoiserie (gri.vwä′zer.i): a lewd act; lewd and lascivious behavior.

grobianism (grō′bi.a.nizm): rudeness; boorishness.

gromatics (gro.mat′iks): the science of surveying. 1.

grues (grōoz): Robert Louis Stevenson's word for Little Willies and other such gruesome rhymes.

grummel (grum′el): sediment; dregs. 2.

grumph (grumf): grunt. 44.

Grundyism (grun′di.izm): prudish conventionalism.

grunge (grunj): something bad, inferior, ugly, or boring.

grylli (gril′i), (pl. of *gryllos*): a comic combination of animals and or of animal and human forms in Greco-Roman glyptic arts, esp. in intaglios.

Gryllus (gril′us): a genus of Old World crickets.

guarana (gwä′ra.nä): a Brazilian climbing shrub yielding caffeine from leaves and bark; a paste made from it; an astringent drink from the paste.

gufa (gōo′fa): a round boat made of wickerwork used in ancient Mesopotamia.

guffer (guf′er): the eelpout. 44.

guffin (guf′in): an awkward person. 21A. (pl.) Very large feet. 35.

guggle (gug′l): the windpipe. 21A. A sound of guggling, a gurgle. 25.

THE FABULOUS HUNT OF THE JACKAROO

Do you recall the jackaroo
   Who left his sheep at home
To hunt the wily kangaroo
   That skulks through frosty Nome?

(Would he have went had he but knew,
   As many might explain,
That *several* sorts of kangaroo
   Bound on the bounding main?—
The walleroo—the poteroo—
   The kangaroo again?)

He sat in shade of gamdeboo
   To rest him from his search.
Although the tree wore gingham blue
   In readiness for church,
She stayed at home; 'twould never do
   To leave him in the lurch.

He shook his jug of hoochinoo,
   And offered her a quaff,
And sang, and played the digerydoo
   To make the good tree laugh.

Then up there swam a gillaroo,
   And much that trout did please them;
They fed it bones of cockatoo
   So its insides could squeeze them.

A square-egg-laying gillygaloo
   Refused in manner curt
To lay a square egg for the two—
   She said that it would hurt.

A wolf leaped out with tingling cry—
   A fearful kabaru!
The jackeroo prepared to die,
   And uttered pililoo.

Up jumped a sleepy kinkajou,
   And bit that wolf in twain,
And gently kicked the jackaroo,
   And went to sleep again.

The jackaroo when home he came
   Brought nary a kangaroo.
His sheep baaed welcome all the same
   With lullilulliloo.

---

guignol (gi.nyol′): puppet; a puppet show. (cap) The main character in a French puppet show.

guitguit (gwēt′gwit): any of several small tropical American honey creepers.

gula (gū′la): the upper front of the neck, next to the chin; the gullet. In some insects, a plate forming the lower surface of the head. In architecture, one or more moldings having a large hollow; also, an ogee, or S-shaped curve.

gulosity (gū.los′i.ti): greed; gluttony.

gummastic (gum.mas′tik): an aromatic resinous sap obtained from mastic trees; mastic.

gunation (goo.nā′shun): in Sanskrit grammar, a strengthening of the simple vowels by prefixing an *a* element to each.

gundi (gun′di): a short-tailed rodent, about 8 inches long, related to the porcupines, cavies, chinchillas, etc.

gup (gup): an exclamation of reproof, derision, or remonstrance. 1. In India, gossip.

gurk (gurk): a fat person. 44.

gurl (gurl): to growl; howl. 44A.

gurly (gur′li): rough; boisterous; also, surly. 44A.

gurt (gurt): a trench; drain. Also, dial. Eng. var. of *great.*

guss (gus): in mining, a dragrope. 41.

gussie (gus′i): swine; pig. 43.

gutling (gut′ling): a glutton. 2.

guttatim (gu.tā′tim): drop by drop (used in prescriptions).

guttle (gut′l): to gormandize.

gyascutus (jī′as.kū′tus): an imaginary beast with legs longer on one side than the other, so that it walks easily, but in only one direction, on steep hillsides.

gyle (gīl): a brewing. The beer produced at one brewing. Malt in the process of fermentation added to stout or ale.

gymnophobia (jim′no.fō′bi.a): fear of nudity.

Gymnotus (jim.nō′tus): a genus of South American cyprinoid fishes that sometimes includes the electric eel.

gynecocentric (jī′ni.ko.sen′trik): centering on or in the female, as a *gynecocentric* society.

gynecophobia (jī′ni.ko.fō′bi.a, jin′i-): morbid fear of women.

gyneolatry (jī′ni.ol′a.tri, jin′i-): worship of women.

gynesic (ji.nes′ik): pert. to femaleness.

gynocratic (jī′no.krat′ik, jin′o-): pert. to government by women.

gynotikolobomassophile (jī′.not′i.ko.lō′-bo.mas′o.fīl, jin′ot-, -fil): one who likes to nibble on women's earlobes.

gyromancy (jī′.ro.man′si, jir′o.-): divination by walking in a circle until falling from dizziness, the place of the fall determining one's fortune.

gyropigeon (jī′ro.pijun): a clay pigeon or similar target.

gyrovagues (jī′ro.vāgz): monks who wander from monastery to monastery.

H

haboob (ha.boob′): a violent dust storm or sandstorm of northern Africa or India.

habromania (hab′ro.mā′ni.a): extreme euphoria.

Hadrosaurus (had′ro.sô′rus): a genus of heavy herbivorous dinosaurs found in the Cretaceous of North America that attained a length of over thirty feet.

haecceity (hek.sē′i.ti): thisness; specificity. The character of being here and now.

Haemanthus (hi.man′this): a genus of African herbs often called *blood lilies* or *blood-flowers.*

haffle (haf′l): to stammer; also, to quibble. 13.

hafter (haf′ter): one who makes or fits hafts or handles.

hagia (hā′ji.a): holy things; specif. (cap), the consecrated bread and wine in the Eucharist.

hagiolatry (hag′i.ol′a.tri): the worship of saints.

hagiophobia (hag′i.o.fō′bi.a): morbid dread of holy things.

haikai (hī′kī): an often playful type of Japanese verse or prose cultivated in the later feudal ages.

hairif (hâr′if, har′if): goose grass or other kinds of cleavers. 13.

Hakka (häk′kä): a distinct strain of the Chinese people in southeastern China.

hala (hā′la): a common Pacific-island screw pine whose fiber is woven into coarse mats.

halieutics (hal′i.ū′tiks): fishing.

haliography (hal′i.og′ra.fi): description of the sea.

halituous (ha.lit′ū.us): related to breath, vapor, exhalation.

hallelujatic (hal′i.loo.yat′ik): pert. to or containing hallelujahs.

halma (hal′ma): in ancient Greece, the long jump with weights in the hands—the first exercise of the pentathlon.

halobiotic (hal′o.bī.ot′ik): relating to the total oceanic flora and fauna.

halomancy (hal′o.man′si): divination by salt.

halophile (hal′o.fīl, -fil): an organism flourishing in saltwater.

hals, halse (hals): the neck, throat, windpipe. A pass or defile. 13.

hamartiology (ha.mär′ti.ol′o.ji): that part of theology which treats of sin.

hamartithia (ham.är.tith′i.a): proneness to mistakes.

hamartiophobia (ha.mär′ti.o.fō′bi.a): fear of sin or sinning.

hamble (ham′bl): to cut off the balls of dogs' feet to make them useless for hunting. To limp. 1.

hamiform (hā′mi.fôrm): hook-shaped.

hamirostrate (hā′mi.ros′trāt): having a hooked beak.

hamman (ham′an): a building or room for bathing; a Turkish bath.

hamus (hā′mus): in biology, a hook or curved process.

hanif (ha.nēf′): a pre-Islamic hermit of Arabia who lived a wandering ascetic life and professed a vague form of monotheism.

hankle (hang′kl): to fasten; entangle; twist. 13.

haole (hä′o.lā): a white or a foreigner in Hawaii.

Hapi (hä′pi): in Egyptian religion, one of the four genii of Amenti, the region of the dead. Also, Apis, a sacred bull believed to be the embodiment of Ptah, father of gods and men. Also, the Nile, represented as a fat man, flower-crowned, and wearing a loincloth.

haplography (hap.log′ra.fi): the inadvertent omission in writing of adjacent and similar letters, syllables, and words, as *intusuception* for *intussusception.*

haptodysphoria (hap′to.dis.fôr′i.a): the unpleasant sensation some feel when touching peaches, cotton, or such surfaces.

harageous (ha.rā′jus): rough and bold; stern, cruel. 1.

haramaitism (har′a.mā′i.tizm): the Hindu practice of child marriage.

hardock (här′dok): the burdock.

harengiform (ha.ren′ji.fôrm): herring-shaped.

hariolation (har′i.o.lā′shun): the act or practice of deduction; guesswork. Ventriloquism.

harlock (här.lok): burdock; prob. corruption of *charlock* or *hardock.*

harmine (här′min): a white crystalline alkaloid found in harmel seeds.

harmonicon (här.mon′i.kon): a harmonica. An orchestrion.

harmoniphon (här.mon′i.fon): an obsolete wind instrument with a tone resembling that of the oboe.

harpactophagous (här.pak.tof′a.gus): predatory—used esp. of insects.

harpaxophobia (här.pak′so.fō′bi.a): fear of robbers or of being robbed.

harpocratic (här′po.krat′ik): pert. to silence.

harquebusade (här′kwi.bus.ād′): a discharge of fire from one or more harquebuses.

hassar (has′er): any of several catfishes of the Orinoco and its tributaries, remarkable for their nest-building habits and their ability to travel some distance on land.

hasta (hus′ta): symbolic positions of the fingers and hands employed in iconography and in dramatic dancing.

hatchel (hach′el): an instrument with long iron teeth, set in a board, for cleansing flax or hemp.

haustrum (hôs′trum): a recess in the colon.

haver (hav′er): an oat; esp., volunteer or uncultivated oats. Tall oat grass. (hā′ver): To hem and haw. 40A. A comrade or associate. In Scots law, the holder of a deed.

havier (hăv′yer): a castrated deer.

havior (hāv′yer): property. 1. Behavior; demeanor. 10.

haya (hā′a, hā′ya): an arrow poison used by natives on the west coast of Africa, said to be derived from sassy bark.

haybote (hā′bōt): in English law, wood or thorns allowed a tenant for repair of hedges or fences; the right to take such material.

haznadar (haz.na.där): in Turkey, a treasurer.

heald (hēld): in weaving, a harness or heddle.

hebetant (heb′i.tant): making dull, as blunting the cutting edge of a knife.

hederaceous (hed′er.ā′shus): growing ivy.

hederate (hed′er.āt): to decorate with ivy.

hederiferous (hed′er.if′er.us): *hederaceous.*

hederigerate (hed′er.ij′er.āt): pert. to ivy; ivy-covered.

heeze (hēz): hoist, exalt. 14.

heinie (hī′ni): the buttocks. 21. (cap) A German, German soldier, German airplane, or the like. 22A.

helcotic (hel.kot′ik): ulcerated.

helicity (hi.lis′i.ti): in nuclear physics, the direction of the spin of an elementary particle.

heliochrome (hē′li.o.krōm): a photograph in natural colors.

heliolater (hē′li.ol′a.ter): a sun worshiper.

heliophilous (hē′li.of′o.lus): attracted by sunlight.

Heliornis (hē′li.ôr′nus): a genus of finfoots consisting of a single species, the sun-grebe.

heliosis (hē′li.ō′sis): sunstroke.

helispheric, helispherical (hel′i.sfer′ik, -i.kal): winding, like a spiral, on a sphere.

hellanodic (hel′a.nod′ik): an official at an Ancient Greek game or combat, serving as a herald or judge.

hellhag (hel′hag): an evil old woman; a hellcat.

hellkite (hel′kīt): a fierce bird of prey; an extremely cruel person.

helminthology (hel′min.thol′o.ji): the study of worms, esp. parasitic worms.

helminthophobia (hel.min′tho.fō′bi.a): fear of worms.

helosis (hi.lō′sis): the condition of having corns.

helotomy (hi.lot′o.mi): the cutting of corns.

hemeral (hem′er.al): in geology, pert. to the time range of a particular fossil species. Pert. to a period of time during which a race of organisms is at the apex of its evolution.

hemeralopia (hem′er.a.lō′pi.a): a condition in which one can see well only at night.

hemeraphonia (hem′er.a.fō′ni.a): a condition in which one can hear or speak only at night.

hemipenis (hem′i.pē′nis): one of the paired sex organs of lizards and snakes.

henhussy (hen′hus.i): a man who does housework.

henotic (he.not′ik): harmonizing, pacific.

HASSAR: A CATFISH THAT BUILDS NESTS AND WALKS ON LAND

I met a dear old catfish as I walked the road to Vassar;
She dropped a humble curtsey, and said, "Sir, I am a hassar;
And begging of your pardon, sir, I've trudged a weary way,
And sun is hard on catfish in the middle of the day;
So would you be so kind, sir, as to help me build a nest
Where I can stretch my aching fins and take a fishy rest?"
"With pleasure, Madam," I replied; and as I laid a heap
Of straw she knelt, and prayed, "Dear Lord, I lay me down to sleep."
And as she slept I lit the straw, and soon I had her basted.
As sweet a piece of catfish as a fellow ever tasted.

---

hent (hent): to seize, lay hold of, carry off. 9, 11.

heptaglot (hep′ta.glot): using seven languages. A book in seven languages.

Heptameron (hep.tam′er.on): a French collection of tales, modeled upon Boccaccio's *Decameron.*

herbulent (hur′bū.lent): containing herbs.

heraism (hē′ra.izm): faithfulness in marriage.

heresiography (her′i.si.og′ra.fi): a treatise on heresy.

heresyphobia (her′i.si.fō.bi.a): hatred of heresy.

herl (hurl): a barb of a feather used in dressing artificial flies. A fly so dressed.

herle (hurl): a heron. 44.

hern, herne (hurn): a corner, a nook. 11.

heroogony (hē′ro.og′o.ni): a genealogy of heroes.

herpetoid (hur′pi.toid): like a reptile. 52.

herse (hurs): a harrow. 2. A harrow-like battle formation. A frame for drying skins. A spiked portcullis; a hearse. 2. (cap) A Greek goddess of the dew.

hestern (hes′tern), hesternal (hes.-tur′nal): pert. to yesterday. 1.

hesychastic (hes′i.kas′tik): soothing, calming—said of a style of ancient Greek music. Also, pert. to the 14th-century *Hesychasts,* who believed they could see a divine light by gazing at their navels.

het (het): dial. past and past participle of *heat.*

heterize (het′er.īz): to transform.

hetero (het′er.ō): attracted to members of the opposite sex; not homosexual.

heteroclite (het′er.o.klīt): deviating from ordinary forms or rules; irregular, anomalous, abnormal. One that deviates in this fashion. In grammar, a word of irregular inflection.

heterogene (het′er.o.jén): heterogeneous.

heterogony (het′er.og′o.ni): in botany, the state of having two or more hermaphrodite or perfect flowers. In biology, the alternation of generations between the sexual and the asexual.

heteropathic (het′er.o.path′ik): morbidly or abnormally sensitive to stimuli.

Heterophagi (het′er.of′a.jī): the altrices, birds having their young hatched in a very helpless condition, so as to require care for some time.

heterophobia (het′er.o.fō′bi.a): fear of or aversion to those of the opposite sex.

heterotaxis (het′er.o.tak′sis), heterotaxy (het′er.o.tak′si): abnormal arrangements, as of organs of the body, geological strata, etc.

heterotelic (het′er.o.tel′ik): existing for something else; having an extraneous end or purpose—contrasted with *autotelic.*

heterotopic (het′er.o.top′ik): in medicine, relating to a shift in position, as of an organ or growth.

heterotropic (het′er.o.trop′ik): in physics, showing different properties in different directions—not isotropic.

heuretic (hoo.ret′ik): the logic of discovery.

hexaglot (hek′sa.glot): using six languages. A book in six languages.

hexameron (heks.am′er.on): the six days of creation.

hexamerous (heks.am′er.us): in botany and geology, having six parts.

hia (hē′a): the hawk parrot.

hiant (hī′ant): gaping.

Hibernicism (hī.bur′ni.sizm): Irishness; an Irish trait.

hidrotic (hī.drot′ik): causing sweating. A medicine that causes sweating.

hield (hēld): a slope or incline. 1. To incline, tilt, be favorable. 2. To decline, droop. 4. To yield, turn away. 1.

hierography (hī′er.og′ra.fi): descriptive writing on sacred subjects.

hieromachy (hī′er.om′a.ki): a dispute between ecclesiastics.

hieromancy (hī′er.o.man′si): divination by interpreting sacrifices.

Hilaria (hi.lā′ri.a): a genus of grasses of the southwestern United States and Mexico, incl. the curly mesquite grass of Texas.

hilding (hil′ding): a base wretch or jade; mean, cowardly. 9.

hilum, hilus (hī′lum, -lus): in botany, a scar on a seed (as a bean) where an ovule is attached to the stalk. In anatomy, a notch in a bodily part suggestive of a hilum.

hindermate (hin′der.māt): a mate who is a hindrance rather than a help.

hinnible (hin′i.bl): able to whinny. 52.

hipe (hīp): a throw in which a wrestler lifts his opponent from the ground and throws him on his back. To throw by means of a hipe.

hippiater (hip′i.ā′ter): a horse doctor.

hippiatric (hip′i.at′rik): pert. to the diagnosis and treatment of diseases of the horse.

hippocaust (hip′o.côst): the burning of a horse in sacrifice.

hippocerf (hip′o.surf): a monster combining horse and stag.

hippocrepiform (hip′o.krep′i.fôrm): horseshoe-shaped.

hippomania (hip′o.mā′ni.a): a passion for horses.

hippometer (hi.pom′e.ter): an upright with a movable arm to measure the height of a horse.

hippophagan, hippophagous (hi.pof′a.gan, -gus): eating horseflesh.

hippophile (hip′o.fīl): a lover of horses.

hippopotomonstrosesquipedalian (hip′o.pot′o.mon′stro.ses′kwi.pi.dā′li.an): pert. to a longer than sesquipedalian word.

hipsy (hip′si): a drink made of wine, water, and brandy.

hirci (hur′si): armpit hair.

hircinous (hur′si.nus): having a goaty smell.

hircismus (her.siz′mus): a smell as of a goat.

hirmos, hirmus (hur′mos, -mus): in the Eastern Church, a verse used as a standard rhythmic and melodic pattern for troparions, hymns, or canticles.

hirondelle (hir′on.del): a swallow.

hirple (hur′pl): a limp. To hobble, walk with a limp. 44A.

hirsel, hirsle (hur′sl): a herd, flock, pasture ground; a large number or quantity; to arrange as in flocks. 44A. To hitch along; slither; move with a rustle or restlessly. 44.

hirsutorufous (her.sū′to.roo′fus): red-haired.

historionomer (his.tôr′i.on′o.mer): one versed in the laws or principles governing historical phenomena.

histrio (his′tri.ō): a stage player or dancer. 1.

hobbadehoy, hobbledehoy (hob′a.di.hoi, hob′l-): a youth entering manhood.

hoddypeak (hod′i.pēk): a fool. 1.

hodiernal (hō′di.ur′nal): of this day.

hodman (hod′man): a hod carrier; a hack; assistant.

hodophobia (hod′o.fō′bi.a): fear of road travel.

hoggerel (hog′er.el): a boar of the second year; a yearling sheep in its first fleece; a yearling colt. 2.

hoitzitzillin (hoit.zit.zil′en): a showy American bird.

hoker (hō′ker): scorn; derision. To scorn, mock. 1.

holagogue (hol′a.gog): a medication that removes all trace of a disease.

holarctic (hol.ärk′tik, hōl-): pert. to the Arctic regions collectively.

holluschick (hol′us.chik): a young male fur seal; a bachelor.

holmgang (hōm′gang): a duel, esp. one fought on an island.

holocryptic (hol′o.krip′tik): wholly concealing; incapable of being deciphered without a key.

holodactylic (hol′o.dak.til′ik): in classical prosody, having all its feet (except the last) dactyls; said of a hexameter.

holomorphic (hol′o.môr′fik): in mathematics, designating a certain function of a complex variable. Of crystals, symmetrical in form as regards the two ends.

holophrasis (ho.lof′ra.sis): a whole phrase or idea expressed in one word.

holus-bolus (hō′lus.bō′lus): all at once; altogether.

homichlophobia (hō′mi.klo.fō′bi.a): fear of fog.

homilophobia (hom′i.lo.fō′bi.a): fear of sermons.

homodox (hom′o.doks): having the same opinion. 1.

homogeny (ho.moj′e.ni): in biology, correspondence between parts or organs due to descent from the same ancestral type.

homogony (ho.mog′o.ni): of a plant, the state of having one kind of flower, with stamen and pistil of equal length, as distinguished from heterogony.

homophobia (hō′mo.fō′bi.a): fear of sameness or monotony.

homotaxis, homotaxy (hō′mo.tak′sis, -si): similarity in arrangement. In geology, similarity in order of arrangement of stratified deposits.

homuncle (ho.mung′kl): a homunculus.

hondo (hon′dō): a broad, deep gully or dry gulch.

hoochinoo (hoo′chi.noo): an alcoholic beverage distilled from boiled farina and flour by the Hoochinoo Indians of Alaska.

hordaceous (hor.dā′shus): pert. to barley.

horme (hôr′mi): vital energy as an urge to purposeful activity.

horography (ho.rog′ra.fi): the making of clocks, watches, sundials, etc.

horral (hôr′al): a kind of small wheel or caster. 44.

horreum (hôr′i.um): in antiquity, a building for storage, esp. of grain.

horrisonant (ho.ris′o.nant): horrible-sounding.

hortensian (hor.ten′shi.an, -shun): grown in a garden.

hospodar (hos′po.där): a governor of Moldavia and Walachia under Turkish rule.

hougher (hok′er): one that hamstrings cattle; specif., one of a band of 18th-century lawbreakers in Ireland.

housal (houz′al): pert. to the house; domestic. 1.

housebreak (hous′brāk): housebreaking. 1.

housel (hou′zl): the Eucharist or the act of administering or receiving it. To administer the Eucharist to. 9.

hoveler (hov′el.er, huv-): a coast boatman who does odd jobs in assisting ships. His boat. 41.

hoven (hō′ven): of an animal, afflicted with bloat; to bloat.

howadji (hou.aj′i): in the East, formerly, a traveler or merchant, merchants being the chief travelers there.

howel (hou′el): a cooper's plane for smoothing the insides of casks. A rounded cut above and below the croze in a barrel stave.

hoyman (hoi′man): one who owns or navigates a hoy, or small coastal vessel.

huck (huk): short for *huckabuck*, a kind of textured weave. Dial. English for *hook*. The hip, haunch. 11. To higgle; bargain. 2.

huckle (huk′l): to haggle. 1. To bend. 13. The hip, haunch.

hui (hoo′i): a firm or partnership. 38. An assembly united for a common purpose. 38A.

hulster (hul′ster): a lurking place. 11.

hulu (hoo′loo): a tuft of brilliant yellow feathers from the o-o, a bird of Hawaii.

humdudgeon (hum.duj′un): an imaginary illness or pain; a complaint about nothing. 25A.

humicubation (hū.mik′ū.bā′shun): the act of lying on the ground, esp. in penitence.

hummel (hum′l): hornless—of cattle; awnless—of grain; to separate from the awns—of barley. 17A.

hup (hup): a word used to urge on a horse, or to command it to turn to the right. 44A.

hurlbat (hurl'bat): an ancient weapon that was whirled to increase the force of a blow. 1.

hurley-hacket (hur'li.hak'et): a wobbly horse-drawn carriage; downhill sledding. 7A.

hurst (hurst): a grove or sandbank (often used in place names).

hushion (hush'un): a stocking without a foot; hence, a useless creature. 44.

huttoning (hut'n.ing): the manipulation of a dislocated or stiff joint.

huzzard (huz'erd): a yellow fly used in angling.

hwyl (hū'el): fervor, excitement. 41C.

hyalescence (hī'a.les'ens): the state of becoming or appearing hyaline, or glassy.

hyalography (hī'a.log'ra.fi): the art of writing or engraving on glass.

hyblaean (hī.blē'an): honeyed; mellifluous.

hydragogue (hī'dra.gog): a cathartic that causes a copious watery discharge from the bowels.

hydrogel (hī'dro.jel): a gel in which the liquid is water.

HOW THEIR NEIGHBORS ENVIED THEM!

Because of chronic *hemeraphonia*,
Jack Spratt could hear in darkness only*—
Which in his view made matrimony a
    Quite tolerable state, though lonely.

His wife sang all day long off-key;
    He might have wished the woman dead,
But when he could have heard her, she
    Was silently asleep in bed.

And she, because of *hemeralopia*,
    Could never see a thing till night,
Yet found her handicap Utopia—
    For Jack was not a pleasant sight.

On scale of one to twenty, he
    Might rate a two, if lights were dim;
But by the time that she could see,
    He had the covers over him.

He heard no plaints *ad hominem;*
    She saw no scowl or sullen mien,
And so between the two of them
    They licked the marriage platter clean.

*Some say that hemeraphonia is the ability to *speak* only at night—but that would spoil my story.

---

hydromica (hī'dro.mī'ka): any of several varieties of muscovite that are less elastic and more unctuous than mica.

hydrophobophobia (hī'dro.fō'bo.fō'bi.a): fear of hydrophobia.

hydropic (hī.drop'ik): characterized by swelling and imbibation of fluid. Eden.ic. Dropsical.

hydrotelluric (hī'dro.te.loo'rik): the acid hydrogen telluride.

hyetography (hī'i.tog'ra.fi): the scientific description of the geographical distribution of rain.

hygiolatry (hī'ji.ol'a.tri): fanaticism about health.

hygiology (hī'ji.ol'o.ji): the science of hygiene.

hygrology (hī.grol'o.ji): the branch of physics that deals with humidity.

hygrophobia (hī'gro.fō'bi.a): fear of liquids.

hylactic (hī.lak'tik): pert. to barking. 52.

hyle (hī'li): in philosophy, matter, or whatever receives its form or determination from outside itself. (cap) The name given by the Manicheans to the Regent of the World of Darkness.

hylogenesis (hī'lo.jen'i.sis): the beginning of matter.

hylophagan (hi.lof'a.gan): wood-eating.

hylotheist (hī'lo.thē'ist): one who believes that matter is God.

hymenogeny (hī'mi.noj'i.ni): the production of artificial membranes by contact of two fluids.

hymnography (him.nog'ra.fi): the composition and writing of hymns.

hypaethral (hi.pē'thral, hi-): open to the sky.

hypantrum (hi.pan'trum): a notch on the neural arch at the anterior ends of the vertebrae of certain reptiles.

hypengyophobia (hī.pen'ji.o.fō'bi.a): fear of responsibility.

hyperbatic (hī'per.bat'ik): pert. to transposed word order (as "tolled the bell" for "the bell tolled").

hyperdulia (hī'per.doo'li.a): veneration of the Virgin Mary as the holiest of mere creatures.

hyperesthesia, hyperesthesis (hī'per.es.thē'zhi.a, -zi.a, -zha; -thē'sis): a state of exalted or morbidly increased sensitivity.

hyperhedonia (hī'per.hi.dō'ni.a): abnormal pleasure from any sensory perception.

hypermimia (hī'per.mim'i.a): excessive gesticulation while talking.

hyperthermalgesia (hī'per.thur'mal.jē'zhi.a, -zi.a): abnormal sensivity to heat.

hyperthetical (hī'per.thet'i.kal): in classical prosody, pert. to an interchange of position between a successive long and short syllable in a verse of mixed rhythm. In philology, pert. to transposition of a sound or letter from one syllable to an adjoining syllable.

hypertridimensional (hī'per.trī'di.men'shun.al): having more than three dimensions.

hypnoetic (hip'no.et'ik): pert. to mental processes of a logical form or nature, but not involving consciousness of logic nor effort to think logically.

hypnopedia (hip'no.pē'di.a): sleep-learning, sleep-teaching.

hypnophobia (hip'no.fō'bi.a): morbid fear of sleep.

hypobulia (hī'po.bū'li.a): difficulty in making decisions.

hypochonder (hī'po.kon'der, hip'o-): the abdomen just below the rib cartilages; the hypochondrium. 1.

hypogeal (hī'po.jē'al, hip'o-): subterranean, as *hypogeal* ants or beetles.

hypogelody (hī'po.jel'o.di, hip'o-): underground surveying, as of mines.

hypomnematic (hī'pom.ni.mat'ik, hip'om-): consisting of notes or memoranda.

hypophobia (hī'po.fō'bi.a, hip'o-): fearlessness.

hyporadius (hī'po.rā'di.us, hip'o-): in zoology, a barbule on the feather shaft.

hyporchema, hyporcheme (hī'pôr.kē'ma, -kēm, hip'ôr-): an ancient Greek choral song and dance usu. in honor of Apollo or Dionysus.

hyporchesis (hī'pôr.kē'sis, hip'ôr-): among the ancient Greeks, the choric dance to which the hyporchema was sung.

hypostigma (hī'po.stig'ma, hip'o-): a point in punctuation, orig. used with the value of a comma.

hypostyptic (hī'po.stip'tik, hip'o-): moderately styptic, or contraction-producing; a mild styptic.

hypothymic (hī'po.thī'mik, hip'o-): low in thymic functions such as immunological responses.

hypotyposis (hī'po.tī.pō'sis, hip'o-): vivid, picturesque description.

hypsiloid (hip'sī.loid, hip.sī'loid): resembling in form the Greek letter Y, upsilon.

hypural (hī.pū'ral): pert. to or designating the bony structure that supports the fin ray in the ordinary fishes.

hysteranthous (his'ter.an'thus): of a plant, developing leaves after the flowers have expanded.

hystricine (his'tri.sīn, -sin): pert. to porcupines.

I

iambographer (ī.am.bog.ra'fer): a writer of iambic verse. 52.

iatraliptic (ī.at'ra.lip'tik): treating disease by anointing and friction.

iatramelia (ī.at'ra.mēl'ya): medical negligence.

iatrogenesis (ī.at'ro.jen'i.sis): the occurrence of a disease through the medical activity of the physician.

iatrology (ī.a.trol′o.ji): the science of healing; a treatise on it.

iatromisia (ī.at′ro.mis′i.a): dislike of doctors.

iatrophobia (ī.at′ro.fō′bi.a): fear of going to the doctor.

iba (ē′ba): a medium-sized Philippine tree, prized for its roundish greenish-white fruit.

Ibo (Ē′bō): a Negro people of the lower Niger.

icaco (i.kak′ō): the coco plum.

Iceni (ī.sē′ni): a tribe of Britons that, under its queen Boadicea, revolted against the Romans in the 1st century A.D.

ichneutic (ik.nū′tik): pert. to tracking or trailing. 52.

ichnogram (ik′no.gram): a footprint.

ichnolatry (ik.nol′a.tri): the worship of idols.

ichnolite (ik′no.līt): a fossil footprint.

ichnology (ik.nol′o.ji): the study of (generally fossilized) footprints.

ichthyomancy (ik.thi.o.man′si): divination with fish offal.

ichthyophobia (ik.thi.o.fō′bi.a): fear of fish.

icker (ik′er): an ear of corn. 44.

iconoduly (ī.kon′o.dū.li): veneration of images.

iconomatic (ī.kon′o.mat′ik): pert. to the stage of writing between picture writing and phonetic writing.

icosian (ī.kō′si.an): relating to twenty.

ictic (ik′tik): caused by a blow; abrupt. Also, pert. to medical stress.

idalia (ī.dā′li.a): a large red-and-black butterfly of the eastern United States. Its caterpillar feeds on violets.

iddat (i.dät′): a period of several months in which a Moslem widow or divorcée may not remarry.

ideaist (ī.dē′a.ist): an idealist; a Platonist.

ideate (id′i.āt): to form an idea; to have or work through ideas.

idiogamist (id.i.og′a.mist): one capable of coitus only with his wife.

ideogenous (id′i.oj′i.nus): mental in origin.

idiograph (id′i.o.graf): a trademark.

idiolalia (id′i.o.lāl′ya): a mental state characterized by the use of invented language.

ideopraxis (id′i.o.prak′sis): the putting of ideas into effect.

idiostatic (id′i.o.stat′ik): pert. to a method of measurement of electricity without employing auxiliary electrification.

Ido (ē′do): an artificial language, devised in 1907; a modified form of Esperanto.

idoneous (i.dō′ni.us): apt; suitable.

idorgan (id′ôr.gan): a morphological unit consisting of a group of cells composing an organ, but without possessing the characteristics of an individual or colony.

ignavia (ig.nā′vi.a): idleness; laziness.

ignescent (ig.nes′ent): emitting sparks of fire when struck by steel; scintillating; becoming inflamed; inflammatory.

ignify (ig′ni.fī): to set on fire; to burn.

ignigenous (ig.nij′i.nus): producing or yielding fire.

ignipotent (ig.nip′o.tent): having power over fire.

ignoscency (ig.nos′en.si): forgiveness; a forgiving nature.

iiwi (i.ē′wi): a Hawaiian bird with brilliant red feathers, once used for regal capes.

illability (il.a.bil′i.ti): infallibility.

illaqueation (i.lak′wi.ā′shun): the act of ensnaring, entrapping, catching. 52.

illation (i.lā′shun): an inference or conclusion.

illicitator (il.lis′i.tā.ter): an auctioneer's shill. 22.

illinition (il′i.nish′un): a smearing or rubbing in or on; inunction.

illinium (i.lin′i.um): an element of the rare-earth group.

illision (i.lizh′un): a striking against something.

illium (il′i.um): an alloy of nickel, chromium, copper, manganese, silicon, and tungsten, used esp. for laboratory ware.

illth (ilth): the condition of being poor and miserable. The opposite of wealth.

illutation (il′ū.tā′shun): a mud bath.

imaginate (i.maj′i.nat): to imagine. 52. Imaginary. 1. To change (an insect) to an imago. 52.

imbibition (im.bi.bish′un): absorption, saturation, steeping.

imbosk (im.bosk′): to hide, conceal.

immanity (i.man′i.ti): monstrosity. 1.

immarcescible (im′är.ses′i.bl): indestructible, imperishable. 52.

immeability (im′i.a.bil′i.ti): want of power to pass or flow; impassableness.

immer (im′er): ever (German).

immerd (i.murd′): to cover with ordure.

immie (im′i): a marble, esp. one streaked with color.

imminution (im′i.nū′shun): diminution.

immorigerous (im′ôr.ij′e.rus): rude, boorish.

immund (i.mund′): unclean; filthy.

immundicity, immundity (i.mun.dis′i.ti, -mun′di.ti): uncleanliness, filth. 1.

impacable (im.pā′ka.bl): not to be pacified; implacable.

impanate (im.pā′nāt): containing (as Eucharistic bread and wine) the body of Christ without change in any substance.

imparl (im.pärl′): to consult; discuss. 1.

impatible (im.pat′i.bl): that cannot suffer or be suffered. 1.

impavid (im.pav′id): fearless.

impeccant (im.pek′ant): sinless.

impedient (im.pē′di.ent): (one) that impedes.

impeditive (im.ped′i.tiv): tending to impede; obstructive.

impertinacy (im.pur′ti.na.si): erroneous for *impertinency.*

impetulant (im.pech′oo.lant): not petulant.

impi (im′pi): a body of Kaffir warriors or native armed men.

impletion (im.plē′shun): state of being full; that which fills, a filling. Fulfillment, as of prophecy. 1.

implex (im′pleks): involved, intricate, complex.

imprese (im.prēz′): historically, a device or emblem; the sentence usu. accompanying it; a motto, proverb, or maxim. 1.

improlificate (im.pro.lif′i.kāt): to impregnate.

INIA, MINIA: A COUNTING SONG

Inia, minia, one two three,
Inia, minia, out blows he—
Seven-foot whale with a long long snout,
First he is Inia, then he's out.

Inia, minia, one three two,
Inia, minia, out goes who?
Seven-foot whale with a seven-foot spout,
First he is Inia, then blows out.

---

impropriate (im.prō′pri.āt): in English law, to transfer monastic properties to lay control.

impropriatrix (im.prō′pri.āt′riks): a female impropriator (one that takes over an ecclesiastical property).

improvvisatore (im.prov.vē′za.tō′ri): one who recites his own improvised poetry.

impudicity (im.pū.dis′i.ti): immodesty.

imsonic (im.son′ik): onomatopoeic.

imu (i.mōō): in Hawaii, a baking pit dug in the sand.

inaniloquy (in.a.nil′o.kwi): an idle and garrulous bit of chatter.

inaugur (in.ô′ger): to inaugurate. 52.

inauration (in.ô.rā′shun): the act of gilding.

inby (in′bī′): inwardly, within; nearby, beside. An inner room. 44.

incalescent (in.ka.les′ent): growing warm or ardent.

incameration (in.kam′er.ā′shun): an addition to papal property.

incarn (in.kärn′): to become covered with flesh; to heal over.

incastellate (in.kas′te.lāt): to change into, or make like, a castle. 1.

incatenate (in.kat′i.nāt): to fetter; to restrain with chains.

incoalescent (in.ko.a.les′ent): not coalescing. 52.

incommiscible (in.ko.mis′a.bl): incapable of mixing or blending; immiscible.

inconnicity (in.ko.nis′i.ti): unsuitableness; ineptitude.

incrassate (in.kras′āt): in plants or animals, thickened and swollen. To thicken, inspissate. 1.

increpation (in.kri.pā′shun): criticism; censure.

incruental (in.krōō.en.tal): bloodless.

incuss (in.kus′): to impress, inspire. 1.

indican (in′di.kan): a colorless glucoside, the source of natural indigo.

indicatrix (in′di.kā′triks): indicator; specif. *Dupin's indicatrix,* a limiting form in mathematics.

indicavit (in.di.kā′vit): in English law, a writ of prohibition for removal of certain cases affecting tithes from the ecclesiastical to the common-law courts.

indiscerptibility (in.di.surp′ti.bil′i.ti): the state of not being subject to dissolution.

indocible (in.dos′i.bl): unteachable.

inearth (in.urth′): to inter.

inenarrable (in′e.nar′a.bl): indescribable, ineffable.

inequable (in.ek′wa.bl): not uniform, even, tranquil; not equable.

inermous (in.ur′mus): without thorns or prickles, as some leaves.

infaust (in.fôst): unlucky. 52.

infibulation (in.fib′ū.lā′shun): the sewing up of the genitals to prevent sexual intercourse.

OR PERHAPS A PELTOGRAM

Do you recall that florid, convoluting,
  Declamatory old professor
Who spent a fustian lifetime substituting
  The greater lexeme for the lesser?

    (When others spoke of ''idle chatter,'' he
    Said, ''More precisely, *inaniloquy.*'')

That hippopotomonstrosesquipedal
  Altiloquenter? For the birds!—
(And yet he won the William Morris Medal
  By never using little words.)

    (He reached his peak in verbal self-indulgence
    When milking cows—which he called
    ''*vaccimulgence.*'')

At last those Golden Stairs he had to climb.
  He capered up in dithyramb,
And left behind him on the sands of time
  Not footprints, but an ichnogram.

---

inficete (in′fi.sēt): dull; unfunny; humorless; deadly serious. 52.

infracostal (in′fra.kos′tal): below the ribs.

infrapose (in′fra.pōz): to place beneath.

infucation (in.fū.kā′shun): the putting on of makeup.

infumate (in′fū.māt): to smoke, as a fish.

infuscate (in.fus′kāt): obscured; specif., darkened with a brownish tinge—said of the wings of insects.

ing (ing): a low-lying pasture. 42A.

ingannation (in.ga.nā′shun): deception; fraud.

ingestar (in.jes′tar): a large 17th-century decanter.

ingle (ing′gl): a fire; a fireplace. An angle, a corner. 52. To cajole, wheedle. A catamite. 1.

ingluvious (in.glōō′vi.us): gluttonous.

ingustable (in.gus′ta.bl): tasteless.

inhearse (in.hurs′): to put in a hearse or coffin. 52.

Inia (in′i.a): a genus of dolphin-like cetaceans of the Amazon and its tributaries, with but one species, seven feet long and having a long snout.

inition (in.ish′un): initiation; beginning. 1.

inkle (ing′kl): a kind of linen tape or braid; also, the thread or yarn from which it is made. To have an inkling of. 13.

inlagary (in.lā′ga.ri): the legal restoration of the rights of criminals. 1.

innascible (in.nas′i.bl): without a beginning.

in petto (in pet′tō): in the breast; not yet made public.

insanable (in.san′a.bl): incurable.

insecable (in.sek′a.bl): indivisible.

insecution (in.si.kū′shun): a following after; close pursuit. 1.

inshallah (in.shal′a): in Arabic, ''God willing.''

insuetude (in′swi.tūd): unaccustomedness. A state of disuse. 52.

insulse (in.suls′): tasteless, flat, insipid.

insussuration (in.sus′e.rā′shun): a whispering in the ear; insinuation. 1.

intactable (in.tak′ta.bl): imperceptible to the touch.

intempestive (in.tem.pes′tiv): untimely; inopportune.

interaulic (in′ter.ôl′ik): existing only between two royal households.

intercrop (in′ter.krop): to grow two or more crops simultaneously in the same ground.

interdigitate (in′ter.dij′i.tāt): to interlace the fingers.

interfenestration (in′ter.fen′es.trā′shun): the space between windows. The placing of windows.

interfret (in′ter.fret): the interaction between two wind currents, frequently producing such effects as a mackerel sky.

intergern (in′ter.gurn): to snarl back. 1.

interjaculate (in′ter.jak′ū.lāt): to ejaculate parenthetically, interject.

interlacustrine (in′ter.la.kus′trin): between lakes.

interlucation (in′ter.lū.kā′shun): the thinning out of trees in a forest to let in light.

intermundane (in′ter.mun′dān): existing between stars or planets.

internecion (in′ter.nē′shun): mutual destruction; massacre. 52.

interneural (in′ter.nū′ral): in anatomy, between the neural arches or neural spines.

interpilaster (in′ter.pi.las′ter): in architecture, the space between two pilasters.

interpunction (in′ter.pungk′shun): act of interpointing; punctuation.

intersert (in′ter.surt): to interpolate, insert.

intersidereal (in′ter.sī.dēr′i.al): interstellar.

intersilient (in′ter.sil′yent): emerging suddenly in the midst of something. 1.

interstadial (in′ter.stā′di.al): a halt, with minor oscillations, in the advance or retreat of an ice sheet.

interstrial (in′ter.strī′al): between striae—grooves, strips, or lines.

intertessellation (in′ter.tes′i.lā′shun): an intricate design, as mosaic.

intertill (in′ter.til): to till between the rows of a crop.

intervallic (in′ter.val′ik): pert. to an interval.

intervert (in′ter.vurt): to turn to an improper course; misuse, esp. embezzle. To change, invert.

intorsion (in.tôr′shun): a winding, bending, or twisting, as of the stem of a plant.

intrapial (in′tra.pī′al): in anatomy, within the pia mater, which connects the brain and spinal cord.

intrathecal (in′tra.thē′kal): in anatomy, within a sheath. Under the membranes covering the brain or spinal cord.

intropression (in′tro.presh′un): pressure acting within. 52.

introsusception, intussusception (in′tro.su.sep′shun, in′tus.-): the reception of one part within another. Invagination.

introvenience (in′tro.vēn′yens): the act of coming in; entering.

intumulate (in′tū′mū.lāt): to bury.

inturgescence (in′ter.jes′ens): a swelling.

inumbrate (in.um′brāt): to shade. 52.

inusitate (in.ūz′i.tāt): obsolete.

inustion (in.us′chun): burning; cauterization.

invalescence (in.va.les′ens): the state of being an invalid.

inviscate (in.vis′kāt): to make viscid; to entangle, as an insect, in a sticky substance.

invultuation (in.vul′chōō.ā′shun): witchcraft in which a wax image is melted or stuck with pins to cause death or injury to the intended victim.

ipsedixitism (ip′se.dik′sit.izm): dogmatism.

ipseity (ip.sē′i.ti): self-identity; selfhood.

irade (i.rä′de): a decree of a Mohammedan ruler, as formerly of the Sultan.

irenark (ī′re.närk): a Roman official corresponding to a justice of the peace.

irenicon (ī.ren′i.kon): a statement that attempts to harmonize conflicting doctrines, as in theology.

iridize (ir′i.dīz): to point or tip with iridium, as a gold pen.

irpe (urp): a grimace or bodily contortion (as used by Ben Jonson).

irreptitious (ir.rep.tish′us): creeping stealthily.

irriguous (i.rig′ū.us): irrigated; watered. 9. Serving to irrigate, water, moisten.

irrisory (i.rī′so.ri): derisive.

irrorate (ir′o.rāt): to bedew, moisten. 1. In zoology, covered with minute grains, appearing like sand, or with small specks of color.

irrugate (ir′u.gāt): to wrinkle. 1.

irrumation (ir.ōō.mā′shun): oral stimulation of the penis; fellatio.

isagoge (ī′sa.gō′ji): a scholarly introduction to a branch of research.

iscariotic (is.kar′i.ot′ik): traitorous.

ischiatic (is′ki.at′ik): pert. to the region of the ischium, or seat bone; ischial. Affected with sciatica. 1.

ischidrosis (is′ki.drō′sis): suppression of the secretion of sweat.

isocheimal, eisocheimic (ī′so.ki′mal, -mik): pert. to an imaginary line connecting places having the same mean winter temperature.

isocracy (ī.sok′ra.si): a system of government in which all have equal political power.

isocrymal (ī′so.krī′mal): isocheimal.

isodiabatic (ī′so.dī′a.bat′ik): pert. to the equal transmission of heat to or from a substance.

isogenous (ī.soj′e.nus): having a common origin.

isonomic (ī′so.nom′ik): pert. to equality of law or rights.

isopectic (ī′so.pek′tik): an equiglacial line drawn through points where ice begins to form at the beginning of winter.

isoperimetrical (ī′so.per′i.met′ri.kal): in geometry, having equal perimeters.

isophorous (ī.sof′er.us): in medicine, having the visual axes of the two eyes in the same horizontal plane.

isopsephic (ī′sop.sef′ik): equal in numerical value. Also, one of two or more isopsephic verses.

isopycnic (ī′so.pik′nik): of equal density; passing through points at which the density is equal.

iter (ī′ter): an eyre, or circuit, orig. of certain justices in England; the record of the proceedings during an eyre. 6. In Roman law, the right to pass over another's property by foot or horseback. In anatomy, a passage.

izle (ī′zl) (usu. pl.): a speck of soot; a spark. 43.

J

jacchus (jak′us): a kind of marmoset.

jacent (jā′sent): recumbent.

jackaroo, jackeroo (jak′a.rōō, jak′e-): in Australia, a green hand on a sheep ranch; in the western U.S., a cowboy.

jacoby (jak′o.bi): the purple ragwort.

jactancy (jak′tan.si): boasting, bragging.

jadu (jä′dōō): conjuring; magic; fortune-telling.

jager (yä′ger): a hunter; a huntsman. (cap) A German or Austrian rifleman.

jaggish (jag′ish): tiddly.

jagua (häg′wa): the inaja, a tall Brazilian palm having immense spathes used for baskets, tubs, etc. In the Caribbean, the genipap tree or its orange-sized fruit.

jako (jak′ō): the gray parrot.

jama (jä′ma): a long Indian cotton gown.

jambee (jam.bē′): an East Indian rattan cane; the tree from which it is made.

jamdani (jam.dä′ni): a flower-patterned muslin.

jami (jä′mi): in Turkey, a principal or central mosque.

jampan (jam′pan): in the hill country of India, a sedan chair carried by four men.

janiceps (jan′i.seps): a two-headed monster facing opposite ways.

Janiculum (ja.nik′ū.lum): a hill on the west bank of the Tiber, opposite the seven hills of Rome.

jannock (jan′uk): leavened oatmeal bread. 13. Candid, pleasant, liberal. 11.

jarbird (jär′burd): the nuthatch.

jarble (jär′bl): to wet; bemire. 13.

jargogle (jär.gog′l): to befuddle. 1.

jargonelle (jär′go.nel): an early variety of pear.

jarl (järl): to quarrel. Historically, a Danish or Norse chieftain below the king.

jasey (jā′zi): a wig of jersey or of a similar yarn. 13.

Jataka (jä′ta.ka): stories about incarnations of Buddha.

jauk (jôk): to trifle or toy with. 44.

jawab (ja.wäb′, -wôb): in India, an answer or reply. Also, a building corresponding to another.

jazerant (jaz′er.ant): armor made of overlapping metal pieces, like fish scales.

jeel (jēl): jelly. 44. Damage, mischief. 55. var. of *jheel*.

jejunator (jej′ōō.nā′ter): one who fasts. 52.

jelab (je.läb′): a hooded jacket of North Africa.

jemadar (jem′a.där): an officer in the army of India equivalent to a lieutenant in the English army.

jenna (jen′a): Paradise, in the Mohammedan religion.

jennerize (jen′er.īz): to vaccinate; immunize.

jentacular (jen.tak′ū.lar): pert. to breakfast.

jeopard (jep′erd): to put in jeopardy.

jereed (je.rēd′): a blunt javelin used in military games in Muslim countries; also, a game played with it.

jerque (jurk): to search (a vessel) for unauthorized goods, etc. 41.

jerrican (jer′i.kan): a five-gallon jug. 13.

jessamy (jes′a.mi): jasmine. 2. A dandy, fop.

jheel (jēl): in India, a pool or marsh left after inundation; a rain puddle. Jelly. 44.

jhool (jōōl): in India, trappings for a horse, elephant, etc.

jhow (jou): a tamarisk of India, used for basket making.

jibble-jabble (jib′l.jab′l): nonsense chatter.

jigamaree (jig′ma.ri): something fanciful or ridiculous.

jimp (jimp): slender; trim; also, scant. Barely; scarcely. 15A. To cut short; skimp. 13.

jingal (jin′gal): a long, heavy musket, or rude cannon, fired from a rest, often with a swivel, formerly used in central Asia.

jingbang (jing′bang): a crowd; shebang (only in ''the whole *jingbang*''). 21.

jirble (jur′bl): to spill (a liquid) by jolting or shaking; hence, to pour from one vessel to another. 44.

jism (jizm): semen. Pep; vigor. 21.

jiti (jē′ti): a woody Asian vine, the Rajmahal creeper, which yields hemp.

jiva (jē′va): in Hinduism, the life energy, vital principle; individual soul.

jixie (jik′si): a two-seated cab. 23.

jobation (jo.bā′shun): a scolding; a long, tedious reproof. 26.

jocker (jok′er): a tramp who takes with him a boy to beg and steal. 32A.

jocoque, jocoqui (ho.kō′kā, -ki): a preparation of sour milk; buttermilk. 35A.

jocoserious (jok′o.sē′ri.us): mingling mirth and seriousness.

jojoba (ho.hō′ba): a small tree of southwestern North America, with oil-bearing, edible seeds. 35A.

jokul (yō′kool): in Iceland, a mountain covered with snow and ice.

jollop (jol′up): a fowl's dewlap, or wattle.

jookerie (jook′er′i): trickery; swindling. 44.

joola (joo′la): a Himalayan rope suspension bridge.

joom (joom): in Bengal, the cultivation of forest land by burning and then sowing it with mixed crops.

jornada (hor.nä′tha, -näda): a full day's travel with no stops. In Mexico, as a land measure, as much land as can be plowed in a day. 35A.

jorum (jō′rum): a large wine jug or bowl. 26.

josser (jos′er): a fool, simpleton. 23.

jotation (yo.tā′shun): palatalization.

jouk (jouk): an obeisance; a trick; a shelter. To roost; sleep; dodge; hide. 44A.

jowter (jou′ter): a peddler or hawker, esp. of fish. 13.

Ju (joo): blue or white porcelain of the Sung dynasty.

Jubal (Joo′bal): in the Bible, a son of Lamech. He is called the father of those who play the harp or organ.

jubbah (joob′ba): a long garment worn in Mohammedan countries by both sexes.

jube (joob): a screen separating the chancel of a church from the nave; also called *rood screen*. A lozenge like the jujube.

jucundity (joo.kun′di.ti): pleasantness. 1. Jocundity. 52.

jumart (joo′mart): the fabled offspring of a bull mating a mare or jenny, or of a horse or ass mating a cow.

jumelle (joo.mel′): paired; jugate.

jumentous (joo.men′tus): having a strong animal smell, as that of horse urine.

juncous (jung′kus): full of, or resembling, rushes.

jupe (joop): a man's shirt or jacket; a woman's blouse or skirt. 44.

jupon (joo′pon): a tight-fitting garment like a shirt, often paddled and quilted and worn under medieval armor. Also, a late medieval jacket similar to the surcoat.

jussel (jus′el): in cookery, a hodgepodge. 1.

justaucorps (zhoos′to.kôr): a fitted coat or jacket; specif., a man's knee-length coat with flaring and stiffened skirts worn in the late 17th and early 18th centuries.

juvenate (joo′ve.nāt): in the Society of Jesus, a two-year course of instruction for junior members.

juzgado (hoos.gä′do, -thō): hoosegow; jail. 35A.

THE JAKO, THE JARBIRD, AND THE JUMARTS

A jako and a jarbird were appalled one day to see
A pair of jumarts jouking in a jacaranda tree.
One jumart was the offspring of a bull upon a mare;
The other had a cow for ma, a Percheron for père.

The jako and the jarbird were not snobbish in the least,
Nor cared about the parentage of any bird or beast,
But feared the branches were too frail to hold such massive things.
Besides, a jumart shouldn't fly—it hasn't any wings.

Those jumarts got the jako and the jarbird so jargogled,
They thought and *thought* and THOUGHT, and still their intellects were boggled.
They jawed, they jibble-jabbled, and they even jarled a wee,
But could not solve the problem of that jumart jigamaree.

So jocoseriously they decided to get soused,
In hopes they'd sleep the whole thing off before the time they roused.
And sure enough, when they had slept, and woke at break of dawn,
They checked and found they were correct; the jumarts both were gone.

K

ka (kä): the Scottish jackdaw. In ancient Egypt, the immortal soul.

kaama (kä′ma): a hartebeest.

kabaya (ka.bä′ya): a loose cotton Malayan tunic.

kaberu (ka.bä′roo): the Abyssinian mountain wolf.

kachina (ka.chē′na): the spirit of a departed Hopi Indian, or some representation of it.

kadein (ka.dīn′): a member of the imperial Turkish harem.

kadoodle (ka.doo′dl): to romp; cavort.

Kaf, Qaf (käf): in Moslem cosmology, a mountain range supposedly encircling the earth, home of a bird of great wisdom.

kaffiyeh (ka.fē′ye): a Bedouin headdress consisting of a square kerchief bound around the head with a cord.

kaha (kä′ha): the proboscis monkey.

kahuna (ka.hoo′na): in Hawaii, a medicine man or high priest; also a master artisan.

kai (kä′i): to the Maoris, food. 56.

kai-kai (kä′i.kä.i): among the Maoris, feasting; to feast. 56.

kaikara (kī.kä′ra): the demoiselle crane.

kailyard (kāl′yärd): a school of writing characterized by sentimental description of Scots life and much use of Scottish dialect.

kaivakuku (kä′i.va.koo′koo): Papuan police hired to protect the crops. 56.

kaki (kä′ki): the Japanese persimmon. The New Zealand stilt-bird.

kakidrosis (kak′i.drō′sis): disagreeable body smell.

kakistocracy (kak′i.stok′ra.si): government by the worst elements of society.

kakkak (kak′kak): in Guam, a small bittern.

kakorrhaphiophobia (kak′or.a.fē′o.fō′bi.a): fear of failure.

kala (kä′la): a black bulbul of India, often kept as a cage bird.

kali (kä′li): the glasswort. Alkali; potash. 1. A carpet of extra length used in the center of Persian rooms. (cap) In the Hindu poem *Nala and Damayani,* an evil genius who causes Nala to gamble his kingdom away. (cap) In Vedic myth, one of the tongues of the fire-god Agni.

kalium (kä′li.um, kal-): potassium.

kalogram (kal′o.gram): a monogram using one's name rather than initials.

kalon (kal′on): the beautiful—frequently with an implication of moral as well as aesthetic beauty.

kamala (ka.mä′la, kam′e.la): an East Indian tree. The orange-red powder from its capsules, used as a vermifuge.

kamalayka (kam.a.lā′ka): a waterproof shirt made from seal guts.

kameel (ka.mēl): an African giraffe.

kamerad (kä′mer.ad): to surrender. 26. (cap) Comrade—used as an appeal for quarter by German soldiers in the First World War.

kamichi (ka.mē′shi): the horned screamer, a South American bird with a hornlike projection on its forehead.

Kanaloa (kan.a.lō′a): one of the principal gods of the Hawaiian pantheon.

kankedort (kang′ke.dôrt): in Chaucer's works, a critical state or affair. 1.

kantele (kan′te.lä): an ancient five-stringed Finnish harp.

kapa (kä′pa): tapa, the bark of the paper mulberry; hence, tapa cloth. Cloth or clothes in general. 38.

karao (ka.rä′o): in Hindu law, a widow's marriage to her brother-in-law. Concubinage.

karimata (kä.ri.mä′ta): a whistling, two-headed Japanese arrow.

kaross (ka.ros′): a simple square garment or rug of animal skins used by native tribesmen of southern Africa.

kasida (ka.sē′da): in Arabic, Persian, and related Oriental literature, a poem of a laudatory, elegiac, or satiric character.

katabasis, catabasis (ka.tab´a.sis): a going or marching down or back; a military retreat.

katar (ka.tär´): in India, a short dagger with a handle of two parallel bars and a cross grip.

kathenotheism (ka.then´o.thi.izm): polytheism with one ruling god.

kathisophobia (kath´i.so.fō´bi.a): fear of sitting down.

katun (ka.tōōn): among the Mayans, twenty years.

kava (kä´va): an Australian pepper used to make an intoxicating drink. The drink so made.

Kavi, Kawa (kä´vi): the ancient language of Java, parent of Javanese.

keb (keb): a ewe that has lost her lamb. To bear a stillborn lamb. Also, a sheep tick, *ked*. 43.

ked (ked): a sheep tick.

kedogenous (ke.doj´i.nus): produced by worry.

keek (kēk): an industrial spy. A peeping Tom. 21.

keelivine (kē´li.vīn): a pencil having black lead. 43.

keest (kēst): sap; substance; marrow. 44.

keet (kēt): a guinea fowl; esp., a young guinea fowl.

keeve, kieve (kēv): a vat or tub, as a brewer's mash tub. (Also *kiver, keever*.) A rock basin hollowed out by water. 41.

kef (kef): tranquility induced by drugs. Indian hemp.

---

*WARNING AGAINST
AN EARLY-GROWING PEAR*

Seek not, seek not, lest mind and life you jeopard—
Seek not, I say, to pluck the jargonelle.
It grows in jungles where the feral leopard,
The jackal, and the naked savage dwell.

And if you needs must brave those floors of marble,
Those dusty deserts, and those huddled rocks,
Wear rubbers—else your Sunday boots you'll jarble;
And take a jerrican to hold your sox.

The houris touch it to their tongues in jenna;
The blessed angels wear it in their hair.
Why's Satan still in exile in Gehenna?
Because he sold his soul to bite that pear.

No letter of this warning dare you garble;
Recall it as you stand there in the stocks:
Wear rubbers—else your Sunday boots you'll jarble;
And take a jerrican to hold your sox.

Kefti (kef´ti): pert. to ancient Crete; an ancient Cretan; a Keftian.

keiri (kē´ri): the wallflower. 1.

keld (keld): a spring or fountain; the still part of a body of water. 13.

kell (kel): a caul; specif., a net cap worn by women. 13.

kellion (kel´yun): a monastery housing not more than three monks and three lay persons.

kelly (kel´i): ver. of *killie, killy*. A stiff hat, esp. a derby. 22. The topsoil removed in order to secure clay for brickmaking. A kind of green associated with the Irish.

kemb (kemb): comb. 11.

kemp (kemp): a coarse hair. 1. A champion; a warrior or athlete. 43. A harvesting contest; to compete in harvesting. 44.

kempt (kemt): neatly kept; trim.

kench (kench): a bin where fish or skins are salted. To install a kench. 32.

kennebunker (ken´i.bung´ker): a kind of large suitcase. 36A.

kenophobia (ken´o.fō´bi.a): fear of empty or open spaces.

kenspeckle (ken.spek´l): conspicuous. 44.

kerana (ke.rä´na): a kind of long Persian trumpet.

kerasine (ker´a.sin): horny; corneous.

keraunoscopia (ke.rô.no.skō´pi.a): divination by thunder.

kerdomeletia (kur´do.me.lē´shi.a): excessive attention to wealth.

kerygma (ke.rig´ma): preaching; the proclamation of the gospel.

ket (ket): filth, rubbish. A good-for-nothing person. 13.

keta (kē´ta): the dog salmon.

ketupa (ke.tōō´pa): a fish owl.

kex (keks): the dry, usually hollow stem of cow parsnip, wild chervil, and the like.

khet (ket): in Egyptian religion, the mortal, corruptible body, in contrast to the *sahu*, or spirit body.

Khubur (koo´bōōr): in Babylonian religion, a river that had to be crossed to reach the underworld.

khuskhus (kus´kus): the sweet-scented root of an Indian grass used in the manufacture of mats or screens.

kibbling (kib´ling): cut-up fish used as bait in Newfoundland.

kibe (kīb): as used by Shakespeare, a crack in the flesh caused by cold; to affect with kibes.

kife (kīf): prostitutes; male homosexuals. To rob. 21.

killie, killy (kil´i): the killifish, often used as bait.

killow (kil´ō): graphite. 1.

kinch (kinch): a noose or twist in a cord. To fasten a noose on the tongue of (a horse). 17A.

kinclunk (kin.klungk´): per Alistair Reid, the sound of a car going over a manhole cover.

kinesiatrics (kin´i.si.at´riks): a mode of

treating disease by appropriate muscular movements.

kinesodic (kin´i.sod´ik): in physiology, conveying motion or motor impulses—applied esp. to the spinal cord.

kinesophobia (kin´i.so.fō´bi.a): fear of movement.

kingling (king´ling): a small or petty king.

kinic, quinic (kin´ik, kwin-): pert. to cinchona bark.

kinology (ki.nol´o.ji): the physics of motion. 52.

kip (kip): half a ton—1,000 pounds.

kipe (kīp): an osier basket for catching fish.

kippage (kip´ij): commotion, confusion, excitement. 44.

kiri (kē´ri): a *knobkerrie*.

kissar (kis´ar): the five-stringed Abyssinian lyre.

kitsch (kich): a rather second-hand, synthetic, and self-conscious emotion; anything (as certain art, literature, etc.) that gives rise to such emotion.

kitling (kit´ling): one of the young of an animal; a whelp. 1. Kittenish; petty; inexperienced. A young cat or kittenish person. 17A.

kittereen (kit´er.én): a two-wheeled one-horse carriage with a movable top.

kitthoge (ki.thōg´): a lefty. Left-handed; awkward. 51, 32.

kiva (kē´va): in Pueblo architecture, an underground ceremonial chamber.

kivu (kē´vōō): the tsetse fly.

kleagle (klē´gl): a high-ranking official in the Ku Klux Klan.

Klepht (kleft): one of the Greeks who formed communities of brigands after their country was conquered by the Turks in the 15th century.

kleptic (klep´tik): thievish.

kleptocracy (klep.tok´ra.si): rule by thieves.

klippe (klip´i): a coin struck with a square-shaped or lozenge-shaped rim.

klipspringer (klip´spring´er): a small African antelope with big ears.

knag (nag): a knot in wood; a wooden peg; a short spur from a tree trunk.

knaggy (nag´i): knotty, rough.

knapple (nap´l): clapboard. 18A.

knez (knez): a Slavic prince or duke.

knibber (nib´er): a male deer beginning its first antlers.

knickknackatory (nik´nak´a.tō´ri): a collection or storehouse of knickknacks.

knissomancy (nis´o.man´si): divination by incense burning.

knittle (nit´l): var. of *nettle*. A string or cord for tying or fastening. 1.

knobkerrie (nob´ker´i): a short club with a knobbed end used as a missile weapon by the aborigines of South Africa.

knop, knosp (nop, nosp): an ornamental knob, as on the stem of a goblet or the shaft of a candlestick; a boss. An ornamental ball or tuft of contrasting color on yarn, thread, or cloth. A projection up or out; a hill. 44C.

knub, nub (nub): a knob; to thump, nudge. 11. Waste silk produced in winding threads from a cocoon.

knubby, knubbly (nub′i, -li): abounding in, or covered by, knubs.

ko (kō): a Chinese liquid measure. (cap) A dark clay Chinese porcelain produced in the 12th century.

kob, koba (kob, kōb, -a): an African antelope related to the water buck.

kobo (kō′bō): a Nigerian penny.

kobold (kō′bold, -bōld): in Germany, a mischievous domestic spirit. A gnome living underground.

koi (koi, kō′i): in Japan, the carp.

koimesis (koi.mē′sis): in the Eastern church, a commemoration of the death and assumption of the Virgin Mary.

kokam (ko.käm′): the slow loris of the Philippines.

koko (kō′kō): any of several araceous plants inc. the taro, cultivated in tropical West Africa for their starchy, edible roots.

kokomo (kō′ko.mō): a drug addict, esp. of cocaine. 21.

kokophobia (kō′ko.fō′bi.a): fear of exhaustion.

kokum (kō′kum): pretended sympathy. 23.

kompology (kom.pol′o.ji): boastful speech.

kona (kō′na): a storm of southerly or southwesterly winds and heavy rains in Hawaii.

konimeter (ko.nim′e.ter): an instrument for measuring dust in the air.

koochahbee (koo′cha.bi): a California Indian dish made from fly larvae.

koomkie (kōōm′ki): a female elephant that has been trained to decoy wild males.

koph, qoph (kōf): the 19th letter of the Hebrew alphabet, representing the sound of English *k,* or *q* in *qu.*

kora (kō′ra): the water cock, a large gallinule bird of southeastern Asia and the East Indies. (cap) An almost extinct Hottentot dialect.

kore (kō′rā): in Maori mythology, the primordial void or first cause of the universe. 56. (cap) In Greek mythology, Persephone, daughter of Demeter.

korova (ko.rō′va): calfskin.

koto (kō′to): a long Japanese zither having 13 silk strings.

kotukutuku (ko.tōō′kōō.tōō′kōō): the New Zealand fuchsia.

Krama (krä′ma): the aristocratic or courtly form of Javanese speech. (not

cap.) The wine mingled with water used in Eastern Orthodox churches in celebrating the Eucharist.

krasis (krā′sis, krä′sis): dilution of the Eucharist wine.

kratogen (krat′o.jen): a dormant area next to one beset by earthquakes.

kreatophagia (krē′a.to.fā′ji.a): the eating of raw meat.

krieker (krē′ker): the pectoral sandpiper.

krypsis (krip′sis): the secret exercise by Christ as a man of his divine powers.

kuku (kōō′kōō): the New Zealand fruit pigeon.

kurveyor (ker′vā′er): in South Africa, a traveling salesman who carts his goods.

kyack (kī′ak): a packsack to be swung on either side of a packsaddle. 35C.

kyacting (ki.ak′ting): clowning while at work. 21.

kylie (kī′li): a boomerang having one side flat and the other convex. 53.

kymatology (kī′ma.tol′o.ji): the science of waves and wave motion.

kyphotic (ki.fot′ik): hump-backed.

Kyrie (kir′i.e, kē-): short for *Kyrie eleison,* ''Lord have mercy on us,'' used in various offices of the Eastern and Western churches.

kyrine (kī′rén): any of a class of basic peton-like substances, obtained by hydrolysis of gelatin, casein, etc.

L

laaba (lä′ba): a storage platform high enough to be beyond the reach of animals. 37B.

labefy (la′be.fī): to weaken or impair. 52.

labia (lā′bi.a): pl. of *labium,* lip.

Labrosaurus (lab′ro.sô′rus): a genus of dinosaurs, related to *Megalosaurus,* from the Colorado Jurassic.

lacca (lak′a): a resinous substance from a scale insect esp. cultivated in northern India, used in the making of shellac, etc.

lacertian, lacertilian (la.sur′shun, -ser.-til′yun): lizard-like.

lacrimando (lak.ri.män′dō): in music, lamenting; plaintive—used as a direction.

lactary (lak′ter.i): a dairy house. 52.

lactescent (lak.tes′ent): of plants, having a milky look; becoming milky. Secreting milk. Yielding latex.

lactivorous (lak.tiv′or.us): living on milk.

ladrone (la.drōn′): a rogue; blackguard; slattern. 44A. In Spanish-speaking countries, a thief, highwayman.

lagarto (la.gär′tō): an alligator.

lagnosis (lag.nō′sis): satyriasis.

lagopous (la.gō′pus): in plants, having hairy rhizomes suggestive of the foot of a hare.

Lagopus (la.gō′pus): a genus of northern game birds comprising the ptarmigans and the red grouse.

lagostic (la.gos′tik): having rabbitlike ears.

laine (lān): an open tract of arable land at the foot of the Downs, in Sussex.

lairwife (lâr′wīf): in old English law, a fine against a married woman for adultery.

lairy (lâr′i): earthy; filthy. 1. Miry. 43.

Lais (lä.ēs′): a hetaera who lived during the Peloponnesian War and was regarded as the most beautiful woman of her age.

Lakme (läk′mi): an Anglo-Indian opera (1885) by Delibes.

lallophobia (lal′o.fō′bi.a): fear of speaking.

lalo (lal′ō): the powdered leaves of the baobab tree, used in Africa in soups.

lamellirostral (la.mel′i.ros′tral): having a bill with transverse toothlike ridges inside the edges, as a duck.

lametta (la.met′a): foil or wire of gold, silver, or brass.

lamin (lam′in): a thin plate or scale. An astrologer's charm consisting of such a plate.

lampadomancy (lam′pad.o.man′si): divination by means of the flickering flame of a torch.

lampas (lam′pas): an ornamental textile fabric with a somewhat elaborate pattern, used chiefly for upholstery.

HOW TO TELL THE SCOTTISH FROM THE EGYPTIAN KA

The ka, deemed deathless on the teeming Nile,
In Scotland moulders in but little while.
Come, rain down tears for that poor Scottish ka—
He caws his little caw, and gangs awa′;
Though sometimes rather he may gang awô,
And not awä, when he has cawed his caw.

The Scottish ka's a jackdaw. Don't forget
That jackdaws are entirely formed of *khet,*
The ''part corruptible,'' Egyptians say.
That is, the Scottish ka is mortal clay
(Or mortal clô, or maybe mortal clä;
In any case, it's bad news for the ka).

Not so the ka of Egypt; through and through
The lucky creature's essence of *sahu.*
The flesh has fled, and spirit is the whole.
(Egyptians say *sahu,* and mean the soul.)
Souls have no gang awäing, gang awôing;
They hang around the place, and keep on cawing.

I find that travel fuddles. When I stay
In Scotland, and espy a ka, I pray.
Were I in Egypt, and a ka I saw,
I'd try to pray, but probably I'd caw.

lamprophony (lam′pro.fō′ni, lam.-prof′o.ni): loud, ringing speech.

lancepesade (lans′pi.zäd, -pe.zäd): a lance corporal. 7.

lancinate (lan′si.nāt): to tear, stab, lacerate.

landlooker (land′look′er): a timber surveyor. 32.

landloper (land′lō′per): one who runs about the land; a vagabond; a renegade.

languescent (lan.gwes′ent): becoming languid or fatigued. 52.

laniation (lā′ni.ā′shun): the act of tearing in pieces. 52.

> THE ZAMBIAN KWACHA'S WORTH 100
> NGWEES (PRONOUNCED NGWAYS)
>
> O you kwacha!
> Once I've gotcha
>   I'll have a hundred ngwees!
> A kwacha's smaller
> Than a Yankee dollar . . .
>   But it ain't hay these days.

lant (lant): urine, esp. stale urine used in manufacturing. 1.

lanx (langks): in ancient Rome, a large metal platter.

laparohysterosalpingooophorectomy (lap′a.ro.his′ter.o.sal′ping.o.o.e.fo.-rek′to.mi): surgical removal of the female reproductive organs.

laparoscope (la′pa.ro.skōp): an instrument inserted through the intestinal wall for direct medical examination.

lapicide (lap′i.sīd): a stonecutter.

lapidify (la.pid′i.fī): to turn into stone.

lapling (lap′ling): one who particularly enjoys reclining on women's laps.

lappaceous (la.pā′shus): in botany, resembling a burdock burr; echinate.

lappage (lap′ij): the amount that surfaces or layers overlap.

lari (lä′ri): money consisting of silver wire doubled, either twisted into the form of fishhooks or straight. Hook money. (cap) A suborder of Charadiformes, including the gulls, terns, jaegers, and skimmers.

larigot (lar′i.got): a shepherd's pipe or flageolet.

larmoyant (lär.moi′ant): tearful.

laroid (lar′oid, lā′roid): pert. to gulls.

larve (lärv): larva.

laryngophony (la′ring.gof′o.ni): the sound of the voice as heard through a stethoscope placed upon the larynx.

lasket (las′ket): on ships, an eye formed on a headrope for attaching a piece of canvas to the foot of a sail. A latching.

lassipedia (las′i.pē′di.a): a case of tired feet.

lat (lat): a pillar in some Indian Buddhist buildings; also, a gold coin of Latvia.

latericeous, lateritious (lat′er.ish′us): brick-red; resembling brick.

lateropulsion (lat.er.o.pul′shun): a sidewise way of walking, as from Parkinson's disease.

latescent (lā.tes′ent): becoming, or being, hidden from view, as a *latescent* meaning.

latibulize (la.tib′ū.līz): to hibernate.

laticostate (lat′i.kos′tāt): broad-ribbed.

Latinitaster (la.tin′i.tas′ter): one who has a smattering of Latin.

latipennate (lat′i.pen′āt): broad-winged.

latria (la.trī′a): the highest kind of worship, given to God only.

latrobe (la.trōb′): a kind of stove that heats the room above too.

latus (lā′tus): side.

lau-lau (lou′lou): meat and fish wrapped in leaves and baked or steamed. 38.

laureole (lô′ri.ōl): spurge-laurel. 1.

Laurus (lô′rus): a genus of trees comprising the laurel, bay laurel, bay tree, etc.

lavolt, lavolta (la.vōlt′, -a): an old dance for two persons, consisting largely of making high springs. 1.

lav (lav): short for lavatory.

lavor (lav′er): basin, laver.

lawk, lawks (lôk, -s): minced form of *Lord,* used esp. in surprise. 11.

layboy (lā′boi): a papermaking-machine attachment that delivers sheets in piles.

leal (lēl): faithful; loyal; true. Genuine, correct. 5.

leam (lēm): a gleam of light, radiance. To shine forth; gleam. 44A. A drain in a fen. 13. To remove (nuts) from the husk.

leat (lēt): an artificial trench for water, esp. one leading to or from a mill. 13.

lecanomancy, lecanoscopy (lek.a.no.-man′si, -nos′ko.pi): divination by gazing fixedly at water in a basin.

lech (lech): a prehistoric monumental stone. A lecher. 21.

lectual (lek′chōō.al): bedridden.

Ledum (lē′dum): a small genus of shrubs of cold regions, as the Labrador tea and the marsh tea. (not cap) A plant of this genus.

leeangle, liangle (lē′ang′gl): a heavy weapon of the Australian aborigines having a sharp-pointed end bent at right angles to the shank.

legulian (leg′ū.lē′an): a lawyer, pettifogger. Lawyerlike (used pejoratively).

legumen (li.gū′men): a legume.

legumin (li.gū′min): vegetable cassein.

Leipoa (lī.pō′a): a genus of Australian mound-building birds of mixed white, brown, black, and gray plumage. The adults are about two feet long.

lelotrichous (le.lot′ri.kus): smooth-haired.

lemel (lē′mel): metal filings.

lenify (len′i.fi, lēn-): to assuage; soften. 52.

lenitic (li.nit′ik): living in quiet waters.

lenitude (len′i.tūd): the quality of being lenient. A lenient action.

lentando (len.tän′dō): in music, becoming slower; retarding—used as a direction.

lentiginous (len.tij.i.nus): freckly.

lentiscus (len.tis′kus): the mastic tree. A preparation of its leaves, used as an adulterant of sumac.

lentitude (len′ti.tūd): slowness; sluggishness; languor.

lentoid (len′toid): lens-shaped.

lentor (len′tôr): tenacity; also, sluggishness.

lenvoy (len.voi′): to bid farewell.

lepid (lep′id): pleasant; jocose; charming. 52.

lepidosiren (lep′i.do.sī′ren): a dipnoan eel-shaped fish inhabiting the swamps and tributaries of the Amazon and La Plata.

leptorrhinian (lep′to.rin′i.an): having a long thin nose.

lerret (ler′et): a powerful sea boat with sails and oars, used in the English Channel.

lesed (lēst): damaged; injured. 18A.

lethiferous (le.thif′er.us): deadly; destructive.

leucomelanous (lū.ko.mel′a.nus): pert. to a light complexion with dark hair and eyes.

leucous (lū′kus): white, blond—applied esp. to albinos.

levoduction (lev′o.duk′shun): a leftward movement, esp. of the eye.

lexiphanic (lek′si.fan′ik): interlarded with pretentious words; bombastic.

li (lē): in China, as a measure of weight, a decigram; as a measure of distance, a millimeter, kilometer, or centiare. In Chinese philosophy, correct behavior as the expression of inner harmony.

Liassic (li.as′ik): in geology, pert. to the Lias, the oldest division of the European Jurassic system.

liberticidal (li′bur′ti.sī′dal): destroying or tending to destroy liberty.

licca (lik′a): a West Indian tree.

lich (lich): a body; esp., a dead body, a corpse. 17A.

licitation (lis′i.tā′shun): the act of selling or bidding at auction.

lieve (lēv): lief.

ligger (lig′er): a counterpane, coverlet; a float that usu. consists of a bundle of reeds with baited line attached for pike fishing; a footpath (as a plank) across a ditch or drain. 13.

liguration (lig′ū.rā′shun): a greedy licking or devouring. 52.

ligyrophobia (lij′i.ro.fō′bi.a): fear of loud noises.

lilaceous (lī.lā′shus): like the color lilac.

lilapsophobia (lī.lap′so.fō′bi.a): fear of tornadoes.

liliaceous (lil′i.ā′shus): like or pert. to lilies.

lill (lil): in music, one of the holes of a pipe or other wind instrument. 44. A very small pin. To loll; said of the tongue. 11.

limaceous, limacine (lī.mā′shus, līm′a.sin): pert. to slugs.

Limax (lī′maks): the genus containing the typical slugs.

limberham (lim′ber.ham): a supple-jointed person; one who is obsequious. 1.

limbous (lim′bus): with slightly overlapping borders—said of a suture.

limen (lī′men): the borderline of awareness.

limicolous (lī.mik′o.lus): living in mud.

limitrophe (lim′i.trōf): adjacent; on the frontier.

limity (lim′i.ti): a limit. 1.

limivorous (li.miv′o.rus): swallowing mud for the organic matter contained in it.

limnophilous (lim.nof′i.lus): living in freshwater ponds.

limosis (lī.mō′sis): a morbid desire to eat chalk. Any insatiable craving for food.

Limulus (lim′ū.lus): the commonly used generic name of the king or horseshoe crab.

lin (lin): the linden. Flax; linen; to stop; desist. 11. In Chinese mythology, a female unicorn.

lincture (lingk′cher): a thick cough syrup to be licked or sucked.

lind, lynde (lind): the linden.

lindo (lin′dō): any of several bright-colored South American tanagers.

lingel, lingle (ling′gl): a shoemaker's thread; a little thong of leather. 44.

linguacious (lin.gwā′shus): loquacious.

linonophobia (lin′on.o.fō′bi.a): fear of string.

linous (lī′nus): pert. to, or in, a line. 52.

liparoid (lip′a.roid): fatty.

lipectomy (li.pek′to.mi): the surgical removal of fat.

lipogram (lip′o.gram): a written passage in which specified letters of the alphabet are avoided.

lipography (li.pog′ra.fi): the inadvertent omission of a letter, syllable, etc. in writing.

lipper (lip′er): ripply waves; light sea spray. In whaling, a piece of blubber used for wiping the deck. A tool for forming the lip on glass containers. To wipe with a lipper. 13.

THE LIRIPOOP AND HIS LIRIPIPE

A liripoop (read *nincompoop*)
    Affected silly clothing,
Quite unaware folks called him ''stupe,''
    And looked on him with loathing.

One day he donned a liripipe,
    And rudely he was baited
When strolling in his hood and stripe,
    Liripipionated.

Some kids, cheered on by kin and kith,
    Soon had his life at risk.
They pummeled him in every lith,
    They kicked him in the lisk.

And when he sought to loppet off,
    They threw him in a ditch,
Where still his hood he would not doff,
    Though beaten to a lich.

They laid him in a litten dim,
    Nor guessed, those guttersnipes,
The saints in heaven welcomed him
    All wearing liripipes.

---

lippitude (lip′i.tūd): soreness or bleariness of the eyes.

lipsanography (lip′sa.nog′ra.fi): the study of relics.

lipsanotheca (lip′sa.no.thē′ka): a shrine or container for relics.

liration (lī.rā′shun): a ridge (as on some shells) resembling a fine thread or hair.

lirella (li.rel′a): an elongated spore structure in lichens that has a furrow along the middle.

liripipe (lir′i.pīp): a medieval hood, esp. one worn by academics. 6.

liripoop (lir′i.pōōp): a trick. A silly ass. Also, a liripipe. 6.

lirp (lurp): a snap of the fingers; to snap them. 1.

lis (lēs): in heraldry, a fleur-de-lis.

lish (lish): active; agile; quick. 43.

lisk (lisk): the groin. 11.

lissen (lis′en): a cleft dividing the seam of a rock. A support for a beehive. A strand of rope. 11.

lissotrichous (lis′o.trik′us): having straight hair.

literatim (lit′er.ā′tim): letter for letter; literally.

lith (lith): a joint or limb; a bodily member. A division or segment, as of an orange. 44A.

lithoglyph (lith′o.glif): an engraving on stone, esp. on a gem; an engraved stone.

lithoid (lith′oid): like a stone.

lithomancy (lith.o.man′si): divination by stones or stone charms.

lithophagan, lithophagous (li.thof′a.gan, -gus): swallowing stones or gravel. Burrowing in rock.

lithophane (lith′o.fān): porcelain impressed with figures that are made distinct by transmitted light, as in a lampshade.

---

lithotripter (lith′o.trip′ter): a medical device that shatters stones in the kidney by shock waves without injuring surrounding tissue.

litten (lit′en): a churchyard or cemetery. 2.

littlin (lit′lin): a young or small child or animal. 43.

liturate (lich′er.āt): spotted. To blot out, erase. 1.

litus (lī′tus): in Frankish and some German medieval law, one of a class between the free man and the slave or serf.

llanero (lya.ner′ō): a cowboy or herdsman in South America.

loa (lō′a): a kind of African filiarial worm infecting humans, and transmitted by the bite of a fly.

lochus (lō′kus): a small division of an ancient Greek army, of about 100 to 200 men.

logan, login (lō′gen): a stretch of still water in a river or bay. 28.

loganamnosis (lō′ga.nam.nō′sis): preoccupation with trying to recall forgotten words.

loggin (log′in): a bundle, as of straw.

logodaedaly (lō′go.ded′a.li): verbal legerdemain; wordplay. 52.

logolept (lō′go.lept): a word freak.

logology (lo.gol′o.ji): the science of words. 52.

logomachy (lo.gom′a.ki): contention about or by means of words.

loka (lō′ka): in Hindu mythology, a world; sphere; universe.

loke (lōk): var. of *lawk.* A private road; a lane; a blind alley. 13.

lollock (lol′uk): per Mrs. Byrne, a large lump.

lollop (lol′up): to loll, lounge, slouch about. To proceed with a bouncing or bobbing motion. 13.

Loma (lō′ma): a people of the border regions of Liberia, Sierra Leone, and the Republic of Guinea. (not cap) A broad-topped hill. 35A.

lomi-lomi (lō′mi.lō′mi): a vigorous massage used by Hawaiians to relieve pain and fatigue.

---

*YOUNG MAN'S PLEA OF NOT GUILTY
TO A VERY LONG WORD*

What—did I trap her? No.
What—have I kissed her? No.
What—were we palping? No.
All was correct with me.
    She'll say the same.

She's had a *laparo-*
            hystero-
        salpingo-
            o-o-forectomy?
I'm not to blame.

longe (lunj): var. of *lunge*. A long rope used to lead a horse in training. A place, usu. a ring, for training horses. The *namaycush*.

longicaudal (lon'ji.kô'dal): long-tailed.

longiloquy (lon.jil'o.kwi): long-windedness.

longimanous (lon.jim'a.nus): long-handed.

longinquity (lon.jin'kwi.ti): remoteness. 52.

longipennate (lon.ji.pen'āt): long-winged.

longirostral (lon'ji.ros'tral): having a long jaw.

loob (lōōb): the slimy dregs of tin ore; the trough containing them.

loof (lōōf): the palm of the hand; the inside of a cat's paw. 43A.

lopper (lop'er): curdled milk; a blood clot; slush; curdled. 5. To curdle. 12, 13.

loppet (lop'et): to walk or run awkwardly. 13.

lorikeet (lor'i.kēt): a small brightly colored parrot of the Malay archipelago.

lorimer (lor'i.mer): a maker of bits, spurs, and metal mountings for bridles and saddles.

loro (lō'rō): the monk parrot. The parrot fish.

lotic (lō'tik): pert. to or living in actively moving water.

Lotophagi (lo.tof'a.jī, -jī): in the *Odyssey*, a people who subsisted on the lotus and lived in the dreamy indolence it induced.

lotophagous (lo.tof'a.gus): lotus-eating.

louche (lōōsh): squinting. Oblique, devious, sinister.

loury (lou'ri): var. of *lowery*, overcast.

loutrophoros (loo.trof'er.os): in ancient Greece, a vase used for transporting ceremonial bathwater for the bride and groom.

lovertine (luv'er.tēn): one addicted to lovemaking.1.

lowmen (lō'men): dice loaded to turn up low numbers.

loxotic (lok.sot'ik): in medicine, slanting, distorted.

loxotomy (lok.sot'o.mi): in amputation, an oblique section.

loy (loi): a long narrow spade used in Ireland. A tool for digging postholes. 32.

lubric (lōō'brik): lubricious. 52.

luce (lōōs): a pike, esp. when full grown. In heraldry, a fleur-de-lis. A lynx. 1.

luciferous (lōō.sif'er.us): affording physical or mental illumination.

lucifugous (loo.sif'u.gus): avoiding light.

lucivee (lōō'si.vi): a lynx (corruption of *loup-cervier*).

luciferous (loo.krif'er.us): profitable; lucrative.

luctation (luk.tā'shun): a struggle; endeavor. 1.

luctiferous (luk.tif'er.us): mournful; sorry. 52.

lud (lud): var. of *lord*. (cap) A legendary king of Britain.

ludicropathetic, ludicroserious (lōō-'di.kro.pa.thet'ik, -sēr'i.us): ludicrous and either pathetic or serious at once.

ludification (lōō'di.fi.kā'shun): the act of deriding.

luggar (lug'er): any of several large Asiatic falcons of dull-brown color.

luggy (lug'i): a small wooden pail or dish with a handle. 44A.

lulliloo (lul.i.lōō): to welcome with cries of joy.

lum (lum): a chimney; a sink; pool; pond. 11. An area of softness in a coal seam. 30.

lunt (lunt): smoke, esp. of a pipe; a torch; to kindle, light. 44A.

lupanarian (lōō'pa.nâr'i.an): pert. to brothels.

lupulus (lōō'pū.lus): the hop plant.

lura (lōō'ra): in anatomy, the orifice of the infundibulum of the brain.

lurry (lur'i): something, as a formula or a canting speech, repeated by rote; a confused throng or aggregation; a jumble of sounds, tumult. 10. To drag; worry; hurry. 11. Var. of *lorry*.

lusk (lusk): lazy; a lazy person. 11. To loaf; idle; skulk. 1.

lusory (lū'zer.i): sportive; playful; composed in a playful style.

lutarious (lōō.târ.i.us): living in mud.

lutescent (lōō.tes'ent): yellowish.

lutulence (lōō'tū.lens): muddiness, turbidity.

lychnoscopic (lik'no.skop'ik): pert. to a low side window of medieval churches.

lycopode (lī'ko.pōd): powder of lycopodium, the club moss known also as ground pine, ground fir, etc.

Lycopsis (lī.kop'sis): a genus of bristly herbs, inc. the wild bugloss.

lygophilia (lī'go.fēl'ya): love of darkness.

lygophobia (lī'go.fō'bi.a): fear of darkness.

lymacatexis (lī'ma.ka.tek'sis): preoccupation with dirt.

lypophrenia (lī'po.frē'ni.a): sadness for no known reason.

lyssophobia (lis'o.fō'bi.a): morbid dread of hydrophobia.

M

mab (mab): to dress sloppily; a slattern. 1.

Macaca (ma.kä'ka): a genus of Old World monkeys, the macaques.

macaco (ma.kä'kō): any of several lemurs, as the black lemur and the ring-tailed lemur.

macarize (mak.a.rīz): to laud; declare happy or blessed.

machi (mä'chi): in Japan, a town or commercial center.

machinal (ma.shē'nal): pert. to machines.

mackalow (mak'a.lō): goods held in trust by a foster parent for the child. 7A.

macrobian (ma.krō'bi.an): long-lived.

macrodactylic (ma'kro.dak.til'ik): long-fingered.

macrology (ma.krol'o.ji): redundancy.

macromastic (ma'kro.mas'tik): having excessively developed mammary glands.

macrophobia (ma'cro.fō'bi.a): a fear of long waits.

macrosmatic (mak'rz.mat'ik): having a supersensitive nose.

macrotome (ma'kro.tōm): an instrument for making large sections of anatomical specimens.

macrotous (ma.krō'tus): having large ears.

mactation (mak.tā'shun): sacrificial murder.

OR AT LEAST MAKE UP AFTERWARDS

Since women take *mariticide*
  In stride
(I understand the merest bride
  Can do it):
While husbands hear that word and flinch,
For their own wives might in a pinch
  Go to it;

Since women, though, cannot abide
  Uxoricide,
Whence certain of their sex have died
  Unknowing—
Have vanished from the ones they love,
Nor stood upon the order of
  Their going;

Since dead by either word is just
  As dust;—
Let me suggest, to be discussed,
  A moral:
Can't men be more *uxorious*,
And wives more *maritorious*?
To drive uxoricide away,
To keep mariticide at bay—
  Don't quarrel.

---

macuta (ma.kōō'ta): an old west African coin or unit of value.

madefaction (mad'i.fak'shun): wetting.

madrasah (ma.dras'a): in India, a Mohammedan university.

maffle (maf'l): to stammer; blunder. To confuse. 2.

mafflin (maf'lin): a simpleton. 13.

mafoo, mafu (ma.fōō'): in China, a groom or stable boy.

magadis (mag′a.dis): a Greek dulcimer. A Lydian flute on which octaves could be played.

magger (mag′er): var. of *mauger*. 9.

magian (mā′ji.an): magical. (cap) One of the Magi, a priestly order of ancient Medea and Persia.

magiric (ma.jī′rik): pert. to the art of cookery. 52.

magister (maj′is.ter): a medieval title given to a person in authority or to a licensed teacher.

magnetopause (mag.net′o.pôz): the boundary between the terrestrial and the interplanetary magnetic field.

maha (mä′ha): the Ceylonese langur, a long-tailed monkey. Also, the sambar deer.

Mahadeva (mä′ha.dē′va): Siva.

maholi (ma.hō′li): a long-eared African lemur.

maieusiophobia (mä.ū′si.o.fō′bi.a): fear of childbirth.

mainour (mā′ner): in old English law, stolen goods found on the thief.

maja (mä′ha): a Spanish belle of the lower classes.

majagua (ma.hä′gwa): a small tropical tree yielding a durable fiber.

majestatic (maj′es.tat′ik): majestic. 1.

maki (mak′i): a lemur.

makimono (mäk.i.mō′nō): in Japan, a picture, picture story, or writing mounted on paper and usu. rolled in a scroll.

mako, makomako (mä′kō, mä′ko.-mä′kō): a New Zealand tree.

malacissation (mal′a.si.sä′shun): the act of making something soft or pliable.

malacodermous (mal′a.ko.dur′mus): soft-skinned.

malactic (ma.lak′tik): emollient; tending to soften.

malaxator (mal.ak.sā′ter): a machine for grinding, kneading, or stirring into a pasty or doughy mass.

malentendu (mal′än′tän.dū): misunderstood; a misunderstanding.

maliferous (ma.lif′er.us): harmful; unhealthy, as certain climates.

malik (mal′ik): in Hindu law, an owner, a proprietor.

malleate (mal′i.āt): to hammer; to beat into a plate, sheet, or leaf, as a metal. 52.

malleolus (ma.lē′ō.lus): the rounded lateral projection on the bone of the leg at the ankle.

malmaison (mal′mä′zen′): any of various tender greenhouse carnations with large, fully double, usu. pink flowers.

malmy (mä′mi): clayey, chalky soil. Soft; warm and sticky, as weather. 44C.

malneirophrenia (mal.nī′ro.frē′ni.a): depression following a nightmare.

malo (mal′ō): in Hawaii, a loincloth worn by men. An ornamental royal girdle.

malum (mä′lum): pl. *mala*. An offense against right or law; evil, wrong.

mamamouchi (mä.ma.mōō′chi): in Molière's *Le Bourgeois Gentilhomme*, a bogus Turkish title. One with such a title.

mameliere (mam.el.yâr): in medieval armor, one of two round plates, or a single plate, covering the breasts.

mamelon (mam′i.lon): a low, rounded hill.

mameluco (mam′i.lōō′kō): in Brazil, a mestizo.

mammock (mam′uk): a shapeless piece; a scrap. 11.

mammonism (mam′un.izm): devotion to wealth; worldliness.

mammothrept (mam′o.thrept): a spoiled child; lit., a child brought up by its grandmother.

manal (man′al): pert. to the hand.

manavelins (ma.nav′el.inz): leftovers; odds and ends. 59.

manbote (man′bōt): in Anglo-Saxon and old English law, compensation paid to a lord for the killing of his man.

manchet (man′chet): a wheaten bread of the highest quality. 9. A spindle-shaped roll of manchet. A piece of white bread. 11A.

mancinism (man′si.nizm): left-handedness.

mancipate (man′si.pāt): enslaved. To enslave or restrict. 1.

mandillion (man.dil′yun): a loose outer garment of the 16th and 17th centuries, as a soldier's sleeved cloak or a servant's sleeveless garment.

mandola (man.dō′la): a 16th- and 17th-century lute with a pear-shaped body, the ancestor of today's smaller mandolin.

mandom (man′dum): a word used by Browning for *mankind*.

mandra (man′dra): in the Eastern church, a monastery.

manducatory (man′dū.ka.tôr′i): related to or adapted for chewing.

manerial (ma.nē′ri.al): manorial. 52.

mang (mang): to lead or go astray. 43.

mangonize (mang′go.nīz): to traffic in slaves. 52. To furbish up for sale. 1.

maniaphobia (mä′ni.a.fō′bi.a): fear of insanity.

manipulandum (ma.nip′ū.lan′dum): in psychology, something to be manipulated.

manit (man′it): the amount of work done by one worker in one minute; a man-minute.

mannie (man′i): a little man; in affectionate use, a boy or lad. 44A.

mansuete (man.swēt′, man′swēt): tame; gentle; kind.

manteel (man.tēl′): a cloak or cape; a mantle. 1.

mantology (man.tol′o.ji): divination. 52.

manucaption (man.ū.kap′shun): a former system of law serving a purpose similar to bail, or writ for the production in court of an alleged felon.

manucaptor (man′ū.kap′ter): one who takes responsibility for the appearance of an accused in court and for defending him.

manuduction (man′ū.duk′shun): guidance as by the hand; direction. A guide; an introduction.

manuductor (man′ū.duk′ter): director, esp. of a band or choir.

manurement (ma.nūr′ment): cultivation. 1.

manustupration (man′ū.stū.prā′shun): masturbation.

maquillage (ma′ki.yäzh): makeup.

Mara (mä′ra): in Teutonic folklore, nightmare taken as a demon, usu. female. In Buddhist mythology, the spirit of evil and enemy of the Buddha. In the Bible, the name claimed by Naomi, meaning bitter. Also (not cap.) a rodent of Patagonia related to the cavies.

marcato (mär.kä′to): in music, marked, emphatic; accented.

marcescible (mär.ses′i.bl): liable to wither or fade.

marcidity (mär.sid′i.ti): state of witheredness, decay, exhaustion. 1.

maremma (ma.rem′a): in Italy, low marshy maritime country, which in summer is so unhealthy as to be uninhabitable. The miasma of such a region.

margaritaceous (mär′ga.ri.tā′shus): pearly.

margent (mär′jent): a margin; border; brink; edge. 9.

margosa (mär.gō′sa): a large East Indian tree having a bitter bark used as a tonic.

maricolous (ma.rik′o.lus): inhabiting the sea.

marigenous (ma.rij′i.nus): produced in or by the sea.

marikina (mar′i.kē′na): the silky tamarind.

mariticide (ma.rit′i.sīd): murder of a husband by his wife; a wife who kills her husband.

maritodespotism (mar′i.to.des′po.tizm): domination by the husband.

maritorious (mar′i.tôr′i.us): excessively fond of one's husband; female equivalent of *uxorious*.

markhor (mär′kôr): a wild goat of mountainous regions from Afghanistan to India.

markka (märk′ka): the gold monetary unit of Finland.

marlet (mär′let): a martin or a swift. 1.

marlock (mär′lok): to frolic; sport; a frolic. 13.

marmarize (mär′ma.rīz): to convert (limestone) into marble.

marouflage (ma′rōō.fläzh): the process of painting on canvas and then gluing the picture to the wall.

marrano (ma.rä′nō): a Jew or Moor in medieval Spain who professed Christianity to escape prosecution.

martyrium (mär.tir′i.um): a building or chamber used by early Christians as a burial place. A place where the relics of martyrs are stored.

marum (mar′um): cat thyme. Also, var. of *marram,* beach grass.

marver (mär′ver): a flat slab (as of metal, stone, or wood) on which a gather of glass is rolled, shaped, and cooled.

maschaliphidrōsis (mas.kal.i.fi.drō′sis): heavy sweating of the armpits.

mascle (mas′kl): male. 1. A steel plate, esp. of lozenge shape, used in series on 13th-century armor.

mashallah (mash.al′a): an Arabic exclamation, signifying "What wonders has God wrought!"

mashugga (ma.shoog′a): crazy.

maskoid (mas′koid): like a mask. A masklike carving on ancient Mexican and Peruvian buildings.

masticic (mas.tis′ik): pert. to mastic.

mastigophobia (mas′ti.go.fō′bi.a): fear of punishment.

mataco (ma.tä′kō): a three-banded armadillo, the apar. (cap) A people of Bolivia, Paraguay, and Argentina.

matamata (mä′ta.mä′ta): a turtle of the rivers of Guiana and northern Brazil, reaching a length of three feet, with rough shell and long neck. Also, any of several South American trees.

matanza (ma.tan′za): a slaughterhouse. 35C.

matchy (mach′i): fit for matching or mating.

matelassē (mat′la.sā): decorated with markings like quilting; a fabric so decorated.

matelotage (mat′lo.täzh): the hire of a boat. The communal living of West Indian buccaneers in the 18th century.

mathesis (ma.thē′sis): learning; mental discipline, esp. in mathematics.

matico (ma.tē′kō): a shrubby tropical American wild pepper. Also, its leaves, used formerly as a stimulant and hemostatic.

matra (mä′tra): in Sanskrit and other Indian languages, a unit of metrical quantity.

matric (mä′trik): pert. to a matrix.

matripotestal (mä′tri.po.tes′tal): pert. to maternal control.

matronize (mā′tro.nīz): to make into or like a matron. To chaperone.

mauger, maugre (mô′gr): in spite of, notwithstanding. 9. Ill will; spite—often used as a mild imprecation. 1.

maugh (môg): a brother-in-law; a son-in-law; a companion. 13.

maut (môt): var. of *malt.* 44A.

maxilliped (mak.sil′i.ped): one of the mouth appendages of crustaceans.

mazological (mä′zo.loj′i.kal): pert. to mammiferous animals.

mazomancy (mä′zo.man′si): divination by interpretation of a baby's nursing.

mazophilous (ma.zof′i.lus): mad about breasts.

mbori (em.bôr′i): a fever and hemhorragic disease, a mild form of surra, affecting camels.

meable (mē′a.bl): readily penetrable.

meacock (mē′kok): an uxorious, effeminate, or spiritless man. 1.

meak (mēk): a long-handled hook or scythe. 13.

mease (mēz): to pacify, calm. 44A. A measure for counting herrings, varying in different localities. 14.

mechanograph (mi.kan′o.graf): a copy of an artwork, produced by mechanical means.

mechanomorphism (mi.ka′no.môr′fizm): the belief that the universe can be explained mechanically.

mechanophobia (mek′a.no.fō′bi.a): fear of machines.

meconology (mek′o.nol′o.ji): the study of opium.

meconophagism (mek′o.nof′a.jizm): addiction to opium.

meda (mē′dā): var. of *mide, midewiwin.*

medalet (med′l.et): a small medal.

medicaster (med′i.kas′ter): a medical charlatan or quack.

mediety (mi.dī′i.ti): the half; moiety. 6A. Middle or intermediate part. 1. Moderation, temperance.

meech, miche (mēch, mich): to move in a furtive or cringing manner; to skulk, sneak; to complain, whine. 11.

meechy (mēch′i): sneaky, dishonorable.

megalonisis (meg′a.lō′ni.sis): a tendency to exaggerate.

Megalonyx (meg′a.lon′iks): a genus of large extinct Pliocene and Pleistocene toothless mammals of North America.

megalophobia (meg.a.lo.fō′bi.a): fear of anything large.

megalophonous (meg.a.lof′a.nus): having a loud voice.

megatype (meg′a.tīp): an enlarged copy of a picture or negative.

mehari (me.hä′ri): a kind of swift dromedary once used by the French army in Algeria.

meinie (mān′i): a family, household; a herd. 1.

meizoseismal (mī′zo.sīz′mal): pert. to the maximum destructive force of an earthquake.

mel (mel): honey. Also, a subjective unit of tone pitch.

melangeur (me.län.zhur′): a machine for making chocolate syrup.

melanochroic (mel.an.o.krō′ik): pert. to Caucasians having dark hair and pale complexions.

melanous (mel′a.nus): having dark skin and black hair.

melcryptovestimentaphilia (mel.krip′-to.ves′ti.men′ta.fil′i.a): a fondness for women's black underwear.

melic (mel′ik): of or pert. to song.

meline (mē′lin, -lin): canary yellow. Also, made up of or resembling badgers.

melisophobia (mel′is.o.fō′bi.a): fear of bees.

melittology (mel.i.tol′o.ji): the scientific study of bees.

mell (mel): the last cut of grain in the harvest; a feast at the close of harvest; a hammer or mallet made of wood; a booby prize; to join; to join in combat (usu. with *with*). 13.

melliloquy (mel.lil′o.kwi): sweet speech.

melodion (mi.lō′di.on): a keyboard musical instrument of graduated metal rods, sounded by a revolving metal cylinder.

melogram (mel′o.gram): a graphic record showing the tones of successive syllables, words, phrases, sentences, etc.

melograph (mel′o.graf): a contrivance for recording the order and length of musical notes by recording the action of the keys of a keyboard.

melolog (mel′o.log): a declamation with musical accompaniment.

melomania (mel′o.mā′ni.a): inordinate passion for music.

melophobia (mel′o.fō′bi.a): hatred of music.

melopeia (mel′o.pē′a): the art of inventing melody; melodics; melody.

melote (mi.lō′ti): a monk's hair coat. 1.

Melursus (mel.ur′sus): the genus consisting of the sloth bear.

menacme (mi.nak′mi): the part of her life in which a woman menstruates.

mendaciloquy (men′da.sil′o.kwi): lying as a fine art.

mendicity (men.dis′i.ti): begging; mendicancy.

menilite (men′i.līt): an impure opal of a dull brown to gray color.

mennom (men′um): a minnow. 44A.

menology (mi.nol′o.ji): an ecclesiastical calendar of festivals honoring saints and martyrs. A register of saints.

menophania (men′o.fā′ni.a): false menstruation.

menticide (men′ti.sīd): brainwashing.

mentimutation (men′ti.mū.tā′shun): a change of mind.

mentulate (men′tū.lāt): having a large penis.

meracious (mi.rā′shus): unadulterated; pure.

meraculous (mi.rak′ū.lus): slightly dirty.

mercative (mur′ka.tiv): pert. to trade or commerce.

merdaille (mer.dīl′): the rabble.

merdivorous (mer.div′o.rus): dung-eating.

merenda (mi.ren′da): a snack between meals.

meritmonger (mer′it.mung′ger): one who expects salvation as a reward for good works.

merkin (mur′kin): the female pubis; a wig for it. 3A.

merorganization (mer.ôr′gan.i.zā′shun): a partial organization. 52.

merse (murs): land near water. 43. To immerse. 52.

mersion (mur′zhun): immersion. 1.

merulator (mer′ū.lā′ter): a wine bibber.

merycism (mer′i.sizm): the chewing of regurgitated food, or of the cud.

mesophilic (mez′o.fil′ik): thriving or growing best in medium temperatures.

mesothetic (mez′o.thet′ik): intermediate.

Messalian (mi.sāl′yun): a Euchite, one of an ecstatic, mendicant, vagrant Christian sect of the 4th to 8th century, which believed man's congenital devil could be expelled only by unremitting prayer.

mestee (mes.tē′): strictly, an octoroon; loosely, a half-caste.

metabasis (mi.tab′a.sis): in rhetoric, a transition from one subject or point to another. In medicine, a change in a disease, its symptoms, or treatment.

metabatic (met′a.bat′ik): pert. to the transfer of heat or any form of energy.

Metabola (mi.tab′o.la): a division of the insects that undergo a metamorphosis.

metad (me.täd′): a small field rat.

metagnostic (met′ag.nos′tik): unknowable.

metagrabolize (met.a.grab′o.līz): to mystify. 58.

metalepsis (met′a.lep′sis): in rhetoric, substitution by metonymy of one figurative sense for another.

metaleptic (met.a.lep′tik): pert. to a metalepsis. Also, designating a muscle having synergetic action with another muscle.

metallochrome (mi.tal′o.krōm): a coloring or ring produced on metal by the electrolytic decomposition of copper, lead peroxide, etc.

metallogeny (met′l.oj′e.ni): the branch of geology dealing with the origin of ore deposits.

metanalysis (met.a.nal′i.sis): the evolution of words into new elements (*a napron* into *an apron*) or their misdivision (*selfish* into *sell fish*).

metaplast (met′a.plast): a form made by a change in the letters or syllables of a word.

metayer (met′a.yā): a sharecropper.

metempirical (met′em.pir′i.kal): pert. to concepts outside human experience.

metempsychosis (met′em.sī.kō′sis): the transmigration of souls.

metemptosis (met′emp.tō′sis): the suppression of a day in the calendar to prevent the date of the new moon being set a day too late. The suppression of the bissextile day once in 134 years.

metensomatosis (met′en.sō′ma.tō′sis): the migration into one body of different souls.

meteoromancy (mē′ti.er.o.man′si): divination through thunder and lightning.

meterstick (mē′ter.stik): a device for leveling or measuring cargo.

metic (met′ik): in ancient Greece, a settler; immigrant; at Athens, an alien resident who had some civil privileges.

metical (met′i.kal): a coin of Mozambique.

metopomancy (met′o.po.man′si): divination by examination of the face.

metoposcopy (met′o.pos′ko.pi): the art of discovering character from the markings of the forehead.

metrician (mi.trish′un): a writer or student of verse.

metromania (met′ro.mā′ni.a): a mania for writing verse.

metrophobia (met′ro.fō.bi.a): hostility toward poetry.

meum (mē′um): mine, as in *meum and tuum*, ''mine and yours.'' (cap) A genus of European herbs of the carrot family.

meuse (mūz): a gap or hole, as in a hedge or wall, through which wild animal is accustomed to pass. A loophole.

meute (mūt): a mew or cage for hawks.

mezonny (mi.zon′i): money spent on drugs. 21.

miche (mich): a loaf of bread. 1. To pilfer. 1. To lurk; grumble secretly; play truant. 11.

michery (mich′er.i): theft; cheating. 1.

mico (mē′kō): a marmoset, esp. the black-tailed marmoset of parts of tropical South America.

microbiotic (mī′kro.bī.ot′ik): of a seed, surviving dormant for not more than three years. Also, pert. to the microscopical flora and fauna of a region.

microlipet (mī′kro.lip′et): one upset by trifles.

microlithic (mī′kro.lith′ik): pert. to a tiny blade tool used in the paleolithic culture.

micromastic (mī′kro.mas′tik): having abnormally small breasts.

microstudy (mī′kro.stud′i): a study of a minute, specific, or minor part of a subject.

microtia (mī.krō′sha): smallness of the ear.

microtome (mī′kro.tōm): in biology, an instrument for cutting sections, as of organic tissues, for microscopic examination.

mide, midewiwin (mē′di, mi.di′wi.win): a once-powerful secret religious organization among the Ojibway Indians. A member of this organization.

milder (mil′der): to molder, decay. 13.

militaster (mil′i.tas′ter): an insignificant military man. 1.

mim (mim): affectedly shy. To act in a mim fashion. 11.

mimographer (mi.mog′ra.fer): a writer of mimes, in which scenes from life were represented in a ridiculous manner.

mimography (mi.mog′ra.fi): the art of reducing gestures or sign language to writing by means of symbols.

mimp (mimp): a pursing of the mouth or lips; to speak or act affectedly or mincingly. 44B.

mimsey (mim′zi): prim; prudish. 11.

minargent (mi.när′jent): a white alloy of copper, nickel, tungsten, and aluminum.

minauderie (mi.nôd′ri): (usu. pl.) Coquetry.

mingy (min′ji): stingy; mean. 26.

miniate (min′i.āt): pert. to the color of minium; to paint red.

minimifidianism (min′i.mi.fid′i.an.izm): the condition of having a minimal amount of faith.

minionette (min′yun.et): small, delicate. 1. In printing, a type size.

minium (min′i.um): red lead.

mino (mī′nō): in Japan, a cape or overcoat of straw, rushes, or the like, worn by peasants.

miny (mī′ni): pert. to a mine.

minyan (min′yun): in Jewish religion, a quorum, or number necessary for conducting public worship, consisting of not less than 10 males above the age of 13. (cap) Pert. to a prehistoric Greek civilization noted for its pottery.

Mirabel (mir′a.bel): a witty gentleman in Congreve's *Way of the World*. (not cap) A kind of plum.

mirabilia (mir′a.bil.i.a): wonders; miracles.

mirador (mir′a.dôr): a watchtower; a turret or window with an extensive outlook. The color reddish-orange.

mird (murd): to meddle; toy amorously; try. 44.

mirific, mirifical (mi.rif′ik, -rif′i.kal): working wonders; wonderful.

misapodisis (mis′a.pō′di.sis): a dislike of undressing in front of others.

miserotia (mis′er.ot′i.a): aversion to sex.

misocainia (mis′o.kī′ni.a): hatred of anything new or strange.

misogallic (mis′o.gal′ik): hating the French.

misomania (mis′o.mā′ni.a): hatred of everything.

misopedia (mis′o.pē′di.a): hatred of children, esp. one's own.

misophy (mis′o.fi): hatred of wisdom.

misopolemic (mis′o.po.lem′ik): hating war.

misoscopy (mi.sos′ko.pi): hatred of beauty or sights in general.

misotheism (mis′o.thē′izm): hatred of gods.

misotramontanism (mis′o.tra.mon′ta.- izm): hatred of the unknown.

missa (mis′a): (Latin): Mass, as *Missa bassa,* Low Mass, etc.

missionate (mish′u.nāt): to proselytize.

missis, missus (mis′iz, -uz): a married woman. Informally, one's wife.

mistetch (mis.tech′): a bad habit. To teach bad habits to. 13.

mistle (mis′l): mistletoe. 52.

mitrophobia (mī′tro.fō′bi.a): fear of hate.

mixogamy (mik.sog′a.mi): a surplus of male fish at spawning time.

Mixosaurus (mik′so.sôr′us): a genus of swimming reptiles of the Triassic Age similar to *Ichthyosaurus* but with less fully developed paddles.

mixoscopy (mik.sos′ko.pi): peeking at sexual intercourse from hiding.

mizzy (miz′i): a bog or quagmire. 11.

mneme (nē′mi): the persistent or recurrent effect of past experience of the individual or of the race.

mnesic (nē′sik): pert. to *mneme.*

mobby (mob′i): an alcoholic drink made from sweet potatoes in the West Indies. Fruit juice for distilling brandy; the brandy.

moch (mok, mōk): a moth. 44.

mogadore (mog′a.dôr): a ribbed silk or rayon fabric, used esp. for neckties.

moggan (mog′un): stocking; esp. a long stocking without a foot. 44.

mogigraphia (moj′i.graf′i.a): writer's cramp.

mogilalia (moj′i.lā′li.a, -lāl′ya): painful speech; stuttering.

mogo (mō′gō): an aboriginal stone hatchet.

moho (mō′hō): a Hawaiian honey eater having yellow breast feathers. (cap) A point at a depth ranging from about 3 miles beneath the ocean floor to about 25 miles beneath the continental surface where the earth's materials change from the crust to the mantle.

mohr (mōr): a gazelle of northern Africa with 11 or 12 prominent rings on its horns.

moider (moi′der): to throw into an unsettled state; perplex, bewilder, distract; to talk incoherently; to wander about in a confused manner. 13.

moiré (mô.rā, mwä′rā): a watered, clouded, or frosted appearance of silk, paper, rocks, or metals. To give such an appearance to (a surface).

moirologist (mwä.rol′o.jist): in Greece, a hired mourner.

moit (moit): var. of *mote; usu.* pl. A piece of stick or other matter found in wool.

OF MUGGETS AND MIRRORS

When muggets aren't the entrails of a calf or of a sheep,
They're lilies of the valley (you'll admit that's quite a leap).
Yet when I see the stranger in the mirror on the wall,
The difference in muggets seems no difference at all.

---

mojo (mō′jō): the *majagua.* A voodoo charm or amulet. 35A. (cap) An Arawakan people of northern Bolivia.

moki (mō.ki): the bastard trumpeter fish. A native raft made of bundles of rushes, flags, or dried flower stalks of flax. 56. (cap) Var. of *Moqui,* a branch of or another name for the Hopi Indians.

moko (mō′kō): the Maori system of tattooing. Also, a Maori tattoo of spiral grooves rubbed into the skin with a small instrument resembling an adz.

moko-moko (mō′ko.mō′kō): a common small lizard of New Zealand.

moky (mō′ki): foggy; misty. 11.

Mola (mō′la): the genus consisting of the sunfish.

molendinaceous (mo.len′di.nā′shus): resembling a windmill, as certain vegetable fruits or seeds.

moliminous (mo.lim′in.us): massive; momentous; also, laborious. 1.

mollescence (mo.les′ens): the state of softening, or tending to soften.

mollitious (mo.lish′us): softening; luxurious; sensuous.

mollitude (mol′i.tūd): softness. 52.

molossic, molossus (mo.los′ik, -us): in classical prosody, a foot of 3 long syllables. (cap) A genus of mastiff bats.

molybdomancy (mo.lib.do.man′si): divination by dropping molten lead on water.

molysmophobia (mol′is.mo.fō′bi.a): fear of dirt or contamination.

mome (mōm): a blockhead. 9. A cavilling critic. 1. A buffoon. 60.

mommiology (mom′i.ol′o.ji): the science of mummies. 52.

momo (mō′mō): the short-eared owl of Guam.

monachal (mon′a.kal): monastic.

monachist (mon′a.kist): monkish.

monadology (mō′na.dol′o.ji): the theory that the universe is composed of monads, or individual units. Monadism.

monepic (mo.nep′ik): consisting of one word or of sentences of one word.

monial (mō′ni.al): a nun.

monoblepsia (mon′o.blep′si.a): vision normal when but one eye is used, but indistinct with two. Also, color blindness for all but one color.

monocrotic (mon′o.krot′ik): of the pulse, having a simple beat and forming a smooth, single-crested curve on a sphygmogram.

monoculous (mo.nok′ū.lus): one-eyed.

monodelphic (mon′o.del′fik): pert. to the placental mammals.

monoglot (mon′o.glot): familiar with but a single language.

monogony (mo.nog′o.ni): asexual reproduction.

monokini (mon.o.kē′ni): a bikini without the top.

monolatry (mo.nol′a.tri): the worship of but one among several gods.

monophasic (mon′o.fā′zik): of electricity, single-phase; of an animal, having a single period of activity followed by a period of rest in each 24 hours.

monophobia (mon′o.fō′bi.a): fear of being alone.

monophylite (mo.nof′i.līt): one who believes that mankind developed from a single parent form.

monophysite (mo.nof′i.sīt): one who maintains that there was but a single nature in Christ, or that the human and divine in Him constituted but one composite nature.

monostrophe (mon′o.strōf′i): a poem in which all the stanzas are of the same metric form.

monotic (mo.not′ik): affecting a single ear, as a sound.

monotriglyph (mon′o.trī′glif): in architecture, intercolumniation with only one triglyph over the space between two columns.

monotropic (mon′o.trop′ik): visiting only a single kind of flower for nectar.

monstration (mon.strā′shun): demonstration. 1.

monstricide (mon′stri.sīd): the slaying of a monster.

monteith (mon.tēth′): an 18th-century silver punch bowl. A kind of polka dot handkerchief.

montigenous (mon.tij′e.nus): produced on a mountain.

Montjoy (mont.joi′): a medieval French battle cry. 1.

mool (mōōl): mold; dry earth. (often pl.) a grave or its earth; to crumple; bury. 44C.

mopsical (mop′si.kal): like a spoiled child; pettish. 1.

mopus (mō′pus): a small coin. 23. (usu. pl) Money. 13.

mora (mō′ra): in Roman and civil law, a culpable delay. In Sparta, an army division. Also, a poisonous tree of the Amazon valley.

morcellate (môr′si.lāt): to divide into small pieces.

moreta (mo.ret′a): a salad with garlic.

morganize (môr′ga.nīz): to kidnap as insurance against a security leak.

moriform (môr.i.fôrm): shaped like a mulberry.

morigerous (mo.rij′er.us): obsequious.

mormaor (môr.mā′er): the ruler of one of the seven provinces into which medieval Scotland was divided. 44.

Moro (mō′rō, mo′rō): any of several Muslim peoples of the southern Philippines, or their languages.

morology (mo.rol′o.ji): nonsense; foolishness.

morosaurian (môr′o.sô′ri.an): one of a genus of large dinosaurs found in Jurassic strata in Colorado and Wyoming.

morosis (mo.rō′sis): moronity.

morph (môrf): a sound unit in language.

morphous (môr′fus): having a definite form.

morpunkee (môr.pung′ki): in India, a long, paddle-powered pleasure barge.

morro (môr′ō): a round hill or point of land; hence, *morro castle,* a castle on a hill.

morth (môrth): in Teutonic tribal law, murder (as by poison or witchcraft) that cannot be extenuated.

mortling (môrt′ling): wool taken from a dead sheep. 9.

mortress (môr′tres): a kind of soup or pottage, made of either bread and milk or various kinds of meat. 1.

Mosaism (mō′zā.izm): the religious and legal system attributed to Moses. Attachment to the Mosaic system.

mosasaurus (mō.sa.sôr′us): a genus of large, extinct, aquatic, Cretaceous fish-eating lizards.

motatorious (mō′ta.tôr′i.us): constantly active.

moted (mō′ted): filled with motes.

motet (mo.tet′): a polyphonic choral composition on a sacred text.

motitation (mō′ti.tā′shun): a quivering movement. 52.

moulleen (mōō.lēn′): a hornless cow; a muley.

moxibustion (mok′si.bus′chun): cauterization by moxa, the downy covering of a kind of dried leaf.

moyle (moil): a kind of shoe or slipper. In mining, a kind of wedge or drill.

mpret (em.pret′): title of the ruler of Albania, 1913–1914.

mubble-fubbles (mub′l.fub′ls): a fit of depression. 1.

mucedinous (mū.sed′i.nus): pert. to mold or mildew.

mucid (mū′sid): musty; slimy; mucous.

mucket (muk′et): any of several freshwater mussels esp. used in button manufacture.

muckmidden (muk′mid′en): a dunghill.

muculent (mū′kū.lent): slimy; moist and viscous; full of mucus.

mudge (muj): budge; move. 44.

muffineer (muf′i.nēr): a dish for keeping muffins hot.

mufflin (muf′lin): the long-tailed titmouse.

muga (mōō′ga): a kind of silk made from the cocoons of an Indian moth. The caterpillar producing this silk.

mugget (mug′et): entrails of a sheep or calf. 2. The woodruff; the lily of the valley. 13.

mukkus (muk′us): a dull, stupid person. 21.

mulada (mū.lä′da): a drove of mules. 35A.

mulierose (mū′li.er.ōs): woman-crazy.

mulita (mōō.lē′ta): the mule armadillo.

mulk (mulk): in Turkey, land that is the absolute property of its owner.

mullein, mullen (mul′en): any herb of the genus *Verbascum,* incl. the common mullein and the moth mullein.

mulley (mool′i, mōōl′i): var. of *muley,* hornless.

mulm (mulm): organic sediment that accumulates in an aquarium.

mulse (muls): wine boiled and mixed with honey.

multanimous (mul.tan′i.mus): mentally multifaceted.

multiloquy (mul.til′o.kwi): talkativeness.

multiversant (mul′ti.vur′sant): protean; assuming many forms. 52.

multure (mul′cher): a toll or fee for the grinding of grain at a mill. 10.

mumblecrust (mum′bl.krust): a toothless person; a beggar.

mumpish (mump′ish): sullen; sulky.

mumpsimus (mump′si.mus): a bigoted adherent to exposed error. A fixed prejudice. 9.

mumruffin (mum′ruf′in): the long-tailed titmouse. 30.

mumu, muumu (mōō′mōō): a woman's loose-fitting dress, usu. brightly colored and patterned, adapted by the Hawaiians from the ''Mother Hubbard'' dress provided by the missionaries.

Munchausenism (mun-chouz′n.izm): the habit of telling extravagant fictions as truth.

mund (mund): in early English law, the right of protection or guardianship, as over a widow or orphan.

mundatory (mun′da.tôr.i): a towel or cloth used to cleanse ecclesiastical vessels used in Holy Communion.

mundify (mun′di.fī): to cleanse; deterge.

mundil (mun′dil): a turban ornamented with an imitation of gold or silver embroidery.

mundle (mun′dl): a stick for stirring. 2.

mundungus (mun.dung′gus): vile-smelling tobacco. 9. Waste, trash. 1.

munity (mū′ni.ti): a granted right or privilege. 52.

munjeet (mun.jēt′): Indian madder, a herb used in dyeing.

muriphobia (mū′ri.fō′bi.a): fear of mice.

murlin (mur′lin): *badderlocks.* 50. A round basket with a narrow opening. 44.

murly (mur′li): crumbly—used esp. of soil. 11.

Musa (mū′sa): a genus of perennial herbs, incl. the common banana.

muscoid (mus′koid): mosslike.

musculus (mus′kū.lus): a muscle.

museographist (mū.zi.og′ra.fist): one who writes about or classifies objects in a museum.

muskimoot (mus′ki.mōōt): among certain Indians, a sack for holding pelts.

musquashroot (mus′kwôsh.rōōt): the water hemlock. The musquash weed. The fall meadow rue. 32.

mussitation (mus′i.tā′shun): a muttering.

mustee (mus.tē′): *mestee.*

mutch (much): a head covering. 17A.

mutescent (mū.tes′ent): becoming mute or silent, as a final syllable.

mutuum (mū′chōō.um): a loan of things to be restored in kind. A contract for such a loan.

mux (muks): mess; botch. 11.

myall (mī′ôl): any of various Australian acacias having hard, fragrant wood. An uncivilized native of Australia. Wild, uncultivated.

mycoid (mī′koid): fungoid.

mycophagy (mī.kof´a.ji): the eating of fungi, as mushrooms.

mycterism (mik´ter.izm): in rhetoric, sneering derision.

mymy (mī´mī): an aboriginal hut; a bed. 53.

myophobia (mī´o.fō´bi.a): fear of mice.

SOME OF MY BEST FRIENDS ARE MULES

I don't deny I'm mulierose,
But this is also true:
Though mules and I are very close,
I'm fond of women too.

---

myoxine (mī.ok´sīn, -sin): pert. to dormice.

myriadigamous (mir´i.a.dig´a.mus): many times marrying or married.

myriologue (mir´i.o.log): in Greece, an extemporaneous funeral song composed and sung by a woman on the death of a close friend.

myriorama (mir´i.o.rama, -rä´ma): a picture made up of several smaller pictures combinable in many different ways.

myriotheism (mir´i.o.thi.izm): polytheism.

mysophobia (mī´so.fō´bi.a): fear of dirt; molymsophobia.

mystacial (mis.tā´shal): mustachial; pert. to a mustache.

mystagogic (mis.ta.goj´ik): pert. to one who initiates or interprets mysteries (as the Eleusinian mysteries), or to the practice of interpretation of mysteries.

mytacism (mī´ta.sizm): excessive or incorrect use of the letter *m* or its sound.

mythogony (mi.thog´o.ni): the study of the origin of myths.

mythogreen (mith´o.grin): a yellowish-green color of low saturation and high brilliance.

mythopoetic (mith´o.po.et´ik): making or giving rise to myths; mythopoeic.

N

nagaika (na.gī´ka): a thick, tightly twisted whip, used by Cossacks.

nagana (na.gä´na): in South Africa, a disease of livestock transmitted by the tsetse fly.

nagsman (nagz´man): a man who rides horses in a sales ring.

Naia (nā´a): var. of *Naja*.

nais (nā´is): a naiad; river nymph.

naissant (nā´snt): newly born or about to come into being; nascent.

Naja (nā´ja): a genus of elapine serpents containing the cobras.

namaqua (na.mäk´wa): a long-tailed African dove. (cap) One of a Hottentot people in southwest Africa.

namaycush (nam´ā.kush): a large trout, reaching 20 pounds, of the lakes of northern Africa. 37.

nanoid (nā´noid): having an abnormally small body; dwarfish.

nanosecond (nan.o.sek´und, -unt): one billionth of a second.

nanpie (nan´pī): the magpie. 30.

naology (nā.ol´o.ji): the study of holy buildings.

naos (nā´os): a temple or shrine. (cap) A star in the constellation Argus Navus.

naperer (nā´per.er): an officer of a royal household in charge of table linen.

napoo (na.pōō´): in British soldiers' slang, no more; all finished; dead. To be done for; die. To put an end to; kill.

naprapathy (na.prap´a.thi): a medical treatment by manipulation of strained ligaments.

naras, narras (nar´as): a South African desert shrub with melonlike fruit of a pleasant flavor.

narr (när): to growl or snarl, as a dog. 2. A legal declaration. 1, 28.

narra (nā´ra): a timber tree of the genus Lingoum; also, its hard wood, which takes a fine polish.

nasillate (nā´zi.lāt): to speak or sing through the nose.

nast (nast): filth; dirt. 13.

natalitial, natalitious (nā´ta.lish´al, -us): natal. 1.

natterjack (nat´er.jak): the common toad of western Europe.

natuary (nā´chōō.er´i): a ward or division of a hospital, set off for women in childbirth.

naulage (nô´lij): payment for sea freight.

naumochy (nô´mo.ki): in ancient Rome, a mock sea battle, or the theater in which it takes place.

nauropometer (nô´ro.pom´e.ter): an instrument for measuring a ship's heeling at sea. 52.

nauscopy (nôs´ko.pi): the pretended power of discovering ships or land at a great distance.

navicella (nav´i.sel´a): any vessel-shaped ornamental object, as one for holding incense.

navicert (nā´vi.surt): a certificate exempting a noncontraband shipment from search or seizure by British patrols.

nealogy (ni.al´o.ji): the study of young animals.

neanic (ni.an´ik): youthful. Specif., constituting the pupal stage of insect development.

nebby (neb´i): given to impertinent interference; spiteful. 45.

nebneb (neb´neb): acacia bark used in tanning.

Nebo (nē´bō): in the Babylonian religion, god of wisdom and agriculture. In the Bible, the mountain in Moab from which Moses saw the land of Canaan.

nebulaphobia (neb´ū.la.fō´bi.a): fear of fog.

nebulium (ne.bū´li.um): a hypothetical chemical element formerly inferred from certain lines in the spectra of nebulae.

nebulochaotic (neb´ū.lo.kā.ot´ik): hazily confused. 60.

necation (ni.kā´shun): a killing. 1.

necrologue (nek´ro.log): an obituary.

necromimesis (nek´ro.mi.mē´sis): the pretence or delusion of being dead.

necroponent (nek´ro.pō´nent): one temporarily in charge of a household after a death.

necyomancy (nes´i.o.man´si): divination through the summoning of Satan.

nedder (ned´er): an adder. 2.

neddy (ned´i): a donkey. A life preserver. 21.

neele (nēl): darnel, an annual grass found as weeds in cornfields and other cultivated grounds. 29. An eel. 1.

neem (nēm): the *margosa*.

neep (nēp): a turnip. 11A.

neer (nēr): a kidney. 11.

neese, neeze (nēz): to sneeze. 43.

nef (nef): a 16th-century clock in the form of a ship, having mechanical devices to simulate astronomical movements. A table utensil for napkins, salt, etc., in the shape of a ship. 6. The nave of a church. 1.

negritude (nē´gri.tūd): the distinctive qualities or characteristics of blacks.

neif (nēf): in law, one born a serf; a native. Also, var. of *nieve*.

nelipot (nel´i.pot): barefoot.

nema (nē´ma): a roundworm, eelworm, nematode.

nematocide (ni.mat´o.sīd): a chemical used to destroy roundworms.

Nemertinea (nem´er.tin´i.a): a class of carnivorous, mostly marine worms ranging in length from a fraction of an inch to many yards.

nemo (nē´mō): a radio or television broadcast that originates outside the studio.

nemophilous (ni.mof´i.lus): forest-loving.

nemoral (nem´o.ral): pert. to a wood or grove.

nenta (nen´ta): a chronic nervous disease of grazing animals in South Africa, similar to loco disease.

neocracy (ni.ok´ra.si): government by inexperienced people. 52.

neography (ni.og´ra.fi): any new system of writing. 52.

neolith (nē´o.lith): a neolithic stone instrument.

neolocal (nē′o.lō′kal): living away from the families of either spouse.

neomenia (nē′o.mē′ni.a): the time of the new moon; also, the festival of the new moon. (cap) A genus of marine mollusks having a thick, turgid body, and the foot represented by a narrow groove.

neomnesia (nē′om.nē′zha): a clear memory of recent events.

Neophron (nē′o.fron): a genus of Old World vultures, named for a legendary Greek who has turned into one.

neoplasm (nē′o.plazm): in medicine, any abnormal new formation or morbid growth.

neoplastic (nē′o.plas′tik): pert. to a *neoplasm,* or to *neoplasty.*

neoplasty (nē′o.plas′ti): in surgery, restoration of a part by a plastic operation.

neorama (nē′o.rä′ma): a panorama of the interior of a building, seen from within.

neossology (nē′o.sol′o.ji): the study of young birds.

neoteinic (nē′o.tī′nik): pert. to prolonged adolescence.

nephalism (nef′a.lizm): total abstinence from spirituous liquor.

nepheligenous (nef′i.lij′i.nus): emitting clouds, esp. of tobacco smoke.

nephology (ni.fol′o.ji): the study of clouds.

nephroid (nef′roid): kidney-shaped.

nephrosis (ni.frō′sis): a degenerative condition of the kidneys.

nepotation (nep′o.tā′shun): living high. 1.

nepotic (ni.pot′ik): pert. to a nephew or nepotism.

nerval (nur′val): a salve for the sinews. Pert. to the nerves; neural.

nervine (nur′vīn, -vin): having the quality of affecting the nerves; soothing nervous excitement. A nerve tonic. An orchid of the genus *Cypripedium.*

nes, nese (nes, nēz): nose. 5.

nesh (nesh): soft; tender. Timid; delicate; weak. Dainty; fastidious. To make or become soft. 1. To act timidly (with *it*). 13.

nesiote (nē′si.ōt): inhabiting an island.

neskhi (nes′ki): cursive Arabic script used in writing scientific and esp. religious books.

neurocoele (nū.ro.sēl): the cavity or series of cavities in the interior of the central nervous system.

neuromimesis (nū′ro.mī.mē′sis, -mi.-mē′sis): neurotic simulation of organic disease.

neurotropic (nū′ro.trop′ik): having an affinity for nerve tissues, as a drug or poison.

neurypnology (nū′rip.nol′o.ji): the branch of science that treats of sleep, partic. hypnotic sleep; hypnology.

nevel, nevell (nev′el): a fisticuff. To beat with the fists. 43.

ngoko (en.gō′kō): a dialect used by Javanese when speaking to social inferiors.

ngwee (en.gwā′): a Zambian coin equal to ¹⁄₁₀₀ of a kwacha.

nibber (nib′er): one who or that which puts a nib on, as on a pen. A tool for nibbing a pen.

nibby-jibby (nib′i.jib′i): a narrow margin, as in making a train.

nicker (nik′er): one of the 18th-century London brawlers noted for breaking windows with halfpence. A fabulous water monster; a nix. To snigger; to neigh. 43B.

nickle (nik′l): the green woodpecker. 30.

nicotian (ni.kō′shan): a user of tobacco.

niddle-noddle (nid′l.nod′l): having an unstable nodding head; nodding; to nod or wobble.

nidge (nij): var. of *nig.* Also, to shake, quiver. 52.

nidget (nij′et): idiot; fool. 9. A kind of horse-drawn cultivator. To till (soil) or to mix (manure, etc., with soil) with a nidget. 30.

nidicolous (ni.dik′o.lus): reared in a nest.

nidifugous (ni.dif′ū.gus): leaving the nest soon after birth.

nidulate (nid′u.lāt): to make a nest.

niente (ni.en′ti): nothing (Italian).

nieve (nēv): the fist; hand. 10. Also, a female *neif.*

nievie-nievie-nick-nack (nē′vi.nē′vi.-nik′nak): a children's choosing game. 45.

niffle (nif′l): a trivial or worthless person or thing. To steal in small quantities. 11A.

nific (nī′fic): pert. to *nife,* the hypothetical core material of the earth, supposed to be nickel and iron.

nig (nig): short for *nigger, renege.* To dress (stone) with a sharp-pointed hammer.

nikhedonia (nik′i.dō′ni.a): pleasure derived from the anticipation of success.

nikin (nik′in): a very soft creature. 1.

nim (nim): to filch, steal. 9.

nimb (nim, nimb): a nimbus or halo.

nimious (nim′i.us): in Scots law, excessive; extravagant.

nimmer (nim′er): a thief, pilferer.

nimtopsical (nim.top′si.kal): one of Benjamin Franklin's 228 words for "drunk."

nipperkin (nip′er.kin): a quantity of liquor of not more than a half pint. 9.

nisse (nis′e): in Scandinavian folklore, a friendly goblin or brownie that frequents farm buildings, similar to the German *kobold.*

nither (nith′er): to humiliate, debase. To shiver, tremble as with cold. 17. Var. of *neither, nether.* 11.

nithing (nith′ing): a coward; niggard; dastard. 9.

nobilitation (no.bil′i.tā′shun): the act of ennobling. Ennoblement.

nocake (nō′kāk): Indian corn pounded into a powder.

noctivagation (nok.tiv′a.gā′shun): night wandering.

noctuary (nok′chōō.er′i): a diary of nighttime activities.

nodose (no.dōs′, nō′dōs): knotty; knobbed.

nodulous, nodulose (nod′ū.lus, -lōs): having nodules.

noematachograph (no.ē′ma.tak′o.graf): an instrument for measuring complex reaction time.

noematic, noetic (nō′i.mat′ik, no.et′ik): apprehended only by the intellect; given to purely intellectual reason.

noemics (no.ē′miks): the science of understanding.

noily (noil′i): pert. to short fiber removed during the combing of a textile fiber and spun into yarn for cloth.

noli-mi-tangeretarian (nō′li.mi.tan′je.-ri.tā′ri.an): a rigid, unbending person.

nolition (no.lish′un): adverse action of will; unwillingness.

nomancy (nō′man.si): divination by letters of the alphabet.

nomic (nom′ik, nō′mik): in spelling, traditional as opposed to phonetic. Customary; conventional.

nominy (nom′i.ni): rhyming doggerel. A rigmarole; a wordy tale. 13.

nomology (no.mol′o.ji): the science of the laws of the mind.

nomothetic (nom′o.thet′ik): giving or enacting laws; legislative.

nonda (non′da): a kind of Australian tree, or its edible, plumlike fruit.

none (nōn): by ancient Roman and Eastern canonical reckoning, the ninth hour of the day. A religious office recited in the Roman Catholic Church.

nonic (nō′nik): in mathematics, a curve or quantic of the ninth degree.

noology (no.ol′o.ji): the study or science of intuition.

noop (nōōp): a rounded prominence, as the point of the elbow. 44. The fruit of the cloudberry. 13.

nooscopic (nō′o.skop′ik): pert. to the examination of the mind.

nordcaper (nôrd′kā′per): a right whale.

norsel (nôr′sel): a short line for fastening fishnets or fishhooks.

norward (nôr′ward): northward.

nosocomephrenia (nos.o.kō′mi.frē′-ni.a): depression from a prolonged stay in the hospital.

nosocomium (nos′o.kō′mi.um): a hospital.

nosoconology (nos′o.ko.nol′o.ji): the study of hospital administration.

nosophobia (nos′o.fō′bi.a): abnormal fear of disease.

nostology (nos.tol′o.ji): the study of senility.

nostomania (nos′to.mā′ni.a): overwhelming homesickness.

nostrificate (nos.trif′i.kāt): to accept as one's own.

notaeum (no.tē′um): the upper surface of a bird's body.

notandum (no.tan′dum): a thing to be noted, or an entry of it; a note; memorandum.

nothosomia (noth′o.sō′mi.a): the act of calling someone a bastard.

novendrial (no.ven′dri.al): lasting nine days; a nine-day festival.

novercaphobia (nō′ver.ka.fō′bi.a): fear of a stepmother.

novilunar (nō′vi.lōō′nar): pert. to the new moon.

novitial (no.vish′al): pert. to a novice. 52.

novitious (no.vish′us): recently invented.

nowel (no.el′, nou.el′): Noel. 9. The inner part of a mold for casting a large hollow object.

Nox (noks): Roman goddess of the night.

noxa (nok′sa): in medicine, something that exerts a harmful effect on the body.

noyade (nwa.yäd′): drowning, usu. of many persons at once. To put to death by drowning.

nubiferous (nū.bif′er.us): producing or bringing clouds.

nubigenous (nū.bij′e.nus): produced by clouds.

nubilate (nū′bi.lāt): to cloud; obscure.

nucal (nū′kal): pert. to a nut.

nucha (nū′ka): in anatomy, the spinal cord; the nape of the neck. 1. In insects, the hind part of the thorax.

nuciverous (nū.siv′er.us): nut-eating.

nucleomitaphobia (nū′kli.o.mit′a.fō′bi.a): fear of death by nuclear weapons.

nuddle (nud′l): to thrust with the nose, as in suckling; to press close, nuzzle. 11.

nudiped (nū′di.ped): having feet without a natural covering (as of hair or feathers).

nudiustertian (nū′di.ū.stur′shun): pert. to the day before yesterday.

nugacity (nū.gas′i.ti): triviality; futility.

nullibicity, nullibiety (nul′i.bis′i.ti, -bī′e.ti): the state of being nowhere. 52.

nullifidian (nul′i.fid′i.an): a skeptic; an unbeliever. Skeptical.

nulliparous (nu.lip′a.rus): pert. to a woman who has never borne a child.

nullo (nul′ō): a game in which the player undertakes not to take a trick.

numble (num′bl): pert. to the numbles, edible entrails of deer. 9.

numerophobia (nū′mer.o.fō′bi.a): fear of numbers.

nummamorous (num.mam′er.us): money-loving.

nummary (num′er.i): pert. to coins or money.

nunch, nuncheon (nunch, nun′chun): a light midmorning or midafternoon refreshment, as of bread, cheese, and beer. 2.

nundine (nun′dīn, -din): a market day held every ninth day according to ancient Roman reckoning.

nuptaphobia (nup′ta.fō′bi.a): fear of marriage or weddings.

nursle (nur′sl): to rear, bring up.

nutricism (nū′tri.sizm): symbiosis in which one organism nourishes or protects another with no apparent reciprocal benefit.

nuzzer (nuz′er): in India, a ceremonial gift to a superior.

nyanza (nyan′za): in Central Africa, any large body of water; a lake or river.

nychthemeron (nik.thē′mer.on): a period of 24 hours.

nyctalopia (nik′ta.lō′pi.a): night blindness.

nyctophobia (nik.to.fō′bi.a): dread of the night or darkness.

Nymphea (nim.fē′a): the true water lily; synonymous with *Castalia*.

Nyx (niks): Greek goddess of the night.

O

oam (ōm): steam, warm air. 44A.

obambulate (o.bam′bū.lāt): to walk about, wander. 52.

obdormition (ob.dôr.mish′un): numbness and anesthesia caused by a pressure on a nerve; the condition of a limb when it is "asleep."

obduce, obduct (ob.dūs′, -dukt′): to cover with, cover over. 1. To conduct an autopsy.

obequitation (o.bek′wi.tā′shun): the act of riding about on a horse. 1.

oblati (ob.lā′ti): those (esp. in the Middle Ages) who have offered themselves and their property to the church.

oblatration (ob.la.trā′shun): railing, reviling, scolding. 1.

obley (ob′li): a small flat cake or wafer, esp. of altar bread.

obliviscent (ob′li.vis′ent): forgetful.

obmutescent (ob′mū.tes′ent): becoming or staying silent.

obnubilate (ob.nū′bi.lāt): to cloud; obscure. 52.

obolary (ob′o.ler′i): very poor; having only small coins. 60.

obreption (ob.rep′shun): act of creeping upon with secrecy or by surprise. 1. The fraudulent obtainment or attempt to obtain a dispensation (from ecclesiastical authorities) or a gift (from the sovereign).

obreptitious (ob′rep.tish′us): obtained by trickery or by concealing the truth. 1.

obrogate (ob′ro.gāt): to supersede one law by another.

obrotund (ob′ro.tund): nearly spherical, but with one diameter slightly exceeding the other.

observandum (ob′ser.van′dum): a thing to be observed. (pl. *observanda*.)

obsidional (ob.sid′i.on.al): pert. to a siege; besetting.

obsignation (ob′sig.nā′shun): formal ratification. 52.

obstipation (ob′sti.pā′shun): extreme constipation. 1.

obstringe (ob.strinj′): to constrain or bind. To put under obligation. 52.

obstupefy (ob.stū′pi.fī): to stupefy.

obumbrate (o.bum′brāt): to shade; darken; cloud. 52. To adumbrate. 1. Darkened, as by shadow; also, concealed beneath a protecting part, as the antennae of certain insects.

obus (ō′bus): an artillery shell.

obvallate (ob.val′āt): walled in or around.

obvention (ob.ven′shun): an incidental or occasional gift or offering.

obvolve (ob.volv′): to enwrap. 52.

occecation (ok′se.kā′shun): blindness; going blind.

occiduous (ok.sid′ū.us): going down, as the setting of a heavenly body. 52.

occision (ok.sizh′un): slaughter.

ochlesis (ok.lē′sis): medically, a morbid condition induced by the crowding together of many persons, esp. sick persons.

ochone (o.kōn′): alas—an Irish and Scottish exclamation of lamentation.

ochroid (ok′roid): like ocher, esp. yellow ocher, in color.

octarius (ok.târ.i.us): one-eighth of a gallon; a pint.

octogild (ōk.to.gild): in Anglo-Saxon law, a pecuniary compensation for an injury, coming to eight times the determined value of the injury.

od (od): a minced form of *God*. Also, a force once believed by some to underlie hypnotism, magnetism, etc.

oda (ō′da): a room in a harem.

odaler, odaller (ō′dal.er): among early Teutonic peoples, one who owns heritable land.

oddman (od′man): an arbiter having the deciding vote; umpire. Also, *oddsman.*

oddsman (odz′man): an umpire, arbiter.

odontalgy, odontalgia (od.on. tal′ji, -ji.a): toothache.

odonterism (o.don′ter.izm): the chattering of teeth.

odontic (o.don′tik): pert. to the teeth.

Odontoglossum (o.don′to.glos′um): a genus of showy American orchids, incl. the baby orchid of Guatemala. A plant of this genus.

ON THE IMMEMORIAL WORSHIP OF ASSES: A KYRIELLE

Now hangs occiduous the sun;
All things must end that have begun—
Save this, that sounds eternally:
Ass-worshipping onolatry.

I hear the mourners wail "Ochone"
Who soon are one with them they moan.
Macrotous Spirit, hear the plea
They utter in onolatry!

From shade of atom bomb and missile
They pray to You Who champ the thistle.
As ass to Ass they bend the knee
In asinine onolatry.

---

odorivector (o.dor′i.vek′ter): a substance that gives off a smell.

ods bobs (odz bobz): a minced form of the oath "God's blood." 10.

odylic (o.dil′ik): pert. to *od.*

odynophobia (o.din′o.fō′bi.a): fear of pain.

oecodomic (i.ko.dō′mik): architectural.

oeillade (oo.yäd′): a flirtatious glance; an ogle.

oenanthic, enanthic (i.nan′thik, en.an′-): pert. to a certain acid found in wine.

oenomancy (ē′no.man′si): divination by the color or other peculiarities of wine.

oenophilist (i.nof′il.ist): a lover of wine.

ogdoad (og′do.ad): the number eight; a group or set of eight.

Ogygia (o.jij′i.a): the island on which the sea nymph Calypso kept Odysseus for seven years.

Ogygian (o.jij′i.an): pert. to Ogyges, first king of Thebes, or to a flood said to have occurred during his reign. Extremely ancient.

ohia (o.hē′a): any of several myrtles of the genus *Metrosideros,* such as the lehua and the Malay apple.

oikology (oi.kol′o.ji): the science of housekeeping; household economics.

oikophobia (oi.ko.fō′bi.a): fear of one's own home.

oillet (oi′let): an eyelet. 9.

oke, oka (ōk, -a): Turkish and Egyptian measures of weight.

olamic (o.lam′ik): eternal; infinite.

oldwench (ōld′wench): the triggerfish of the Atlantic and Indian oceans.

oleiferous (ō.li.if′er.us): producing oil.

olent (ō′lent): fragrant.

olid (ō′lid): smelly.

olidous (ō′li.dus): olid, smelly. 52.

oligogenics (ō′li.go.jen′iks): birth control.

oligophagous (ō.li.gof′a.gus): eating only a few specific kinds of foods.

oligophrenia (ō′li.go.frē′ni.a): mental deficiency.

oligoria (ō′li.gôr′i.a): cessation of interest in former associations.

oligotokous (ō′li.got′o.kus): laying fewer than four eggs.

olitory (ō′li.tôr′i): a kitchen garden. 9.

olivet (ol′i.vet): an olive grove. 1. A bogus pearl.

om (ôm): a mantra used in the mystical contemplation of the cosmos.

omadhaun (om′a.thôn): a fool; simpleton; idiot. 51.

ombrology (om.brol′o.ji): the branch of meteorology that deals with rain. 52.

ombrometer (om.brom′i.ter): a rain gauge.

ombrophilous (om.brof′i.lus): thriving in the rain, as some plants in humid tropics.

ombrophobia (om.bro.fō′bi.a): fear of rain.

ombrosalgia (om′bro.sal′ji.a): pain or discomfort connected with rain.

omneity (om.nē′i.ti): allness.

omnigenous (om.nij′i.nus): of all types and kinds.

omniligent (om.nil′i.jent): reading constantly and indiscriminately.

omniparient (om′ni.par′i.ent): the source or origin of all. 52.

omnitude (om′ni.tūd): universality; allness.

omnivalent (om.niv′a.lent): in chemistry, capable of combining with any atom of another element.

omophagic (ō′mō.faj′ik): pert. to the eating of raw flesh.

omoplatoscopy (ō′mo.pla.tos′ko.pi): divination by study of a cracked shoulder blade.

omphacine (om′fa.sēn): pert. to unripe fruit.

omphaloid (om′fa.loid): resembling a navel.

omphalomancy (om′fa.lo.man′si): prediction of the number of children a woman will have by the number of knots in the umbilical cord of her first. **omphalopsychite (om.fa.lop′si.kīt):** a *Hesychast.*

omphaloskepsis (om′fa.lo.skep′sis): meditation while gazing at the navel.

Ona (ō′na): one of a Chonan people of Tierra del Fuego off the southern tip of South America.

ondoyant (on.doi′ant): wavy.

oneirocritic (o.nī′ro.krit′ik): an interpreter of dreams.

oneirodynia (o.nī′ro.din′i.a): a nightmare.

oneirotaxia (o.nī′ro.tak′si.a): confusion between fantasy and reality.

oneirotic (o.nī′rot′ik): pert. to dreams.

oniomania (ō′ni.o.mā′ni.a): a mania for buying things.

onlocholasia (on.lok′o.lā.zhi.a): shopping as a means of relaxation.

onolatry (o.nol′a.tri): the worship of asses.

onomantic (on′o.man′tik): pert. to divination by means of names.

onomasticon (on′o.mas′ti.kon): a vocabulary or collection of names or nouns.

onomatomania (on′o.mat′o.mā′ni.a): preoccupation with words and names.

onomatophobia (on′o.mat′o.fō′bi.a): fear of hearing a special name.

ontal (on′tal): in philosophy, pert. to real, as opposed to phenomenal existence or being; noumenal.

onychomancy, onymancy (on′i.ko. man′si, -i.man′si): divination by means of the fingernails.

onychophagy (on′i.kof′a.ji): fingernail-biting.

onymatic (on′i.mat′ik): pert. to nomenclature.

oolly (ool′i): in India, a lump or loop of iron, when taken as a pasty mass from the crucible.

ooid, ooidal (o′oid, -al): egg-shaped.

oom (ōōm): in South Africa, an uncle.

opacate (o.pā′kāt): to make opaque, darken.

ophelia (o.fēl′ya): a hybrid tea rose with salmon-yellow flowers. A reddish purple color. (cap) A genus of small burrowing worms. (cap) The daughter of Polonius in *Hamlet.*

ophelimity (ō′fi.lim′i.ti): satisfaction; the ability to provide it.

ophic (of′ik): of or relating to snakes.

ophicleide (of′i.klīd): a deep-toned brass wind instrument replaced by the tuba about 1850.

ophidiophobia (o.fid′i.o.fō′bi.a): fear of snakes.

ophioid (of′i.oid): pert. to snakes.

ophiomancy (of′i.o.man′si): divination by means of snakes.

ophiophagan, ophiophagous (of′i.of′-a.gan, -gus): feeding on snakes; one that feeds on snakes.

ophryitis (of′ri.ī′tis): inflammation of the eyebrow.

ophthalmophobia (of′thal.mo.fō′bi.a): fear of being stared at.

opianic (ō′pi.an′ik): pert. to a certain bitter, crystalline, aldehyde acid.

opimian (o.pim′i.an): pert. to a famous Roman wine of 121 B.C., when *Opimius* was consul.

opiparous (o.pip′ar.us): sumptuous. 9.

opisthograph (o.pis′tho.graf): a manuscript written on both sides.

opisthoporeia (o.pis.tho.pôr′i.a): involuntary walking backward.

oppidan (op′i.dan): pert. to town as opposed to country. A townsman. At Eton, a student who boards in town. 1.

oppidum (op′i.dum): in the Roman Empire, a provincial town, not self-governing, as London when under Roman rule.

oppignorate (o.pig′nor.āt): to pawn.

oppilation (op′i.lā′shun): the state of being stopped up. An obstruction.

opsablepsia (op′sa.blep′si.a): inability to look another in the eye.

opsigamy (op.sig′a.mi): a late marriage.

opsimathy (op.sim′a.thi): education late in life.

opsonium (op.sō′ni.um): food used as a relish. 52.

optophobia (op′to.fō′bi.a): fear of opening one's eyes.

opsophagist (of.sof′a.jist): a fastidious eater; an epicure.

opuscule, opuscle (o.pus′kūl, -pus′l): a small or petty work.

oquassa (o.kwas′a): a small, rather slender trout found in Maine.

oragious (o.rā′jus): stormy. 52.

oralogy (o.ral′o.ji): the science of the mouth and its diseases.

orarian (o.râr′i.an): pert. to the seashore; a coast dweller. (cap) An Eskimo or Aleut of the Bering Sea coastal region.

orbation (ôr.bā′shun): lack of parents or children; bereavement.

orbell (ôr′bel): a small circular place. 1.

orbific (ôr.bif′ik): pert. to the creation of the world.

orchesis (ôr.kē′sis): the art of dancing, as in the ancient Greek chorus.

orchestic (ôr.kes′tik): pert. to dancing.

orchestrion (ôr.kes′tri.on): a device with stops capable of imitating a variety of musical instruments.

orchestromania (ôr.kes′tro.mā′ni.a): a passion for dancing.

orchidectomy (ôr′ki.dek′to.mi): castration.

orectic (o.rek′tik): pert. to the desires; hence, impelling to gratification, appetitive.

oreillet (ôr′e.let): a covering for the ear.

oreography, orography (ôr′i.og′ra.fi, o.rog′ra.fi): the branch of geography that deals with mountains; orology.

orexigenic (o.rek′si.jen′ik): whetting the appetite.

orexis (o.rek′sis): desire, appetite. The feeling and striving aspect of the mind as compared with the intellectual.

orgia (ôr′ji.a): orgies.

orgillous (ôr.gil′us): var. of *orgulous.*

orgue (ôrg): in military history, one of the long, thick timbers behind the gateway of a fortress or castle, to be let down in case of attack. Also, an old-time piece of ordnance having a number of barrels arranged side by side.

orgulous (ôr′gū.lus): proud, haughty. Hence, showy; splendid.

orignal (o.rēn′yal): the American moose.

orismology (ôr′is.mol′o.ji): the science of defining technical terms.

orle (ôrl): in heraldry, a band following the outline of the shield inside the edge. The metal rim of a shield.

ornis (ôr′nis): the bird life of a region.

ornithoid (ôr′ni.thoid): birdlike.

ornithon (ôr′ni.thon): an aviary.

ornithophilous (ôr.ni.thof′i.lus): bird-loving; said specif. of plants pollinated through the agency of birds.

ornithorhynchous (ôr′ni.tho.ring′kus): having a beak like a bird.

ornithorhynchus (ôr′ni.tho.ring′kus): a creditor—i.e., "a beast with a bill." 23A (cap) A genus of egg-laying mammals incl. only the platypus.

oro (ôr′ō): gold; sometimes, in Spanish American countries, specif. U.S. money. (cap) In Polynesian religion, the god of fertility, procreation, and war.

orra (ôr.a): odd; not matched; good-for-nothing. 44.

orthobiosis (ôr′tho.bi.ō′sis): normal life; life according to accepted hygienic and moral principles.

orthodromics (ôr′tho.drō′miks): the act or art of sailing by the great-circle route.

orthology (ôr.thol′o.ji): the art of using words correctly.

orthophobia (ôr′tho.fō′bi.a): a distaste for propriety.

orthophony (ôr.thof′o.ni): voice training.

orthopter (ôr.thop′ter): a flying machine with flapping wings.

orthoptic (ôr.thop′tik): pert. to the treatment of defective vision or bad visual habits.

orthotectic (ôr′tho.tek′tik): in geology, pert. to the results of directly magmatic processes, as the segregation of an ore body from molten material.

orthotetrakaldekahedron (ôr′tho.tet′ra.kal.dek′a.hē′dron): the truncated octahedron.

orthotic (ôr.thot′ik): pert. to erect posture; standing upright.

orthotomic (ôr′tho.tom′ik): in geometry, cutting at right angles.

ortive (ôr′tiv): pert. to the time of rising; eastern. 52.

oryctology (o′rik.tol′o.ji): the science of things dug from the earth. 1.

oryzivorous (ôr′i.ziv′o.rus): rice-eating.

osela (o.sel′a): a silver or gold medal representing a bird, presented each New Year's Day by the 16th-century doges of Venice to the Venetian noble families.

---

*IT ALL DEPENDS
ON THE SUFFIX*

Beth emerged from bath of bubble,
Sweet of scent and tempting trouble.
From the pigpen Hank, her neighbor,
Rushed still reeking from his labor.
Beth would not be kissed by Hank;
She informed him that he stank.
Hank to pen retreated dolent:
He was olid, she was olent.

---

osmagogue (oz′ma.gog): stimulating to the sense of smell.

osmonsology (oz′mon.sol′o.ji): the study of the sense of smell.

osmophobia (oz′mo.fō′bi.a): fear of smells.

osphresiophilia (os.frē′zi.o.fil′i.a): love of smells.

ossature (os′a.cher): the skeleton. 52. In architecture, the framework.

osso buco (os′ō bōō′kō): marrow bone of veal. A Milanese dish consisting of leg of veal with rice cooked in saffron sauce.

ostent (os′tent, os.tent′): a significant sign; portent. A manifestation. Ostentatious display.

ostreophagy (os′tri.of′a.ji): the eating of oysters.

othergates (uth′er.gāts): in another manner. 4.

otiant (ō′shi.ant): unemployed, idle. 52.

otiation (ō′shi.a′shun): leisure, idleness. 1.

otosis (o.tō′sis): inability to hear correctly.

ouakari (wa.kä′ri): a South American monkey with silky hair and a short tail like a baboon's.

ouf (ouf): a dog's bark; woof. An exclamation of impatience.

ouph, ouphe (ouf): an elf or goblin.

outfangthief (out′fang.thēf): in medieval English law, the right of a lord to try one of his vassals for thievery, even if caught outside his manor.

outgang (out′gang): departure; also, a road out. 43.

outgrabe (out.grāb′): squeaked.

outrance (ōō.träns′): the utmost or last extremity.

outrecuidance (ōō′tre.kwē′dens): extreme self-conceit; presumption.

outrooper (out´rōōper):   an auctioneer. 1.

overslaugh (ō´ver.slô):   in England, exemption from one military duty by being assigned a more important one. In the U.S., a sandbar. Also, to hinder, obstruct, pass over for appointment. 41.

ovivorous (o.viv´e.rus):   egg-eating.

owala (o.wä´la):   a tropical African tree with seeds yielding a lubricant.

ower (ō´wer):   dial. version of *over*.

owler (ou´ler):   someone who hoots like an owl; a prowler. 2.

owling (ou´ling):   formerly, in England, the smuggling of wool or sheep from the country.

oxgang (oks´gang):   an English unit of land measure. 1.

oxycanthous (ok´si.kan´thus):   having sharp spines or thorns.

oxyesthesia (ok´si.es.thē´zi.a):   extreme sensitivity to touch.

oxyosphresia (ok´si.os.frē´zi.a):   extreme sensitivity to smell.

oxyphony (ok.sif´o.ni):   in medicine, shrillness of voice.

oxyrhynch (ok´si.ringk):   a crab having a pointed rostrum.

oxyrhynchous (ok.si.ring´kus):   pert. to a large superfamily of crabs, incl. the spider crabs. Sharp-snouted; sharp-billed.

oyer (oi´er):   in law, a criminal trial conducted by a particularly authorized judge. The hearing of a document read in court. A copy of the instrument given rather than read to the petitioning party.

ozostomia (ō´zo.stō´mi.a):   bad breath.

P

pabular, pabulous (pab´ū.lär, -lus):   pert. to pabulum. 52.

pabulation (pab´ū.lā´shun):   food; fodder; the providing of them.

pacable (pā´ka.bl):   pacable.

pacate (pā´kāt):   appeased; pacified. 1.

pachinko (pa.ching´kō):   a Japanese slot machine.

pachycephalic (pak´i.si.fal´ik):   thick-skulled.

paco (pä´kō):   an earthy-looking ore, consisting of brown oxide of iron with minute particles of native silver.

paction (pak´shun):   an agreement; a compact; a bargain. 44A.

padella (pa.del´a):   in Italy, a shallow dish used for fat or oil, in which a wick is placed for burning.

padmasana (pad.mä´sa.na):   statue base shaped like a lotus flower.

paedophobia (pē´do.fō´bi.a):   fear of dolls.

paeanism (pe´a.nizm):   the singing or chanting of paeans.

paggle (pag´l):   to hang loosely, sag.

pagophagia (pag´o.fā´ji.a):   a program of eating ice to help offset iron deficiency.

pahmi (pä´mi):   the bobac (a marmot of eastern Europe and Asia), or its fur.

pahoehoe (pa.hō´i.hō´i):   in Hawaii, lava that has cooled in ropy forms.

paideutic, paideutics (pä´dū´tik, -s):   pedagogy.

paigle (pā´gl):   the cowslip, or oxlip. The cuckooflower. The stitchwort. Any of several crowfoots. 13.

paillette (pal.yet´):   spangle.

paizogony (pī´zo.gon´i):   love play— *paraphilemia, sarmassation.*

paktong (pak.tong´):   a Chinese alloy of nickel, zinc, and copper, resembling German silver.

paladin (pal´a.din):   one of the twelve peers of Charlemagne's court. Hence, a knight of the Round Table; a knight errant.

palafitte (pal´a.fit):   a pile-built structure used by neolithic lake dwellers.

palama (pal´a.ma):   the webbing on the feet of aquatic birds.

palame (pa.lä´me):   a Greek measure of length, 3.937 inches.

paleanthropic (pal´i.an´throp´ik):   pert. to a genus of homonids often incl. the Neanderthals.

paleocrystic (pal´i.o.kris´tik):   pert. to ice of ancient origin.

paleogenetic, palaeogenetic (pal´i.o.ji.-net´ik):   originating in the past.

paleomnesia (pal´i.om.nē´zhi.a):   a sharp memory for the far past.

Paleotherium (pal´i.o´thē´ri.um):   a genus of extinct tapir-like mammals, of which one species was as large as a rhinoceros.

paletiology (pal´i.ti.ol´o.ji):   the explanation of past events by the laws of causation, as in geology.

paletot (pal´ō.tō):   a man's or woman's loose overcoat.

palfrenier (pal´fre.nēr):   a groom. 9.

palification (pal´i.fi.kā´shun):   the driving of piles or posts into the ground to make it firm. 52.

palilalia (pal´i.lāl´ya):   the ailment of helplessly repeating a phrase faster and faster.

palilogy (pa.lil´o.ji):   in rhetoric, the repetition of words for emphasis.

palinoia (pal´i.noi´a):   the compulsive repetition of an act until it is perfect.

palla (pal´a):   among the Romans, a loose outer garment for women formed by wrapping or draping a large square of cloth.

pallah (pal´a):   the impala.

palmigrade (pal´mi.grād):   plantigrade.

palmiped (pal´mi.ped):   web-footed. A web-footed animal.

palo (pä´lō):   a pole, stick; in Spanish America, used in the names of trees. 35B.

palpebrate (pal´pi.brāt):   to wink.

paludamentum (pa.lōō´da.men´tum):   a military cloak worn by a Roman general; also, the imperial cloak.

palustral (pa.lus´tral):   living in marshy places; marshy; pert. to marshes. Malarial. Paludal.

palycrotic (pal´i.krot´ik):   of the pulse, having a complex or multiple beat and forming a curve with several crests on a sphygmogram.

pament, pamment (pam´ent):   in brewing, the tile or brick used for paving malting floors.

pampootee (pam.pōō´ti):   an Irish moccasin of untanned cowhide.

pampre (pam´per):   in sculpture, ornamentation of vine leaves and grapes.

panade (pa.nād´):   a large knife or dagger. 1.

Panagia (pa.nä´ji.a):   literally, the All Holy—the most common epithet of the Virgin Mary. A ceremony observed in honor of her assumption. (not cap) A medallion of the Virgin Mary, worn by bishops.

pancheon (pan´chun):   a large flaring shallow vessel variously used, as to set milk for cream. 41.

pancratic (pan.krat´ik):   pert. to a pancratium, an ancient Greek athletic contest. Having all or many degrees of power (said esp. of an adjustable eyepiece for a microscope).

pandal (pan´dal):   in India and Ceylon, a shed, esp. a temporary one; a booth; bower; arbor.

Pandean (pan.dē´an):   pert. to the god Pan.

pandiculation (pan.dik´ū.lā´shun):   a stretching and stiffening, esp. of one's trunk and extremities (as when fatigued or drowsy).

pandita (pan.dē´ta):   a priest of the Philippine Moros.

pandle (pan´dl):   a shrimp. 30.

panduriform (pan.dū´ri.fôrm):   having an indentation on both sides, like a violin.

pandy (pan´di):   a hit on the palm, as with a cane. 45.

panela (pa.nel´a):   low-grade brown sugar.

panivorous (pa.niv´o.rus):   bread-eating.

pannage (pan´ij):   in English law, the feeding of, or right to feed, swine in a wood; also, the fee for it. Food (as chestnuts, etc.) for swine in a wood or forest.

panstereorama (pan.stēr´i.o.räma):   a relief map of a town or country.

Pantagruelian (pan´ta.grōō.ĕl´yan):   ribaldly satirical, with great exaggeration.

pantanemone (pan′ta.nem′o.ni): a windmill with two semicircular vanes.

pantarbe (pan.tärb′): a precious stone supposed to shine like the sun and act as a magnet on gold. 52.

panthophobia, pantophobia (pan′tho.-fō′bi.a, pan′to-): fear of suffering and disease.

pantisocracy (pan′ti.sok′ra.si): a Utopian community (imagined by Coleridge, Southey, etc., in their youth), in which all rule equally.

pantler (pant′ler): in a great household, the servant in charge of the bread and the pantry. 9.

panto (pan′tō): short for *pantomime*. 26A.

pantological (pan′to.loj′i.kal): pert. to a systematic view of all knowledge.

pantophagous (pan.tof′a.gus): omnivorous.

panurgy (pan′er.ji): universal skill or craft.

papaphobia (pā′pa.fō′bi.a): dread of the pope or of popery.

papaverous (pa.pav′er.us): pert. to the poppy.

papilionaceous (pa.pil′i.o.nā′shus): butterfly-like.

papiopio (pä′pyō.pyō): the young of the ulua, a Hawaiian fish.

papyrography (pa′pi.rog′ra.fi): a process of multiplying copies of writings, etc., by use of a paper stencil and corrosive ink.

parabolanus (par.a.bo.lā′nus): in the early church, a monk who treated contagious diseases.

parabolize (pa.rab′o.līz): to speak in parables. Also, to make parabolic, as a mirror for a telescope.

Parabrahm, Parabrahman (par′a.bräm, -brä′man): in the Hindu religion, the supreme, absolute, nameless, impersonal principle.

paracenastic (par′a.si.nas′tik): relating to one of the two projecting wings of the skene of a Greek theater.

paracentesis (par′a.sen.tē′sis): in surgery, the puncture of a cavity of the body with an instrument, to draw off effused fluid; tapping.

paracentral (par′a.sen′tral): lying near a center or central part.

TONGUE-TIED LOVER

The jackal on the prowl cries, ''Pheal!''
A-hunt for dearer prey,
The boar in rutting time cries ''Fream!''
The stag on oestral day
Cries ''Troat!'' . . .
Would I, dear, so could squeal!—
Would I could scream!—
But pheal, and fream, and troat
Lock in my throat.

---

parachronism (pa.rak′ro.nizm): a chronological error, esp. one in which a date is set late.

paraclete (par′a.klēt): an aide, legal helper. (cap) The Holy Spirit as intercessor.

paracoita (par′a.ko.ē′ta): a female sexual partner.

paracoitus (par′a.ko.ē′tus): a male sexual partner.

paracrostic (par′a.kros′tik): a poetical composition in which the first verse contains, in order, the first letters of the following verses.

paradiddle (par′a.did′l): a certain roll of the snare drum.

paradromic (par′a.drō′mik, -drom′ik): running side by side; following a parallel course.

parageusic (par′a.jōō′sik): relating to abnormality of the sense of taste.

paragoge (par′a.gō′je): the addition of a sound or syllable to the end of a word.

paragram (par′a.gram): a pun, esp. one made by changing the first letter of a word.

paragraphia (par.a.graf′i.a): aphasia in which the patient writes unintended words or letters.

paralalia (par′a.lāl′ya): a speech disorder marked by distortion of sound.

paralepsis (par′a.lep′sis): in rhetoric, a passing over with brief mention so as to emphasize the suggestiveness of what is omitted.

paralian (pa.rāl′yan): a dweller by the sea. 1.

paralipomena (par′a.li.pom′e.na): passages that are deleted, but added as a supplement.

paralipophobia (par′a.li.po.fō′bi.a): fear of responsibility.

parallelepiped (par′a.lel′i.pī′ped): a six-sided prism with parallelogram faces.

paralogic (par′a.loj′ik): illogic.

paralogist (pa.ral′o.jist): one who uses reasoning that begs the question.

paramimia (par′a.mim′i.a): a pathological misuse of gestures.

paramimiographer (par′a.mim′i.og′ra.-fer): a collector or writer of proverbs.

paranymph (par′a.nimf): a best man; bridesmaid; advocate.

paraphasia (par.a.fā′zhi.a): aphasia in which the patient talks volubly but misuses words.

paraphilemia (par′a.fi.lē′mi.a): love play; paizogony.

paraphrast (par.a.frast): a paraphraser.

paraphrenic (par′a.frē′nik, fren′ik): pert. to any of the paranoid disorders, but usu. excluding paranoid schizophrenia.

parapraxia (par′a.prak′si.a): faulty or blundering action.

---

paratamous (pa.rat′a.mus): pert. to a bird's upper jaw.

parathesis (pa.ra′thi.sis): in grammar, the setting of a second word beside the first as an adjunct term (''Jesus *Savior*''); apposition. A parenthesis. 1.

parathetic (par′a.thet′ik): parenthetic. 1.

paratonic (par′a.ton′ik): retarding movement or growth.

parenesis (pa.ren′i.sis): advice; counsel; an exhortatory composition.

parenetic (par.i.net′ik): advisory, consulting.

parentate (pa.ren′tāt): to perform funeral rites, esp. for a relative. 1.

parepithymia (par.ep.i.thīm′i.a): distorted cravings due to mental illness.

paretic (pa.ret′ik): pert. to paresis, or paralysis. One who is paretic.

pargasite (pär′ga.sīt): the mineral hornblende.

pari (par′i): in textiles, the weight of raw silk before it is degummed.

parisology (par′i.sol′o.ji): intentional ambiguity.

parison (par′i.son): a gob of partially shaped molten glass. A receptacle in a bottle-making machine that releases the exact amount of metal needed for making a bottle. In rhetoric, an even balance between the members of a sentence.

Pariti (pa.rī′tī): a small genus of tropical trees with entire cordate leaves and yellow flowers, as the *majagua*.

paroemia (pa.rē′mi.a): a proverb.

parorexia (par.o.rek′si.a): perverted appetite, demanding strange foods.

parral, parrel (par′al, -el): in ships, the rope loop or sliding collar by which a yard or spar is held to the mast in such a way that it may be hoisted or lowered. To fasten by means of a parrel.

parrhesia (pa.rē′zhi.a): in rhetoric, boldness or freedom of speech.

parten (pär′ten): to impart; partake. 1.

parthenic (pär.then′ik): pert. to a virgin or virginity.

parthenolatry (pär′thi.nol′a.tri): the worship of virgins.

parthenology (pär′thi.nol′o.ji): the study of virgins and virginity.

Parthenopean (pär′thi.no.pē′an): pert. to Parthenope, a Siren who threw herself into the sea after failing to beguile Odysseus by her songs. Also, pert. to a large genus of spider crabs.

parthenophobia (pär′thi.no.fō′bi.a): fear of virgins.

partimen (pär.ti.men): a disputatious lyrical poem composed by Provençal troubadors.

partiversal (pär.ti.vur′sal): in geology, dipping in different directions, as at each end of an anticlinal axis.

parturifacient (pär.tū.ri.fā′shent): inducing childbirth. A medicine to induce childbirth.

parvanimity (pär.va.nim′i.ti): pettiness; meanness; a petty or mean person.

parviscient (pär.vish′ent): uninformed.

pash (pash): to throw violently, crush; a crushing blow; a heavy fall of rain or snow. 11A.

pasigraphy (pa.sig′ra.fi): any system of writing using signs to represent ideas rather than words. Loosely, any artificial language designed for universal use.

pasilaly (pa′si.lā′li): a universal language. 52.

passade (pa.sād′): a turn of a horse backward or forward on the same spot.

Passiflora (pas′i.flôr′a): a genus of mainly tropical and mostly tendril-bearing American vines with showy red, white, or purple flowers, incl. the passion flower. (not cap) A plant of this genus.

patache (pa.tash′): a tender to a fleet of sailing vessels.

patata (pa.tä′ta): the potato. The sweet potato.

patavinity (pat′a.vin′i.ti): local or provincial words, pronunciations, or expressions, and their use.

paterissa (pat′e.ris′a): a crosier surmounted by a small cross from whose base issue two serpents.

patesi (pa.tā′zi): in Babylon, a ruler of a Sumerian city-state who combined the religious and the secular chieftaincies; a priest-king.

patharmosis (path′är.mō′sis): mental adjustment to one's disease.

pathematic (path′i.mat′ik): pert. to emotion; emotive. 52. Pert. to disease.

pathic (path′ik): passive; suffering; also, a passive participant; a catamite. 52.

pathognomic, pathognomonic (path′og.nom′ik, -no.mon′ik): characteristic of a particular disease (as a symptom).

pathognomy (pa.thog′no.mi): the study of the signs of human passions. Medically, the science of diagnosis.

pathomimesis (path′o.mi.mē′sis): the act of malingering.

pathophobia (path.o.fō′bi.a): fear of disease or germs.

patible (pat′i.bl): the transom of a cross; the cross itself. Sufferable; tolerable. 52. Capable of suffering; capable of being acted on. 1.

patibulary (pa.tib′u.ler′i): pert. to the gallows or hanging.

patinate (pat′i.nāt): to coat or become coated with a patina.

patripotestal (pa.tri.po.tes′tal): pert. to paternal authority.

patrix (pā′triks): a pattern or die to form matrixes.

patrocinate (pa.tros′i.nāt): to patronize.

patroclinous (pa.tro.klī′nus): having characteristics inherited from the father.

patrology (pa.trol′o.ji): the branch of historical theology treating of the teachings of the Fathers of the Christian church.

patronate (pā′tro.nāt): the right, duty, and jurisdiction of a patron; patronage.

patronomatology (pat′ro.nō′ma.tol′o.ji): the study of patronymics.

patronymic (pat′ro.nim′ik): strictly, a name formed from that of the father; generally, a surname handed down in the paternal line.

pauciloquy (pô.sil′o.kwi): brevity in speech.

pauldron (pôl′drun): a piece of armor covering the shoulder where the body piece and arm piece join.

pavid (pav′id): timid; fearful. 52.

pawk (pôk): a clever device; a trick or wile. 44. Impertinence; an impertinent person. 42.

peage (pā′ij): a toll. 2.

pean (pēn): a kind of heraldic fur. Var. of *peen*.

pearlin, pearling (pur′lin, -ling): a kind of silk or thread; pl., trimmings of this; also, clothes trimmed with it. 44A.

peart (pērt, pyurt): dial. var. of *pert*. Brisk; active; flourishing.

peba (pē′ba): a small armadillo, ranging from Texas to Paraguay and having nine movable bands of scutes.

peccatiphobia, peccatophobia (pe.ka.ti.fō′bi.a, -to.fō′bi.a): fear of committing or having committed a crime.

peckerwood (pek′er.wood): a woodpecker. In parts of the south, a poor white.

pectoriloquy (pek.to.ril′o.kwi): the distinct sound of a patient's voice heard in auscultation, usu. indicating a morbid change in the lungs.

pectous (pek′tus): pert. to pectin.

pectus (pek′tus): the breast of a bird. The lower surface of the thorax of an insect.

peculium (pe.kū′li.um): in Roman law, property held by a subject at the pleasure of the male head of a household.

pedalier (ped′a.lēr): the pedal keyboard of an organ, harpsichord, pianoforte, or piano.

pedality (pe.dal′i.ti): a measuring by paces; a going on foot. 52.

pedantocracy (ped′an.tok′ra.si): government by pedants.

pedetentious (ped′i.ten′shus): proceeding gradually or cautiously. 52.

pedial (ped′i.al): asymmetric.

pediculophobia (pi.dik′ū.lo.fō′bi.a): fear of lice.

Pediculus (pi.dik′ū.lus): a genus of true lice, incl. the common forms infesting man.

pedigerous (pi.dij′er.us): having feet.

pediluvium (ped′i.lōō′vi.um): a foot bath.

pedimanous (pe.dim′a.nus): having feet like hands.

pediophobia (pē′di.o.fō′bi.a): fear of dummies, dolls, puppets, mannequins, etc.

pedology (pi.dol′o.ji): the study of soil.

peele (pēl): the rhebock, a South American antelope.

peelee (pē′li): in croquet, a ball which is peeled.

peen (pēn): the sharp end of the head of a hammer or sledge opposite the face.

peesweep (pē′swēp): the lapwing; the greenfinch. 30.

peever (pē′ver): a stone used in hopscotch; the game hopscotch. 44.

peirameter (pī.ram′i.ter): an apparatus for measuring the amount of power necessary to haul a truck or carriage over a given way.

peirastic (pī.ras′tik): fitted for trial; experimental; tentative.

peisage, pesage (pā′sij, pes′ij): formerly, in English law, a toll charge for weighing avoirdupois goods, except for wool; also, the right to impose such a toll. 1.

pelargic (pi.lär′jik): pert. to storks; storklike.

pelfed (pelft): robbed; pilfered; despoiled. 1.

pell (pel): pelt; to pelt; also, a garment lined with skins or fur. 1. A roll or record of parchment. 6.To hasten; hurry.2.

pellas (pel′as): the small cheese-shaped fruit of the dwarf mallow.

pellate (pel′āt): to tend to separate, to repel mutually.

pelmatic (pel.mat′ik): pert. to the sole of the foot.

pelmatogram (pel.mat′o.gram): a footprint.

pelology (pi.lol′o.ji): the study of mud and its therapeutic applications.

pelta (pel′ta): in Greek antiquity, a small light shield.

peltast (pel′tast): a soldier of ancient Greece armed with a pelta.

pelvimeter (pel.vim′i.ter): an instrument for measuring the dimensions of the pelvis.

penduline (pen′dū.lin, -lin): pendulous—applied to birds that build hanging nests.

penelopize (pe.nel′o.pīz): to undo and redo to gain time.

penetralium (pen′i.trāl′yum): the most secret or hidden part.

peniaphobia (pē′ni.a.fō′bi.a): fear of poverty.

peninsulate (pen.in′sū.lāt): to form into a peninsula.

pennanular (pi.nan′ū.lar): nearly ring-shaped.

penniform (pen′i.fôrm): feather-shaped.

penotherapy (pē′no.ther′a.pi): the regulation of prostitutes to control venereal disease.

pensum (pen′sum): a task, esp. one set as punishment in school.

pentacrostic (pen′ta.kros′tik): a set of verses containing five acrostics of a name, one in each of five divisions.

pentaglot (pen′ta.glot): using five different languages. A pentaglot book.

pentalpha (pen.tal′fa): a five-pointed star.

pentapolis (pen.tap′o.lis): a union, confederacy, or group of five cities.

Pentelic (pen.tel′ik): pert. to Mount Pentelicus, near Athens, where the fine white marble of the Parthenon was quarried.

penteteric (pen′ti.ter′ik): recurring every five years.

pentheraphobia (pen′ther.a.fō′bi.a): fear of one's mother-in-law.

pentice (pen′tis): a penthouse. 9.

peotomy (pi.ot′o.mi): amputation of the penis.

peperino (pep′er.ē′nō): dark-colored volcanic detritus containing crystals of minerals and fragments of rock.

percussor (per.kus′er): a doctor's hammer, used in examining patients.

perduellion (pur′dū.el′yun): in Roman law, treason.

perdure, perendure (per.dūr, pur′-en.dūr): to last, continue to exist.

perdurant (per.dū.rant): very long lasting.

perendinate (pe.ren′di.nāt): to postpone until the next day, or indefinitely.

perennate (per′en.āt): in botany, to be perennial.

perflation (per.flā′shun): the act of blowing through; ventilation.

perfluant (per.floo′ant): flowing; flowing through; as, a *perfluent* battery.

perfrication (pur′fri.kā′shun): a thorough rubbing; the rubbing in of ointment.

perfuse (per.fūz): to suffuse or sprinkle with, or as with, a liquid.

pergameneous (pur′ga.mē′ni.us): like parchment.

perhiemate (per.hī′e.māt): to spend the winter. 1.

peri (per′i): in Persian mythology, an imaginary being like an elf or fairy. A very beautiful person.

periastrum (per′i.as′trum): that point in the real orbit of a binary at which the stars are nearest together.

perichareia (per′i.ka.rē′a): violent rejoicing.

perichoresis (per′i.ko.rē′sis): in theology, the reciprocal existence in each other of the three persons of the Trinity, or the human and divine natures of Christ. *Circumincession.*

periclitation (per′i.kli.tā′shun): the act of exposing to danger.

periculous (pe.rik′ū.lus): perilous. 1.

periegesis (per.i.i.jē′sis): a description of an area.

periergy (per′i.ur′ji): excessive care. 1.

perigon (per′i.gon): a round angle.

perigraph (per′i.graf): an inexact description or drawing. An instrument for drawing outlines of bones.

perijove (per′i.jōv): the point in the orbit of a Jovian satellite nearest the center of the planet.

periople (per′i.ō′pl): the thin waxy outer layer of a hoof.

periplus (per′i.plus): a voyage or trip around, as an island or coast. An account of such a journey.

perispheric (per′i.sfer′ik): exactly spherical; globular.

perissological (per′is.o.loj′i.kal): relating, in old rhetoric, to a superfluity of words.

peristerophilist (pi.ris′ter.of′i.list): a pigeon fancier.

peristrephic (per′is.tref′ik): turning around; rotatory.

perkin (pur′kin): a kind of weak cider.

perlaceous (per.lā′shus): pearly; resembling pearl.

perlustration (pur′lus.trā′shun): a thorough survey or examination, as of a museum or set of documents.

permiscible (per.mis′i.bl): capable of being mixed.

pernancy (pur′nan.si): in law, the receiving of rent or profit.

pernoctation (pur′nok.tā′shun): an all-night vigil.

peroral (per′or.al): via the mouth.

perpilocutionist (pur′pi.lo.kū′shun.ist): one who talks through his hat.

perqueer (per.kwēr′): by heart, perfectly; perfect, accurate. 7A.

perruquier (pe.rōō′ki.er): a wigmaker or dealer in wigs.

perscrutation (pur′skrōō.tā′shun): subjection to scrutiny or close examination.

perseity (per.sē′i.ti): self-sufficiency.

persicary (pur′si.kâr′i): a herb of the genus *Persicaria*—sometimes called *lady's thumb.*

persico, persicot (pur′si.kō): a liqueur made from brandy flavored with the kernels of peaches, apricots, etc.

persienne (per.zi.en′): a kind of painted

or printed cotton or silk, orig. from Persia.

persifleur (pur′si.floor): one given to persiflage or banter, esp. about matters usu. considered as serious.

perstringe (per.strinj′): to find fault with; criticize. To touch upon lightly or in passing. 9. To dull the vision of. 1.

pertusion (per.tū′zhun): a perforation; the act of punching or piercing.

perula, perule (per′ū.la, -ōō.la, per′ōōl): one of the scales of a leaf bud. A basal projection in certain orchid flowers.

pervicacity (pur′vi.kas′i.ti): extreme obstinacy; wilfulness. 52.

pervulgate (per.vul′gāt): to publish. 52.

petalism (pet′a.lizm): in ancient Syracuse, banishment for five years. Ostracism.

petardeer, petardier (pet.ar.dēr′): a soldier who manages a petard. 6.

petronel (pet′ro.nel): a large carbine or pistol used in the 16th century and early 17th century by horse soldiers.

pettichaps (pet′i.chaps): a European warbler.

pettitoes (pet′i.tōz): the feet of a pig, often used as a food; toes or feet, esp. those of a child. An insignificant person or thing. 1.

peyton (pā′ton): a smokeless gunpowder containing nitroglycerin and guncotton.

phagomania (fag′o.mā′ni.a): madness marked by insatiable hunger.

phalacrosis (fal′a.krō′sis): baldness.

Phalaris (fal′a.ris): a small genus of American and European grasses with rather broad flat leaves and a dense head of flowers, incl. canary grass and ribbon grass.

phaneromania (fan′er.o.mā′ni.a): a morbid compulsion to pick at a skin growth, bite the nails, etc.

phanic (fan′ik): manifest; apparent.

pharmacophobia (fär′ma.ko.fō′bi.a): fear of drugs or medicine.

pharmic (fär′mik): pert. to drugs or pharmacy. A student of pharmacy. 48.

pharology (fa.rol′o.ji): the art or science of lighthouses or signal lights.

pharyngology (far′ing.gol′o.ji): the science of the pharynx and its diseases.

phasic (fā′zik): pert. to a phase or phases.

phasis (fā′sis): phase. The first appearance of the new moon. An aspect; a mode or manner of being.

phasm (fazm): an appearance, as a meteor or an apparition. 8A.

Phasma (faz′ma): the type genus of Phasmatidae, a family of running insects incl. the stick insects and the leaf insects.

pheal (fēl): the cry of the jackal on the hunt.

phelloplastic (fel′o.plas′tik): a figure or model in cork.

phemic (fē′mik): pert. to or like speech.

phenakistoscope (fen′a.kis′to.skōp): an optical toy resembling the *zoetrope*.

phenicopter (fen′i.kop.ter): a flamingo.

Pherecratic (fer′i.krat′ik): in prosody, a logaoedic tripody acatalectic, of a dactyl and two trochees. Get it?

Phigalian (fi.gāl′yun): pert. to Phigalia, a city in the Peloponnesus; as the *Phigalian* sculptures of the 5th century B.C., now in the British Museum.

philalethe (fil′a.lēth′i): one who enjoys forgetting.

philauty (fi.lôt′i): self-love; selfishness. 1.

philematology (fil′i.ma.tol′o.ji): the art of kissing.

philhellene (fil′he.lēn′): a friend of Greece or of the Greeks.

philiater (fil′i.ā′ter): one interested in medical science.

philocalist (fi.lō′ka.list): a lover of beauty.

philodox, philodoxer (fil′o.doks, -er): one who loves his own opinions; a dogmatist.

philogynist (fi.loj.i.nist): a lover of women and womankind.

philomathic (fil′o.math′ik): loving learning. 52.

philopena (fil.o.pē′na): a game in which a man and a woman each try to claim a forfeit from the other by fulfilling certain conditions, as being the first to cry "philopena."

philophobia (fil′o.fō′bi.a): fear of loving or being loved.

philopolemic (fil′o.po.lem′ik): loving argument or controversy.

philornithic (fil′ôr.nith′ik): bird-loving. 52.

philosity (fi.los′i.ti): the degree of body hair.

philosophastering (fi.los′o.fas′ter.ing): pseudo-philosophizing.

philosophicopsychological (fil.o.sof′i.ko.sī′ko.loj′i.kal): philosophical and psychological in one.

philotherian (fil′o.thēr′i.an): fond of animals.

phit (fit): a sound suggesting that of a rifle bullet.

phlebotomize (fli.bot′o.mīz): to let blood by opening a vein; to bleed (one).

phlegmagogue (fleg′ma.gog): a medicine for expelling phlegm.

phlogogenetic (flō′go.ji.net′ik): causing inflammation.

phobophobia (fō′bo.fō′bi.a): fear of fear.

Phoca (fō′ka): a genus of seals now restricted to the harbor seal and a few closely related forms.

phocine (fō′sēn): pert. to the seals.

phoenixity (fi.nik′si.ti): the state of being a paragon, a model of one's kind.

phon (fon): a unit for measuring sound.

phonasthenia (fō′nas.thē′ni.a): hoarseness.

phoniatrics, phonistry (fō′ni.at′riks, -nis.tri): the scientific study and treatment of voice defects.

phonogram (fō′no.gram): a character or symbol representing a word, syllable, or single speech sound.

phonophobia (fō′no.fō′bi.a): fear of noise or of speaking aloud.

phoronomic (fôr.o.nom′ik): pert. to kinematics, the science of the motions or elements of bodies.

photology (fo.tol′o.ji): photics, the science of light.

photophobia (fō′to.fō′bi.a): fear of light.

photophony (fo.tof′o.ni): the transmission of sounds by the modulation of light beams and their reconversion into sound.

phrenesiac (fre.nē′zi.ak): subject to delirium or brain fever.

phronesis (fro.nē′sis): practical wisdom, prudence.

phrontistery (fron.tis′ter.i): a place for study and contemplation.

phrygium (frij′i.um): a helmet-like white cap, worn in the early Middle Ages by the popes at nonliturgical ceremonies.

phthiriophobia (thir.i.o.fō′bi.a): fear of lice.

phthisozoics (tiz′o.zō′iks): the art of destroying noxious animals.

phycography (fī.kog′ra.fi): description of algae or seaweeds.

phylacter (fi.lak′ter): phylactery. 1.

phylarch (fī′lärk): in ancient Greece, the chief ruler of a phyle, or tribe. The commander of the cavalry furnished by each tribe. In the Asiatic provinces of the Roman Empire, the accepted head of a tribal division.

phyllary (fil′a.ri): one of the involuted bracts in a cluster of sessile flowers.

phylliform (fil′i.fôrm): leaf-shaped.

phyllomancy (fil′o.man′si): divination with leaves.

phyllophorous (fi.lof′o.rus): leaf-bearing.

phyloanalysis (fī′lo.a.nal′i.sis): a study of the psychology of society.

phylon (fī′lon): a tribe or race; a genetically related group.

phyma (fī′ma): in medicine, an external nodule; a skin tumor.

physagogue (fiz′a.gog): a medicine to induce expulsion of gas from the bowels.

physianthropy (fiz′i.an′thro.pi): the study of the constitution and diseases of man, and their remedies. 52.

physiogony (fiz′i.og′o.ni): the theory of the origin of nature.

physiolatry (fiz′i.ol′a.tri): nature worship.

physis (fī′sis): nature; that which grows or becomes.

physitheism (fī′zi.thē′izm): the belief that God has a physical form.

phytivorous (fī.tiv′o.rus): feeding on plants; herbivorous.

phytolithology (fī′to.li.thol′o.ji): the paleontology of plants; paleobotany.

phytoma (fī.tō′ma): the vegetative substance of plants.

phytophagous (fī.tof′a.gus): *phytivorous.*

phytophil (fī.to.fil): one fond of plants, or feeding on plants.

pia (pē′a): a perennial herb of East India, Australasia, and Polynesia, cultivated for its large, starch-yielding root.

piacle (pī′a.kl): a heinous offense; a crime; sin; guilt. Also, a sacrificial rite; an expiatory offering. 1.

pial (pī′al): pert. to the pia mater, the connective tissue investing the brain and spinal cord.

pianino (pē′a.nē′nō): pianette.

pianteric (pī.an.ter′ik): fattening food.

Piarist (pī′a.rist): a clerk of the Scuole Pie (religious schools) founded at Rome early in the 17th century.

piation (pī.ā′shun): the act of atoning, expiating. 52.

piatti (pi.ät′i): cymbals.

piccadill (pik′a.dil): a flaring collar worn at the back of decolleté gowns in the 17th century.

pickedevant (pik′de.vänt): a Vandyke beard. 1.

picosecond (pī′ko.sek.unt, -und): one thousandth of a nanosecond; one trillionth of a second.

picqueter (pik′e.ter): one who bunches artificial flowers.

pictorical (pik.tôr′i.kal): pictorial. 52.

picuda (pi.kōō′da): the great barracuda.

pidan (pi.dän′): Chinese duck eggs aged in brine.

piet, piot (pī′et): the magpie; like a magpie—piebald, chattering. A piebald horse. A chatterbox; a saucy person. The water ouzel. 44.

piff (pif): an exclamation.

pightle (pī′tl): a small field or enclosure. 30.

pignorative (pig′no.rā′tiv): pledging; pawning. 52.

pika (pī′ka, pē′ka): any small gnawing mammal of the family Ochotonidae inhabiting high mountains in Asia and western North America, related to rabbits, but having small ears, rudimentary tail, and relatively short hind legs.

pikel, pikle (pik′l): hayfork; *pightle.* 13B.

pilaf, pilaff (pi.läf′, pi.laf′): a Turkish dish of rice combined with meat and other vegetables and seasoned with herbs.

pilar, pilary (pī′lar, pī′lar.i): pert. to hair; hairy.

pilau, pilaw (pi.lô): var. of pilaf, pilaff.

pilch (pilch): an outer garment made orig. of skin and fur and later of leather or wool. An infant's diaper cover. A light child's saddle. A saddle cover. 1. To pilfer; filch. 2.

pilcher (pil′cher): an Elizabethan term of contempt. 1.

pilgarlic (pil.gär′lik): formerly, a bald-headed man; now, a poor sort of fellow.

pili (pē′li): the edible nut of a Philippine tree, *Canarium ovatum,* or the tree itself. In Hawaii, twisted beard grass. Also, pl. of *pilus,* a hair or hairlike structure in botany and zoology.

pilikea (pē.li.kē′a): trouble, in Hawaii.

pililoo (pil′i.lōō): in hunting, a cry of distress.

pillet (pil′et): a pellet; a small pill.

pilliwinks (pil′i.wingks): an instrument of torture for the thumbs and fingers. 6.

piloerection (pī′lo.i.rek′shun): the standing of hair on end.

pilwillet (pil.wil′et): the American oyster catcher. 28.

Pimenta (pi.men′ta): a small genus of tropical American aromatic trees of the myrtle family, incl. the allspice tree. Pimento. The black pepper.

pimola (pi.mō′la): an olive stuffed with pimiento.

Pimpinella (pim′pi.nel′a): a large genus of herbs of the carrot family, incl. the anise and the burnet saxifrage.

pinacoid (pin′a.koid): a crystal form with two faces parallel to two axes.

pinacotheca (pin′a.ko.thē′ka): a picture gallery.

pincette (pin.set′): a small pair of pincers, tweezers, or forceps used in surgery.

pincpinc (pingk′pingk): an African warbler.

pindy (pin′di): gone bad; tainted. 13.

pingle (ping′gl): to strive or struggle, esp. for a living; to trifle, esp. with one's food; a struggle; effort. 17A. A small piece of enclosed ground. 2.

pinguefy (ping′gwi.fī): to fatten; to make fat or greasy; to enrich (the soil). 52.

pinguidness, pinguitude (ping′gwid.nes, -gwi.tūd): fatness; obesity; oiliness.

pinic (pī′nik): pert. to or obtained from the pine.

pinnet (pin′et): a pinnacle; a pennant. 44. A pin; a pint. 13.

Pinus (pī′nus): the largest and most important genus of coniferous trees.

pipa (pē′pa): the Surinam toad.

piperacious (pip′er.ā′shus): pert. to the *Piperaciae,* a family of tropical plants having aromatic herbage.

pipistrel, pipistrelle (pip′is.trel): the brown bat of Europe.

pipple (pip′l): to murmur, as the wind or rippling water. 1.

pir (pir): a Mohammedan saint or his tomb.

pirl (purl): var. of *purl.*

pirlie (pur′li): anything small, esp. the little finger (also *pirlie-pig*); a money box. 44.

pirn (purn): any of various devices resembling a reel. 44A. A twitch or nose ring for a refractory animal. 11.

pirner (pur′ner): one who winds thread or yarn on pirns.

pirnie, pirny (pur′ni): a little *pirn,* or bobbin. 44.

pishaug (pish′ôg): a female or young sea duck—surf scoter. 36.

pishogue (pi.shōg′): sorcery; witchcraft. 50.

pisk (pisk): the common American nighthawk.

pisky (pis′ki): var. of *pixy.* Also, a moth.

pissabed (pis′a.bed): any of various wild plants, as the dandelion, with diuretic properties.

pistic (pis′tik): pure; genuine.

pistolade (pis′to.läd): a pistol shot or wound. To fire on with pistols. 1.

pistology (pis.tol′o.ji): the study of faith.

pithecological (pi.thē′ko.loj.i.kal): pert. to the study of apes. 52.

pithiatism (pith′i.a.tizm): a forceful suggestion.

pitpit (pit′pit): a *guitguit.* Also, having a rapid succession of slight sounds of unvarying quality and stress.

Pittosporum (pit′o.spôr′um): a genus of evergreen trees and shrubs of Asia, Africa, and Australasia, often having fragrant white or yellow flowers succeeded by berries, as the laurel. (not cap) A plant of this species.

pituitous (pi.tū′i.tus): consisting of, resembling, or discharging mucus.

pixillation (pik′si.lā′shun): stop-motion photography that gives live actors the appearance of jerky movement associated with cartoon characters.

placet (plā′set): an expression of approval or vote of assent.

placophobia (plā′ko.fō′bi.a): fear of tombstones.

plafond (pla.fond′): in architecture, a ceiling formed by the underside of a floor. Also, contract bridge.

plaga (plā′ga): in animals, a stripe of color.

plancier (plan.sēr′): in architecture, the underside of a cornice; a soffitt.

planeta (pla.net′a): among Romans, a cloak that enveloped the person, leaving the face free.

planiloquent (pla.nil′o.kwent): straightforward in speech.

planiped (plā′ni.ped): barefoot; a barefoot person.

planomania (plā′no.mā′ni.a): a passion for the bohemian life.

planta (plan′ta): the sole of the foot. The back side of the shank of a bird's leg. The first joint of the tarsus of an insect. An anal clasping leg of a caterpillar.

plantigrade (plan′ti.grād): walking on the sole with the heels touching the ground, as bears and people.

plantocracy (plan.tok′ra.si): government by planters.

plaquette (pla.ket′): a small plaque. In anatomy, a blood platelet.

plastron, plastrum (plas′trun, -um): a metal breastplate. A protection for the breast of a fencer. A trimming for the front of a woman's dress. The starched front of a man's shirt.

plateresque (plat′er.esk): pert. to a 16th-century Spanish architectural style with rich ornamentation suggestive of silver plate.

platic (plat′ik): not exact; imperfect—said in astrology of the imperfect conjunction of two planets.

platinize (plat′i.nīz): to cover, treat, or combine with platinum.

platitudinarian (plat′i.tū.di.nâr′i.an): full of platitudes.

platonize (plā′to.nīz): to conform to Platonic principles. To render Platonic; idealize.

platycephalic (plat′i.si′fal′ik): tending toward flatness of the crown of the head.

plaustral (plôs′tral): of or relating to a wagon or cart.

plebicolous (pli.bik′o.lus): courting the favor of the common people. 52.

plegometer (pli.gom′e.ter): an instrument to measure and record the force of blows.

pleionosis (plī′o.nō′sis): exaggeration of one's own importance.

pleniloquence (pli.nil′o.kwens): talking to excess.

plenipotence (pli.nip′o.tens): the quality of being invested with authority to transact business. 52.

plenist (plē′nist): pert. to the theory that every part of space is full of matter. One who believes in this theory.

pleochromatic (plē′o.kro.mat′ik): pert. to the property of some crystals of showing different colors when viewed in the direction of different axes.

pleon (plē′on): a crustacean's abdomen. The terminal segment of a king crab.

pleonaxia (plē′o.nak′si.a): avarice.

Plesiosaurus (plē′si.o.sôr.os): a genus of marine reptiles of the Mesozoic, having a very long neck, a small head, and all four limbs developed as paddles for swimming.

pleurodynia (plur′o.dī′ni.a): a sharp pain in the side, usu. located in the rib muscles.

plex (pleks): to form a plexus or network; to make plexiform.

plexure (plek′sher): a weaving together; that which is woven together.

plicative (plik′a.tiv): capable of being folded.

plimp (plimp): to take part in an event so as to write about it, as George Plimpton does—a *Time* magazine coinage.

plock (plok): an imitative word.

plonk (plongk): cheap table wine.

plouk, plook (plook): a pimple. 44A.

plousiocracy (ploo′si.ok′ra.si): plutocracy.

ployment (ploi′ment): the act of forming a column from a line, in the military.

pluffer (pluf′er): a shooter; marksman. A popgun. 43.

pluffy (pluf′i): puffy; fat; fluffy. 17A.

plumassier (plū.ma.syā): a dealer in ornamental plumes or feathers.

plumbeous (plum′bi.us): consisting of, or resembling, lead; leaden; the color of lead.

plumbic (plum′bik): pert. to, or containing lead.

plumcot (plum′kot): a hybrid between the plum and the apricot.

plumigerous (ploo.mij′er.us): feathered.

plumiped (ploo′mi.ped): having feather-covered feet. A plumiped bird.

plummer (plum′er): a pillow block or bearing block. Var. of *plumber*. 1.

plumper (plum′per): something held in the mouth to fill out the cheeks; also, a false bosom. A heavy blow. 21.

plurennial (ploo.ren′ial): lasting for many years. A long-lived plant.

plushette (plush.et′): an inferior kind of plush.

plutomania (ploo′to.mā′ni.a): madness for money.

pluviograph (ploo′vi.o.graf): a rain gauge.

pluviophobia (ploo′vi.o.fō′bi.a): fear of rain.

pneumonoultramicroscopicsilicovolcanoconiosis (nū.mon′ool.tra.mī′kro.skop′ik.sil′i.ko.vol.kan′o.kō′ni.ō.sis): a lung disease caused by inhaling fine particles of silicon dust.

pnigophobia (nī′go.fō′bi.a): fear of choking, as during sleep.

po (pō): in English folklore, an impish spirit. 1. In Polynesian mythology, the realm of darkness and the dead.

pobby (pob′i): puffed up; swollen. 13.

pochette (po.shet′): a handbag. A small envelope of transparent paper for holding stamps.

poculation (pok.ū.lā′shun): the drinking of wine, spirits, etc.

poculiform (pok′ū.li.fôrm): cup-shaped.

podger (poj′er): a small taper rod used to align rivet holes.

podgy (poj′i): softly fat; pudgy.

poditti (po.dit′i): an Australian kingfisher.

podobromhidrosis (pō′do.brom′hī.drō′sis): sweatiness and smelliness of the feet.

poe (pō′i): the parson bird of Tahiti, which has two tufts of white on its throat.

poecilonymy (pē′si.lon′i.mi): the use of several names for one thing.

poeticule (po.et′i.kūl): a poetaster.

pogamoggan (pog′a.mog′an): a club used as a weapon or ceremonial object by various American Indian peoples.

pogoniasis (pō′go.nī′a.sis): excessive growth of beard in a man, or any such growth in a woman.

pogonology (pō′go.nol′o.ji): a treatise on beards.

pogonophobia (po.gō′no.fō′bi.a): fear of beards.

pogonotomy (pō′go.not′o.mi): shaving.

poikilothymia (poi.kil′o.thim′i.a): extreme fluctuations of mood.

poimenics (poi.men′iks): pastoral theology.

polacca (po.lak′a): the polonaise, a stately Polish dance developed from the promenade.

polacre (po.lä′ker): a vessel with two or three masts, having sails usu. in one piece and square, but occas. lateen, used in the Mediterranean.

polder (pol′der): land reclaimed from the sea.

polemology (pol′i.mol′o.ji): the study of war.

polemoscope (po.lem′o.skōp′): an opera or field glass arranged for seeing objects not directly before the eye.

polenta (po.len′ta): in Italy, a thick porridge of corn meal, semolina, barley, or chestnut meal.

poliosis (pō′li.ō′sis): premature graying of the hair.

pollicitation (po.lis′i.tā′shun): a promise. 52. In civil law, an unaccepted promise or offer.

pollincture (po.lingk′cher): preparation of a corpse for interment or cremation. 1.

polony (po.lō′ni): a polonaise.

poltina (pol.tē′na): a Russian silver coin equivalent to 50 kopecks or half a ruble.

poltophagy (pol′tof′a.ji): the prolonged chewing of food, reducing it to a semiliquid state.

polychrestic (pol′i.kres′tik): having many uses.

polyemia (pol′i.ē′mi.a): a condition marked by an excessive amount of blood in the system—plethora.

polygenic (pol′i.jen′ik): pert. to a group of genes that collectively control aspects of inheritance.

polygenous (po.lij′i.nus): containing many kinds, as of elements or rocks—a *polygenous* mountain.

polygonous (po.lig′o.nus): having many angles and sides; polygonal.

polygyral (pol′i.jī′ral): having, or pert. to, many cycles, rounds, or whorls.

polyhemic (pol′i.hēm′ik): pert. to *polyemia*.

polylemma (pol′i.lem′a): a dilemma with several solutions, all undesirable.

polylogy (po.lil′o.ji): verbosity.

polymeric (pol′i.mer′ik): in chemistry, consisting of the same elements in the same proportions by weight, but differing in molecular weight.

polymicrian (pol′i.mik′ri.an): compact.

polymythic (pol′i.mith′ik): having to do with the inclusion of many or several stories or plots in one narrative or dramatic work.

polynesic (pol′i.nē′zik): in medicine, occurring in different spots or in sporadic patches like islands.

polyonomous (pol′i.on′o.mus): synonymous. Also, having many names.

polyorama (pol′i.o.rä′ma, -ram′a): a view of many objects; also, a kind of panorama with a dissolving view.

polyphagous (po.lif′a.gus): subsisting on a moderate variety of foods.

polypharmic (pol′i.fär′mik): containing many drugs.

polytopic (pol′i.top′ik): occurring in many places.

polytropic (pol′i.trop′ik): visiting many kinds of flowers for nectar—used of an insect.

pomato (po.mā′tō): a fragrant, succulent, tomato-like fruit, produced by grafting tomato scions on potato plants.

pomatum (po.mā′tum): a perfumed unguent, esp. for the hair; pomade. To dress (as hair) with pomatum.

pombe (pom′be): in Africa, a kind of beer made from grain, usu. from millet. Also, a Tibetan chief.

pombo (pum′bō): a chief or headman in Tibet.

pommage (pom′ij): the substance of apples crushed by grinding as in making cider. Cider. 1.

ponent (pō′nent): western; occidental.

ponerology (pō′ne.rol′o.ji): a branch of theology dealing with the doctrine of evil.

pong (pong): a hollow ringing sound. On the British stage, to improvise to cover up a fluff.

ponophobia (pō′no.fō′bi.a): fear of overwork.

pontage (pon′tij): a bridge toll.

pont-levis (pont.lev′is): a drawbridge.

poogye (pōō′gi): the Hindu nose flute.

poon (pōōn): an East Indian tree that yields hard, light wood used for masts, spars, etc.

poorwill (pōōr′wil): a bird of the western United States and Mexico, like but smaller than the whippoorwill.

popinary (pop.i.nâr.i): a short-order cook.

popination (pop′i.nā′shun): the frequenting of bars or taverns.

popoloco (pō′po.lō′kō): to the Nahuatl Indians, one who speaks a barbarous or foreign language. (cap) A people of southern Pueblo, Mexico.

porcelanic (pôr′se.lan′ik): resembling porcelain; said of certain rocks.

poriomania (pôr′i.o.mā′ni.a): wanderlust.

porismatic (po.riz.mat′ik): in geometry, pert. to a proposition that affirms the possibility of finding conditions that will render a certain problem either indeterminate or capable of innumerable solutions.

pornerastic (pôr′ne.ras′tik): licentious.

pornocracy (pôr.nok′ra.si): government by whores.

pornogenarian (pôr.no.je.nâr.i.an): a dirty old man.

pornophobia (pôr′no.fō′bi.a): fear of prostitutes.

Poro (pō′rō): a native secret society in Sierra Leone, having only men as members.

porotic (po.rot′ik): promoting the formation of a callus.

porphyrogene (pôr′fir.o.jēn): born to the purple; royal born.

porphyrophobia (pôr′fi.ro.fō′bi.a): fear of purple.

porraceous (po.rā′shus): resembling the leek in color; leek-green.

porrect (po.rekt′): extended horizontally, stretched out. To extend in this fashion.

portglave (pôrt′glāv): one of a Livonian religious order of knights in the first half of the 13th century.

portlast (pôrt′last): the porpoise. 52. The upper edge of a gunwale. 1.

portmantologism (pôrt′man.tol′o.jizm): a blending of two or more words into one.

portreeve (pôrt′rēv): in early England, the official charged with keeping the peace in a port or market town.

porwigle (pôr′wig′l): a tadpole, pollywog. 1.

posada (po.sä′da): in Spain, a hotel or inn.

posole (pō′sōl): in Spanish America, a dish or thick soup composed of meat, hominy, garlic, and chili.

posology (po.sol′o.ji): in medicine, the science of doses. In mathematics, the doctrine of pure quantity.

postcibal (pōst′sī′bal): after dinner.

posteriad (pos.tēr′i.ad): posteriorly, in anatomy and zoology.

posticous (pos′ti.kus): posterior. In botany, situated on the outer side of a filament—said of an extrorse anther.

postil (pos′til): a marginal note or comment, specif. of the Bible. To make marginal notes.

postillate (pos′ti.lāt): to postil. To preach by expounding Scripture verse by verse, in regular order. 52.

postliminium (pōst.li.min′i.um): the law under which things taken by the enemy in war are returned afterward to the previous ownership.

postscenium (pōst.sē′ni.um): the back part of the stage of a theater; the part behind the scenes.

potagerie (po.taj′e.ri): garden vegetables and herbs; a kitchen garden.

potamic (po.tam′ik): pert. to rivers.

potamophilous (pō′ta.mof′i.lus): river-loving.

potassic (po.tas′ik): a combining form of potassium.

pote (pōt): a stick or rod for poking or stirring; a poker; a kick or push with the foot. 21.

potichomania (pō′ti.sho.mā′ni.a,po′ti.-ko-): a craze for imitating painted porcelain ware by coating the inside of glass vessels.

potomania (pō′to.mā′ni.a): dipsomania. Delirium tremens.

potoroo (pot′o.rōō): a rat kangaroo.

pott (pot): a size of paper—12½ × 15″ for writing paper, 13 × 16″ for printing paper.

pottah (pot′a): in India, a certificate of tenure; title deed; lease.

potvalor (pot′val′er): boldness or courage resulting from alcoholic drink.

potwaller, potwalloper (pot′wôl′er, -wol′up.er): prior to the Reform Act of 1832, an Englishman whose qualification for voting was that he boiled (walloped) his own pot—i.e., was a householder.

pouze (pōōz): refuse from cider-making.

pozzy-wallah (poz′i.wol′a): a jam lover. 23.

practic (prak′tik): *practice* in various senses. 9. Practical. Practiced; also, cunning, shrewd. Requiring skill or experience. A practical man, as opposed to a student or theorist.

prana (prä′na): in the Vedic and later Hindu religion, life breath; the life principle.

pranayama (prä′na.yä′ma): certain Yoga exercises.

pratal (prä′tal): pert. to, growing in, or living in, meadows.

pratiloma (prat′i.lō′ma): contrary to custom—said in India of a marriage in which the man is of a lower class than the woman.

pratityasamutpada (prä′ti.tya.sa.mut.pä′da): in Hindu philosophy, the chain of causation.

pravity (prav.i.ti): depravity. Badness or foulness; physical deformity. 9.

praya (prä′ya): beach; strand; specif. (cap), in Hong Kong, a road bordering the shore.

preagonal (pri.ag′o.nal): just before death.

preantepenultimate (pri.an′ti.pi.nul′-ti.mit): fourth from the last.

precentral (pri.sen′tral): in anatomy and zoology, situated in front of the central furrow of the brain.

preception (pri.sep′shun): a preconception; presumption; a precept; command. 1. Instruction by a preceptor. 52. In Roman law, the taking, as of a legacy, before the distribution of the estate of the testator.

precibal (pri.cī′bal): before dinner.

preconize (prē′ko.nīz): to proclaim; publish; commend publicly; summon publicly.

predacean (pri.dā′shun): a carnivorous animal.

predal (prē′dal): predatory; plundering.

predella (pri.del′a): a step on which an altar is placed; a painting or sculpture on the face of a predella; a portable altar of marble, etc.

predicant (pred′i.kant): one who preaches; a preacher; specif., a preaching friar; a Dominican. Preaching; addicted to preaching.

preferent (pref′e.rent): exhibiting or enjoying preference.

premial (prē′mi.al): of the nature of a reward. 52.

premorse (pri.môrs′): ended abruptly, as if bitten off.

premundane (pri.mun′dān): antedating the creation of the world.

prender (pren′der): in law, the right to take something without its being offered.

preominate (pri.om′i.nāt): to forecast by omens.

prepend (pri.pend′): to consider, premeditate. 1.

presbyophrenia (prez′bi.o.frē′ni.a, pres-): female senility attended espec. by loss of memory.

prester (pres′ter): a priest or presbyter. (1, except for *Prester John,* a legendary Christian priest and king in the Middle Ages).

preterhuman (prē′ter.hū′man): beyond human, more than human.

prevene (pri.vēn′): to come before, precede. 52. To forestall, prevent. 1.

prickmadam (prik′mad′am): the stonecrop, a mosslike herb used in gardens.

prickmedainty (prik′mi.dān′ti): affectedly nice; a goody-goody. 44A.

pridian (prid′i.an): pert. to the day before yesterday. 52.

prill (pril): a stream, rill. In mining, an ore selected for excellence. To turn sour; to get drunk. 41A.

primigenous, primigenial (prī.mij′i.nus, prī′mi.jē′ni.al): first created or formed; original; primary, primal. 52.

pringle (pring′gl): to tingle annoyingly; to cause a tingle.

Priscian (prish′i.an): a grammarian; a grammar.

priss (pris): to act or dress in a prissy or fussy manner—usu. with *up*. 27.

proa (prō′a): a Malaysian sailing outrigger.

probal (prō′bal): approved, probable. 52.

probouleutic (prō′bo͞o.lo͞o′tik): pert. to previous deliberation.

procacious (pro.kā′shus): pert; petulant; insolent.

proceleusmatic (prō′se.lo͞oz.mat′ik): inciting; animating; encouraging (esp. applied to a song). In prosody, a foot of 4 short syllables; pert. to such a foot.

procellas (pro.sel′as): a tool for imparting a characteristic shape to the neck of a forming bottle or other object as the work is rotated.

procellous (pro.sel′us): stormy.

procerity (pro.ser′i.ti): tallness; height. 52.

prochronism (prō′kro.nizm): the referring of an event to an earlier date than the true one.

prociduous (pro.sid′ū.us): in medicine, prolapsed.

proctalgia (prok.tal′ji.a): a pain in the rear; pygia.

prodelision (prō′di.lizh′un): elision of the initial vowel of a verse.

proditorious (prō′di.tôr′i.us): traitorous. Apt to betray secret thoughts.

proemptosis (prō′emp.tō′sis): the addition of a day to the lunar calendar at intervals of about 310 years.

profectitious (prō′fek.tish′us): derived; in Roman law, pert. to inherited property.

proficuous (pro.fik′ū.us): profitable; useful. 52.

profulgent (pro.ful′jent): in poetic use, shining forth; effulgent.

progenerate (pro.jen′er.āt): to beget.

progeria (pro.jēr′i.a): premature senility.

projicient (pro.jish′ent): serving to bring an organism into relation with the environment.

prolegeron (pro.lej′e.ron): the period of life in which a woman can bear children.

prolegomena (prō′li.gom′i.na): preliminary remarks.

prolepsis (pro.lep′sis): anticipation.

proletaneous (prō′li.tā′ni.us): having many children.

prolecide (prō′li.sīd′): the killing of offspring.

promic (prom′ik): in the theory of numbers, designating a number of the *form* $x + x^n$ where x and n are positive integers.

promulge (pro.mulj′): to promulgate, publish, make known.

pronaos (pro.nā′os): the outer part of an ancient Greek temple forming a portico or vestibule, immediately in front of the cella or *naos*.

pronovalence (prō′no.vā′lens): inability to have sexual intercourse except lying down.

propale (pro.pāl′): to divulge. 9.

propense (pro.pens′): leaning or inclining toward; favorably disposed; favorable, partial. 9.

prophoric (pro.fôr′ik): enunciative. 52.

propination (prō′pi.nā′shun): the act of drinking to someone's health.

proplastic (pro.plas′tik): the art of making molds for castings; pert. to this art.

propugnator (prō′pug.nā′ter): a defender; vindicator.

prorhinal (pro.rī′nal): in front of the nasal cavities.

prosaist (pro.zā′ist): a writer of prose. A prosaic person.

prosneusis (pros.nū′sis): in a nuclear eclipse, the angle of position of the part of the moon first obscured.

prosoma (pro.sō′ma): in zoology, the anterior division of the body, esp. of a mollusk.

prosonomasia (pros′o.no.mā′zhi.a): a nicknaming by punning on the real name.

prosophobia (prō′so.fō′bi.a): fear of progress.

prosopic (pro.sop′ik): pert. to the face.

prosopography (pros′o.pog′ra.fi): description of the face or personal appearance.

prosopolepsy (pros′o.po.lep′si): acceptance of persons, esp. prematurely, from their appearance. 1.

prosopolethy (pros′o.po.lē′thi): inability to remember faces.

protactic, protatic (pro.tak′tik, -tat′ik): telling or explaining beforehand, as the plot of a play; introductory.

protagon (prō′ta.gon): a powder mixture of lipides from the brain.

protophytology (prō.to.fī.tol′o.ji): the study of unicellular plants.

Protorosaurus (prō′to.ro.sôr′us): a genus of upper Permian reptiles resembling lizards and attaining a length of several yards.

protreptic (pro.trep′tik): an exhortation. 52. Persuasive; doctrinal.

protutor (pro′tū′tor): in civil law, one who acts as tutor or guardian without legal appointment.

provection (pro.vek′shun): advancing; advancement. 1. In philology, the carrying forward of a final sound or letter to a following word, as *a nickname* for *an ekename*.

provine (pro.vīn′): to layer.

proxenete (prok′si.nēt): a marriage broker; a procurer.

prud'homme (pro͞o′dum′): orig., a wise or prudent man. Now, specif., a member of a French industrial arbitration board, or Conseil des Prud'hommes.

pruriginous (proo.rij′i.nus): tending to, or caused by, prurigo, a chronic inflammatory skin disease.

prytaneum (prit.a.nē′um): in ancient Greece, a public building consecrated to Hestia, goddess of the hearth, in which the chief officials met and dined, and where official hospitality was extended.

psaphonic (sa.fon′ik): planning one's rise to fame.

psellismophobia (sel′is.mo.fō′bi.a): fear of stuttering.

HOGAMUS, HIGAMUS

When Churchill told us that democracy
Is an infernal bother—
Of governments, the worst that there could be
(Except for any other)—

He might have had *monogamy* in mind.
What man would stay on track
Except that, having left it, he might find
That there was no way back?

Show me a man who's not philogynous,
And I will show again
A mewling meacock any prudent puss
Would leave out in the rain.

An eye should wander; that's the way of laughter,
And speeds slow-beating hearts;
It's when the rest gets up and wanders after
That all the trouble starts.

Though womankind must surely feel more cheery
To know men prize them,
Use *one* for practice, and the rest for theory:
Idealize them.

Mazophilous, crurophilous are fine
To stir temptation;
But skip the human—stick to the divine;
Try sublimation.

(The author was moved to add the following postscriptum):

Misogynists wish Eve were still a rib;
Philogynists love even Women's Lib.

psephology (si.fol′o.ji): the study of elections.

psephomancy (sef′o.man′si): divination by pebbles.

pseudandry (sūd′an.dri): female use of a male pseudonym.

pseudautochiria (sū.dô.to.kī′ri.a): murder disguised as suicide.

pseudepisematic (sū′di.pis′i.mat′ik): an animal colored like its prey or its surroundings.

pseudoantidisestablishmentarianism (sū′do.an′ti.dis′e.stab′lish.men. târ′-i.a.nizm): pretended opposition to the withdrawal of state support from an established church.

pseudocyesis (sū′do.sī.ē′sis): false pregnancy.

pseudography (sū.dog′ra.fi): incorrect writing, printing, or spelling.

pseudogyny (sū.doj′i.ni): male use of a female name, as taking it at marriage.

pseudolalia (sū′do.lāl′ya): nonsense talk; the uttering of meaningless speech sounds.

pseudomancy (sū′do.man′si): intentionally fraudulent divination.

pseudomania (sū′do.mā′ni.a): the neurotic assumption of guilt by one who is innocent.

pseudomnesia (sū′dom.nē′zhi.a): memory for things that never happened.

pseudophonia (sū′do.fō′ni.a): a suicide disguised as murder.

pseudorhombicuboctahedron (sū′do. rom′bi.kū′bok.ta.hē′dron): an Archimedean solid with 26 faces.

Psidium (sid.i.um): a genus of tropical American trees of the myrtle family, incl. the common guava.

psilanthropy (si.lan′thro′pi): the doctrine of the merely human existence of Christ.

psilology (sī.lol′o.ji): empty talk.

psilosophy (sī.los′o.fi): superficial or fake philosophy.

psilotic (sī.lot′ik): pert. to the falling out of hair.

psithurism (sith′ū.rizm): a whispering sound, as of wind among leaves.

psittaceous (si.tā′shus): parrotlike.

psomophagy (so.mof′a.ji): the swallowing of food without thorough chewing.

Psoralea (so.rā′li.a): a genus of herbs and shrubs of the pea family common in the western United States, incl. the breadroot.

psychagogic (sī′ka.goj′ik): attractive, persuasive, inspiring. Having to do with psychagogy, a method of influencing behavior by suggesting desirable life goals.

psychalgia (sī.kal′ji.a): mental anguish.

psychasthenia (sī.kas.thē′ni.a): a neurosis involving indecision, doubts, and phobias.

psychiasis (sī.kī′a.sis): spiritual healing; religious healing for the soul.

psychiater (sī.kī′a.ter): a psychiatrist.

psychonosology (sī.ko.no.sol′o.ji): the study or science of psychogenic ailments.

psychrophile (sī′kro.fīl): an organism thriving at a relatively low temperature.

psychrotherapy (sī′kro.ther′a.pi): the use of cold water in medical treatment.

psychurgy (sī′kur.ji): mental energy.

ptarmic (tär′mik): provoking sneezing; sternutative.

pteric (ter′ik): pert. to or like a wing.

pteriodology (ter′i.o.dol′o.ji): the study of ferns; *filicology*.

pteroid (ter′oid): fernlike. Winglike.

pteronophobia (ter′o.no.fō′bi.a): fear of being tickled by feathers.

pterygium (ti′rij′i.um): a film on the eye.

ptochocracy (to.kok′ra.si): rule by the poor.

ptochogony (to.kog′o.ni): the production of poverty.

ptochology (to.kol′o.ji): the study of poverty.

pucelage (pū′sel.ij): virginity. 1.

pucelle (pū.sel′): maid; damsel; virgin. (1, exc. as an appellation for Joan of Arc.) Prostitute. 1.

pud (pud): Forefoot; paw; hand. Vulgar slang for penis.

puddee, puddy (pud′i): a measure of capacity in Madras.

pudder (pud′er): pother. 11.

puddingwife (pood′ing.wīf): a large, handsomely colored, wrasselike fish of Florida, Bermuda, and the West Indies. A woman skilled in making puddings, or sausages. 11.

puddock (pud′uk): dial. var. of *paddock*, toad.

pudge (puj): a puddle. A pudgy person or thing. 26.

pudiano (poo′dyä′no): the *puddingwife*.

pudu (poo′doo): a small reddish deer of the Chilean Andes having simple antlers resembling spikes, and standing only 12 or 13 inches high.

puericulture (pū′er.i.kul′cher): the science of bringing up children. Prenatal care.

pugger (pug′er): a worker who mixes and stirs wet material to make brick, enamel, etc.

puggi (pug′i): in India, a tracker, esp. one of a caste trained to track criminals.

puggle (pug′l): to poke a rod through or into; to clear out or stir up by poking.

puist (pwist): in comfortable circumstances. 43.

pulicious (pū.lish′us): pert. to or abounding with fleas.

pulsion (pul′shun): a pulsing. 1. The act of driving forward; propulsion—opposed to *suction* or *traction*.

pultaceous (pul.tā′shus): of porridge-like consistency; pulpy.

pulvil (pul′vil): cosmetic or perfumed powder. 9.

pulvinar (pul.vī′ner): cushion-like. A cushioned seat at a public spectacle.

puna (poo′na): a bleak, desolate region. In South America, the higher Andes; also, mountain sickness. In Peru, a cold mountain wind.

punaluan (poo′na.loo′an): pert. to a marriage of several brothers to several sisters.

punction (pungk′shun): a pricking; a puncture. 1.

pundonor (pun′do.nôr): a point of honor.

pungle (pung′gl): to pay up, pony up, contribute—usu. with *up*.

puniceous (pū.nish′us): bright-red or purplish-red.

punnet (pun′et): a shallow basket for displaying fruit or flowers, esp. strawberries.

punquetto (pun.ket′ō): a young punk. 1.

punta (pun′ta): in fencing, a point; a pass.

puparial (pū.pā′ri.al): pert. to the outer shell of a pupa.

pupilarity (pū′pi.lar′i.ti): the years before puberty.

purana (poo.rä′na): in Hinduism, astronomical knowledge—third of the four shastras, or categories, of sacred knowledge. The other three are the cosmogonic, theological, and physical.

purdy (pur′di): disagreeably self-important; surly. 11.

purl (purl): to twist, twine. 9. To spin, revolve. 44A.

purlicue (pur′li.kū): a peroration; to perorate. 44A. The space between the thumb and forefinger extended. A curlicue at the end of a word.

purpurate (pur′pū.rāt): purple-colored; royal. To empurple. A salt of purpuric acid.

purpureal, purpureous (per.pū′ri.al, -us): purple.

purpuric (per.pū′rik): pert. to a nitrogenous acid related to uric acid and obtained as an orange-red powder.

purseproud (purs′proud): haughtily proud of one's wealth.

puteal (pū′ti.al): in ancient Rome, a well curb. 1.

putid (pū′tid): rotten; fetid; worthless.

putredinous (pū.tred′i.nus): proceeding from putrefaction; stinking; rotten.

putti (pōo′ti): cupids in sculpture and painting.

puture (pū′cher): food for men or for animals; hence, in old English law, the customary right of keepers of forests, and some others, to take food from the land of certain tenants.

putz (puts): among the Pennsylvania Dutch, a crèche.

puxy (puk′si): a quagmire; swampy ground. Hence, a difficult situation; a quandary. Swampy; miry. 13. Ill-tempered; snappish; puckish. 32.

pycnotic (pik.not′ik): pert. to pycnosis, a degenerative condition of a cell nucleus.

pygal (pī′gal): pert. to the region of the rump.

pygia (pij′i.a): a pain in the rear; *proctalgia*.

pyknic (pik′nik): stout; fat-bellied; round; squat. A pyknic person.

pyroballogy (pī′ro.bal′o.ji): the art of throwing fire; the science of ballistics. 1.

Pyrola (pir′o.la): a genus of short-stemmed herbs, called *wintergreen* in England and *false wintergreen* or *shinleaf* in the United States.

pyromantic (pī′ro.man′tik): pert. to divination by means of fire or flames.

pyrophanous (pī.rof′a.nus): becoming translucent or transparent when heated.

pyrophobia (pī′ro.fō′bi.a): fear of fire.

pyrophone (pī′ro.fōn): a musical instrument in which the tones are produced by flames of gas.

pyrophonous (pī.rof′o.nus): pert. to the pyrophone.

pyrotic (pī.rot′ik): pert. to heartburn.

Pyrrhonic (pi.ron′ik): pert. to the doctrines of Pyrrho, a skeptic philosopher of ancient Greece.

pyrrhotism (pir.o.tizm): the characteristic of having red hair.

pysmatic (piz.mat′ik): interrogatory.

Pythiambic (pith′i.am′bik): Pythian verse (dactylic hexameter) followed by an iambic dimeter or trimeter.

pythogenic (pī′tho.jen′ik): producing, or originating in, decomposition and filth.

Q

qabbalah (kä′ba.la, ka.bä′la): cabala—secret or occult doctrine; a system based on Búber doctrine.

qadi (kä′di): cadi.

qoph (kōf): the 19th letter of the Hebrew alphabet.

qua (kwä): as, in the role of. Also, the night heron. 30.

qua, quaa (kwä): a quagmire.

quab (kwäb): one of several small fishes, incl. the eelpout and gudgeon. Something immature or unfinished. 1.

quackle (kwak′l): to quack.

quaddle (kwä′dl): to grumble; a grumbler. 13.

quadragene (kwä′dra.jēn): a person of forty, or in their forties.

quadragesimal (kwa′dra.jes′i.mal): consisting of 40. A 40-day fast. Pert. to Lent.

quadratrix (kwad.rā′triks): in geometry, a curve used in determining the area of other curves.

quadratum (kwad.rā′tum): in medieval music, a natural. A breve.

quadratus (kwad.rā′tus): any of several muscles, used for rotating the thigh outward, pulling the lower lip down or laterally, etc.

quadrifurcation (kwäd.ri.fer.kā′shun): a branching into four parts.

quadriga (kwad.rī′ga): a Roman chariot drawn by four horses abreast, together with the horses. The four horses alone; less often, the chariot alone.

quadrigamist (kwad.rig′a.mist): one who has married four times, or who has four spouses concurrently.

quadrigenarious (kwäd′ri.je.nãri.i.us): consisting of four hundred.

quadripennate (kwäd.ri.pen′āt): four-winged.

quadrumana (kwa′drōo′ma.na): a group of mammals comprising the monkeys, lemurs, baboons, and apes.

quaesitum (kwi.sī′tum): something sought or desired. In mathematics, the true value.

quaestuary, questuary (kwes′choo.âr′i): undertaken for money. One whose first consideration is profit.

quag (kwäg): a quagmire. To quake or quiver. To sink (someone or something) in a quag. 2.

quakebuttock (kwāk′but′ok): a coward. 2.

qualtagh (kwäl′täk): the first person one sees on waking or leaving home on a special day. 55.

quandong (kwän′dong): an Australian tree; also its edible fruit or nut.

quannet (kwan′et): a flat file with a handle at one side, used for making combs.

quant (kwant, kwänt): a pole for propelling a punt. To punt with such a pole.

quap (kwap): to heave; throb; palpitate. A throb, palpitation. 13.

quaquaversal (kwä′kwa.vur′sal): turning or dipping in every direction; specif., in geology, dipping from a center toward all points of the compass, as in a dome. A quaquaversal dome or ridge.

quar (kwär): to fill; choke; block. 2. To curdle. 4.

quardeel (kär′dāl): a cardel, or cask, used by Dutch sailors.

quarenden (kwôr′en.den): in England, a deep-red, early apple.

quarentene (kwor′en.tēn): a furlong; a rood. 6.

quarl (kwôrl): a large brick or tile, esp. one used to support melting pots for zinc. A jellyfish. 52. To curdle. 1.

quarternight (kwôr′ter.nīt): halfway between sundown and midnight.

quarterpace (kwôr′ter.pās): a staircase platform where the stair turns at a right angle.

quartodeciman (kwôr′to.des′i.man): one of a sect of early Christians who celebrated the Pascual on the date of the Jewish Passover.

quassation (kwa.sā′shun): a shaking; a beating. 52.

quatercentenary (kwä′ter.sen.ten′a.ri, kwā′-): a 400th anniversary. 52.

quatercousin (kwä′ter.kuz′in, kwā′-): *catercousin*. 1.

quaternary, quaternate (kwa.tur′nā.ri, kwä′ter.nāt): arranged in sets of four, as *quaternate* leaves.

quatorzain (kat′er.zān): a poem of 14 lines, such as the sonnet. (The verse below is *not* a quatorzain.)

WEDE IS MY NICKNAME, AND YOU CAN GUESS WHO QUEDE IS

Now quap and quop, my heart! The east
　Again to quarternight gyres 'round.
Stilled is the ever-moaning queest;
　The quiller sleeps without a sound.
The quackle of the duck has ceased;
　The quis dreams, nesting on the ground.

So queme!—but ah, what quags beneath?
　What quelches through the queachy glede
And quiffs and quetches—seeks to quethe?
　Must my next qualtagh be dread Quede?
(The Qs, you see, bring quaving teeth
　To quaggly old quakebuttocks Wede.)

---

quatre (katr, kä′ter): a card, die, or domino having four spots, or pips.

quatuorvirate (kwä′tōo.ôr′vi.rāt): an association of four men. 52.

quawk (kwôk): caw, screech. 11. A night heron. 32.

queach (kwēch): thicket. 13B.

queachy (kwē′chi): boggy, marshy. 13B. Forming a dense growth; bushy. 4.

quede (kwēd): evil; also, an evil person. Specif., (cap), the Devil. 1.

queechy (kwē′chi): sickly, puny. 13.

queest (kwēst): a ringdove, wood pigeon.

queesting (kwēs′ting): bundling—said of sweethearts who occupy the same bed without undressing.

queet (kwēt): ankle. 44.

queeve (kwēv): a twist or turn, as in a road. To twist or turn. 13A.

queezmadam (kwēz′ma′dam): an early variety of pear. 11.

quelch (kwelch): to make a sucking or gulping sound; to squelch. 11A.

quelquechose (kel′ke.shōz): a mere trifle; a nothing.

quemado (ki.mä′dō): a district that has been burned. 34B.

queme (kwēm): pleasant, agreeable. 2. To suit, satisfy. 1.

quercitannic (kwur′si.tan.ik): relating to the tannin of oak bark.

querimonious (kwer′i.mō′ni.us): querulous.

querl (kwurl): twirl; coil. 28.

quern (kwurn): a small handmill for grinding spice.

quetch (kwech): to break silence; utter a sound. 11A.

quethe (kwēth): to speak, tell. (1, except in past tense *quoth*). Clamor, cry; a will, testament.

quiapo (ki.ä′po): a water lettuce of the Philippines.

quia-quia (kē′a.kē′a): the cigarfish.

quica (kē′ka): a small South American opossum.

quiff (kwif): a puff; whiff. For some in Britain, a prominent forelock. A girl. 21.

quiller (kwil′er): a fledgling. 1. A machine for transferring yarn from spools to quills; the operator of such a machine.

quincentenary (kwin′sen.ten′a.ri): a 500th anniversary.

quincentennial (kwin′sen.ten′i.al): pert. to 500 years. A quincentenary.

quinic (kwin′ik): pert. to or obtained from cinchona bark.

quinoa (ki.nō′a): a pigweed of the high Andes or its seeds, ground for food and widely used as a cereal in Peru.

quinology (kwi.nol′o.ji): the science of the cultivation of the cinchona tree, and the chemistry and medical use of its bark.

quinquarticular (kwin′kwär.tik′u.lär): relating to five articles or points, particl. (in religion) those in dispute between Arminians and Calvinists.

quinquertium (kwin.kwur′ti.um): an athletic meet in which each contestant participates in five different events; a pentathlon. 1.

quinse (kwins): to carve. 1.

quintessentialize (kwin′ti.sen′sha.liz): to extract the quintessence of.

quintroon (kwin.trōōn): a person 1/16 black—the offspring of an octaroon and a white.

quirl (kwurl): a curl. To bend; coil; twist.

quis (kwis): the European woodcock.

quisquillious (kwis.kwil′i.us): trashy; rubbishy. 52.

quisquose (kwis′kwōs, -kōs): perplexing. 44.

quizzacious (kwi.zā′shus): bantering; given to quizzing. 52.

quo (kwō): something received in an exchange.

quoddity (kwod′i.ti): quiddity—used derisively. 52.

quodlibetic (kwod.li.bet′ik): consisting of or like quodlibets—purely academic. Given to quodlibets, or academic discussion.

quop (kwop): to throb. 2.

quotennial (kwo.ten′i.al): annual. 52.

quoz (kwoz): something queer or absurd. 1.

R

rab (rab): master, teacher—a Jewish title of respect.

rabiator (rab′i.ä.tor): a violent man. 44 (52).

rabic (rab′ik): pert. to rabies.

raca (rä′ka): a term of reproach used by the Jews of the time of Christ, meaning ''fool.''

rach (rach): a hunting dog. 10.

rackett (rak′et): an old wind instrument of the bassoon kind, having a double-reed mouthpiece and a wooden tube, bent upon itself, with ventages but no keys.

radicant (rad′i.kant): rooting from the stem, as common ivy.

radicate (rad′i.kāt): to plant firmly; to establish solidly. 2.

radiesthesia (rā′di.es.thē′zi.a): the claimed ability to detect underground water by means of a divining rod; dowsing.

radiolucent (rā′di.o.lōō′sent): permeable to radiation.

radiopraxis (rā′di.o.prak′sis): the use of ultraviolet rays or x-rays in medicine.

rafale (ra.fal′): a rapid burst of artillery fire, consisting of several rounds.

raff (raf): riffraff. Rubbish. 11.

rafty (raf′ti): rancid; stale or musty. 4.

ragarock (rag′a.rok): a kind of rock 'n' roll using an Indian melodic form.

raggee (rä′gi): an East Indian cereal grass whose ground seeds make a somewhat bitter flour.

raggle (rag′l): a groove cut in masonry, esp. one to receive the upper edge of a flashing above a roof. To cut such a groove. A rag; shred. 52.

rais (rīs): a Muslim ship's captain. A Muslim chief. (cap, n. pl.) A Mongoloid people of Nepal.

raisonné (rā′zo.nā): logical; arranged systematically.

raith (rāth): a quarter of a year. 44.

ramage (ram′ij): the boughs or branches of a tree. 9. Wildness, courage. Wild, shy. 1.

A QRIOUS COLLECTION, BUT KIND OF QT

A Q in most words should be followed by U,
But once in awhile it is not.
To find Q without U, simply follow my Q—
I'll show you a few of the lot.

There's *Qabbala*—mystical meanings attached
To Scripture by certain old Jews;
And *Qadarites*—sheiks whom the Moslems dispatched
For having claimed freedom to choose.

There's *Qadi*—a judge who apportions a loaf
By guessing Mahomet's intention.
There's one little letter (ק) that answers to *Qoph*—
Another old Hebrew invention.

There's *Q-boat*—a warship disguised as a botch;
And *Qantas*, an airline to watch.
New York has a mayor, I think, name of *Qoch*,
Though maybe the spelling is *Kwôch*.

*ק. The nineteenth letter of the Hebrew alphabet, sounding like our *k* or *qu*.

---

ramarama (rä′ma.rä′ma): a New Zealand myrtle sometimes cultivated for its curiously wrinkled leaves and pale pink flowers.

rambooze (ram.bōōz′): wine and sugar mixed (in winter) with ale and eggs, or (in summer) with milk and rose water. 52.

ramentum (ra.men′tum): something scraped off; a shaving. One of the thin, brownish, chaffy scales borne upon the leaves or young shoots of many ferns.

ramfeezled (ram.fē′zld): worn out; exhausted. 44.

ramiferous (ra.mif′e.rus): bearing branches.

rammish (ram′ish): lustful; lewd. Rank in smell or taste. 11. Violent; untamed. 43. To rush about as if frenzied. 43.

rampacious, rampagious (ram.pā′shus, -pā′jus): rampageous; given to displays of recklessness; wild, unruly.

ramus (rā′mus): (pl. *rami*). A branch. In biology, one of several bones, incl. the posterior part of the lower jaw and a branch of the pubis. Also, a branch of a nerve, a barb of a feather, etc.

rana (rä′na): prince—a title of some of the native rulers of India. (cap) A large genus of tailless leaping amphibians, incl. the frogs.

ranaria (pl. of *ranarium*) (ra.när′i.a): places for keeping or rearing frogs.

rance (rans): a dull red Belgian marble with blue-and-white markings. A prop or support; to prop. 44A.

rancer (ran′ser): a tool that enlarges or shapes holes or smooths bores; a worker who uses such a tool; a reamer.

rangatira (rang.a.te′ra): a Maori chief; a leading citizen. 56.

ranic, ranine (rā′nik, -nīn): pert. to frogs.

ranivorous (ra.niv′o.rus): frog-eating.

rantipole (ran′ti.pōl): a reckless, sometimes quarrelsome person. Wild; unruly. To behave in a wild fashion. 52.

rantism (ran′tizm): ranting. 1.

ranula (ran′ū.la): a cyst formed under the tongue by the obstruction of a gland duct.

rastik, rastick (ras′tik): any of various hair dyes.

ratafee, ratafia (rat′a.fi, -fē′a): a fruit-flavored liqueur, gen. with a taste of bitter almond.

ratal (rā′tal): the amount at which a person is rated with reference to tax assessment.

ratamacue (rat′a.ma.kū): in drumming, a figure more difficult than the paradiddle.

rataplan (rat′a.plan): the sound of rhythmic beating, as a drum or a galloping horse. To make such a sound.

ratch (rach): a notched bar with which a pawl or click works to prevent reversal of motion. A blaze on an animal's face. In sailing, to reach. 1.

ratchel (rach′el): stone in small fragments; gravel; gravelly subsoil. 11A.

ratihabition (rat′i.ha.bish′un): ratification, sanction.

ratten (rat′en): to steal tools from an employer as a way of enforcing trade union demands. 40A.

rawn (rôn): roe; spawn. Also, a female fish, esp. a herring or salmon.

raya (rā′a): the East Indian broadbill, a sluggish duck with a rather wide flat bill. Also, a subject Christian peasant under the Ottoman Empire.

razee (ra.zē′): a wooden ship reduced in class by having her upper deck cut away, as a seventy-four cut down to a frigate. A razeed chest, book, or the like. To razee.

razoo (ra.zōō′): a razzing; a racket. 22.

rea (rē′a): a female defendant in a court trial (fem. of *reus*).

reable (ri.ā′bl): to rehabilitate. 40A.

reasty, reasy (rēs′ti, rē′zi): rancid. 2.

reaver, riever (rē′ver): one that takes away by stealth or force.

rebia (rē′bi.a): a gold coin of the Ottoman Empire in the 19th century. A Turkish silver coin.

reboantic (reb′o.an′tik): reverberating.

rebullition (reb.ul.lish′un): a boiling up again. 1.

recadency (ri.kā′den.si): a relapse. 52.

RUMBELOW, RUMBELOW

Oh, did you know the rumbelow,
Rumbelow, rumbelow—
Oh, did you know the rumbelow
Who lived in Drury Lane?

She'd chug-a-lug her ratafee,
Ratafee, ratafee,
She'd chug-a-lug her ratafee,
And chug-a-lug again.

Rambooz to her was mother's milk,
Mother's milk, mother's milk,
Rambooz to her was mother's milk,
And never weaned was she;

Rumgumption was her middle name,
Middle name, middle name,
Rumgumption was her middle name,
A shilling was her fee.

Once in there came a rantipole,
Rantipole, rantipole,
Once in there came a rantipole,
And ordered her to bed;

"I give to you the old razoo,
The old razoo, the old razoo;
I give to you the old razoo,
For sir, we are not wed."

A round ribroasting gave her he,
Gave her he, gave her he,
A round ribroasting gave her he,
And of it she did die;

Ramfeezled by her weary life,
Weary life, weary life,
Ramfeezled by her weary life,
She rose up to the sky.

And oh, how happy we should be,
We should be, we should be,
And oh, how happy we should be
Were she but redivivus;

We'll no more know a rumbelow,
Rumbelow, rumbelow,
We'll no more know a rumbelow
So excellent to swive us.

---

recalesce (rē′ka.les): to release heat, as a metal when cooling.

recaptor (ri.kap′tor): one who recaptures; one who takes a prize that had been previously taken.

recension (ri.sen′shun): a scholarly editorial revision.

receptary (ri.sep′ta.ri): accepted as fact but unproved; a postulate. A collection of recipes.

recheat (ri.chēt′): a blast on the horn to call the hunting hounds. 9.

reclivate (rek′li.vāt): s-shaped; sigmoid.

recoct (ri.kokt): to recook; to redo.

rectalgia (rek′tal′ji.a): proctalgia.

rectigrade (rek′ti.grād): moving in a straight line.

rection (rek′shun): in grammar, the influence of a word that requires another word to be placed in a certain case or mood.

rectopathic (rek′to.path′ik): easily hurt emotionally.

recubation (rek′u.bā′shun): recumbency. 1.

reculade (rek′ū.läd): a retreat.

recussion (ri.kush′un): repercussive action.

redan (ri.dan′): a fortification having two faces that form a salient angle.

redargution (red′är.gū′shun): orig., reproof; later, refutation. 52.

reddition (re.dish′un): restoration; restitution; surrender. Formal restitution by judicial confession.

redditive (red′i.tiv): in grammar, corresponding; correlative.

redhibition (red′hi.bish′un): the return of defective merchandise to the seller.

redintegrate (re.din′ti.grāt): to renew. To be restored to a previous condition.

redition (ri.dish′un): returning, return. 1.

redivivus (red′i.vī′vus): revived; living again.

redubber (ri.dub′er): in history, one who buys, alters, and resells stolen cloth.

reduct (ri.dukt′): to reduce. 1. To deduct. 11.

redux (rē′duks): indicating return to a healthy state.

reechy (rē′chi): rancid. 2.

reeden (rē′den): of or like a reed. 52. Reedy. 1.

reem (rēm): the wild ox mentioned in the Old Testament. To cry, shout. 1.

reese, reeze (rēs, rēz): to become rancid. 2. To scorch. 1.

refocillation (ri.fos′i.lā′shun): revival; refreshment. 52.

refrangible (ri.fran′ji.bl): capable of being refracted, as rays of light.

refrangent (ri.fran′jent): refrangible.

regalian (ri.gāl′yan): pert. to regalia; regal.

reif (rēf): robbery; plunder. 44A.

reiver (rē′ver): a raider. 44.

rejessed (ri.jest′): reattached jesses to (a hawk).

rejunction (ri.jungk′shun): a reuniting. 52.

relata (ri.lā′ta): a group of related things.

religate (rel′i.gāt): to tie together. 52.

remanet (rem′a.net): in law, the postponement of a case. In the British Parliament, a bill carried over to another session.

remeant (rē′mi.ent): returning. 52.

remiped (rem′i.ped): having feet or legs used as oars, as certain crustaceans and insects. A remiped animal.

remontado (ri.mon.tä′dō): a Filipino who has renounced civilization and "fled to the mountains."

renable (ren′a.bl): fluent; eloquent; glib. 2.

renascible (ri.nas′i.bl): capable of rebirth. 52.

renidification (ri.nid′i.fi.kā′shun): the building of another nest.

renifleur (ren′i.floor): one who derives sexual pleasure from body odors.

rennet (ren′et): an old form of apple. 41.

reparationist (rep′a.rā′shun.ist): one who believed in reparation to ex-slaves.

repartimiento (rā.par′ti.mi.en′tō): in the Spanish colonies of America, a grant, esp. of Indian forced labor.

repertorium (rep.er.tôr′i.um): an index, catalogue, or collection. A storehouse, repository.

repristinate (ri.pris′ti.nāt): to revive; to restore.

reptatorial (rep′ta.tôr′i.al): creeping, as a reptile.

repullulate (ri.pool′yoo.lāt): to bud or sprout again; to recur, as a disease. 52.

resiccant (res′i.kant): drying up; causing to dry up. 1.

resiccate (res.′i.kāt): to make dry again. 1.

resile (ri.zīl′): to draw back, recoil; retract.

resipiscent (res′i.pis′ent): changing the mind and heart; reforming; returning to a sane, sound, or correct view.

restis (res′tis): a pair of nerve fibers on the dorsal surface of the medulla oblongata.

restringent (ri.strin′jent): binding; astringent; styptic. 52. A restrictive word. 1. In medicine, an astringent or styptic.

retorsion (ri.tôr′shun): var. of *extortion*.

retrad (rē′trad): backward or posteriorly.

retrochoir (ret′ro.kwīr): the space in a church behind the high altar or choir enclosure.

retrocollic (ret′ro.kol′ik): pert. to the back of the neck.

retrocopulation (ret′ro.kop′u.lā′shun): copulation from the rear.

retromancy (ret′ro.man′si): divination by looking back over the shoulder.

retromingent (ret′ro.min′jent): urinating to the rear; an animal that does so.

retter (ret′er): one who soaks or exposes to moisture (as flax, hemp, timber). 52.

retunded (ri.tun′ded): beaten or driven back; rendered impotent, weak, or useless. 1.

reus (rē′us): a male defendant in a court trial.

revalescent (rev′a.les′ent): convalescing.

revalorize (ri.val′o.rīz): to restore the value of a monetary unit.

reve (rēv): to muse in revery. 52.

revehent (ri.vē′hent, rev′i.hent): carrying back.

revellent (ri.vel′ent): causing revulsion; revulsive.

reverso (ri.vur′sō): the reverse, or left-hand page of a book or folded sheet of paper; a verso. The reverse, as that which appears when something is seen from opposite to the usual direction.

rhabdophobia (rab′do.fō′bi.a): fear of being punished or severely criticized.

rhapsodomancy (rap.so.do.man′si): divination by poetry.

rhema (rē′ma): a verb; word; term.

rheme (rēm): any semantic unit or element of a speech.

rheocrat (rē′o.krat): a kind of speed controller for an electric motor.

rheophile (rē′o.fīl): living in rivers or streams.

rheotan (rē′o.tan): an alloy of copper, zinc, nickel, and iron.

Rhiannon (ri.an′on): the Great Queen or Mother Goddess of Welsh mythology, whose three birds could sing the dead to life or the living to death.

rhigosis (ri.gō′sis): a sensation of cold.

rhinocerical (rī′no.ser′i.kal): gorged with money, rich. 9.

rhinocerotic (rī′no.si.rot′ik): pert. to or resembling a rhinoceros.

rhinophonia (rī′no.fō′ni.a): marked nasal resonance in speech.

rhinoplasty (rī′no.plas′ti): a nose job; nasoplasty.

rhipidate (rip′i.dāt): fan-shaped.

Rhodian (rō′di.an): a native or inhabitant of Rhodes. Pert. to Rhodes, or to the Knights of Rhodes (Hospitallers).

rhombicosidodecahedron (rom′bi.kos′i.do.dek′a.hē′dron): an Archimedean solid with 62 faces.

rhonchisonant (rong′ki.sō′nant): snorting; snoring.

rhopalism (rō′pa.lizm): a rhopalic.

rhyophobia (rī′o.fō′bi.a): fear of filth.

rhyparography (rī.pa.rog′ra.fi): the painting or literary depiction of mean or sordid subjects.

rhysimeter (rī.sim′e.ter): an instrument for measuring the velocity of a fluid, current, a ship's speed, etc.

rhytiphobia (rī′ti.fō′bi.a): fear of getting wrinkles.

rhytiscopia (rī′ti.skō′pi.a): neurotic preoccupation with facial wrinkles.

riancy (rī′an.si): state of one laughing, smiling; gaiety; brightness.

ribble (rib′l): to remove seed from (flax) by combing before the flax is retted.

ribroasting (rib′rōs′ting): a sound beating; a thrashing.

ricercare (rē′cher.kä′rä): a fugue-like composition; an elaborate fugue.

rident (rī′dent): laughing or broadly smiling; riant. 52.

ridotto (ri.dot′ō): a public entertainment consisting of music and dancing, often in masquerade, introduced from Italy and very popular in England in the 18th century. An arrangement or abridgement of a musical composition from the full score.

riem (rēm): in South Africa, a thong; a strap. A pliable strip of rawhide, used for twisting into ropes, etc.

rifacimento (ri.fach′i.men′tō): a remaking or recasting; an adaptation, esp. of a literary or musical composition.

rigation (ri.gā′shun): the act of wetting.

rigescent (ri.jes′ent): growing stiff or numb.

riggot (rig′ot): a half-castrated male animal, esp. a horse. 11. A gutter. 13.

rignum (rig′num): the horsemint *Monarda punctata*.

rincon (ring.kŏn′): a small circular valley, usu. one containing a house. 35A.

rindle (rin′dl): a rivulet; brook, runnel. 11.

ripa (rī′pa): a bank of a river, beyond which the waters do not normally flow. A ptarmigan. 52.

ripal (rī′pal): riparian. 52.

ripieno (rip′yä′no): in music, a supplementary instrument or performer.

riroriro (rē′ro.rē′rō): the gray warbler of New Zealand.

rishi (rish′i): a Hindu mystic or mystical poet.

risoluto (rē′so.loo′tō): resolutely and with marked accent—a direction in music.

risorial (ri.sō′ri.al): pert. to or producing laughter.

risp (risp): the stem of such plants as peas and strawberries. A coarse kind of grass. 43. A sound of risping; a carpenter's file; a tirling pin; to rasp; turl; a metal bar on a house door, rubbed with an attached ring to draw attention. 44.

risper (ris′per): in South Africa, a caterpillar.

rissel (ris′el): the common red currant.

rissle (ris′l): a stick, staff, or pole. 17A.

rist (rist): to engrave, scratch, or wound; insurrection; also, resurrection; an ascent (of ground) or increase (of price). 1.

ritornel, ritornelle (rit′ôr.nel): a short instrumental passage in a vocal composition, often a refrain. Also, an instrumental interlude between the parts of an opera or a tutti passage in a concerto.

rix (riks): dial. var. of *rush;* a reed.

rixation (rik.sā′shun): a quarrel. 52.

rixatrix (riks.ā′triks): a termagant, scold. 1.

roborean (ro.bō′ri.an): oaken; stout; strong. 1.

robur (rō′ber): the British oak.

rocambole (rok′am.bōl): a European leek or wild garlic, cultivated as a flavoring ingredient.

rocca (rok′a): a fortress, hold, donjon, keep.

rochet (roch′et): a medieval outer garment, usu. short-skirted, worn by men or women. A loose cloak; a frock. 49. A close-fitting ecclesiastical vestment, worn by bishops in certain ceremonies; hence, a bishop. 1. The red gurnard, a fish with fanlike pectoral fins.

rock-cistus (rok.sis′tus): the rockrose.

rockoon (ro.kōōn′): a small rocket fired from a balloon.

rogan (rō′gan): a kind of wooden bowl or receptacle, as for holding maple sap. 12.

roid (roid): rough; unmanageable. 11. Riotous; frolicsome. 44.

rokelay (rok′e.lā): a knee-length coat, buttoned in front, worn after 1700. 44A.

roky (rō′ki): foggy, misty. 13B.

roleo (rō′li.ō): a contest at birling logs.

rolley (rol′i): a lorry. 41. Formerly, any of various vehicles drawn by horses or by hand. 53A.

Rom (rom): a male gypsy.

rondache (ron.dash′): a round shield carried by medieval foot soldiers.

rondle (ron′dl): a rung of a ladder. 1. In metallurgy, the crust on molten metal in the crucible.

rone (rōn): a clump of briars or bushes. 2. A rainspout. A small patch of ice. 44.

ronyon (ron′yun): a mangy or scabby creature. 1.

roodle (rōō′dl): in poker, one of a round of hands played after a player has won a round with an esp. high hand. The pot limit is usu. doubled.

rootle (rōō′tl): to root, as a pig. 52.

roral, roric, rorulent (rō′ral, -ik, -ū.lent): dewy.

THE MISTAKEN GRATITUDE OF THE GODDESS RHIANNON′S BIRDS (WHO CAN SING THE DEAD TO LIFE, OR THE LIVING TO DEATH)

Three birds flew down, and perched among the ramages
Extending in the greenwood from a robur.
They sat there calculating legal damages.
(I listened from below, and I was sober.)

It seems the Mother Goddess, great Rhiannon,
Had sent them on a mission to a Scot.
But he had died while eating cold colcannon;
So, sensibly, they finished off the lot.

They found that spud-and-cabbage mix so tasty
That though they'd come to sing the man to death
Rhiannon's order now seemed over-hasty;
And so instead they sang him back to breath.

For dereliction in their duty to her,
The goddess fired them; and they plan to sue her.

---

rosal (rō′zal): rosy. 1. Belonging to the Rosales, an order of 25 plant families incl. those of the plum, pea, saxifrage, and stonecrop.

rosella (ro.zel′a): a vividly colored Australian parakeet. A European who works bared to the waist (from the scarlet color of his skin). 53. A sheep that has shed a portion of its wool. 20.

rosen (rō′zen): consisting of, or resembling, roses; rosy. 1.

roser (rō′zer): a rosebush. 1.

rosinante (rō′zi.nan′ti): a broken-down horse, nag—called after Don Quixote's bony horse.

rosmarine (ros.ma.rēn′): sea dew. Also, a sea animal fabled to climb rocks by its teeth to feed on the dew. A walrus. 1.

rosorial (ro.zō′ri.al): pert. to the rodents; gnawing.

ross (ros): rubbish; waste. 1. The rough exterior of bark. To strip the bark.

rosser (ros′er): a logger who smooths the wood on one side of logs so they can be dragged more easily, or who peels bark from pulpwood by hand to avoid waste. An attachment for a circular saw to remove scaly and gritty bark.

rostel (ros′tel), **rostellum** (ros.tel′um): a small beak. In orchids, a small projection beneath the retinacula. The sucking beak of lice; more rarely, the beak of true bugs. In certain parasitic worms, a forward extension of the head bearing hooks.

rostral (ros′tral): pert. to a rostrum.

rotch (roch): the dovekie, a small, short-billed auk of the Arctic.

rotchet (roch′et): a vestment.

rouky (rōō′ki): foggy, misty. 44A.

rounce (rouns): the apparatus that moves the bed of a hand printing press under the platen; the handle of this apparatus. To flounce about, fuss. A card game in which jacks are trumps.

rowlet (rou′let): a little roller. 52.

rowlyrag (rou′li.rag): a dark gray stone.

rowy (rō′i): of uneven texture or appearance; streaked.

rox (roks): to decay, rot. 13.

roxy (rok′si): decayed; softened. 13.

ruana (rōō.ä′na): a viol instrument used in India.

rubai (rōō.bä′i): a Persian quatrain.

rubedinous (rōō.bed′i.nus): reddish.

rubific (rōō.bif′ik): causing redness, as of the skin; rubefacient.

rubiginous (rōō.bij′i.nus): rust-colored; rusty.

rubineous (rōō.bin′i.us): ruby-red, rubious.

ructation (ruk.tā′shun): the act of belching. 52.

rudenture (rōō.den′cher): in architecture, a cabling.

rudge (ruj): dial. var. of *ridge*.

ruelle (rōō.el′): the space between the bed and the wall. 1. In 17th- and 18th-century France, a morning reception held in the bedroom; hence, a select gathering.

rugulose (rōō′gū.lōs): finely wrinkled.

rukh (rōōk): in Kipling, a forest, jungle.

rumbelow (rum′bi.lō): a refrain in old songs, esp. sea songs. 52. A prostitute. 1.

rumgumption (rum′gump′shun): keenness; shrewdness. 43.

rumtifusel (rum.ti.fū′sel): a supposed beast, flat as a laprobe, which attracts human prey by its resemblance to a rich fur coat, and in a trice sucks out their flesh.

runcation (rung.kā′shun): the removal of weeds. 1.

runch (runch): charlock; jointed charlock or wild radish. 43.

rundle (run′dl): a step of a ladder; a rung. Something that rotates about an axis, as a wheel. One of the pins of a lantern pinion. The drum of a windlass or capstan.

runnet (run′et): the contents of the stomach of an unweaned calf or other animal, used for curdling milk. Also, obs. form of *rennet*.

runnion (run′yun): a scurvy wench.

rupestrian (rōō.pes′tri.an): composed of rock; inscribed on rocks.

ruptuary (rup′chōō.âr′i): a plebean; a commoner. 52.

rurigenous (rōō.rij′i.nus): born in the country. 52.

ruskin (rus′kin): a receptacle, as for butter, made of bark; also, butter kept in a ruskin. 13.

rustre (rus′ter): in medieval armor, a metal scale of oval or lozenge shape.

rutaceous (rōō.tā′shus): pert. to Rutaceae, a family of herbs, shrubs, and trees, often glandular and strong-scented.

rutcher (ruch′er): something that moves with a crunching or shuffling noise. 52.

rutin (rōō′tin): a yellow crystalline glycoside found in various leaves and flower buds. It is used in medicine to strengthen capillary blood vessels.

ruttle (rut′l): a rattle; a gurgle, as the breath of one dying.

S

sabbatia (sa.bā′shi.a): the sabbat—in medieval demonology a midnight assembly in which demons, sorcerers, and witches celebrated their orgies. (cap) A genus of smooth, slender North American herbs incl. the marsh or sea pinks.

sabbulonarium (sab′ū.lo.nâr′i.um): a gravel pit. The digging of gravel, or a wage paid for such digging.

sabeca (sa.bek′a): an ancient instrument, prob. a kind of harp, mentioned in the Bible.

sabretache (sā′ber.tash, sab′er-): a leather case or pocket sometimes worn, suspended on the left from the saber belt, by cavalry.

saburration (sab′e.rā′shun): application of sand to the body as therapy; arenation.

saccade (sa.kād′): a quick, violent check of a horse by a single twitch of the reins. A sudden strong pressure of a violin bow, causing strings to sound simultaneously.

saccadic (sa.kad′ik): jerky, twisting.

sacellum (sa.sel′um): in ancient Rome, an unroofed space consecrated to a divinity. A small monumental chapel in a church.

Sacheverell (sa.shev′er.el): a kind of blower once used on stoves.

sacket (sak′et): a small sack or wallet; also, a small, stupid, or rascally person. 44.

sacrificant (sak.rif′i.kant): one who offers up a sacrifice.

Sacripant (sak′ri.pant): a boastful coward, from the name of a king of Circassia (in Boiardo's *Orlando Innamorato*) whose charger was stolen from between his legs without his knowing it. 52.

sadda (sad′a): a book of Zoroastrian writings.

Sadducaic (sad′ū.kā′ik): pert. to the Sadducees, a priestly sect of the Jews that flourished from the 2nd century B.C. to the latter part of the 1st century A.D.

sadr (säd′r): the lotus tree. (cap) A star in the constellation Cygni.

saeculum, seculum (sek′ū.lum): a long time. A generation.

saeter (sē′ter): a meadow or a mountain pasture. 61.

saeterious (si.tēr′i.us): pert. to a *saeter*. 61.

saffian (saf′i.an): a kind of leather made of goatskins or sheepskins tanned with sumac and dyed with bright colors.

sagaciate (sa.gā′shi.āt): to get along; thrive. 34A.

sagene (sa.jēn): a network. 52. A fishing net.

saginate (saj′i.nāt): to pamper; fatten.

sahu (sä′hōō): in Egyptian religion, the spirit body, in contrast to the *khet*.

sai (sä′i): the capuchin monkey.

said (sa.ēd): a kind of ketch common in the Levant.

sain (sān): to cross (oneself); to consecrate. To save from evil by invocation or blessing. 10. Poetically, to heal.

saj (säj): an East Indian tree. Its wood, widely used for construction.

sakeen (sa.kēn′): an ibex of the Himalayas.

sakkara (sa.kä′ra): the color mouse gray.

salago (sa.lä′gō): any of several Philippine shrubs of the genus Wikstroemia; also, their bast fiber, used for making bank-note paper and other strong papers.

salatorial (sal′a.tôr′i.al): pert. to a ritual prayer of Muslims.

salimeter (sa.lim′e.ter): an instrument for measuring the amount of salt in a solution; a *salinometer*.

salinometer (sal′i.nom′e.ter): *salimeter*.

salnatron (sal.nä′tron): crude sodium carbonate.

salsuginous (sal.sū′ji.nus): growing naturally in soil impregnated with salts.

saltimbanco (sal′tim.bang′ko): a mountebank; a quack. 9.

saltimbocca (sal′tim.bok′a): scallops of veal rolled up with ham, cheese, etc.

salvific (sal.vif′ik): tending to save or to secure safety.

saman (sä′man): the rain tree. In India, furniture; stores; equipage; baggage.

sambo (sam′bō): an Indian or mulatto and black half-breed. (cap) A black, often used disparagingly.

sambouka (sam.bōō′ka): var. of *sambuk*.

sambuk (sam′book): a small Arabian dhow.

sambuke (sam′būk): an ancient shrill-toned harp. A bagpipe. A hurdygurdy.

sammy (sam′i): damp, clammy. 11A. A ninny; simpleton. 13. (cap) A U.S. soldier. 21.

Samsam (sam′sam): a Malayan-Siamese people on the west coast of the Malay peninsula.

san (san): a sibilant letter (ꟼ) of the primitive Greek alphabet. By shortening, sanatorium. A plant similar to hemp, also called sunn.

sanable (san′a.bl): capable of being healed or cured.

sanative (san′a.tiv): having the power to cure or heal; curative.

sanctanimity (sangk′ta.nim′i.ti): holiness of mind. 52.

sandek, sandik (san′dek, -dik): one who holds the Jewish infant during circumcision.

sandever, sandiver (san′di.ver): scum cast up in glassmaking—glass gall.

sanglot (sän.glō′): in singing, a sobbing grace note.

sanguify (sang′gwi.fī): to produce blood; to change into blood. 1.

sanguinivorous, sanguivorous (sang′-gwi.niv′o.rus, -gwiv′o.rus): feeding on blood.

sans-culottic (sanz′kū.lot′ik): radical; Jacobinic; uncouth for lack of breeches.

santon (san′ton): a Muslim saint; a dervish or hermit regarded as a saint.

sapan (sa.pan′): the heartwood of the sappanwood tree, formerly used as an astringent.

saponacity (sa′po.nas′i.ti): soapiness. 58.

sapphism (saf′izm): lesbianism.

saprophilous (sa.prof′i.lus): thriving in decaying matter, as certain bacteria.

saraad (sa.räd′): in early Welsh law, a fine for injury, payable in cattle.

sarcel (sär.sel′): a pinion feather of a hawk's wing.

sarcelle (sär.sel′): a teal. 39A.

sarcle (sär′kl): a hoe. To weed. 1.

sarcodic (sär.kod′ik): pert. to or resembling protoplasm.

sarcophagic, sarcophagous (sär′ko.faj′ik, -kof′a.gus): feeding on flesh.

sarcophilous (sär.kof′i.lus): fond of flesh.

sardanapalian (sär′da.na.pāl′yun): having a luxurious, effeminate nature.

sardel, sardelle (sär.del′): a sardine.

sark (särk): a shirt; a body garment for either sex. To cover with sarking. 11.

sarmassation (sär′ma.sā′shun): love play, *paizogony*.

sarmassophobe (sär.mas′o.fōb): one who dreads love play.

sarment, sarmentum (sär′ment, -.men′tum): in botany, a cutting; a scion; a slender, prostrate, running shoot.

sarna (sär′na): among the Kols of India, a sacred grove.

Sarsar (sär′ser): in Muslim countries, a whistling, violently cold, deadly wind.

sart (särt): the town dwellers of a native race in Turkestan. Also, var. of *soft*. 11.

sasin (sä′sin): the black buck, or Indian antelope.

sasine (sä′sīn, -sin): in Scots law, seizin, or possession of feudal property; also, the formality by which it is acquired.

satanophany (sä′ta.nof′a.ni): possession by the devil.

sati (sut′i): var. of suttee, the former practice of a Hindu widow cremating herself on her husband's funeral pyre. The cremated widow. (cap) In Egyptian religion, the queen of the gods, depicted with cow's horns.

sation (sā′shun): a sowing or planting. 1.

satisdiction (sat′is.dik′shun): the condition of having said enough. 59.

satispassion (sat′is.pash′un): in theology, a satisfactory level or amount of suffering.

satrapess (sā′tra.pes): a female sa-trap—a petty ruler or subordinate official in ancient Persia. Hence, a woman in a responsible administrative or executive position.

savate (sa.vat′): a form of boxing in which blows may be delivered with the feet.

sawder, soft sawder (sô′der): to flatter. Flattery. 26.

sawney (sô′ni): a fool; simpleton; naively foolish; silly; to talk blandishingly. 26A.

saxcornet (saks′kôr.net): a small sax-horn.

saxify (sak′si.fī): to petrify, turn into stone.

saya (sä.ya): in the Philippines, a woman's outer skirt, tied at the waist with a tape and extending to the ankles.

scacchic (skak′ik): pert. to or like chess.

scaddle (skad′l): noxious; cruel; timid; skittish; mischievous; thievish. To run off in fright. 11. Injury; mischief; confusion. 2.

scaldabanco (skal′da.bang′ko): a fervent debater or preacher. 1.

scall (skôl): a scabby disease, esp. of the scalp.

scamander (ska.man′der): to wind, meander, as the Scamander river in Asia Minor.

scamell, scammel (skam′l): the bar-tailed godwit.

scaphism (skaf′izm): in ancient Persia, execution by exposure to the sun, head and limbs being smeared with honey to attract insects.

scapple (skap′l): var. of *scabble*.

scapulimancy (skap′ū.li.man′si): divination by the study of a shoulder blade, usu. as blotched from the fire.

scarabee (skar.a.bi): a scarab, or dung beetle.

scarebabe (skâr′bāb): a thing to scare a baby; a bogy.

scarious (skâr′i.us): in botany, thin and membraneous in texture, as a bract.

scarrow (skar′ō): a faint light or shadow; to shine faintly. 44.

scatch (skach): a stilt; a crutch. 1. A kind of oval bit for a bridle.

scatomancy (skat′o.man′si): divination by the study of feces.

scat-singing (skat′sing′ing): the improvising or repeating of meaningless syllables to a melody.

scatula (skach′e.la): in pharmacy, a flat rectangular box used for dispensing powder and pills.

scaturient (ska.choor′i.ent): gushing forth; full to overflowing; effusive.

scauper, scorper (skô′per, skôr′per): one of various tools used in wood engraving, line engraving, jewel chiseling, etc.

scaurie (skô′ri, skä′ri): a young gull; esp., a young herring gull. 44.

scaurous (skô′rus): thick-ankled.

scavage, scavenge (skav′ij, -inj): the act of scavenging. In old English law, a toll duty exacted of merchant strangers by mayors, sheriffs, etc. for goods shown or offered for sale.

scavager (skav′a.jer): scavenger.

scaw (skô): var. of *scall*. 43.

scena (sē′na): *skene*.

scenography (si.nog′ra.fi): the art of perspective.

schesis (skē′sis): the general disposition of the body or mind; habitude. 1. In rhetoric, the citing of an opponent's mental set as tending to invalidate his arguments.

scete (skēt): *skete*.

schizothemia (skiz′o.thē′mi.a, skit′so-): digression by a long reminiscence.

BUT COWS ARE "KINE" IN ENGLAND?

A picnic is a pasture feast,
  A pyknic is a fat-stuff;
But nothing care we two, at least,
  That *this* stuff leads to *that* stuff.

So we shall splore among the cows,
  And on the grass sit stodging;
If lambs come bounding as we smouse,
  Let others do the dodging.

Let others jog, their waists to shear—
  Slipe lipids off by diet;
We'll lean against some Jersey's rear,
  And sloam in God's own quiet.

Let others scuddle; let them strain,
  And fitness pamphlets study;
Though we grow squaddy, we'll remain
  As seely as a scuddy.

While they do push-ups on the lea,
  And play the cockalorum,
Our briskest exercise will be
  A hand of snipsnapsnorum.

---

schlenter (schlen′ter): in South Africa, an imitation, as an imitation diamond.

schnitz (shnits): sliced dried fruit, esp. apples.

schoenobatist (ski.nob′a.tist): a tight-rope walker.

schola (skō′la): in ancient Rome, a school or meetingplace for associations.

schola cantorum (skō′la kan.tō′rum): a singing school; specif., the choir or choir school of a monastery or a cathedral. The part of an ecclesiastical edifice reserved for the choir.

scholia (skō′li.a): scholarly notes, specif. insertions by the editors in Euclid's *Elements*.

schorl , shorl (shôrl): tourmaline, esp. of a common black iron-rich variety. Any of several dark-colored minerals other than tourmaline. 9.

schorly, shorly (shôr′li): containing or

mingled with schorl, or with black tourmaline, a gemstone.

schrik (shrik): in South Africa, a sudden fright; panic.

scialytic (sī′a.lit′ik): shadow-dispersing.

sciaphobia (sī′a.fō′bi.a): fear of shadows.

sciapodous (sī.ap′o.dus): having very large feet, as the Sciapods, a fabulous Libyan people who used their feet as sunshades and umbrellas.

sciatheric (sī′a.ther′ik): pert. to a sun-dial.

scincous (sing′kus): like or pert. to skinks; scincoid.

scintle (sin′tl): to stack (molded brick) with spaces between to allow ventilation for drying. To set (brick) in a wall so as to produce a rough quality. Brick so stacked or set.

sciography (sī.og′ra.fi): a superficial study.

sciophyte (sī′o.fīt): a plant that endures the shade or thrives in it.

sciopticon (sī.op′ti.kon): a magic lantern.

Sciot (sī′ot): pert. to the isle of Chios. A native or inhabitant of Chios.

sciotheism (sī′o.thē′izm): belief in disembodied spirits as effective agents in human affairs.

sclerema (skli.rē′ma): hardening of bodily tissue, esp. the subcutaneous tissue.

Scleria (sklē′ri.a): a genus of sedges. The American species is often called nut grass.

scob (skob): a rod or splint of wood, esp. a thatch peg. 41.

scobby (skob′i): the chaffinch. 13.

scobicular (sko.bik′ū.lar): sawdust-like.

scobs (skobs): raspings of ivory, hartshorn, metal, or other hard substances.

scoleciphobia (skol′es.i.fō′bi.a): fear of worms.

scolecophagous (skol′i.kof′a.gus): worm-eating.

Scomber (skom′ber): the genus containing the common Atlantic mackerel.

sconcheon, scuncheon (skon′chun, skun′chun): in architecture, the part of an opening from the back of the reveal to the inside face of the wall.

scoon (sko͞on): to skip a flat rock across water. 11.

scopa (skō′pa): an arrangement of short stiff hairs on an insect that functions like a brush in collecting something (as pollen).

scopiferous (sko.pif′er.us): furnished with one or more dense brushes of hair.

scopophobia (skop′o.fō′bi.a): fear of being seen.

scordatura (skôr′da.to͞o′ra): an unusual tuning of a stringed instrument for some special effect.

scortation (skôr.tā′shun):   fornication.

scote (skōt):   a prop; chock. To prop. 13.

scotography (sko.tog′ra.fi):   the process of producing a picture in the dark; radiography.

scotoma (sko.tō′ma):   in medicine, a blind or dark spot in the visual field.

scotomy (skot′o.mi):   dizziness with dimness of sight. 1.

scotophobia (skot′o.fō′bi.a):   fear of darkness.

scovel (skuv′el):   a mop for sweeping ovens. 13.

scraffle (skraf′l):   scramble; struggle, wrangle. 13B.

scranch (skranch):   to crunch. 11A.

scrannel (skran′el):   slight; thin; lean; weak; poor. 9A. Harsh; unmelodious.

scrappet (skrap′et):   dim. of *scrap*.

scray (skrā):   a frame to hold textiles, as for drying. A bush. The common tern. 29A.

screeve (skrēv):   to write (as begging letters); to draw on a sidewalk, in order to attract passers and elicit charity. 21.

scride (skrīd):   to creep; to crawl on all fours. 11.

scringe (skrinj):   to cringe; flinch. To flog the water in fishing. 11. To squeeze or rub with force; to pry, search. 13.

scriniary (skrin′i.er.i):   a keeper of archives.

scripee (skrip.ē′):   one to whom land scrip is issued.

scriptor (skrip′ter):   one who writes; a scribe.

scripturient (skrip.choor′i.ent):   having a desire to write or a passion for writing.

scritch (skrich):   screech. 10.

scrivello (skri.vel′o):   an elephant's tusk, esp. one weighing less than 20 pounds.

scrog (skrog):   scrubby land—used usu. in pl.; the blackthorn; any stunted shrub or bush. 49. The crab apple.

scroop (skrōōp):   to creak, grate; to sound like silk; the rustle of silk. 13A.

scrotiform (skrō′ti.fôrm):   pouch-shaped.

scrouge (skrouj, skrōōj):   to squeeze together; crowd, press. 26.

scrow (skrou):   a cutting from a skin, used for making glue. A schedule or list; a scroll (pl.) Writings. 1.

scrump (skrump):   something shriveled or undersized; to shrivel. 13A.

scrutineer (skrōō′ti.nēr):   an examiner, as of votes at an election.

scruto (skrōō′tō):   a kind of trapdoor in a theater stage.

scry (skrī):   outcry; shout. 11. To descry; to practice crystal gazing. 9. A kind of sieve; to sift. 2.

scuddle (skud′l):   hurry, scuttle. 11.

scuddy (skud′i):   naked; a naked child. 44.

scuft (skuft):   cuff; buffet. 13.

sculp (skulp):   An engraving; a piece of sculpture; to engrave. 1. To sculpture. 58. (var. of *scalp*) To break (slate) into slabs. The skin or pelt of a seal, esp. a young seal. To remove this (skin).

scuppet (skup′et):   a small spade or shovel. 13.

scutiferous (skū.tif′er.us):   shield-carrying. Bearing scutes or scales, as reptiles.

scutum (skū′tum):   among the Romans, an oblong, leather-covered shield, esp. for heavily armed infantry. A bony, horny, or chitinous plate of an insect. One of the two lower valves of the movable shell plate of a barnacle.

scybalum (sib′a.lum):   a hardened fecal mass.

scye (sī):   *armscye*.

seave (sēv):   a rush; a rushlight. 42.

sebago (si.bā′go):   the landlocked salmon.

sebastomania (si.bas′to.mā′ni.a):   religious mania.

secability (sek′a.bil′i.ti):   divisibility. 52.

secernent (si.sur′nent):   separating; secreting. Something that secretes or promotes secretion.

secernment (si.surn′ment):   the act of separating, distinguishing, discriminating. The act of secreting, as mucus.

secesh (si.sesh′):   secessionist. Secessionists collectively. 23.

sectary (sek′ta.ri):   a zealous adherent of a sect. (often cap) A nonconformist.

sectiuncle (sek′ti.ung′kl):   an insignificant sect. 52.

sective (sek′tiv):   capable of being cut; sectile.

secundation (sek′un.dā′shun):   the act of making (one) lucky or prosperous.

secundo (se.kun′dō):   secondly; in the second (year).

secundogeniture (se.kun′do.jen′i.cher):   the state of being second-born, esp. among sons. The inheritance of a second son.

sedile (si.dī′li):   a seat in the chancel near the altar for the officiating clergy during intervals of the service.

sedilia (si.dil′ya):   pl. of *sedile*.

seeksorrow (sēk′sor′ō):   one who finds pleasure in sadness or pain.

seely (sē′li):   blessed, happy: good, kind: innocent, harmless; weak, poor, wretched; simple, timid, foolish, silly. 10.

seesee (sē′si):   a small Asiatic sand partridge.

seg (seg):   an animal castrated when full grown. 14. Sedge; the iris. 11A.

segger (seg′er):   a boaster, braggart. 1.

seghol, segol (se.gōl′):   in Hebrew grammar, a vowel sign (∴) written below its consonant and nearly equivalent to English *e* as in *set*.

seinsemblers (saɴ′säɴ.blä):   falsies.

seity (sē′i.ti):   a quality peculiar to oneself; selfhood; individuality.

sejoin (si.join′):   to separate. 52.

sejugate (sej′ōō.gāt):   to sunder.

sejunction (si.jungk′shun): separation. 1.

selcouth (sel′kōōth):   marvelous; wonderful. 9. A marvel; a wonder. 1.

selenian (si.lē′ni.an):   pert. to the moon.

selenophobia (si.lē′no.fō′bi.a):   fear of the moon.

selion (sel′yun):   in early England, one of the strips or ridges in which land was plowed in the open-field system.

sella (sel′a):   in Roman antiquity, a seat, saddle. In anatomy, a saddle-shaped portion of the sphenoid, a compound bone at the base of the cranium.

sellar (sel′er):   pert. to a depression in the middle line of the bone at the base of the cranium, lodging the pituitary body.

sematology (sem′a.tol′o.ji):   the study of the relation of signs, or words, to thought. 52.

semeiological, semiological (sē′mi.o.loj′i.kal):   pert. to the study of signs.

semese (se.mēs′):   half-eaten. 52.

semic (sem′ik, sē′mik):   pert. to a sign.

semiped (sem′i.ped):   in prosody, a half foot.

semiustulate (sem′i.us′chōō.lāt):   half burned.

semordnilap (se.môrd′ni.lap):   a word that spells another word in reverse; "palindromes" spelled backward.

sempervirent (sem′per.vī′rent):   evergreen. 52.

sempster (semp′ster):   var. of *seamster*, tailor.

sendal (sen′dal):   a thin silk fabric used in the Middle Ages.

sennight (sen′īt):   the space of seven nights and days; a week. 9.

senocular (sen.ok′ū.lar): having six eyes.

sensific, sensificatory (sen.sif′ik, -a.tō′ri):   producing sensation.

sensor (sen′ser):   sensory.

sensum (sen′sum):   in philosophy, an object of sense, or content of sense perception; a sense datum.

sententiarian (sen.ten′shi.er′i.un):   an aphorist. A discourse full of meaning or wisdom.

sepicolous (si.pik′o.lus):   inhabiting hedges or hedgerows.

seppuku (sep.pōō′kōō):   in Japan, suicide by disembowelment; hara-kiri.

septangle (sep′tang′gl):   a heptagon.

septemplicate (sep.tem′pli.kāt):   one of seven copies.

septenate (sep'ti.nāt): divided into seven parts—said of leaves.

septentrionate (sep.ten'tri.o.nāt): to point north. 52.

septile (sep'tīl, -til): pert. to a septum, or partition—in anatomy, to the partition between the nostrils.

septimanal (sep.tim'a.nal): weekly.

septimanarian (sep'ti.ma.nâr'i.an): in a monastery, a monk who served in certain capacities for a week.

septimole (sep'ti.mōl): in music, a group of seven notes to be played in the time of four or six of the same value. Septuplet.

septophobia (sep'to.fō'bi.a): fear of decaying matter.

septulum (sep'tū.lum): a small septum—partition, membrane.

serang (se.rang'): the boatswain of an East Indian crew; also, the skipper of a small native boat.

serenitude (si.ren'i.tūd): serenity. 1.

sereno (si.rā'nō, -rē'nō): in Spain, serene. Also, a night watchman.

seri (sē'ri): var. of *siri*. (cap) An Indian people of the state of Sonora, Mexico.

serictery (si.rik'ter.i): the silk-producing gland of a caterpillar or other insect larva.

sermocination (ser.mos'i.nā'shun): a form of rhetoric in which one immediately answers one's own question. 52.

sermuncle (sur'mung'kl): a short sermon.

serriped (ser'i.ped): having serrated feet.

serrurerie (se.rur'e.ri): highly finished work in wrought iron.

sertulum (sur'tū.lum): in botany, a collection of scientifically studied plants. Having the flower cluster arising from a common point; an umbel.

sertum (sur'tum): a scientific treatise upon a collection of plants.

seruke (si.rook): a bloodsucking fly of Nubia and the Sudan, remarkable for its long sucking organ.

servation (ser.vā'shun): preservation. 52.

sesquitricentennial (ses'kwi.trī'sen.ten'i.al): a four hundred and fiftieth anniversary.

sestole (ses'tōl): a group of six equal musical notes performed in the time ordinarily given to four of the same value, and written in three groups of two. A sextuplet.

setal (sē'tal): in zoology and botany, pert. to any slender, typically rigid or bristly and springy organs or parts of animals or plants.

setarious (si.târ'i.us): resembling a bristle.

seth (seth): in India, a merchant or banker.

seton (sē'tn): in medicine and veterinary medicine, one or more threads or horsehairs or a strip of linen introduced beneath the skin by a knife or needle to form an issue; also, the issue.

set, sett (set): in Scots law, the constitution of a burgh. A spot in a river where nets are set. A tartan pattern.—44A.

sevocation (sev'o.kā'shun): the act of calling apart or aside. 52.

sewen (sū'en): a British trout regarded as a subspecies of the sea trout.

sexangle (seks'ang'gl): a hexagon.

sfumato (sfoo.mä'tō): of a painting, having hazy outlines, shades, and colors.

sgabello (zga.bel'ō): an octagonal Italian Renaissance chair.

shaconian (shā.kō'ni.an): one who believes Bacon wrote Shakespeare's plays.

shadoof (sha.doof'): a counterpoised sweep used in Egypt and nearby countries for raising water.

shaftsbury (shafts'ber'i): a gallon jug of wine.

shaganappy (shag'a.nap'i): a thread, cord, or thong of rawhide.

shahzadah (sha.zä'da): son of a shah.

shamal (sha.mäl'): a northwesterly wind over Mesopotamia and the Persian Gulf.

shamateur (sham'a.ter): one pretending to be an amateur.

shandry (shan'dri): short for *shandrydan*, an old-fashioned chaise or gig. A rickety vehicle.

shandy (shan'di): wild in mirth or fancy; boisterous; visionary. 13. To discourse in the manner of Sterne's Tristram Shandy.

shanker (shang'ker): one whose work consists of making or fastening on shanks.

shapoo (sha.poo'): a wild mountain sheep of Kashmir and Tibet.

shardborn (shärd'bôrn): born in dung.

shastra (shas'tra): in Hinduism, the four classes of scriptures known as *sruti*, *smriti*, *purana*, and *tantra*. Also, technical treatises on religious or other subjects.

sheal (shēl): a shelter; to shelter. 17A.

shebeen (she.bēn'): an illegal drinking establishment; a speakeasy; to keep a shebeen. 47A.

shee, sidhe (shē): an underground fort or palace of the fairies in Gaelic folklore. A general name for the fairyfolk of Ireland.

sheel (shēl): shovel. 44.

shelta (shel'ta): a secret jargon of tinkers and kindred classes, still to be found in Britain and Ireland.

Shen (shen): the name of the Christian God as adopted by some Chinese Protestants.

shend (shend): to protect or defend. To punish, revile, put to shame and confusion; to injure, ruin. 10. To worst, as in battle. 1.

sheng (sheng): in China, a province divided into districts. A Chinese wind instrument, with music produced both by exhaling and inhaling. A Chinese measure.

shep (shep): short for shepherd. 2.

shereef, sharif (she.rēf'): an Arab prince or chief.

sherryvallies (sher'i.val'iz): chaps, leggings. 52A.

shet (shet): dial. var. of shut.

sheugh (shūk): to make ditches or drains; to cover over. A ditch; gully. 44A.

shevel (shev'el): to distort or be distorted; to walk waveringly. 43.

shewel (shoo'el): a scarecrow, esp. one made of feathers tied to a string. 11.

shicker (shik'er): a drunk; a drunkard. 21.

shikasta (shi.kas'ta): a Persian hand in which correspondence and sometimes manuscripts are written.

shillaber (shil'a.ber): a shill, a decoy. 22.

shillibeer (shil'i.bēr): a horse-drawn omnibus. A hearse, with seats for mourners.

shilpit (shil'pit): feeble, puny, worthless, stupid. 44.

shintiyan (shin'ti.yan): wide loose trousers worn by Muslim women.

shinty (shin'ti): shinny. 43A.

shippo (ship'ō): in Japanese art, cloisonné enamel on a background of metal or porcelain.

shippon (ship'un): a cow barn. 14.

shish (shish): a prolonged sibilant sound. To shish, esp. for the purpose of quieting.

shitepoke (shīt'pōk): any of various herons, esp. the green heron or night heron.

shoad (shōd): in mining, a fragment of vein material removed by natural agencies from the outcrop, and lying in the surface soil.

shode (shōd): the top of the head; the parting of the hair there. 1.

shog (shog): to shake, jog, jolt; a shake, jog, jerk. 10.

shole (shōl): a plank or plate placed beneath an object to give increased bearing surface or to act as a protection.

shoneen (shō'nēn, sho.nēn'): a would-be gentleman who puts on superior airs; a snob; a toady. 51.

shott (shot): a shallow salty lake in one of the closed basins of northern Africa.

shram (shram): to shrink or shrivel with cold; to be numb. 13.

shroff (shrof): in the Far East, a money changer or banker. To inspect coins.

shtreimal (shtrī'mal): a tall round fur cap.

shud (shud): a shed. 4.

sialogogic (sī'a.lo.goj'ik): promoting the flow of saliva.

sicarian (si.kâr'i.an): an assassin.

sicarious (si.kâr'i.us): murderous.

sicca (sik'a): a coining die. A newly coined rupee; hence, any silver (coin) in excellent condition.

siccaneous (si.kā'ni.us): of soil, dry, unwatered. 52.

siccar (sik'er): dial. form of *sicker*.

sicchasia (si.kā'zhi.a, -zi.a): nausea.

sice (sīs): the number six on a die; the throw of six. 9. A sixpence. 23.

sicker (sik'er): secure; trustworthy; firm and well established. Securely; safely. 44A. Trickle, ooze. 11A. To assure, secure, pledge. 9.

sicsac (sik'sak): the crocodile bird of Egypt.

sideration (sid'er.ā'shun): a sudden attack of disease for no known cause; erysipelas. 1. The use of green manure in agriculture.

siderodromophobia (sid'er.o.drō'mo.fō'bi.a): fear of train travel.

siderographist (sid'er.og'ra.fist): one who engraves steel.

sideromancy (sid'er.o.man'si): divination by regarding stars or watching burning straw.

sidi (sē'di): a title of respect given to an African Mohammedan, usu. to one in authority.

sidy (sī'di): pretentious. 26.

Sif (sif): in Norse mythology, the wife of Thor and the guardian of the home.

sifaka (si.fak'a): any of several diurnal lemurs of Malagasy that have a long tail and silky fur and are of a usu. black and white color.

siffilate (sif'i.lāt): to whisper.

sigillate (sij'i.lāt): decorated with seal-like markings. To seal.

sigillography (sij'i.log'ra.fi): the study of seals.

signaletics (sig'na.let'iks): the science of making or using signalments.

sika (sē'ka): the Japanese deer, or any closely allied deer of the eastern Asiatic mainland. (cap) A subgenus of the genus *Cervus*, comprising these deer.

sike (sīk): a small stream, esp. one that dries up in summer; a ditch; trench; drain; a gully; ravine. 43A. A sigh. 2.

Sikinnis (si.kin'is): in Greek antiquity, an orgiastic dance of satyrs.

sile (sīl): to drop, drip; to subside. 2. To strain, filter; a strainer. 2.

silentiary (si.len'shi.er'i): one appointed to keep order and silence.

sillar (sēl'yär'): building material, chiefly Mexican, consisting of blocks of clay cut from a natural clay deposit and differing from adobe in not being pugged or molded.

siller (sil'er): var. of silver. 43.

sillock (sil'uk): a young coalfish. 44.

silphium (sil'fi.um): an extinct plant, perhaps the laswerwort, used medicinally by the ancient Greeks. (cap) A large genus of North American herbs having coarse heads and yellow flowers.

simba (sim'ba): to the Bantus, a lion.

simbil (sim'bil): an African stork with bronzy back and white underparts.

simblot (sim'blot): in weaving, the harness of a drawloom.

sime (sīm): a monkey. A rope or frame of straw. 42.

Simia (sim'i.a): a genus orig. incl. most apes and monkeys, but now confined to the Barbary ape.

simity (sim'i.ti): pug-nosedness.

simous (sī'mus): snub-nosed. Concave; snub. 1.

sinapis (si.nap'is): a white mustard, charlock, or other weedy herb of the subgenus Sinapis.

sinapize (sin'a.pīz): to powder or sprinkle.

sinarchism (sin'är.kizm): a Mexican counterrevolutionary movement seeking a return to early Christian principles, and opposing communism.

sind (sind): to rinse; wash out; quench; drench. 4A. A rinsing; a drink to wash down solid food. 43.

sinistrogyrate (sin'is.tro.jī'rat): inclined or moving toward the left.

sinople (sin'o.pl): ferruginous quartz of a blood-red or brownish-red color, sometimes with a tinge of yellow.

sinsyne (sin'sīn): since that time; ago. 44A.

siphonage (sī'fon.ij): the action or use of a siphon.

sipid (sip'id): tasty, flavorful.

sipple (sip'l): tipple. 44A.

sircar (ser.kär', sur'kär): in India, the government, the supreme authority. Also, a house servant.

sirenic (sī.ren'ik): siren-like; fascinating, melodious; deceptive.

sirgang (sur'gang): an Asiatic, long-crested jay, called also the Chinese roller.

siri (si'ri): betel.

siserara (sis'er.âr'a): a severe blow; a violent scolding. 11.

sist (sist): a stay of legal proceedings, or an order for such a stay. To bring into court; summon. 44A.

sistle (sis'l): to whistle with a hissing sound.

sithe (sīth): dial. var. of sigh. A journey; conduct; course of life; chance, mishap; time. 1.

sitophobia (sī'to.fō'bi.a): fear of eating.

situal (sich'ōō.el): positional.

sizar (sī'zer): a student (as in the universities of Cambridge and Dublin) who receives an allowance, formerly for serving other students.

sizarship (sī'zer.ship): the position or standing of a sizar.

sizz (siz): a hissing sound. To hiss.

sizzard (siz'erd): heat with high humidity. 27.

sizzen (siz'en): childbed. 7A.

skaddle (skad'l): short for skedaddle. 32. Var. of *scaddle*.

skag (skag): a low-decked boat for duck shooting. To shoot from a skag. A cigarette. 21.

skedge (skej): the common privet.

skeeg (skēg): lash; flog; slap. 44.

skeel (skēl): a pail, bucket, or tub. 2.

skegger (skeg'er): a young salmon in the stage when it has dark transverse bands on its sides; a parr.

skelder (skel'der): to cheat, panhandle. A cheat, panhandler. 60.

skelb (skelb): a splinter; slice. 44.

skelp (skelp): a strip of wrought iron for making a hollow piece or tube. To form into skelp. A splinter, scratch. To strike, drive with blows; to perform in a lively fashion; to beat, as a clock. 49.

sken (sken): squint, stare. 13.

skene (skē'ni): in the ancient Greek theater, the structure behind the orchestra, facing the theatron.

skep (skep): a kind of farm basket, or the quantity it holds; a bowl-shaped ladle; a coal scuttle. 42.

skerry (sker'i): a rocky isle; an insulated rock or reef. 44A. A kind of potato. 45. A punt seating two. 1.

skete (skēt): any settlement of Eastern Orthodox monks, called *sketiotai*, who form a loosely knit religious community, living outside their monastery in cottages.

skillagalee (skil'a.ga.li): a worthless coin; a thin broth or porridge. 13C.

skilly (skil'i): skilfull; skilled. 43. Skillagalee.

skilpot (skil'pot): the red-bellied terrapin.

skimmington (skim'ing.tun): one publicly impersonating and ridiculing a henpecked or disgraced husband or his shrewish or unfaithful wife. A boisterous procession intended to ridicule such a husband or wife. 13.

skinker (sking'ker): one who serves liquor; a tapster. 9. A drinking vessel. 1.

skite (skīt): a sudden glancing blow; a trick, a prank; an offensive person; to move hurriedly. 11. To strike an object with a glancing blow; ricochet, skip. 44. Boast, brag. 53.

skittler (skit′ler): one who plays skittles.

skivered (skiv′erd): skewered; impaled. 44A.

skivie (skiv′i): silly 44.

sklent (sklent): to slant, cast aspersions, fib, balance sidewise; a slant, untruth, side glance. 43.

slade (slād): a hillside; a cave; a flat piece of bogland. 11A. A sledge. 11. To slide; glide. 13. The sole of a plow.

slaister (slās′ter): to smear; bedaub; to do dirty or sloppy work; to do anything clumsily or untidily or carelessly; to idle. 43A. A mess. 43. To beat; flog. 13.

slampamp (slam′pamp): a medley; rigamarole; trick. 1.

sleech (slēch): silt, slime, or ooze from rivers or the sea, esp. as used for manure. 11A.

sleechy (slēch′i): oozy, slimy. 11A.

slipe (slīp): a thin, narrow strip, esp. of land. Wool removed from skins by using lime. A sleigh, a sled. 13. To peel, pare, strip. 44D. To glide or slip away. 44C.

slish (slish): in Shakespeare, a cut, slash. To slish.

slobber-chops (slob′er.chops): a slobberer.

sloka (slō′ka): a distich having two lines of 16 syllables each or four octosyllabic hemstichs—the chief verse form of the Sanskrit epics.

sloke (slōk): any of var. edible marine algae, as sea lettuce and Irish moss. 50. Slime or scum in water. To sneak away. 11.

sloom, sloam (slōōm, slōm): to slumber, doze; become weak and flaccid; decay; swoon; move slowly and silently; drift. 2.

slougher, sluffer (sluf′er): in medicine, that which becomes encrusted with a slough. A sloughing agent.

slote, sloat (slōt): a former device for moving persons or scenery above or below a theater stage.

slowcome (slō′kum): a lazy person. 21.

sloyd (sloid): skilled mechanical work, as in carving; specif., a system of manual training based on one in Sweden.

slub (slub): a mess, a mire. 11A. To muddy, mire. 11. A slubbed roll of cotton, wool, or silk.

slubber (slub′er): to darken, obscure, skim cursorily; mire, slime. 11A.

slubby (slub′i): muddy. 11A.

sluit (slōōt): in South Africa, a ditch or gully, usu. dry, produced when heavy rains form a crack in sun-baked soil.

smabbled (smab′ld): killed in action. 21.

smatch (smach): to smack. 1.

smatchet (smach′et): a small, contemptible fellow; also, an unmannerly child. 44.

smearcase (smēr′kās): cottage cheese. 32.

smee (smē): a pintail duck. 32. A smew. 41. A widgeon; pochard.

smeeth (smēth): mist, haze; to screen with mist. 13.

smeu, smeuth (smū, smūth): the willow warbler. 44.

smew (smū): a merganser of northern Europe and Asia, smallest of the mergansers and one of the most expert divers of all ducks. A widgeon, pollard, pintail duck.

smich (smich): the stonechat. 31.

smicker (smik′er): to smile amorously; smirk. 5.

smilet (smīl′et): a little smile.

smolt (smōlt): smooth; calm; clear; bright. 4A.

smoot (smōōt): a narrow passageway; to move stealthily. 42A.

smouse (smouz): to eat with gusto; to feast. In South Africa, an itinerant peddler.

smout (smōōt): to work at odd jobs in a printing establishment. One who smouts. Also, var. of smolt.

smur, smurr (smur): a mist or cloud. Drizzle, mist. 11.

snarleyyow (snär′li.you): a dog. 21.

snash (snash): insolence; gibing. 44A. To talk insolently. 44.

snast, snaste (snast, snāst): a candlewick. 2.

snath (snath): the handle of a scythe.

snathe (snāth): var. of snath. To lop; prune. 5A.

snead (snēd): a scythe handle or shaft; a snath. 11.

sneap (snēp): to chide, chasten; spy; sneak. 11. To blast or blight with cold; nip. 9.

sneath (snēth): dial. var. of snath.

sneesh (snēsh): snuff; a pinch of snuff. To take snuff. 49.

sneest (snēst): taunt; sneer.

sneg (sneg): cut. 44.

snig (snig): a small eel. 13. To chop off; jerk; to drag on a rope or chain, as a log. 11. To sneak; pilfer. 21.

snipsnapsnorum (snip′snap′snō′rum): a card game with this name.

snoach (snōch): to snuffle. 11.

snod (snod): trim, smooth, neat; to make so. 43A.

snoga (snō′ga): a Sephardic synagogue.

snollygaster, snollygoster (snol′i.gas′ter, -gos′ter): per Sen. Charles Mathias, a monster that sought to prevent Maryland blacks from voting after the Civil War. Used by President Truman for a politician with no principles.

snooger (snōō′ger): in marbles, a close miss.

snum (snum): vow; declare; "vum." 12.

snurge (snurj): to avoid an unpopular job. 23.

sny (snī): the upward curve of a plank, esp. toward the bow or stern of a ship; to bend upward. To cut. 1.

S STANDS FOR SCOBBY, SEESEE, SHITEPOKE, SQUACCO . . .

Of certain birds that start with s I'll sing a pretty song,
And you are welcome, if you wish, to sit and sing along.
The first is shorter than a span, but longer than a half-inch;
The British call it *scobby*, but it's better known as chaffinch.
The second lives in Inja. If you take a gun and cartridges,
Perhaps you'll bag some *seesees*, which your friends will swear are partridges.
The *shitepoke* is a heron that's embarrassed as the deuce
Because its name includes a word that's not in decent use.
Another heron spreads its wings from Shanghai to Monaco,
And since it's always squacking, the Italians named it *squacco*.
Brazilians have a heron too, of curvature rococo,
That bites if called a bittern, but will bow if called a *soco*.
In Asia there's a crested jay that, moulting, changes color;
When green it is a *sirgang*, and when blue a Chinese roller.
Our widgeon, pollard, pintail duck, exposed to English view,
Will drop those silly Yankee names, and call itself a *smew*,
Or else a *smee*. (The Scots have got a warbler known as *smeu*.
Another *smew's* a diving bird—a jolly good one, too.)
I overheard a Brit and Scot who thought they were alone chat
About a *smich*, and that was rich—I knew they meant a *stonechat*.
The saddest of the *s*'es is the bird that ends this ditty,
The *squonk*. It's always full of warts, and weeping from self-pity.

---

snye (snī): a natural channel that bypasses rapids or a waterfall.

soboliferous (sō′bo.lif′er.us): producing shoots or suckers.

socage (sok′ij): a form of land tenure in medieval England, obtained by service, such as military service.

soce (sōs, sos): comrades, friends—used as a form of address. 9.

soceraphobia (so′ser.a.fō′bi.a): fear of parents-in-law.

Socinianism (sō.sin′i.an.izm): a 16th-century doctrine of Faustus Socinus, who denied the Trinity, the divinity of Christ, and the personality of the Devil.

sociophobia (sō′si.o.fō′bi.a): fear of friendship or society.

socle (sok′l, sō′kl): in architecture, a molded projection at the foot of a wall or beneath the base of a column or pedestal. In cooking, a rice or bread base that allows elaborate garnishing of a dish.

soco (sō′kō): any of several Brazilian herons, esp. certain night herons and bitterns.

sodaic (so.dā′ik): pert. to or containing soda.

sodder (sod′er): dial. var. of solder.

sog (sog): boggy ground; to soak, saturate. 11A. To drowse. 11.

solano (so.lä′nō): a hot, oppressive east wind of the Mediterranean, esp. on the eastern coast of Spain; also, such a wind bringing rain.

Solanum (so.lā′num): a large genus of herbs, shrubs, or trees, incl. the potato, the eggplant, the Jerusalem cherry, and the horse nettle.

soldatesque (sôl′da.tesk): soldierlike; marauding.

Solen (sō′len): a genus of razor clams. (not cap) A clam of that genus.

solenium (so.lē′ni.um): in zoology, a *stolon*.

soli (sō′li): having only one performer in each part—a direction in choral and orchestral music.

Solidago (sō′li.dā′go): a large genus of chiefly North American herbs, the goldenrods.

solidum (sol′i.dum): the dado of a pedestal. A whole; an entire sum.

solidus (sol′i.dus): the oblique stroke (/) sometimes used in fractions (5/8), in expressing sums of money £4/12/6), and in and/or (either *and* or *or*). A gold coin of Roman antiquity. A medieval money of account.

soliped (sō′li.ped): having a single hoof on each foot, as a horse.

sollar, soller (sol′er): in mining, a platform in a shaft, esp. between a series of ladders. To install such a platform.

somnifugous (som.nif′ū.gus): driving out sleep.

somniloquacious (som′ni.lo.kwā′shus): given to talking in one's sleep. 52.

somnipathy (som′nip′a.thi): hypnotic sleep.

somnolism (som′no.lizm): hypnotic drowsiness.

sonorescent (son′o.res′ent): capable of emitting sound when acted upon by light.

soodle (sōo′dl): to saunter; stroll. 13.

sook (sōok, sook): Scot. & dial. var. of *suck*. A call for cattle and hogs. In the Muslim East, a booth or market.

sookie (sōo′ki): a call to cattle. 11.

sooterkin (sōo′ter.kin): a kind of false birth, which Dutch women are fabled to produce by sitting over their stoves; fig., an abortion, an abortive scheme.

sophister (sof′is.ter): a sophist. In Oxford and Cambridge, a student in his second or third year.

sophistic (so.fis′tik): sophistical. The art, method, or doctrine of a sophist or Sophist. Sometimes, sophistry.

sophomania (sof′o.mā′ni.a): a delusion of being exceptionally intelligent.

sophophobia (sof′o.fō′bi.a): fear of learning.

Sordello (sôr.del′ō): the title and chief figure of a philosophical and narrative poem by Browning.

sordor (sôr′der): refuse, dregs; also, sordidness.

sorema (so.rē′ma): in flowers, a mass of imbricated carpels forming a compound pistil, as in the magnolia.

sorner (sôr′ner): a sponger. 44A.

sorra (sor′a): A blessing; bad cess; sorrow. 47.

sortance (sôr′tans): agreement. 1.

sortita (sôr′tē′ta): an issuing forth; a coming or going out. In opera, an entrance aria. A postlude.

sorus (sō′rus): in ferns, one of the clusters of sporangia forming so-called fruit dots on the fertile fronds. In parasitic fungi, any mass of spores bursting through the epidermis of a host plant. In lichens, a heap of brood buds on the thallus.

sosh (sosh): drunk; intoxicated. A jag; as, to have a *sosh* on. A small quantity; a dash. 11.

soss (sos): a call to food addressed to dogs or swine. 11. Slop, swill; also, to lap. 44C. Heavily; also, to plunge, thump. 17B.

sotadic (so.tad′ik): a scurrilous, often lewd, satire, usu. in verse, named for the Greek poet Sotades. Also, palindromic verse.

sottise (so.tēz): stupidity.

soum, sum (sōom, sum): the area of pastureland that will support a fixed number of stock; the number of cattle that can be pastured in a given area. 47B.

sous-entendu (soo′zäN′täN.dü): something hinted at but not openly expressed.

souter, soutar (sōo′ter): shoemaker, cobbler. 43.

souterrain (sōo′te.rān): an underground passage or chamber.

spadassin (spad′a.sin): a swordsman; duelist; bravo.

spadille (spa.dil′): the ace of spades.

spadonism (spä′do.nizm): eunuchry. 52.

spadroon (spa.drōon′): a sword lighter than the broadsword. 9. Cut-and-thrust swordplay.

spale (spāl): a splinter or chip of wood. 13.

spalpeen (spal.pēn′, spal′pin): a scamp; a rascal (often used playfully); a boy, a mere lad. 51.

spalt (spalt, spält): to split off; chip. Liable to split; brittle. 11.

spaneria (spa.nēr′i.a): a scarcity of men.

spanogyny (spa.noj′i.ni): a scarcity of women.

spasmatomancy (spaz′ma.to.man′si): divination by watching the twitching of a body.

spatchcock (spach′kok): a fowl split and grilled immediately after being killed. So to prepare a fowl.

spatiate (spā′shi.āt): to stroll, ramble.

spatilomancy (spat′i.lo.man′si): divination by observation of the droppings of animals.

spatrify (spat′ri.fī): to besmirch; sully.

spatulamancy (spat′ū.la.man′si): divination by examining the shoulder blade of a sheep.

spawl (spôl): spittle; to spit. 9. Var. of *spall*, a chip or flake from a piece of stone or ore.

speckioneer (spek′i.o.nēr): in whaling, the inspectioneer, or chief harpooner.

spectroheliokinematograph (spek′tro.-hē′li.o.kin.e.mat′o.graf): a camera for taking motion pictures of the sun.

spectrophobia (spek′tro.fō′bi.a): fear of looking in a mirror.

speel (spēl): to climb, mount; the act of climbing or mounting. 44.

sperling (spur′ling): a smelt; a sparling. 13. A young herring. 28.

spermology (sper.mol′o.ji): the branch of botany dealing with seeds.

sphacelate (sfas′e.lāt): to become gangrenous.

sphagnicolous (sfag.nik′o.lus): growing in peat moss.

sphenography (sfi.nog′ra.fi): the art of writing in or deciphering cuneiform characters.

spial (spī′al): espial; watch. 1. A spy, a scout. 9.

spiegelschrift (spē′gel.shrift): mirrorwriting.

spiff (spif): spiffy; to spruce (up). 21. Push money, paid to a salesman to push certain goods. 23.

spiflicated (spif′li.kā′ted): intoxicated. 11.

spiflication (spif′li.kā′shun): the act of astonishing, bewildering, confounding. 58.

spig (spig): short for *spigotty*.

spigotty (spig.o.ti): a Spanish American, esp. a Mexican—usu. taken to be offensive. 21.

spik (spik): *spigotty*. 21.

spiloma (spi.lō′ma): a birthmark.

spindrift (spin′drift): sea spray.

spink (spingk): the chaffinch. 31. The common primrose; cuckoo flower; maiden pink. 44C.

spintry (spin′tri): a male whore.

spinulescent (spin′ū.les′ent): in botany, having small spines; somewhat spiny.

spirated (spī′rāt.ed): corkscrew-shaped.

spissitude (spis′i.tūd): density; viscosity.

spitchcock (spich′kok): var. of *spatchcock*. Also, to treat summarily; to handle roughly.

splanchnology (splangk.nol′o.ji): study of the viscera.

splenial (splē′ni.al): pert. to the splenium or the splenius muscle. Also, pert. to a thin splint-like bone of the mandible of many submammalian vertebrates.

splodge (sploj): var. of *splotch*.

splore (splōr): a carouse, merrymaking; to carouse; to brag. 44.

spodogenous (spo.doj′i.nus): pert. to or due to waste matter.

spodomancy (spō′do.man′si): divination by ashes.

spoffish (spof′ish): fussbudgety. 21.

spoffokins (spof.o.kinz): a prostitute pretending to be a wife.

spongology (spon.gol′o.ji): the study of sponges.

sponsal (spon′sal): spousal.

sponsalia (spon.sā′li.a): a formal betrothal.

spoom (spōōm): of a boat, to run before the sea or wind; to scud. 1.

sporabola (spo.rab′o.la): the trajectory of a falling spore.

sporange (spo.ranj′): a plant's spore-case, within which asexual spores are produced.

Sporozoa (spō′ro.zō′a): a large class of parasitic protozoans with a life cycle usu. involving alternation of sexual and asexual generation, incl. many causing diseases such as malaria.

spoucher (spōōch′er): a utensil for bailing water; a bailer. 44A.

spousal (spous′al): marriage, nuptials. 1. Relating to or celebrating marriage.

spousebreach (spous′brēch): adultery. 1.

spraints (sprānts): otter dung. 41.

sprangle (sprang′gl): to struggle. 7A. To sprawl; spread out; straggle; a strangling mass, as a *sprangle* of mistletoe. 11. To cause to sprangle or straggle. 11A.

sprent (sprent): to run, leap; spring, sprint, catch; a hasp; a prune. 43A.

sprew (sprōō): a South African starling of glossy plummage. In medicine, thrush; sprue.

springal (spring′al): a medieval engine for hurling missiles. 6.

sprunt (sprunt): a spasmodic movement; a spring, leap; active, brisk, spruce. 1.

spumescent (spū.mes′ent): like foam; foaming.

spurcidical (sper.sid′i.kal): foul-mouthed.

spurgall (spur′gôl): a gall or wound from a spur.

spurtle (spur′tl): a spurt; a trickle; to flow in jets, trickle. A stick for stirring porridge and the like; a sword. 44A.

sputation (spū.tā′shun): spitting.

squabash (skwa.bash′): to crush, esp. by criticism; a crushing blow. 26B.

squabbish (skwä′bish): thick, fat, heavy.

squacco (skwak′ō): a small crested heron that breeds in parts of Asia, Africa, and southern Europe.

squaddy (skwäd′i): squat; fat and heavy. 11A.

squail (skwāl): a counter that is snapped at a mark in the center of a board in the game of squails.

squaliform (skwäl′i.fôrm): shark-shaped.

squaloid (skwä′loid): sharklike.

squarson (skwär′sun): formerly, a landed proprietor who was also a clergyman of the Church of England—used in ridicule. *(Squire + parson.)*

squelette (ske.let′): a thin wood veneer used in making match boxes; a skillet.

squench (skwench): to quench. 11.

squidge (skwij): a squelching sound.

squidgereen (skwij′e.rēn): a short, insignificant person. 21.

squinny (skwin′i): squint; peep. 4. Squinting, peering. Slender; thin; long and narrow. To weep or fret.

squireen (skwīr.ēn′): a petty squire; a gentleman in a small way.

squonk (skwongk): an imaginary, wart-covered bird that weeps in self-pity.

sraddha (sräd′da, shräd′da): in Hinduism, a rite or ceremony in which balls of rice are offered to ancestors, as after a birth.

sri (shrē): in India, fortunate, glorious, holy, as a king or divinity.

stablestand (stā′bl.stand): in old English law, the fixed position of one about to shoot his bow or slip his dogs in deer hunting.

stactometer (stak.tom′e.ter): a pipette of small bore for counting drops.

staddle (stad′l): a small tree or sapling, esp. a forest tree. The lower part of a stack, as of hay; the supporting framework or base of a stack; to form into staddles. A support, staff, crutch. 1. A stain. 13.

stadial (stā′di.al): pert. to a stadium or a stadia.

stagflation (stag.flā′shun): persistent inflation combined with stagnant consumer demand and relatively high unemployment.

staggard, staggart (stag′erd, -ert): the male red deer in its fourth year.

stagiary (stā′ji.er.i): a resident canon; a law student.

stagnicolous (stag.nik′o.lus): inhabiting stagnant water.

staith (stāth): a landing stage or wharf for transshipment. 42.

stamin (stam′in): a coarse woolen cloth usu. dyed red and used for undergarments. An undergarment for penitents made of harsh stamin.

standage (stan′dij): privilege of or room for standing, as of cattle, or a fee paid for it.

stanniferous (sta.nif′er.us): containing tin.

starken (stär′ken): to make stiff or inflexible.

stasibasiphobia (stas.i.bas.i.fō′bi.a): fear of standing or walking.

stasiphobia (stas′i.fō′bi.a): fear of standing upright.

stasivalence (stas′i.vā′lens): inability to have sexual intercourse except when standing.

statal (stā′tal): pert. to a state.

stathmograph (stath′mo.graf): an instrument for measuring the speed of trains or projectiles.

staurolatry (stô.rol′a.tri): worship of a cross or crucifix.

staurophobia (stô′ro.fō′bi.a): dread of a crucifix.

staxis (stak′sis): in medicine, a dripping; specif., hemorrhage.

stean, steen (stēn): a stone. 44C. A vessel of stone. 11A. To line (as a well or cistern) with stone, brick, or the like.

steganographist (steg′a.nog′ra.fist): a cryptographer.

stelar (stē′ler): resembling or pert. to a stele, or pillar.

stellification (stel′i.fi.kā′shun): glorification.

stellionate (stel′yun.āt): in Roman and civil law, any fraud not set apart by a special name.

stemple, stempel (stem′pl): in mining, a crossbar of wood in a shaft serving as a step, or as a support for a platform or roof. A strut, as a spur timber. 41.

stend (stend): a spring, bound, stride, rearing-up; a stick to distend a carcass. To stend. 44A.

stenopaic (sten′o.pā′ik): having a narrow opening—applied specif. to certain optical devices. Also, using such devices.

stenophobia (sten′o.fō′bi.a): a fear of narrow things.

stenosis (ste.nō′sis): a narrowing of bodily tubes, cavities, or orifices.

stent (stent): extent; bound; to extend, stretch; outstretched, tight. 44A. A compound for holding a surgical graft in place. Dial. var. of stint; also, past and past participle of *stend*.

stentorophonous (sten'to.rof'o.nus): very loud-voiced.

stephane (stef'a.ni): a headband, narrowing toward the temples, in statues of the divinities.

stercoricolous (stur'ko.rik'o.lus): living in dung.

stereognosis (ster'i.og.nō'sis): the art of learning the weight of a solid by handling it.

sterquilian (ster.kil'yun): pert. to a dunghill; filthy.

sthenia (sthi.nī'a, sthē'ni.a): strength, vigor.

sthenic (sthen'ik): in medicine, strong, active, as a *sthenic* fever. In psychology, indicative of strength and vigor; as the *sthenic* emotions.

sthenobulia (sthen'o.bū'li.a): strength of willpower.

stibbler (stib'ler): a horse grazing on stubble. A gleaner. A probationer. 44.

stibium (stib'i.um): antimony.

sticcado (sti.kä'dō): a kind of xylophone.

stichomancy (stik'o.man'si): divination based on passages from books.

stigonomancy (stig'o.no.man'si): divination by writing on tree bark.

stillatitious (stil'a.tish'us): falling in drops; drawn by a still. 52.

stillicidious (stil'i.sid'i.us): constantly dripping.

stillion (stil'yun): a cradle for vats in a brewery.

stimulose (stim'ū.lōs): having stinging hairs.

stingo (sting'gō): sharp or strong liquor, esp. ale or beer; stinging quality; zest; zip. 21.

Stipa (stī'pa): a widely distributed genus of grasses incl. feather grass, bunch grass, silky grass, porcupine grass, etc.

stirious (stir'i.us): icicle-like.

stirpiculture (stur'pi.kul.cher): the breeding of special stocks; animal eugenics.

stive (stīv): dust; smoke; the floating dust in flour mills caused by grinding. 13. A stew. 52. To keep close and warm; stifle. 2.

stob (stob): a stake or post; a gibbet; to pierce, stab. 11.

stocah (sthō'ka): an idle fellow; a menial attendant. 51.

stoccado (sto.kä'dō): a stab; a thrust with a rapier or in fencing. 9.

stochiology (stok'i.ol'o.ji): the art of conjecture or guesswork.

stodge (stoj): to stuff full, as with food. To mix or stir up together. To tramp clumsily. A thick, filling food (as oatmeal or stew). A dull, stupid person, idea, or literary work.

stodger (stoj'er): a large, heavy person or thing. 11. An old fogy. 26.

stola (stō'la): a long robe worn by women of ancient Rome.

stolo (stō'lō): a runner; a shoot; a branch growing at or near the base of the parent plant; a *stolon*.

stolon (stō'lon): in botany, a *stolo*. In zoology, an extension of the body wall, from which buds of new zooids develop.

stook (sto͞ok): a shock of corn. 37A. A shock of small grains, beans, etc. 41B. A pillar of coal standing as a support in a coal mine. 41. A handkerchief. 23.

stooker (sto͞o'ker): one who works at arranging (as grain or hay) in shocks. 40A.

stoop-gallant (sto͞op'gal'ant): humbling; that which humbles. 1.

storge (stor'je): parental affection; the instinctive affection that animals have for their young.

storify (stō'ri.fī): to narrate or describe in story. To arrange in stories, as beehives.

storiology (stō'ri.ol'o.ji): the study of folklore.

stot (stot): a young horse. 1. A young bull or ox, esp. one that is three years old; a castrated bull. 5A. To bounce, rebound, jump; stammer; stagger; lurch. Also, a leap in dancing. 43. Swing, rhythm. 44.

stote (stōt): var. of *stoat*.

stoundmeal (stound'mēl'): gradually; from time to time; now and then. 1.

stramineous (stra.min'i.us): like straw; valueless.

stratephrenia (strat'i.frē'ni.a): neurosis associated with military service.

strathspey (strath'spā): a Scottish dance, lively but slower than a reel; its music.

stratonic (stra.ton'ik): pert. to an army. 52. (cap) Pert. to the 3rd century B.C. Greek Strato or his naturalistic philosophy.

stremma (strem'a): in Greece, two measures of land quantity, each less than an acre.

strephographia (stref'o.graf'i.a): mirror-writing; *spiegelschrift*.

strephonade (stref'on.ād): a love song.

strephosymbolia (stref'o.sim.bō'li.a): a perceptual disorder in which objects appear reversed.

strepitant (strep'i.tant): noisy; clamorous.

strepitoso (strep'i.tō'sō): noisy, impetuous—a direction in music.

strepor (strep'ôr): strident or clanging sound; noise.

stria (strī'a): a faint or minute groove or channel; a minute band, as of color.

striga (strī'ga): a striation. In architecture, a flute in a column. In botany, a pointed, rigid, hairlike scale or bristle.

(cap) A genus of seed plants living as root parasites.

striggle (strig'l): a trail—"the hurt mouse left a *striggle* of blood."

Strine (strīn): an Australian way of slurring words, as "air fridge" for "average" and "fraffly" for "frightfully."

strinkle (string'kl): to sprinkle. 5A.

striola, striolet (strī.ō'la, strī'o.let): *stria*.

strobic (strō'bik): spinning, as a top.

strockle (strok'l): a shovel with a turned-up edge used by glassworkers.

stroil (stroil): couchgrass, or certain other weeds with creeping rootstock.

stromatology (strō'ma.tol'o.ji): the study of stratified rock formation.

stromb (strom, stromb): a mollusk or shell of the genus Strombus, as the king conch.

stromboid (strom'boid): pert. to the genus Strombus.

strow (strō, stro͞o): disturbance; turmoil. 44D. To strew. 9.

stroy (stroi): destroy. 1.

strubbly (strub'li): untidy; unkempt. 12.

strue (stro͞o): to construe.

studdle (stud'l): to stir up so as to muddy. 13. A prop in or about a loom. 1. A prop or stud used in timbering a mine shaft.

studia (stū'di.a): schools. (pl. of *studium*.)

studium (stū'di.um): an institute where people from all parts of the world come to study any subject, as a medieval university.

stufa (sto͞o'fa): a jet of steam issuing from a fissure in the earth.

stulm (stulm): an approximately horizontal passageway in a mine; an adit, *aditus*.

stultiloquy (stul.til'o.kwi): foolish talk; babble. 52.

stumpage (stum'pij): uncut timber; its value; the right to cut it.

stupration (stū.prā'shun): violation of chastity; rape. 1.

stupulose (stū'pū.lōs): covered with fine short hairs.

stuss (stus): a gambling game like faro, in which the banker wins on splits.

styan (stī'an, stīn): a stye on the eye. 5A.

stygiophobia (stij'i.o.fō'bi.a): fear of hell.

stylagalmaic (stī'la.gal.mā'ik): resembling caryatids, ancient Greek columns in the shape of women.

Stylaster (stī.las'ter): a genus of delicate, usu. pink, hydroid corals. (not cap) Any coral of this genus.

styryl (stī'ril): the univalent radical found in certain derivatives of styrene, etc.

suability (sū'a.bil'i.ti): capacity to be sued.

suant (sū′ant):   smooth; regular; placid; grave; demure. 11.

suasible (swā′si.bl, -zi.bl):   capable of being persuaded; easily persuaded.

suaviation (swä′vi.ā′shun, swā-):   a love kiss.

suaviloquy (swa.vil′o.kwi):   soothing, agreeable speech.

subacid (sub.as′id):   slightly tart.

subah (sōō′ba):   a province or division of the Mogul Empire, or its government. The ruler of such a province—short for *subahdar*.

subahdar (sōō′ba.där):   in India, a viceroy. Also, the chief native officer of a native company in the former British Indian army.

subalary (sub.ā′la.ri):   under the wings.

subarrhation (sub′a.rā′shun):   betrothal by the bestowal, on the part of the man, of marriage gifts or tokens upon the woman.

subboreal (sub.bō′ri.al):   cold, just short of freezing.

subderisorious (sub′di.rī.sō′ri.us):   mildly ridiculing.

subdititious (sub′di.tish′us):   (something) put secretly in the place of something else.

subdolous (sub′do.lus):   somewhat crafty or sly.

subduct (sub.dukt′):   subtract, deduct, remove.

subduple (sub′dū.pl):   in mathematics, subdouble, in the ratio of 1 to 2.

suber (sū′ber):   in botany, cork tissue; also, the outer bark of the cork oak.

subfusc (sub.fusk′):   lacking brightness or appeal. Somewhat dusky. Drab, dingy.

subhastation (sub′has.tā′shun):   a public sale or auction. 52.

subingression (sub′in.gresh′un):   a hidden entrance. 52.

subintelligitur (sub′in.te.lij′i.ter):   a meaning implied but not specifically stated. 52.

subrision (sub.rizh′un):   the act of smiling. 52.

subsannation (sub′sa.nā′shun):   derision. 1.

subsemifusa (sub′sem.i.fū′sa):   in medieval music, a thirty-second note.

substaquilate (sub.stak′wi.lāt):   to defeat, overwhelm.

substruct (sub.strukt′):   to build or lay beneath.

subtegulaneous (sub′teg.ū.lā′ni.us):   indoor. 52.

subterfluous (sub.tur′flōō.us):   flowing or running under or beneath.

subumbonal (sub′um.bō′nal):   situated beneath or forward of the umbones of a bivalve shell.

subverse (sub.vurs′):   to subvert. 52.

succedaneous (suk′si.dā′ni.us):   pert. to one who serves as a substitute. Substituted; supplementary.

succentor (suk.sen′ter):   one who sings the close or second part of (a verse), as in responsive singing. A precentor's assistant, esp. in some monasteries and cathedrals.

succiduous (suk.sid′ū.us):   ready to fall; falling.

succiferous (suk.sif′er.us):   feeding on plant juices. 52.

succursal (su.kur′sal):   subsidiary; auxiliary, as a *succursal* church, a *succursal* bank.

succus (suk′us):   juice; specif., in pharmacy, the expressed juice of fresh drugs for medicinal use.

succuss (su.kus′):   to shake violently. In medicine, to perform succussion upon (a patient).

sudarium (su.dâr′i.um):   a sweat cloth or handkerchief, specif. the one with which St. Veronica wiped the brow of the dying Christ. 1.

sudder (sud′er):   in India, chief—applied to several government departments and chiefs. The headquarters of the provincial or rural districts. (cap) The Indian Supreme Court.

sudor (sū′dôr):   sweat; perspiration; exudation.

Suevi (swē′vi):   the Suevians, or Swabians, inhabitants of part of Bavaria, Germany. Also, the Germanic horde from east of the Rhine that overran France and Spain early in the 5th century.

suffrago (su.frā′gō):   the tarsal joint—sometimes called the knee—of a bird.

suggilate (sug′ji.lāt):   to beat black and blue; to defame.

suilline (sū′i.līn):   piglike.

suji (sōō′ji):   in India, wheat granulated but not pulverized.

sull (sul):   a plow; to plow. 2. To sulk. 35.

sulla (sul′a):   a European herb valued for forage, and cultivated for its pink flowers under the name French honeysuckle.

sumbooruk (sum′boor.uk):   a small swivel-cannon carried on the back of a camel.

summage (sum.ij):   a former toll on goods carried on horseback.

sumpitan (sum′pi.tan):   in Borneo, a blowgun for poison darts.

sumpsimus (sump′si.mus):   a strictly correct grammatical usage replacing an error.

supellectile (sū′pe.lek′til):   pert. to furniture.

superalimentation (sū′per.al′i.men.tā′shun):   overfeeding, once prescribed for certain diseases.

superbiate (su.pur′bi.āt):   to make arrogant, haughty.

supercalifragilisticexpialidocious (sū′per.kal.i.fraj.i.lis′tik.eks′pi.al′i.dō′shus):   a nonsense term that might be rendered as ''highly educable in atoning for great and delicate beauty.''

supercrescence (sū′per.kres′ens):   a parasitic organism.

superlation (sū′per.lā′shun):   glorification, stellification.

supernacular (sū′per.nak′u.lar):   first-rate; as, a *supernacular* wine. 52.

superseptuagenarian (sū′per.sep′tu.aj′e.nâr′i.an):   one who is over seventy.

superstruct (sū′per.strukt):   to build over or on; to erect on a foundation.

supervacaneous (sū′per.va.kā′ni.us):   needlessly added; redundant.

supinovalent (sū′pi.no.vā′lent):   unable to perform sexual intercourse except when supine.

suppulpation (sup′ul.pā′shun):   the act of winning affection by caressing.

supputate, suppute (sup′ū.tāt, -pūt):   to reckon, compute. 1.

supracostal (sū′pra.kos′tal):   above the ribs.

sural (sū′ral):   pert. to the calf of the leg.

surbated (ser.bāt′ed):   bruised, made sore—said esp. of overworked feet.

surculation (sur′kū.lā′shun):   the act of cutting off suckers; pruning.

surculus (sur′kū.lus):   a shoot from the roots or the lower stem of a plant; a sucker.

surdity (sur′di.ti):   deafness.

surnap (sur′nap):   a cloth with towels spread, for use in washing at formal banquets.

surra, surrah (sōōr′a, sur′a):   a severe Old World disease of domestic animals, marked by edema and anemia, transmitted by the bite of certain insects.

surrejoin (sur′ri.join):   in law, to reply as a plaintiff to a defendant's rejoinder.

surreption (su.rep′shun):   fraudulent means; underhanded methods; a surreptitious getting; a coming unperceived. 1.

suspercollate (sus′per.kol′āt):   to hang by the neck. 58.

suspirious (sus.pir′i.us):   breathing heavily; sighing.

sussultatory (su.sul′ta.tō.ri):   of an earthquake, characterized by up-and-down vibrations of large magnitude.

susu (sōō′sōō):   a blind dolphin-like cetacean, about eight feet long, inhabiting the larger rivers of India.

susulike (sōō′sōō.līk):   resembling the susu.

susurrous (su.sur′us):   rustling; full of whispering sounds.

sutile (sū′til):   done by stitching. 52.

sutteeism (su.tē′izm):   suttee. (See *sati*.)

sutter (sut′er):   var. of *souter*.

suttle (sut′l): to act as a sutler. 10. In commerce, light—designating the weight of packed goods when the weight of the container has been deducted.

swallet (swol′it): an underground stream; also, an opening through which a stream disappears underground.

swan-upping (swän-up-ing): nicking of the beaks of the swans on the Thames to show ownership by the Crown or certain corporations.

swape (swāp): a pole or bar used as a lever or swivel. A long steering oar used by keelmen on the Tyne.

swaraj (swa.räj′): in India, political independence; national self-government.

swarth (swôrth): skin; rind; sward; turf; a crop of grass or hay. 11. To produce greensward. 11A. Apparition; wraith. 13. Swarthy; swarthiness.

swartrutter (swôrt′rut′er): a trooper of one of the bands in blackface and black garb that harassed the Netherlands in the 16th and 17th centuries.

sweal (swēl): to burn; singe; scorch. 11.

swelp (swelp): corruption of "*so help* me God."

sweven (swev′en): sleep; a vision seen in sleep; a dream. 9.

swillbowl (swil′bōl): a drunkard.

swingle (swing′gl): a wooden instrument like a large knife, about two feet long, used for beating and cleaning flax. A scutcher; the *swiple* of a flail; a flail-like cudgel; a spoke-like lever used for turning the barrel in wire drawing, etc.; to clean with a swingle. Swing, to swing. 11A.

swink (swingk): labor, drudgery; to labor, toil, slave. 10.

swiple, swipple (swip′l): the part of a flail that strikes the grain in threshing; a *swingle.*

swipper (swip′er): nimble; quick. 2.

swither (swith′er): to doubt, waver, hesitate. Hesitation; quandary; agitation. 44A. A faint. 13. A rush. To whiz; to rush; also, to fall down. 17A. To scorch. 44D.

swow (swou): to swoon, faint. 1. To swear, as "I swow." 28B. Sough. 11.

syagush (syä.gōōsh′): the caracal, a lynx of Africa and southern Asia.

sybotic (sī.bot′ik): pert. to a swineherd or his employment.

syce (sīs): in India, a groom or attendant.

sycomancy (sik′o.man′si): divination by figs.

sylloge (sil′o.ji): a collection; a compendium.

sylvestrian (sil.ves′tri.an): sylvan. 52.

symbolaeography (sim′bo.li.og′ra.fi): the art of drawing up legal documents.

symbolography (sim′bo.log′ra.fi): symbolic writing or designs.

symbolum (sim′bo.lum): a symbol; a creed. The Apostles' Creed.

symphoric (sim.fôr′ik): accident-prone.

synactic (si.nak′tik): acting together; cumulative in effect.

synallagmatic (sin′a.lag.mat′ik): imposing reciprocal obligations in civil law; bilateral.

synanthous (si.nan′thus): bearing flowers and leaves that appear at the same time.

synartetic (sin′är.tet′ik): in Greek prosody, metrically continuous.

synaxis (si.nak′sis): an assembly met for worship, esp. in the early church. A congregation gathered for a liturgical service. An early part of the divine liturgy of the Eastern Church.

syncretical (sin.kret′i.kal): pert. to the reconciliation of conflicting beliefs, esp. religious beliefs; also, to egregious compromise. Pert. to any grammatical case that has absorbed the function of others, as the Greek genitive or the Latin ablative.

synderesis, synteresis (sin′der.ē′sis, -ter-): inborn knowledge of the primary principles of moral action.

syndesmology (sin′des.mol′o.ji): the anatomy of ligaments.

syne (sīn): next; then; later; since. 44A.

synectic (si.nek′tik): joining; connecting; (of a cause) immediate. 52. In mathematics, *holomorphic.*

syngenesophobia (sin′ji.nes′o.fō′bi.a): fear of relatives.

synodite (sin′o.dīt): a friend or companion.

synonymicon (sin′o.nim′i.kon): a dictionary of synonyms.

synomosy (si.nom′o.si): a political association.

synovia (si.nō′vi.a): in anatomy, a transparent, viscal lubricating fluid secreted by membranes of bursae, articulations, and tendon sheaths.

synsacrum (sin.sā′krum): in birds, dinosaurs, and pterosaurs, a solidly fused series of vertebrae in the pelvic region.

syntality (sin.tal′i.ti): the inferred behavioral tendencies of a group, acting as a group, which correspond to personality in an individual.

syntectic (sin.tek′tik): wasting; melting away.

synthermal (sin.thur′mal): having the same degree of heat.

syntomy (sin′to.mi): brevity.

syntropic (sin.trop′ik): repeated symmetrically without being reversed, as the ribs of one side.

syrma (sur′ma): in the classical theater, a trailing robe, worn esp. by tragic actors. (cap) A star in the constellation Virginis.

syrt (surt): a quicksand; bog. 52.

syssitia (si.sish′i.a): the practice among the Spartans and Cretans of eating the one chief meal of the day at a public mess to promote discipline and good habits.

T

tabardillo (tab′är.dēl′yō): a form of typhus fever occurring esp. in Mexico.

tabasheer, tabashir (tab′a.shēr): a siliceous mass in the joints of the bamboo, valued in the East Indies as a medicine—called also *sugar of bamboo.*

tabefy (tab′i.fī): to waste away gradually. 52.

tabella (ta.bel′a): a medicated lozenge or tablet.

tabetic (ta.bet′ik): pert. to, or affected with tabes.

tabi (tä′bi): a cotton sock, usu. white, having a thick sole and a separate part for the big toe, once commonly worn by the Japanese. (also pl.)

tabific (ta.bif′ik): producing tabes; wasting.

tabinet, tabbinet (tab′i.net): a poplin made chiefly in Ireland. A dress of this material.

tableity (tab.lē′i.ti): the abstract concept of which a table is the concrete.

tache (tach): a spot, stain. 1. A fault. 9. A characteristic. 11. To attach. 2. Var. of *teach.* 2. One of the evaporating pans in sugar making.

tacheography (tak′i.og′ra.fi): speedwriting.

tachydidaxy (tak′i.di.dak′si): quick teaching.

tachylalia (tak′i.lāl′ya): rapid speech.

A ROSE BY ANY OTHER NAME

L.P. Beria*
Could not have hysteria,
And Jackie Onassis
Cannot have tarassis—
The words disagree
Genderally.

That's been the idea
Since the tritavia
Of my tritavia;
Been drilled in us
Since the tritavus
Of my tritavus.

Different name—
Symptoms the same.

*Lavrenti Pavlovich Beria ran the OGPU for Stalin.

---

tachyphrasia (tak′i.frā′zhi.a, -zi.a): extremely voluble speech, sometimes resulting from emotional disturbances.

tacket (tak′et): a nail or tack. 1. A hobnail; also, a hobnailed shoe; to strengthen or fasten with tackets. 17A.

tactor (tak′ter): in zoology, a tactile organ; specif., a feeler or antenna or a tactile corpuscle.

tactus (tak′tus): sense of touch; touch.

taenifuge (tē′ni.fūj): a medicine for getting rid of tapeworms.

taffle (taf′l): tangle. 17A.

taha (tä′ha): a South American weaverbird with black and yellow plumage in the male.

tahali (ta.hä′li): to Arabs, an adornment to be worn.

Tai (tī): a family of languages in Southeast Asia, incl. Thai, Lao, and Shan. A group of tribes in Burma and Thailand. (not cap) Any of several brilliant crimson Japanese porgies.

taiaha (tä′i.a.hä): a long light staff or club adorned with red feathers or dog's hair, carried by Maori chiefs as a sign of authority and used as a two-handed striking weapon. 56.

t′ai chi ch′uan (tä′i.chē′choo.än): a Chinese system of physical exercises similar to shadow boxing.

talao (ta.lä′o): in Kipling, a low flat ground; a plain.

tali (tä′li): in India, a gold piece tied about a bride's neck by the groom and worn by her during his lifetime.

taligrade (tal′i.grād): walking on the outer side of the foot, as the great anteater.

tallet (tal′et): a hayloft; attic. 2.

talliate (tal′i.āt): to impose a tax.

talo (tal′ō): a starchy tuber of the Pacific islands; taro.

tambaroora (tam′ba.rōō′ra): a dice game in which equal amounts are subscribed to a pool, the winner paying for drinks for all the others. 53.

tamis (tam′is): tammy.

tammy (tam′i): a kind of woolen or woolen and cotton cloth, often highly glazed, used for gowns, linings, curtains, etc. A strainer, or sieve, made of this material; a tamis. To strain through a tammy. A tam-o′-shanter.

tampan (tam′pan): a venomous South American tick.

Taniwha (tan′i.hwä): a lizard-like monster of Maori legend. 56.

tankle (tang′kl): a sound louder and less acute than that represented by "tinkle."

tanling (tan′ling): one tanned by the sun. 52.

tannate (tan′āt): a salt or ester of tannin.

tannometer (tan.om′e.ter): a device for determining the strength of a tanning liquor by drawing it through hide.

tao (tou, dou): in China, a road, way; fig., the absolute; truth; right conduct. In the Philippines, a peasant.

tapen (tāp′en): of tape. 52.

taphephobia (taf′i.fō′bi.a): fear of being buried alive, or of cemeteries.

taphephilia (taf′i.fil′i.a): fondness for funerals.

tapinophobia (tap′i.no.fō′bi.a): fear of being contagious.

tarassis (ta.ras′is): the male equivalent of hysteria.

Tarpeia (tär.pē′a): in Roman legend, a maiden who betrayed the citadel to the Sabines for the promise of "what they wore on their arms," meaning their gold bracelets. They threw a shield on her and killed her.

tarsiatura (tär′si.a.tū′ra): a kind of mosaic woodwork.

tascal (tas′kal): formerly, a reward for information about stolen cattle. 44.

tasco (tas′kō): a kind of clay for melting pots.

tash (tash): stain; soil; also, fatigue; disgrace. 44A. An East Indian fabric containing much gold and silver thread.

tasher (tash′er): one who stains, soils, disgraces. 44A.

taskit (tas′kit): fatigued; fagged. 44.

tasimeter (ta.sim′iter): an instrument for measuring minute extensions or movements of solid bodies by the changes of pressure produced.

taslet, tasse, tasset (tas′let, tas, tas′et): in a body of armor, one of a series of overlapping metal plates that form a short skirt.

tassie (tas′i): a small cup. 44A.

tath (tath): the dung of sheep and cattle; the coarse grass growing near manure; to manure by pasturing sheep and cattle. 2.

tauromorphic (tô′ro.môr′fik): shaped in the form of a bull—said of vases found in several early Mediterranean cultures.

tautegory (tô′te.gō′ri, -ger-i): expression of the same thing with different words.

tautoousious (tô′to.us.i.us): exactly the same.

tautophony (tô.tof′o.ni): repetition of sound.

tavell (tav′el): a bobbin on which silk is wound.

Taxodium (tak.sō′di.um): a genus of tall, deciduous trees, incl. the common bald cypress of the southern United States.

tchin (jin): in pre-communist Russia, rank; persons of rank. Var. of chin, a Chinese weight.

tead (tēd): var. of toad. 43.

teagle (tē′gl): dial. var. of tackle.

teap (tēp): a ram. 11.

technicon (tek′ni.kon): a gymnastic device for developing the hands for piano or organ playing.

technophobia (tek′no.fō′bi.a): fear of technology.

teck (tek): a ready-made cravat imitating a four-in-hand. Var. of teak, also of tec, short for detective.

tecnogonia (tek′no.gō′ni.a): childbearing.

tectal (tek′tal): pert. to the dorsal part of the midbrain, the tectum.

tectiform (tek′ti.fôrm): roof-shaped, tent-shaped.

tectorial (tek.tō′ri.al): in anatomy, forming a covering; resembling a roof.

ted (ted): a toad. 44. To put a serrated edge on, as on a scythe. 30. To dung, manure; to spread out.

Tedeschi (te.des′ki): in Italy, Germans.

tedesco (te.des′kō): in music, "the German style."

teenage (tēn′ij): brushwood used for fences and hedges. 13.

teer (tēr): to plaster; daub. To stir up colors. 44.

teetertail (tē′ter.tāl): the spotted sandpiper.

teg (teg): a sheep in its second year, or its fleece (var. of tag). Formerly, a doe in its second year; also, a woman.

tegmental (teg.men′tal): pert. to a tegument; covering.

tegumen (teg′ū.men): in zoology and botany, a tegmen or integument, such as the tough, leathery forewing of certain insects or the inner coat of a seed.

teil (tēl): a European linden, or lime tree.

teknonymy (tek.non′i.mi): the custom in certain savage tribes of naming the parent after the child.

telamnesia (tel′am.nē′zhi.a, -zi.a): loss of memory for long past events.

telarian (te.lâr′i.an): web-spinning. A web-spinning spider.

telegnosis (tel′eg.nō′sis): supposed occult knowledge of distant events.

telenergy (tel.en′er.ji): a display of force or energy without contact—applied to mediumistic phenomena.

teleophobia (tel′i.o.fō′bi.a): fear of definite plans, or of religious ceremony.

Teleosaurus (tel′i.o.sô′rus): a genus of crocodilian reptiles of the Jurassic having a long and slender snout and platycelous vertabrae.

telepheme (tel′i.fēm): a telephone message. 52.

telephote (tel′e.fōt): an apparatus for producing photographic images of distant objects.

telestic (ti.les′tik): mystical.

telestich (ti.les′tik, tel′i.stik): a poem in which the consecutive letters of the lines spell a name; a form of acrostic.

Tellima (te.lī′ma): a genus of herbs, incl. the false alumroot.

Telina (te.lī′na): a genus of marine bivalves, often handsomely covered.

tellural (te.lū′ral): pert. to the earth. 52.

tellurate (tel′ū.rāt): a salt of telluric acid.

telurgy (tel′ur.ji): the hypothetical action of one's thought upon another person by means of some unknown form of energy.

temeration (tem′er.ā′shun): violation, desecration. 1.

tempean (tem.pē′an): beautiful and charming.

temporaneous (tem′po.rā′ni.us): temporary. Temporal. 52.

temse, tems (tems, -z): a sieve. To sift. 11.

temulence (tem′ū.lens): drunkenness.

temulous (tem′ū.lus): intoxicated. 52.

tenaille (te.nāl′): in fortifications, an outwork in the main ditch between two bastions.

tenaillon (te.nāl′yun): a work constructed on each side of a ravelin in a fortification.

tendance (ten′dans): bestowal of attention; ministration; watchful care. Also, service done to gain favor.

tenent (ten′ent): a tenet. 1. In zoology, adapted for clinging. 52. Var. of tenon, tendon.

tenney (ten′i): var. of tenné, an orange or bright brown color in heraldry.

tentable (ten′ta.bl): temptable.

tentacula (ten.tak′ū.la): tentacles (pl. of *tentaculum*).

tenterbelly (ten′ter.bel′i): one whose gluttony distends his belly. 1.

tentiginous (ten.tij′i.nus): sensuous, lascivious. Also, stiff or strained.

tentigo (ten.tī′go): priapism; also, satyriasis.

tenture (ten′cher): wall decoration, esp. paper. 52.

tephramancy (tef′ra.man′si): divination by studying ashes from an altar.

tephrosis (ti.frō′sis): incineration.

tepidarium (tep.i.dâr′i.um): a warm room for a bath.

tepor (tē′per): gentle heat; tepidness.

teratophobia (ter′a.to.fō′bi.a): fear of having a deformed child.

teratoscopy (ter′a.tos′ko.pi): divination by watching monsters.

terdiurnal (ter′dī.ur′nal): thrice daily.

terebinthine (ter′e.bin′thin): turpentine. 1. Pert. to turpentine, or the terebinth tree, which yields it.

Terebra (ter′i.bra): a genus of marine gastropods, incl. the auger shells.

terebration (ter′i.brā′shun): a boring or drilling; a perforation; a pain. 52.

terek (ter′ek): a sandpiper, breeding in the far north of eastern Europe and Asia and migrating to South Africa and Australia.

tergeminal (ter.jem′i.nal): thrice twin; in botany, forking with three pairs of leaflets.

termen (tur′men): the outer margin of a triangularly shaped wing of an insect.

termin (tur′men): an Algerian measure of length, varying approx. from 2 to 4 inches.

Terminalia (tur′mi.nāl′ya): a Roman festival held on Feb. 23 in honor of Terminus, god of landmarks. A genus of tropical trees and shrubs with entire leaves clustered at the end of the branches, as the Malabar almond. (not cap.) The final segments of the insect abdomen modified to form the external genitalia.

termitarium (tur′mi.târ.i.um): a termites' nest.

termon (tur′men): land belonging to a religious house in Ireland; church land, exempt from secular imposition.

terp (turp): a large artificial mound in the Netherlands providing a refuge for a prehistoric people in a seasonally flooded area.

terriginous (te′rij′i.nus): earthborn; produced by the earth.

tersion (tur′shun): the act of cleaning by rubbing. 52.

tertian (tur′shun): occurring every third day.

tertiate (tur′shi.āt): to examine the thickness of the metal of a piece of ordnance in three places. To do or perform for the third time. 1.

tessaraglot (tes′er.a.glot): one who speaks four languages. Speaking in, written in, or versed in four languages.

testamur (tes.tā′mer): in English universities, a certificate of proficiency.

testar (tes′ter): a West Indian clingfish.

testatum (tes.tā′tum): in law, that portion of the purchase deed which contains the statement of the consideration, covenants for title, and the operative words.

teste (tes′ti): in law, the witnessing or concluding clause of a writ or other precept. Also, a statement used to indicate that what immediately follows is the authority for what precedes.

testudinarious (tes.tū′di.nâr′i.us): like a tortoise shell; arched; vaulted.

testudineous (tes′tū.din′i.us): slow, like a tortoise.

tetradrachma (tet′ra.drak′ma): in ancient Greece, a silver coin of the value of four drachmas. A weight equiv. to 265 grams.

tetralemma (tet′ra.lem′a): an argument analogous to a dilemma but presenting four alternatives in the premise.

Tetrao (tet′ra.ō): a genus of grouse now restricted to the capercaillie (cock of the wood) and closely related forms.

tetrapolis (tet.rap′o.lis): a group or confederation of four cities or towns.

tetraskelion (tet′ra.skēl′yun): a figure having four arms or rays, as the swastika.

tetricity (tet.ris′i.ti): austerity; harshness; gloom. 52.

teutophobia (tū′to.fō′bi.a): fear of Germans or things German.

tew (tū): a state of worried agitation; a stew. To fuss, worry; to work hard. 11A. To beat, belabor; pull, haul. 2.

tewel (tū′el): a hole; a bore; a vent; esp. a pipe, funnel, or chimney, as for smoke. 1.

textorial, textrine (teks. tō′ri.al, teks′-trin): pert. to weaving. 52.

thalassochemistry (tha.las′o.kem′is.tri): the chemistry of the sea.

thalassophobia (tha.las′o.fō′bi.a): fear of the sea.

thalassotherapy (tha.las′o.ther′a.pi): treatment of disease by sea baths, sea air, etc.

thalian (tha.lī′an): pert. to comedy; comic.

thalpotic (thal.pot′ik): pert. to the sensation of warmth.

thanatoid (than′a.toid): deathly; resembling death. Deadly, as a poisonous snake.

thanatology (than′a.tol′o.ji): the study of the effects and treatment of approaching death.

thanatomania (than′a.to.mā′ni.a): suicidal mania. Also, death by autosuggestion.

thanatophobia (than′a.to.fō′bi.a): dread of death.

tharm (thärm): an intestine; the belly. Twisted gut; catgut. 2.

thasophobia (thas′o.fō′bi.a): fear of being seated.

theantropism, theantropy (thi.an′tro.pizm, thi.an′tro.pi): the state of being both god and man. Also, the ascription of human attributes to the Deity.

thelyotokous (thel′i.ot′o.kus): producing only female offspring.

thelymachy (thi.lim′a.ki): war by or among women.

thelyphthoric (thel′if.thôr′ik): corrupting to women.

theocrasy (thi.ok′ra.si): a fusion of the divinities of different religions in the minds of worshipers.

theody (thē′o.di): a hymn praising God.

theogony (thi.og′o.ni): the generations or genealogy of the gods.

theologicophobia (thē′o.loj′iko.fō′bi.a): fear of theology.

theomagical (thē′o.maj′i.kal): pert. to divine wisdom, esp. to miracles claimed to be performed by divine help.

theomancy (thē′o.man′si): divination by the responses of oracles supposed to be divinely inspired.

theomicrist (thi.om′i.krist): one who makes light of God or of divinity.

theopathetic, theopathic (thē′o.pa.-thet′ik, -path-ik): pert. to the experience of the divine illumination.

theophagic, theophagous (thē′o.faj′ik, thi.of′a.gus): practicing theophagy—the sacramental eating of a god, often in the form of an animal.

theophanic (thē′o.fan′ik): pert. to a physical manifestation of a god to man, esp. by incarnation in a human body or appearance in a human form.

theophobia (thē′o.fō′bi.a): phobia against God, or gods.

thereanent (ther′a.nent): with reference to a certain matter.

theriacal, theri.al (thi.rī′a.kal, thēr′i.al): medicinal.

therianthropic (thēr′i.an.throp′ik): combining animal and human form, as the centaur.

theriomancy (thēr′i.o.man′si): divination by observing wild animals.

theriomimicry (thēr′i.o.mim′ik.ri): imitation of animal behavior.

thermotic (ther.mot′ik): pert. to or caused by heat.

theroid (thēr′oid): resembling a beast in nature or habit.

therology (thi.rol′o.ji): the study of mammals; mammalogy.

theromorphic (thēr′o.môr′fik): pert. to an order of primitive reptiles, Pelycosaura, resembling mammals and often having a sail-like crest along the spine.

thersitical (ther.sit′i.kal): loud-mouthed, scurrilous.

thesmothete (thes′mo.thēt): a lawgiver, legislator.

thestreen (thes′trēn): last night. 44.

thig (thig): to beg, borrow. 44A.

thiller (thil′er): the horse that goes between the thills of a vehicle and supports them; also, the last horse in a team, called thill horse.

thirl (thurl): a hole, as for a window. To perforate, drill. 2. To pierce, as with emotion. To subject to thirlage. 62.

thirlage (thur′lij): A requirement that certain tenants carry their grain to a particular mill and pay for the grinding. 62.

thoke (thōk): to lie abed; to idle. 13.

thoral (thō′ral): pert. to a bed; hence, nuptial. 52.

thrack (thrak): to burden; to pack full. 4.

thrail (thrāl): flail. 13.

thrapple (thrap′l): var. of thropple.

thrave (thrāv): a bundle; a quantity; a crowd. 11. A measure for unthreshed grain. 41.

thraw (thrô): throe, agony; a twist or wrench; ill-humor, anger; to be in pain. 44, 44A, 44B, 44C.

Thrax (thraks): in ancient Rome, a Thracian; hence, a gladiator armed like a Thracian.

threap, threep (thrēp): to scold; chide; to affirm, urge acceptance of; to wrangle, haggle; to complain, insist; the act of threaping. 44C.

threed (thrēd): var. of thread. 2.

threne (thrēn): lamentation; threnody; dirge. 1.

threpsology (threp.sol′o.ji): the science of nutrition.

threpterophilia (threp′ter.o.fil′i.a): fondness for nurses.

threptic (threp′tik): pert. to the feeding of insect offspring, esp. among social insects, as ants.

thribble (thrib′l): triple; threefold.

thrid (thrid): var. of thread, esp. the verb. 5.

thrimble (thrim′bl): to handle, esp. to test for quality, or with hesitation; to fumble; to squeeze; to wrestle. 43A.

Thrinax (thrī′naks): a genus of North American fan palms incl. the thatch palm. The leaves are used for thatches, fans, etc.

thrion (thrī′on): the fig-leaf garb of Adam and Eve.

thrip (thrip): a threepenny piece. 26A. To snap (one's fingers) softly. To twitch slightly. Var. of thrips.

thropple (throp′l): the throat, windpipe—esp. used of a horse. 11A.

thurl, thurle (thurl): var. of thirl. 4.

thwaite (thwāt): forest land cleared and converted to tillage, or used as a meadow (chiefly used in place names of England).

thylacine (thī′la.sīn, -sin): a flesh-eating marsupial of Tasmania, slightly larger than a fox and looking like a dog.

tiarella (tī′a.rel′a): a little tiara. (cap) A small genus of chiefly North American herbs having a slender raceme of delicate white flowers, as the false bitterwort.

ticca (tik′a): in India, for hire, as a ticca carriage.

tice (tīs): an enticement. In cricket, a kind of pitched ball. To entice. 2.

tid (tid): the right time or season; mood, humor; ill-temper; to time. 44A. Fond; tender. 13.

tidology (tīd.ol′o.ji): the science of tides.

tift (tift): a puff or gust of wind; a whiff, a sniff; hurry, breathlessness; a state, condition, or mood. 43. To put in order. 2. To pant. 13.

tignum (tig′num): a building material.

tikka (tik′a): in India, a leaf spot of the peanut caused by a fungus.

tikker, ticker (tik′er): a form of interrupter of electric current used in the early days of radio as a detector of continuous waves.

tikolosh (tik′o.losh): a South African water spirit in the form of a little man, friendly to children.

tillot (til′ut): a cloth for wrapping fabric.

tilly (til′i): composed of, or pert. to, till, or clay. Something added for good measure. 51.

timbrology (tim.brol′o.ji): the study of postage stamps.

timon (tī′mon): helm; rudder. 1. (cap) The hero of Shakespeare's Timon of Athens; hence, a misanthrope.

timoneer (tī′mon.ēr): a helmsman. 52.

timothy (tim′o.thi): short for timothy grass.

tinamou (tin′a.moo): a bird of southern Brazil and Argentina similar to the partridge.

tingent (tin′jent): having the power to tinge. 1.

tink (tingk): a tinkle; to tinkle. To tinker. 5.

tintamarre (tin′ta.mär): a confused uproar; din. 9.

tirl (turl): a bout or turn, as at drinking; something that revolves, as a turnstile or wheel; to strip the covering from, divest, unroof; to make a rattling sound with a door latch; to twirl. 44A.

tirocinium (tir′o.sin′i.um): apprenticeship. A band of raw recruits.

tither (tīth′er): one who collects, pays, or advocates the payment of tithes.

tiver (tiv′er): red ocher. 4.

tjaele (chā′li): permafrost.

tmema (tmē′ma): a segment; a section. 52.

tnoyim (tnoi.im): a Jewish engagement party, or a marital agreement made at such a party.

toatoa (tō′a.tō′a): a striking New Zealand evergreen tree with whorled branches, often cultivated for ornament.

tock (tok): an African hornbill.

toco, toko (tō′kō): a flogging, thrashing; sometimes a tongue-lashing. 23. A large South American toucan.

tocophobia (tō′kō.fō′bi.a): fear of pregnancy or childbirth.

toddick (tod′ik): a very small quantity.

toison (twa.zoN′): a sheep's fleece.

toke (tōk): a puff on a cigarette, espec. a marijuana cigarette. 22.

toko (tō′kō): in the Dutch East Indies, a shop or store, usu. one kept by Chinese.

tolpatch (tol′pach): in Carlyle's works, a foot soldier.

toluic (to.lū′ik, tol′ū.ik): pert. to four isomeric acids.

tolutiloquy (tol′ū.til′o.kwi): a voluble speech.

tombolo (tom′bo.lō): a bar or reef of sand or gravel connecting an island to the mainland.

tomium (tō′mi.um): the cutting edge of the bill of a bird.

tomnoddy (tom′nod′i): a simpleton. A kind of puffin. 44A.

tomomania (tō′mo.mā′ni.a): a mania for surgery.

tonant (tō′nant): making a thundering noise.

tondino (ton.dē′no): a metal disk for striking a coin. A small *tondo*.

tondo (ton′dō): a circular painting. A sculptured medallion.

tonga (tong′ga): a light two-wheeled carriage in India, drawn by one horse. A creeper living on the surface of other plants, used in Malaysian folk medicine. Formerly, a pharmaceutical drug containing tonga. (cap) Any of several Bantu-speaking peoples in parts of East Africa.

tonish, tonnish (ton′ish): stylish, chic.

tonitruophobia (to.nit′roo.o.fō′bi.a): fear of thunder.

toom (toom): empty. 45. Lank; lean; lacking wit; empty-sounding; a dumping ground. 44. To empty, pour. 43. Leisure; spare time. 1.

tootlish (toot′lish): childish; muttering, as an aged person. 11.

topia (tō′pi.a): a mural of Roman times representing fanciful landscapes.

toph (tōf): tufa; travertine; porous rock. A Hebrew musical instrument resembling a timbrel.

tophaceous (to.fā′shus): gritty, sandy, rough, stony.

topolatry (to.pol′a.tri): worship of a place, or excessive reverence for it. 52.

topomancy (tō′po.man′si): divination by land contours.

topophobia (tō′po.fō′bi.a): a morbid fear of certain places.

topopolitan (tō.po.pol′i.tan): limited to a certain area (as opposed to cosmopolitan).

torcel (tôr′sel): the larva of the South American botfly, living beneath the human skin.

torcular (tôr′kū.lar): a wine press. 1. A surgeon's tourniquet.

toreumatography (to.roo′ma.tog′ra.fi): a description of work wrought in metal by embossing, chasing, etc.

torfaceous (tôr.fā′shus): turflike. 52.

toril (to.rēl′): in bullfighting, a corral from which the bull enters the ring.

torminous (tôr′mi.nus): afflicted with the gripes.

toro (tō′rō): a bull. A cowfish. A food fish of the tropical American coasts, the cavalla. A New Zealand tree with reddish wood used for inlaying.

torotoro (tō′ro.tō′rō): a kingfisher of New Guinea, having an orange beak.

torp (tôrp): a croft; a small leased farm. Short for torpedo, torpedoman.

torpescent (tôr.pes′ent): becoming torrid.

torpify (tôr′pi.fī): to make torpid; stupefy.

torpillage (tôr′pi.yäzh): electric shock treatment.

torrefy (tôr′i.fī): to heat; to dry or roast by a fire; scorch.

torrentine (tôr′en.tin, to.ren′tin, -in): torrential. 52.

torse (tôrs): a torso. Twisted spirally.

torta (tôr′ta): a flat heap of moist, crushed silver ore ready for further processing.

tortility (tôr.til′i.ti): the state of being twisted, coiled, or twistable.

tosh (tosh): bosh; sheer nonsense. Tidy; neat. To make tidy. 44.

tossel (tos′el): var. of tassel. 2.

tossut (tos′ut): the tunnel of an igloo.

tosy (tō′zi): slightly intoxicated; also, snug; comforting. 44.

tota (tō′ta): the grivet monkey.

totora (to.tō′ra): a tall South American cattail having shoots edible when new, and reedy stems yielding fiber useful for making fences, boats, etc.

tottle (tot′l): dial. var. of toddle; to walk with short tottering steps, as a child.

touse, towse (touz): a noisy disturbance; ado, fuss; to pull or handle roughly; to dishevel. 11.

towdie (tou′di): a young hen that has not yet laid; a young unmarried girl. 44.

toxicoid (tok′si.koid): like poison.

toxophily (tok.sof′i.li): love of archery.

toze (tōz): to tease, comb; to pull about, esp. in disentangling. 9.

tozee (tōz′i): in the Scottish game of curling, the mark aimed at by players who hurl heavy stones along a smooth stretch of ice.

trabea (trā′bi.a): a type of Roman toga with a border of colored stripes.

tractoration (trak′to.rā′shun): a former process of drawing two small rods of different metals over an affected part of the body to reduce pain or local inflammation.

tradal (trād′al): commercial.

traditive (trad′i.tiv): pert. to tradition; transmitted or transmissible by tradition.

traduction (tra.duk′shun): defamation; slander. Also, the repetition of a word or term with a change in sense for rhetorical effect. Something transmitted; esp., a tradition.

tragacanthin (trag′a.kan′thin): in chemistry, a substance obtained from certain gums that swell to form a gel.

tragicomipastoral (traj′i.kom′i.pas′-tor.al): pert. to or combining tragic, comic, and pastoral poetry. 52.

traik (trāk): to waste away, break down. To stroll, lounge, follow; a plague, pest;

a fatiguing journey; flesh of a sheep that died by accident or disease; a fatiguing tramp or journey. 44A. Fatigue, misfortune. 1.

traiky (trā′ki): exhausted; wasted away. 44A.

traiteur (tre.tur′): a restaurateur.

tralatitious (tra.la.tish′us): metaphorical; figurative; as the primary and *tralatitious* meanings of a word. Also, passed along; handed down from generation to generation; traditional.

tralucent (tra.lū′sent): translucent. 1.

trampot (tram′pot): in milling, the step supporting the lower end of a millstone spindle.

trank (trangk): an oblong piece of skin from which glove shapes are cut.

tranky (trang′ki): a small undecked sailing vessel used in the Persian Gulf.

transfuge (trans′fūj): a deserter; an apostate. 52.

transilience (tran.sil′yens): the quality of passing, as by a leap, from one thing to another, marked by abrupt change or variation.

translucid (trans.lū′sid): translucent.

translunar (trans.loo′ner): in or toward the direction of the moon.

transpontine (trans.pon′tīn, -tin): on the other side of the bridge; specif. in London, south of the Thames. Resembling cheap melodramas once popular there.

THESTREEN

"Pray tell me why women
Are like a persimmon?"
A lad thestreen did pipe.
And I answered thestreen,
"They're astringent when green,
But remarkably sweet when ripe."

---

transshape (trans.shāp′): to transform.

transumption (tran.sump′shun): a transference; a metaphor. 1.

transvase (trans.vās′): to pour out of one vessel into another.

transversus (trans.vur′sus): in anatomy, any of several small transverse muscles.

transvert (trans.vurt′): to change or turn about; transform. 1.

trape (trāp): traipse. 2.

trappoid, trappous (trap′oid, -us): pert. to traprock.

traulism (trô′lizm): a stammering or stuttering.

traumatophobia (trô′mat.o.fō′bi.a): fear of injury.

travale (tra.val′, tra.val′i): a vibrant sound produced by rubbing the head of a tambourine with a wet finger or thumb.

tremellose (trem′e.lōs): gelatinous.

tremolant (trem′o.lant): having a vibrant, tremolo note, as certain organ pipes. Such a pipe.

trenchermate (tren′cher.māt): a messmate, eating companion.

trendle (tren′dl): a circular object, as a wheel, hoop, or spindle; a trundle. 52. A large, round, shallow tub, trough, or vessel. 13.

trental (tren′tal): in the Roman Catholic Church, a series of thirty masses for the dead, celebrated one daily, or formerly sometimes all in one day.

trepidity (tre.pid′i.ti): a state of alarm or trembling agitation; trepidation.

tresaiel, tresayle (tres.āl′, tres′īl): a grandfather's grandfather. 6.

tressure (tresh′er): a headdress, as a caul or ribbon; an arrangement of hair; coiffure. 1. A double-orle design within the border of a heraldic bearing. An additional border or ornamental enclosure in numismatology.

tret (tret): at one time, a weight allowance to purchasers for waste or refuse.

trewsman (trōōz′man): a Highlander. 44.

trialogue (trī′a.log): a colloquy between three persons.

tribometer (trī.bom′e.ter): an instrument for measuring sliding friction.

tricerion (trī.sē′ri.on): a three-branched candlestick symbolizing the Trinity.

trichology (tri.kol′o.ji): the science treating of the hair.

trichotillomania (trik.o.til′o.mā′ni.a): insane desire to pull out one's hair.

trigamy (trig′a.mi): bigamy plus one.

trigintal (trī.jin′tal): trental.

trigonal (trig′o.nal): triangular.

trigrammatic, trigrammic (trī′gra.mat.ik, trī.gram′ik): pert. to a three-letter inscription or a three-line figure.

trihemeral (trī.hem′er.al): lasting three days. 52.

trilith, trilithon (trī′lith, tril′i.thon): a monument consisting of two upright megaliths carrying a third as a lintel.

trillet (tril′et): a slight trill.

trillibub (tril′i.bub): tripe; a trifle. 2.

Trillium (tril′i.um): a genus of herbs with short rootstocks and an erect stem, chiefly North American, incl. the wakerobin.

trimenon (trī′me.non): a three-month period.

trinervate (trī.nur′vāt): trineural; three-nerved.

tringle (tring′gl): in architecture, a narrow straight molding, usu. of square section; a fillet. A low guardrail on a gun platform to keep the trucks of the gun carriage from running off.

tringoid (tring′goid): pert. to the sandpipers.

trink (tringk): a kind of fishing net. 1. A trench; channel. 44.

Trinkgeld (tringk′gelt): a gratuity, pourboire, tip.

trioctile (trī.ok′til): the aspect of two planets with regard to the earth when three octants (135°) apart.

triodion, triodium (trī.ō′di.on, -um): in the Eastern church, a liturgical book containing the offices from the fourth Sunday before Lent to Easter eve.

trior (trī′er): a person appointed by law to try challenges of jurors; (var. of *trier*).

tripennate (trī.pen′āt): having three sets of leaves on each side of a common leafstalk; tripinnate.

triphibious (trī.fib′i.us): at home in the sea, on the land, or in the air.

triphony (trif′o.ni): in medieval music, diaphony for three voice parts.

triplasian (trī.plā′zhun): threefold. 52.

tripody (trip′o.di): in prosody, a unit of three feet.

trippant (trip′ant): of a heraldic lion or other beast, walking with the farther forepaw raised; passant.

tripsis (trip′sis): the act of giving a shampoo or a massage. Also, in medicine, the act of rubbing or grinding to a very fine powder; trituration.

tripterous (trip′ter.us): three-winged, as certain fruits or seeds.

triptote (trip′tōt): a noun having only three cases.

tripudiation (trī.pū′di.ā′shun): dancing, rejoicing. 52.

trisection (trī.sek′shun): the division of a thing into three parts.

trisectrix (trī.sek′triks): in geometry, a curve that trisects an arbitrary angle.

triskaidekaphobia (tris′kī.dek′a.fō′bi.a): morbid fear of the number 13.

trispast, trispaston, (trī′spast, tri.spas′ton): an ancient machine with three pulleys acting together to raise great weights.

tristiloquy (tris.til′o.kwi): a dull, gloomy speech or way of speaking.

trisulcate (trī.sul′kāt): having three furrows, forks, prongs, or the like.

tritagonist (trī.tag′o.nist): in ancient Greek plays, the third-ranked actor.

tritavia (trit′a.vē′a): a great-grandmother's great-grandmother. 6.

tritavus (trit′a.vus): a great-grandfather's great-grandfather. 6.

trithing (trī′thing): one of the three administrative jurisdictions into which the county of York, in England, is divided; a riding. The name was also given to divisions in colonial Pennsylvania and Long Island.

troat (trōt): the cry of a buck in rutting time. To troat.

troca (trō′ka): a top shell used to make pearl buttons.

trochilic (tro.kil′ik): the science of rotary motion. 1. Pert. to rotary motion.

trochiscus (tro.kis′kus): a kind of tablet or lozenge.

trochomancy (trō′ko.man′si): divination by studying wheel tracks.

troco (trō′kō): an old English game played on a lawn, using wooden balls and cues; also called lawn billiards.

trogue (trōg): in mining, a wooden trough, forming a drain (var. of trough). 30.

troilism (troi′lizm): three-way sex.

troke (trōk): to barter or negotiate; a barter; trash. 44.

trollylolly (trol′i.lol′i): a song refrain, suggesting careless gaiety. Coarse lace.

tromba (trom′ba): a trumpet, or an organ stop imitating the tone quality of a trumpet.

trophaeum (tro.fē′um): a Greek or Roman monument commemorating a victory.

tropophobia (trō′po.fō′bi.a): fear of change.

tropophilous (tro.pof′i.lus): thriving under seasonal changes, as of temperature or humidity.

trucidation (trōō′si.dā′shun): slaughter.

trummel (trum′l): a round tin box for cake or bread. 28.

trusion (trōō′zhun): act of pushing or shoving. 52.

trussell (trus′el): the upper or reverse die used in coining. 1.

trutinate (trōō′ti.nāt): to weigh; balance; consider.

truttaceous (tru.tā′shus): pert. to or like a trout.

tsine (tsīn): the banteng, a wild ox of the Malay peninsula and archipelago.

tsiology (tsi.ol′o.ji): a dissertation on tea.

tsuba (tsōō′ba): the metal guard of a Japanese sword, often elaborately decorated.

tubar (tū′ber): tubular.

tubicinate (tū.bis′i.nāt): to blow a trumpet.

tucky (tuk′i): the common spatterdock, or yellow water lily, of North America.

tui (tōō′i): a New Zealand honey eater, predominantly glossy black with white markings. It is a notable mimic and often kept as a cage bird. Also called parson bird.

tumeric (tū.mer′ik): var. of *turmeric*.

tump (tump): a small rise of ground; a mound, molehill, etc.; a clump of vegetation, esp. one making a dry spot in a swamp. 30.

tumulate (tū′mū.lāt): to entomb.

tunk (tungk): rap; thump. 11.

tupman (tup′man): a man who breeds or deals in rams. 13.

turbitteen (tur′bi.tēn): a type of Oriental frilled pigeon.

turfite (turf′īt): a horse-racing addict. 26.

turkle (tur′kl): turtle. 11.

turmeric (ter.mer'ik): an East Indian herb; its aromatic rootstock, used in powdered form as a condiment, esp. in curry powder.

turncock (turn'kok): a stopcock with a plug that is turned in opening and closing.

turp (turp): to rub with turpentine. 21.

turriculate (tu.rik'ū.lāt): having, or formed like, a turret.

tussal (tus'el): pert. to a cough.

tussive (tus'iv): *tussal.*

tute (tūt): to tutor. 58.

tutrix (tū'triks): tutoress. 52.

tuza (tōō'sa, tū'za): a pocket gopher, common in Mexico.

tuzzymuzzy (tuz'i.muz'i): a garland of flowers, nosegay. 9.

twangle (twang'gl): to twang. 52.

twank (twangk): to sound like a twang sharply cut off; to slap smartly.

twattle (twät'l): to talk idly; chatter, prate, twaddle. 13.

tweel (twēl): a clay covering for the mouth of a glass furnace. Also, Scot. var. of *twill.*

twiddlepoop (twid'l.pōōp): an effeminate-appearing man.

twink (twingk): the chaffinch. 31. A wink, a twinkling; to wink, to twinkle; to punish, thrash. 13.

twinter (twin'ter): a sheep two years old; also applied to cattle and horses. 44C.

tychism (tī'kizm): a theory of evolution which holds that variation may be purely fortuitous.

Tychonic (tī.kon'ik): pert. to the 17th-century Danish astronomer Tycho Brahe or his system of astronomy.

tyg (tig): a ceramic drinking cup with two or more handles.

tymbal (tim'bal): var. of timbal.

tymp (timp): the mouth of a blast-furnace hearth.

typhonic (tī.fon'ik): pert. to a typhoon.

typtology (tip.tol'o.ji): the theory or lore of spirit rappings.

tyromancy (tī'ro.man'si): divination by watching the coagulation of cheese.

U

uakari (wa.kä'ri): *ouakari.*

uayeb (wa.yeb'): in the Mayan calendar, the five days added at the end of each year to complete 365 days.

uberty (ū'ber.ti): fruitfulness; plenty.

ubiety (ū.bī'e.ti): the quality or state of being in a place. Location. The abstract quality of whereness.

ubiquarian, ubiquitarian (u'bi.kwâr'i.an, -bik'wi.târ'i.an): ubiquitous. 52. (cap) One of a school of Lutheran divines which held that, Christ being omnipresent, his body is everywhere, esp. in the Eucharist.

ucalegon (ū.kal'e.gon): a neighbor whose house is on fire.

udometer (ū.dom'e.ter): a rain gauge.

ufologist (u.fol'o.jist): a student of flying saucers.

ughten (ut'en): morning twilight. 1.

uitlander (oit'lan'der, ut-): formerly, in South Africa, a foreigner, esp. a Briton residing in the Transvaal or the Orange Free State.

ula (ū'la): the gums.

ulcuscle, ulcuscule (ul'kus'l, ul.kus'kūl): a little ulcer. 52.

uliginose, uliginous (ū.lij'i.nōs, -nus): muddy; oozy; swampy. Also, growing in many places.

ultion (ul'shun): revenge. 1.

ultraantidisestablishmentarianism (ul'tra.an'ti.dis'es.tab'lish.men.târ'i.a.nizm): Gladstone's reported term for extreme opposition to sundering the relationship between state and established church.

ultracrepidarian (ul'tra.krep'i.dâr'i.an): presumptuous.

ultrafidian (ul'tra.fid'i.an): gullible.

ultroneous (ul.trō'ni.us): spontaneous; voluntary.

ulu (ōō'lōō): an Eskimo woman's knife resembling a food-chopper with a crescent blade. An Indian grass used for forage.

ulua (ōō.lōō'a): any of several large fishes of Hawaiian waters highly prized for food and sport.

umble (um'bl): singular form of *umbles* (var. of *numbles*).

umbrette (um.bret'): an African wading bird allied to the storks and herons.

umbriferous (um.brif'er.us): casting a shade; umbrageous.

umu (ōō'mōō): in Polynesia, a native earth oven or baking pit for cooking food wrapped in leaves.

Una (ōō'na): a lovely lady in Spenser's *Faerie Queene* intended as a personification of Truth.

unau (ū'nō, ōō'nou): the two-toed sloth.

uncular (ūng'kū.lar): avuncular. 52.

underfong (un'der.fong): to undertake; receive; sustain. 1. In Spenser, to entrap.

undernim (un'der.nim): to perceive; understand; undertake; rebuke; seize. 1. In Spenser, to ensnare; circumvent; trap.

underspurleather (un'der.spur'leth'er): a humble attendant or underling. 9.

undinism (un'din.izm): the arousal of erotic thoughts by the sight, sound, or touch of water.

unicity (ū.nis'i.ti): uniqueness.

unicum (ū'ni.kum): a thing unique in its kind; esp. a sole existing exemplar (as of writing).

unigenous (ū.nij'i.nus): in biology, being of one and the same kind.

unthrid (un.thrid'): unthread. 9A.

untrowable (un.trō'a.bl): incredible. 1.

upasian (ū.pā'zhun): deadly, as the sap of the upas tree of Java.

upbreak (up.brāk'): to break up or open. To force a way up or to the surface.

URVAS ARE CRABBY ABOUT AMBROSIA

In ancient days the Asian mongoose Urva
   Climbed high Olympus on a quest for crab,
His food of choice. He came across Minerva,
   And asked her if she'd rustle up a dab.
But stay-at-home Minerva thought he meant
   Ambrosia, which delights immortal gods.
She brought a bowlful, to his discontent;
   They parted angry, and are still at odds.
Ambrosia? Pooh! For Urva, uberty
Means *crab;* and I wholeheartedly agree.

---

upeygan (ōō.pā'gan): the black rhinoceros.

uranism (ū'ra.nizm): male homosexuality.

uranography (ū.ra.nog'ra.fi): a description of heaven; the science of describing the heavens and the heavenly bodies.

uranophobia (ū.ra.no.fō'bi.a): fear of heaven or the sky.

urbacity (er.bas'i.ti): excess of pride in one's city.

urbicolous (er.bik'o.lus): living in a city.

urethrophobia (ū.rē'thro.fō'bi.a): aversion to the urethra.

urimancy (ū'ri.man'si): divination by the examination of urine.

urning (ur'ning): a male homosexual.

Uro (ōō'rō): an Indian of a tribe of primitive culture, living in western Bolivia.

ursal (ur'sal): churlish; bearish in disposition. 52.

ursoid (ur'soid): bearlike.

urson (ur'son): the Canada porcupine.

Ursus (ur'sus): a genus now commonly restricted to the European brown bear and its allies, incl. the American grizzly bear.

urubu (ōō'rōō.bōō): the black vulture.

urus (ū'rus): a large, long-horned wild ox of the German forests, now extinct, believed to be the ancestor of the domestic ox.

urva (ur'va): the crab-eating mongoose of southeastern Asia. It has black fur with white at the tip of each hair, and a white streak extends from the mouth to the shoulder.

ustion (us'chun): cauterization. 52.

V

vaccary (vak′a.ri): a cow or dairy building; a cow pasture. 2.

vaccimulgence (vak.si.mul′jens): the milking of cows.

vacuist (vak′ū.ist): one who maintains that nature has vacuums.

vade (vād): to go away, leave. (52, except as Latin imperative—*go hence! Depart!*)

vagitus (va.jī′tus): the cry of the just-born.

vairé, vaireé (vā.rā′): pert. to a fur (prob. squirrel) much used in medieval times to line and trim robes. Also, pert. to a heraldic representation of fur.

valence, valency (vā′lens, vā′len.si): power; importance; value. In chemistry and physics, the degree of combining power of an element or radical.

valeta (va.lā′ta, -lē′ta): a dance in slow waltz time.

vali (val′i): a governor general of a vilayet, an administrative division of Turkey. (cap) In Norse mythology, the son of Odin and avenger of Balder. Var. of *Bali*.

vallary (val′a.ri): designating a palisade crown of gold bestowed by the Romans on the soldier who first surmounted the rampart and broke into the enemy's camp. Such a crown in heraldry.

vallum (val′um): a Roman rampart, esp. one set with a palisade or stakes. Also, the combination of earthworks and ditch that follows the line of Hadrian's Wall in Britain.

vancourier (van′koo.rēr): an advance man. 9.

Vanda (van′da): a genus of Indo-Malayan orchids. (not cap) A plant of this genus. A pale purple to pale reddish-purple color.

vanfoss (van′fos): in fortifications, a ditch for defense usu. filled with water.

vanillism (va.nil′izm): a morbid skin condition caused by handling vanilla.

vaniloquy (va.nil′o.kwi): a vain and foolish speech.

vannet (van′et): in heraldry, an open scallop shell.

vapulation (vap′ū.lā′shun): the act of beating or flogging.

vare (vār): a weasel. A staff, a wand. 1.

varicelloid (vâr′i.sel′oid): resembling chicken pox.

varietist (va.rī′e.tist): one who varies from the norm in attitudes, habits, desires, etc.

variole (vâr′i.ōl): something resembling a smallpox marking; a small pit.

varsal (vär′sal): dial. corruption of *universal*.

varsovienne (vär′so.vyen): a dance similar to the polka or mazurka, popular in the 19th century.

vasal (vā′sal): pert. to an anatomical vessel, as a vein or artery.

vastation (vas.tā′shun): devastation. 1. Purification through fire.

vates (vā′tis): among the Gauls, a learned class of soothsayers, prophets, and seers.

vaticide (vat′i.sīd): the murder of a prophet.

vaultage (vôl′tij): a vaulted place; an arched cellar.

Vayu (va.yoo′): in Vedic mythology, the wind-god. In the Sanskrit epic Ramayana, the father of Hanuman, the monkey god.

vectitation (vek′ti.tā′shun): the act of carrying or being carried. 52.

vega (vā′ga): in Spanish America and the Philippines, a fertile meadow.

Vega (vē′ga): a brilliant star in the constellation Lyra.

vegete (vi.jet′): lively, healthy; flourishing. 52.

velarian (vi.lâr′i.an): in ancient Rome, the awning of an amphitheater.

veliferous (vi.lif′er.us): carrying or bearing sails.

veligerous (vi.lij′er.us): pert. to a larval mollusk in the stage where it has developed its velum, a swimming organ.

A WORD OF APPRECIATION FROM AN AMATEUR OF THE CLASSIC TONGUES

There's something fine in Latin. Something—oh, How should I say it? Something like . . . you know . . .
Well, *fine!* Like, I could call a man
(A sucker, say)—an *ultrafidian!*

And Greek's great too. They've even got a noun For "neighbor with a house that's burning down"! I kid you not. They turn the firehose on, And shout across, "Hi there, *ucalegon!*"

I'm for the classics. Like . . . you'll think I'm loony . . .
But honey, just you listen. You're my *unicumissimus*—my very most unique!
Hey, Latin's good for grammar. So is Greek.

---

velitation (vel′i.tā′shun): a minor battle; a skirmish.

vellicative (vel′i.kā′tiv): in medicine, causing to twitch.

velocimeter (vel′o.sim′e.ter): an apparatus for measuring speed, as of machinery or vessels, or esp. of projectiles.

venditation (ven′di.tā′shun): a display as if for sale. 52.

veneficious (ven′i.fish′us): acting by poison; used in poisoning or in sorcery. 52.

venenation (ven′i.nā′shun): the act of poisoning. The condition of being poisoned.

veneniferous (ven′i.nif′er.us): bearing or transporting poison.

venin (ven′in): poison. 1. Any of a class of toxic substances in snake venom.

venireman (ve.nī′re.man): a juror.

ventoseness (ven.tōs′nes): flatulence, windiness. 52.

ventripotent (ven.trip′o.tent): fat-bellied; also, gluttonous.

venust (vi.nust′): beautiful; elegant; Venus-like. 1.

verbasco (ver.bas′kō): the *mullein*.

verbicide (vur′bi.sīd): the mangling of words.

verbigerate (ver.bij′er.āt): to talk; chat. 1. To be unable to stop repeating words.

verbophobia (vur′bo.fō′bi.a): fear of words.

verd (vurd): green, greenness, freshness. 9.

verecund (ver′i.kund): bashful, modest.

veridical (vi.rid′i.kal): truthful, veracious, genuine.

veriloquy (vi.ril′o.kwi): truthful speech.

vermeology (vur′mi.ol′o.ji): the study of worms. 52.

verminophobia (vur.min.o.fō′bi.a): fear of vermin.

vernality (ver.nal′i.ti): the state of being springlike. 52.

vernant (vur′nant): flourishing, as in spring; vernal. 52.

verset (ver′set): a short verse, esp. one from the Bible, the Koran, or some other book regarded as holy.

versor (vur′sor): in geometry, the turning factor of a quaternion (if, unlike me, you know what *that* means).

verutum (vi.roo′tum): a short spear or dart carried by the Roman light infantry.

vervel (vur′vel): a ring attached to a bird's leg for securing the bird to its perch.

vespertilian (ves′per.til′yun): batlike.

vespertine (ves′per.tīn, -tin): pert. to the evening.

vespoid (ves′poid): pert. to the wasps.

vetitive (vet′i.tiv): prohibiting; having or pert. to the power of vetoing.

vettura (vet.too′ra): an Italian four-wheeled carriage; a hackney coach.

vetturino (vet′too.rē′nō): one who drives a vettura or has one for hire.

vetust (vi.tust′): venerable from antiquity; ancient; old. 52.

viaggiatory (vi.aj′i.a.tō′ri): traveling; restlessly moving around. 52.

viagram (vī′a.gram): a chart produced by a *viagraph*.

viagraph (vī′a.graf): an instrument on wheels used to determine the relative smoothness or roughness of pavement surfaces.

viameter (vī.am′e.ter): an odometer to measure distance on roads.

viator (vī.ā′tor): a traveler.

vibex (vī′beks): a linear bruise.

vibratiunculation (vi.brāt′i.ung′kū.lā′shun): a slight vibration. 52.

viduous (vid′ū.us): widowed; bereaved. 52.

vigesimation (vī.jes′i.mā′shun): the act of killing every twentieth man. 52.

vihara (vi.hä′ra): in ancient India, a pleasure garden, esp. the precincts of temples and monasteries; hence, a Buddhist monastery or temple.

vill (vil): in the feudal system, a township, or division of a hundred. Hence, a village. A villa. 1.

villanella (vil′a.nel′a): an old rustic dance; its music. An Italian rustic song, precursor to the stricter canzonet and madrigal.

villanette (vil′a.net): a small villa. 52.

villeggiatura (vi.lej′i.a.too̅′ra): a stay at a villa; occasionally, the villa itself.

vimineous (vi.min′i.us): pert. to twigs; woven of twigs. Producing long slender twigs or shoots.

vinal (vī′nal): of or from wine; vinous.

vindemial (vin.dē′mi.al): pert. to a vintage.

vindemiation (vin.dē′mi.ā′shun): a gathering of grapes for wine, or a harvesting of fruit.

vinea (vin′i.a): in Roman warfare, a shedlike structure serving as protection to besiegers.

vinification (vin′i.fi.kā′shun): the conversion of fruit juice into alcohol by fermentation.

vinny (vin′i): moldy. 53.

vinquish (ving′kwish): dial. var. of vanquish, a wasting disease in sheep, attributed to feeding on certain plants. 44.

vint (vint): a card game similar to auction bridge.

vintry (vin′tri): a place where wine is sold or stored.

violescent (vī′o.les′ent): tending to a violet color.

VIGESIMATION

Vigesimation's not just *hurting,*
  But *killing* every twentieth
Man captured. So I count your flirting
  As mere vigesimation, Beth.

Yet though you slay but one in twenty,
  And boast how merciful you've been,
I fear the damage done is plenty
  To those residual nineteen.

---

viparious (vī′pâr′i.us): a mistaken form of vivacious in the sense of "tenacious of life." 52.

viperine (vī′per.īn, -in): pert. to a viper; venomous.

vire (vīr): an arrow feathered so as to acquire a rotary motion.

virent (vī′rent): green; not withered. 52.

viridarium (vir′i.dâr′i.um): a garden in an ancient Roman villa.

virilescence (vir′i.les′ens): among certain animals, the acquiring of characteristics more or less like those of the male, often observed in barren or old females.

viripotent (vir′i.pō′tent): of a man, sexually mature.

virole (vi.rōl′): in heraldry, a ring surrounding a bugle or hunting horn.

viron (vī′ron): a circuit; to environ, encircle. 1.

virose (vī′ros, vī.rōs′): virulent; poisonous.

vis (vis): a brief visit. 1. Vis-a-vis. 52. Force, vigor.

viscin (vis′in): a clear, sticky, tasteless substance from the sap of the mistletoe or holly.

visne (vēn, vē′ni): vicinage; in law, venue.

vison (vī′sun): the American mink.

vitilitigate (vit′i.lit′i.gāt): to wrangle. 1.

vitiosity (vish′i.os′i.ti): viciousness; depravity.

vitricophobia (vit′ri.ko.fō′bi.a): fear of one's stepfather.

vituline (vit′ū.līn, -lin): pert. to a calf, or veal.

vivandier (ve′van′dyā): in continental armies, esp. the French, a sutler.

vivandière (vi.van′dyâr): a female sutler.

viviparous (vī.vip′a.rus): producing living young.

vivisepulture (viv′i.sep′ul.cher): the practice of burying people alive.

vocabulation (vo.kab′ū.lā′shun): selection or use of words. 52.

Volapuk (vō′la.puk): an international language, based on English, developed in the 19th century.

volery (vol′er′i): a large birdcage; an aviary; the birds in an aviary; a flight or flock of birds.

volitient (vo.lish′ent): exercising free will.

voltigeur (vôl′ti.zhur): a sharpshooter in the French military. 1. A tumbler, leaper, vaulter.

volucrine (vol′ū.krīn, -krin): pert. to birds.

volumnist (vol′um.nist): one who writes a volume.

voortrekker (fōr′trek′er): in South Africa, a pioneer; esp. (cap) a Boer who trekked from the Cape Colony to the Transvaal in 1834–37.

voraginous (vo.raj′i.nus): pert. to a gulf; hence, devouring. 52.

vorago (vo.rā′gō): a gulf; an abyss.

vorant (vō′rant): in heraldry, (a creature) shown in the act of devouring.

vorticism (vôr′ti.sizm): in post-Impressionist art, emphasis on the complexity of modern civilization, incl. machines.

vortiginous (vôr.tij′i.nus): moving rapidly around a center; vortical; whirling.

votaress, votress (vō′ta.res, vō′tres): a female votary. A woman voter. 52.

vouchee (vouch′i): one called into court to warrant or defend a title. One cited as an authority or sponsor.

vouge (voo̅zh): a long-handled, halberd-like weapon of the later Middle Ages.

vraisemblance (vrā′sän′bläns): the appearance of truth; verisimilitude.

vrille (vril): in aviation, a deliberate spinning nose dive.

vuggy (vug′i): pert. to vugs, small unfilled cavities in a lode or in the rock around it.

vulnerative, vulnific (vul′ner.ā′tiv, vul.nif′ik): causing wounds.

vulpecular (vul.pek′ū.lar): pert. to a fox, esp. a young one; vulpine.

W

wabby (wä′bi): the red-throated loon.

wabe, (wä′bi): the huisache, a shrub of the southern U.S. and tropical regions, bearing fragrant flowers used for making perfume.

wabeno (wô.bē′nō): a magician; specif., one of a class of shamans among the Ojibway Indians.

wack (wak): damp; clammy. 44.

Waco (wā′kō): an Indian of a small tribe of the Wichita confederacy in Texas.

wadget (waj′et): a little bundle. 11.

waggel (wag′el): a black-backed gull in immature plumage. 30.

waghalter (wag′hôl′ter): a rogue, rascal; one likely to be hanged. 1.

wagwag (wag′wag): a polishing device used by watchmakers.

walla-walla (wôl′a.wôl′a): an unintelligible sound produced by many people talking at once. (cap) An Indian people of the Pacific Northwest; a city of Washington state.

wallydrag (wāl′i.drag, wol-): the youngest of the litter; the runt. 44.

wally-gowdy (wāl′i.gō′di, gōōd′i): in endearment, a precious jewel or ornament. 44.

walm (wälm): to well up, gush forth. 9.

wamefoo, wamefu (wām′fōō): a bellyful. 43.

wampee (wäm′pi): the pickerelweed. 35.

wampus (wäm′pus): a heavy, stupid, sluggish person; sometimes, a person objectionable for any reason. 21.

Wanderjahr (vän′der.yär, wän′der.yär): a year of traveling before settling down.

waniand (wä′ni.and): the waning moon, regarded as unlucky. 1.

wankapin (wäng′ka.pin): an American lotus, the water chinquapin. Its edible nutlike seed.

wantwit (wänt′wit, wônt′wit): a fool; foolish, idiotic.

wappenschaw (wap′en.shaw): a rifle-shooting contest. 44.

wappenschawing (wap′en.shô′ing): a military muster or review. 44.

wapperjawed (wäp′er.jôd): having crooked jaws, or sometimes an undershot jaw. 28.

waringin (wor′in.jin): a common fig tree of India, with inedible fruit.

warmouth (wôr′mouth): a freshwater sunfish of the eastern United States.

wase (wāz): a wisp or bundle of hay or straw; a pad, as of straw to support a burden on the head. 2. A torch. 1.

waterchat (wâ′ter.chat): any of numerous South American flycatchers. A forktail.

wayman (wā.man): a shipwright who prepares and lays launching ways. A laborer who lays tracks or keeps them in repair.

wayzgoose (wāz′gōōs): in Britain, a printers' annual holiday or entertainment.

weanel (wēn′el): weanling. 2.

weatherfend (weth′er.fend): in Shakespeare, to defend from the weather; to shelter.

wede (wēd): shrivelled. 11. To be or become mad; to be wild with anger or desire; to rage. 1.

weet (wēt): the call of any of several birds, as the European sandpiper; also, the bird itself. A sound imitative of the cry of a small bird. To weet.

weeze (wēz): to ooze. 44C.

wegotism (wē′got.izm): excessive use of the editorial *we*. 58.

wem (wem): a spot, stain, flaw. 10.

wergild (wur′gild): in Anglo-Saxon and Germanic law, the price paid by a killer's family to the family of the victim to prevent a blood feud.

wey (wā): any of several local British measures of weight. Also, to move; agitate. 1.

whabby (hwä′bi): *wabby*.

whally (hwä′li): having a light-colored iris. 52.

whangdoodle (hwang′dōō′dl): an imaginary creature of undefined character. 58A.

whata (hwä′ta): a storehouse, usu. thatch-roofed, built on posts capped with inverted cones to prevent rats from getting in. 56.

wheeple (hwē′pl): the drawn-out shrill cry of certain birds, as the curlew or plover. To utter such a cry.

wheetle (hwē′tl): to chirp or whistle shrilly. 44A.

wheft (hweft): a nautical pennant.

wherret (hwer′et): hit, box, slap. 11. Var. of *worrit*.

whid (hwid): a word. 3A. Lie, fib. 44A. A silent, rapid motion; to move silently. 47.

whigmaleery (hwig′ma.lē′ri): a knick-knack; whim; vagary. 44A.

whinchacker (hwin′chak′er): a small European singing bird that frequents grassy meadows; the whinchat.

whipjack (hwip′jak): a beggar pretending to have been shipwrecked; a vagabond.

whiskerino (hwis′ker.ē′no): a whisker-growing contest. 21.

whiskin (hwis′kin): a shallow drinking bowl. 1.

whisp (hwisp): a low sound as of puffing, rustling, or sprinkling; to whisp. Also, var. of *wisp*. 11A.

whisterpoop (hwis′ter.pōōp): a blow, buffet. 11.

whuff, whuffle (hwuf, hwuf′l): to emit whuffs or whiffs; of a dog or horse, to breathe with noisy whiffs.

widdifow (wid′i.fōō): a rogue, *waghalter*. 1.

wiff (wif): wife. 1.

windhover (wind′huv′er): the kestrel. 30.

wingmanship (wing′man.ship): skill in flying. 52.

winklehawk (wing′kl.hôk): a rectangular rent in cloth. 28.

winze (winz): a vertical or steeply inclined passageway connecting one mine working place with another at a different level.

wisket (wis′ket): a basket; esp. a straw provender basket. 13.

witchety (wich′e.ti): a grub—the chief food of the marsupial mole. 53.

witney (wit′ni): a heavy, woolen fabric, napped and shrunk, used for coats and blankets.

wittee (wit′i): a wife who is encouraged in unfaithfulness by her husband. 60.

wittol (wit′ul): a man who encourages his wife's infidelity. 9.

witzchoura (wi.chōō′ra): a woman's mantle with large sleeves and deep falling collar, fashionable in the reign of George IV.

witzelsucht (vit′sel.sookt): an emotional state involving futile attempts at humor.

woader (wō′der): one who employs the blue dye woad; a woadman.

wobbegong (wob′i.gong): in New South Wales, the carpet shark.

wod (wod): dial. var. of *would;* obs. past tense of *wade*.

wonga, wonga-wonga (wong′ga, wong′ga.wong′ga): a woody vine with loose panicles of yellowish white flowers; a narrow-leaved cattail; a large pigeon with very white flesh. 53.

wonk (wongk): one who studies excessively (perhaps *know* spelled backwards). 21.

wooer-bab (wōō′er.bab): a garter tied below the knee as a love knot. 44.

woom (wōōm): to the Cantonese, beaver fur.

wootz (wōōtz): a steel made anciently in India in small crucibles; the oldest known process for making fused steel.

worricow (wur′i.kōō): a bugaboo, hobgoblin; esp. (cap) the Devil. 44A.

worrit (wur′it): worrier; worry; to worry. 11.

wou-wou (wou′wou′): the silver gibbon, an ashy-gray species of Java. The agile gibbon, a dark-brown species of Sumatra.

WANDERJAHR

Young I began my Wanderjahr;
  A gibbous moon was climbing.
I blew it smoke from my cigar,
  And set about my rhyming.

I rhymed in country and in town,
  In bed and in the loo;
I rhymed for princess and for clown,
  I rhymed for Worricow.

But words to them were walla-walla;
  They cried, ''Your rhymes are whacko;
Besides, you bring into the hall a
  Miasma of tobacco.''

Old I returned from Wanderjahr;
  The moon hung waniand;
Dead as the butt of my cigar
  The rhymes were in my hand.

The moon will wax and climb encore;
  Yet here, until they end me,
I'll puff my rhymes out, grateful for
  A hut to weatherfend me.

wowf (wōof): wild; crazed. 44.

wowser (wou′zer): one who is censoriously hostile to minor vices. 26.

wrasse (ras): any of numerous edible, marine, usu. brilliantly colored, spiny-finned fishes of the family Labridae, allied to the parrot fish.

wrig (rig): the feeblest member of a brood or litter; a puny child, or the youngest child of a family. 44. To wriggle. 2.

wull (wul): dial. var. of will.

wuntee (wun′ti): a lone ole buffalo bull.

wurrus (wur′rus): the *kamala*.

wuther (wuth′er): var. of whither, n. & v. 13. A sharp blow; flurry. To hurry; rush; bluster; to tremble; totter. 44. To hurl; shake. 44C.

wuzzy (wuz′i, wooz′i): var. of woozy.

wyliecoat (wī′li.kōt): an undervest or petticoat; a nightdress. 44A.

wype (wīp): the lapwing. 4.

X

Xanthippe (zan′tip′i): the shrewish wife of Socrates.

xanthoderm (zan′tho.durm): a member of a yellow-skinned race.

xanthodont (zan′tho.dont): one with yellowish teeth.

xanthomelanous (zan.tho.mel′a.nus): pert. to races having an olive or yellow complexion and black hair.

xanthophobia (zan′tho.fō′bi.a): fear of the color yellow.

xanthoproteic (zan′tho.pro.tē′ik): relating to xanthoprotein, a yellow substance formed by action of hot nitric acid on albuminous or protein matter.

xanthyocyanopsia (zan′thi.o.sī.a.nop′-si.a): a form of color blindness in which one sees only yellows and browns.

xat (zat): a carved post in front of certain Indian houses.

xenagogue (zen′a.gog): a guide. 52.

xenagogy (zen′a.gō′ji): a guidebook. 52.

xenial (zē′ni.al): pert. to hospitality, or relations between guest and host.

xenium (zē′ni.um): a present given among the ancient Greeks and Romans to a guest or stranger.

xenodochium (zen′o.do.kī′um): in the Middle Ages, a home for the disabled and friendless.

xenodochy (zen.o′do.ki): hospitality.

xenoepist (zen′i.pist): one who speaks with a foreign accent.

xenomancy (zen′o.man′si): divination by study of the first stranger to appear.

xenomania (zen′o.mā′ni.a): a mania for things foreign.

xenophobia (zen′o.fō′bi.a): fear of strangers or foreigners.

xeromyron (zi.rom′i.ron): a dry or stiff ointment.

xeronisus (zi.ron′i.sis): inability to achieve orgasm.

xerophagy (zi.rof′a.ji): the strictest Christian fast, in which only bread, salt, water, and vegetables may be eaten; observed chiefly in the Eastern churches during Lent or esp. Holy Week.

xerophobous (zi.rof′o.bus): of plants, easily succumbing to drought.

xibalba (hi.bäl′ba): in the Mayan religion, the underworld; the abode of the dead.

xiphopagus (zi.fop′a.gus): a monster consisting of twins joined at the abdomen.

Xiuhtecutli (he′oo.ta.koo′tli): the Aztec fire god.

xoanon (zō′a.non): in ancient Greece, a primitive image of carved wood.

xylite, xylitol (zī′lit, zī′li.tol): an alcohol obtained as a sirupy liquid by reduction of xylose.

xylographer (zī.log′ra.fer): one who makes prints from the natural wood grain.

xylology (zī.lol′o.ji): the part of the study of trees that treats of the gross and the minute structure of wood.

xylomancy (zī′lo.man′si): divination by pieces of wood.

xylophobia (zī′lo.fō′bi.a): fear of wood or of forests.

xylopolist (zī.lop′o.list): one who deals in wooden objects.

xylopyrography (zī′lo.pī.rog′ra.fi): the art of producing pictures or designs by burning or scorching wood with hot instruments.

xyresic (zī.res′ik): sharp as a razor.

xystus (zis′tus): in Greek and Roman architecture, a long open portico, used in winter or in stormy weather for athletic exercises. Incorrectly, a walk lined with trees.

THEY WERE BOTH XANTHODONTIC, TOO

In a xystus, shrew Xanthippe
  Fell in love with Socrates.
Nag in love with aging hippy—
  Hippy hipped on shrew Xanthippe—
In the name of all that's dippy,
  What are we to make of these?
In a xystus, shrew Xanthippe
  Fell in love with Socrates!

Y

yabber (yab′er): talk; jabber; language; esp., the broken English of the Australian aborigines. 53.

yabbi (yab′i): the *thylacine*.

yabbie, yabby (yab′i): a small burrowing crayfish found in creeks and water holes in Australia.

yaboo, yabu (ya.boo′): a strong, hardy pony bred in the mountains of Afghanistan.

yaff (yaf): to bark; yelp; scold. 44.

yaffle (yaf′l): To yaff. 44. An armful, handful; the green woodpecker. 11.

yagua (yä′gwa): a Puerto Rican palm resembling the royal palm. Also, its thick woody leaf. (cap) A Peban Indian dwelling along the Amazon in northeastern Peru.

yahoomanity (ya.hoo.man′i.ti): the supposedly boorish mass of humanity.

Yahwism (yä′wizm): the worship of Yahweh (Jehovah). The use of Yahweh as a name for God.

yair (yär, yâr): an enclosure for catching salmon. 43.

yapok (ya.pok′): the water opossum.

yapp (yap): a style of bookbinding in which a limp cover is bent over the edge without being cut at the corners.

yarb (yärb): herb. 11.

yardang (yär′dang): a sharp-crested ridge carved by wind erosion.

yardwand (yärd′wänd): a yardstick.

yark (yärk): var. of *yerk*. 2.

yarwhelp (yär′hwelp): the bar-tailed godwit. 31B.

yati (yat′i, yut′i): a Hindu ascetic; a devotee.

yatter (yat′er): chatter, clamor. 44A.

yaud (yôd, yäd): a workhorse, esp. a mare; also, a jade. 43.

yauld (yôd, yäd, yäld): alert, able-bodied; also, sharp, as weather. 43.

yaya (ya.yä′): any of several tropical trees, inc. the gum-yielding copa of Panama, the lancewood of Puerto Rico, and the chaparro of Belize.

ydromancy (id.ro.man′si): divination using water.

yed (yed): fib; wrangle. 44.

yede (yēd): to go, proceed. 10A.

yehudi (ye.hoo′di): a British gremlin, so-named because it is always fiddling around.

yeld (yeld): (of a cow or ewe) barren; having slipped her young; not old enough to bear; giving no milk. 44D.

yeme (yēm): to take care of; heed; observe. Solicitude. 1.

yerk (yurk): to make ready; prepare. 2.

yestern (yes′tern): yester. 9.

yette (yet′i): to grant; concede. 1.

yeuk, yewk, yuke (yook): itch. 43.

yex (yeks): sob. 1. Hiccup; cough. 11.

yez (yēz, yiz): you (pl.). 51.

yirn (yurn): whine; grimace. 47.

yiver (yī′ver): eager; greedy. 1.

ylahayll (il′a.hāl): bad luck to you. 1.

ylespil (il′es.pel): the hedgehog. 1.

ynambu (ē′nam. bōō): a large kind of *tinamou.*

yocco (yok′ō): a Colombian plant allied to the *guarana,* and, like it, yielding caffeine from the bark and leaves.

yojan (yō′jan): a Hindu unit of distance equal to about 5 miles.

yperite (ē′per.īt): mustard gas.

ypsiliform (ip.sil′i.fôrm): Y-shaped.

ythe (ēth): a wave of the sea. 1.

yuca (yōō′ka): cassava.

yukkel (yuk′el): the green woodpecker. 30A. The flicker. 28.

yupon (yōō′pon): var. of yaupon, a species of holly native to the southern United States.

Z

zaman (sä′man): the rain tree.

zambo (zam′bō): *sambo.*

zambomba (tham.bom′ba): a crude musical instrument made by inserting a stick through parchment stretched over a widemouthed earthen jar, and sounded by rubbing the stick.

Zan (zan): an old Doric name for Zeus.

zander (zan′der): a pike perch of central Europe, allied to the walleyed pike.

zante (zan′ti): the smoke tree, or fustet; its wood.

zapateado (thap′a.ti.ä′dō): a Spanish tap dance.

zaptiah (zap.tē′a): a Turkish policeman.

zarzuela (thär.thwä′la): a 17th-century Spanish variety of operetta or vaudeville, mixing songs and dialogue.

zati (zä′ti): the bonnet monkey.

Zea (zē′a): a genus of large grasses, incl. Indian corn. (not cap) Formerly, a diuretic made from elements of Indian corn.

zebrula (zē′broo.la, zeb′roo.la): a cross between a male zebra and a female horse.

zedland (zed′land): the English countries of Devonshire, Dorsetshire, and Somersetshire, where Z replaces S in colloquial speech.

zedonk (zi.dongk): the offspring of a male zebra and a female donkey.

zeist (zē′ist): in medicine, one who supports the theory that pellagra is the result of a diet of corn.

zelophobia (zel′o.fō′bi.a): fear of jealousy.

zemi (sā′mi): among the extinct Taino Indians of the Greater Antilles and the Bahamas, a spirit or supernatural being. Also, an object believed to be the dwelling of a spirit and hence to possess magic potency.

zemmi (zem′i): the great mole rat.

zenography (zi.nog′ra.fi): the study or description of the surface of the planet Jupiter.

zester (zes′ter): a small rake-like tool used to shave the top layer from an orange or lemon.

zetetic (zi′tet′ik): seeking; proceeding by inquiry.

zeticula (zi.tik′ū.la): a small withdrawing room.

ziara, ziarat (zi.ä′ra, zē′a.rät): a tomb of Muslim saint; hence, a shrine.

zibetum (zib′i.tum): civet from the zibet, a civet cat of India.

zieger (zē′ger): a cheese made from whey, consisting principally of albumin.

Zigeuner (tsi.goi′ner): a gypsy.

zimb (zimb, zim): a large two-winged fly of Abyssinia, resembling the tsetse, and very destructive to cattle.

zimentwater (zim′ent.wô′ter): a kind of water found in copper mines; water impregnated with copper. 52.

zimme (sim′i): a gem.

zimmi, zimmy (zim′i): a *dhimmi.*

zizz (ziz): an imitative syllable.

zoanthropy (zo.an′thro.pi): a monomania in which one believes oneself changed into an animal and acts accordingly.

zobo (zō′bō): a kind of Asian cattle, supposedly a cross between the zebu and the yak, used for its flesh and milk.

zoetic (zo.et′ik): pert. to life; living; vital.

zoetrope (zō′i.trōp): a toy in which figures on the inside of a revolving cylinder are viewed through slits, and appear to be a single animated figure.

zogo (zō′gō): among the Miriam-speaking people of the Torres Strait, a sacred object of magic potency.

zoiatrics (zō′i.at′riks): veterinary medicine.

Zoilean (zo.il′i.an): having the characteristics of Zoilus, a bitter, envious, unjust Greek critic who lived in the 4th century B.C.

Zoilism (zō′i.lizm): carping criticism.

zomotherapy (zō′mo.ther′a.pi): a raw meat diet as a treatment for tuberculosis.

zona (zō′na): a zone or band. A girdle; a layer.

zonda (zon′da): a hot wind of the Argentine pampas.

zonesthesia (zōn′es.thē′zhi.a, -zha): a feeling of restriction about the waist.

zonulet (zō′nu.let): a little girdle; a zonule.

zoodynamics (zō′o.dī.nam′iks): the science that treats of the vital powers of animals.

zooid (zō′oid): in zoology, an entity that resembles but is not wholly the same as an individual organism, as a phagocyte or sperm cell having locomotion.

zoolite (zō′o.līt): a fossil animal.

zoopery (zo.op′er.i): experimentation on the lower animals.

zoophobia (zō′o.fō′bi.a): fear of animals.

zoophorous (zo.of′er.us): in classical architecture, a frieze having continuous relief sculptures of men or animals or both.

zoopraxiscope (zō.o.prak′si.skōp): an early form of motion-picture projector.

zoopsychologist (zō′o.sī.kol′o.jist): a student of animal psychology.

zoosemiotics (zō′o.sem′i.ot′iks): the study of communication between animals.

zoozoo (zōō′zōō): the ringdove. 30.

zorillo (zo.ril′o, so.rē′ō): a tropical American shrub or small tree with a skunk-like odor.

zortzico (zôr.sē′kō): a song or dance in quintuple or sextuple time, common among the Basques.

Zu (zōō): in Babylonian mythology, an evil storm-god in the form of a black bird.

zubr (zōō′br): the European bison or aurochs.

zuche (zōōch): a tree stump. 1.

Zugzwang (zoogz′väng): a chess dilemma where any move will weaken the player's position.

zuureveldt (zur′velt): in South Africa, a tract of land covered with coarse grass.

zygal (zī′gal): H-shaped.

zygomancy (zī′go.man′si): divination by weights.

zymometer, zymosimeter (zī.mom′i.ter, zī′mo.sim′i.ter): an instrument measuring fermentation.

zypthepsary (zip.thep′sa.ri): a brewery.

zyxomma (zik.som′a): an Indian dragonfly. Also, the last word in several dictionaries.

Zyzzogeton (ziz.o.jē′ton): a genus of large South American leaf hoppers. The last word in this glossary.

APPENDIX A: MEANING OF THE NUMBER KEYS

1. Obsolete.
2. Obsolete except dialectal.
2A. Chiefly obsolete except dialectal.
3. Obsolete or dialectal.
3A. Obsolete slang.
4. Obsolete except dialectal, England.
4A. Obsolete except the north of England.
4B. Obsolete except Scotland and the north of England.
5. Obsolete except Scotland.
5A. Obsolete except Scotland and dialectal, England.
6. Obsolete except historic.
6A. Obsolete except in law.
7. Obsolete except military.
7A. Obsolete, Scotland.
8. Obsolete except heraldry.
8A. Obsolete or archaic.
9. Archaic.
9A. Archaic and dialectal, England.
10. Archaic and dialectal.
10A. Pseudoarchaic.
11. Dialectal.
11A. Chiefly dialectal.
12. Dialectal, United States.
13. Dialectal, England.
13A. Dialectal, Sussex.
13B. Chiefly dialectal, England.
13C. Dialectal, England, and slang.
14. Dialectal, England and Scotland.
15. Dialectal, north of England and Scotland.
16. Dialectal, north of England, Scotland, and Ireland.
16A. Chiefly Scots dialectal.
17. Dialectal, England, Scotland, and Ireland.
17A. Scotland and dialectal, England.
17B. Chiefly Scotland and dialectal, England.
18. Dialectal except Scotland.
18A. Obsolete, Scotland.
19. Dialectal, Sussex.
20. Dialectal and slang, Australia.
21. Slang.

21A. Dialectal and slang.
22. United States slang.
22A. United States and Canadian slang.
23. English slang.
23A. Australian slang.
23B. Australian slang and dialectal.
24. School slang.
24A. Scottish slang.
25. English prison slang.
26. Colloquial.
26A. Colloquial, England.
26B. Colloquial, Scotland.
27. Colloquial, United States.
28. Local, United States.
28A. Local, chiefly United States.
28B. Chiefly local, United States.
29. Local, United States and Canada.
29A. Local or dialectal, England.
30. Local, England.
30A. Local, Scotland.
31. Local, England and Scotland.
31A. Local, Australia.
31B. Local, England and Ireland.
32. United States.
32A. Thieves' language, United States.
33. United States and Scotland.
33A. Northern United States.
34. Northern United States and Canada.
34A. Chiefly southern United States.
34B. Texas.
35. Southern United States.
35A. Southwestern United States.
35B. Chiefly southwestern United States.
35C. Western United States.
36. Massachusetts.
36A. Maine.
37. Vermont.
37A. New England.
37B. Alaska.
38. Hawaii.
38A. Hawaii and New Zealand.
39. Pennsylvania.
39A. Louisiana.
40. Alabama, Louisiana, and Mississippi.

40A. Chiefly England.
41. England.
41A. Cornwall.
41B. England and Cornwall.
41C. Wales.
42. North of England.
42A. Chiefly north of England.
43. North of England and Scotland.
43A. Chiefly north of England and Scotland.
43B. North of England; Scotland, dialectal.
44. Scotland.
44A. Chiefly Scotland.
44B. Chiefly Scotland and dialectal, England.
44C. Scotland and dialectal, England.
44D. Scotland and dialectal.
45. North of England, Scotland, and Ireland.
46. England, Scotland, and Ireland.
47. Scotland and Ireland.
47A. Chiefly Scotland and Ireland.
47B. Scotland and northern Ireland.
48. College slang.
49. Scotland and Ireland; dialectal, England.
50. Ireland.
50A. Chiefly Ireland.
51. Anglo-Irish.
51A. Anglo-Indian.
52. Rare.
52A. Rare, United States.
53. Australia.
53A. England and Australia.
54. New South Wales.
55. Isle of Man.
56. New Zealand.
57. Regional.
58. Humorous.
58A. Humorous, chiefly United States.
59. Slang, chiefly nautical. Also, nonce.
60. Nonce. Also, old slang.
61. Shetland and Orkney Islands.
62. Scots and Old English law.

APPENDIX B: — -MANCY

To Webster's Second, -*mancy* (from Greek *mantis*, divination) is "a combining form denoting divination, esp. by means of a (specified) thing, as in aleuro*mancy*, chiro-*mancy*, necro*mancy*."

The rhyming list had been put to bed with ninety-one -*mancy* words in it—a very adequate supply, it seemed to me—when I came across one hundred and fifty in Paul Dickson's *Words*. There were fifty-eight that I did not have, and he let me use them. Here they are, listed alphabetically, with abbreviated definitions:

The word	*That is, divination by*
aichomancy (ā′ko.man.si)	sharp points.
alomancy (al′o.man′si)	salt.
amathomancy (a.math′o.man′si)	walking.
amniomancy (am′ni.o.man′si)	a newborn's caul.
anthomancy (an′tho.man′si)	flowers.
anthropomancy (an′thro.po.man′si)	human entrails.
apantomancy (a.pan′to.man′si)	objects appearing haphazardly.
arithmancy (ar′ith.man′si)	numbers.
aspidomancy (as′pid.o.man′si)	a trance while seated on a shield in a magic circle.
astromancy (as′tro.man′si)	the stars.
brontomancy (bron′to.man′si)	thunder.
cartomancy (kär′to.man′si)	dealing cards.
causimomancy (kô.sim.o.man′si)	flammability. (The longer some object takes to ignite, the better the outlook.)
chaomancy (kā′o.man′si)	clouds and airborne apparitions.
cheiromancy (kī′ro.man′si)	palmreading.
cledonomancy (kled′o.no.man′si)	interpreting mystical utterances.
conchomancy (kong′ko.man′si)	seashells.
cromniomancy (krom′ni.o.man′si)	onions on the Christmas altar.
cryptomancy (krip′to.man′si)	hidden signs.
cubomancy (kū′bo.man′si)	dice.
daphnomancy (daf′no.man′si)	the crackle of a laurel branch on a fire.
demonomancy (dē′mun.o.man′si)	the help of demons.
dririmancy (drir′i.man′si)	dripping blood.
elaeomancy (i.lē′o.man′si)	a liquid surface.
empyromancy (em.pir′o.man′si)	fire.
graphomancy (graf′o.man′si)	handwriting.
hippomancy (hip′o.man′si)	the neighing of horses.
hyomancy (hī′o.man′si)	the hyoid, or tongue bone.
iconomancy (ī.kon′o.man′si)	images.
idolomancy (ī.dol′o.man′si)	idols.
labiomancy (lā′bi.o.man′si)	lip-reading.
libanomancy (lib′a.no.man′si)	the smoke of incense.
logomancy (log′o.man′si)	magic words.
machairomancy (ma.kī′ro.man′si)	knives or swords.
macromancy (mak′ro.man′si)	the largest thing at hand.
maculomancy (mak′ū.lo.man′si)	splotches, stains, spots.
magastromancy (mag′as.tro.man′si)	astrological magic.
margaritomancy (mar′ga.rit′o.man′si)	pearls.
meconomancy (mek′o.no.man′si)	drug-induced visions.

The word	*That is, divination by*
micromancy (mī′kro.man′si)	the smallest thing available.
moromancy (mor′o.man′si)	nonsense.
nephelomancy (nef′el.o.man′si)	clouds.
nephromancy (nef′ro.man′si)	the kidneys.
nomancy (no′man.si)	the letters of a name—onomancy.
odontomancy (o.don′to.man′si)	the condition of the teeth.
ololygmancy (ō′lo.lig.man′si)	the howling of dogs.
omphalomancy (om′fal.o.man′si)	the navel.
ornomancy (ôr′no.man′si)	the flight of birds.
osteomancy (os′ti.o.man′si)	bones.
pegomancy (peg′o.man′si)	fountains.
pessomancy (pess′o.man′si)	clothes-brushing.
phyllorhodomancy (fil′o.rō′do.man′si)	rose leaves.
pneumancy (nū′man.si)	blowing.
sphondulomancy (sfon′dū.lo.man′si)	spindles.
stercomancy (stur′ko.man′si)	the seeds in dung.
stolcheomancy (stol′ki.o.man′si)	a random pick from a book of poetry.
stolisomancy (stō′lis.o.man′si)	one's manner of dressing.
topomancy (top′o.man′si)	the terrain.
tyromancy (tī′ro.man′si)	cheese.

A Note about Appendices C and D

After the body of this book was finished, Paul Dickson mentioned to me that a man named Rudy Ondrijka had assembled a tremendous collection of words ending in *-mania* and *-phobia*. I wrote to Mr. Ondrijka, and he sent me his manuscript, defining more than 450 maniac and more than 850 phobic words. With the most uncalled-for and welcome generosity, he said that though the manuscript had been prepared for publication, I was welcome to use as many of his words in my book as I found convenient. I wish I could use them all. Since that is impossible, I have chosen, to save space, only those words that have definitions less than a line long.

APPENDIX C: — -MANIA

A mania is a morbid impulse or derangement concerning something, and when it is used as a suffix the something is defined by the root word to which the mania is appended. A mania may be a maniacal desire to *do* something—*nepiomania*, for instance, is an overwhelming desire to have a child—or an equally maniacal passion *for* something; *pizzamania* is an obsession with pizza. I do not know why manias are less abundant than phobias; theoretically, one would have the other as its opposite.

The following list represents a little more than a quarter of the manias that Rudy Ondrijka has assembled for his forthcoming book. (I refer to the book as Ondrijka's ''Manias and Phobias,'' which may not be his final title.) None of the paltry seventy-one manias in my rhyming list is included here. In a few cases I have modified Mr. Ondrijka's definitions slightly to save space.

anagramania (an'a.gra.mā'ni.a): the anagram craze.

apimania (a'pi.mā'ni.a): obsession with bees.

autophonomania (o'to.fō'no.mā'ni.a): suicidal insanity.

balletomania (ba.let'o.mā'ni.a): passionate addiction to ballet.

brychomania, brycomania (brī'ko.-.mā'ni.a): the grinding of teeth in insanity.

cataromania (ka.ta'ro.mā'ni.a): an uncontrollable urge to curse.

copromania (kop'ro.mā'ni.a): an obsession with feces.

decubomania (di.kū'bo.mā'ni.a): an urgent desire to lie down.

desanimania (des'an.i.mā'ni.a): Amentia, or mindless insanity.

doromania (dôr'o.mā'ni.a): a morbid desire to give presents.

economania (i.kon'o.mā'ni.a): a mania for economy.

emetomania (i.met'o.mā'ni.a): a compulsive drive to vomit.

entomania (en'to.mā'ni.a): obsession with insects.

epairomania (i.pi'ro.mā'ni.a): insane elation.

eremiomania (er'i.mi.o.mā'ni.a): obsession with stillness.

erythromania (i.rith'ro.mā'ni.a): excessive and uncontrollable blushing.

grammania (gra.mā'ni.a): a mania for correct grammar.

guinnessmania (gin'es.mā'ni.a): the urge to set a world record.

hedonomania (hi.don'o.mā'ni.a): obsession with pleasure.

hieromania (hi'er.o.mā'ni.a): religious madness; sebastomania.

hippomania (hip'o.mā'ni.a): extreme fondness for horses.

hodomania (hō.do.mā'ni.a): abnormal desire to travel.

hymenomania (hī'men.o.mā'ni.a): an inordinate desire to deflower a virgin.

hypnomania (hip'no.mā'ni.a): a mania for sleep.

ichthyomania (ik'thi.o.mā'ni.a): an obsession with fish.

ideomania (id'i.o.mā'ni.a): an obsession with ideas.

jumbomania (jum'bo.mā'ni.a): fascination with mammoth dimensions.

lalomania (lal'o.mā'ni.a): obsession with speech.

malaxomania (mal'ak.so.mā'ni.a): a wild craving to knead the flesh of a woman.

mammathigmomania (mam'a.thig'mo.-mā'ni.a): a compulsion to touch a woman's breasts.

nominomania (nom'in.o.mā'nia): a mania for naming.

nudomania (nū'do.mā'ni.a): morbid desire to go nude.

onychotillomania (on'i.ko.ti.'o.mā'ni.a): neurotic picking at the nails.

orchidomania (ôr'kid.o.mā'ni.a): a craze for orchids.

ornithomania (ôr'ni.tho.mā'ni.a): a craze for birds.

pareunomania (par'ū.no.mā'ni.a): a compelling need for sexual intercourse.

phrenomania (frē'no.mā'ni.a): acute mania; delirious mania; collapse delirium.

phronemomania (frō'ni.mo.mā'ni.a): an obsession with thinking.

phytomania (fī'to.mā'ni.a): a mania for collecting plants.

polemomania (pō'li.mo.mā'ni.a): a rage for war.

polkamania (pōl'ko.mā'ni.a): a mania for dancing the polka.

pteridomania (ter'i.do.mā'ni.a): excessive enthusiasm for ferns.

resomania (rē'so.mā'ni.a): uncontrollable desire to gather things.

selenomania (si.lē'no.mā'ni.a): maniacal symptoms induced by moonlight.

studimania (stū'di.mā'ni.a): abnormal devotion to a hobby. Hedonism.

stupemania (stū'pi.mā'ni.a): insanity with symptoms of stupor.

succubamania (suk'ū.ba.mā'ni.a): intense desire by a woman to lie under a man.

titillomania (tit'i.lo.mā'ni.a): a morbid desire to scratch.

tomomania (tō'mo.mā'ni.a): a craze for needless surgical operations.

tristimania (tris'ti.mā'ni.a): melancholia.

uxoricidomania (uks.ôr'i.sī'do.mā'ni.a): obsession with killing one's wife.

uxoromania (uks.ôr'o.mā'ni.a): a strong desire to have a wife; desire for one's wife.

videomania (vid′i.o.mā′ni.a): infatuation with television.

yakomania (yak′o.mā′ni.a): a chattering of youngsters—and older people too.

zoomania (zo.o.mā′ni.a): a morbid love of animals.

APPENDIX D — -PHOBIA

In Greek, *phobia* means fear or dread that contains a strong element of loathing; in its present-day suffix form the loathing often has the upper hand. Strictly, like mania, it should be suffixed only to Greek roots; popularly, however, it is added freely to any substantive, and is frequently a tool of word play, as in "absenceophobia: fear of having the heart grow fonder," or "agateophobia: fear of losing one's marbles." Rudy Ondrijka's 850-word collection of phobias has many of the punning kind, and some are represented in my abbreviated selections below, but most are of the more conservative variety. You will see the others when Mr. Ondrijka's book appears—and it cannot be too soon.

agateophobia (ag′a.to.fō′bi.a): fear of insanity.

agonologophobia (a′go.no.log′o.fō′bi.a): fear of sports language.

agrizoophobia (ag′ri.zo′o.fō′bi.a): terror of wild animals.

aichurophobia (ī.ker.o.fō′bi.a): fear of points.

alektorophobia (a.lek′tôr.o.fō′bi.a): fear of chickens.

alphabetophobia (al′fa.bet′o.fō′bi.a): fear of things in alphabetical order.

amoebaphobia (a.mē′ba.fō′bi.a): fear of being infected with amoebae.

amnesiophobia (am.nē′zi.o.fō′bi.a): fear of amnesia.

anablepophobia (an′a.blep′o.fō′bi.a): fear of looking up at high places.

angelstreadophobia (ān′jelz.tred′o.fō′-bi.a): fear of places where fools rush in.

angrophobia (ang′gro.fō′bi.a): fear of anger.

anophelophobia (a.nof′e.lo.fō′bi.a): fear of hurting the woman in sexual intercourse.

antlophobia (ant.lo.fō′bi.a): unwarranted fear of floods.

antrodermatophobia (an′tro.dur′ma.-to.fō′bi.a): fear of acne.

anuptophobia (a.nup′ta.fō′bi.a): fear of being a spinster.

argumentophobia (är′gū.men′to.fō′bi.a): fear of arguments.

arsonophobia (är′son.o.fō′bi.a): fear of being set on fire.

astrologophobia (as′tro.log′o.fō′bi.a): fear of your birth sign.

astrophingophobia (as′tra.fing′go.fō′-bi.a): fear of insecurity.

atelophobia (atel′o.fō′bi.a): fear of imperfection or incompletion.

auchmophobia (ôk′mo.fō′bi.a): fear of disorder, disarray, or confusion.

aurophobia (ô′ro.fō′bi.a): fear or dislike of gold.

auroraphobia (ô.rō′ra.fō′bi.a): fear of the northern lights.

autophobophobia (ô′to.fō′bo.fō′bi.a): fear of one's own fears.

bagophobia (bag′o.fō′bi.a): fear of wrinkled panty hose.

bathmophobia (bath′mo.fō′bi.a): fear of stairways or steep slopes.

blissophobia (blis′o.fō′bi.a): fear of ignorance.

botanophobia (bo.tan′o.fō′bi.a): intense dislike of plants and flowers.

boustrophobia (boō′stro.fō′bi.a): fear of cattle.

bozophobia (bō′zo.fō′bi.a): fear of blind dates.

cacistophobia (kak′is.to.fō′bi.a): fear of the worst.

callophobia (kal′o.fō′bi.a): fear or hatred of beauty.

calyprophobia (ka.lip′ro.fō′bi.a): fear of mystery, hidden or obscure meaning.

carnophobia (kär'no.fō'bi.a): abnormal aversion to a meat diet.

catapedaphobia (kat'a.pē'da.fō'bi.a): fear of jumping from even the slightest elevation.

cataphobia (kat'a.fō'bi.a): fear of falling.

chionomophobia (kī'o.no.mo.fō'bi.a): fear of snow.

chiraptophobia (ki.rap'to.fō'bi.a): fear of being touched by hands.

chirophobia (kī'ro.fō'bi.a): fear of hands.

chlorephobia (klor'i.fō'bi.a): fear of, or aversion to, the color green.

chronometrophobia (kron'o.met'ro.fō'bi.a): fear of clocks.

chrysophobia (kris'o.fō'bi.a): fear of gold or wealth.

cnidophobia (nī'do.fō'bi.a): fear of stings.

coimetrophobia (ko'i.met'ro.fō'bi.a): fear of cemeteries.

comapocophobia (kom'a.pok'o.fō'bi.a): fear of being shorn of hair.

cometaphobia (ko.met'a.fō'bi.a): fear of long hair.

conistraphobia (kon'is.tra.fō'bi.a): fear of slovenly places or untidiness.

cosmophobia (koz'mo.fō'bi.a): fear of cities.

crunchophobia (krunch'o.fō'bi.a): fear of shaking hands with weightlifters.

cryophobia (krī'o.fō'bi.a): fear of frost and ice.

cymophobia (sī'.mo.fō'bi.a): fear of sea swells or waves.

cyprinophobia (sīp'ri.no.fō'bi.a): fear of lewd women.

demophobia (dē'mo.fō'bi.a): dislike of crowds or people.

dendrophobia (den'dro.fō'bi.a): fear of big trees.

dentophobia (den'to.fō'bi.a): fear of dentistry.

diaperophobia (dī'a.per.o.fō'bi.a): fear of being alone with an infant.

didymophobia (did'i.mo.fō'bi.a): fear of twins.

dinophobia (din'o.fō'bi.a): fear of dizziness or of whirlpools.

dishpanophobia (dish'pan.o.fō'bi.a): fear of being caught red-handed.

doxophobia (dok'so.fō'bi.a): fear of expressing opinions or receiving praise.

dysphobia (dis.fō'bi.a): fear of knowing what to fear.

enetephobia (en'i.ti.fō'bi.a): fear of pins.

enterophobia (en'ter.o.fō'bi.a): fear of intestines, intestinal diseases.

epistagmophobia (ep'i.stag'mo.fō'bi.a): fear of nosebleeds.

equinophobia (i.kwī'no.fō'bi.a): fear of horses.

ergolatrophobia (ur'go.lat'tro.fō'bi.a): fear of overdevotion to work.

fechtenophobia (fek'ten.o.fō'bi.a): fear of fights.

feefifofumophobia (fē'fī'fō'fum'o.fō'bi.a): fear of giants on beanstalks.

friggaphobia (frig'a.fō'bi.a): fear of Fridays.

geniophobia (jē'ni.o.fō'bi.a): fear of chins.

genitophobia (jen'i.to.fō'bi.a): fear of the genitals.

genuphobia (jen'ū.fō'bi.a): fear of knees.

giraffaphobia (ji.raf'a.fō'bi.a): fear of sticking your neck out.

googoophobia (goo'goo.fō'bi.a): fear of baby talk.

groanophobia: (grōn'ō.fō'bi.a): aversion to puns.

gyrephobia (jīr'fō'bi.a): fear of being encircled, or enclosed, by other people.

halophobia (hal'o.fō'bi.a): fear of saltiness or salty flavors.

hedysophobia (hed'i.so.fō'bi.a): fear of sweetness or sweet flavors.

herpetophobia (hur'pi.to.fō'bi.a): dread of reptiles.

hormephobia (hôr'mi.fō'bi.a): fear of shock.

hybophobia (hī'bo.fō'bi.a): fear of hunchbacks.

hylophobia (hī'.lo.fō'bi.a): fear of forests.

hypertrichophobia (hī'per.trik'o.fō'bi.a): fear of hair on the body.

hypophobia (hī'po.fō'bi.a): lack of fear.

ichnophobia (ik.no.fō'bi.a): fear of footprints.

iconophobia (ī.kon'o.fō'bi.a): hatred of images.

isopterophobia (ī.sop'ter.o.fō'bi.a): fear of termites.

ithyphallophobia (ith'i.fal'o.fō'bi.a): female fear of the erected phallus.

Jonesophobia (jōnz.o.fō′bi.a): fear of not keeping up.

kyphophobia (kī′fo.fō′bi.a): fear of stooping.

lachanophobia (la.kan.o.fō′bi.a): fear of vegetables.

laliphobia (lal′i.fō′bi.a): in persons with a speech impediment, fear of speaking.

leucophobia (loo′ko.fō′bi.a): fear of white.

ligyrophobia (li′ji.ro.fō′bi.a): fear of loud noises.

limnophobia (lim′no.fō′bi.a): fear of lakes.

lipophobia (lip′o.fō′bi.a): fear of getting fat, or of fat people.

logophobia (log′o.fō′bi.a): fear of study, speech, words.

lycanthrophobia (li.kan′thro.fō′bi.a): fear of werewolves.

lycophobia (lī′ko.fō′bi.a): fear of wolves.

mageiricophobia (ma.jī′ri.ko.fō′bi.a): fear of having to cook.

melanophobia (mel′a.no.fō′bi.a): fear of the color black.

millstreamophobia (mil′strēm′o.fō′bi.a): fear of barbershop quartets.

mitrophobia (mī′tro.fō′bi.a): fear of hats or head coverings.

mnemophobia (nē′mo.fō′bi.a): fear of memories.

mycophobia (mī′ko.fō′bi.a): unreasoning fear of mushrooms.

myrmecophobia (mur′mi.ko.fō′bi.a): dread of ants.

nagophobia (nag′o.fō′bi.a): fear or hatred of backseat drivers.

nosocomephobia (nos′o.kō′mi.fō′bi.a): fear of hospitals.

nuciphobia (nū′si.fō′bi.a): dread of nuclear warfare.

obesophobia (o.bē′so.fō′bi.a): fear of gaining weight.

octophobia (ok′to.fō′bi.a): fear of the figure eight.

odontriatrophobia (o.don′tri.at.ro.fō′bi.a): fear of dentists.

ommatophobia (om′a.to.fō′bi.a): fear of eyes.

oneirophobia (o.nī′ro.fō′bi.a): fear of dreams.

oompahpahphobia (oom′pa.pa.fō′bi.a): fear of German marching bands.

ophthalmophobia (of.thal′mo.fō′bi.a): aversion to being stared at.

ornithophobia (ôr′ni.tho.fō′bi.a): fear of birds.

osphresiophobia (os.frē′zi.o.fō′bi.a): a morbid aversion to odors.

ostraconophobia (os.tra′kon.o.fō′bi.a): fear of shellfish.

pantaphobia (pan′ta.fō′bi.a): absolute fearlessness.

penguinophobia (pen′gwin.o.fō′bi.a): fear of tuxedos.

phaphaphobia (faf′a.fa.fō′bi.a): fear of stutterers.

phasmophobia (faz′mo.fō′bi.a): fear of ghosts.

phemophobia (fē′mo.fō′bi.a): fear of voices.

philemaphobia (fil′i.ma.fō′bi.a): intense dislike of kissing.

philosophobia (fi.los′o.fō′bi.a): dread of philosophy or philosophers.

phyllophobia (fil′o.fō′bi.a): fear of leaves.

plastiphobia (plas′ti.fō′bi.a): fear of credit cards.

pnigerophobia (nī′jer.o.fō′bi.a): fear of smothering.

podophobia (pō′do.fō′bi.a): fear of feet.

poinephobia (poi′ni.fō′bi.a): fear of punishment.

prepuciophobia (pri.pū′si.o.fō′bi.a): fear of being circumcised.

primesodophobia (prī′mi.sod′o.fō′bi.a): the female's fear of first sexual intercourse.

psellismophobia (sel′iz.mo.fō′bi.a): fear of stammering or stuttering.

pteronophobia (ter′o.no.fō′bi.a): fear of feathers or being tickled by them.

pterygophobia (ter′i.go.fō′bi.a): fear of flying; also of airplanes.

qwertyuiophobia (kwur′tī.i.o.fō′bi.a): fear of touch typing.

rhacophobia (rak.o.fō′bi.a): fear of tattered garments.

runcophobia (rung′ko.fō′bi.a): fear of weeds.

satanophobia (sā′tan.o.fō′bi.a): dread of the devil.

saurophobia (sô′ro.fō′bi.a): fear of lizards.

scelerophobia (sel′er.o.fō′bi.a): fear of criminals.

selachophobia (si.lā′ko.fō′bi.a): fear of sharks.

semnologophobia (sem'no.log'o.fō'-bi.a): fear of moralizing.

senilisophobia (si.nil'i.so.fō'bi.a): fear of senility.

septophobia (sep.to.fō'bi.a): fear of decaying matter.

shushophobia (shush'o.fō'bi.a): fear of librarians.

sophobia (sof'o.fō'bi.a): fear of learning.

spheksophobia (sfek'so.fō'bi.a): fear of wasps.

synophobia (sin'o.fō'bi.a): fear of togetherness.

tachistothanatoophobia (ta.kis'to.than'-a.to.fō'bi.a): fear of head-on crashes.

taurophobia (tô.ro.fō'bi.a): fear of bulls.

threnotophobia (thren'o.to.fō'bi.a): fear of dirges or funerals.

tomophobia (tō'mo.fō'bi.a): fear of surgical operations.

tremophobia (trem'o.fō'bi.a): fear of trembling or shaking.

trypanophobia (trip.a.no.fō'bi.a): fear of inoculations or injections.

typhlophobia (tif'lo.fō'bi.a): fear of blindness, blind people, or going blind.

tyrannophobia (ti.ran'o.fō'bi.a): fear and hatred of tyrants.

undulaphobia (un'jōō.la.fō'bi.a): fear of water beds.

urophobia (ū'ro.fō'bi.a): fear of urination.

vestiophobia (ves'ti.o.fō'bi.a): fear and hatred of clothing.

villophobia (vil'o.fō'bi.a): fear of hairy people.

vitricophobia (vit'ri.ko.fō'bi.a): fear of or hatred for a stepfather.

xenoglossophobia (zen'o.glos'o.fō'bi.a): fear of foreign languages.

xyrophobia (zī'ro.fō'bi.a): fear of razors.

Index
First Lines of Verses

Aboard, Laertes, and my blessing carry, 19
A Cockney named I. Asimov, 34
A Crystal and a Prism, 553
A fair entellus in a banyan swung, 578
A Fish dreamed the sea had turned dry as the shore, 577
After neighbors' wives you neigh, 15
A gremlin Brits call the yehudi, 646
Ah, Cloe, the animal kingdom's a-teem, 7
Aida relish cymbal-smack, 21
A jako and a jarbird were appalled one day to see, 594
A liripoop (read nincompoop), 598
"Alliteration's artful aid," 375
Although informal speech is free, 48
A Mädchen met a Nazi, 100
A man in my town, Cal y-clempt, 102
Among the flags did Moses lie, 334
A mouse of my acquaintance in seven days was fed, 17
An aging Paris avocat, 49
An aging lawyer of Paree, 49
An alto, trained in Esperanto, 643
A needless vowel this—it's heard, 41
A nimiety of gin, 419
A picnic is a pasture feast, 626
A poetry writer named Brodsky, 34
A Q in most words should be followed by U, 621
A Quad, I'm told, is a quadril-, 463
As planet gyres about its sun, 308
As spread my waistful span (io), 34
A stomach pump's required to rescue, 428

Bacchus a boil vexing Jupiter's thigh? . . . , 29
Because of chronic hemeraphonia, 590
Beth emerged from bath of bubble, 609
Blessed Shepherd, 41
By Louis' side in royal tumbril, 135

Call me a Gussie, a Grice, Globaloney, 585
Capricious, upsy-downsy sweet, 30
Charles Dickens was caught by the devil, 412
Consider now the Quark, which is, 31

Damned be that beast who, as he ***** on others, 39
Dear ewe, dear lamb, I've l thee; we, 43
Don Juan, 35
Don't tell me no grammatic rules:, 436
Doth steam from coffeemaker bellow, 222
Do you recall that florid, convoluting, 592
Do you recall the jackaroo, 586

Enjambment doesn't—say who may—, 3
Eve, fear not lest through my dissent, 126

Feeling sick, 395
For words to warn the wicked world, 166
For Jim's scant thought no style could be too terse, 8
For planets forsaken, 447
Friend John, whose (:) was removed, 46

Get gets around. Get also gets the air, 28

God be his judge: that passive, zealous Quaker, 41
God holds a dialogue with me, 8
Great Demogorgon, on a daggly day, 574

Had I butt nude, 163
Haikus show I.Q.'s, 31
He **** for gold, 38
He said, "Thou art ugly as e'er man did see," 19
Her lambent gaze came up, a full moon rising, 582
How dangerous it is to think!, 358
How do I love thee? Let me count the ways, 19
How sad, how sad that I must say, 27
How singular some old words are, 48

I am Mars, and you are Venus, 45
I don't deny I'm mulierose, 605
I dreamt of a corrigible, nocuous youth, 8
I felled my words as trees fall . . . fanned their stout, 560
I find it curiositive, 92
If a boy, 12
If love be fine, as some contend, 25
If Pegasus, 37
If you're ab-, 9
I have a little philtrum, 244
I'll meet you at the circus where the beasts all sit and rhyme, 43
Illogic I abhor, 169
"I'll pay for lunch this time," I hear you say, 27
I love the girls who don't, 144
I love to watch the flocks, 180
I'm aware a, 303
I met a dear old catfish as I walked the road to Vassar, 588
I met a wise antelope, born in a zoo, 39
I met on a tram in exotic Siam, 5
I met some swollen words one day, 44
In ancient days the Asian mongoose Urva, 641
In a xystus, shrew Xanthippe, 645
Inia, minia, one two three, 591
Insinuate, 39
In your demeanor there's a dream, dear friend, 45
I saw quasars in the night, 113
I scarce recall when first you said hello, 35
I seldom stretch beneath a bough, 6
It all just happened? No intent? 164
It is unth-, 37
It's written in each piscine part, it's stamped upon the whole fish, 563
It was a lovely love affair, 191
I've knocked her to the sidewalk and I've taken all she's got, 17
"I was a stranger, and you took me in," 25
I was prodigal with time, 218
I was recently warned by a girl in Algeria, 45
I would that my palate were pat in, 15

Jogger, jog, and runner, run!, 491

Let us wonder, while we loiter, 110
Lie down once more where once we kissed, 49
Love's a game, 36
Love's lost its glow, 37
L.P. Beria, 635

Macaulay tells us Byron's rules of life, 36
Meg's fashion in passion, though warm, 'll, 42
Mute as a mackerel, darling, I am, 15
My amnesty to all, 127
My Chinese Miss is dainty as a Chinese fan, 16
My dear's dear kitchy-koo am I, 9
My idol!—Your idle, 344
My television set is snowing snow, 20
My tongue can't handle 'amn't I,' 48
My weight, sir, you must not survey, 41

No hu-, 12
None recalls that I am there, 28
Now, a little while, 41
Now hangs occiduous the sun, 608
Now may the heavens open up, and pour, 33
Now quap and quop, my heart! the east, 621

Of certain birds that start with s I'll sing a pretty song, 630
Of Clerihew Bentley, 89
Of truths I knew, 157
Oh, did you know the rumbelow, 622
O mangy cat, O scruffy cat, 357
One acts, one's acted on. (I ment-, 47
One fury alone has God found inexpungeable, 16
On Sundays, 12
O pendant stalactite, 13
O some may promise riches, 14
O try, O try a triolet, 25
Our love will never dwindle, being never, 16
O you kwacha, 597

Pray tell me why women, 639
Pygmies? Weren't they little guys, 8

Quoth I to me, "A chant royal I'll dite, 23

Rick Ballad (God him pity!), 32
Roads are muddy, 298

Said Ann, "Kiss not, sir—any, 41
Say, **** man in thy ***** cot, 39
Scribble a dribble a, 35
Seek not, seek not, lest life and mind you jeopard, 595
Seek out the Elbow Ingle, 583
Send my dear a cowslip, send my dear an oxlip, 552
She who, when young and fair, 36
Since women take mariticide, 599
Solomon Grundy, Monday ****, 39
Swing and sway with me, my dear, 565

"T?," 11
Tarantara, tarantara, off the hunters ride, 17
The Apple which the Snake supplied, 286
The bard who Hippocrene for gin gave up, 7
The cry of a cat's meow, 289
The dryad Ariadne used for play den, 38
The drunken Species homeward reels, 47

The fire, the ash, 13
The four eng-, 37
The hartebeest grows beastly, and his heart starts beating fast, 241
The heaving of her maiden breast, 8
The hermit crab lives safely curled, 315
The hominid avoids, 118
The jackal on the prowl cries "Pheal!", 611
The ka, deemed deathless on the flowing Nile, 596
The kind of sorcerer folks call an obeah, 259
The Latin teacher need not explicate, 50
The Male (or Lesser) Praying Mantis is, 16
The Mrs. kr. Mr., 43
. . . then she from laving, 26
The opposition candidate, 47
The qualities rare in a bee that we meet, 36
There's scandal out in Birdland. One morning Mr. Fuffit, 584
There's seldom been a man I knew, 9
There's something fine in Latin. Something—oh, 642
The rich eat steak, 250
The ∂ on his diurn ∂l rounds, 46
The vows that I exchanged with she, 49
The zobo is a cross between the zebu and the yak, 646
This yellow bird, who loves to frisk in, 558
Though *, well gone ** ***, may ****, 40
Three birds flew down, and perched among the ramages, 624
Time befriends, 42
Toadfish, croaker, hogsucker, happily swimming, 31
To abort little Willy, 36
To die a critic will be tough, 26
Tweedledum Tweedledee, 35

Vigesimation's is not just hurting, 643
Virgin Mary, meek and mum, 108

What? Do you in a thumbnail sketch? I may go, 26
What—did I trap her? No, 598
When all the world grows honest, 13
When announcers announce, 385
When Charon ferries me across the Styx, 18
When Churchill told us that democracy, 618
When I ******* to be a father, 38
When I was a larva, 14
When I was keen and young as you, 29
When muggets aren't the entrails of a calf or of a sheep, 603
When my craft first set to sea, 570
When reading the obits, I frequently say, 325
When stomping victims in a mugging, 49
When the praying mantis, 201
When the whole blamed caboodle has gone up the spout, 22
When you sin, friend, know that later, 94
Why doth the eyeless fellow cry, 41
Wild boars and lions haul Admetus' car, 9
Would * saw proof of God's restraint, 40

You'd be a poet, but you hear it's tough, v
Young I began my Wanderjahr, 644
You're beautiful, you're sweet, 36
You there, watching, 13
You whose joy is intellect 'll, 581